FAMILY, MARRIAGE, AND PARENTHOOD

Contributors

HOWARD BECKER

DON MARTINDALE

ARNOLD S. NASH

RICHARD A. SCHERMERHORN

MANFORD H. KUHN

READ BAIN

JOSEPH K. FOLSOM

EDGAR S. GORDON, M.D.

HARRIET R. MOWRER

HOWARD F. BIGELOW

RAY D. OWEN

ELIZABETH GENTRY

KATHARINE WHITESIDE TAYLOR

SVEND RIEMER

AMEY E. WATSON

FRANK D. WATSON

JOHN S. BRADWAY

ROCKWELL C. SMITH

THOMAS D. ELIOT

MABEL A. ELLIOTT

JAMES H. S. BOSSARD

T. J. WOOFTER

REUBEN HILL

Family, Marriage and Parenthood

SECOND EDITION

Edited by
HOWARD BECKER
UNIVERSITY OF WISCONSIN

and
REUBEN HILL
UNIVERSITY OF NORTH CAROLINA

With the Editorial Assistance of
MARGUERITA STEFFENSON
WINONA STATE TEACHERS COLLEGE

D. C. Heath and Company
BOSTON

GEORGE E. MAYCOCK

Library of Congress Catalog Card No. 54-8793

Preface

Family, MARRIAGE, AND PARENTHOOD herewith makes its bow in a second edition; the first, which appeared in 1948, required no alterations in basic plan, but at many points current research findings necessitated changes in detail. Our contributors, all of whom return with this edition, have tried, in so far as possible, to take account of recent happenings. Three of our contributors, Mowrer, Kuhn, and Folsom, have consented to add their recent articles critical of the Kinsey Reports in the form of an Appendix. Their promptness and generosity in making these articles available, as well as similar courtesies by the editors of *Social Problems,* the journal in which the critiques initially appeared, are hereby appreciatively acknowledged.

We have tried to keep textbook purposes clearly in view. A textbook is not a treatise. It is or should be designed to make tested knowledge available and assimilable. The scope of tested knowledge about family matters is vast — so vast, indeed, that an adequate textbook can perhaps best be written by a group of specialists following a unified plan. The plan of this book represents an effort to combine the better features of both the traditional type of course and the newer variety pointed toward preparation for marriage.

Family, marriage, and parenthood are here dealt with as webs of social interaction. It is of course impossible to avoid consideration of the many necessary factors setting the conditions under which such webs are woven, and many of the chapters deal with these factors. When all is said and done, however, family structure is a matter of social organization, marriage is a social institution, not a "private affair" of merely biological or even of "companionship" character, and parenthood involves far more than germ plasm.

Most of the specialists dealing with social interaction are sociologists or their near kin, social and cultural anthropologists. Our purpose in editing this symposium, however, has not been technically sociological in character; in fact, it might be better to speak of purpose*s,* for we hope that the result of our labors is a "double-barreled" text. Students are interested in more than strictly sociological analysis; family problems are very much in their minds. "The old order changeth," and a great deal that was once unchallenged is now questioned. No one can accuse the student of being cheaply utilitarian if he persistently seeks answers to problems that may soon be his own — or perhaps are so already.

The "double-barrel," so to speak, becomes even more obviously necessary when we realize that in family matters popular misconceptions abound, and everyone from the video hucksters to the drugstore pulp sellers helps to spread them. This text endeavors to counteract the most harmful.

Interest in family problems is also generated by widespread misgivings about the role of "reason" in human conduct. Several parts of the present text raise the very real question as to whether family, marriage, and parenthood can give much place to cold calculation. Firmly grounded inhibitions should not and cannot be lightly cast aside. Moreover, sentiment, as distinct from maudlin sentimentality, has its very real place.

Again, among the more prominent of family problems is the question of romance *versus* realism in courtship and marriage. The text makes clear in several chapters that at other times and places no such fallacious contrast existed and that, Hollywood to the contrary, it need not exist in modern American life.

Both in the problematical and in the more definitely sociological aspects, many of us have had our interest in the family aroused by striking differences between various contemporary countries. Several chapters in the text deal with topics relevant to this interest.

Sharply focused on the problematical is the discussion of physical factors in marriage, and the conclusions are enlightening. In particular, the physiological bias with reference to marital adjustment is shown to be — a bias. Many divorces, for example, occur when both partners are sexually adequate. Anti-Kinsey?

Strangely enough, problems of parenthood are often linked with this same physiological bias. Parental affection is sometimes thought to be wholly instinctive, but children may be welcome or unwelcome. Unless both parents are properly prepared to be parents in the social sense, there is no assurance that the training they impart will provide the basis for mature and integrated personality.

Parental affection has just been referred to almost as though it were all-sufficient, but at several points in the text it is made clear that affection is not enough to guarantee a properly functioning family. Even though disguised or otherwise named, discipline there must be. Planned or unplanned, budgets are a reality. In our society school, community, and church have their institutional claims on the family, and *vice versa*. How, given these considerations, can the family enterprise be kept solvent? All the answers cannot be provided, clearly enough, but several chapters in the text may be of much help.

Anyone giving a course in the family, marriage, and parenthood can well be a sociologist by virtue of his specialized training, but he must also have at his command, at least in the form of a text, the chief contributions of related disciplines: biology, medicine, economics, and so on. If we are to do justice to all our students, we must somehow combine the services of physiologist, physician, psychiatrist, social psychologist, sociologist, home economist, and other professional workers.

The problem-solving talents of the social technologist are supplemented in this text by the analytical tools of the specialized sociologist whenever it becomes necessary, *viz.,* our oft-repeated assertion that no courtship or marriage setup can be properly analyzed if the persons concerned are regarded as self-contained entities. In many respects of crucial significance for family conduct, "human nature" is extremely variable, changing from society to society. Chapters One, Two, and Six do much to make this plain, but evidences are sprinkled throughout.

All the collaborators were aware of the double purpose of this nevertheless unified symposium, and we wish to thank them for the gratifying manner in which they have carried out their share of the task. Further, for vitally important assistance, "above and beyond the call of duty," our hearty appreciation is extended to Marguerita Steffenson, Dean of Women at Winona State Teachers College, Minnesota. Her name might well have appeared on the binding rather than merely on the title page. Mottoes are no longer fashionable, but if they were, we might well choose *E pluribus unum*.

HOWARD BECKER
REUBEN HILL

Contents

vii

PART FOUR

Problems of Parenthood and Family Administration

PART FIVE

Family Crises and Ways of Meeting Them

PART SIX

Prospects for the Future

Illustrations

Tables

Chapter One

Interpreting Family Life in Context

HOWARD BECKER

NEVER FORGET THAT THERE IS A CULTURAL CONTEXT

Demagoguery in politics, today as yesterday, includes the practice of taking statements of opponents out of context and using them to yield meanings directly opposite to those actually intended. In sectarian controversy men have used Biblical texts in ways foreign to their real meaning; the context was ignored by both the controversialists and their hearers. Even scholars and scientists have been known to wrench phrases, sentences, or paragraphs from their settings and exhibit them as appalling examples of the stupidity or sheer ignorance of someone belonging to another school of thought, whereas due heed to the context might have reduced the argument to much ado about nothing.

Speaking technically: In studying the family, marriage, and parenthood, we run some risk of forgetting that these are all aspects of societies and, as such, functionally bound up with many other clusters of social actions. Societies, composed of social-action clusters, can be viewed as embodiments of systems of value. Such cultural systems provide the contexts within which otherwise meaningless fragments of conduct become interpretable. Convenient terms for comprehensive value-systems are "sacred" and "secular."

To make certain that these vitally important cultural contexts are not overlooked, it seems necessary to devote a good deal of attention to them at the very beginning of this book. Naturally, context and content are inseparably interwoven; the full context will appear only when the entire book has been read. It follows, then, that *this first chapter will not be completely understood,* even after several preliminary readings, by the student who has not done a good deal of work in the fields covered. Only when the detailed presentations of Martindale (which may be read *first*), Nash, Schermerhorn, Kuhn, Bain, Hill, and others have been absorbed will the implications of what is here said become apparent. At the same time, these detailed presentations may not make as much sense as they might unless the broader outlines have been at least partially assimilated. Mark, the "broader outlines"! It is much more important to devote study time to these than to the memorizing of minor details — at least, in the beginning.

The student should therefore come back to this chapter repeatedly; by thus weaving back and forth between the general and the particular he will be able successfully to interpret what he reads. Separate items will take on relevance, and the coherence so essential to genuine comprehension will gradually be revealed. Memorizing may then take care of itself.

I

VALUES ARE HUMAN VALUES

Let us start with the values that interweave to form the "sacred" and "secular" contexts to be used for interpretative purposes. How do values play their part in human conduct?

Man is a valuing animal. From at least the time of the ancient sages whose sayings have come down to us, and almost certainly long before then, those who have watched the doings of their fellows have taken account of the striking differences between the two-legged creature shivering beside the fire and the other inhabitants of the earth. The other animals, to be sure, carry out rudimentary acts of valuation, but man alone has developed the power of adequate speech.[1] Man talks, and talking, he weaves a network of symbols that simultaneously helps him to master some aspects of the world about him and to work into the texture of his personality strands of conduct intertwined with value-objects defined as good and bad, right and wrong, helpful and harmful, useful and useless, proper and improper, holy and profane, blessed and cursed, and so on and on.[2]

The concomitants thereof are everywhere apparent: among all peoples are encountered cherished habits, time-honored ways of doing things, usages, customs, standards, folkways, proverbial wisdom, folklore that enshrines hallowed practices, shrewd counsel about ways of getting on in the world, laws written and unwritten, and vaguely or sharply outlined patterns for living the good life — all bearing the verbal labels affixed to them by their maker, man.

Nowhere does man's tendency to develop and define his values appear more strikingly than in the family. As shown by Martindale in the next chapter, many other animals cluster together in little networks which may justifiably be called families, but only "man the talker" has used these networks effectively in establishing and transmitting socially defined values. These values are transmitted, learned, and shared — that is, they are parts of culture as that term is used by today's social scientists. More will later be said about this, but here it is enough to point out that *human* life is inseparably bound up with what Tylor called "that complex whole which includes knowledge, belief, art, morals, law, custom, and any other capabilities and habits acquired by man as a member of society" — i.e., with culture.

From its very beginning, of course, all life involves activity of one sort or another, and this activity flows in various channels, deep or shallow as the case may be. In many ways the channels tend to serve the needs of the organism — even our heavy stress on culture, on what man has made by hand or tongue, should not cause us to lose sight of this! — but the needs

---

[1] The question as to whether or not animals have "language" does not here concern us, for in any case the most ardent advocate of "animal language" would grant that such language is very rudimentary indeed. This of course says nothing about the basic difference between signals and significant symbols, but see G. H. Mead, *Mind, Self, and Society* (Chicago: University of Chicago Press, 1934), pp. 61–68.

[2] Those interested should consult Florian Znaniecki, *Cultural Reality* (Chicago: University of Chicago Press, 1919), and Howard Becker, "Supreme Values and the Sociologist," *American Sociological Review*, 6, 2 (April, 1941), especially pp. 157–163.

of the human organism are not at first clearly defined. What may be called "need-dispositions," to use a recent term here, are acquired in and through processes of definition by learning, for man has no instincts sufficiently automatic to carry him even a little way in the bustling, confusing world in which he must live out his life. The various ways in which he comes to "act like a human being" can be conveniently epitomized in five stages.

The initial stage of any human activity is a more or less vague impulse or craving which manifests itself in restless trial-and-error seeking. The possibilities of gratifying such undefined needs are manifold, and exploratory responses are made to many different stimuli; eventually the one particular kind of stimulus which gives the greatest gratification is found. A new-born infant, for instance, certainly becomes hungry soon after birth but does not know that he is hungry. He is restless, and he may suckle vigorously on whatever comes within range of his mouth, stopping at intervals to give vent to loud wails. If he is to survive, his restlessness must be recognized as a need for food. When the restlessness has been repeatedly stilled by feeding, the child comes to relate his hunger-feeling with food, and his vague "knowledge" that he is hungry is evidenced by the special kind of wailing or other sign of tension to which he gives vent.[3] His undefined need has become a learned need; his impulse has been defined; he has acquired a need-disposition. The second stage of the activity is thereby reached.

Following this, he seeks food whenever he is hungry, and frequent gratification soon instills a habit with all the qualities pointed out by Dewey:

> . . . that kind of human activity which is influenced by prior activity and in that sense is acquired; which contains within itself a certain ordering or systematization of minor elements of action; which is projective, dynamic in quality, ready for overt manifestation, and which is operative in some subdued subordinate form even when not obviously dominating activity.[4]

In other words, the third stage of the activity has been attained; the learned need has become dynamic and is fully incorporated in the overt activities and latent tensions of the child. Habit-attitude and value-object have been successfully paired, and through repeated pairing they have become inseparably wedded.

Habitual definition of elementary cravings, then, is part of the process by which the child begins to become fully human, by which the biotic individual is transformed into the social person. But it is only part. The sufficient factor is found in the specific type of definition which is found only in "man the talker." The fourth and essential stage is one in which social actions in the strict sense manifest themselves, actions having significance communicable by means of words or other symbols. Continuing to illustrate by reference to feeding, let us analyze a social action which looks like the setting up of an almost mechanical routine but which actually represents the taking

---

[3] Many mothers — and fathers too, for that matter — will testify and demonstrate that they can tell the difference between an infant's characteristic cryings when angry, tired, hungry, or wet.

[4] John Dewey, *Human Nature and Conduct* (New York: Holt, 1922), pp. 40–41.

over of a role, the playing of a part in a social cast of characters; namely, the process by which the child learns to feed itself. (In presenting this analysis we are anticipating the chapter by Read Bain, where a fuller treatment will be found, but logical presentation compels us to say something about role-assumption here.)

VALUES AND ROLES

Suppose that a mother who is not markedly "modern" in the sense of using no corporal punishment (the reason for the qualification will appear a bit later) has a youngster named Bobby. This young man has arrived at that age where he is expected to do something himself about conveying food from his porringer to his mouth. One morning his mother sets him in the highchair with the porringer on the tray, his fist firmly clutching his new loop-handled spoon. Thinking that perhaps "imitation" will solve the problem, she sits opposite him and goes through the motions of conveying food to her own mouth. Soon, however, she discovers that Bobby does not imitate in any such way; there is no infallible instinct to lend aid. He looks at her with his mouth open and drooling slightly at the corners, bangs the spoon on the tray, playfully flourishes it about, and finally throws it on the floor.

Not one of the mother's methods of teaching Bobby to feed himself seems to work very well. The upshot is that she gives vent to a little irritation, not being a "modern" mother, and slaps Bobby sharply on the wrist just as he is about to throw the spoon on the floor for the nth time. He looks at her, taking in the whole configuration — not merely the slap but also the maternal frown and like traces of displeasure. Among these are what Mead calls "vocal gestures," for when the mother slaps Bobby's wrist she says, indulging in the usual baby talk, "Bobby, na, na."

His chin puckers up, a few tears begin to gather, but in spite of these evidences of remorse nothing happens which fits the mother's definition of the situation. The spoon is still being flung on the floor, and each time "Bobby, na, na" and the slap on the wrist are repeated until she finally gives up in despair and starts to go about her usual household duties. Casting one fleeting look over her shoulder as she passes through the doorway, she witnesses Bobby's redefining of the situation. The spoon is brandished once more and seems on the verge of making another trip to the floor. Just as this is about to happen, however, the hand is suddenly checked almost as though the wrist had been slapped, the child is heard to mumble something which can be interpreted as "Bobby, na, na," and the spoon descends into the porringer and then begins its uncertain journey toward the waiting mouth.

This anecdote, for all its triviality, actually illustrates the means by which children acquire those definitions of needs in terms of social action — i.e., conduct assigned meanings communicable to others by means of significant symbols — characteristic of genuinely *human* beings. Bobby has manifested toward his own conduct the actions of the parent. He is talking to himself, symbolizing himself as an object. To put it differently, he represents in himself a value defined in the same way for himself as it is defined by someone else. He is, if you will, inhibiting himself — "Bobby, *na, na.*" In this self-checking action the words spoken represent of course only one aspect of a functioning whole. Why? Because in addition to the words there are all the kinesthetic sensations attached to the sudden arrest of spoon-flourishing, with its wrist-slapping accompaniment and, perhaps, even a mind's eye picture of the maternal frown and other evidences of nervous tension. The self-inhibition is simultaneously other-prohibition.

All in all, then, Bobby is acting toward himself, in however fragmentary and inadequate a way, as his mother was acting. He has assumed the role of the parent with regard to his own conduct. Social actions, from this standpoint, are dramatic performances in which a part is taken over, a role is assumed. Naturally, all connotations of deceit or disguise in "part-playing" or "role-assumption" are barred; the child *is* the mother, for the time that he is playing her part, with reference to his own conduct. Bobby is checking himself, disciplining himself, in maternal terms; he has manifested the actions of the mother toward his own behavior, and it thereby becomes a social action — the fourth stage of the activity.

Not much "mere habit" or "habit as such" about this sort of thing! Only an organism possessing significant symbols, those of speech in particular, can redefine needs in terms of social actions. Man is an animal defining values in special and precise ways because man is a talking animal.

SELF AND OTHER

Fifth in this presentation of the interrelation of needs and values is what may be called sociative needs $\rightleftharpoons$ self-and-other defined values. In simpler terms, as man talks and uses other symbols, he not only crystallizes values in relation to social actions but also endows himself with a self. The mere taking over of a small bit of a single role, however, yields only a fragment of a potential self. The child engages in social actions in the sense of assuming roles in and through significant symbols, but this does not necessitate an integrated self and a clearly differentiated other. He can be said to associate with and dissociate from others only when he can distinguish between self and other.

At first he cannot do this; as Milne puts it in "Busy":

> I think I am a Ticket Man who's selling tickets — please;
> I think I am a Doctor who is visiting a sneeze;
> Perhaps I'm just a Nanny who is walking with a pram;
> I'm feeling rather funny and I don't know *what* I am.*

As time goes on, a whole collection of such fragmentary roles accumulates: father roles, sibling roles, roles of intimates and acquaintances of every sort and description, roles of any number of differing organisms such as puppy-dog confidants or "Gallopoff, the talking pony," or even of inanimate objects such as dolls, taxicabs, or boats which are given the attributes of personality. Slowly, as various roles are played with greater or less dexterity, and as the

* Taken from *Now We Are Six,* by A. A. Milne, published and copyrighted (1927) by E. P. Dutton & Co., Inc., New York.

child learns to skip from one role to another, his world begins to attain some semblance of order; that is to say, he knows what he is expected to do in the appropriate situations and hence begins to achieve a relatively close-knit, unified self.

In many parts of Western society, one of the ways in which integration of the self begins to become manifest is when the child shows interest in and capacity to play organized games. In such games he is not playing with a projected aspect of his self in thoroughly egocentric fashion. Games force him to associate and dissociate with others as others, to take part in a set of sociative actions (sociation = [as]sociation and/or [dis]sociation). As a definite self develops, definite others likewise develop, and *vice versa;* sociation then becomes possible. By inducing the child to take part in a system of actions in which others are involved as others distinct from his self as a totality and not as a random assortment of roles, the organized game serves a highly useful purpose. Moreover, the game usually makes it necessary for the child to stay within the limits of his play role for a time sufficient to allow the whole set of actions to run its course; here again self-and-other development is furthered. *Sociative* social action is greatly facilitated by the game.[5]

Such games may at first be very simple. In hide-and-seek, for instance, there are only two roles, hider and seeker, and when the child can learn to hide and stay hidden until caught, and then really to seek and keep on seeking in spite of the temptation to relapse into the hider's role, sociative action patterns are built up that do much to solidify the core of an organized self. This is of course a gradual process. Those who have had experience with children know how difficult it is to keep the child in one given role for any length of time; organized game-playing must be *learned*. Before this has come about, the child will be hider for thirty seconds and then will suddenly shift over into the role of seeker before he has been found at all, and thus the game will go on, back and forth, without any rhyme or reason, until slowly a little persistence in the retention of the assigned role is acquired.

In addition, explicit norms of fairness-unfairness soon emerge. As the child begins to take part in more and more complex games, the patterns of which are kept in force by the example and precept of other children, the more or less dependable and predictable sort of personality regarded as the desirable variety in our own society — and, with due allowance, in any society — distinctly appears.

This is in large part the result of multiple role-playing and the accompanying stress on intricate rules. Take, for example, participation in a complex organized game such as baseball. Here you have a situation in which, say, the child is playing catcher or first baseman or pitcher. But, to play any single position well, the child must play, in a certain sense, the role of everyone else on his team and of at least three or four of the opposing team. In other words, the child must have among his own potential actions certain readi-

---

[5] There are many definitions of social action, but those by Znaniecki and Weber are probably most frequently quoted. In order to avoid quibbling in a chapter that is not designed as part of a text on systematic sociology, no definition is directly offered here.

nesses to respond that he can project on other people. This means that he has to know what the first baseman would do under the appropriate circumstances, so that if as pitcher he sees a player taking a long lead off first base, he throws to the first baseman with the reasonable expectation that the first baseman will know what to do with the ball when he gets it, because the child in question (the pitcher) knows what to do with the ball if he were to get it while playing the first baseman's role. All this amounts to saying that to play well any organized game, and particularly those involving teamwork, the player must possess a rather well-organized self in which the shifting back and forth from one role to the next has become relatively easy. The player reckons not only with others but also with himself.

The Child's Self and the Older Generation

Call to mind, now, the fact that the play of children is not a matter of entire indifference to parents or other representatives of an older generation. Even if there is no positive approval of certain kinds of play, there must be at least tacit consent. Further, in those societies where children do not play organized games as we know them, there is still the effort to engage in adult activities without bearing adult responsibility, without being even potentially blamable for the certain failures, contradictions, or injuries that would result if adult standards were rigidly applied. Older persons therefore judge the permissibility of such juvenile activities; here again there must be at least passive toleration. In one society, it may be quite all right for the merest toddlers to "play" at the sexual activities of adults whose close quarters they share, whereas in another the most rigid prohibitions against "genital rehearsals" may prevail — but in either case "older and wiser heads" maintain the controls. Organized role-taking (of which play is a sub-variety) therefore runs its course under the more or less watchful oversight of culture carriers whose greater age has given them a head start in defining the proprieties.

Moreover, those phases of juvenile conduct escaping the oversight of the guardians of the general proprieties of the society as a whole still tend to be patterned by the example of older age-groups. This, incidentally, is one of the many reasons why "diaper determinism" is nonsense. What is diaper determinism? Well, for example, the assertion that certain Russians are highly aggressive because during infancy they were swaddled so tightly that for the rest of their lives they give vent to the rage generated while they were babies. The same has been said of Germans and Japanese, but not, apparently of Italians. The latter (remember Mussolini?) seem to have been aggressive without benefit of tight diapers. Perhaps they patterned their conduct along the lines exemplified by older Italians, some of whom thought of themselves as conquering Romans, or as members of the Black Hand.

But to return to the more relevant: the six-year-old youngster who becomes a tag-along member of a delinquent gang is doing his best to take over the roles so impressively played by the "hard guys" who feel their chins hopefully for excuses to shave. Among the various roles to which he aspires is that of loyal gangster; he absorbs a moral code the reverse of that enjoined

in his home circle, but still a moral code. The "rat" or "squealer" is loathed;
the "tough egg," on the contrary, stands only a little lower than the angels.
Note, at this point, that the "hard guys" and "tough eggs" are in no way
indifferent to what goes on among the smaller fry; they see to it that gang
virtues are inculcated — if not systematically, at least steadily. Here again the
older members of a functioning group point to or provide the models of
approved personality, and also label the unworthy or despised in unmistakable
ways.

Whether in a given society as a whole or in an imperfectly integrated
aspect thereof, it can be said that under all circumstances the web of childhood experience is woven out of strands spun by forerunners. The personality patterns which slowly take form, the selves which gradually integrate,
have their models approved or at least tolerated in the more intimately
surrounding clusters. Among these models those exerting the most powerful impress on the child's personality have to do with social actions defined in all essentials by elders mindful of the proprieties peculiar to the
cluster in question. When at last Bobby has approximated the conduct
of the approved models, he has become, in our terms, a socialized personality.

Social actions in general, and sociative actions in particular, are rarely, if
ever, mere mechanisms devoid of "moral" content. Praise and blame, in
stronger or milder forms, are woven into their very fabric. Learning to eat
properly, playing with other youngsters, and a hundred and one other childhood activities are charged with *normative* meaning. Here has been the
great contribution of Freud and the other exponents of functional psychiatry; through their efforts we have learned how the most apparently insignificant muscle-twitch, such as a facial tic, may be inseparably and essentially
bound up with inner conflict arising from failure to play adequately the
roles required by a given value-system. When Bobby grows up to be a "normal" man assuming successfully the roles appropriate to his walk in life, he
will *ipso facto* be free of gross external evidences of "maladjustment" because all his needs and values, and the situations helping to define them, are
relatively harmonious. Tensions not readily noticed either by Bobby or others will exist within him, to be sure, for no personality ever completely fits
the models of the surrounding society, but he will still represent the "man
as he should be" in *his* social world.

MEANS TO ENDS

Which social world? Obviously we could distinguish a great many, as
Martindale does in the next chapter, but for the purpose of setting a context for analysis of the family, just two types will be presented: sacred and
secular societies. Before discussing these, however, it is necessary to characterize the means and ends they embody — or rather, which their interwoven
members embody.

This reference to "members" calls once more to mind the fact that *only
out of the ceaseless shuttling to and fro of social actions do societies take*

form. Families are woven of familial conduct, states of political conduct, and so on. There are no societies that exist over and above their constituent members. Convenience alone prescribes the use of "society" as a noun.[6]

It therefore seems wise to continue for a bit longer the essentially social-psychological method of presentation followed thus far. In order to make clear what is meant by "sacred" and "secular," attention must first be focused on four types of means followed by the members of any society in attaining their ends. More than four can doubtless be distinguished, but for the present purposes these are enough: (1) expedient rationality, (2) sanctioned rationality, (3) traditional nonrationality, and (4) affective nonrationality.

(1) Expedient rationality is that kind of conduct in which the actor seeks to attain values by any means regarded as conforming to the principles of economy of effort, efficiency, and absence of undesirable consequences. (This has also been called instrumental rationality, but it seems best to avoid "instrumental" because of its connections with Dewey's instrumentalism.) "Doing things in the way that is thought to be easiest in the long run" is a useful paraphrase.[7] Social action may be termed expediently rational when it is completely centered upon means viewed by the actor as adequate for the attainment of ends which he conceives to be unambiguous.

From the standpoint of the detached observer looking at what the actor is doing, and possessing greater knowledge of the relevant facts, the means chosen to attain a given end may be wholly inadequate, and the end itself may be self-contradictory. So long, however, as the actor defines the means as sufficient and the end as consistent, the conduct must be called expediently rational. A military commander, for instance, may count upon the certainty of victory if his strategy and tactics are shaped in a certain way; his conduct is expediently rational even though, as the detached observer may know, defeat is certain. Rommel at El Alamein counted on victory, and the detached observer, studying Rommel's battle plan, would have agreed that within the range of the facts *knowable to Rommel,* he was right. But Montgomery knew all that Rommel did, and more too!

Expedient rationality makes use of *any* means for the achievement of the end. It has therefore been suggested that it should be called unlimited or unrestricted rationality. For example, if the social action is combat and the need is annihilation of the opponent, the value may be defined in such a way that, as it were, "no holds are barred." Anything from poison to terroristic inducement of insanity may be held suitable. Utter ruthlessness therefore may be the farthest reach of expedient rationality. *Why* the opponent should be destroyed is another matter, lying in the realm of ends. Once the end is accepted, however, expedient rationality may warrant the choice of the atomic bomb as means, for this lies in the realm of *how.*

Another instance: suppose a man wants to avoid being drafted for mili-

---

6 Howard Becker, *Systematic Sociology on the Basis of the* Beziehungslehre *and* Gebildelehre *of Leopold von Wiese,* hereafter cited as Wiese-Becker (New York: Wiley, 1932), pp. 78–93.

7 From this it should be clear that "expedient" is being used in its original, etymological sense: *"expedire,* to free the feet, to release or extricate." No blameworthy meaning attaches to it.

tary service, and carefully calculates "the best way" to do it. He was once divorced from his wife, but she is willing to remarry him and bear a child. This is done. The man is placed in a deferred category, and when the war is over he divorces his wife again. The end was attained by the use of a given means viewed as satisfactory for that purpose and regarded as having no undesirable aftereffects. Whether or not the later results and other aspects of this action are desirable for the future welfare of the major actor is, again, another matter; if he originally defined his needs and values in so egocentric and hedonistic a way that the action was viewed as having no regrettable consequences, his conduct was expediently rational.

"Cold-blooded calculation" in the choice of means is therefore the hallmark of expedient rationality. The maxim, "The end justifies the means," is frequently invoked, even by those who are not egocentric, in defense of this kind of conduct. As to whether or not the maxim is true we need not here concern ourselves; the plain fact is that many men, in effect, have echoed Cavour: "Ah, signor, we should be great rascals had we done for ourselves what we have done for Italy."

(2) Hard on the heels of this, we may single out sanctioned rationality as a type in which the principles of economy of effort and so on are followed as far as a certain limit; *this limit is set by the character of the end itself.* Although the action may, for instance, be combat and the purpose the annihilation of the opponent, action and purpose may be integrally bound up with a code of sportsmanship. Many American soldiers when first encountering Japanese in World War II were themselves killed because of their readiness to "give the guy a break." Their conception of a fair fight kept them from plunging the bayonet into a Japanese groveling on his face — with the consequence that the groveler disposed of both his sportsmanlike conqueror and himself with one grenade. The value-system of the Marquis of Queensbury suffered speedy eclipse when the risks of observing it were fully realized. But while it lasted, the restraint it imposed provided an excellent example of what we have here elected to call "sanctioned rationality," in indication of the fact that ends of certain kinds provide sanction for only certain means. "Strangleholds are barred."

Charity, love, *agapé,* or *caritas,* the topmost value in the Christian scale, offers another illustration. The attempt to convert men to Christianity by force was long a basic example of the contradiction of means and ends. The contemporary Christian cannot sanction violence for this purpose. In "religions of the sword" such as Mohammedanism, however, allegiance to Allah may be induced by physical coercion, although deceit and some other means are excluded.

(3) As a counterweight to expedient rationality and sanctioned rationality we may also distinguish traditional nonrationality. This is marked by the dominance of means over ends or by a state of affairs in which actions formerly regarded as mere means become ends in themselves. Practices once of strictly utilitarian character are elevated to the level of ceremonials or rituals.

Traditional nonrationality is not solely a matter of the remote, the faraway, the medieval, or the so-called primitive; the modern world affords many instances. Indeed, the vital significance of tradition is often obscured because it is interpreted in antiquarian fashion. Actually, *traditio* meant merely to carry over, to transmit. Bobby was "traditioned" by his mother as to the "right" way to feed himself. We get language by tradition, manners by tradition, morals by tradition.

What we said earlier about the activity of older culture carriers in socializing the child is also relevant here. The imparting of a system of social norms, of symbolically stated values amalgamated with social actions, is a universal process, beginning afresh in every generation but always channeled by the example of persons who themselves have been "traditioned" within essentially the same system. We can nowhere find a society that does not develop basic agreements about alternative ways of acting and pass them on by tradition. A "fact" of social life in any society, however small and however "primitive," is the defining of approved and disapproved modes of conduct. The roles of hero and villain, so to speak, are traditionally delineated, and every youngster is told, and told repeatedly, that he is expected to be a hero.

Usually only certain members of a society are responsible for setting the models of good conduct, and their choices are made in the light of what they think and feel to be for the best interests of all concerned. Beyond doubt they make mistakes, but so great is man's capacity for self-justification that these mistakes are rarely admitted. Instead, they are draped in the same ennobling veil that is cast over genuinely beneficial decisions. Depending on the foresight, special privileges, and dispassionateness of the controlling group, the limits of what is thought to be for the good of all may be broad or narrow. Nevertheless, no matter how greatly such limits may favor those who have staked them off, with the lapse of time the favoritism is forgotten or obscured. Those whose personalities are shaped in accordance with such models necessarily take the inequities of tradition for granted; traditional nonrationality lies at the very base of a large proportion of social actions even among the "enlightened" members of any society.

Further, it must be borne in mind that tradition is not always inequitable. The young are often shielded from the disastrous consequences to which the uninhibited pursuit of imperfectly defined needs and values would inevitably lead — "inevitably," given the standards of the society in question. Realizing this when maturity is reached, those who have been thus "traditioned" come to feel a reluctance to depart from the ways of the tradition-bearers. Such reluctance powerfully reinforces the unwillingness or inability to change which the taken-for-granted always carries with it. "It was good enough for father, and it's good enough for me" — here again there is traditional nonrationality.

(4) Another counterweight of the rationalities is what may be called affective nonrationality. It is definitely a catchall term, including as it does everything from outbursts of love or hatred to the unquestioning, emotionalized acceptance of a leader who proclaims, "Ye have heard it said by them of old time . . . but I say unto you . . ."

Let us begin with the outburst variety. An irate husband swinging an axe on a woodpile because the coffee was cold is indulging in an emotional discharge or — to speak more precisely — in an affective release. Manifestly it is virtually impossible to find examples of the *purely* affective, for as we have seen, very little if any human conduct, in our sense of "human," is empty of symbolic reference. The purely affective would be the nonsymbolic — i.e., it would not be social action in any sense. After all, the fact that the axe was used on the woodpile rather than on the wife responsible for the clammy coffeepot means that a way of expressing temper permitted by the given society was followed; in that sense, then, the action had a definite symbolic content. Hence the empirical manifestations of affective nonrationality usually occur in close connection with one or more of the other three types: expedient and sanctioned rationality, and traditional nonrationality. It may be said, however, that when it is encountered as the *chief* phase of an action it represents a fairly complete fusion of means and ends; even analytic separation is often impracticable.

Affective nonrationality is also evident in the phenomena of the "mania," revival, fad, or style. The dancing mania which followed the Black Death gripped a large proportion of the peasantry and townsfolk of Central Europe, but it soon passed away almost everywhere, leaving behind only the phrase "Saint Vitus' dance," thereafter applied to a radically different but similarly uncontrollable manifestation. The tulip mania of seventeenth-century Holland left multitudes impoverished and vaguely wondering what evil spirit had caused the obsession with mere tulip bulbs and the heaps of gold they supposedly represented. The great Kentucky revival of 1800 led to scenes in which crawling circles of men "barked the Devil up a tree" and women "had the jerks" so violently that "their long hair cracked like a whiplash," but only feeble traditional traces have remained. The zoot-suit fad of the early nineteen-forties caused riots in many parts of the United States; today it is well on the way to becoming a remote memory. The Fanny Hatrack style of woman's dress prevalent in the United States during the middle nineteen-twenties has silently slipped away; but what impassioned oratory, for and against, it called forth while it was still with us! The sudden fanatical attachment to an innovation, and the surging emotions that attachment calls forth, can properly be placed among the manifestations of affective nonrationality.

Still another aspect of affective nonrationality is that of charismatic leadership, of the capacity to evoke awe, devotion, and unquestioning obedience. The Greek word from which "charismatic" derives means "grace" in the New Testament, but it has now been expanded far beyond its narrower theological meaning and in present sociological usage denotes simply the possession of extraordinary qualities.[8] These qualities may be many and varied; Mohammed owed a large part of his grip on Abu Bekr and other early disciples through his terrifying ability to "throw fits" and recount the visions he had seen while out of the flesh. Joseph Smith was a prey to hallucinations

---

[8] The range of literature on this topic is vast, as every informed student knows. Here, therefore, I cite only one of my own recent studies, *German Youth: Bond or Free* (New York: The Grove Press, 1946), chapter 4, "Proclamation: 'He Spoke as One Having Authority.'"

which he took for reality, and these plus his oratorical powers dragged in his train such men as Brigham Young, whose sober good sense in other matters is abundantly attested. Illustrations of this kind should not be taken to mean that the charismatic leader is always a religious leader — far from it. He may exercise his sway in many other fields: Jeb Stuart, Custer, and Patton in the military; John McGraw, Leo Durocher, and Knute Rockne in the athletic; Sylvia Pankhurst, Susan B. Anthony, and Carrie Chapman Catt in the feminist; Hitler, Mussolini, Stalin, Churchill, and Roosevelt in the political.

The minimum definition of charisma, in effect, has already been stated: it is an extraordinary quality of an individual which commands the emotionalized obedience of others. The most pressing problem of a charismatic leader is to verify and perpetuate his charisma, whether through miracles, the cult of hero-worship, feats that regenerate trust in his leadership, or by otherwise gratifying the impulses of his followers.

While it endures, the relation between leader and led is a personal one based on belief and confidence in "extraordinariness." A leader having this quality needs no administrative aides, no officialdom in the usual sense, relying as he does on his band of personal disciples or henchmen held together by the affective intensity of their belief in his charisma.

In contrast with both sanctioned rationality and traditional nonrationality, this kind of affective nonrationality is not only extraordinary but also, in its implications at least, revolutionary. "Charisma is the great revolutionary power in traditionally engulfed epochs." [9] Old value-systems are shattered; and out of the fragments, with a few pieces added, new ones are formed. Needs and values are re-defined, but the historical cleavage is never as complete as the innovators originally intended. Why? Because, to reiterate, it is virtually impossible to find examples of the *purely* affective. As I have put it elsewhere:

> Occasionally, of course, there comes some great image breaker. . . . Even these "extraordinary" or "uncanny" men, however, never make a clean break with the past; Mohammed and Buddha, to name no others, proclaimed their teachings with the sounding board of tradition behind them. . . . The charismatic leader must derive his . . . "gift of grace" from a source regarded as legitimate by . . . [those who follow] in his footsteps. Joseph Smith without a Biblical tradition and Protestant sectarianism is simply unimaginable, but given these and like essentials, the Book of Mormon finds its martyrs and its triumphs. Eventually, to be sure, all-powerful routine makes sedate ceremonial out of ecstatic deliverance, and tradition, temporarily set in second place, resumes its ancient sway, changed in outward seeming but inwardly the same.[10]

Many charismatic phenomena, therefore, have a heavy traditional or sanctioned content; one can say only that in some cases the affective element plays the preponderant part in the social actions of leaders, followers, or both.

[9] Max Weber, *Wirtschaft und Gesellschaft* (Tübingen: Mohr [Paul Siebeck], 1922), p. 141.
[10] Howard Becker and Reuben Hill, eds., *Marriage and the Family* (Boston: Heath, 1942), p. 11.

There is a striking resemblance to certain aspects of what Mead has called "I" conduct, for here too there may be a large proportion of affective nonrationality. Further comment on this correspondence, however, would carry us far beyond the confines of the present chapter.

Leaving the topic of affective nonrationality, and epitomizing: (1) expedient rationality is unrestricted in the means adopted; (2) sanctioned rationality has ends of sorts that inevitably bar certain means; (3) traditional nonrationality elevates means to the rank of ends; and (4) affective nonrationality manifests a coalescence of means and ends.

The Ends Themselves

What human beings really want in life has been the subject of debate from time immemorial, and the debate shows no signs of diminishing intensity. "One man's meat is another man's poison" is occasionally all too true. To be sure, broad uniformities within given societies can readily be detected, and even between one society and another there is frequently more agreement about essentials than we ordinarily suspect; but the difficulty of getting unity on the ends men *should* pursue is still notorious. Those who merely try to say what ends they *do* pursue have trouble enough.

Moreover, there is very little common ground when the question arises as to *why* men seek certain ends. One thinker may say that the ends are fixed by God, and that man simply uses his natural reason in choosing the good and abhorring the evil. Another will agree that God has fixed the ends, but that man has nothing to do with choosing the ways in which he will strive for them, or whether he will strive for them at all — predestination takes care of all that. Still another rejects God and all His supposed works, and pins his faith on Evolution or Nature or Progress; man blindly struggles for survival, or follows his biological impulses, or automatically seeks to move onward and upward.

If we try to single out just one capacity through which ends may be sought, we still find no agreement. Reason, for example, may be regarded as a divinely implanted principle, or as a weapon in the struggle for existence, or as a mere veil covering obscure urges that would be victorious in any case, or as the outcome of an evolutionary process of which Man the Reasoner, *homo rationalis,* is the culmination.

This is no inconsiderable array, certainly, but it could be very much longer. Whether or not we put them in words, in one way or another we all hold beliefs about the "why" of man's supreme ends and his struggles to attain them which in most if not all instances are quite as arbitrary as any in our list. It is impossible to carry on even the ordinary affairs of life without some kind of reference, implicit though it may be, to what Wells called "first and last things." [11] Those of us who think otherwise simply deceive ourselves.

To choose a trite but searching illustration, life can be brought to a slow or sudden halt in a thousand and one ways, from prolonged fasting to jump-

[11] H. G. Wells, *First and Last Things: A Confession of Faith and Rule of Life* (London: Cassell, 1918).

ing off a plane without a parachute. Most of us prefer to live, however, and hence consciously or unconsciously act in accordance with this preference. An inquiring reporter asking "Why do you want to go on living?" would ordinarily get only the mouthing of platitudes, blank stares, or impatient evasions in reply. That life *is* worth living is so deeply rooted an assumption for most of us that talk about it seems superfluous or even ridiculous. Nevertheless, with sufficient persistence our reporter could certainly extract enough from his victims to fill a column, and when analyzed everything in it would be found to bear upon the "why" of man's supreme ends and their pursuit.

Reading such a column, few of us could avoid taking sides. If we succeeded in being impartial, it would only be because of an interest in scientific detachment. Such an interest is highly specialized, hard to acquire, and hard to maintain. Indeed, only as we take over the role of scientist, together with *its* value-system, can such detachment be successfully practiced, and then only for short periods of time. Doing the scientific handstand is a part-time job.

This being true, there is no intention of denying the fact that scientists walk and sit and lie down like other people most of the time. Each of us decides, in one way or another, what the "chief end of man" is and why it should be sought. While we are carrying on our professional roles, however, no such decision need be made. The "good" scientist is merely the man who succeeds in maintaining his detachment as well and as long as others who follow his calling. In other words, he succeeds in predicting, time after time, what happens next in his chosen field of research, and in systematizing his method so that others can use it regardless of the ends they may pursue.

Hence, in discussing the ends of human conduct there is here no faintest idea of saying why they are ends — if and when they are. Nor is there the remotest suggestion as to whether the most prominently mentioned human capacity through which ends may be sought — namely, reason — in any of its forms *finally* governs man's activities. Contrariwise, there is no assertion that man is *basically* irrational or even nonrational. The most that can be said is that in some ascertainable situations rationality seems to govern and in others it does not. Beyond this, the scientist as scientist, like Pilate washes his hands of the whole matter. How long they stay washed or how often they have to be washed present interesting *psychological* and *sociological* problems, but they have little to do with the *logical* demands of the pursuit of science.

As the scientist sees him, man's strivings for his supreme ends are classifiable as search for (1) security, (2) response, (3) recognition, and (4) new experience.[12] Moreover, these strivings, classified in this *general* way, are inseparable from the ends themselves; no useful working distinction is possible, and none will hereafter be made. "End" will be used to signify both. Further, all discussion of ends here presented is on the assumption that they are *always* culturally defined. What men want is what they *learn* to want.

---

[12] Obviously, these old Thomas and Znaniecki categories have had a long and checkered sociological career. It is perhaps too much to hope that they will be taken *only* in the senses hereinafter discussed. Cf. Florian Znaniecki, *Social Actions* (New York: Farrar and Rinehart, 1936), chaps. 1–3, and accompanying bibliographies.

This point can hardly be overstressed. What security or response or recognition or new experience actually means to the persons who pursue such ends cannot be known unless their cultures are known, and in particular, unless the more important value-systems of those cultures are known. It is for this reason that some social scientists have suggested reference to "goals" rather than to "ends," their idea being that the culturally limited character of the former is obvious, whereas the latter always implies independence of any given cultural context. The mere substitution of one of these words for another solves nothing, however, more especially as there seems to be little agreement on what is obvious or what is implied. The fourfold classification of ends is simply a convenient way of sorting culturally defined human strivings into baskets few enough to be easily surveyed and at the same time sufficiently numerous to relieve the observer of the necessity of jamming too much into one or two. Preliminary sorting done, the contents of this basket or that may be more thoroughly inspected, and perhaps it will be found that no single basket properly accommodates some items. The ultimate test is predictive, and the amount of specificity sought in prediction determines which classification is most suitable. Rarely if ever will it be enough to say that a given personality type, for example, seeks security; the answer must usually be in terms of what section or layer of such-and-such a society, in what kind of culture, at about what time, a certain variety of security is sought. In short, the striving for ends must be interpreted in context, and with a view to prediction.

Security. Security as a supreme end may mean that "eternal peace in God" of which Goethe spoke, or it may mean simply a state of affairs in which men know where their next meal is coming from and have roofs over their heads. Not only is there this wide latitude in the meaning of security within Western culture, for example, but there is in addition the great variety introduced by the highly diversified meanings peculiar to the other cultures now extant, to say nothing of those which have passed off the scene. Nevertheless, security as one term in a fourfold classification will serve our purposes well enough as long as we do not place upon it a burden heavier than it was intended to bear.

To be avoided, for instance, is the use made of it as an implied universal goal in Adler's "inferiority complex." *All* human beings supposedly lack security, however much they may strive for it, and therefore suffer from a sense of failure and consequent inferiority which accounts for all their conduct. Barely distinguishable from this is Karen Horney's tracing of *all* mental ills to basic insecurity. No such attractive but untrustworthy thesis is advanced here; social actions, with their symbolically defined values, are far too complex to admit of single-factor "explanations." If we can say with some assurance that in societies of certain types men seek ends more readily classifiable under the heading of security than under any or all of the other three headings, such a classification may prove to have predictive utility; if not, other analytic tools must be used.

Response. Response likewise includes a great deal. The mystic ecstasies of Saint Teresa were centered upon the experiencing of divine love mediated through Christ as Eternal Bridegroom. The patronage of Park Avenue pet shops rests in large measure on the assumption that life with a responsive Fido assumes meaning which it otherwise lacks. Response in these forms falls outside the realm of ordinary experience, but ties of kith and kin, friendship, courtship, marriage, and scores of other familiar relations have large — sometimes overwhelmingly large — response components.

In this connection also our use of the response category does not commit us to those supposedly universal explanations of human conduct offered, for example, by orthodox Freudians. Much use can be made of Freud's conceptions of the ends men seek without binding the social scientist to the more fantastic formulas of the psychoanalyst. Some societies demonstrably give larger scope to social actions focusing upon response than do others; this being the case, the use of the tool is warranted.

For instance, although beyond question security was and still is significant in Mormon affairs, the nature of the social organization of the Latter Day Saints between the 1840's and the 1890's gave response a very prominent place. This response, as the evidence clearly shows, cannot merely be labeled "lustful." The Mormons, apart from a few pathological members, seem to have been very much like the rest of mankind in their response strivings; mutual love, conjugal devotion, parental affection, and similar components of sociation in small, intimate human groupings were widely manifest. In other words, the family even when polygamous remains a major channel for practically all kinds of response.

Recognition. As is clearly the case with security and response, recognition may not only be closely intertwined with other ends but also ramifies in many directions. Napoleon's single-minded pursuit of military fame is in point, as is likewise the notorious striving of American clubwomen for space in the society columns. No matter how high the status of a given person may be, it is always possible for him to regard others as at least potential rivals. Spurred by such a threat, human beings may enter upon courses of conduct which would be quite incredible if ample documentary evidence did not compel belief.

Historians make more use of the recognition category than do most other social scientists, and this is entirely understandable in view of the types of "famous" events and personalities with which they have traditionally concerned themselves. The sociologist cannot make such sweeping use of recognition as a goal of social action, but it must undeniably be granted a prominent place. Many a parent has faced the problem of how to handle the family show-off. Youngsters not only want to be recognized as worthy of affection or attention but sometimes insist on getting much more than their share — to the point, indeed, where the other children, if there are any, may make common cause against papa's pet or mama's little darling. If parents are unwise, animosities may be built up which make for family discord throughout the entire lifetimes of its members.

Show-offs are to be found everywhere, even though the unkind term may not be used. What would military organization be like without the stripes, the brass, the bars, and stars, and the rest of the display paraphernalia?

Americans and Russians seem to besprinkle themselves more liberally with such decorative devices than do the French and British, for example; does this mean similar contrast in exhibitionistic traits? Yes? But what of the relatively sober and restrained academic garb of the American scholar as over against the almost gaudy attire of French academicians? Is it not apparent that recognition must always be interpreted as a component, and in a context, of social actions which are not attributable to any single instinct or raw need?

New Experience. New experience is the last of our four pigeonholes. Apparently somewhat more limited in range than the first three, it is nevertheless a kind of end clearly evidenced in societies of every type. The restless adventurer may have little in common with the scientist persistently extending the frontiers of knowledge, but the ends they seek are in some ways remarkably similar. Of course, new experience may be found at a quite different level: the gourmet forever on the lookout for novel recipes and the fashion devotee incapable of resisting the temptation of "the very latest" fall in the same category.

Oddly enough, no body of psychological, psychiatric, or social-psychological theory has been built around the indisputable fact of the lure of novelty. Further, there has been little attention to the ever-present human interest in "luck" as a source of novelty. Yet we all know how largely gambling, racing, and dozens of other evidences of interest in the novelty arising from the relatively unpredictable have figured in human life the world over. New experience is a useful, albeit unexplored, category in the study of ends.

Who, for instance, has not been impressed by the eager interest of a child when taken on a visit to the zoo, and who has not been struck by the rapidity with which that interest wanes when the experience is too frequently repeated? Judicious spacing of the visits so that some charm of novelty can be generated afresh is a technique that many parents soon acquire. Such techniques for making old experience seem new are part of the repertory of anyone who has learned his way about in the social world.

Some persons, to be sure, are so strongly attracted by novelty that they will not put up with substitutes. Travel agencies of every kind flourish accordingly, to choose only one example, and for many persons it soon becomes a case of "We went to the Grand Canyon last year; let's go to Bermuda this time."

Further, vicarious new experience of this kind is eagerly sought by those who must stay at home or are otherwise compelled to accept a substitute "just as good as the original." Travel authors, with their personalized tales of the strange and the faraway, attract their myriads of readers.

THE FUSING OF ENDS

Like all the other ends, however, new experience may lead to or be mixed with polar opposites. The fictional adventurer who struggled his way into a remote nook of what may have been Tibet found intense gratification in the new experience of Shangri-la, but when that queer but idyllic community had been left behind and the road of return had unaccountably vanished, Shangri-la became the "lost horizon" of a nostalgic story.

In these pages, the story leads to this point: few if any social actions are classifiable with reference to any single end. Recognition laps over into response or new experience, and even new experience may have a bearing on security. The most that can be said, where concrete instances of end-seeking activity are concerned, is that greater emphasis is laid on one end as over against another. Unless this is clearly realized, fruitless and essentially unscientific argument will be the only outcome. If, *in a given context,* a high proportion of social actions can be successfully predicted by directing attention toward demonstrable concentration by the actors upon certain ends, to the relative neglect by those same actors of other ends, the purpose of the classification has been achieved.

SACRED SOCIETY AS CONTEXT

"If in a given context . . ." With perhaps wearisome frequency, the analysis of needs, values, means, and ends thus far presented has referred to societies as contexts. Further, we have specified those contexts as interpretable in terms of "sacred" and "secular" value-systems and other social and cultural phenomena bound up with such systems. The point has finally been reached where the closer characterization of "sacred societies" and "secular societies" becomes possible. Only when this has been done can the bearing of the present chapter on family, marriage, and parenthood be clearly seen.

Foremost is the fact that societies are simply larger networks of sociation within which families as smaller networks find their appropriate place. Moreover, it must be recalled that sociation is a shorthand way of designating association and/or dissociation with others *as others* in and through roletaking involving the use of significant symbols. In other words, sociation is a label for social actions in which selves and others intercommunicate. This means, of course, that societies as networks of sociation take form only out of the continual interweaving of social *actions*.[13]

"Sacred" likewise refers to conduct, for it points to inability or unwillingness to respond to the new, particularly at the symbolic level peculiar to the *human* being. For us, social action has sacred traits when an aversion to change is manifested. True, this aversion is more strongly marked in some circumstances than in others, and there are certain kinds of nonsymbolic and imperfectly symbolized behavior in which the explicitly sacred aspects are very slight although much resistance to change is evident. Omitting further discussion of this qualification, however, let it be repeated that societies that impress upon their members modes of conduct making for a high degree of resistance to change are for us sacred societies.

From this it should be clear that "sacred" is here being used in an entirely warranted but precise and limited sense; it simultaneously means

[13] See Wiese-Becker, *op. cit.,* pp. 78–93.

somewhat more and somewhat less than do "religious" and other words frequently thought synonymous with it.[14]

A set of distinctions that may sometimes be useful splits sacred into holy, ritualistic, loyalistic, intimate, commemorative, moralistic, fitting, and appropriate. This roughly represents an intensity range from zeal for martyrdom on behalf of the holy to quiet humor on behalf of the appropriate.

Only the holy has a definite "religious" bearing in the sense of orientation toward what is held to be the supernatural. Here, and *nowhere* else, sacred as an inclusive term necessarily has to do with a god or gods, the divine, and so on. Throughout the rest of the range the emotionalized resistance to change that is of the essence of the sacred may have no reference to religion in the supernaturalistic sense (and to which sense religion is here restricted).

The ritualistically sacred, for example, may have little or no definitely religious meaning. There are technical, economic, and bureaucratic rituals. Granted, these may often have a heavy nonrational content, but who would restrict the realm of the nonrational to that of religion? English legal ceremonial, with its wigs and woolsacks, is certainly ritualistic, but it is not significantly supernaturalistic. *It is sacred, but not holy.*

The same may be said of the loyalistically sacred. Patriotism is often a powerful sentiment; men have gladly died for the sake of loyalty to a flag. Solemnity may surround its symbolism, but rarely is this solemnity identified with that manifesting devotion to the supernatural. The same is true of other varieties of the loyalistic; attachment to a Scottish clan, for example, was never evocative of the reverence that is peculiarly holy.

The bonds of the intimately sacred afford still another example. What have long been called "primary groups" provide ample scope for the sacrednesses of friendship, parental and filial affection, romantic and conjugal love, and similar ties. Yet the intimate as such is not the same as the holy, however much the latter has been drawn upon as reinforcement of the former.

Even where the commemoratively sacred — which in some respects is merely affirmation of continuing intimacy, real or imagined — is concerned, there is no necessary link with the holy. Atheists have been known to commemorate departed relatives with tombstones inscribed "Sacred to the Memory of. . . ." And of course there is a great deal of commemoration that is less intensely intimate than bereavement ceremonial: birthdays and so on.

The moralistically, fittingly, and appropriately sacred, lumped together as folkways and mores, have long been familiar in American sociology, and need not detain us here at any length. It is enough to say that they represent the sacred in lessening degrees of intensity, and that for the majority of the Western world today, what is right, decent, proper, suitable, or customary does not necessarily partake of the holy. *The pursuit of sacred ends often includes religion, but is by no means confined to religion.*

[14] "*Sacred* as meaning having such a character that is protected by law, custom, tradition, human respect, or the like, against breach, intrusion, defilement, or profanation." *Webster's Dictionary of Synonyms* [Springfield, Mass., 1942], pp. 721–722. Cf. Becker and Barnes, *Social Thought from Lore to Science,* hereafter also cited as *STFLTS* (2nd ed., Washington, D. C.: Harren Press, 1952), "1951 Commentary on Value System Terminology," pp. i–xxii.

Sacred societies imbue their members with ends most readily classifiable under security, response, and recognition, with security in many cases uppermost. The means by which these ends are sought are chiefly of traditionally nonrational and sanctioned rational types. This statement needs further elucidation, and this can best be provided by describing, first, what have long been called traditional or folk societies,[15] and second, what may here be designated as sanctioned or prescribed societies.[16]

THE FOLK SUBDIVISION OF SACRED

The best examples of folk societies are to be found in the old-fashioned, backward, or even primitive parts of the world. Regions where custom is strong are of course likely to be remote from the highroads of commerce and the hum of communication; that is, folk societies are ordinarily isolated.

To be sure, the isolation is not merely a question of the land under the feet of the folk in question; but even at the merely geographical level, the absence of disturbing changes may enormously enhance the effect of isolation. When occasional natural catastrophes such as flood, fire, or drought do not interrupt the even round of events, conduct readily becomes stereotyped. Feast days come and go, planting and harvest seasons succeed each other, birth and death replenish and diminish the ranks of the members, and routine is lord of all. From the fish racks of the Faroes to the yam plots of the Trobrianders, folk societies show a startling uniformity of essential function; the more obvious patterns are so diverse that the unwary may be deceived, but the weave is fundamentally similar.

But as the inhabitants of Iceland discovered not so long ago, an island once remote in the purely geographic sense may suddenly become a bustling crossroads when man's ways of traveling change. What really constitutes the isolation of a folk society, in other words, is the lack of relations with neighbors, a point made by Semple when, taking her cue from the old term *vicinage* meaning neighborhood, she spoke of *vicinal* isolation. A people has a twofold location, an immediate or geographical one, based on its actual territory, and a mediate or vicinal one growing out of its relations with other peoples. The first is a question of the spot on the globe where it happens to be located; the other, of its position with reference to neighbors round about. Vicinal position necessarily has geographical location as a substratum, so to speak, but vicinal position may be greatly changed — again the example of Iceland — with no change whatever in geographical location. When air travel supersedes ocean travel, certain regions, in terms of time-cost distance, are no longer in the same place! Hence, vicinal isolation is nothing more than extreme limitation of facilities for direct communication.

Over and above this sheer absence of effective contacts with peoples rep-

---

[15] We have long spoken of folksong, folktale, and folklore, but ordinarily in a sense less inclusive than that of folk society, for this takes in *all* noncivilized or partially civilized peoples.

[16] This is the first use I have made (1948) of the "folk-prescribed" subdivisions of sacred, and, so far as I know, it is the first explicit systematic use by anybody.

resenting contrasting or even distinctly differing ways of life, folk societies are likely to be *socially* isolated. When a straying neighbor "gets outside his own bailiwick," he sometimes finds that barriers to social intercourse may be higher than mountains and deeper than seas even though folk meets folk face to face. Just a few little differences in accent or dress or gesture may put the newcomer in a world as socially remote as that of our familiar man from Mars, and perhaps even colder.

To vicinal and social isolation must be added a third kind; namely, *mental*. The members of different folk societies think and feel differently. The patterns of logic are not entirely arbitrary, and neither are man's emotions, but the combinations of mental processes functionally effective in the conduct of one folk may contrast so radically with those characteristic of another that the unschooled observer may wonder which if either of the two is "really human."

The contrast of course derives from the fact that vicinal and social isolation have furthered the development of strongly contrasting symbolic systems which may initially have differed from each other in only slight measure.[17] The absence of intercourse with other peoples permits small variations to increase in geometric ratio, until finally once mutually intelligible dialects of the same language, for instance, may pile up differences to the point where only the skilled philologist can discover that they were ever related. Language and logic are closely interwoven, and for this as well as for many other reasons sharply divergent folk mentalities may emerge.

The cumulative force of tradition, linguistic or otherwise, is powerfully aided by absence of the written word. Even when folk societies are not wholly nonliterate, the art of writing is often restricted to a select few who use it for quite limited purposes. Total or partial nonliteracy makes for domination by tradition in many ways. Everything regarded as important in the past of a given folk, for example, must be passed on by word of mouth, and this leads to the memorizing of long ballads and epics which, by their combination of meter, alliteration, assonance, paired balance, acrostic pattern, rhyme, or whatnot, make possible almost unvarying repetition. The grooves of language and of thought soon become so deeply channeled that it is virtually impossible to pass beyond their confines. Traditional oral transmission and folk mentality flow along together.[18]

Similarly contributing to traditional control is the prevalence of kinship bonds in folk life. Indeed, some writers claim that "kinship society" is prior to all other principles of organization, and their claims are in considerable degree borne out by the amazing intricacy of many kinship terminologies. Some dwellers in folk societies have as many as three hundred ways of labeling their various relatives, whereas in this modern day, with its small family units as over against the mammoth kinship clusters of earlier periods, we think that we are doing well when we can identify a few second cousins. Enmeshed in a maze of relatives, what wonder is it that the children growing

---

[17] Divergence, the opposite of Goldenweiser's concept of convergence.
[18] See Becker and Barnes, *STFLTS*, chap. 1, "Social Thought of Preliterate Peoples."

up in folk societies acquire binding types of conduct in the form of codes of propriety, ceremonials, "thou shalts" and "thou shalt nots," and a thousand and one other accustomed traditions? The inner countenance, so to speak, is wrinkled, creased, and seamed by the endless repetition of stock grimaces called for by the limited repertory of roles in the drama of sociation. Standard situations and scenes recur again and again, and the parts must be played in the traditional way or not at all. In other words, a folk society has many universals and few alternatives.[19]

This limiting of the range of conduct is also evident in the modes of gaining a livelihood. The minute division of function, ridiculed as "Man number 63 screws on nut number 807," characteristic of much contemporary life, is significantly absent. To be sure, even the folk society has its specialists, as Linton pointed out, but any folk specialist is "master of one trade *and* jack of all." He may be the wood carver or the flint flaker *par excellence,* but in case of need he can still wield the digging-stick or the spear. If he is a teller of tales or a "ghostly man" passing the time of day with familiar spirits, he may be somewhat set apart from his fellows, but except in extreme cases he is rarely as insulated as the professional writer, cleric, or other member of the "learned professions" in our society. That is to say, the traits characteristic of the mentality of a particular folk are likely to be widely diffused among its members because occupational compartments are not watertight.

The power of tradition in folk societies is also enhanced by the necessity of what may be called apprenticeship. Learning the skills necessary in the struggle for sustenance requires long and painstaking effort. The modern expedient of going to school or of hiring a guide or instructor cannot be resorted to by a folk member. Instead, he must kowtow to the "old-timers." If the elders impart their cunning and sleight they demand conformity; in many folk societies the rebel is an outcast, and the outcast quickly becomes a corpse. Once the more or less willing conformist has mastered the mysteries of his craft, he has by the same token established action patterns of great complexity and persistence; and when these are adequately embodied in the symbolic standards of his society, and particularly in speech, the character and life policy of the economic man-as-he-should-be are clearly outlined. Once this result is reached, any disturbance in the traditional way of getting a livelihood, or in any other key practice, encounters stubborn resistance.

With this in view, it becomes relatively easy to understand the folk society's self-imposed social and mental isolation *vis-à-vis* the stranger; there is deep dislike of the person who concretely represents the forces of change. When he is genuinely a stranger on the human plane, he is necessarily an "other-than-expected-fellow" — the Chinese villager's term for the outlander who as such is inevitably crude, disconcerting, barbaric. Any breach of the everyday routines is disquieting, for the mere sight of conduct in conflict with tradition tends to call forth "upset" feelings of a kind that would seize upon any thoroughly "set" personality engaging in actions so blameworthy in the eyes of his own folk. The homebody imagines himself doing the detestable things perpetrated by the "furriner" and "gets all stirred up inside."

[19] Ralph Linton, *The Study of Man* (New York: Appleton-Century, 1936), pp. 272–287.

This disapproval of the stranger of course extends far beyond the realm of queer appearance and unfamiliar gesture. Strange speech, for example, is always striking in its oddity, its "outlandishness"; an old proverb has it that "Whoever speaks two languages is a rascal." This aptly represents the feeling of the custom-bound member of a folk society when "jabberers" or "people who just go bar-bar-bar all the time" apply the wrong names to everything. Name and thing are identified; the use of other words is thought unnatural.

The stranger is also expected to have "common sense." In a folk society, common sense is sense because it is common, and an added warrant of its validity is provided if it is couched in proverbial terms. The stranger who cannot pass out the coins of ancestral wisdom, worn smooth by centuries of use, is necessarily beyond the pale. "Stories are told to stupid children, but proverbs are taught to the clever" is a maxim that in substance guides the elders in folk societies. The proverb is common sense raised to the nth degree, and to doubt this compressed wisdom, or even to be unfamiliar with it, is the mark of the witless or the wanton. Sages of folk societies coin new proverbs continually, but they are accepted as proverbs because their makers already bear the character of sages, and this character is acquired only by copious outpouring of traditional formulas.

The uninterrupted dominance of use and wont is made easier when the ties of familiar locality reinforce the bonds of vicinal, social, and mental isolation, kindred, livelihood, apprenticeship, tongue, and lore. Homesickness does occur. Men grow their way into landscapes, so to speak, and a severe wrench is felt when the native place is left behind. If our bearer of a folk personality tills the soil, he becomes with the passage of time so deeply rooted in the particular plot over which he labors, and which embodies so much symbolism, that shift to another with which he has not the same intimate relation brings with it the disturbance of deepset action patterns and a feeling of uneasiness or even distress. "For such a man, the neighboring valley, or even the strip of land at the other end of the village, is in a certain sense alien territory." [20] To speak with Granet, the "occasions" and "emblems" with which his personality is functionally interrelated are indissolubly linked with the "sites" of his lifelong surroundings.[21] Exploiting the once well-known play and the familiar song, it may be said that "the old homestead" is not simply so-and-so many acres, for the reason, among others, that "the old oaken bucket" is not simply a wooden pail.

DIAGNOSTIC QUESTIONS REGARDING SACRED SOCIETY OF PRIMARILY FOLK TYPE

Discussion of these and other general traits of folk societies might go on indefinitely. To be brief and still serve present purposes, however, it is

[20] Robert E. Park, E. W. Burgess, and R. F. McKenzie, eds., *The City* (Chicago: University of Chicago Press, 1925), p. 18.
[21] Marcel Granet, *La Pensée Chinoise* (Paris: La Renaissance du Livre, 1934), pp. 119, 127, 151–160, 173–208.

enough to list a few questions almost certain to be asked by any sociologist trying to determine the frequency and intensity of folk traits (together with a few of "prescribed" variety) in certain smaller American communities:

I. Intensity of kinship bonds

A. How many relatives can the ordinary member of the society readily list? What proportion is this of those that he actually has?

B. How strong is his genealogical interest? Can the name and place of birth of a large number of grandparents, great-grandparents, etc., be readily given?

C. What proportion of living relatives has the member actually seen in the past five years?

D. With what proportion of relatives are at least annual meetings (dinners, reunions, etc.) held?

E. To what extent is identity felt with blood kin? With in-laws, second cousins, and so on?

F. What are the attitudes toward divorce and illegitimacy within the family? To what extent do these attitudes rest on religious or related prescription?

G. How frequently are letters and gifts exchanged between relatives?

H. Are christening, baptism, confirmation, and like "rites of passage" [22] family affairs?

I. To what extent do children visit relatives? Is there any sense of family responsibility for orphans?

J. What degrees of relationship are in evidence at family marriages, funerals, and similar "rites of passage"? How great is the time-cost distance typically traveled? What is the defined significance of such travel?

K. Is the practice of burial in the family plot maintained? Are the tombstones of traditional character? Of religiously prescribed character?

L. Do the members of the family (collateral and affinal relatives as well as lineal or blood kindred) belong to the same religious body? By explicit prescription?

M. Is there a family homestead, or are there commonly revived memories of one?

N. To what extent are names and birth dates recorded in Bibles or similar places of family inscription?

O. How large is the realm of family symbolism and family secrecy? How much does conversation turn on allusions understood only by family members?

P. Are relatives, friends, or banks most generally named as executors of wills?

Q. When money is loaned to relatives, is it loaned with or without interest?

R. To what extent is mutual aid practiced among relatives in moving, housebuilding, sewing, nursing, and the like?

[22] This Van Gennep term is better translated as "ceremonies of transition" — transition from one stage of the life-death cycle to another. Unfortunately, some literalist gave us "rites of passage" for "rites de passage," and now we must put up with it.

II. Intensity of friendship and neighborhood ties

A. All questions concerning participation in "rites of passage" are also pertinent here.

B. Are there many lifelong friendships between members of the same or opposite sexes in the locality?

C. Are money and property freely loaned back and forth between friends? As taken for granted, or by explicitly quoted prescription? Is interest or rent charged?

D. How frequent are visiting relationships between friends or neighbors?

E. To what extent are friendship and neighborhood mutual-aid practices in evidence?

III. Locality relations

A. All questions concerning participation in "rites of passage" are pertinent here, as are also those pertaining to friendship, mutual aid, etc.

B. Within what area is the typical member of the society referred to by first name, nickname, or in similar familiar terms?

C. What proportion of the persons in the circle of acquaintanceship are "familiar-name acquaintances"?

D. What proportion of community members were born within it? In the case of those who are not native, from how far away did they come? How long ago? And why? What are the general attitudes toward them?

E. What is the range of calling or visiting relationships? To what extent does residence determine neighboring? With whom are social visits carried on? How? [23]

---

[23] The full outline should be provided, but sections IV–VII, given in this footnote, are of less direct relevance for illustrative purposes:

IV. Livelihood patterns

    A. How freely is family land alienated? Is there any communal opposition to the splitting up of ancestral land? Is there a nuclear or homestead parcel of land which would cause loss of status if sold outside the family?

    B. What is the scope of the "cash nexus," i.e., how consistently can it be said that "everything has a price"? For what services are wages or fees ordinarily refused? If so, why?

    C. In employment and trade, are community members disproportionately preferred as workers, merchants, etc., to outsiders? What is the general attitude toward the local banker or moneylender? Does his calling evoke any general approval or disapproval? What is the local significance of such attitudes?

    D. What occupations yield high social status? Is the amount of actual or potential income a determining factor? Do certain occupations yielding low income carry high status? If so, by unspoken tradition or by direct prescription?

    E. What proportion of young people voluntarily choose the occupation of their parents? During depressions is outside help or governmental relief freely sought? Do those who accept relief lose community status? If so, in what ways?

V. Political participation

    A. Are there determinable interrelations between stable family life, friendly and neighborly connections, approved economic activities, and community leadership?

    B. Is any political party thought of as particularly respectable or the reverse? Why? By prescription, or as taken for granted?

    C. How extensive is the attendance at community political and administrative meetings?

Even those of limited social experience should be able to call to mind American societies almost poles apart in the answers returned to some such list of questions. Possum Trot in Alabama and Plainville in Missouri show a high degree of inability or unwillingness to change, and this manifestation of sacredness is primarily of folk rather than of prescribed derivation. Many other folk societies of essentially the same character are still to be found all over the world; indeed, the great majority of mankind still sociates in sacred contexts of markedly folk variety. Even in centers of rapid secularization such as New York, Chicago, and Los Angeles, folk nooks and corners abound: orthodox Jewish communities on the East Side and on Maxwell Street, Molokan "pilgrims of Russian Town," Mexican "Jalopy Parkways" in California cities, and transplanted Deep South villages in Harlem or along South Park Boulevard provide instances.[24]

Certainly the construct "folk society" as a subdivision of sacred is only one among the many tools necessary for a complete sociological kit; its use alone will not assure a finished job. Nevertheless, it serves a useful purpose in trimming away nonessentials, for recognizable shapes are thereby revealed. When we can see the rough outlines of one general context within which the family functions, we can refine our analysis considerably.

What are the principal purposes in attending? Is there a contrast between purposes as verbally stated and as unverbalized? If so, what are the reasons for the contrast?

D. Is political officeholding generally acknowledged to be an indication of high community status?

E. What proportion of those eligible to do so cast votes? Can light or heavy voting, as the case may be, be attributed to community conflicts, special-interest groups, and so on?

F. Is corruption in political office in evidence? If so, how is it defined? How regarded?

VI. Educational institutions

A. Are local schools preferred to those outside, no matter what the differing extent of "educational advantages" may be? By pupils? By parents?

B. Are the models of leadership set before school children drawn from or illustrated by community members? Do school children define "what I'd like to do when I grow up" in ways approved by the community?

C. How zealous are local school boards in making certain that teachers have "correct," i.e., community-sanctioned, attitudes? Are "local products" preferred for teaching positions? Is honorific status accorded schoolteachers?

VII. Religious sanctions

A. How wide is the scope of supernaturalistic controls? Are forms of recreation, dress, child training, etc., under specific religious sanction in the form of direct prescription?

B. Are nonchurchgoers subject to scorn, ostracism, or ridicule?

C. Are guilt-feelings manifest among those church members who do not follow the precepts of their religion? When was the last revival, retreat, novena, or similar manifestation of faith? How was it regarded by the community as a whole? Were local leaders identified with it?

D. What is the traditional attitude toward Sunday school, parochial schools, or similar types of religious education? The prescribed attitude?

E. Is old age held in special reverence? How does age-stratification in the religious organization compare with the proportion of persons in different age groupings in the community at large?

F. Is tradition of special religious significance? If so, by direct prescription, or simply as taken for granted?

[24] See the bibliography at the end of this chapter.

THE PRESCRIBED SUBDIVISION OF SACRED

Sacred societies, as already noted, have two subdivisions, and we have termed the second "prescribed." [25] The clearest examples of this are to be found where sanctioned rationality operates to the fullest extent; namely, where a definite body of dogma calls forth, sets up, or maintains a totalitarian kind of social structure. The Geneva theocracy of Calvin, the Jesuit state of Paraguay, and, by intention at least, Fascist Italy, Nazi Germany, and Soviet Russia are among the most prominent of many instances.

The sanctioned rationality marking the choice of means within these sociative networks may be placed in the service of radically differing ends. Although both the society of Geneva and the society of Paraguay were presumably devoted to the "greater glory of God," the former centered chief attention upon spiritual recognition and security, with economically individualistic ends playing a very large although at first subordinate part. In contradistinction, the society of Paraguay granted a very prominent place to spiritual response, but at the same time developed a collectivist economy stressing mutually rather than individually achieved security. How fundamentally Fascists, Nazis, and Communists have differed in their final ends is a question that might lead to hair-splitting, but it would appear that racial recognition has had little place in the Fascist and Communist mentalities.

However this may be, the basic feature of sanctioned rationality is evidenced in all the cases mentioned, for the ends forbade the use of certain means. The devout Calvinist could acquire no spiritual recognition by indiscriminate charity, for the doctrine of stewardship directly barred means of this kind.[26] The Paraguayan Jesuits resorted to force very rarely, and then only in direct need. When they did resort to it, frank acknowledgment was made of the violation of principle, and extreme penance was almost uniformly imposed.[27] Whatever else Fascists might do, no concessions could be made to economic liberalism or to parliamentarism, for corporative unity, the supreme end of mutually achieved recognition and security symbolized by the *fasces,* would thereby be basically flouted. The genuinely fanatical Nazi really did keep himself free of "racial taint," for otherwise how could he have been granted recognition by his omniscient Führer? The convinced Communist sincerely thinks that he scorns the use of "bourgeois" means for reaching the utimate goal of a classless society in which security, response, recognition, and new experience combine to fill the Marxian prescription of "From each according to his ability, to each according to his needs."

Given the highly contemporary character of the Russian illustration, it is plain that prescribed societies must not be thought of as being of interest to antiquarians only. Indeed, the fact that the element of prescription in any such society stands in the foreground should not blind the observer to the large amount of tradition which can be brought up to date, as it were, by

25 See p. 21.
26 See Max Weber, *The Protestant Ethic and the Spirit of Capitalism* (New York: Macmillan, 1930), *passim.*
27 J. S. Geer, *The Jesuit State of Paraguay* (Nürnberg: Krische, 1928), *passim.*

incorporation in a prescribed formula. The Fascists, to single out only one of our instances, made liberal use of symbols that had long been traditional; they were simply infused with new life by appropriate sanction. The same could be said of Nazi Germany; [28] and Soviet Russia in recent years has certainly done much to incorporate every presumably "dialectic" and beneficial tradition from the time of Ivan the Terrible onward into the prescribed ideology.

This is one of the chief reasons why the notion of geographic isolation makes little sense as the exclusive determinant of sacred phenomena. Of scant use even where sacred societies of traditional type are concerned, it fails utterly when confronted by the great sacred units operating under prescription in the modern world.

Vicinal isolation, however, may prove quite relevant, for restrictions on travel readily bring about situations in which near neighbors are separated as effectively as though impassable oceans lay between them.

Social isolation likewise plays its part in generating prescribed mentality. Protestants may have as little access to the real intimacies of a Catholic community as do Jews, and conversely, the term "Jesuitical" carries with it a degree of reproach, in some outspokenly Protestant communities, reminiscent of the eighteenth-century ostracism of "the man in black." [29] By isolating the sacred stranger [30] of this type from effective contact with those addicted to contrasting prescriptions, unwillingness or inability to change is maintained in full force.

Part and parcel of social isolation, in most instances, is mental isolation, and in this regard prescribed society differs not a whit from folk society. Nazi totalitarianism in its heyday promulgated the slogan "We think with our blood," with such telling effect that the logical patterns evident among large sections of the German population — and not the most fanatical alone — made it very difficult for the outsider to establish any mutually intelligible universe of discourse. Anyone properly schooled in the Soviet version of the Marxian dialectic thinks along lines which set his mentality widely apart from anything current in Western circles. Because overt acts are never taken as they stand, but are always subjected to imputation of motives,[31] the amount of suspicion and hostility which may arise among those mentally isolated by prescription would be unbelievable if evidence of societal paranoia of this kind were not all too abundant.

Prescribed societies are frequently literate; hence the peculiar reinforcement of sacred traits stemming from absence of the written word is not always at hand. Instead, reinforcement may issue from the very fact that a *limited* kind of literacy is systematically maintained. Suppression of opposing doctrine can of course take place in societies that have no books to burn,

[28] Howard Becker, *German Youth: Bond or Free* (New York: The Grove Press, 1946), chap. entitled "The Accomplishment of Perversion."

[29] Cf. the chapter entitled "The Man in Black" in George Borrow's *Lavengro*. And what of passage after passage in *The Bible in Spain?*

[30] Wiese-Becker, *op. cit.,* pp. 322–344.

[31] See my chapter, "Interpretative Sociology and Constructive Typology" in Gurvitch and Moore, eds., *Twentieth Century Sociology* (New York: Philosophical Library, 1945), esp. part I.

but literary bonfires have unquestionably helped to hold many prescribed regimes in power. Extreme measures of this sort are not always necessary, for control of press, radio, and other means of mass communication may simply drown out the opposition. In any event, the formulation of a body of doctrine and its according-to-plan inculcation by creed, catechism, sermon, speech, editorial, "news" broadcast, and the like is of the essence of control technique in a prescribed society.

Kinship in the ordinary sense plays little part in such control, but in broader meaning it may be highly significant. The "Pan" movements of every sort stress unities which, although not necessarily of racial character, rely heavily on common religion, tongue, "political destiny," or culture. The racial dogmas of the kind involved in Nazism or Nipponism of course present a clearer analogy to the sacralizing [32] effects of kinship ties. No miracle, therefore, is the intense solidarity engendered by such aids in prescribed societies.

Ways of gaining a livelihood are frequently brought within the scope of prescription by invoking the idea that a society is an organism in which the humblest cells (members) have functions necessary in the highest degree for the life of the whole.[33] The Fascists and Nazis unweariedly rang changes on this theme, and to a considerable extent succeeded in overcoming the effects of the minute division of labor.

In prescribed societies strangers are often physically in evidence to an extent far greater than in folk societies, but genuine intercommunication on an intimate plane may nevertheless be rare. Conducted tours, whether commercial or government-sponsored, usually bring the outsider into only superficial touch with the people among whom he moves.

The use of unfamiliar language may not set the stranger apart in a prescribed society, but the use of any language to voice a disapproved ideology inevitably does. Hence we might change the already-quoted maxim to read "Whoever is familiar with two *ideologies* is a rascal"; it simply does not do to quote with equal facility and relish from Adam Smith *and* Josef Stalin, or from Churchill *and* Malenkov. The wise man in a prescribed society is he who expounds orthodox doctrine with fluency and force, and quotes opponents only to refute their devilish designs. Common sense, in other words, is prescribed orthodoxy.

The bonds of locality, so powerful in sacred societies of folk variety, operate in a different way where the prescribed type is concerned. For example, there is a strong contrast between eras "when patriotism was a hearty parochial love of the native land rather than a reedy hurrah for a tinsel-bedecked, brand-new national state,"[34] and those when chauvinistic loyalty to the German nation canceled out love for Westphalia. In other words, the ties of territory are likely to be intertwined with abstractions: nation, empire, Fatherland, God's country, Worker's Homeland, or Celestial King-

[32] See footnote 39 if the meaning of this term is not self-evident.
[33] Becker and Barnes, *STFLTS*, pp. 664–692.
[34] Howard Becker, *German Youth: Bond or Free* (New York: The Grove Press, 1946), p. 86.

dom.[35] Social actions evoked by reference to such territorial abstractions may be quite as fatefully decisive for other conduct as are those linked with the relatively tiny plots of soil for which homesickness in its more specific meaning can be felt.

This sketching of the more prominent features of prescribed societies might go to much greater length, but our immediate purpose is to present only enough to provide meaningful context for the study of the family. For example, it should take little effort to see that family, marriage, and parenthood can never exist in their own right in certain prescribed societies; they must always be subservient to the larger demands of the totalitarian structure.

From what has just been said, it might be thought that prescribed societies are always exclusively dominated by traits to which, in particular, the ordinary American would strenuously object. That this tends to be the case is doubtless true, but it must never be forgotten that we as Americans accept many prescriptions as beneficial. The Declaration of Independence, the Constitution (and especially the Bill of Rights), the oath of allegiance, and the Four Freedoms all have their prescribed aspects.

Indeed, the later discussion of stable secular societies deals with the essential functions served by tradition or prescription, or both, in keeping these societies in that state of moving equilibrium which alone can be called stability in our rapidly changing world. Final, essentially unquestioned loyalties there must be if social change is not to issue in extreme social disorganization, and prescription has much to do with generating those loyalties in any modern society.

THE RISE AND COURSE OF PRESCRIPTION

At this point there may well arise the question, "How are prescribed societies generated?" as well as the closely related query, "What antecedent conditions make the emergence of prescription possible?" Fully adequate answers would of course enable us to seize the elusive master-clues of history, "to get the feel of the fur on the tail of the world," but no such adequacy is hoped for, here or elsewhere. Moreover, the few hints that can be offered here are limited by the space available, but even fragmentary hints may be better than nothing.

Prescriptions are often not much more than systematic verbalizations of tradition. Over long centuries a large stock of proverbs and similar condensations of folk wisdom having sociative bearing accumulates. This lore is eventually put into some sort of order by patient systematizers, and may even be compressed into relatively brief formulas from which, by deduction, subsidiary doctrines running more or less parallel with prevailing social actions may be derived. In other words, prescription may arise in such a way that it does little more than underscore tradition. The priestly codes of the Old Testament are instances of exactly this sort of process.

[35] Cf. Wiese-Becker, *op. cit.,* chaps. 42–45.

In other cases, however, prescriptions break like volcanic eruptions out of traditional ground that has been turned into a "shatter zone," full of faults and fissures, by powerful shocks and pressures. Again the Old Testament provides illustrations: the eighth-century prophets proclaimed their doctrines under the stress of potential or actual catastrophe. The sway of tradition had either brought on crisis or proved unable to meet it, or both, and the prophets set themselves in conscious opposition to the established society of their day. That their saving formulas partook of what has been called "reactionary radicalism" [36] is of little moment here; significant for the present analysis is the fact that they attempted to break with the prevailing traditions of their times.

Such Old Testament examples can be matched, in all essentials, by many others, not excepting dozens drawn from the modern period. In every case there will be found a streak of affective nonrationality in both leaders and followers of the new prescription, and this can usually be characterized as charismatic. Extraordinary or even "uncanny" men are often the only members of a society who can crack its traditional crust.

The answers to the questions, then, can be phrased thus: "Prescriptions may be the result either of gradual systematization or sudden charismatic reformulation of older conceptions"; and "Either societal continuity long enough to permit the rise of prescription out of tradition, or the threat of societal discontinuity issuing from crises of various kinds, is the necessary precondition."

Finally, note that the impact of affective nonrationality necessary to break the cake of custom may be so great that the only persons capable of exerting it are those who in personality makeup are of a type unable or unwilling to formulate prescriptions of clear-cut character. Adolf Hitler provides an excellent example: only as systematic interpretations were provided by Goebbels, Rosenberg, and other subsidiary prescribers was the new creed brought into forms that could be readily imparted to the rank and file. Without an array of faithful disciples who put the aphoristic utterances of the master into easily intelligible form, it would be impossible for most charismatic leaders to exert any marked effect on the masses. That is to say, affective nonrationality is ordinarily transmuted into the sanctioned rationality characteristic of prescribed societies only by undergoing formulation and systematization at the hands of persons having deductive powers, inclinations, or opportunities greater than the man initially responsible for shattering traditional restraints.

For a time it often happens that the sanctioned rationality thus brought to the fore is belligerently anti-traditional where the *old* tradition broken up by the affective eruption is concerned. Sooner or later, the sanctioned rationality of prescription calls to its aid a body of *new* tradition. Eventually the implicit or imperfectly verbalized controls of the new tradition may prove more powerful in sustaining the prescribed society than are the explicit, precisely worded doctrines and dogmas with which it began and which it continually improves and restates.

The conclusion to be drawn, for our purposes, is that prescribed societies

[36] Becker and Barnes, *STFLTS*, pp. 124, 314.

never remain merely prescribed if they continue as societies for any length of time. What may be termed a folk-prescribed type is soon generated. Surveying societies the world around, moreover, it is evident that although nowadays the greater number which can be labeled as sacred are of folk-prescribed variety, it is also evident that most examples falling into this intermediate category have more folk than prescribed components. Further, although societies of almost pure folk type are occasionally to be found, it is nearly impossible to find comparably pure examples of the prescribed. After all, however, this is only what might be expected from what we know of the way in which human personalities are elicited and molded. No society, prescribed or otherwise, ever starts from scratch.

SECULAR SOCIETY AS CONTEXT

Attention now turns to another main type of sociative network, already frequently mentioned but not yet adequately described; namely, secular society. It also subdivides into two varieties, which may be called unstable and stable, or normless and principled.

Even when discussing the kind marked by extreme instability, however, there is a certain contradiction involved in calling it a secular society, for in terms of our analysis, a *completely* secular society would not be a society at all. That is to say, secularization would ultimately result in the appearance of a heterogeneous assembly of human units having no goals in common; instead of a value-system with ends in some respects accrete,[37] there would be only a systemless mass of utterly discrete ends pursued at random.[38] So entirely secular and disorganized an aggregate has not made its appearance anywhere and, we make bold to say, will not do so. The most that can be said of any society is that it is highly secularized or is secularizing rapidly,[39] for sacred residues always remain or are regenerated in some form. Furthermore, the bonds that make a collection of mere human beings into a society — that is, into a coherent, continuing, self-perpetuative, and relatively self-contained social unit — are basically of sacred character. This means that a stable secular society could with almost equal warrant be designated as an adaptive sacred society,[40] a point of which more will be made later. As long

---

[37] Accrete, in this context the opposite of discrete, is a botanical term meaning fused or grown together. It seems permissible to borrow it for sociological purposes.

[38] Cf. Talcott Parsons, *The Structure of Social Action* (New York: McGraw-Hill, 1937), *passim*.

[39] Hence strict consistency would call for "a secularizing society" and "a sacralizing society," or "secularization" and "sacralization." The emphasis on *process* thereby resulting, moreover, would be advantageous. Incidentally, note that "sacralization" is now an anatomical term meaning the fusion of pelvic vertebrae. Witticism aside, however, it seems that it may justifiably be used in a sociological sense as well, for the *os sacrum,* the fused vertebrae forming the posterior wall of the pelvis, was a bone offered in sacrifice. In other words, the sacrum had a function in a certain kind of sacred society.

[40] Elton Mayo has long made use of an "established-adaptive" dichotomy. His established society is quite similar to sacred society of both folk and prescribed varieties, and his adaptive is much the same as what is here termed stable secular society. He does not, however, pay much attention to *unstable* secular society, and there is no real place for it in his classification.

as these and forthcoming qualifications are taken into account, however, no great harm is done by clipped terminology.

A secular society is one in which resistance to change is at a minimum or, to say the very least, where change in many aspects of life is usually quite welcome. In this special sense, "secular" is the photographic negative of "sacred," and therefore should not be taken as a mere synonym for profane, godless, or irreligious, all of which mean considerably more *and* less.[41] Briefly, societies which endow their members with a high proportion of action patterns leading to readiness to change are secular societies.

The ends most frequently pursued by such persons are chiefly classifiable under new experience, recognition, and response, with new experience, obviously enough, dominant in most instances. The means furthering such ends are primarily of expediently rational and affectively nonrational character.

SECULAR INSTABILITY

In order to make this abstract formulation reasonably concrete, let us begin by describing secular societies marked by much instability and its accompanying focus on expediency and affective appeal.

The clearest instances are to be found in centers of culture contact. These are very often sections of great cities standing at the crossroads of commerce and communication.[42] In other words, secular societies are ordinarily *accessible* — the antithesis of isolated.

This accessibility is by no means an affair of geography alone, for although sea, land, and air combine in various ways to further the antlike swarming of the metropolis, change in the technical culture may suddenly bring about accessibility where isolation previously prevailed. Iceland and air travel have already been mentioned, but for an earlier period the shift of Chicago from a remote fur-trading post to the world's greatest railway center is likewise relevant. Accessibility is largely man's making, not nature's.

Clearly, however, the neighbors round about any given people undergoing secularization must be so situated and disposed that vicinal accessibility prevails. This is tantamount to saying that highly secularized centers are almost necessarily cosmopolitan; all sorts and descriptions of people come together and succeed in communicating after a fashion. *Koiné* Greek, the *lingua franca,* pidgin English, Spaniola, "OK" American (otherwise known as Occupation English), or similar palavers flourish luxuriantly. Linguistic accessibility, as it were, comes into being.

41 In particular, secular as used here does *not* have the blameworthy meaning which most Catholics and many Protestants assign to it when speaking of "modern secularism."

42 This is of course the reason why Redfield uses "urban" as the antithesis of "folk." It must be noted, however, that certain varieties of the city show no high incidence of secularization. What of folk-prescribed cities such as Lhasa, Benares, and Mecca, or prescribed cities such as Fascist Rome, Communist Moscow, and Nazi Munich? Redfield obviously means only one type of city; namely, the highly secularized variety. This being the case, why not say secular instead of urban? Further, it is not mere pedantry to point out that rural is the correct antithesis of urban, and that some rural societies, past and present, show a low incidence of sacredness. Sacred-secular is a less ambiguous dichotomy.

Further, in a secular society the devices of communication have ordinarily advanced to the point where the roaring voice of Stentor the herald is not the only way of spanning the gap between groups. The knotted string quipu which aided in the uniting of the empire of the Incas, the Egyptian papyrus with its reed-penned symbols, the penny post, the far-writing telegraph, the telephone, the wireless dot-and-dash, voice or face — all these methods have helped in varying degree to make possible or to increase vicinal accessibility.

Moreover, they have helped to generate social accessibility, which is another trait of a markedly secular society. Where it fully prevails, there are no rigid social barriers cutting off one segment of the society from another.

The upshot is that vicinal and social accessibility come to be linked with mental. Any secular society is necessarily "open-minded." The open-mindedness may consist not only in easy-going disregard of matters once held sacred, but also in their ostentatious flouting. "Anything for a thrill" — which represents the fusion of means and ends characteristic of affective nonrationality — is often the outspokenly admitted maxim. Figuratively put, the walls of mental isolation have completely crumbled; the result is not only accessibility but also normlessness.

Secular societies, now everywhere in evidence, were quite rare in the remoter historical record, and nonexistent, it may well be assumed, among man's earlier clusters of sociation. It is for this reason, and for this alone, that secular here follows sacred, for as the discussion of prescribed societies may have shown, there is ample evidence that societies once strongly secular may be poured back into sacred molds. Recall the references to Nazi Germany; many others will readily come to mind.

Kinship, however interpreted, figures to a dwindling degree in secularizing societies; the rapid shrinking of kinship vocabularies is a consequence. Along with this goes a decline in the social control exercised by kindred, for the household shrinks to the immediate marriage group and its scanty roster of offspring. The most effective of all modes of imparting tradition — continual daily precept and example by a large number of intimately sociating tradition-bearers — no longer functions. Grandparents do not occupy a "west room" or gable end,[43] and the voice of Aunt Matilda, heard only during infrequent visits, goes unheeded. Instead of the reverent imitation of elders, ancestors, or other traditional models, there is the prairie-fire spread of style among contemporaries. "Shirt-tail out" changes to "shirt-tail in" almost over night, the switch from skirt to blue jeans and back overrides parental protest, and the Tubular Torso yields to the New Look. The social scene changes so rapidly that there are few standard situations; parts in the social drama cannot be played in traditional or sanctioned ways, and continual improvisation takes place under the sway of convenience and emotional pull. Reversing the sacred formula, a secular society has many alternatives and few universals.

The farflung range of conduct thereby made possible is strikingly evident in the modes of gaining a livelihood. Competition has wide scope even when

[43] Here reference is to Irish and German examples: see Conrad Arensberg, *The Irish Countryman* (New York: Macmillan, 1937), and Howard Becker, "Peoples of Germany," in T. C. T. McCormick, *Problems of the Postwar World* (New York: McGraw-Hill, 1945).

monopoly capitalism is well to the fore, and minute subdivision of function
is the rule. Specialties are uppermost, and the sage who incorporates all
knowledge available in his society in his single person is replaced by the library which finds its only unity in its card catalogue. Technical vocabularies
of mutually unintelligible character become a matter of course.

Moreover, although the skills necessary for economic survival presuppose
special training, technical instructors and handbooks replace the guild masters and the graybeards. The action patterns that are established do not interweave with all portions of the personality; the technical man is distinct
from the family man, the religious man, and so on, even though the same
skin holds them all. The consequence is that action patterns which are of
great importance from the standpoint of effective economic functioning, for
instance, can be changed by the person concerned without a comprehensive
change in his other conduct. To be sure, change of action patterns is difficult enough under any circumstances, but when action patterns are frac-
tional, as it were, the principle of divide and conquer can readily be applied.
The member of a secular society is therefore "set" in only some of his ways;
for the rest, he has a high degree of "freedom from"; [44] that is, a minimum
of specific social constraint. In such a society the normal personality, speaking
statistically, is unintegrated; "the left hand knows not what the right hand
doeth."

When secularization has gone a long way, the stranger becomes attractive to many persons, for the relative scarcity of over-all habits and the continual contact with new sensual values lend charm to the exotic. This is particularly true of the leisured classes in a secular society, for they lack even the
routine stabilizations of the time clock, the punch press, and the assembly
line. Instead of unwillingness or inability to respond to the new, there is frequently unwillingness or inability to *refrain* from responding to the new.
Change of scene, dress, friends, and marital partners becomes virtually
compulsive among that small proportion of a secular society which pays
the costs — or if one prefers, reaps the advantages — of ultrarapid secularization. Here again the result is normlessness in high degree.

Be it noted that the stranger is present not only in the more obvious form
described above, but that everyone is in some sense a stranger. Anonymity
is the rule: the subway patron, the taxi driver, the newsboy, and the chain
store manager are units, not names. The social control exercised by intimates
who knew one's whole family "way back when" is lacking, and Mrs.
Grundy is strangely silent.

Silent likewise is the voice of the sage; his proverbs no longer pass as
current coin. Instead, there appears the vendor of "wisecracks" — here today
and gone tomorrow. The old turns of speech drop out of use; slang replaces
them, and slang in turn occasionally yields to the studied novelty of "double-
talk." If it does not so yield, it is in any case destined to be outmoded by
still newer slang.

Another significant aspect of secular societies is the importance of the

[44] This comes from Nietzsche's aphorism: "Free *from* what? What is that to Zarathustra? Clear
shall your eye tell me, Free *to* what?"

written word. The unspoken understandings or tacit agreements, the eating of salt or the breaking of bread, the ceremonial utterance, are all replaced by the lawyer's whereases, the marriage license, the will with its witnesses and possible contestants, the passport, and the notary public's seal. The chanted ballad yields to the pulp thriller, and the long life-histories of garrulous oldsters are supplanted by the "true story" and "confession" magazines. Heroic sagas are replaced by sacred books, and these in turn by increasingly secular commentaries on sacred books.

In a secular society, the ties of locality diminish in importance; as Stephen Leacock wryly put it, "I remember, I remember the house where I was born" becomes "I wish I could remember the flat where I was born." In normal times, May 1 and October 1 are not betrothal festivals or reapers' frolics, but moving days; the landlord must redecorate "or else." The upshot of this is that the home is increasingly hotel-like in character: it is a mere secular stopping-place changed without emotional reluctance — indeed, with gratification.

Supernaturalism may be quite prevalent in a secular society, but the cults that promise the Limitless Whichness and All the Works, from eternal youth to painless dentistry, are not of *traditionally* religious reference. Affective non-rationalisms abound, but they must bear the saving label of "scientific." Genuine science of course has great power and influence, but among its practitioners few are called but many are chosen. That is to say, the prestige of science in a secular society is so great that scientific quacks flourish like the green bay tree.

Here again it would be possible to go on for a long time. Secular societies, in *our* civilization, are chiefly urban,[45] and whole libraries have been written on urban sociology. If the reader will take another look at the outline on pages 24–27, reversing the implications of many of the questions asked, he can lend more meaning to the impressionistic comments just presented.

Secular Stability Is Linked with Principle

Manifestly, what has here been said about secular societies has focused on the unstable extremes. Turning to the more stable, it can be said with some confidence that stability is directly linked with the functioning of both tradition and prescription, and that security, in particular, comes to seem an end more important than new experience. The misoneism, neophobia, or dislike of the new, which is characteristic of extremely sacred societies, may not be strongly in evidence; but the philoneism, neophilia, or liking for the new, which runs rampant in rapidly secularizing societies, is held in check.

The source of the check is always some sacred practice, precept, or principle. Democracy, to choose a highly relevant example, is self-evident only to the heirs of a transmuted Greco-Roman tradition, Christianity in certain

45 But to repeat: not all urban societies are secular, nor are all rural societies sacred. Refer to footnote 42.

versions, or the natural rights philosophy of the eighteenth century Deists [46] —
and frequently of all three together, with other sacred components thrown
in for good measure. To say this is not to challenge the validity of democracy as a form of social and political organization, for its pragmatic work-
ability may — and in the estimation of the writer does — justify most of the
arguments put forward in its behalf. It may well be possible that democracy,
as a kind of stable secular society in moving equilibrium, may sometime
reach the point where the sacred elements which called it into being and
which still sustain it will be left behind — but that point has not yet been
reached. Moreover, when it is reached for any given generation, other traditions and prescriptions will lend to the new democracy whatever stability it
may possess, for from them will be derived the essential guiding principles,
adaptable but by no means opportunistically so.[47]

In the field of family relations the same analysis seems to hold. Precisely
why a family *should* be democratically organized, with family councils entered into by co-equal husband, wife, and maturer children, is not self-
evident to persons outside the pale of modern Western European middle-
class, and perhaps, more specifically, *American* middle-class ideology.

That ideology takes for granted, among other things, the desirability of
family harmony and, by the same token, family continuity. From the standpoint of the well-being of society as a whole, there can be little doubt that
such harmony and continuity are of the highest value. But is it possible to
talk about the well-being of society *as a whole* without making a host of
unproved and as yet unprovable assumptions? [48] The married pair coming
together merely for the purpose of legalized copulation and its attendant
gratifications of response and new experience are expediently achieving these
ends, which for them are discrete, well enough. To convince them of the
desirability of rearing acceptable citizens for an on-going democracy, or active
participants in a humanitarian and essentially Christian ethic, or contributors

[46] This is the essential reason why Sorokin found it necessary to insert an "idealistic" intermediary stage between his "ideational" and "sensate" societies. In saying this, however, there
is no necessary agreement with his choice of "idealistic" periods — fifth-century Greece and
thirteenth-century Western Europe. Unless societies wholly disintegrate — and this rarely
occurs short of internal or external conquest — a set of "idealistic" factors is always operative.

[47] To talk about the possibility of an "organized secular society," therefore, is to recognize that
norms ultimately deriving from sacred sources provide the possibility of organization. Here
reference is to the article by W. L. Kolb, "The Objective Possibility of an Organized Secular
Society," *The Southwestern Journal*, 2, 3 (1946), pp. 161–169. Kolb phrases his hope for an
organized secular society in part as follows: "If . . . the persons of a secular society share
a system of relatively well-defined but flexible and non-specific norms, lawmaking becomes
an attempt to define and control changes in action patterns in the light of these ultimate
values. Recognizing that rapid change makes impossible the growth of specific tradition out
of general tradition, attempts would be made to forge a common definition of the new situation of . . . varying individual group definitions, all of which, however, share a common
orientation toward a system of ultimate norms." What Kolb is saying is that rigid, narrow,
traditional nonrationality provides no basis for stability in periods of rapid change, but that
some kinds of sanctioned rationality may. Folk societies and hardshelled prescribed societies
go under, but it is perhaps possible for societies having broad general prescriptions, plus
secular adaptability, to survive. Kolb is right.

[48] Cf. Kolb, *op. cit.*

to the lofty cultural values of music, poetry, and art, would necessitate appeal to ultimate values which are perceived only by those trained to perceive them. The family can never be grounded on a self-contained companionate providing its own inherent justification; [49] to be genuinely a family — which is to say, to be a social institution [50] — in any society there must be functional reference to a system of accrete ends transcending the merely expedient and affective. In other words, the form of the human family never rests on a purely biological basis, and all of its various forms, including the "democratic," are bound up with sacred considerations which to the social scientist are by no means self-evident. Here again there is no intention of calling into question the pragmatic warrant of the modern monogamic equalitarian family. The only purpose is the underscoring of the indispensable sacred traits of *any* normative aspect of a stable secular society — i.e., a secular society based on principle.[51]

THE NORMATIVE REACTION TO NORMLESSNESS

Highly interesting in connection with both unstable and stable varieties of secular society are the functions exhibited by affective nonrationality. In the unstable type, the fusing of new experience as end with affective nonrationality as means not infrequently reaches the point where some members will "try anything once," or "don't know where they are going but they're on their way." Such a condition of relative normlessness, however, soon becomes intensely disquieting to other members for whom future security, continuing response, and assured recognition also constitute supreme values. These other members therefore give expression to *their* affective nonrationalities in ways which simultaneously serve, although in varying degree, all four major ends. New experience as such is not sought, but rather there is an effort to achieve *new experience compatible with other goals*. Normlessness calls forth demand for norms, although in most instances this demand is vague, and sometimes may not be put into words at all.

The society of part of rural New York state, for instance, had undergone extensive secularization [52] by the time of Joseph Smith's boyhood. Freak gospels, clashing ways of life, and itinerant prophets made their disconcerting appearance even in quiet village communities. The countryside had undergone revivals so frequently that evangelists referred to it as "burnt out." Relative normlessness prevailed, and many persons longed agonizingly for a new way of life which would grant equal claim to "new" and "way of *life*."

Certainly the little cluster of followers around the charismatic Smith

---

49 As Burgess and Locke seem to imply in *The Family: From Institution to Companionship* (2nd ed., New York: American Book Co., 1953).

50 Wiese-Becker, *op. cit.*, pp. 401–407, 565–571.

51 Which, as already noted, might quite as well be called an adaptive sacred society. Cf. footnote 40.

52 In the early nineteenth century parts of New York State were still of semifrontier character. Add to this the complications of Erie Canal hell-raising, Shakerism, vociferous civil war among the sects of Protestantism, the roving of tramp printers and garrulous peddlers, the upheavals following the war of 1812, and many other occurrences, and it becomes plain that a rural society may manifest a considerable degree of secularization.

valued their new experience highly, but his teachings, in spite of their confused and fragmentary character, also provided assurance of fellowship and well-being within an on-going community of the faithful. The successive migrations which that community undertook consolidated both the Mormon hope and the Mormon determination, and the United Order finally set up in the valleys of the Rocky Mountains testified to the fact that a highly sacred society may emerge from conditions of marked secularization.

The affective nonrationality finding vent in miscellaneous cults, sects, "intellectual" fads, and passionately espoused ideologies may therefore serve both as a solvent of remaining sacred components lending a rapidly secularizing society whatever stability it still possesses, and as a precipitant of new sacred deposits around which stable structures rapidly crystallize. Normlessness, in short, tends to call forth its own antidote: "the most that can be said of any society is that it is highly secularized or is secularizing rapidly, for sacred residues always remain or are *regenerated* in some form" (page 33).

CHANGING PERSONALITIES IN A CHANGING WORLD

Time and again attention has been called to the fact that societies are woven out of social actions. A corollary of this is that social actions issue from actors whose personalities in turn are constituted by the socially assigned roles they play and the ways in which they play them. It follows, therefore, that additional light may be thrown on needs, values, means, ends, and the contexts of sociation by viewing some of the personality types relevant to a crucial phase of the total analysis and description. This phase may be limited, for present purposes, to personality types appearing in conjunction with change from primarily sacred to primarily secular society. Examples are abundant, for social and cultural anthropologists, social psychologists, and sociologists have in recent years devoted a large share of their attention to precisely these phenomena.[53]

To begin with, change from sacred to secular ordinarily takes much more than one generation, but having registered awareness of this fact we shall proceed as though in most instances only one or two generations are involved. Further, there is no intention of setting forth more than a few prominent traits of each of the type personalities, and these will be sketched merely as types, not as "real" individuals. Still further, only seven types will be presented, although it would be entirely possible to isolate several more.

Unadjusted or Amoral. First in logical order, but not necessarily in actual sequence, is the amoral or unmoral personality exemplified in many slum, trailer camp, and "defense town" children. Frequently the offspring of parents themselves rooted in tradition and prescription, these children "just ain't never had no bringin' up." The rapidity of the societal transition has been so great that their behavior follows channels that are defined poorly

[53] Cf. my article, "Processes of Secularisation," *Sociological Review* (British), 24 (April–July, and October, 1932), pp. 138–154, 266–286. See also my articles on sociology appearing in the *Encyclopaedia Britannica Yearbook* from 1941 to now, as well as in the special EB volume, *Ten Eventful Years*, 1937–1946.

if at all by the available symbolism, consequently their responses are erratic and frequently unpredictable. "Broken homes," when they have been broken early and completely enough to deprive children of adequate and socially approved formative influence on personality growth, often turn out similar products.

Such children are not disorganized or maladjusted; they are unorganized, unadjusted. Never having been properly inducted into the web of self-and-other relations peculiar to a given society or an important part thereof, it is difficult if not impossible to tell what they are likely to do next. The poorly defined needs of the moment are the only ones that govern; there is little or no power of postponement, of inhibition, and the child gyrates from one minute to the next very much on the basis of whether he happens to be hungry, sleepy, or what not, at this time or that. The amoral personality is not really a personality, for the person, strictly speaking, is capable of playing social roles consistently and hence predictably.

Maladjusted or Demoralized. The second of our types is the demoralized. Here there has been some incorporation of sacred controls, but the collapse of the old society, or the loss of its buttressing pressure through migration, tears up the props of personality. The resulting conduct is, in some cases, almost as unpredictable as that of the wild youngsters just mentioned. The bestial traits displayed by juvenile gangsters who have undergone such demoralization took place among Thomas and Znaniecki's uprooted Polish peasants carelessly thrust into the stony soil of South Chicago. The family conduct appearing among the demoralized frequently falls outside of all traditional and prescribed bounds. Incest, for instance, is a word frequently encountered in the social casework records of such areas.

Partially Adjusted or Segmental. More frequent is partial demoralization, which we may here call segmental. The person in question is held in leash in some segments of his personality by economic or military routine, let us say, but is almost wholly unchecked in other segments. The placing of various segments of conduct in watertight compartments, so characteristic of a highly secular society, of course increases the likelihood of uncontrolled segmental manifestations in some of them. When to this is added the impersonality and anonymity prevalent in big cities, often the focal point of secularization in modern life, there results a state of affairs in which "anything goes."

Societies undergoing rapid change cannot maintain an accrete value system. Ends conflict with each other, and the means to them involve contradictions so serious that personalities are sometimes saved from going to pieces altogether only by resorting to compartmentalization and its segmental accompaniments. For instance, where family life has been defined in ways which cannot be made to fit the total situation, we may encounter the gangster who is a loving husband and father when at home and a coldblooded bombthrower when acquiring the money to keep his home going.

It is probably fair to say that in a society like our own the path of least resistance, in a great many cases, is the path taken by the segmental personality. The achievement of some degree of consistency as between the varying social roles thrust upon the participant in a rapidly secularizing social world is occasionally very difficult. It requires a considerable measure of reflection, ability to focus on essentials, and sincerity with others *and* oneself — all of them capacities not automatically provided by "nature."

It is perhaps because of this difficulty in achieving personal unity that highly secularized societies are shot through with affective nonrationality of cult and "ism" type. Where tradition has lost power and sanctions wane in strength, sheer expediency comes to seem terrifyingly futile as a means of reaching the chief ends of life. As a result there is frenzied search for relief from the confusion of segmental conduct by almost any channel leading to adequate affective release, satisfying emotional outlet.

In-between Adjusted or Marginal. Fourth in our list is marginal social action. Sometimes the transition from old sacred to new secular is of such character that a few members of the old society are, as it were, "left hanging in the air." Their accent, gestures, color, diet, or other easily noticeable traits bar them from ready acceptance in the new society, and yet they have wandered so far away from the old that return is impossible. Parents may find their marginal children so unaccountably strange, for example, that living together in the same family becomes impossible.

The possessors of marginal personalities are often highly self-conscious and alert; the equivocal position in which they are placed forces them to be planful, adaptable, and reflective. They frequently resort to sheer expediency in the attainment of their ends, and among these ends recognition and security often loom large. Response in forms suitable to stable family life is often slighted, with the result that marriage either is not entered upon at all or yields satisfaction for only a short time.

If possessed of marked native ability, such marginal personalities sometimes achieve, in the battle for recognition and security, positions of considerable prominence. Moreover, they may occasionally develop charismatic traits and thereby secure mass reinforcement. Interesting, to say the least, is the fact that many of the leaders of the Nazi movement, from Hitler down, were clearly marginal.

If the marginal man is not of a type finding relief in aggressive self-assertion, but has expressive ability, he may manage to get along reasonably well in secular society. Many great poets such as Dante, Heine, Burns, Shelley, and Poe have been marginal men in one way or other. Often, of course, the marginal man is unable thus to express himself outwardly, and he therefore develops a fantasy environment of daydreams. Eventually he may retreat so far into an inner world that he cannot find his way back. His problems have been "solved" by insanity. Even when this final disaster does not come about, his marginal traits may become so firmly fixed that he could never adapt to the new society even if barriers were removed; he is then permanently marginal.

Such persons often do much to speed up social change, for their inferiority feelings demand it; they are permanent neophiliacs. There is not only inability to refrain from responding to the new, but also aggressive activity in furthering it. The permanently marginal are always among the outstanding advocates of "a new world tomorrow." Further, so far as criticism of existing conditions may bring about change at a slower rate, marginal men have played leading parts, for they are likely to be vigorous critics of both foes *and* friends. The sacred-to-secular shift is sometimes difficult to understand if the role of the marginal man is overlooked.

Uncritically Adjusted or Regulated. A fifth result of transition from sacred to secular is found in the regulated personality, of which the once famous Babbitt and the 200 per cent American offer classic examples. The regulated person so whole-heartedly abandons his own standards, and so uncritically adopts the new, that secular patterns almost at once acquire sacred significance. The regulated man has simply exchanged one set of absolutes for another, although in many cases there has been an intermediary period of demoralized or marginal character. In almost all instances, moreover, regulated conduct is also segmental. This arises from the fact that uncritical espousal of everything thought worthy or advantageous in the new secular world means that the segmental conduct which is one of its most striking features is likewise espoused. " 'When in Rome, do as the Romans do,' and do it completely, irrevocably, without doubt or hesitation" — such is the regulated man's all-sufficing credo.

Fretfully Adjusted or Decadent. The decadent personality, sixth of the types presented, manifests in well-marked form some of the more extreme consequences of secularization. In some respects similar to the demoralized personality, or even to the segmental, the decadent is even more strikingly akin to the amoral. The chief difference is that decadence as here presented is chiefly found among persons of the leisure class whose status shields them from the more immediately disastrous consequences of their erratic conduct.

Everything that was previously said about the compulsive search for variety is applicable here, and we need not expand much further. It should be pointed out, however, that unwillingness or inability to *refrain* from responding to the new not only brings feverish, hither-and-yon restlessness, but also is dogged by boredom. After all, the capacities of the human organism for response to fresh stimuli are limited, and the decadent readily grows "tired of it all." Marriage partners may be changed with Hollywood frequency, but eventually old experience can no longer be made to seem new. Children may be welcome for a time as playthings, but when they turn out to be as bent on new experience as are their parents, and to be quite as indiscriminate in their choice of expedients and affective thrills, they become too troublesome to be amusing. The plain fact is that nothing is more elusive than the bluebird of happiness if directly pursued, and a sense of baffled futility and maddening monotony overtakes its too zealous votary.

This extreme susceptibility to change frequently means that the tempo and volume of change reach a crescendo. The more one is a beneficiary of change, so to speak, the more one *must* be a beneficiary of change. The more frequent the relief from boredom by new sensual or other stimulation, the more frequent *must* be the relief from boredom. The process is never-ending, and in many of the decadent personalities encountered we find a sense of maddening monotony, a feeling of futility, and a desire to do anything rather than what one is doing at the moment. Neophilia in extreme form dominates. There is no saving routine; there is no work ethic. The result, of course, is that history is a cemetery, not of aristocracies as such, as Pareto mistakenly thought, but of decadent personality types who, in particular, are utterly unable to carry on the duties of responsible marriage and parenthood.[54]

Tight-Rope Adjusted or Liberated. Seventh and last of these personality types epitomizing, as it were, various modes and rates of the shift from sacred to secular is what may be termed the liberated. It will be recalled that in discussing stable and unstable secular societies the statement was made that the stable kind might with almost equal warrant be designated as "adaptive sacred society." This warrant issues out of the fact that stability derives from a value-system which, in its essential aspects, is devoted to ends that are in some measure accrete, fused, in harmony with each other. Members of such a society do not, figuratively speaking, jump on their horses and ride off in all directions at once; they do not pursue, where the key phases of their personalities are concerned, a chance collection of discrete ends. In important respects, but not necessarily in all respects, they are at one with themselves and their society. Any society that is not utterly totalitarian, however, makes allowance for inconsistency. If inconsistency is too strong a term, let us then say that such a society permits the pursuit of ends which would be mutually exclusive if treated as absolutes rather than as relative goals subject to considerations of balance, mutual adjustment, or the like. At bottom, this means that the liberated man is the sort of person who without serious loss of integrity more or less successfully "makes the best of both worlds."

The liberated man possesses a stout set of working principles, or even prejudices; unlike the decadent personality, he refuses to "try anything once." He is not the first by whom the new is tried, nor yet the last to lay the old aside. His key needs and values have been imparted in a sacred context of folk or prescribed variety, thus inducing refusal or reluctance to change in these crucial respects, but in these crucial respects only.

In matters which the liberated man regards as nonessential, change may not only be welcomed but actually sought for eagerly. Basic family relations, friendship and intimacy, community life, religion, and even politics may all be tinged with conservatism, but at the same time ways of getting a living, of dealing with nature, of conducting affairs with outsiders, may be marked by readiness to accept or bring about innovation. The new as such is not esteemed under any and all circumstances, but neither is it always scorned. Neophobia and neophilia balance each other, so to speak, which is one reason why the liberated personality has elsewhere been termed "the tight-rope walker adjusted."

The rapid transition from one value-system to another frequently brings with it, as William James and Teggart have pointed out, the release of latent or potential energies previously held in check. This release may accelerate the disorganizing tendencies which sudden change always calls forth, with

---

[54] P. A. Sorokin, *Social Mobility* (New York: Harper, 1927), chaps. 21, 22, has some interesting remarks on decadent personality types. So also has Niles Carpenter, *The Sociology of City Life* (New York: Longmans, Green, 1931), chaps. 6–10, 13, 14.

resulting demoralization, but if the new value-system is more complex and/or adequate to the total situation than was the old, there may be genuine liberation in the sense of a surge of creative power. Accordingly, Thomas and Znaniecki's description and analysis of "the creative man" in most respects coincides with the present treatment of the liberated personality type.

A point of much importance with regard to liberation is that the flood of energy is at least partially held within channels leading to the higher levels of achievement of secular society. The channels are rarely those of expediency alone, although certainly success in the modern world demands due heed to expediency. Beyond this, however, there must ordinarily come about a broadening of traditional or sanctioned channels which permits the use of the released energies in directions not deviating greatly from those first followed.

The result is that the liberated man, unlike the marginal, is more or less in accord with the new secular world. The marginal man either withdraws from a social reality too much in conflict with the ends to which he is devoted, or else attempts to overcome it by expediency or shatter it by revolt. The liberated man, in contrast, is likely to follow a policy making full use of the opportunities existing in secular society for the attainment of his ends, or at the most to propose only modification of that society. The marginal man is inclined to be idealistically aloof, cynical, or revolutionary. The liberated man, although not necessarily lacking in idealism, works with what he has at hand, has confidence in the worthwhileness of his own efforts, and is an advocate of gradual change or, at the very least, does not engage in revolution for revolution's own sweet sake. His principles call for *orderly* liberation.

It sometimes happens, of course, that liberation is a temporary matter. Adaptation to the new society may be so complete that the energies of release are soon dammed up again, and a variety of regulated man makes his appearance, the type called the Philistine by Thomas and Znaniecki.

In those cases, however, where a balance between release and the reorganization of personality within a secular framework is achieved, the new equilibrium is dynamic, and the liberated man remains liberated. Such persons have acquired a value-system which is flexible without sacrificing supreme ends of essentially sacred character. In other words, they have become mentally accessible and mobile without falling prey to normlessness; they have met the crisis which a shift from the rigidly sacred to the secular always generates without becoming permanently disorganized.

It should be pointed out, however, that in the contemporary world, liberated men are not, typically speaking, likely to be great creative geniuses in the field of expression. Poetry, music, drama, the fine arts, and other manifestations of the expressive culture are at present judged great only when they are the product of inner struggle. The marginal man or even the segmental man is therefore more likely to be expressively successful in modern secular society than is the liberated man. The latter, on the other hand, is better fitted to undergo the discipline of science, or even to be a secular "man of action," than is the marginal man or any of the other types. The reason for this seems to be that such pursuits demand personalities that are considerably individualized and mentally mobile, but that are not so extremely mobile in their affective aspects as are those suited to the directly expressive arts.

The liberated man is in a state of moving balance on a tightrope twisted out of both sacred and secular strands. The other personality types have not effected the combination of sacred and secular — a combination which requires skill, good luck, and sustained effort. Apart from a few ventures, past and present, in liberal education, there has been no planned production of liberated men. This is not at all surprising, for there is little knowledge of how to produce them and little genuine demand for their production. Moreover, it is extremely difficult even to discuss liberation, for most of us like to fancy ourselves liberated. *We* never have blind prejudices, but only firm principles, and *we* never either stubbornly resist or carelessly welcome change, for *we* are always eminently reasonable and intelligently adaptable.

Nevertheless, it seems clear that the liberated man is not entirely a product of the imagination, even though the examples which can be found in real life usually have some marginal, segmental, regulated, and even decadent or demoralized traits as well. The fact that an element is rarely if ever found in nature except in mixture with other elements does not mean that it cannot be isolated by proper analysis.

The upshot of these considerations seems to be that the really Good Life, in any day and generation, cannot be lived without a Good Society and the Good Personalities intertwined with it.

RETROSPECT AND PROSPECT

We now have before us some rough indications of the ways in which human needs and values grow and intertwine, of the development of genuinely human conduct in and through sociation, of the means and ends of sociative endeavor, of the main contexts within which this endeavor may run its course, and of the kinds of personality that produce and are produced by the transition from sacred to secular. Let it again be noted that the path from one polar societal type to the other is not a one-way street; all around us can be seen evidence of the fact that societies, even "modern" societies, can journey from secular to sacred. Historical priority and ease of exposition and illustration alone have governed our choice of the sacred-to-secular route; we are not advocating such a route, much less drawing it on the social map as a philosophy of history.

With our universe of discourse thus established, we can now turn to the various chapters of our text with some hope of seeing the forest as well as the trees. The polar types constructed here will not be explicitly mentioned with any great frequency from this point on, but between them a great many of the topics dealt with will nevertheless oscillate. Rarely, however, will the pendulum reach the extremes of ultra-sacralization or ultra-secularization. To change the figure: most family affairs in most parts of the world now significant for us represent a mixture of the contrasting kinds of sociation, and our fellow contributors to this symposium are well aware of that fact.

Nevertheless, they have carried on their analyses within much the same frame of reference, for they know that little can be done with a mixture unless there is some knowledge of what its different ingredients are.

Moreover, the succeeding chapters are also oriented toward the study of what the family does — i.e., what its functions are — in a world that has been shifting back and forth between sacred and secular for a long time. These functions, in the American sociological tradition, are commonly held to be seven: (1) reproduction of population; (2) protection and care of the child; (3) economic production of family goods and services; (4) socialization of the child; (5) education of the child; (6) recreation; and (7) affectional interaction. If the student in reading the text will perpetually ask himself this question: "What are the differences in the way each of these functions is carried on when a society is sacralizing and when it is secularizing?" he will have done much to organize his thinking about the family in a lastingly useful way.

In the chapter on the future of the family the seven functions above listed are surveyed with special reference to the conclusions about them that can justifiably be drawn from the preceding portions of the text. Before that chapter is reached, however, the student should have made up his own mind about the problems raised and, it is to be hoped, will also have decided what he intends to do about them as they affect him personally. Science speaks in the declarative mode, not in the optative or imperative. It relieves no one of the responsibility of running his own life. If he shirks that responsibility, life will run him.

SELECTED READINGS

ARENSBERG, CONRAD M., *The Irish Countryman* (New York: Macmillan, 1937).

——, and KIMBALL, SOLON T., *Family and Community in Ireland* (Cambridge: Harvard University Press, 1940).

BECKER, HOWARD, *German Youth: Bond or Free* (New York: The Grove Press, 1946), chaps. 1, 4.

——, "Processes of Secularisation," *Sociological Review* (British), 24 (April–July, and October 1932), pp. 138–154; 266–286.

——, *Through Values to Social Interpretation* (Durham, N. C.: Duke University Press, 1950), chaps. 4 and 5.

BECKER, HOWARD, and BARNES, HARRY ELMER, *Social Thought from Lore to Science* (2nd ed., Washington, D. C.: Harren Press, 1952), Vol. I, chap. 1, and notes.

CARPENTER, NILES, *The Sociology of City Life* (New York: Longmans, Green, 1931), chaps. 6–10, 13, 14.

LEONARD, OLEN, and LOOMIS, C. P., *Culture of a Contemporary Rural Community: El Cerrito, New Mexico* (Washington, D. C.: U.S. Department of Agriculture, Rural Life Studies, I, November 1941).

MINER, HORACE, *St. Denis: A French-Canadian Parish* (Chicago: University of Chicago Press, 1939).

MUNCH, PETER, "Cultural Contacts in an Isolated Community: Tristan da Cunha," *American Journal of Sociology*, 53, 1 (July 1947), pp. 1–8.

REDFIELD, ROBERT, *The Folk Culture of Yucatan* (Chicago: University of Chicago Press, 1941).

——, *The Primitive World and Its Transformations* (Ithaca, N. Y.: Cornell University Press, 1953).

RUBIN, MORTON, *Plantation County* (Chapel Hill, N. C.: University of North Carolina Press, 1952).

SANDERS, IRWIN T., *A Balkan Village* (Lexington, Ky.: University of Kentucky Press, 1949).

SOROKIN, P. A., *Social Mobility* (New York: Harper, 1927), esp. chaps. 21 and 22.

——, ZIMMERMAN, C. C., and GALPIN, C. J., eds., *A Systematic Source Book in Rural Sociology* (3 vols.; Minneapolis: University of Minnesota Press, 1930), Vol. I, Readings 11–13, 18, 25, 35, 38, 39, 41–51, 68; Vol. II, Readings 83, 86, 91, 113, 117, 119, 122.

WEST, JAMES, *Plainville, USA* (New York: Columbia University Press, 1946).

TOPICS FOR DISCUSSION OR REPORTS

1. Describe and analyze some American folk society, such as that found in the remoter Appalachians. What is the proportion of sacred and secular traits?

2. Read a standard text on urban sociology. Show how, if at all, it increases your knowledge of secularizing processes.

3. "Primitive" societies, peasant societies, and similar sociative units are tremendously diverse in many of their features. What justification, if any, is there for putting such societies toward the sacred pole of a sacred-secular scale?

4. Study some society of heavily prescribed character, and ask these questions, among others: "To what extent do the prescriptions in force derive from folk traditions? From other traditions? From prior prescriptions inside and outside the society?"

5. Read John Dewey's *Human Nature and Conduct* (New York: Holt, 1922) and other similar treatments of habit. Do they provide any basis for the assumption that habits, in Dewey's sense, may be closely linked with standards, norms, and like value-formulations? To what extent are traditions habits? Are *all* habits of potentially sacred character? How does habit as defined in the text differ from the Dewey usage?

6. Read P. A. Sorokin's discussion of the effects of mobility in chapters 21 and 22 of his *Social Mobility* (New York: Harper, 1927). What corroborative or contradictory evidence from your own experience can you add?

7. Try to find a good example of a stabilized or stabilizing secular society. What are the sources of the norms, etc., to which stabilizing influence can justifiably be attributed? Can you state these norms as general principles?

8. Collect information about the "wild boys" of post World War I in Russia, waifs and strays resulting from the Spanish Civil War, children of wandering families in the Dust Bowl migrations of the 1930's, refugee and DP youngsters after World War II, or child migrants in Korea. What personality types can you distinguish?

9. Discuss the nature of constructed types, using chapter 2 of Becker, *Through*

Values to Social Interpretation (Durham, N. C.: Duke University Press, 1950), as a point of departure. Relate the discussion to the types set forth in the present text.

10. Compare the treatment of means and ends in this chapter with related treatments in Talcott Parsons, *The Structure of Social Action* (New York: McGraw-Hill, 1937), and Florian Znaniecki, *Social Actions* (New York: Farrar and Rinehart, 1936).

11. Taking Willard Waller's *The Old Love and the New: Divorce and Readjustment* (New York: Liveright, 1930) as a starting-point (particularly chapter 4, "Why the Bohemian Adjustment Is Unsatisfactory"), describe the emergence of demoralized, segmental, marginal, regulated, and liberated personality types among the divorced.

12. Survey a number of contemporary novels and short stories with the purpose of discovering and analyzing the decadent personality types therein depicted. Useful authors are Fitzgerald, Hemingway, Faulkner, *et al.*

13. Try to use the five sets of "pattern variables" in Talcott Parsons, *The Social System* (Glencoe, Ill.: Free Press, 1951), in the analysis of values affecting the family. What predictive utility do these variables have?

14. How can "the shift from sacred to secular" be related to the sociological analysis of social control and of social change?

15. Show how J. H. S. Bossard and Elinor H. Boll's *Ritual in Family Living* (Philadelphia: University of Pennsylvania Press, 1950) relates to the discussion of family sacralization in Becker and Hill, *Marriage and the Family* (Boston: Heath, 1942), pp. 110–111.

Chapter Two

The Variety of the Human Family*

DON MARTINDALE

MAN as organism is first and last a living thing. Man and the microbe that may bring his death are only very distant relatives, but the same stuff of life is in both. With the monkey in the zoo, the alley cat, the rat, the flea, the microbe, man shares the distinguishing characteristics of all life: the capacity to take nourishment, to grow, to adapt to the physical environment, to reproduce. Among his closer relatives in the animal world, man numbers the gorilla, the chimpanzee, the old-world monkey. Even the fine points of his genealogy have been traced with fair exactness.[1]

The human family is built about the very things man shares with all life: food, growth (of the young), adaptation (of young and old), reproduction. It was inevitable that when man came to probe into the mystery of his lost origins he should search the biological world for clues.

In tracing the evolution of his hand, his upright posture, the arrangement of his shoulders, man has had a high degree of success. Even the differences between the human races have been explained as minor variations of a single animal species.[2] Can he do the same for the family? To phrase the question differently: Is there a protohuman family out of which the wide variety of contemporary forms have arisen? If there is, many of the doors closed to the sociologist will open as if by a master key.

The Search for the Protohuman Family

The search for a protohuman family would seem, reasonably enough, to begin with man's nearest relatives. But students have by no means stopped here. In the call of a bird, the trill of a frog, the curious dance of a salamander, they have found "courtship" patterns. In the dam of a beaver, the burrow of a prairie dog, the nest of a bird, they have discovered "home building." In the protection of its cubs by a mother wolf, the hatching of the eggs and feeding of its young by a mother bird, they have discerned analogies to the education of human children. Some thinkers, in fact, carry the search for clues back to the "social" insects: the ants and the bees.

---

* It is suggested by the editors that the instructor weigh carefully the advisability of having the student read this chapter *first* and Chapter One *second*. Pedagogically there are some advantages in having the concrete thus precede the abstract.

[1] Man belongs to the order of *Primates*, which is divided into three suborders: the *Lemuroidea, Tarsoidea,* and *Anthropoidea.* He belongs to the family *Hominidea* of which *Homo sapiens* is the single extant representative. For a sketch of the biological evolution of man see William Howells, *Mankind So Far* (New York: Doubleday, 1945).

[2] Howells, *op. cit.,* chap. 24.

The search for a protohuman family is far more difficult, however, than the search for a protohuman animal form. The animal form, at least, is an immediately tangible thing of flesh and blood or, at the very least, of fossil remains. A family, by contrast, is the result of a series of actions between the persons composing the group. It is an organized action *pattern,* and such patterns are not turned up by the spade of the archaeologist.

For analytic purposes two major types [3] of behavior may be distinguished. Behavior is *instinctive* [4] when it is directed toward fixed goals, when these goals or objects are biologically determined, and when the behavior pattern is hereditarily transmissible. The migration of birds south in the fall of the year, the return of the spawning salmon to fresh-water streams, the spontaneous croak of a frog in the spring, are examples of instinctive behavior.

By contrast, behavior is *noninstinctive* when it is undefined as to goal, when it is conditioned, in whole or in part, by other than biological factors in its execution, and when it must be learned. Though only a small part of noninstinctive behavior is "conscious" or "rational," rational action is the most extreme antithesis of instinctive behavior. The man who goes on a vacation has little in common with the migrating bird or spawning salmon. He chooses among possible vacation spots; he calculates his resources; he adjusts his stay to his time and general interests; and at the last moment his wife may change her mind. Without a road map he might get hopelessly lost in a way the migrating bird or spawning salmon never could. Similarly, a family resting on an instinctual basis will be objectively fixed, biologically structured, and hereditary; a family resting on a noninstinctual basis will be variable in pattern and subject to a range of adjustment in which accident and learning play significant parts.

The search for clues to a protohuman family may now be phrased in more exact terms. It is a search for a central core of instinctive actions — for a rough series of generalized drives. Furthermore, total behavior patterns of man and animal must be compared. Isolated similarities may be quite misleading. The "promiscuity" of a wren, the "homosexuality" of a pair of male chimpanzees in the absence of females, may bear little resemblance to comparable practices among men. The assumption that they are "natural" because they are found both among animals and men may be irrelevant.

---

[3] For the utility of "type constructs" in social science see Howard Becker, "Interpretative Sociology and Constructive Typology," in *Twentieth Century Sociology,* edited by Georges Gurvitch and Wilbert E. Moore (New York: The Philosophical Library, 1945), and also his "Constructive Typology in the Social Sciences," *Contemporary Social Theory,* edited by H. E. Barnes, Howard Becker, and Frances Bennett Becker (New York: Appleton-Century, 1940), pp. 17–46, or his *Through Values to Social Interpretation* (Durham: Duke University Press, 1950), chap. 2 and pp. 189–247.

[4] The term "instinct" has been one of the most ambiguous in the literature of psychology and social psychology. Here the term is restricted to behavior that takes a special form about fixed classes of objects. A vague tendency, an undefined drive, a general need or urge is *not* an instinct.

INSECT SOCIETIES

The societies of the so-called "social" insects show a marvelous internal division of labor. A beehive, for example, is organized about the activities of the queen bee. The drones, once they have served the purpose of supplying spermatozoa for the eggs, are useless and usually die off in winter when food is scanty. The multiple activities of the hive, the construction of the intricate "cells," gathering the honey, the secretion of wax, guarding the hive, even the feeding of a special food that turns larvae that would otherwise be sterile workers into queens — all these are done by the workers. The hive functions as a communally guarded storehouse, nursery, and honey factory.[5] This community, however, organized with a completeness that would arouse the envy of the most absolute dictator, is only in external form in any way comparable to human society. Human society, too, has a division of labor and an integration of many activities into a working whole, but there the similarity ends. Before it is even grown, the larva is determined to be a worker or a queen by its diet. The physical structure that leads to the construction of the hive does not have to be learned — it is transmitted by the germ plasm of the insect. Instinctive behavior *par excellence!*

BIRD FAMILIES

The activities of birds toward their young sometimes seem to display a rather amazing intelligence. The bush turkey of the Solomons, for example, lays its eggs in heaps of vegetable matter and sand. The heat from the rotting vegetation serves to incubate the eggs. The blunt end of the egg points upward; the feathers of the fledgling point backward; and when the chick hatches, every move serves to force it up and out of its natural incubator.[6] The bush turkey appears to have solved the problem of hatching its eggs without undergoing the inconvenience of sitting on the nest. Again, the robin seems to display real skill with her sculptured nest; the oriole appears to be a first-rate weaver when she contrives her silken bag on a swaying bough. And the naive hunter is amazed when he finds himself deceived by the pretended disability of a mother partridge as she lures him away from her young. All these things are so ingenious as to seem not only intelligent but also consciously planned.

These actions, however, are uninspired by awareness or conscious intention. While there is great variation between the various species of birds with respect to ways of mating, nest building, egg hatching, or feeding, the behavior of any one species is biologically fixed. The fledgling hatched in an incubator and reared under artificial conditions reproduces the exact details of the life of its forest parents. Skills do not need to be learned but emerge

[5] H. G. Wells, Julian S. Huxley, and C. P. Wells, *The Science of Life* (New York: Literary Guild, 1929), pp. 1162–1199.
[6] *Ibid.*, p. 1225.

complete with maturation. Sexual receptivity is periodic, appearing as the result of seasonal changes in the physiological processes of the bird.[7] The sequence of activities that constitutes the family arises automatically without learning. A sparrow does not learn new techniques from the nest of a robin; a crow is never tempted to append its nest like the oriole to the swaying branch-tips of a tree.

In the bird there is far greater latitude for accident and variation than is found among the "social" insects. There is, too, a surplus of energy that is expressed in play. Still, the fundamental behavior pattern involved in the family activities of the bird is biologically fixed and hereditary. It is definitely of the instinctive type.

MAMMAL FAMILIES

In contrast to the birds, mammals show a tremendous increase in capacity for learning. Beyond instinctive ways of behavior new "learned" patterns, habits, appear. Yet little can be gained from the study of the dam of a beaver, the tunnel of a prairie dog, the den of a mountain lion or fox. Sexual activity is in most cases confined to a special season. The inception of physiological changes in the mammal serves as a trigger mechanism to set off a chain of responses in which each response is linked to the preceding one in an invariable sequence. The peculiar house, hutch, den, or shelter is biologically determined in the species.

Interesting differences marking them off from other forms are nevertheless displayed by mammals. The period of gestation becomes longer. The time required for maturation is greater. There are fewer young, and this permits more "individual" attention. The latitude for individual variation on inherited behavior almost imperceptibly widens. And finally, learning, in the form of individual adjustment, learned responses, habits, can be discovered.[8]

PRIMATE FAMILIES OTHER THAN HUMAN

The chief characteristic of the primate order is its simplicity and "generalization," or lack of specialization (that is, the animal is not limited to one purpose, as may be seen by comparing the hand to a hoof, a paddle, a claw). Most of the order lives in trees, and the whole of the order has characteristics resulting from life in trees, including upright posture and the tendency toward a generalized hand with a refined development of the power of grasp. Generalization is apparent, too, in the fact that mating is not restricted to a limited period, but occurs in monthly cycles throughout the year.[9] Above all, the further one moves up the scale of primate complexity the larger the brain capacity.[10] Again, the period of complete de-

[7] *Ibid.*, p. 1231.
[8] *Ibid.*, pp. 1239–1252.
[9] For a complete list of primate characteristics see Howells, *op. cit.*, pp. 44–93.
[10] For a tabulated listing of primate brain measurements see Robert M. Yerkes and Ada W. Yerkes, *The Great Apes* (New Haven: Yale University Press, 1934), p. 478.

pendency on the mother is increasingly lengthened. The lemur is completely dependent for a few days, the monkey for a matter of weeks, the ape from three to six months, man a year; maturity is attained by the lemur in a year, by a monkey in from two to three years, by an ape in eight to twelve years, and by man in from twelve to fourteen years.[11]

From the lack of specialization of the primate order consequences of great significance to family patterns follow. It becomes inaccurate to speak of a *sex instinct*. Sex urge or drive would be better, for sexual activity is possible almost continuously throughout the year. As might be expected, the primates display an amazing amount of general sexual play.[12]

Both the male and the female primate are always to some degree in a sexually excitable condition, and the stimuli that can release their sexual responses are enormously varied. Any member of the social group, old or young, will stimulate sexual responses in another. A monkey will, as Hamilton has shown, also attempt to use kittens, puppies, foxes, and even snakes as sexual objects.[13] Sexual interest, in fact, seems to be one of the major bases, if not the most important basis, of more or less permanent male-female relationship.[14] The long period of dependency serves to bind parents and young together for a longer period.

Even the briefest survey reveals the wide diversity of family organization among the primates. The howler monkey studied by Carpenter in Panama[15] lives in groups of from four to thirty animals, occupying jungle areas with which they are identified by a process of mutual avoidance. The adult males act as defenders and protectors of the group as a whole, sometimes intervening in quarrels between the young, leading the monkey band on their noisy treks through the jungle. Other than such rough dominance by males there is no distinct organization in the howler bands; there are no distinct families. Copulation with the females during receptive periods is continuous and indiscriminate; the howler is genuinely promiscuous.

Quite another picture is afforded by the baboon. In Zuckerman's study, it was observed that the dominant males tended to build up harems which they defended to the death. At times when the proportions of males to females were roughly equal and when the males were of equal strength, a situation approaching monogamy appeared. Ordinarily, however, the dominant males gathered about them as many females as they could effectively defend. Thus the total family group consisted of the male overlord, his females and their young, and one or more bachelors which attached themselves to the family group.[16] The bachelors, in spite of an air of superb in-

---

[11] For a tabulated listing of primate brain measurements see Robert M. Yerkes and Ada W. Yerkes, *The Great Apes* (New Haven: Yale University Press, 1934), p. 568.

[12] S. Zuckerman, *The Social Life of Monkeys and Apes* (New York: Harcourt, Brace, 1932), p. 238.

[13] *Ibid.*, p. 238.

[14] *Ibid.*, p. 213.

[15] C. Ray Carpenter, "A Field Study of the Behavior and Social Relations of Howling Monkeys (*Allouatta palliata*)," *Comparative Psychology Monographs*, 10 (1934), pp. 1–68.

[16] Zuckerman, *op. cit.*, p. 227.

difference, seemed to join the groups out of general sexual interest and were not always disappointed.[17]

In his native habitat the baboon does not seem to be as territorially bound as the howler monkey. During the day the large bands split up into solitary individuals or family groups and forage in the fields and plantations: by night they assemble in bands to sleep on the cliffs.

The gibbon of Siam [18] is monogamous, displaying a different family pattern. Groups ranging from two to six live within and defend areas of the forest. Gestation takes about seven months, during which copulation continues uninterruptedly. Infancy is prolonged; the infant gibbon is seldom out of contact with its mother for the first six weeks. The adult male's role seems to be primarily protective, and he may even intervene in intergroup quarrels. The young gibbons, brother and sister, intermate; sometimes a young male may even replace the father as sexual partner of the mother.

In his African setting, the chimpanzee is gregarious and nomadic. "Individuals are associated in groups of two to a score, in which there ordinarily appear an adult male, one or more adult females, and a varying number of individuals between infancy and adolescence." [19] Food and shelter are readily available and the groups rove about building individual nests each night and living off the fruits of the jungle. Both monogamous and polygynous families occur, with polygynous patterns appearing more frequently. The remoteness of the areas and the shyness of the creatures have prevented systematic observation of the relative permanence of such families. The family life of the gorilla is roughly equivalent to that of the chimpanzee.[20]

In summary, the primates other than man are confined to tropical areas where food is plentiful. They live on fruits, berries, grubs, and vegetable matter, evidently without using special food-gathering techniques. There is, furthermore, at present no way of judging whether the territorial bands or groups of apes are instinctive or habitual, though the presence of a "territorial" instinct in birds has been proved.[21] The closest approach to shelter or house building among the apes is the crude "nest" built by chimpanzees and gorillas.[22] Perhaps more significant is the fact that the crude sleeping platforms of the chimpanzee are built for a single night, fitting into no permanent house pattern; the young sometimes build them in play. There is a decided difference between the various apes in the amount of time spent in the trees. The gibbon spends a majority of its time in arboreal activities; the chimpanzee spends about half its time in the trees; the gorilla

---

[17] *Ibid.*, pp. 226–229.

[18] C. Ray Carpenter, "A Field Study in Siam of the Behavior and Social Relations of the Gibbon (*Hylobates lar*)," *Comparative Psychology Monographs*, 16 (1940), pp. 1–212. See also Yerkes and Yerkes, *op. cit.*, pp. 47–110.

[19] Robert M. Yerkes, *Chimpanzees* (New Haven: Yale University Press, 1943), p. 40.

[20] Yerkes and Yerkes, *op. cit.*, pp. 195–561; see also H. C. Bingham, "Gorillas in a Native Habitat," *Carnegie Institution of Washington Publications*, 426 (1932); also H. W. Nissen, "A Field Study of the Chimpanzee," *Comparative Psychology Monographs*, 8, 1 (1931).

[21] Wells, *op. cit.*, p. 1007. Carpenter, however, has done a great deal to demonstrate gibbon territoriality. See *op. cit.*

[22] Yerkes and Yerkes, *op. cit.*, pp. 222–228.

is at best a clumsy acrobat. The gorilla, however, can stand erect and walk bipedally far more easily than the chimpanzee or orangutan.

Of more interest are the "psychic" characteristics of the apes. The chimpanzee shows a definite fondness for rhythmic bodily movements and sometimes performs crude dances. While the gorilla has not been observed to dance, rhythmic pounding and beating is common. All the apes are gregarious and more seem to prefer group life, although as an ape grows older he is frequently solitary. Yerkes quotes Kohler with approval: "A chimpanzee kept in solitude is not a real chimpanzee at all."[23] Rudimentary leadership based on size and strength appears in all the apes. The group is usually dominated by a male. While gibbons are found normally in single families, groups of families are found among both chimpanzee and gorilla. Finally, there seem to be distinct temperamental differences among the apes. The gibbon appears shy, timid, gentle, good-natured, easily stirred to emotional response, quick to express resentment or anger; the chimpanzee is active, excitable, impulsive, and buoyant, with intense emotional responses — temper tantrums are not unusual; the gorilla appears calm, deliberate, reserved, seems to repress or inhibit emotional response, and is on the whole brooding and moody.[24]

Yerkes and Yerkes note[25] that the term "instinct" seldom occurs in the literature concerning the chimpanzee. It does, in fact, tend to vanish from the literature concerning all the primates other than that about man. In place of biologically inherited instincts the monkey and, more particularly, the ape tend to inherit less specialized drives or tendencies. One result of this is the formation of varying sized groups, another the multiple forms of sexual play. Most marked of all is the amount of learning, sociability, and emotional response. Family types range from promiscuous to monogamous. There is, however, no indication that any one kind of primate "employs" more than one kind of family form except where celibacy is forced on "bachelor" baboons, or monogamy results from an under-supply of females, or physical dominance leads to varying degrees of subordination.

The Human Family

The most general survey of the characteristics of the human family indicates how far it has departed from a set of instinctively fixed actions.

Man lives under every variety of climatic condition from tropic to desert and from desert to pole. He does not simply accept his environment but has positive and even aggressive attitudes toward it. He molds it to suit his needs. His house may be built out of skins, snow, bark, wood, stone, grass, mud, steel, or glass. He secures his own food supply through cultivation. He utilizes an amazing array of implements and instruments. Man's social life, too, is amazingly complex — sexual, political, economic, and many other elements are compounded in ways that rarely are twice the same.

[23] Yerkes and Yerkes, *op. cit.*, p. 45.
[24] See *ibid.*, pp. 552–561, for a tabular comparison of the great apes.
[25] *Ibid.*, p. 236.

If instinctive and noninstinctive behavior patterns are thought of as polar types,[26] the families traced fall on a scale. While insect societies represent an extreme case of instinctive social grouping, the families of human beings

TABLE I

A Tabular Comparison of Biological Families

FAMILY	COMPONENTS OF THE FAMILY				
	SEXUAL BASIS	SOCIAL* GROUPING	SOCIAL DOMINANCE	ECONOMIC† STATUS	BEHAVIOR‡ PATTERNS
Insects	None after fertilization has occurred	Bee hive or ant hill	Ant Warriors	Communal economy	Instinctive
Birds	Temporary mates during mating season	Nest	Pecking order	——	Instinctive
Mammals	Mating promiscuous during rutting period	Herds, Packs, and Pairs	Strongest mammal	——	Instinctive Some learning manifest
Howler Monkey	Promiscuous	Unorganized bands	Dominant males	No communal solution	Largely instinctive
Baboon	Polygynous	Groups of families	Dominant males	No communal solution	Instinctive Some learning
Gibbon	Monogamous	Single family group	Strongest ape, usually male	No communal solution	Instinctive Some learning
Chimpanzee	Monogamous	Single family group	Strongest ape, usually male	No communal solution	Instinctive Some learning
Gorilla	Monogamous	Single family group	Strongest ape, usually male	No communal solution	Instinctive Some learning

* Nothing comparable to a consanguinal family is apparent.
† Except in the case of the insects, a few birds, and mammals, nothing approaching a pure communal solution to economic problems can be discerned.
‡ No definitive study of instinct has been made among apes. A certain amount of crude education is discernible.

represent an extreme case of noninstinctive social grouping. It is noteworthy that as the role of instinct in behavior diminishes there is increased scope for generalized drives, needs, or tendencies which not only permit but require individual adaptation and the increased application of intelligence. For

[26] The concepts "instinctive behavior" and "noninstinctive behavior," as used here, are deliberately constructed one-dimensional types. See Howard Becker and Robert C. Myers, "Sacred and Secular Aspects of Human Sociation," *Sociometry,* 4 (Aug., 1942), 5 (Nov., 1942), pp. 207–229, 355–370.

a fixed problem with a single unlearned solution, there appear general problems capable of many solutions.

The search for a biological prototype of the human family, for a core of purely instinctive modes of behavior, has failed. The explanation of the human family has to be found in the nature of noninstinctive behavior patterns.

THEORIES OF FAMILY ORIGINS

To say that the search for a protohuman family has hitherto failed does not mean that the human family had no "origins"; it had to begin sometime, somehow. Moreover, it is clear that the human family took its various forms step by step with the emergence of noninstinctive behavior. This does not mean of course that the family is in any way "unnatural." Noninstinctive behavior is as "natural" as instinctive behavior.

Since it is so vital to an understanding of the family, noninstinctive behavior deserves closer analysis. It has been shown to be based on generalized drives. Furthermore, an area of indeterminateness surrounds the action. Within this indeterminate area a variety of equally effective adjustments is possible. The most crucial question that can be asked with reference to noninstinctive behavior is, "Why, when many actions were possible, did this particular one occur?"

In the ape it was noted that "instincts" had largely vanished and in place of these were general needs, which were satisfied in a rough hit-or-miss fashion. The nest of a chimpanzee was extremely crude by comparison with the beehive. But no infant bee ever demonstrates the virtuosity of a young chimpanzee who constructs a crude counterpart of the nest in play. The chimpanzee's nest affords significant insight into the nature of noninstinctive behavior. Without fixed instincts to predispose him to a single invariable chain of responses, his actions become not responses at all but solutions of problems. The limiting conditions of the action are found in the satisfaction of the need in terms of the plasticity of the environment. The plasticity of the environment, in turn, must be interpreted in terms of the intelligence of the animal. The general needs of the ape are easily satisfied in a propitious environment; hence his solutions are quite crude and do not indicate any *extended* intelligent application — but intelligent they are.

The essential characteristic of noninstinctive behavior is found in the amount of intelligence [27] involved in the given case. Types of noninstinctive behavior may be constructed in these terms for the purposes of analysis.

The rat in the maze tries every available possibility, repeating the same actions over and over many times and at last achieving success by accident.

[27] "Intelligence" is here used in the sense of the capacity of the creature to adapt its behavior to new circumstances. Whenever the new situation is interpreted as a problem and adaptation takes the form of the organization of means to ends, the application of intelligence is indubitable. The apes show a marked capacity for such problem-solving. The only definitive difference between the intelligence of ape and man is the use by man of "significant symbols." See George H. Mead, *Mind, Self, and Society* (Chicago: University of Chicago Press, 1934).

Through many trials the maze is at last "learned" and the rat runs it swiftly and unerringly. The pattern of behavior consists in *random effort, leading to unthinking habit*. If this is set up as the lower limit of noninstinctive behavior in terms of the amount of intelligence involved, the most complete antithesis is the reflective action of a man at those times when he consciously plans a course of behavior in terms of an anticipated result. Between these extreme types of noninstinctive actions (random effort leading to unthinking habit and conscious planning and experiment) a number of intermediate types can be distinguished.[28]

Human actions do not occur singly. They are grouped and patterned in various ways. For this reason institutions and even total societies have been analyzed in terms of the kinds of actions that go into their composition. A society or family in which *traditional* and *sanctioned* actions predominate may be called a *sacred* society or family; a society or family in which *rational* actions predominate may be called a *secular* society or family.[29]

When the American housewife goes to the market and buys at the store that sells the product most cheaply, and when, further, her purchase is made in terms of a carefully calculated family budget, she is behaving *rationally,* and her behavior is a part of a *secularized* pattern. When the Irish countryman goes to the village and trades only at the shop the owner of which has married a kinsman, he is behaving *traditionally;* his action is a part of a *sacred* pattern.

It is instructive to note that the predominant drift in times covered by written history has been from *sacred* to increasingly *secularized* types of social adjustment. The family has been deeply affected by such transformations.[30]

These considerations as to the nature of noninstinctive behavior are of great importance to the problem posed in the first section of this study. When the search for a protohuman family has not gone back to the biological world for an instinctive model it has sought for a common *sacred* family pattern, assuming that from it contemporary family types may have arisen.

The only safe conclusion that can be drawn from older studies of the family is that as a form of noninstinctive behavior it was, from the beginning, capable of assuming varied patterns. We should, perhaps, not speak of the "origin" of the "human family" but of "origins" of "human families" — recognizing that from the beginning of his differentiation from other animals man was a peculiarly plastic and adaptable kind of ape. The first family patterns no doubt originated in random activity that became fixed in unthinking habits. When such unthinking habits are socially transmitted — forced on the young or "learned" by the young — the patterned actions are traditional.

[28] See Chapter One for a full description of the various types of social action. Here we simplify.
[29] See Howard Becker and Harry Elmer Barnes, *Social Thought from Lore to Science*, hereafter also cited as *STFLTS* (2nd ed., Washington, D. C.: Harren, 1952), chap. one, by Becker.
[30] Becker-Barnes, *op. cit.,* trace some phases of this general increase of secularization. It should be noted, however, that *new* sacred types may emerge when least expected. Witness Nazi Germany: it had many features of a highly sacred society.

In at least one respect man's development, in spite of minor setbacks, has been continuous. Though the downfall of great civilizations testifies to the loss of techniques and tools *en masse,* once men have discovered or invented new tools they have tended, by and large, to extend the use of them. Man's forebears left the jungle and slowly through invention populated the planet — finally even boxing up a tropic atmosphere inside a house of snow in the Arctic wastes.

When man learned to speak, his capacity for varied adaptation to his fellows and to his environment expanded so terrifically that he was forever to be set apart from other animal forms. The first human families could hardly have been based on anything other than unthinking habits socially transmitted. They were traditionalistic sacred types. Change must have occurred as a result of discovery and invention — brief flashes of rational insight that extended one man's control over others or the control of the group as a whole over the environment. In part the development of man has been his continuous advance into an environment he has made (or partially made) himself.

Nonliterate Families (Sacred Types)

The old illustrative method, miscalled "comparative," was not so much method as license. It drew its pictures of the family in the way the Greeks depicted the centaur — adding the torso of a man to the body of a horse and turning him loose on the wings of a bird. Illustrative studies of the family sketched in this eclectic style have been almost wholly rejected.[31]

A study of older theories calls attention, however, to the purposes of the various actions that make up the family. The actions that occur between members of the family or between the family and the wider social group may be sexual, affiliational, economic, magico-religious, esthetic. Some or all of these types of actions may be present and vital to the continued existence of the given family.

One of the most glaring errors of the older theories was the failure to take account of the total effect of all these actions as they were interrelated in the special case. Ordinarily, the minimum-essential social actions that must be taken into account are the sexual, the internal affiliational (those relating the parents to each other and to the young), the external affiliational (those relating the family to the wider group), and the economic. Magico-religious and esthetic actions are at times important, but it is not always necessary to reckon with them.

It should be noted that, in characterizing actions as sexual, affiliational, or economic, the emphasis has shifted to the defined *needs* the actions fulfill or the *purposes* they serve rather than the degree to which they are affective, traditional, sanctioned, or expedient.

On the basis of the sex relationship families have been classed as follows: (1) *promiscuous,* when every female is available for sexual purposes to every

---

31 Howard Becker sums up the case against this methodology in "Interpretative Sociology and Constructive Typology," *Twentieth Century Sociology,* edited by Georges Gurvitch and Wilbert E. Moore (New York: The Philosophical Library, 1945), p. 93, footnote 39.

male and vice versa; (2) *group marriage,* when two or more brothers (kin by blood or classification) marry two or more sisters; (3) *polygynous,* when one man has two or more wives; (4) *polyandrous,* when one wife has two or more husbands; and (5) *monogamous,* when one husband has one wife.

In terms of affiliational dominance of the parents over the young and one parent over the other, families have been classed as (1) *genocratic* or *gerontocratic,* when the old men of the group are collectively dominant over the females and the young; (2) *patriarchal,* when the eldest male is affiliationally dominant; (3) *matriarchal,* when affiliational dominance rests in the woman.

In terms of the affiliations within and between the family and other groups of society, families have been classed thus: (1) *conjugal,* the immediate linkages between husband, wife, and children; and (2) *consanguinal,* the family based on a more or less extended kinship system. The chief types of consanguinal family are: (a) the *clan,* or *matrilineal clan,* when relationship is traced through the mother; (b) the *gens* or *patrilineal clan,* when relationship is traced through the father; and (c) *mixed,* when kinship follows some other principle.[32]

In terms of its economic functions the conjugal or consanguinal family may be classed as (1) *autonomous,* when it constitutes a self-sufficient economic unit, or (2) *heteronomous,* when it constitutes a part of a larger economic pattern.[33]

Too much attention has been paid to the classification of families on the basis of isolated traits; too little has been paid to the evaluation of the families as wholes. The classification of families as *nonliterate* (when the people did not possess writing) and *literate* (when the art of writing existed), *sacred* (when the actions that composed them were primarily traditional and sanctioned) and *secular* (when the actions composing them are increasingly affective and expedient), was a major step in the new direction.[34] This approach looks beyond the individual traits to the total family.

As has been indicated, the drives that underlie human behavior do little more than indicate the general problem. They do not predispose man to the choice of one rather than another means for its solution. The solutions of recurrent needs, however, are not random but patterned — this time patterned by "habit." The longer the period of infancy and dependent youth the greater the opportunity for the young to learn the habits of the parents.

A society built of such unthinking habits and not subject to intrusive outside influence tends to demonstrate a high degree of internal solidarity and a strong resistance to change — though adaptation to an advantageous set of intrusive conditions may occur dramatically, as in the case of the Comanche,

---

[32] The ideas of affiliational dominance and kinship are sometimes implied by the use of the terms *matrilineal* and *patrilineal* for the principle of descent, and of *patriarchate* and *matriarchate* for the systems that result. Furthermore, "clan" is often used without qualifying adjectives, and may mean simply the "relatives." These usages should not confuse the problem of tracing descent in the consanguinal family with the problem of affiliational dominance.

[33] For an extended classification of kinship systems see John Lewis Gillin and John Philip Gillin, *An Introduction to Sociology* (New York: Macmillan, 1942), chap. 9, pp. 205–245.

[34] See Chapter I for the extended description of the approach and the bibliography thereto appended for further explanatory studies.

who changed from a peaceable plateau people into raiders in a relatively short time.[35]

Left to themselves *nonliterate* peoples (and their families) are essentially conservative — tending to grow into their traditions rather than out of them. Innovation, of course, occurs constantly, and the accumulation of small changes in traditional behavior patterns eventually transforms the society. For the people within the society, however, there is often no awareness at all of change.[36]

The examination of a few nonliterate societies may serve the purpose of illustrating some of the varieties of sacred families. Since they represent long-established patterns from which slow internal adjustment has tended to eliminate antithetical elements, they indicate some of the ways in which sexual, affiliational, economic, and religious actions may be continued in stable patterns.

The Ovimbundu Family

The Ovimbundu of Benguela, South Africa, live primarily by agriculture.[37] The social structure in the past centered in two systems: (1) the Ovimbundu (those who do not eat flesh), who were commoners; and (2) a nobility (royal households of Imbangala stock). The line between these strata has tended to be blurred by intermarriage. The contemporary Ovimbundu peoples are divided into tribes feudatory to larger ones. The office of king centralized religious, political, and civil judiciary functions. The basic social unit is the village (*imbo*) under a headman (*sekulu*) who is technically the patriarch of the village.

The Ovimbundu household consists of a man, his wives (the family is polygynous), and their children. The household (*ocikumbu*) consists of domestic animals and possessions as well as persons. Each wife, with her own hut, granary, chickens, and fields, forms the core of an autonomous economic unit. The wives are ranked — the first having pre-eminence.

Nearly all villages belong to a single *epata* or extended family. The two main kinship groupings are the *oluse* (paternal line) and *oluina* (maternal line). The *oluse,* consisting of local residence units,[38] controls education of children, ownership and inheritance of land, village office, and village worship (including agricultural festivals). The *oluina* dominates negotiable property, family observances, and rituals for specialized economic goods.

---

[35] See Abram Kardiner, *The Psychological Frontiers of Society* (New York: Columbia University Press, 1945).

[36] Under such circumstances there may be a gradual intensification of the problems of a community that paves the way for the sudden dramatic rise of a charismatic leader — that is, not all crisis situations are a result of pressures from outside the community. Change, when it occurs, may be revolutionary, followed by the slow entrenchment of the followers in the categories established by the leader. See Chapter I.

[37] See Gladwyn Murray Childs, *Umbundu Kinship and Character* (London: Oxford University Press, 1949).

[38] *Ibid.,* pp. 42–45.

The Family in Lesu

A considerably different integration of family into social structure is illustrated by the Melanesians of New Ireland. Relatively propitious land and sea conditions make the gaining of a modest livelihood fairly easy. Pigs, taro, yams, banana, and pawpaw are staples supplemented by coconut, betel nuts, sugar cane, dates, breadfruit, and sago.[39]

The village, the primary locality unit, divides into hamlets consisting of from two to eight households with communal cooking facilities and, in some instances, with a men's house and a cemetery. Socially the village is organized into moieties and clans. Lesu has two: the Telenga (fishhawk) and Kong kong (eagle). The clans are composed of extended maternal families. Residence is matrilocal.[40]

At marriage, which cuts the lines of moiety and clan, the maternal clan functions as a unit. The child is a member of the mother's clan, which regulates education and property inheritance. The preferred marriage for a man is with the daughter of his father's sister's daughter's daughter. As in most sacred societies, sexual organization is pervasive. Women may not enter the men's house or attend its feasts and dances. Brush-clearing is a male activity, planting and cultivating female; cooking is a female prerogative, fishing and pig-hunting are male.

Among the contrasts with the family of the Ovimbundu are the importance of a matriarchal and matrilocal principle, basic differences in the relative economic independence of the household, and a different distribution of educational responsibility. These contrasts are definite enough to make it very clear that sacred societies or their components, although similar in many important respects, are often dissimilar in others.

The Trobriand Family

The family of the Trobriand Islanders described by Malinowski [41] stands in marked contrast to those already sketched. The islanders live in villages under the jurisdiction of a chief of noble blood. There is a sharp division of labor: the men do the heavier work of planting yam tubers, mending fences, housebuilding, fighting; the women do the lighter tasks, household work, weaving.[42]

The consanguinal family is matrilineal. The conjugal family is of two types: that of the chief, polygynous; of the commoner, monogamous. In contrast to the Lesunese, however, the man does not live in the wife's house but the wife in the man's. The maximum effect of the matrilineal clan is therefore prevented by a patrilocal principle of residence.

Economically the consanguinal family is autonomous, the conjugal family

---

[39] Hortense Powdermaker, *Life in Lesu* (New York: W. W. Norton, 1933).
[40] An excellent example of matrilocal residence among American Indians is afforded by the pueblo-dwelling Zuñi.
[41] Bronislaw Malinowski, *The Sexual Life of Savages* (New York: Halcyon House, 1929).
[42] *Ibid.*, p. 35.

is heteronomous, i.e., the conjugal household receives its yearly supply of yams from the wife's clan. The chief receives no tribute from his villagers, but each year the clans of his many wives contribute a share of the yams to his household. The vast stores of yams thus built up are used by the chief to finance wars, ceremonies, and expeditions.

The society is remarkable for the exceptional sexual freedom it tolerates. Sexual experiments among very young children are not uncommon. At adolescence the sexes are segregated, and young men live in "bachelor" houses. By this time temporary sexual liaisons are formed and broken. Marriage usually follows more or less permanent premarital liaisons, the motives being quite definite. A man cannot achieve full status in the community until he is married. Furthermore, the support of the household comes from a yearly gift of yams of the girl's clan. The final control of the clan over a displeasing marriage consists in withholding the support of the household.

Children are welcome among the Trobriand Islanders, and the roles of maternal uncle and father are the reverse of our own. Child training is accomplished with a maximum of ease. The child steps, at last, of his own volition from the situation of premarital sexual license into a monogamous adult role within which he is expected to be "faithful."

Marriage depends only upon the consent of the wife's clan. Divorce is as simple; the wife simply packs her belongings and returns home. With his economic support lost, the husband usually tries by means of gifts to win her back.[43]

The casual, free-and-easy aura that surrounds sex in the Trobriand Islands contrasts with the restrained attitude of the Ovimbundu, who ignored it when possible, and the Lesunese, who were quite ambivalent about it. A significant difference, too, is found in the way matrilineal descent and patrilocal residence tend to counterbalance each other. Affiliational dominance in the society is patristic.

The Eskimo Family

The economics of the Eskimo are all-absorbing; he is eternally preoccupied with the problem of survival.[44] So completely has he solved the environmental problem as he defines it, however, that little trading is done with the outside. While retaining some sentiment for the local area where he was born,[45] he may migrate over very long distances. Travel, in fact, is almost second nature.[46]

There is no definite political structure among the Eskimos. A chieftain is usually appointed for a single hunt, but his authority returns to its original status once the hunt is over.[47] The family is small and simple; it constitutes

[43] Bronislaw Malinowski, *The Sexual Life of Savages* (New York: Halcyon House, 1929), p. 146.
[44] Ruth Bunzel, "Economic Organization of Primitive Peoples," in Franz Boas, *General Anthropology* (Boston: Heath, 1938), p. 335. For a general survey of Eskimo economics see Alexander Goldenweiser, *Anthropology* (New York: Crofts, 1937), chaps. 6, 7.
[45] Bunzel, *op. cit.*, p. 340.
[46] Goldenweiser, *op. cit.*, p. 74.
[47] Goldenweiser, *op. cit.*, p. 376.

a self-sufficient economic unit with a division of labor typical of a hunting family.

Both polyandry and polygyny occur among the Eskimos, though polygyny is more frequent. The family lives in a common snow house sleeping on blocks of ice covered with skins. While indoors, heated to a considerable degree of warmth by burning animal oil, the family is naked, for the clothes are removed on entrance.

The Eskimos are ordinarily exceptionally mild.[48] Revenge takes the form, normally, of a wrestling match or a songfest.[49] The general friendliness is nowhere more completely illustrated than in the treatment of strangers, for no Eskimo would allow an acceptable stranger to remain long in his house without lending him a wife.[50]

In contrast to the families outlined so far, that of the Eskimo is simple. It is not integrally linked with a large kinship system nor with a political structure. The family is an autonomous economic unit which may be polyandrous or polygynous; sexual hospitality is widely practiced.[51]

The Atimelang Family

Du Bois' study[52] of Atimelang in Alor in the Netherlands East Indies provides still another example of the sacred family. Affected by the Australian landmass, Alor has a monsoonal climate with a wet season from January to March. With the gradual cessation of the rains, the sequence of crops from corn to rice and beans, followed by sweet potatoes and finally cassava, gives order to socio-economic life. At the end of the period, the land is burnt over and communal hunts for wild pigs are undertaken.

The villages of these former head-hunters are built around dance places of patrilineal lineages (*hieta*). These are surrounded by graves of prominent dead. The lineage houses are expressions of patrilocal residence.[53]

The kinship system has three groupings. The first patrilineal lineage, consisting of descendants of the eldest brother, is called the Eldest House. Descendants of other brothers form the Middle Ones and the Youngest House.[54]

A second kinship grouping is found in the Male Houses. These relationships are recognized as the grouping of the given person's mother's brother and male descendants (Male House I), the father's male house (Male House II), the mother's male house (Male House III) — there are six in all. The third grouping is the Female House, consisting of all bilaterally

---

[48] But see Peter Freuchen, *Eskimo* (New York: Horace Liveright, 1931).

[49] Goldenweiser, *op. cit.,* p. 95.

[50] Reichard, in Boas, *op. cit.,* pp. 436, 481.

[51] See Paul-Emile Victor, *My Eskimo Life,* translated by Jocelyn Godefrai (New York: Simon & Schuster, 1939), for a day-to-day account of the life of the Greenland Eskimo.

[52] Cora Du Bois, *The People of Alor* (Minneapolis: University of Minnesota Press, 1944).

[53] For an almost complete antithesis see Reo Franklin Fortune, *The Social Organization of Dobu* (London: George Routledge and Sons, Ltd., 1931).

[54] In Dobu there is said to be such suspicion of male descent that even the children may not be buried in the same cemetery as the father.

reckoned kin not included in the above. It is made up of persons from whom supplementary ceremonial and "financial" assistance may be expected.

Marriage may be monogamous or polygynous. Taking a second wife is conditional upon considerable "financial" success, and it is only the older men who manage it. Marriage to any known kin is considered improper. Since the kinship system is relatively simple, marriage possibilities are wide. Mother-son, father-daughter, brother-sister relations are tabooed as incestuous.

Two major economic patterns intertwine among the Atimelangers. Women are theoretically responsible for cultivation and own all vegetable food, regardless of how much land and work by males is involved.[55] They therefore have very real power. On the other hand, men control the active "financial" system, operating with pigs, gongs, and kettledrums.[56] Such "currency" is invested primarily in the purchase of wives, burial feasts, and the building of lineage houses. The "financial" transactions may be complex enough to drag over two generations.

Interrelations between Families Studied

These five nonliterate families may serve to illustrate the way sexual, affiliational, economic, and other actions are patterned in a given family type. They indicate, too, the danger of taking any one trait apart from its context in the family and in the culture. Monogamy was found among the Ovimbundu, Trobriand commoners, and Atimelangers. In each instance the family was economically dependent (heteronomous). Polygyny appeared among the Eskimos, Ovimbundu, and the nobles of the Trobriands. In the case of Eskimo and Ovimbundu, the conjugal family was economically independent (autonomous); among the Trobriand nobility, polygyny had an important status as well as economic value. Polyandry appeared as an occasional marriage type among the Eskimos. Affiliational dominance was variously located in the family, the kinship system, or the village. The nature of the affiliational dominance and its location had an important effect on the type of relation that existed between family members and family and society. Premarital chastity was in no two cases given the same evaluation. Perhaps more significant than anything else, the qualities of personality valued in a given family were nowhere identical. The Trobriand Islander is genial, hardworking, convivial; the Eskimo, sturdy, self-reliant, and friendly; The Ovimbundu is extraverted, expansive, aggressive, balanced in judgment, and dignified; the Atimelanger is mistrustful and introverted, with low self-esteem.

While these five family types are too few to be made the basis of sweeping generalizations, they do indicate some of the factors that must be considered if one is to discuss the family with any precision.

The older theorists talked frequently of *promiscuity*. Yet no people

---

[55] In general, female ownership of land and dominance of maternal relationships are correlated. This is in process of breaking down the importance of paternal lines and male houses.

[56] "Financial" success is not reckoned in terms of subsistence, but with respect to ceremonial exchanges that mediate other ceremonies.

studied thus far have been proved to be "promiscuous." Even the ideas of "group marriage" are subject to some doubt, for there is some disagreement as to whether or not "group marriage" is actually present in the Australian tribes to which it has been ascribed, and a clearcut case is hard to find. Again, the assertion has frequently been made that monogamy always is bound up with the institution of private property. In none of these families sketched here was this true. Most significant of all is the fact that in no case was the family without a definite form. Each has its own specific rules and conditions and its own definitions of crimes and punishments.

LITERATE FAMILIES: SECULAR TYPES

The terms "sacred" and "secular," "nonliterate" and "literate," have been used as though they were parallel. This is only roughly true. It is difficult, *but by no means impossible,* to find a nonliterate society that is fairly thoroughly secularized. Such in fact were the Comanche, who developed into a raiding group on the fringe of advancing white culture. Expedient calculations had almost replaced the traditional patterns of the plateau.[57] Similarly, it is possible for peoples to possess writing and still to represent predominantly sacred-type societies. Such were India, China, and Europe in the early stages of our Western heritage. Writing, in fact, may be a conservative force — such was the function of all "sacred" texts. Consequently, it may be said that in many instances writing facilitates the growth of what have been called, in Chapter One, prescribed societies. Oral transmission of sacred prescriptions is often amazingly effective, but the written word is even more so. Granting that affective nonrationality always remains or emerges in some form, the final test of secularization is always the degree to which expediently rational calculation has replaced custom-bound and sanctioned behavior.

However, in the progressive "rationalization" of human society, a development that has by no means been linear but has been filled with discontinuities, writing has a peculiar significance. It is to a large degree a rational invention in itself. It holds the face of the present before the mirror of the past. Even when the text is "sacred" and "inviolable" it tends to grow, if by no other means, but the addition of bitter commentaries on the lack of congruence of the times with the ways of the fathers. Moreover, secularizingly destructive controversies about the exact meaning of a given prescription are likelier to arise if the prescription has been set down in writing.

A written record of the accumulated wisdom of the ages is more trustworthy than the span of the old man's memory. The recording of statistics, property settlements, and tax assessments permits government on an unprecedented scale. The codification of rules of social conduct, the transmission of messages through other than an intermediary — all these things and many others are possible with writing. As a net result, the presence of writing tends, by and large, toward an increasing rationalization of human actions.

The significance of writing as a secularizing agency can be seen by ex-

[57] Abram Kardiner, *op. cit.*

amining the problem of taboo. It is quite unnecessary, in explaining "taboo," to assume the existence of sexual jealousy, substitute symbolism, ambivalence, and all the rest. Social actions originated in the establishment of unthinking habits. The social transmission of these habits occurs because the young find it convenient to conform and acquire them or the old find it convenient to impose them. The unthinking accumulation of traditional actions is quite automatic. Training consists in the acquisition by the young of the body of traditional actions of the society. It is precisely offense against these traditions that is "taboo." The theological and magical interpretations of both tradition and taboo given by the society are often quite incidental.

No public force has been set up to enforce the taboo. The breaking of it may occasion only horror, or it may be punished by a solemn decision of the elders. The punishment may in turn become traditionalized.

With the development of writing, violations of taboos may be re-defined as crimes. Punishments may be set down in a criminal code. The action now is universalized, standardized, and calculable in a new sense. In fact, the criminal may even weigh the advantages of the offense against the probability of the punishment in terms of a conception of reasonable risks.[58]

Among the secularizing traits that writing makes possible are the development of larger economic units such as would not be possible without some means of accounting; the replacement of a system of mores by legal codes with a consequent standardization of punishments; the appearance of contractual relations based on written documents maximizing the calculation of specific social relationships. In addition, the development of a monetary medium of exhange, if it has not already developed, is hastened, and this monetary medium of exchange in turn permits the translation of a wide diversity of values into standard units of value — "everything has a price." But the list is almost endless, for ultimately hardly a single sphere of human activity will remain untouched.

The more secularized the society, the more difficult becomes the job of analyzing the family in terms of the sum of the influences that play upon and within it. The nonliterate family, ordinarily, is located in a small unified culture. The nonliterate rarely comes in contact with more than a few hundred people during his entire life, and the effective society within which he lives may be far smaller than this. The secularized family is quite another story. So complex are the influences that may play upon it that they are almost impossible to list. Its members may participate in different groups and share with these groups values violently clashing with those held by parents or siblings. In many other ways the secularized family may be pressed on every side by competing appeals and conflicting interpretations. Remote changes in the far parts of the world may influence its economic status. The persons linked within it may wonder, in fact, whether there is anything certain beyond "death and taxes."

In contrast to the survey of nonliterates, where something approximating a total estimate was possible, the best that can be hoped for in examining a few

---

[58] This picture is, of course, oversimplified, but there is much "white-collar" crime which matches it closely.

types of literate families outside the United States is to isolate a small number of the major influences that play upon them.

The Irish Countryman

The Irish countryman studied by Arensberg [59] comprises small farmers concentrated in the south and west of Ireland. The typical farm is from fifteen to thirty acres in size. Rye, oats, potatoes, and turnips are grown. Pasture is kept, and hay is provided for a few milk cows. Pigs and chickens round out the economy, which is largely self-sufficient. Only the sale of cows brings money income to the household.

The division of labor between the sexes centers in the house and "haggard" (the family yard). The wife does the housework, takes care of the yard, the chickens, the milking, the churning. The man does the heavier work: mending walls, repairing, field planting, cutting peats in the bog for winter fuel. The children are early apprenticed to father and mother in the chores and work of the farm.

Two types of affiliational distinction run through the family of the countryman. By convention a woman cannot inherit the land, which must if possible be inherited by a son — preserving the land in the family name. Women are subordinate in the scheme, but are economically essential in the completion of the farm work, and affiliationally essential for the production of sons. The other affiliational division is that of old and young, between whom much reverence and mutual respect is shown.

Marriage is of central significance to the whole system. It is arranged through an intermediary. It sets in motion the most crucial transitions of the society. The "boy" becomes a man. The old folks move into the special "west" room — the most hallowed part of the house. The sibling family is dissolved at this time, for other daughters and sons emigrate from the home. The dowry serves to compensate father, sisters, and sons for their loss.

Before one of the boys is married and settled on the parental farm, the countryman tries to make provision for his other children. If possible, the boys are apprenticed to a tradesman in the town. The girls are married to prosperous farmers or to tradesmen in the village.

Provision for his children makes heavy financial demands on the countryman. He tends to hold on to the farm long; hence "boys" continue to grow older, and fret at the reluctance of the father to step down. Marriage occurs late; the system enforces celibacy and virginity.

Folk traditions and beliefs about the "good people" (the fairies) are strong and persist in spite of the fact that the public schools and the Catholic church preach against the fairy cult. But the Irish countryman is in transition. Folk beliefs are steadily "picked to pieces" in the schools. If the surplus youth were not able to emigrate, they would tremendously depress the subsistence level. The picture is that of a peasant tending to become a farmer — a sacred family in the process of being secularized.

[59] Conrad M. Arensberg, *The Irish Countryman* (London: Macmillan, 1937).

The Japanese Family

In his survey of the manner in which Japanese sociology flourished after the Meiji restoration in 1868, Becker notes that though Japan has a rich variety of family types Japanese scholars have largely ignored them:

> The family furnishes important and interesting object-matter for concrete study, but up-to-date economists like Shiro Kawata and moralists like Kimio Hayashi have almost monopolized the field. The only sociological treatments worth noting are Teizo Toda's *Studies of the Family* (1927) and *Family and Marriage* (1935). When we take account of the fact that the family is one of the most important, constant, and universal of groups, and that Japan offers a rich profusion of family types, this neglect seems hard to justify. Hence we must rely chiefly on studies by Westerners.[60]

During the feudal era, tea-drinking had gradually been reduced to a ceremony in which the tea-drinker and his guest sat cross-legged in a relatively bare room sipping tea that had been precisely prepared. Host and guest joined in the contemplation of an art object such as a painting, a vase, a symbolic arrangement of flowers. After the Meiji, the government revived the Tea Ceremony and Flower Arrangement — making them symbols for the grandeur of Japan. The Japanese code of feudal ethics, *Bushido,*[61] "The Way of the Warrior," was also cultivated afresh. The Samurai (feudal warriors of Japan) were erected into ideals of Japanese manhood. The ethic of loyalty to the feudal chief was translated into the ideal of loyalty to the emperor. The highest expression of the loyalty was *hara-kiri,* ceremonial disembowelment.

The partially Westernized Japanese consist of university teachers, government bureaucrats, members of the foreign legation, and people brought up under the tutelage of missionaries. Even in the case of university professors and civil servants, however, the influence of *shukan* (custom) is strong. The people are devoted to their native costume, and prefer to sit cross-legged and without shoes. Ceremonial gifts of symbolic jellybeans are exchanged on customary occasions. Gratitude to a host is expressed by a ceremonious quotation from a twelfth century writer. The Tea Ceremony is a daily festival.

In the home and in society the Japanese man is completely dominant. The wife cannot argue, discuss ideas, or talk seriously with her husband. The Japanese woman is not a hostess, and can accompany her husband only on those occasions strictly required by custom. Her duty is always to act in accordance with custom, functioning as a servant of husband and children. She is not allowed to associate with men before marriage. Marriage is accomplished by agreement between the men involved. A woman of dignified

---

[60] Becker and Barnes, *STFLTS*, p. 1170 (by Becker). The discussion by Becker, it should be noted, and the general discussion in this section are based upon pre-Pearl Harbor conditions in Japan. Under American Military Government, large-scale changes took place in postwar Japan, and there is much evidence to show that these changes are regarded as more than temporary.

[61] See Inazo Nitobe, *Bushido, The Soul of Japan* (New York: Putnam, 1905).

status cannot work or earn money. The only schools of higher education for women in Japan are run by missionaries. Though peasant girls are utilized in the cotton factories, their presence is not voluntary but by agreement with the parents. The girls are confined to dormitories, and all spare time is devoted to schooling them in tradition and the arts of homemaking. At the end of the period the girl is returned to her parents. This arrangement brings in a small income to the family and supplies cheap labor for the factory.

The Japanese male has far more latitude than the woman. He is master of the household, its representative in society. For him the universities are open. His standard sexual outlet is the geisha, who is trained in the arts of dancing, love-making, singing, and entertaining.

It is rather ironic that the system of state capitalism tends to destroy the autonomy of the family. Industry requires the aggregation of proletarian workers. Urban centers that result create markets for farm products and turn the peasants into farmers. Correlated with such economic specialization is a differentiation of governmental function, and modern bureaucratic government tends to transform the feudal functionary into a civil servant. All these factors have tended to secularize the life of the Japanese man and woman.[62]

The Hindu Family

While the Hindu family is undergoing a transmutation,[63] it is interesting to look back at the family as it was in a system that is now slowly crumbling. The family was inseparably bound up with the affiliational order; that order, in turn, was inspired by Hindu religion.

Affiliationally, India was divided by a system of castes which consisted of occupationally closed, mutually exclusive, and endogamous strata to which general honorific qualities were attached. The castes of India (*jati*) were, in turn, organized into four larger "colors" (*varnas*).[64] One general theory advanced to explain the origin of this social structure is that the word *varna* originally denoted the distinction between the Aryan (who came as a white conqueror into ancient India) and non-Aryan (the dark substratum of the native population) and that later Brahmanic interpretation invented the *jati* system to distinguish the castes actually found in practice.[65] Whatever the origin, there were four *varnas*.

At the top of the social system were the *Brahmans,* and these constituted not only a *varna* but also a caste. Then came the *Kshatriyas*. These were not a definite united caste. The name *Kshatriya* was simply a collective one assumed by such castes and families as were then dominant. In like manner the *Vaishyas* were not a caste. The name was merely a collective one comprehending the landed classes, cattle-keeping tribes, and clans of men engaged

---

[62] For a general cultural background of contemporary Japan, see G. B. Sansom, *Japan, A Short Cultural History* (New York: Century, 1932).

[63] See Frieda Hauswirth, *Purdah: The Status of Indian Women* (New York: Vanguard, 1932), chaps. 9–15.

[64] S. V. Ketkar, *The History of Caste in India* (Ithaca: Taylor & Carpenter, 1909), chap. 5.

[65] Pandharianath H. Valavalkar, *Hindu Social Institutions* (London: Longmans, Green, 1939), p. 298. The word *Aryan*, it should be noted, derives from the word meaning *honorable*.

in commerce. The name *Shudra* is applied, as a collective one also, to various castes engaged in commerce and skilled trades, unskilled labor and household service, and other occupations held to be low.[66]

The two hundred million Hindus in India are divided into more than three thousand castes, most of these in turn having subcastes. The Brahmans alone have over eight hundred.[67]

The patriarchal Hindu family, consisting of male descendants, was located within the endogamous caste and bound together in a belief in progressive transmigrations of the soul. The system was further enhanced by the fact that only the male son could perform those rituals necessary to the transmigrations of the soul. The significance of marriage lay in the fact that a son was essential to family continuity.[68] A girl, on the other hand, was an economic liability. She left the house at puberty under a system of child marriage; hence she was of little use at birth or later. Infanticide of females was common.[69]

The son was most carefully awaited and carefully attended, and greatest care was devoted to his education under a Brahman teacher, a *guru*. The education of the woman, however, was slighted or omitted completely. She would be lost to the household anyway. The woman could attain salvation only through her husband, who was her god and teacher (*guru*) in all things.[70] So important was the need for a son that if the woman was barren, provision was made for polygyny. Finally, after the death of the husband the woman was expected to follow him to death on the funeral pyre or, failing that, to remain a widow for life.[71]

In its original form the genocratic patriarchal family constituted an integral economic unit; recently, however, the industrialization of the country has made inroads on its autonomy. The system of child marriage and female infanticide is gradually being legislated out of existence. In most places, at present, the *nautch* girl and *devadasi* have been eliminated. The strong tendency completely to seclude the women (the purdah) has been weakened. In one form or other the Hindu family is becoming secularized.[72]

The Latin American Families

The Spaniards and Portuguese came to the New World as conquerors; the main outline of the Latin American scene is in no little measure due to this fact. Generally speaking, the agricultural land is carved into huge estates, *latifundios*. In 1910 seven thousand families in Mexico owned nearly all the good land; 7 per cent of the population of Chile controlled the tillable soil.[73] This in turn has led to the sharp distinction between the extremely rich and

[66] Ketkar, *op. cit.*, p. 99.
[67] *Ibid.*, p. 5.
[68] Hauswirth, *op. cit.*, p. 52.
[69] *Ibid.*, chap. 7.
[70] *Ibid.*, p. 28.
[71] *Ibid.*, chap. 7.
[72] *Ibid.*, chaps. 9–15.
[73] Samuel Guy Inman, *Latin America* (New York: Willett, Clark, 1937), p. 158.

extremely poor.[74] It is the foundation, too, of the official contempt for labor that characterized the *hidalgo*.[75] Business has been largely dominated by foreign concerns.

The Iberians carried with them over the ocean a dynamic scheme of antithetical ideas about marriage, family, and sexual love. Catholicism enjoined celibacy and virginity as the highest service to God. Marriage had to be sanctioned by the church; it was eternal and irretractable. Birth control or even the thought of birth limitation by any means was sinful. As a direct contrast to this scheme the ideal of romantic love had developed. "The Romance misses no opportunity of disparaging the social institution of marriage and of humiliating husbands."[76] While the church officially enjoined eternal fidelity, the ideal of romantic love centered about adultery.[77] While the priesthoods and nunneries were sworn to celibacy and religious chastity, the development of concubinage in the clergy was a favorite theme of Boccaccio and Rabelais.[78]

The Mohammedan conquest of Spain, with the resulting diffusion of the ideals of polygyny and the seclusion of women, furthered the isolation of the romantic pattern in its Christian context. The more remote the lady became, the more irresistibly attractive. The more virtuous she was, the more valuable as an erotic object. The refinement of a dual standard of morality: of chaste secluded virgins, or dashing polygynous gallants, took place in this context. The higher the barriers about sex the more intense the passion — such was the "paradox of the Western attitude."[79]

This complex of ideas was transferred to the New World, and while the missionaries taught the ideas of monogamy, celibacy, continence,[80] the upper-class Iberians developed a flourishing system of concubinage and polygyny. The operation of a dual standard was never more marked. Not until well in the twentieth century has the Latin American woman been enjoying anything remotely approaching genuine freedom.[81]

Not the least of the differences between North and South America is the manner in which the two continents were conquered. The northern continent was secured by a constant flow of immigration and internal growth that displaced the Indian populations; the southern continent was secured by the spread, over the surface of the Indian populations, of a ruling hierarchy. This has resulted in the pressure of partially Westernized native peoples on the social order of South America.

[74] *Ibid.*, p. 159.
[75] *Ibid.*, p. 160. This is well summarized by Freyre: "But predominant over all these antagonisms was the more general and the deeper one: that between master and slave." Gilberto Freyre, *The Masters and The Slaves,* translated by Samuel Putnam (New York: Knopf, 1946), pp. 79–80.
[76] Denis de Rougemont, *Love in the Western World,* translated by Montgomery Belgion (New York: Harcourt, Brace, 1940), p. 25.
[77] *Ibid.*, pp. 4–5.
[78] For the development of concubinage in Brazil see Freyre, *op. cit.,* p. 85.
[79] De Rougemont, *op. cit.,* p. 299. For a more detailed account of the evolution of romantic love, see chap. 4, pp. 117–120.
[80] Freyre, *op. cit.,* pp. xxv, 107.
[81] *Ibid.*, p. 206.

In this connection, the study by Robert Redfield [82] of the folk culture of Yucatan has great significance for students of Latin American family life.

Yucatan lies between the modernized area of the northwest and the city of Merida. It is a Hispano-Indian culture devoted to the cultivation of maize, and of henequen from which sisal fiber for bags is made.[83] The maize is grown for home consumption; the henequen is grown for export and ties the economy of Yucatan with that of the outside world.

The study compares the city (Merida), the town (Dzitas), the peasant village (Chan Kom), and the tribal village (Tusik) in terms of race and class, Spanish and Indian cultural elements, cultural organization, economic problems, social problems, and religion. Interesting differences appear between these communities.

In the city, Spanish descent carried positive prestige, Catholic elements were weakened, the culture was highly diversified, mobile, and modernized, money was a true medium of exchange, individual ownership of land was universal, marriage choices were spontaneous and based on the conception of romantic love, the Church was an association competing with other organizations, and folk practices were commercialized.

At the other extreme, namely, the tribal village, Spanish descent had negative status, the practice of Catholic ritual was more pervasive (and more modified in the direction of folk custom), commercial dealings within the group were almost completely absent, marriage was arranged by the patrilineal consanguinal family, the symbols of the church were more venerated, religion was practiced as a communal affair, and folk custom was a genuine expression of the socio-psychic life of the tribe.

The town and urbanized villages showed gradations between these extremes.

The value of the study lies in the insight it affords into the dynamics of the secularization of Hispano-Indian societies and families. In the tribe the consanguinal family is strong and effective. Marriage occurs by arrangement; the interests of the solidarity of the consanguinal family are paramount; property is owned corporately; monetary exchange between tribal members is almost absent. The consanguinal family is economically self-sufficient. While premarital chastity is not insisted upon, the "arranged" marriages are stable and even adultery is not grounds for a break in the family group.

All these elements tend to change as the family is traced in progressively urbanized centers. In the city the consanguinal family vanishes; marriage is individualistic and based on romantic choice; property is owned individually; divorce is frequent. In short, at least some of the Hispano-Indian families are tending to follow the model sketched as characteristic of the ruling stratum.[84]

[82] Robert Redfield, *The Folk Culture of Yucatan* (Chicago: University of Chicago Press, 1941).
[83] *Ibid.*, p. 6.
[84] *Ibid.*

The Chinese Family

The China in which the old-style family flourished was based on an agricultural economy. In contrast to the society of India, it never had hard and fast divisions of class.[85] The affairs of the emperor were administered by a body of scholars, the *literati,* who were skilled in the arts of calligraphy and learned in the sacred texts. These officials were chosen on the basis of competitive examinations open to everyone. The bureaucratic structure that resulted prevented the growth of a fixed nobility.[86]

The occupations of China carried varying degrees of prestige. Scholarship was the most honorable of occupations, farming ranked next, followed by craftsmanship and commerce. Actors, prostitutes, eunuchs, and slaves were regarded as socially inferior.[87]

The religion of the ordinary person was eclectic and tolerant — it was an "ethical" religion rather than a "salvation" religion like Mohammedanism or Christianity.[88] Two doctrines of popular religion were of great importance to the family. It was believed that two principles operated in the universe, known as *yin* and *yang.* "The *yin* stands for Earth, the moon, darkness, evil, and the female sex. On the *yang* side are Heaven, the sun, light, fire, goodness, and the male sex."[89] The other doctrine was that of the "five loyalties," which formulated explicitly the modes of conduct proper between prince and minister, father and son, older brother and younger brother, husband and wife, and friend and friend.[90] All recognized patterns of social conduct have specific religious sanction. And since the duty of son to father extends beyond death, a man and his ancestors are joined in a common socio-religious order.

The Chinese family was the specific affiliational unit that embodied these socio-religious principles. The consanguinal family normally lived in a single household. It consisted of the grandparents, the sons, grandsons, and grandchildren. It was genocratic; decisions were made by the older males.[91] It was an economically autonomous unit, normally engaged in agriculture. Often the oldest male in one of the larger families was the sole authority in a small village. In all cases the union between family and local political authority was close.

The son was essential to the family. He represented its *yang,* its hope. The rituals essential to the cult of ancestor reverence had to be performed by the son. Woman, on the other hand, represented sin, darkness, and earthbound passion (*yin*). The first importance of a woman was the possibility of a son, and this was too important a problem to be left to chance

85 Kenneth Scott Latourette, *The Chinese, Their History and Culture* (New York: Macmillan, 1946), p. 685.
86 *Ibid.,* pp. 685–686.
87 *Ibid.,* p. 687.
88 See Latourette, *op. cit.,* pp. 607–646. For a general sociological analysis see Becker and Barnes, *STFLTS,* chap. 2.
89 Latourette, *op. cit.,* pp. 647–648.
90 *Ibid.,* p. 669.
91 *Ibid.,* p. 687.

by the consanguinal family — marriages were arranged by the parents, often when the children were quite young.

In addition to ordinary marriage there was a system of concubinage that was not contingent upon the barrenness of the bride. The concubines were two types: those acquired with legal formality, and those purchased — often prostitutes from a brothel. Again, the imperial harem duplicated on a larger scale the constellation of the family. In the imperial harem there were a number of classes of concubines: the consort, three concubines of the first rank, nine of the second rank, twenty-seven of the third rank, eighty-one of of the fourth rank.[92]

The slaves in China, at the time, were largely composed of daughters sold by poor families to the rich (to be used as servants) or to the brothels. These girls were taught singing, dancing, and playing the guitar-like *p'i-pa*. Many of them hoped eventually to buy their way out of the houses. Some were purchased by husbands who were not satisfied with the marriages-of-convenience arranged by the parents in their anxiety to secure an heir.[93]

The status of the woman in the Chinese family was decidedly inferior to that of the man. The five loyalties, the ancestor cult, the doctrines of *yin* and *yang,* all reiterated the importance of the male. Girls were a liability and were lost to the family at marriage. Furthermore, the girl was not given any sort of formal education while schools, often taught by mandarins who had not been fortunate enough to get places in the government, were established for the boys. The wife had no property of her own, and achieved definite status only at the birth of her son.[94]

This old Chinese family which, Latourette remarked, "performed the functions which in the modern Occident are associated with sickness and unemployment insurance, old-age pensions, and life insurance,"[95] is passing away. The reasons for this are multiple: modern couples are leaving the consanguinal household, concubinage and slavery are no longer legal, divorce has been made easy, education (in the form of the public school) has been opened to women as well as men, women have been granted suffrage. All of these changes were well under way before the rise of Communism; they have now speeded up slightly.[96]

DYNAMICS OF FAMILY CHANGE

In contrast to the families of nonliterate peoples, which could be outlined within small compass, it has been possible only to trace a few of the central features of the literate families. This in itself calls attention to one significant difference between literate and nonliterate families; namely, difference in the complexity of the elements that play upon the family structure.

While no complete treatment of the problem is possible here, some of

[92] Florence Ayscough, *Chinese Women* (Boston: Houghton Mifflin, 1937), p. 35.
[93] *Ibid.,* pp. 92–99.
[94] Latourette, *op. cit.,* pp. 678–680.
[95] *Ibid.,* p. 666.
[96] *Ibid.,* p. 685.

the dynamic principles underlying the transformation of the family from a sacred to a secular type can be noted. In all of the five literate family types traditional and sanctioned patterns were disintegrating; rational calculations, sometimes accompanied by outbursts of affective nonrationality, were taking their place. Reference to the summary chart, Table 2, may prove helpful.

The consanguinal family tended to be weakened or to vanish altogether. With its disappearance, marriage by arrangement disappeared — there was no longer a larger group vitally concerned in the conjugal grouping and

TABLE 2

A Tabular Comparison of Human Family Types

LOCALE OF FAMILY	COMPONENTS OF THE FAMILY				
	CONJUGAL FAMILY	CONSAN-GUINAL FAMILY	AFFILIATIONAL DOMINANCE	ECONOMIC STATUS	EDUCATION
Ovimbundu	Polygynous	"Oluse"	Elders of Tribe	Autonomous	Elders
Lesu	Monogamous and Polygynous	Clan	Maternal Males	Autonomous	Parents and Clan Elders
Trobriand	Monogamous and Polygynous	Clan	Males of Clan	Heteronomous	Maternal Uncle
Eskimo	Polyandrous and Polygynous	None	Patristic	Autonomous	Parents
Atimelang	Monogamous and Polygynous	Male House	Patristic	Heteronomous	Primarily Parents
Irish	Monogamous	None	Patristic	Autonomous	Public School
*Japanese	Monogamous	None	Patristic	Heteronomous	Public School
†Hindu	Monogamous and Polygynous	Gens	Elders	Autonomous	Brahman
Latin American	Monogamous Unofficial Polygyny	None	Patristic	Heteronomous	Public School
†Chinese	Monogamy and Concubinage	Gens	Elders	Autonomous	Public School

* The Japanese family represented here is by no means characteristic of the whole of Japan. It represents rather its most "Westernized" type.

† In the case of both Hindu and Chinese families the explanation centered about the old-style family that is now rapidly disappearing.

securing its own group interest in its control of the marital arrangements. Related to the disappearance of marriage for convenience, individual choice by the mates began to play an increasing role in the marriage. Marriage, too, became contractual; divorce, more simple and frequent.

Economically, in the change from sacred to secular the family ceases to be autonomous. The members of the family are incorporated in an expanded economic order. Other economic changes are apparent in society at large: the disappearance of barter, the appearance of a monetary system of exchange, the disappearance of the fair, the appearance of the market. The peasant becomes a farmer; the trader becomes a retail merchant; the artisan becomes a factory worker or a semiskilled laborer. The land ceases to be corporately owned. Group property becomes private property or the property of a contractual corporation.

Affiliationally, in the change from sacred to secular striking differences appear. Ultimate political control ceases to be local. It tends to be appropriated by a special organization — the town, county, or state government. The sexes tend to achieve equality. Taboo is replaced by law; custom is replaced by formal regulation. Education ceases to be a family affair and becomes the business of a specially planned school. The differences between age groupings are narrowed. The groups of the community (social organizations) become purposeful associations.

In all these spheres the range of rational choice continually widens; sexual, affiliational, economic, religious, and esthetic actions are less traditionalistic and sanctioned, and more subject to rational examination and individual choice. At times these choices are swayed by affective nonrationality.

The variety of family forms found in both nonliterate and literate societies constitutes both a promise and a warning, for the evidence unmistakably proves that while there is no one solution to sexual, affiliational, economic, and religious problems, these solutions are never unpatterned. The family can be changed and the hope of improvement need never be abandoned — this is the promise.

Yet there is an implicit warning in this very variety of family forms. Each culture has achieved its own patterned solution — a solution that it guards most jealously. The amount of variation within a pattern is carefully delimited, and individual transgression of culturally defined limits may subject the individual to scorn and contempt, excommunication, imprisonment, exile, or death. The community strikes back at the deviate.

The dream that unfettered freedom, sexual, economic, and social, is the solution to all human problems, the dream that man was born free and society has enchained him, the dream that human nature is "good" and institutions have corrupted it, are dangerous fantasies. Logically these notions are akin to the argument that since the earth resists the feet, walking would be perfect if there were no earth at all. But the earth and the friction of the ground to the foot are *necessary conditions* of walking; and existing social patterns are *necessary conditions* of social life.

The patterned solutions of family problems characteristic of any given culture constitute its conventional modes of behavior. These conventions are not only supported by specific punishments (spearing, drowning, imprisonment, exile, etc.) but by the structure of personality. Even if the delinquent offender is not discovered he is often stricken with guilt-feelings leading to cynicism, bitterness, disgust, progressive degeneration, and suicide. The internally secure and balanced individual is normally the one who achieves his individuality and freedom through the behavior patterns of his culture.

Thus, while the study of family varieties holds out the promise of change for betterment, *it carries the warning that ill-considered change may have far-reaching destructive effects on individuals and society.*

New Directions

The literature on the family is vast; it has been possible only to sample it here. Yet in tracing families from biological to literate a number of general characteristics are evident.

The family is a behavior pattern which must be analyzed in terms of the characteristics of behavior. In the analysis of insect and animal families a distinction was drawn between instinctive and noninstinctive types of behavior. When the biological family was evaluated in these terms, it held little promise for the discovery of a protohuman family.

A review of nonliterate and literate family types reveals that no two families are quite the same. This lends support to the suggestion that there were probably many family types from the very beginning of man's history. Furthermore, these earlier families could hardly have been anything other than sacred types based primarily on traditional actions.

It seems clear that families have changed from the beginning. In times of written history this change has been, with many notable setbacks, a change from sacred-type families resting on tradition and sanction to secular-type families within which a high degree of rational calculation is possible. Sexual, affiliational, economic, religious, and esthetic actions have all been increasingly rationalized.

In spite of the voluminous literature on families of the world, however, much of it, for lack of a trustworthy scientific method, is useless; it is only recently that the study of the family has come into its own.

One approach to analysis of the family that seems to hold genuine promise is that of Howard Becker and Robert Redfield, who have approached the problem comparatively on the basis of the type-constructs sacred and secular and folk and urban.[97] Such types necessitate (a) the re-

97 Both Becker and Redfield were influenced in the use of the terms *sacred* and *secular* by the lectures of Robert E. Park at the University of Chicago. See footnote 3 of Howard Becker and Robert C. Myers, "Sacred and Secular Aspects of Human Sociation," in *Sociometry,* 5 (Aug., 1942). "To the best of our knowledge, the first sociological use of the terms *sacred* and *secular* was made by Robert E. Park in his lectures at the University of Chicago. Our use of these words is an adaptation rather than a strict 'Parkian' interpretation, and stems from Howard Becker, *Ionia and Athens: Studies in Secularization* (unpublished doctoral dissertation supervised by Park, University of Chicago, 1930), and 'Processes of Secularisa-

fined study of individual family traits, while (b) they permit an evaluation of the specific family as a whole, and (c) they lead to scientific evaluations of the dynamics of family change. The superiority of this approach to the older anthropological and sociological approaches is twofold: (1) it avoids the meaningless classification of family traits; and (2) it permits prediction, and perhaps control, of family trends.

The same problem is approached in another fashion by Kardiner and his associates.[98] Their method consists in the acceptance of the uniqueness of the particular culture and applying to it of a revised version of psycho-analysis. The primary object of analysis, in terms of this method, is the individual family member. The child is particularly important, for the nature of the culture, in the final analysis, rests upon the traditions the child assimilates. His personality embodies many of the features that typify the culture.

The child is analyzed in terms of three behavior categories: *key integrational systems, projective systems,* and *reality systems.*

Key integrational systems consist of those phases of the child's training crucial to his development; viz., maternal care, nursing, sphincter control, emotional response, sibling attitudes, marriage, etc. The *projective systems* of the culture consist of "ultimate rationalizations," such as religion, magic, folklore, etc. The *reality systems* are those specific bodies of knowledge, those skills and techniques that give the people mastery over their material and social environments, such as boat building, wood carving, weaving, pottery making, scientific knowledge, and the like.

In surveying family types it has been stated that different families produce special personalities. Various writers have asserted that the Eskimo is self-reliant and good humored; the Kwakiutl of Vancouver island is ambitious and competitive; the Trobriand Islander is generous and sexually easy-going; the Dobuan is suspicious and devious. The method of study proposed by Kardiner and his associates may permit a more exact analysis of the manner in which these personality types are developed. The family is the first school of personality. It is often the context within which personality assumes its characteristic shape, and sometimes the context within which personality achieves its most complete realization.

The analytical method of Kardiner, consisting of an analysis of individual adjustment, ideology, and scientific knowledge, of training, ideas, and activities promises more than the old illustrative method which isolated single

---

tion,' *Sociological Review* (British), 24 (April, July, and October, 1932), pp. 138–154, 266–286."

The terms *sacred* and *secular* as used by Park were in turn based upon the concepts *Gemeinschaft* and *Gesellschaft* of Ferdinand Tönnies. As used by Becker the terms *sacred* and *secular* are considerably expanded beyond their original employment by Park. For a fuller description see Becker and Myers, *op. cit.,* and Chapter One of this book.

Redfield uses the terms *folk society* and *urban society* instead of *sacred* and *secular.* It should be noted, moreover, that Redfield's terms *folk* and *urban* are far more restricted in application than the terms *sacred* and *secular* as used by Becker and could not be employed, for example, for the analysis of trends in contemporary civilizations. By contrast see Section V of Becker and Myers, *op. cit.,* for the analysis of the forces at work in prewar Germany, or Becker, *German Youth: Bond or Free* (New York: The Grove Press, 1946).

[98] Abram Kardiner, *op. cit.*

traits from their specific contexts in family and community and "compared" these; it was incapable of explaining either the diversity of the traits or the significance of the special case.

These two developments in the field of genuinely comparative study — the *type analysis method* of Becker and Redfield and the *social-psychological method* of Kardiner and his associates — are complementary. The one aims at precise scientific knowledge of the basic patterns of family structure and change; the other aims ultimately at a more complete understanding of personality. New vistas may be opened by these new directions that the study of the family has assumed.

SELECTED READINGS

ARENSBERG, CONRAD M., *The Irish Countryman* (New York: Macmillan, 1937).

AYSCOUGH, FLORENCE, *Chinese Women* (Boston: Houghton Mifflin, 1937).

BECKER, HOWARD, *Systematic Sociology on the Basis of the* Beziehungslehre *and* Gebildelehre *of Leopold von Wiese* (New York: Wiley, 1932), chaps. on small groups — 39–40.

——, "Constructive Typology in the Social Sciences," in *Contemporary Social Theory,* edited by Harry Elmer Barnes, Howard Becker, and Frances Bennett Becker (New York: Appleton-Century, 1940).

——, *German Youth: Bond or Free* (New York: The Grove Press, 1946).

——, *Through Values to Social Interpretation* (Durham: Duke University Press, 1950), chaps. 2, 4, and 5.

BECKER, HOWARD, and BARNES, HARRY ELMER, *Social Thought from Lore to Science* (2nd ed., Washington, D. C.: Harren, 1952).

——, and USEEM, RUTH HILL, "Sociological Analysis of the Dyad," *American Sociological Review,* 7 (1942), pp. 13–26.

BENEDICT, RUTH, *Patterns of Culture* (New York: Penguin, 1946).

BOAS, FRANZ, *General Anthropology* (Boston: Heath, 1938).

BRIFFAULT, ROBERT, *The Mothers* (New York: Macmillan, 1927).

CARPENTER, C. RAY, "A Field Study in Siam of the Behavior and Social Relations of the Gibbon (*Hylobatas lar*)," *Comparative Psychology Monographs,* 16 (1940).

CHILDS, GLADWYN, *Umbundu Kinship and Character* (London: Oxford University Press, 1949).

DE ROUGEMONT, DENIS, *Love in the Western World* (New York: Harcourt, Brace, 1940). Translated by Montgomery Belgion.

DEWEY, JOHN, *Human Nature and Conduct* (New York: Holt, 1922).

DU BOIS, CORA, *The People of Alor* (Minneapolis: University of Minnesota Press, 1944).

FORTUNE, REO FRANKLIN, "The Social Organization of Dobu," reprinted from *Sorcerers of Dobu,* pp. 1–93 (London: George Routledge & Sons, Ltd., 1931).

FREUD, SIGMUND, *Totem and Taboo* (New York: Dodd, Mead, 1912).

GOLDENWEISER, ALEXANDER, *Anthropology* (New York: Crofts, 1937).

HAUSWIRTH, FRIEDA, *Purdah: The Status of Indian Women* (New York: Vanguard, 1932).

HOWELLS, WILLIAM, *Mankind So Far* (New York: Doubleday, 1945).

INMAN, SAMUEL GUY, *Latin America* (rev., New York: Harcourt, Brace, 1942).
KARDINER, ABRAM, *The Psychological Frontiers of Society* (New York: Columbia University Press, 1945).
KETKAR, S. V., *The History of Caste in India* (Ithaca: Taylor & Carpenter, 1909).
LATOURETTE, KENNETH SCOTT, *The Chinese, Their History and Culture* (New York: Macmillan, 1946).
MAINE, HENRY SUMNER, *Ancient Law* (New York: Holt, 1888).
MEARS, HELEN, *The Year of the Wild Boar* (Philadelphia: Lippincott, 1942).
NISSEN, H. W., "A Field Study of the Chimpanzee," *Comparative Psychology Monographs,* 10 (1934).
NITOBE, INAZO, *Bushido, The Soul of Japan* (New York: Putnam, 1905).
POWDERMAKER, HORTENSE, *Life in Lesu* (New York: Norton, 1933).
REDFIELD, ROBERT, *The Folk Culture of Yucatan* (Chicago: University of Chicago Press, 1941).
SANSOM, G. B., *Japan, A Short Cultural History* (New York: Century, 1931).
VALAVALKAR, PANDHARINATH H., *Hindu Social Institutions* (London: Longmans, Green, 1939).
WELLS, H. G., HUXLEY, JULIAN, and WELLS, C. P., *The Science of Life* (New York: Literary Guild, 1929).
WESTERMARCK, EDWARD, *The History of Marriage* (London: Macmillan, 1921).
YERKES, R. M. and ADA W., *The Great Apes* (New Haven: Yale University Press, 1943).
ZUCKERMAN, S., *The Social Life of Monkeys and Apes* (New York: Harcourt, Brace, 1932).

TOPICS FOR DISCUSSION OR REPORTS

1. Discuss the role of instinct in subhuman family types.
2. What is the effect of a "rutting" period upon the family organization of subhuman animal forms?
3. Emotion has been described as the reaction that occurs as a result of the frustration of the usual activities of the organism. What relevance does this statement have for Westermarck's theory that monogamy is an inevitable result of masculine jealousy?
4. The thesis has been advanced that human families most probably have had multiple origins. What arguments can you advance for and against this?
5. Artificial insemination has been proved practical for human beings. Would you class the general application of this practice as a sacred or a secular tendency? Why?
6. Which of the family types sketched is most comparable to the present-day American family? In what respects?
7. Read the account of the Kwakiutl in Ruth Benedict's *Patterns of Culture.* Analyze the family form in terms of the concepts of this chapter.
8. In what respects do the apes display a greater fixity of instinctual endowment than human beings? What effect does this have on the respective families?
9. Discuss the role of learning in the human family.
10. To what extent do sacred and secular family types tend to be self-sufficient economic units? How do you account for the difference?

11. Discuss the thesis that the institution of private property has been the primary instrument of the evolution of the family.

12. What are the advantages of the "historical" method of family study? What are its limitations?

13. In the histories of various peoples families have changed in spite of the fact that the members of the families have been satisfied. How do you account for this fact?

14. Discuss some of the ways in which the family institutions have been inter-related with other institutions of given societies.

15. What is meant by a constructed type (see footnote 26) of family? Describe a constructed type of sacred family, of secular family.

16. Compare the simplified treatment of sacred and secular found in this chapter with that presented in Chapter One. What advantages or disadvantages arise from the difference in the emphasis on affective nonrationality as manifested in a secular society — especially of the normless or unstable type?

Chapter Three

Ancient Past and Living Present

ARNOLD S. NASH

MARRIAGE HELPS TO INSTITUTIONALIZE THE FAMILY

EXHIBITED in and represented by the phrase "marriage and the family" is a certain minimum and ever-present pattern: each family, whatever form it may take, has its origin in that particular union of men and women, either singly or collectively, that we call marriage. Indeed, one of the few definite conclusions to emerge from the extensive anthropological and sociological investigation and research initiated by Sir Henry Maine's pioneering work of nearly a hundred years ago is that marriage has its origin in the family and not *vice versa*. In fact, the tendency nowadays is to define marriage in terms of the family by saying that marriage is that institutionalizing union, temporary or permanent, between a man and a woman that persists beyond the acts of procreation and birth of the offspring to the time when the child or children of the union can fend for themselves. The modern democratic conception of marriage as a union based on mutual affection and with the intention of permanence is a very recent idea.

By using in the active mood a transitive verb like "institutionalize" we do not wish to suggest that marriage is a sufficient factor for the emergence of the family. Indeed, quite the opposite tends to be true; historically, marriage arises out of the development of the family only as soon as the individual family has the required measure of continuity. It is then already an institution, *implicitly;* marriage merely represents a more *explicit* kind of institutionalization.

The family can be institutionalized by various means. It may be by religious or legal sanction, or it may be even by mere community consensus. Without such implicit or explicit institutionalization the family is simply an organized group of no great continuity. In other words, it is not a family at all.

The origin of marriage cannot be found in mutual affection since a husband and wife may separate, as in many tribes they do, after the child or children have reached independence. Neither does sexual drive of itself account for the emergence of marriage, since the history of concubinage, prostitution, and the like indicates how the attempt to satisfy the sexual impulse can be made independently of the permanent or semipermanent ties associated with marriage. It seems most likely that in the early development of the human race those parents who did not develop the practice of nurturing their young simply lost them, and hence they failed to propagate themselves. Thus it is in a biological fact — the lengthy duration of the period of helplessness of the human infant — that a union of a man and a

84

woman sufficiently permanent to be called a marriage has its origin. Moreover, it is another biological fact — only the human female can bear children — that in its turn conditions the form the institution of marriage takes.

ANCIENT AND MODERN MARRIAGE AND SOCIETY

Within the range of these biological necessities the human race has worked out the multitudinous types of the noninstinctive social group that we call the family. In other words, marriage and the family in human society are what they are because man, although biologically conditioned, yet has a capacity for creativity so that repeatedly he invents something new and unexpected. No culture known to historians or sociologists more clearly illustrates this truth than that of North America at the present time. Man can mold marriage and the family, not because he can change the biological conditions just referred to but because in a particular cultural context he can direct and to some extent (as in the case of birth control and planned parenthood) effectively regulate them. Thus, to understand marriage and the family in North America is to understand that particular complex of "inner" human drives and "external" social conditions which we call North American culture. Yet this in its turn can be comprehended only in the light of its past, and that is the evolution of a particular version of European culture transferred to the wide-open spaces of the North American continent and left to develop within that geographical environment. Well before we reached the twentieth century this version of European culture had been radically transformed. What began as a peculiar synthesis of free enterprise in economics, representative democracy in politics, and sectarian Protestantism in religion has now changed almost beyond recognition. But society, like man, can never break away completely from its origins. Indeed, the resemblance goes further. The psychiatrist finds that he has to take his analysis back to earlier stages in human development, especially periods of crisis such as birth and puberty, if he would understand the sickness of his patient. Similarly, anyone who would understand the maladjustments of our contemporary society must go back to its earlier and formative — what we usually call revolutionary — stages. That process of itself will not furnish such an inquirer with complete understanding; but without it even a partial understanding will be denied him. It is for this reason among others, and not only for the purpose of so-called academic completeness, that in this book explicit attention is being given to the historical aspects of marriage and the family.

Moreover, the Protestant-capitalist-democratic form of the family, whose evolution in America we have witnessed since the days of the early pioneers, was not created *ex nihilo*. Like Topsy, it just grew; but it grew out of the chaos left in the sixteenth century by the collapse of the medieval synthesis of Western Europe.[1] Upon a universal economic basis (feudalism) there

[1] Within recent years a voluminous literature has arisen on this subject. A student who wishes to study the question might begin with:
H. J. Laski, *The Rise of Liberalism* (New York: Harper, 1936); R. H. Tawney, *Religion and the Rise of Capitalism* (New York: Harcourt, Brace, 1926); A. N. Whitehead, *Science and*

was built a universal church (Catholic), a universal law (Roman), a universal art (Gothic), a universal metaphysic (scholastic theology), a universal code of honor (chivalry), a universal ethic (Greco-Christian), and a universal language (Latin). But this society, too, had its origins. It was the outcome of the impact of the Judaic-Christian tradition, in the dress of Greco-Roman culture, upon the Teutonic barbarians who provided the human material out of which feudal society, and therefore Western civilization, was ultimately molded.[2]

In our historical analysis the farthest we can penetrate is to the part played by the Hebrew, Greek, and Roman traditions in laying the spiritual and intellectual, if not the ethnic, foundations of Western civilization. If we seek to go back farther we enter Europe at the dawn of its history, reaching preliterate and therefore "prehistorical"[3] societies.

To consider the historical origins — as distinct from the sociological or biological origins — of the contemporary family is to examine the part played by marriage and the family in the life of the ancient world. That subject, however, is inexhaustible and, for our purpose, not immediately profitable since we can limit ourselves to such a study only so far as light is thrown on the marriage and family patterns of later Western civilization. Although it would be misleading to overemphasize the resemblances between the three strands that make up our rope, yet we can take courage since there are certain common features in their origin and development which will at many points lighten our task.

In the first place, each of the three cultures pass successively from pastoral nomadism to urban trade and commerce through an intermediate stage of settled agriculture. Secondly, each culture repeats to a considerable extent the same pattern of struggle for freedom against tyranny, since each society was a "class" society as a direct outcome of the existence of a slave economy. Thirdly (and from the standpoint of this chapter the most important resemblance), each of the three cultures presents the family[4] in its patriarchal form as the type that predominates amid the changes and chances of war and peace, famine and prosperity, that made up its chequered history.

THE HEBREW FAMILY

About two thousand years before the beginning of the Christian era there were substantial population movements in what we now call North Arabia. Certain nomadic tribes moved with their goods and chattels, flocks and herds, to settle in northern Mesopotamia. Within two centuries the whole

---

the *Modern World* (New York: Macmillan, 1925); Reinhold Niebuhr, *Beyond Tragedy* (London: Nisbet, 1938); ——, *The Nature and Destiny of Man* (New York: Scribner's, 1941–43).

[2] On this whole question see Part I of *The Making of Europe* by Christopher Dawson (New York: Sheed & Ward, 1945).

[3] I am using here the usual framework of ideas for which the distinction between prehistory and ancient history is the discovery of writing. For a review of some of the results of writing and its concomitant, accounting, see the previous chapter (pp. 67–68) by Don Martindale.

[4] Our word "family" is derived from the word used by the Romans to designate the group of members of a man's household who lived under his roof.

area between the Mediterranean coast line and the upper Tigris was dominated by a people known in the Old Testament as the Amorites. This people produced, on the one hand, the first dynasty of Babylon, the most illustrious member of which was the famous Hammurabi; and, on the other hand, in all probability the Hebrew patriarchs.

What we know of their early history is full of speculation. The name by which they first call themselves is B'ne Israel (the sons of Israel). Yet their tradition has it that Israel himself was a descendant of the desert sheik, Abram, to whose independence of thought and action they owed their origin as a self-conscious group. According to Genesis, Chapter 11, however, it was still another ancestor, Terah, the father of Abram, who initiated the original move northwards from the ancestral home at Ur.[5]

It is not until the lapse of six or seven centuries that we enter history proper. Then these desert nomads were driven by a scarcity of food from what we now call Palestine into Egypt, where they ended as slave laborers in the extensive building operations of, most probably, Rameses II. Thanks to the imagination and leadership of one of their number, Moses, who stood in a peculiar relation both to the Egyptian ruling class and to the desert clans of Palestine, they were liberated, according to the most recent archaeological findings, about 1290 B.C. and became, to use the modern phrase, displaced persons. Under the leadership of Moses they finally escaped to the peninsula of Sinai. There for the first time they were welded into a real inner unity and became something more than the loose religious federation of previous years. Indeed, the events which took place in the Sinaitic desert and with which the name Moses has been associated in their thought and feeling, were so epoch-making that ever afterwards all their ethical codes and social customs, with their underlying theological basis, were ascribed to this period. Fundamental to all their future activity was a bond or covenant to the effect that although other gods may exist, their allegiance was to the god who had declared himself to them at that time, Yahweh.

These desert tribes, living a nomadic pastoral existence, journeyed north and fought the more civilized tribes occupying Palestine. They did not find the task easy, for the native inhabitants had erected lines of forts to safeguard the strategic routes. The most that the Israelites could do was to filter gradually into the hilly parts of the country and settle in scattered communities, each under the government of a sheik or elder. Gradually, as a result of intermarriage with the natives during intermittent periods of peace and conquest of the valleys during war, and after sundry battles and skirmishes, the country as a whole came under Israelite control. Finally by about 1000 B.C. the whole area, now based economically on a settled agriculture, came under the political control of one king, David, with his capital at Jerusalem. This consolidation was of short duration. Under his grandson

[5] J. H. Breasted, *The Conquest of Civilization* (New York: Harper, 1926), pp. 215 ff., gives perhaps the most readable of authoritative reconstructions of this period, but W. F. Albright, *From the Stone Age to Christianity* (Baltimore: Johns Hopkins Press, 1940; see especially pp. 140 ff.), gives the most recent archaeological knowledge. For reasonably recent sociological interpretation, see Max Weber, *Ancient Judaism,* trans. by H. H. Gerth and Don Martindale (Glencoe, Ill.: The Free Press, 1951).

the kingdom split to form two separate kingdoms — Israel in the North and Judah in the South. During this period and for the next few centuries we have the usual development of an agricultural country under the impact of trade, until there appears a commercialized society built on the town, with the usual glaring inequalities between rich and poor, and a resulting class struggle. Religiously considered, the most important aspect of this struggle was the outcome of the clash of the two cultures: the nomadic, brought by the wandering tribes, and the urban of the settled inhabitants. We can say that the Yahweh worship of the former provided the nomadic and sacred side of the dialectic, and the Baal worship of the latter furnished the urbanized and secular side of it.

In the meantime powerful empires had arisen in Egypt and Assyria. Palestine proved a cockpit and in 734 B.C. the upper classes of Israel, having made the mistake of organizing a coalition against the all-powerful Assyrians, were deported and lost to history. Just over a century later a new empire, Babylon, defeated both Assyria and Egypt, and the inhabitants of Judah became a subject people. They rebelled unsuccessfully against their overlords in 586 B.C., when they too were carried off into captivity. There they stayed until Babylon in her turn collapsed before the Persians under Cyrus, who allowed the remaining Jews to return to their homeland, still however as a subject people. They remained under Persian rule until Alexander the Great occupied their country after his defeat of the Persians. From this time onward the Jews were increasingly under the influence of Greek culture. This Hellenizing was to some extent halted when they recovered their independence in 165 B.C., but that did not last long, for they came under the sway of Rome through Pompey's victories in the Near East in 65 B.C.

Such in outline is the essence of the political and economic history of the Hebrews. Plainly, marriage and the family among a tribe of desert nomads under the patriarchal authority of a sheik is radically different from what it was during a period of self-government and urbanized trade under a typical oriental monarch like Solomon. That too is vastly different from what it was under the Greek rule of Alexander nearly seven centuries later. Yet there were many features that remained unchanged, and it is with those that we are here concerned.

In the earliest stages of Israelite history the family was matrilineal [6] but, as with all tribes living a nomadic life, the domestication of cattle and the development of a pastoral economy soon led to the emergence of the patriarchal family.

Until recently the general assumption was that matrilineal ideas exercised a strong influence on the thought and practice of the Hebrews during the historical period, i.e., from the time of Abram onwards. But during the past few years the overwhelming ascendancy of patriarchal ideas has been increasingly recognized and the influence of matriarchal conceptions has been almost completely dismissed. For example, E. B. Cross [7] and many others thought they detected in the Old Testament several instances of *beena* or

[6] See E. B. Cross, *The Hebrew Family* (Chicago: University of Chicago Press, 1927), chap. 1. Indeed, this stage goes so far back that to be accurate we should perhaps call it prehistory.
[7] *Op. cit.,* pp. 16 ff.

Sadica marriage, a form of marriage where at regular intervals the husband visits his wife who meanwhile continues to live with her own kin. Now these instances of apparent matriarchy, for that is what the existence of *beena* marriages indicates, are explained [8] in terms of a completely different set of ideas, as a form of marriage called *Errebu.* Here the husband is adopted by his father-in-law usually until such time as the bridegroom is considered to have discharged his obligation to furnish his bride's father with the appropriate *mohar* or "compensation gift."

Moreover, in addition to being patriarchal the Hebrew family was individual in that it consisted of a well-defined household of husband, wife or wives, concubines, children, grandchildren, and servants. Such a family, bound together by common interests, could readily function as a mobile group in its search for food and pasture.[9]

From this time onwards the patriarchal character of the family increased. If a wife committed adultery, her husband was empowered to determine whether the death penalty should be inflicted. A father's authority over his children was almost unlimited, for although he could not sell his daughter as a slave to a foreigner or condemn her to a life of prostitution, yet he could barter her as a slave to a fellow Israelite. But such a state of affairs did not mean that the father could govern the family as he wished. He may not have had an elaborate scheme of codified laws to serve as a rein on his masculine and paternal whims and in accordance with which his judgments were to be given, but he did have to reckon with the collected wisdom of tradition represented by the word *mishpat.* Translated literally it means "judgment" or "justice" but in actual fact it was construed by the Israelites as having more content than either of these abstract nouns has with us. For example, used with the verb "to keep" it meant for them legal ordinances.[10] Indeed *mishpat* was "the distillate of the accumulated rules of right conduct forming part of the clan's traditional heritage." [11]

That property rights played an important role in molding Hebrew thought and practice is evident too from the levirate, a custom which outlasted all the political upheavals we have just examined.[12] The brother of any man who died childless was expected by public opinion to marry his deceased brother's widow in order that his brother's name and estates might be preserved. As the centuries wore on, the custom was modified and loopholes were introduced, though that it had not disappeared by the time of Jesus is evident from the account of his famous controversy with the Sadducees concerning the life after death.[13]

It is hardly to be questioned that we have here a definite illustration of

[8] See E. Neufeld, *Ancient Hebrew Marriage Law* (London: Longmans, 1944), chap. 2, and note in particular the footnote references on p. 63.
[9] See the story of the clash between the servants of Abraham and Lot, Genesis 13:2–12.
[10] W. O. E. Oersterley and T. H. Robinson, *Hebrew Religion: Its Origin and Development* (New York: Macmillan, 1931), p. 283.
[11] Howard Becker and Harry Elmer Barnes, *Social Thought from Lore to Science,* hereafter also cited as *STFLTS* (2nd ed., Washington, D. C.: Harren, 1952), p. 116.
[12] For a conclusion to the contrary see E. B. Cross, *op. cit.,* p. 162.
[13] Matthew 22:23–30. By 1869, however, certainly so far as American Judaism is concerned, the practice was formally declared to have lost all meaning and force.

the general truth that in a pastoral and agricultural economy children are a distinct asset, whereas in an economy built on trade and commerce the contrary is more likely to be true.[14] For the same reason the Hebrew family tended to be polygynous in the case of the more wealthy sheiks like Jacob. This custom again carried with it such residual tenacity that it was continued well into the Middle Ages. However, once urbanized life was reached, the force of economic necessity for the bulk of the population was so strong that polygyny was the exception rather than the rule. Moreover even in the earlier pastoral times and during the days of the monarchy the practice of polygyny was restricted to the wealthy and more powerful leaders, the desert sheiks or warrior kings. This, as with the vast majority of tribes and races that allow polygyny in theory, is only to be expected since it is a limitation born of biological and economic necessity. With some qualification due to the differential in birth rate between males and females and to the apparently natural longevity of women as compared with men, the number of menfolk in a tribe equals that of the womenfolk. Although governmental stability is not seriously upset if the members of the ruling class have more than their share of the women available, it is clear that no society, the sex urge being as strong as it is, could long endure as a stable entity if any serious attempt were made by a substantial proportion of the males of a community to introduce polygyny as a widespread practice. Inevitably, therefore, this biological fact of the virtual equality in number of the sexes makes customary the practice of monogamy.

Last but by no means least is the weight of religious conviction in favor of monogamy. Old Testament scholars up to about a decade ago were so overwhelmed by the fashion in which evolutionary ideas had illuminated the study of the literature and history of the Hebrews that they tended to assume only too readily that all the practices and beliefs they studied were the expression of regular and orderly development. Thus they detected, so they thought, a steady evolution in Hebrew religious beliefs from animism to fetishism through polytheism to henotheism and then on to monotheism. Similarly they tended to construe Hebrew teaching about immortality as evolving from no faith at all in human existence after death to a belief in man's shadowy existence in the darkness of Sheol, then a doctrine of rewards and punishments, and finally a belief in the resurrection. Marriage and the family were seen as following a similar pattern from group marriage through polygamy to monogamy.

But it is now being increasingly recognized that a fruitful idea is not necessarily a key to unlock all doors. Indeed the contrary may be true; if we try it too often, it may break the lock! To be more literal, it is now evident that we cannot understand the Old Testament unless we recognize the existence of a pattern of ideas that keeps reappearing as a dominating theme and that shows no signs of evolving from lower to higher levels. The "idea" of God in his relation to man and the world as Creator is one of these patterns. Another is the notion that a monogamous marriage is in accord-

---

14 A conclusion well illustrated by contrasting the attitudes towards children in colonial and in contemporary America.

ance with the will of Yahweh. It is clear from archaeological evidence that this conviction is at least as old as Abram's contacts with Babylonian civilization,[15] and from the time of Abram onward both lawmaker and historian in the Old Testament records regard any departure from monogamy as a regrettable even if on occasion an inevitable step.

Moreover, economic factors contribute towards the predominance of monogamy, since in every society marriage is an expensive business. Indeed, from the standpoint of our Western approach to life, we often tend to think that among the ancient Israelites the bride was "bought." Thus the statement has been made that "outright purchase was the rule."[16] In a sense that is true, since a valuable gift called the *mohar* had to be given as a kind of compensation to the bride's family. But it was not purchase in the sense that a slave was purchased. Among recent scholars to work on this problem is Millar Burrows.[17] He argues that the primary purpose of marriage among the Israelites was to continue the husband's family. This meant that another family had to be induced to give up one of its female members to be a bride. A "compensation-gift" accomplished this end; thereby it created an obligation and sealed a contract between the two families. Burrows concludes that although economic development caused this procedure to look formally like a commercial transaction, the value of the *mohar* as a gift or present remained essentially the same. Thus during the nomadic period when Isaac's future wife, Rebekah, was betrothed to her spouse-to-be, her mother, Milcah, and brother, Laban, received valuable presents from Abram's emissary.[18] Her son, Jacob, in his turn too, met with considerable economic difficulty before he was able to satisfy the stringent financial conditions laid down by Laban, his future father-in-law. Jacob had to work for fourteen years to pay off his "debt."[19] However, as the centuries passed and the softening influence of civilized life began to operate, even the appearance of a primitive cash transaction was modified.

The introduction of a period of betrothal[20] prior to the actual wedding as the real terminus of the marriage negotiations represented the equivalent to the engagement period of modern Western civilization. The parallel is not exact, since if the betrothed woman had sexual relations with a man the crime for which she was punished was adultery. Evidently betrothal was regarded as a solemn *contract* of marriage rather than, as engagement is with us, a *promise* of marriage. Nevertheless, we undoubtedly see in this practice and the set of customs arising, the forerunner of many of our modern

---

[15] The code of Hammurabi assumes that marriage shall be monogamous, although under certain circumstances, such as childlessness or the illness of his wife, a man may take another one or a concubine. There seems to be more than an echo of Babylonian influence in Abram's relation with Hagar, his wife's Egyptian maid (Genesis 16:1 ff.).

[16] Becker and Barnes, *STFLTS*, p. 115.

[17] See his valuable monograph on this point, *The Basis of Israelite Marriage* (New Haven: American Oriental Society, 1938).

[18] Genesis 24:50–53.

[19] Genesis 25:1–28.

[20] See E. Neufeld, *Ancient Hebrew Marriage Law* (London: Longmans, 1944), chap. 9, for a discussion of betrothal.

usages. By the time we approach the Christian era the formality of betrothal was regarded as completed only when the bride-to-be had been presented with a small coin or a written promise of marriage. In each case at least two witnesses had to be present, and a benediction was pronounced at the conclusion of the ceremony by a rabbi or, if he were absent, by some elderly male relative. The actual wedding followed some time later. After a very simple religious ceremony, again before witnesses and again completed by the benediction pronounced by a rabbi, if present, and if not, by one of the male witnesses, the wedding party proceeded to their equivalent of the wedding breakfast of our era. In parentheses, one might note that the influence of Jewish ideas in forming the set of Christian marriage codes and customs was reciprocal. The Jews in the Middle Ages substituted the wedding ring instead of the coin while, as in the Christian community, the presence of an officiating minister became no longer optional but a necessity. In short the Jews, who had always given a religious content to the meaning of marriage and the family, now formally expressed that conviction by changing what was a private family ceremonial into a public religious service.

The Jews developed an elaborate code to govern what did and what did not constitute a valid marriage. From one angle a concubine was not a legal wife, yet under certain conditions the child of a concubine and even of a slave could be counted legitimate. But it was legitimacy with a difference, as indicated by the story of Hagar and her child by Abram, Ishmael. Sarah, Abram's legal wife, was willing to regard Ishmael as her legitimate son [21] until somewhat unexpectedly her own child, Isaac,[22] was conceived.

Legal marriage among the Hebrews was generally within the kinship, i.e., it was endogamous. Gradually the prophetic tradition, having taken marriage as one battleground upon which it could contend for Judaism as a universal religion, won out, as the insertion of the Book of Ruth as an authentic book in the Jewish Bible plainly indicates. Ruth was a heathen, a Moabitess; yet she was destined to become through her grandson David the ancestress of the Messiah of Israel. This pastoral love story was written after the exile as a protest against the policy of the authorities who sought to implement the teaching of the Book of Deuteronomy:

> An Ammonite or a Moabite shall not enter into the assembly of the Lord; even to the tenth generation shall none belonging to them enter into the assembly of the Lord for ever.[23]

Although the tendency was towards endogamy, yet there were many prohibited degrees of relationship within which marriage was ruled out. Originally they were introduced as prohibitions during the life of the wife. Thus a man

---

[21] Genesis 16:1 ff.

[22] *Ibid.*, 9:5–10.

[23] Deuteronomy 23:3. For an excellent but brief exposition of the significance of the Book of Ruth see the article by James Strahan in *A Commentary on the Bible,* edited by A. S. Peake (London: T. C. & E. C. Jack, 1924), pp. 271–272. For a contrary interpretation based upon the contention that the book was written before the exile, see *Marriage Laws in the Bible and the Talmud* by L. M. Epstein (Cambridge, Mass.: Harvard University Press, 1942), pp. 151 ff.

could not marry his half sister or his daughter-in-law. Later on, the range of these degrees of prohibited relationships was gradually extended; especially was this true as exogamy replaced endogamy in the relations between the Israelites and surrounding tribes and neighboring nations.[24] These prohibitions were destined to have considerable influence on Anglo-Saxon matrimonial law. Another point at which Jewish thought and practice have contributed to the character of Western marriage was on the all-important question of consent. No marriage was deemed valid unless both parties freely gave their agreement.[25] Presumably it was for this reason also that although a boy or girl could be betrothed before puberty, yet the marriage contract could not be regarded as legal until after that age had been reached, i.e., thirteen for a female and fourteen for a male. Moreover, this was no mere legality; a girl had the power to negate her betrothal made before puberty if after she had reached her fourteenth year she did not wish to abide by the arrangement previously made on her behalf by her father.

No aspect of marriage and the family indicates so clearly as divorce the changes wrought under the combined influence of political and economic development and the work of the prophets. From patriarchal times the husband had virtually unlimited freedom in giving his wife a bill of divorcement.[26] Public opinion, however, in a community that took the family so seriously as did the Jews, naturally acted as a strong brake upon any casual use of the simple formula "I divorce thee." Moreover, under the influence of prophets like Hosea and Malachi, strong opposition to divorce as such began to appear.[27] The wife was not so fortunate as the husband. Indeed, the only way she could get a divorce was by persuading her husband to divorce her.[28]

Jesus introduced a completely different and revolutionary standard of marriage and family life. Indeed, he went far beyond the teaching of the strictest school of rabbis, that of Shammai, and introduced a new test of inward loyalty that transcended any attempt to translate it into legal codes or social customs.[29]

Less than a generation after the death of Jesus, the Jews revolted against Rome, their capital was destroyed, and its inhabitants scattered. Marriage and the family like all else in Jewish life and culture was to be molded from henceforth within a completely Greco-Roman setting, and to this we must now turn.

[24] For an excellent précis of this process see Willystine Goodsell, *A History of Marriage and the Family* (New York: Macmillan, 1934), p. 62.

[25] It was for this reason that the Jews ruled out valid marriage as a possibility for the insane or the feebleminded.

[26] Deuteronomy 24:1 ff.

[27] See M. Mielziner, *The Jewish Law of Marriage and Divorce in Ancient and Modern Times* (Cincinnati: Bloch, 1884), chap. 15, and D. W. Amram, *The Jewish Law of Divorce According to the Bible and the Talmud* (Philadelphia: Amram, 1896), chap. 5.

[28] Mielziner, *op. cit.,* p. 118.

[29] Perhaps the most useful interpretation, in short compass, of New Testament teaching is the chapter "Marriage and the Family in the New Testament," by C. H. Dodd and Alan Richardson, in *Education for Christian Marriage,* edited by A. S. Nash (New York: Macmillan, 1940).

MARRIAGE AND THE FAMILY IN GREEK CULTURE

Prior to the opening years of the present century it was generally assumed that Western civilization had originated in Greece, but over the last forty years this assumption had been overthrown by the archaeological researches in Crete initiated by Sir Arthur Evans. These investigations have shown that the first real civilization to appear within the geographical limits of Europe existed during the Bronze Age on the island of Crete. Going back to the year 2500 B.C., it reached its heyday about a thousand years later. Our knowledge of it is still imperfect; for example, although we know that the Cretans used writing extensively, the linear script on the archaeological remains has not yet been fully deciphered. Still, the main outlines of Cretan or, as it is more usually called, Minoan history are clear. The leading center of this civilization was at Knossos, where the Cretans built a huge palace on the Egyptian model. They were skillful seamen and their commerce and culture had spread by 1600 B.C. to the islands and the part of the mainland that we now call Greece, giving rise to the Mycenaean civilization.

It is this civilization that Homer depicts in legendary form but there is certainly a definite historical core within the mythical stories of the *Iliad* and the *Odyssey*. Our greatest debt at this point is to the German-American archaeologist, Heinrich Schliemann, whose excavations in Asia Minor laid bare the ruins of ancient Troy and who initiated the investigation of ruins of the Mycenaean civilization on the Greek mainland.

This civilization was early subject to pressure and subsequent invasion from more primitive and pastoral tribes living in the plains to the north along the banks of the Danube. The exact details are matters of speculation from meager historical knowledge but the most probable reconstruction is that the vanguard of Ionians, a blue-eyed, fair-haired people speaking an Indo-European language, had intermarried with the aboriginal stock even prior to 1600 B.C. It is more than possible that this hybrid stock provided the biological bearers of Mycenaean cultures. In any case a second wave of Greek nomads, the Achaeans, pushed south and largely dispossessed their kinsmen who had begun to live in towns. The Achaeans soon learned the art of seamanship and began to trade along the shores of the Aegean Sea. This policy proved their undoing, for it left their cities open to yet a third wave of Greek-speaking nomads, the Dorians, who completed the process whereby the Greek tribes occupied the Greek mainland, the isles of the Aegean Sea including Crete, and the coast of the neighboring Asia Minor.[30]

Some of the Achaeans fled to the coast of Asia Minor and founded settlements there; others occupied the islands scattered up and down the Aegean Sea. They came to be known as Asiatic Ionians. By the seventh century B.C.

30 For attempted reconstructions of the course of the Greek invasions see J. H. Breasted, *The Conquest of Civilization* (New York: Harper, 1926), and W. G. de Burgh, *The Legacy of the Ancient World* (New York: Macmillan, 1924). Chap. 4 of Becker and Barnes, *STFLTS,* and Part I of *A History of Western Philosophy* by Bertrand Russell (New York: Simon & Schuster, 1945) should be consulted also for some illuminating analyses of the influence of geographical dispersion on social practices and beliefs.

these three groups of Ionian, Achaean, and Dorian stock became a self-conscious cultural entity, calling themselves the Hellenes, with a common language, Greek. Politically they were self-governing city-states with extensive trading relations, both by sea and by land, with each other and with the countries bordering on the shores of the Mediterranean.

As one would expect, the Ionian cities on the Asiatic mainland developed, under the stimulus of oriental culture, the first signs of the intellectual virility we associate with the glory that is Greece. Athens, however, had to wait more than a century to achieve her imperishable fame. In the early years of the fifth century B.C. all the Greek cities were engaged in a series of exhausting but finally successful wars against the Persian Empire. Athens now became the economic center of the Hellenic world, a position that was reflected in the burst of intellectual genius of which Socrates is the outstanding example. Unfortunately the animosities between the rival city-states had already evoked a series of civil conflicts — the so-called Peloponnesian War — that proved even more devastating than those against the Persian Empire. Indeed the peninsula had no real peace until the independent city-states were forced into a compulsory unity under Philip of Macedonia. His son, Alexander the Great, brought the whole of the eastern Mediterranean and Asia up to the gates of India under Greek control and Greek influence. After Alexander's death, his empire slowly disintegrated; the armies of its scattered parts were helpless against the disciplined legions of Rome. In 146 B.C. Greece became a Roman province under the once proud name of Achaea. As T. R. Glover points out,[31] she was not to recover her freedom from a foreign yoke until A.D. 1834.

The ancient Greek family was, practically speaking, an urbanized family. This fact was reflected in the family structure. Like the Hebrew family, it was patriarchal; but unlike the Hebrew family during so many centuries of the formative period of its history, the Greek family legally speaking was monogamous. Marriage to concubines, however, was permitted, and the influence of property rights together with the desire to ensure the survival of the family had the same effect as among the Hebrews. If a legal wife failed to bear children, the offspring of the concubine became the residual legatees of the estate. The similarity between the Greek and Hebrew views of the family does not terminate at that point, for there was in Greece an institution much like the levirate, whereby if the head of a family died leaving no sons then the heiress — daughter or widow — became the wife of the nearest male relative.

Again, as in the Hebrew family, the Greek father had almost unlimited authority over his children. His power, indeed, was more complete than among the Israelites. As in Rome, he had the right to decide whether a child after its birth should be accepted as a member of his family or whether it should be rejected and condemned to exposure and death.[32] If the new-born child, especially if it was a girl, was physically handicapped or disfigured, this

---

[31] *The Ancient World* (New York: Macmillan, 1935), p. 275.
[32] Both Aristotle and Plato argued in favor of this practice. See C. Schmidt, *The Social Results of Early Christianity* (London: Isbister, 1889), pp. 51 ff.

fate was usually its lot. Moreover, the Greek father's power over his children
was more extensive than that of the Hebrew father, in that no Greek son or
daughter had power to veto the father's choice of spouse.

The husband's authority over his wife was equally unquestioned. At law
she was not a person and therefore her property, even her dowry, belonged
to her husband. This philosophy of ownership expressed itself at every point
in the process whereby the Greek girl became a wife. The family was regarded as a means to safeguard property ownership, and to this whole system religious sanction was given by the institution of the family altar, with
the father as the priest to offer sacrifices to the spirits of the ancestors. Marriages were arranged for the perpetuation of the family and its ancestral
rites. Betrothal was a purely business and legal affair, but the wedding itself
involved an elaborate religious service conducted by the bride's father. Then
the custody of the bride was granted to the bridegroom and she became a
member of his family with the right to participate in its rites. From that
time onwards she was under her husband's control. In some cities like Sparta
she could move freely, but in others like Athens she could walk in the streets
only if veiled and even then only at her husband's pleasure. Regarded as an
inferior being, she had little social life with her husband even in her own
home; indeed, she was scarcely more than a housekeeper whose children
were legitimate. To compensate for the lack of any affection based on friendship and common intellectual pursuits with his wife, the Greek husband
sought the company of the *hetairae,* who were little more than cultured
prostitutes.

This state of affairs meant that in matters of divorce the Greek wife had
even fewer rights than among the Hebrews. Almost her only safeguard
against being cast off by her husband for any passing whim or fancy was
that if her husband divorced her he had to give back her dowry to her father
or, if the latter was dead, to the male relative to whom she was committed.
In addition, the ex-husband might be compelled to pay alimony as long as
his former wife remained unmarried.[33] These conditions, to the property-
loving Greek, were usually sufficient to make any husband thinking of a
divorce pause before taking that step and instead to find some other method
of dealing with his problem. He was usually able to do so except in the two
cases where there was some corresponding property interest at stake. The
first was adultery and the second was lack of legal issue. The very foundation of Greek life and culture was being undermined either if a husband did
not know whether his wife's child was his legal heir or if he had a wife who
could not give birth to children.[34]

As with the Jews, the only real way in which the Greek wife could get
a divorce was by persuading her husband to grant her one. In theory she

[33] C. B. Gulick, *The Life of the Ancient Greeks* (New York: Appleton, 1902), p. 125. My colleague, Professor Wallace Caldwell, rightly points out to me that the view of the Greek
family presented in this and the previous paragraph must be severely qualified if it is to
apply to the Spartan family or to the proletarian family of Athens.
[34] Where the situation was unfair in particular was that in view of their ignorance of the
physiology of conception the Greeks like the Hebrews simply assumed that failure of the
wife to conceive was always her "fault."

could get a divorce by proving that his conduct was prejudicial to the life of the family — another instance of the Greek concern with the family rather than with the individual man or woman — but in practice that was rarely possible. In any event, she had little encouragement to seek a divorce, since thereby she lost her social standing and had to go to the home of her nearest male relative so that she could worship once more at her own family's ancestral shrine.

To complete our picture of the politico-economic setting in which the family in the ancient world found itself, we must turn now to Rome.

Marriage and the Family in Ancient Rome

Unlike the Hebrews and the Greeks, very little is known of the Romans prior to the eighth century B.C. Rome was then a village inhabited by Latin-speaking tribes who in the sixth century B.C. were conquered by a tribe from the immediate north, the Etruscans. In 509 B.C. the Romans recovered their independence and set up a republic governed by a senate drawn from the land-owning aristocratic farmers, the patricians, together with two consuls who were members of the senate but in whose election the plebeians, i.e., artisans and other workers, had a voice. In the early years of the fifth century severe economic unrest precipitated a readjustment in political power whereby tribunes elected by the plebeians were given a considerable share in the government. As a cure for the increasing economic distress that this political readjustment failed to alleviate, Rome then embarked on a policy of imperialistic expansion. Despite initial setbacks, the whole of the Italian peninsula came under her control through victories over the Gauls in the north, the Samnites in the south, and the Greeks, defending Tarentum, a Greek city still farther to the south.

During this period the economic and spiritual foundations of the Roman family, as indeed the whole of Rome's cultural life, were being laid. For example, about this period the Romans adopted the Greek alphabet so that they could put into writing their own language, Latin.[35] Again, it is scarcely an exaggeration to say that the forms of law and methods of procedure that regulated Roman life and thought in the fifth century B.C. are expressed, although in modified form and on a larger scale, in the "civil" code promulgated by Justinian twelve hundred years later.

The divisive tendencies within Greek culture had proved almost too much for the military safety of the city-states when that security was imperiled by the Persian onslaughts. Alexander the Great, in spite of his brilliant accomplishments, did nothing to produce any really cohesive principle of unity. Perhaps like Plato he recognized that to achieve an adequate basis for a wider loyalty than the city-state he would have to destroy the Greek conception of the family. That was a world he did not try to conquer. The Roman leaders, on the other hand, were much more fortunate. From the earliest time the Roman family was regarded not as a rival to the state but as its

[35] F. Poland, E. Reisinger, and R. Wagner, *The Culture of Ancient Greece and Rome* (London: Harrap, 1926), p. 77.

mirror and therefore its training school. A most apt illustration of this attitude is given in Virgil's epic, the *Aeneid*. From a Roman standpoint the action of Aeneas in leaving Dido with whom he was in love and marrying Lavinia whom he did not love, was perfectly intelligible. Indeed, if he had done otherwise and so followed the inclinations of his own desire and not the good of the state, he would not have been the ideal Roman hero.

The authority of the Roman father over his family transcended even that of his Greek counterpart. It extended over the persons and goods of his sons as well as over his wife and his unmarried daughters, and it lasted as long as the patriarch was alive. Although he had to consult his peers among his relatives before he could condemn to death any of those in his power, the final decision in theory if not always in practice lay with him. The only way a son could achieve *patria potestas* (absolute authority) was by marriage. A daughter, too, escaped from her father's *potestas* (or, if he was dead, from that of her guardian) only by marriage. She then became subject to her husband's *potestas* with the status of a daughter. Moreover, only those who would have been in the *potestas* of a male had he lived were legally recognized as his kin. Thus a son, for example, was not regarded at law as a relative of the members of his mother's family.

Nevertheless the position of a Roman matron of free birth [36] was much more dignified than that of her Greek counterpart. Although she could not appear in court as a claimant since she had no legal status, nevertheless she had considerable social prestige in public and in her own home.[37] She could help her husband entertain friends and even assist at the family altar. Before marriage, too, the Roman girl had some liberty denied her Greek sister, e.g., she could, in theory, withdraw from a betrothal arranged by her father.

The actual wedding among the patrician class was either a religious ceremony at the home of the bridegroom conducted by a priest in front of witnesses or a lay ceremony based upon what appears to be a symbolical sale of the woman to the man. Among plebeians a procedure not unlike our marriage at common law was adopted: if a woman had lived with a man as his wife for a year and if she had not left him for longer than three days, then automatically she became his legal wife and came under his *potestas*. In each case, however, the prestige of the Roman matron in her own home-to-be was symbolized by her remark to her husband as she was lifted over the threshold of her new home: "Where thou art lord, I am lady."

As one would expect, this relationship between husband and wife was calculated to preserve the bond upon a more monogamous level than did the Greek family pattern. Moreover a free citizen could live in a legalized union with a plebeian woman, this relationship being called *matrimonium non justum*. The children of such a union would be regarded as his by custom

---

[36] Marriage among the Romans was subject to limitations depending on the status of the two parties, e.g., a woman marrying a husband of lower rank continued to remain, with certain qualifications, under the *potestas* of her own father. See Goodsell, *op. cit.*, pp. 121–122.

[37] See W. W. Fowler, *Social Life at Rome* (New York: Macmillan, 1909), pp. 145 ff., for an elaboration of this point.

but not by law, and hence they could not inherit his property as his children. There seems to have been no equivalent to the Greek *hetairae,* and concubinage in the ordinary sense was strongly condemned by public opinion until after the rapid expansion of the Roman Empire that followed the final defeat of Carthage in the middle of the second century B.C.

Rome soon became the mistress of the whole Mediterranean basin, and the resulting political and economic repercussions were linked with substantial changes in the pattern of Roman family life. Divorce before the Punic Wars, for example, could be obtained only with great difficulty. Indeed the wife had no rights at all, and only in the case of proved adultery could the husband divorce his wife without the permission of his own and his wife's male relatives. After the Punic Wars the situation was radically changed, and divorce became a mere commonplace. By the days of Augustus the resulting problem was so acute that he passed a law depriving adulterers of half their fortune and forbidding them to marry each other.[38] His policy represented a real attempt to grapple with a state of affairs which, as he recognized, would ruin the empire. For example, in the earlier centuries adultery by the wife was sufficient cause for death at the hands of her husband, but if he were guilty then there was no corresponding punishment. Augustus sought to change all this by treating the two sexes equally and by making divorce more difficult to obtain. The law was honored, nevertheless, more in the breach than in the observance. Divorce was actually granted on the most trivial grounds, and Augustus' legislation proved to be a mere dead letter. Even women had so much latitude that there is little exaggeration in Seneca's oft-quoted and bitter comment that Roman women counted the years not by consuls but by husbands.

Undoubtedly among the chief reasons for this radical re-orientation of Roman society to divorce was the increasing wealth that came to Rome's coffers from plunder and tribute. Another factor was the power delegated to the patrician wife when her husband was away on some military or political errand for the imperial government. Inevitably marriage itself, under social pressures occasioned by these changed conditions, altered its character. It became merely a matter of consent; the wedding became less and less a religious rite and, most important, the wife, being now able to own property, remained a member of her own family so that she was no longer under the power of her husband.

Parallel to these revolutionary changes was a disinclination to marry at all. This of itself was indicative of the plight into which the empire had fallen at the height of its military power. Ancient family ideals no longer served to challenge the practices of a generation to whom a decline in moral standards was simply a matter of course. Marriage was no longer regarded as a matter upon which the dignity and honor of the state ultimately depended. Both men and women, following only the personal gratification of their own desires, chose illicit affairs rather than marriage with its legal and

[38] Jerome Carpocino, *Daily Life in Ancient Rome* (New Haven: Yale University Press, 1940), p. 94.

moral and civic responsibilities. In short, marriage tended to disappear [39] to such an extent that Julius Caesar initiated a series of rewards as an incentive to the adoption of the marital state. But the canker had eaten too far into the fabric of Roman society. The sickness was too deep for financial inducement, direct or indirect, to have a profound effect. Augustus Caesar soon realized that Rome faced a crisis not only in her attitude towards marriage but also in her economic life and in her political ideals. The empire had lost its nerve, for the crisis was one of faith. Whether his attempt, to use his own words, "to establish the republic safe and sound on its foundations" was doomed to failure from the very outset is a problem of speculation to be left to the philosophically minded political historian. What we do know is where his efforts failed [40] Christianity succeeded. The faith that conquered the Roman world substituted for Augustus' plan the conviction that in the death and resurrection of a crucified carpenter was to be found the key to the understanding of the universe. Here is not the place to try to ascertain why the Christian church finally prevailed. What information we have is from the New Testament writers and early Church Fathers, all of whom were concerned with what they conceived to be far more important matters than the rise and fall of an empire, even if that empire was Rome. As for the pagan writers, they really tell us nothing. Indeed, as the famous Lecky remarks:

> There is no fact in the history of the human mind more remarkable than the complete unconsciousness of the importance and the destinies of Christianity, manifested by the pagan writers before the accession of Christianity.[41]

In the light of our concern with marriage and the family, the important thing is that all the writers [42] who have grappled with the problem of why Christianity succeeded have recognized that Christian belief and practice about marriage played a most significant part in the result.

MARRIAGE AND THE FAMILY IN THE EARLY CHRISTIAN ERA

Christianity began as a sect within Judaism but in less than a generation after the death of Christ it was clear to Jew and Christian alike that the new wine of the Christian faith was too potent for the old wineskins of the tradi-

---

[39] Many parallels have been drawn between the decay of civilization in the Roman Empire at this time and its fate during the present era. At no point does the parallel seem more obvious than in the field of marriage. The head of the London School of Economics, Sir Alexander Carr-Saunders, wrote a few years ago: "It is as certain as anything can be that, where families are voluntary, a community, in which marriage is regarded as it is today in Western civilization, will die out." *World Population* (Oxford: University Press, 1936), p. 256. Substitute the words "Roman Empire" for "Western civilization" and it might be Seneca writing. For a more optimistic interpretation of current trends in family life see Hill's chapter, pp. 773–806.

[40] For a fascinating analysis of the significance of Augustus' attempt see Part I of C. N. Cochrane's *Christianity and Classical Culture* (Oxford: Clarendon Press, 1940).

[41] In his *History of European Morals* (London: Watts, 1924), p. 142.

[42] Perhaps the most useful among recent reviews of the various answers to this problem can be found in H. J. Randall, *The Creative Centuries* (London: Longmans, 1945), chap. 24.

tional Jewish religious scheme. Marriage was one of the first social institutions to receive a new orientation. Judaism allowed polygamy but the early church espoused monogamy and the strictest rules about divorce. The ambiguity in the records of the teaching of Jesus occasioned then, as it does today, considerable confusion about the possibility of divorce where adultery had been committed.[43] At other points — and those the more fundamental — the early church followed the best insights of the Old Testament. Marriage was instituted by God for his purposes and not as a means of legitimizing sexual satisfaction. Here St. Paul's teaching [44] was plainly inconsistent both with traditional Judaism and with the teaching of Jesus. For St. Paul the marital state as compared with celibacy was but a second best. This teaching dogged the Christian church for centuries, though there is no warrant for it in the teaching of Jesus. Undoubtedly St. Paul, like the early Church Fathers who followed him, was so overwhelmed by the licentiousness of the corrupt society around him that he often tended to regard sex itself as evil. Yet even in his most pessimistic moods he never completely adopted the view that sex as such is to be condemned. Indeed the most striking quality about St. Paul's and early Christian teaching as a whole is its inconsistency: marriage might be a remedy for sin, but the union of husband and wife in marriage was also a symbol of the union between the risen Christ and the Christian community. Thus the family was an image of the church.

In the light of these somewhat contradictory beliefs the early Christians tried to work out a philosophy and practice of Christianity in the Roman Empire. They regarded themselves as pilgrims in a strange land, and if martyrdom was to be their lot so let it be. In the strength of this faith they lived and died. Slowly, indeed almost imperceptibly, they wrought a great transformation through all ranks of Roman society. H. J. Laski has recently analyzed the victory of Christianity by pointing out that [45] Christianity conquered because it removed the sense of moral frustration that beset all classes and races in the Empire; the masses felt bitterly the injustice of life, and the intellectual elite suffered from a paralyzing frustration of mind.[46] Moreover Christianity spoke in universal terms to all the diverse races and tribes that made up the empire. By A.D. 300, as Diocletian found out, Christianity was too powerful among officers and administrators to be coerced out of existence by persecution. In 312 Christianity was placed on a legal equality with other tolerated religions of the empire, and its confiscated property was restored.[47]

Until the Christian church was legally tolerated by the Empire — and indeed for almost a century afterwards — the influence of Christianity upon marriage and the family was mainly indirect. The members of the church carried on, seeking to express their philosophy of marriage within the framework of the marriage codes of Roman law and custom. Their greatest con-

---

[43] According to Mark 10:11–12 and Luke 16:18 divorce under any circumstances was excluded, whereas according to Matthew 5:31–32 an exception is possible.

[44] 1 Corinthians 7:1 ff.

[45] *Faith, Reason, and Civilization* (London: Gollancz, 1944), chap. 5.

[46] *Op. cit.*, p. 29.

[47] Contrary to what is usually said (e.g., by Goodsell, *op. cit.*, p. 160), Christianity was not *established* then "as the official religion of the empire." That came much later.

tribution undoubtedly was in attacking abortion, infanticide, and child exposure. To the Christian all life was holy. Had not the Lord of the Universe in the person of Jesus of Nazareth bought every human soul and was not every individual therefore of infinite worth whether in the womb or out of it? The church leaders soon found out that preaching and ecclesiastical censure were not enough. The practices against which they inveighed had been illegal for years. Only gradually, and that after some centuries, did the practices finally disappear.

In the matter of child exposure the Christian emperors, like their pagan predecessors, had to recognize that it was much easier to get laws passed than to get them obeyed. So it was with divorce. Moreover the early church had no common mind on the question until the Council of Arles in A.D. 314. Generally speaking, the Christian emperors followed the method of their predecessors: they made divorce financially difficult. If the wife was proved to be the guilty party, she lost the marriage settlement granted to her by her husband. If the husband was proved guilty, then he had to surrender his wife's dowry. In the absence of either dowry or settlement then a quarter of the guilty party's property was forfeited.[48]

The rigidity of the above arrangements was qualified, however, at one or two points. As celibacy increased in popularity, divorce was granted without the financial penalties just described if one of the parties concerned wished to take up life in a monastery or a nunnery. In addition, the wife could claim divorce without penalty if her husband was absent for more than five years, and her husband could claim divorce by good grace, as it was called, if there seemed good reason to believe that children could not be born of the union. At this point the early church was echoing the conviction common to the three types of marriage pattern already described, to the effect that a primary purpose of marriage was the procreation of children. The celibate life, however, was universally regarded among the early Fathers as more worthy in the sight of God than the marital state. One legislative result of this conviction was that the legal penalties, somewhat vainly imposed by Augustus Caesar in an attempt to discourage celibacy and childlessness, were removed.

At one further point the Christian church strongly encouraged the tendency, already present in social life, whereby the authority of the father declined. As we have seen, during pagan times the wife was achieving an independent juridical status. But it was not then for the highest reasons. Christianity, by affirming that in Christ there was neither male nor female, furnished both an intellectual and a moral justification that pagan Rome lacked for improvement in the status of women.

Moreover, the increasing severity of laws against infanticide and infant exposure symbolized a radical diminution in the power of a father over his children. During the reign of the pagan emperors the sale of free children into slavery was increasingly discouraged. By the time of Diocletian and

[48] *The Institutes of Justinian,* translated by J. T. Abdy and Bryan Walker (Cambridge: University Press, 1876), p. 463.

Maximian it was forbidden, but Constantine allowed an exception in the case of parents who were too poor to bring up their children properly.[49]

In summary, the influence exerted by Christianity on the Roman Empire weakened the Greco-Roman family by encouraging celibacy and by teaching that loyalty to the family, like that to the state, was of less importance than loyalty to Christ and the church; but it strengthened the family upon the plane of personal relationship — as distinct from that of legal enactment — by emphasizing the worth of monogamy and lessening paternal authority.

SELECTED READINGS

ALBRIGHT, W. F., *From the Stone Age of Christianity* (Baltimore: Johns Hopkins Press, 1940).

BREASTED, J. H., *The Conquest of Civilization* (New York: Harper, 1926).

BURROWS, MILLAR, *The Basis of Israelite Marriage* (New Haven: American Oriental Society, 1938).

CALDWELL, W. E., *The Ancient World* (New York: Rinehart, 1937).

DE BURGH, W. G., *The Legacy of the Ancient World* (New York: Macmillan, 1924).

GOODSELL, WILLYSTINE, *A History of Marriage and the Family* (New York: Macmillan, 1934).

LECKY, W. E. H., *History of European Morals* (London: Watts, 1924).

MACE, DAVID R., *Hebrew Marriage* (London: Epworth, 1953).

MENDELSOHN, I., "The Family in the Ancient Near East," in *The Biblical Archaeologist*, 11, pp. 24–40.

MILLER, WALTER, *Greece and the Greeks* (New York: Macmillan, 1941).

NEUFELD, E., *Ancient Hebrew Marriage Law* (London: Longmans, 1944).

PEAKE, A. S., *A Commentary on the Bible* (London: Jack, 1924).

POLAND, F., REISINGER, E., and WAGNER, R., *The Culture of Ancient Greece and Rome* (London: Harrap, 1926).

SCHMIDT, C., *The Social Results of Early Christianity* (London: Isbister, 1889).

TROELTSCH, ERNST, *The Social Teaching of the Christian Churches* (London: Allen and Unwin, 1931).

WEBER, MAX, *Ancient Judaism,* trans. by H. H. Gerth and Don Martindale (Glencoe, Ill.: The Free Press, 1951).

TOPICS FOR DISCUSSION OR REPORTS

1. Discuss the influence of urbanized life upon marriage and the family in the three cultures considered in this chapter.
2. Write an essay on the history of the Greek family.
3. Describe the influence of the spread of the Roman Empire on marriage and the family in Rome.
4. What remnants of the Hebrew, Greco-Roman, and early Christian marriage patterns are to be found in the customs and marriage laws of your state?

[49] Abdy and Walker, *op. cit.,* p. 458.

Chapter Four

Family Carry-Overs of Western Christendom

RICHARD A. SCHERMERHORN

THE MIDDLE AGES is a child reared by an old man," declared Antoine Augustin Cournot. This penetrating comment gives us a clue to the development of European society after the Dark Ages. The child in the metaphor represents the Teutonic tribes with their artless, simple-minded, and free-spoken customs, while the old man symbolizes the merging of classical and Christian ideals, codified into law and incorporated into the institutions of both church and society. Or to change the figure, the child could be called the sacred group which gradually modified its conduct because of migration into areas where rules and regulations from the defunct Roman secular community were operating on new ground. Here it will help us to think of the analogy of a map drawn on a broad scale. On such a map a river may appear to be a straight line between two points, and in a sense it is true to say that the river proceeds from A-town to B-town quite directly. But a surveyor's map which traces the detail of the river may show that at times it has many meanderings and turnings, that here and there it curves back on itself, so that it proceeds very unevenly from one town to another. Thus while we can say that the evolution of the European family is in general from the sacred to the secular, we must also recognize that there have been many interruptions of its even course and its irregular flow needs charting.

Let us begin by getting a bird's-eye view of these deviations which we shall discuss in more detail below. First of all came the migrations of tribes in which kinship bonds were changed in form and gradually broken down; then there was the change in sexual dominance which accompanied it; there was intermarriage with other groups; there was change in the type of economy; military safety and security required reshaping of the community; rigid regulation followed such attempts at security; new currents of thought from the Orient and from Moorish Spain flowered into the heresy of Catharism and the romantic ideal of medieval chivalry; Christian authoritarianism attempted to hold the impulses of man in line; towns and cities sprang up in which individualistic and bourgeois existence replaced the old feudal culture; the Renaissance with its new confidence in science and reawakened appreciation of classical ideals turned attention to this-worldly matters, while the Reformation, on its side, secularized the legal basis of marriage. All these twistings and turnings occurred before the European family was finally transformed from a type predominantly sacred to its later secular form. Since our major concern is with the European family before colonial settlements in America, the Renaissance movement will receive little attention; but its major importance must not be forgotten.

The Early Barbaric Family

Before the Roman invasions of Western Europe and long after, the continent was peopled by innumerable tribal units of Teutonic origin such as Goths, Norsemen, Franks, Danes, and Saxons. Although no written records of their life exist, many of their customs are inferred from sagas or from legal records of the historical period. There is some evidence that the most ancient family type among these tribes may have been brother-sister marriage similar to that of the nonliterates of Hawaii.[1] On the whole, however, the most common form was probably the matriarchal family with the children cared for by the mother, since the father was unknown or unrecognized.[2] Early Russia, too, had a matriarchate; brother-sister incest was not tabooed. Women had many rights including choice of husbands, and there was a strong tie between brother and sister.[3] Echoes of the early period are found in the rule of the *Sachsenspiegel,* a thirteenth-century compendium of Teutonic laws, which states flatly that "no child is illegitimate as regards the mother,"[4] as well as in the fact that woman received a high place in German respect; her wisdom was prized as almost magical.[5] (Is there a trace of this in Goethe's famous lines, *Das Ewig-Weibliche zieht uns hinan* — "The eternal feminine draws us upward"?)

Following the dawn period of the family came the organization of kinship groups into clans (*Sippen*) grouped around the female line.[6] By the time the Romans came into contact with the Teutons, this had changed so markedly that the *Sippe* or clan included kindred descended from the grandchildren of two common ancestors.[7] What brought about the shift of emphasis is not certain; but continual migration, bringing close culture contacts with other tribes, undoubtedly had its effect. This bilateral descent differed from the Roman practice of tracing the line through the males only (agnation). The *Sippe* or clan kept order and punished crimes. Married women still belonged to their old sib after marriage.

With the coming of intertribal hostility and continual warfare with the Romans, woman assumed a more and more subordinate function in the group. It is axiomatic that a military society will give a higher status to men than to women, and this influence soon made itself felt. Before long, the eldest male gradually became chief protector and organizer of the clans and

---

[1] Karl Lamprecht, *Deutsche Geschichte* (7 vols.; Berlin: Gaertner, 1902), 3rd ed., Vol. 1, p. 90.

[2] *Ibid.*, pp. 91–92. See also F. Müller-Lyer, *The Family,* translated by F. W. Stella Browne (New York: Knopf, 1931), p. 216.

[3] Elaine Elnett, *Historic Origin and Social Development of Family Life in Russia* (New York: Columbia University Press, 1926), pp. 1–2.

[4] Lamprecht, *op. cit.,* p. 101.

[5] J. J. Bachofen developed the theory in the nineteenth century that a matriarchal society with its "mother-right" preceded the patriarchal universally. Although this theory is not accepted by anthropologists today, it appears to apply for Teutonic groups.

[6] Lamprecht, *op cit.,* p. 93.

[7] Willystine Goodsell, *A History of Marriage and the Family* (New York: Macmillan, 1934), rev. ed., pp. 191–192.

this power became identical with that of a war lord.[8] The barbarian Goths, Franks, and Saxons entered their heroic age led by bold military chieftains whose triumphs were celebrated in saga and epic.[9] The constant movement of peoples brought a weakening of clan solidarity and an increase of personal loyalty to a war lord; with it came also the growth of more or less vigorous conjugal rather than consanguine relationships. At first these ties were not too strong, for bigamy and polygyny were perhaps natural results of the free and easy life pursued by the chiefs.[10] The tribes or political units needed the strength of masculine power; and this power, freed suddenly from old kinship restraints, was ungovernable. Abductions and marriage by capture were common among Goths, Norsemen, Langobards, Franks, and Alemanni.[11] Among the Russians of the same general period adultery, wife capture, and sexual relations of fathers with daughters-in-law were also common.[12]

The capture of women became prevalent and continued up to the sixth century. Teutonic tribes in the early Christian era regarded abduction and betrothal as practically synonymous. In Anglo-Saxon law it was a respectable marriage, while widows in the Frankish kingdom asked King Lothar's protection against abduction. Survivals appear in wedding ceremonies in southern Germany and Austria even in the twentieth century.[13] Later, a payment in settlement for abduction of the bride appeared, and finally the bride price remained while the abduction vanished or became a fiction. This bride price gave the bridegroom the power of protection over the bride and eventually it was called the *mundium* (*muntehe*) or power over the bride herself. This power, transferred from the father to the bridegroom upon payment of the bride price, became an exclusive right of the husband from the time of the fifth or sixth century. The *mundium* became generalized and finally meant the right of the father over both the wife and the children. Only after this was there undisputed blood relationship between father and children;[14] and with its coming, patriarchalism took over the field. It is therefore correct to say that Teutonic patriarchalism was joined and merged with the Roman patriarchalism, one with the *mundium,* and the other with the *potestas* (power of father over wife and children). As Lamprecht boldly declares, "It is the patriarchal peoples who have made history and still make it."[15] With the return of unilateral descent (though now in the male rather than the female line) inheritance of property by the sons became the regular practice instead

[8] Lamprecht, *op. cit.,* p. 95.

[9] For the heroic ages of barbarians, see Arnold Toynbee, *A Study of History* (6 vols.; London: Oxford University Press, 1934), Vol. 1, pp. 19, 58, 62, 65; Vol. 2, pp. 89–95. The original source for this interpretation is H. M. Chadwick, *The Heroic Age* (Cambridge: University Press, 1912).

[10] Lamprecht, *op. cit.,* p. 96.

[11] Müller-Lyer, *op. cit.,* pp. 219–220.

[12] Elnett, *op. cit.,* pp. 8–9.

[13] Lamprecht, *ibid.,* pp. 112–113.

[14] *Ibid.,* pp. 113–115.

[15] *Ibid.,* p. 99.

of the former custom of having the property revert back to the community. Primogeniture (right of the first born son to family property) remained an alternative.[16]

THE MEDIEVAL FAMILY AND CLASS STATUS

The turbulent conflicts of chieftains and tribes before Charlemagne called for patterns of stability and order suitable to the times. Politically this took the form of feudalism, a hierarchy of vassals with king or emperor at the apex; economically it took the form of the manor or landed estate, a barbarian modification of the Roman villa.[17] Military chiefs became the new aristocrats or lords[18] while below them were the villeins and serfs who performed the agricultural labor. The manorial village had usually from ten to forty households. A lord with only one manor was lowest of the ruling class, while dukes, counts, and viscounts often had hundreds. Later as the church came into the picture an episcopal manor or monastery often had thousands of manors. When a noble or church held as many as this, it would be called a domain.[19] Over all would be the power of the king to whom the various nobles owed their loyalty and service.

From this time to the seventeenth century, family life became a function of class position. At the bottom of the scale were the slaves (chiefly domestics), who were not allowed to have family relations, then the serfs, who were bound to the land and who could marry only with the lord's consent.[20] Along with this was a curious form of endogamy whereby no serf could marry outside his manor without both the permission of his lord and the payment of a fee called *formarriage*.

The life of the villein and serf[21] fitted perfectly the memorable phrase of Hobbes, being "solitary, poor, nasty, brutish, and short." He owned but little personal property, had nothing to call his own outside of his family and a few necessities, could be transferred from one lord to another when property changed hands, and was forced to spend many weeks of the year working in the lord's *demesne* (that portion of the manor where all crops belonged to the lord alone). The cottage in which he lived was a wretched, one-room affair, purposely built without chimneys so that no baking could be done except at a common center. Smoke from cooking filled the house and could

---

[16] *Ibid.*, pp. 121–122.

[17] Carl Stephenson, *Medieval History,* Europe from the Second to the Sixteenth Century (3rd ed., New York: Harper & Bros., 1951), chaps. 8, 9, and 10. For the relation of the villa to the manor, cf. pp. 144–145. For two main types of the manor, cf. p. 200.

[18] James Westfall Thompson, *Economic and Social History of the Middle Ages (300–1300)* (New York: Century, 1928), p. 739. For the class system of England during this period, see H. D. Traill and J. S. Mann, editors, *Social England* (6 vols.; London: Cassell, 1902–1904), Vol. 1, pp. 182–183.

[19] *Ibid.*

[20] *Ibid.*, p. 745; E. Lipson, *The Economic History of England* (7th ed., London: Adam & Charles Black, 1937), Vol. 1, chap. 2.

[21] Here considered together in spite of technical differences. As Stephenson says, "Actually all lived under the same regime," *op. cit.*, p. 203. The use of the term "peasant" from here on will refer to one of these two classes without entering into details of the system.

escape only through the door. In the summer it was possible to cook out-doors and avoid the smoke. Beds were nothing but heaps of straw and for the most part the peasants slept in their clothes.[22] The wife worked with her husband in the field whenever she could spare time from the care of children and cooking at home. Children were plentiful and wives died early. Manners were so rough as to sound fantastic in our age. In hot weather, men often worked naked beside women in the grain fields, and at times they would even appear in the towns unclothed. Monogamy was the rule, not at first because of any legal prescription but because the support of more than one wife was impossible. (Incidentally, monogamy is the most frequent form of marriage even in modern countries where plural marriage is lawful.)

The lot of the villein was somewhat better but only slightly so. He lived on the borderline, the lowest of freemen or the highest of serfs. Actually he was a former free landowner whose property was so small that he accepted conditions of protection very much like the serf's. But he became dependent individually while serfs could be brought under protection a whole com-munity at a time. The lord could not use the labor of the villein beyond a certain limit and the latter could leave personal property to his heirs. Fre-quently he was allowed to take any surplus crop to the village market and sell it at whatever price it would bring. Thus he could occasionally save money. But otherwise he was to all intents and purposes a serf. The liberties we take for granted were won only after centuries of struggle.

In England when a villein died custom determined what happened to his land (immovable possessions) and goods (movable possessions). The best beast went to the landlord, this tax being known as the *heriot,* the sec-ond best went to the priest as *mortuary,* and the necessary (or sometimes best) tools went to the heir. The word "loom" in old English meant "tool"; so these were called "heirlooms." The rest of the property was split three ways: one third to the widow, one third to the children, and the last third bequeathed by a will. If there were no children, half went to the widow and half as bequeathed.[23]

The peasant family (and indeed that of higher classes as well) was plagued with high mortality. The general age at death in the medieval period was forty-two as compared with seventy-two today. About three or four children out of twelve lived to maturity.[24] Often the family was divided because the children of a single household had to serve different manors.[25] If a son went into a monastery, into orders, or to school, the father had to pay a fine to the lord. If the tenant had no children at his death, the lord

---

[22] Thompson, *op. cit.,* p. 742.
[23] George Caspar Homans, *English Villagers of the Thirteenth Century* (Cambridge: Harvard University Press, 1941), pp. 133–134. This is one of the all-too-few American sociological studies using historical evidence. Just why it is that American sociologists should be allergic to history is a question that is not easily answered, but that they are allergic is not in doubt. Homans' book has many other merits, of course!
[24] Thompson, *op. cit.,* p. 178.
[25] G. G. Coulton, *The Medieval Village* (Cambridge: University Press, 1926), p. 14.

claimed everything he had.[26] So important were children to his economic life that the serf, to avoid going childless, was permitted to lend his wife to a neighbor and thus have offspring.[27] So great was the power of the lord over the serf and his marriage relations that in many manors the *jus primae noctis* was enforced. According to this procedure the lord had the right to spend the first night with the bride of the serf unless the latter would pay a fine.[28]

Still higher in the scale were the freemen who owned land but also owed military service to the lord, which the serf did not.[29] Although the freemen were better off economically, their families were more unstable because of the constant danger that the husband and father might be taken by war. It is probable that the marriage and family laws of the period were chiefly applicable to those either in this class or above it. Free status is implied, for example, in the fact that among the Anglo-Saxons the father had the right to guardianship over property of children received from maternal kindred and also over the usufruct, "rents and perquisites," although this did not apply to the son's earnings.[30] The arranging of marriages for the daughter was also the prerogative of the father among the Anglo-Saxons up to the eleventh century,[31] and for the most part on the Continent as well. When the child was born, it was brought to the father before it had eaten food, and he had the right to say whether it should live or not. After the child had eaten food, however, the father lost this right.[32] No child born out of wedlock had any rights of inheritance,[33] a rule which did not apply to higher nobility or royalty.

According to old English custom there were two forms of inheritance, partible and impartible. Partible inheritance divided the property equally among the sons or, if there were no sons, among the daughters. Impartible inheritance prescribed the bestowal of property to a single son. Each of these types of inheritance had two subforms. Partible inheritance provided either that the property be divided among the sons so that each would farm only his *own* share (*gavelkind*) or else that the land be held jointly and farmed cooperatively (joint ownership). Impartible inheritance led to the bequeathing of property to the *youngest* son in some cases (called borough-English); this was apparently on the theory that the oldest could take care of himself, and implied that the eldest brother would manage the property until the heir was of age. In other cases it meant that the property reverted to the *oldest* son (ordinary primogeniture). There are records of areas which changed from borough-English to primogeniture and others which reversed the process, so that it is difficult to tell which was earlier. Sociologically, partible and impartible inheritance are important, for they give evidence of two main family types which were probably brought to England from the Continent, where they remained separate much longer. Partible inheritance of the joint ownership type existed in Kent and is attributed to the Jutes or Franks. It appears to have been a Norman custom common in

---

[26] *Ibid.*, pp. 250, 364 n.   [29] Thompson, *op. cit.*, p. 745.   [32] *Ibid.*, pp. 192–193.

[27] *Ibid.*, p. 250.   [30] Goodsell, *op. cit.*, p. 195.   [33] *Ibid.*, p. 192.

[28] *Ibid.*, pp. 464 ff.   [31] *Ibid.*, p. 195.

Auvergne and Nivernais, France, down to the nineteenth century, where a family owned joint land for hundreds of years. The other form, impartible inheritance, appeared in all parts of Europe as well as England but implied a different type of family held together by the eldest son, who had the duty of keeping up both the family name and the family property. Le Play, the French sociologist, refers to these as the joint family and the stem family respectively.[34]

In pre-Carolingian times the Frankish chiefs often exchanged wives and concubines while the richer ones had a considerable harem. Normans were notorious for capturing girls in their raids, violating them, and passing them from hand to hand.[35] Charlemagne had four legitimate wives and five or six concubines as well as other temporary mistresses.[36] This set certain precedents for the behavior of the privileged classes, customs difficult to erase.

In Russia after the Tartar conquest the higher class women were shut up in *terems* (similar to the harem) and eventually came to have less freedom than their lower class sisters.

Even down to the time of Ivan the Terrible in the sixteenth century three marriages were allowed to upper class Russians. The second and third had no nuptial benediction and a fourth brought prohibition of Holy Communion for eighteen years. Ivan himself did not keep this rule but took for himself any woman he wanted.[37]

During both Merovingian and Carolingian times it was common for the rich noble or king to have a distant part of the house set aside for women's quarters. This section was called the *gynaeceum* where wives, concubines, and servant girls (who also bore children to their lord) were quartered.[38] It must not be supposed, however, that the *gynaeceums* were centers of idleness; in fact their chambers were the original home of cloth-making and weaving in Europe [39] and hence their influence on later economic development was considerable. Many of the arts and industries later taken up and developed by the guilds had their origin in the *gynaeceums,* and the tradition of women workers persisted even into those close corporations.

Although the Christian church from early times sanctioned monogamy and the bishops frequently fought the practice of polygamy, bigamy, or concubinage,[40] the change was slow for two reasons. In the first place the church had to cope with recalcitrant and stubborn barbarians who had considerable political power and used it to buttress their established customs. Furthermore, the priesthood came more and more from barbarian ranks; it was too much to expect of these newly inducted prelates that they would

[34] Homans, *op. cit.,* pp. 110–126.
[35] Paul Lacroix (Pierre Dufour), *History of Prostitution,* translated by Samuel Putnam (New York: Covici Friede, 1931), p. 675. Stephenson notes marked economic limits to polygyny, *op. cit.,* pp. 47–48.
[36] *Ibid.,* p. 697.
[37] Elnett, *op. cit.,* pp. 28, 37.
[38] Lacroix, *op. cit.,* pp. 661–662.
[39] *Ibid.,* p. 667.
[40] *Ibid.,* pp. 673–674.

proceed harshly against nobles and kings of their own language and culture. The early popes did not use language that was strictly monogamous, and the church sometimes allowed bigamy under certain conditions; for example, if the wife had an infirmity.[41] The Council of Vermene in 752 said that a man might marry again if his wife refused to go on a journey with him and he did not return. Sterility was sufficient cause for bigamy with some church authorities.[42] And among the Jews there was also some concession to public sentiment in this regard, some Jewish authorities holding that the husband might marry again if his wife were captured forcibly, deserted, refused to go on a pilgrimage to Jerusalem, or refused relations.[43] In the same century Eastern church authorities found it necessary to publish the Nicene Canons against bigamy, thus furnishing evidence of their struggle to enforce monogamous practice.[44] Furthermore, in both the Merovingian and Carolingian epochs, the illegitimate child did not offend the public conscience.[45] Indeed, many noblemen and other male members of the upper classes openly boasted of having "sired goodly numbers of sturdy bastards."

THE INFLUENCE OF CHRISTIANITY

During the early Middle Ages, the church gave rise to two tendencies which were to have a powerful effect on the relations between the sexes. The first was to regularize marriage relations and stabilize the family; the second was to extend the ascetic ideal and celibacy. Along with the latter came the view of woman as a sinful daughter of Eve and sexual relations as essentially degrading.

From the fourth and fifth centuries the church acted against abortions, infanticide, child exposure, and divorce.[46] It also promoted a doctrine, most surprising to the Romans, that unfaithfulness in the marriage vow is as sinful in men as in women. Adultery was condemned regardless of whether the party were husband or wife. This rule, while it protected the wife as well as the husband, was apparently honored more in the breach than in the observance,[47] though it was appealed to as a court of last resort. The church also tried to protect the family by improving custodial relations of widows and minor children under a lord who might dissipate the property; it used its influence also to prevent marriage of very old and very young by family arrangement.[48]

[41] Israel Abrahams, *Jewish Life in the Middle Ages,* 2nd ed., enlarged and revised by Cecil Roth (London: Edward Goldston, 1932), p. 133.

[42] *Ibid.,* p. 133.

[43] *Ibid.*

[44] William Smith and Samuel Cheetham, *A Dictionary of Christian Antiquities* (2 vols., Boston: Little, Brown & Co., 1875), Vol. 1, p. 205, cited in Abrahams, *op. cit.,* p. 134. The Abrahams book abounds in such revealing details.

[45] Thompson, *op. cit.,* p. 262.

[46] Goodsell, *op. cit.,* pp. 177–179.

[47] *Ibid.,* pp. 175–177.

[48] Thompson, *op. cit.,* p. 676.

Another interesting case is the way in which the church opposed primogeniture. Old Teutonic law allowed for partible inheritance or an equal division of land among the sons, but feudalism changed this to primogeniture because otherwise it would have been impossible to keep the feudal estates together. Germany never wholly accepted this arrangement but it was prevalent nearly everywhere else.[49] The church, however, was very definite in resisting the trend toward primogeniture; it advocated the right of female inheritance to fiefs as well as equal division of land among sons. Since this helped to break the feudal power of the nobles and princes, it is suggested by Thompson that there may have been mixed motives involved, for the dissipation of feudal estates could lead to a *beneficium* (endowment) of lands to churches or monasteries and it would make sale easier.[50] It also enabled male members of noble families to enter orders or the cloister without the obligation of caring for their property. Thompson estimates that within three hundred years, 12 per cent of the princely houses, 36 per cent of the counts, and 80 per cent of the lesser noble families lacked heirs to carry on the family line because of sons entering the priesthood.

Feudal custom allowed marriage of blood relatives in order to keep and extend the property of families, and here again the church was firmly opposed. Not only was marriage of consanguinity forbidden by ecclesiastical law but marriage of affinity also; that is, marriage to relatives of either father or mother. In addition to this, marriage by spiritual affinity was likewise prohibited. Those who had spiritual affinity were defined as all those who had participated together in the rites of baptism or confirmation.[51] Thus the church law helped not only to abolish incest but also to break up and dissipate large holdings. The "prohibited degrees" laws were also most important in defining divorce relationships.

To stabilize family relationships, the church opposed divorce from early times, basing its antagonism on the saying of Christ in the Gospels[52] where the only exception allowed is for cause of adultery.[53] Some of the early Church Fathers made other exceptions such as apostasy, idolatry, or covetousness.[54] During the early Middle Ages there was some divergence in the application of the rule, and several grounds for divorce were recognized in some of the *Poenitentiales* or manuals for instruction of the laity. Even divorce by mutual consent was allowed a place,[55] undoubtedly because of the reluctance of the barbarians to accept too stringent a doctrine. Not until the twelfth century was the law fully codified and enforced, prohibiting divorce except through a bishop's court.[56]

[49] Thompson, *op. cit.,* p. 714.
[50] *Ibid.,* p. 677.
[51] Goodsell, *op. cit.,* pp. 174–175, and Thompson, *op. cit.,* p. 677.
[52] Matthew 5:32.
[53] In Mark 10:11, where Christ opposes divorce without qualification, modern scholars are generally of the opinion that we have more nearly the original statement, but higher criticism was unknown in the Middle Ages and there was simply an awareness of discrepancy between the two statements.
[54] Goodsell, *op. cit.,* p. 180.
[55] *Ibid.,* p. 212.
[56] *Ibid.,* pp. 212–213.

In the Council of Trent the church proclaimed marriage a sacrament; now there were but two conditions on which a husband and wife might go separate ways. (1) *Divortium a vinculo matrimonii* maintains that the original marriage was null and void, not a true marriage. Reasons for annulment are: some previous verbal contract of marriage in which the oath was given in words of the present tense; affinity or consanguinity to the seventh degree; spiritual affinity. (2) *Divortium a mensa et thoro* is simply a separation of the two partners without the right to remarry. The bond of *vinculum* remains, while the separation is "from bed and board." This is permitted because of adultery, apostasy, heresy, or cruelty.[57] This twofold treatment of the problem is of fundamental importance, since it has defined the attitude of the Roman Catholic Church from that day to this. It must be emphasized that neither of these two is divorce in the twentieth-century meaning of the term; for in the latter the marriage bond, once established, is broken. In canon law neither of these is a divorce in that sense. The first is an annulment, which declares that the marriage was not valid in the first place and hence there was no bond. The second is a separation order which retains the reality of the bond in spite of the fact that the partners are separated; under no conditions may either one of them break the bond. Hence we shall speak of them henceforth as annulment and separation.

The question may naturally arise why in case of annulment the previous contract to marry had to be in the present tense. Apparently there was some doubt about the betrothal ceremony (which was accepted among Teutons as binding) where the promise was given to marry in the future, and the church wished to emphasize that this was not a true marriage. However, much difficulty arose over the fact that many of the European languages did not make such a clear distinction between present and future tense as the Latin, and much confusion resulted from the rule, with the privileged upper classes taking advantage of it.[58] The various degrees of affinity also gave rise to many abuses, for in case of doubt it was not hard to discover or get witnesses to prove such affinity.[59] Dispensations were also allowed to those who had violated one of the various laws of annulment, but it was possible for only the very wealthy to obtain these.[60] In spite of these many difficulties it is certain that the church laws helped to strengthen the family tie and thus to bring order into marriage relations. The battle with the secular kept up steadily until the Council of Trent in 1563, when concubinage and marriage by mutual consent were finally and officially banned by the church.[61]

Another powerful trend in the church was asceticism. The Christians after Augustine were driven to suppress and deny the natural sexual impulses for many reasons: because of competitive pagan cults that boasted of self-control

[57] *Ibid.*, p. 213. See also Elliott's discussion in a later chapter, pp. 671–672.
[58] G. D. Howard, *History of Matrimonial Institutions* (3 vols.; Chicago: University of Chicago Press, 1904), Vol. 2, chap. 11.
[59] *Ibid.*, p. 59.
[60] Goodsell, *op. cit.*, p. 214.
[61] Müller-Lyer, *op. cit.*, p. 234.

vastly superior to that of the Christians; ecclesiastical writers from Paul to the Church Fathers definitely regarded marriage as a second-best state, a concession to the mere demands of the flesh; the thoroughgoing dualistic doctrine of body and spirit in Neoplatonism specifically designated the body as evil and the spirit as good, this doctrine finally merging into Christian theology. Both St. Jerome and St. Augustine expounded the superior purity of celibacy and placed marriage lowest in the scale of virtue. Theodore Schroeder refers to this development as "erotophobia" and asserts that it grew up along with its close associate, misogyny.[62] The Church Fathers called woman everything from the "organ of the devil" to a "scorpion ever ready to sting."

In Russia, Christianity brought subjection of women as a result of Byzantine asceticism. From this time on, the female sex was regarded as unclean in much of the church doctrine.[63]

A sixth-century provincial church council forbade women from receiving the Eucharist in their naked hands. In a number of choirs women were replaced by eunuchs. The Council of Macon (585) decided by one vote that women had souls, but in the Russian church women were not classified as human beings till the time of Peter the Great.[64] (They are still prohibited from going behind the altar in an Orthodox church.) Nevertheless the doctrine grew up that women were equal with men in the spiritual realm but not in the temporal world. Woman was responsible for the Fall and was the gateway to hell unless man kept tight rein on his impulses. The best assurance of doing so would be the total avoidance of women. This rule soon became a regular demand made upon the higher clergy, although it took much longer before it was applied to the lower orders.

In 385 Pope Siricius first decreed the rule of celibacy for the clergy; it was called forth according to the pope's own testimony by the immorality of vowed priests and virgins. The decree was not popular, however, and was annulled by the Trullan Council in 680 which allowed all priests, deacons, and inferior clergy to have conjugal relations, except that the *digami* or twice-married were not admitted to orders. From that time to the eleventh century, the ascetic ideal was in open warfare with the desire of many of the clergy either for marriage or for some form of concubinage.[65] From the ninth to the eleventh century the clergy were engaged in so much licentiousness that it became an open scandal. Caricatures, statues, friezes, and arabesques on churches and monasteries depicted monks and nuns indulging in sexual excesses, although these were destroyed in postmedieval times by later churchmen.[66] The hierarchy became more and more concerned with the problem and finally Pope Gregory VII re-enacted the celibacy legislation

[62] Theodore Schroeder, "The Evolution of Marriage Ideals," in E. B. Reuter and J. R. Runner, eds., *The Family,* Source Materials for the Study of Family and Personality (New York: McGraw-Hill, 1931), p. 107.

[63] Elnett, *op. cit.,* pp. 22–24.

[64] Theodore Schroeder in Reuter and Runner, *op. cit.,* p. 107.

[65] George Cross, "Celibacy, Christian," in *Encyclopedia of Religion and Ethics* (New York: Scribner's, 1928), Vol. 3, pp. 273–274.

[66] Lacroix, *op. cit.,* pp. 691–693.

in 1073. It was confirmed by the Lateran Council in 1215 and has been the official policy since that time.[67]

A series of decisions in the Eastern or Orthodox church from Justinian in 528 to Leo the Philosopher in 900 led to a somewhat different outcome. From 900 to the present day the rule has been that monks are not allowed to marry but the lower orders of the secular clergy (who serve regular parishes) are free to do so. This prevents them, however, from rising to higher office in the church, for bishops are selected only from the monks who are bound by the vow of chastity. Among the Uniat churches (observing the same Byzantine rite as the Orthodox but submitting to the authority of Rome) the rule is the same: inferior clergy only may marry.[68]

Three tendencies in the Roman Catholic Church were finally crystallized into the social structure. These are (1) living according to the *lex naturae* or law of nature; (2) asceticism, applying at first to the monks only; (3) ecclesiasticism, which embodied the theocratic ideal and applied to the ordained clergy. Of the three, asceticism was recognized as the power which was potent to revivify the others, because reform movements so often began from ascetic sacrifice and enthusiasm.[69] From these three elements arose a hierarchy of ranks: first the laity, then the religious orders, and finally the priesthood. The first has the duty of propagating the race and institutionalizing natural impulse into the marriage relationship. As we have seen, asceticism finally captures both the monastery and the church. The corollary is that the life of celibacy is considered higher than the marriage estate and social activity is divided into two spheres of social ethics, one for priests and monks (a higher ethic), and one for laymen. Morality for laymen, both in domestic and in political affairs, is simply a special field of natural and human law under the dispensation of the Fall. Patriarchalism likewise is traced to the Fall and belongs to the church militant rather than the church triumphant.[70] Lewis Mumford is therefore not far wrong when he claims that the church fostered both chastity and fertility, each extreme being complemented by the other.[71]

On the other hand the church undoubtedly raised the standards of marriage practice, promoted monogamy and faithfulness to vows, opposed di-

[67] Cross, *op. cit.*

[68] Henry Charles Lea, *History of Sacerdotal Celibacy in the Christian Church* (2 vols., New York: Macmillan, 1907), 3rd ed. revised, Vol. 1, pp. 93–97. Also *The Catholic Encyclopedia, An International Work of Reference on the Catholic Church*, ed. by Charles G. Hebermann and others (15 vols.; New York: Robert Appleton Co., 1907–1914), Vol. 3, p. 488, article "Celibacy" by Herbert Thurson. Parenthetically it is interesting to notice that hereditary tendencies appeared in the Orthodox church of post-Petrine Russia (after Peter the Great, who ruled from 1689 to 1725). Under this new trend the priesthood often passed from father to son in the same parish, resulting in a priestly and bureaucratic caste system. The parish priest was even obliged to marry by tradition and the wife was supposed to be the daughter of a priest. The celibate rules of the Roman church avoided this rigidity.

[69] Ernst Troeltsch, *The Social Teachings of the Christian Churches* (New York: Macmillan, 1931), p. 239.

[70] *Ibid.*, p. 288.

[71] Lewis Mumford, *The Condition of Man* (New York: Harcourt, Brace, 1944), p. 113.

vorce, and helped to promote the ideal of good will. It urged the lower classes to humility and obedience, the upper classes to paternalism and solicitude for those under their care, and thus broadened the family ethic.[72] And one service which it performed is usually forgotten: it provided in the cloister a haven for the unmarried. Owing to the frequent wars of the times, the sex ratio was low and medieval society had to find a place for excess women.[73]

THE POSITION OF WOMEN

It must not be assumed that because most of Europe had reached a patriarchal society at the beginning of the historical period this entailed absolute subjection of women. Just as family conditions are a function of class status, so are the rights of the individual before the law — whether man or woman.[74] The supremacy of the male was functional, having to do with the military service he owed to the king or overlord. This did not mean that males alone inherited property; if the eldest son in England had no male heir, his property went directly to his daughter.[75] An estate owed military obligations to the king and therefore if a widow were left with an estate, it was to her advantage to marry again, although the king would see to it that she did not marry a lord who was hostile.[76] England of the sixth century allowed the wife to have half the property on the death of her husband and even the power to leave him for good cause with her half of the property and her children.[77]

In the literature of feminism there appears a constant reference to the fact that in English common law the wife is not a person at all, being merged in the legal personality of her husband. The authority for this statement is always Blackstone, the famous commentator on English common law. Recently Mary Beard has asserted that this opinion is largely fallacious because Blackstone was quoting from common law of a late period — the sixteenth or seventeenth century; furthermore Blackstone disregards not only the common law of an earlier period but equity and statute law which modified the legal status of women to a marked degree.[78] The studies of Maitland in the origins of English law make it quite clear that women had innumerable rights under the law which were not dependent in any way upon those of men; a woman had the right to own land or chattels, sue in the courts, and act as attorney either for herself or for her husband.[79]

[72] Troeltsch, *op. cit.*, p. 295.
[73] Thompson, *op. cit.*, pp. 711–712.
[74] Mary Beard, *Woman as Force in History* (New York: Macmillan, 1946), p. 178.
[75] *Ibid.*, p. 179.
[76] *Ibid.*, p. 182.
[77] *Ibid.*, p. 183.
[78] *Ibid.*, chaps. 4–7.
[79] *Ibid.*, p. 192. Frederick Pollock and Frederick W. Maitland, *The History of English Law Before the Time of Edward I* (2 vols., 2nd ed., Cambridge: Cambridge University Press, and Boston: Little, Brown & Co., 1899), Vol. 1, p. 482.

After she was married she nevertheless had her *maritagium* (land granted by her father as a sort of dowry upon marriage or before marriage) and the right to maintenance. Under the rule of equity, trusts (estates or other property given to the keeping of a trusted individual) were more and more often put in women's hands and thus removed from the power of the common law, which would recognize the husband's right over his wife's property.[80]

On the other hand, it would be false to deny that women on the whole held a subordinate position everywhere in the Middle Ages, at least till commerce and industry transformed towns into cities (twelfth century).[81] A decree of the Council of Toledo says that the husband is obliged to chastise his wife to a moderate degree unless he is a priest, in which case he may be more harsh.[82] In England, even though women might possess titles and property by inheritance, they could not sit in parliament.[83] It is true that they had more privileges in church law than under the newly codified common law, which took away their right to make wills, for example.[84] Among the upper classes even as late as the fifteenth century a husband is praised in a famous book of etiquette for knocking his wife to the ground and kicking her nose till it was broken when his wife scolded him in public.[85] A woman's position was largely due to local custom and the force of her own personality. It often fluctuated between an idealized elevation and a low debasement,[86] not wholly unlike its condition ever since.[87]

CHIVALRY AND THE ROMANTIC IDEAL

Feudal knighthood arose partly from the retainers of a Teutonic war chief, partly from special bands of horsed warriors which helped to beat off the Saracen invaders from Spain. By the beginning of the eleventh century these knights were very numerous in all parts of Europe, some of them being freemen who accepted service with a lord, some of them owning landed estates. Those who belonged to some of the great military orders were like a

---

[80] *Ibid.*, p. 202.
[81] Henri Pirenne, *Medieval Cities,* tr. by Frank D. Halsey (Princeton: Princeton University Press, 1925), p. 104.
[82] G. G. Coulton, *Medieval Panorama* (New York: Macmillan, and Cambridge: University Press, 1938), p. 615.
[83] *Ibid.*, pp. 617–618.
[84] *Ibid.*
[85] *Ibid.*, p. 617.
[86] *Ibid.*, p. 622 (see quotation by Eileen Power).
[87] Mary Beard's remarkable work noted above is a strong corrective of the older half-truths about woman's subjection in English common law. It also leaves the reader with the impression that woman's status as a whole was remarkably high throughout European history. This can be proved only by a careful selection of proof texts, and that is precisely what she has gathered. The obvious disadvantage of this method is that it can be countered with similar ones, equally true and even more numerous. Furthermore, Mrs. Beard fails to bring out an essential point, that woman's status was higher from the thirteenth to the fifteenth centuries as a result of industrial changes.

priesthood, dedicated to celibacy like the priests; they had the sword of the flesh, while the priests had the sword of the spirit. And like the priests, the knights owed allegiance to no country but only to their superiors, dukes, counts, barons, kings, or the emperor and the pope.[88] As long as they were fighting the Saracen, they had a social function well recognized by all. But with the expulsion of the Moors, they began to relax in idleness, to become rapacious and violent. The coming of the crusades near the beginning of the twelfth century might have afforded an opportunity for reforms, but it simply gave new opportunities for licentiousness. By this time the number of *ribaudes* (camp followers or troopers' girls) grew by leaps and bounds. Chroniclers of that age say that each crusaders' camp had its brothel. They relate too that crusaders imitated the Moslems and set up harems with slave girls purchased in Asia.[89] Scott was not falsifying history when he emphasized, in *Ivanhoe,* the licentiousness of Brian de Boisguilbert.

Back home in the castle, life was dull and monotonous for the lady. Her marriage to her lord was prearranged, usually for financial reasons, and there was rarely any love between them. Like most women of her day, the noble lady could read little.[90] She could either take out her resentment on the servants or look forward to one of the two great events in her life: the arrival of traveling knights or the visit of a minstrel or troubadour. To the lady marooned in the castle, these occurrences assumed much more than ordinary importance.[91] Around these two figures the ideals of chivalry and romance were woven. The heroic deeds of the knights gradually came to be performed not only for honor but for the love of a fair lady; and many a knight had his lady. She in turn, having had days, months, or even years to dream of the perfect knight who would some day be her lover, encouraged her knight to deeds of bravery and heroism, partly as a compensation for lack of ardor in her husband, partly as a simple projection of an adolescent ideal (for every noble girl married early).[92] Marriage and courtly love became two separate realms insulated from each other.

The other arrival at the castle, the troubadour, reinforced the tendency toward a more romantic conception of love. He sang a curious poetry which magnified unhappy love and glorified love outside marriage. The love that was perpetually unsatisfied and the praises of a fair lady who ever said "No" became a symbol of a higher and more aristocratic way of life available to the knights but not to the common people.

There are many evidences that the poets and troubadours, particularly in Provence, were believers in the Catharist heresy. According to this secret

[88] Thompson, *op. cit.,* pp. 722–723.

[89] Lacroix, *op. cit.,* p. 731.

[90] Coulton, *op. cit.,* p. 627. Coulton thinks, however, that noble women were probably more literate than men (in reading romances). They also were the main church-goers.

[91] Thompson, *op. cit.,* p. 720.

[92] Mumford, *op. cit.,* p. 113. Apparently the *chansons de geste* were stories primarily for men, but the Arthurian legends had a more feminine audience if not authorship. Cf. H. O. Taylor, *The Medieval Mind* (2 vols., 4th ed., London: Macmillan, 1927), Vol. 1, chap. 24, esp. p. 581.

doctrine, which comes from Manichaeism in Asia Minor,[93] the soul is divine or angelic but is imprisoned in created forms of matter. Since God is love and the world is evil, man's task is to escape from the world and the demands of the flesh. This faith was "lyrical" in its essence; that is, it was not subject to rational, impersonal, or objective exposition. It was a combined experience of enthusiasm and dread, representing the invasion of the world by the divine love which was to release the soul from its prison. The neophyte before joining the Catharist order had to vow to devote himself to God as revealed in the new belief, never to lie or swear, to avoid touching his wife if he were married (absolute chastity), to eat no animal flesh, and to keep his faith a secret forever. This last vow was necessary for protection because the heresy was savagely attacked by the church. In order to avoid revealing their belief, the Catharist troubadours would sing of the love of their lady (a circumlocution for their cult). Hence by employing the language of love with its frankly sexual symbols, they would appear to be extolling the romance of chivalry, although secretly they would intend to extol the love of the divine. This ambiguity was not apparent to their listeners but only to themselves.

One thing, however, the troubadours did not conceal, and that was their dislike of orthodox Christianity; they were singing of a higher and more abandoned love than the priests could know. It is already apparent that Christian marriage imposed on the pagan an intolerable strain, particularly among the upper classes. Hence the troubadours were one with their courtly hearers in opposition to the clergy and their strict ideas about the marriage bond. The mingling of these two strains of opposition created among the nobility and all those addicted to the ways of chivalry a cult of Eros or passionate love finally embodied in the Tristan myth which found its way all over the Continent. When the Catharist scaffolding had dropped away, there remained an edifice of romantic thought which became the common property of the knighthood and nobility — a strange mingling of heretical ideas and courtly embroidery. It is therefore instructive to review briefly the ideology which resulted.

It became the view of the romantics that ordinary human love was a poor thing compared with passionate love, that marriage was a concession to ordinary love and was a kind of second-best state.[94] True love was an obsession of the mind, a subjective state of intense feeling beyond the canons of good and evil; in fact this feeling became its own justification because in the course of passionate love one was conquered by an irresistible force greater than himself and could consequently have no control over his actions. Romantic love was a destiny and should not be opposed; it was antagonistic to the ordinary norms of life, leading to a clash with the social order often pursued to the death. Of course there was something higher about a love which led to a union beyond death, a tragedy which was embodied in later European drama, the novel, and opera. This "esthetic ideal

---

[93] There is some evidence, also, that Moorish thought transmitted to Provence may have influenced the romantic belief.

[94] Notice how opposites meet. The celibate clergy held the same view in a different context.

posing as a moral ideal" was at first circulated only among the upper classes
through forms of etiquette and manuals of instruction for young ladies; but
with the rise of the towns and the imitation of aristocratic mores by the
middle classes the new form of love became more and more popularized,
sometimes taking a frankly sensual form as in the *Cent Nouvelles Nouvelles*
and "l'esprit gaulois," and later exchanging the final tragedy for a happy
ending which made it more acceptable to a wider public. Eventually the
romantic idea became a necessary prelude to marriage and was merged with
the orthodox conception of the married state, thus becoming all things to
all men.[95] Although this conception was not influential with the early
American colonists, it became more widely disseminated as soon as the
pioneers had won for themselves sufficient leisure to read European plays
and novels, and its popularity has been thoroughly reflected in American
literature, drama, and cinema.

THE RISE OF TOWNS AND CITIES

During the period of the crusades (eleventh to thirteenth centuries) prosperity was increasing and serfdom waning as more and more peasants
bought their freedom.[96] Money rent became easier for the lord to exact than
labor rent with its supervision; free tenancy increased. Towns arose, sometimes on the border of feudal villages, sometimes in new locations. They were
chiefly composed of two types of traders and merchants: those who sold the
products of others such as wine, grain, and merchandise; and those who were
artisans and sold their own products.[97] Schmoller declares that the rise of the
medieval city marked a turning point far more important than the later industrial revolution, which was only its "secondary consequence." [98] Certainly
its importance for the family was equally great, for it was in these larger
centers of population that individual relations began to predominate over
those of class. The freedom of self-government and liberation from feudal
duties meant that in town the so-called classes were politically though not
socially equal, and a new aristocracy of wealth began to appear.[99] It may be
true that the *bourgeoisie* or middle class were at first a separate status group,
but in another sense they created an atmosphere in which a kind of classless
society was born, with universalistic ideologies that came to flower in the
French Revolution. Even though that universalism was often specious, it

---

95 For full details of this development see Denis de Rougemont, *Love in the Western World*
   (New York: Harcourt, Brace, 1940), Vols. 1–4; also J. Huizinga, *The Waning of the Middle
   Ages* (London: Edward Arnold, 1927), chaps. 4–6.
96 Thompson, *op. cit.,* pp. 761–762.
97 *Ibid.,* p. 771. Pirenne suggests that a number of these traders and merchants came from displaced agricultural workers pushed off the land with the population increase after the
   tenth century. *Op. cit.,* pp. 117–118. For population pressure in the twelfth and thirteenth
   centuries see his *Economic and Social History of Medieval Europe* (London: Kegan Paul,
   Trench, Trubner & Co., 1936), p. 68.
98 Quoted in Thompson, *op. cit.,* p. 765.
99 *Ibid.,* p. 779.

formed the seed of the new urban society which gave its stamp to the modern world. As more labor was needed in the cities, the serf had an outlet and an escape. If he stayed for a year, he usually secured his freedom [100] according to the old German aphorism *Stadtluft macht frei* ("city air makes man free").

Since the artisans formed the great bulk of the city population, their homes were more or less representative of the period. The medieval urban household was both a home and a workshop; it included relatives, industrial workers, and domestics. Apprentices and journeymen lived as part of the family of the master craftsman, sharing both common labor and common food. These households had large dormitories to sleep in and a great hall to eat in, as well as workrooms where both men and women plied the trade under the tutelage of the master craftsman.[101] The latter with some of his workers, both men and women, belonged to the guilds, which were not only powerful economically but also politically.

The results of this new life were that both women and children took far more part in industry and community life than they did from the sixteenth century to the Industrial Revolution; for from the Renaissance and Reformation to the eighteenth and succeeding centuries, the home became increasingly divorced from the workplace and the housewife began to lose touch with the outside world.[102] The youngest sons of the family often served as night watchmen in the medieval city.[103] Here also the guardianship of all minors passed from the family as such. The city had primary guardianship over its dwellers.[104] By the fourteenth century the father still had some guardianship over the wife and the right to punish the children, but the girl began to get the right to choose her husband instead of having him selected by arrangement with the family.[105] The artisan family of the period was a miniature economic monarchy within the larger authority of the city. Wife and children, apprentices and factors (all who shared the same bread), were under the power of the *Brotherr* or employer. At the same time they were allowed much individual freedom which was not permitted in the great merchant families.[106] The latter, for the most part, went in for gaudy display of luxuries, silks, and finery so as to outdo the aristocracy. Indeed, except in Italy during the early Renaissance, the status of women of the merchant class did not improve markedly.

In the artisan families of the medieval cities, women gained more prominence than at any other time in European history, with the possible exception of the twentieth century. Women also engaged extensively in trade; in the days of Edward I (thirteenth century) we are told that Wallingford had fifty women traders.[107] Women were admitted to the barber-surgeon guilds

[100] *Ibid.,* p. 781.
[101] Lewis Mumford, *The Culture of Cities* (New York: Harcourt, Brace, 1938), p. 35.
[102] *Ibid.,* p. 114.
[103] Lamprecht, *op. cit.,* Vol. 4, p. 230.
[104] *Ibid.,* pp. 243–244.
[105] *Ibid.,* pp. 245–246.
[106] *Ibid.,* p. 246.
[107] Ephraim Lipson, *op. cit.,* Vol. 3, pp. 359–361.

in England, they did most of the brewing, and they had a liberal share in the wool industry as sorters, packers, carders, spinners, weavers, and dyers. The term "spinster" for an unmarried woman goes back to the close relation between these women and the spinning industry.[108] On the Continent from the time of Louis IX (thirteenth century) the silk industry and the making of gold thread were carried on solely by women, who had as many as five corporations organized with masters, workers, and apprentices, all women. The masters or mistresses (*maîtresses*) of these guilds elected *prudes-femmes* (trusted women) to represent them in the council just as the masculine guild masters chose *prud'hommes* (trusted men); and although the women's guilds were formally under the supervision of a *prud'-homme*, this seems to have been a polite fiction.[109] In fifteenth-century France, the most important trade for women was that of *lingère* (linen draper). The guilds engaged in the manufacture of linen cloth were both religious and economic and were entirely unsupervised by men.[110] Unlike some of the other guilds, these placed no limit on the number of apprentices; so the bourgeois often entered their daughters to save them from the perils of *l'oisiveté* (leisure).[111] The king issued rules that no woman of bad reputation should be admitted. If any one of them became immoral after working on the job, she was to be expelled from lodging or public meeting with others of the same trade though not from engaging in the industry.[112] Apparently the practices of this guild became popular because they were adopted for the silk industry in Lyon, Toulouse, and Tours in the fifteenth and sixteenth centuries.[113] By this time a guild of this type began to be a substitute for the cloister in providing a place for the surplus female population.

In Paris from 1292 to 1300 there were something like eighty trades open to both sexes. It was common for the widow of a master to keep his power over his workers until she died, though usually another took charge.[114] The two sexes did not enjoy equal privileges through most of France but in Paris they were more nearly equal.[115] By the sixteenth century women in many French cities were working in large numbers of trades. At the time of the Huguenot migration to England, English masters took on Huguenot women in great numbers. Women and girls either brought a knowledge of the trade or worked until they learned it, much to the discomfiture of their male colleagues who complained that women were taking bread out of the mouths of men.[116]

A vein of communalism ran through the urban life of the Middle Ages,

108 *Ibid.*, p. 442.
109 H. Hauser, "Le travail des femmes aux XVe et XVIe siècles," *Revue internationale de sociologie* 5 (1897), pp. 338–339.
110 *Ibid.*, p. 339.
111 *Ibid.*, p. 340.
112 *Ibid.*, p. 341.
113 *Ibid.*, p. 343.
114 *Ibid.*, p. 344.
115 *Ibid.*, pp. 345–346.
116 Lipson, *op. cit.*, p. 500.

some of it inherited from the feudal estate. Public bakeries supplemented the food of the home; public cookshops were also fairly common, catering to the richer *bourgeoisie;* and most bathing was done in public bath-houses.[117] These bathhouses came to be the centers of easy sociability where neighbors gathered for light conversation.[118] Apparently there was no false modesty here, for we are told that men and women bathed together without the formality of clothing.[119] In fact an Italian writer of the period complained that boys and girls in their teens ran naked to the public baths through the streets. Before the end of the medieval period the bathhouses came to have a bad name as hangouts for women of easy virtue.[120] In addition, houses of prostitution were officially established by many cities as a method of protecting the daughters of the *bourgeoisie,* since the understanding was that no girls in the houses could come from the immediate locality.[121] These brothels, built with tax funds, were put in charge of a prominent citizen who saw to it that there was no disorder. The profits were shared by both the religious and lay authorities.[122] In French and German cities the public houses of prostitution were used for hospitality extended to important guests.[123] A serious outbreak of syphilis at the end of the fifteenth and beginning of the sixteenth centuries revealed the danger of these customs, so that with the aid of the Catholic Reformation many of the houses were closed.[124] At the same time the acceptance of public policy for licensed prostitution grew to be current practice.

THE RISE OF THE BOURGEOIS FAMILY

By the fifteenth and sixteenth centuries, more and more guilds were excluding women [125] and female wages dropped lower and lower. At the end of the fourteenth century the ratio of women's wages to those of men had been about three to four. It dropped to a ratio of one to two in the fifteenth century and still lower in the sixteenth. Thus the nearer society came to modern industrialism, the lower was the salary of women.[126] As national states took over more and more of the political power wielded by the cities, common people participated less in government and the family became increasingly a private affair, separated from community life. On the woman's side this was the result of gradual exclusion from industry

---

[117] Mumford, *op. cit.,* p. 41.

[118] *Ibid.,* p. 47.

[119] Emile Durkheim, review of Max Bauer, *Das Geschlechtsleben in der deutschen Vergangenheit* (Leipzig: Seeman, 1902), in *L'Année Sociologique* 7 (1904), pp. 438–440.

[120] Mumford, *op. cit.*

[121] Durkheim, *op. cit.*

[122] Geoffrey May, "Prostitution," in *Encyclopedia of the Social Sciences* (New York: Macmillan, 1933), Vol. 12, p. 554.

[123] *Ibid.*

[124] *Ibid.,* p. 575.

[125] Arthur W. Calhoun, *A Social History of the American Family from Colonial Times to the Present* (Cleveland: Clark, 1917), Vol. 1, p. 16.

[126] Hauser, *op. cit.,* p. 349. Although these figures are from smaller centers, it is inferred that they applied elsewhere.

while on the man's side it meant a growing separation of the home from the workshop. To complete the circle, the increasingly private character of the house led to a relaxation of interest in public affairs. Concomitant with these changes came a change in the home itself; instead of the rude furniture of the medieval period there was an increase in such bric-a-brac as vases, rugs, metal work, curtains, and the like, and from now on the burden of "keeping house" grew heavier.[127] Paraphernalia for taking care of children also developed; such items as toys, cradles, toddlers, and children's books became more common in the sixteenth century.[128]

Although the feudal order remained in force in Germany and central Europe longer than it did in the West,[129] many changes in family life were appearing there, first because the law of primogeniture was poorly observed and estates were continually redivided until the noble families were impoverished, and second because of the influence of the Reformation. The middle class habit of marrying girls at an early age — fourteen or thereabouts — was observed.[130] Just as in medieval times, the girls who were married in their teens began the round of childbearing almost immediately and wife mortality was very great. There was also absolute resignation to dying by disease, for medical remedies were rude and meager.[131] Likewise in England during Elizabethan times girls were married at fifteen or sixteen; and younger sisters were not allowed to marry first, for the older girls would be considered spinsters by the age of twenty. Some were even married before puberty and were made to wait before taking up their duties as wives and mothers.[132] In Germany the habit of betrothal long before marriage, which had come down from early Teutonic times, was continued in Luther's day. The custom was given the full support of the reformer himself, who went so far as to say that betrothal was just as binding as marriage. In opposition to the Roman Catholics, he declared that betrothal was binding even though the man had relations with someone other than the betrothed; after a man had plighted his troth, he was obliged to keep it forever.[133] Very frequently ceremonial betrothal was arranged before marriage, and after the occasion the betrothed were referred to as husband and wife, with the sexual privileges of marriage allowed. This practice was carried over to the American colonies in some instances.[134]

With the changed conditions of newer bourgeois existence, the position of women began to sink once more. The loss of economic status may have been primarily responsible, and yet the Reformation itself tended to accentuate the trend. Luther thought that woman's place was in the home, and

[127] Mumford, op. cit., p. 115.
[128] Ibid., p. 215.
[129] J. S. Schapiro, Social Reform and the Reformation (New York: Longmans, Green, 1909), pp. 56–58.
[130] Calhoun, op. cit., p. 19.
[131] Bartholomew Sastrow, Social Germany in Luther's Time, Memoirs translated by Albert D. Vandam (Westminster: Constable, 1902), p. 8.
[132] Calhoun, op. cit., p. 34.
[133] The Works of Martin Luther (Philadelphia: Holman, Castle Press, 1915), Vol. 2, p. 266.
[134] Calhoun, op. cit., pp. 35–36.

he glorified her household duties.[135] He judged the goodness of a wife by her obedience and said of his own that she was "more" compliant and obedient than he had "dared to hope" although he admitted that absolute obedience was not a woman's nature. Following up this realistic honesty he wrote that if he married again, it might be better to carve an obedient wife out of stone; for he doubted whether any were really obedient.[136]

With the Reformation the legal position of marriage began to shift its base, for in Protestant theory and practice this was a civil affair. Luther believed that marriage was a "worldly, extrinsic thing" which was valid with or without the sanction of any church.[137] Since the Scriptures do not support the doctrine that marriage is a sacrament, Luther thought of it as primarily a matter of civil contract[138] and this view was also adopted by Calvinists and other Protestants. For the Roman Catholic rule about forbidden "degrees" of consanguinity, Luther proposed the law of Leviticus which prohibited natural consanguinity only to the second degree.[139] He also contended that marrying unbaptized persons should be allowed, quoting the example of Augustine's Christian mother Monica, who was married to the pagan Patricius.[140] Probably the most bitterly contested step taken by the Protestants was allowing the clergy to marry. Since Luther taught that marriage was morally superior to celibacy, he felt that he ought to practice what he taught and consequently married a former nun, Katharine von Bora.[141] Though at first this step was regarded even by Protestants as too radical, at length it became more or less standard practice in the Protestant community.

As soon as it became evident that marriage was to be placed on the basis of civil contract, the divorce problem became acute. For if marriage was to be regulated by the state without church control, the state could also regulate the conditions of divorce, with the church as an adviser only. Luther himself hated divorce and even said that he would prefer bigamy (as he did in the cases of Henry VIII and Philip of Hesse). He contended that the Scriptures allowed divorce for adultery only[142] but he thought the Catholic Church was wrong in not allowing remarriage. At the same time he shows clearly between the lines of his writings that he wanted a more satisfactory answer for the problem of divorce and was searching for a new principle.[143] In general the reformers held to the view that the Catholic stringency about divorce promoted immorality among the common people while making it comparatively easy for those with money to obtain dispensations or elaborate

---

[135] *Ibid.*, p. 24.
[136] Arthur Cushman McGiffert, *Martin Luther, The Man and His Work* (New York: Century, 1911), pp. 286–287. A church historian who perused these lines remarked dryly that Luther could hardly qualify as a model husband.
[137] Calhoun, *op. cit.*, p. 25.
[138] Luther, *op. cit.*, Vol. 2, p. 257.
[139] *Ibid.*, pp. 264–265. (See also Leviticus 18:6 ff.).
[140] *Ibid.*, pp. 265–266.
[141] McGiffert, *op. cit.*, p. 283.
[142] Matthew 5:32.
[143] Luther, *op. cit.*, Vol. 2, pp. 271–272.

legal grounds for annulment in a way impossible to the poor. With regard to grounds for divorce, sentiment was somewhat divided; nearly everywhere, adultery was considered sufficient cause, and to this were added desertion, cruelty, insanity, and incurable disease.[144] The number of divorces steadily increased, not merely because of the change in church doctrine but perhaps chiefly as a result of the growing individualism of bourgeois life.[145]

During the sixteenth century there appears to have been a further relaxation of sexual mores. The passing of the convent in Protestant countries made the problem of extra women much more acute,[146] particularly since they found less work outside the home. No great stigma was attached to illegitimacy among the middle classes of central Europe because there was no estate involved as in the case of the upper classes.[147] Some of the sects arising in the Reformation era encouraged loose sexual practices. The Anabaptists at Münster under King John Becold even set up polygamy. John himself had fifteen wives and Jan Wilhelms, a follower, had twenty-one.[148] The Brown sect of the Anabaptists, founded in England, encouraged bundling with other men's wives,[149] and this practice was carried over to the American colonies, since the Pilgrims were an offshoot of the Brownists.

Perhaps some distinction should be drawn between the emphasis of Luther and that of Calvin on worldly pleasures. Luther himself was not a Puritan; he loved games and entertainments, enjoyed convivial company, and liked to see the young dancing or performing in theatricals.[150] On the other hand, Calvin and the Puritans who followed his doctrine thought man's worldly calling so important that work should occupy his major time and all other things should be sacrificed to diligence in business. The Puritans withdrew from community revelry and sought to have their chief pleasures more simply at home. There sprang up a negative concept of the home in which the Puritans conceived it as the place where the family could isolate itself from social pleasures like dancing, the theater, and music.[151] Since Puritanism was a merchant and money-making culture with a sense of religious mission, it placed primary emphasis on the activity of the man engaged in business, and allowed less and less time for the arts of love, which were as superfluous as the other arts. This naturally reduced courtship to a secondary place and heightened the importance of bargaining for an economically successful marriage. It also tended to lower the position of women to a place somewhat lower than they had had in the late medieval period. The outstanding Puritan reformer John Knox went so far as to publish in 1558 a volume, *The First Blast of the Trumpet Against the Monstrous Regiment of Women*. Much of it was directed against Mary of Scotland, whom he denounced bitterly as stepping out of the place reserved for her

144 Frank H. Hankins, "Divorce" in *Encyclopedia of the Social Sciences*, Vol. 5, p. 179.
145 Calhoun, *op. cit.*, p. 27.
146 *Ibid.*, p. 34.
147 *Ibid.*, p. 20.
148 *Ibid.*, p. 44.
149 *Ibid.*
150 McGiffert, *op. cit.*, pp. 298–308.
151 Calhoun, *op. cit.*, pp. 38, 40.

sex to rule over others. Unsatisfied with this invective, he went on to give wholesale condemnation of women, quoting Scripture, philosophers, Church Fathers, and writers from the Greek period to his own day in proof of the sin and foolishness of woman, who should recognize her subordinate place under the rule of the man.[152] Children too had to recognize their place. In Calvin's view, they were to be ruled with a rod of iron and kept submissive; disobedience could be punished even with death (as prescribed by the Old Testament).[153] Judging from the evidence at hand, there is little to show that this harsh rule was often put into actual practice.

The Italian Renaissance, spreading northward, led to increasing refinement. Books of etiquette were popular, for the new *bourgeoisie* aspired to higher social position.[154] Among aristocratic circles in the Italian cities women were given many new rights and privileges, particularly education in arts and letters, and social life was much freer than it had been in previous generations. There is little to show that this change affected the common people. Courtly manners, however, finally made their way northward into France and the northern countries, where they finally flowered in the salon life of the seventeenth and eighteenth centuries. Under this new sensitiveness the older habits of the nobles, who ate like peasants in the Middle Ages, gradually began to take on a somewhat more aesthetic tone.[155] The romantic ideal became greatly strengthened until Castiglione went so far as to say that a court lady should love the man she was going to marry.[156] This was still an exception to the general rule of marriage by convenience, although it showed which way the wind was blowing. On the other hand, the legal status of woman was not raised any higher and in some respects was even lowered, since the dower (or right of the wife to one third of the husband's property at his death) was no longer considered obligatory. This meant that the husband could now leave his entire property to someone else if he chose to do so.[157]

SUMMARY

From the barbarians who roamed the forests of Europe before the coming of the Romans to the colonists who set sail from England for the shores of America was a development of a millennium or more (600–1600 A.D.). Matriarchalism gave way to patriarchalism, while the consanguine form, after a period of transition, was supplanted by a permanent conjugal pattern. Migration and the wandering of people brought the need for a stricter control on behavior. At first this was enforced by the warrior chief, who

[152] Helen C. White, *Social Criticism in Popular Religious Literature of the Sixteenth Century* (New York: Macmillan, 1944), p. 161.

[153] Calhoun, *op. cit.,* p. 47.

[154] Goodsell, *op. cit.,* p. 253.

[155] Charles Seignobos, *The Evolution of the French People,* translated by Catherine Alison Phillips (New York: Knopf, 1932), pp. 228–229.

[156] Count Baldesar Castiglione, *The Book of the Courtier,* translated by Leonard Eckstein Opdycke (New York: Horace Liveright, 1929), p. 222.

[157] Goodsell, *op. cit.,* pp. 257–258.

became an overlord, but soon he was joined by priests who added supernaturalistic controls from another society. The merging of these two streams
resulted in organization along fairly rigid lines [158] and led to the strange
mingling of surging impulse and hoary restraint so peculiar to feudalism.
After a few wild struggles, the European family settled down (or reverted)
to another form of the sacred society in the manor or feudal village, where
it was as effectively isolated from the outside world as in the days of preliterate tribesmen.

It was, however, an isolation with a difference, for in place of the old
homogeneous tribe there was now a series of social levels or classes with
poverty and enforced monogamy among the serfs accompanied by polygamy
or concubinage in the nobility or royal houses. The institutional controls
of the church exerted pressure on the privileged classes until their forms of
marriage were more in line with the monogamous ideal and divorce was
more and more severely restricted. At the same time celibacy among the
clergy became more and more prevalent until it was accepted practice in the
Roman Catholic Church and on the higher levels of ecclesiastical orders in
the Orthodox Church.

The upper classes, having as always more mobility than the lower, began
to break the mold once more as the knights of the various orders cam-
paigned in Spain and took up the crusades. This connected them with new
currents of thought and incidentally opened up new roads of travel for the
troubadours. The romantic ideal entered Europe and gave increasing vitality
to chivalry; in turn this ideal became a rival of the church for the allegiance
of the nobility. At the same time strange new customs from the East also
undermined the stability of the aristocratic family. A current of unrest arose
which swept away from its moorings the ship of marriage so safely an-
chored in the quiet harbor of feudalism. Trade and commerce began to
flourish and the lower classes were caught up into the current; it took them
into the new towns and cities, where they became free citizens for the first
time. As they set up their guilds, a new form of urban family came into
existence where man and woman worked often side by side. As woman
entered the industrial world, her status rose, and the older forms of arranged
marriages were modified among the new middle class. It appeared for a
time as though she would win her emancipation, but the time was not ripe.
Wages were lowered and early capitalism removed the home from the workshop. Before long wage labor began to displace guild labor, and men became
the chief breadwinners. Woman retreated to the home again where now
her tasks increased with the newer household furnishing. With the Reformation came a new sacralizing of the home in terms of the individualistic
ideal and a renaissance of the older Pauline ideas about the subordinate
status of women and the "obedient" wife.

Marriage soon became in Protestant countries an individual contract

---

[158] See Howard Becker, "Processes of Secularisation: An Ideal-Typical Analysis with Special
Reference to Personality Change as Affected by Population Movement," *Sociological Review*
(British), 24 (April–July, and October, 1932), p. 149, for a generalized account of rigid
reorganization accompanying high mobility.

regulated by the state instead of a sacrament; divorce, too, was consequently subject to political authority, although in practice it was available chiefly to the male. Protestant clergy now followed the marriage practices of the laity and celibacy was rejected. Furthermore, the Puritan form of Protestantism gave such impetus to trade and worldly callings as divine duties that it regarded all natural pleasures as sinful. Children must therefore be literally whipped into shape or else their natural bent to evil would cause them to step aside from the path of duty. With all this harshness and severity, there was at the same time a fundamental integrity of purpose, and for both clergy and laity, freedom of conscience was coupled with the fear of divine retribution. Haunted by a sense of an illimitable future and goaded by an inner voice that would not let them rest, the Puritan family embarked on the voyage to the New World.

SELECTED READINGS

BEARD, MARY R., *Woman as Force in History*, A Study in Traditions and Realities (New York: Macmillan, 1946), chaps. 4, 6, 7–11.

CALHOUN, ARTHUR W., *A Social History of the American Family*, From Colonial Times to the Present (Cleveland: Clark, 1917), Vol. 1, chaps. 1–2.

COULTON, G. G., *Medieval Panorama*, The English Scene from Conquest to Reformation (New York: Macmillan, and Cambridge, England: University Press, 1938), chaps. 45–46.

DE ROUGEMONT, DENIS, *Love in the Western World* (New York: Harcourt, Brace, 1940), Books I and IV.

ELNETT, ELAINE, *Historic Origin and Social Development of Family Life in Russia* (New York: Columbia University Press, 1926), chaps. 1–4.

GOODSELL, WILLYSTINE, *A History of Marriage and the Family* (New York: Macmillan, 1934), chaps. 6–7.

HASTINGS, JAMES, ed., *Encyclopedia of Religion and Ethics* (New York: Scribner's, 1928), Vol. 3, "Celibacy, Christian," by George Cross.

HEBERMANN, CHARLES G., and others, eds., *The Catholic Encyclopedia*, An International Work of Reference on the Constitution, Doctrine, Discipline and History of the Catholic Church (New York: Appleton, 1907–1914), Vol. 3, "Celibacy," by Herbert Thurson.

HOMANS, GEORGE CASPAR, *English Villagers of the Thirteenth Century* (Cambridge: Harvard University Press, 1941), chaps. 8–15.

HUIZINGA, J., *The Waning of the Middle Ages*, A Study of the Forms of Life, Thought and Art in France and the Netherlands in the XIVth and XVth Centuries (London: Arnold, 1927), chaps. 4–6.

KEYSERLING, HERMANN A., ed., *The Book of Marriage* (New York: Harcourt, Brace, 1926), Pt. 2.

LEA, HENRY CHARLES, *History of Sacerdotal Celibacy in the Christian Church* (2 vols; 3rd ed. revised, New York: Macmillan, 1907).

MÜLLER-LYER, F., *The Family*, translated by F. W. Stella Browne (New York: Knopf, 1931).

Pirenne, Henri, *Economic and Social History of Medieval Europe* (London: Kegan Paul, Trench, Trubner & Co., 1936).

——, *Medieval Cities,* tr. by Frank D. Halsey (Princeton: Princeton University Press, 1925).

Pollock, Frederick, and Maitland, Frederick W., *The History of English Law before the Time of Edward I* (2 vols., 2nd ed., Cambridge: Cambridge University Press, and Boston: Little, Brown & Co., 1899), Vol. 1.

Reuter, E. B., and Runner, J. R., eds., *The Family,* Source Materials for the Study of Family and Personality (New York: McGraw-Hill, 1931), chap. 5.

Seligman, E. R. A., and Johnson, Alvin, eds., *Encyclopedia of the Social Sciences* (New York: Macmillan, 1933), Vol. 5, "Divorce," by Frank H. Hankins.

—— Vol. 3, "Chivalry," by F. J. C. Hearnshaw.

—— Vol. 12, "Prostitution," by Geoffrey May.

Stephenson, Carl, *Medieval History,* Europe from the Second to the Sixteenth Century (3rd ed., New York: Harper & Bros., 1951), chaps. 8, 10, and 11.

Stern, Bernhard J., ed., *The Family Past and Present* (New York: Appleton-Century, 1938), Sec. 3.

Taylor, H. O., *The Medieval Mind* (2 vols., 4th ed., London: Macmillan & Co., Ltd., 1927), Vol. 1, chap. 24.

Thompson, James Westfall, *An Economic and Social History of the Middle Ages (300–1300)* (New York: Century, 1928), chaps. 25–28.

TOPICS FOR DISCUSSION OR REPORTS

1. Compare the views of family development by stages in Burgess and Locke, *The Family,* pp. 18–22 and the one given by Müller-Lyer, *The Family,* chap. 9. How do they compare with the account given here?

2. Read Goodsell's *History of Marriage and the Family,* chap. 6, noting the origin of our present wedding ceremony, and write an essay on how present practice reflects medieval customs.

3. See Mary Beard's work, *Woman as Force in History,* especially the section on the medieval period, and compare her view of the status of women with that of Coulton in his *Medieval Panorama,* chap. 45.

4. Write a paper on the rise of the romantic ideal, its modern manifestations, giving your own criticism. For guidance consult De Rougemont, *Love in the Western World,* and J. K. Folsom, *The Family and Democratic Society,* especially index items on Love and the Romantic complex.

5. On the changing family type in Russia both pre- and post-revolutionary, compare Elnett's *Historic Origin and Social Development of Family Life in Russia* with Fannina W. Halle's *Women in Soviet Russia.* For a short introduction and orientation note Burgess and Locke, *The Family,* chap. 6.

6. Write a paper on the joint and the stem family. See G. C. Homans' *English Villagers of the Thirteenth Century,* chap. 8, for inheritance related to the joint family and the stem family. Then see the account of both types of family in Zimmerman and Frampton, *Family and Society.*

7. Prepare a report on divorce in medieval times and today. For changes in European divorce customs see Coulton, *Medieval Panorama,* chap. 46, and article "Divorce" in the *Encyclopedia of the Social Sciences.*

Chapter Five

American Families Today: Development and Differentiation of Types

MANFORD HINSHAW KUHN

THE WESTERN HERITAGE

COLONIAL families in America, while reflecting a variety of frontier conditions, were also shaped by historical factors and events which characterized the previous development of Western civilization. Some of these were intricate and complex and even, in some instances, self-contradictory in nature. Others were simpler and more direct and occasionally represented mutually converging trends.

As an example of the former type of historical influence, examine the impact of Christianity on the colonial family. From the teachings of Jesus came certain rather inchoate notions about the equality of the sexes and still others emphasizing the irrevocability of marriage, though the latter are somewhat mitigated by the unmistakable attacks on the formalism of all institutions. From Paul, on the other hand, came a generally negative view toward sex, correlated with notions of the inferiority of women. Paul saw marriage as a mere concession to man's basic weakness. The contrast is more apparent when we remember that the analogies used by Jesus in his teachings were most frequently ones drawn from family life — fatherhood, brotherhood, and the like — strong indications from the standpoint of projective psychology, that Jesus put extremely high value on family relationships.

The early Christians followed Paul's teachings in these respects more than they did those of Jesus. Their leaders' attitudes toward sex were strongly negative and women were, in their view, accorded only a subsidiary position. Perhaps it is fairer to say that the position of women in the early Christian groups tended to reflect their position in the larger society probably more than it reflected Paul's views. At any rate, the early Christians, while they were more influenced by Paul, nevertheless continued quite universally to marry and to raise families. It remained for the later church to develop important alternative patterns of celibacy on the basis of Paul's teachings. In fact it was four hundred years before even the clergy were prohibited from marrying. But in these four hundred years, the aversion toward sex on the part of the Christian Fathers increased, and with this came a greater and greater identification, in their attitudes, of women with sex, so that as the negative view toward sex grew the status of woman diminished,[1] partly in reaction to the contrasting Roman patterns.

---

[1] For a brief account of this increasing antipathy toward sex and womankind see Willystine Goodsell, *A History of Marriage and the Family* (rev. ed., New York: Macmillan, 1934), pp. 160–164.

In the earliest days of Christianity marriage had been a lay ceremony. Century by century it came to include more religious form but not until 1164 did the Church officially proclaim marriage to be one of the sacraments.[2] The Renaissance, the rise of Protestantism, the commercial revolution, and the growth of individualism all converged to make marriage a civil rather than church affair and served to make the middle class family over into a property institution, not by stripping marriage and the family of all "Christian" implications but by reinterpreting them in the new, peculiarly Protestant, framework of "worldly asceticism," in which they were instrumental to the individual's general purpose of accumulating property as evidence of the grace of God.[3]

So much for a necessarily oversimplified example of one of the more complex and inwardly contradictory historical currents which molded and shaped the family of colonial times. An example of a simpler and more direct kind of influence is that of factors making for patriarchal organization of the family. It is not germane here to discuss the ways in which patriarchal power differed among Hebrew, Greek, Roman, and Teutonic cultures since that has already been done in previous chapters. It is only pertinent to note that the families in each of these otherwise differing societies were every one in their several ways patriarchal. Feudalism brought to the fore its own peculiar brand of the patriarchate. While there were a few instances, notably in the late Roman republic and among some of the Germanic tribes, of relative equality of husband and wife, yet most of the historical influences shaping the colonial family were, convergingly, patriarchal in character.

The early settlers in this country thus did not start life on the new continent entirely fresh. While they brought with them only sparse material equipment for coping with rigorous frontier life, they did bring a weighty baggage of culturally inherited ideas. They were highly individualistic when compared with people of the previous, feudalistic era, and yet they placed a high value on family life. This family life was in large measure patterned for them by their culture. They were monogamous and patriarchal; and they were intolerant of anything which tended to disrupt either of these sets of attitudes. They were, as we shall see, mixed in their assumptions regarding women and sex. And again, as we shall discover, they thought of the family as a double-edged instrument — a means of accumulating property and a device for enlarging the Kingdom of God.

A FRAME OF REFERENCE FOR COMPARING FAMILY PATTERNS

The early colonists, though a large portion of them came from remarkably similar segments of English society, differed sufficiently in their patterns of family relationships to make it worth our while to compare and

[2] Goodsell, *op. cit.,* p. 222.
[3] See Max Weber, *The Protestant Ethic and the Spirit of Capitalism* (New York: Scribner's, 1930).

contrast them. In so doing we shall focus our attention on certain significant aspects of family life and values. In the first place, we shall endeavor to picture the *role and status of the members within each type of family configuration,* in terms of the functions of the father, mother, and child, the patterns of power and permissibility (subordination and superordination), and any notions of intrinsic or ultimate worth attributed to the individual. Here we shall be dealing with the family as if it were a little, self-contained society.

In the second place, we shall sketch the *functions of the family with respect to the larger society of which it was a part.* To what degree was the family assigned the functions of inducting the child into the culture and of preparing him for participation in society? What tasks of economic production and consumption were given to the family to perform? What were its religious functions? What recreational activities were essentially family affairs? To what extent was the social control of individual behavior left in the hands of the family? Here, in this section, we will examine the family in terms of its place in the over-all society.

And finally, we shall try to delineate what might be called the *ideology of the family.* By this term we mean that complex of (for them, at least) somewhat consistent ideas by which participants explained to themselves the basic meaning and purpose of marriage and family relationships. This can be approximated through a study of the documents which bear directly on it, but it may also be approached through an examination of the interrelationships of the family with other social institutions (church, school, state, and economic institutions). An understanding of family ideology can be furthered by investigating the significance to the people themselves of their sex notions and their attitudes on morality. And, finally, a consideration of the central meanings which people attached to such patterns as their approved methods of choosing mates or their ways of meeting the problem of marital dissolution will increase our grasp of this group philosophy of marriage and the family. Through such an analysis of direct and indirect hints at a family ideology, we can piece together the operative conception a people had of the interrelationships among the individual, the family, and society.

Didactically it may be profitable to summarize in outline form this frame of reference which we will use as a tool for comparisons:

I. Role and status of family members:
   A. Functions of father, mother, child
   B. Patterns of subordination and superordination
   C. Any notions of intrinsic, ultimate value attributed to members or any category of members
II. Functions of the family:
   A. Educational
   B. Economic
   C. Religious
   D. Recreational
   E. Social control

III. Ideology of the family:
    A. Basic meaning or purpose attributed to marriage and family re-
       lationships, as implicit in
       1. Interrelationships of the family with other institutions such as
          the church, the school, the state, and business
       2. Sex and morality attitudes
       3. Patterns of choosing mates and of meeting marital dissolution

THE NEW ENGLAND PURITAN FAMILY

Without question the culture of Puritan New England had more to do
with the shaping of our national culture than did that of any other colonial
region or that of any subsequent immigrant group. Our governmental structure and our attitudes toward it, our methods of business enterprise and our
national habits of thrift and industriousness associated with them, our instrumental approach to institutions and the corollary idiosyncrasy of building our highest values (ends) into the very ongoing processes of day-to-day
living (means) — all these and a host more of the attributes of our cultural
ethos received their distinctive stamp from the peculiar configuration of
folkways and mores which was Puritan New England. This is no whit less
true of the family as an institution in our culture. The frantic alternation
between taut sexual prudery and blatant self-indulgent "wolfism," the contradiction between woman as a subservient creature and woman as a co-
equal companion, the contrast between the notion that a present generation
of youths, juvenile delinquents all, is going to the devil, and the notion
that our children, properly and gently trained, will transform society —
these are not new culture paradoxes with us; we were anticipated in these
paradoxical notions by the cultural ambivalences of the Puritans of New
England, and the same basic family attitudes which brought these about
three hundred years ago continue in some measure to operate today. What
manner of institution was this New England family?

Role and Status of Members

The father in the New England Puritan family was unmistakably the
head. This patriarchal position he held as a result of English common law,
secular practice, and traditional sanctions, and also as a consequence of his
particular heritage of religious doctrine. The wife was distinctly subordinate
to her husband in matters of ownership of property, major decisions of policy, inheritance, and the like. Her activities were circumscribed and the
notion that she was the "weaker vessel" was generally affirmed. This pattern
of headship of the husband and subordination of the wife is one with which
the average elementary school child in our society has become familiar
through his repeated study of American history.

What is generally not so well recognized, however, is that this is merely the point from which the newly arrived Puritan family *started*. This simple set of assumptions regarding status was soon to be modified by three inter-related sets of factors. First, there were new roles required in the new country. The tasks of clearing the land, building the houses and barns, mak-ing the farm and household tools and the like, were tasks that had to be carried on over and above the ones which were required for day-to-day liv-ing, such as raising, gathering, and cooking the food (and preserving the surplus for winter use), spinning, weaving cloth, dyeing, making the cloth-ing, chopping firewood, and the thousand and one other activities made necessary by a self-sufficient family economy characterized by extreme scar-city. Women were forced by the exigencies of the situation to help in the heavier jobs as well as to carry on their unusually arduous household rou-tines — all this in addition to the bearing of great numbers of children. This extension of woman's role unquestionably had a very important part in the modification of her status from the simple one of subordination to her hus-band to one in which the wife, though still dominated theoretically by her husband, was in many respects actually his co-equal.

Second, the implicit, functioning conception that *the family — rather than the state or some other institution — is the organizing center for society* necessarily had its impact on the position of woman. That New England Puritan society was essentially family-centered is a point which has been for too long underestimated [4] and one to which we shall return when we con-sider the ideology of this family. Here it is only important to note that such a conception, even though it was largely unconscious, had an automatic effect of making woman's role take on far greater significance than it could have in a state-centered or church-centered society, especially in those days when church and state were traditionally affairs dominated by men. The effects of this conception on woman's role were no doubt exaggerated by the absence in the New World of outwardly imposed government on the one hand and the lack of a complex class structure on the other — things which in England had constituted for the Puritan such a large (and men-acing!) part of his social milieu.

Third, the growing individualism of the time was responsible in some measure for increasing woman's status. This individualism was the product of several factors. Protestantism laid great stress on individual worth, in-dividual moral responsibility, and individual rather than corporate relation-ships with God. Concomitantly, the rise of commercial relationships and capitalism began to break down all the old, settled, feudal relationships that rested on inherited, ascribed, and group-sanctioned status, and to build up in their stead relationships of a highly individualistic sort resting on per-sonally achieved status. In its turn, the rugged Northern frontier provided a set of social conditions which operated, convergent with Protestantism and capitalism, to heighten the importance of the individual relative to other social categories. The net result of these various emphases on individual per-

[4] The analysis of Puritan society as extremely family-centered has been made recently by Ed-mund S. Morgan in his *The Puritan Family* (Boston: Boston Public Library, 1944), pp. 78 ff.

formance was to give woman, whose role in colonial life was obviously so extremely important, an even more augmented status.[5]

That the early Puritans considered children to be sinful and depraved is well known. It is also common knowledge that their children were given useful and often arduous tasks very early in life by contemporary standards. Work was indeed thought to be one of the best ways by which the young child might begin to depart from his natural sinfulness. Education, particularly in learning the Scriptures, was another remedy employed to drive out original depravity. Finally, if the child persisted in his evil ways, he was to be treated with sternness and physical punishment. This complex of ideas seems to indicate that the child in early New England had a very low and servile status in the family.

Such a conclusion, however, would be inaccurate. While it is true that the relation between parent and child had the trappings of formality and emotionlessness in many respects, yet there are many indications that this was more apparent than real. Although the new-born child was held to be sinful, he did represent a soul to be saved. As Puritanism became a more settled way of life, the children born to Christian families came more and more to be regarded, probably unconsciously, as the chief potentialities for the increase of the Kingdom of God, for the Puritans soon began to ignore the nonbelievers about them as prospects for evangelism. Nor was the religious aspect the only one making for a high valuing of the child. The worldly asceticism of Puritanism centered around the gaining of property as an evidence of the grace of God. The most important consequence of this idea was to enhance the family as a property institution. Now a child was not only a worker helping to increase the goods of the family; he was also a future heir to the accumulated property — he made the continuity of the family possible.

It is thus to be expected that the actual status of the child in the New England family was somewhat confused and contradictory. The popular stereotype is that the colonial Puritan child had the supposed sin quite literally beaten out of him. Yet there is really no convincing evidence that he was corporally punished any more regularly or severely than is the contemporary American child. Again, the general notion today is that the father ruled the entire family with a very firm hand, made all the basic decisions, and stood for no opposition. Yet, again, there are many indications that children at a very early age were treated as individuals; that is, their differing temperaments and desires were respected. In fine, one must conclude that the pattern of role and status in the New England family represented

[5] If it strikes the reader as self-contradictory to cite in one and the same analysis the "family-centeredness" and the "individualism" of a society such as that of colonial New England, then it is because he is accustomed to thinking in absolutes and polarities. In Puritan New England individualism and family-centeredness were not antithetical polarities that tended to cancel each other, however inevitable that might seem to be purely from the standpoint of logic. On the contrary, each was a reaction — and in the same direction — from the class-categorized social, political, and economic structure of feudalism. Perhaps another way to put it would be to say that this society tended to break up into family molecules in those respects in which it was not expedient to go all the way to complete individualism.

a compromise between that of the historically established patriarchate and that of equalitarian individualism.

Functions of the Family

The self-sufficiency of this family is so familiar to us that here we need only remind ourselves that this is probably the area in which the contemporary American family differs most markedly from its New England precursor. Today educational, economic, religious, recreational, and control functions have come to be performed by differentiated agencies outside the family. It is, doubtless, in the economic realm that the shift has been most marked. The contemporary family is dependent on one or more workers who perform rather highly specialized tasks, tasks which are performed outside the home. The New England household was, contrariwise, a cooperative economic unit, producing all kinds of raw materials and transforming these into finished products, most of which were consumed by the family itself.

This difference between the New England colonial family and the contemporary family has been overstated, however. The difference is attributable more to rural-urban differences than to differences brought on by historical changes. The New England village family was by no means as self-sufficient as the rural family. Conversely, the contemporary rural American family has not lost nearly so many of its functions as has the contemporary city family.[6] One should not take this to mean, however, that there have been few changes from the New England rural family to the contemporary one. The family-centered barn-raisings, quilting bees, and husking bees as examples of cooperative economic and recreational activities; the shearing, combing, spinning, dyeing, weaving, and tailoring of wool into clothing for all the members of the family as an example of the hosts of economic self-sufficiency activities; the Bible reading and family prayers as an example of family religious functioning; the training of children as chiefly a family affair — all these and many more examples could be cited to show how remarkably the New England rural family differed from the contemporary rural American family.

Ideology of the Family

The family was undoubtedly the most important institution in Puritan society. Both government and religion as institutions were subsidiary to it. The state and other governmental units merely did whatever was left over after family control had been exerted. And as for religion, there had come with Protestantism a close linkage with economics; these two were intertwined, principally in the functioning of the family. While it was the individual who received a "call" to some vocation, it was his family that advised him regarding the genuineness of this "calling," and it would be largely a family rather than an individual affair once he went into it.

[6] This point will be developed later in this chapter in another connection.

The Puritan revolted against marriage as a religious sacrament. It was a strictly civil affair and for a time marriages by a preacher were not allowed. And again the Puritan allowed divorce, which neither the Roman Church nor the Church of England had permitted. However, these two things do not mean that the family had become separated from religious practices. On the contrary, we have already seen that it carried on many religious functions and that it was even regarded as the nucleus out of which the growing Kingdom would emerge. No; the emergence of civil marriage and divorce reflected the fact that the individual and the family were really held to be above the church, so much so in fact that there was not going to be any acknowledgment that the church had a right to marry people or for that matter that it had a right to keep them married against their wishes.

FAMILIES IN THE MIDDLE COLONIES

While it has been possible to treat the New England family as a single phenomenon owing to the remarkable homogeneity of the people who settled in the colonies there,[7] it is by no means as simple to describe marriage and family behavior in the Middle Colonies. The people who came to live in the colonies lying between New England to the north and east and Maryland to the south came from very diverse cultures in Europe and hence had widely different family patterns. There were the Dutch Walloons, the Swedes, the French Huguenots, the Germans (who came to be called Pennsylvania Dutch), the Welsh, the Moravians, the Quakers, the Scotch Presbyterians, English Puritans, English conformists and royalists, Catholics, and a variety of other groups, each with distinctive family characteristics of its own. Nor did the differences tend immediately to merge and fade away, for the ways of life differed tremendously — from life on the great Hudson River estates to that of New York and Philadelphia artisans and tradesmen. It would be impossible within the scope of this chapter to treat each family type separately. Instead we shall look very briefly at one of these, the Quaker family. The Quaker family is chosen not because it is in any sense a typical or average pattern for the Middle Colonies, for there was no "central tendency" among these diverging patterns. It is chosen, rather, because (a) the Quakers were for a time a dominant group in a great section of these colonies and (b) the Quakers are commonly confused with the Puritans in their family ways, whereas actually there are many interesting and important contrasts.

Role and Status in the Quaker Colonial Family

While the Quakers were like the Puritans in holding as central values industry, sobriety, and thrift, they did so for quite different reasons. They

---

[7] The colonies of New England were settled almost entirely by English. There were a few Huguenots and Ulster Scots but their numbers were almost negligible. Of course not all the English were Puritans, but the Puritan family tended to be the prototype.

were this-worldly rather than other-worldly even in their theology, making much of their peculiar doctrine of "that of God in every man." This "seed of God in man" idea led to a very different attitude toward behavior than that held by the Puritans. For the Quaker, sin was the absence of goodness, a result of neglect in "nourishing the seed"; for the Puritan, sin was an active, malignant, growing thing. This difference is of more than philosophic importance, for it led to differences in attitudes among the members of the family. For example, parents treated children with much the same consistent firmness and respect that the horticulturalist treats a growing plant. Further, since "that of God" was within the individual at the start, there was not the harshness which seemed to characterize the relationships of some Puritans toward their children, a harshness predicated on the assumption that the young child was possessed by the devil. Quaker family relationships were, to use the Quakers' own term, "tender," a term intended to convey the ideas of incomparable value and mutual respect but certainly nothing of sentimentality. That the Quakers put their children to work at a very early age there can be no doubt, but they seem not to have been accused, as were the Puritans, of having "sweated" their children. This is probably attributable more to the greater success with which the Quaker parent internalized in his child the goals of work and diligence than to any great difference in the amount of work done by the Puritan children and the Quaker children.

Thanks to their unique theological outlook, the Quakers were far more democratic in their family relations than were the Puritans. The dignity of each individual was for them a nonpareil value, and it followed that there were less implicit status gradations in the family according to such things as differences in age and sex. Parents and children, father and mother, brother and sister, the older and younger, all were on a fairly level plane of family regard and esteem. Parents, it is true, had many weighty responsibilities in the rearing of their children, but the network of rights and duties was an evenly balanced system among the members of the family circle. Right dealing, industriousness, and concern for others were ends in themselves rather than, as among the Puritans, instrumental activities aimed at claiming the grace of God. This kind of presentism among the Quakers was in itself an exponent of the value placed on the dignity of each individual in the family, regardless of his age or sex.

Functions of the Quaker Colonial Family

It is not necessary to treat at length the functions of the Quaker family, since they are much the same as those of the New England Puritan family. The chief difference lies in the fact that a greater proportion of the Quakers were tradesmen and business people; hence there was less self-sufficiency and greater specialization and division of labor. Among the farmers, and there were many, there was perhaps somewhat less self-sufficiency, too, than among New England rural families, because transportation and communication were easier and hence more quickly developed. Nevertheless the number of functions performed in the household was very great. The religious function of the Quaker family was, both among the rural and among the urban communities, scarcely separable from that of the more organized "meetings," for the family participated either at home or at meeting as a unit; and religious activity, in many ways undifferentiated from any other activity, was one unbroken continuity. Recreational activities were never recognized as such but were simply epiphenomena of other activities. Governmental and control activities were, again, functions of the family and of the meetings. The Quakers in England had suffered so much at the hands of the state that even when under Penn's leadership they had control of formal government, they were highly ambivalent about what should be their role in participation. This contrasts with the Puritan attitude in which formal government, though subsidiary to family control, was regarded as its adjunct for problems beyond its power or brought about by its breakdown.

The Ideology of the Quaker Colonial Family

It must be clear from the foregoing discussion that there was no sharp delineation between the family and other social institutions in the Quaker community. It is true that the meeting had the responsibility of disciplining miscreant and erring members. This sometimes led to "reading out of meeting" those who persisted in their ways. But the religious meetings were participated in by families rather than by individuals, and any differentiation between religion and family as separate social institutions became visible only when something went awry. So, too, with the economic institutions; the family was the chief economic unit even in trading and business. The conduct of economic activity was a subject much discussed in the family circle, in the meetings for worship, and in the Quaker business gatherings.

In all these respects, the family and the other social institutions were perceived by the Quakers themselves as being one single, rounded whole — the Quaker way of life. It was this way of life — not the family as such — that was conceived by them to be central. And to a great degree this idea was operative, too; for people were repeatedly "moved" to make extended journeys to visit Friends in distant parts, leaving their families for long periods of time in order to express their "concerns" to Quakers elsewhere. So in this respect the Quaker family again contrasts with the Puritan family in that while the Puritan family was unquestionably the dominant institution, the dominant Quaker institution was a comprehensive pattern of life to which the family must at times subordinate itself.

There is another contrast which must be noted. The Puritans after settling in New England did not seem to have a sense of separateness or of being different, while the Quakers in the Middle Colonies did. A story which persists will illustrate this: The Quakers used (and many still use) what was known as the "plain language," which involved the use of the pronouns "thee" and "thine" (the nominative "thou" was never used). One mother had considerable difficulty in making a good Quakeress of her little daughter. Finally, after a series of aberrations on the part of the child, the mother turned sternly and cried at her, "Thee little *you,* thee!" The very use of this different language was, obviously, a minor cause and a major acknowledgment of the sense of separateness from other groups and their ways. The wearing of the Quaker garb is parallel to this. There can be little doubt that the sense of being a people apart had the effect of heightening the solidarity which existed in the family.

The Quakers did not acknowledge the right of government to perform a marriage, and since they had no ministers it might be assumed that they had no way of regularizing the marriage. This is not true, however, for marriage was actually regulated with great care. It was the custom for people to marry themselves, the ceremony taking place in meeting at due time after an announcement of intention to wed had been made. Divorce was unheard of, not because the marriage had any supernatural sanction but rather because the choosing of mates was done with great care and because of the in-group solidarity.

As for attitudes toward sex, the Quakers while living by a very strict code seemed to have had more naturalistic notions than did the Puritans. There is no evidence that the Quaker had morbid ideas such as the Puritan seems to have had. There is no Quaker counterpart to *The Scarlet Letter.* This lack of preoccupation with sex is undoubtedly attributable to the fact that the peculiar Quaker theology failed to engender a sense of guilt or sin, a process which is so distinctive in Puritan thought and behavior.

As to choice of mate, Puritan parents tended to arrange the marriages of their children, the "veto power" being left in the hands of the individuals concerned, while among the Quakers there was individual choice of mate, with "veto power" being left in the hands of parents and the meeting. This generalization is, no doubt, subject to many exceptions, but it does describe fairly well the differences between the two groups in this respect. In neither group was the mate expected — or really allowed — to be outside the group itself. Certainly any Quaker who married someone "outside of meeting" would find himself quickly "read out of meeting." Hence the Quaker individualism in this matter was not so divergent from the arranged marriage of the Puritan as it might first have appeared. Yet the difference does have significance. The Puritan arrangement was aimed at the control of property, its concentration and inheritance, while the Quaker pattern reflected the characteristic individualism of this group, without much reference to property considerations as such.[8]

[8] That the whole Quaker pattern had implications for the acquiring of wealth, however, there can be no doubt. The ideals of industry, sobriety, diligence, and thrift which the Quakers had in common with the Puritans had much to do with this. Then, too, according to Professor Ralph Linton, there was extensive practice of primogeniture among the Quakers in this area. This helps account for the steady accumulation of wealth by the Quakers who remained in areas of original settlement.

THE SOUTHERN ARISTOCRATIC FAMILY

The Old South was settled by groups as divergent as those which came to the Middle Colonies. In fact many of the same European groups contributed to the population of the South as well as to that of New York, Pennsylvania, and New Jersey — Irish, Swiss, Huguenots, Germans, Scots, but with the English always predominating. Only Maryland and Virginia might be said to have been settled almost completely by English, but these two colonies, despite the sameness of ethnic background, had a heterogeneity of population based on the fact that large numbers of convicts were sent to them during the latter half of the seventeenth century. In addition a considerable number of voluntarily indentured servants from the pauper classes in England came over to spend varying numbers of years working out their freedom. Then, too, the pattern of Negro slaveholding developed to add further heterogeneity to the population.

There were two chief reasons for the development of a rather marked pattern of social stratification in the South. One was the point just mentioned — the early establishment of both limited and absolute servitude. This might have had even greater consequence for social stratification than it did were it not for the fact that wives were lacking in the southern colonies, and in the competition for what women there were those of the indentured classes lost out and hence failed to contribute to the perpetuation of a servile caste. On the other hand, the Negroes did marry after whatever fashion was possible under slavery, and their distinctive color served as a badge to set apart a class considered so low as virtually to constitute for a long time a variety of untouchables.

The other reason for the extreme stratification in the South stems from the fact that many of the early English settlers were Cavaliers. It is only natural that royalists would have quite a different outlook than would a group of dissident nonconformists like the Puritans. This is particularly true of the kind of social organization they would expect to build in the New World. The royalist naturally patterned his new social relationships after those he had subscribed to in England, including, of course, the sharp social gradations in status. It was not long before the groups at the top of the social and economic pyramid of power and prestige began to think of themselves as belonging to a noble English lineage. In fact the myth became so common that all classes accepted it as true, and finally the country as a whole came to think of the upper-class Southern family as being a branch of English nobility. It remained for the social historian, Arthur Calhoun, to explode this myth [9] by discovering that the aristocrats of the South came from middle-class English families, just as did the Puritans and the Quakers. Nevertheless, as Thomas and Znaniecki have said, "If men define situations as real, they are real in their consequences," and so this myth has had profound effect in bolstering the lines of class cleavage in the South.

[9] Arthur Calhoun, *Social History of the American Family* (Cleveland: Clark, 1918), Vol. 1.

In the South, as in the Middle Colonies, we will devote our attention to one family, in this case the aristocratic family. The reader must again be reminded that this family is in no sense typical of the family in general in the South. No average is possible when the actual families differed so markedly in their organization, economic patterns, interrelations with other families, systems of role and status, and the like. The aristocratic family was chosen because of the importance of the aristocracy throughout Southern history.

Role and Status of Family Members

The aristocratic family in the colonial South was extremely patriarchal, especially when compared with the Puritan or the Quaker family. In this as in other matters the prototype was the English manorial estate with its lord. As the pattern of large holdings developed, the family tended to take on some of the characteristics of the great family or extended family, with more than two generations and one conjugal pair living together. As this came about, the head of the family increased his dominance over men of younger generations, married as well as unmarried. The functions of the head were largely to plan and supervise and to make ultimate decisions of policy if any were necessary. Again, however, he attempted to model his life after that of the English gentleman, so that the Southern master became more and more a man of leisure.

His wife, though definitely subordinate to him, was mistress of the household and in this capacity she wielded a great deal of authority. Circumscribed though she was by the "protective" patterns related to the double standard of morality — an idea which held sway in the Old South to a far greater degree than elsewhere in the colonies — she nevertheless came in many instances to have, de facto though never de jure, even greater power than did her husband. This came about partly by default as the master developed more and more his emulated patterns of leisure, partly by the nature of social organization as the household came to play such an important part in the functioning of the plantation. Certainly her role in the intrigue of marrying off her children to "proper" mates among the kindred aristocracy made her a key figure in the family. And as leisure patterns developed in the South in this class, much of the planning and management of the constant round of entertaining fell to her.

The children were definitely subordinate. Their role was chiefly to learn how to be ladies and gentlemen. As the arduous physical work was taken over more and more by the lower caste, the children were relieved of all hard work and grew up chiefly in leisure. This is, of course, in direct contrast to the roles of children in Puritan and Quaker groups to the north. The double standard impinged early and at many points on the lives of the oncoming generation to the end that girls were largely subordinate to boys of their own age groups. While subordinate in the family, children of this elite were heavily indoctrinated with a sense of superiority to others in the population, and furthermore their whole training was such as to make them constantly aware that their subordination even in their own families was merely temporary.

Functions of the Family

The Southern aristocratic household was early the epitome of self-sufficiency. While in New England and in the Middle Colonies village and town soon grew up with attendant specialization and division of labor wearing away some of the functions of the farm home, in the South the system of tobacco culture and later of cotton culture brought about larger and larger plantations. This fact in turn tended to preclude the development of town specialization, thanks particularly to the transportation problems involved. Hence the Southern plantation developed within itself techniques and specialists to meet virtually all its needs. Many a plantation did its own carpentry, brick and stone masonry, metalwork and forging, milling, barrel making, dyeing and weaving, and so on. There was, accordingly, much less commerce within the region itself than in the other colonies, and trade was principally with England. Hence roads remained relatively undeveloped and rivers were used instead, since they led to the sea and thus to shipping points.

Education was chiefly a matter of informal and unconscious training within the family itself. It consisted chiefly of learning the "forms, postures, and graces." In New England by contrast, education meant chiefly learning to read, which in turn meant learning to read the Scriptures. Learning the Scriptures was part of the way toward salvation. Now the teaching of reading is more easily turned over to a specialized agency, the school, while the social *savoir faire et dire* is more reliably taught in the home itself. Hence the South developed formal schooling later than the other colonies.

The principal religion of the aristocratic South (apart from Maryland, where Catholicism was important) was that of the Church of England as one might expect in a royalist group. It was a more ceremonial and ritualistic practice than that of the Puritan or certainly than that of the Quaker, and as a consequence it impinged less on actual behavior except to bolster and sustain the prestige of the upper class. It was not by any means so closely tied in with the family as an institution as was the religion of the Puritans or the Quakers, but on the formalistic side it had even more influence, in that a marriage had to be performed by a minister of the established church and divorce was not allowed. The home performed few religious rites compared with the home in Puritan New England. However self-sufficient the home in the Old South was economically, it must be said that it relied religiously on a distinct and discrete social institution, the established church.

The principal social control exerted on members of the aristocracy was that of the family. In this the Southern elite parallel the Puritan and Quaker groups. Government was more or less at the apex of the social hierarchy as it had been in royalist England. Probably its principal function may be said to have been the freezing of the status quo, the preservation of the classes and their prerogatives in this New World brand of feudalism, and the disciplining of aberrant members of the lower classes.

Ideology of the Family

The dominant social institution, if it may be properly termed an institution, in the colonial South was that of class. The owning class, actually a very small proportion of the population, was quite literally a kind of extended clan inasmuch as it was made up of a number of families who treated the class as an endogamous unit. Hence the members of the upper class were soon fairly closely related to each other by blood. The family was the principal agency by which the upper class was perpetuated. This the family accomplished both by controlling marriage and by controlling inheritance (the latter chiefly through primogeniture). In fact the very folkways which constituted class behavior were really identical with the folkways of family behavior.

The attitudes toward sex could be defined as elastic as far as men were concerned but as approaching the Puritanic as applied to women's behavior. This meant that those women involved in extramarital relations with men of the aristocratic class must necessarily belong to the lower classes. Women of the Negro slave class were, for example, defined as accessible and acceptable as sexual objects for men of the aristocracy. Naturally, the society did not regard offspring of these unions as belonging to the upper class. Whatever other functions they may have served, these sex attitudes may be regarded as functional adjuncts to the class system. They made possible escape from uncongenial and unsatisfying arranged marriages as far as the men were concerned, and they tended greatly to reduce sex as a value as far as women were concerned, thus operating as (inside) controls on their behavior in the interests of class maintenance.

It must not be concluded, however, that the Southern aristocratic family remained insulated against the notions of democracy which were so predominant in the rest of the colonies during the late colonial period. It must be remembered, for example, that Thomas Jefferson was from one of the upper class families of Virginia, nor was he the only one of his type by any means. The results of democratic ideology were quite visible. Primogeniture died out or was abolished by law. It became possible for ministers other than those of the established church, or even in some cases civil justices of the peace, to perform the marriage ceremony. There even came to be a somewhat more equalitarian relation within some of the upper class families. Nevertheless the typical pattern of the Southern aristocratic family is that pictured in the above analysis.

COMPARISON AND SUMMARY

Despite the fact that all three of the family types we have had under consideration had their origins in English culture and English middle class culture at that, we have discovered some marked differences among them. Consider the matter of status within the family for example: The Quaker family probably approximated equality of status as closely as it could in the face of the limitations imposed by basic biological age and sex differences. The Southern upper class family, on the other hand, developed rather extreme gradations of status within the family paralleling the marked stratification in the society as a whole. The New England Puritan family was somewhere in between these two extremes. While there were some very real (and growing) elements of equalitarianism within the Puritan family, there was still a hang-over from English common law in the generally inferior status of women, and there was also undoubtedly a lower status for children predicated on the Puritan theology of original sin and infantile depravity.

All three of the families were, by our contemporary standards, self-sufficient. This is a relative matter, however, and again the three families differed among themselves both in the degree and in the types of self-sufficiency. In an over-all sense the aristocratic Southern family had the most self-sufficing household establishment, while the Quaker family in the Middle Colonies had the least — thanks to the early growth of trade, interdependence, and urbanization. Yet if this generalization is construed to apply to the satisfaction of *all* man's needs (rather than just his "economic" needs) within the orbit of family activity, then it needs qualifying and amending. The South had, for example, probably the most distinct and differentiated religious activity of the three, instead of being on this score, as in economic matters, familially self-sufficient. The Quaker family, contrariwise, was most able to get on without the use of a formal governmental pattern to assist it in matters of social control. Perhaps it is best, then, to leave this area of comparison at the point at which we entered it — with a reiteration of the observation that in comparison with the contemporary American family the colonial family of whatever type was self-sufficient.

As to the ideology of the family, each of these three groups tended to revolve around the family as its major institution. In each case there was a close relation between the family on the one hand and the accumulation and maintenance of property on the other. In each case there was a close relation between the family and the processes of social control of individual behavior. In each case whatever recreation was available in the society was virtually a monopoly of the family. One must conclude that these three groups were extremely familiocentric.

The Quaker family had the most naturalistic attitude toward sex and manifested the least hypocrisy toward it. The other two groups differed mainly in the points at which sex was repressed and the points at which cultural rationalizations reconciling the (to us) obvious contradictions were called for. All three groups exercised in one way or another more group control over choice of mate than we do today. All three rigorously inhibited separation and divorce of married partners, though the Puritans at least made divorce possible.

In the New World it clearly seems to have been the family which held society together. The family was the kernel of new social organization. And, lacking a well differentiated set of social institutions, it devolved upon the family to provide patterns for meeting virtually all the basic human needs —

needs for shelter, food, sex gratification, warmth, protection, social control, recreation, community welfare, and the like — as well as the one basic need which families in every society must provide for — the care of the young. The saga of the American family since colonial times, to which we now turn, is characterized by the differentiation and development of relatively separate and distinct institutions (with corollary social organization) to meet many of these needs.

The American Family in the Nineteenth Century

The most important factors affecting the family in the nineteenth century were these: (1) the westward movement of the frontier; (2) the rapid growth of urbanization; (3) the concomitant development of industrialization; (4) the spread of mass education; (5) Victorianism and the genteel tradition; (6) successive waves of mass immigration. These did not all operate in the same direction in affecting the family. Some tended to perpetuate one or another of the aspects of the colonial family. Others brought about sudden and cataclysmic changes.

The Frontier

The obvious effect of the frontier was to perpetuate and often even accentuate among frontier families the pattern of familial self-sufficiency. Families leaving for the West forsook areas where there was a growing differentiation of labor and an increasing specialization for areas in the "wide open spaces" where the family again had to meet virtually all the needs of its members. Secondly, the movement to the frontier was more of a mass movement than a group movement; that is, it was a movement of individuals and individual families, rather than cultural groups (as had been most often the case in colonial settlement).[10] The consequence was that the families were much more "on their own" and were somewhat inhibited in resorting to the usually spontaneous forms of community cooperation. Thirdly, the frontier struggle — forest clearing, conflict with the Indians, plowing the sod, living in sod houses, exploitation by unscrupulous land promoters, grappling with disease, floods, fires, storms, etc. — was such that each individual member was called upon to do his utmost, regardless of age or sex. Hence the frontier brought both an individualism and an equalitarianism in family member roles to an extreme not found in the early colonial families. Fourthly, this individualism, plus the plenitude of economic opportunity and the relative classlessness of the frontier, resulted in a pattern of freedom in choosing a mate, not much tempered by any residual group control or "veto power" by the family. And, finally, the usefulness even of children in proportion to their cost resulted in a net reproduction rate a fourth to a half greater than that of regions from which these families had come, so that the frontier was everywhere a place of large families.

[10] This is of course only relatively true. In some instances whole frontier communities were settled by a single cultural group.

Urbanization

The nineteenth century in America was one of tremendous growth both in size and in number of cities. In 1790 there were only twenty-eight cities in the United States in the bracket of 2500 to 10,000 population; by 1880 there were 872 in this classification. In 1790 there were no cities 100,000 or over; yet by 1880 there were 20. The over-all picture is even more startling: in 1790 there were only 33 cities in the United States; by 1880 there were 1054! While the population of the country as a whole was growing at a phenomenal rate, the *proportion* of the total population which lived in cities was approximately five times as great in 1880 as in 1790.

The effects of this growing urbanization on the American family were tremendous. In the first place the city's very existence is always predicated on specialization and interdependence. The family in cities thus lost much of its old colonial and frontier self-sufficiency, both in the narrow sense of economic subsistence and in the broad sense of providing patterns in lieu of separate social institutions. In the second place the city with its heterogeneity of peoples, the qualities of anonymity and impersonality which it imparts, and its generally instrumental and secular atmosphere converged to make the family much more of a secular and much less of a sacred institution. In the third place the wide assortment of secondary groups and specialized interest activities brought about a heightened individualism and equalitarianism in the roles played by family members. In the fourth place the rapid mobility, general rootlessness, unfavorable living conditions, and many other factors tended to increase the amount of family disorganization. And, finally, the high costs of children relative to their usefulness brought about small families and a growing proportion of childless families.

Industrialization

Closely interrelated with the rapid growth of cities was the development of the factory system. Chiefly to be noted here are its consequences in the directions of furthering the equality of women and of detaching "bread-winning" from family activity as such. The first employees of the earliest factories (mills) were chiefly women and children. As soon as women were given alternatives to the economic security of marriage, they began to take on added status *within* the family. No longer was it possible for husbands to treat their wives as mere chattels. Furthermore, many of the products of factories were taking the place of home-produced (chiefly woman-produced) goods, thus freeing the wife from some of the drudgery which was her lot under colonial and frontier conditions.

As the locus of work shifted from the home to the factory, the nature of family relationships began to change. The family was no longer a business enterprise. It began to be more of an equalitarian, consuming group. Emphasis was starting to shift unavoidably to the distinctive wants and needs of each individual member. The patriarchal pattern began to disappear as the need for a "foreman" disappeared.

It should also be noted that the rise of industrialization brought with it the rise of a whole new group — a middle class composed of white collar clerical, professional, and technical workers as well as tradespeople and others engaged in the control and distribution of the fabulous production of the new factories. The families in this class were much more equalitarian and individualistic in their family member roles than were those of the laboring class.

Education

A factor the consequences of which tend to converge in the same general direction with those of urbanization and industrialization is the spread of mass education. This had its inception in the democratic ferment during the period of the Revolution, but the movement itself developed gradually through the century and did not really get under way until the last half. Mass education tended to contribute to the flow of population from rural to urban areas by making rural youths aware of the advantages of city life and employment and also by making possible a selection of the more able individuals in rural areas in recruiting the ranks of the emerging middle class of white collar and professional people.

More important, perhaps, was the effect of mass education on the status of women. Education, like a factory job, was for a woman a rung in the ladder leading toward emancipation from the hitherto inexorable fate of getting married and accepting whatever that entailed. Education, early available to girls as well as to boys, even made possible the achieving of a job of a more socially esteemed sort than that of a mere factory worker.

And finally, mass education, wherever it was beginning to be established, made available another avenue of social mobility. This tended to disrupt class lines, if they were forming, and to cause a more thorough mixing of the heterogeneous elements in the population. This in turn tended to reduce the variety of families in America toward a common denominator, shaking them loose somewhat from traditional and cultural uniquenesses.

Victorianism and the Genteel Tradition

Encompassed in these terms are a number of ideas. One is the idea of sexual prudery coupled with that of the double standard of sexual morality. A second is a sense of complacency, smugness, and "all's right with the world" as it is or at least as it is going. A third, closely related to the second, is the concept of automatic progress — "upward, ever onward, down the ringing grooves of time." And, finally, there is the idea of gentility, of being a gentleman or a lady, of being reticent or silent about tacitly agreed-upon subjects which are uncomfortable and unpleasant. Over the whole is spread the haze of romance. Thus characterized, Victorianism, contradictory as it may seem, was an important part of the mood of the century, for the United States as well as for England. It was a product partly of the intoxication brought on by the tremendous expansion of the century and partly of an attempt to stabilize the patterns for living by tying the new culture in with the old. Its impacts were particularly felt by the family and by education.

As a *Weltanschauung* it served partially to stem the rising tide of individualism, equalitarianism, and disorganization in the family, and to set up a number of graded, "genteel" roles and statuses within the family which people might "properly" play. It contained myths which functioned to relieve, temporarily, tensions within the family brought on by the frictions of a rapidly changing society.

As a body of convention interwoven with myth, it was never completely subscribed to, either by our society or by that of England. It was always being attacked by notions of naturalism, realism, and cynicism. Samuel Butler's *The Way of All Flesh* might be taken as a type example of reaction to it. Victorianism was, however, so widely accepted that it took an intellectual revulsion covering the first two decades of the present century to rid our outlook effectively of its vestiges, and even yet many of them are with us more or less unconsciously. In fact, considerable respect for the positive achievements of Victorianism is today manifest.

Immigration

The nineteenth century witnessed a mass influx of peoples into this country that is to be counted one of the great population movements of world history. The early part of this immigration was of people from the northern and western parts of Europe, where culture patterns were enough like those of England to enable people to make adjustments and become assimilated in a reasonably short period of time and with relatively little tension and conflict. This generalization applies to their family patterns as well as to other aspects of their culture. During the latter part of the century, however, and during the first decade and a half of this one, the bulk of the immigration was from eastern, central, and southern Europe, from the Orient, and from other areas where the culture was sharply different from that of the original settlers of this country. One of the consequences was to increase greatly the already important heterogeneity of patterns of marriage and family life. Another consequence was to "kick upstairs" a great many people who were in the laboring class, especially since the bulk of the later migration was composed of people without skills who settled in the larger American cities in search of economic opportunity of any sort. This upward social mobility served to enhance the growth of individualism and equalitarianism in family role playing, for it had the effect of tending to free people somewhat from the encrustments of their traditional cultural definitions of family behavior.

THE FIRST HALF OF THE TWENTIETH CENTURY

We are too close to the era just ended to see it clearly and in perspective, particularly since its family is our family, both the one that nurtured us and, if we are married, the one we are in process of establishing. Nevertheless, certain things stand out sharply as having influenced the shape of the contemporary American family: (1) the sexual revolution; (2) further extension of mass education; (3) continued urbanization; (4) the spread of mass production; (5) continued increase in the employment of women; (6) the hardening of class lines; (7) rapid fluctuations in economic opportunity; (8) war.

By sexual revolution we mean not only various types of reaction against Victorian sexual restraints, such as the inquiring approach epitomized by writers like Ellis, Freud, and Kinsey; we also mean the mingling of the sexes in a wide variety of activities, from tavern drinking to pursuit of the Ph.D. degree, in which the sexes were once rigorously segregated or in which participation was limited to one or the other of the sexes. Since sexual restraint has in the past been an adjunct of the patriarchate, the diminishing of the keep-quiet attitude toward sex has undoubtedly had the effect of pushing the status of woman toward a position more nearly equal to that of man. The mingling of the sexes has had much the same effect.

Coinciding with this are the effects of furtherance of mass education, continued urbanization, spread of mass production, and continued increase in the employment of women. Each has contributed its bit to greater individuation in the family, more equality of status, and beyond a doubt to family disorganization as it is contemporaneously defined. It is highly significant that today approximately 25% of all women of working age are gainfully employed and that approximately that same percentage of the total working force is made up of women. Although women are still discriminated against in employment and, once employed, their wages may be no more than half those of men for equal work,[11] the fact that so large a proportion is employed has a very significant relationship to the high status of woman in both American family and society.

Just what the impact will be of the closing of class lines it is impossible to tell yet, but in general we know that loss of social mobility is associated with a development of a graded series of statuses in the family. We know that as classes become less open-ended, individualism and equalitarianism tend to diminish.

In this connection it may be well to mention the effects of the great depression of the 'thirties. Other than making for increased stratification in general, the depression resulted in a diminished status for women both within the family and in society. The proportion of women employed kept going upward during the period, it is true, but the number of women entering the professions actually diminished.

That the effects of the two great wars have been important as far as the family is concerned no one can deny, but it is difficult to assess these effects with any accuracy. In this as in other matters war seems merely to have

[11] A recent survey of earnings of members of the National Federation of Business and Professional Women's Clubs gives further evidence, if any is needed, of the relatively low level of employed business and professional women's earnings. Forty-five per cent of the 160,000 respondents reported earnings of less than $3,000 a year. Reported in the Des Moines *Register*, June 29, 1953, p. 2.

speeded up processes already at work in peacetime society — such as the
entry of women into industry, loosening of the sex mores, individuation of
family members, etc. It is common to assume that war causes a great disintegration of parental control over children. It has been claimed that the
juvenile delinquency which becomes so alarming both during and after
modern war is merely something which escapes cultural notice during peacetime. However, the great mobility of people and the innumerable family
separations which take place during war unquestionably contribute to rootlessness and demoralization of many families.

In summary, regarding the history of the family during the first half of
the twentieth century it may be said that the processes at work are similar
to those which were at work during the last century, though some of these
are now working at a much faster rate. The convergence of consequences
still seems to be in the general direction of individuation, intrafamily democracy, further stripping of function from the family, and increased family disorganization (at least as measured by divorce, family conflict, and other
indices).

THE LIVING HERITAGE

We have now traced the development of the American family from
colonial days to the present. It remains for us to take stock of the contemporary family to discover if anything remains of the colonial and frontier
family traits. It is obvious at once that much does remain. For example,
there are elements of the patriarchal pattern in virtually every socioeconomic
level, in every gradation from the extremely rural to the extremely urban
family, and in every cultural region. Again, there are still alive a good many
remnants of Puritanism, of religious control of marriage and family patterns,
of tendencies toward family self-sufficiency, of strong opposition to divorce,
of high valuing of large families, and of eulogizing the rural family way of
life. Many of these are mainly verbal and rationalizing and do not regulate overt behavior to any great degree. But how can we explain the persistence of these even when they are confined to fantasy, ceremony, and
verbalization?

It has become customary to explain persistences of this sort in terms of
the *culture lag*. This phrase means that not all parts of a culture change at
the same rate of speed, that nonmaterial culture changes less rapidly than
material and technical culture, and that there is considerable resistance to
change in the realm of ideas. As one writer put it, we tend to explain emerging fact with outworn symbol. Now, however valid this idea may be in
general, we do not need its quasi-mystic concept of inertia to explain the
persistence of certain colonial and frontier patterns in a considerable number
of contemporary families. The explanation is much simpler and more naturalistic. It is simply that colonial and frontier patterns have persisted among
rural families because *these patterns tend to be functional in the rural
situation*. The rural family has tended to be large, for example, as were
colonial and frontier families, not from the inertia of the folkways but be-

cause children are useful on the farm. The second step in the explanation is this: the rural family has reproduced at such a heavy rate as to be constantly exporting population to towns and urban areas. Furthermore it has characteristically furnished far more recruits to the professional classes than has the urban working class family. Conversely, urban areas in general and professional classes in particular have not been reproducing at a rate sufficient to replace themselves in the population. All this means that the rural family is still exercising an influence throughout society because normally people are never more than one or two generations removed from a farm background and often enough they themselves have been reared on the farm. We are accustomed to think chiefly of the urban influences on rural life; it is quite possible that the more significant influences are the other way round.

It is obvious that in many ways the heritage from the colonial and frontier families is indeed a *living* heritage. In many parts of rural America the reproduction rate is as much as one and a half times that necessary to replace the present rural population but in many large cities the rate is as little as three fourths that necessary merely for replacement. In fact in the largest cities approximately half the married couples are childless. Yet the urban proportion of the population is increasing and the rural diminishing. There is thus a constant flow from the country, where patriarchal and self-sufficiency patterns are functional, to the city, where presumably other patterns prove more congenial to the adults but less so to child bearing and rearing.

It is necessary to note, however, that rural life is changing. We are now entering the era of high mechanization of farming operations. This is the day of combines, pick-up balers, electric milkers, battery brooders, and the like. Thanks to this mechanization, there is greatly lessened usefulness for children on the farm. Farm families are becoming smaller, more equalitarian, and given to less participation in formal religious activities. As these trends progress patterns paralleling those of the colonial and frontier eras will become less operative.

Five Divergent American Family Types

Now that we have completed our drastically compressed view of the development of the American family and have examined the dynamics of its heritage, it is necessary to look more closely at what we have been calling "the contemporary American family." When we do so, it becomes apparent that such a term is a very general one indeed, referring in reality only to central tendencies — modes — in family behavior patterns. In reality there are a great variety of contemporary American family types. It is unfortunate that we do not have careful, objective, descriptive studies of families in all the various dimensions of variations — rural-urban, top-to-bottom socioeconomic class, highly mobile to highly immobile, top-to-bottom educational level, highly isolated to highly participating, autocratic-democratic-anarchistic range of child-rearing programs, etc. Until we have more studies we shall not know even roughly what the range variation is on any one of these scales.

It is obvious, however, that there is a great deal of variation. While we limited our view of colonial society to three important groups, because each was dominant in one way or another in its own particular region and also dominant in subsequent developments, yet we are all aware that America was settled not by three but by literally scores of diverse ethnic and nationality groupings. Furthermore the peculiar conditions of adaptation in various regions of the country contributed their share to deviations in the direction taken in the development of the family. And, again, the growth of more distinct social classes here and there and in the whole country in the last few years has done its bit to contribute to differentiation. Finally, the volatile processes of collective behavior, operating as a consequence of frustration, crisis, and cultural breakdown, have contributed a variety of native cults, sects, and social movements, each with its own implications for family type differentiation and variation. It is not surprising that despite the factors making for mutual assimilation and homogeneity we find a welter of differences in the contemporary American family. Let us look at some of the families which have been studied, in order to see what some of the differences are:

The Middletown Family

Robert and Helen Lynd, in their re-study of Muncie, Indiana,[12] give a picture of the Muncie family in which three important characteristics stand out. The first is the general reluctance with which the family deals openly and consciously with anything connected with sex. "Sex is one of the things Middletown has long been taught to fear." This is in contrast with actual behavior, for to have had sexual relations prior to marriage appears to have become more common for members of both sexes in the business class than to have remained a virgin. Furthermore there is a considerable amount of prostitution in Muncie, a constantly rising sale of contraceptives, a growth of frank talk in the younger generation, and other indices of cultural trends contradictory to the pattern of general fear and avoidance of sex.

The second characteristic that stands out is the tendency of adults and youths each to be immersed in a subculture of its own. This gap between the two generations seems to the Lynds to be becoming more distinct. Adult controls over adolescent behavior appear to have been weakening. As a result the parents tend to disapprove of a great deal of the conduct of their teen-age children, calling it "fast," "sexy," "bold," "sophisticated," "immoral," and the like. Curiously, much of the so-called "sophistication" in dress and provocative appearance and demeanor has reached down even into the lower grades — in such matters as bright nail polish, permanent waves, etc. The revolt of high-school-age youth is typified in the "clubs" (really

12 Robert and Helen Lynd, *Middletown in Transition* (New York: Harcourt, Brace, 1937), chap. 5.

illegal sororities) to which the girls — particularly girls from business-class homes — belong and which operate to frustrate parental control and heighten competition in dress and other matters.

The third characteristic is another division into subcultures — this time the subcultures of the two sexes. Assumptions are made regarding what is right for members of each sex to do. Other assumptions are made regarding the intrinsic temperamental and personality differences between the two sexes.

> Men are expected to perform certain social functions and to behave in certain ways, and another set of expectations rules the lives of women. Men get the living, i.e., earn the money to buy the living for the family; they pay for the children's education and the family's leisure, as well as for food, clothing, and shelter. They are the representatives of the family in civic affairs, the government surrogates, the paid religious leaders, the doctors, the lawyers. They handle certain practical affairs — repairing the car or buying the tickets to Florida. Women look after affairs within the household; they care for the small children, and rear and teach the children, always with male authority in the background in the form of the father who comes home at night or the male superintendent of schools. They select the family's social life. They represent the family in aesthetic activities and in many unpaid civic activities of a refined or charitable sort.
>
> But this culture says not only that men and women do different things; they *are* different kinds of people. Men are stronger, bolder, less pure, less refined, more logical, more reasonable, more given to seeing things in the large, but at home needing coddling and reassurance, "like little boys." Women are more delicate, stronger in sympathy, understanding, and insight, less mechanically adept, more immersed in petty detail and in personalities, and given to "getting emotional over things." [13]

The Lynds point out that there has been some change in this, particularly in woman's role, but they indicate that the change has not altered the basic assumptions of intrinsic differences between the two sexes.

The Ozark Family

In striking contrast to the family in Muncie, Indiana, is the family in the folk society of the Ozarks.[14] Muncie is a growing, middle-sized industrial city in the heart of a prosperous agricultural region in the Middle West. Its life is increasingly caught up in the whole pattern of industrialization and commerce of the northeastern United States. Its population has several heterogeneous elements. Changes in population size, methods of earning a living, intellectual outlook, and the like have been fairly rapid over the past few decades. In the Ozark Highlands, on the other hand, there is a society

[13] *Ibid.*, pp. 176–177.
[14] Material for this discussion of the Ozark family is drawn from *Family and Society* by Carle Zimmerman and Merle Frampton (New York: Van Nostrand, 1935), chaps. 9–14; and from *The Ozarks* by Vance Randolph (New York: Vanguard, 1931).

very similar to that which existed on the frontier. Strictly speaking there
has been no urbanization and the whole area has been until the last few
years almost completely cut off from the main stream of American life with
its swift changes and rapid secularization. The population, though stemming from diverse colonial settlements of Scotch-Irish, German, and English groups in Pennsylvania, North Carolina, and Virginia, has become
homogeneous through long-continued isolation and in-marriage. The dominant cultural heritage has been that of the English with added accretions
of hill-folk invention. Cultural change has been slow, almost to the point
of becoming nonexistent.

The family is the keystone of the entire social organization in the Ozarks.
Subsistence farming on semi-isolated hill farms is the basic way of life, and
this farming is a familial pursuit. The father is definitely the head of the
family. Women and children, however, play important roles in the family
enterprise. They take care of the cows, chickens, and garden, and in addition during the period of field planting, cultivation, and harvest, they work
alongside the men, performing many of the same tasks. The adult male role
is characterized by "virility," masculinity, temper, and decisiveness. The adult
female role is best characterized by the Southern white stereotype of "the
purity of white womanhood." Her role is to marry, to bear many children, to
be loyal and subservient to her husband, to cook and keep house, in addition
to the other functions already mentioned. The principal cultural dictum regarding children is that they develop and maintain respect for their parents
and loyalty to the family as such. They must be circumspect in their play and
recreation, and later they must accept adult supervision of their courting.
Their principal activities are those connected with the family enterprise —
subsistence agriculture.

The assumptions regarding the intrinsic differences between men and
women are as important as they are in Muncie. Connected with this are a
perpetuation of the double standard and an extreme degree of certain varieties of sexual restraint. The gaps between man's world and woman's world
and between the adult world and the youth world, so evident in Muncie,
are, however, not present here in most significant matters. This is to be accounted for by the fact that they are all immersed to varying degrees in the
major activity of farming.

The Ozark region is one of a barter rather than a money economy. In
fact trade of any kind is subordinate to the general pattern of family self-
subsistence. This fact, together with the low ratio of resources to population,
primitive state of technology, and a relatively low (psychological) standard
of living, conspires to bring about a low plane of living as far as material
goods are concerned. In Muncie an income as low as that of most Ozark
families would be conducive to family disorganization and would require
formal welfare agency help. Thanks to the closer correlation between aspiration and achievement in the Ozarks than in Muncie, however, and thanks
also to the indigenous informal patterns of mutual aid, the low level of
material goods does not contribute to family disorganization in these highlands. In fact the Ozark family manifests more solidarity than most family

types, urban *or* rural, in the United States. Children are, in general, loyal to parents and family throughout the life cycle. The most capable boy becomes the new head of the family but the others are either kept on the home farm or are helped to set up farming nearby if possible. The rest drift down to the lowlands and detach themselves from Ozark society.

Controls over those who remain hill people are chiefly familial in character. It is true that religion, which is an important factor in control, is maintained as a separate institution, and yet there are ways in which religion is intertwined with the family. The preacher, for example, is supported mainly by living with one family after another; and then, too, participation in religious activities is by family groups. "Getting saved," it is true, is obviously an individual affair, but the social control by individualistic "salvation" in the periodic revival meetings is far less significant than the day-to-day sustaining process of certain aspects of religion to the familistic mores.

Other than religion there are no nicely discrete and visible social institutions such as characterize the culture of Muncie. Functions performed by these in Muncie are discharged in the Ozarks largely by the family as a virtually all-embracing institution.

The Negro Mother-Centered Family [15]

Thanks to the special characteristics of the institution of slavery, the African culture of the Negro was almost completely obliterated. This was particularly true of that culture which related to the family, its structure and role definitions. As a result the Negro family in the United States started to rebuild on the basis of the most elementary and basic characteristic of the family — the mother-child relationship. Slavery as a system of property and exchange rights was not consistent with an inviolable right of Negro husband and wife to live together permanently. On the other hand slavery *was* consistent with the idea of producing many Negro children; whether sired by white or black fathers, legitimately or illegitimately, made little difference.

In this kind of situation the Negro mother usually took sole responsibility for the upbringing of her children. The biological father was not only not expected to play the role of social father of the child; he was in one way or another often actually prohibited from playing such a role. Nor did the culture provide, as it sometimes does in primitive societies, a father surrogate in the form of an uncle. The Negro mother was not simply the head of the family; she was the center — the core — of the family. Neither marriage customs nor marriage laws protected her by providing her with a responsible husband who would be a father to her children.

After the end of slavery a number of factors were favorable to the continuation of the mother-centered family among Negroes. Among these were low economic status (which made legal marriage often out of reach

---

[15] For the material on this type of family the present author is indebted chiefly to E. Franklin Frazier's definitive work, *The Negro Family in the United States* (Chicago: The University of Chicago Press, 1939).

financially); the indifference of the Southern courts toward Negro rights (especially, here, the rights of the Negro mother); and the institutionalizing, in some measure, of the older patterns of the mother-centered family. To these might be added a number of other factors, among them the continued right of sexual accessibility to Negro females exercised in some areas by white males. Today it is estimated that perhaps as many as one third of all Negro families are, in greater or lesser degree, matricentric in character. The matricentric family can be found among rural, village, and urban Negroes.[16] If there are any additional factors making for its survival, many of them have to do with the increased mobility of the Negro, which often means that adult Negro males are apt to drift around in search of work, treating their marriage bonds, if any, very lightly, and leaving their wed and unwed mates to shoulder the burden of child rearing.

This pattern is not unadapted to life on a cotton farm. There the pattern is apt to be enlarged to include a family tending toward the extended type. In such instances the grandmother will be the definite head of the house, while the daughters (with or without husbands) and their children live with her and under her control. In the rural South such a family works together as a unit, maintains its solidarity, and develops a strong *esprit de corps*. The children are indulged, perhaps not weaned for several years, and as a result of this and the family solidarity they become strongly attached to the mother and grandmother. Sometimes the husbands are not present in the family precisely because this attachment has become so strong that the daughters have refused to leave home and go with their husbands to set up new establishments.

At the other end of the scale, in the cities, the mother-centered family is very ill adapted. There is no common work activity for the whole family. Instead the family head must spend a great proportion of time away from the family in order to provide its sustenance. The impersonality, individuation, and anonymity which are so characteristic of city life tend to dissolve family loyalty and loosen the mother's control over her children. The common result is family disorganization and breakdown. There is little tendency among such urban families for the matricentric family to extend to include three generations. If anything there is a tendency to drive distinctly apart the two generations which it does attempt to contain.

Since the mother-centered family is found in such diverse contexts, it is impossible to discover any common functions of the family or common ideology. In fact the role-playing of the family members is by no means a constant in this family as one goes from the rural sections through small town communities to metropolitan centers. Perhaps the only generalization that can be made with any assurance is that as a pattern mother-centeredness (i.e., this type of family) is much more characteristic of the lower class, whether in rural or urban areas. As income, education, and similar indices increase, this pattern disappears. In other segments of Negro so-

16 Since it has come to be a stereotype in some quarters that the Negro family *in general* is matricentric, it should be made quite clear at this point in the discussion that this is not true. It is but one of three or four types of contemporary Negro family organization.

ciety patriarchal patterns have had a fairly long history and in still others the democratic type of family structure has come to be dominant, but neither one of these is of interest to us here.

What does concern us is the fact that the dominant culture did not prescribe the role for the father except in a negative sense. This left his function largely in the realm of more or less casual sex gratification. That the need for permanent personal intimacy did not immediately result in the stabilizing of married-pair relationship is attributable to a variety of economic and other cultural factors and to the possibility of achieving some modicum of this intimacy in the relationships between mother and child. But in the city where individuation precludes the establishing of this intimate mother-child relationship, the mother-centered family pattern has not been adaptive or functional. That it continues to appear in urban Negro life is mainly due to the continued importation of Negro people from rural areas into urban communities.

The Mormon Polygynous Family [17]

The practice of polygamy ("polygyny" is the more precise term) was initiated by a "revelation" which Joseph Smith, founder of the church, had in 1843 when the group was centered in Nauvoo, Illinois. Polygyny was not practiced openly until the group had migrated to Utah. It was doctrine promulgated largely from New England and New York State where the culture had strongly sanctioned monogamy and had hedged this prescription with firm taboos regarding any sort of deviation or alternative pattern. Its introduction has been explained in a variety of ways: that the economic conditions of the western frontier made children highly useful, that the proportion of women was far greater than that of men in the Mormon group, and so on. The sex-ratio theory is discounted by the church itself; the church explains its rise by the recognition that "myriads of souls of men" were waiting in heaven to be born into this world — a phase in ontogenesis which is pictured as involving development both on earth and in heaven. There is no doubt that economic factors were favorable, though there is dispute regarding the sex ratio.[18]

It is estimated that plural marriage was practiced by from 2 to 4 per cent of the members of the Mormon Church from 1843 to 1890, in which year it was officially abolished under extreme pressure of federal legisla-

---

[17] The discussion of this family type is based chiefly on the unpublished Ph.D. thesis of J. E. Hulett, Jr., *The Social and Social Psychological Aspects of the Mormon Family* (Madison: University of Wisconsin Library, 1939). See also his article, "Social Role and Personal Security in Mormon Polygamy," *American Journal of Sociology*, 45 (Jan., 1940), pp. 542–553. Other sources include P. W. Tappan's unpublished Ph.D. thesis, *Mormon-Gentile Conflict* (Madison: University of Wisconsin Library, 1939); and an unpublished paper by W. W. Scott, "Mormon Polygamous Marriage in a Monogamous Background," prepared for Professor Howard Becker's seminar in Systematic Sociology, 1946.

[18] Much of this dispute hinges on the question whether the influx of converts from Britain, Germany, and the Scandinavian countries was evenly balanced as to sex or whether it was made up predominantly of women.

tion. After this happened, a group split off which have continued the teaching and practice of polygyny. Disowned by the church, their members excommunicated, this group have generally been referred to as the "Fundamentalists." These people are to be found mainly in isolated parts of southern Utah and northern Arizona. Thanks to their isolation they continued to practice plural marriage undisturbed until the practice came to light during World War II under the scrutiny of Selective Service officials. Because of the illegality of the practice, the antipathy of the mores in the larger society to its practice, and the consequent covertness of the pattern, it has not been possible to make a definitive study of it as a contemporary phenomenon. We know much more about its historical traits when it was an open practice. That it is such a divergent method of meeting the needs of the family situation makes desirable its treatment here in preference to the treatment of several other family types about which we know more but which are much less divergent in character.

We must remember that while the practice of having plural wives is fairly common in many other societies, its appearance in our society puts it in quite a different context. Where polygyny is found elsewhere it is in a context which sanctions its practice and provides for each oncoming generation a set of ready-made rules, developed by accretion and winnowing from trial-and-error experimentation over a long period. These rules govern the role and status of each family member and prescribe the nature of his relationships with other members. The idea of polygyny among the Mormons seems to have been modeled originally after Old Testament accounts of early Hebrew polygyny. The accounts which tend to define the roles of family members were, however, extremely sketchy and those which did exist were essentially inapplicable to the social situations in which the Mormons found themselves. The only relevant role definition, one which fitted fairly well into the traditions of our society and which was functional in the frontier situation, was that of the patriarch. This left the definition of the other roles and statuses within the family to be developed by social interaction of the personal-social sort (to use Kimball Young's term), virtually unguided by supporting cultural norms and constantly under antagonistic pressure from the relevant culture of the larger society.

As might be expected, this brought about a wide variety of types of adjustment to this form of family structure. In the larger picture the patriarchal dominance persisted, chiefly because it had extreme religious sanction. The father was really the sole means of salvation for his wives. In actuality even this broke down in a number of instances because of the long-continued absence of the father from any particular mother-children family group (for separate establishments for each wife had come to be the rule).

The pair-marriage ideal undoubtedly played its part in bringing about a trend toward an institution of favorite wife (which in turn meant for all practical purposes "head-wifeship"). In many cases head-wifeship devolved upon the first wife, but again the norms of the larger society together with unstandardized interaction operated to vary the pattern and to base headship upon personal favor and attraction. An understanding of this can be heightened by applying the concepts of dyadic, triadic, middle-sized, and larger group interaction (developed by Howard Becker) to the personal-social interaction going on here. The larger society sanctioned the dyad as a model or ideal of marriage interaction. But the critical interaction going on in the Mormon polygynous family was frequently of the unstable triadic sort; for example, the relation among the husband, the last-wife-married, and the wife-before-the-last; or the relation among husband, youngest wife, and next youngest wife; or that among husband, most physically attractive wife, and next most physically attractive wife; or that among husband, most fertile wife, and next most fertile wife; or that among three dominant wives, when the husband was of a weak sort or preoccupied with other matters. The usual course of triadic relations is to develop toward the pair-plus-subordinate or pair-plus-outsider situation. This is heightened where the outside culture sanctions the pair situation alone, and where people go into marriage guided by ideals, whether consciously or unconsciously held, that glorify the pair relation in marriage. The Mormon marriage tended to be a series of pair, and temporarily triadic, relationships.

The plural wife was in varying degrees self-supporting. The husband might provide those necessities which had to be purchased or at least obtained from outside this little establishment — or he might not. If the wife were in partial or complete disfavor, she might be left to take complete care of herself and her children. Or it might be that thanks to the operation of the monogamous prototype the husband might fail to make public recognition of any but his first wife and this ideal of monogamy was always a ready-made rationalization for giving much economic support to none other than the one favorite wife.[19] Favoritism in open discrimination tended, however, not so much toward the all-or-none principle but toward subtle gradations. All-or-none acceptance as wife was usually reserved for the more covert aspects of companionship between husband and wife. In some instances failure to support wives was due not to favoritism but to business ineptitude on the part of the husband.

The wife's principal role was that of mother. But she also had the task of running the home with its economic activities as a going concern — planning the jobs, assigning the tasks, and so on. She also was responsible for religious instruction in the home when the husband was elsewhere. Another role which she played was that of "helpmeet" to her husband. This involved all kinds of personal service and was regarded as status-giving rather than burdensome. The favorite wife often managed to make a monopoly out of some of these services. Frequently it was the care of his Sunday clothes, but there were other roles which she monopolized to a greater or lesser degree, such as being the week-end wife, the social hostess, the lawful wife, and the principal adviser. Often the husband tried to spread these favors more equitably but was blocked by the operation of dominant traits in his favorite wife, working themselves out through unstandardized, personal-social interaction with the other wives.

[19] Legally wives after the first had no status in inheritance, and this also applied to their children who were in the eyes of the law illegitimate.

What held the Mormon polygynous family together? The role of the Mormon religion in sustaining the solidarity of the Mormon family has been made clear. The fact that mother and children functioned as an economic unit also made for solidarity within this unit of the family. Control within the family was tied in with the larger quasi-legal control of the church in the person of the father. The established legal government of the state and nation was at odds, however, with the plural-wife family. Its continuation had been made possible only by isolation from the areas of operation of this government. Thus isolated the polygynous family undoubtedly acquired a good many stable and standard definitions of roles and statuses within the family. About these we can only surmise. We know that societies have a way of developing such standard definitions in order to avoid conflicts and stresses and in order to give individuals security they so persistently crave.

The Old Order Amish Family [20]

The Amish were originally a Swiss Anabaptist group which, driven by religious intolerance from Switzerland, settled in the Upper Rhineland. From there they came in colonial days (in the early 1700's) to eastern Pennsylvania. The major settlement is on a rough triangle of 150 square miles of rich limestone plain lying just east of Lancaster. There are other smaller settlements of the Old Order (or House) Amish in Delaware, Virginia, Ohio, Indiana, Illinois, Iowa, and elsewhere. These people are, and since their beginning have always been, an agricultural people. Farming is intimately interwoven into their way of life. They are a separatist, nonconforming people, epitomized by their strong adherence to the admonition of II Corinthians 6:14, "Be ye not unequally yoked together with unbelievers: for what fellowship hath righteousness with unrighteousness? and what fellowship hath light with darkness?" They are set apart by their religious beliefs and attitudes, their aloofness from the processes of formal government, their language and garb, their social exclusiveness, their patterns of in-marriage, and their avoidance of certain types of modern technology. Their philosophy is one of passive resistance, and in time of war they are conscientious objectors.

In many ways they are strikingly like the colonial Quakers described above. Both groups are heirs to the Anabaptist traditions of mysticism (the belief in the immanence of God), nonviolence, separatism, and individualism. That the Quaker way of life became more or less dissipated and the Quakers came to be much more assimilated than the Amish is attribut-

[20] The discussion of the Amish family is based on the excellent study by Walter M. Kollmorgen, *The Old Order Amish of Lancaster County, Pennsylvania,* U. S. Department of Agriculture, Bureau of Agricultural Economics, Rural Life Studies No. 4, 1942, and on the present author's own observations of the Amish near Kalona, Iowa. See Manford Kuhn, "Fam'ly Impact on Personality," chap. 5 in *Problems in Social Psychology,* J. E. Hulett, Jr., and Ross Stagner, editors (Urbana: U. of Illinois Press, 1952); and a chapter in a symposium on personality and culture (F. L. K. Hsu, editor) to be published in 1954.

able in an overwhelming degree to the fact that farming was rigidly maintained by the Amish as part and parcel of their life. This could not have happened had not the Amish developed in their earlier history a pattern of continually assimilating new and more effective techniques *of agriculture,* a pattern which contradicts their rigid resistance to all other forms of assimilation. This enabled them to achieve and maintain a comfortable and even prosperous level of living, a reward which has helped them continually to compensate for their renunciation of the shifting goals of "the world." But more fundamentally it has been the basis for maintaining their extremely strong family and community solidarity in that farming is a family (and secondarily a community of interfamily) enterprise.

The father is unquestionably head of the house. He plans all the farming operations, makes all the major decisions, and is in general the patriarch we have come to expect in a family which is engaged as a unit in the operation of a farm, particularly a self-sustaining farm.[21] The mother, occupying a status distinctly lower than that of her husband, still has standing well above that of the children. She cans and preserves enormous quantities of fruits and vegetables, makes garments for the entire family, quilts, embroiders, and the like. She has the responsibility of preparing the great mounds of food required for the periodic religious meetings and for the occasional cooperative activities such as barn-raisings. The children are treated with tenderness mixed with respect as well as firmness. They are given farm work to do at a very early age, and since this fits in with the universal aim of becoming farmers with which they have been indoctrinated, their early responsibilities are regarded as status-giving rather than as onerous tasks.

The fortnightly religious services are held, in rotating fashion, in the houses (or in the case of the less-well-off, in the barns) of members. The religious leaders are not a separate, trained group but rather are simply members who have been chosen to perform these functions and who must carry them on in addition to their regular farming activities. Religion, family, and community are inseparably interwoven. Control over individual behavior is religio-familial in character and, in view of the well-nigh complete separatism of these people, it is very effective. Probably the most effective technique is that of "shunning." Erring members are, when being shunned, fed and cared for separately. They are treated with kindness but are not spoken to.

The youth group of teen age is apparently the critical group as far as potential threat to Amish solidarity is concerned. Boys and girls of this group have strong desires to have and use the proscribed automobile, to frequent the forbidden movie theater, and to do many other things of which the community deeply disapproves. As soon as they marry (and they marry at relatively early ages) they seem to settle down into the old grooves of traditional culture.

[21] The Amish farm is amazingly self-sufficient, though the trend is somewhat away from this extreme. Yet the Amish farm is typically also a commercial farm producing at least one and usually several cash crops.

A Reconsideration of the Problem of Family Types

We have surveyed five widely divergent family types in the United States. Some are patricentric while others are in varying degrees matricentric; some are self-sufficient economic units while at least one is caught up in highly interdependent economic processes; they range from a fair degree of individuation to a high degree of individual submergence in family or familio-community control; and so on. We must now look at some of the common underlying social forces which are impinging on these families.

There are recent comers to Muncie from the hill country of the South. There are on the other hand more and more visitors to the Ozark Highlands from the Muncies throughout the country. Furthermore, radio, movies and television are bringing folk culture into the mainstream of American life. Negroes, in turn, are on the move to the North and West; while contrariwise the cotton culture of the rural South is on the way out and industrialization and urbanization are moving in. Negro levels of education and other indices of Negro assimilation are rising. Mormon polygyny has been pushed into a few tiny islands of seclusion; and now with the growth of good roads, communication, industrialization, and urbanization these islands are no longer secluded. The Old Order Amish are being drawn — by the commercialized aspects of their agriculture, by the spread of consolidated public secular education, by the shortage of nearby land, by the rapid spread of transportation, and by the growth of cities — into more and more participation with the outside society, regardless of their principle of the "unequal yoke." In our survey of five divergent family types we did not begin to cover the range of family diversity along the many scales on which we need to measure this diversity, but we did discover that forces are at work which are constantly tending to reduce the differences which exist. The diminution of that proportion of the population engaged in agriculture is apparent. The rapid growth of nationwide networks of transportation and communication is visible. There is in process a continual expansion of mass education. And finally there is a still increasing pattern of geographic mobility. All these factors are working in the same general direction — that of ironing out differences in family function and family structure on the one hand, and on the other that of making more distinct and discrete from family function and structure the institutions (and corollary associations) of religion, government, recreation, community welfare, economic production, and education.

The Family: Institution or Companionship?

Another attribute of the trends as these have affected the family has been the emergence of the *individuated person* in a relatively *democratic* (as opposed to a patricentric, matricentric, or filiocentric) type of family structure and organization. This has been particularly true of the family in the great new and growing middle classes. This evolution toward individuation and democracy coupled with a stripping from the family of the functions which it had in colonial, frontier, and rural situations (functions of economic, religious, educational, recreational, and other self-sufficiency) has, beyond a doubt, heightened the degree to which family relationships depend on *companionship* for their ultimate validity in the eyes of family members.

This has led Burgess and Locke [22] to conclude, in a very provocative hypothesis, that the family as an institution is withering away in favor of a family that rests on mutual companionship. This is an over-stated, partial truth. A social institution has generally been regarded by sociologists and other social scientists as having two aspects: that of group consensus regarding the manner in which some basic human need may be acceptably gratified; and that of traditional sanction buttressing the group consensus. As continuous social change and growing interdependence become increasingly the major characteristics of Western society, the second aspect of social institutions becomes of lesser and lesser importance. This is just as true of government, economic production and distribution, recreation, education, and the rest as it is of the family. If the family is ceasing to be an institution, so too are the other chunks of culture which we have called social institutions. But in each case the aspect which is waning is that of tradition and not that of group consensus. More and more the whole structure of Western culture is coming to rest on public opinion. Universals, to use Linton's terminology, are being replaced by alternatives, it is true, but even these alternatives must rest in the last analysis on group acceptance, and group acceptance is gauged not so much by adherence to the traditional and sacred but by the needle pointer of public opinion.

Nor has the family actually been stripped down to the sheer element of companionship. It continues to function in highly important fashion in regulating sex behavior, in rearing and educating children, and in channeling the function of economic consumption.[23] Nor is there any important trend toward stripping the family of these residual functions. And when the family is seen as a whole, companionship takes shape more as an accessory in the discharge of these functions than as an end held purely for itself.

---

[22] See the analysis by E. W. Burgess and Harvey J. Locke, *The Family: From Institution to Companionship* (2nd ed., New York: American Book Co., 1953), and Reuben Hill's comments in the final chapter of this book, pp. 773–806.

[23] This last point needs underlining. Sociology and economics have both been "culturally blind" to consumption as a highly important aspect of the functioning of the economic process. Almost all theoretical economics treats economic endeavor as that of the production and distribution of goods and services, thus almost completely ignoring consumption. The family, not the individual, is the unit of consumption, even this emerging, individuated, democratic, middle class, urban family. One of the chief activities in this family is organizing and effectuating consumption of goods and services.

A CONSTRUCTED TYPOLOGY FOR FAMILIES

Analytically considered, the family types we have been considering are not sociological or scientific, i.e., predictive, types at all, but are rather types of an historical nature, applicable only to historically unique and nonrepeatable families in their particular setting in time, space, and culture. Types of this sort are useful chiefly in the preliminary exploration which is designed to discover hypotheses. These types are, in effect, rough averages or composites derived from the study of varying families within each of the five groups which we considered.

The sociologist has at his disposal another form of typology, formulated by Max Weber and developed in this country by Howard Becker.[24] This is ideal or constructive typology. In understanding constructed types, a number of points must be kept in mind. (1) A constructed type is an abstraction and does not refer to "real," "existing," or historically unique families. (2) It may represent an extreme on a scale rather than an average. (3) It may be useful in setting up scales instead of as a final step in scientific prediction and control; the scales can then be used in quantification procedures.

We are interested, in the sociology of the family, in constructing types which will aid us in the prediction and control of success in marriage. So far, in attempting to predict the outcome of marriage, sociologists have measured individual traits and traits held in common by the pair. In order to weight these traits so that we may properly understand their significance in any given marriage situation, we need a typology of the family according to role-playing, both actual and intended. Accordingly the following six-dimensional construct is suggested:

1. The People-Centered Family
2. The Things-Centered Family
3. The "Idea-Sentiment-Complex"-Centered Family
4. The Activities-Centered Family
5. The Status-Centered Family
6. The Family Turned In on Itself

It will be noted that each one of the above actually suggests *two* constructed types rather than one, i.e., each one is, as stated, at one extreme end of a scale, and implies its opposite, not stated, at the other end. It will also be noticed that these types refer to aspects of the family that are *culturally relevant in any society*. Furthermore they are peculiarly appropriate for studying the family in a society the culture of which has come to rest on fluctuating pointers of public opinion rather than on the static norms of tradition.

---

[24] See H. E. Barnes, Howard Becker, and F. B. Becker, eds., *Contemporary Social Theory* (New York: Appleton-Century, 1940), chap. 2, "Constructive Typology in the Social Sciences," by Howard Becker; Georges Gurvitch and Wilbert E. Moore, eds., *20th Century Sociology* (New York: Philosophical Library, 1945), chap. by Howard Becker, "Interpretative Sociology and Constructive Typology," pp. 70–95; Howard Becker, *Through Values to Social Interpretation* (Durham, N. C.: Duke University Press, 1950), chaps. 2, 4, and 5.

And finally it will be noticed that they are relevant to the *individual's* aims and goals for the functioning of his family as well as to an external appraisal of the major role-playing that is actually going on. Hence they can be used to measure divergence between actual and intended role-playing, something which would undoubtedly be of significant aid in refining our present techniques for predicting marital success.[25]

CONCLUSION

We have in shorthand fashion described some of the changes that have taken place in the American family since colonial times. Note has been made of some of its many diversities and of some of the many factors at work which were bringing about these diversities. It is obvious that the family always exists in some social setting and in some kind of cultural context. Sometimes the family is so inclusive that it is almost coterminous with its society and culture; in other instances, and particularly under the influence of urbanization, industrialization, and specialization, it becomes much less important within the scope of the larger whole. But whatever the context, it always has an important functional relationship with the particular type of family structure and organization with which it coexists.

SELECTED READINGS

ANSHEN, RUTH, ed., *The Family: Its Function and Destiny* (New York: Harper, 1949), chaps. 1-9.

BARNES, H. E., BECKER, HOWARD, and BECKER, F. B., eds., *Contemporary Social Theory* (New York: Appleton-Century, 1940), chap 2.

BURGESS, E. W., and WALLIN, PAUL, *Engagement and Marriage* (Philadelphia: Lippincott, 1953), chap. 1.

CALHOUN, ARTHUR, *A Social History of the American Family* (Cleveland: Clark, 1919), 3 vols.

FRAZIER, E. F., *The Negro Family in the United States* (Chicago: University of Chicago Press, 1939).

GOODSELL, WILLYSTINE, *A History of Marriage and the Family* (rev. ed., New York, Macmillan, 1934).

HOSTETLER, JOHN A., *Amish Life* (Scottdale, Pa.: Herald Press, 1952).

HULETT, J. E., JR., "Social Role and Personal Security in Mormon Polygamy," *American Journal of Sociology* 45 (Jan. 1940), pp. 542-553.

LANDIS, JUDSON T. and MARY G., *Readings in Marriage and the Family* (New York: Prentice-Hall, 1952), chaps. 1-5.

LYND, ROBERT and HELEN, *Middletown in Transition* (New York: Harcourt, Brace, 1937), esp. chap. 5.

MORGAN, EDMUND S., *The Puritan Family* (Boston: Boston Public Library, 1944).

[25] No more detailed statement than is denoted in the phrasing of each type will be attempted here. The next step of course is to make as denotative as possible every referent involved in each type. This could be made more refined through the panel technique. Then would come the building of questionnaire or observational scales to use in rating families.

Randolph, Vance, *The Ozarks* (New York: Vanguard, 1931).

Whitney, Janet, *John Woolman, American Quaker* (Boston: Little, Brown, 1942).

Winch, Robert F., *The Modern Family* (New York: Henry Holt, 1952), chap. 2.

Zimmerman, Carle, *Family and Civilization* (New York: Harper, 1947).

TOPICS FOR DISCUSSION OR REPORTS

1. What are the evidences that in Puritan New England there was behind the sexual restraint a rather important preoccupation with sex? Account for this in any way that you can.
2. Describe some of the types of families, other than those of the Quakers, to be found in the Middle Colonies. How did they differ among themselves?
3. Attempt an analysis to discover what relation exists between status differentiation within the family and the particular pattern of social stratification which exists in the surrounding society. How would you go about this?
4. Apply the outlined frame of reference (used in comparing colonial families) to the five contemporary families described in this chapter. Construct a chart with parallel columns for each of the five types of family. Fill in any spaces left blank by absence of information in this chapter with information gained through your own perusal of sources.
5. Collect case histories which will enable you to describe the Northern, white, urban, middle-class family, its structure and organization.
6. Do the same for the Northern, white, metropolitan-suburban, upper-class family.
7. Collect from newspapers and magazine articles five or six examples of normative evaluation of contemporary family trends. Make explicit any implicit assumptions about a "golden era" of the family at some point in history. Check any factual data used against that given in this or some other sociological work on the family. Sort into types any examples of contemporary "myth-making" regarding family change which you encounter. What effects on actual family behavior does such myth-making have?
8. Carefully put together concise statements which will make the six constructed types (which are suggested in this chapter) more denotative. Test these on a panel of "judges."

Chapter Six

Producing Marriageable Personalities

READ BAIN

WHY PEOPLE MARRY

"No, daddy, when I grow up I'm going to be a plain lady like Mother."

Thus did my handsome four year old daughter reject my proposal that she train for the Follies chorus.

"I'm going to have five little children," she continued.

"That's lovely," I replied appreciatively; "and who is going to be the father of your babies?"

"Why, you, daddy."

This is the way families begin. . . . People do not marry because it is their social duty to perpetuate the institution of the family or because the preachers and Mrs. Grundy both recommend matrimony or even because they fall in love. . . . They marry because they lived in families as children and still cannot get over the feeling that being in a family is the only proper, indeed the only possible way to live.

First impressions are strong impressions. Adults cannot help reliving the kind of life they knew in childhood. . . . By the time her [his daughter, or any child] worldly knowledge has progressed far enough to make her critical about the family, it will be too late for her to change her basic feelings. Whether she likes it or not, her emotional bias toward family living will be so strong that she cannot overcome it.

. . . Utopian systems of marriage make a fundamental blunder [by ignoring] that marriage begins in infancy. . . . The most perfect system fails if it does not meet the expectations formed in childhood.[1]

THIS is the way Levy and Monroe began their wise and interesting little book, which you should read. You already have learned that the family is found in all societies and that it has the same general function in all of them, although its structure and the particular ways it functions differ widely in various societies and in the same society at different periods. Still, the basic function is the same. In the family men and women satisfy their sex impulses in a socially approved manner. They bear children, who are then consciously and unconsciously adjusted to social living. Roughly, this early learning is both positive and negative: what to do, think, and feel, and what *not* to; prescriptions and proscriptions, requirements and taboos (prohibitions). Children learn to define their world as is customary in their culture.

[1] John Levy and Ruth Monroe, *The Happy Family* (New York: Knopf, 1938), pp. 3–6.

Certainly our own society is no exception. From the above quotation, we can draw several conclusions which will be discussed more fully later. Among them, and perhaps the most inclusive one, is the idea that what happens to the person in infancy and childhood is everlastingly important. Upon this, most students of personality are agreed. Thus, what happens to the child in the family will affect for good or ill everything that later happens to him in his other social relationships. Children begin, usually, by loving and emulating their parents; later, they become critical of them. Most of them will marry because marrying is customary in our culture. Most of them will be happy in marriage — or at least not too unhappy to bear it! Most of them will have children and rear them somewhat as they were reared, though fortunately many will do a better job than their parents did.

The student should never forget that ours is a rapidly changing and highly heterogeneous society. There are many classes of people, many competing types of ideas and behavior, in all the major social institutions. New technological devices, new scientific and artistic ideas and ideals, new social regulations require each successive generation to make new adjustments. The family is not immune from this rapid change, but its basic structure and functions are probably more stable than those of some other institutions, such as the economic, religious, and political. During your lifetime, our system of monogamy, free choice of mates, naming and rearing of children in the parental home, birth control (planned parenthood), divorce, and family affection probably will not change much. The theme will endure, though there doubtless will be many minor, and perhaps some major, variations on the theme. In economics, however, you are likely to see radical changes in free enterprise, the distribution of wealth, and the production and distribution of goods; in politics, you are likely to see an ever increasing dominance of the federal government, the "surrender" of "absolute sovereignty" and the growth of the United Nations, or possibly the development of two or more colossal and contending imperialistic states; the present supernaturalistic basis of religion may largely disappear and the conflicting Christian groups may become more united.

The family will probably continue pretty much as we know it. People will fall in love and court each other, perhaps with somewhat different techniques, "lines," and forms of love-making, but in the end they will marry, settle down, rear their children, and be proud and fond of them and their grandchildren. There is considerable similarity in the family pattern within each recognizable segment of our culture. For example, we can meaningfully speak about upper, middle, and lower class families; Negro, white, Catholic, Protestant, Jewish, "educated," rural, urban, and so on, though probably there are more differences among the upper, middle, and lower class families within each of these categories than there are differences between the categories themselves. There is an over-all similarity in the family patterns of all categories; this is what distinguishes our family institution from that of the Middle Ages or the Chinese.

Dr. Levy's little girl wanted to have five children with her father for the

papa. Many little girls talk this way. It doesn't indicate some deep, dark, Freudian impulse toward unconscious incest. Rather it shows they have learned the culture patterns of family life. They have played with dolls and like babies; they know "where babies come from"; they like their mothers and want to be like them; the best father they know is their own.

Parents react differently to such childish ideas. Many, perhaps most, fear their children will marry "too young"; they try to "run" their lives even after they are married; they can't bear to see them "grow up"; they strictly oppose "college" marriages. Fortunately, some parents are wiser than this. They want their children to marry young and to get their desired number of children while the mother is still under thirty. To this end, they are willing (and sometimes able) to help financially.

There are both general and unique ways of looking at social behavior. The latter often seem more important, colorful, and interesting, but when carefully analyzed, they do not seem so "unique." The scientist helps us to understand the apparently unique by demonstrating that it is a specific instance of a general pattern. This leads to our next topic.

SCIENCE AND PERSONALITY

Normal (and even abnormal) people behave in more or less predictable ways. Were this not true, social order would be impossible. People usually keep their "dates" and other appointments and behave as expected. Most natural phenomena show enough orderliness to permit common-sense predictions about them. Scientific predictions are merely more generalized and accurate than those of common sense. While specific events never correspond *exactly* either to common sense or scientific predictions, there is usually enough correspondence to insure better adjustments than otherwise would be possible. Scientific generalizations (rules, "laws") are obviously much better than common sense for dealing with physical and biological phenomena. In fact, some "common-sense knowledge" turns out to be nonsense when tested.

This is especially true of social phenomena. While we do not have as much or as accurate scientific knowledge about them as we do about the physical-biological world, we have enough to know that a good deal of social "common sense" is actually nonsense. This is especially true of what we know about "personality." Many of our ideas about social behavior are based on ancient traditions and superstitions, irrational fears, and unwarranted assumptions. Common ideas about luck, miracles, race differences, sex, love, and the rearing of children are good examples.

We are rapidly increasing and improving our scientific social knowledge in all fields. Therefore, if you want to apply the available scientific knowledge to your own marriage and family problems, you will have to keep on studying after you leave college. Otherwise, you will be hopelessly behind the times in a very few years. All the sciences, physical, biological, and social, are constantly finding new knowledge applicable for producing better families.

Though we seriously need more scientific social knowledge, it is now definitely erroneous to assert that we know nothing about human nature, that it's all one big gamble, that good common sense is all you need, or that we must let nature take its course. On the contrary, there is general agreement among social scientists regarding the nature of human nature (personality), how it develops, gets "sick," how some personality defects are caused, how they may be prevented, and even cured.

There are still many people who scoff at the scientist who attempts to tell them anything about their marital problems or how to rear their children, especially if the scientist is unmarried or has no children. Women seldom refuse the services of an obstetrician because he has not borne a baby nor do we reject the knowledge of the astronomer because he has not been to the moon. In connection with family problems, however, many people still trust in common sense, custom, "instinct," or astrology rather than the knowledge of the scientist and the specialist in family behavior. It is a serious thing, of course, to try to influence other people's lives, but all parents and teachers are doing it, willy-nilly. It is highly important that they should be trained to make as few mistakes as possible. It is equally important that they should be able to recognize problems which they themselves cannot solve and be willing to employ the expert services of those with better training and more experience in dealing with personality problems. Family counseling and child guidance are new professions, but the competent people in these fields are rapidly increasing. You shouldn't run to such people for every little thing, but if you are having serious family trouble, you should make use of their services.[2]

While early family experiences are frequently the cause of later marital and parent-child problems, we now know that we are not doomed by our past experiences to continue forever as we are. We now know it is false to think you cannot change human nature. It is closer to the truth to say that you cannot prevent human nature from changing. Everything we do, say, think, and feel changes our personality to some degree, and also the personalities of those with whom we are interacting. The cumulative result of these minor changes may be very great, may even produce dramatic and apparently uncaused changes in personality. Therefore it is important to change our habits if they are not serving us well. We are constantly doing this by using our common sense; in serious instances, we may need the uncommon sense of science. The mark of an educated man is the ability to change his mind and behavior easily and quickly in order to make a better adjustment to the problems of life.

A SOCIOLOGICAL THEORY OF PERSONALITY

Personality has always been one of the most interesting things in man's experience, which is another way of saying man has always been, still is, and probably will always be, most interested in himself. Consequently he has elaborated many theories to explain why he acts as he does and "how

2 For addresses of marriage counselors in your vicinity, write to Dr. Robert W. Laidlaw, Secretary, American Association of Marriage Counselors, 270 Park Ave., New York, N. Y., or to the Family Service Association of America, 192 Lexington Ave., New York, N. Y.

he got that way." This everlasting mystery of man has been explained by almost every factor you can think of: food, climate, topography, heredity, environment, race, sex, endocrine glands, body form, conditioned responses, intelligence, economic activity, technology, religion, art, instincts.[3] You can see that these explanations are vague, overlapping, and more a matter of emphasis than anything else. They can all be classified as Physical, Biological, and Cultural theories.

None of them, nor all of them together satisfy the sociologist. He of course rejects any theory of personality which relies upon supernaturalistic or occult factors. He regards personality as a natural phenomenon to be explained by the general methods and theories of natural science. He recognizes that all the factors mentioned, and many more, are involved in the development and functioning of personality but he rejects all theories which are oversimplified and place too much emphasis on any single factor. He admits that all these factors condition and limit the development of personality, but he believes the basic clue to personality, mind, consciousness, culture itself, is the fact that *human beings interact with each other by various means of communication*. Most personality theorists have emphasized the fact that man reacts to things outside of him (physical, biological, and "supernatural"), or to things inside of him (genes, glands, muscles, reflexes, instincts, drives, etc.). There is an element of truth in this, of course, and the sociologist is not unmindful of it; but he thinks the essential clue to personality is *interaction between persons*. He notes that most of our reactions to the external environment — all the physical, biological, and cultural phenomena to which we can respond — are conditioned by the habits we previously have learned from our interactions with other people.

A baby is not born human; he is merely a squirming piece of protoplasm — a little animal, in short. He has no mind, no intelligence, no morals, no personality. He has a fairly well organized set of biological structures, however, and the potentialities for becoming human. These factors are what differentiate him from all other animals. They will be discussed briefly in a moment. He always is born into a culture. He is conceived as a result of social (and biological) interaction between two personalities; he remains in culture all his life, interacting with persons who have minds, morals, and intelligence.

His personality must develop within the limits imposed by (1) his own biological nature, (2) the physical universe, and (3) the culture into which he is born. All three factors are inextricably interrelated, and he is constantly interacting with all of them, being modified by them and to a slight degree modifying them. You now see why "heredity *versus* environment"

---

[3] "Instinct" in one form or another, which is closely related to "heredity," is one of the most persistent types of explanation, though most social scientists have seriously criticized it in recent years. One of the most comprehensive treatments is L. L. Bernard, *Instinct: A Study in Social Psychology* (New York: Holt, 1924). See also A. P. Weiss, *A Theoretic Basis of Human Behavior* (Columbus, Ohio: Adams, 1925) and E. B. Holt, *Animal Drive and the Learning Process* (New York: Holt, 1931) — both hard reading! A good discussion of this whole subject is found in H. E. Barnes, Howard Becker, and F. B. Becker, eds., *Contemporary Social Theory* (New York: Appleton-Century, 1940), pp. 329–430.

is a meaningless question over which men have wasted, and still waste, oceans of ink and millions of words. There are some specific traits, of course, which can be attributed mostly to heredity or to environment; but when the question is stated as an inclusive proposition, it is silly. Both are indispensable for the production and persistence of personality. In a sense, the cultural factor is most important, since there is ample evidence that personality disintegrates as a result of social isolation and never develops if the newborn baby does not interact with other persons.[4]

It is also true that the effects on personality of the physical and biological factors are always mediated by culture. The physical and biological world is more stable, is more nearly "given," so far as the newborn child is concerned, than his cultural world. His responses to the physical and biological world are more fixed and final than his responses to culture, and in all cases are limited by the culture he has acquired. To this slippery question we now turn.

PHYSICAL AND BIOLOGICAL LIMITS TO PERSONALITY

While sociologists stress social interaction as the basic factor in personality, to ignore the importance of other factors would be as unscientific as to assume that race, native intelligence, or any other single factor is the sole or most important factor. We do not know precisely what effect the physical environment may have on culture and therefore, indirectly, on personality. Does living in the desert, in the mountains, or on the ocean shore, directly affect personality? It is obvious that culture determines to a large extent what uses man can make of the physical resources of an area. He can overcome some of the limitations of physical nature, but not all. He must have water, certain chemicals, and air. Gravitation is always a barrier to some things he wants to do — and a great help to others. Temperature sets limits. So do the fertility of the soil and other earth-crust resources. He can overcome some of these limitations to some extent, but always as a result of cultural innovations (including all technological devices) and always at some personality price, since the kinds of social organization and social interaction necessary for his purposes will affect personality. This is all so obvious that we can skip it. The biological limits are more difficult to appraise. Much of this book is devoted to various aspects of this question as it pertains to the family.

One way to approach the problem is to mention (1) those biological factors which differentiate man from other mammals and then (2) those that differentiate individuals from each other.

All members of the human race, which includes the erroneously named white, yellow, and black races, have certain hereditary characteristics which

[4] Arnold Gesell, *Wolf Child and Human Child: A Narrative Interpretation of the Life History of Kamala, The Wolf Girl* (New York: Harper, 1941); Robert M. Zingg, "Feral Man and Extreme Cases of Isolation," *American Journal of Psychology*, 53 (Oct., 1940), pp. 487–517; Kingsley Davis, "Extreme Social Isolation of a Child," *American Journal of Sociology*, 45 (Jan., 1940), pp. 554–565.

make them *capable of culture*. Other mammals, including the higher apes, lack these or possess them to such a slight degree that they have not developed culture and presumably cannot. The most important of these human traits are: (1) unspecialized hand with opposable thumb; (2) upright carriage (this and his unusual hand enable man to manipulate objects skillfully, from the crudest tools to the most delicate instruments); (3) a head with movable eyeballs and a torso with rotating and bending hips which allow him to look up and down and even behind his back; (4) exceptionally acute hearing; (5) a highly unspecialized and conditionable central nervous system; (6) a relatively unspecialized and highly conditionable muscular system; (7) a complex and highly conditionable vocal apparatus; (8) a long growth period. There may be many other less obvious differences, such as endocrines, blood constitution, and protoplasmic plasticity, about which we know little today. Comparative biochemistry is not a highly developed science.

These are the biological traits which make man, not superior, or higher, but *different* from other animals. While he has many traits in common with them, he is more adaptable and not so much limited by his instincts, reflexes, and specialized structures. Because of his unspecialized auditory-vocal structures, he can develop a highly complex system of symbolic communication; because of his unspecialized hands, brain, and neuromuscular system, he can make and use tools, thus implementing his communicational culture with "material" culture. These traits also give him his powerful memory, imagination, self-consciousness, and inventiveness.

You will note it has not been said that the difference between man and the other animals is that man can learn, or that he is a conscious, rational, intelligent, moral being, or that he has a soul. To some degree, the higher animals have all these traits. There are even wide differences in the intelligence of individual rats, fishworms, and amoebas, and all of them may have souls if any of them do. These biological traits make it possible, and usually inevitable, for man to acquire *culture and personality*. This is mainly what differentiates him from other animals. A normal human being has these eight traits in varying amounts. They limit his development and his ability to acquire culture but because of man's highly unspecialized and conditionable biological nature, the limit is almost unlimited. There are nearly ten billion cells in man's cortex; he has several thousand muscles; his ability to learn specific reactions is theoretically the permutations of these astronomical figures. It is untrue that you can't teach an old dog new tricks if the "dog" is a man who has the habit of learning. Men go on learning as long as they live, and the cortex is almost the last part of the body to deteriorate from old age; the muscles, tendons, bones, heart, blood vessels, eyes, and kidneys grow old much earlier. "Never too old to learn" is almost true.

The factors that give us our biological individual differences are such things as race (sub-race, or species-variety), sex, size, body-form, age and rate of aging, hair-and-eye color and structure, skin color and texture, reaction-time, coordination, hairiness, anatomical defects, susceptibility and resistance to disease, blood-type, and native intelligence — to name only a few of the hundreds of individual differences. These are all more or less hereditary or at least genetic, though it is also true that personal and cultural experience modifies all of them.

We all know that height and weight are affected by health, food, clothing, and exercise. Rate of aging, and especially one's reaction to it, is also influenced by one's life experiences, though long life seems to be largely genetic.[5] Most defects are certainly the results of disease, accident, and habituation rather than "bad" genes. Disease resistance is greatly increased by good food, clothing, housing, and proper exercise, to say nothing of immunization. Reaction-time and coordination can be improved by training — within limits. Hairy legs and faces can be shaved; kinky hair straightened and straight hair curled and any kind of hair colored any color; secondary sex traits can be minimized or accentuated; even body size and shape can be modified by dieting and illusion-producing devices such as height of heels, girdles, shoulder-pads, colors, and horizontal-vertical stripes. Intelligence as measured by the tests obviously depends to a great extent on social conditioning, though there is ample evidence that biological differences exist. Whether these are genetic or variational or acquired, it is often impossible to tell.

Perhaps the great concern about whether intelligence is "inherited" calls for some generalized statement about biological traits. This is the way it looks to me. All biological traits can be classified as follows:

> I. Genetic: (1) hereditary, (2) variational;
> II. Acquired: (1) congenital, (2) postnatal.

All the main species-characteristics are hereditary — eyes, legs, livers, etc., although there are always some variations in these large hereditary structures. Some specific small traits are also definitely heritable, such as the famous Hapsburg lip and many family traits, blood-types, certain defects, and so on, though in such cases the fact of genetic variation is also observable.

We say some things are as like as peas in a pod, but the fact is that no pea, in the same or another pod, was ever *exactly* like any other pea. In fact, there is no reason to assume that any object in the universe, from atoms to stars, is *exactly* like any other similar object nor does it remain *exactly* the same for any successive instant. That some things are sufficiently similar to be treated as identical makes science possible. What we call "continuous," i.e., not heritable, variations are the unique elements in biological traits.

By "acquired" biological traits, I mean all those which result from the development of the genetic factors. They depend upon such things as food, temperature, pressure, disease, hormones and other chemicals, accident, habituation, quantity and quality of air, water, and so on. Such influences from conception to birth are congenital; those after birth, postnatal. Remembering this simple scheme will prevent much confusion. All factors are constantly interactive, but it is possible in some instances to separate

---

[5] See Read Bain, "The Ages of Man," *American Sociological Review* (June, 1945), pp. 337–343, and especially the cited references.

them by scientific analysis and experiment. All kinds of scientists are constantly trying to do this and their findings are mutually helpful for further research.

Thus, no two babies are ever *exactly alike,* not even identical twins (born from the same ovum), nor are any two babies ever born into *identical* social situations. Culture is changing all the time and the child is changing all the time, both biologically and socially. The biological factors, genetic and acquired, set limits to the personality traits he develops. So also do the cultural patterns into which he is born and in accordance with which he must develop. You do not produce Chinese personalities in Muncie, Indiana, nor urbanites in the mountains of Appalachia.

There is a cultural as well as a biological meaning for all the terms mentioned above. Take *maleness.* First we note that there is no such thing as absolute maleness — it is a constructed biological type. Some males have many "female" biological traits — few whiskers, narrow shoulders, broad hips, short legs, etc.; some females are quite "masculine." This is still more marked when we consider personality traits. The main biological function of the male is to fertilize ova, and of the female, to bear and nurse children; but their social functions vary widely from culture to culture and within the same culture at different times. To be a male in a cannibal tribe is very different from being an American campus male. Some of the males who read this will change the baby's diaper and scrub the kitchen floor; some of the females may cut out appendixes, go to Congress, and pilot airplanes. As for size, color, deformity, beauty, and intelligence, biological though they be, their meaning and significance depend upon the social definition of the situation.

Two other biological factors influencing personality must be mentioned, though only briefly. The first is maturation. We speak about people being emotionally, intellectually, and biologically mature. By the first two adverbs, we mean they have grown up, are able to behave in what we call an adult manner.[6] By the third, we mean the growth stages through which the individual goes from the embryo till death. (The geneticist and histologist use it in a more restricted technical sense which need not concern us.) Ignoring the prenatal stages, we know that babies are incapable of acquiring certain behavior patterns until they reach certain stages of biological growth, though it would be dangerous to assume that what goes on around them does not affect their behavior when they finally reach the point in growth, or maturation, where certain types of behavior become possible.

For example, you may talk to your baby till you are black in the face, but it won't talk much to you until it is about a year old. Try as you may, it won't walk much before that either, and if "it" is a boy and fat, even later. The same is true of sphincter control, teething, eye-and-hand coordination, ability to think abstractly, adolescence, and so on. You can't rush nature; in these matters, it is wise to let nature take its course. In fact, there is considerable evidence that personality maladjustments may result from the efforts of proud parents to force development on the child. Of course, there is

[6] See our discussion of emotional maturity in chap. 16, pp. 456–458.

considerable difference in the rate of maturation; some children are precocious, some are slow. The wise and competent parent is one who does the right thing at the right time.

Another biological factor that may have significance for personality development is body-form. This is an ancient idea at least as old as Hippocrates. In modern times, Kretschmer did some scientific work on it and recently W. H. Sheldon has amassed a large amount of data and interpreted them in a very interesting and plausible manner.[7] If Sheldon is right, he has made a great contribution to our understanding of human personality.

Whatever may be the verdict of science on Sheldon's work, we certainly err when we treat all personalities as if they were identical. There is no satisfactory scientific classification of personality types. It is pointless here even to enumerate those that have been proposed. The essential idea is that the type of personality that can develop in a given culture varies according to the biological characteristics of the person. These are due to heredity, genetic variation, congenital conditioning, and postnatal factors all interacting. Endocrine balance, body-form, race, infantile sexual conditioning, and instincts have all been used to explain the common-sense observation that people are different as well as funny.

We conclude that the cultural conditioning of biological factors seems to be more important for personality development than the biological factors alone. Biological factors undoubtedly limit a person's achievement but they never wholly determine either the selection of his goals or his success. It is true there are many round pegs in square holes, but both the pegs and the holes are largely the product of culture. Intelligence tests may measure native intelligence, but they also measure opportunity, health, interests, goals, education, race and class traits, and all the influences that have transformed the squirming baby into a human personality. All persons have a different genetic equipment, different cultural conditioning, and a different personal history. All these factors are vastly complex. To ascertain their respective influences in particular cases is impossible at present. It will require many years of research by all the natural sciences and we probably shall never completely succeed.

It is difficult if not impossible to give a concise and wholly acceptable definition of personality, but this one is ventured: Personality is all the habits of acting, speaking, thinking, and feeling acquired by responding to the physical, biological, and cultural environments through symbolic interaction with other similarly produced personalities.

---

[7] W. H. Sheldon, *Varieties of Human Physique* (New York: Harper, 1940) and *Varieties of Temperament* (New York: Holt, 1942). See also Aldous Huxley, "Who Are You?" *Harper's Magazine* (Nov., 1944), pp. 512–522, for a very readable and fair presentation of Sheldon's system.

To Talk Is Human

Now that we know the sociologist's conception of personality and the general relations between personality and the physical, biological, and cultural environments, let us see just how the newborn baby becomes human. Communication is the key. To talk is to be human. Reading, writing, and mathematizing are really shorthand or symbolic ways of talking. A newborn baby is much like the other higher mammals and, aside from learning to talk, he always remains so. His biological systems for eating, breathing, breeding are much like theirs; his circulatory, muscular, nervous, and excretory systems are about the same. Like them, he can learn and vocalize and, also like them, he has no instinct to imitate.

Animals can make and respond to sounds, but why do they never learn to talk? Because they lack the biological characteristics which differentiate man from other mammals. The child, after four or five months of maturation, begins to vocalize incessantly. It is the nature of the animal and it seems to please him as much as it does his proud parents; perhaps more, because his first habit of vocalizing, bawling, is a bad one and continues long after he begins to vocalize for fun. However, if he never cries, he will never talk. The finest oration or aria is but a modification of the infantile cry. About the time he begins to gurgle and google and "da" and "ma," he also begins to manipulate his hands, toes, and toys. Some of these sounds become attached to, associated with, or conditioned to certain objects. Now he can communicate — but a dog or cat can do this. The main difference is that the baby soon knows more words than any animal ever learns. Still, the baby can't talk; his communication, like that of the dog, is merely a series of simple conditioned responses, what Mead calls a "conversation of gestures." [8] It is about like two dogs making differential physical and vocal responses to each other when fighting or playing. There is no sense of self, no personality; it is merely face-to-face stimulus and response.

It won't be long, however. Particular sounds become attached to particular objects and actions. Among these are those applying to mother and father. In his random vocalizing, "ma" and "da" are easy, natural, and frequent sounds. Mother's words to and for him are also established as conditioned responses. Now there is a rudimentary verbal distinction between himself and others as there was an earlier and still more rudimentary nonverbal distinction between himself and other objects through manipulating his hands and feet and other things. Since he can hear himself and likes to vocalize and the family is ever alert to stimulate him, he gets a lot of verbal exercise. When he learns his own name and the names of others, and "eyes," and "nose," and "mama's nose," etc., he is close to talking, has almost become a person; he, like his ball, is now an object with a name, and other people also have names. Some day, while he says ball-ball-ball just for the fun of vocalizing, a ball is put in his hand; or he mutters "mama-mama," and mama suddenly ap-

[8] George H. Mead, *Mind, Self, and Society* (Chicago: University of Chicago Press, 1934), pp. 63–64.

pears. Now the miracle has happened: a conditioned response is established between a mere sound and something not present to his senses, the vocal sign has become a symbol with a "referent"; now the vocable has meaning. He can talk, and the endless flood of culture pours upon him.

BECOMING HUMAN: SELF-WORDS AND ROLE-TAKING

C. H. Cooley long ago showed the significance of self-words, names of others, and personal pronouns in the development of consciousness of self and other selves.[9] Some children have more difficulty than others in learning self-words properly — why, we do not know. The effects of early language habits on personality development and socialization merit serious research. Such things as "baby talk," improper grammar and pronunciation, poor enunciation, confused personal pronouns, humor, fantasy ideas, pitch, nasality, tempo, tonality, phrasing, etc., should be thoroughly investigated.

When the child says "baby's ball" or "my ball," he has a sense of self; when he says "your ball" and "his ball" properly, he has a sense of other selves. Now he can be called a self, a person, a human being; he has a personality, or the beginning of one. Vocal play continues but "something new has been added." He talks to himself and makes other selves (including many "not-selves") talk to him and to each other. He personifies everything; he now is a person — and a poet. His word-play is dramatic and his object-play is dramatized. He invents roles of others for himself to play; he makes everything "talk"; he says "my" and "mine" with explosive force; he says his own name and the names of his own things with caressing, contented, almost smug satisfaction. His sense of self is powerful, possessive, coercive; he is the world's worst (and best) egotist; he can do everything — that can be done with words. Growing up consists largely of curbing, and thus socializing, this childish ego. Many of us never quite make it. Parents should realize that many of the apparent fantasies and "lies" of children are merely verbal play, not the real fantasies and lies of later years which indicate personality maladjustment.

Mead believes that when the child can distinguish verbally between himself and others, he also responds to his own words as others respond to them, or similarly. He tends to modify his own responses according to the anticipated responses of others. Mead calls this "communication by significant symbols" — true human communication. Now the child has a mind and is a person. He is an object to himself. He can talk to himself as he does to others; that is, he can think, since he can assume the role of others and respond to his own talk as he imagines, or "thinks," others will respond to it. The conversation of gestures which characterizes animal interaction has become a conversation of significant symbols, *meanings,* which, so far as we

[9] C. H. Cooley, "A Study of the Use of Self Words by a Child," *Psychological Review* (Nov., 1908), pp. 339–357; Read Bain, "The Self-and-Other Words of a Child," *American Journal of Sociology* (May, 1936), pp. 767–775; Otto Decroly, "Comment l'enfant arrive à parler," *Cahiers de la Centrale,* Vol. 8, pp. 1–306; Barnes, Becker, and Becker, *Contemporary Social Theory* (New York: Appleton-Century, 1940), pp. 337–349.

know, is possible only between persons. This is conscious "transactional" behavior without which there is no culture and no human personality.[10]

PERSONALITY: PRODUCT AND PRODUCER OF CULTURE

We have seen how the nonhuman baby is transformed into an intelligent human being under the limitations of the physical, biological, and cultural environments. We have emphasized that he can become human only by interacting with others, but we have not discussed cultural limitations.

It is meaningless to ask whether society or the person comes first or which is the "more important." They come together; both are indispensable and they continue to be interdependent. In a sense, society and person are both abstractions; the sense-observable reality is the interactions of persons: the words, gestures, actions, and the deduced feelings, attitudes, values, goals, hopes, fears, and expectancies to which we give names from observing the behavior of others.

The baby is born into an already existing culture which provides the general patterns for his personality development. Within the limits imposed by the physical environment and his biological potentialities the culture determines what kind of person he will become: his language, food, moral, and other habits — all the kinds of social behavior he may acquire.

On the other hand, no two personalities are the same, for the reasons given above. Since no person can acquire all the available culture, the kind of personality one becomes depends upon his biologically conditioned and limited personality type, what kinds of social types he interacts with, what aspects of the total culture affect him. While there is some difference of opinion about the meaning of personality types, most sociologists agree that social types are the characteristic learned and stereotyped roles found in a given culture. Personality type usually refers to the distinctive manner in which persons perform their social roles. For example, one teacher (social type) is urbane, kindly, and patient (personality type); another is provincial, harsh, sarcastic, and short-tempered. Some students explain such differences by stressing biological factors: body-form (Sheldon), endocrine differences, effects of disease or injury, and so on. Others emphasize childhood experiences, family conditioning, crises, and other social factors.

These two sources of conditioning (biological and personal-social) are always involved. There are various ways of classifying personality types, no one of which is wholly satisfactory, but that they do exist and are important in the selection and definition of one's social type and his performance of various social roles seems incontrovertible. This is a fruitful field for research. Everyone adds a little to culture though we all receive much more than we add. Some make apparently great contributions — artists, scientists, statesmen, inventors, "leaders" in all fields, but analysis of specific contributions always shows the contributor was almost wholly dependent upon the an-

[10] John Dewey and Arthur F. Bentley, *Knowing and the Known* (Boston: Beacon Press, 1949), especially chaps. IV, V, XII. This book is for able students — but don't be too modest — try it.

tecedent culture. For the most part, man is a culture producer by combining, criticizing, reordering, and reinterpreting elements which already were in the culture before he was.[11]

It is fruitless to ask whether the mind is in the brain, or the organism-as-a-whole, or the soul. If our analysis is correct, it isn't in anything; it is an abstraction, a name for the behavior of organisms that respond to themselves as objects at the same time they respond to the anticipated responses of other objects, animate and inanimate. Our minds are thus not only in ourselves, but also in other selves, other objects, in books and music and machines, in everything for which we have significant symbols.

Individual psychologies are unable to give a logical explanation of social behavior. To start out with mind-as-individual, as a pre-existent entity, and then derive mind-as-social from instincts, compound reflexes, association of ideas, insight, etc., ends in confusion — an explanation that doesn't explain. Our sociological analysis starts with the conception that mind and personality are social. The social self is a datum, an observable entity with a history, in the same sense that the cortex is an entity. Our assumption is that man is a vocalizing animal whose vocables become symbols which stimulate both himself and others. This is possible because of the great similarity in the neuro-muscular systems of men. This is an observable fact. Thus, communication by significant symbols, socially conditioned speech habits, the learned distinction between self and others, and symbol-mediated role-taking furnish the necessary and sufficient basis for a sociological concept of personality.

So far we have been concerned with the nature and origin of personality. Now we shall turn briefly to the conditioning of the personality in the already existent culture into which the child is born. Here we are primarily concerned with personality as a cultural product rather than as a culture producer. We shall deal with this process in (1) the family, (2) primary and secondary groups, and (3) institutions, with some suggestions as to how family experiences are related to each.

CULTURAL DETERMINANTS OF PERSONALITY

The Family

All children are born into a family, or into a situation in which the necessary functions of the family are performed. We are concerned here with children in the normal, American, mid-twentieth-century family, by which we mean a monogamous father-mother-sibling group dwelling in a household, interacting with each other, with neighbors, friends, relatives, and with outside groups and social structures according to the folkways, mores, customs, traditions, laws, and regulations of our culture.

[11] See Howard Becker, *Systematic Sociology on the Basis of the* Beziehungslehre *and* Gebildelehre *of Leopold von Wiese* (New York: Wiley, 1932), pp. 331–334, on the "liberated man." See also C. H. Cooley, "Genius, Fame, and the Comparison of Races," reprinted in *Sociological Theory and Social Research* (New York: Holt, 1930), pp. 121–159. This invaluable essay was first published in 1897.

Each individual family is uniquely different from every other one but there are so many similarities between families that many family types can be found. There is no one best way to classify families, though presumably there is a best classification for each particular purpose. It is assumed that personality develops somewhat differently in each type of family. This is discussed more at length in other parts of this book and we are learning more about it all the time. Some classifications cut across all segments of our culture; some refer to particular segments. At this point, we want to emphasize that while the different types of families tend to produce personality similarities within each type, these are relatively superficial. All types of families in our culture meet the basic and fundamental requirements for normal personality development in the same general way, though the details of methods, means, and results vary widely. What happens to the child in all types of families affects the kind of adjustment he finally will make in his local and larger societal groups. In the vast majority of cases, he is a normal person, that is, he is able to get along in society.

Some of the family types with which you are already familiar are upper, lower, and middle — which usually has an economic reference; patriarchal, matriarchal, and equalitarian — who is "boss"; and a whole series of dichotomies like Negro-white, rural-urban, educated-uneducated, suburban-slum, rich-poor, native-immigrant, Protestant-Catholic, and Jewish-Gentile. The same general things happen to children in all these families, but the specific ways of thinking, feeling, and acting, the sum total of which is personality, differ widely. These various types of families merely represent somewhat specialized ways of dealing with various aspects of our total culture. Just how will the personalities of the children differ in Catholic and Jewish families, supposing the families are closely comparable in all respects except that they are orthodox Catholic and Jewish families? No one can now say with any scientific certainty. The same is true of the hundreds of possible combinations of family types just mentioned.

What, if any, is the correlation between family types and personality types? Do family types select or create certain personality types? Is the similarity (if it exists) in successive generations due to biological or cultural factors? What is the incidence of various types of mental diseases in various family types? Hundreds of such questions can be asked but few certain answers can be given at present. Roughly, we can predict that certain personality traits will develop in certain types of families: Jewish and Catholic families affect the religious ideas, food habits, and language habits of their children differently; upper class families are more likely than lower class families to send their children to college and prepare them for professions; and so on. So in considering the general factors mentioned below, we must always remember that the actual behavior patterns will all be noticeably different as between members of different types of families and even between members of the same family, all of whom are limited and conditioned by different biological and cultural factors.

These are some of the things, then, which all children learn — though somewhat differently — in all families: how to talk; what are proper food and excretory habits; how to play games; what is good and bad, reasonable and unreasonable; what people and goals are admirable and unworthy; how and when to express anger; how to love, laugh, and wear clothes; and many other actions and attitudes which make up the personality. Because of his conception of himself, which comes from interaction with other people in (and out of) the family, a child's later life may be influenced significantly if he is an only, a favorite, or an unwanted child; oldest, youngest, sickly, or healthy; only boy in a family of girls, or vice versa; if his siblings are near his own age, or far removed; if his parents love each other and, if not, if one or both try to find an affectional substitute in the child; if there is parental death or divorce; if a parent who has failed to achieve a goal tries to realize it vicariously through the child (and there is a success-counterpart of this projection process); if the child has a sense of insecurity, is filled with irrational fears, indulges in too much fantasy and other unrealistic modes of behavior; if he is pampered too much; if he is disciplined too harshly; and literally hundreds of other things. Not a great deal is known about the specific effects of such family situations, but most authorities agree that the general pattern of personality is fairly well formed by eight or ten years of age.[12]

Mother-child and father-child relations are of great importance. One of the major needs of the child (after proper food, sleep, clothing, and health care) is affection. The parents are the main source of such security, especially in infancy and early childhood. The socializing process that goes on in language acquisition, play, self-other distinctions, and all the formative experiences of childhood are more closely linked with the mother than with any other single person during the first three or four years of the child's life. If the parent does not love the child, or is too busy or too tired, or ill, or ignorant, or unhappy, the emerging personality of the child is endangered. Or the mother may love the child unwisely and too much; — she may *smother* rather than *mother* him.

Another basic need of the child is to explore, to learn how to handle himself, to run, climb, and take chances. He needs to measure himself against other children of his own age, to incur the risks of interacting with other developing personalities. If the mother loves him too much, is too fearful he will get hurt, or dirty, or sick, or lost, or learn bad habits, he may never learn enough self-reliance or gain the breadth of experience necessary for adequate adulthood; he may remain tied to his mother's apron strings all his life. This is one of the possible effects of parent-child fixation. There are many others we cannot go into here.[13]

The child also needs praise and encouragement and appreciation. If the family members are always belittling, teasing, and frustrating him, the child will have difficulty in acquiring the self-respect a normal person must have. Parents with insight and understanding help develop self-reliant children.

[12] See Duvall, Gesell, Levy, Blatz, *et al.,* in bibliography at end of chapter.
[13] For more on this, consult the index on parent-child fixation and parent-child relations; also, Read Bain, "Needed Research in Parent-Child Fixation," *American Sociological Review* (Apr., 1945), pp. 208–216; also chap. 16 of this book, pp. 462–465.

It is true that the child must learn how to face trouble and failure, but such experiences should be part of his normal exploring and competing with others who are his equals. In general, and especially while he is young, he should have more successes than failures, and more praise than blame. Unmerited praise and blame, however, are equally bad. When things go wrong, he should have sympathy and understanding and be helped to deal adequately with the situation when he is again confronted with it. He must be taught early to value facts, to face reality, and to respect the rights and property of others.

Wise parents will teach the child to become as independent of them as possible as quickly as possible, but they must not overdo this principle. They must not be so anxious to make him a good person or superior child that they violate the facts of maturation; they must not demand grown-up behavior before the child has had time to develop it. If they attempt to enforce their too ambitious plans by shaming, nagging, condemning, and punishing the child, he may respond by regressive conduct (crawling into his shell, lying, daydreaming, etc.) or by aggressive conduct (fighting, breaking things, stealing, etc.). Similar effects may come from similar relations with his siblings or other children.

There are hundreds of family experiences that may seriously affect the child's personality for weal or woe. An only child may be unhappy if other children he knows have brothers and sisters. A second child may be hated by an older sibling who resents the attention the new baby necessarily must receive. A girl in a family of boys may become a tomboy in self-defense or a regressive weak sister in despair. A boy in a family of girls may become a holy terror or a spoiled, tyrannical sissy. Parents who are too old or too young may neglect, spoil, or ignore their children. Maids may have a bad influence. Usually, however, even when adverse social conditioning is present, it seldom does permanent and severe damage to the personality. Fortunately, man is a tough and adaptive animal. He can take a lot and still pull through. Most families lay a sound foundation upon which the later personality can be built. The close personal-social relations with parents, relatives, and siblings give the general definition of the personality which, although modified by subsequent contacts with culture, becomes the basic personality structure.

Primary and Secondary Groups

Primary groups are those in which the social interactions are relatively enduring, personal, informal, unspecialized, and affectional; sentimental rather than mental, and ends in themselves rather than instrumental means to other ends. The family, play group, elementary school, fraternity, club, gang, and friendship groups are examples. In such groupings, the social contacts are face to face and the significant symbols deal largely with common-human and personal-social relations that are concrete, immediate, and filled with rich, deep, personal, and individual meaning. The bonds are those of intimate sacredness, hence "privatized" values, stereotypes, folklore, and tradition flourish in primary groups. Much of the communication is based upon the mutual interpretation of subtle gestures of voice and body.

People understand each other and have insightful and intuitive experiences which they often attribute to instinct. They know how the others will react. Families have a little private vocabulary, pet names and nicknames, special terms for tabooed objects, private histories, characteristic gestures, and so on. The socialization is largely unconscious, uncritical, and merely accepted. There may be considerable authoritarianism, ethnocentrism, and all-or-nothing types of reaction. While the control is not highly formalized, it is coercive none the less, and usually a ritualistic pattern is clearly observable.

Secondary groups are those in which the social interactions are relatively transient, formal, impersonal, abstract, specialized, utilitarian, and instrumental rather than affectional. Political parties, the large urban congregation, denominational church membership, the American Sociological Society, the National Association of Manufacturers, the C.I.O., etc., are examples. Cooley stressed the fact that the moral principles developed in primary groups are generalized and organized so as to govern secondary group behavior also. Among these primary group ideals and attitudes are such traits as honesty, honor, tact, loyalty, kindliness, humor, courtesy, neighborliness, generosity, sympathy, gratitude, and love. Generalized for larger impersonal secondary groupings, these principles become such things as justice, patriotism, piety, diplomacy, charity, and international good will.

Cooley emphasized the socially constructive aspects of the primary group influence on the larger society, using democracy and Christianity as examples. This is true, but there is another side to the story. The family and other primary groups may stress such attitudes as self-centeredness, authoritarianism, intolerance, lying (to children and hence by them), cruelty, fear of strangers, jealousy, greed, and self-asserted superiority. The generalized secondary group manifestations of these may be ethnocentric attitudes regarding race, class, and religion; chauvinistic patriotism, imperialistic political and economic exploitation, bigotry, intolerance, and undemocratic behavior of all kinds.

All groups cannot be put into one of these two classes as easily as the above discussion might indicate. Many have both primary and secondary characteristics in varying degrees. Such are sometimes called intermediate groups. The actual number of such mixed-type (intermediate) groups probably greatly exceeds the number of relatively "pure" primary and secondary groups as defined in this section. All three are "constructed types."

The student will recognize the similarities between Becker's sacred and secular societies (Chapter One) and Cooley's primary and secondary groups, especially when one realizes that primary group ideals are not always socially beneficial as Cooley seems to imply. Becker shows that sacred and secular societies have both good and bad characteristics. So do primary and secondary groups.[14]

[14] C. H. Cooley, *Social Organization* (New York: Scribner's, 1909), chaps. 3–5 inclusive. See Louis Wallis, *Egoism* (Chicago: University of Chicago Press, 1905), for a brief exposition of how these ideas are related to Christianity.

Institutions

Institutions, like all other social structures, are concepts derived from sensory experiences. Certain classes of groups are found in all societies. We assume they exist because they satisfy basic human needs. While the specific ways of satisfying these needs vary widely in time and space, the needs themselves are relatively permanent and universal. However, these "specific ways" can be generalized. Each class of groups always has some specialized physical equipment (symbolic and utilitarian), specialists, and a set of ideas and practices (here called "ideology"). These are the means by which the basic needs are satisfied. This whole complex of structures and functions comprises the "institution."

Ten such classes of groups can be recognized, so we have at least ten major institutions: Artistic, Economic, Educational, Familial, Medical, Political, Recreational, Religious, Scientific, and Welfare. In some societies, the institutions may not be clearly differentiated, e.g., the "primitive" religious specialist also may be "teacher," "scientist," "doctor," and "social worker," but the basic needs for these services are there — and are met in some fashion. The overlapping of such functions is also observable in our own society, but most groups and specialists usually can be classified under a particular institution. The following table is a schematic outline of the above paragraphs.[15]

THE STRUCTURE OF SOCIAL INSTITUTIONS

TEN MAJOR INSTITUTIONS	BASIC NEEDS	EQUIPMENT		SPECIALISTS		IDEOLOGY	
		UTILITARIAN	SYMBOLIC	BASIC	DERIVED	"OLD"	"NEW"
4. Family	Control of sex Care of children Love	Furniture Clothes Housing Utensils	Rings Pictures Heirlooms "Home"	Home econo- mists Family service Researchers	Obstetri- cians Pediatri- cians Architects	No divorce Patriarchy Duty Sex taboos	Divorce Sex equal- ity Freedom Sex educa- tion

All societies regulate sexual behavior and the rearing of children. They provide intimate personal relations between spouses which go far beyond sexual access. Symbolic objects are those that have greater sentimental than intrinsic or utilitarian value. "Home" is more than housing and a "ring" is "worth" more than it costs.

A basic specialist is an authority on the family, a professional, whereas derived specialists are professionals from other institutions, e.g., lawyers, doctors, architects who "specialize" as domestic relations judges, pediatricians, and dwelling house designers. This "borrowing" of specialists illustrates the constant interaction and interdependence of all the institutions. What goes on in each institution affects all the others in many ways. All social life is an organic unity.

[15] For a similar approach, see F. Stuart Chapin, *Contemporary American Institutions* (New York: Harper, 1935), especially chap. 2.

The "Old" and "New" factors often indicate tensions within the ideology of an institution. The "New" are not necessarily better than the "Old"; they are different. Some segments of a society may be dominated by "Old" ideas long after other segments have adopted "New" ones, thus causing conflict. Attitudes and practices related to birth control and sex education are examples. "Ideology" should not be confused with "ideals" or "what should be." It refers to *all* the ideas and practices which are socially sanctioned and condemned in a given society at a given time.

Parents and children constitute the *nuclear* family group. Other groups which mediate between the nuclear and other groups of other institutions may be called *peripheral*. Often they are pressure groups. For the family, the P.T.A., mothers' clubs, Big Brother and Sister organizations, etc., are examples.

The child's early experiences are important for his later social adjustments. This was stressed by Freud and is emphasized by the notion of Basic Personality Structure: ". . . the constellation of personality characteristics which appear to be congenial with the total range of institutions comprised within a given culture." [16] While these investigators worked mainly with nonliterate societies, their findings are probably applicable to our own. The child's basic orientation to the major institutions, his experience with their equipment and adjustment to their specialists and ideologies largely determine his later social behavior.

What he learns in the family greatly influences what he learns outside of it, what such learning means, and what his basic personality structure becomes. Being well adjusted to his own family may cause poor adjustment outside of it. Suppose he has not played much with other children, has always "had his own way," been "babied," "petted," and "spoiled." He is well adjusted to parents and siblings and they to him. Everyone is happy. Then he is suddenly thrust into school. The teacher doesn't talk and act like his parents; he doesn't know how to play; he and his playmates do not "speak the same language." His personality is inadequate to deal with these new and rapidly changing situations.

When the child begins to escape from the home, he soon finds many other statuses and roles which differ from those he knows; the standards and modes of approval and disapproval also differ. However, he quickly learns that these "others" have much in common. From *my* parents, *our* preacher, *our* milkman, he soon develops *generalized* concepts of parents, teachers, preachers, etc. This is what G. H. Mead calls "generalized others." They are also called "social types," statuses, and roles. The child has had some preparation for this in the "role-taking" play described above. This is soon increased by contacts with many new primary and secondary groups. Social types like patriot, honest man, criminal, etc., are ethicalized versions of generalized

[16] Abram Kardiner, *The Individual and His Society: The Psychodynamics of Primitive Social Organization* (New York: Columbia University Press, 1939), pp. 12, 126–134; A. Kardiner, Ralph Linton, Cora Du Bois, and James West, *Psychological Frontiers of Society* (New York: Columbia University Press, 1945); Cora Du Bois, *The People of Alor: A Social-Psychological Study of an East Indian Island* (Minneapolis: University of Minnesota Press, 1944).

others. Adequate adjustment to these social patterns of rights and duties, learning what is expected and what to expect of various social types, is what "being human" means; this is socialization.

In a heterogeneous and rapidly changing society like ours, the child is confronted with many institutionally defined inconsistencies, contradictions, and conflicts. While there are differences between upper and lower class families, immigrant and native-born, Negro and white, Catholic and Protestant, etc., generally speaking, the family patterns are more stable and consistent than is the case with many other institutions.

There are not only conflicts *within* the various institutions but also *between* them. The church, home, and school may teach brotherhood and love, but the political institution teaches war and hate, the recreational and economic institutions teach conflict and competition, while science and education teach that many of the child's early religious ideas about the world and man are false or doubtful. Thus his total personality is a complex of many institutionally defined selves, some of which are logically and actionally incompatible. He is a different person to different people. His age-mate ("gang") self might shock his mother, Sunday School teacher, and Boy Scout leader. Do you behave at college exactly as you do at home and in the home town? In varying degrees, our institutional selves are bound to contain some inconsistencies and contradictions and "inner" conflicts. This should be a good cue to say a few words about conscience.

CONSCIENCE FORMATION AND PERSONALITY CONFLICT

Since personality is formed and functions through the interactions of group-defined selves, conflicts between group-demands are an integral part of the personality. One often feels, and even behaves, in ways contradictory to the demands or impulses of the other segments of his personality. The recognition of such conflicts and the dis-ease and "pain" it gives, is what we mean by guilt-feelings and the pangs of conscience. Conscience is thus a social product and the producer of socially approved behavior. If one were living in a completely unified culture to which he was thoroughly adjusted, he would never feel guilty, sinful, or shamed, and would not be conscious of a conscience.

There never has been any such society or any such persons, though people vary widely in the degree and intensity both of their maladjustment and their consciousness of it. Guilt-feelings may be expressed in many ways: by rationalization, affect-transfer, daydreams, wishful thinking, ambivalence, fantasy, compensation, and other so-called "mask-mechanisms" including psychosomatic illness. Or the person may deal realistically with his maladjustment and acquire new behavior patterns that resolve the conflict — that is, patterns which are consistent with the conflicting segments of his personality. This is more easily said than done, but is approximated by most of us.

So long as a person is able to play his various roles properly, with no serious sense of guilt or conflict and with acceptance by others, so long as he can make quick and adequate transitions from one role to another, he is "normal." This generalized habit of appropriate role-playing is what integrates and unifies a personality. No one is ever completely integrated; there is always some unadjustment, maladjustment, and even disorganization in some aspects of most personalities, especially when considered in relation to other segments of one's own personality, the personalities of others, or to various institutional aspects of his society. This is particularly true in a rapidly changing, heterogeneous society like ours.[17] When one's role-transitions or use of significant symbols are so inadequate that normal people regard his behavior as a menace to himself or others, he is judged to be abnormal, antisocial, criminal, or insane. Probably more socially abnormal behavior is the result of defective social conditioning than of genetic biological factors.

The moral is clear: sound personality development requires considerable consistency between the ideals, goals, folkways, mores, interests, and activities of the family and those of the outside community. If the family patterns are greatly different from those of other institutions, the parents should fortify the child with habits of understanding and generosity which will enable him to make adequate adjustments to other segments of society. He must be taught to disagree agreeably and to change his ideas and actions quickly and easily when that is necessary. He should not give up his own ideas and ideals for light and transient reasons, but all people have to change their minds about many things. In the meantime, people should know how to take the roles of others and see the other fellow's point of view well enough to avoid being socially objectionable and personally miserable. If we want freedom for ourselves, we must be willing to grant it to others.

THE GOOD PERSONALITY

Most students agree that the basic personality is pretty well defined by the age of eight or ten or even earlier. We have briefly reviewed some of the main factors involved in this definition. Perhaps we can summarize the whole process under the two apparently contradictory concepts, stability and change.

A personality is a more or less stable, socially organized set of habits. Habit systems, like all energy systems, manifest varying degrees of inertia, inflexibility, and repetitiveness. Social systems, even more than personalities, exhibit this relative fixity. This is suggested by such terms as cake of custom, folkways, mores, usage, convention, conformity, cultural continuity, tradition, and social heritage. This relative stability of social phenomena makes social order, social organization, and hence prediction possible, whether at the level of common sense or of science.

The child's personality at eight or ten, therefore, gives us some basis for predicting his probable future. If he is healthy, happy, and bright, he is likely to continue so. If he has a vocabulary of significant symbols and habits of role-taking adequate for a ten year old, the chances are good that he will do as well as an adult. If he gets along well with children and adults, when he

---

[17] Read Bain, "Cultural Integration and Social Conflict," *American Journal of Sociology* (Jan., 1939), pp. 499–509; C. H. Cooley, *Social Organization* (New York: Scribner's, 1909), chaps. 30–33 inclusive, on disorganization.

is adult he will probably get along with adults and children. If he can manage his mind, emotions, and body well in childhood, he is likely to do so as an adult. This is the basis of the proverb about the bent twig.

If this — were all, life would be a pretty bleak affair. We would be the victim — or the beneficiary — of the accidents of birth and social conditioning. If life were no more than a mechanical, deterministic, completely predictable series of events, men would be sheer automatons. Obviously this is not the case. It takes both stability and change to make a personality. We have indicated that all people are unique in some respects, that this basic biological variability is differentially affected by the postnatal cultural, biological, and physical environments. Human protoplasm is highly plastic, conditionable, and capable of learning. Were this not so, there would be no point in education, change would be impossible, and society would soon stagnate. We all know people who made a bad start but a strong finish, sickly children who became healthy adults, people who flunked as freshmen but made good records as seniors, and so on. We have even seen people whose adult personalities undergo remarkable transformations: introverts becoming extraverts; religious people becoming atheists; bankers becoming painters (Gauguin); radicals becoming reactionaries; and the reverse of such cases.

Intensive study of such instances usually reveals that most of them are not really exceptions to the generalization that early personality definition remains relatively stable. They are rather cases of personality conflict in which one segment of the personality has been repressed or dominated by other segments. It now asserts itself as a result of cumulative habit-changes, or impulses generated by the conflict, or biological changes, or other factors very difficult to analyze. Dramatic overturns of personality always have a history which usually begins in early childhood. What seems strange at first becomes reasonable and almost expected when we know the facts. Many returns to the faith after a life of sin and departures from the faith (all kinds of faith) can be explained by early conditioning.[18] The point here is that the personality can and does change and sometimes such changes are quick and spectacular. Dramatic religious conversions are good examples.

We can now state some traits of the "good personality." Both change and stability are necessary and inevitable. Instead of being contradictory, they are mutually beneficial in producing an adaptive culture and an adaptable person. If cultural or personal change is too rapid or too intense, the stabilizing habit-systems of the person are either not formed at all or are disorganized or even destroyed. If this happens to enough people in a short period of time, the whole society or some segment of it may become unstable. Learning usually requires the breaking of older habits of thinking and acting and the making of new habits. To be sure, some people continue to think the same and act differently, or vice versa, but such behavior usually results in confusion and conflict, in unadaptive or maladaptive conduct. A proper balance between stability and change is necessary for the effective adaptation of both personalities and cultures. Too much or too little of either produces trouble. Old Aristotle's idea of the golden mean is still sound doctrine.

[18] Franz Wittels, "Economic and Psychological Historiography," *American Journal of Sociology* (May, 1946), pp. 527–532.

Bearing in mind all that has been said above, we suggest that one has a good or effective personality in our culture when he can make adequate social adjustments while retaining enough plasticity and spontaneity to deal effectively with novel situations. He lives in a dynamic and changing world. He must be at home in both primary and secondary groups; he must be able to withstand the slings and arrows of outrageous fortune; he must, in most things, though not in all, be not the first by whom the new is tried, nor yet the last to lay the old aside; he must know how to make a good living and live a good life; how to give and receive love like a mature person; how to marry and be happy and raise children who are better than their parents. In short, he must be a liberated personality (see pages 44–45).

Early Personality and Successful Marriage

This chapter tries to emphasize that *personality development in the family is basic to all later personality development and social adjustment.* Thus we end on our beginning note: how early personality patterns influence later success and failure in love, marriage, and parenthood. As you study the later chapters, remember what you have learned in this: that early personality patterns are involved in all the topics the other authors discuss. In this chapter only seven broad topics can be even briefly discussed: (1) the habit of happiness; (2) emotional balance and fear; (3) attitudes toward sex; (4) parent-child and child-parent fixation; (5) vicious circles and vicious cycles; (6) the principle of similarity; and (7) modification of childhood patterns.

The Habit of Happiness

One thing upon which most students of the family agree is that happiness in marriage is highly correlated with the happiness of the families in which the spouses were reared. While there are many exceptions, in general the chances are better for happy and successful marriage if both spouses come from families in which the parents were happy and loved each other and the children in a normal and socially well-adjusted way. This means that being happy and well adjusted is a socially acquired personality structure.

Terman has compiled a list of personality traits that show statistically significant correlations with unhappiness in marriage. These are (not in order of importance): being touchy; grouchy; losing temper easily; being critical and careless of others' feelings; rebellious at discipline; expressing dislikes without restraint; being sensitive to praise and blame; a self-doubter; domineering toward opposite sex; having little interest in other people or social welfare; unconventional toward religion, drinking, and sex; excitable; happy or sad without apparent cause. The traits which had the highest correlation with marital happiness (in order) are: superior happiness of parents; marked childhood happiness; no conflict with mother; firm, but not harsh, home discipline; strong love for mother and father; no conflict with father, parental frankness about sex; infrequent and mild childhood punishment; discipline that is tactfully imparted and that consequently elicits cooperation; a healthy attitude toward sex.[19]

Note two things: first, all these traits are defined early; second, the traits in the first list make for happiness, while those in the second point toward unhappiness. The unhappy child is poorly socialized: he cannot take the role of others; he lacks insight and understanding; he is in conflict with socially approved culture patterns. The happy child is the opposite: he is other-centered, not self-centered; love, cooperation, and social approval are the basic patterns of his personality. He has acquired the habit — or better habits — of happiness, and they carry on into his later marital and other forms of social behavior.

What does the child need to develop this pattern of personality? He probably will be a happy child, and therefore a happy adult, if he is born because he is wanted — which means he is planned for. He must be loved and taught how to love others, be praised, be secure, be disciplined firmly, but not harshly, have a chance to play and explore, have what his friends have — which means rights and privileges as well as things. His parents are considerate of his welfare and pleasure. They do not believe children should be seen and not heard. They take an interest in his interests and talk to him and treat him like a responsible person — no baby talk, fairy stories, lies, teasing, shaming, humiliation. They do not treat him as a toy or an object of perverted humor. They protect him from people who treat children unwisely and from the ordinary adult worries which do not immediately concern the child: financial troubles, father's problems at the office, mother's difficulties with the neighbors, etc.

The child will not be happy if he is excluded from things that do concern him. A happy childhood does not mean the child is never unhappy. If there is sickness or death in the immediate family, or if a pet dies, good parents will help the child to face the facts without undue emotional stress and strain. Perhaps one of the best tests of the good parent is the manner in which he handles the big and little crises and tragedies of childhood. Lies, false promises, bribes, encouragement of violent grief, and harsh punishment are some of the wrong ways; sympathy, love, explanation, change of scene and interest, tenderness, and healthy-mindedness help to establish the habit of happiness. Parents who are not happy seldom rear happy children. Practice beats precept. The unhappy parent is too much wrapped up in his own woes to deal constructively with the crises and problems of his unfortunate and unhappy children.[20]

Terman does not mention that happy people usually have a well developed

---

[19] Lewis M. Terman, et al., *Psychological Factors in Marital Happiness* (New York: McGraw-Hill, 1938), chap. 14. Ernest W. Burgess and Leonard S. Cottrell, Jr., *Predicting Success and Failure in Marriage* (New York: Prentice-Hall, 1939), working independently confirm most of Terman's findings. Read both books.

[20] For a beautiful account of how an engineer and his wife reared *eleven* happy and healthy children, all of whom married happily, see Lillian E. Gilbreth, *Living With Our Children* (New York: Norton, 1928; 1951 rev.). She gives many concrete techniques for dealing with everyday problems.

sense of humor. Healthy, normal, well adjusted people usually laugh a lot. Seeing a joke, especially when it is on you, involves taking a role. Laughter is one of the commonest and best means of relieving tension. Wit and humor are verbal habits which, like speech and table manners, are usually acquired unconsciously. A sense of humor is learned. People who have similar humor habits are likely to get along together. It is as important for children to have a good sense of humor as it is to have a good education. A good sense of humor makes us laugh with people, not at them.

EMOTIONAL BALANCE AND FEAR

People who have the habit of happiness, who are normally socialized, are likely to be well balanced emotionally. Most people talk about the emotions, such as fear, love, and remorse, as if they were things or innate biological entities of some kind. It is also common to regard "intellectual" and "emotional" as opposites.

Actually, "emotion" is merely a name for one element in response to any stimulus. It is the biological mechanism by which the organism releases enough energy to produce movement. This is always true of any action, whether thinking or throwing; enough energy must be released to overcome the inertia of the organism or the blockage which results when there are several possible ways of responding to a stimulus. Thus, if we are confronted by a stimulus which experience has defined as dangerous, there are several possible things to do. The simplest is to run away or to remove the danger. If we choose, that is, respond according to our past experiences, to run away, the emotional feeling we have is often called fear; if we fight, we say the emotion is anger or rage.

Emotion is a generic type of behavior like digesting and breathing. It is instinctive in the sense that all higher mammals have the capacity to release differential amounts of energy under various conditions. Emotional behavior is generic and hereditary but not specific; we have to learn what to fear, hate, love, or be angry at, as well as how to express these emotions. We have to emote to act, whether we are solving problems or knocking each other down. The opposite of "intellectual" is therefore not "emotional"; it is ignorant, unintelligent, or irrational. The opposite of "emotional" is apathetic, inactive, unmoved. What people usually mean when they say "he got emotional" is that he acted, verbally or overtly, in an irrational, unadaptive, maladaptive, or socially disapproved way.

What we mean by "emotional balance" is that the organism is moved enough to release sufficient energy to insure an adequate adjustment. This implies that we have defined the situation accurately (according to our culture) and responded to it properly (according to our needs and society's demands). Emotional balance, then, is always socially defined. When the necessary behavior is habitual, automatic, and routine, relatively little emotion (energy) is required; novel situations, crises, conflicting habit patterns, whether of action or thought or feeling, require more energy (more emotion). Emotional unbalance means that because of improper definition of the situation or conflicting elements in our personality, either too much or too little energy is released or our resultant behavior is such that our response is inadequate either personally or socially and we are unadjusted or maladjusted. Such inadequate behavior habits acquired in childhood may remain part of the personality for years. The more conscious of his maladjustment the person becomes, the more intense the internal and external conflict is and the more "emotionally" the person behaves. The fears of childhood may become the phobias of adulthood and give rise to chronic worry, anxiety, and even neurotic behavior (too much emoting).

Fear itself is a necessary type of adaptive behavior but children should be taught to fear only fearful things and not to fear them too much or too little. Likewise, an indispensable companion to rational fear should be adequate habits of dealing with the fearful situation: how to avoid it or master it. We now know that too much emotion, which merely means that more energy is released than can be utilized in adaptive action, is damaging to the organism. It upsets digestion and excretion, causes headaches, and if sufficiently prolonged may cause psychosomatic diseases such as stomach ulcers, asthma, or even heart disease. Boys whistling in the dark, shouting, or running are merely using up the excess energy of fear. When you are emotionally excited, it is sound sense to do something which requires a lot of energy.

It is rational to fear contagious diseases and busy crossings; but if the child is made too fearful, if he is unable to do anything or go anywhere because he is too much afraid of germs or cars, the result is emotional unbalance. On the other hand, if he does not have enough fear and is too ignorant of possible ill consequences, his behavior is also inadequate. Fear arises because his desire to cross the street is blocked by his knowledge that he may get killed; so he gets "emotional." If he has emotional balance, he gets just emotional enough to cross carefully without being plagued for hours afterward by fear of death or maiming. When prudent street crossing has become automatic, the emotional content of the act is minimal and its adequacy is maximal.

Much emotional unbalance is the result of irrational fears. In our culture, one of the commonest is fear of fear or rather fear of being thought afraid. It frequently is deeply repressed and produces unconscious conflict which keeps the person chronically overemotional, with the ill results referred to above; or it may produce foolhardy, impulsive, dangerous behavior. A common form of emotional unbalance is overcompensation, which makes a person try to convince himself and others that he really is not what he seems. The timid man tries to appear brave; the stupid man, brilliant; the little man, "big," by being blatant, aggressive, and dictatorial. They protest too much and seldom fool anyone but themselves.

Overcompensation is often the result of an inferiority feeling which frequently is due to an irrational fear that one isn't normal or equal to others. If fear is really unfounded or due to some unfortunate combination of circumstances such as failure at first trial or marked social disapproval or lack of parental guidance and sympathy, and if one does not overcompensate, he may undercompensate and escape from reality into daydreams, avoidance of social interaction, sulking, self-doubt, self-pity, and other forms of withdrawal.

Excessive reading, writing, music, or collecting may be the child's reaction to morbid fears. If he is fortunate enough to gain social approval for his withdrawal activities, the original emotional unbalance may be transformed into normal behavior. The same may be true of the overcompensating, aggressive, attention-getting child. The quarreling bully may later become the champion prize-fighter, big leaguer, military hero, or adventurous explorer.

Emotional unbalance sometimes arises as a result of defective social conditioning in connection with eating, sleeping, managing excretion, and playing with other children. The result may be a moody, irritable, unsociable adult unfitted to become a good spouse and parent. A person who has food antipathies or is too fastidious about food, who does not sleep well and hence does not get proper relaxation, whose bowels are always bothering him, may be a difficult spouse and parent. Children who fight, sulk, and too easily get their feelings hurt may show similar traits as adults.

Much emotional unbalance is due to discipline — too little, too much, too severe, too lenient, too erratic. One parent may condone what the other condemns. The parents should agree on discipline and then adhere to their plan. Security, knowing what to expect, in discipline is as important as security in affection. Parents should not try to control the child by irrational fears or threats which they and the child know will never be carried out. Few parents nowadays threaten their children with the bogeyman or the policeman or the reform school, but many do frighten them with germs, vitamins, traffic, threats of not loving them, or with being a disgrace to the family and never amounting to anything.

If the basic personality is to function effectively in adulthood as lover, spouse, and parent, it is highly important that it be conditioned in childhood to deal with all its problems in a realistic, emotionally balanced manner. It must be protected from irrational fears and emotional imbalance.

ATTITUDES TOWARD SEX

Healthy-minded attitudes toward sex are highly important for happy marriage. Perhaps no other aspect of our culture is so much surrounded with irrational fears, ignorance, taboo, and emotional imbalance. Instead of helping their children to achieve a socially and personally adequate set of sex habits and attitudes, many parents actually contribute to the child's sexual maladjustment. An atmosphere of secrecy and fear and shame frequently surrounds this subject. If parents attempt to "tell" their children, they often lack the proper knowledge and vocabulary. If they have the knowledge and vocabulary, they themselves often lack a healthy-minded attitude toward sex. The result is that they deliver untimely, erudite lectures in sepulchral tones which the child does not understand or which leave him confused. A proper sex education consists not only of information but also of proper emotionally toned attitudes acquired in the same matter-of-fact way as proper speech and manners. The child should never be able to remember when he did not know the essential anatomical and functional differences between males and females, how babies are born, and that all children grow up and fall in love, get married, and have children just as father and mother did. Boys and girls should learn naturally and easily what menstruation is and how it is cared for, as well as the proper names and functions of the sex organs of both sexes. Euphemisms, baby talk, and circumlocutions are sure to produce mental and emotional confusion. A person who can be shocked by the questions and actions of a child is not fit to be a parent. A parent who lies and evades and hushes, permitting his child to grow up in ignorance and fear about one of the most imperious and important aspects of his life, is a poor parent. His general approach to these problems should be as frank and commonplace as his approach to questions that deal with the circulatory or solar system.

Very young children sometimes have "love affairs." These should be treated with respect and sympathy. It is thoughtlessly cruel to use these first experiences to tease and humiliate the child or to have adult "fun." Being able to love, to give and receive affection, is a habit. Children should see and hear their parents expressing affection for each other and should participate in it themselves. Expression of affection should not be confined to gift-giving and doing things for each other; it should include appropriate physical and verbal behavior. Parents should set the pattern by word and deed in educating their children in heterosexual love. Parents who use such terms as "puppy love," "infatuation" and "silly boy-and-girl affairs" are laying the groundwork in their child for cynicism and future unhappiness in marriage. These general remarks apply to the preadolescent and adolescent years as well as to early childhood. If the early years are properly handled, parents are less likely to have the humiliating experience of being regarded as strangers by their adolescent children. Children naturally turn to the able parent for guidance and sympathetic understanding when they are faced with difficult problems. The failure of parents to keep the avenues of communication open between themselves and their children, the inability to take a child's-eye view of things, is largely responsible for "adolescent rebellion" and problem children — who later become emotionally immature and inadequate adults. In no phase of personality development in our culture are serious difficulties so likely to occur as in the realm of sexual and affectional behavior.

PARENT-CHILD AND CHILD-PARENT FIXATION

By "fixation" is usually meant some compulsive, irrational, and maladaptive centering of attention and feeling on some object or activity. If one is "all bound up" in it, we say he has an obsession or mania. An example would be a golf addict who neglects his family and business for golf. If one were negatively fixated on golf, he would fear and hate it and make a nuisance of himself trying to break people of the bad habit of golfing.

If you have read the article referred to in footnote [13], you will understand what is meant by positive, negative, and ambivalent parent-child and child-parent fixation. The main thing to bear in mind is that the first term refers to the abnormal person. In parent-child fixation, it is the parent who is the emotionally unbalanced person, who exhibits the compulsive, irrational, unadjustive behavior. A child afflicted with such a parent is likely to respond to the social situation by developing a fixation on the parent, which of course may be positive (excessive love, identification, dependence) or negative (hate, rejection, rebellion, contempt) or ambivalent (a mixture of love and hate). You can see many possible combinations of these fixation patterns. There is very little scientific evidence regarding their number, their intensity, or their effects upon the developing personality of the child or upon his later life-adjustments. However, there is a good deal of common sense and case-study evidence that such relationships do exist and that they do influence later behavior especially with reference to marriage and parenthood.

You should be warned that people frequently use these terms very loosely and thus probably exaggerate (in thought) the prevalence, intensity, and after-effects of family fixations. We should be careful not to confuse normal, strong love and affection with fixation, whether between spouses or siblings or both. Most parents love their children very much and are loved deeply in return. This is not fixation. By fixation, we mean that the love or hate must be so obsessive, compulsive, and irrational that it produces maladjustment in the fixator and often in the fixated. The following remarks are tentative and deal with only a few of the more common forms of fixation and some of the more obvious (alleged) effects.

It is likely that parent-child fixation more often develops when there is discord or misunderstanding between the parents; also, and partly because of this, that mothers are fixators more often than fathers. If a man does not like his wife, he can more easily find an affectional or other substitute than can a woman who does not like her husband. He can have outside affairs, drink, play golf or poker, or devote himself to his business. Such opportunities are increasingly available to unhappy wives, of course. Often, however, such antagonistic parents, who may be unconscious of their dissatisfaction with each other, will consciously or unconsciously compete with each other for the affection and loyalty of their children. If there are two children, they may tacitly take one each. The result may be, let us say, that the mother has a positive fixation on her daughter, the father on his son (or vice versa), which the children reciprocate. This may result in the two children having negative fixations on each other, the father having a negative fixation on his daughter (who is "on her mother's side") and the mother having a negative fixation on her son ("papa's boy"). If children return the positive parental fixations, they may have negative fixations on the opposite-sexed parent. You can see how these patterns would vary if the parents should fixate the opposite-sex children; or if each parent should fixate both children; or if one parent only should fixate both, or only one, the other parent perhaps finding his substitute or escape from the family discord in some of the outside activities mentioned above. Probably in all such cases we would find more ambivalence than clear-cut cases of love and hate.

In all cases where both parents are competing for the love of the children, the mother has a great advantage in the earlier years. The fixations thus formed may last throughout the life of the child or result in adolescent rebellion, one outcome of which might be a transfer of the positive child-mother fixation to the father and the development of a negative child-mother fixation. Or, in rebelling against the mother, the child might become merely a normal person, which I suppose is what happens in most cases; or he might develop a negative attitude toward the mother and punish her by carousing, flunking, or irregular sex behavior, or in many other possible ways. He may also be punishing himself because he feels guilty for deserting and disturbing his mother. Similar patterns would develop, with differences of course, if the rebel were a daughter escaping from a fixating mother, or son or daughter escaping from a fixating father.

There is some evidence to support the belief that mother-child fixation is much more common than father-child fixation. Freudians believe reciprocal positive mother-son and father-daughter fixations are not only common but to some degree universal in all cultures and that all other types of fixation, positive, negative, and ambivalent, are unconscious transfers from these basic instinctual Oedipus and Electra complexes. My guess is that in our culture mothers fixate daughters more often and more intensely than they do sons; and fathers, sons. I also think the amount and intensity of parent-child and child-parent fixation is greatly exaggerated and is diminishing.

A parent-child fixation is thus a symptom of a personality defect in the parent which usually has its origin in the parent's childhood. Without taking the time to analyze how a positive mother-son fixation may have developed and how it may affect the mother (who is the maladjusted person), let us see how it may affect the child. She is abnormally fearful something may happen to him; she cannot bear to have him out of her sight; she makes all his decisions. Later, she cannot let him go away to school, or suffers terribly if he does; she cannot endure seeing him fall in love and get married — she breaks up his romances; if he does rebel and marry, she becomes the interfering mother-in-law and hates (often unconsciously) his wife. She may induce him to hate his father and avoid and fear all women except herself. She binds him to her with the silver cord, which should be called the rusty iron chain of perverted mother-love. She may permit him some male friends, though often she is jealous even of these. If she succeeds in isolating him from the opposite sex, she may lay the basis for later homosexual love — the only kind of affectional relationship of which he is capable. You can work out possible effects of similar mother-daughter fixation, and father-son, or father-daughter, whether positive or negative.

Young children are relatively defenseless against such monopolistic "smother-love." Our boy in the pattern described above may never grow up, may fail to attain the independent self-directing personality and emotional balance necessary for his various adult roles. He may become a permanent sissy; his decisions may always be colored by what mother will think; he cannot leave mother to go to college, or to a job, or to get married; or he may rebel against her by "raising Ned." If he marries, he may always be telling his wife "how mother does this" or "what mother thinks." You figure out how a positive mother-daughter fixation may affect the life-pattern of the girl.

Parents who have failed to achieve their life-goals sometimes try to do it vicariously through their children. This is called parental projection. For example, a mother who wanted to be a teacher but married unhappily instead, may try to compel one of her children to go into teaching, even though the child has no interest in teaching nor aptitude for it. Another form of projection is the attempt to make the child carry on the parent's work. This is probably more common in the case of father-son relations than in the other parent-child combinations. You can see that such parental projection would be more likely to occur in cases of parent-child fixation and that the fixating parent is compensating.

Most such projections probably do the children no harm if they are interested in what the parent wants them to do and have the necessary qualities for success. Most parents who have such ambitions for their children are able to adjust themselves to the situation if the children do not fall in with the plan. Some parents, however, are not able to subordinate their own desires to the best interests of the children. They compulsively and obsessively try to force the child to do what he cannot do or does not want to do. This may be one of the main sources of the "round-peg-square-hole" behavior so common in our society. The parent is more interested in himself than he is in the child. He tries to make the child like what the parent likes: he regiments him in recreation, religion, school, work — in everything. Thus the child has no sense of freedom and may fail to develop the habit of happiness so essential for later success in marriage and the other activities of adulthood.

Vicious Circles and Vicious Cycles

By a vicious circle we mean maladjustive behavior which is accentuated the longer it is practiced. A vicious cycle is similar except that it appears in successive or alternate generations.

Almost all types of defective personality definition may be vicious circles. Take the case of the smothering mother. The child is unable to do what other children do. This calls forth care, protection, and indulgence on the part of the mother, which makes the child still more dependent and inadequate: a vicious circle. If the child tries to escape the dominating mother by rebelling, he may do bad things. The worse he becomes, the more the mother suffers; the more she suffers, the worse he becomes. He feels guilty. He both hates and loves her (ambivalence), and often does things that hurt himself (one of the ways by which people try to relieve guilt-feelings). This also hurts her, which makes him feel more guilty, which makes him punish himself and her, more severely: a vicious circle.

Vicious circles are bad habits. They arise because the person is trying to meet some need, relieve some tension, solve some problem. They are bad because they do not work; the more they are repeated, the more automatic, compulsive, and maladjustive they become. They are not due to natural cussedness, or original sin, or any deliberate attempt of the child to make a nuisance of himself. They all have a history. If our analysis is correct, the causes are more often social than biological.

The real question is what to do about them. The best remedy is prevention. Many little habits of children which annoy parents are really trivial and will disappear as the child grows up unless the parent makes an issue out of them by nagging, punishing, shaming, and so on. If the child has his basic needs satisfied, many bad habits will never develop. If they do, the proper procedure is to ignore them if they are trivial, find out what need the child is trying to satisfy if they are serious, and then provide a socially approved substitute. Ordering and forbidding is usually ineffective; it merely aggravates the difficulty. Suggestion, indirection, substitution, diversion of attention, example, are better ways than bearing down on the child. Matter-of-fact, quiet, kindly, reasonable treatment will get better results than emotionally charged threats and angry punishment, whether physical or verbal. Excessive masturbation, for example, may be due to the fact that the child's natural curiosity about sex has never been satisfied; unhealthy attitudes toward sex may have been acquired from parents or others; he may have been prevented from learning how to satisfy his needs for excitement, adventure, recognition, and affection. Because his energy cannot express itself in satisfying interaction with others and socially approved manipulation of objects, it becomes centered on himself as an object; he manipulates himself rather than other objects and plays imaginary roles rather than real ones.

If vicious circles do develop and the parents do not know how to handle them, they should seek expert advice. Many parents are unable to recognize the existence of vicious circles, to say nothing of being able to analyze and remedy them. Often they themselves are an essential element in the problem. They cannot carry out the doctor's directions except by breaking their own vicious circles. Problem parents produce problem children; to cure the children the parents first must be cured.

There are at least two classes of vicious cycles: alternation and repetition. As an example of the first, let us take a child who has been the victim of severe and harsh discipline. He rebels against it and later coddles and indulges his children. They are inadequately socialized and suffer later in their play groups and social life, in school, in business, in marriage. So they discipline their children too much; the children hate them and rebel, and the vicious cycle is repeated. Extreme religiosity may thus produce extreme aversion to religion; drunkenness, teetotalism; thrift, wastefulness; love of school, hate of school; and so on till the next generation, when the opposite extreme develops.

The vicious repetition cycle also may be illustrated by harsh discipline. The child thus treated manages to make a fairly adequate adult adjustment. He now treats his own children the same way, on the theory that it was the harsh discipline which made him succeed. So with the Santa Claus myth, or baby talk, or any other type of behavior which the parent may have been able to take and still succeed but which may damage or ruin the child who is different from the parent or who has to adjust himself to changes in the culture or the family's status.

Vicious cycles are broken only when their victims are able to develop personalities which neither repeat the parental pattern nor react violently against it. Such adjustment is possible because we are able to learn by experience and through books, friends, teachers, scientific-mindedness, and fortunate group influences. All the factors that make for normal social adjustment are involved in breaking a vicious cycle.

THE PRINCIPLE OF SIMILARITY

Folklore and proverbs say, and many people believe, that opposites attract: tall men marry short women; the plump person wants a skinny spouse; blondes fall for brunettes; brilliant men prefer dumb wives. Here is a clear case of common sense that is mostly nonsense. When you begin to count cases, you soon see that the opposite is closer to the truth: people who are similar tend to marry, or at least a considerable degree of personal and cultural similarity is necessary for happy and successful marriage. (See the chapter on "How Mates Are Sorted.") As we have shown, the personality traits which make people like or dislike each other are largely learned in childhood. Even if some early patterns are later modified, often the change is only skin deep. In old age or in crises, the earlier patterns may reassert themselves and produce behavior which appears unaccountable.

For example, a man who had an intense positive mother-fixation as a child may rebel, marry, and be happy (apparently). However, in some crisis (death of a child, loss of position, trouble with his wife) he may run home to mother or take up some substitutive form of positive or negative compensation for his mother-fixation: drink, religion, club life, desertion, absorption in business, or what not. His wife may be totally unable to understand what has happened to make a man whom she thought she knew behave so strangely. Then there are people whose love affair goes awry and who marry someone the exact opposite of the first lover — "on the rebound," we say. Such marriages often are unhappy. We have very little tested scientific knowledge about such matters but we are beginning to know enough about them to make it a fruitful field for research.[21]

There are some happy marriages, of course, in which "opposites" do seem to attract or at least to get along. Take the case of a dominant male married to a submissive female, or vice versa. Both are inadequately socialized but their personality deficits complement each other by meeting each other's neurotic needs. An egocentric male who thinks he really is more clever than he is may require a beautiful but dumb wife whose relative inferiority continually reinforces his illusion. This may not be a good example of opposites attracting since our male in this case is really not too bright himself. Perhaps we can modify our principle of similarity by saying there are apparent exceptions to it in the case of people with personality quirks which are opposite but complementary. Two people who are similar in their abnormality — excessive egocentrism, for example — obviously will not be happy even if they marry. While the principle of similarity seems sound in general, for normal people, it obviously does not apply to all people. Most of the assorta-

[21] Merl E. Bonney, "Parents as Makers of Social Deviates," *Social Forces* (Oct., 1941), pp. 77–87; Arnold W. Green, "The Middle Class Male Child and Neurosis," *American Sociological Review* (June, 1946), pp. 31–41.

tive matings are due merely to proximity in social and geographical space. Well-to-do people marry well-to-do people because they are thrown with them; and so with the bright, the stupid, the educated, and the various religious, racial, and urban-rural classes. Catholics and Protestants may marry and be happy if they are sufficiently secularized or tolerant in their religious ideas so that the differences really do not mean much to them. It is the meaning of opposite traits that determines the outcome. Many people get into later marital trouble because they have underestimated the significance of the dissimilar personality traits of the other party. They are not as objective and secularized as they thought they were. Assortative mating, like family fixation, needs a great deal of intensive research before we can make valid generalizations.

MODIFICATION OF CHILDHOOD PATTERNS

Some readers may be disturbed because they feel that their chances for happy marriage are lessened because of early childhood experiences. If you should have such misgivings, remember that we have also emphasized that human nature is very plastic and capable of being changed. Man is a learner; he begins to learn before he is born and continues till he dies. By taking thought and proper action he can make many modifications in his behavior within the limits imposed by his biological nature and the culture within which he lives. There are almost infinite unrealized possibilities within these limits. These possibilities are greater, of course, for generations than for particular persons, but very few of us even remotely approach our limits of possible achievement.

By taking advantage of what we can learn from what others have learned, we can solve most of our problems fairly well and rear our own children better than we were reared. One whose parents were unhappily married and whose childhood was badly confused may marry and be happy and rear his children to be healthy and happy and socially well adjusted. We can break vicious circles and vicious cycles.

If you have suffered because of a parent fixation, you very probably will never fixate your children; you may even love them normally and constructively. If you were made miserable by irrational fears, threats, and erratic parental treatment, you may be honest and consistent and considerate in dealing with children. It is sometimes true that parents who had a bad break make the best of spouses and parents. They have a keen personal sense of what was wrong with their own childhood and protect their own children from a similar experience. Although they have recovered from their own maladjustment, they know at what cost this was done and are able to save their children from having to repeat their own struggle.

People who have had a bad start but make a strong finish are the real people. They have learned the kind of truth that makes us free; they help mankind to approach more closely his age-old goal of the good and more abundant life.

SELECTED READINGS

BALDWIN, BIRD J., and STECHER, LORLE I., *The Psychology of the Preschool Child* (New York: Appleton-Century, 1927).

BLATZ, WILLIAM E., and BOTT, HELEN, *Parents and the Preschool Child* (New York: Morrow, 1929).

BÜHLER, CHARLOTTE (PEARL GREENBERG and ROWENA RIPIN, trs.), *The First Year of Life* (New York: Day, 1930).

BURGESS, ERNEST W., and COTTRELL, LEONARD S., JR., *Predicting Success or Failure in Marriage* (New York: Prentice-Hall, 1939).

COOLEY, CHARLES H., *Human Nature and the Social Order* (New York: Scribner's, 1902).

DAVIS, EDITH A., *The Development of Linguistic Skill in Twins, Singletons with Siblings, and Only Children from Age Five to Ten Years* (Minneapolis: University of Minnesota Press, 1937).

DEWEY, EVELYN, *Behavior Development in Infants: A Survey of the Literature on Prenatal and Postnatal Activity, 1920–1934* (New York: Columbia University Press, 1935).

DUVALL, EVELYN RUTH, *Family Living* (New York: Macmillan, 1950).

GESELL, ARNOLD, et al., *The First Five Years of Life* (New York: Harper, 1940).

GESELL, ARNOLD, and ILG, FRANCES L., *The Child from Five to Ten* (New York: Harper, 1946).

LANDIS, JUDSON T. and MARY G., *Building a Successful Marriage* (New York: Prentice-Hall, 1948).

LEVY, JOHN, and MONROE, RUTH, *The Happy Family* (New York: Knopf, 1938).

LEWIS, M. M., *Infant Speech: A Study of the Beginnings of Language* (New York: Harcourt, Brace, 1936).

McCARTHY, DOROTHEA A., *The Language Development of the Preschool Child* (Minneapolis: University of Minnesota Press, 1929).

MEAD, GEORGE H., *Mind, Self, and Society,* Introduction by C. W. MORRIS, ed. (Chicago: University of Chicago Press, 1934).

NAGGE, JAMES WILLIAM, *Psychology of the Child: Mental and Physical Growth* (New York: Ronald Press, 1942).

PIAGET, JEAN, *The Language and Thought of the Child* (2nd ed., New York: Harcourt, Brace, 1932).

SHELDON, WILLIAM H., and STEVENS, S. S., *The Varieties of Temperament: A Psychology of Constitutional Differences* (New York: Holt, 1942).

SHIRLEY, MARY M., *The First Two Years: A Study of Twenty-five Babies* (Minneapolis: University of Minnesota Press, vol. I, 1931; vols. II, III, 1933).

SKIDMORE, REX A., and CANNON, ANTHON S., *Building Your Marriage* (New York: Harper, 1951).

TERMAN, LEWIS M., et al., *Psychological Factors in Marital Happiness* (New York: McGraw-Hill, 1938).

THOMAS, WILLIAM I., and THOMAS, DOROTHY SWAINE, *The Child in America* (New York: Knopf, 1928).

WALLER, WILLARD, rev. by REUBEN HILL, *The Family: A Dynamic Interpretation* (New York: Dryden Press, 1951).

W:NCH, ROBERT F., *The Modern Family* (New York: Holt, 1952).
YOUNG, KIMBALL, *Personality and Problems of Adjustment* (New York: Crofts, 1940).

TOPICS FOR DISCUSSION OR REPORTS

1. What similarities and differences are there in child personality development in the "upper" and "lower" classes in your community?
2. Criticize Mary Shirley's "Laws" (volume III, p. 216).
3. Report on the most interesting chapter in *The Child in America*. Why does it interest you? How much of it is still sound?
4. How many *kinds* of "sense of humor" can you think of? Illustrate each.
5. What vicious circles do you have? How did they develop? What ones have you "broken"?
6. What will you do (and not do) to your children that your parents did (and did not) do to you? Why, for each specific item?
7. List all the conflicts you can *within* and *between* the ten major institutions.
8. Why are young people more concerned about money (or are they?) than any other single factor (except love — or is it?) when they think about marriage?
9. Make a list of your ten best and ten worst personality traits. Get a close friend to do the same, i.e., list *your* traits, without knowing you have made such a list. Explain the differences between the lists.
10. Observe a five to nine months' old baby as much as you can. Is it human? Does it distinguish between its self and other selves? Does it talk? Does it vocalize?
11. What are your five most intense irrational fears? How did you get them? How do you think they will affect your behavior as spouse and parent?
12. Describe your sex education up to age twelve. How will you handle this problem with your children? Be specific — a complete program.
13. Read five articles on parent-child fixation written since 1945. What are the major agreements and disagreements between them?
14. Analyze the divorce that you know most about.
15. Analyze the most dramatic case of adolescent rebellion that you know about.
16. Write all the proverbs, adages, and wise-cracks you know (don't ask anyone, or "read up" on it) pertaining to love, marriage, and parent-child relations. Mark them "true," "false," or "partly true." Then write in some detail your reaction to your list.
17. How different (or similar) have the (boys) (girls) been in your three most intense love affairs, or "cases"? How do you explain this?
18. Did you ever imagine or wish that one of your parents was not really yours? How do you account for this?
19. Describe and try to explain the most unjust treatment you ever got from one of your parents; from a brother; a sister; a teacher.
20. Observe a kindergarten for several days. List the main adjustment problems. Is it likely that they are connected with conflicts between the home and school situations? Are there any differences between boys and girls in this respect?

Chapter Seven

Steps in Love and Courtship

JOSEPH K. FOLSOM

WHAT is true love? How can it be found? Should love be a prerequisite for marriage? *Must* its thrills and inspiration eventually wear off?

Such are the questions in the minds of young people facing marriage. This chapter will not provide ready-made answers but rather a background of information and suggestive ideas which will help the student work out his own answers. These, in the last analysis, must be individual.

We shall first analyze love psychologically, that is, mainly in terms of individual experience and behavior; then sociologically, that is, in terms of the group and the relations between persons. But both analyses will be sociological in a broader sense, namely in the sense that we shall recognize the constant influence of the cultural environment. By this we mean the general context of customs, mores, social values, and common ideas that surrounds every person and gives pattern to his development despite the enormous variations of personal circumstances.

THE PSYCHOLOGY OF LOVE

The Psychoanalytic Conception of Love

According to the psychoanalytic conception of love advanced by Freud and his disciples, all love is derived from one great source — the libido, a kind of reservoir of love energy which is constant within any one individual. The libido is said to have *cathexis* (attachment, concentration) on various objects. The average individual develops sequentially through several stages of cathexis: autoerotism, narcism (love of self), and object-cathexis (love of an outside object). The stage of object-cathexis may be subdivided into: first (although not in all cases), a love of the parent of one's own sex (homosexual stage); second, love of parent of opposite sex; and third, the mature love of an outside person of the opposite sex.

A person can have his libido development arrested at any of these stages, and become fixated upon any object. Thus the narcist, whose love of others is said to be only in reflection of self-love, the homosexual, and the man who cannot fall in love with a marriageable woman because of emotional ties to his mother, represent arrests of development. Likewise, a person's love may become stubbornly fixated upon a person of opposite sex who cannot or will not marry him. Normally the libido moves on or shifts to a new object, till one is found which is completely satisfying. Love which cannot shift itself when circumstances render its present object hopeless is regarded as neurotic.

All cultures have an incest-taboo which not only forbids sexual relations with parents or other near-of-kin, but may make the individual ashamed of feeling even a desire for such intimacies. Normally parent fixation comes at an age before the sex drive is developed in its mature specialized form, and is outgrown before adolescence with its maturing sexuality. Yet many, and perhaps to some extent all persons, experience some conflict between the incest-horror taught by society and their inner feelings toward their parents. To escape this shame or horror they repress into the "unconscious" any sexual feeling toward parents, and this repression is a common source of neuroses or nervous disorders. Likewise, homosexual urges are often repressed, with resulting emotional disturbances, because our society also places a strong shame-and-horror taboo upon this kind of love.

Oedipus was the mythological Greek king who unwittingly killed his father and married his mother. On discovering these facts he destroyed his eyesight in horror and shame and abdicated his throne. This legend is regarded by Freud as symbolizing a common, if not universal, experience in the development of human beings. The mother-fixated man is said to have an Oedipus complex (see Chapter Six, pp. 197–199). The woman whose love is fixated on her father is said to have an Electra complex (from the heroine of tragedies by Sophocles and Euripides). These two complexes constitute the "family romance." When serious and intense they are usually repressed, and give rise to various emotional maladjustments whose true origin is not recognized without the help of psychoanalysis.[1]

A Conception of Love in Terms of the Learning Process

The actual observations made by psychoanalysts upon the development of human personalities are of outstanding scientific value. But the language and figures of speech used by this school of thinkers to explain their findings are in many ways misleading.

Years before psychoanalysis came to the fore, more orthodox psychologists had worked out the basic principles of *learning*. A school called "behaviorism" later came into being and pictured more clearly the physiological details of the learning process. Yet psychologists busied themselves so much with the observation of minute details that they left the really important problems to be shouldered by the psychoanalysts. This writer has great respect for the actual findings of psychoanalysis but prefers to describe them in more parsimonious terms.

The psychoanalytic conception is too hydraulic: it makes one think of a fluid under pressure in pipes, with alternative outlets; of an increase of flow through one channel with a mathematically corresponding decrease through another channel. This conception is misleading in several ways.[2]

First, the various behavior patterns called love do not originate in one homogeneous form of mental or emotional energy but rather in several dis-

---

[1] J. C. Flügel, *A Psychoanalytic Study of the Family* (London: Wolff, 1926); William Healy, August F. Bronner, and Anna M. Bowers, *The Structure and Meaning of Psychoanalysis* (New York: Knopf, 1930).

[2] Joseph K. Folsom, *Social Psychology* (New York: Harper, 1931), chaps. 2–5.

tinct drives and reflexes. These develop through maturation and learning into an integrated system of behavior, but they are not integrated at the beginning. Second, the sequences of cathexes, the shifting of love reactions from one object to another, are determined by external circumstances as well as by inner development. Certain types of experience are well-nigh universal, such as finding familiar persons after being alone and frightened, enjoying contested or forbidden fruits through temporary hiding, discovering the different sensory qualities of the sexes and different individuals. Other experiences are almost universal within a given culture, such as the stereotyped pictures of male and female attractiveness displayed as art and advertising. Still others are individually peculiar. Third, there is no constant quantity of love in general. Love does not have its own special budget of bodily or mental energy. The functioning of the sexual organs may have upper and lower limits of frequency, but these limits are wide, and sexual excitement is only a part of the total love complex. Fourth, the cultural environment restrains and directs the development of love, as Freud has pointed out, but it does so in a more positive and specific way than Freud would admit, and different cultures produce very different results. The newer psychoanalytic thinkers, for example, Horney, Fromm, and Kardiner, recognize the different patterns of personality and of love produced by various cultures.[3]

Needs, Learning, and Desires

Let us bear in mind the *creative* principle which pervades all nature — that elements combine to form a compound or a whole which has very different characteristics from any of the elements which enter into it. A rose is made, chemically, of two invisible gases and charcoal. It nourishes upon soil and manure. Yet it is still a rose. A beautiful poem may be written by a man when he is drunken and insane. Nevertheless it is a beautiful poem. Love, even though it is built out of physiological processes, is nevertheless love!

The organism, animal or human, is in many ways like a machine. It is a machine which operates in such a way as to perpetuate itself as long as possible and to reproduce itself. In other words, it "lives." Its continued operation requires that the needs which develop during this process of living shall make themselves felt, and thereby cause the organism to change its operation in such ways as to satisfy the needs. And so it has developed sense organs to feel the needs, and a nervous system to carry these reports of need, organize them, and deliver them to reaction organs (muscles and glands) which act in such ways as to bring about the needed changes. This total process, involving transmission through the nervous system, is called "behavior."[4] The total behavior system may be analyzed into three parts. (1) The appetitive system

---

[3] Abram Kardiner and Ralph Linton, *The Individual and His Society* (New York: Columbia University Press, 1939).

[4] "Life" is more than "behavior." It includes vital processes not involving transmission through the nervous system, such as metabolism and growth. The entire living process of plants is non-behavioral in the strict sense.

takes care of chemical shortages or surpluses, satisfies needs arising within the life process itself. It includes feeding, drinking, excreting, warmth-seeking, resting or sleeping, and sexual excitation. (2) The defensive system takes care of outward menaces, satisfies emergency needs created by the environment. It includes various patterns of withdrawing, rejecting, struggling, and escaping movements, with inner visceral reactions designed to lend all possible power to those movements. (3) There is a great volume of random, surplus activity, involving every muscle and organ, which at first is completely chaotic but comes gradually to be organized and trained into more specific patterns in the service of the appetitive and defensive systems.

The felt needs which arouse the appetitive system are generally pleasant while they are being slowly reduced or changed or while there is prospect of their satisfaction; hence there are many and often prolonged periods of pleasure during the operation of appetitive behavior. When it is blocked, its feelings (hunger, sex need, etc.) become unpleasant and intensify the drives toward finding satisfaction.

On the other hand, the felt needs which arouse defensive behavior must have quick and immediate relief, or else they lead to strong unpleasant emotions: anguish (the emotional element of pain), disgust, anger, or fear. Since there is commonly some delay and frustration in meeting these needs, defensive behavior is attended by many periods of unpleasant emotion. These defensive and unpleasant emotions always have the immediate right of way in the nervous system over the appetitive and pleasant feelings. If a fear stimulus is present together with a sex stimulus or hunger, the fear will always prevail — until it is substantially relieved. Fright quickly stops digestion and produces temporary sexual impotence. The appetitive and defensive systems operate through two structurally distinct branches of the nervous system.

Whatever object or situation is frequently perceived while needs are being reduced or satisfied becomes an object of desire; that is, the organism tries to approach, possess, or create such an object or situation. This is the principle of satisfaction, which is the key to the learning process. We tend to continue or repeat that which was satisfying or that which immediately accompanied satisfying experience. Through this process the child comes to love his mother as an object.

All learned connections or linkages (conditioned responses, etc.) are sometimes termed "habits." But the word "habit" has a tradition about it which is misleading. It tends to imply to most readers that repetition is the main principle of learning and personality formation. Practice does make perfect, but it does not always make enthusiasm for the thing practiced. The boy who attends military school learns military habits, that is, he can perform certain series of movements more and more quickly and accurately; he learns to carry out orders with a certain form and tempo. But "habit" includes not only the linkage of one movement to the next but also the less obvious emotional linkage by which the whole series is started or stopped. If our boy does not learn the simple habit of being pleased or satisfied with military life, all his practice in the detail of its execution will be comparatively useless as soon as he gets into a nonmilitary environment. Whole masses of laboriously acquired habits, such as playing the piano or speaking a foreign language, may be neglected and unused for years because we no longer gain satisfaction from using them. One of the major contributions of psychoanalysis is that it gives this principle of satisfaction, as distinguished from the principle of mere repetition, its proper importance by showing how it controls the major trends and decisions of the individual's life.

The Feeling Elements of Love and Their Origins

"Love" is a broad, loose term for several different patterns of behavior. These patterns belong mostly to the appetitive system and to surplus activity which is brought into its service, and they are all pleasurable, except under prolonged deprivation of objects. They are all learned patterns, to the extent at least of having discovered persons as sources of satisfaction and hence of having developed desires which have persons as objects. "Love" may be broken down and the elements classified in many different ways, with as much or as little detail as we wish. This writer has found helpful a simple analysis which considers first the feelings or emotional states which are involved in love experiences, and second, the objects and situations which arouse these feelings.

Three main types of feeling are involved in love. (1) The first type of feeling we shall call *tenderness*. It seems to involve sensations arising from the skin, particularly that of the chest, face, and inner surface of the arms,[5] and its motor expression or drive is toward skin contacts with the object, with light pressure and slow gentle movements. The feelings involved in nursing or being nursed, cuddling, and the nonerotic kiss may be placed under this heading. These reactions form a group which is allied with the biological functions of feeding the infant and protecting the child or weaker person. Probably the feelings in the protégé or nursling are somewhat different from those in the protector or mother, and this might be the basis for a subclassification. Followers of Rank lay stress upon the supposed feelings of the fetus in utero. There seems to be a common denominator of all these feelings so far as we can observe, imagine, or record them: pleasure associated with sensations of light, warmth, and restful contact.

(2) Second is *erotic feeling,* also known as *eroticism,* sexual excitement, lust, or just plain "sex." Probably what many people call "physical attraction" belongs here. This feeling seems located primarily in the genital areas, although some introspectors report that it spreads during the extreme excitement of sexual intercourse until the whole body seeems to tingle with it. It can rise to higher intensities than can tenderness, and its drive is toward a contact involving heavier pressures and more or less friction, particularly with the genital areas. It arises in childhood long before the sex organs are fully matured. It is accompanied by an increased blood supply to the sex organs, but the feeling may be present for some moments before tumescence or erection takes place.

(3) The third type of feeling is a very broad category which we may call

---

[5] Floyd W. Allport speaks of "sensitive zones" and "sensitive zone reflexes"; *Social Psychology* (Boston: Houghton Mifflin, 1924), pp. 67–69.

joy. Its prototype is seen in the gleeful delight of the young child when surprised by finding a lost toy or a person who is playfully hiding from him. Feelings in this group do not seem to be tied up with skin sensations. They are aroused by visual and auditory perceptions and olfactory and muscular sensations; as personality develops, they become linked very much to mental images and ideas. Introspection does suggest a localization of joyful feelings in the interior of the chest and partly in the muscles.[6] A joyous person tends to breathe deeply and sometimes rapidly, and often feels a pleasant muscular urge to run and jump ("exultation," "going wild," etc.). Laughter, and even weeping, are other expressions. Some of these reactions, especially those which are called "excitement" (heart acceleration, etc.) belong to the defensive system. But they operate under such conditions that they are pleasant rather than disagreeable. Joy involves a great deal of random or surplus behavior. It is often an experience of sudden relief from anger, fear, or anguish, occurring when these defensive reactions have achieved a sudden success. The most intense joys are obtained by subjecting the organism to some form of tension or "suspense" with some unpleasant feelings, and then quickly changing the situation to one of pleasure-producing stimuli (the roller-coaster pattern). The sudden redirection of energy takes the form of laughter, shouting, dancing, and other surplus movements, sometimes weeping — all quite pleasant.

When the source of joy is something upon which we must concentrate with eyes, ears, or thinking processes, the reaction is likely to be less violent in the muscular realm but perhaps even more intense as to visceral reactions or inner feelings. Of this character are the "serenity" and "ecstasy" of contemplating something beautiful or something totally satisfying to the whole personality. These feelings sometimes take the form of "thrills," which seem to be some kind of reaction in the chest or abdomen, often accompanied by a moderate muscular tonus and extreme alertness of the sense organs.

Feelings of the class called "joy" are especially characteristic of "romantic love." This supreme passion is a total love containing also tenderness and eroticism, but with the latter held in leash. Quite significantly, romantic love is said to be in the heart. This writer elsewhere has called it "cardiac-respiratory love."

Weeping and tears are falsely conceived by most persons, who regard them as a danger signal in others and as something to be ashamed of in themselves. Indeed, laughter and weeping are close together in pattern and easily changed, one into the other. Weeping is not an accompaniment of the most intense period of suffering or unpleasantness but is, rather, characteristic of the "coming-out-of-it" stage. It indicates that the tension may have been reduced and the person is already on the way toward joy or calm. Tears are emotional convalescence.[7] If one can accept them in himself, and not develop secondary shame or guilt reactions, they can be a source of real pleasure. This

---

[6] Joseph K. Folsom, *The Family: Its Sociology and Social Psychiatry* (New York: Wiley, 1934), pp. 68–69. The term "cardiac-respiratory love" is applied to certain among the joyful feelings.

[7] Frederick L. Lund, *Emotions* (New York: Ronald Press, 1939), p. 305.

idea is contrary to Anglo-Saxon culture, but we are seeking to understand realities. Some other cultures, especially the Russian, tend to accept the "enjoyment of tears" as natural and therapeutic.

On the borderline between tears and cheerful joy there is a feeling which is profoundly moving and inspiring. It is found in homesickness or nostalgia as well as in love of a person. This feeling is especially apt to be attached to a love-object of long acquaintance. We might call it "nostalgic love." Then there is a gay and playful feeling which enters into many, and perhaps at times all love relations. There is the calm pleasure which we call "sense of security" and which is commonly produced by the mere presence of friends, relatives, or persons upon whom we are dependent, without excitement or physical contact. There is the outburst of grateful feeling which occurs when the protector has rescued us when we were in fear or other suffering. There is the excitement of falling in love with a new person, and the deeper, richer excitement which occurs at the height of romantic love. It is impossible here to describe or classify all these types of joy adequately in terms of feeling; hence we have noted them partially in terms of the situations which commonly arouse them. We must remember, however, that the linkage of any feeling to any situation is a matter of individual learning. A description of a given situation or object may recall different feelings to different persons, while any carefully described feeling will not suggest the same situation or object to all persons.

We have, then, tenderness, possibly of two or more kinds, erotic feeling, and joy of several kinds. When strong feelings of all these three types are integrated and directed toward the same object and that object is a person, we have total love, or the state known as "being in love." In this state, the several feelings reinforce one another. The keystone, however, is the joy element. Joy is aroused to an intense pitch by the very idea of the tender and erotic relationships even when those feelings themselves are not present in high degree. Eroticism is often held in the background — sometimes merely anticipated or deferred — and the present concentration is upon the sheer delight of contemplating the experience. One kisses one's beloved, and there is a momentary tenderness and perhaps erotic feeling, but the chief pleasure comes from the thought that "she (or he) really kissed me"; it is a response to anticipation and memory and imagination more than to present sensations.

The Objects of Love Feelings

The feelings which enter into love may become linked to any stimulus itself not linked to defensive behavior or unpleasant emotions, which, as we have seen, always hold right of way over appetitive behavior and pleasant emotion. One can fondle a well-worn smoking jacket with a feeling of tenderness; one can arouse erotic feelings through mere friction; and one can feel rapturous joy on hearing a symphony. Indeed, a child may cry out with delight when his favorite dish appears, "I love ice cream!" Yet for our purposes here, let us reserve the word "love" for cases where a person (other than self), either directly or through some symbol, is the object of the feeling.

When we say that love has an object, we are thereby implying that love is learned and not inborn. The capacity to have the feelings of love is of course inborn. Also, the linkage of these feelings to certain simple stimuli is inborn. A stimulus is any condition which produces a sensation; it may be merely noise or light or warmth. But an object is something which has some external unity, which the subject must learn to perceive and recognize even though it sends forth different combinations of stimuli at different times. The object must be sensed in several different settings, and its recognition thus requires learning or conditioning. The infant is born with a tendency to enjoy milk and warmth, but there is nothing *in him* at birth which predisposes him to love his mother rather than some other similarly behaving animal. But that part of his environment which is his mother has characteristics which will almost inevitably cause her to become a perceived object and a loved object. So, also, there is no "instinct" to love the opposite sex as such (unless, perhaps, in some animals smell furnishes a clue to its identity). Young human beings have their erotic impulses guided toward the opposite sex by teachings of their elders. They have to learn to identify the opposite sex — and this requires learning many visual details which vary with costume. Most people do finally achieve heterosexual love. Even if this outcome were absolutely universal, however, as it decidedly is not, such heterosexuality would not be proved inborn or instinctive. Certain linkages are universally learned.[8]

A love-object may be a specific person, or any person of a given class. In many persons there is a tendency to feel some tenderness toward almost any child who might fit into a broad description. Men in a frontier community may tend to feel erotic toward almost any woman.

To say that a given person is the love-object and to state which of the feelings are involved, and how much of each, does not tell the whole story. The object always is perceived in some setting, and often through some indirect medium. Tenderness may be aroused by the picture of one's absent parent or spouse. Erotic feeling may sometimes require actual touch; at other times the mere sight of the exciting person is sufficient; sometimes a mental image briefly dwelt upon serves to arouse the feeling. The joy element may be aroused to a high degree by a telegram coming from one's beloved announcing his or her forthcoming arrival at the station.

A given object may be linked to only one of the types of love feeling, or to two, or to all. After a person has experienced total love, the feelings themselves tend to become interlinked through the object as a "bridge," so that in the future there may be an increased tendency for any object of partial love to become an object of total love. This is the natural course of development, but it may be blocked by personal or cultural inhibitions. Our traditional Euro-American culture has tended to prevent the natural integration of love feelings in the male. It has been subtly but effectively suggested to him that he would not feel tenderness toward the prostitute or

[8] A naive observer seeing *all* the automobiles emerging from a certain country road covered with blotches of mud might reason that the cars were all made that way. On studying further he would learn that the uniformity he observes lies in the environment and not in the nature of cars.

other woman who aroused extreme erotic feeling, and that toward his wife he should feel great tenderness but only a restrained eroticism.[9] Yet when a man is emancipated from this tradition he finds it very easy and natural to love the same woman with both extreme tenderness and extreme eroticism, and finds that each feeling reinforces the other. A pair of unmarried lovers caress each other with the intention of indulging only their tender feelings, when suddenly they find themselves consumed with erotic desire. A married couple at the height of sexual excitement find themselves suddenly overwhelmed by a feeling of tenderness, and suspend the erotic process for a few moments in order to concentrate upon that tender feeling.

In all cultures, however, including that of our most uninhibited social sets, there is an incest-taboo which prevents tenderness from becoming erotic in the case of a brother-sister or equivalent relationship. Some cultures prevent brother-sister incest by tabooing even ordinary social contacts and tender expression between them. Among the Trobrianders it is bad form to invite a man on the same expedition with his sister or any female related to him through the female line. With his father's sister or other patrilineally related females he may have great freedom, including sometimes sexual intercourse. In our culture we encourage a strong brother-sister tenderness and inhibit the erotic feeling which might develop out of this by inculcating a deep inner horror of such incest.

Our traditional Puritan culture also introduced inhibitions which prevented the integration of love feelings in women. In them eroticism was discouraged much more than in men. Yet many found it, sometimes through homosexual relations or autoeroticism; sometimes it was unexpectedly aroused by the mere presence of some male who would be unacceptable as a husband. Sometimes the erotic remained quite generally repressed beneath a barrier of shame and fear. When erotic feeling did arise, instead of reinforcing joy, it led to its inhibition. The joyful feeling of sheer delight in the presence or companionship of a man was discouraged from mixing with sexual feelings. Yet the natural development is toward such a mixture.

Thus cultural values and taboos guide the love feelings toward objects and away from objects. Freud acknowledged this point, but failed to elaborate on it with the specific detail which is warranted. The development of the average person's love life is not so much a process of inner maturation as it is the acquisition of a cultural pattern from without, with the specific details and objects supplied by his peculiar individual experience. The total experience of each individual is a unique history, duplicated by no one else, not even a twin brother or sister brought up with him.

In general, people finally marry partners who in most respects resemble themselves more than does a person selected at random. In some traits there is a mere random degree of resemblance. In no traits has it been found that

[9] Perhaps it would be more accurate to say that the traditional male did occasionally develop extreme erotic feeling toward his wife, at least enough to permit sexual intercourse, but that he was not free to make use of many facilitating stimuli which occurred in purely erotic relations. The couple had to behave in a restrained manner, with a certain coolness and modesty even during sexual love-making, with the result that copulation was either less frequent or less satisfying than it would otherwise have been.

people tend to marry their opposites, despite popular myths to that effect, except that they usually marry the opposite sex.[10]

Much ink has been used in writing books about how man's love differs from woman's love. There do appear to be certain inborn sex differences in the rhythm of sexual desire, in the ease of its stimulation, and in various glandular and emotional factors. But these factors have about as much bearing upon total love life as the particular wood out of which a piano is built has to do with the tune which is being played upon it. Most of the folklore and literature about sex differences in love is a commentary upon some particular culture with its differential education of the sexes, and not as it purports to be a description of biological sex differences. Men and women are innately capable of the same feelings and the same object-attachments.

The Love Focus: Ambivalence, Fetishes, Idealization

We often do not love a whole person, and we seldom love him in complete independence of the environmental background of our relationship. Figure 1 illustrates this. The inner rectangle represents a person who is a love-object

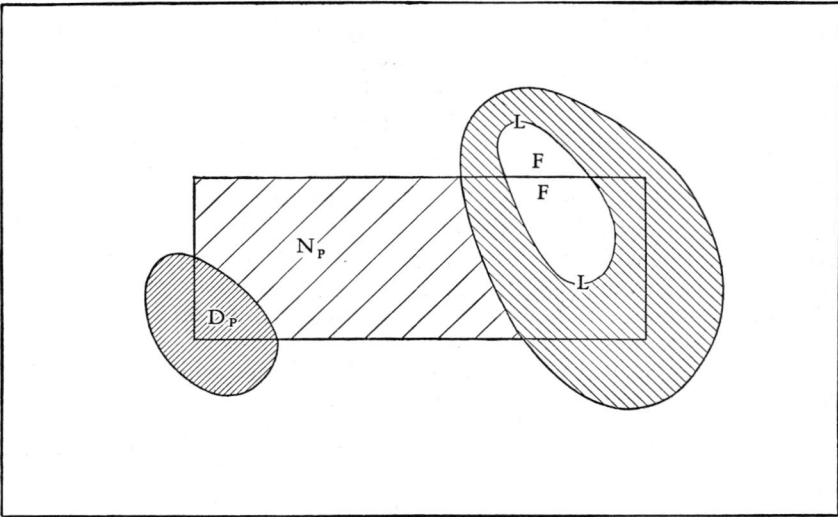

FIGURE 1. HOW SOCIAL SITUATIONS AFFECT AMBIVALENCE

The outside rectangle represents the environmental background of a love-object; the small rectangle represents the love-object itself. LL, the part of the whole situation which arouses strong love feelings. N_p, the part of the love-object neutral to the observer's feelings. D_p, source of unpleasant feelings. FF, the love focus.

of the observer. The remaining area of the outer rectangle represents the background. The unshaded ellipse LL represents the part of the whole situation which arouses strong love feelings. It is analogous to the area illuminated

[10] See pp. 261–262 for fuller data on homogamy.

by a spotlight. Some of the person-object and also some of his circumstantial environment are illuminated by our love. On occasion, these environmental features could serve as a bridge to transfer love to another person. A part of the person-object, represented by the light shading N_p, is neutral to our feelings. Still another part, represented by the dark shading D_p, may be a source of unpleasant feelings. Of course these "parts" are not meant in a spatial, physical sense. They are circumstances or characteristics. The focal bright area (LL) may be structured, with items of greatest potency at the center (FF) and somewhat less essential items toward the periphery. We may speak of the focus of a person's love as this area or group of characteristics and circumstances (some of them concretely tied up with a given object-person, others somewhat abstract and separable from the object) which has greatest potency to arouse his love feelings.

Fiction is replete with stories of men who loved peasant girls or South Sea maidens but found that their love waned when they brought them into a different environment. A wife may love three fourths of her husband, while the one fourth of him which is drunken, abusive, or flirtatious not only leaves her love cold but rouses her anger feelings to considerable pitch.

The term "ambivalence" is frequently used by psychologists to denote the existence of opposite feelings toward the same object. This is often treated as an example of the mysterious complexity of the human mind and as evidence of the need for the intricate concepts of psychoanalysis to unravel it. The matter might be much more simply conceived, however, by analyzing external objects and situations. It may be that the problem is mainly there. The writer's conception is that we do not feel love and hate toward the same identical segment of reality. If we dislike some particular group of personal characteristics or circumstances, we come to enjoy them only by re-education (reconditioning), which takes time. But if at the very next moment we find ourselves pleased by apparently the same object, then we are really seeing the object in a different setting, we are focusing our attention on a different piece of the larger situation.

If we are compelled to look at the larger picture which contains both pleasure-giving and annoying features and cannot narrow our attention, then our reaction tends to become either pleasant or unpleasant, and the unpleasantness, except when it is at a low intensity, has the power to dominate and drive out the pleasure. The two do not readily mix.

A young woman was debating whether to marry the man who for some time had been courting her. When she saw him as someone who loved her, a kind, dependable person who would tolerate her faults, take her away from the boredom of living with her mother, make possible a "nice" wedding and a new social prestige among her friends, and save her from the danger of becoming an old maid, she was joyful and eager. But when her attention turned to the facts that this man had many annoying, untidy relatives, that he was careless with money, especially through overgenerosity to friends who imposed upon him and would probably intrude themselves frequently in their new home, and when she compared his patient but undramatic love-making with that of a more "glamorous" man who had formerly been interested in her, she felt anxiety and her love was cooled.

The several types of love feeling may have somewhat different foci, although concentrated upon the same object sufficiently to make total love possible. To develop total love to the utmost, it would be helpful if each could know specifically the foci of the other's feelings. Often the lover is in serious doubt. If the woman, for example, wishes to awaken the maximum tenderness in the man, shall she behave somewhat like a child, or be somewhat motherly? When erotic feeling is in order, shall she dress to approximate some of the females pictured in *Esquire,* or shall she "go peasant"? If she wants to awaken the supreme thrill of joy, shall she keep him in suspense about a date and then surprise him with a sudden and eager Yes; or shall she keep him always feeling secure, and contrive many meetings in the moonlight?

The answers to these questions are individual; let not anyone be guided by generalized "advice to the lovelorn" or armchair statements about what "most men like" or "the way to get a woman." The way to one man's heart may be through his stomach, but to another's it may lie through his nose, his eyes — or even through his intellect! Popular literature advises men that women prefer the masterly and dominating male, but men will do better to study individual women. Of course each person has limits to the traits he can exhibit. He must be himself; otherwise he may purchase temporary love at the expense of later disillusionment. But each person has a certain range of behavior and appearances consistent with his personality.

Specialized foci of erotic feeling are often called fetishes. In extreme cases a fetish may be preferred to a person-object. Thus there are some men who are sexually more excited by a woman's handkerchief or highheeled shoe than by the whole body or personality of any particular woman.[11] These cases are rare. Much more common are cases of mere erotic emphasis upon some part of the body or clothing or some type of behavior which, if the accompanying desire is gratified by the loved person, only serves to intensify total love for that person. Sometimes ideas and total situations may play the role of fetishes. One subject reported an erotic feeling from the sight of a particular locale along a familiar road, another from the idea of a man and woman working together as equals upon an intellectual task, quite apart from the image of particular persons. Fetishism applies also to the noneroeotic love feelings. It is the "irrational" element in falling in love as when one "falls for" a certain gesture, odor, or tone of voice.[12]

Love brings with it a tendency to idealize the object and to become blind to characteristics which otherwise would be annoying or disturbing. One should be aware of his blind spots in contemplating his beloved. Yet sometimes the outside observer may think there is blindness when the lover has really acquired a positive attachment to the supposedly unpleasant trait. Characteristics which are neutral or only superficially annoying may become reconditioned into pleasure stimuli by the positive power of the love.

Disillusionment may be due not only to the cessation of a blindness but also to the appearance of some trait which the loved one had really kept in

---

[11] For an illustration of compulsion in love focus see the next chapter, pp. 248–249.
[12] See Vernon Grant, "A Fetishistic Theory of Amorous Fixation," *Journal of Social Psychology* 30 (1949), pp. 17–37.

concealment during an earlier period. Again, it may be due to an actual change of the loved one in a direction displeasing to the lover.

Time Sequence of Feelings: Love Histories

The so-called "realistic" theory to the effect that any given love relationship must blossom and then decline has many supporters. One person put it this way: Love is like an arrow shot high into the air. If the initial force is great enough, the projectile may not come down to earth until death. If the initial force is weak then the lovers outlive their love.

To guess the future of a love relation from the intensity or quality of feeling at its high point is impossible. When a person puts his hand on his chest and solemnly avers "I am in love," we may as well rate it 100 per cent. Yet he cannot mathematically compare this with a former love. It is merely that he has an "all-out" feeling, perhaps like that of former occasions, and the intensity is probably as great as his physiological constitution and health at the time will allow. To be sure, the lover may recognize a difference in the quality or proportion of the different feelings between this and former loves. But all this comparison furnishes no clue as to the future outcome.

The only way to guess the outcome is to consider the personalities and the circumstances rather than to weigh the feelings. The present feelings *will* change; that is sure. Their changes will depend upon factors entirely outside the feelings themselves.

In Chapter Eight (pp. 268–274) are given the results of the best prediction studies now available as to the success or failure of marriage. These studies attempt to predict total happiness in marriage, and not precisely the feelings of love between the partners; the predictions depend mainly upon the separate characteristics and backgrounds of the two persons and not upon their similarity, dissimilarity, or their feelings or relations to each other.

Jessie Bernard has shown that happiness in marriage tends gradually to decline with the years, reaching a low point on the average at about eleven years after marriage, a still deeper low point at about twenty-three years, and then rising somewhat in old age.[13] Here again we are dealing with marital happiness, which is always love plus other factors. Sometimes the other factors constitute a "minus" influence which detracts from the love. We might be more intelligent in planning for marital happiness if we knew more about the spontaneous course of love by itself. To date it has not been feasible to isolate this phenomenon from its institutional context. Love is everywhere culturally channelized and controlled.

Hamilton found that of 1358 love affairs reported by his 200 mature subjects 15 per cent led to marriage; 26 per cent were terminated by external circumstances such as spatial separation, death, marriage to another person, interference of third persons; 54 per cent were terminated by their own weaknesses (dissatisfactions, lack of reciprocity, quarrels, transfer of affection to another person apart from marriage, drifting apart); and 4 per cent were still

[13] "Factors in the Distribution of Success in Marriage," *American Journal of Sociology*, 40 (1934), pp. 49–60.

in effect. But the sample included many adolescent affairs. Only 14 per cent of all the affairs involved complete sexual intercourse, and 34 per cent were without any demonstration of affection.[14]

Kirkpatrick and Caplow have provided some most interesting data as the result of a questionnaire answered by 399 University of Minnesota students, describing 896 "serious love affairs."[15] At the time of the report about 6 per cent of all those affairs had developed into engagement or marriage, 22 per cent were still continuing but without engagement or marriage, and 72 per cent had terminated. In the standard instructions, four grades of emotion were named: "dislike," "indifference," "attraction," "love." The "regular" curves for the terminated affairs ended somewhere near the point of "indifference." Questions about the degree of physical intimacy were deliberately avoided. By selecting ready-made curves or drawing in their own curves, the students indicated that 69 per cent of the terminated affairs were of the "regular" type (gradual rise to a peak followed by a gradual fall of emotion). Eleven per cent were of the "cyclical" type (several ups and downs of feeling); 17 per cent were of irregular types (such as long plateaus of "attraction" preceded or followed by a peak of "love," or a dip into "dislike" followed by a rise to "love"). Three per cent were represented by a straight line, meaning the same level of emotion throughout the duration. Of all the definitely specified causes assigned for the break-up of affairs, 42 per cent were "mutual loss of interest," 46 per cent were the interest of *one* party in a third person, 12 per cent the influence of parents or friends. There were considerable sex differences here, to be described later.

Four types of readjustment after the break in the affair were distinguished. (1) The majority (59 per cent) showed a simple, slow, and steady further decline of feeling; (2) about 15 per cent showed an upsurge of affection for the lost love-object after the break; (3) about 11 per cent reported a sudden drop to "dislike"; (4) about 15 per cent reported several ups and downs before a dead level of indifference was reached. Sex differences in the features so far mentioned were relatively small. The most common emotional state after the break was "mixed regret and relief" (21 per cent of responses). Other feelings included "indifferent," "relieved," "hurt," "satisfied." Only 5 per cent of the responses were "bitter," 3 per cent "angry," 3 per cent "crushed." Women more often reported "hurt" and "crushed," men more often "indifferent" or "satisfied," but there were no important sex differences in any of the other feelings. On the whole, the evidence "suggests that at least half the students' love affairs investigated do not involve serious emotional traumas."

In one study involving one thousand engaged couples, it was found that

[14] G. V. Hamilton, *A Research in Marriage* (New York: Boni, 1929), chap. 10.
[15] Clifford Kirkpatrick and Theodore Caplow, "Courtship in a Group of Minnesota Students," *American Journal of Sociology,* 51 (Sept., 1945), pp. 114–125; and "Emotional Trends in the Courtship Experience of College Students as Expressed by Graphs with Some Observations on Methodological Implications," *American Sociological Review,* 10 (Oct., 1945), pp. 619–626. Through their consistency with verbal evidence and other results, the graphic techniques of curve-selecting and curve-drawing to describe emotional experience were found to have satisfactory validity.

about 24 per cent of the men and 36 per cent of the women had broken one or more previous engagements. About 15 per cent later broke their current engagements.[16] Broken engagements result from causes which may be classified as superficial attraction, separation, parental influence, cultural divergence, and major personality problems. Under cultural divergence may be placed the case in which one partner is in transition from a lower to a higher social class. Personality problems include cases where a person is prone to fall in love with someone whose characteristics he does not really wish in a married partner; such as "the young man who bitterly resents the continued domination of his mother, but who becomes engaged to a domineering woman, only to break the engagement at the last minute." [17]

In a study of college girls, Albert Ellis found substantial positive correlations among these variables: early beginning, frequency, and intensity of love attachments, and strong sex desires.[18] Seventy-three per cent of 500 girls reported that they "usually" remained infatuated for less than a year, 42 per cent that they usually remained in love less than a year. But when considering the *most-loved* male so far in their lives, the median subject at the time of reporting had been in love or infatuated with him for at least two years; 36 per cent were at the moment engaged or married to this man, an additional 43 per cent were still on friendly terms with him, and only 21 per cent had ceased contact with him. As a result of this greatest love 70 per cent were "very" happy; 50 to 70 per cent had increased ambition and energy, no desire to hurt the partner or to be hurt by him, and no feeling of inferiority to him. The compulsive, "human bondage" type of love relation seemed uncommon.[19]

Of these 500 girls, 58 per cent said that at least once in life they had been infatuated with two males at the same time, and 25 per cent that they had been *in love* with two males simultaneously.[20] The commonness with which this experience is admitted may seem an amusing contrast with the popular theory that the female, whatever her outward behavior, is innately and emotionally monogamous. But actually, it is only a reminder that we cannot compare the amorous natures of the two sexes without considering the social situations in which they are placed. The demand for young women is greater than the supply of them, for they are sought not only by the fairly equal number of men of their own age, but also by many older men as well. But above the age of forty there is a marked surplus of women in ratio to their potential male partners, and now it is in the male breast that the potential-

---

[16] Ernest W. Burgess and Harvey J. Locke, *The Family: From Institution to Companionship* (New York: American Book Co., 1953), pp. 417–422.

[17] Burgess and Locke, *op. cit.;* and Charlotte A. Cooper, unpublished study, University of Chicago, Department of Sociology.

[18] "Some Significant Correlates of Love and Family Attitudes and Behavior," *Journal of Social Psychology* 30 (1949), pp. 3–16.

[19] Albert Ellis, "A Study of the Love Emotions of American College Girls," *International Journal of Sexology* 3 (1949), pp. 15–21.

[20] Ellis, "A Study of Human Love Relationships," *Journal of Genetic Psychology* 75 (1949), pp. 61–71. The subjects applied the label "infatuation" to more numerous, briefer, lighter, and earlier attachments, but sparingly to any attachment existing at the time of reporting.

ity for plural love is more apt to be aroused to actuality. Furthermore, love feelings are not the same thing as erotic desires, and erotic desires are not the same thing as sexual acts. The more we can keep an open mind about the nature of the male and the female and about the intricate complex of motives inside of other human beings, the better we shall get along, and the more we shall help to dispel prejudice and bitterness.

The natural course of love is to endure and strengthen; the breakdowns are accidents, and like other accidents they are due largely to carelessness. Whether justifiably or not, we are careless of love when we subordinate it even for a time to some other motive such as anger, pride, fear, self-assertion, curiosity, pure sex, or the love of some other object. Of course there are limits: should one, for example, sacrifice one's actual health to the stubborn ignorance of a partner? The test of a couple's compatibility is not to be found in some quality of present feeling or in objective similarity of positive interests, but in their flexible capacity to harmonize their love with their other needs, with a minimum of frustration and sacrifice.

In reply to certain naïve opinions by young people who have had no continuous experience, it may be stated categorically that if intercourse is mutually satisfying, people do not get tired of it merely because it is with the same person week after week and year after year. The tendency is rather the reverse — toward increased satisfaction if other factors do not interfere. Moreover, the erotic satisfactions constitute a powerful binding force which holds many couples together despite much conflict in other areas. The tender feelings also thrive upon the familiar and do not seek new objects.

The more pessimistic views sometimes expressed are based on observations of: (1) cases where sex and/or tenderness never do attain complete mutual satisfaction; (2) cases where conflict over nonsexual matters has aroused so much anger and hostility that the partners have developed emotional blocks against seeking sexual relations with each other; and (3) cases where one or both persons have tried and found an extramarital love relation so satisfying that they have been willing to risk the alienation of the spouse. Frustration is the common denominator in all these three types of cases — definite frustration with its defensive, unpleasant emotions which injure the love — not a process of "wearing out" or "getting tired," as suggested by the advocates of free love.

If there is any spontaneous decline of feeling, it applies to certain feelings under the heading of "joy." The excitement which characterizes the early stages of "being in love" usually becomes less prominent, whether in or outside of marriage. Familiarity does not breed contempt, nor even indifference; it does seem to breed a certain calmness. It is sometimes wrongly assumed that the only way to restore the earlier state of feeling is to find a new object. But this assumption overlooks two other variables: time factors, and the setting in which the object is observed. It seems that the cooling off of romance is at least partly a reduction in the frequency or duration, or both, of intense feelings, and not always a decline in the intensity of a feeling when it is felt. In the early stages of romance much time is spent in daydreaming about an absent loved one. The lover is in a sense in love with his own day-

dreams of the object. In one reported case the lover found himself somewhat relieved when his beloved, whom he had been seeing every day, departed to a place where he could see her only every month. He could now
enjoy pure daydreams without the strain of arranging the daily date and
rendezvous. This was not direct evidence of mental ill-health, but could
readily have developed into a quite serious maladjustment. So-called "hebe-
phrenic schizoids" live a blissfully happy inner life, to all appearances, while
consorting only with themselves.

After marriage the love-object is usually more available. Actual contacts
occupy more time, daydreams less. Yet it may become a source of disappointment to the lover, and of chagrin to the object, that the object can be present
for considerable periods of time without being the center of attention and feeling. The lover, of course, has duties, and must make an adjustment that permits him or her to work even though the beloved is near. For a while there
are periods of excited attention to the beloved, interspersed with long periods
in which he or she is calmly taken for granted. The periods of excitement
grow less frequent and perhaps less prolonged. Yet many couples find that
if situations resembling those of courtship come again — absences, departures, arrivals, vacations together, eating in strange places, and so forth —
thrills may again appear from time to time. Familiarity breeds calm, but it
may be in large part the familiarity of the setting, the environment. Some
thought should be given to the possibility of changing the setting rather
than the object. (Naturally, too much thought acts as a preventative of
thrills; a certain spontaneity must be preserved.)

But there is still another resource, within the general class of joyful feelings, which gains rather than loses power with the lapse of years. It is seldom
recognized explicitly by psychologists, but it has received plenty of recognition from poets and song writers. It would hardly be called excitement, but
it can be as intense as any excitement of romantic newness; and it also has
its thrills. It is the sentiment we have called nostalgic love. It is akin to homesickness — a passionate yearning for the old and familiar after an actual or
imagined separation therefrom.

The Romantic Complex

Romantic love is a total love dominated by the element of thrill or excitement, but it is more than that. It is a total pattern of love behavior and relationship which is said to have come into our Western culture with the
Moorish occupancy of the Iberic peninsula, the French troubadour complex
of the twelfth and thirteenth centuries, and the Celtic myth of Tristan and
Iseult. (See our earlier discussion, "Chivalry and the Romantic Ideal,"
pp. 117–120.) Characteristics of the pattern are: (1) individual freedom and
social irresponsibility in choice of partner, sometimes with ideas of predetermined "affinity" or mysterious destiny; (2) exclusive concentration of feeling upon one love partner; (3) the man's preparedness to seize and take the
woman, if necessary, from any other possessor; (4) the honoring of love,
sometimes by unnecessary sexual restraint, sometimes by a glorified adultery

(but the erotic feeling is never allowed to have an independent value); (5) idealization, aesthetic appreciation, and worship (but yet possession) of woman by man; (6) adventure and braving of dangers in the process of courtship; (7) aesthetic and dramatic settings for courtship.

Sociologists have long believed that the romantic complex, while contributing new values to our culture, has also greatly intensified the problems and pains of modern marriage. Although its European advent dates from the twelfth century or even earlier, romanticism gained new power and diffusion with the late nineteenth century and its age of individualism. The popular magazine, the short story, and the motion picture have found romantic plots the best material for the vicarious satisfaction of the masses of the people. In America especially, with its democracy, its mobility of population, and its breakdown of family authority, young people have been encouraged to follow the caprice of their feelings in choosing a life partner. Young marriages with insufficient foresight have contributed to the high divorce rate. Romance in earlier days connoted extramarital love (ideally, and to a large extent actually, without sexual intercourse). Marriage was arranged; hence only outside of marriage could people make true love choices. But in modern days romance has come to be the ideology of the marriage choice itself. It has received aid and encouragement from our traditional mores because it apparently helps to keep sex within marriage and to relegate eroticism to an inferior level in the scale of values, subordinate to the great moving thrills of excited love. Actually the romantic complex may have helped to break down the traditional sex mores, but if so that has been an indirect result. The romantic idea in its complete form stands for monogamous love but does not demand the indissolubility of marriage. The net influence in America seems to have been to channel marital discontent into the pattern of divorce and remarriage, which some have called "serial polygamy," as against the older and more European pattern of "simultaneous polygamy."

Of course the American love ideal is extreme romanticism in courtship with two qualifications: (1) abstention from intercourse until after marriage, and (2) lifelong sexual fidelity to one *and the same* partner. Romanticism as understood in continental Europe is rather more a total way of life without these two qualifications. It is against this European background that we must view Denis de Rougemont's [21] scathing denunciation of romance as a whole, calling it the "cult of passion." He ascribes to it a large part of the evils and suffering of the modern world, and even views nationalism and war as "the transplanting of passion into politics." He recommends, instead, "Christian love and marital fidelity." He admits that fidelity is also irrational or "absurd" in Tertullian's sense, that is, a value or faith chosen for its own sake. But fidelity, he says, is constructive, for it values a particular person, the chosen partner, and the relationship to that partner, rather than a particular kind of feeling; it is concerned with objective realities more than with a dream. Unlike many American moralists, de Rougemont is concerned

---

[21] Denis de Rougemont, *Love in the Western World* (New York: Harcourt, Brace, 1940). This book gives also a useful factual history of the romantic ideology.

not so much with degrees of physical intimacy as with a broader ethical issue: is it better to live opportunistically, finding values in whatever life happens to offer from time to time, or to set oneself a goal, to take a stand, to limit one's experiences for the sake of the chosen goal? He urges the latter scheme of values, which he calls creative, and attacks "the general belief in spontaneity and manifold experience."

Are de Rougemont's recommendations relevant to America? They deserve our thoughtful consideration, but for a somewhat different reason than in Europe. It may be that there is a basic conflict within our version of the romantic complex. Is it humanly possible to condition people so intensely to the romantic way of thinking during youthful courtship and then to demand that this attitude shall be finally put aside after the honeymoon or that two distinct personalities (the partners) keep in perfect step with each other as they gradually settle down to conjugal love?

The remedy for marital disillusionment is not only to avoid setting up illusions in courtship but also to use such art and skill within marriage that some of the alleged illusions become realities. This can be done, and other chapters of this book will suggest ways and means. The major criticisms of American love life made by thoughtful scholars pertain mostly to the way love is handled after marriage and to the conditioning which parents give to their children. Thus many authorities agree that (1) American husbands are preoccupied with business and do not give enough actual time and thought to comradeship with their wives; (2) there is too little *psychological* intimacy between American husbands and wives, too little appreciation between mature men and women as persons, apart from erotic attraction, too much differentiation of their interests; (3) too much — or the wrong kind — of domination of American boys by their mothers; (4) a tendency of each sex to treat the spouse, in some way or other, as a child.[22]

Perhaps one of the most neglected needs of the courtship period is that for rich, understanding contacts with people who are already married. Our social customs tend to separate adolescents sharply from adults and to preoccupy them with the problems of their current adolescent world. Courting couples would do well to spend more time discussing and investigating realistically the problems of married life. It is surprising how little those already married will really talk to the unmarried youth. They leave this too much to the professors. Every young person should have the opportunity to observe and understand a number of happy and successful marriages. Ideals which are set up in terms of these concrete observations are less likely to be illusions.[23]

[22] See for example David L. Cohn, *Love in America* (New York: Simon and Schuster, 1943); Karl Menninger, *Love Against Hate* (New York: Harcourt, Brace, 1942). Hugo Beigel has analyzed the history and function of romantic love and concludes that in its genuine form it has not harmed but has "saved monogamous marriage from complete disorganization" — "Romantic Love," *American Sociological Review*, 16 (1951), pp. 326–334.

[23] The Peckham Experiment (for better health and family living) in England holds as part of its philosophy that the married and unmarried age groups should mingle more freely in social activities. James H. Pearce and Lucy H. Crocker, *The Peckham Experiment* (London: G. Allen and Unwin, 1944).

Love and Frustration

There is a strange tendency among some thinkers to consider love, especially romantic love, as a product of the frustration of one of its elements — the erotic desire. This idea is contained in the brilliant and trenchant work of the late Professor Willard Waller. He calls it "the dynamic conception of love."[24] Love is a striving — of the total person — toward another person as object. It is biological in origin, cultural in pattern. Once it has passed the initial stages, it has a powerful momentum which tends to carry it on to its goal, which is the completion of the sexual act. But any striving when blocked generates ideation and emotion. Our culture always blocks this love striving, and the result is the powerful emotion of romantic love.

The writer questions Waller's concept of romantic love as a product of frustrated erotic love. He also questions de Rougemont's related thesis that the essence of the modern romantic complex is to impose obstacles to love in general in order to experience the intensified feeling that comes from frustration. These ideas, like orthodox psychoanalysis, tend to disregard the concrete physiological processes in favor of some abstract concept of love as a homogeneous force, readily transmutable from one form into another.[25]

People can (as Waller admits) have frequent and thoroughgoing sexual satisfaction, either with the romantic beloved or with another person, and at the same time remain in an intense state of romantic love. Literature and mythology do not create obstacles to love merely in order to intensify it. Their function is also to provide a vicarious satisfaction to persons who are, by circumstances beyond their control, already frustrated. At the same time, there are always plenty of people who are enjoying romantic or erotic love, or both, to the fullest through frequent satisfactions. Neither they nor the unsatisfied would introduce any additional obstacles in real life if they had the power. Fiction and myth, with their imagined obstacles to satisfaction, serve to beautify the *inevitable* frustrations of living and thus reduce tension.

When any strong desire is frustrated, anger and aggression are apt to arise. To say that the frustrated feeling is *transmuted* into the feeling of anger or that the energy of the frustrated desire becomes the energy of the aggression, is in the writer's opinion a false metaphor. There are yet no known laws as to what kind or how much of a frustrated desire will result in what kind or how much of a frustration reaction. The result depends on individual learning and the cultural situation.

When de Rougemont, then, links modern war with the "transplanting of passion into politics," he misconceives the nature of the relation but recog-

[24] Willard Waller, *The Family: A Dynamic Interpretation,* rev. by Reuben Hill (New York: Dryden Press, 1951), pp. 198–199.

[25] Theodore Reik, a pupil of Freud, now denies Freud's thesis that love is "an aim-inhibited form of the sex urge." He says that love is an amalgamation of the sex urge, the need to conquer, and the need for affection. See his *Psychology of Sex Relations* (New York: Farrar and Rinehart, 1945). Vernon Grant, in "A Major Problem of Human Sexuality," *Journal of Social Psychology* 28 (1948), pp. 79–101, points out that the prestige of Freud and Havelock Ellis eclipsed the previous work of Albert Moll, who held that affection is an independent drive and not a sublimation of the sex drive.

nizes its existence and importance. His misconception leads him to single out a certain type of love as bad or dangerous because, he supposes, it is peculiarly likely to be transmuted into aggression.

The real problem of the Western world is not that of a bad kind of love versus a good kind. It is rather how to widen the opportunities for the harmless satisfaction of all kinds of love. All kinds (that is, types of love feeling) are good. It may prove wise to have separate objects for tenderness, eroticism, and joy within certain limits; but in any case, the supreme satisfaction which human experience recommends is total love directed to one person-object. (By satisfaction is meant adequate frequency and duration of satisfying situations.) Adequate satisfaction does not weaken love desire except momentarily. Indeed, the tendency is to repeat the pleasure-giving act more happily and constructively after an appropriate interval. Adequate satisfaction enriches and increases the volume of love feelings and reduces the stimulation to aggression and anger. If war, as de Rougemont suggests, is stimulated by frustrated love, perhaps the world would better not try to curb love of any kind but try to facilitate all the natural and harmless satisfactions. It is highly suggestive to compare the general nature of the objects of human emotion and interest in Germany of the 1930's with the same in France of the 1930's (or France during most of this century). It may be that the emotional conditions which are dangerous from the standpoint of defense against an aggressive neighbor will be the safest and healthiest if and when they can be cultivated on an international scale. The last word has not yet been said about what constitutes "national decadence."

But this merely states the problem and suggests the general direction of its solution. The details will have to be worked out slowly, tolerantly, thoughtfully, and democratically. Here is a great opportunity for youth. Any sudden and blanket emancipation of sex, such as Russia attempted in 1917, will defeat its own ends. Likewise, no solution will be satisfactory which regiments everyone into the same pattern of love life. De Rougemont's ideal of fidelity and devotion to a person as such may well prove to be the highest and most constructive value. But to choose and cultivate a value successfully is to link to it our strongest pleasant feelings, including also the erotic. Human beings will not in the long run be loyal to a value which is clothed with a sense of effort and renunciation or even of perpetual moderation and calm. De Rougemont is really recommending a better focus for our feelings, but he weakens his appeal by seeming to condemn the feelings themselves. If he were a psychologist as well as a discerning historical sociologist, he would know that feelings are linked to their objects and foci by the conditioning process, which is partly and perhaps increasingly under the control of organized education, and that even adult persons can to some extent be "reconditioned," that is, emotionally re-educated.[26]

[26] Daniel A. Prescott, *Emotion and the Educative Process* (Washington: American Council on Education, 1938).

The Sociology of Love: Courtship

Love in the Social Group

When love is thought of simply as feelings of the individual subject directed toward various person-objects, the possible variations are almost infinite, because the linkages are acquired and not inborn. Human beings live in groups, however, and certain things are true of group living whether the members of the group are Hottentots, Wisconsin farmers, New York suburbanites, or howler monkeys. For example, all groups develop leaders and followers and rules of possession. The very nature of the group narrows the range of possible behavior, but it also enriches and intensifies experience within these limits.

The chief force which leads love feelings to become fixated upon a person as object, and thus to become true love, is the reciprocal activity of the object itself. We love someone who does, or did, or might love us. In the remainder of this chapter we shall think of love as a relation between persons and not merely as the behavior and feelings of each person separately.

It has been said that "two is company, three a crowd." But choice is always made from a larger group, which also in some ways furnishes an audience and at the same time chaperonage. Even friendly gossip contributes to the positive values of courtship. In the "Middletown" of 1890, the Lynds tell us,[27] young people went about a great deal in groups of one sex, the two sexes occasionally mingling. Today "pairing-off" is permitted and even artificially stimulated. Drive through the suburbs and recreation areas around New York or Detroit on a Sunday afternoon when most people are at leisure, and later do the same in a relatively populous area of the southern Appalachians. A striking difference will be noted. In the first region the heterosexual pair will be a most common sight, in the latter it will seldom be seen. Modern urban society demands and also supplies more privacy for the pair than did our traditional society; it also forces people to depend more upon pair relationships for love and lighter companionship. Through privacy an individual may be simultaneously engaged in several pair relationships of considerable feeling, and nobody but himself may know the whole picture. Some of these may be competitive, but only the individual at the center is conscious of the competition. In the simple, small-community life of years ago, in "sacred societies," the individual probably had more numerous bonds of tender and friendly affection than he does now. He loved and was loved by his relatives, his neighbors, his community, in a sense which is not true today. This distributed affection may have given him a sense of security which made romantic or other intense pair-love less imperative. On the other hand, pair-love was under stricter surveillance. Courtship was a serious business and being alone with a person of the opposite sex was apt to be regarded as evidence of sexual intercourse or else a conscious step toward marriage.

[27] Robert S. Lynd and Helen M. Lynd, *Middletown, a Study in Contemporary American Culture* (New York: Harcourt, Brace, 1929), pp. 111, 138, 283.

Competition and Property in Love Relations

Rivalry and jealousy are essential characteristics of group life. Rivalry is always governed by some code of rules. It results finally in the object which was struggled for becoming the property of the winner. After that, the attempt of another person to gain it is a trespass rather than rivalry and awakens the reaction of jealousy.[28] Why is not love a "free good" like the water in the river and the air we breathe? Is not its alleged scarcity an artificial one created by certain cultures? If a man wants love there is probably always a woman in the group who wants it too, and thus supply can always be equated to demand with no more effort than a little searching. The immediate answer is, of course, that we value exclusiveness and monogamy. But monogamy is always violated to some extent; why has man not learned in all these years to modify this ideal just enough to secure the more free and abundant love which would thereby be possible?

Possessiveness in love relationships has deeper roots than those springing from any particular culture. It may be said to be "subcultural." This does not mean that it is inborn in individual human nature, but that it springs from the essential nature of groups and the balance of biological forces. It is found among animals, which have no values or ideals.

In order to prevent the development of possessive attitudes, there needs to be much more of a good thing than merely enough to go around. Many animals as well as humans hoard and guard private supplies of life's various goods even though the total supply under this system of decentralized storage far exceeds the active needs of the moment. A person learns that by the device of property ownership he avoids the risk of having to search for something at the moment when he particularly needs it. When any of our important needs are satisfied by a person, then the possession of that person, under an adequate system of rules and penalties, makes us feel somewhat more secure against that person's being taken by another or running away during our absence. Slavery is the crude form of man's possession of man, but marriage, betrothal, and even the agreement to "keep steady company" are all in various degrees expressions of this basic human group-elicited tendency to stake out claims.

The same competitive forces act upon females, and whether there are just enough men to go around or less than enough, the women also try to gain possessive rights and thus security. But the net result of these two processes — the competition of men for women and the competition of women for men — is to place the sexes in a very unequal position. In nearly all human and mammalian societies, males dominate females and are the more active competitors. This inequality is due fundamentally to the superior physical power of the male. For example, only the human male can perpetrate rape. This male superiority is not necessarily great in degree nor is it true of every individual and on all occasions. But social interaction processes

---

[28] Kingsley Davis, "Jealousy and Sexual Property," *Social Forces*, 14 (1936), pp. 395-405

often build up and establish a great social difference on a moderate and fluctuating biological difference. If one individual conquers another at the first encounter, or on the majority of occasions, he develops habits of domination and the conquered develops habits of submission. They may continue to live by these habits even after the ratio of their physical strength has changed. The same principle holds for groups and classes of individuals. Among humans these patterns of interaction tend to become cultural and thus even more to crystallize the status of individuals.

Males, it is usually held, have more intense or frequent sexual needs and this is thought to account for male possessiveness and aggression. Among most mammals, indeed, the female sex desire is periodic (see pp. 52–54), whereas the male seems to be in a state of readiness over much longer periods of time. With apes, however, the periodicity is less distinct, and with human beings, for all practical purposes, absent. Sexologists generally believe that the human female, when not inhibited through cultural teachings, has on the whole as much sexual need as the male. There is reason to believe, however, that the male's need remains at a more constant level and shows less tendency to fluctuate.

To speculate further regarding differences in sexual need is unnecessary, for stronger individuals usually succeed in organizing a group in such a way as to give their satisfactions priority, whatever be the nature of the desire to be satisfied. The sex need, although often intensely felt, is not a matter of life and death to the individual; it *can be* inhibited, and *is* inhibited as a result of interaction processes. In many animal groups there is a surplus of females, but even then the males share unequally in the sexual opportunities and are under the power of one dominant male, or form a hierarchy of status. Among howler monkeys the sex ratio within integrated groups is about three males to seven females. Yet there are large numbers of additional bachelor males outside the groups.[29]

Because of this domination of males over females and of stronger males over other males, the actual frequency of coitus enjoyed by different individuals would seem in many groups to bear little relation to their differences in need. Our pattern of monogamy doubtless brings us nearer to a fair distribution in this respect than did the patriarchal-polygynous pattern of many other human societies, but there are still injustices and unsolved problems.

Similar patterns of competition and conflict, attempted and actual possession, occur in human bisexual groups where sexual intercourse is ruled out by the mores and where the stakes are friendship, "petting," romantic love, and the ego satisfactions of courtship.

There is still another reason why love is competitive and possessive. It is that members of any group are very unequal in their average desirability to members of the opposite sex, which means severe competition for the favors of the more attractive.

[29] C. R. Carpenter, "A Field Study of the Behavior and Social Relations of Howling Monkeys," *Comparative Psychology Monographs,* 19 (1934), pp. 1–168. See also S. Zuckerman, *The Social Life of Monkeys and Apes* (New York: Harcourt, Brace, 1932).

Rating and Dating

Whatever may be the elements of desirability — and there are always several: general attractiveness, money, social power or prestige, beauty, physical strength, love-making ability, or other characteristics — every group is bound to form a ranking of its members from greatest to least desirability. A sex ratio of 100 males to 100 females provides no guarantee against competition, rivalry, and jealousy. The normal result of the often smooth-running but inexorable competitive process is that the high ranking males secure high ranking females, and so on down the scale. In coeducational colleges with a fraternity system, the hierarchy reveals itself through a structure composed of high and low ranking fraternities, with the independents still lower down. The high groups are enabled to have their pick of members while the lower ones have to take second choices, although members of the top cliques may seem more attractive only because of the prestige of their organization. The same stratified social structure and related processes occur in a one-sex group where the stakes are merely prestige, power, and friendship.

In coeducational groups the stakes of competition, of course, are the outward symbols of favor, such as invitations to social affairs, being seen together publicly, and so on. A certain amount of romantic love-making and some sex relations doubtless take place behind a veil of secrecy and are not so much controlled by the competitive process. Still, the things that are most wanted of the opposite sex are very much tied up with visible symbols.

Studies have shown that persons at the top of the scale of desirability have more dates than those lower down. They have to refuse many invitations, while the less fortunate may have few. Fraternities and sororities crystallize status. "Here you have been 'dating' with A-1 sorority girls all year, and now you bring around a 'barb' to the house. What's the matter anyway?" Thus the fraternities control their brothers' social relations with girls in the interest of preserving the hierarchy.

Among the low ranking, of course, an invitation or initiated friendship must always be faced with the thought that "he (or she) really wanted somebody else but took me as second choice." Poverty, long hours spent in earning money, and a sense of inferiority conspire to make the "dating" of low ranking persons with each other less frequent and presumably less satisfying than the "dating" at the top. We might ask, Why do not the socially underprivileged assert themselves and build up a courtship culture appropriate to their situation? Sometimes they may, but there is always reluctance to identify oneself with an inferior group. In America, especially, one always hopes to rise. So instead of taking a lunch basket on the streetcar to a public park with a boy of her own humble status, the girl of inferior status will prefer to wait "dateless" in the hope that a more popular boy will invite her to the dinner at the Washington.

Yet the outcome is not always happy for those at the top of the scale. Waller describes one case in which two "top" persons married largely because they were "tops," had little in the way of common interests, and lived through many years of unhappy marriage.[30]

The mental conflict involved in making decisions and the knowledge that someone's feelings are going to be hurt burden the more sensitive upper-class "daters." Moreover, some of the most popular, who possess wealth or prestige or attractive appearance, often wonder whether their partners really value them for "themselves." A person's later married life is much influenced by the position he held on the desirability scale before marriage. The more popular of two spouses may be exposed to more temptations toward extra-marital love, with the result that the other partner may be more in danger than otherwise of developing jealousy. Or again, the more popular may carry over into marriage habits of expecting various attentions and concessions to which he or she was formerly accustomed.

The romantic theory is that people really choose their partners because of something unique and supremely qualitative. Modern freedom of court-ship is supposed to give opportunity to find the "one and only." Yet it is doubtful whether young people whose choices are controlled by a competitive situation, where persons are rated and ranked, are really more free than those who are guided by their parents. In both cases competitive forces are present which limit the choice of the individual, however free he may feel. The breadth and soundness of choice may be increased if the group is not too homogeneous and does not concentrate its approval upon some one type of desirable personality.

The writer asked a number of college girls to describe their "ideal man." Some presumably described a person with whom they were already in love, others evidently described abstractions. The significant thing is that the descriptions of about half of the girls approximated a recognizable stereotype.

Brilliant mind and strong interest in intellectual things. A "smoothie." Dresses well, dances well, has poise, can take his liquor, has good line of small talk. A man of action — must be doing interesting work and really getting somewhere in it (without reference to money). Modern, sane attitude toward sex — and thorough knowledge, though not necessarily firsthand. Personal charm — attractive smile or small mannerisms, physical appeal though not necessarily good-looking, rather tall, virile. A good companion — shares intellectual interests and enjoys plays, concerts, pictures, etc. Large sense of humor.

The other half of the girls deviated widely from this stereotype in several directions. One wanted a man who had some of the standard qualities but was also "a philosopher and writer, rather absent-minded, not particularly careful of the style of his clothes and appearance, musical but not a good singer, very gay and with a great sense of humor, firm religious beliefs, very brave, with capacity to go against his environment and produce reforms, delicate worshiper of wife." Another wanted a powerful man with perfect health, a shrewd businessman, mathematician, and practical handy man, who

[30] Waller, *op. cit.*, 363–379. See also Kuhn's more intensive analysis below, pp. 257–261.

compliments his wife "not by his attentions and verbal expressions as much as by his disregard of other women." The girls differed greatly in the extent to which physical and aesthetic characteristics entered into their concept of the attractive male. With some the description was almost half physical, with others physical details were barely mentioned.

There are several studies of men's ideals of women, but they are mostly in the form of a ranking of general traits and not comparable with the detailed descriptions of men just quoted. Both sexes want health, honesty, intelligence, ambition, and good disposition. Six hundred Wisconsin students of both sexes agreed on the following as the most important factors in choosing a mate: dependable character, emotional stability and maturity, pleasing disposition, mutual attraction, good health, desire for home and children.[31] One finding of the statistical studies, however, is important although it is not "news": men rank beauty much higher in the scale of values desired in a mate than women rank handsomeness.[32] Thus there enters into the rating of women by men a factor which has little to do with personality or ability. The demand for beauty and youth has some bearing on the "mating gradient" elsewhere described; that is, the tendency of men to marry "downward" and thus leave an unmarried residue of highly capable and educated women.

A fairer distribution of love and friendship, and wiser marriages, would be achieved through (1) a more equalized initiative in courtship; (2) more independence (even with the help of a little ridicule) from the worship of the standardized types and ideals portrayed by advertising and the movies and from narrow standards set up by one's particular group; and (3) education of both sexes toward a wider range of appreciations, especially of the male sex toward appreciation of personality traits apart from youth and beauty.

Bargaining and Exploitation in Courtship

Waller emphasizes the feature of exploitation in modern courtship. This he defines as the "sort of utilization of another which, in accordance with conventional standards, would be called unjust or unfair." [33] Three kinds of alleged unfairness or exploitation appear.

First, exploitation may result from the unequal status of the two persons in the scale of general courtship desirability. This results in unequal bargaining power. When a high ranking boy "dates" with a low ranking girl, he may disappoint her, break dates, give her last-minute or relatively undesirable invitations, and go with other girls — and yet may find her waiting upon his convenience because she has no other opportunities. Sometimes he may demand sexual intercourse from her as a tacit condition for continuing the relationship, while he could not do so with a higher placed girl. Likewise, an at-

31 Reuben Hill, "Campus Values and Mate Selection," *Journal of Home Economics* (Nov., 1945), p. 556.
32 Ray E. Baber, *Marriage and the Family* (New York: McGraw-Hill, 1939), p. 149. Wayne C. Neely, "College and University Students' Ideals of Family Life, 1929 and 1936" (mimeographed paper; author at Hood College).
33 Waller, *op. cit.*, p. 244.

tractive girl may, in various ways, "use" an unprepossessing suitor while she is seeking or enjoying more thrilling relations with a more glamorous male. Exploitation of this type is a part of the larger problem of social justice, of which courtship is only one phase, and may be evaluated in two different ways.

We might hold that people normally expect treatment according to their status and bargaining power and that when one enters into companionship or affection with a person of higher status he is choosing, of his own free will, a relation which he knows must be somewhat different from the bond between persons of similar status. If the lower placed person raises his status through the relation or secures advantages other than pure affection or companionship, we, and the partner, may be in doubt as to his motives and as to the strength of the love element in them. We may see a clearer value in a love tie which does not change the status of the parties nor bring supplementary advantages.

On the other hand, we may feel that the correction of social injustices is so important that every human relation, including courtship, should be subject to that general aim. We may imply that "mixed motives" on the part of the lower placed person are natural and legitimate and that it is the love of the higher placed person which should be tested for its "purity" by his willingness to be generous or even to lower his status.

A general adherence to the second scale of values would probably tend to reduce the actual number of love relations between persons of unequal status. It would make the high-status persons more cautious and might prevent many relations which have positive values to the persons concerned although they do not look good to outsiders. Yet this adherence might also help somewhat to bring about the broader democracy which would eventually make for happier love relations in general. Perhaps the dilemma is best regarded as a challenge to youth to work out a code which is between these extremes and which meets the realities of the day.

A second type of exploitation or injustice is that which exists between the sexes as such, either in society at large or within a particular class.

In a milieu where the acceptable men wishing dates or marriage are much fewer than the women, men often use to good advantage their greater bargaining power. Waller cites one instance of this: women students at summer school paying expenses, lending cars, and giving themselves sexually to the fewer and younger men students.[34] In the country at large the surplus of females is only two per cent. But men in general have the advantage — through their greater possession of money, power, and specialized ability; their lesser risks in the sexual relation; the custom of male initiative in courtship; the freedom of the man to take either a woman younger or economically poorer than himself or a woman of his own age or status; the power of leading men to exclude other men from effective competition for mates through service in the army or in remote industries; the ability of such isolated men to satisfy sexual needs without total love or responsibility. Under these circumstances it is not surprising that women sometimes seem mercenary in courtship and yet sometimes appear to be a surplus commodity which

[34] *Ibid.,* p. 247.

can be had cheaply. Until men and women have equality of economic opportunity, their sociosexual relations will be complicated by economic factors, and the justice of the noneconomic relations will be as difficult to evaluate as it currently is.

In a particular locale one sex often feels itself aggrieved or exploited by the other sex in general, so that there is a great deal of sex antagonism expressed in the one-sex group toward the other sex even though individually some of its members are in love. For example, there is the hostile attitude of the boys in some former men's colleges toward girls recently admitted to these colleges. The girls are felt to be on the average less attractive than girls of comparable groups, but this is not the real reason for the hostility. Often it is due to a very peculiar group process which might be called "sour grapes." There are not enough girls to go round; they add only a limited amount of courtship opportunity to what the boys already have; and if the boys were really to go after them it would lead to rivalries and competition, disrupting the traditional, temporarily homosexual *esprit de corps* of the male group. Male groups especially have this spirit of internal loyalty, resembling that of a labor union. They ridicule and otherwise punish those members who dare to go forth and seize advantages for themselves which the whole group cannot enjoy. On the other hand, at some western universities girls are reported to have acted as a group in setting up "dating" standards to prevent the unlimited encroachment upon their study time which free competition brings.

A third type of alleged exploitation often occurs when the two individuals are unequally involved as to their feelings. One tries to make the other fall in love while he cannot or will not allow himself to feel so deeply. In such cases, Waller says, the principle of least interest prevails. The one who loves most is at a disadvantage in all the other give-and-take relations of the courtship. Unequal bargaining power has been created by the difference in feeling.

The present author, however, is undecided in such cases as to who is being exploited. We must know more about the actual satisfactions and frustrations of the two partners. One partner may feel much more of romantic or excited love, while the other tries to reciprocate in the form of tenderness or sex. Tenderness in such a case may take the form of an intense compassion or sympathy. Should we judge the fairness of a love relationship by the balance of external advantages — the little services, conveniences, and inconveniences which the parties render each other? Again, should we assume that where petting or erotic feelings are involved the man is always the getter and the woman the giver? Should we assume that the partner who has no other love relation at the time is being exploited by the one who has? That this partner who has only one love loves more intensely or totally than the other? These questions cannot be answered dogmatically. They require study of the individual case, and they suggest the need for working out codes of values as yet unformulated.

Although standards of justice and the criteria of exploitation seem variable and uncertain, some definiteness could be gained by emphasizing the criteria of honesty and kindness. Many of the cases of alleged exploitation described by Waller seem to contain the element of fraud or deception. A bargain can sometimes be unjust even if both parties freely accept it with open eyes. It can be much more definitely unjust, however, if one of the parties deceives the other as to what he is giving. This simple working code might be helpful: Be honest about your feelings, do not pretend to love more than you do, do not promise what you do not intend to fulfill or what you are not sure you *can* fulfill. See that the other knows your code and attaches no false meanings. If it is the custom to say "darling," you may say it, but first make sure that the other person lives in this same culture and entertains the same meaning. Be sensitive to the needs of the other. Do not deal with her (or him) by formula. You may produce a heartache or a serious trauma [35] in your partner by doing something which seems to you perfectly just. You have a certain responsibility for every person who enters a love relationship with you.

"Circulation" and Possession

In our secular society it is more than ever desirable that young people should "circulate" until they find a relationship which will pass both the emotional and the intellectual test; that is, a relationship in which there is total love and also a degree of mutual suitability that will appeal to a reasonable judgment. This may take more time and involve more trial and error than does courtship in a simple, highly sacred society. Honest exploration of friendship does not necessarily mean exploitation. Young people with a social conscience will be careful to avoid hurting, they will not deceive each other, they will defer formal engagement until they both feel certain.

Engagement has very different meanings in different cultures, and in our varied American culture it means different things to different couples and within differing social sets. It does, however, seem to have a common denominator. Where it is entered by free choice, it marks off the preliminary experimental period from the later period of exclusiveness, and in some respects is a trial marriage. According to our traditional Victorian mores, kissing and what we might now call "light petting" were supposed to begin at engagement, while "body petting" and intercourse were reserved until after marriage. Before engagement the lover had no "rights" over his beloved that would prevent her receiving attentions from another also. After engagement he (or she) might properly show jealousy. Even before engagement, however, there were steps and degrees. In our traditional culture there was commonly a period of "going steady" before the formal engagement, which was sometimes covered by a verbal agreement between the partners and was sometimes merely a habit. But this also is really a feature of the universal tendency toward possessiveness as a means of partial security in a competitive field. Even when youth are frankly "circulating" among several partners, there is the tendency to recognize and expect others to recognize that "Mary belongs to John" for some particular time. It may be for this evening, or for this house party, or indefinitely until one of them wants to make a change.

[35] Waller, *op. cit.*, p. 249.

Even when they are both absolutely free to change partners at will, this freedom is difficult to exercise unless both want it at the same time, and the one who wants it first commonly feels need of an excuse and a suitable opportunity for the change.

Kirkpatrick and Caplow [36] in comparing the first, second, and third affairs of a given person where that was possible, found that the men rated their first affairs as somewhat more "exclusive" than the women rated theirs, and the men also increased much more rapidly in exclusiveness with succeeding affairs. Men rated later affairs as substantially more "important" than earlier ones; women did so only to a very slight extent. Men reported considerably more "melancholy" than did women. Ratio of pleasant to unpleasant emotions decreased with succeeding affairs in the case of the men, increased in the case of the women. In this Minnesota sample the men more often than the women reported jealousy, "feeling trapped," and "giving in on important theoretical or moral issues for fear of losing him or her." The authors suggest that in the college situation men have an economic hurdle to cross before they can marry, so that the deeper involvements give them more anxiety while they give the women more security.

Present-day conditions call for a code of courtship mores in which possessiveness is completely eliminated in the pre-engagement period and less rigid even after engagement. When a person lived, moved, and had his being in a single community and group, the conditions encouraged a certain exclusiveness of devotion. Where people are moving about and each participates in several unrelated activities and groups, it is not unnatural to develop some degree of affection toward more than one person of opposite sex. The sailor who has a girl in every port is an object of jest. But this stereotype represents, on a physical level, patterns common to other levels of social relations in our modern highly mobile society. This pattern is in conflict with old-fashioned communal mores and also with the romantic ideal in its modern form. Herein lies one of the chief "unrealisms" of the romantic cult. Since under modern conditions one's social relationships are easy to hide, mental conflict often arises in the individual. Shall he tell his partner that he is also interested in somebody else? Perhaps the partner already suspects but prefers to preserve the illusion of exclusiveness. Even in relation to one's fiancé or principal partner this problem may arise because some persons, no matter how intensely loved, cannot feel secure and happy unless they are the exclusive object of affection. Individual cases should be handled according to their peculiar conditions, but the general effort, if there is to be adjustment to the tide of social change, should be toward greater frankness, honesty, and less rigid standards of exclusiveness.[37]

[36] Waller, op. cit.
[37] Reference is made here to the affection and companionship of courtship, not to sexual intercourse.

Courtship under Modern Conditions: Delayed Marriage

According to Waller, the "dating complex" differs from the "true court-ship" of the "normal," traditional community in that the "dating" group is (1) postponing marriage (usually because of the time required to finish education and become economically independent), and (2) placing, in consequence, more emphasis upon present satisfactions as distinguished from the remoter aim of choosing a spouse and preparing for marriage. Normal court-ship is a series of steps each of which brings the partners closer to each other and also closer to the wedding. Normal courtship also has its false leads and its failures, but these are minimized by the responsible attitudes enforced through the watchfulness of the community. In our traditional Euro-Ameri-can culture strong heterosexual love (whether or not it involves sexual inter-course) is supposed to belong to marriage with such exceptions as are thought necessary for selection of the partner. In other words, courtship is supposed to exist purely for the sake of marriage. But in many modern situations, such as that of college life, the necessary postponement of mar-riage leads to the pseudo courtship pattern of "dating," the purpose of which is immediate personal satisfaction of love needs. If marriage comes out of dating, well and good, but if not, let us enjoy it for its own sake — so runs the thought. This, according to Waller, explains the exploitation and the cruel one-sided breakings off, the traumas and heartaches, the cynical de-fenses built up by the two sexes in their own groups against such disappoint-ments, the valuation of thrills and isolated experiences, the arts of coquetry and light love, the "line," the high valuation of the dramatic or glamorous personality as distinguished from the more prosaic person of good back-ground and ability, and the willingness to go very far with sexual stimula-tion with a minimum of possessiveness and exclusiveness.[38]

There are those who think of this pseudo-courtship as a pathological con-dition which would be largely remedied if we could spare young people the economic necessity of postponing marriage. The present author is inclined to view the problem in a somewhat different light. First, this particular "dating" pattern is not peculiar to college youth, who marry on the average at about twenty-seven and twenty-five. Many of these features also characterize the courtship of less educated urban youth, who will marry at twenty-five and twenty-three. Second, statistics of success do not show young marriages to be superior; those contracted below twenty-one and twenty are definitely un-promising.[39] Third, the complexity of modern life calls for more time and more trials to find the ideally suitable mate. Instead of saying that modern conditions force an "unnatural" postponement of marriage, it would be just as correct to say that old attitudes call for an unnatural hastening of marital choice, which would be all the more unnatural under modern conditions. These old attitudes are based (1) on the early maturing of sexual need, coupled

[38] Waller, op. cit., chaps. 9, 11. See Kuhn's criticism of Waller's views on dating as pseudo-courtship below, cf. fn. 24, p. 259.

[39] Hornell Hart and Ella B. Hart, Personality and the Family (rev. ed.; Boston: Heath, 1941), pp. 122–131.

with the dangers, especially to the girl, of premarital intercourse, and (2) on the nature of competition in a primary group, which causes individuals to hasten to possess whatever seems desirable "before someone else gets it." These motives to get people settled down into their permanent roles as early as possible and to keep sex relations within marriage may be important; but there are also other values which must be recognized in a democracy. Democracy calls for the maximum opportunity for individual development, even at the risk of partial sacrifice of some other values.

In a moderate-sized urban community where organizations and contacts are numerous and flexible, there is opportunity for a wide variety of courtship patterns to suit the needs of different individuals. This opportunity can be realized by helping all individuals to use the organizations of the community and to circulate in a variety of groups. It is not realized when persons invest their whole courtship life in some particular group or under the aegis of some one institution. The "rating and dating" complex is a special case of such limited investment. So far as college youth have other contacts outside, the factors so thwarting to the low ranking people, described by Waller, are mitigated.

Some have pointed out the need for parental subsidies and unrestricted employment of young married women to enable youth to marry earlier. Floyd Dell has pointed out the need for an unhurried courtship, with non-exclusive petting as well as companionship in order to give opportunity for the complete development of heterosexual feelings before choice must be made. He feels that young people, of their own volition, do not wish to hurry to complete sexual fulfillment.[40] On the other hand, Groves and others point out the risk of "becoming fixated on the petting level." [41] Many young women, especially, have interpreted the newer freedom to mean a great deal of extreme sexual stimulation by several partners, and they feel that by barring complete intercourse they are staying within safety and the mores. The later marriage problems of some women who have had this experience often lead the counselor to feel that they would have done better to keep their relations more Platonic until they were ready for complete intercourse.

Almost anything that is said about the advantages and the risks of various courtship practices is true — for some persons — and very untrue for others. Indeed, in the development of the love life, one person's meat is another's poison. The real problem is to be able to diagnose the peculiar needs of an individual. One girl should be helped to keep friendship Platonic; another needs help to let herself go. Some should be warned that marital failure and divorce are very devastating experiences. Yet another may need the idea that divorce is always possible and not disgraceful, in order to save her from the perpetual indecision of an overcautious nature. There are risks involved in petting. There are also risks — to some persons — in a rigid and uncompromising refusal of it.

The prolongation of the courtship period and its becoming to some extent an end in itself and not merely something subservient to marriage are a

[40] Floyd Dell, *Love in the Machine Age* (New York: Farrar and Rinehart, 1930).
[41] Ernest R. Groves, *Marriage* (rev. ed.; New York: Holt, 1941), p. 86.

natural part of the democratic trend. They are analogous to the present trend in attitudes toward the child; namely, recognizing the ultimate values in the present life of the child at every age instead of regarding childhood merely as a means of adult life. The writer suggests that if we throw aside the old attitude that courtship exists only for the sake of marriage, we shall have a better chance of improving marriage. The newer conception would be that love and companionship between the sexes are in general desirable for their own sake, that their dangers should be dealt with constructively, and that out of this total network of friendly and affectionate relations marriage may arise as a more complete and perfect pattern — whenever any given pair of partners is ready for it.

When 1600 high school and college students were asked to give their three most important reasons for dating, 41 per cent of the reasons had to do with affection and choice of mate, 34 per cent with the educational motives of "learning to adjust," "gaining of poise or ease," and 25 per cent with fun, getting to social affairs, prestige, and necking.[42] Waller's sharp distinction between dating and "true courtship" seems to several more recent observers to be somewhat unrealistic. Indeed, the participants themselves recognize various stages from the first "playing of the field" to the altar, such as a stage of "being pinned" which in some colleges is a kind of engagement to become engaged. But they and many sociologists now feel that even the earlier stages of dating activity are constructive and educational rather than socially useless or harmful as Waller's theory implied. This writer prefers to use the term "courtship" for the entire social activity, recognizing that those who participate in it at any one time represent all stages of commitment and many combinations of motives. Then any one unit of this courtship activity is a "date." As Lowrie says, "A first appointment between two teen-age children or the last prearranged meeting of an engaged couple before marriage are both dates." We can go farther. Many busy husbands and wives today have to make dates with each other to insure themselves of the uninterrupted pleasure of their own companionship. Is this a symptom of the decay of marriage, or is it perhaps the kind of "spice" which many marriages need?

Social Planning for Courtship

The view just outlined implies that society should take a more positive and constructive responsibility for courtship. If it decides that certain practices must be forbidden in the interests of the general welfare, it should be equally alert to give positive aid to practices it finds desirable. Society may act through the medium of government or any other of its institutions and through the voluntary organization of young people themselves.

To this writer, four broad social needs are evident. First is the need for more initiative in courtship by women. Second is the need for removing all restraints upon the employment of women (such as the bans on married

[42] Samuel H. Lowrie, "Dating Theories and Student Responses," *American Sociological Review* 16 (1951), pp. 334–340.

teachers) so that mate selection and the time of marriage will be less dependent upon the economic fortunes of the man. Third is a need for the organized cultivation of wider acquaintance between the two sexes, to reduce the number of lonely and socially isolated persons and to help even socially active persons to keep out of the ruts of traveling with only one social set. Fourth, there is need for a greatly increased number of trained counselors to help the individual apply available knowledge and resources to his or her own case.

The third need is not discussed elsewhere in this book and warrants fuller discussion here. Professional matchmaking is an old, old institution. Chinese parents used it to find appropriate mates for their children. It is still in vogue among some Jewish groups in this country; the *schatchen* is not yet extinct. In general, however, matchmaking has seemed inconsistent with romance and free choice of partners and has become almost obsolete. Yet it may be that the preservation of the values which romance introduced requires the development of a modern, democratic equivalent for matchmaking.

The idea has been in some disrepute because of the various commercial agencies which advertise and offer to find partners for lonely persons. Naturally it is the more unattractive persons or those isolated from the channels of acquaintance who have resorted to marriage bureaus.[43] "Dating bureaus" have been tried at many colleges, and many have failed. Still the idea persists and crops out in newer and more ambitious forms, because the need for some such service is great and is increasingly felt. The most ambitious experiment known so far to the writer was "Introduction, a Service for Sociability,"[44] in Newark, New Jersey, from 1941 to 1946.

Such special agencies, however, form only a small part of the social machinery which could be used. Many churches and many kinds of clubs and societies have served the purpose of widening acquaintance, and they are well fitted to do so because they attract members in relation to some specialized interest and not merely to the general desire to meet somebody. But these organizations could be far more effective (1) if they would plan their activities to give time for the free mingling of people in an atmosphere which is both educative and attractive and (2) if they would through leaders or other key persons give more attention to the study and guidance of individual members. In one NYA group on work projects it was reported that the wider acquaintance between the sexes and within each sex was one of the chief values obtained by the program. Several organizations in the same community might join to set up a clearing house for recreational interests and personal acquaintance, operated by a part- or full-time secretary, and having an attractive reception room where people could wait and be introduced. This would be a worthwhile project for a council of social agencies, a local church federation, or a council representative of a whole community.

[43] See Lee R. Steiner, *Where Do People Take Their Troubles?* (Boston: Houghton Mifflin, 1945), for a firsthand investigation and serious criticism, from a professional social-work point of view, of practically all these agencies. Newark's "Introduction" (see below) is, however, commended.

[44] Operated largely by volunteer service, under the leadership of Mrs. Elizabeth Wells Puth.

The function of social introductions is of course performed by many existing organizations and customs, which tend to bring together persons of similar social status, religious affiliation, and the like. They should, however, be supplemented by agencies which will bring together people of similar individual interests or complementary personality needs, cutting across these other social classifications. It is somewhat risky to marry a person of very different social status or cultural background. But a moderate and sometimes an extreme difference in these respects may be safer than marriage to a person who cannot share one's most cherished interests and ideals, *if* one can be reasonably sure that these interests and ideals are permanent.

Changing Mores and Individual Adjustment

Many other changes in courtship practices have been suggested. For example, girls now have more devices for taking the initiative in courtship than they formerly had. It is thought that if these were made more frank and honest and that if the stigma which attaches to feminine aggressiveness were entirely removed, we should probably get a better matching of partners. John F. Cuber has cited evidence of considerable change in urban areas during the decade 1933–1943 toward (1) women taking initiative in arranging dates or suggesting the form the date should take, (2) women paying expenses of recreation and the "Dutch treat," (3) less feeling of possessiveness as well as greater physical intimacy during the courtship stage, (4) the single standard of morality.[45]

The Kinsey report [46] showed that during the 22 year period from about 1923 to about 1945, premarital intercourse increased somewhat among males of grade school education but did not change among males of the college level. The report estimates, however, that from a third to a half of the intercourse which males used to have with prostitutes replaced itself by increased premarital acts with companions or other girls. Obviously the total number of such acts must be the same for the two sexes, but many lines of evidence indicate that these premarital acts are now spread out through a wider segment of the female sex rather than concentrated among a marked and labeled few.[47]

There were certain more definite and significant findings in the Kinsey report. (1) There have been definite increases in petting at all social levels,

[45] "Changing Courtship and Marriage Customs," *Annals of the American Academy of Political and Social Science,* Sept., 1943.

[46] Alfred C. Kinsey, Wardell B. Pomeroy, and Clyde E. Martin, *Sexual Behavior in the Human Male* (Philadelphia: Saunders, 1948).

[47] See, for example, Terman's sample of cases in which female virginity at marriage declined steadily from 85 per cent among the women born before 1890 to 32 per cent among the women born since 1910. Lewis M. Terman and Associates, *Psychological Factors in Married Happiness* (New York: McGraw-Hill, 1938), chap. 12. Other studies giving similar results are described in Joseph K. Folsom, *The Family and Democratic Society* (New York: John Wiley and Sons, 1943), chaps. 11 and 14. Much of the increased premarital intercourse seems to be "with future spouse"; this is borne out by the recent Burgess and Wallin study.

and on the college level an increase in petting that goes to the point of sexual climax. (2) Petting is much more prevalent in the college than the grade school social stratum, and is also much more approved there. (3) People on the grade-school level both were and are more likely to have premarital intercourse, and although they do not pronounce it virtuous they feel it is more natural and excusable than the prolonged petting of the college level.

It is a serious mistake to think that something is right and good just because people do it, or do it more than they did before. There have been fashions and changes of custom which history later showed to be injurious. This writer believes that it is possible to discover universal ethical principles, harmonious with science and religion, standing above the so-called relativity of particular cultures and codes. His approach to this would resemble that of F. S. C. Northrop in *The Meeting of East and West*.[48] There is no space for this here. But in surveying courtship forms and behavior, we cannot escape the fact that, while practice is never the same as the ideal, there are also striking variations in ideals and values: values sincerely held by the serious people, the law-abiding people, the churchgoing people, even if we limit ourselves to traditional Christian societies. Comparison between past and present is apt to be somewhat indefinite, but we can make some very clear and definite comparisons between social classes, religious and ethnic groups, regions and nations, existing at the present time. Kinsey compared not only practices but sex beliefs and values of three American social strata. From less statistical evidences, such as used by anthropologists, we know that an unmarried couple seen in the woods has very different meanings according to whether it occurs among Greek, Roumanian, Russian, Swedish, or Irish peasants, among Italian or Jewish minorities in the United States, among Deep South Negroes, Kentucky Highlanders, or Bostonian weekend mountaineers. The differences lie in the facts which are inferred and also in how the inferred facts are evaluated.

Some years ago Judge Ben Lindsey proposed "companionate marriage," a new law which would permit divorce by joint consent to a childless couple, but after pregnancy would require the usual divorce procedure of an innocent party's proving the other party guilty of adultery, desertion, cruelty, etc. He proposed to combine this with complete legalization of contraceptive information. He thought that these measures would help youth to shorten the biologically unnatural postponement of sex life and to make an honest tryout of their compatibility, without the guilt of premarital intercourse or the guilt of ordinary divorce procedures in case of failure.[49] Lindsey's proposal created quite a stir in its day. If we hear little of such proposals today, it is not because the need for some such arrangement is any less, but because the need is being partly met by other, less honest-and-above-board methods. It is very difficult to change laws in this field. Also, the formal moral commandments change very slowly if at all: probably we shall always declare that "unchastity is wrong." But in the meantime, subtly and gradually, the

[48] New York: Macmillan, 1947.

[49] Ben B. Lindsey and Wainwright W. Evans, *The Companionate Marriage* (New York: Boni and Liveright, 1927). See also Chapter Twenty-three of this book, on divorce.

terms used in these legal and moral pronouncements change their definitions. "Cruelty" in the divorce court is not what it used to be; "chastity" now seems to mean to many people anything short of the complete sexual act; even "monogamy" can be defined in more than one way. The permissiveness of parents, the tolerance of friends, and even the interpretations of judges change more readily than the text of the law or the code.

Behavior statistics by themselves may mix several different though simultaneous social trends. Thus Kinsey suspects that the real trend is toward less premarital intercourse in America because our intense social climbing process is putting more and more people into the upper and middle class categories where female virginity at marriage is prized, prostitution despised, and yet extreme sexual stimulation through petting condoned. At the same time there may be an increasing tolerance of premarital intercourse for those who are engaged or in love. If so, this would not be anything very new. It might be like the bundling [50] customs of our colonial ancestors or the courtship customs of several highly educated European peoples.

Now that, with the help of Kinsey and others, we have heard so much about physical sex behavior, we may be able to turn our attention to other and more delicate aspects of love and courtship. Are there any mores or standards about how one may, should, or should not express love through words, gifts, and services? Emily Post offers some advice, but we need something deeper. Perhaps this is a field for individual values, but there is a great opportunity here for a group, a college community, etc., to formulate certain values which might make its emotional life run more smoothly. For example, should one ever keep a dating partner guessing about the nature and extent of one's other involvements, if any? Is it kind to break any relationship abruptly? When partners have reached a certain degree of feeling for each other, should there be a permanent loyalty expressed by always keeping in contact and speaking no evil of each other no matter what happens otherwise? What rights does engagement or marriage give one to interfere with the friendships of one's partner? What should be done with love letters? Is it civilized to celebrate a new love affair by tearing up the pictures and souvenirs of a former partner? Would we all be happier if we expressed love in words whenever we felt it toward anyone whatsoever, but without expecting anything in return or using any other mode of expression? By what principles may we classify information about friends as "confidential" and preserve it as such? Should we try to bring together two friends who are hostile or jealous or misunderstanding toward each other? Is there any situation which cannot be improved by sitting the persons involved around a table to talk it out?

It is quite unnecessary to "confess" one's past as a matter of principle. Where both partners have tolerant, scientific attitudes, a mutual revelation of life histories may enrich and deepen their relationship. One should be guided by the partner's feelings, perhaps finding out with the help of a counselor what the partner *really wants* to know. The "frankness" which most matters is to be honest with the partner about one's present attitudes and be-

[50] Baber, *op. cit.*, pp. 94–97.

liefs and intended way of life and about anything else which can really affect the partner's decision or welfare.

It is not meant that rigid rules can be made about these matters, but they are the kinds of problems that need to be discussed much more than they have been. This writer suspects that there are more acute moral dilemmas and psychological conflicts over these questions of *communication, honesty,* and *multiple loyalties,* than over questions of the degree of bodily intimacy.

Are all morals then "relative"? No, not if we believe in the democratic way of life, in the things toward which mankind has been struggling through ages, in the things for which millions have died and are still dying. If we do so believe, then there is a certain inner personal morality which endures through changing social codes. It may be summed up thus: to have no good thing for yourself at the hurt or unfair expense of another; to be honest — not least, intellectually honest; to break a custom only when you are willing that others should do the same when you are placed in the position of disadvantage; to use no human being as a means, but to respect everyone as a person worthy of the greatest possible development.

SELECTED READINGS

BABER, RAY E., *Marriage and the Family* (2nd ed., New York: McGraw-Hill, 1953), chaps. 4–7, 17.

BREEN, MARY J., *Partners in Play* (New York: Barnes, 1936).

BROMLEY, DOROTHY DUNBAR, and BRITTEN, F. H., *Youth and Sex: A Study of 1300 College Students* (New York: Harper, 1938).

BURGESS, ERNEST W., and COTTRELL, LEONARD S., JR., *Predicting Success or Failure in Marriage* (New York: Prentice-Hall, 1939).

——, and LOCKE, HARVEY J., *The Family: From Institution to Companionship* (2nd ed., New York: American Book Co., 1953).

——, and WALLIN, PAUL, *Engagement and Marriage* (Philadelphia: Lippincott, 1953).

COHN, DAVID L., *Love in America* (New York: Simon and Schuster, 1943).

DELL, FLOYD, *Love in the Machine Age* (New York: Farrar and Rinehart, 1930).

FLÜGEL, J. C., *A Psychoanalytic Study of the Family* (London: Wolff, 1926).

FOLSOM, JOSEPH K., *The Family and Democratic Society* (New York: Wiley, 1943), chaps. 11, 14.

HART, HORNELL and ELLA B., *Personality and the Family* (rev. ed.; Boston: Heath, 1941), chaps. 1, 4–8.

HOLLINGSHEAD, A. B., *Elmtown's Youth* (New York: Wiley, 1949).

LUND, FREDERICK L., *Emotions* (New York: Ronald Press, 1939).

MEAD, MARGARET, *Male and Female* (New York: Morrow, 1949).

MERRILL, FRANCIS E., *Courtship and Marriage, A Study in Social Relationships* (New York: Sloan, 1949).

ROUGEMONT, DENIS DE, *Love in the Western World* (New York: Harcourt, Brace, 1940).

STEINER, LEE R., *Where Do People Take Their Troubles?* (Boston: Houghton Mifflin, 1935).

Terman, L. M., *Psychological Factors in Marital Happiness* (New York: McGraw-Hill, 1938).

Waller, Willard, *The Family: A Dynamic Interpretation,* rev. by Reuben Hill (New York: Dryden Press, 1951), chaps. 6–12, 25.

TOPICS FOR DISCUSSION OR REPORTS

1. Write a case history of a love relation.
2. Get several fellow students to write anonymous introspective reports upon the feelings of love when at high intensity.
3. What items of outward behavior are regarded as tests of love? Make a list. Do you know of any case in which one partner tried to "test" the other's love? Describe what happened.
4. Compare our conceptions and valuations of love and of emotion with those expressed in the literature of other prominent nations such as Great Britain, France, and Russia.
5. Write up one or more cases in which a person tried to maintain two or more simultaneous relations involving strong affection.
6. Analyze several current motion pictures as to their treatment of love and courtship.
7. Analyze one or more cases of ambivalence of feeling. Do these support the thesis advanced in the text about ambivalence?
8. Study the story plots in magazines of the "true story" type. What generalizations can you make about them?
9. Describe one or more cases of disillusion or disappointment in love. What effects do these experiences have on the personality and later behavior?
10. Analyze the effect of reading a romantic story or seeing a romantic movie upon (a) a person who is in love, (b) a person not in love.
11. Describe the courtship mores and customs of (a) your home community, or the circle in which you have your social life, (b) your college community. How much of the "rating and dating" pattern appears?
12. Read a good description of courtship customs in some primitive society or an advanced society other than ours, and compare them with our own.
13. Describe cases of jealousy and possessiveness found in friendships within the same sex. What light do these cases throw upon the problem of jealousy in heterosexual groups?
14. Compare the first and second Kinsey reports. Are the standards of scientific impartiality the same? What have the reviews in the professional as distinct from the popular publications been like?

Chapter Eight

How Mates Are Sorted

MANFORD HINSHAW KUHN

Do YOU expect to marry? Nearly everyone in his late teens and early twenties not only intends to marry but spends an enormous amount of time talking, thinking, and daydreaming about the kind of mate he expects to choose and the kind of family he hopes to have. This is not surprising when we consider how important the outcome is to the later course of anyone's life. It is even more understandable when we consider that the youth, whether boy or girl, has had his basic purposes and intentions molded by *family living*. His own parental family, a constellation comprised of a host of deeply ingrained and intermeshing habits working within and between its members, is the most important model he has for picturing his future pattern of life. If his deepest needs and wishes have been satisfied in this parental family situation, he has an almost irrepressible need to establish his own family when his growing independence severs most of the ties with his parental family. It is as natural, then, to spin dreams about the choice of a mate as it is to spin dreams about the choice of a vocation. In fact, the two problems are often so related that neither can be considered alone.

But can you really "decide" whether or not to marry? Can you "choose" your wife or husband? Can you "plan" a wise and stable marriage? There is much less choice involved than is commonly believed. A number of factors narrow the range of conscious choice, factors which are not essentially different from those involved in any other aspect of human behavior. We may place them in three broad categories: (1) Personal and temperamental traits are first in the list; these result from the interplay of inherited predisposition and early childhood experiences, probably forming the framework on which most later attitudes and purposes are built. (2) *Inter*personal factors come next; these are the precipitate of interaction during the immediate period of courtship. (3) Then there are *im*personal factors of three principal varieties: (a) spatial and occupational limitations upon choice — such as vicinally (inexactly, geographically) imposed isolation; (b) limitations resulting from the peculiarities of population structure and sex ratio; (c) cultural permissives, cultural preferences, cultural prescriptions, and similar shadings of cultural prohibitions with respect to marital choice and in terms of status in the group. It should be noted that all these types of factors tend to limit conscious choice without themselves becoming conscious or subject to conscious control or alteration. From this standpoint there is a grain of truth in the romantic doctrine that "Some one person is destined by the stars in their courses to be my mate." Is not every person limited (that is, somewhat "predestined") in settling the problem of whether or not to marry, in choosing a mate, in planning intelligently for a happy marriage, by such factors as his vicinal position, his parents' vocational and economic group, his inherited intelligence, as well as by his traits of temperament and physique as they have been modified by early childhood experiences?

This is not, however, a fatalistic or deterministic philosophy which would rule out the exercise of intelligent choice and rational planning. On the contrary, it is precisely through bringing certain limiting processes to one's conscious attention that he is able to be reasonable rather than romantic in the choices he does have the capacity to make. In short, we can marry wisely only if we understand wherein wisdom is possible.

In this chapter we shall discuss the processes involved in leading people to choose various types of mates, and the consequences to marriage stability and success of such "choices." But first we shall look at those persons who fail to marry at all, for just as in any other branch of scientific inquiry we can learn much about typical behavior from studying that which is atypical — and failure to marry is distinctly atypical in our society.

FAILURE TO MARRY

"We are the most married nation on earth," as professors assert repeatedly to their classes on the family, and yet about one person in ten never marries. That so many should fail to marry is surprising when we consider how habituated to and dependent upon family roles each of us comes to be through the conditioning experiences which we undergo as children — at the very time in our lives when our personalities are being basically shaped and molded. How can we account for this one person in every ten, particularly when we note further the fact that his married friends exert pressure upon the unmarried individual in many subtle ways, the most obvious effect of which is to exclude him from the circle? Parents and relatives begin to volunteer subtle but insistent advice when he remains unmarried beyond the age of twenty-five (this is even more true for young women than for young men). Even the cultural restrictions on freedom of behavior of single women become more obvious and probably more keenly felt by them when most of their friends have married. There are places where they may not go unescorted. Finding a socially acceptable living arrangement becomes more complicated. In smaller localities the single person, male or female, is forced into a pattern of living so different from that of the rest of the community that he is soon aware of not "belonging."[1] And finally he who does not marry must face, more or less alone, the problem of dealing with sexual drives, with the understanding that most of the ways alternative to marriage of getting release and gratification for these drives are highly disapproved by our society. What, then, are the reasons why some people never marry?

Paradoxically, one of the processes leading to nonmarriage is identical

---

[1] See, for example, Robert and Helen Lynd, *Middletown in Transition* (New York: Harcourt Brace and Co., 1937), p. 147: "Middletown is a marrying city. The unmarried members of the research staff, coming from New York with its larger proportion of young bachelor men and women, felt the pressure of pairwise activity. One felt it all the way from such simple matters as the dearth of pleasant places to eat if one did not have a home, through the customary activities that constitute 'spending the evening' in Middletown."

with that process which is most potent in leading people to marriage. It is the process which causes adult attitudes and behavior patterns to result largely from childhood experiences. Usually, as we have seen, this tends to bring people to marry, but in the case of an unhappy childhood, one in which basic wishes and needs remained unsatisfied and frustrated, the carry-over to adulthood will often include hostile attitudes toward marriage and family life or in other cases toward members of the opposite sex. It is probably well that such people do not marry in great numbers, for when they do, they often play roles which lead to an inordinate amount of conflict — roles which at times are carried over from the patterns of intense conflict followed by parents and at other times occur simply by the continual expectation of frustration from family life, conditioned by unfortunate early experiences. This reason for not marrying is one of the personal and internal factors limiting marriage over which there is little conscious control. After all, one cannot choose his parents, nor even his childhood experiences!

Some people do not marry because the objects of their sexual and affectional drives are those of their own sex. It is a "common sense" assumption in our society that interest in the opposite sex "comes naturally" — in other words, is innate — and that homosexuals are biological freaks or "queers." This assumption is no longer held among biologists, psychiatrists, and psychologists. The more tenable picture would seem to be this: the heterosexual direction of the sexual drive is not implicit in the drive itself, especially since the individual of either sex is even somewhat bisexual in organic equipment. The direction of the sexual interest is acquired as a result of conditioning. The drive is without object at the outset, and the various processes by which it becomes attached to an object are as yet imperfectly understood (see the previous chapter, pp. 215–217, for a summary of what we do know about love focus). It seems likely that we all tend to identify ourselves with those of our own sex at some time or other in childhood or youth, but most of us pass through more or less culturally standardized experiences in which our love drives become firmly directed toward those of the opposite sex. Some people, whether from constitutional or circumstantial causes, remain attached to the homosexual class of love-objects. When homosexuals, or "inverts" as they are sometimes called, do marry the results are usually tragic. Consequently it is well that these people, too, do not ordinarily marry. Here again we are dealing with personality factors over which a person has little or no control — in the ordinary sense of the word "control."

Other personality variations which may, in specific situations, disqualify people for marriage are too numerous to list here. There are people who tend to recede from all social relations and dwell in worlds of fantasy within themselves. Others are inordinately suspicious. The actions of still others are of a highly compulsive nature.

A person may upon occasion feel "compelled" to marry a certain individual. In one such case a college student found that the mate she felt compelled to marry did not share her compulsion, but even this did not stop her from attempting to bring about what seemed, for reasons she could not give, to be inevitable. This one-sided affair dragged on for quite a time until the man finally married another girl. Even this did not put an end to the first girl's compulsions. She attempted to interfere, manipulating friends and acquaintances in an endeavor calculated to alienate the two.

In another instance of compulsive behavior a marriage did take place, but its unstable character points up our notion: namely, that by studying factors which generally lead to nonmarriage we can learn a great deal about the factors which make for success and stability in a marriage relationship. In this case a girl from a very respectable and well-known family felt compelled to marry a boy who was far beneath her social status. The object of her choice was of an acquiescent disposition, and though he was not at all emotionally involved with her, her attention, compulsive though it was, was exceedingly gratifying to his ego. They eloped, but her family's disapproval and all the other objections to the match which her compulsion had led her to ignore at the outset finally operated not merely to neutralize but rather to reverse her emotional set. Coming to hate her husband as compulsively as she had previously wished to marry him, she even tried to murder him. Of course, as Waller and Hill put it,[2] "love at first sight" has a certain compulsive quality, but it is not ordinarily so extreme as in the above instances.

Some people remain so emotionally attached to their parents that they can never bear the thought of renouncing this affection in order to marry. They are said to have "mother fixations" or "father fixations." Fortunately such types are much more rare than during the Victorian era when the cultural norms tended to sanction this kind of personality development. Then there are those who are more or less the opposites of these parent-fixated individuals. After rebellious and negativistic childhoods, they remain so negativistic and uncooperative as adults that, happily for society, they never find mates with personalities pleasing enough to suit them. And there are those who, being egocentric, love themselves so much that no one else can offer effective competition.

Then there are those whose physique or health has some quirk which makes marriage unlikely. Unmarried men in our society are probably shorter, on the average, than married men, because of the group among them who are unmarried because they are short. This difference should tend to increase because the rising emphasis on dancing makes height more and more of a selective factor in a young woman's choice of a mate. Others do not marry because of chronic illness — and of course there are those who imagine illness because they are not married! Some have muscular or skeletal disabilities.[3] Others are unattractive in form, homely of feature, or lacking in grace of movement.

[2] Willard Waller, *The Family: A Dynamic Interpretation,* rev. by Reuben Hill (New York: Dryden Press, 1951), p. 200.

[3] The marriageability of men with physical disabilities is likely to increase somewhat as a result of the war. More than half of all families in the United States, according to Wilma Donahue and Clark Tibbitts in their article, "The Task Before the Veteran and Society," *Annals of the American Academy of Political and Social Science,* 239 (May, 1945), p. 1, now include one or more disabled persons. The commonness of physical disability, the war-caused imbalance of the sex ratio, the increasing employability of men with disability because of planned programs designed to that end — all of these will converge to increase a physically disabled man's chances of marrying.

So far we have been concerned with those whom Waller terms "rejected types." It should be kept clearly in mind that those who are rejected types in our society would not necessarily be scorned in other societies. Standards of beauty, of health, of "normal personality," and the like are largely culturally determined and hence vary from one group to another. For example, a hairy upper lip on a young woman is considered a mark of beauty in certain southern European groups, while in our society millions of dollars are spent annually to remove any suggestion of such hair. Standards of desirability are never completely determined by the culture, however, and much of their content in any individual's thinking is unique and subjective. Hence a rejected type in a certain social group in Kankakee might be acceptable to a different group in Kokomo. The "rejected type" theory, while not absolute, does help us to explain why some people never marry.[4]

A large portion of those who fail to marry would be rather poor marital risks anyway. Yet a great many people who are bad risks do manage to get married, and again, many who are good risks do not. How may we account for the fact that certain persons of charm, intelligence, emotional balance, and emotional independence from infantile attachments fail to marry?

This is to be explained, partially at least, by the fact that there are a number of other strongly held values in our society which in certain instances tend to conflict with the value of marrying and establishing a family. Ambition to be professionally successful is an example. Careers are often interfered with by marriage and the establishment of binding and restricting family relationships. The length of the training period for entrance into a profession often results in delaying marriage until all of one's friends of the opposite sex have already married.

Not only the training for a career but also the nature of the career itself may contribute to the nonmarriage rate. For example, the kinds of work which women usually undertake are those in which there are very few men. Table 3, on the facing page, is a table of occupations which women most frequently enter, showing the disproportionate number of women in such pursuits. The occupations traditionally entered by women are precisely those offering the least chances of finding husbands.

Furthermore there are a number of cultural factors which help to explain why some good marital risks never marry. One such is the discrepancy between the courtship situation and the marriage situation. Almost all those who fit smoothly into the courtship situation, as it is defined in our society, get married, but they are not necessarily good marital risks. The reverse of the last remark is also true — not all good marital risks fit smoothly into the courtship situation and those who do not, run a grave risk of not having a chance to marry. Movies, dances, and moonlight drives (the courtship situation) are a far cry from holding a job, keeping a house,

---

[4] The concept of rejected type should be used with caution, however, for some people fail to marry because of *chance* factors and then as they grow older take on undesirable personality traits from their bitterness over failure to marry. To explain such cases as "failure to marry because of rejected type" would be a gross error. The causal sequence is the other way round in such instances.

rearing children, and meeting frequent crises of all varieties (the marriage-and-family situation).

Another factor responsible for many persons' not marrying has to do with the dizzy height of our American standard of living, perhaps more as it is observed by young people through the movies than in life in their own city blocks. A good many young people regard as essential deep freezes, station wagons, television sets, phono-radio-recorder combinations, electric ranges, electric food mixers, a ranch-style house, and a host of other such items. For them, ability to have these at the very start is a prerequisite of marriage.

TABLE 3

Distribution of Men and Women in Selected Occupations [5]

Occupation	% Male	Men	Women
Teachers	24.3	247,716	772,044
Social and Welfare Workers	35.7	24,868	44,809
Trained Nurses and Student Nurses	2.1	7,509	348,277
Librarians	10.5	3,801	32,546
Religious Workers	25.4	8,798	25,874
Telephone Operators	5.4	10,697	189,002

That they are out of reach of most young couples is obvious when we consider that in the prosperous year 1952 only 25 per cent of the "spending units" (chiefly families) received as much as $5000 or more in income! [6] This discrepancy between what they have been led to expect and what they find possible keeps a number of young people from marrying.

To sum up with respect to nonmarriage: personal, interpersonal, and impersonal factors operate to keep some persons from marrying. In the living tissue of life it is virtually impossible to disentangle one pure type of factor (e.g., a purely personal factor) from another type. Look, for instance, at the high-standard-of-living illustration cited immediately above: one set of cultural norms conspires to instill the high standard (goal) of living in all of us reared in America, but conditions in society often preclude the attaining of this standard. Some of us have attributes and resources of personality to bridge this gap between aspiration and achievement in order at the same time to achieve other culturally inspired goals such as getting married; others lack such a flexibility of personality. Aside from this lesson pointing up the interwoven character of processes at work on these three levels, the most important result of our survey of reasons for failure to marry — and this has probably occurred to you already — is the suggestion of the hypothesis that these very reasons also have something to do with instability *within* marriage. We shall return to this point later.

[5] See the *16th Census of the United States: 1940, Population, Vol. 3, The Labor Force, Part 1;* U. S. *Summary,* Table 58, pp. 75–80. Figures for 1950 were not yet available (June, 1953), but undoubtedly the proportions have not changed remarkably.

[6] See "Selected Preliminary Findings of the 1953 Survey of Consumer Finances," *Federal Reserve Bulletin,* 39 (March, 1953), pp. 217–218. Forty-three per cent of the spending units received less than $3000!

Factors Affecting Mate Selection

Personality traits are rarely if ever desirable or undesirable in an absolute and universal sense. As we mentioned, each group has its own norms of desirability which its members come to look upon as absolute and imperative. Then, too, every person, through his unique personal-social experiences [7] in areas of behavior which are not culturally standardized, develops subjective ideals, standards, and tastes with regard to what he deems desirable in a mate.[8] The degree to which any of these standards operates, however, depends on whether members of the opposite sex who would qualify under such standards are *available*. You will not really choose a mate from all the members of the opposite sex in America who happen to fit your consciously or unconsciously held standards. You will, rather, be forced to select your marriage partner from among those with whom you come in contact. Briefly this means that we must now consider what effects occupational contiguity, residential propinquity, and social contacts have on mate selection, for these are obviously of prime importance to the question of availability of potentially suitable mates. Crosscutting these factors is that of the sex ratio in any particular grouping. We shall first consider in detail this problem of the sex ratio as it affects marriage.

The Sex Ratio as a Factor in Mate Selection

How many of each sex are there in each group in which you participate? This is an important question for a number of reasons. A young man will be, generally speaking, *less* "choosy" if there are more young men than young women in the group from which he must choose a mate, and a young woman in the same group will tend to be *more* particular in her choice. This means that the size of a courtship group and the sex ratio (usually expressed in number of males per 100 females) have to be considered in connection with any evaluation of the importance of desirable personality traits.

The sex ratio undoubtedly has an important effect upon the number of marriages in any given group. Even at birth the number of males per 100 females is not exactly equal; there are ordinarily 104 males born for every 100 females. The most serious imbalance in the sex ratio exists between three different types of population: (1) geographical divisions, (2) rural-urban divisions, and (3) divisions between socioeconomic classes.

The West has attracted more men than women of marrying age. New England has for some time had a sex ratio for its total population lower than that of the other regions of the nation and thus less favorable to a high marriage rate. In 1950 the number of males per 100 females in the entire coun-

---

[7] For a discussion of the concept "personal-social" see Kimball Young, *Personality and Problems of Adjustment* (2nd ed., New York: Appleton-Century-Crofts, 1952), pp. 6, 124–125.

[8] Folsom has discussed some aspects of this problem of individual preferences, Chapter Seven above, pp. 231–232.

try was 98.6, while in Massachusetts the ratio was 93.8.[9] The South is some-what better off, but even so the ratio does not equal 100. In Georgia, for example, the sex ratio was 96.2, while for urban nonwhites it was a dismal 83.3.[10] Texas had a sex ratio of 100.4, only slightly poorer than Colorado's, which was 100.8. The superiority of the West appears to decrease with each decade. California's sex ratio in 1950 was only 100.1, although Washington had one of 106.0 and a whopping 128.0 for the 20–24 age bracket or rural farm whites! This imbalance means that men have a scarcity value in New England and that women have a scarcity value in the Northwest. The implications of the sex ratio for the problem of marriage versus nonmarriage have been studied by Ogburn.[11] He finds that the highest percentage of married persons will be found not in a population with a sex ratio of exactly 100 but in one having a considerable excess of men, perhaps having 115 or 120 to 100 women. Ogburn also finds that men are little affected by the sex ratio as far as their ultimate chances of marrying are concerned, while women are considerably affected. Men are probably marriageable because of economic qualifications; women's marriageability largely depends on the marriage market.

Cities attract young women from the country to a greater degree than they attract young men. Table 4 indicates the disproportionate number of

TABLE 4

A COMPARISON OF RURAL AND URBAN SEX RATIOS [12]

Area	Sex Ratio of All Classes of the Population in Each Area
United States, 1950	98.6
Urban	94.6
Rural Nonfarm	103.6
Rural Farm	110.1

females in the urban population. Metropolitan Boston had, for example, a sex ratio of 92.7. It must not be concluded, however, that the situation is universally poorest in the urban Northeast. Colorado Springs had a dismal ratio of 83.6, while Chicopee, Mass., had a surprising ratio just under 108! Metropolitan San Francisco (including Oakland) appears to have one of the most favorable ratios of any city in the country, with a ratio of 102.3. Thus while the young woman residing in a city has, generally speaking, less chance of marrying than does the young woman on a farm,[13] obviously some cities are better supplied with men than are others. Others may have a modest sex ratio for the entire population, while having a very favorable one for the relevant groups and brackets. Seattle, for example, had a ratio of 100.9, but for single persons fourteen years and over, the sex ratio in 1950 was 130!

[9] These figures and all other figures for 1950 are from the *17th Census of the United States: 1950, Preprint of Vol. 2,* U. S. Government Printing Office, 1952.
[10] This indicates a marked sex differential in Negro migration.
[11] See E. R. Groves and W. F. Ogburn, *American Marriage and Family Relationships* (New York: Holt, 1932), chap. 13.
[12] From the *17th Census of the United States: 1950, Preprint of Vol. 2, Part 1,* Chapter B, pp. 107–108.
[13] This situation is becoming more rather than less serious, apparently, for the urban sex ratio was 98.1 in 1930, 95.5 in 1940, and 94.6 in 1950.

During the Second World War sex ratios changed rapidly. The induction of fifteen million men into the armed forces brought about, first of all, a sudden shift of men from the parts of the country in which they lived to the fairly concentrated regions where they were trained; and secondly, the removal of many overseas, which temporarily lowered the sex ratio of the whole country. In addition to this there were wholesale shifts of the civilian population to centers of war production. While figures of interstate migration are available, statistics indicating the shifts in sex ratio are lacking. We can be sure, however, that the large number of men killed in action, the establishment of permanent armed forces several times the size of previous peacetime forces, and the gains made by urban populations will conspire to establish sex ratios in many areas which will be unfavorable to high marriage rates.

There is a low sex ratio among the upper socioeconomic classes and a high one among the lower classes. This is borne out by comparing the sex ratios of working-class residential districts with those of upper-class residential districts. Rapid shifts in economic opportunity give rise to a large semifloating population of unattached workingmen. Young women normally engage in teaching, nursing, or other occupations in which there are few men, and they tend to move up the socioeconomic ladder. Those young women born at the top of the ladder tend to remain at home, while the young men of that class frequently must leave in order to enter business.

Actually, the sex ratio impinges on one's fate with respect to marriage only in terms of his own little social world, which is never coextensive with a region, a city, or an economic class. In a primitive society, the young men designated as eligible to marry a particular young lady are often clearly defined. In our highly mobile society (from both a vicinal and a social standpoint), such definitions are at best hazy and highly elastic. Frequently a young woman, because of her particular vocation or because of her participation in certain types of leisure-time activities, may have several times as many potential and actual young men friends as her equally attractive sister who has chosen a vocation and/or avocation in which there are very few men. In this instance, neither region nor rural-urban difference nor socioeconomic class has anything directly to do with the difference between the sex ratios of the respective social worlds of the sisters.

RESIDENTIAL AND OCCUPATIONAL PROPINQUITY

The notion of a limited social world from which each must select his mate [14] has proved valuable to us in our analysis of the operation of the sex ratio on mating. It is a very valuable frame of reference for the study of mating, for it enables us to see how impersonal factors (such as the culture, war, unemployment, etc.) impinge on the individual in a very personal way. We can use this frame of reference in explaining how residence and occupation bear upon marital choice.

[14] Waller put it this way: "One does not select a wife from the whole group of possible wives, but only from the group of women he knows." *Op. cit.*, p. 204.

Even though today's world has shrunk tremendously from yesterday's because of conveniences such as the automobile, the airplane, the radio, and the like, each person's little social world is still made up in good measure of people who live quite close to him. Consequently, the person chosen for a mate is more likely to live close to one than far away. Bossard, in a study of five thousand consecutive Philadelphia marriages occurring in the first five months of 1931, found that more than a third of these marriages were between people who lived within five blocks or less of one another, while over half were between people who lived within twenty blocks.[15] Several studies have confirmed Bossard's finding that propinquity is a factor in mate selection. The most recent is that by Marches and Turbeville on marriages in Duluth. Table 5 gives a summary of their findings.

TABLE 5

DISTRIBUTION, CUMULATIVELY, OF THREE HUNDRED CONSECUTIVE MARRIAGES BY RESIDENTIAL PROPINQUITY BEFORE MARRIAGE IN DULUTH IN 1952 [16]

Number of Blocks Apart	Number of Cases	Per Cent
Same address	17	5.67
Within one block	24	8.00
Within two blocks	34	11.33
Within three blocks	46	15.33
Within four blocks	53	17.66
Within five blocks	62	20.66
Within ten blocks	93	30.99
Within fifteen blocks	112	37.32
Within twenty blocks	128	42.65

That the influence of propinquity may even be increasing in most communities despite the steady growth of individuation and mobility is indicated by a comparison of two studies of residential propinquity prior to marriage in New Haven. Ruby Jo Reeves Kennedy summarizes this comparison in a table showing cumulative percentages of those who marry, having lived at specified distances from one another before marriage.

Her findings, and the findings of more recent studies,[17] indicate that nationality, ethnic, religious, and other social groupings are responsible for a good share of this tendency to choose a mate living in the same general area. It is a mistake, then, to consider residential propinquity *per se* as a direct factor favoring marriage or as a "cause" operating in marital choice. It is not mere physical nearness but social nearness that is significant. Social nearness is compounded out of meanings derived from *social* contexts, not from distances in feet. Social meanings stem not only from national groupings but

[15] J. H. S. Bossard, "Residential Propinquity as a Factor in Marriage Selection," *American Journal of Sociology*, 38 (Sept., 1932), pp. 219–224.
[16] Joseph R. Marches and Gus Turbeville, "The Effect of Residential Propinquity on Marriage Selection," *American Journal of Sociology*, 58 (May, 1953), p. 594.
[17] A. C. Clarke, "An Examination of the Operation of Residential Propinquity as a Factor in Mate Selection," *American Sociological Review*, 17 (Feb., 1952), pp. 17–22; G. J. Schnepp and Louis A. Roberts, "Residential Propinquity and Mate Selection on a Parish Basis," *American Journal of Sociology*, 58 (July, 1952), pp. 45–50.

also from socioeconomic classes and from occupational groupings, both of which relate to residential propinquity.

We have already seen, in connection with the problem of nonmarriage, the tendency of men and women to get into occupations limited chiefly to one sex. This should prepare us for the fact that people tend to marry those

TABLE 6

CUMULATIVE PERCENTAGE DISTRIBUTION OF RESIDENTIAL PROPINQUITY
BEFORE MARRIAGE IN NEW HAVEN, IN 1931 AND 1940 [18]

Number of Blocks Apart	Per Cent	
	1931	1940
Same address	9.05	9.92
Within five	33.30	35.79
Within ten	55.44	55.48
Within twenty	64.43	76.31
Over twenty	35.59	23.69

within the same occupation. An early study [19] found that the number of marriages occurring within occupations (in the native American group) was 2.8 times as high as would be expected from the operation of chance factors alone. Another study [20] indicates that the higher an individual is in the occupational scale the less subject he is to vicinal contacts in the choice of mate.[21] Unlike the effect of residential propinquity, that of occupational propinquity is important to marriage choice even toward the top end of the occupational ladder. The tendency is for women doctors to marry doctors, women engineers to marry engineers, and women lawyers to marry lawyers. Of course this cannot work the other way around, for there are very few women in these higher professions. Each occupational group isolates itself to some extent through the social distance which it establishes between itself and other groups — a social distance which serves to augment its "collective ego" figuratively speaking. This isolation augments intragroup marriage. Social distance and its consequent group isolation result in limiting the single person's little social world largely to those of the same occupational group as himself. If this has a moral it is largely directed toward women rather than men. Women seeking to marry men with similar occupational and other interests ought to avoid what is traditionally "woman's work" and invade occupations which men have always attempted to relegate to themselves. This is not an easy thing to do, for men use all kinds of devices to keep certain occupations for themselves. For example, the attitudes which many doctors and medical students take toward the woman medical student, whom they often term, with a certain amount of contempt, "a hen medic,"

[18] Ruby Jo Reeves Kennedy, "Premarital Residential Propinquity and Ethnic Endogamy," *American Journal of Sociology,* 48 (March, 1943), pp. 580–584. This table is from page 581.
[19] Donald Marvin, "Occupational Propinquity as a Factor in Marriage Selection," *Quarterly Publication of the American Statistical Association,* 16 (Sept., 1918), pp. 131–150.
[20] A report of this study by Daniel Harris is to be found in the *New York Times,* April 8, 1934.
[21] See also the study by Richard Centers, "Marital Selection and Occupational Strata," *American Journal of Sociology,* 54 (May, 1949), pp. 530–535, which shows substantial occupational endogamy.

are enough to distract her mind and make it very difficult to complete the arduous training required.

MATE SELECTION IN THE COLLEGE SITUATION

As a factor affecting mate selection, the college situation is, in a sense, only a special combination of factors we have already considered. If vicinal proximity of and by itself has any influence, then the small college in particular offers an opportunity *par excellence* for this factor to operate. Even the large university is often a rather closely knit community from the standpoint of its physical plant — its dormitories, laboratories, and classroom buildings. But this factor is made significant, again, as in the case of residential areas in urban communities, by factors that determine *social* nearness and distance. Attending a college or university is in itself an occupation, so that vicinal proximity is given meaning by the underlying factor of occupational propinquity. Then, too, the relative sameness of their socioeconomic class backgrounds gives college students more interest in common, more likelihood of speaking a "common language," and a greater sharing of common "social definitions of the situation" — all of which quite obviously facilitate heightened participation and social interaction.

While recognizing that college students tend to come to a large extent from a relatively small stratum of the outside society, we would be blinding ourselves to important factors in mate selection if we were to ignore the existence of stratification on the college and university campus. However narrow in comparison to the breadth of stratification in our outside society the segments from which college and university students are drawn, there nevertheless exists on most campuses a fairly complex class structure, indigenous to the college itself and considered as a little society.[22] This class structure, on the one hand, tends both to reflect and magnify the relatively slight class differences in the larger society from which the students came and, on the other, to be a function of goals, many of them conflicting, peculiar to the campus in question.

There has been much over-simplification of this problem of social stratification in connection with descriptions of courtship patterns on college campuses. It has frequently been assumed that fraternity affiliation and football feats are the principal factors in placing the individual on the college social scale. It is further assumed that this scale has virtually universal recognition on each campus and that those who do not accept its validity consciously and overtly are merely those who rank low on that scale and who are thus manifesting nothing more than a "sour-grapes psychology" when they maintain they do not subscribe to the values such a scale objectifies.

We must remember that no generally acceptable set of concepts has been developed for describing the social stratification which exists in the larger American society. Our society is multivalued, and many of the gradients

---

[22] See Willard Waller, *op. cit.,* pp. 148–157 for discussions of social gradations with respect to courtship on college campuses.

measured in terms of some of these values cut right across gradients expressing others. While monetary success, for example, is unquestionably the
strongest value, professional, service, and skill successes often carry little
money reward, although they have their effects on social stratification. So,
in a similar fashion, each little campus "world" is multivalued and it is thus
in the nature of a value judgment to assume that one cluster of values (in
this case, fraternity and football values) with its attendant objectification in
terms of a social hierarchy is the only, the "real," basis for social gradation
which everyone "really" accepts.

Waller suggested [23] that everyone on a college campus is pegged somewhere on a "rating scale" with respect to dating, an idea all of a piece with
his notion of a "scale of courtship desirability." This suggestion presup-
poses, implicitly or explicitly, a single value or else a cluster of consistent
values in accordance with which the individual can be measured. To demonstrate the validity of this construct it is not enough to show that a few individuals have numbers of dates all out of proportion to the number which
the average student has or that many individuals have virtually no dates at
all; one has to go ahead and show that a single set of standards is operating
on a campus-wide scale in such a way as to bring about these differences in
dating and courtship popularity. Because of the multivalued character of the
campus such a single scale is obviously nonexistent.

Instead of advancing the hypothesis that social stratification on American campuses is a function of the football-and-fraternity complex, we ought,
if we are to derive predictive results from it, to use this hypothesis to build
a constructed type. In conjunction with this constructed type we might then
set up several other constructed types, for there are many of the six or seven
hundred colleges in this country in which neither the football complex nor
fraternity life plays a very significant part in the scaling of individual and
group status and, moreover, the peculiar roles of this sport and this form of
social life vary significantly from one period to another on any one campus.
(Consider as an example the contrasting position of fraternities on many
campuses in the "Joe College" era of the "Roaring 'Twenties," the subdued
period of the "Depression 'Thirties," and the V-12 period of the "War
'Forties.") We might, for instance, quite properly construct other types
relative to social stratification around the following themes: the fraternity-
less college, the football-less college, the "crowd" — or spontaneous and shifting social grouping — college, the religion-centered college, the "educational
mission" college, the "streetcar" college, and the like.

Against this background of general values varying from campus to
campus and from one era to another on any particular campus, are a welter
of standards of the multifold congeniality groups. These groups, while always reflecting or reacting to the values of the dominant culture and more
immediately to the values implicit in the particular cultural atmosphere of
the campus in question, nevertheless have unique and distinctive values of
their own. They get themselves going around a tremendous variety of interests and activities — card playing, movie following, common religious inter-

[23] *Op. cit.*

est, "social consciousness" or "social cause" of some variety (e.g., Marxism, world federalism, Zionism, trade unionism), riding, hosteling, record playing, revolt, Freudianism, malicious gossiping, dating, shooting pool, common crisis experiences (celebrated in their retelling), discussions of sex, and an almost endless list of others, singly or in a variety of combinations and sequences. Each of these groups has its own unique values and goals. These affect the picture of the ideal mate. Thus it is highly unreasonable to presume that there is a single scale of courtship desirability [24] along which every student on a campus is pegged. There are, rather, as many scales as there are differing groups, and it is in these groups that the individual's popularity is made or broken.

That those high on the scale of their little social worlds should tend to pair off with partners similarly rated is an obvious probability. But social interaction is much more complex than even this indicates. Such a mechanical "rating" view presumes a behaviorism that is entirely external, overt, and observable. Actually it is "selves" [25] that are in interaction, not biological organisms. The significance of this is that each self "works over" other persons' estimates, status ascriptions, expectations, and assumptions regarding himself in both his internal feeling and thinking processes and in his overt responses. Thus the "rejected type" which Waller makes a great deal of is really a very complex phenomenon indeed, and not simply someone who fails to "rate." Externally he may be virtually indistinguishable from someone who rates rather high on the scale. The difference lies in his own picture of himself — the role he considers himself to be playing — and this picture of himself in turn is a response to the roles of others which he has internalized and made a part of himself. We never react to purely biological entities. We are basically responding to other people's pictures of themselves as these are communicated to us and as we reconstruct them in accordance with our own conceptions of our own selves. In a society whose culture is as discontinuous, split, conflicting, and internally contradictory in its status and role assignments as that of an American college campus, this notion of "interaction of selves" is highly important. Without it, we cannot scientifically understand the "ratings" of any person on the scale of "courtship desirability."

But there are other problems of assortative mating relative to status and role on the college campus. Coeducational colleges would seem to be ideal mating agencies, for they serve to throw young men and women of marriage-

---

[24] Or "rating scale." I skirt here Waller's sharp distinction between dating and courtship. No such sharp distinction exists in actual behavior. Any such interpretation (that there is a basic difference) is apt to arise in the individual's mind *after* the fact. It is perhaps more descriptive to put the whole matter as John F. Cuber has done in his article, "Changing Courtship and Marriage Customs," in the *Annals of the American Academy of Political and Social Science,* Vol. 229 (Sept., 1943), p. 32, when he writes that the man-woman relationship is one which for the partners "is its own excuse for being." Samuel H. Lowrie, in his research article, "Dating Theories and Student Responses," *American Sociological Review,* 16 (June, 1951), pp. 334–340, demonstrated through ingenious questioning the fallacy of the distinction between dating and courtship.

[25] G. H. Mead, *Mind, Self and Society* (Chicago: University of Chicago Press, 1934).

able age together in an atmosphere of leisure and considerable freedom. In fact, most coeducational colleges have been referred to at one time or another as "marriage mills." Nevertheless, a number of factors have resulted in a rather high nonmarriage rate among college graduates. One of these factors is related to the pattern of "getting established" or "on one's feet" before a young man marries. If he plans to enter a profession a young man may expect to spend a number of years in graduate or professional school after graduating from college. Even if his ambition does not require him to pursue postgraduate training, he usually expects to spend a few years working before marrying. A young woman, on the other hand, is usually ready to marry upon graduation. But she must face the fact that most of the young men she had known in college are not ready to marry.[26] She is also handicapped by what Popenoe calls the "mating gradient," or the tendency for a young man to marry someone of lower intelligence, educational achievement, or social status than his own, while a young woman, on the other hand, plans to marry someone at least as educated, intelligent, and of as high social status as herself. The result is that many a young man postpones marriage so long that he never gets married or, if he does marry, chooses a young woman who either did not go to college or did not complete her college course, while many a young college-trained woman can find no one who meets her exacting requirements and is, at the same time, ready to marry. This situation is serious for young women, for their chances of marriage decline rapidly after the age of twenty-five, in contrast with the fact that men can delay marriage for a considerable time without seriously reducing their ability to find mates.

The actual situation is even darker than this would indicate, for women who are able to go to college are, on the average, from higher socioeconomic strata than are the men. This is attributable to the assumption, by no means dead, that college training is a useful investment in professional training as far as young men are concerned but is primarily a luxury for the principal purpose of adding "polish" and "culture" and maintaining high social status as far as young women are concerned.

Obviously the sex ratio must be taken into account in any discussion of the influence of college life on marriage selection. During World War II coeducational colleges and universities were filled almost exclusively with women students. In the postwar period, under GI benefits and otherwise, men quite literally repossessed American campuses, making the sex ratio almost, but not quite, as badly out of balance in the direction of male preponderance as it had been in the other direction during the war. While the postwar imbalance was more favorable to marriage than the wartime type, other factors have intervened, notably the Korean war and the consequent stepped-up draft. Thus for the past five or six years the sex ratio

---

[26] For a discussion of "dalliance" which this anticipated postponement of marriage leads to, see Waller, *op. cit.*, pp. 141–143. That college men undergo considerable strain as a result of this postponement is indicated in the findings of Clifford Kirkpatrick and Theodore Caplow as reported in their article, "Courtship in a Group of Minnesota Students," *American Journal of Sociology*, 51 (Sept., 1945), pp. 114–125.

on college and university campuses has greatly restricted the operation of colleges as "marriage mills." Here again the interrelated character of factors affecting marital choice and rate is evident.

HOMOGAMY

The term *homogamy* is often used as a synonym for *assortative mating*. We shall use homogamy more narrowly to mean the tendency to mate with a member of the opposite sex having a similar or related personality trait, while assortative mating in our usage includes, additionally, mating with a person from the same vicinity, having the same cultural or social background, belonging to the same socioeconomic class, having a similar vocation, and the like.

Both terms were first used in connection with biological studies of lower animals. When the concept of homogamy is carried over into the description of human mating, considerable care must be taken to understand the inherent differences between human mating and the mating within subhuman species. These differences stem principally from the fact that the human being lives, as we have pointed out, in a world largely defined for him by the evaluations, meanings, norms, and standards of his particular group. The human being is much more malleable, more teachable, and governed far less by biologically determined ways of behaving than are the subhuman animals. This learning ability gives to the human being an adaptability which lower forms of life do not have, but in making his daily adaptations man finds it easiest to take over the ready-made patterns of attitudes and behavior with which his group in the past has met similar situations. Such group custom has something to do with the Chinese taste for ancient eggs and the American delight in malted milk. It may not be as obvious, but it certainly is as true, that custom similarly has to do with the choice of a mate, even in such matters as stature, weight, and the like. Less than fifty years ago the most attractive and desirable type of young woman was buxom almost to the point of being fat. Twenty years ago the most attractive type of young woman was thin and curveless. Whether a young man married a fat young woman in the 1890's or a thin young woman in the 1920's and early 1930's depended not nearly as much upon whether he himself was fat or thin (biological assortative mating) as upon whether or not he stood high or low on some scale of desirability (cultural assortative mating).

In our society people tend to marry those of approximately the same ages. This is sometimes cited as evidence that biological assortative mating is operative among human beings. Yet among the Plateau Indians a young man married a rather old woman as a rule.[27] Thus group tradition and custom are to a large extent determinative in this aspect of mating too.

Every culture singles out certain personality traits for emphasis, and these in turn alter the mating tendencies of the group of marrying age. The preference for light-skinned mates among American Negroes a few years ago is

---

[27] From a lecture by Dr. Ralph Linton.

a case in point. Now that the Negro is more conscious of his own race, many reports suggest that very dark-skinned people rank highest in the scale of courtship desirability, at least among certain segments of Negro society.

A number of studies have been made of assortative mating among human beings: studies of height, age, weight, physical defects, hair color, eye color, intelligence, and temperament. These tend in many cases to support the biological hypothesis that like marry like, that there is much homogamy. The highest correlation found in these studies is that between married partners with respect to intelligence, some studies finding an r of as high as plus .70. All these studies, however, ignore the fact that group meanings remake biological impulses, and until studies are made comparing assortative mating in one cultural group with mating in another, the results of these earlier studies cannot be interpreted with any validity.

To generalize even for our own particular society is dangerous if we do not take into account the wide variety of factors (even other than the biological factors and the cultural factors we have discussed) which bear upon mating choices. For example, the statement is frequently made that people tend to marry those of approximately the same ages as themselves. Yet after a few years of the depression of the 1930's the age of males at marriage had gone up considerably while the age of females remained about the same as that in the predepression years, indicating that the postponed marriages of the first years of the depression had resulted in men marrying women considerably younger than the ones they would have married had there not been a depression to interrupt the normal course of mating.

Yet it would be untrue to say that there is *no* physical or biological aspect of assortative mating in our species. Such an aspect certainly exists but becomes so completely modified through experiential factors that it cannot be isolated in the adult's behavior. One young man reported to this writer that young women were attractive or not to him almost entirely on the basis of the shape of their feet. The biological determinist would undoubtedly assert that this man's criterion stemmed from a basic biological homogamous mating tendency. The orthodox Freudian, too, might find "phylogenetic components" in this and cases of more segmentalized foot-fetishism. This is pure nonsense. Whatever biological vestiges there are in the original nature of man as regards homogamy are completely remade and channeled by the individual's social experiences and by his culture.

In connection with our analysis of homogamy of physical traits we must consider the tendency of people to marry others of the same "racial" skin color. The popular notion is that this preference is an example of homogamy in its original sense — that is, that choosing a mate having the same "racial" skin color is an expression of "instinctive," innate "human nature." To the sociologically and anthropologically sophisticated this is of course both naive and absurd. One has only to go to Hawaii or to Brazil to discover the incongruousness of the assumption that racial endogamy is instinctive. But first let us get a general framework for viewing the whole problem of intermarriage before we analyze the problem of interracial marriage in greater detail.

INTERMARRIAGE

In no society is choice of mate left to the individual without regulation by the group or groups of which he is a member. A common fallacy is to regard marriage regulation as being more or less a product of so-called "higher civilization," with the assumption that marriage among nonliterate peoples is virtually unregulated. Actually, many nonliterate groups regulate choice of mate and marriage to a much greater degree than we do. In fact, our individualism, romanticism, heterogeneity of cultural norms, and urbanization, with its consequent dissolving of primary-group norms and its accentuation of impersonal, touch-and-go relationships, have freed marriage from many of its earlier sacred regulations.[28] There is a tendency for racial, religious, national, educational, and regional groups, and socioeconomic classes to be endogamous in our society. Many people, however, do marry across such lines, and it is these marriages which we wish to consider here.

Not all such marriages are equally cacogamous,[29] that is, bad marriages from the standpoint of the group's norms. In fact, the interclass marriage of the lowly office clerk, for example, to his millionaire employer's daughter receives some approval, albeit mixed with disapproval. We might rank types of intermarriage [30] in order of decreasing cacogamy as follows: (1) interracial marriage; (2) internationality, interclass, and interfaith marriages; (3) inter-educational-group marriage; (4) inter-regional marriage.

INTERRACIAL MARRIAGE

Marriage between races is cacogamous in this country for three basic reasons: (1) Interracial marriage is also intercaste marriage. The caste line between races in this country varies in its rigidity, depending on the region and on the particular races involved, but is probably universally present in some degree. It is most rigid in the South between blacks and whites. (2) Interracial marriage is usually also interclass marriage. Each race has its own culturally defined ways of doing things, and each class within a race has its own subculture. These customs of a class within one race are not at all identical with the customs of a corresponding class within another. If the classes involved in an interracial marriage do not correspond — e.g., middle-class white with lower-class black — the divergence in group traditions and customs is even greater. (3) Underlying and ramifying through the caste divi-

---

[28] The distinction between sacred and secular has already been developed in Chapter One by Professor Howard Becker. One of the aspects of this distinction most relevant to our discussion here has to do with the rationality of the means-ends relationship in any institutional form; see pp. 8–14.

[29] Robert K. Merton, "Intermarriage and the Social Structure: Fact and Theory," *Psychiatry*, 4 (Aug., 1941), pp. 361–374.

[30] The social scientist's use of the term "intermarriage" is the opposite of its popular usage. It refers to marriage of persons belonging to different groups — groups ordinarily *endogamous;* popularly it is used to mean marriage within a group which is ordinarily *exogamous.*

sion between the races is the pseudo-biological myth of racial superiority, with its equally fallacious corollary, the notion that children of interracial marriages have traits biologically inferior to those of either race involved.

Why do people marry across racial lines in our society, if all these impediments exist? No categorical answer to this question can be given. Baber suggests that the reasons for such marriages are the same, in most instances, as those underlying marriages which are racially endogamous, namely, "love, propinquity, mutual interests, etc." [31] This is probably true, but more intensive case-history and psychoanalytic studies of individuals involved in such marriages would probably reveal some significant differences between these individuals and those making more acceptable marital choices. One thing should be said in support of Baber's comment, however: our romantic doctrines have idealized the mysterious and the strange, giving an interracial relation a value which a racially endogamous relation cannot have. Nevertheless, temperament and experiences which produce negativism in the child and rebellion and bohemianism in the young adult probably have a part in such interracial choices on the part of whites. Furthermore, social pariahship of a member of the white race, for whatever reason, undoubtedly explains why he crosses race lines in the selection of a mate. The fact that there are several times as many white women who marry nonwhite men as there are white men who marry nonwhite women suggests a further factor; namely, that fear of not finding a mate at all and the taboo against women's taking the initiative in selecting a mate lead such women to accept nonwhite mates. White men everywhere have assumed sexual access to nonwhite women on an extramarital basis, and the motives of nonwhite men in marrying white women may sometimes involve retaliation not only for this situation but for the existence of the whole caste system as well.

Interracial marriages usually result in the partners' becoming outcasts of both races. Friends desert them; they may not be able to go together to restaurants and theaters or on trains; hotels may not accept them; permanent dwelling places may be hard to find. Probably the hardest of these to accept is the loss of friends. Certainly this loss has tremendous implications for the stability of married life, for a marriage is not a self-contained thing; its inner solidarity is closely related to its outer ties, and secure relations with mutual friends rank high. The inner relations of a marriage across racial lines are also in jeopardy. The difference in cultures represented by the two is almost sure to lead to conflict over views and ways of doing things. Many of us blame our spouses for our own misfortunes and inner conflicts; this habit becomes even more pronounced when marked distinctions of color and culture differentiate mates, offering convenient hooks on which to hang petty grievances and displeasures. Furthermore, the desire for a family is a tremendously solidifying factor in a marriage, and the knowledge of the racially mixed couple that their children will probably be outcasts militates against having them. If children are born, their ostracism may become a

[31] See Ray E. Baber, "A Study of 325 Mixed Marriages," *American Sociological Review,* 2 (Oct., 1937), pp. 695–716, or his *Marriage and the Family* (New York: McGraw-Hill, 1939), pp. 160–173.

grievance which one parent projects on the other, perhaps thus aggravating an already growing conflict.[32]

OTHER FORMS OF MIXED MARRIAGES

Marriages across national, religious, regional, educational and socio-economic class lines all involve differences in culture. Baber found in his study of several types of intermarriage that lack of happiness was directly related to "degree of difference in culture or color." This becomes especially serious in the light of the fact that intermarriages frequently involve the crossing of more than one boundary. For example, internationality marriages are often interfaith marriages, interracial marriages are often internationality marriages, inter-educational class marriages are often inter-socioeconomic class marriages. There are even some marriages which cross several of the normally tabooed boundaries — racial, religious, national, educational, and socioeconomic.[33] Two people, highly matched as to cultural background, ordinarily find relatively large areas of conflicting interests and irritations. When the two come from differing milieus, the probability of conflict and dissension is drastically increased.

Of course, some young people are much more emancipated from their social backgrounds than others, but most emancipated people find that they thought they were more emancipated than they really are. After all, as a character in Willa Cather's *Shadows on the Rock* said, "One has but one set of memories and he cannot get another." These memories bear the imprint of our milieu — whether we like that fact or not — and they form a screen through which all present experiences must pass and through which such experiences assume significance for us. Thus no one can rid himself of the imprint of background to any greater extent than he can rid himself of his memories. This fact ought to be seriously considered before the romantic dictum that "Love scales all barriers" is accepted.

Do not conclude from this that the romantic complex has swept aside all tendencies to choose a mate from within one's own national, religious, racial, or other cultural grouping. Kennedy's study, referred to above in connection with our discussion of residential propinquity, seems to indicate that the tendency for such cultural groups to be endogamous is probably increas-

---

[32] What few statistics there are on Negro-white intermarriage may be found in Gunnar Myrdal's *An American Dilemma* (New York: Harper, 1944), vol. 2, pp. 1360–1361.

[33] It is not implied here that assortative mating (in terms of matching of social and cultural backgrounds) is an "all-or-none" phenomenon. On the contrary, "mixed" marriages are usually "assortative" or "matched" with respect to *some* social or cultural factors — sometimes several. Panunzio, in his study of intermarriage in Los Angeles, found that interracial marriages were most frequently *intra*cultural. In connection with our general thesis that no single or particular factor in assortative mating operates alone to "cause" or determine marital choice but always, rather, in interaction with other factors, it is interesting to note that Panunzio found interracial marriage rates reflect not only culturally defined social distances but also the sex ratios of the particular ethnic groups involved. See his article, "Intermarriage in Los Angeles, 1924–33," *American Journal of Sociology*, 47 (Mar., 1942), pp. 690–701.

ing to some extent in some urban communities, where, it has been assumed, the touch-and-go type of relations between the sexes has done most to dissolve the ties these groups have had in the past.[34] A study of rural groups in one part of Minnesota discovered that in this area most marriages were endogamous with respect to nationality and religious groupings.[35]

A study much more far-reaching with respect to the variety of factors involved in assortative choices has been made by Burgess and Wallin in connection with their study of one thousand engaged couples.[36] In their sample, drawn from the Chicago metropolitan area and made up of whites mainly from business and professional class homes falling economically into the middle and upper-middle classes, they found that the couples were assortatively matched to a marked degree with respect to nativity of parents (whether native, mixed, or foreign-born), place lived in during childhood, and degree of education attained. Other significant findings regarding assortative matching of social characteristics included: similarity of pairs with respect to social status and cultural homogeneity of parents; similarity of members of engaged couples in religious affiliation and behavior; similarity of members of engaged couples in religious affiliation and behavior; similarity of members of engaged couples respecting their early family relationships (happiness of parents' marriage, attitude of subject when a child toward the father, attachment to siblings); similarity of each of pair in extent and type of social participation; similarity in courtship behavior, in conceptions of marriage, and the like.

Thus these studies show the surprising fact that, in the face of pressures which work against the conscious acceptance of endogamy as an ideal for ethnic, religious, and other groups within our society (pressures such as the "melting pot" ideal, the doctrine of romance, the egalitarianism and individualism of our ideology), still assortative mating (in this case, endogamy) continues as a most important factor in most marital choices.

Nowhere, however, are the discontinuities and conflicting norms of our culture more evident than in this realm. The final result — that of inmarriage — is obviously achieved at a very considerable cost in terms of inner conflict and difficulty in achieving personality integration, for young people often learn about these endogamous pressures the hard way; that is, they experience these pressures through parental opposition to their early romantic choices. Thanks to the heterogeneity of our society, these early love affairs are frequently exogamous in character. In the process of experimentation the choices finally become significantly assortative with respect to social factors.

[34] Kennedy, *op. cit*. But see John L. Thomas, "The Factor of Religion in the Selection of Marriage Mates," *American Sociological Review*, 16 (Aug., 1951), pp. 487–491, for negative evidence on this.

[35] Lowry Nelson, "Intermarriage among Nationality Groups in a Rural Area in Minnesota," *American Journal of Sociology*, 48 (Mar., 1943), pp. 585–592. See also Hildegard B. Johnson, "Intermarriages between Pioneers and Other Nationalities in Minnesota in 1860 and 1850," *American Journal of Sociology*, 51 (Jan., 1946), pp. 299–304.

[36] Ernest W. Burgess and Paul Wallin, *Engagement and Marriage* (Philadelphia: Lippincott, 1953).

THE UNCONSCIOUS IMAGE AS A FACTOR IN MARITAL CHOICE

From psychoanalytic theory, particularly that related to the notion of the Oedipus complex, has come the idea that people are *deeply affected in their choice of mates by unconscious images of one or other of their parents,* images implanted through identification and attachment as a result of deep emotional experiences in childhood sometimes described as the "family romance." Without accepting this theory as a whole, we can yet set up the hypothesis that a great many persons are guided in their mate selection by images which remain unconscious and unverbalized, stemming from events which lie deeply buried in their past lives, repressed from consciousness because they also relate to conflicting unpleasantnesses, dislikes, disgusts, and even hatreds which, if called to consciousness, would mar their present idealizations of those with whom they fall in love. These images can be traced back to our first love-objects, our parents and our brothers and sisters, to preadolescent and adolescent love affairs, and to a myriad of other experiences not related to love at all.

The difficulties in testing such an hypothesis are many and great. In the first place, what is an image? Is it a configuration, a whole of some sort? Or is it reducible to a list of discrete and separate traits which a person seeks in a mate? Does it refer primarily to physical characteristics or, rather, to attitudinal and emotional factors or, finally, to some kind of meaningful combination of physique and temperament? But perhaps the most difficult question is, just what relation does this theory of the unconscious image presume to exist between the covert and unconscious image and the overt and conscious features of the mate chosen?

If it is assumed that an image is the mere sum of the list of traits which one unconsciously wishes to find in a mate and that these traits, if not physical, are at least overtly enough expressed to be measurable, then the recent studies of Robert Winch and those of Anselm Strauss are testings of the hypothesis.[37] Without going into their somewhat differing approaches to this problem, we may summarize their findings by saying that most people do have "ideals," consciously held, by which they tend to choose mates and that there is some indication that these choices may also have some relation to the types of family contexts from which these persons come. The emphasis in these "ideals" seems to be greater on those traits which are related to physique. The relationships indicated by statistical manipulations of questionnaire data are relatively small but several of them have, none the less, statistical significance. These findings of Winch and Strauss are a meaningful

---

[37] See Robert F. Winch, "Further Data and Observations on the Oedipus Hypothesis: the Consequence of an Inadequate Hypothesis," *American Sociological Review,* 16 (Dec., 1951), pp. 784–795. This contains a bibliography of the author's other writings on the subject. Anselm Strauss, "The Influence of Parent-Images upon Marital Choice," *American Sociological Review,* 11 (Oct., 1946), pp. 554–559; and his article, "The Ideal and Chosen Mate," *American Journal of Sociology,* 52 (Nov., 1946), pp. 204–208.

addition to our knowledge of the manner in which assortative mating operates, even though the investigations are admittedly only of an exploratory nature.

Nevertheless it is necessary to point out that Winch and Strauss have implicitly answered the questions we raised about the nature of images and their relation to conscious, overt thought and behavior in ways which are not acceptable to the psychoanalyst. The latter would question any one-to-one relationship between the unconscious image and traits consciously sought for in a mate. Although we can accept the findings of Strauss and Winch as significant in terms of their own explicit and implicit hypotheses, we must, however, await extensive depth-psychological investigation to test the assumption that an *unconscious* image is an important factor in the selection of a mate.

While we await such a study we can make some fairly good conjectures. The unconscious character of the image the psychoanalysts assume for us is relative to the emotional intensity of our early childhood relations with one or other of our parents. In short, the more intense that set of attachments, the more neurotic we were and are, and the more compulsive and irrational we are in our choices of mates. But the net result in this is identical with that of the operation of romantic love. Therefore when we sing, "He's — I don't know — he's just my Bill," or rhapsodize about that phantasm, "Laura," we are not necessarily giving unconscious lip-service to the equally unconscious image within us; we may be only "in love with love." At any rate the findings cited above regarding assortative mating with respect to social characteristics seem to indicate a rationality not to be expected if the assumed unconscious image really exerted a *determining* influence in the choice of mate. This is a serious matter. If we are not conscious of the factors which enter into our choice of mates, we have little or no control over that choice. Fortunately this is only partially true, but it deserves extended consideration and we shall return to it after we have considered the problem of predicting marital success.

Assortative Mating and the Prediction of Marital Happiness

Two significant pioneer studies of marital happiness, one by Ernest W. Burgess and Leonard S. Cottrell, Jr.,[38] and the other by Lewis M. Terman and associates,[39] exploratory though they confess to be, have provided a great deal of information regarding the relation between marital choice and marital happiness. They have brought refined statistical techniques to bear upon the complex background and personality factors on the one hand, and upon the equally tangled factors which constitute marital happiness on the other.

From his study of 792 couples, Terman's conclusions were, most significantly, that marital happiness is a function of personal temperament which stems back to innate constitutional factors and the experiences of early child-

[38] *Predicting Success or Failure in Marriage* (New York: Prentice-Hall, 1939).
[39] *Psychological Factors in Marital Happiness* (New York: McGraw-Hill, 1938).

hood. He found that *those who had highest marital happiness scores had had the happiest childhoods,* generally speaking. The moral of this is rather obvious, that a major consideration in selecting a mate who will be a good marital risk is to discover whether or not he is a happy person, and to follow this up by finding whether or not his childhood was a happy one.

Burgess and Cottrell, in their study of 526 couples, found significant corroboration of the old generalization that similar family backgrounds make for a happy marital adjustment. They constructed a statistical device whereby they could measure the similarity of family backgrounds of husband and wife with respect to each of the following: (1) religious preferences of parents of each, (2) participation in church, (3) educational status, (4) occupation of father, (5) socioeconomic status of parents, (6) social status in the community. They combined the scores on each of these into a single index of background similarity for each couple. Table 7 shows only the highest and lowest groups

TABLE 7

INDEX OF SIMILARITY IN FAMILY BACKGROUND AND ADJUSTMENT [40]
(Percentage distribution)

Index of Similarity in Family Background	Adjustment			Number of Cases
	Poor	Fair	Good	
19 to 21 (lowest)	41.1	27.7	31.2	141
28 to 30 (highest)	22.7	20.2	57.1	119

with respect to indices of background similarity as these indices relate to marital adjustment. Roughly only 31 per cent of those pairs having the most dissimilar backgrounds had a good marital adjustment, while about 41 per cent had a poor adjustment. At the other end of the similarity scale where there was most similarity of background between mates, about 57 per cent had a good adjustment in marriage while less than 23 per cent had a poor adjustment.

Burgess and Cottrell found that background factors of the husband were of more importance to marital adjustment than were those of the wife. They found that childhood and adolescence spent in the country were more conducive to marital adjustment than was city rearing.

Another discovery was that close attachment of the husband to his parents and absence of conflict with them were significantly correlated with good marital adjustment. Terman's findings were essentially the same as these. But much more significant was the discovery that *marital adjustment between husband and wife correlated highly with their own ratings of their parents' marriages.* This, again, is essentially the same as Terman's findings.

Only children were found to be poor risks, as were youngest children, while eldest children and members of families of four or more children were found to be good marital risks. Marriages between only children and only children had the lowest average marital-happiness ratings, while marriages between eldest children and eldest children had the highest rating.

The age at which to marry has been the subject of much controversy. Hart

[40] Abbreviated from Table 40, Burgess and Cottrell, *op. cit.*, p. 84.

and Shields [41] have taken the position as a result of their study that the ideal age for marriage is twenty-four for women and twenty-nine for men. Popenoe [42] has criticized this position, and Himes [43] argued in favor of much earlier marriage. Hill and Christensen, in a study made at the University of Wisconsin,[44] found that men *wanted* to get married about the age of twenty-five, while women *wanted* to get married about twenty-three. In the light of all this, it is interesting that Burgess and Cottrell found marriages in their sample to have generally low adjustment scores when either partner involved was less than twenty-two at marriage, and that Terman found essentially the same thing in his study. As for differences in age between husband and wife, husbands of the same age as their wives or from one to three years older proved the best risks. Here, let us note parenthetically, we undoubtedly see the effects of culture preferences in operation. We "expect" the husband to be a year or two older than his wife. We "expect" people to wait until they are twenty-two or twenty-three to get married. These cultural expectations are really preferences. They operate, as Durkheim puts it, with the appearance of "exteriority and constraint" but they are also internalized into the person's expectations regarding his *own* behavior.[45]

One of the most significant findings of the Burgess-Cottrell study was that educational status was highly correlated with marital adjustment. Those who had gone only to grade school had the poorest adjustment while those who had had graduate or professional training beyond college had the highest average adjustment scores. Educational status was, however, but one attribute of the participating or socialized person. If he had many friends and participated regularly in religious and other activities, indications were good that he was high on adaptability and therefore a good marriage risk.

Occupations involving a high degree of vicinal mobility were found to be negatively correlated with marital happiness. The jokes about the traveling man may be more than jokes!

[41] Hornell Hart and Wilmer Shields, "Happiness in Relation to Age at Marriage," *Social Hygiene,* 12 (1926), pp. 403–410.

[42] Paul Popenoe, "Early Marriage and Happiness," *Social Hygiene,* 12 (1926), pp. 544–549.

[43] Norman Himes, *Your Marriage: A Guide to Happiness* (rev. ed.; New York: Rinehart, 1940), chap. 9, "The Case for Early Marriage."

[44] Reuben Hill, "Campus Values and Mate Selection," *Journal of Home Economics* (Nov., 1945), pp. 554–555.

[45] This is but one aspect of the problem. Others remain to be explored. Studies of the relations between personal appearance and age at marriage (see S. J. Holmes and C. E. Hatch, "Personal Appearance as Related to Scholastic Records and Marriage Selection in College Women," *Human Biology,* 10 [1938], pp. 65–76; E. W. Burgess and Paul Wallin, "Personal Appearance and Neuroticism as Related to Age at Marriage," *Human Biology,* 16 [Feb., 1944], pp. 15–22) may suggest some hypotheses. For example, women rated more attractive tend to marry earlier. This may be correlated with the working of romantic love as opposed to the more culturally assortative factors in mating. As the Burgess-Cottrell prediction study clearly shows, this would make for less adjustment in marriage. Then again the correlation of beauty with age at marriage may also be related to certain narcissistic factors in the woman's personality which again are unfavorable for marital adjustment. Or finally it may simply be that early marriages are unsuccessful because, on the average, they indicate that insufficient opportunity was allowed for personality testing, culture matching, and the development of companionship.

Wives were found to have higher marital adjustment scores when they taught school before marriage. For the wife to have been employed in domestic or unskilled work was, on the other hand, a distinct handicap as far as adjustment in marriage is concerned.

Burgess and Cottrell found another very significant factor in connection with choice of mate; namely, the importance of parental approval of mate choice. The approval of the husband's parents appears, furthermore, to be of more importance to future marital adjustment than is the approval of the wife's parents.

These studies need further corroboration and extension, of course, but we begin to get a picture of what is significantly rational in mate selection. The person who is a good risk (of either sex) is the person who is happy and has been happy all his life. He is attached to his parents and has had little conflict with them. He comes from a "good" (i.e., socially approved) background and from a happy family. Preferably he is neither an only child nor the youngest child. He has a high educational status, he is a participant in approved organizations, and he has friends. He is twenty-two years old or older, and his occupation is such that he is subject to community and neighborhood controls. These attributes, however, are pertinent to the individual as such and not to the assortative character or matching of the pair. They seem to presume an *intrinsic* validity of individual traits to adjustment in marriage.

More recent research in the prediction of marital adjustment appears to question this assumption and to indicate that assortativeness has more to do with marital happiness than does the presence or absence of particular traits in the individual. Furthermore, the extended study of a thousand engaged couples by Burgess and Wallin — though it corroborates previous studies showing homogamy in such physical characteristics as height, weight, health, and physical attractiveness and though it discovers a certain degree of homogamy in many personality traits (as measured by the Thurstone Neurotic Inventory and as scored in self-ratings) — concludes nevertheless that "upon the basis of present evidence 'cultural likeness' appears more important than 'temperamental or personality similarity' in marital selection," for the measures of assortativeness with respect to religious affiliation and behavior, cultural background, courtship behavior, conceptions of marriage, and social participation were much more significant statistically.[46] From all that we already know about social interaction it is reasonable to suppose that an increasing knowledge of assortativeness will yield more predictive results than will studies of individual traits assumed to be "intrinsically" favorable to marital adjustment. In this connection we ought to remind ourselves that physical, personality, and even background characteristics become meaningful in social interaction only as groups assign them meaning or act *as if* they are real and significant.

[46] E. W. Burgess and Paul Wallin, *Engagement and Marriage* (Philadelphia: Lippincott, 1953). See especially pp. 204–211.

CRITIQUE OF THE PREDICTION STUDIES

While the Terman and Burgess-Cottrell studies in prediction of marital adjustment achieve positive correlations of roughly 0.50 between scores on their respective sets of items and their measures of marital adjustment, the authors admit that these correlations are only moderate. Despite the fact that, in as complicated a field of behavior as this, such correlations are very significant, it must be remembered that the *square* of the correlation coefficient more nearly represents the percentage of causal relationships discovered. In other words these investigators have discovered approximately 25 per cent of the factors at the time of marriage which are related to marital adjustment.

Can we expect that the use of this method will reduce more and more of the problem of marital adjustment to prediction? Burgess and Wallin studied a large sample of engaged couples with the hope of improving predictability. Since the earlier studies of Terman and Burgess-Cottrell were of samples of already married couples, this new study of engaged couples at least answers questions regarding the validity of findings of the earlier studies.[47] It is possible that out of similar studies will come the discovery both of new variables in personality and cultural background and also new techniques of combining and weighing those already discovered. Since the Terman, Burgess-Cottrell, and Burgess-Wallin samples are drawn from a rather narrow segment of the population — white, urban, professional, middle-class — some new and productive hypotheses might be gained from similar studies of other segments — rural, upper and lower class, Negro, and the like — hypotheses which might augment predictability somewhat. We must not expect, however, that highly accurate prediction of marital adjustment is in immediate prospect, highly significant though these initial investigations have been. In any particular pair, marital adjustment is not so much a matter of discrete traits of personality and separable items of background culture as it is a matter of the adjustment of the multifold *common and complementary roles* which each member plays, expects to play, and expects the other to play. It is through functioning in these distinctive roles that personality traits and background items become meaningful in intrapair interaction. It is in these roles that personality, society, and culture meet. Here is the crux of the whole significance of assortative mating, for matching with respect to social context has meaning at the human level only if the particular social context in question has prepared or failed to prepare the members of the pair to play parts that will be mutually and reciprocally satisfying. (For more detail on this point see Chapter Eleven, "Getting Along in Marriage," pp. 341–365.)

The difficulty is that roles are hard to describe and measure objectively and accurately. Professor Burgess and his associates have attempted to solve this problem by supplementing their questionnaire and statistical methods of

---

[47] *Ibid.* Chaps. 15–16. The gain is not notable.

prediction with various interview and case study analysis techniques, but so far the increase in predictability has not been notable.

A technique seemingly adapted for use in approaching this problem of delineating roles is that of the psychodrama, developed by J. L. Moreno.[48] In the psychodrama, both actual and intended roles can be acted out before observers, and, moreover, this dramatization can be done either with "stand-ins" or real courtship or marital partners playing the complementary parts. The exploration of roles and role expectations through pencil-and-paper tests is suggested in the researches of Strodtbeck, Jacobson, Yi-Chuang Lu, and Rose.[49] Through the use of such techniques of investigation, it ought to be possible to assign "role-weighted" values to certain responses on the prediction questionnaires that Terman, Burgess and their associates have worked out, to the end that prediction is both culturally and personally oriented.

We are now ready to return, as we promised, to the problem of unconscious and irrational factors in mate selection. If man is inherently and incurably irrational in his choice of mate, studies like those of Terman and of Burgess and Cottrell are of little avail in bringing about successful choices of mates. Much of the difficulty, however, is a *cultural irrationality,* if we may coin a phrase. An individual is expected to marry because of love. This love is held to be irrational ("Love is blind"). This very irrationality is approved. If a young person gives consideration to rational factors in the choice of a mate, he is often looked upon as too calculating and conniving to be in love; hence he will not "live happily ever after," for only those who fall, and fall too hard to think, enjoy that prospect.

To take into account the matching of roles in making a choice of a mate violates the notion that there is "some person destined by the stars in their courses to be your mate." This romantic search for one's soul mate must have nothing to do with such mundane and practical considerations as educational status or childhood background. Our increasing urbanization has been partly responsible for our emphasis on romantic love, for it has impersonalized and segmentalized relationships on the mate-selection level as well as on other levels, and this has made mystery a more and more common attribute of all affairs between young men and women.

Man, however, is not just an irrational creature. He is both rational and irrational. In the realm of mate selection it is possible to choose one's mate on a fairly rational basis and then fall madly in love with him. Some may hotly contest this, but it is still true. We now have the beginnings of blueprints for rational mate selection, and most young people value highly enough the prospect of happiness in marriage to consult these blueprints once they become convinced that rational choice and marital happiness are

[48] See J. L. Moreno, "Psychodramatic Treatment of Marriage Problems," *Sociometry,* 3 (Jan., 1940), pp. 1–23.

[49] Fred L. Strodtbeck, "Husband-Wife Interaction Over Revealed Differences," *American Sociological Review,* 16 (Aug., 1951), pp. 468–473; A. H. Jacobson, "Conflict of Attitudes toward the Roles of the Husband and Wife in Marriage," *American Sociological Review,* 17 (April, 1952), pp. 146–150; Yi-Chuang Lu, "Predicting Roles in Marriage," *American Journal of Sociology,* 58 (July, 1952), pp. 51–55; Arnold M. Rose, "The Adequacy of Women's Expectations for Adult Roles," *Social Forces,* 30 (Oct., 1951), pp. 69–77.

related. Once they see that love is not the only requisite of happiness there is reason to believe they will begin to look before they leap.

There are, of course, many who are so biased or so unconsciously motivated that it does them no good to look, for they cannot see what there is to see because of quirks in innate temperament and early experiences. You can discover whether you are a biased or detached person by marking down in a notebook every instance in which a good friend does something which surprises you, something you had not expected him to do. Detached and healthyminded people are seldom surprised by other people's actions. Extremely biased persons not only are frequently surprised by what their friends do but also by what they themselves do in certain social situations. They not only do not understand their friends — they do not understand themselves. Such people should examine their motives for doing what they do. The motives they have been giving themselves are not the ones which are operating. They should examine their sensitive spots and their disgusts. Behind these they may find something amazing; namely, that those wishes which they despise in other people are precisely the ones operating in themselves. Such a discovery is painful and may require the help of counselor, psychiatrist, or psychoanalyst. Unfortunately, he who does not have some perspective of himself, including his weaknesses and shams and the ways other people look upon him, will never be happy or adjusted in life — either in or out of marriage.

SELECTED READINGS

ADAMS, ROMANZO, *Interracial Marriage in Hawaii* (New York: Macmillan, 1937).

BABER, RAY E., *Marriage and the Family* (2nd., New York: McGraw-Hill, 1953), chaps. 4, 5, 6, 7.

BARRON, MILTON L., *People Who Intermarry* (Syracuse: Syracuse University Press, 1946), especially Part I.

BURGESS, ERNEST W., and COTTRELL, LEONARD S., JR., *Predicting Success or Failure in Marriage* (New York: Prentice-Hall, 1939).

BURGESS, ERNEST W., and WALLIN, PAUL, *Engagement and Marriage* (Philadelphia: Lippincott, 1953), chaps. 3–13.

FOLSOM, JOSEPH K., *The Family and Democratic Society* (New York: Wiley, 1943), chaps. 12, 16.

LANDIS, JUDSON T., and LANDIS, MARY G., *Readings in Marriage and the Family* (New York: Prentice-Hall, 1952), parts IV and V.

LOCKE, HARVEY J., *Predicting Adjustment in Marriage: A Comparison of a Divorced and a Happily Married Group* (New York: Henry Holt, 1951).

MERTON, ROBERT K., "Intermarriage and the Social Structure: Fact and Theory," *Psychiatry,* 4 (Aug., 1941), pp. 361–374.

STRAUSS, ANSELM, "The Influence of Parent-Images upon Marital Choice," *American Sociological Review,* 11 (Oct., 1946), pp. 554–559.

TERMAN, LEWIS M., and associates, *Psychological Factors in Marital Happiness* (New York: McGraw-Hill, 1938), particularly chap. 9.

WALLER, WILLARD, *The Family, A Dynamic Interpretation,* rev. by Reuben Hill (New York: Dryden, 1951), chap. 11.

WINCH, ROBERT F., *The Modern Family* (New York: Henry Holt, 1952), chap. 15.

TOPICS FOR DISCUSSION OR REPORTS

1. Give illustrations from your own experience of parental opposition to early love affairs brought about because the loved person was not of the same class, nationality, religious, educational, or other "standing."
2. Describe the formal and informal pressures, if any, brought to bear within your religious group to bring about endogamous marriages. Which of these are rewards and which are punishments?
3. From your acquaintances, give brief sketches of two or three marriages across religious lines. In what ways has this affected the marriages? What differing solutions have the couples worked out?
4. Describe the various standardized roles in the courtship situation in American society. Compare these with the expected roles of the partners in the marriage situation. Does the playing of the courtship roles seem likely to enable a person to make a rational choice of marriage partner?
5. Sketch briefly some marriages which have been surprising to you. How do you explain these surprising choices of mates? Do your surprises reflect romantic or assortative matching ideas on your part?
6. Give as much as you can of the early life history of someone who married across racial lines. Do these early experiences shed any light on the reasons for culminating a cacogamous marriage?
7. Analyze a movie or a novel in which a married couple experience conflict. List the ways in which the couple were not properly matched as to background or temperament. Was their marriage justifiable in your opinion?
8. Enumerate the eligible members of the opposite sex in your "little social world" and in the circles of your best friends. What conclusions do you reach regarding the number of eligible partners an individual ordinarily has? How does the sex ratio in your circle of acquaintances compare with the city or state in which you live?
9. What effects has your college education (with its attendant social experiences) had on the roles you expect to play as a partner in marriage? What effects has it had on your expectations of roles in your partner?
10. Using illustrations from life, show any concrete effects of participation in outside community life on marital adjustment and solidarity.

Chapter Nine

The Engagement: Thinking about Marriage

MANFORD HINSHAW KUHN

WHAT DOES IT MEAN TO BE ENGAGED?

THE conservative and respectable New York newspapers carry, in their society pages, a picture of a young woman together with her parents' announcement of her engagement to be married. Perhaps the announcement lists briefly the schools of high social standing that the young lady has attended. It may also describe the gathering where the engagement was announced. That the families expecting to be brought together in the future marriage are represented in the social register and that considerable family fortunes are involved are matters left unannounced, but they are nevertheless generally understood.

Throughout our society, are engagements simply slight variants on this theme? In Plainville, James West found that engagements are, in contrast to the above type, highly *secret* affairs.[1] Only the immediate families of each of the pair know of the approaching marriage. Even in communities much less rural and isolated than Plainville, the engagement while not secret may be simply a scarcely perceptible aspect of the growing emotional involvement of two people who have been "going steady." Then again, in many individual cases, an engagement may have largely the function of cloaking sexual exploitation of one of the pair by the other, or, in other cases, a camouflage mutually worn in order to gain freedom from community sex regulations and controls.

From the foregoing it is obvious that a good deal of ambiguity and haziness surrounds not only the act of becoming engaged but the very state of being engaged. What does it mean to be engaged? Perhaps no situation in any society is ever completely defined by the symbols which relate to it, but the engagement situation in our society is one which is left almost completely *undefined* by its symbols. The symbols are commonly the wearing of a ring or fraternity pin, the announcement of engagement at a party and in the newspaper, exclusive courtship over a long period of time, the words "I love you. Will you marry me?" and so on. The significance or meaning of engagement, however, is not at all standardized or universal. While the symbols remain fairly constant throughout our society the meaning varies from couple to couple. Even more striking is the fact that *the functions which the engagement period fulfills are not regulated by the formal customs of our society*. In this respect modern America differs from most other societies. This will be appreciated when we survey the varying customs and functions of the betrothal among groups other than our own.

[1] James West (pseud.), *Plainville, U. S. A.* (New York: Columbia University Press, 1945), pp. 201–202.

FUNCTIONS OF THE BETROTHAL IN OTHER SOCIETIES

For those who are inclined to view social institutions as products of economic determinism, the Manus people in New Guinea are an interesting primitive group whose patterns of behavior, including those surrounding the betrothal, would seem at first glance to confirm this doctrine. The Manus' adult life is characterized by continuous trading of dogs' teeth, shell money, pigs, and oil.[2] It will be no surprise, then, to the economic determinists in our midst to find that among the Manus the engagement is primarily a property arrangement between families. Not only do the young pair have nothing to do with the selection, but they must also avoid each other completely during the engagement period. Their names, and even words which resemble their names, are taboo to each other. They are usually betrothed before puberty, by a payment of dogs' teeth and shell money from the father and relatives of the future husband to the father and relatives of the future wife. The betrothed girl spends much of the engagement period in activities connected with the approaching wedding ceremonies, but these are really trading rituals concerned more with property exchanges than with the personal relation being created. Actually this relation is not, strictly speaking, a highly personal one, for husband and wife live together as virtual strangers.

What is the essential function of the engagement among the Manus? Certainly it is not that of preparing a couple for future companionship and cooperation, nor is it a way of insuring sexual compatibility. Among these people neither companionship nor sexual compatibility between the married couple is of any recognized importance. What is tremendously important, however, is the Manus system of investment and trading. In this complex of property exchanges, the adult's mind is preoccupied and his daily work is centered. *The essential function of the Manus engagement period, then, is to transform the undisciplined and carefree youngster who has little interest in property or debts into an adult whose chief concern will thenceforth revolve around almost diurnal gift investments and property repayment.*

There is, it must be admitted, an indirect way in which the Manus engagement prepares for marriage in the sense in which we in our society are accustomed to think of marriage preparation: since engagement and marriage represent heavy investments not only of the immediate family of the pair but also of a wide circle of their relatives, and since the endurance of the match is necessary to insure the wisdom of such investments, the property ceremonies of the betrothal do have as their by-products some rather obvious social pressures which tend to hold the pair together. On the other hand, the almost universal estrangement between husband and wife among the Manus seems to result in large part from blame projected from each partner on the other for having to give up a carefree childhood to assume the worries and anxieties attendant upon this amazingly property-centered adulthood. Remote, indeed, seem these psychological and social processes from those related to engagement among ourselves, but perhaps this contrast enables us

---

[2] Margaret Mead, *Growing Up in New Guinea* (New York: Morrow, 1930).

to perceive a little less dimly the processes involved in our own engagement period. It ought also to enable us to see how overly particularistic the economic determinism dogma is; for our society like that of the Manus is heavily preoccupied with commercial activity, yet the engagement in our society has little to do either with property or with trading except as it operates among the tiny few at the top of our socioeconomic pyramid.

In Samoa [3] the courtship and marriage patterns which are followed contrast sharply with those we have described among the Manus of New Guinea. Samoan courtship consists of sexual and affectional experimentation in surreptitious "love under the palms," secret night meetings in the house of the girl's family, elopement, or the more open and proper "sitting before the girl" in the presence of her parents. *Formal engagement is of importance mainly for those of higher rank.* Among most Samoans there is little emphasis upon it, nor is there any expectation of faithfulness either before or after marriage. Where rank is of no concern, choice of mate belongs to the young lovers and is therefore not a strictly parental affair as among the Manus. Here is a society whose individualism in love and in mate selection approaches that of our own. The economic determinist, may we repeat, would expect the Manus, who have a materialistic set of values which in many ways closely parallels our own, to resemble us in such patterns as love and engagement mores more closely than do the Samoans, but quite the opposite is the case.

Among the Trobrianders [4] of northwestern Melanesia the engagement ceremony involves the boy and the girl's parents rather than the girl herself. It consists of a request by the girl's parents for a gift from the boy; by this request they signify their consent to the match. The engagement period is not distinctively one of sexual experimentation, for this has preceded the engagement in a stage of semipromiscuity, during which, however, each succeeding alliance is longer and of an increasingly serious nature. The engagement, then, is but one of several steps leading from a free and easy sexual experimentation to a monogamous relationship. However complex and multifarious the functions of engagement may be elsewhere, its sole function among the Trobriand Islanders, seemingly, is to begin the process of giving social approval to the match.

This premarital license may seem somewhat shocking to us who are accustomed to think of social approval of courtship and engagement as presupposing chastity. That the Trobrianders are wont to give approval to a match only after the couple has been living together for some time should only deepen our understanding of the mutability of socially sanctioned values and standards. Our astonishment at the variability, from one society to another, of man's behavior patterns is exceeded only by our amazement at contradictions from group to group in what is held to be right and what is looked upon as wrong.

Sometimes these antitheses in moral codes occur even between neighbor-

[3] Margaret Mead, *Coming of Age in Samoa* (New York: Morrow, 1930).
[4] Bronislaw Malinowski, *The Sexual Life of Northwestern Melanesia* (2 vols.; New York: Liveright, 1929).

ing tribes, as for example between the Pedi and the Thonga.[5] Among the Thonga the unmarried girl may have sexual relations without censure, but once she is married she must remain faithful to her husband. Among the neighboring Pedi, on the other hand, unmarried girls must remain strictly chaste but after they have married and borne a child they may have sexual relations with men other than their husbands. Among the Pedi the engagement is contracted before birth in some instances, and very early in any case, in order to insure sexual abstinence prior to marriage.

In pre-Westernized China all considerations of purely personal pleasure and eroticism were subordinated in the highest possible degree to those of classically moral obligations and relationships between father and son, husband and wife, and elder and younger brothers.[6] Marriage was not an institution providing primarily for the channeling of sexual drives. Rather was it an affair principally of providing an ancestral line with male children to venerate the ancestors and give the clan continuity. The betrothal was an arrangement between the families of a pair brought about by a mediator (who was used in order to avoid losing face in case the suit was rejected, and also in order to be able to discuss the good personal qualities of the two without self-praise). There is a Chinese saying that a good marriage is one between those whose "doors face each other," that is, whose station in life is the same. Thus in China there was little or no attempt to use betrothal to someone of greater wealth or status as a means of climbing socially, as is the case occasionally in our own society. The betrothal ceremony itself was a family affair, consisting of an interchange of numerous presents and family records. The man did not see his mate, in theory at least, until her veils were removed for the first time at the conclusion of the wedding ceremony. *Thus Chinese engagement was an affair of the family and the group; that is, it was a mechanism to put the nascent family in its proper place in the continuing context of familial and societal relationships.* It was not designed to serve as a period of personality testing, for the matching of personalities was expected to be assured through the highly standardized set of experiences — resulting from the rigid, universal, and continuous observance of the socio-moral code of relationships — which each member of the pair, coming from the same station in life, had passed through.[7]

The Western world stands somewhere between the extremes of such societies as Old China and the Manus on the one hand, with their rules minimizing and even forbidding association between the two mates-to-be, and

---

[5] William I. Thomas, *Primitive Behavior* (New York: McGraw-Hill, 1937), pp. 257–258.

[6] Richard Wilhelm, "The Chinese Conception of Marriage," in *The Book of Marriage,* edited by Herman Keyserling (New York: Harcourt, Brace, 1926). For an interesting and concise statement regarding the changes wrought in engagement and related marriage patterns in the last few years, see E. W. Burgess and H. J. Locke, *The Family* (New York: American Book Co., 1945), pp. 51–56.

[7] Japanese culture is in many respects a derivative of Chinese culture. It is interesting, therefore, to note that the engagement in contemporary Japan is more like that of pre-Westernized China than is the pattern in most parts of contemporary China itself. For a brief discussion of the pattern of contracting marriage in Japan, see J. F. Embree, *The Japanese Nation* (New York: Rinehart, 1945), pp. 159–162.

of such groups as the Samoans, on the other hand, whose not very monogamous "love under the palms" starts well before marriage and often continues well after. Yet Western civilization really encompasses a number of
groups, each with its own culture and its own mores which prescribe right
ways of behavior during courtship and engagement. Among the Scots, for
example, there has long been a custom of "handfasting," or living together
for a time before marriage in order to test whether or not the match is a
fertile one — the marriage being concluded only if the girl becomes pregnant.[8] This custom still persists, although only among certain of the lower
classes. Similar customs prevail, at least in some strata of the population, in
Wales, Ireland, and Germany.

   Ancient German law looked upon intent to marry as the equivalent of
marriage, so that we find some confusion and ambiguity between betrothal
and marriage prior to the Christian epoch. Among people without status or
property, betrothal and wedding ceremonies were omitted, but the law
looked upon these ceremonies as necessary when property and rank were
involved. Even here there was disagreement as to whether betrothal meant
the conclusion of a marriage, of which the wedding ceremony was only a
confirmation, or whether it meant only the intention to wed at some future
date. Finally the betrothal and wedding ceremonies were united, but the
custom of living together before marriage continued despite this, at first in
all classes, later only in the lower layers of society.[9]

WHAT IS THE ENGAGEMENT FOR?

   From our vantage point which now overlooks not only our own but
several non-Western societies as well, we are able to see that the engagement
varies in function from one group to another. The functions it may perform,
in one society or another, are extremely diverse in character, ranging all the
way from trial marriage, with all its intimacies, to a system of taboos and
avoidances requiring virtual cessation of all relations of all kinds between the
betrothed pair. We can distinguish at least six possible functions of engagement: (1) It may serve to take one or both of the mates-to-be out of sexual
"circulation" and to provide a period of exclusiveness — with or without
sexual intimacy — prior to marriage. The equating of the exclusive right to
the mate with property rights, which grows out of this period of exclusiveness, may and usually does have the effect of making the consequent marriage more solid and permanent. (2) The engagement period may constitute
a trial marriage in which the two live together, testing mutually pleasing
characteristics in an attempt to determine whether or not the match should
be permanent. (3) The engagement period may be one of culturally enforced
sexual abstinence, on the assumption that this denial will build anticipation
and intensify the loyalty between the pair. (4) The engagement may serve

[8] See Edward Westermarck, *The Future of Marriage in Western Civilization* (New York: Mac-
    millan, 1936), chap. 6; also Norman E. Himes, *Your Marriage: A Guide to Happiness* (rev.
    ed.; New York: Rinehart and Co., 1940), p. 105.
[9] William Graham Sumner, *Folkways* (Boston: Ginn, 1907), pp. 405–406, 412.

no purpose with respect to personality testing or sexual experimentation, existing merely as a concomitant of economic processes and readjustments respecting property arrangements, in which case the ensuing marital relation itself is usually more or less an epiphenomenon of property rights and property exchanges rather than a focal point of gratification, affectional response, and close-knit companionship. (5) Betrothal is often a way of celebrating or symbolizing the placing of a new pair relation in terms of an elaborate network of reciprocal family, clan, or gens, moiety, tribal, locality, or other group relations. As a required ceremony it provides the group with a means of scrutinizing new matches before they have become final and permanent. (6) By defining a new match in terms of status or rank, the engagement may operate to control mobility from one social class to another and to make apparent under what conditions "marrying upwards" in rank is permissible.

The betrothal cannot serve all these purposes at once in one and the same society, for some of these functions are obviously the opposites of others. Just why each society selects one or two of these for emphasis, and looks upon groups emphasizing others as "ridiculous," "immoral," or both, can be discovered only when engagement is considered against the whole configuration of social institutions of each group.[10] The engagement, like any other social institution, must fit in or be consistent with the other institutions in a society, and yet at the same time it must satisfy as fully as possible the basic, universal, common-human needs which are its reason for being. Running through the other purposes of engagement which we have just surveyed are aspects which indicate the basic human needs which give rise to engagement everywhere. One of these basic needs is that of having group sanction and approval when one begins to take on an adult role as a mature member of the group. The other basic need comes from the necessity of cushioning the sharp transition from youth to adulthood and parenthood, from the state of single irresponsibility to that of married responsibility.

THE ENGAGEMENT IN OUR SOCIETY: SACRED OR SECULAR?

Our society differs from those we have briefly mentioned in that the engagement in the primitive and Oriental societies we have noted is in each case rather rigidly patterned and prescribed. The forms and functions of the engagement in American society are in the realm of what Ralph Linton calls cultural "Alternatives," while in most other societies they are "Universals." [11] Much of the manner and meaning of the engagement, in other words, is left — in our society — to individual and pair definition, while in most societies the engagement is more narrowly defined culturally. It is character-

---

[10] The personification of society in this statement is, of course, a mere figure of speech. It is used to indicate "manifest functions" as distinguished from "latent functions." For this distinction see Robert Merton, *Social Theory and Social Structure* (Glencoe, Ill.: Free Press, 1949), chap. 1.

[11] Ralph Linton, *The Study of Man* (New York: Appleton-Century, 1936), pp. 272–287.

istic of secular societies [12] that much behavior falls in the realm of Alternatives. The peculiar significance of this generalization lies in the fact that in a secular society there is possible a more consistent and more continuously adaptive relation between means and ends. In a sacred society the institutional form is the universally prescribed means by which certain basic needs are gratified. The form has acquired a "sacred" character; that is, the form (means) has become an end in itself. This has often reached such a degree that the need to which the form is supposed to minister is obscured by the social sanction applied to the form itself.[13]

In our highly secular society, marriage and family relationships have changed rapidly in function in the last century or so. While they once represented a coalescence of functions and satisfactions relating to a wide range of human behavior — economic, religious, educational, recreational, and other behaviors — today they center increasingly in the satisfaction of the wish for affectional response and companionship. As this becomes more and more characteristic of the marriage relationship, it becomes increasingly advantageous to have alternative, instrumental patterns both for testing and for building pair solidarity and companionship in the *pre*-marital relationship.

Actually, of course, our society is only relatively, not absolutely, secular in character. It is obvious that marriage and family have by no means lost all their sacred, sanctioned, traditional forms. It is, however, probably true that the engagement as such in our society has gone much further over into the realm of Alternatives than have marriage and the family. The purpose of this discussion has been to point out the potentially adaptive character of the secularization of the engagement. To the degree that we have cultural Alternatives in this area of behavior, to that degree is it possible for us to adjust to the changing functions of marriage and the family.

The Pair Relation as Such

In our highly individuated, highly differentiated, highly anonymous society it is not surprising to find that a young man and a young woman increasingly value their relationship for itself and not as an instrument aimed at some covert or future end. What is surprising, however, is that in the face of this emphasis we have paid so little attention, as observers, to the pair relation as such. What is the nature of this relationship which is so highly valued by the participants? We can profitably think of the love pair as being in some ways simply a special case of the dyad, or social group having only two mem-

---

[12] For a discussion of sacred and secular societies and means-ends relations, see Chapter One. See also Howard Becker, "Sacred and Secular Societies Considered with Reference to Folk-State and Similar Classifications," *Social Forces,* 28 (May, 1950), pp. 361–376.

[13] For a relevant analysis of means-ends relations as these have to do with social forms, see Howard Becker, *Through Values to Social Interpretation* (Durham, N. C.: Duke University Press, 1950), chap. 4, "Interpretative Sociology and Constructive Typology," and his *German Youth: Bond or Free* (New York: The Grove Press, 1946) from which most of the illustrations in the chapter cited are drawn.

bers. The dyad has a number of characteristics common to all its forms: the friendship pair, the sexual pair (to which classification the engaged pair belongs), the generation pair, the common-interest pair, and others.[14]

> There are fluctuations in dyadic intimacy based solely upon certain peculiarities of the pair *as such*, peculiarities of this smallest of all groups. This is much more important than it at first appears. A great deal that is regarded as the result of love or friendship or family life or business interests is simply the product of pair-formation and pair-habituation. Many actions of those in love are ascribed to that amiable weakness when as a matter of fact they really arise out of the dyadic pattern, for in larger groups similarly united by erotic bonds these peculiarly dyadic features cannot be discerned.[15]

Now, engagement serves as a formal second or middle stage in the development of a dyad, to which courtship represents the initiation and marriage the culmination. Not ordinarily until the engagement period does the relation between the pair begin to involve their total personalities. In this period each begins for the first time to identify himself with the other, to equate his ego with the relationship, and to regard a possible disruption of the dyad as a form of self-destruction.

The alternations, among engaged couples, of euphoria and dysphoria, of feelings of oneness and of lovers' quarrels, we are in the habit of regarding as peculiarly germane in love affairs, whereas in fact *they are largely the result of the intimate interaction which characterizes all dyads.* The alternating positive and negative feelings reflect: (1) the organic cycles of tension and mood within each of the pair; (2) the frustrations brought by each upon the other (a) by the very intimacy and exclusiveness of the pair relation and (b) by the positive and negative reactions of each to the thousands of distinctive and unique personality traits possessed by the other; (3) the transference of love and the projections of antipathy from one member to the other as displaced from relationships lying outside the pair relations; and finally, (4) the alternating idealization (overestimation) and devaluation of each other depending on whether lifelong expectations of what a mate should be like (i.e., anticipated common and complementary roles) are fulfilled or foiled, either by the mate himself or by trivial circumstances which sustain or deflate the glorified image of the ideal mate, or promote or frustrate the will to equate this image with the actual mate.[16] These alterna-

---

[14] In this discussion of the pair the present author is indebted chiefly although not exclusively to Howard Becker, *Systematic Sociology on the Basis of the* Beziehungslehre *and* Gebildelehre *of Leopold von Wiese* (New York: Wiley, 1932), particularly pp. 511–515; and to —— and Ruth Hill Useem, "Sociological Analysis of the Dyad," *American Sociological Review,* 7, No. 1 (Feb., 1942), pp. 13–26. The student will profit by referring to these sources for "small-group" analysis *outside* the laboratory or psychodramatic theater.

[15] Wiese-Becker, *op. cit.,* pp. 512–513.

[16] See Becker and Useem, *op. cit.;* also J. L. Moreno, "Interpersonal Therapy and the Psychopathology of Interpersonal Relations," *Sociometry,* 1 (July, 1937), pp. 9–76, referred to by Becker and Useem, particularly in connection with the "ups and downs" of feelings in close relationships.

tions, which pull the pair together and then drive them apart, are common to all pairs, in greater or lesser degree depending upon the amount of intimacy and exclusiveness involved in the relationship and upon the extent to which the *total* personalities of the two are involved.

In the growth of pair solidarity, memories of certain incidents and common experience come to have meaning out of all proportion to other past events of life for the two, so much so in fact that they may be said to symbolize the unity of the pair for each other. For the love pair these shared memories may be of a dance, a moonlight ride, a romantic walk through the woods in the spring; often they have to do with the chance meeting which brought them together for the first time, colored by the "what ifs" surrounding life had not the accident of fate thrown them together. These shared memories, however, may also stem from crises which at the time were very painful — the opposition of her parents to the affair, a shortage of money which threatened to cause his leaving the school they were attending, an automobile accident which kept them from returning home from a date until dawn, when irate and unsympathetic parents proved more upsetting than the accident itself.

More often, these rapport devices consist not of whole scenes reconstructed from the shared past, but rather of words and phrases that act as a kind of sign language. Short-circuiting the need to renarrate the past events, a symbol from this special language serves to let loose in each of the members emotions conducive to solidarity, unity, and rapport. The use of such highly emotionalized symbols of identification when among other friends is also conducive to pair rapport, since those who are not members of the pair notice, consciously or unconsciously, the inflection used, the accompanying facial changes, the inadvertent look at each other, and the like, which almost certainly give away, even to strangers, the emotions which are called up by them. When this happens, even outsiders begin to treat the two as a unity, and since each of us tends to play the role assigned to him by others, pair rapport is greatly strengthened by such attitudes.

There is, of course, usually some divergence between the pair's pattern of behavior in public and in private. The public pattern must conform within certain limits to the culturally standardized customs. In private, although the group's standards and expectations still operate to some degree, the interaction is more likely to reflect the peculiar patterns of the two persons involved. The extent of divergence between public and private patterns of interaction depends in large measure upon how congenial the group's standards and patterns are to the two personalities — in short, upon how conventional the two are. The greater the congruence between public and private patterns of interaction — that is, the more the couple's "front" corresponds to its core of interaction — the greater the probability of the stability and continuation of the pair's rapport; for rapport has its roots in outside relations as well as in internal unity, and marked differences between public and private patterns of interaction make for strain. Again we are dealing with an aspect of the engagement period which is found generally in dyadic relations, although the amount of time which engaged couples spend by themselves makes possible the development of more completely private ways of behaving than are found among many other types of dyads.

Pair solidarity may in individual instances reach pathological proportions, especially when the couple spends an inordinate amount of time together alone. Tensions develop unconsciously from the overclose intimacy, providing pair solidarity with a kind of automatic regulator — which, however, may not function properly if either of the pair has a tendency to repress such tensions until they explode. As pointed out by an old German anecdote, human beings, like porcupines, cannot huddle too closely together for warmth without damaging their skins.

THE PAIR AND THIRD PERSONS

Each member of the pair usually carries into the period of the engagement one or more other pair relations. In an earlier day, characterized by a stable, sacred, primary society, an engaged person had broken off all companionate relations with eligible members of the opposite sex, usually well prior to the engagement. In our mobile, anonymous, touch-and-go society, it is not at all uncommon for people to carry along in some fashion or other these pair relationships which had been formed prior to the engagement. Indeed it is often the case that pair relations with "outsiders" get started *during* the engagement. These "outside" affairs received a great deal of public attention during the war and were generally thought of as purely wartime aberrations, but like a good many social phenomena they seemed products of the war because they have been much more visible. In actuality these quasi-subsidiary pair relations have become a typical adjunct of the engaged pair relation.

It must not be imagined, however, that the only pair relations having important consequences for the engaged couple are those with other potential mates. Here again what are commonly supposed to be peculiar attributes of the (in this case, "disloyal") love affairs are for the most part attributes of the dyadic relation itself. A young man engaged to be married may have a strong pair relationship with his mother, his father, a brother or sister, a friend of his own age and sex. While none of these possibilities represents in our society an appropriate heterosexual love object for him, yet pair relationships with one or more of these will have consequences for relations between his fiancée and himself — consequences most often not essentially different from those engendered by an outside love affair. The pair relationship between any persons tends typically to have an exclusive, all-or-none quality with respect to the emotions and loyalties of the two people. Hence the coexistence of another pair relationship involving only one of the partners tends to constitute a threat to each relation unless and until some form of accommodation is evolved.

In our attempt to understand the course of dyadic development in the engaged pair, it is important to note the ways in which outside dyads impinge on the relationship between the two. There are three general types of interaction possible in this social configuration: (1) In the first, there is compartmentalization, purposeful or not, of the two or more dyadic relations. (a) If purposeful, one person in each of the pair relationships attempts to keep one pair relation hidden from the person involved in the other. (b) On the other hand, the dyadic relations may lie within two different "social worlds," so that the compartmentalization is gratuitously afforded by the nature of the social situations. (2) In the second general type of interaction, the two pair relations are quite socially visible and tend actively to compete for the loyalties and attachment of the one person common to the two. (3) In the third type, one of the persons either (a) attempts to "move in," or (b) is pulled in, to the other dyadic relation to form a three-person group, a triad.

In order to avoid strengthening the popular impression that interfering outside love affairs are generically and qualitatively different from other dyadic relations in affecting a couple's rapport development, we will illustrate each of these general types with a single case in which examples lie outside the realm of what is commonly spoken of, with much innuendo, as "the triangle."

A young woman, Roberta S., was employed as stenographer by a brilliant young woman lawyer, Miss P. In the course of three years, this had become much more than an employment relationship. The two had come to discuss virtually all their personal affairs with one another and had developed a high degree of rapport and solidarity. Roberta became engaged to marry George R., a young businessman in the city whose business activity happened by chance to be peculiarly open to the scrutiny of Roberta's woman employer. Although he knew of the employment relationship George was quite unaware that many of his business affairs were visible to the lawyer or that there was a close personal relationship between the lawyer and his fiancée. Roberta for her part kept secret the fact that she and her employer exchanged mutual confidences. Miss P., a somewhat older single woman, leaned heavily on Roberta for counsel and mutual support. More or less unconsciously she regarded the approaching marriage as a direct threat to her own emotional security, for it would deprive her of her confidante. Consequently she tended to use to his detriment the information about George's business. Consciously she recognized that this might be true and occasionally attempted to compensate for this unconscious tendency by trying to take "an unbiased view" toward the young man in question. All in all, however, her relations with Roberta were such as to intensify the alternating positive and negative feelings in the latter with respect to both pair relationships.

Roberta had had an earlier most platonic attachment with a professor while at college. She had done brilliant honors work in psychology, her major field. Her work had come to the attention of Professor B., the head of the psychology department when she was a junior, and in her senior year she had been given a research assistantship, an honor usually reserved for graduate students. As a product of this year's work a paper under their joint authorship was published in one of the psychological journals. Despite Dr. B.'s extreme protests Roberta turned down the invitation to return to the university to do graduate work as a fellow, and accepted instead the position of stenographer, hoping to enter law school later. Three years later, the university received a sizable foundation grant with which to pursue research in the very area in which she had been most interested. Dr. B. pleaded with her on several occasions, and with her fiancé George R. more than once, to postpone the marriage for two or three years in order that she might return to the university as a graduate student to help with the research projects. Though this proposal was turned down, the final decision came after much discussion and alternation feelings which had significant impact on the rapport of the engaged couple.

A third triadic relationship which affected this couple involved Roberta's father. She was the youngest of three children and the only child to continue to live at home with her parents. She was throughout childhood the special favorite of her father, a prominent professional man in the community. When she became engaged to George, her mother, who had professional ambitions for her daughter, had been rather cool to the idea of this match, but her father had been quite pleased. During the course of the engagement he had many genial talks with the couple. On three or four occasions he had motored them to Chicago to see plays and had managed in one way or another to accompany them to see several "Big Ten" football games. He frequently discussed their future plans with them and in these discussions he always seemed to evolve ways of injecting his own role into their future lives. He and George seemed to "talk the same language." It was inevitable, however, that the young couple's plans occasionally conflicted with his. When they went places without him or when they made plans for marriage that conflicted with his plans for them, he characteristically felt hurt and became cool and aloof. When this happened he would turn to his wife for emotional solace, support her arguments in opposition to the marriage, or in other ways show his petulance. In sociological language we might say that he tried very hard to make the developing dyad into a triad, an attempt which was alternately welcomed and rebuffed, but these alternations in the moods reflecting them had repercussions in all of the dyads involved in this particular affair.

In this sketch, we have, for simplicity, ignored the outside dyadic relations in which the young man in question was enmeshed. Suffice it to say that the couple finally developed considerably stronger pair rapport than that which characterized any of the other pair relations in which each of them was involved.

It must be apparent by now that the developing pair relation between the two engaged persons does not take place in some vague, inchoate context of "outside social relationships." Instead it weaves itself, in large part, into the texture of other highly personal attachments, particularly dyads, which have distinctive patterns and "boundaries" of their own. As any two-person relation develops in this kind of configuration, it is bound, from time to time, to take on the character not of a dyad but rather of a triad,[17] in that part-

[17] In the treatment of the triad, which follows, the author is again, as with his treatment of the dyad, chiefly indebted to Wiese-Becker, *op. cit.*, esp. pp. 521–530. Their analysis of the triad should be read by every serious student of sociology or social psychology. The distinctive character of three-person groups has been unwarrantedly neglected by observers of social interaction.

ners in other pair relations get involved in one way or another in the intra-pair interaction.

The striking characteristic of the triad is that it tends to be an unstable social grouping. Anyone who has observed the behavior of a group of three children playing together over an extended period must certainly have noticed the tendency of that group to devolve into a dyad plus an outsider. This is as surely true of adult triads as it is of triadic play groups among children.

The principle of least interest, first enunciated by E. A. Ross[18] and more recently elaborated upon by the late Willard Waller,[19] probably operates with greater effect in the three-person group than it does in the two-person group, in the analysis of which Waller made such widespread application of it. It is very rare that a three-person group is characterized by an equality of interest and loyalty among all three members. There is, almost inevitably, one person among the three who wants to bring the other two together, while the other two, though they may be almost equally paired with the first, have only moderate and varying degrees of interest in one another, mitigated by the jealousy they may feel toward each other over their desires for exclu-siveness with the first. Or, as in the instance of Roberta's father, in the case cited above, one person of the three may be trying to "crash" the exclusive-ness of the pair relation existing or developing between the other two. Again, one of the three may dominate each of the other two, individually; in fact he may use as a principal device for domination the playing of the affections of one against those of the other, with all that may involve in the way of disequilibria of loyalties and attachments. In any one of these instances it must be apparent that the person characterized by the least interest in the other two is in a position to exploit one or both of them. In fact, he who has the least interest in either of the other two is in a position to use on that person the most potent control device of all — that of exclusion — provided he sufficiently possesses the loyalty of the third person.

It is in the nature of the triad, then, that its existence is tenuous, its struc-ture unstable and precariously balanced. Its cohesion is constantly threatened by potential jealousy and intrigue, by power plays and ostracism. Note that whatever comes to operate as a symbol of identification for only two of the three is automatically an exclusion symbol for the third. Certainly "the course of true love never did run smooth," not because that is the nature of true love but because that is the nature of a developing dyad of any sort, caught in a welter of other dyads for whom the new relation is but a threat of third-person disturbance to the rapport of pair relations.

How Well Matched? An Exploration of Assortativeness

In our society the main purpose of the engagement is to facilitate, by allowing a certain intimacy and privacy, the testing of personalities in order

---

[18] For the first statement of it, see the first edition of his *Principles of Sociology* (New York: Century, 1921), p. 136.

[19] *The Family*, rev. by Reuben Hill (New York: Dryden Press, 1951), pp. 190–192.

to see how well suited mates are to each other. This is more important than in the case of the formation of other dyadic relations, inasmuch as marriage is less revocable and lasts longer than do most other pair groupings. Such a period of exploration is more important in our society than in most others because of our emphasis on individual choice of marriage partner in a social universe characterized by extreme heterogeneity of cultural elements and extreme mobility from class to class. In societies in which there is little heterogeneity and class mobility, there is little likelihood of getting a mate whose background is radically different from one's own, and hence the chances that any personality in a given social class will "jibe" with any other are reasonably good. It is usually in just such societies that parental judgment plays the decisive part in mate choice, thus minimizing the effects of the sex-frustrated love blindness of late adolescence which has been responsible for so many of the unsound marital choices in our society. The function of engagement for us, then, is a concomitant of our individualism and romanticism.

For those of you who are engaged and who seek some objective method of measuring your adjustment to each other, we have included in Appendix A, pp. 807–822, Reuben Hill's adaptation for self-administration of the engagement success inventory devised by Burgess and Wallin for their recent study of 1000 engaged couples in Chicago.[20] This is a test which you can administer and score yourselves. It has the merit of enabling you to compare your adjustment score with those of several hundred engaged and married couples to whom the test has been administered. The questions are phrased to uncover the degree of articulation in the roles, congruent or complementary, which the members of the pair are playing with respect to one another. In the section on agreements, the test may even uncover some of the roles which one or the other of the members intends to play or expects the other to play but may in varying degrees find lacking in the relationship. It seems necessary, however, to warn the reader that in our society quantification and numerical measurements have acquired a kind of magical prestige. This scale has limited but significant validity for *the group studied* by Burgess and Wallin. It would be wrong to impute a high intrinsic predictive value to the numerical score in any *single case,* and particularly so if the social background of each member of the pair differed significantly from the backgrounds characterizing the Burgess-Wallin sample. The best way for an individual couple to use this scale, we think, is to treat it as a guide with which to explore their own congruent, intended, and possibly incongruent roles. This suggestion is not made in order to afford an easy rationalization to those with low scores but high in "heady love" who seek to cover up the ill assorting of their cultural backgrounds and their more down-to-earth purposes, if any, in order to justify the culmination of their physical desires. The suggestion is made, rather, that serious people may more rationally judge their developing adjustment in engagement against the stuff of which their particular marriage, if it takes place, will be made.

A number of aspects of nonquantitative personality testing and explora-

[20] Ernest W. Burgess and Paul Wallin, *Engagement and Marriage* (Philadelphia: Lippincott, 1953), pp. 306–309.

tion are worth surveying. Perhaps the most important is the experiment in mutual problem-solving which occupies so much time in the engagement period, in which the couple plan for the future both of the engagement and of life after marriage. The present, too, as a day-to-day experiment in more intimate living, is a course that must be charted afresh by each pair, particularly with respect to sexual conduct. Then there is the process of testing, consciously or unconsciously, whether or not friends, relatives, and other people who "matter" approve of the match, a process particularly important in the first part of the engagement period. Finally, there are the inevitable mixed feelings and doubts that arise from all this personality testing; these must be weighed, sometimes directly but usually indirectly and inadvertently, in order to ascertain whether or not the engagement should be broken. Here are the important aspects of engagement — not the thrills, which arise primarily from the surprise and novelty of new experiences, and which a great many mistakenly look forward to as the meaning of engagement. The thing that really matters is the problem-solving — the solving of differences and the finding of areas of agreement — and the growth of a synthesis of wishes through the establishing of a common universe of discourse and the sharing, through it, of past experiences, present desires, and future plans.

Mutual Planning: A New Necessity

When our society was predominantly a rural one, the family was an economic unit, with each member highly important to the well-being of the whole in the matter of making a living. From a very early age children were taught to do highly useful tasks, the girls being taught to cook, to sweep, to dust, to sew, to care for babies, and the like, whereas the boys were depended upon to feed animals, to chop wood, to help in the haying and the threshing, to run errands, to milk, and what not. In short, children began, often as early as the fourth or fifth year, to do tasks which they would do for the rest of their lives. Furthermore, they not only were preparing for adulthood, but were performing tasks economically useful at the time, a fact which greatly augmented the training process. In this situation, children were prepared, beginning at a very early age under the direct and continuous supervision of their parents, not only to perform tasks highly important in the economics of their own future family relations, but also to perform them in a cooperative way. Of the two elements of training the latter was perhaps the more important, for it taught them how to work together, and nothing is more significant in marital relations than the capacity for joint functioning, no matter what the task at hand.

Nowadays, in our largely urban society, the family is no longer the economic, religious, educational, or recreational unit of society. Today it takes far more time and patience to teach a child to do the household tasks than to do them continuously oneself. Indeed, from the standpoint of immediate efficiency there is no reason to teach a child these "chores," for they are neither so numerous nor so onerous that the adults cannot accomplish them in a fairly short time with the help of such conveniences as vacuum cleaners, washing machines, electric mangles, and food mixers. The shrinking size of the home and family and the lack of outside "chores" have done their part in changing the housekeeping picture. Clothing is now mostly ready made, canning is done mainly in factories, bread is baked in bakeries. To the urban child, milk comes from bottles, eggs from cartons, and cows and chickens exist largely as illustrations in picture books. Girls seldom learn homemaking at home. In fact, even that proportion of girls who take home economics courses in high schools or in colleges is quite small. It is a fad of our times that a young woman must act as if she never expected to marry until she is definitely engaged, and hence most young women pretend, consciously or unconsciously, that they plan to carve out careers for themselves. Those who do take home economics courses stoutly maintain that they are planning to teach or to be dietitians; and very few college students, men *or* women, are even so brave as to confess openly that they are studying child psychology for the purpose of being more understanding fathers or mothers.

Indeed, it may be said that our society does not adequately prepare children and youths for the roles they will be expected to play as adults. Our culture has a sharp discontinuity in patterns between those prescribing childhood and youthful behavior and those describing adult behavior. In most societies the child is inducted gradually into adult culture, in practice as well as through precept. There is for persons growing up in these societies no sharp transition in this process which the sociologists call socialization. In our society, as it becomes increasingly dependent on a highly complicated technology and a correspondingly complex specialization in the professions, and as the home is stripped of its educational functions, there is an increasing chasm between the world of the pre-adult and that of the adult. This is as true of family living as it is of one's professional life.

It is therefore far more necessary today than formerly for couples to prepare for marriage during the engagement period. This preparation must include a great deal more conscious planning than formerly, for those who lived a hundred years ago had developed a "second nature" regarding homemaking by the time they were ready to marry. Moreover, there are far more choices to be made by couples today than there used to be, since specialization and differentiation in every aspect of life have complicated almost every situation — whether to live in the city or in the country; whether to build, buy, or rent; whether to have no children, a few children, or many children; whether to live charily in order to build up security for old age or to live in the present "in order to get the most out of life"; whether to find recreation separately or together; whether to make the home a canning, baking, gardening, sewing, woodworking center of almost self-sufficient proportions (à la Borsodi), or to find a one-room apartment for sleeping headquarters only.

The final choice made in any one of these instances will reflect in no small measure the backgrounds of the persons involved. So, though it may not have occurred to you before, mutual planning is an excellent way of testing the assortativeness of the match. But mutual planning is not simply a way of testing for the matching of personalities and the backgrounds of which they are so largely products. Mutual planning is, more significantly, simply an aspect of purposive role-playing — the very stuff out of which pair solidarity emerges. And finally, mutual planning is not something which is peculiar to the engagement period. It is, rather, a most important ingredient of role-playing throughout life.

Exploring Other Aspects of Personality and Social Role

To know thoroughly the various facets of a prospective mate's personality before becoming engaged would be desirable, but most lovers do not. Nor should they be too severely blamed for this, for the courtship situation in our society is very highly standardized and stereotyped, making possible an easy masking of distinctive personality traits through the assumption of the highly stylized and generally accepted courtship role.

Consequently, if a young lover is to find out the significant features of his prospective spouse's personality, he must do so during the engagement. Fortunately, the code makes it possible to learn much about family background during engagement, inasmuch as it allows each member of the pair to visit the family of the other. In such direct acquaintanceship much more can be learned than through mere verbal description by the prospective mate, for the matching of family backgrounds is to some extent a matter of "feel" and not alone the finding of similarity in incomes, educational achievements, religious interests, and other easily verbalized data. There is nothing mystical about this "feel," for it represents an unconscious or semiconscious sensing of similarity or strangeness in ways of behavior. Furthermore, getting acquainted with the beloved's parents and brothers and sisters enables one to evaluate more clearly the significance of the loved one's own personality traits and thus to mitigate the blinding effects of romantic love. No opportunity to visit with the affianced's parents and siblings should be missed — even though the ordeal may seem somewhat painful at first.

The engagement period, with its intimate living, also makes it possible for each to discover significant personality differences. Many of these are not uncovered by the Burgess-Wallin test we recommended above. Often these have to be *experienced* in the intimacy of the engagement, rather than rationally arrived at through conscious thought and discussion. Differing likes and dislikes in literature, drama, music, house furnishings, and architecture may seem trivial during the free and easy period of "dating," but during engagement they can be seen in somewhat the same perspective in which they will be seen after marriage. The greater the intimacy and the exclusiveness of a relationship, the greater is the importance of little traits of character, little likes and aversions, little twists and idiosyncrasies of manner, gait, speech, bearing, haircut, wearing of clothing, shine of the shoes, little differences in habits of cleanliness, orderliness, promptness, and the like. Far more important, of course, are such items as a difference in life philosophies, disparity in fundamental life wishes, and divergence as measured on the introversion-extroversion scale, particularly as these shape the roles played and the roles expected.

Although, we repeat, many of these differences must be experienced in the give-and-take of role-playing in order to be evaluated, much can be determined as to the advisability of the match by way of the give-and-take of mutual discussion. If some topic brings, to one or both, reticence and unwillingness to talk, it ought to be examined with a great deal of care, for little can be successfully hidden behind reticence or secrecy in the marital relationship. "We don't talk about that" may make a nice cloak for a highly charged emotional situation in a song hit, but unfortunately in married life the intense emotion breaks forth almost inevitably in bitter talk and tears. Early discussion and analysis of sensitive spots serves to anesthetize them — in some cases, for life.

Major personality defects should be detected during the engagement if they have not been discovered before. Parent fixation, inferiority complex, acute alcoholism, criminaloid tendency, mental imbalance, chronic ill health (imagined or otherwise), extreme egocentricity, and negativism are all decided handicaps, any one of which is more than the average marriage can bear. As Himes points out, marriage cannot be a successful reform school, nor, for that matter, can the engagement period.

There is a great danger that the conventional courtship masks which hide distinctive characteristics of temperament may extend through the engagement period and thus make impossible any attempt at evaluation of differences. One way to avoid this is to engage in activities which involve frequent crises of one kind or another, for anyone who is confronted by a crisis is thrown off his usual, habitual ways of reacting and tends to expose his basic traits. It is difficult if not impossible to advise what to do in order to be confronted with crises. Most of us avoid them whenever we can. It remains true, however, that many a girl has seen a new and sinister side of a lover's character when a puncture occurred and the spare turned out to be flat. Perhaps the most sensible thing to do is to minimize the time spent in the conventional amusements, such as the movies and dancing, in order to seek out mutually interesting but less conventional pursuits-in-common, such as hobby cookery (how do you behave when you scald your thumb?), distance canoeing, ornithological photography, and the like. And remember — it isn't cricket to set a trap which will be a crisis for your partner but not for you! The main point of matching for background and personality congruence is not to see how your mate suits you, but *to see how you mutually suit each other as you cooperate in joint functioning of all kinds.* It makes a great deal of difference both in engagement and in marriage where your point of reference lies — whether it is in yourself and in your own little selfish whims, fancies, and foibles or whether it is in the mutuality of the relationship with a mate whose personality is at all times considered fully as important and (with respect to being "pushed around" and experimented upon) as inviolable as your own.

How Long Should an Engagement Be?

"When should we get married?" is a mutual question asked almost daily by many engaged couples. There are multitudinous considerations involved here, such as the amount of money a couple ought to have, the kind of job the breadwinner should have, his prospects for immediate advancement, whether to live with in-laws for a time, whether the wife-to-be ought to continue working, whether to wait until all in-laws approve more heartily. Laying these aside for the moment, however, there is a fundamental question which ought to be considered first, the answer to which is not subject to as many qualifications as the answers to these highly relative problems. This is a question which faces every engaged couple, whether or not they are confronted with any of the questions just mentioned. The question is "Does a long engagement have any values *per se?*"

Most people will answer "No" almost immediately to that question, for it is common in our society to regard long engagements as an evil. Most parents advise their sons and daughters against long engagements. The force of ritual and ceremony in our culture operates to shorten the period of engagement, for an engagement that is to be a long one is frequently not announced with the usual party, and the period itself often has fewer parties and showers for the bride-to-be. Yet if we consider for a moment the major function of the engagement period in our society — to provide for personality testing and exploration — we come to the conclusion that the short engagement is not entirely desirable, since it may not allow enough time for this process of matching and experimentation to take place. Furthermore, we have to admit that an engagement which is one continuous whirl of gay parties is ordinarily a poor preview of the kind of life to be experienced after marriage. Instead of encouraging the unmasking of the courtship "front," which is really made to order for just such a round of social appearances, the members of the pair are encouraged to maintain the fiction of courtship days.

We now have some definite evidence that long engagements are to be preferred over short ones. Burgess and Cottrell, in their study of 526 couples, discovered that couples whose engagement was less than three months had a much poorer adjustment than those who were engaged for from three to eight months, and the latter, in turn, were more poorly adjusted than those engaged anywhere from nine to twenty-three months. The best-adjusted couples were found to be those whose engagements had lasted two years or more. Half of those having had an engagement of less than three months had a poor marital adjustment, according to the Burgess-Cottrell method of rating, while only 11 per cent of those whose engagement lasted two years or longer had a poor marital adjustment. On the other hand, while only about one fourth of those engaged for less than three months had good marital-adjustment scores, almost two thirds of those engaged two years or more had a good adjustment.[21] The study of 792 couples by Terman and associates, published somewhat earlier than the Burgess-Cottrell study, indicates essentially the same thing. In this study the mean happiness scores went up steadily in relation to length of engagement, those having been engaged five years or longer having the highest scores.[22] While some of the differ-

---

[21] Ernest W. Burgess and Leonard S. Cottrell, Jr., *Predicting Success or Failure in Marriage* (New York: Prentice-Hall, 1939), pp. 167–168.

[22] Lewis M. Terman and associates, *Psychological Factors in Marital Happiness* (New York: McGraw-Hill, 1938), pp. 198–200.

ences in Terman's study are not statistically significant, their corroboration by the Burgess-Cottrell study gives them enhanced validity.

These findings, as Burgess and Cottrell point out, give further support to the principle that companionship rather than romantic love forms the best sustaining force for a long-lasting mutually satisfying marital relation. The notion that boy-girl relationships should be allowed to mature over a period in time is antithetical to the romantic dogma that love (usually at first sight) is "all that matters." [23]

The Problem of Sex in Engagement

Perhaps one of the foremost reasons why a short engagement is considered superior to a long one is that a brief engagement tends to enable the couple to avoid having to face the problem presented by the drive toward greater and greater sexual intimacy during the betrothal period. The problem of sexual intimacy is a very difficult one for an engaged couple to solve.

On the one hand, the mores allow a great deal of physical intimacy not condoned in ordinary "dating." On the other hand, sexual intercourse prior to marriage is condemned, although the natural conclusion to physical caressing is the completed sex act. All the physical processes set in motion by caressing and mutual fondling press toward that conclusion. To stop short of complete sexual union is accomplished only by the operation of strong inhibitions established early in youth — inhibitions which are largely implanted as a result of the working of the mores.

Certain widespread notions in our society have tended to work in a direction opposed to that of the mores of chastity in the engagement period; otherwise these compulsives would be much more universally effective not only in preventing premarital sexual intercourse but also in ending the inner conflict which occurs in the minds of engaged couples.

These notions come from various sources and often have little in common except their result — to mitigate the effects of the mores. One of them is the notion that long-continued caressing without the culmination of the sex act results in inability either to complete the act or to enjoy it — in short, that sexual foreplay ceases to be foreplay and becomes the sexual aim or end. Another notion is that a couple in love and intending to marry is psychologically wedded and hence can go ahead to culmination of that love. A third notion prevalent in our society is that the main cause of unhappiness in marriage is sexual incompatibility, and that to avoid an unhappy marriage one should engage in sexual intercourse with a prospective mate prior to marriage in order to test sexual harmony of the match.

These notions have varying amounts of validity. Certain people do seem to develop an interest far greater than normal in sexual foreplay, so that this interest interferes with or completely blocks the culmination in sexual union. We are not sure, however, how this abnormality develops or what propor-

[23] Burgess and Wallin, *op. cit.,* apparently do not take length of acquaintance or of engagement into account in computing the engagement success score.

tion of couples are subject to it. It is highly probable that improper sex education during an impressionable period and the adult attitudes resulting therefrom are in the main responsible for the development of such abnormality. If the attitudes remain healthy, frigidity and impotence will not develop.

The fallacy in the notion that a couple in love, being psychologically wedded, is entitled to sexual relations is obvious, of course. Marriage is a concern not only of the pair but also of the group. The ceremonies express society's approval of the match; and incidentally, these rites have a significant effect on the future solidarity of the match, lending stability and reinforcement to the inner unity through public understanding and public defining of the relationship. Without this public recognition family stability is impossible, and without family stability children, society's main concern, become foundlings or otherwise wards of the state.

The notion that most marital unhappiness stems from sexual incompatibility is completely erroneous. It is equally fallacious to suppose that trial intercourse, under conditions of surreptitiousness, fright, and discomfort, will give any real indication as to the possibilities of mutual sex harmony. True, the thrill and the novelty of the experience may counterbalance the unfavorable conditions in some instances, but it is certainly not fair to say, if the act under such conditions turns out to be painful and unenjoyable, that this is a result of sexual incompatibility. Sexual harmony is usually the result of mutual adjustment taking place over an extended period of time, and cannot be said either to exist or not to exist at the outset. Furthermore, most sexual incompatibility is not physical but is, rather, the result of attitudes; and attitudes are ordinarily capable of being brought into mutual adjustment. So the difference between sexual harmony and sexual incompatibility becomes only one of degree on an attitudinal scale.

The importance of these and similar notions, however, has little relation to their logical validity; *it results, rather, from the fact that they have been and are being believed in and accepted as true. This makes them a part of social reality and as such they are real in their consequences;* namely, in mitigating the inhibiting effect of the mores of premarital chastity and continence.

Perhaps more important than these notions, each of which has a kind of pseudo-rationale, is the basic paradox in our culture regarding sex. On the one hand we live in a world highly supercharged with sex stimuli. A company could scarcely sell toothbrushes without using pictures of semi-nude women in the advertisements. From our literature, movies, radio programs, from our popular songs, our jokes, our Sunday supplements, these sex stimuli bombard us. On the other hand we are prudish to the extreme in a wide variety of matters relating to sex. There are restricting taboos on every hand. These operate particularly with respect to the manifestations of any overt visible *responses* to the rain of stimuli.[24] This cultural discrepancy has a profound effect on the thinking and behavior of young men and women. Sensing the hypocrisy in the implied notion that the gay, bright

[24] For a particularly apt characterization of this set of cultural contradictions, see John McPartland, "Footnote on Sex," *Harper's Magazine* (March, 1946), pp. 212–214.

world of sex all about us is merely make-believe, they are in a quandary over what significance the verbal mores have. Many of them simply begin to ignore the mores.

Terman found a steady decline in the percentage of virgins (of both sexes) at marriage of those born before 1890 onward to those born since 1910.[25] He also found that the ascertainable difference in marital happiness between those who were virgins at marriage and those who were not is less significant than is ordinarily believed. It is also of interest that he found those marrying late (between the ages of twenty-five and twenty-nine) had less premarital sex experience than those marrying earlier.

Kinsey found that 70.5% of the males in the United States are involved in premarital intercourse in the late teens.[26] He found, however, that the rate of premarital intercourse varied markedly by educational level (which he used as index to class level); among those who finally attained only eight years or less of formal education the incidence of those involved in premarital intercourse was 81.2 per cent during the late teens, while those who had gone one or more years to college had an incidence of 38.8 per cent during the same period. But while Kinsey's findings converge with Terman's in general regarding the incidence of premarital intercourse, Kinsey did not find (as Terman did) that this incidence is increasing.

Burgess and Wallin, in their study of a sample comprising a thousand engaged couples and a follow-up of six hundred sixty-six of these as married couples, found the incidence of premarital intercourse to have been increasing but to have leveled off somewhat for those born since 1910.[27] Nearly half of the six hundred twenty-eight couples about which they collected these data had practiced intercourse with each other before marriage. Those who had previously had sex relations with others were more likely to have intercourse with the engagement partner. Burgess and Wallin attempted to discover whether there is any relationship between having sexual intercourse during the engagement and scores on their engagement success test. They found only a very small relationship, and were, in addition, unable to say whether the intimacy could be interpreted as "causal" with respect to the slightly lower score.

Burgess and Wallin found no correlation between length of time of "going steady" and intercourse during premarital period, but they did find a small relation between length of engagement and occurrence of premarital intercourse.

Some years ago Hornell Hart suggested that a young couple avoid the drive toward premarital sexual intercourse by minimizing the amount of time they are alone together, by spending more of their time with friends, and by setting definite limits past which it is mutually agreed they shall not go in their caresses. Norman Himes believed that a better solution lay in early marriage. The early marriage principle, however, runs into a contra-

[25] Terman and associates, *op. cit.*, chap. 12.
[26] A. C. Kinsey, W. B. Pomeroy, and C. E. Martin, *Sexual Behavior in the Human Male* (Philadelphia: W. B. Saunders, 1948), pp. 248–249, 350.
[27] Burgess and Wallin, *op. cit.*, chap. 11, "Sex and Engagement."

diction. Not only does it sometimes impose heavy burdens on the subsidizing parents (who of recent years, among the relatively fixed income groups, have been squeezed by inflation), but we have already seen that *long* acquaintance, courtship, and engagement are correlated with success in marriage. Early marriage is thus a definite risk unless it fulfills these requisites, and this it seldom can do.

A fatal mistake is made in assuming that since such a large number of young couples break the formal code of engagement behavior, no consequences are entailed by so doing. On the contrary, whenever two people break this code and go on to the culmination of the sex act they take upon themselves the entire responsibility for its consequences. Should pregnancy result or should they be apprehended, they are treated in much the same way they would be if there were no such divergence between code and general practice. The everybody's-doing-it argument may be influential in bringing about the breaking of the code, but after the code is broken this argument often recedes from consciousness, *while the code demands and receives its pound of flesh in the form of a feeling of guilt.* Codes are curious, because they are both outside and within each of us, and while it is often possible to evade the external aspects of a code, it is very rarely possible to avoid the internal consequences of such evasion.

PLANNING THE SIZE OF THE FAMILY

In this day when the size of the family is much more subject to control than previously, it is important for an engaged couple to discuss rather thoroughly with each other their ideas about how many children they desire, how widely spaced they wish them, and when they want the first one. This discussion is worth while, not because it leads to blueprints which will be followed in absolute detail, but rather because the two have to reach some kind of initial understanding of each other's general point of view regarding family size. From this initial understanding many a tack is usually taken as the winds of fortune and the zephyrs of fancy change, but once the understanding is achieved the changes of course and direction are made together and not separately. It is particularly important to discuss plans with respect to children if one of the pair does not desire any at all. All couples who are planning to marry ought to consider the findings of Burgess and Cottrell regarding the relation between the wish for children and the presence or absence of them on the one hand, and marital adjustment on the other. These authors found those without children but desiring them to be the best-adjusted group. Only about 10 per cent of these had a poor adjustment, while almost two thirds had a good adjustment. Twenty per cent of the couples having and desiring children had a poor marital adjustment score, while almost half of them had a good adjustment. Exactly 55 per cent of the couples having and desiring no children had a poor adjustment, while only slightly more than 20 per cent had a good adjustment. Those having children against the wishes of one or both had the poorest record of all, two thirds having a poor adjustment and only a trifle over 11 per cent of them having a good adjustment.[28] While it is possible that the desire not to have children may be subsequent to marital maladjustment in some cases, it remains probable that those who enter marriage with a mutual desire for children have a markedly better chance for marital adjustment than those couples of which either one or both do not desire children. Certainly, failure to reach an understanding before marriage regarding whether or not to have children is a mistake which ought to be avoided.

Regarding the number of children to have, few couples can plan with any definiteness during the engagement. As Himes pointed out, the girl's expressed hopes for a large number of children ought not to be taken too seriously by the boy (just as, incidentally, his daydreams about the mansion they'll build to house them ought to be considerably discounted by the girl). A good many girls plan to have a "dozen" but end up having only two or three.[29]

The spacing of the children, too, is a problem which usually cannot be decided with much definiteness in the engagement period but can be discussed to advantage. Both the number of children and the spacing of them are affected by group patterns; each couple tends to pattern after others in the size and spacing of its family. Again, the economic prosperity of each family has an important effect on the spacing of children, for during periods of depression or unemployment middle-class families, in particular, tend to postpone the next baby until times get better. It is well for engaged couples to recognize these and other factors which in the future might affect the carrying out of their present plans.

One of the most salutary effects of planning for children is that in this way engaged couples begin to be dimly aware of their coming responsibilities and duties as parents. Probably much more important than spinning dreams about the number of children they hope to have and the spacing of these children is the engaged couple's discussion of the proper ways to teach, discipline, and care for the children they desire. Through this discussion the two are enabled, if they are wise, to get good glimpses of very fundamental patterns within each other's personalities; for one's philosophy of child rearing is usually a basic character trait, stemming as it does from one's own early upbringing and thus reflecting even one's parents' philosophy. Terman, it will be remembered from the preceding chapter, found that happiness in marriage is closely related to childhood happiness, which in turn is correlated with a firm but not harsh discipline experienced in childhood. These are very crucial points, which ought to be kept in mind during the mutual testing of the engagement period and particularly in the discussion of child training and discipline. If one of the pair has experienced a childhood of severe and harsh discipline, he is not only a poor risk as a partner but he may likewise make a very poor parent.

---

[28] Burgess and Cottrell, *op. cit.*, pp. 260–261, 414. Burgess and Wallin, *op. cit.*, chap. 21, "Children and Marital Success," find the *attitude of wanting children* to be the crucial factor. The presence of, or number of, children has no apparent relation to marital success.

[29] The Burgess-Wallin study, *op. cit.*, pp. 704–706, indicates that the number of children desired tends to *increase* rather than decrease after marriage, however.

CULTURAL CONTRADICTIONS AND INNER DOUBTS

One of the dogmas held by the cult of romance is that once you have fallen in love you are no longer subject to doubts and misgivings: either you *know*, intuitively, that you are in love, or what you are experiencing is not true love at all. Like a good many other notions surrounding romantic love this is misleading. Any two people who endeavor to solve mutually the variety of problems presented in the whole panorama of the life which is facing them are almost sure to find areas of disagreement and misunderstanding. The application of the romantic standard in such an instance only results in the mass production of large mountains out of quite ordinary molehills, for it means that the slightest misunderstanding between the two challenges the basic validity of the whole relationship. This is decidedly unwarranted and unrealistic. An engaged couple will do well to accept at the outset the fact that they doubtless will have not only occasional misunderstandings but also concomitant inner doubts and frequent emotional ambivalence as well. They must therefore begin at once to judge the quality of the relation between them, not on the basis of the presence or absence of absolute agreement and harmony, but rather on the significance of the clashes and doubts that will undoubtedly arise, and to set up some kind of machinery for ironing out minor disputes and inner conflicts.

One way to acquire a healthy, balanced view toward these inevitable difficulties is to survey carefully the aspects of the engagement itself which make for ambivalence and doubts. First of all, the engagement often comes at a time when the young man or young woman is still struggling for independence and heterosexuality, while clutching at the security of the old parental dependence and the responses of a transitory homosexual relation. This struggle alone is sufficient to generate a whole host of doubts, mixed feelings, and inner conflicts, and when the weighty problems of an approaching marriage are added to it, the result is sometimes a serious strain upon the resiliency of the personality. Usually this struggle dies as one "grows up."

In the second place, the dream or image of a perfect mate, which has been built up throughout childhood and youth by highly emotional relationships of identification with, and idealization of, a parent, sibling, or other hero, is of necessity altered into congruence with the worldly and somewhat imperfect characteristics of the actual mate-in-the-flesh. This is never a pleasant process, and few there are who can go through it without pangs of disappointment. There are always times when one suffers more from nostalgia for the original dream image in its pristine purity than from frustrated desire for the actual mate, and there is frequently ensuing ambivalence as to the advisability of looking further for a more perfect incarnation of the dream mate. This, too, is in most cases a transitory source of inner doubt.

In the third place, a kind of circularity is frequent. Here inner strife is projected outwards in the form of a lovers' quarrel; but thanks to the operation of the romantic dogmas regarding the import of misunderstandings, this reacts to augment the original inner conflict — and so on back and forth until both inner and outer conflict have reached major proportions. This circularity is rendered inoperative by understanding the mechanisms which are at work — the romantic notions, the projections of inner conflict, and the internalization of outer quarrels.

Fourth, there is often a carry-over, from the prebetrothal courtship period into the engagement itself, of certain patterns and attitudes of exploitation described by Folsom in Chapter Seven. In most cases, unfortunately, there is nothing transitory about these attitudes, and it is not uncommon for them to be carried on into the marriage relation. They operate to block mutuality and to destroy the "sharing in" of the relation. The insidiousness of these attitudes is greatly enhanced by the fact that they are usually not consciously recognized. They can be dealt with only if they can be brought out into the open where they can be thoroughly examined. This calls for constant and scrupulous self-searching and for inner honesty.

Fifth, inner conflicts are the internal counterpart of the pulling and hauling among the various dyadic groups to which each member of the engagement pair belongs. Some of these "outside" loyalties are strong, yet must be broken or moderated if the engagement pair solidarity is to develop. Triadic relations, attempting to bridge these external conflicts, wax and wane, leaving their consequences chiefly in the form of doubts and inner strain.

Finally, inner conflict arises from the fact that engagement is in some ways a hybrid between the courtship situation with its dalliance and free and easy play on the one hand, and marriage with its assumption of adult responsibilities on the other. The conflicting definitions of the situation involved in engagement lead directly to mixed feelings and inner struggles, and there is probably no remedy for this ambiguity in our culture patterns. Why? Because culture is a thing which cannot be repealed or enacted, but must grow and change through generations by tiny accretions and infinitesimal erosions.

Elopement: Psychic and Social Flight

Mixed feelings are obviously a normal accompaniment of the testing process with which we have been concerned during so much of this chapter. When one is in the throes of inner conflict there is usually a drive to find mental escape through some means or other. There are two such escapes available: one is elopement, and the other is the breaking of the engagement.

It may seem strange to some that we consider elopement as an escape from inner misgivings, yet in a good many instances that is exactly what it is, even though conflict with parents is usually the apparent cause. The latter, in such cases, results largely from a projection of the inner conflict. Like any mental escape, such elopement is psychically unhealthy because it is illogical, unrealistic, and inappropriate to the situation at hand. It therefore does not solve the problems but leads the two to shut their eyes to them and to postpone the solution. Inner conflicts are only temporarily anesthetized by flights of this sort. Married life often acts like a dash of cold water to reawaken these inner tensions. At this point they are often projected toward the partner, probably resulting in flight again, this time one from the other.

There are two important objections to elopement, aside from those connected with its frequent function as an escape mechanism. One is that, coming as it usually does before the engagement has been publicly announced, elopement by-passes the engagement period with its valuable testing, matching, and experimentation in intimate living, and thus denies the two those important values which come from the engagement's *gradual* mental preparation for marriage. The other objection is that "running off to get married" often angers parents and friends. This is not surprising, since it is usually the parents from whom the couple is ostensibly running away. Since it often represents a complete severing of ties which act in most cases as outer supports of a couple's inner solidarity, it bodes ill for the continuity and stability of the relationship. As we have previously noted, an important function of the engagement is to provide a test of public approval and of friends' approval, since "outside" acceptance of the couple is highly important to its continued well-being. If they have eloped and have thus cut themselves off from a large number of close friends annd relatives, they will often find themselves alone together far more than they wish.

BREAKING AN ENGAGEMENT

The breaking of the engagement, too, may represent an attempt to escape from the doubts and misgivings which have arisen from the engagement situation in and of itself. Such doubts do not necessarily have anything directly to do with the poorly matched characteristics of the two personalities involved or the suitability of the relation. There are some persons who can never quite bring themselves to go through with all that is involved in engagement and marriage — among other things, with the severance of early ties and the renunciation of dependence upon parents, *plus* the development of an exclusive loyalty to the mate-to-be. For these the breaking of an engagement, like the elopement, is often not a realistic solution but an escape from the same mental quandary. The difference is merely in the direction chosen for the escape.

If the couple, after testing the relation, have found it lacking in congruence and mutuality, the breaking of the engagement may of course be a logical solution. The possibility of breaking the relationship without excessively drastic results, particularly without bringing down the opprobrium of the community, is one of the major reasons for having an engagement period at all.[30] How to distinguish between doubts arising from genuine ill-matching and those coming from intrinsic aspects of "growing up" and the complete changing of one's role and status is, however, a severe test of judgment. Those who make this distinction the most intelligently are those who

---

[30] For a study of the variety of patterns of interaction in courtship, see C. Kirkpatrick, and T. Caplow, "Courtship in a Group of Minnesota Students," pp. 79–80 in *Readings in Marriage and the Family,* edited by J. T. and M. G. Landis (New York: Prentice-Hall, 1952). See also Burgess and Wallin, *op. cit.,* chaps. 8 and 9.

have come, through reading and through intelligent introspection, to recognize the earmarks of endogenous doubting and to understand its sources within themselves.

The breaking of an engagement is rarely an easy matter even in those instances in which ill-suitedness thoroughly justifies it. Almost inevitably, significant amounts of identification and idealization have gone on and the self of each has expanded to include the other person, so that the breaking of the relation is like divorce or bereavement in that it represents a certain amount of disintegration of the self. As in divorce or bereavement, hostile and aggressive attitudes formerly directed toward the mate become directed toward one's own ego, resulting in melancholia and in extreme cases in suicidal attempts. For mental health and balance, those caught in the situation of a broken engagement ought to interest themselves as deeply as possible in vocational or avocational pursuits which have an intrinsic appeal to them. They ought also to impose upon themselves restrictions, at least for a time, with respect to becoming embroiled in new affairs in order to avoid the "rebound" with its well-known blindness and irrationality. Himes's suggestion that those who decide to break an engagement would do well to seek a change of scene may in some instances be good advice while in others it may be bad. When there is a tendency toward melancholia, to withdraw somewhere into solitariness is an invitation to suicide. Normally, however, getting away from old scenes and friends who call to mind the broken relation is very helpful to one who desires to forget. But far better is it to have little or nothing to forget, and therefore to have no need to imitate Jim of Huckleberry Finn fame by inscribing on the walls of the prison house, "Here a captive heart busted." Therefore, be engaged not too well, but wisely.

SELECTED READINGS

BECKER, HOWARD, *Systematic Sociology on the Basis of the* Beziehungslehre *and* Gebildelehre *of Leopold von Wiese* (New York: Wiley, 1932), pp. 511–514.

——, *Through Values to Social Interpretation* (Durham, N. C.: Duke University Press, 1950), chaps. 2 and 4.

——, and USEEM, RUTH HILL, "Sociological Analysis of the Dyad," *American Sociological Review,* 7, No. 1 (Feb., 1942), pp. 3–26.

BROMLEY, DOROTHY DUNBAR, and BRITTEN, F. H., *Youth and Sex: A Study of 1300 College Students* (New York: Harper, 1938).

BURGESS, ERNEST W., and COTTRELL, LEONARD S., JR., *Predicting Success or Failure in Marriage* (New York: Prentice-Hall, 1939), chap. 10.

——, and WALLIN, PAUL, *Engagement and Marriage* (Philadelphia: Lippincott, 1953).

KINSEY, ALFRED C., POMEROY, WARDELL B., and MARTIN, CLYDE E., *Sexual Behavior in the Human Male* (Philadelphia: W. B. Saunders, 1948).

LOCKE, HARVEY J., *Predicting Adjustment in Marriage: A Comparison of a Divorced and a Happily Married Group* (New York: Holt, 1951).

TERMAN, LEWIS M., and associates, *Psychological Factors in Marital Happiness* (New York: McGraw-Hill, 1938), chap. 12; see also pp. 197–201.

Thomas, William I., *Primitive Behavior* (New York: McGraw-Hill, 1937), chap. 10.

TOPICS FOR DISCUSSION OR REPORTS

1. Describe the personality and background characteristics of two or three upper-middle class couples who kept their engagements secret. Does this give any insight into the function of publicly announcing the engagement?
2. List the ways in which the engagement in our society operates to exert group control over individual behavior. Then make a list of the aspects of engagement which seem to you to represent nonfunctional cultural lag.
3. Would American marriages have more stability if betrothals were arranged by the parents rather than by couples themselves? Discuss the other relative merits of such arranged marriages as contrasted with those based on romantic love and individual choice. What general elements in our cultural ethos run counter to the idea of parental arrangement of marriages?
4. Suppose you were given the power to change our mores and our patterns of behavior during the engagement. In what ways would you alter them: (1) with respect to sexual intimacy; (2) as regards the custom of spending much time at movies and dances; (3) by adding activities which will continue after marriage; and (4) with respect to length of engagement and early marriage?
5. Examine your answers to questions under topic 4 above. Which of the modifications you have suggested are actually possible at present thanks to the wide range of cultural Alternatives? Which are impossible, and for what reasons? What do you conclude regarding the possibilities for a *rationally* planned engagement in our (relatively) secular society?
6. How much of one's past affairs and intimacies should one tell his mate before marriage? Discuss the pros and cons of this problem.
7. In how far is it possible or desirable to keep the engagement pair relation compartmentalized and separated from the other dyadic relations in which each of the pair is involved?
8. Give a brief life history of someone whose courtship included two or more broken engagements. Does this personality sketch give any clues to the explanation of this type of behavior?
9. Write a case history of a married couple of your acquaintance who eloped to marry, emphasizing any problems which seem to stem from missing the engagement period of mutual testing.
10. Set up a model for a research project in which you suggest possible methods for testing the congruence of common and complementary, actual and intended roles of engaged couples. Explore the possibilities of measuring the significance of personality traits and background factors for specific types of role-playing.

Chapter Ten

Taking Physical Factors into Account

EDGAR S. GORDON, M.D.

THE SIGNIFICANCE OF PHYSICAL FACTORS

IN any consideration of the problems involved in preparation for marriage, the physical factors must of necessity receive a large share of attention, since the success or failure of the marriage venture may be determined to a considerable degree by the knowledge and adaptability of both partners in this phase of their relation. The exact relative importance of the combined physical factors is difficult to state, and varies in the opinions of various observers. It is a matter of common observation, however, that marriage partnerships which are based chiefly or exclusively upon physical attraction have a poor chance of success. Indeed, most qualified students of the family feel that the temperamental, intellectual, and spiritual elements are perhaps of more fundamental importance than sexual attraction and compatibility. It is probably wisest to consider the latter as only one supplementary building block in the stability of the marriage partnership. Terman and his associates, on the basis of their extensive study, state: "Our data indicate that the influence of the sexual factors is at most no greater than that of the combined personality and background factors, and that it is probably less." [1] This study shows with equal clarity that partners who are psychically and socially well mated are likely to show a high degree of tolerance for the things that are unsatisfactory in their sexual relations. This it would be as erroneous to overestimate as it would be to underestimate the importance of sex as a determining factor in marital happiness.

In spite of this conservatism in estimating the role played by all the combined physical factors, it is true that many marital unions have been broken by sexual incompatibility either as the dominant or as an important contributing cause. It is probable that a large portion of these tragedies might be averted if marriage partners would make an earnest attempt to understand all phases of the marital relation, including the physical phases.

The pattern of behavior of both male and female animals in regard to sexual matters is remarkably constant throughout the animal world (with, of course, some minor species variations).[2] This behavior is the resultant of such an intricate mixture of psychical, emotional, physical, and endocrine factors that the clear-cut delimitation of the role played by any one of these components becomes virtually impossible. As our knowledge in this field has broadened, however, it has become increasingly apparent that the development of all phases of this entire pattern in both sexes is the result of endocrine or chemical changes, brought about in response to some unexplained

[1] Lewis M. Terman and associates, *Psychological Factors in Marital Happiness* (New York: McGraw-Hill, 1938), p. 376.
[2] See Martindale's discussion of the family pattern of animals, pp. 50–56.

and predetermined stimulus present in the individual from birth and probably from conception. This unknown factor appears to be the chromosome pattern which is established when the sperm cell enters the ovum. Further, the differentiation of tissues into male or female, as it occurs in embryonic life, is a response to the directing force of the chromatin arrangement in the fertilized ovum.[3]

During embryonic growth, certain groups of cells become isolated at various stages for the development of special functions. Among these are the collections of cells on either side of the midline, in the region later to be occupied by the kidney, which grow and differentiate into the sexual apparatus. By inspection, at this early stage, it is not possible to identify the sex of the embryo, since the sex organs of both sexes develop from identical structures and the differentiation occurs so slowly that for a considerable period no structural differences are apparent. Indeed, even in adult life each structure in the organs of one sex has a homologue in the opposite sex, as, for example, Fallopian tubes and vas deferens, penis and clitoris, ovary and testis, scrotum and labia majora, etc.

The fully developed sex organs of either sex remain more or less functionless throughout the period of childhood. During this time the individual is sexless in the physiological sense, except in so far as social customs make boys and girls aware of their differences. At puberty, the sexual phase of life begins through the increased activity of the sex glands, which in turn are stimulated to this new function by the pituitary gland, located at the base of the brain. We are still ignorant of the factors responsible for this sudden spontaneous activity. It tends to occur somewhat earlier in girls (twelve to thirteen) than in boys (fifteen to seventeen), but in each case the physiological and psychological changes are parallel, resulting in the well-known differences between the adult man and the adult woman.

For a period of thirty to forty years, the behavior of both sexes is normally conditioned by the powerful force of the sex drive, which attains full maturity with completion of the pubertal changes. This is the reproductive period of life, during which the desire for children expresses itself most strongly, the period when both men and women develop their greatest drive of efficiency and productiveness. In woman the age at which the decline in reproductive capacity begins (the menopause or climacteric) usually varies from forty to fifty-five. It is often accompanied by severe emotional changes which, in association with the cessation of certain physical functions, may make this a difficult period. In men, a climacteric may also occur, although it is much less common. Physical capacity for reproduction often declines in intensity at fifty to sixty years, but authentic instances of fatherhood at ninety-five have been recorded.

THE ANATOMY AND PHYSIOLOGY OF SEX: MALE

The testis, or male sex gland, is a rounded and elongated organ about the size of a small walnut, located normally in a pouch of skin called the

[3] See Owen's discussion, pp. 423-430.

scrotum. (See Figure 2.) Each testicle is suspended by a spermatic cord which contains the blood vessels and nerves necessary to supply the testicle, and the vas deferens or excretory duct by means of which the spermatic fluid is conveyed to the outside. Since the left spermatic cord is somewhat longer than the right, the left testicle normally hangs slightly lower. The course of the spermatic cord is of great importance. It passes upward from the scrotum and over the top of the pubic bone, where it lies just beneath the skin. From here it passes through an opening in the muscles of the abdominal wall, thence into the lower abdominal cavity, where it turns downward next to the urinary bladder and to the prostate gland, at which point the vas deferens, joining with some other ducts, empties into the urethra or urinary passage leading away from the bladder. Of particular importance is the defect in the abdominal muscles through which these structures pass, since loops of intestine have a tendency to protrude through this opening

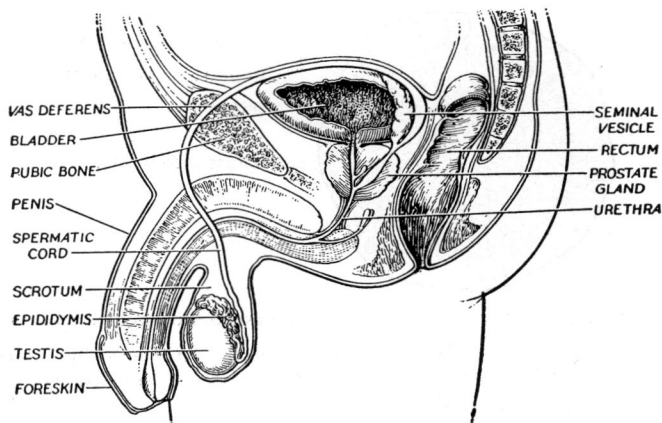

FIGURE 2. ANATOMY OF THE MALE REPRODUCTIVE ORGANS

and to follow the course of the spermatic cord into the scrotum, thus causing a hernia, or rupture. Such an accident must be surgically repaired by closing the mechanical defect, which has usually become somewhat enlarged, in the abdominal wall. This operation in the hands of an inexperienced surgeon is attended by grave danger, since any interference with the integrity of the spermatic cord, which normally passes through that opening, may lead to damage of the blood supply to the testicle on that side, thereby producing atrophy and loss of function.

The testis is composed of two types of cells, each with a specific function The first of these, known as the seminiferous tubules, is the glandular tissue, the function of which is the production of sperm cells or spermatozoa. The second type, the interstitial cells, elaborates the male sex hormone which, acting upon all the cells of the body by virtue of its wide distribution through the blood stream, causes the well-known secondary sex characters of the male, such as deep voice, beard, broad shoulders, etc.

The cells of the seminiferous tubules as seen through the microscope are arranged in rosettes, and the maturing sperm cells may be viewed in all stages of development, from the parent cells around the periphery to the mature spermatozoa in the open portion of the gland. These tubules empty into an elaborate system of ducts, which eventually lead the sperm cells to the outside. Chief among the components of this duct system is the epididymis, an extremely coiled and convoluted tube about eighteen to twenty feet in length, constituting a definite soft, rather stringy mass lying immediately alongside the testicle. This tube serves to conduct the spermatozoa from the seminiferous tubules to the vas deferens, a larger tube about eighteen inches in length, which then connects with the urethra and so to the outside.

The spermatozoa are extremely minute, actively moving (motile) cells. They average about one twentieth of a millimeter or one five-hundredth of an inch in length, and their intense moving about (motility) is due to

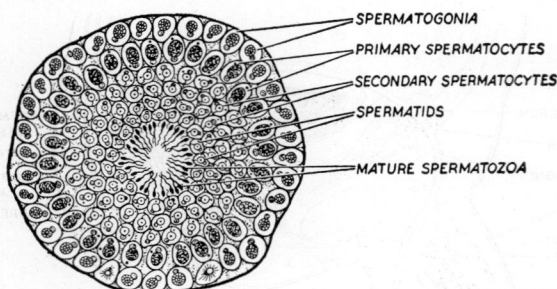

FIGURE 3.   SECTION OF TESTIS SHOWING SPERMATOGENESIS

The successive stages in the maturation of sperm cells are represented by (1) the original parent cells (spermatogonia), and (2) the subsequent development stages (primary spermatocytes, secondary spermatocytes, and spermatids).

the propellerlike motion of their tails. Spermatozoa are inactive until they are brought in contact with the fluid from the prostate gland and seminal vesicles. These combined secretions form the semen in which the sperm cells are actively motile. At each normal ejaculation of semen from 200,000,000 to 400,000,000 spermatozoa may be released.

The prostate gland is a structure about the size of a walnut located at the opening of the urinary bladder and surrounding the urethra as it leaves that organ. The secretion of this gland is a milky fluid which is one of the important constituent parts of semen; its function is probably to activate the spermatozoa to intense motility. The secretion accumulates during normal resting conditions in the branching, irregular gland spaces, and is discharged at the time of ejaculation by contraction of muscle cells scattered throughout the gland. Prostatic fluid is expelled through small openings into the urethra at the point near where the ducts leading from the testes and seminal vesicles also enter. Thus a mixing of secretions from these three sources occurs at this point.

The seminal vesicles are folded, irregularly shaped tubular pouches, each one about six inches in length, but coiled in such a manner that in their natural condition each one is about three inches long. There are two such vesicles, one on each side of the midline. Their secretion, like that of the prostate, is expressed during ejaculation and is an important constituent of semen chiefly because it contributes toward the motility, vigor, and endurance of the spermatozoa.

The penis is the copulatory organ of the male, and as such it must fulfill two functions: (1) it must convey the semen to the outside; and (2) it must be capable of assuming sufficient rigidity to permit the deposition of spermatozoa within the female genital tract.

The ejaculatory ducts bringing the secretions from the testes, seminal vesicles, and the prostate gland all empty into the urethra, which serves both as a urinary passage and as a genital opening. The second function is accomplished by means of three elongated, intricately subdivided blood sinus spaces, each provided with a valvelike mechanism at the outlet in the form of con-

FIGURE 4.   STRUCTURE OF SPERMATOZOON

stricting bands of muscle. Under conditions of sexual excitement, nerve impulses are conducted through the pelvic nerves to these muscle fibers; the outlets to the sinuses mentioned above are thereby constricted and a sharp rise in pressure, due to the continued inflow of blood and a simultaneous obstruction to outflow, then results. The entire penis therefore becomes distended and turgid, and assumes the rigid form commonly recognized as an erection. With the passing of sexual excitement the outflow of blood from these special sinuses is released, and the organ again becomes relaxed and flaccid, reassuming its original size.

The skin surface of the penis is richly supplied with sensory nerve endings of a special type, a fact which is probably correlated with the tactile sensitivity of the genital area. Such nerve end organs are especially abundant in the foreskin of the penis, the surgical removal of which by circumcision commonly leads to a diminution in this special type of tactile sensation.[4]

The testes form in embryonic life, high in the abdomen, in close proximity to the kidney; only in the seventh month of pregnancy do they descend into the scrotum, where they remain throughout life. During its migration, the testis is accompanied by the various nerves, blood vessels, and excretory ducts which have formed with it and which are necessary for its function. By migrating to a site outside of the body cavity proper, the testis enters an environmental temperature lower by several degrees than that found in its original location. This is apparently an important detail, since testicular degeneration characterized by a cessation of the spermatogenic

4 This operation is performed chiefly for hygienic reasons since it insures greater cleanliness of the underlying skin surface. Among people of orthodox Jewish faith circumcision of male infants is a religious ritual.

function follows the return of the testicle to the abdominal cavity or the artificial raising of its environmental temperature for a prolonged period. The interstitial cells which produce the male sex hormone appear to be more resistant to degeneration resulting from an elevated temperature. Under certain abnormal conditions, the descent of the testes into the scrotum is either delayed or prevented by factors which are not clearly understood, and under such circumstances testicular function is impaired to such an extent that sterility results in adult life if treatment is too long delayed.

Testicular function in the male is maintained at its normal level through constant stimulation by hormones secreted by the pituitary gland at the base of the brain, located in the center of the skull. If the pituitary gland is removed from experimental animals, or if it is accidentally destroyed in human beings, sexual function promptly diminishes; the testes become small, atrophic, and functionless. Extracts of pituitary glands will prevent this degeneration and will even restore function if atrophy has not proceeded to an irreversible point. Although the same general type of mechanism exists in the female, the entire function of the ovary is a cyclic one characterized by the regularly recurring menstrual flow. In the male, on the contrary, there is no good evidence that any such cycle exists, and the entire pituitary-testicular relationship appears to be without significant fluctuations.

The exact mode of action of the male sex hormone is very poorly understood in spite of the fact that the chemical nature of this substance is known. The reasons for the onset of adolescent changes at about fifteen or sixteen years of age and the means by which these changes are effected still remain very much of a mystery. After remaining in a physiologically dormant state for many years the stimulus to activity arises, probably in the pituitary gland. The ensuing growth and functioning of testicular cells produces profound anatomical, physiological, and psychical changes. By virtue of the male sex hormone poured into the blood stream by the interstitial tissue, a great spurt in growth takes place, the larynx changes to produce a low-pitched voice, hair begins to grow on the face and other parts of the body, the shoulders broaden, muscles enlarge, and the relative proportions of body weight made up by muscle increase sharply. The genital organs and all accessory structures develop rapidly, and in the psychical sphere, an awareness of the sexual urge begins to appear, coupled with the first evidences of masculine energy and aggressiveness. Thus do we recognize the transition stage in a boy's life known as puberty.

Ignorant as we still are concerning most of the forces involved in this general pattern, it is nevertheless possible to induce these changes prematurely, to increase their intensity, or to start them going if they have been abnormally delayed, by the administration of male sex hormone. Restoration of spermatogenic function is obviously quite another problem, since the testicle itself must produce the cells. In short, effective medical assistance may be offered in the production of a more masculine male, in appearance at least; but the restoration or improvement of his capacity to procreate is a more difficult matter, and one which is less often accomplished.

THE ANATOMY AND PHYSIOLOGY OF SEX: FEMALE

The ovaries, or female sex glands, are small rounded, flattened bodies about one inch in diameter located in the pelvis, one on either side of the midline and immediately adjacent to the womb or uterus. Like the testes in the male, the ovaries serve a double function: that of producing the primary sex cells or ova for reproduction, and the endocrine function of manufacturing the female sex hormone, the chemical substance which, discharged directly into the blood stream, is responsible for the secondary sex characteristics of the female. The cyclic nature of female sex activity is well known because of the monthly recurrence of uterine bleeding, and there is an increased understanding of the complicated mechansims responsible for these phenomena.

At the time of birth the ovaries occupy the same relative anatomical positions that they retain throughout adult life, and each one contains approximately 15,000 to 30,000 potential or undeveloped ova, each one of which is capable in later life of maturation into a ripe cell susceptible of fertilization. It is probable that no new ova are formed after birth, although it is known that multiplication of these sex cells (oogonia) continues until shortly before birth. Since during the normal sexually active life of a woman (from the age of thirteen to forty-five, a total of thirty-two years) only about four hundred of these cells come to maturity, the wide margin of safety provided by nature is apparent. Under normal conditions one ovum reaches maturity for each menstrual cycle, so that twelve to fifteen are usually discharged during a period of one year.

After remaining in a quiescent and functionless state for about eleven to fourteen years after birth, the ovaries gradually acquire a rhythmic form of activity which continues for thirty years or more. The awakening of function is in response to stimulation from the pituitary gland, but little is known about the onset of the entire series of changes recognized as puberty. This period of life is characterized by a sudden acceleration of physical growth of the whole body, by a change in body proportions from those of a child to those of a mature woman, and by the appearance of adult psychical and emotional patterns. The simultaneous maturation of the sex organs marks the initiation of reproductive fertility.

All these changes, so far as can be determined, are initiated and maintained (potentiated) by the female sex hormone (estrone), a chemical substance produced by certain cells in the ovary, surrounding each ovum as it matures in anticipation of fertilization. Pituitary stimulation of the ovary in turn occurs by means of a hormone called the pituitary gonadotropic hormone (meaning gonad-stimulating). In the absence of this stimulation, as in surgical removal of the pituitary in animals or its destruction by disease in human beings, ovarian function likewise ceases, thereby clearly indicating the dependence of the latter on the functional integrity of the pituitary as a driving, stimulating force.

Each month, under the influence of the gonadotropic hormone, one ovum assumes a predominant position and begins to ripen. This process consists in the rapid multiplication of the surrounding accessory cells to form a follicle or fluid-containing space. This follicular fluid, together with the female sex hormone it contains (estrone), is manufactured by the cells of the follicle, and it completely surrounds the developing ovum. Estrone is poured into the blood stream and thereby reaches all parts of the body. It is even excreted in the urine, the exact amount at any one time depending upon the amount being produced in the ovary.

At about twelve to fifteen days after the beginning of the last menstrual period, or roughly midway between periods, the ripening process in the ovary reaches its peak, the intrafollicular pressure causes the whole structure to rupture, and the fluid and ovum escape, occasionally with slight pain and bleeding. The ovum is immediately passed into the dilated end of the Fallopian tube and starts on its journey to the uterus. In the ovary, at the site of rupture, new cells begin to grow which have an extremely important func-

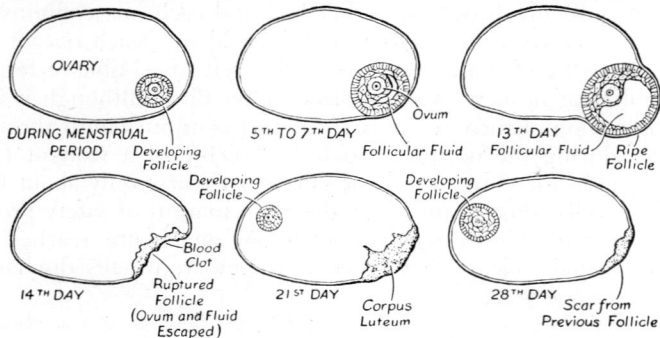

FIGURE 5. CYCLE OF OVARIAN CHANGES

tion. Because of their yellow color, this new structure is called the corpus luteum and the hormone it produces is known as progesterone. This substance has a profound effect upon all parts of the uterus: the womb lining, or endometrium, is microscopically changed to permit reception of the embryo, if fertilization occurs, and the stimulating action of estrone on the muscle is somewhat counteracted to produce a quieting effect.

The Fallopian tubes, one on each side, are hollow muscular tubes, each about four inches in length, the function of which is to conduct the ovum to the uterus after it has been discharged from the ovary. One end therefore communicates with the uterine cavity, while the free end, dilated into a pocket, partially surrounds the ovary by means of fimbriated or fingerlike projections. Since the ovum has no power of locomotion by itself, it must be propelled down the tube by means of wavelike muscular contractions, similar in type to those which move food materials through the intestines. In normal reproduction, sperm cells entering the uterus find their way into the Fallopian tubes and propel themselves through the entire distance up to the ovary, so that fertilization of the ovum usually occurs well up toward the free end of the tube. Cell division and growth of the embryo follow immediately, so that at the end of five to seven days (the normal length of time for passage into the uterus), the developing embryo has already progressed to a many-cell stage.

The uterus is a hollow pear-shaped muscular organ which measures about three inches long, by two inches wide, by one inch in thickness. It lies in the midline, in the pelvic cavity between the urinary bladder and the rectum. Its function is that of providing a space for growth of the fertilized ovum during the entire period of gestation. Its blood supply is very rich and becomes even more abundant during pregnancy in order that the embryo may receive adequate nutrition. The muscular wall measures from half an inch to an inch in thickness in various portions, and increases very strikingly during pregnancy, since it must provide a large part of the motive force which finally expels the infant during the process of birth. The muscle is of the "smooth" variety, which means that its contraction is not under voluntary control, but rather is determined by activity of the autonomic nervous system.

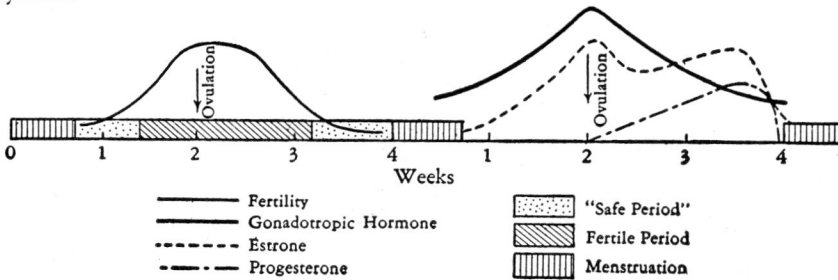

FIGURE 6. BLOOD HORMONAL VARIATIONS IN THE MENSTRUAL CYCLE

The uterine lining or endometrium is of unusual interest, since its microscopic structure varies in a cyclic manner under the direct control of the ovaries, through the action of the female sex hormone. In a normal young woman, a large part of this tissue sloughs away about every twenty-eight days; the bleeding so produced is recognized as the menstrual flow. During the succeeding twenty-eight days it is then necessary to build up an entirely new endometrium preparatory for another menstrual period. This occurs as a result of the growth stimulus of estrone acting on the remaining portions of endometrium which have not been removed. For the first two weeks of the cycle, beginning even before the bloody discharge has ceased, these cells begin to grow and multiply at a remarkable rate of speed. During all this time the follicle in the ovary is ripening and the hormone from the follicular fluid is being poured into the blood stream. Following ovulation, at about mid-period the entire picture changes. The ovary is now producing not only estrone, but progesterone; the latter arising in the corpus luteum which is growing at the site of the old ruptured follicle. Progesterone predominates in the hormonal effect, so that all tissues of the body come under its influence. Among these is the endometrium, which now changes its character toward a condition that will make possible the implantation and full maintenance of the young embryo in case fertilization occurs. This phase also lasts for two weeks, during which the endometrial layer grows even thicker until finally, if no embryo arrives, the corpus luteum begins to grow smaller, its production of progesterone and estrone ceases, and the amounts of these two hormones in the blood fall sharply. It is believed that this sudden change in blood concentration precipitates the onset of the menstrual flow, which then proceeds to complete destruction and removal of the endometrium — and a new cycle is begun. Menstrual bleeding may therefore be considered as a spontaneous abortion of an ovum which has failed to be fertilized.[5] When fertilization does occur the corpus luteum is thereby prevented from regression in size; it grows larger instead. The changes in blood hormone concentration which usually bring on bleeding are thereby prevented, and no menstrual period ensues. It is chiefly the functional ade-

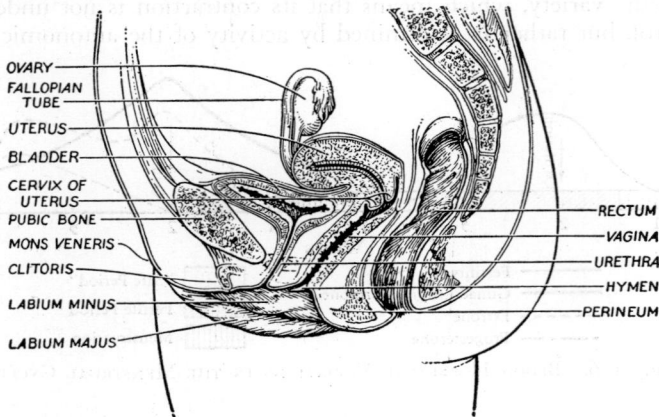

FIGURE 7.   ANATOMY OF THE FEMALE REPRODUCTIVE ORGANS

quacy of the corpus luteum that maintains the integrity of the growing embryo during the early weeks of pregnancy.

The uterus may be grossly divided into a lower portion or cervix and an upper portion or body. The cervix is the canal which opens into the vagina, thus forming a passage for egress of the menstrual discharge and for the entrance of sperm at the time of fertilization. It also acts as an important barrier since it is dilated slowly and with considerable difficulty, during childbirth. The cells in the cervical glands do not participate to any significant degree in the cyclic changes characteristic of the endometrial glands higher up in the uterus. These glands are, however, exposed to infection by a multitude of bacteria which normally inhabit the vagina. Ordinarily such infections do not increase to serious proportions, but they may cause a discharge from the vagina, known as leucorrhea.

[5] Vaginal bleeding may occur even if ovulation has not preceded it, although such a flow probably should not be called a menstrual flow since the mechanism of its production is different. "Anovulatory flows," as they are called, may occur rather often in normal women, although there is no easy way to recognize them. Fertilization during such a cycle would obviously be impossible.

The vagina is a membranous, elastic tube from five to seven inches in length lying between the bladder in front and the rectum behind. It serves three important functions, all of which are purely mechanical: (1) it is the passageway of escape for the menstrual discharge; (2) it is the female organ of copulation; and (3) it acts as an important part of the birth canal. Its upper or inner end terminates in a blind pouch into which the cervix of the uterus projects, and its lower or outer end forms the opening in the external genital organs lying in the lower part of the vestibule.

The vagina is lined by layers of cells which resemble very closely the cells of the skin, but they are constantly bathed by a mucoid secretion and, in addition, they are under the influence of the female sex hormone. It is possible by examining these cells microscopically, therefore, to observe cyclic changes which parallel those already described in the endometrium. An acid reaction is normally maintained in the vagina, chiefly due to the lactic acid produced by the normal bacterial residents of the area. This acidity serves a useful purpose in sharply limiting the growth of pathogenic or harmful bacteria, since most organisms in this category cannot tolerate such acidity. It also provides an environment in which spermatozoa cannot long survive. They are therefore promptly killed unless they can gain quick access to the protection of the cervical canal of the uterus.

Surrounding the external opening of the vagina is a membranous fold which narrows the orifice in degrees varying in different individuals. This is the hymen, usually intact in a newborn female infant and nearly always ruptured at the first sexual intercourse. It is not infrequently ruptured in childhood or adolescence, however, either as a result of accidental injury or during a medical examination for difficulties involving the sex organs. In addition, it may be injured by masturbation or by manipulation for relief of itching or irritation. It is therefore obvious that a diagnosis of virginity cannot be made with certainty by examination of the hymen — a fact which often assumes considerable medico-legal importance.

Complete blocking of the vaginal orifice by a hymen having no opening sometimes occurs, and usually makes surgery necessary, inasmuch as the onset of menstrual periods results in the damming back of the flow. Rupture of the hymen at intercourse may be attended by some bleeding, and occasionally by slight pain.

The external genital organs of the female, called collectively the vulva, consist of the larger lips or labia majora, the lesser lips or labia minora, and the clitoris. In a newborn female child, the large labia are in contact and their folds constitute the entire portion of the genitals visible from the outside unless the structures are separated. During adolescence, however, the smaller labia enlarge somewhat and become visible as thin projections of tissue between the larger folds. If the smaller labia are separated, the almond-shaped space between them is known as the vestibule into which open the urethra above and the vagina below.[6]

[6] Two important pairs of glands also open into the vestibule. These are Bartholin's glands, whose ducts open into the labia on either side, and Skene's glands, opening on either side of the urethral orifice. Their respective functions are not definitely known, but probably

The clitoris is located at the upper end of the vestibule, at the point where the two labia minora come together. The labia even form folds of tissue which cover the clitoris above and below. It is the female homologue of the penis in the male, and the folds of skin covering it correspond to the foreskin of the penis. It is composed of erectile tissue and under sexual excitement becomes enlarged and turgid. Because of its particularly rich supply of tactile nerve endings, as is also the case with the penis, it is the chief site of erotic sensation in the female. It is largely because of pressure and friction on the clitoris during the sexual act that the intense pleasurable sensation is produced. Indeed, this structure has no other known function. It is erroneous, however, to believe that the clitoris represents the sole concentration of erotic sensation, since this function is distributed throughout a considerable area involving the labia, the vestibule, the vagina, and even the breasts.

Some mention should be made of the external structures surrounding the outlet of the vagina. Above the clitoris, and therefore overlying the pubic bone, is a pad of fatty tissue which in the adult is covered with coarse and usually curly hair. This is the mons veneris, and the distribution of hair is typically triangular with the base directed upward. In addition, some hair is distributed down over the larger labia. This hair pattern or escutcheon is different from that of the male, since in the latter the upper hair line tends to extend upward in a point to the navel, and downward over the fore and inner surfaces of the thighs. Below the vaginal opening, the skin surfaces of the larger labia flatten out and join to form the fork or fourchette, a term used to designate the skin surface immediately behind the opening. The area between the vagina and rectum is called the perineum, and may be damaged rather badly at times by tears at childbirth. For this reason the operation called episiotomy is frequently performed as a preventive measure.

The breasts may be classed as organs of reproduction because they not only play an important part in the reproductive process but also because the changes they undergo parallel those in the uterus. The breasts may be looked upon as glandular structures functioning specifically in the production of milk. This role is not apparent, however, except during pregnancy, when a great many endocrine or hormonal factors cause marked structural changes which bring about the secretion of milk. Under normal conditions, the breast tissue of a postadolescent or adult female passes through cyclic changes much like those described for the uterine lining. These fluctuations are in response to estrone, progesterone, and possibly even pituitary hormones. Many young women are regularly aware of swelling, tenseness, tenderness, and even intense pain in their breasts at certain stages in their menstrual cycle, most commonly in the four to seven days just prior to the onset of flow. Such cyclic changes begin at the time of puberty, and continue throughout the reproductive period of a woman's life. Extensive observations have established conclusively that these glands are under as direct control of the ovarian hormones as is the uterus itself. In addition, the nipples are sup-

---

involve the production of lubricating mucuslike fluid when they are stimulated by sexual excitement. Infections in this region may also attack these glands — of these, gonorrhea is undoubtedly the most serious.

plied with abundant nerve endings, and contain also some erectile tissue identical with that of the penis and clitoris. The breast region in general and the nipples in particular may therefore be classed as erogenous zones, through which tactile stimulation may produce sexual excitement.

The Nature of the Sex Drive

Sexual excitement is a strange and interesting phenomenon, universally present throughout all animal species and undoubtedly responsible for their continued survival. Its components are both psychical and physical. There are certain important differences between the two sexes in relation to the assertion of the sex impulse. In both sexes certain erogenous zones are well recognized. These involve the sexual organs themselves, the breasts in the female but not in the male, and to a certain extent the mouth, lips, and tongue in both. Excitation of these areas by all forms of stimuli, but especially by contact, pressure, or friction initiates emotional responses of a special type which are recognized as sexual excitement. As a part of this response the sexual organs themselves undergo temporary changes preparing them for intercourse. Thus, erection of the penis in the male and the production of abundant lubricating secretion by the glands of the female external genitals are reflex responses to such stimulation, and their occurrence leads logically to sexual intercourse as the end result.

Sexual behavior can be readily observed in most of the lower animals, but the lack of creative intelligence, reasoning, and memory reduces the sexual act to a powerful uninhibited reproductive force. In man, on the other hand, the presence of the same intellectual attributes and the recognition of standardized patterns of social conduct have profoundly changed sexual expression. In short, the entire approach to sexual matters has been altered for human beings by the very nature of the psychosocial elements involved.

In the male are concentrated those elements of aggressiveness and strength which have come to be associated with the initiation of sexual activity, whether it be the simple finding of a mate and consummation of the legal procedures necessary to make the partnership acceptable in the eyes of society, or the actual performance of the sexual act. This aggressive behavior may have its true origin in the male sex hormone itself. Indeed, the effect of experimentally subjecting laboratory animals to the action of this hormone leads us to believe that this is true. In any case, the will and ability to initiate sexual activity are accompanied by a high degree of susceptibility to stimuli, both psychical and physical, which is conspicuously lacking in the female. Young men, in whom the sexual drive is most acute, are normally filled with an abundance of sexual energy so changeable in its manifestations (labile) and so close to the surface that only insignificant stimuli are necessary to bring the entire reaction to the level of consciousness, and so lead to the initiation of a whole sequence of responses.

The frequency with which this fact is put to use in everyday affairs in our culture is striking and often is not appreciated. As a basic force in human conduct this principle is involved in the theater, the movies, the burlesque show, in magazine stories, in advertising of a multitude of common products, in women's styles, and in every aspect of our heterosexual social customs. It asserts itself, in addition, in many other more subtle ways which are often obscure enough to escape recognition.

It is highly probable that women wear silk stockings, revealing skirts, and tight-fitting sweaters largely for their value in attracting and stimulating the male sex. A male burlesque performance, with customary "strip-teasers" and chorus, before a totally female audience, is almost unthinkable; even Margaret Mead's exceptions remain — exceptions. Although these factors have unquestioned survival value for the human species and may be accepted as a part of our normal twentieth-century pattern of life, the hazards should not be overlooked. The inhibitions of our social order serve to create a situation which is nearly intolerable to many young men. Their principles conflict with their sex drives, aroused as the latter are by a constant succession of stimuli from a variety of sources. It is perhaps not surprising that the inhibitions are often not powerful enough. In retrospect we wonder whether in times when modesty of dress and decorum of social behavior were more conservative, the equilibrium between these two powerful opposing forces was as unstable as it is today.

Moreover, the conflict under consideration occurs at precisely the time of life when young people are in greatest need of stability and equanimity, when they are concentrating a maximum of energy and attention on preparing themselves for a place in the general scheme of things. It is perhaps unfortunate that emotional stresses and conflicts usually rise to the most troublesome levels at a time when a minimum of diversion is desirable. Emphasis is being placed today, particularly in academic fields, upon long periods of training; and the days of economic independence, when family responsibilities may be safely tackled, are thereby moved farther and farther ahead. It is probably justifiable, therefore, to consider the problem of sexual adjustment as one of the most insistent and difficult of all those confronting young people of college age. It must be admitted that no satisfactory solution has been found, inasmuch as early marriage is currently held to be out of the question for millions of young people because of economic reasons.[7]

Serious consideration must rightly be given to the problems which confront adolescents and young adults of both sexes as they pass through that vital phase of their lives in which they begin to assume a mature adult outlook on life and in which the patterns for both their social and sexual behavior are largely determined. It is indeed regrettable that such a vast majority of these young people are forced to seek information and advice on a multitude of problems from undependable and often erroneous sources. Unfortunately, many parents feel that this particular responsibility should be relegated to those in charge of the formal education of their children[8] — if

[7] Howard Bigelow, in his treatment of the economics of early marriage, advances the alternative of husband and wife working until the husband completes his professional training. See Chapter XIII.

[8] Although the author does not concur with this view, feeling rather that sex education is a parental function, he nevertheless advocates presentation of these materials in the formal curriculum on the elementary as well as the secondary school levels.

they are willing that they should receive any adequate instruction whatsoever.

The gradual awakening of sexual consciousness at the time of puberty finds most young people ill prepared for its far-reaching consequences. An awareness of differences between the two sexes leads to the necessity for readjustment in social relations which, for many individuals, is not easy. And even more perplexing, all normal healthy young adults discover at this time that they are subject to strange new emotional experiences, the free and full enjoyment of which they naturally seek for biological reasons, but which they soon come to realize are necessarily subject to certain inhibitions established in the course of their early moral training.

By virtue of the inherent sexual lability of his sex, the plight of the young male constitutes a special problem. He is beset by strange and powerful temptations, frequently emanating from the seemingly unrelated stimulation of normal social contacts with the opposite sex, but often arising with seeming spontaneity within himself.

"PETTING"

The whole relationship between adolescents and young adults falls naturally under the critical scrutiny of older people. The insidious transformation of purely social heterosexual relations into sexual experiences is probably inevitable, but the form which it takes depends upon a great many factors. "Petting" is the modern, semislang name for something that has always existed among civilized people. It is a sexual experience and is therefore as natural as any other physical manifestation of sex, but it is not acceptable to the elders of our society for the same fundamental reasons that promiscuous extramarital sexual relations are unacceptable; that is, it is incompatible with our existing organized monogamous society. From the physiological standpoint, petting corresponds in every detail to the love-play which should normally precede sexual intercourse as it occurs under ideal conditions, and therein lies its chief danger, since if carried to its logical conclusion it will always end in intercourse. On the other hand, if the normal sequence of events is interrupted by means of a display of superior will power or by extraneous interference, the resulting emotional turmoil for both individuals may be almost a more difficult experience than the remorse and worry which may follow completion of the entire act. The actual physiological response to this type of stimulation is so clearly that of intense sexual excitement that even the most complete novice has no difficulty in recognizing it as such.

An important moral issue is therefore involved; concerning it many attitudes obviously are possible. It is not the purpose of the present discussion to decide any moral issues, but it may be stated categorically that young people who don't pet are generally much happier and, in the long run, more contented. They are able to escape the extremes of sexual stimulation which can lead only to feelings of guilt and remorse, to the emotional shock or trauma of unsatisfied excitement, or to the worry and fear of consequences. The irresistible progression of sexual excitement when it has once been aroused makes its voluntary interruption extremely difficult, and to escape from the late consequences therefore clearly implies the avoidance of conditions which initiate the early stages of excitement. Many young people actually use a plan of this sort for keeping clear of the "habit" of petting. Others are not able to sublimate this spontaneous sexual energy into non-erotic channels, so that they develop a constantly growing appetite for this exciting outlet. Many mature adults, who can hardly be accused of lacking understanding of these problems, feel that petting turns a fine emotion that should rightly be reserved for the serious relations of mature heterosexual love into cheap exploitation, thrill seeking, and tawdry "comedy" or cynical "humor." If this point of view be accepted, then there is clearly an element of unfairness in participating in a performance which implies the most serious of intentions when only an irresponsible whim or passing fancy is intended.[9]

For the adolescent girl or young adult unmarried woman, the problem can be stated in much the same terms, but the vigor of the initiating stages is usually not so intense because of the slower response of most females to erotic stimulation. Nevertheless, the initiative often actually does come from the female, and because of the instantaneous response of healthy young males to even minor stimuli, girls possess a powerful weapon for arousing the passions of their companions. Undoubtedly some girls use this capacity almost cruelly, without fully realizing what they are doing, and it is only right that they should be permitted to see the entire picture in its true perspective.

Much could be written on the general subject of self-control in relation to sexual function. This is no less desirable for the sexual than it is for all other appetites. Sublimation of sexual desire, or the voluntary redirection of this type of energy into socially approved channels, is not only possible but appears to be successfully practiced by both sexes. It is facilitated by hard physical exertion and by the avoidance of stimuli which naturally arouse erotic thoughts. In general, it is perhaps easier for women than for men. Sublimation is compatible with good health and, within reasonable limits, with satisfactory mental efficiency.

In the interest of a fair perspective on this difficult problem, it must be recognized that there are growing numbers of well-informed adults who believe that a certain amount of premarital "experimentation" is not only justified but advisable. This may take the form of a freedom of sexual intercourse by an engaged couple with the idea of 'testing' their physical compatibility before marriage. It is the author's opinion that this plan is usually derived more from emotional than from intellectual motives, in which the latter is given as an excuse for the former. In view of the remarkable capacity for sexual adjustment in couples with high compatibility in other spheres, such an attitude of sexual freedom is made to appear rather far-fetched. Nevertheless, in the difficult business of advising young people, for the sake of avoiding prudishness, this point of view must be taken into consideration and even discussed seriously and freely. The clandestine and surreptitious nature of extramarital sexual relations attests to their social unacceptability,

[9] See our discussion of exploitation and cynicism, pp. 233–235.

and to the semiguilt that is felt by those who participate in them, regardless of the overwhelming thrill of physical satisfaction that they may provide. Most emotionally mature young adults, if they are motivated by intelligence and if the problem is presented to them fairly in all its aspects, are able to see the wisdom of restraint in their physical relationships prior to marriage, through an emphasis on other types of activity which reduces to a minimum the inevitable temptations.

In young men, the voluntary abstinence from sexual activity results normally in the periodic nocturnal seminal emission of "wet dream," which is in reality a spontaneous orgasm, occurring usually during sleep and frequently attended by an erotic dream. Although similar mental activity occurs in young women, there is nothing to correspond to the discharge of semen. Nocturnal emissions are strictly normal, and may be experienced at intervals of from one to six weeks or longer, often with considerable regularity. Their frequency diminishes or they disappear completely when or if a normal sexual outlet is found.

Masturbation is the other common form of release from sexual tension, practiced so universally by both sexes that it must be considered almost normal. Unfortunately many young men and women have been severely and unnecessarily frightened by the thought of broken health and even insanity which will "surely" follow this habit. This idea, actually believed at one time, constitutes the greatest danger from masturbation. This danger is entirely illusory, and reassurance on that fact is often sorely needed. Masturbation must be considered as an undesirable means for sexual gratification, resorted to because of failure to find any other satisfactory outlet or sublimating substitute. The habit usually disappears spontaneously when a normal heterosexual outlet is available.

In some cases, however, it continues into marriage, and thus introduces grave complications into the relations of the spouses. To be condoned when it occurs only occasionally and, as it were, nonhabitually, masturbation should never be counseled, much less encouraged.

COPULATION

Physical relationships between the two sexes have important psychical aspects which often condition the entire response. These are best considered as modifying influences which alter the purely biological function as it occurs in the lower animals. The period of "heat" or "oestrus" in female animals is caused by the high ovarian hormone content of the blood and tissues at the time of ovulation. This is the phase in which sexual desire reaches its peak and the female will willingly accept the male. At other times she will not participate in copulation, and the male in turn is scarcely attracted to the female. Thus a cyclic form of activity results; in modified form this also exists in the human species. A large proportion of women are not aware of any such fluctuation in their sexual feelings, as might be anticipated from the available knowledge of the physiology of ovulation. This is probably due to the modifying influence of the psychical factors already mentioned. Human life is such an intricate network of emotional, intellectual, and physical components that the sexual urge may be stimulated by a variety of influences such as physical contact, visual phenomena, sounds, and even odors; these arouse a train of associations leading to the mental imagery of erotic symbols and sexual fantasies. Physical contact is usually the most potent of all of these, and under normal conditions will initiate the sequence of responses which ends in sexual intercourse, as has already been pointed out in our discussion of petting.

Even though the initiation of sexual contact may originate in some subtle sensory stimulus, the relation soon evolves into a physical one. The physiological consequences of this excitement are started and kept going chiefly through the autonomic nervous system, resulting in a pleasurable sensation of stimulation throughout the erogenous zones. The blood supply to the genital organs of both male and female is greatly increased and the vessels become engorged. The genital glands pour out their mucoid secretion serving to lubricate the parts and also partially to neutralize the acid vaginal reaction. Erectile tissue in both sexes becomes engorged and turgid. The penis in the male becomes much enlarged, and the urethral glands begin to produce a clear mucoid material which is discharged from the urethra in anticipation of intercourse. Under the influence of intense sexual excitement, this fluid in some men contains a small number of spermatozoa capable of fertilizing an ovum, a fact which in itself renders inadvisable the use of coitus interruptus as a contraceptive technique.[10]

Sexual intercourse is not a purely "instinctive" act, but must be learned even by the conceited young male who thinks that he "knows all the answers" or by the girl who prides herself on her "sophistication." Once intercourse has been started, excitement in both partners builds up progressively until the orgasm, an "explosive" emotional release, is attained. Ideally this should occur at precisely the same instant in both individuals, so that the intense pleasure of the experience may be equally shared. Unfortunately this is not always possible — the male usually attaining orgasm before the female. He needs to learn how to restrain his emotions in order to achieve the orgasm simultaneously with his partner.

The orgasm is accompanied in the male by the ejaculation of about a teaspoonful of semen, which represents the combined secretions of testes, prostate, seminal vesicles, and several minor glands of the genital tract. As previously stated, the ejaculate may contain up to 200,000,000 to 400,000,000 sperm cells, most of which, as a rule, are actively motile and normal in structure. At the time of discharge, semen is distinctly viscous, somewhat sticky, cloudy, white in color, and has a characteristic fleshy odor. Upon standing, however, it soon becomes thin and almost water-clear. When the sperm in a single ejaculation are reduced to less than 100,000,000, fertility appears to be somewhat impaired, although the exact relation is not entirely clear.

Orgasm in the male is normally accompanied by a strong thrusting motion which presses the tip of the penis deep into the vagina and allows the

[10] See our discussion of contraception, pp. 336–339.

seminal fluid to be discharged in a pool; in this the cervix of the uterus usually is submerged. Immediately after withdrawal of the penis, the vaginal space is reduced; the motility of the sperm cells then carries them into the cervix in large numbers. It is therefore certain that even immediate removal of the entire vaginal contents by means of thorough douching will not give contraceptive protection, because many cells have already escaped beyond access of the douching fluid. Furthermore (and contrary to current folklore) since the urethral opening is adjacent to the vaginal outlet and does not open into it, the passing of urine immediately following intercourse will have no contraceptive effect whatever.

Orgasm in the female is composed of the same nervous and emotional components as in the male, but there is nothing comparable to the male ejaculation. It must be emphasized that the female orgasm is not necessary for fertility, since countless instances are recorded in which pregnancy followed rape, during which the female not only was devoid of sexual feeling but was actually struggling against the assault. In both male and female the nervous and emotional reactions consist of a progressively rising level of excitement, so striking that all other intellectual functions become temporarily repressed or even blocked out completely. In this state of mind, nothing seems of as great importance as the full attainment of the orgasm. When this point is finally reached there is a sudden sharp release of tension accompanied by a momentary intense sensation of warm, tingling pleasure, followed by the desire for complete, utter relaxation. This latter mood persists for a considerable time, and usually expresses itself in the form of sleep so relaxing that the end result is one of release of sexual tension and of invigoration.

The attainment of a perfect technique of intercourse is so vital to complete marital happiness that it should constitute a goal in itself. It should be emphasized that perfect adjustment rarely occurs immediately and spontaneously, but must actually be the subject of some definite attention.

In most healthy couples who marry during the third decade of life, intercourse is so completely a part of the ceremony of marriage that its occurrence quite early in the honeymoon period is universally accepted as the normal pattern of behavior. It is only right that this should be so, since it marks the culmination in the physical sense of a sequence of events which expresses, both symbolically and in fact, the deep affection of two individuals for each other. Accomplishment of successful intercourse during the honeymoon is enhanced by the release from the moral inhibitions that usually exist before marriage, but is often prevented by a variety of factors ranging from simple fear or embarrassment up to the presence of a menstrual flow or intolerable pain. During the first few weeks or months of married life, young couples may have intercourse nearly every night, but this is gradually reduced to a frequency of one to three times a week, which is then maintained over a period of many years. It is well established that many individuals of both sexes past the ages of fifty or sixty continue to participate in and enjoy sexual intercourse, indicating the degree to which this function becomes centered entirely in the nervous system, divested of all endocrine activity. Indeed, release from the fear of pregnancy often permits a more complete enjoyment unattainable in earlier years.

MUTUAL SEXUAL ADJUSTMENTS

Of the specific maladjustments which require attention, the most frequent is the great difference in speed of attainment of the orgasm by the two partners. The greater spontaneity of the male sex drive, together with the man's usual function of initiating sexual activity, results in his greater ease in arriving at the point of orgasm. If he allows this to occur without any attempt at restraint he will be fully satisfied himself but his wife will be left in a difficult emotional state because of her unsatisfied excitement. Although this situation may occasionally occur in the best-adjusted couples, its repeated occurrence eventually may be responsible for a serious state of "nerves" in the woman, who is left in the semipanicky state of longing for satisfaction. Strange as it may seem, this state of affairs exists in countless homes, and either through prudish modesty or a complete lack of sympathy and understanding, it may continue uncorrected indefinitely. Still more often it is the result of ignorance!

Restraint of emotional excitement on the part of the male is sometimes difficult, and its technique can hardly be described since it is a highly individual matter. In general, this effect may be accomplished by a variety of mental means, as well as by physical means, designed to lessen the stimulation. Circumcision, while it is practiced chiefly for hygienic reasons, usually has the additional effect of slowing down the male reaction, since it removes that portion of the foreskin most richly supplied with nerve endings. The total effect of this operation is therefore beneficial in helping to solve this rather difficult problem. Another item of equal or even greater importance is the balancing effect of a more prolonged period of love-play before intercourse actually begins. This has an exciting effect on both partners, and usually has the desirable end result of bringing the woman's emotional pitch up to a level more nearly approaching that of her husband.

Psychical barriers to free participation and enjoyment of intercourse are frequently present, and are more common in women than in men. Of these, fear of pregnancy probably ranks first as a source of trouble. This fear can be lulled by adequate contraceptive technique, as prescribed by a qualified physician. For members of certain religious groups there is often no adequate solution of the problem. The rhythm technique, which is acceptable to most religious groups, is of some assistance, but it is far from perfect, and in addition restricts sexual activity to certain short periods during the menstrual cycle. If the psychical hazard is to be removed, the important consideration is not only that contraception should be nearly perfect, but that the woman should know it to be so and, therefore, be mentally at ease. Much to be desired, of course, would be a change in the standards of American marriage, plus a more nearly adequate economic system, which would make larger families a goal to be striven for rather than avoided as at present. (See the chapter on "Larger or Smaller Families for America?") Even if the average number of children per family were to be greatly raised, however, the benefits of proper child spacing (see the chapter on "Caring for Mother and Child Before and After") would still make contraception exceedingly pertinent. Moreover, the distressing facts of abortion, as recounted in later sections of this chapter (pp. 335–337) present a moral dilemma which those who oppose birth control can hardly avoid. To be sure, there are other moral dilemmas, and we are far from claiming that contraception has no drawbacks; we are merely trying to see our way with the light that has been vouchsafed to us. But enough of digression; let us return to the main discourse.

Disproportion in the size of genital organs is a difficulty which is often mentioned in cases of sexual maladjustment, but it has been greatly overemphasized. For those cases where the trouble actually did exist, minor adjustments in the technique of intercourse have usually solved the problem.

Disparity in ages between man and wife may be the source of some sexual incompatibility, chiefly because of the gradual decline in the vitality of sexual drive with increasing years in both sexes. Of more significance, however, is each partner's fundamental constitutional level of interest in matters of sex. Disparity in this regard may indeed be quite serious, since a satisfactory solution is difficult to attain.

A more serious problem is the attitude of the maladjusted woman to the sex relation. Frequently she has been instructed about matters of sex in a manner so repellent that she has come to abhor the whole idea; or she has not been instructed at all and has had to learn what little she knows from haphazard, inaccurate, or obscene sources; or her first intercourse may have been a painful or disagreeable experience because her partner failed to show proper consideration for her inexperience and apprehension.

In addition to the above considerations, the whole emotional pattern of many women causes them to be abnormally susceptible to the distracting influences of extraneous sensory stimuli such as radio music, the ringing of a telephone or doorbell, the sound of voices, the fear of being interrupted, or even the ticking of a clock. Any one of a thousand interfering environmental disturbances may prove disturbing to the sex relation. It is perhaps fortunate that absolute perfection usually is not necessary.

THE PREMARITAL EXAMINATION

The wisdom of premarital physical examinations is gradually coming to be widely accepted. Indeed, the recognition of venereal disease as a justifiable basis for prohibiting marriage has caused the certification of freedom from venereal disease to be a legal prerequisite in most states. Unfortunately, the issuance of certificates is too often a perfunctory matter, imposed upon busy physicians who have not the time or patience to do more than the required Wassermann test. Ideally, the examination should be much more thorough; it should consist of a complete physical examination, including in the female a pelvic or vaginal examination, and it should be accompanied by urine analysis and even a blood count. Such measures permit both the man and the woman to enter this new phase of their lives with an intelligent appraisal of their physical assets and liabilities, an appreciation of the dangers of hereditary disease, and an estimate of the ease or difficulty of their raising a family. It may be a great many years before such thorough examinations become generally used, but only by this means can serious chronic and familial diseases be recognized and treated. The vaginal examination should be routine and thorough, with especial attention to the hymen, position and size of the uterus, and condition of the ovaries and tubes.

As a part of this examination, determination of Rh blood type may also properly be included. Although Rh blood incompatibility is not seen with great frequency, its recognition is of considerable importance because of certain reactions in newborn infants and following blood transfusions.

The Rh blood factor, recognized in 1937, was found to be of clinical importance in 1939 by Peters and Wiener when transfusion reactions were first recognized to result from Rh incompatibility. The term Rh was selected by these investigators to indicate the origin of the responsible antibodies in rabbits injected with blood from rhesus monkeys to produce an "antirhesus" serum. The serums so produced were found to contain antibodies which would agglutinate, or cause to clump, the red blood corpuscles of about 85 per cent of the white population and about 92 per cent of the Negro population. Such individuals are said to be Rh positive. The remaining 15 per cent and 8 per cent respectively are referred to as Rh negative. Transmission of these blood types follows a definite inheritance pattern in which the Rh factor is transmitted as a Mendelian dominant by a pair of allelic genes. The Rh distribution of the offspring will then depend upon the types of the parents as well as upon their homozygosity or heterozygosity.

Since naturally occurring Rh isoantibodies have not been demonstrated in humans, any Rh negative individual may be transfused with Rh positive blood provided the recipient has not become sensitized to the Rh factor through a previous transfusion or, in women, through pregnancy with an Rh positive fetus. In either instance, a subsequent exposure may result in a serious transfusion reaction. For this reason, typing of patients with regard to the Rh factor should precede every transfusion, and Rh negative individuals should receive only Rh negative blood. From the practical standpoint, however, it should be noted that only about one in every twenty-five persons so exposed to the Rh antigen will become sensitized, so that it is well recognized that under emergency conditions, such as obtain on the battlefield, these precautions need not be taken. Nevertheless it has now become common hospital practice to include this test as a routine measure. It is especially important in the treatment of all women of childbearing age.

Immunization of an Rh negative mother by an Rh positive fetus during pregnancy may result in another type of disaster. The observation that 90 per cent of cases of the serious and often fatal infant disease known as erythroblastosis occur in Rh negative mothers has led to the establishment of Rh isoimmunization in pregnancy as the cause of this disease, which is more commonly called congenital hemolytic disease. This condition rarely appears in a first-born infant since at least one episode of immunization of an Rh negative mother by an Rh positive fetus is necessary for its production. Following such an exposure, however, subsequent pregnancies may result in congenital hemolytic disease or in stillbirth. When congenital hemolytic disease does occur with the first pregnancy, the cause may almost invariably be established as a previous transfusion with Rh positive blood. This fact serves to emphasize the importance of Rh testing in women of childbearing age and even in young girls, since their chances of bearing normal children may be ruined by the administration of the wrong blood type (see also reference to this phenomenon in Chapter Fifteen).

The premarital examination also offers a splendid opportunity for the acquisition of reliable information concerning contraception and other matters of sexual hygiene about which either the man or woman may be ignorant. Practical knowledge so acquired often supplements theoretical information obtained from a variety of other sources, and may be of great value in making the physical adjustments incident to married life.

FERTILIZATION AND FETAL DEVELOPMENT

Conception takes place under normal conditions when a healthy sperm cell unites with a living ovum. The conditions necessary for fertilization are therefore rather sharply limited, since the ovum is discharged from the ovary at only one definite time in each menstrual cycle. As has already been stated, the actual union between these two cells usually takes place high in the Fallopian tube, so that the first stages in cell division are completed before the embryo even arrives in the uterus. The ease and frequency with which a pregnancy actually follows unprotected intercourse, so far as practical experience is concerned, is probably due to the combined factors of survival of the living ovum in the tube and the survival of actively motile sperm cells within the female genital tract for many days. From these considerations the approximate delimitations of the "safe period" may be stated. If the exact day of ovulation in any normal woman is not known (and there is no easy way to determine this in most cases), she must assume that it may occur at any time from about the ninth to the sixteenth day of the cycle, although the theoretical normal is the fourteenth day, counting always from the first day of the last menstrual flow. If the survival periods of the two cells now be taken into consideration, it is clear that the periods most free from the possibility of conception are the two or three days immediately following cessation of the menstrual flow, and the two or three days immediately preceding the next flow. The latter of these two possibilities remains valid only when the menstrual rhythm is regular, for obviously in an irregular cycle no woman can state with assurance when she will flow, except in so far as she is aware of an approaching period by symptoms she may have learned to recognize. The probability of pregnancy therefore increases as the mid-cycle is approached, with a theoretical maximum on the fourteenth day. It should be emphasized again that even the most rigid observance of this principle is still not infallible, as there are authentic recorded instances of pregnancy having occurred following intercourse during the menstrual flow.

Multiple pregnancies occur in slightly more than 1 per cent of all cases. Twins are found in about one out of eighty, and triplets in one out of 6400 pregnancies. Twins are of two types, the dizygotic, fraternal, or double-ovum type, and the monozygotic, identical, or single-ovum type. The former constitute about 75 per cent of all twin pregnancies and the latter about 25 per cent. The former, as designated, result from the simultaneous fertilization by two sperm cells of two ova coming either from the same ovary or from different ovaries. This state of affairs can be produced only by the simultaneous ovulation of two ova, an occurrence which must be relatively uncommon. Fraternal twins may be of the same or of opposite sex, they have separate placentae, and they do not look more alike than do other children in the same family. Their occurrence appears to be an inherited tendency transmitted through either mother or father. Identical twins, on the other hand, are necessarily of the same sex, usually have only one set of fetal membranes, and resemble each other very closely. They are conceived, presumably, from the fertilization by one spermatozoon of one ovum followed by cell division through several stages, with subsequent separation into two cell masses each of which develops into a complete individual. Occurrence of identical twins is thought to be largely the result of chance.

As has previously been stated, actual fertilization normally takes place well up toward the free end of the Fallopian tube.[11] Cell division has progressed to the "blastocyte" or hollow-mullberry-mass stage, during its passage down the tube over a period of eight to nine days, before it is implanted in the uterine wall. The uterine endometrium has been prepared by the action of progesterone from the corpus luteum in the ovary, so that the environment of the embryo will be satisfactory. The mass of embryonic cells then embeds itself in the endometrium and the maternal cells heal over the gap, thus leaving the embryo completely surrounded by maternal tissues which are richly supplied with blood vessels.[12]

---

[11] Confusion concerning "tubal pregnancy" should be avoided. This term is applied to a gestation which implants and remains in the Fallopian tube. Normal migration down into the uterus during the early stages of cell division is blocked, and further development proceeds in the tube. Since this structure is not capable of distention to accommodate a full-term pregnancy, symptoms are eventually produced. Surgical removal of the affected tube is necessary; if rupture of the pregnancy has occurred, the situation may constitute an acute surgical emergency. Pregnancies can also take place in the ovary or even in the abdominal cavity, completely outside the genital organs. The latter type may even develop to term and must then be delivered by Caesarean section.

[12] The phenomena of skipping a menstrual flow is so regularly associated with the inception of pregnancy, and is so often the announcing manifestation, that the appearance of this sign in a woman of childbearing age is immediately considered to be indicative of pregnancy, regardless of other circumstances, until proved otherwise. This does *not* mean that pregnancy is the only cause for the cessation of menstrual periods in young women. On the contrary, many other causes exist, the exact identification of which is clearly a medical problem. Mention should be made, however, of the influence of emotional and situational factors on this function. Thus many young girls when placed in strange surroundings, as when going away to college, or moving to a strange city, etc., may miss several periods in a row, only to resume a normal rhythm later. On the other side of the picture, it is well known that

Development of the fetus from this point on is a combination of differentiation into various organs and tissues and growth in size. In addition, that portion of the embryonic mass nearest to the uterine wall develops into the placenta, through which nutrition is provided as the fetus grows and matures. During the early weeks the change is chiefly one of differentiation. At two weeks, the parts of the embryo can be made out only with a microscope, and very little is seen suggesting the shape of an infant's body. Within the next week changes are so rapid that a semblance of head and body can be distinguished. The total length of the fetus at this stage, however, is less than an eighth of an inch. By the twenty-second or twenty-third day, the buds which later form hands and feet can be easily identified; and by the end of the fourth week, when the fetus has a total length of more than a quarter of an inch, the head, body, arms and legs can all be seen. At the end of five weeks, fingers and toes are visible, and by eight or nine weeks the body shape and features have become fully differentiated.

An embryo born at three months has the shape of a very minute infant. Its fingernails and toenails are fully formed, the bones are beginning to ossify, the sex can usually be determined, and it will make spontaneous movements if kept warm. By the fifth month its total weight is more than eight ounces, and hair has appeared on the head. At the sixth month, the head is still disproportionately large, and the total weight is about one and one half pounds. A miscarriage at this stage produces an infant which usually attempts to breathe but which invariably fails to survive. At the seventh month the weight is around three pounds, and if delivery occurs at this point the infant moves vigorously but usually does not survive. From this time on, however, the chances for survival increase progressively with each passing day. At full-term birth, as is well known, the weight is usually between six and eight pounds and the length is about eighteen to twenty inches. During the nine calendar months of gestation, the fetus has increased in weight from .000004 gram to about 3250 grams (average), or 812,500,000 times. In fact, during the first month it grows about 1,000,000 per cent.

The function of the placenta is absolutely vital, as evidenced by the prompt death of the infant if its source of nutrition is damaged. The normal, full-term placenta is a circular or oval structure about seven or eight inches in diameter and flattened to an inch to an inch and a half in thickness. The placenta is a part of the product of conception, grows as the fetus grows, and is a mechanism whereby the most intimate connection is effected between fetal and maternal blood streams without any actual interchange of formed blood elements. An intricate system of fetal fingerlike projections, each bearing a blood vessel, interdigitate with similar projections on the maternal side, so that food materials and oxygen can be transferred across the gap to the embryo; carbon dioxide and other waste products are eliminated in the reverse direction. The fetal blood vessels carrying these materials join together progressively into larger vessels until they form very large channels,

some women have a periodic discharge of blood from the vagina after pregnancy has begun. Such a flow can hardly be considered as menstruation, since the mechanism which brings it about is not that of the normal ovarian cycle.

which then reach the fetus by means of the umbilical cord through the abdominal wall at the navel. Obviously, any interference with the integrity of this cord, either at birth or before, is quite as serious to the fetus as is interference with the placenta itself. Since fetal respiration is carried out through the placenta, the infant's lungs are functionless, strictly speaking, until birth. This means that a sudden drastic change in the circulatory pattern occurs in the infant as he emerges into the world. The stimulus to breathe and the actual expansion of the lungs in the first breath appear to be the mechanism which brings about this shift in the respiratory organ from placenta to lung.

As pregnancy progresses, the uterus is forced to increase steadily in size in order to accommodate its growing contents. During the first three months it remains almost entirely within the pelvic cavity, where it encroaches upon the space ordinarily occupied by the bladder and rectum. This fact may serve to explain the constipation and marked increase in frequency of urination so often noted during these early weeks. The uterus soon becomes too large to remain in the pelvis and rises into the abdomen, where it compresses the intestines. It is in close apposition to the abdominal wall so that it is often possible to feel the shape of its contents through the abdominal muscles, and to view the movements of the fetus.

In view of the violent efforts made by the normal nonpregnant uterus to eject anything placed within its cavity, it is perhaps surprising that the growing fetus and its attached membranes are allowed to remain undisturbed. This appears to be the result of hormonal influences acting upon the uterine muscle. Chief among these is progesterone, formed during early weeks of pregnancy by the corpus luteum, but taken over later by the placenta itself. The quieting effect of this substance comes gradually to be neutralized by a rise in the blood level of estrone, which seems to have the remarkable effect of sensitizing uterine muscle to the stimulating effect of the hormone of the posterior pituitary gland (usually "pituitrin"). Thus the irritability of the uterus begins to increase very gradually during the last few weeks of gestation as evidenced by the increasing frequency of contraction pains similar to those of labor itself. This irritability finally reaches such a point that rhythmic contractions occur at progressively shorter intervals until the uterine contents are expelled. This sequence of events, referred to collectively as labor,[13] is still very mysterious in many respects, even to physicians.

VENEREAL DISEASES

Among the factors which interfere with the normal progress of sexual adjustment and procreation are gonorrhea and syphilis, the chief venereal diseases (so named because of the method of transmission through sexual contact). There are other diseases so transmitted, but their occurrence is much rarer, and they do not constitute public health hazards as great as do gonorrhea and syphilis. Both of the latter are extremely serious, largely be-

[13] See the discussion of labor and childbirth in Chapter XV.

cause of their late or ultimate effects rather than because of any great mortality rate occurring during the acute phases of the diseases.

All previous evaluations of the magnitude of gonorrhea and syphilis as public health problems have required revision since the beginning of the "antibiotic" era, approximately coincident with the mid-period of World War II. Indeed the enormous rise in incidence of these two venereal diseases coincident with and characteristic of the war period, provided an outstanding opportunity to test the practical efficacy of penicillin, the first of the antibiotics, which became generally available to the armed forces at that time. This vast experience, supplemented by a number of years of general use in civilian medicine, has revealed such high sensitivity to this agent of the causative organisms in both of these diseases that from 90 to 95 per cent of early cases may be cured promptly by institution of a properly intensive program of treatment. Thus it is apparent that the public health menace they have created in the past has been dramatically reduced. It is erroneous, however, to believe that either of these diseases has been completely conquered and may henceforth be disregarded, as some popular writers have either stated or implied.

Gonorrhea is often if not regularly considered by the average uninformed layman as trivial, "no worse than a bad cold." The actual truth is that gonorrhea may be and often has been a very serious disease. It always possesses the potential capacity to cripple and even to kill its victims. It is no exaggeration to say that in adults gonorrhea is always transmitted by sexual contact, in spite of the popular opinion to the contrary. (A modified form of the disease occurs in little girls, often in epidemic form, in which transmission results from nonvenereal contact.) The organism responsible is a small bead-like body which grows in paired form.

The usual course of the disease consists of the appearance of a discharge of pus from penis or vagina within a matter of twelve to seventy-two hours after sexual contact with an infected person. This discharge is accompanied by local discomfort in the genital region, varying from vague to severe, and most characteristically by an intense burning sensation on urination. There may be general but usually mild signs of infection as well — for example, fever, headache, loss of appetite, and feeling of being ill at ease.

This entire group of manifestations may slowly or quickly clear up, at times with complete cure in so far as any subsequent medical evidence of the disease is concerned. Often, however, a chronic stage follows, characterized by invasion of the prostate gland in the male and Fallopian tubes in the female. So often does this situation occur in medical experience that any person giving a history of an acute gonorrheal infection must of necessity always be considered as a potential candidate for further trouble from the same source.

Subsequent development may lead in any of several directions. The entire infection may subside in this chronic phase and never be heard from again, or it may develop into a second acute episode with serious incapacitating illness. Such a complication is usually due to invasion by the organism of the

Fallopian tubes or ovaries in the female, or the prostate gland in the male, often with abscess formation ultimately necessitating surgical intervention. In the male, a further hazard is the involvement of the epididymis on one or both sides, with swelling, fever, and excruciating pain and tenderness. Any or all of these variations may be attended by sterility — that is, by the permanent inability to have children on the part of either the male or the female.

Although it is impossible to discuss all the complications arising from gonorrhea, mention should be made of the eye infection of the newborn transmitted from the mother at birth, resulting in damage to the infant's eyes which may go on to total blindness. In order to eliminate the possibility of this misfortune, it has now become a legal obligation of every physician in attendance at the birth of a child to place a drop of weak silver nitrate in each eye of the infant to insure against gonorrheal infection. This procedure is enforced regardless of the identity or medical history of the parents.

Medical cure of gonorrhea theoretically involves the complete sterilization of all tissues invaded by the infecting organism. This is the aim of the natural defense mechanisms of the body, but outside assistance is frequently needed. Many drugs have been used for this purpose, and some have been of great value. Of these, the antibiotics, and especially penicillin, have replaced all others, and are so effective that the entire outlook has become immeasurably brighter.

Syphilis, often regarded as one of the great plagues of mankind, possesses perhaps even greater potentialities for human disaster than does gonorrhea. The historical origins of this infection are somewhat uncertain; one version is that it was originally indigenous to the North American Indians and was taken back to Europe at the end of the fifteenth century, carried perhaps by some of the sailors of Columbus.[14]

The infecting organism is a motile corkscrew, called a spirochete, which is remarkably fragile and easily destroyed, considering its virulence and its capacity for transmission from one person to another. The great fragility of this organism is probably responsible for the fact that the disease is rarely transmitted except by direct contact of the infected and the uninfected persons. Rare cases do occur (so-called innocent syphilis) in which the infection has resulted from the use of a towel or drinking cup. In these instances, the living organisms were undoubtedly deposited on the intermediate object only a few minutes before they were transferred to the recipient, since even drying will regularly kill them. Transmission of syphilis without body contact therefore accounts for only an extremely small percentage of all cases (variously estimated at 1 to 8 per cent).

Of the cases communicated by direct contact, sexual intercourse accounts for the largest part; kissing comes second. Syphilis may be transferred from an infected mother to her child in the womb (in utero), in which case the infant is born with congenital syphilis. To the best of our knowledge this

[14] This version is flatly rejected by many students of the history of syphilis, including H. H. Reese. Some scholars point to the Levant, and call the disease "an aftermath of the Crusades."

form of the disease is never the result of a syphilitic infection in the father unless he first gives the disease to the mother. In other words, sperm cells from an infected individual cannot by themselves produce a syphilitic child.

At the point of entrance of the infecting organisms, usually on the genital organs of either sex or the lips, there develops a primary sore known as a chancre. It is a local area of inflammation, over which the skin is broken, and it appears ten to twenty days following the entrance of the infection. It has a hard, indurated consistency and is often described as resembling a button, and it is teeming with spirochetes. These organisms enter the intact skin through a small crack or abrasion, and immediately begin to multiply. They are carried very swiftly (a matter of hours only) to the lymph glands in the region of the chancre. Enlargement of the lymph glands and appearance of the primary sore, many days later, are the first manifestations of the disease, although it has long before involved the entire body. The chancre is usually single and nearly always painless. In the female the lesion may be in the vagina or on the cervix of the uterus, and since it may be insignificant in size, it is hardly surprising that it is often overlooked. When the chancre is on the lip or other extragenital area it may be overlooked or regarded as the result of some other and more benign cause.

About six weeks after the first appearance of the primary sore, a secondary rash usually appears, scattered over most of the body surface. It may masquerade as almost any well-known skin rash, and therefore may be difficult to diagnose with assurance. Mucous membranes all over the body are covered at this time with "mucous patches," which are really identical with the skin lesions except that the surface is macerated. These mucous patches are literally alive with spirochetes and are highly infectious. The secondary stage of syphilis is of the utmost importance from the public health standpoint, since an individual in this condition is a menace to everyone about him. Direct contact is obviously dangerous, but he may in addition infect anything and everything he touches. It is perhaps fortunate, as far as public health is concerned, but equally unfortunate for the infected individual, that the secondary stage is often either completely missing or is so brief and mild that it passes unrecognized. It is typically attended by fever, headache, joint pains, and general discomfort, similar to and often mistaken for the symptoms of "grippe" or "flu." If the secondary stage of the disease is not clinically recognizable, the patient may be completely unaware of his infection until many years afterward when its serious, late effects become apparent.

The tertiary stage of syphilis may occur at any time from a few months to many years after the primary and secondary stages. In this phase, many vital organs are potentially endangered, for it is in this form that the viscera are destroyed. The central nervous system may be involved in many different ways. Paresis or general paralysis (the G.P.I. — general paresis of the insane — of the psychiatrist) is the term applied to general destruction of the higher cortical functions of the brain. Tabes or locomotor ataxia represents the spinal cord lesion due to the effects of the spirochete, in which certain sensory pathways are interrupted with a resulting loss in position sense in the muscles, tendons, and joints.

The heart and blood vessels may be the site of a destructive process which typically either weakens the wall of the aorta, the great artery leading away from the heart, or breaks down some of the heart valves so that this organ is forced to function against tremendous obstacles. The stomach, the lungs, the skin, and the liver are also often the sites of a tertiary syphilitic process; no tissue of the body is immune to the action of these organisms.

The Wassermann reaction has now become familiar to the public because of its widespread application in public health work. It is usually not positive at the time the primary lesion appears, but becomes positive in a progressively larger percentage of cases as the period after infection lengthens. Approximately 96 per cent of infected patients react positively after the fortieth day. This test is not absolutely specific for syphilis, and does not depend upon the infection *per se*. It is frequently positive under certain other clinical conditions, and particularly in spirochetal infections other than syphilis. The availability since about 1906 of the Wassermann test and its various modifications has greatly broadened the attack on the disease. Testing of every patient admitted to most hospitals is now accepted. In addition, testing of all people intending to marry is rapidly being made a legal requirement in most states.

The treatment of syphilis has an interesting historical background. The value of mercury was apparently known to Benvenuto Cellini and to other scientific people of the early sixteenth century. Since the disease was first recognized about this time, it would appear that the gravity of the disease acted as a stimulus to the discovery of a remedy. Modern therapy, however, began with Ehrlich (1910) whose "606" has now become famous. The efficacy of arsenic thereby became known, and its use has been intensively studied and amplified since that time. Generally speaking, our kit of chemotherapeutic agents up to a decade ago consisted of the heavy metals bismuth, arsenic and mercury, and the element iodine. Over a brief period of a year or two, beginning in about 1943, all of these were completely replaced by penicillin. We know that the ideal time to try for a complete cure is in the very early stages. Therapy under these conditions is intensive and consists of the administration by injection of 2,400,000 up to 10,000,000 units of penicillin over a 7 to 14 day period. Complete cure may be expected in 90 per cent of cases with even more cases yielding to longer courses of treatment. The outlook for late tertiary syphilis, regardless of the form it takes, is still not especially bright, due to the serious damage to vital organs already produced by the disease by the time this stage is reached, even though proper treatment may halt its progress.

From the practical standpoint, the ultimate solution of the venereal disease problem may be resolved into at least three phases: (1) prophylaxis for those exposed to venereal infection; (2) prompt recognition and adequate treatment of active cases; and (3) isolation and elimination of sources of dissemination of the diseases. This third point involves, among other things, the destruction rather than the "control" of organized prostitution. Cases of venereal disease must be reported and their isolation from public contact enforced by law. Diagnostic methods must be further improved, and their value so widely disseminated and their use made so accessible to every physician that venereal cases can be identified and treated before they can become a public menace. Only by such a strong attack can we repeat with these diseases the striking record achieved by public health with typhoid fever, diphtheria, and smallpox. Notable progress has been made during the past decade.

Abortions and Miscarriages

The term abortion bears in popular parlance the connotation of a criminal act, but to the medical profession it simply means the expulsion of the embryo from any cause whatsoever between the time of conception and the sixteenth week of pregnancy. If this occurs between the sixteenth and twentieth weeks, it is termed a miscarriage; between the twenty-eighth week and full term it is called premature labor. Because of the unpleasant implications of the word "abortion," all accidental terminations of pregnancy before the period when the fetus has a chance of survival are popularly called "miscarriages."

In general, the spontaneous emptying of the uterus in the early months of pregnancy should probably be looked upon as the organism's method of preventing the maturation and survival of a defective fetus, for fetal death is by far the commonest precipitating cause of spontaneous abortion. This lack of fetal vitality may be a reflection of defective germ plasm transmitted from either the father or the mother or both, or it may result from an accidental anomaly of development which if allowed to continue might produce a freak of some type. Maternal diseases or abnormalities are responsible for some abortions, and it is possible that lead poisoning or chronic alcoholism in the father can produce this result through injury to the paternal germ plasm.

Regardless of the cause, spontaneous premature termination of pregnancy is extremely common. Accurate statistics on this point are obviously difficult or impossible to obtain, but the best estimates indicate that one fifth to one third of all pregnancies end in abortion. It is therefore apparent that this accident is a very common one, usually having as its underlying cause a fundamental biological error of some sort. The part played by injuries to the mother, whether they be physical (falls, body strains, etc.) or emotional (grief, fright), has undoubtedly been greatly exaggerated. Indeed, it seems safe to state that in an overwhelming majority of abortions which appear to have been caused in this way the stage had already been set for the accident by other deep-seated factors, so that the precipitating injury merely initiated the inevitable disaster. If one regards spontaneous abortion in this light — as a protective mechanism — considerable doubt is immediately cast upon the wisdom of medical interference with the process. Such an attitude is not in order, however, where a woman habitually aborts every pregnancy at approximately the same stage. Here the mechanism may be quite different, and appropriate treatment is indicated.

Under any circumstances, spontaneous abortion is a potentially serious event. The only exception to this would be the loss of a pregnancy within the first week or two, the manifestations of which would then be merely profuse vaginal bleeding, usually interpreted by the woman herself as a delayed, abnormal menstrual period. Under almost all other circumstances the event is not one to take lightly. Hemorrhage may be very serious, with the necessity of surgical intervention; a physician should always be consulted.

The dangers of induced or "criminal" abortion cannot be too strongly stated. Voluntary termination of unwanted pregnancies have been conservatively estimated at nearly 700,000 annually in the United States, resulting in the death of many thousands of women — a fact which must be considered, by the way, when discussing the pros and cons of birth control. These deaths result from two chief causes: hemorrhage and infection. Of these, the latter is probably the more hazardous, since most laymen and many professional abortionists do not appreciate the extreme care that is required, even in the most perfectly equipped hospitals, to insure rigid asepsis in executing therapeutic abortions. The uterine cavity provides a perfect culture medium for pathogenic microorganisms, the most feared of which is the hemolytic streptococcus. Unfortunately, it is all too easy for infections to gain access to the uterus through instrumentation of all types. The enormous development of antibiotic therapy during the past decade through employment of penicillin, aureomycin, terramycin, erythromycin and other similar preparations has eased somewhat the extreme anxiety concerning septic complications of abortions induced by instrumentation and has significantly brightened the outlook for victims of these misfortunes. Nevertheless, the threat still exists and serious illness and even fatalities have by no means been completely eliminated even by these improved methods of therapy.

Contrary to much popular opinion, the medical profession does not at the present time possess any form of medication to be administered by mouth or by injection which will induce abortion without grave danger. It must still be performed as a difficult surgical procedure.

The many-sided problem of criminal abortion thus occupies a unique position, demanding the attention of sociologists, law enforcement agencies, the church, the medical profession, and the public in general. Clearly no effective solution has thus far been found, and the evil not only continues but is probably increasing. In an earlier section of this chapter we pointed out that the facts of criminal abortion may be said to pose a moral dilemma. This dilemma might be said to take the form of: "Abortion or contraception?" If the answer is "Neither" — as it sometimes is — further moral problems arise, especially when we note the further fact that the greater number of criminal abortions are performed on married women whose contraceptive techniques are faulty or who do not practice contraception.

CONTRACEPTION

The term "contraception" has been defined as the voluntary prevention of pregnancy without the prohibition of normal sexual relations. Practically speaking, it means a great deal more, since its use permits the control of family size and the spacing of children in harmony with the health and economic resources of the parents. Contraception has contributed greatly to marital happiness in some quarters by dissipating fear of unwanted pregnancies, but individual reactions naturally vary widely. For example, the use of "artificial" contraceptive devices is not equally acceptable to all religious groups. Viewed from the broadest standpoint, therefore, the matter of contraception has economic, physical, emotional, population, and religious aspects so important and far-reaching that it merits some discussion without in any way attempting to deal with its morality or ethics. (Population problems are discussed elsewhere in this book. See Chapter Twenty-Five.)

The real or supposed advantages of contraceptive practice are well known: (1) the safeguarding of the maternal health by optimum spacing of pregnancies; (2) the limiting of family size to a number commensurate with the available economic resources and plane of living; and (3) the prevention of serious emotional disturbances in either husband or wife by eliminating the constant fear of unwanted pregnancies.

The opposition to contraception is based almost entirely on moral or religious considerations. Some people believe that sexual intercourse is intended exclusively for procreative purposes, and that any interference with the fulfillment of this function is unjustified. The acceptance or rejection of this idea by others is currently held to be a matter decided by religious authority or tradition; consultation with spiritual mentors, or private judgment. More than this we cannot fairly say.

All contraceptive techniques have as their ultimate aim the prevention of the access of spermatozoa to the uterus and Fallopian tubes at times when fertilizable ova are present. Of the numerous theoretically possible means of accomplishing this end, only a few will be discussed. First, many of the kinds of contraception possible or known to man are not likely to be used by anyone in our society. Second, many of them have not stood the test of time or are sufficiently impractical to contraindicate their use. Third, it is at present illegal to deal with some of the more reliable types in a book intended for general college and university circulation; only medical and other professional textbooks can legally present information about them. This is of course a farcical restriction in view of the wide dissemination of such information among a large proportion of the American populace, but the ghost of Anthony Comstock is not yet laid. We shall therefore discuss only those kinds of contraceptive technique that are extensively used but which, for various reasons, are unreliable or in other ways of doubtful value or positively undesirable. It should be plainly understood, however, that our failure to mention certain commonly known methods does not necessarily indicate approval of these methods on our part. Consultation with a qualified physician is usually desirable — if contraception is to be practiced.

1. Perhaps the commonest method of contraception in general use everywhere is coitus interruptus, so designated because the act of intercourse is interrupted, immediately before the male orgasm, by withdrawal of the penis and ejaculation outside the vagina. Although this might seem to be a simple and almost ideal solution of the problem, it is by no means satisfactory from any standpoint. Its success is predicated upon the ability of the man to maintain complete control of his actions and be so alert to the fluctuations of his

emotional level that he is able to withdraw at precisely the instant before his orgasm. Instead of being easy, this task is very difficult for most men because they not only arrive unexpectedly at the point of orgasm on occasion, but also because they often are so involved emotionally that although aware of the approaching orgasm they are unable to withdraw in time. A second hazard is the danger of sperm cells in the few drops of seminal fluid which often escape from the penis before the orgasm is reached. Finally, but by no means of minor importance, is the deleterious effect on the nervous and emotional equanimity of both husband and wife which often follows prolonged use of this technique. Both partners develop an insatiable craving for complete and absolute sexual satisfaction which is never possible under these circumstances, since the male orgasm is likely to be most unsatisfactory and the woman is denied any relief whatsoever. Coitus interruptus is therefore not only insecure in its contraceptive efficiency, but it involves certain emotional hazards for those who would practice it faithfully.

2. The "rhythm method" of contraceptive control has already been discussed in connection with ovarian physiology, since it depends upon an accurate knowledge of the time relationships in the cycle of ovarian activity. Stated simply, the time of maximum probability of pregnancy following intercourse in any woman's cycle is at ovulation and immediately thereafter. This is roughly halfway between menstrual periods. This probability then decreases in each direction and reaches a minimum during the preceding and the succeeding menstrual flow. As has already been pointed out, accurate estimation of the safe period depends upon an exact knowledge of the day of ovulation. Although this is usually impossible, approximation becomes possible if the menstrual cycle is regular. Irregularity casts great uncertainty upon the advisability of this technique from the purely physiological standpoint.

A certain small percentage of young women experience a brief sharp pain in the lower abdomen regularly from ten to fifteen days after the beginning of the last menstrual flow. This pain coincides with and is due to ovulation. In certain other women a faint spotting of blood for a few hours at about the same time likewise indicates ovulation. The great majority, however, have no means of exactly identifying the time of this event in each ovarian cycle, and they must therefore depend for contraceptive protection upon the simple rule of allowing unprotected marital intercourse on the first three or four days following and the last three or four days before the menstrual flow. One additional, relatively new technique for establishing the date of ovulation has permitted increased accuracy in utilizing the "safe period" method for many couples. This is the use of the temperature chart employed in the following manner: the woman takes and records accurately her body temperature with a standard clinical thermometer each morning upon awakening and before arising. This may be taken either orally or rectally, the latter probably being somewhat more accurate. Considerable fluctuation, usually within about one degree, is usually noted from day to day, but in a high percentage of women a definite, easily identified and well-sustained rise occurs on the day of ovulation; this persists until a day or two before the onset of the menstrual period. The elevated phase of this curve corresponds to the corpus luteum phase of ovarian activity, and the sharp rise in temperature occurring at about mid-cycle permits identification of the day of ovulation with dependable accuracy. Once established through observation of two or three cycles, the pattern may subsequently be relied upon as fairly consistent for that individual, and the limits of the "safe period" are thereby more dependably recognized. Without careful identification of the event of ovulation, utilization of this contraceptive method must depend upon the basic rules stated above, and with the addition of each day to the basic "safe period," the chances of occasional pregnancies increases. It should be emphasized again that even the most stringent observance of this rule does not provide a guarantee of complete contraceptive protection, probably because of occasional abnormal survival of both ova and sperm in the female genital tract.

Use of the "safe period" for control of conception is acceptable to many members and the official representatives of conservative religious organizations, and presumably to most persons who object to the use of artificial measures of all sorts on moral or aesthetic grounds. Its two chief drawbacks seem to be the unusual care that must be exercised in calculating dates (partly overcome by the "artificiality" of special computing calendars), and the enforced restriction placed on sexual relations for two to two-and-one-half weeks out of every month. It is nevertheless a source of great comfort to many millions of people who are completely sincere in their religious beliefs, and in their eyes its real or supposed disadvantages are completely overshadowed by the moral reassurance it gives.

SELECTED READINGS

BANNING, MARGARET C., "The Case for Chastity," *Reader's Digest,* Aug., 1939.

BUTTERFIELD, OLIVER M., *Sex Life in Marriage* (New York: Emerson Books, 1937).

DELL, FLOYD, *Love in the Machine Age* (New York: Farrar and Rinehart, 1930).

DICKINSON, ROBERT L., *Human Sex Anatomy: A Topographical Hand Atlas* (Baltimore: Williams and Wilkins, 1933).

——, and BEAM, LURA, *A Thousand Marriages* (Baltimore: Williams and Wilkins, 1931).

EXNER, MAX J., *The Sexual Side of Marriage* (New York: Norton, 1932).

Four Great Encyclicals (New York: Paulist Press, no date). This contains a translation of the encyclical on marriage (*Casti connubii*), published Jan. 9, 1931.

HARTMAN, CARL G., *Time of Ovulation in Women. A Study of the Fertile Period in the Menstrual Cycle* (Baltimore: Williams and Wilkins, 1936).

HIMES, NORMAN E., *Medical History of Contraception* (Baltimore: Williams and Wilkins, 1936).

——, *Your Marriage: A Guide to Happiness* (rev. ed.; New York: Rinehart, 1940).

KINBERG-VON SNEIDERN, JULIA, and SUNDQUIST, ALMA, *Sex Hygiene: The Anat-*

omy, Physiology and Hygiene of the Sex Organs, translated by Mary E. Collett (New York: Holt, 1926).

KINSEY, ALFRED C., POMEROY, WARDELL B., and MARTIN, CLYDE E., *Sexual Behavior in the Human Male* (Philadelphia: W. B. Saunders, 1948).

LATZ, L. J., *The Rhythm of Sterility and Fertility in Women* (Chicago: Latz Foundation, 1932).

NEWCOMB, THEODORE, "Recent Changes in Attitudes toward Sex and Marriage," *American Sociological Review,* 2 (Oct., 1937), pp. 659–667.

OGINO, KYUSAKU, *Conception Period in Women* (Harrisburg, Pa.: Medical Arts Publishing Co., 1934).

PARRAN, THOMAS, *Shadow on the Land* (New York: Reynal and Hitchcock, 1937).

TOPICS FOR DISCUSSION OR REPORTS

1. What do recent scientific studies show to be the relative importance of the sexual factor in marriage? How would you characterize the current popular beliefs on sexuality and marriage?
2. What is the mechanism of erection? How does circumcision affect male sexual functioning? From what three internal sources does the male ejaculate come?
3. Describe the process of ovulation. What is the relation of time of ovulation and time of menstruation?
4. Name the three chief functions of the vagina. What is the female homologue of the penis? What three external genital organs of the female collectively make up the vulva?
5. Does our present culture offer more erotic stimuli than the culture of previous generations? What might be regarded as wise public policy with regard to erotic exhibitions such as "strip-teasing"?
6. Why is petting likely to be troublesome? In what sense can it be said to be an unfair practice?
7. State the case for the premarital examination. What can be said in opposition?
8. Describe the process of fetal development, and relate the materials of this chapter to the one on "Caring for Mother and Child."
9. Why are gonorrhea and syphilis such extremely serious diseases?
10. How does the number of induced abortions occurring annually in the United States compare with the number of live births?
11. How does the fact of numerous criminal abortions performed on married women relate to the problem of birth control?
12. What are the three chief advantages commonly claimed for contraception by its advocates? What disadvantages are asserted by its opponents?

Chapter Eleven

Getting Along in Marriage

HARRIET R. MOWRER

MARITAL adjustment has long held the attention of layman and scientist alike. To the layman, whether as a participant in a marriage relationship or as an outsider viewing the marriage of others, the appeal is fundamentally emotional. To the scientist it is a problem for objective study through the use of statistical, clinical, and laboratory techniques out of which will ultimately come a body of generalizations concerning the nature of marriage adjustment and the causes and processes of marital accord and marital discord.

Increasing interest and research during the past few decades have already taken the problem out of the realm of romantic faith, fatalistic acceptance, and arbitrary speculation and have given it some basis, at least, of scientific understanding. No longer is love considered too elusive or ethereal to be studied, the sexual relationship too sacred and personal to be dissected, or marriage success any more inevitably and invariably acquired than perfect health or success in one's job. Through the layman's emotional interest in marriage and the family, translated into his increasing willingness (sometimes eagerness) to offer his emotional experiences to the scientist for study, there has come a highly significant change in outlook toward marital adjustment. This fact has made it possible to lay the foundation for a more nearly complete and a more dynamic understanding of the success and the failure of marital behavior. Statistical, case, and clinical studies resulting in more unbiased findings have combined to help establish a social psychology and sociology of marriage.[1]

MARRIAGE AS INTERACTIONAL BEHAVIOR

As emphasis upon marriage *per se* and divorce *per se* shifted to behavior within marriage and to behavior leading up to divorce (i.e., marital failure), the scientist's attention became fixed upon the persons constituting the relationship. The unique unity, the dynamic relationship between husband and wife, became the focal point. The interplay of the personality of each with the other was described in terms of wishes, attitudes, and sentiments. These three were thought to characterize the personality and to constitute the essential elements in the relation between husband and wife. Adjustment, accordingly, was a matter of concurrence and accommodation between the wishes, attitudes, and sentiments of the two persons. But the explanation of this concurrence and the resultant behavior lies in the genesis of the social-psycholog-

---

[1] Ernest R. Mowrer and Harriet Mowrer, "The Social Psychology of Marriage," *American Sociological Review*, 16 (Feb., 1951), pp. 27-37.

ical elements constituting the personality, because one sees in marriage only the resultant behavior of a long interactional process which begins almost with the birth of the individual. Why is this true?

GENETIC DEVELOPMENT OF MARITAL UNITY

Marriage is essentially an affectional relationship which has its beginning far back in the earliest affectional experience of the child in his family. This experience is commonly with the parent or the parent surrogate. In our traditional family configuration of mother and father and child the mother's main although not exclusive function is to care for the child; the father's, to provide for him. It is natural, then, that the infant's first affectional experience is with the mother or mother surrogate because the infant usually must look to her for the satisfaction of its bodily needs and comforts. During this interidentification between mother and infant there develops a host of unrelated responses of a gratifying affectional, often erotic, nature. Just as the infant's ability to grasp the bottle and to alternately compress and relax the nipple becomes transmitted into an ability to feed himself, so his affectional satisfactions become transmitted into a capacity to express affection toward a particular love object, i.e., the mother. This early relationship is the training ground for the development of attitudes of solicitation and tenderness, the demonstration of affection, sympathy, and understanding — in short, the pleasant aspects of the love experience (see pp. 206–212 for more detail on the genesis of love patterns).

This elemental pattern is modified very early by the superimposition of a second one growing out of the heterosexual character of social relationships. The Freudians maintain that there is a predominant tendency for the child to select the parent of the opposite sex as the object of affection. This somewhat parallels a growing instinctual tendency toward heterosexual selection, according to Flügel.[2] However, another more important factor which determines the child's conception of his affectional role is, as some of the psychoanalysts would agree, that of the heterosexual preferences which parents show toward the child of the opposite sex. This means further reinforcement of the earlier elemental identification pattern in the case of the male child, whereas in the case of the female child it means a shift in the locus of importance and in the nature of the identification. For the girl it is the father who displaces the mother as the ultimate source of affection. This does not mean a discontinuance of the affectional relationship between mother and daughter, but a shift, more or less unconscious, in the preference and predominance of the type of affectional pattern. Likewise it should not be concluded that no close interidentification exists between the father and son, but only that this phase is subordinate to that between mother and son.

The degree to which heterosexual preference is exercised by the parents may depend upon a number of factors, chief among which are the specific family tradition, the cultural pattern, and the essential difference between

[2] J. C. Flügel, *The Psychoanalytic Study of the Family* (4th ed.; London: Hogarth Press, 1931), p. 15.

masculine and feminine emotional experience, this latter being also an adjunct of the cultural pattern. Thus, to illustrate the factor of family tradition, an infant son may be the source of great exultation by the mother (expressed in frank preference) because he is the male child who bears the same given name as an ancestor in preceding generations. From the moment the identity of his sex is made known, the traditional family role is assigned him and the mother's preference is expressed not just in terms of maternal-offspring relations but in terms of the father, grandfather, etc., relation of generations past.

In the popular mind filio-parental relationships have come to be portrayed heterosexually, perhaps because of the influence of the so-called romantic complex upon family relations. Affection is portrayed more tenderly if it exists between father and daughter or mother and son. This may be an expression of the traditional pattern of chivalry and romance in Western culture which assigns to the male the protective role toward the female. It may be more accurately said, however, that the affectional relationship experienced by the child in his family is usually of two kinds, paralleling the heterosexual differentiation between the two parents. It tends on the one hand to be more personal, subjective, infantile, and possessive; on the other, more objective, companionable, and emancipated. These forms lay the groundwork for later marriage interaction and accord.

These pleasant emotions of affectional security and preferential treatment are not the sole components of filial love. Since familial interrelationships are always in flux, new patterns evolve and there is often a shifting of preferential treatment to another member of the family, particularly a sibling. In this shifting rivalries between siblings are inevitable. They develop early toward brothers and sisters in regard to toys, attention from the parents, granting of special privileges, etc. They are often more pronounced between siblings of the same sex and often develop through adolescence and adulthood. Furthermore, it is quite normal for two sisters to see themselves as rivals in a specific instance for a parent's affection, or for a girl to feel hurt at times by her father's attentiveness to her mother. However good-natured this rivalry may be, some elements of frustration and loss of accomplishment are always experienced and it has its unpleasant and ambivalent response components: rivalry, jealousy, insecurity, fear, anger, and rage. In almost every affectional experience in the family these components are found, the degree of their presence depending upon the unique pattern of the individual's evolving social adaptation. For these affectional experiences constitute the child's family romance and are part and parcel of his coming of age, his emotional and social maturation.

FROM FAMILY ROMANCE TO PSYCHOSEXUAL MATURITY

As the child's social world widens and expands from the cloistered realm of his family circle to contacts outside, there comes a shift from parental affectional fixation to love objects in this new world. Here the child is thrown more and more with his contemporaries and it is only natural that his affectional relationships should be transferred to them. One most commonly sees this transference expressed in a chum relationship — a love object of his own sex — for at this time the child experiences the homosexual stage of social and emotional development. Members of the opposite sex are looked upon for the most part with disdain. Boys, for example, think it is "tough" to hate girls and to ridicule their sisters. The confidant is usually, if not always, the pal of one's own sex. Often crushes are developed upon older persons, such as a teacher or counselor, but these probably represent vestiges of parental fixation and constitute intermediate steps in the transition. The significant point is that the affectional identification is made with members outside the family circle. To the extent that a lag exists in the process of transference there is a retardation in the process of emancipation.

Paralleling the physiological maturation of the child, the final stage in the love or affectional life of the individual gradually emerges. The individualistic boy or girl is transformed into a social being dependent upon the favorable opinion of others. Desire for the more elemental affectional satisfaction of the infancy period revives but it is defined and oriented in a cultural setting of heterosexual contacts which eventually lead to a more or less mature heterosexuality of adulthood. Thus in our culture sophistication and maturity become synonymous with heterosexual contacts.

The adolescent often seems to burst forth suddenly to proclaim his new interest in the opposite sex. It is not uncommon for the boy, for example, to seek (unconsciously, of course) the most conspicuous manner of announcing his entrance into this new world. The "new girl" in school or in town becomes the object of his first love and the most sought after by all his pals and, accordingly, the most envied of her sex.[3] The same unconscious motive exists in the selection of an older girl of questionable reputation, probably not for the reason that she seems prettier or more attractive as a stranger but because her conquest provides a more glamorous and spectacular setting for his "coming out" and introduction to this third affectional world which soon is to merge into courtship and marriage. Furthermore, it provides him with an explanation as to why he has not been interested in girls heretofore: "there just weren't any worth noticing." A comparable process takes place on the part of the girl, in which she likewise is attracted to the "new" boy or the older man.

COURTSHIP AS INITIAL MARRIAGE ACCOMMODATION

Courtship, in which numerous love objects are singled out, then becomes significant training for marriage unity just as it does for the personality development of the individual. Each emotional experience with the other sex normally brings the adolescent closer to mature heterosexuality and aids him in testing out his facilities of accommodation. Through the dating experience, the young man or woman learns to rearrange his or her finances, rate dates in terms of status-giving potentialities, develop the pleasant and modify the unpleasant phases of his personality, clarify his dominant wishes, and test

[3] This experience occurs frequently in life-history documents of normal adolescents.

them experimentally. The girl, for instance, who has been taught by her mother to believe that a woman should be waited on hand and foot has the opportunity to find out among other things whether this approach brings out man's protective attitude or whether possibly her mother's training was not practicable after all or whether her relationship with the other sex needs re-definition. Furthermore, she learns when and when not to get too emotionally involved, the give-and-take of close association, the eccentricities of the opposite sex, subordination and superordination, how to overcome frustrations of the ego. In the process she experiences rivalries, jealousies, insecurity, mis-understanding, tenderness, security, exaltation, as she did in intersibling re-lations in her family circle. Thus she progresses another step in the training and management of heterosexual relationships with her contemporaries.

Out of this experience of probing, experimenting, and accommodating, guided and manipulated by the earlier affectional pattern, one love object is selected.[4] After a period of courtship the two persons involved go through a process of confirming their selection of each other. At first the selection is tentative and often characterized by a certain amount of vacillation, but even-tually arrives at a point where sufficient confidence is achieved to declare the relationship publicly (the formal engagement).

Courtship then provides the locale not only for the stabilization of the heterosexual affectional pattern but also for the development of a host of accommodations which become the foundation of marriage relations.[5] At first these accommodations are largely in the realm of recreational interests and activities. Common likes and dislikes discovered in courtship are re-inforced and clarified. A couple, for example, may find that they both like a certain food and together they order it and partake of it in the privacy of the cozy, dimly lighted, favorite restaurant-nook. Here is built up an identi-fication which is based, it is true, upon elemental satisfactions but which later plays an important function in marriage unity. This courtship identification associated with a definitely pleasant response comes to symbolize a unity of feeling which gets its significance not out of the peculiar involved elements (kind of food, locale, etc.), but out of an exclusiveness of association and its components of intimacy and like-mindedness. There is an almost insatiable striving for exclusiveness which provides the prototype for the domestic ar-rangements achieved in marriage (eating and living together, sharing of common facilities, owning and managing a household, etc.).

An accompaniment of this exclusiveness is the mutual achievement of erotic experiences in petting and demonstrations of affection, associated with exchanges of confidence, secrets, future plans, and all the other romantic elements that make up the meaning of love-interaction in our culture.

Marriage thus marks the culmination of the affectional maturation proc-ess which was initiated in the cradle. It is a process characterized genetically,

---

[4] Cf. Anselm Strauss, "The Influence of Parent-Images upon Marital Choice," *American Socio-logical Review*, 11 (Oct., 1946), pp. 554–559.

[5] Cf. E. W. Burgess and Paul Wallin, "Predicting Adjustment in Marriage from Adjustment in Engagement," *American Journal of Sociology*, 49 (1944), pp. 324–330.

as we have seen, by infantilism, possessiveness, ambivalence, idealization, emotional stress, shifting of love objects and loyalties, adventure, enchantment, erotic awakenings, instability, and finally by growing emancipation from inhibitory discipline, verbalization of newly discovered wishes and newly defined goals, and a new orientation in an adult heterosexual world.

THE PROCESS OF ADAPTATION

In agreement with the psychoanalytic principle of the ambivalence of the emotions, especially of love and hate, all social accommodation is a dual process, a combination of two antagonistic processes operating at the same time. According to this principle, two contradictory emotional attitudes toward the same object may exist simultaneously or arise alternately without interfering with one another.[6]

But this process can be explained from the point of view of social psychology by the multiplicity and varied nature of the individual's social contacts. In fact, duality in interaction may be said to grow out of the individual's multiplicity of roles in social participation. All these are not equally important because of different definitions given them not only in the family but also in the larger social group. Thus, personality is a reflection of the role of the individual in the group; that is, the individual as a consequence of group membership obtains a conception of himself which defines for him the kind of role he aspires to in social relationships. But since group membership is plural and not singular and since each group defines the individual's role differently, the individual has as many personalities as there are groups to which he belongs.

Some groups, however, play a more dominant part in the definition of personality than others. The family into which the individual is born furnishes both the first and the most persistent definition of role. The conception of himself developed in the early family becomes the dominant element in the personality and exercises the function of striving to bring some order into the relationships between the several roles developed out of communal living. This statement should not be interpreted to imply that the child has necessarily but one role in the family group. He may have several, depending upon the differential attitudes of the several members of the family. In fact, as a consequence of invidious comparison he may develop a conception of himself antithetical to that conceded him by any member of the family, and this comes to be quite as important in his repertoire of roles as any of the others. Nevertheless one role tends to stand out as more congenial and more important and becomes the dominant one.

Accommodation between roles is a relative matter. Complete identification probably never occurs, but in some instances there is such facility in accommodation that every conflict situation is met with a repertoire of adjustment techniques which readily bring the conflicting elements into control and insure a continued equilibrium between the several roles and the demands which society makes upon the individual. These are the well-adjusted

---

[6] Ernest R. Mowrer, *The Family* (Chicago: University of Chicago Press, 1932), pp. 89, 94.

personalities. In fact the degree of personality adjustment is largely a matter of the facility with which the individual can move from membership in one group to that in another and be accepted in terms of his conception of his role. Thus the well-adjusted personality is that in which there is little or no strain in the interactive relationship between the group definition of role and the individual definition.

Marriage interaction, then, is but a mirror of the interacts of these various roles which go to make up the personalities in an exclusive sphere of social intimacy. Conflicting definitions in our culture, as reflected in the multiplicity of social contacts, introduce ambivalent elements so that in every interact there are both discordant and harmonious, organizing and disorganizing, elements. These become crystallized into two dynamic processes in marriage just as in the personality. There is the process or pattern of accord on the one hand and, on the other, the process of conflict. The adjusted marriage, then, like the well-adjusted personality, is one in which there is an equilibrium between the several roles of the personality and the demands of marriage and in which the dominant role continues to maintain order in a realm of both discordant and orderly elements. The relationship between the minor roles is of little importance, so long as the accommodation between the two dominant roles exercises a controlling force upon the conflicts between these minor roles.

Nevertheless the degree of adjustment in marriages is highly variable because there may be recurrent conflict between the subsidiary role of one person and that of the other. Furthermore, the dominant role of the individual may be of such a character as to facilitate or impede the accommodation between the affectional pattern developed in the early experiences of each of the persons. Thus the well-adjusted marriage is one in which the dominant roles of the two persons do not significantly conflict. This implies an ability and a facility upon the part of the individual to pass from one role to another in the various spheres of marriage interaction. It further implies that each partner is able to play the role which marriage entails without too great a diversity between the marriage partner's conception of his marriage role and his own conception.

Mechanisms of Marriage Unity

Marriage accommodation is a process initiated from the moment a mate is chosen, a process having potentialities of both unity and discord. So far as the accommodations are accumulative, they make for unity; but so far as they are resolved into conflict, they make for discord. What determines whether or not they are accumulative is largely a matter of the relationship between the potential mechanisms of unity.

Accommodation presents a wide range of mechanisms from the early phases of identification, based primarily upon sex attraction, to the later stages of assimilation or fusion of personalities. At the time of marriage there is little more than an emotional tie with another person which, as the Freudians and some sociologists have pointed out, is a substitute for earlier parental affectional ties. But marriage unity is something that has to be achieved, and it is achieved through the interplay of a number of mechanisms, which are in part catalytic agents in the accumulative process toward unity.

The first mechanism through which unity is transmitted is identification. It consists in solidarity of thinking and feeling toward an affectional object so that what one marriage partner experiences is the reflection and counterpart of what the other experiences. This solidarity, based first upon sex attraction, becomes in time overlaid with concrete expression of likeness in behavior so that there is built up a constellation of experiences which symbolize a further conviction of oneness. If identification is not arrested early in marriage, it becomes the basic mechanism in achieving the ultimate pattern of accord. Some writers have pointed out the possible loss of individuality in the operation of identification. It is true, to be sure, that the very essence of marriage is loss of a considerable degree of individuality if the couple achieves any high degree of adjustment or unity, just as the individual loses his individuality as he becomes a member of any group, the degree of individuality lost being correlated with the degree of group solidarity. This does not mean of course that, comparatively speaking, a high degree of marriage unity exists only where there is complete loss of individuality. So long as the individual must of necessity operate in other social relationships than the marriage, he will likewise retain some individuality; and so long as it is confined to these relationships, it does not in any real sense threaten the marriage unity. In fact, even in the marriage relationship itself some degree of individuality tends to be maintained through the differentiation of marital roles. Indeed we might say that sound marriages will attain maximum identification while maintaining at least a minimum of differentiation of personalities.

The second mechanism, differentiation of marital roles, contributes to marital stability in producing an interdependence between husband and wife, both emotional and physical. From the standpoint of ultimate determination, this differentiation tends to emphasize the husband's role as the chief source of economic support and the wife's role as the partner responsible for the care and supervision of the household and the children. On the emotional side the differentiation follows the cultural pattern less closely. Here the peculiar needs of the pair play a more important part in determining the roles each will play, for in modern marriage each person plays not one or two roles but many in the drama of unity. For instance, a wife may be to her husband a mother, a child, a sister, a companion and comrade, a sweetheart, a plaything, a social butterfly, a hostess, a symbol of his economic and professional status, a nurse, a confidant, or a business associate, as well as a wife. In turn, the husband may be in addition a father, a brother, a protector, a lover, a companion, a playboy, or a teacher.

Differentiation makes for unity to the extent to which each marriage partner can with facility and finesse shift from role to role as the occasion demands and yet always play a complementary rather than a conflicting role. For example, a wife who sees herself in a child-father relationship with her husband cannot at that moment satisfy his affectional demand for a mother-son role. Similarly, a wife's role as a social butterfly competes with her husband's demand for a confidant. Lack of ability to adjust to a role comple-mentary to that of the marriage mate is discussed in detail in the next chapter. In most instances it is a reflection of deep-seated personality conflict which makes marital adjustment difficult to achieve.

The effect of the lack of mutually satisfactory differentiation of roles is most vividly seen in cases of sexual inversion, when there is a reversal of husband roles and both husband and wife tenaciously claim the same one. Here the conflict is not directly sexual but is more pronounced in those phases in which the inverted husband comes in conflict with his socially de-fined role. The following case illustrates this point.

Mr. Baker's attitudes and interests are those his wife would normally possess. He likes to cook and his wife resents his considering himself supe-rior in this respect. Each is jealous of the other when one receives compli-ments for a new dessert. Both clash over one another's activity in beautifying the home. Mrs. Baker feels that she is the one to arrange the flowers for the table when dinner guests are expected, but her husband insists that he should do it because he has more artistic ability. Each complains of the other's em-phasis upon personal appearance. He resents her attractiveness and strongly disapproves of the amount of time she spends on make-up. He really wishes to do the same thing and thus projects his guilt-feelings upon her. When she is ill for a day, he suggests that he carry out her plan to launder some of her clothing; here he reinstates the earlier inverted role in which he washed his baby sisters' clothing. He resents the fact that she does not "play up to him," give him presents occasionally, and defer to his wishes more often; and she says that he never sees himself as the giver of attention and affection in any situation.

A third unifying mechanism for the achievement of marriage unity is emulation, in which one of the marriage partners, because of respect and admiration for certain traits and characteristics of the spouse, strives to re-produce them in himself. The emulated spouse, whose ego is thus flattered and gratified, reacts appreciatively. Out of this interactive appreciation fur-ther unity is developed. The mechanism is seen very often in June-December marriages and in those where there is a rather wide divergence in cultural background. Marriages between student and teacher, businessman and sec-retary, well-established physician and nurse, for example, gain much of their unity through the operation of this mechanism. Although it is undoubtedly true that in some instances the emulation is superficial, it nevertheless is a stabilizing element in the marriage relationship. Much of the unifying effect of emulation, particularly in those marriages in which there is considerable diversity in age, grows out of the fact that the age-gap is bridged by the younger mate's achieving through emulation a maturity comparable to that of the other person.

While emulation occurs only in terms of traits possessed by the marriage partner, idealization, another unifying mechanism, assigns to the spouse traits which he does not possess, at least to the degree to which they are attributed to him. In the past, idealization has been portrayed as one of the hazards of marriage on the ground that while it might function in courtship it ceases to function in marriage and becomes the basis for disillusionment and dissatisfaction. This analysis failed to take into account the possibility that the person idealized might respond by acquiring a closer approximation to the idealized portrait. This unifying character of idealization and its reciprocal response is revealed in the love accommodation of Don and Betty:

> Don has been most important in my personality development through suggestion. By keeping before him a certain ideal of me and by expecting certain things from me he has almost completely remade my personality, much to my advantage. He thinks I am sweet, fastidious, feminine, adorable, etc.; he thinks me happy, optimistic, enthusiastic; he thinks me refined, virtuous, moral, intelligent, "cute," clever, and the possessor of a very sparkling personality. It's been a certain strain, but I've had to live up to all that as best I could and it's changed me remarkably.

The reciprocal response to idealization makes it under some conditions a disunifying factor and under others a unifying one. When the reciprocal response is one of acceptance of the idealized definition without any compensating development, the tendency is eventual disillusionment. Conversely, when the idealized person is stimulated to acquire some semblance of the idealized traits, he becomes more in harmony with the expectations and anticipations of the other person and this results in greater unity. It is difficult to conceive of any marriage being successful without some idealization, just as it is unlikely that a painting in which there is not some accentuation of contrasts in color and line will have wide aesthetic appreciation.

Another element which functions in idealization is the presence of a constellation of satisfying experiences knitted together in an affectional-role relationship in which the parts played by husband and wife are complementary and equally satisfying. These experiences blot out or police the unsatisfactory elements so that only the more gratifying phases remain. These tend to cast an aura of diffused satisfaction, even enchantment, around the mate and the entire marriage experience.

Somewhat allied to idealization is enhancement, in which some interest or trait-complex of one marriage partner culturally unacceptable to the other becomes channeled into a form which has social approval and enhances the status of the individual in the eyes of the spouse. In this way the elements of a pattern which previously made for cultural differentiation becomes so recast as to be highly satisfying to both mates and so elevates the stature of the previously subranked mate both in his own eyes and in those of his partner that the entire marriage becomes overcast with the light of this enhanced status. This mechanism is particularly operative in cases where there is considerable difference in cultural background and experiences which might otherwise be expected to lead to marital conflict.

An illustration is provided by the man who, reared in a rural environment, prefers hunting to "social" affairs, likes to dress casually and to avoid the more formal contacts in life. When he later moves to a city he feels out of place. He is married to a woman who, although reared in a small-town environment, has attended college, traveled abroad, and developed interests quite foreign to her husband's, which have remained oriented essentially in a rural background. In the process of adjustment the husband's hunting interests have been redefined in terms of a gentleman's interests in shooting, frequent hunting trips and rifle tournaments where he often wins prizes. These accomplishments enhance his status in the eyes of his wife, who now likes to buy him sportsman's clothing and tell of his activities, and at the same time provide an acceptable formula of being too busy with these activities to participate in those in which his wife engages. Since the character of his hobby is such as to virtually preclude participation on the part of a woman, a culturally accepted demarcation of their leisure-time interests results. Furthermore, what in the earlier period in marriage symbolized cultural diversity and inferiority now becomes a symbol of cultural identification.

Another important part of the unity of any marriage is that which results from interhabituation. Marriage obviously entails the living together of two persons, and living together means that a host of habitual patterns of response are built up upon which the individuals become dependent. There are among other things the household responsibilities and functions which are shared more or less. The setting of the alarm clock the previous night, turning it off in the morning, the sequence of using the bathroom in the morning, the preparation of breakfast, the retrieving of the morning newspaper from the doorstep, the closing of the garage door, bringing in the milk from the backdoor step, are but a few of the myriad of habitual acts which become established in terms of responsibility and expectancy.

But interhabituation is more than simply a matter of responsibilities and conveniences of the household. Habit patterns also become established in the social intercourse between husband and wife — patterns of expectancy and dependency in regard to when each will be in the other's company, availability for social functions and dining out, as dancing and bridge partners, companion and escort to the theater, etc.

Of even greater significance is the emotional aspect of interhabituation. This covers a wide range of reactions which give rise to interidentifying feelings and emotions: the goodnight and morning kisses, the affectionate pat of assurance and understanding, the sympathetic attentiveness to one's trials and problems no matter how small or great without the bother of a detailed explanation of the situation, the amicable chiding of one's forgetting, the confidential talks, the planning of the campaign to impress the boss, the little white lies to protect the other's ego, all these and more, give impetus toward emotional unity.

This emotional interdependence is supplemented by a variety of symbolic elements, some of which may be slightly irritating in some respects and yet if absent would leave a void. These elements usually are physical objects which symbolize pair or dyadic interaction. Thus the way the pictures are hanging in the home, the arrangement of the furniture, the decorating scheme of the familiar walls, the pieces of bric-a-brac, the little plants stuck here and there, the smoking paraphernalia, the sight of familiar bits of the other's clothing such as a pair of house-slippers with the familiar scuff on the heel sitting in their accustomed spot in the room, the bathrobe with the pockets bulging with Kleenex — all of these call out little pangs of feelings of solidarity, each relatively unimportant alone yet in their totality of considerable import.

Waller seems to have had this phase of marriage adjustment in mind when he speaks of the "dead level of marriage interaction." [7] What he fails to take into account is that these essentially unchanging elements do *not* constitute a dead level, because they are dynamically linked with the experiences of the past in which the marriage pair participated and furnish the little emotional satisfactions and pleasures which somehow seem to join with the planning of new activities and adventures which constitute the warp and woof of everyday living.

Interhabituation also involves the development of habits of sexual experience in which the stimuli and recurrent occasions for intercourse become stabilized. That is, frequency, amount of preliminary sex play, time, setting, etc., follow a recurrent pattern, peculiar to the needs of the particular couple. This habituation of the sexual relationship eventually achieved in every successful marriage stands in sharp contrast to the experimental character of sexual adjustment early in the marriage when sexual episodes tend to take variable forms in which there is often more or less uncertainty and fear of unsatisfactory experience on the part of the other marriage partner or else a careless disregard for these satisfactions. There is probably no other area of marriage in which the ego is more protected from rebuff than in the realm of sexual interaction. Some degree of timidity, insecurity, inhibition, misunderstanding, tension, characterizes the period of early sexual adjustment. Once, however, sexual adjustment has achieved a smooth-running pattern, confidence, feelings of contentment and well-being, mutuality, further identification, replace these earlier disturbing and often frustrating elements.

The most significant character of sexual interhabituation is the degree of mutuality achieved in the gratification of the sexual impulse in which each person is both the giver and the receiver, and deviation from this pattern of mutuality tends to make the sexual relationship unsatisfactory. Once this mutuality is achieved it tends to be diffused into the other realms of the marriage relationship so that it becomes an unconscious unifying influence throughout.

The importance of interhabituation as a mechanism, whether physical, emotional, or sexual, is attested by the fact that even temporary separations between spouses in successful marriages are often unpleasant and disturbing because of the interference with the smooth flow of these patterns. This in large part accounts for the elevation of the emotions in the experiences of reunion even though but a short time has elapsed since separation.

[7] Willard Waller, *The Family,* rev. by Reuben Hill (New York: Dryden Press, 1951), pp. 396–398.

ONE UNIVERSE OF DISCOURSE

With the convergence of marital experiences and the interpenetration of personalities in the marriage, assimilation is the natural process. Assimilation is a continuous process of building up likenesses in attitudes, and many of these likenesses are the precipitates of the operations of the other mechanisms of adjustment. Thus assimilation is both a mechanism and a product of marriage adjustment; that is to say, the process of living together and making adjustment to a diversity of needs and demands tends to precipitate a commonness of these needs and demands so that the diversity is eliminated.

Assimilation in marriage is a process, then, in which husband and wife become more and more nearly identical. But since no two human beings ever are identical, complete identity is never accomplished. Theoretically, the higher the degree of assimilation the higher the degree of marriage unity. But it is inconceivable that assimilation of any two human beings could be complete because no two persons could adjust simultaneously in the same way to the same stimuli.

Assimilation, then, is a relative matter and is tempered by the cultural world in which one lives. Differentiation of the sexes and the necessity of adjusting along sex lines to the world outside marriage alone would hold in check any exaggerated degree of assimilation beyond similarity in ideas, habits, traits, attitudes, mannerisms, appearance, etc.

Nevertheless it is significant that a high degree of identity is achieved in successful marriages. It is a matter of common observation, for example, that many husbands and wives bear a striking physical resemblance to each other, both in physical traits and in mannerisms. That similarity in the latter is at least partly the result of close identity of husband and wife over a period of years cannot be denied. How much of the similarity in the former is due to assimilation is, however, difficult to say until more research is done in the field of mate selection. What appears on the surface as assimilation may not be this at all but simply a perpetuation of traits through what may be called the marital selective process.[8]

More or less identity in physical characteristics and mannerisms, accordingly, is not a reliable index of assimilation. It is rather to similarity in ideas, thinking, feeling, and attitudes that one has to look. In this social-psychological world there develops a continuity of meaning and a universe of discourse which has peculiar significance to the married couple. This universe of discourse finds expression in pet names, unique words and phrases, allusions to past experiences, jokes about one's family, etc. Words take on common connotations, and verbal patterns become similar if not identical in character. Even the trend of thought of the married pair often shows a high degree of identity, and emotional reactions to experiences become similar in character. In fact the old adage that one knows a person by the company he

[8] Cf. A. B. Hollingshead, "Cultural Factors in Selection of Marriage Mates," *American Sociological Review*, 15 (Oct., 1950), pp. 619–627.

keeps can be revamped to say that one comes to know a man by becoming acquainted with his wife.

Some writers on the family seem to be concerned lest too great a degree of identity between husband and wife make for frustrations.[9] In fact, from reading Waller's discussion of marriage adjustment one would conclude that the less husband and wife are identified and the more they escape through lodges, religion, vacations, bridge parties, and dancing (the "opiates" of marriage), the happier the marriage will be. He takes essentially the same view toward marriage that the traditional Freudians took toward social life; namely, that culture imposes barriers to the healthy development of the personality. He considers that the very nature of marriage in our culture imposes inevitable frustrations upon the personality. Psychiatrists, psychologists, sociologists, and other students of human behavior generally agree with this view. On the other hand, we must point out that cultural restrictions determine the character of opportunities for individual development and expression; a counterpart of restrictions is definition of opportunities and direction of behavior into socially sanctioned channels that imply equality of opportunity for the expression of inherent needs and desires. The inference, however, that assimilation or close identity of husband and wife results in frustration in personality is not substantiated by valid systematic research with cases either of adjusted marriages or of marital conflict. Any frustration growing out of the marriage relationship is in itself an index of the absence of assimilation.

Clinical study of domestic discord cases by the writer reveals that it is the *barriers* to assimilation which produce personality frustration, and as a consequence frustrations characterize cases of marital conflict. Furthermore, it is of fundamental significance that these frustrations seldom are a product of the marriage but are only accumulated results of early psychocultural-genetic influences which have already channeled the personality into unsatisfying modes of response. Study of adjusted marriages also bears out these findings.

Criticism of marriage and rebellion against one's own marriage are all too often employed by individuals whose personalities have never been adjusted and therefore cannot complement any other personality in the intimate relationship of marriage. Others have never attained emotional maturity and find in their marriage conflicts a rationalization for retarded development. These persons want the security which marriage offers them and yet wish to retain the freedom and independence from responsibility which they have experienced as single persons. The critics, both professional and lay, fail to take into account the fact that the development of a single universe of discourse does not mean that there is no difference of opinion, no flexibility of behavior, no individuality of response, between well-adjusted marriage partners; it means, rather, that these differences are bridged by the mutually developed attitudes, wishes, and satisfactions which provide a groundwork for the expression of differential elements.

9 Waller, *op. cit.*, pp. 339, 421, 440–441, 565, etc.

Some Alleged Factors in Marital Adjustment

Marriage adjustment, functioning through the mechanisms already described, involves the operation of a considerable number of factors, many of which have been analyzed in recent studies. How these factors operate and the relationship of one to another constitutes the crux of the problem of why some marriages succeed and others fail. What are these studies and how well do they answer this fundamental question?

A number of studies, predominantly of a statistical nature, have been made of the factors which make for or against success in marriage. Katharine B. Davis, using the anonymous questionnaire method, in a study of one thousand married women found that when the wife was healthy at the time of marriage, had had no petting or sex relations before marriage, and had had more than a high school education, her happiness in marriage was greatest.[10]

G. V. Hamilton, combining the questionnaire and the interview, studied a group of two hundred married persons, of whom fifty-five were married mates. What he reported as significant for marital success was: the wife physically resembles the husband's mother, has a brother or brothers, has had no sexual intercourse prior to marriage, and both husband and wife have had equal education.[11]

Clifford Kirkpatrick, in a study of the factors in marital adjustment, found that no greater intimacy of the wife with one parent than the other makes for better adjustment on her part and that the husband is happier when he has had no excess or deficiency of women friends before marriage.[12]

Burgess and Cottrell, whose findings were discussed at some length in Chapter Eight, have made an extensive statistical study, having distributed about 7000 questionnaires, of which 1300 returns yielded an analysis of 526 couples, largely from the Chicago area, who had been married from one to six years.[13] No premarital items regarding the sexual factor in marriage adjustment were secured, the researchers deciding to concentrate upon the economic and social aspects of marriage. While some case studies were secured on the sexual factor, there were no statistical data on sex comparable to those on the other factors. In the writer's estimation, this omission detracts from the comprehensiveness of the study and makes for contradictions in the frame of reference.

Terman's subjects in a similar study comprised 1250 couples, of which 792 couples were included in the main experimental group.[14] They were all Californians, three fourths belonged to the business class, the median income was

---

[10] Katharine B. Davis, *Factors in the Sex Life of Twenty-Two Hundred Women* (New York: Harper, 1929).

[11] G. V. Hamilton, *A Research in Marriage* (New York: Boni, 1929).

[12] Clifford Kirkpatrick, "Factors in Marital Adjustment," *American Journal of Sociology*, 43, (1937), pp. 270–283.

[13] E. W. Burgess and Leonard S. Cottrell, Jr., *Predicting Success or Failure in Marriage* (New York: Prentice-Hall, 1939).

[14] Lewis M. Terman, *Psychological Factors in Marital Happiness* (New York: McGraw-Hill, 1938).

about $2300, and about 43 per cent were college graduates. The average length of marriage was 11.4 years, with 12 per cent married more than 20 years and 32 per cent childless. Terman used a seven-point classification: extraordinarily happy, decidedly more happy than average, somewhat more happy than average, about average, somewhat less happy than average, decidedly less happy than average, and extremely unhappy.

Both of these studies used happiness as one criterion of success. The criticism may be raised as to the use of such a criterion: Is happiness a reliable measure of successful marriage? Happiness is so elusive and subjective that some more objective measure should be found. What is happiness to one individual may not be to another, and what is happiness to one couple may not be happiness to another.

Happiness ratings, the authors themselves say, while fairly reliable as a report of the state of feeling of the person toward his marriage, only partially indicate the nature of adjustment in marriage. Thus certain questions were asked which were thought to be indicative of the presence or absence of adjustment; these concerned such points as agreements and disagreements, common interests and activities, demonstration of affection, confiding, satisfaction and dissatisfaction, and feelings of unhappiness. Each question in turn was broken down into a number of subquestions which were taken to measure the extent of the state of interaction and this in turn was taken to indicate the presence or absence of adjustment. For example, the authors considered the most important matters in the first category of agreements and disagreements to be (1) handling family finances, (2) recreation, (3) religion, (4) demonstration of affection, (5) friends, (6) intimate relations, (7) caring for the baby, (8) table manners, (9) conventionality, (10) philosophy of life, and (11) ways of dealing with in-laws. The married person filling out the schedule was asked to check the extent of agreement or disagreement in terms of "always agree," "almost always agree," "occasionally disagree," "frequently disagree," "almost always disagree," and "always disagree." [15] What do these questions actually measure? Do they measure anything more than overt processes in marriage interaction but still leave untouched the covert processes?

BACKGROUND FACTORS

Both the studies of Terman and those of Burgess and Cottrell reveal a host of factors in the family background of husband and wife during their childhood and the period prior to marriage which are thought to influence marital happiness. The finding of a high correlation of marital adjustment with similarity in family cultural background, which would include religious affiliation, seems inconsistent with findings that wide differences in religious affiliation show no relation to marital adjustment. It might be argued that since the couples studied had only been married six years, religious conflicts might not arise until after that time in connection with the religious training of the children. But it is not known how many of these

[15] Burgess and Cottrell, *op. cit.*, pp. 45-49.

couples had children. Furthermore this argument is contrary to what is shown by case studies of cultural conflict in marriage. These show that conflict is likely to emerge in relation to the birth of a child and the selection of the type of baptismal ceremony. One does not know the length of marriage of the couples in relation to the birth of the first child. According to the United States census figures for 1940, the median age of a mother bearing her first child was 22.6 or one year after marriage. How closely the two groups approximate each other is not known.

Knowing what we do about assimilation and marital adjustment, one would assume that a marriage rated happy had a high degree of assimilation, and therefore it is unlikely that conflict because of wide divergence of religious affiliation would arise after six years of marriage if enough assimilation had taken place to cause the couple to rate their marriage as reasonably successful (see also our discussion in the chapter on religion in family life, pp. 608–611). Should conflict arise in this realm at this late date, it would only be a rationalization of other conflicts.

The order of birth was another factor which was taken as showing some significance in marital happiness. Thus it was found by Burgess and Cottrell that a husband not an only child was more favorable to marital happiness; and if an only or youngest married an only or youngest, this constituted the most unfavorable combination. A combination of only and oldest was more favorable than only and youngest, but combinations of oldest with oldest and middle with middle were favorable. Terman's study showed that if the wife were not an only child the marriage had a better chance of happiness.

What effect ordinal position has upon familial interaction is not entirely clear.[16] It has been portrayed by some writers as significant in marital conflict and also in types of personality disorganization,[17] while other writers have attached no significance to it. It would seem that ordinal position is of little or no significance except as it may be a factor in determining role, and in this connection one must take into consideration the meaning which any given ordinal position has in the particular culture in which one lives and in the family tradition in which he is born. Thus any child in a family may have a role which is typically that of the only child or youngest child. *Role,* then, is significant rather than ordinal position, and the meaning of this role in the particular family pattern.

Furthermore, a particular type of escape response, or so-called neurotic behavior, is associated with many early psychogenetic factors, one of which, study of these cases reveals, is the role of youngest in the family. This role, along with the interplay of other factors, produces a unique behavior pattern which impedes, if it does not make impossible, adjustment in marriage. Thus ordinal position in itself is of little or no significance.

[16] Cf. Robert R. Sears, "Ordinal Position in the Family as a Psychological Variable," *American Sociological Review,* 15 (Jan., 1950), pp. 397–401.

[17] Harriet R. Mowrer, "Alcoholism and the Family," *Journal of Criminal Psychopathology,* 3, (1941), pp. 90–99.

ROMANCE AND SEXUAL FACTORS

The nature of the affectional relationship between husband and wife as indicated by the difference in age, duration of the acquaintance, length of the engagement, approval or disapproval of parents, is another realm which has been explored by marital research. It is assumed that there is a relationship between short engagements and so-called romantic love, longer engagements and companionship. An acquaintance of two or more years, the husband older by one to three years or the same age as the wife, an engagement of nine months or more, the approval of the marriage by both parents, were all found to be favorable factors and thought to be indicative of a marriage of companionship as opposed to a marriage based upon romantic love. Romantic love, sex attraction, companionship, rapport, sympathetic understanding, idealization, are so interwoven that it is difficult to separate the components; most marriages have both romantic love and companionship regardless of their success or failure.

Romantic love, it would seem, needs to be redefined in terms of changing mores and a redefinition of the present-day relationship between the sexes. The late Dorothy Dix, who for thirty years conducted an "advice to the lovelorn" daily column, once commented that thirty years ago she received letters inquiring whether it was proper for a girl to help a young gentleman on with his coat; now she receives inquiries as to whether it is proper to go on week-end trips with one's boy friend.

The significance of longer engagements for marital adjustment lies in the fact that since the engagement period is one of initial accommodation, a time sufficiently long to permit these accommodations to take place would make for greater success in marriage (Kuhn's development of this point earlier warrants reviewing). This period would vary considerably from one individual couple to another, depending upon the geographical and psychosocial distance between the pair. Face-to-face contacts would allow for greater possibilities of accommodation than those maintained by letter writing; some personalities are easier to penetrate than others, and some have a greater facility in penetration. It is conceivable, however, that engagements can be of such long duration as to produce loss of interest or apathetic acceptance of the courtship situation as final, but this would depend upon circumstances involved in the particular engagement situation. Seven years, for example, might ordinarily be considered to be in this category; yet in the following case this period seems to have been an asset in later marriage adjustment.

I feel safe in predicting that our union could withstand a separation if that becomes necessary (war). This prediction is based on a rather lengthy courtship. I "went with" my wife off and on for seven years. The off period (in one instance stretching over two years) was caused by various feelings of jealousy and a notion that other pastures are greener, of aversion to settling down too early. Our courtship was fortunately far from serene. We had differences. Now after ten years of having tried both ways, there is still greater contentment living together than apart. There are no serious areas of discord, no wide diversity, and no budding frustration. Family living demands constant adjustment and on past performance my wife seems as eager as I am to make these adjustments intelligently. I feel that we're both emotionally mature enough to make our marriage work.

The sex factor in marriage success has also been statistically investigated. For the most part this research has dealt more with the physical than with the social-psychological aspects. Thus Kinsey's 1948 research, although not a study of sex factors in marriage, deals only with discrete elements of male sexual behavior, their frequency and distribution, and throws little light upon how sex functions in either a social or marital interactional context. The value of the study lies in its revealing contemporary sexual practices which may indirectly affect marital success.[18]

Terman, after examining the returns from husbands and wives upon a mass of sexual items, concludes that only two factors are statistically significant as determiners of marital happiness. These are the relative equality of the sex drives in both spouses and the wife's capacity for orgasm. Factors dealing primarily with the mechanics of the sex act and of the functioning of the sex drive, such as frequency of intercourse, method of contraception, fear of pregnancy, showed little or no correlation with happiness.

These items are significant only as they become transmuted into attitudes toward the sex act, which facilitate or impede sexual satisfaction and happiness in marriage. Whether or not they become carriers or transmitters of accord or discord will to a large degree depend upon the experiences past and future of the husband and wife which define and redefine their meanings to them in the total relationship. Thus it is the capacity to give and receive sexual satisfaction which makes for marital happiness. The giving and receiving of satisfaction implies a mutual satisfaction in which both husband and wife play complementary and interdependent sexual roles.

That the mechanics of sexual intercourse have been overemphasized and the attitudes toward sexual experience neglected by hygienists in the past, there is no doubt. On the other hand, studies which isolate the functioning of sex as a biological urge (a product of chemistry in the organism) and yet contradictorily seek to study it in a concrete personal relationship such as marriage, fall into the same methodological error. That is to say that as a factor in the marriage situation sex cannot be differentiated in its physiological aspects but must always be studied in the light of its dynamic functioning in a socio-psycho-cultural framework. The physiological impulse becomes overlaid with social experiences, expressing itself in demonstration of affection and love, mutual identification and sympathy and companionship as well as in the release of physiological tensions. Sex in general takes on its meaning from the culture in which the individual lives; a culture in which sex is characterized by many conflicting values and notions, superstitions, romantic ideas, inhibitions, guilt feelings, etc. The meaning of sex to the individual, then, is the result of the orientation of his personal feelings, im-

18 A. C. Kinsey, W. B. Pomeroy, and C. E. Martin, *Sexual Behavior in the Human Male* (Philadelphia: Saunders, 1948).

pulses, experiences, attitudes, and wishes within this cultural maze. In marriage one sees the final orientation of this sexual definition and its functioning in relation to another individual. Thus the details of the sexual pattern achieved in marriage vary widely between couples even in the same cultural and social group. The crux of the relationship of the sexual pattern to happy and unhappy marriages lies in the degree of satisfaction which this pattern furnishes to the particular couple involved.

Terman concluded that all the sex factors combined are far from being the one major determinant of success in marriage. These findings are in agreement with those of other studies which demonstrate that sex cannot be considered the basic factor any more than any other of the factors which make up either the adjustment or the conflict pattern.[19] Furthermore, the sexual behavior, as has been pointed out, is so interwined with other aspects of the personality as to make it impossible to divide one from the other. Because of the symbolic nature of marriage behavior one phase becomes both a mirror and a reflection of each of the other phases of the total configuration. What is of more fundamental importance, then, is the total configuration.

SOCIAL AND PERSONALITY CHARACTERISTICS

Certain social characteristics were found to distinguish the happy spouses from the unhappy. These characteristics were taken to represent the degree and character of socialization of the individual. Thus the husband's age, 22 to 30, at marriage, and the wife's, 22 and over, were found by Burgess and Cottrell to make for happy marriage. Terman found it to be husband 22 years and over, and wife 20 and over. Other characteristics were that the husband was older than the wife; that the church attendance of the husband before marriage was two or more times a month, and of the wife four times a month; that both attended Sunday school through adolescence; that the wedding was held in church, in a parsonage, or at home.

Church attendance and affiliation before marriage is taken by Burgess and Cottrell and by Locke as one of the indexes of sociability. The question may be raised as to whether this is true and, if so, how it functions in marital happiness. In this connection, Locke has reported on a study of marital adjustment carried on for five years in Monroe County, Indiana, in which he compared a divorced group and a happily married group.[20] He took two extremes — the divorced (names secured from the courthouse divorce files) and the most happily married (known by a random sample of married persons).

He concluded that affiliation with a church is probably a mark of a sociable personality and is highly associated with marital adjustment; conversely, not belonging to a church is unquestionably associated with unad-

---

[19] Harriet R. Mowrer, *Personality Adjustment and Domestic Discord* (New York: American Book Co., 1936), pp. 149–190; "Sex as a Factor in Domestic Discord," *American Sociological Review*, 1 (Apr., 1936), pp. 252–263.

[20] Harvey J. Locke, *Predicting Adjustment in Marriage* (New York: Henry Holt, 1951).

justment. Furthermore, the later the age at which attendance at Sunday school is stopped, the greater the chances of marital success. For men, going to church through the age of ten is clearly significant for marital adjustment, whereas women have to continue through the age period of 11 to 14 before a clearly significant difference between the happily married and the divorced groups appears. The happily married attended church much more frequently than did the divorced. These findings raise a number of questions which throw contradictory light upon the way in which church attendance becomes a factor in marriage happiness. In the writer's experience with domestic discord cases there have been found few, if any, couples who have not been affiliated with a church. In a considerable proportion, in fact, attendance continued much later than for Locke's couples, so that this attendance should have made for even greater chances of marital happiness than in his cases. How can one explain this apparent contradiction? It might be said that some of these domestic discord cases belonged to a cultural group in which church attendance was a routine and conventionalized experience rather than a mark of a sociable personality. But one might question how much church attendance up to the age of ten is a mark of sociable personality rather than a conventionalized experience. It would seem that in both groups it is rather an index of the functioning of primary-group controls, particularly those of the family. Children go to church because of the direction and pressure of their parents; and when these pressures break down and become diffused, attendance often is less frequent. That girls have to go longer than boys would bear out this interpretation since family controls usually are exerted for a longer period over girls than over boys.

Furthermore Locke is probably dealing with a cultural group (rural and small town) in which primary-group controls operate much more effectively than in urban areas. In some cultural groups church affiliation is so much the accepted pattern that absence of it would set the individual apart from the group as being different and having questionable standards of conduct. His happiness or unhappiness in general would be a reflection of his demarcation from his fellow group-members, which in turn would be reflected in his marriage. This may be what Locke has in mind as a measure of sociability, since the socialized person is more of a conformist. On the other hand, since he is a conformist and a believer in conventional behavior, he would probably be more likely to give his own marriage a higher rating.

Not only certain social characteristics but personality attributes as well have been found to differentiate the happy spouses from the unhappy. Happy wives have been found to be serene, self-confident, benevolent, contented, thrifty, conservative, and interested in "uplift." In contrast, unhappy wives are defensive, escapists (active), critical, romantic, unmethodical, radical, and have neurotic tendencies. Likewise happy husbands have self-confidence, are conciliatory and cooperative, dynamic, benevolent, methodical, and, like the happy wives, conservative. Unhappy husbands are defensive and domineering, passive, escapists (fantasy), unmethodical, and, like the unhappy wives, radical.[21]

[21] Terman, op. cit., pp. 145-164.

Such isolated traits of personality assumed and arrived at through standardized tests and inventories, while suggestive, are highly limited, and their relationship to marital happiness should be accepted with marked caution. At best they are not combinations of traits but elements independently calculated for husband and wife. Since marriage, as has been seen, is an interactional situation, it is the *combination* of traits which is of significance. Furthermore, a trait analysis of personality is static and sterile in that it leaves out of account the organic relationship between traits, and the dynamics of personality development. When the framework in which these traits are supposed to operate is the dynamic interactional marital relationship of husband and wife, then such a static conception is meaningless. The social psychology of marital adjustment is concerned with personality patterns rather than isolated traits and with marital adjustment patterns rather than with isolated and disconnected marital factors. What is significant, then, is the personality in its totality; that is, the whole of the life experiences of the individual considered as a unity rooted in the past and penetrating into the future. It is the functioning of such personality in an intimate interactional relationship with another personality. The fundamental question is: what are the unique patterns of experience which constitute the personality and how do these become dynamically transmitted into those marital configurations which spell the difference between success and failure in marriage?

PROBLEMS OF MARITAL THERAPEUTICS

Trait analysis, whether in application to personality, marriage, or any other field of social interaction, has its limitations as well as advantages. Its chief limitation is that it fails to give a functional and dynamic portrait of the individuals who are successful in marriage; that is, it fails to translate traits and factors into mechanisms of marriage adjustment and describe *how* they operate in a given marriage situation. It is only by inference that they take on significance, and this inference is dependent upon one's particular frame of reference. These segmental items, if taken out of the frame of reference in which they have been placed by their authors, are subject to misuse and misconceptions.

To these marital adjustment studies of the past decade, the student of the family is indebted for clarifying the areas of importance in marital interaction and putting them in a meaningful socio-psycho-cultural framework. Furthermore, the complexity of the data with which one must deal, the handicaps and problems of marital research, the limitations of existing techniques, the tentativeness of social norms and findings — all these are vividly telescoped in these studies. The recognition of these limitations should serve as a flashlight to further research and to counseling and educational programs for marriage success.

As we now generally recognize, one has to look to research for the ultimate control of phenomena, whether physical or social. Just as so-called "cures" in medicine have to wait and go hand in hand with research findings, so the "cures" and "preventives" of marital failures have to await the more valid findings of marital research. As in medicine, the popular mind, overanxious for "cures," is likely to grasp any findings too quickly, too superficially and assign to them meanings and potentialities that were never intended. Likewise it is for the researcher, the clinician, and other students of human behavior to interpret and apply the findings; not for the popularizer to advocate them to the public as a play instrument in the crossword puzzle style.

The neophyte, when confronted with research findings in marital adjustment such as those which deal with a mass of items which can easily be placed in a nontechnical framework, is often inclined to believe that there is only one interpretation of them and so either to accept each item uncritically or to rebel against it. The items or factors are taken individually and pigeonholed into the "right" answers or the "wrong" answers, as proved by research, as a guide to marital happiness. Unfortunately one is likely to be inclined toward that "right" or "wrong" answer which most advantageously suits one's own situation at the moment and which may in many instances become the psychological prop for rationalizations for standards of conduct, ways of behavior, important decisions, etc. Such misconceptions are counteracted only by careful analysis of these factors in the light of a consistent and coordinate theory of marriage such as has been described in this chapter.

What light in general does research throw upon the problem of successful preparation for marriage? Fundamentally, as has been seen, marriage is not a separate and isolated situation calling for a peculiar set of adjustment techniques which can be learned shortly before the wedding. Marriage is another highly important life situation which calls for the same general adjustment techniques which are workable, satisfactory, and satisfying in other life situations.

Education for marriage, then, starts in the early years of childhood: the role of the child in the family — his relationship with his parents, brothers, and sisters — his early attachments, his early sex education, his relationship to the community, his adolescent development and emancipation from family domination, his early love affairs, his sex habits and attitudes, are some of the more important factors which determine his personality and his marriage adjustment. If these factors are such as to impede adjustment, then they can hardly be modified in a short period before the marriage by learning the mechanics of sexual relations, by being given a physical examination, by learning how to budget an income, or through instruction in the "right" attitude toward marriage. All of these may serve some useful function but have little fundamental connection with the mechanisms of marriage adjustment and when used as such becloud the need for more thoroughgoing therapeutics.

The inadequacy of so much of what currently passes as programs of preparation for marriage is in what they do *not* emphasize rather than in what they *do* emphasize. What they do emphasize is more likely to reach and influence those who would make an adjustment anyway, and leave untouched the more important and complex aspects for those who will not be able to make an adjustment without counseling and clinical assistance.

Specifically, the type of earlier sex experience and attitudes toward sex are a part of the personality pattern (not apart from it) and are more fundamental than the knowledge at the time of marriage of the techniques of sexual intercourse. Likewise, a reasonable similarity of ideals, standards of conduct, customs, attitudes toward the economic role of husband and wife, etc., is much more important than the *details* of budget making. Furthermore, a mastery of the mechanisms of adaptability, the ability to meet situations temporarily unpleasant, is more important than uncovering the details of the eccentricity of a distant relative. That is to say, *attitudes* are more important than *mechanics*. Attitudes, because they are highly involved and symbolically interrelated, are slow to change; techniques can be learned quickly and easily.

In other words, preparation for marriage from an educational standpoint is a part of the larger pattern of preparation for life. Instruction, therefore, may well be integrated into the general educational program, the nature of this instruction being determined by the available knowledge, checked and tested, of the factors which make for or against marital success. Since research has shown that primary in the causation of marital conflict are the influences which result in personality maladjustment, educational efforts need to be in the direction of facilitating the development of adjusted personalities. So far as marriage entails the introduction of persons to problems fundamentally like and yet somewhat different from those outside marriage, attention may be directed to these, yet never isolated from the larger educational program.

Medical therapeutics has gone through these stages of development. In the first stage the therapist treated the symptoms of disease; in the second, the disease itself; and at the present time, the patient as well as the disease. Much of marital therapeutics is still in the symptoms stage. As research and therapy converge toward the further understanding and treatment of the functioning personality in the marriage configuration so will they advance the science and art of marital adjustment.

SELECTED READINGS

BOSSARD, JAMES H., and BOLL, ELEANOR S., *Ritual in Family Living* (Philadelphia: University of Pennsylvania Press, 1950).

BURGESS, ERNEST W., and COTTRELL, LEONARD S., JR., *Predicting Success or Failure in Marriage* (New York: Prentice-Hall, 1939), chap. 2.

———, and WALLIN, PAUL, *Engagement and Marriage* (Philadelphia: J. B. Lippincott Co., 1953).

FLÜGEL, J. C., *The Psychoanalytic Study of the Family* (4th ed., London: Hogarth, 1931).

FORD, CLELLAN S., and BEACH, FRANK A., *Patterns of Sexual Behavior* (New York: Harper and Brothers, 1951).

HOLLINGSHEAD, A. B., "Cultural Factors in Selection of Marriage Mates," *American Sociological Review,* 15 (October, 1950), pp. 619–627.

KINSEY, A. C., POMEROY, W. B., and MARTIN, C. E., *Sexual Behavior in the Human Male* (Philadelphia: Saunders, 1948).

LOCKE, HARVEY J., *Predicting Adjustment in Marriage: A Comparison of a Divorced and a Happily Married Group* (New York: Henry Holt and Co., 1951).

LU, YI-CHUANG, "Marital Roles and Marriage Adjustment," *Sociology and Social Research*, 36 (July–August, 1952), pp. 364–368.

MERRILL, F. E., *Courtship and Marriage* (New York: Sloane, 1949).

MOWRER, ERNEST R., *The Family* (Chicago: University of Chicago Press, 1932).

——, and MOWRER, HARRIET, "The Social Psychology of Marriage," *American Sociological Review*, 16 (February, 1951), pp. 27–37.

MOWRER, HARRIET R., *Personality Adjustment and Domestic Discord* (New York: American Book Co., 1935).

SEARS, ROBERT R., "Ordinal Position in the Family as a Psychological Variable," *American Sociological Review*, 15 (June, 1950), pp. 397–401.

TERMAN, LEWIS M., and associates, *Psychological Factors in Marital Happiness* (New York: McGraw-Hill, 1938).

WINCH, ROBERT F., "Further Data and Observations on the Oedipus Hypothesis," *American Sociological Review*, 16 (December, 1951), pp. 784–795.

TOPICS FOR DISCUSSION OR REPORTS

1. Show how the early affectional relationship before marriage makes for or against later marital adjustment.

2. How would you define "average" marital happiness? In what ways would the understanding of this group contribute to an understanding of success in marriage?

3. Analyze three married couples with whom you are familiar distributed in the following classes: "average" happiness, on the verge of divorce, and "very happy." What is the essential nature of the adjustment patterns in each? What are the similarities and differences in these patterns? What is your conclusion as to what differentiates them in degrees of adjustment?

4. What are some of the mechanisms of marital adjustment? Can you show how they operate in a given case with which you are familiar?

5. Note the physical characteristics and mannerisms of fifteen or twenty pairs of spouses with whom you are familiar which are similar. What is your explanation of these similarities?

6. Distinguish between traits and patterns of behavior. In what way is this distinction of importance to an understanding of marital adjustment?

7. List the accommodations made by engaged couples which you have observed. In what way do you think these should facilitate marital adjustment?

8. Analyze your "love affairs" as objectively as you can and as far back as you can remember with a view toward evaluating each relationship in terms of what each contributed to your progress toward affectional maturity.

9. Compare the ideas of romantic love of your own generation with those of your parents' generation.

10. In what ways can "education for marriage" be built upon a foundation of marital research? What would such a program include?

Chapter Twelve

Discords in Marriage

HARRIET R. MOWRER

VARIOUS hypotheses as to the factors making for conflict in marriage have been devised, but a good many of them have proved to be misleading. It was often said that low economic status engenders marriage conflict while high economic status makes for stability. It is now generally agreed that the economic factor as an index of cultural level is of no significance in marital stability and that concepts of what the economic factor really is should be viewed in a broader sociological context than was formerly customary.

Another factor frequently mentioned is that of children. According to data available for 1948, nearly three fifths of divorces were granted to childless couples. But since the peak of the divorce rate was between two and three years of marriage, this is of little significance.[1] As has been said, about all divorce data yield by way of generalization as to children and marital discord is that the longer couples are married, the less likely they are to get divorces and the more likely to have or have had children.[2]

In a recent study of the marital adjustments of a group of college couples, relationship between family size and marital adjustment was found to be a negative one, herein agreeing with the research of earlier writers.[3] Furthermore, according to Jacobson, divorce has increased more rapidly among families with children than among childless couples. Yet it would be quite as illogical to conclude on this basis that children cause divorce as it was previously to cite childlessness as a cause.

Sex adjustment is frequently singled out for discussion with reference to marriage adjustment. Some hold the view that sex is the chief factor, overshadowing all others. Others maintain that sex is of little or no importance, sexual adjustments being achieved spontaneously if the partners are otherwise well mated. Here again, both the clinical and test evidence show that, while sex is important in the marriage relationship, sexual conflict is but one of a combination of causes of marital unhappiness and is not a significant determinant of marriage conflict.

Selection of a particular factor as "fundamental" usually is emotional rather than scientific. Emotional outlooks on marriage tend either to simplify the relation, furnishing only a common-sense approach, or so to color the analysis as to make pessimism the keynote. Thus marital conflict is, on

[1] Paul H. Jacobson, "Differentials in Divorce by Duration of Marriage and Size of Family," *American Sociological Review,* 15 (April, 1950), pp. 235–244.

[2] Ernest R. Mowrer, *Disorganization, Personal and Social* (Philadelphia: J. B. Lippincott Co., 1942), p. 492.

[3] Cf. Reuben Hill, *Families Under Stress* (New York: Harper and Brothers, 1949), pp. 126–128; Ernest R. Mowrer and Harriet R. Mowrer, *Domestic Discord* (Chicago: University of Chicago Press, 1928); H. T. Christensen and R. E. Philbrick, "Family Size and Marital Adjustment," *American Sociological Review,* 17 (June, 1952), pp. 306–312.

the one hand, regarded as the result of a single factor, or on the other, of marriage itself, since "after the honeymoon must come disillusionment and the inevitable first year of conflict," and so on. By the first group therapy is accordingly assumed to be very simple. Families will be more stable if they have children, or more children, or a certain number of children; or marital conflict would disappear if families had larger incomes, or were taught the mechanics of sex adjustment. The second group, however, is opposed to therapy on the ground that it helps keep persons married, whereas their egos would be more healthy if they were separated.

Careful students of the family, however, have increasingly come to approach the subject scientifically. They emphasize *research* into causes of marriage conflict or accord. Here the approach is directed toward an understanding of a general phase of social adjustment, rather than a particular case, a particular factor, or a particular social group. Here it is assumed that only after careful, unbiased studies of many cases (or at least of many recurrent phenomena) can we arrive at a predictive understanding of marriage conflict. Therapy, then, becomes a complicated procedure which must be based upon and be consistent with the research findings (even though prevalent norms always control the therapeutic objective).

The Nature of Marriage Conflict

Marriage conflict can therefore be analyzed into a multiplicity of factors. None of these factors, however, can be regarded as isolated. In fact, they get their significance out of their linkage and typical patterning. Hence we refer to the marriage-conflict *pattern,* and it is with the understanding of this pattern that we are concerned.

Of first significance in this patterning of factors are the personality organizations of the husband and the wife. Statistical studies, case analyses, and clinical treatment of unsuccessful marriages or cases of domestic discord reveal that what makes for or against conflict in marriage is not confined to the factors within the marriage relation as narrowly construed, but also includes elements in the life experiences of the partners. Of prime importance, therefore, are the total life-organizations of the individuals concerned.

Some persons are better able than others to meet the series of situations which marriage initiates because they have already developed a life-organization which provides them with workable adjustment practices. The individual attempts to adjust himself to the demands of marriage in the same way as he has adjusted to previous crisis situations; if these practices are ill adapted to the special problems of marriage, conflict is inevitable. Typical sets of conditions are of course found in every marriage, but these are often dwarfed by persistent personality trends which developed outside the marriage situation.

If, for example, a woman has met every crisis prior to her marriage with the escape mechanism of feigned "illness," she will probably meet the first problem marriage presents in the same way. Again, if a husband has attempted to meet critical situations outside and prior to marriage by excessive drinking, it is likely that he will carry over the same escape technique into his marriage. Once more, if a man up until his marriage has not become accustomed to handling conflicts rationally, he is likely to meet with all sorts of difficulties. He will be in a state of continual conflict, vacillating between contradictory courses of behavior and unable to decide upon either. The clinician often sees this type of man dependent in marriage upon two women; he is unable to give up either because he cannot decide which he prefers.

Merely to say, however, that the individual carries over into marriage the same practices used in meeting past crises is not enough. More fundamental for the student of the family are questions of this order: How do these persistent personality trends and practices develop? It is usually to a peculiar set of family circumstances that the researcher must look. This is not surprising; in the family group the child plays his earliest roles, and there likewise he first achieves status and becomes a person. The role of the child in the family may consequently be expected to have a far-reaching effect on the life-organization of the adult.

Suppose we analyze the family background of the wife who makes exaggerated complaints of "illness" for which there are no physical findings. She is actually in good health, but shows little interest in her children and home, complains that she is "too tired" to go out socially with her husband, etc. What typical set of early family circumstances is found where this type of escape-response pattern occurs? It is most frequently that in which the wife was the youngest child or had the role of the youngest.[4] In modern American society, the youngest child, regardless of sex, tends to be assigned the dominant role. Why? Because the emotional interdependence between the parents and the last-born is allowed to continue without the inevitable break occasioned by the birth of another child.

Frailty was found to be another factor in the development of this escape mechanism. Because of an appearance of frailty, the child may be excused from small unpleasant tasks in which other members of the family engage. The lesson therefore is soon learned: lack of robustness is an asset in getting special consideration. In spite of the fact that his physical condition may show decided improvement, the child may thereafter find it advantageous to pretend illness and incapacity in order to secure the desired coddling.

The pampered child is not always able to carry over his superior family position into his nonfamily relations. Society demands that he grow up emotionally and assume adult responsibilities. Oftentimes he seeks escape from this society-defined role and struggles to retain his earlier family-defined role. One situation after another elicits an escape response until this type of reaction becomes habitual; in every conflict situation he seeks escape from the distasteful elements. In other words, his pampered-child role, forbidden direct expression, continues through the device of illness.[5]

For the person who has evaded every hard problem with an escape mechanism, marriage is the most difficult situation with which he has yet

[4] Harriet R. Mowrer, *Personality Adjustment and Domestic Discord* (New York: American Book Co., 1935), pp. 88–108.
[5] *Ibid.*

had to deal. Among women this is aggravated in many cases by the fact that the marriage itself has been used as a means of escape from an experience which at the time seemed unbearable, such as an unsuccessful love affair or a tiresome job. Marriage thus becomes a crisis situation for which the only available remedy is the escape response. Sex conflict usually develops early in the marriage, since semi-ascetic attitudes toward sex on the part of the wife are often consistent with her pampered role. Where sex has received much attention, only the romantic aspect of the relationship has been attractive. Motherhood may further complicate matters; for example, the child may receive a great deal of attention from the husband; consequently, the wife may feel herself in competition with her own child. In these situations the wife looks about for some escape from the marriage which seems so unpleasant to her in all its aspects. Sickness furnishes the escape; it enables her to reinstate her early family role in a socially approved way. She can maintain the position of wife and mother, and yet be excused from unpleasant responsibilities by playing the role of the "invalid."

This, however, makes for typical conflicts in every realm of the marriage relation. The husband, in such cases, at first usually believes his wife to be genuinely ill, but after repeated visits to numerous physicians he becomes skeptical and less attentive, or even neglectful. Economic conflict often develops out of a succession of doctors' bills. Sex conflict has already been mentioned, but in these cases it takes on a broader meaning and becomes symbolized in a lack of sympathy and understanding, disruption of affection, and loss of identification of interests. This is technically spoken of as a conflict in response relations. Such conflict may develop further: jealousy of the husband's attention to the children or to a member of his family often appears. Cultural conflict results in the husband and wife rarely going to social functions together or engaging in any joint activities. Both then succeed in convincing themselves that their interests never were similar. The wife, becoming more desperate in her attempt to maintain her early role (that of the spoiled child demanding attention and special treatment), may resort to "spells" which disrupt the peace of the household, thereby disorganizing the husband and the children. Thus the observer sees the growth, from childhood through marriage, of many intertwined shoots into a dense marriage-conflict hedge with a definite pattern.

FORMATION OF A PATTERN OF CONFLICT

A second type of marital-conflict pattern, best illustrated by the husband or wife who vacillates in marriage between contradictory courses of behavior and whose personality seems ambiguous and undefined, is characterized by a family background quite different from that typical of the escape response just described. This type can probably best be illustrated by the following briefly summarized case, which is typical in terms of the general pattern:

Outwardly the Allens present a conventional picture of family life. Mr. Allen, a successful professional man, is a graduate of an eastern college. The family owns its own home in an exclusive suburb of a large city. The couple has been married fourteen years and there are two children, both girls. Mrs. Allen belongs to a woman's club, Mr. Allen to various professional and social clubs. When the couple came to the family consultant the husband had just moved to his club and the wife's father was living in the home. The wife complained that her allowance was inadequate and, in a highly emotional state, first blamed the father and then the husband for her unhappiness.

Mrs. Allen, an only child, had an inferior family role in relation to her mother. Her role in relation to her father was not clearly defined, the mother being the dominant person in the family. The mother, a beautiful woman proud of her family connections, was prominent in the social activities of many clubs. Mrs. Allen as a child was not especially attractive, and early got the impression that the mother did not want her friends to know that she existed and, therefore, that she must be ashamed of her. The mother would visit the best department store in the city on shopping expeditions, purchasing the most expensive clothing for herself, and would then take her daughter to the basement department, saying to the saleslady in an undertone, "I want something very inexpensive for *her*." When the child complained of feeling lonely, the mother would tell her, "I stayed home four years after you were born and spent the time with you. I am entitled to a good time now." Rarely was she permitted any play with the children of friends of the family, and when the girl set about to find her own companions they were always pointed out by the mother as "inferior" children. Although quite talented in music, she could not perform if her mother came into the room while she was playing.

The child might have accepted her mother's definition of her had she not been treated differently in other roles. An aunt and a grandmother on the paternal side were fond of the child, spoke of her musical ability, and spent some time talking with her. The aunt paid for her music lessons and, as the girl grew older, purchased some of her clothing. Thus at times these two relatives played the role a mother would normally play. At times the girl felt neglected and abused even to the point of hating her mother; at other times, as she put it, she was simply satisfied to be the daughter of such a beautiful woman. She tried tantrums and then running away from home in an attempt to control the situation, with no success.

Out of the contradictory attitudes of the mother and the paternal relatives there developed a conflict or ambiguity in roles which became the dominant note of the girl's personality. She could be neither inferior nor superior for any length of time, for each role was in contradiction to the other. Furthermore, she was always in the paradoxical situation of being dependent emotionally as well as financially upon both her family and her relatives and, never able to choose between them, of always being placed in the position of defending each to the other. As she grew older there were various vocational preferences, but it is interesting to note that she was never able to make a definite choice and actually engage in any work. So far as religious connections are concerned, she ran the gamut of most of the leading Protestant denominations as well as Catholicism, never remaining affiliated for any length of time with a particular group.

Mrs. Allen claims to have been in love with a man whom she wished to marry, but was unable to do so because her mother considered his family inferior. Mr. Allen was discovered by the mother, and although, Mrs. Allen says, she was not in love with him, it was the mother's influence which finally arranged the match.

The mother has since died, bequeathing her personal belongings, including several pieces of valuable jewelry, to a cousin rather than to her daughter. The aunt too has died, leaving two diamond brooches to Mrs. Allen. With these conflicting elements in the early training of Mrs. Allen no longer present, the casual observer might reason that her situation now might be quite improved, but such is not the case. In marriage Mrs. Allen finds herself in the same paradoxical position as in her early family group. After the death of Mrs. Allen's mother, her father went to live in her home. Although there never was any strong attachment between the father and daughter, the father has assumed an extremely important place in the household. One finds Mrs. Allen between a husband who does not entirely support her or give her complete emotional security, and a father who assumes the role of "helping out" — on occasions even taking over the part of the husband. In other words, the husband is symbolically identified with Mrs. Allen's mother; the father with the aunt and grandmother. Mr. Allen complains that he has lost respect for his wife since he has discovered that she is a person who can never make up her mind. He feels that he as the husband and father should have the dominant role in the household; instead, his father-in-law has gradually usurped his place.

How conflict spreads to other realms of the marriage relationship is again well illustrated in this case. Mrs. Allen, on the advice of her father and unknown to the husband, used money from her allowance to speculate in the stock market, buying stock on margin. She was caught in the crash, and since that time Mr. Allen has scrutinized expenditures and refused his wife access to the checkbook. There have been constant bickerings over financial matters. A great attachment has developed between Mrs. Allen's father and the older girl, the child scarcely noticing Mr. Allen. This only further antagonizes him, inasmuch as his wife has done nothing to remedy the situation although she has taken cognizance of it.

Mr. Allen's behavior in the home as described by the father is interesting and highly significant: "At first there never were any quarrels. Then I started noticing how he acted at the table in the morning. It was not the things he would say to me; none of it was directed to me. It was the way he would snap about the way the table was set. He would say to the maid, 'Can't you bring me a glass of water?' 'Can't I get any service in this house?' Then he would jump up and get it himself." This behavior was of course symbolic of the husband's position in the household and represented his attempt to control the situation.

As time went on Mr. Allen started working late at night and on Sundays, thus avoiding coming home for dinner, and sex conflict also developed. Cultural conflict, however, is more obvious and striking, since the two now belong to entirely different social worlds. Mr. Allen refused to take his wife to social functions; Mrs. Allen was sure that he was ashamed of her. True, her clothes were never attractive, and her grooming was not appropriate for the wife of a successful professional man. This was partly because Mrs. Allen, in direct contrast to her mother (who had so emphasized beautiful clothes for herself), clothed her young daughters extravagantly but showed little interest in her own wardrobe.

Mrs. Allen, when the crisis arose and her husband left the home, characteristically said that she could not choose between her father (i.e., having him move out of her home) and her husband. She felt that what she wanted most to do was to "walk out on both of them"; in other words, run away from the situation.

In the case of the Allens, as in the preceding case, three fundamental characteristics can be isolated. First, we note the continuity of behavior patterns and thought patterns from childhood to maturity. Second, the passing of conflict into the economic, the sex, the response, and the cultural realms of the marriage relation can be observed. Third, factors intertwine in these realms of conflict until each becomes symbolic of conflict in the realm of the other. For example, conflict in response relations or breakdown in the love and affectional relations becomes reflected in and symbolic of cultural conflict; that is, the feeling that their ideals, tastes, and aspirations are entirely different.

Thus has been described the formation of two particular types of marriage-conflict pattern: the escape response, through illness, and the conflicting-roles type. There are a number of other types and, naturally, considerable variation within each type — which, after all, is a construct. What is more fundamental for the student of the family, however, is not so much the classification of types as a clear picture of the *formation* of a type and an appreciation of the complexity of the marriage-conflict pattern regardless of type.

Up until now the discussion has dealt with the conflicts of those persons who enter marriage with life-organizations impeding rather than facilitating marital adjustments. Although these persons constitute a very large proportion of domestic discord cases, they do not constitute the entire group. Many persons may be spoken of as adjusted *until* marriage; that is, they have developed workable methods of getting along in life and have not resorted to substitute devices. Typical conditions are found in the marital situation itself, however, which make for conflict.

Marriage and the Sociocultural Milieu

An analysis of the dynamic relationship between marriage partners requires a consideration of the sociocultural setting of marriage in our Western civilization. Marriage as an institution has been so imbedded in our culture as to make a lack of the relation appear highly undesirable, if not abnormal. Thus the wife and mother have been exalted, the spinster ridiculed and pitied. The bachelor, too, has come in for his share of criticism; he has presumably shirked his responsibilities. That which is most successful, satisfying, and normal in life has long been associated with marriage. In the past, unfortunately, our culture has not distinguished between happy and unhappy marriages in its glorification of the institution; nevertheless, there is the implication that " 'tis better to have married and failed than never to have married at all."

The romanticists (and even those writers on the family who in their emphasis on the antiromantic aspects, nevertheless deal with marriage as an individual matter) have ignored or overlooked the importance of this correspondence to the cultural pattern. They have emphasized blissful blind love before marriage, after which, for the antiromanticists at least, must inevitably come the sudden awakening and the disillusionment of reality. That this "cold gray dawn of the morning after" is present in marked degree in modern marriage, however, is doubtful except in the marriages of the very young who tend to be highly romantic; and in those of persons who have known each other but a few days. Certainly clinical cases do not confirm this romantic or cynically antiromantic conception. Few couples contemplating marriage will refuse to admit that they are occasionally irritated and worried by aspects of their relation making for possible conflicts. This is equally true of those already married, as attested when reviewing their histories. They were willing to "take a chance," and hence preferred a marriage with some risk of conflict to the culturally disapproved life of a bachelor or spinster. In the writer's clinical experience, no one living in domestic discord has ever said, when the question was put to him, that he would not remarry. Likewise, college students' life histories emphasize this desire for marriage, implying the unattractiveness and lower status of any other course.

These same romanticists have pointed out the ceremonial character of the betrothal and the honeymoon to which all married couples to some degree conform. We are after all a ceremonial species. But is marriage governed by many more rules of conduct and by much greater display of sacred sentiment than birth, death, and other "rites of passage"? All have elements in common. Arrival in the world is heralded by one color of ribbon for the boy and a different color for the girl, and by much celebration and real or ostensible rejoicing regardless of planning (or the lack thereof) and of the sex. Most funerals are as carefully prepared and as elaborately executed as the most fastidious weddings. There is the same "front," and perhaps as much sacrifice of savings for the sake of an appearance of "prosperity" and "that well-groomed look." [6] On both occasions the virtues and community status of the participants are exalted.

All this is to say that marriage, like other important life situations, is governed in our culture by its own formal and modified mores and sentiments. Consequently, it is not a unique experience apart from life itself, as the romanticists would have it.

[6] Cf. William M. Kephart, "Status After Death," *American Sociological Review*, 15 (Oct., 1950), pp. 635–643.

Marriage has been pictured as an abrupt and jolting change from the courtship and engagement period. In modern marriage this is no longer true; the transition is a gradual one — particularly where urbanization is far advanced. Couples are thrown together during the courtship and engagement period for a considerable time in varying situations. They are fairly conscious of each other's personality traits, some of the peculiarities of the other's family, and so on. The prospective husband is aware of the type of make-up used by his prospective wife, and of how she looks in a bathing suit and in a housecoat. He has seen her under both favorable and unfavorable physical and psychological conditions. Petting and some sexual play have occurred in a large number of cases, and sex has been discussed — at least to some degree. A premarital relation quite different from that of a few generations ago, true enough; but the student of the family must take account of the changes that demonstrably occur.

With a decline in modern marriage of many of the elements of romanticism and idealization, the presence of which has been emphasized by some writers as an important factor in marriage conflict and disintegration of the family, why then the increasing prevalence of this conflict? Obviously, the romantic phase has been overemphasized as a causative factor in marital conflict, with the result that it has led to the minimizing of the more important but less apparent elements.[7] Thus emotional immaturity, dominant personality trends, lack of adjustment skills, early inhibiting sexual influence, and so on, have been either dismissed too lightly or explained in terms of some aspect of romanticism.

To be somewhat aware of the personality traits of one's prospective partner is one thing; it is quite another, however, to live with and adjust to these traits day by day in marriage. Few persons see or understand the implications involved in what appears overtly as "a slightly unusual situation." (If they did, they would be specialists in personality and marital problems.)

For example, a young woman may realize, as in a case familiar to the writer, that the man to whom she is engaged is attached to his mother, but she fondly envisages the fact that he also is attached to her. She does not see the implications of this mother attachment and how it may affect the husband-wife relation until after marriage, when certain pressures are brought by the parent for a continuation of the childhood responses. She could not foresee the many conflicts, symbolic of this attachment, which would arise in various interactional spheres. How, for example, could the wife have predicted that the mother would make a desperate appeal to the son to continue the relation? Although in robust health she began talking of death, designating which relatives were to have her personal belongings — the significance of which acts the son did not realize. Thus the wife had not been prepared for the rival role into which she was cast by her husband's earlier familial interactional pattern.

Furthermore, most human beings do not seek the unpleasant or analyze a social situation or a personality for troublesome aspects. Therefore, al-

[7] Cf. Hugo Beigel, "Romantic Love," *American Sociological Review*, 16 (June, 1951), pp. 326–334.

though a situation is obviously potential with conflict, it may be viewed optimistically, not because of a romantic complex, but because it is a part of the folkways "never to look for trouble."

The Nature of the Marriage Pattern

Everyone enters marriage, then, with a conception of what this relation will be like. There is first the general conception gleaned from observation of pair interaction in general (see Chapter Nine, "The Engagement," pp. 282–288) and of heterosexual pairs in particular, plus the special traits imposed by the culture of which the observer is a part. On this set of general conceptions is usually imposed another: that based on a particular marriage known intimately to the observer. This marriage may be that of his parents, a close relative, or a friend. This marriage may become the pattern into which, if it is successful, he may wish many aspects of his own marriage relations to fit, or, if it is unsuccessful, not to fit.

Not until after marriage, however, are the details of this vague composite of conceptions worked out. Whereas the partners' conceptions may have appeared quite similar before marriage, the dynamic roles of each in the marriage cannot be foreseen in detail and may prove to be quite dissimilar. In every marriage there is worked out a marital role, or set of roles, for each participant; this constitutes and is constituted by the pattern of interaction in the various spheres comprising the marriage relation. Such a role pattern is not something suddenly achieved or acquired, but is characterized by frequent conflict and accommodation, reaccommodation, and displacement, all of which necessitates experimentation, rejection of some elements, acceptance of others. This is equivalent to saying that some conflict in marriage is normal, just as a certain amount of conflict in personality is normal.

A marital pattern finally achieved becomes the criterion by which the marriage is judged by its participants as satisfactory or unsatisfactory, happy or unhappy. Much interaction within the marriage bond is so intimate and symbolic in character as to be scarcely understandable to an outsider. For example, a bit of conduct at variance with the set pattern may seem trivial to an outsider, while it is of far-reaching concern to the participants because it has a symbolic meaning intelligible only to the two involved.

Because of this exclusiveness no two marriage patterns are alike in exact detail; yet all have common characteristics. This similarity is the result of the fact that interaction takes place in the same spheres regardless of pattern. In fact, it is these spheres or realms of interaction which characterize marriage and give rise to conflict within the relationship itself regardless of the previous personality adjustment of the marital partners.

Granting the presence of fundamental interactions arising from pair relations as such (see Chapter Nine, "The Engagement," pp. 282–288), it can nevertheless be said that other basic processes in marriage derive from the necessities of the sex-response realm of interaction. While sex refers to a physiological impulse it becomes overlaid, except in extreme cases, with social experience, finding expression in demonstrations of affection and the sharing of interests, aspirations, and ideals by husband and wife. This mutual identification, sympathy, understanding, and affection is what is meant by response, and forms the matrix of the marriage relation.

The broadening of sex from its limited physiological sense into response in its affectional sense is of course a variable matter, giving rise to a variety of conflicts. These range from types in which sex appears in much of its original form to others in which it is all but transformed because so charged with sentiment and the emotions of love and affection.

Adjustments in the realm of sex response are linked with processes of accommodation in which at least a few conflicts are inevitable. These conflicts arise out of a wide range of individual differences in sex impulse, notions associated with sex, adolescent development and emancipation from family domination, previous love experiences, sex habits, demands for expressions of affection and solicitation. and the like.

CONFLICT IN THE SEXUAL REALM

Conflict in sexual relations may arise out of biological variation in the sexual impulse, the nature of which is not clear. More frequently, however, such variations are acquired, arising from a host of experiences occurring both within the marriage relation and prior to it. Fear of pregnancy, for example, because of association with the restrictions and unpleasantness of confinement and the pain of childbirth, because of the added economic responsibility, because of health hazards or lack of faith in contraceptive measures, etc., frequently lead to sexual inhibition and restraint on the part of one or both of the marriage partners.

Furthermore, sexual intercourse itself may prove painful, particularly to the woman, and sometimes leads to avoidance, reserve, and fear. Failure to experience sexual relaxation may be related to such fear and pain, or may result from the absence of preliminary love-play and similar negligence. Whatever the source, the irritations accompanying sexual intercourse and the pent-up emotions and tensions throw this phase of marriage into a new and unfavorable light, impeding rather than facilitating the necessary accommodations.

Conflicts in attitudes toward sex, however, do not arise out of experiences in the marriage relation only. In fact, many of the most important conflicts issue from childhood happenings and can frequently be traced to early definitions of sex as unclean and to the lack of sex education. In the minds of many persons, consequently, sex means lewd, licentious, and beastly. The result is that conflict which engenders guilt-feelings often follows any form of sexual experience, leading to complete identification of the two elements.[8] In extreme cases these guilt-feelings even preclude any sexual experience.

Although psychosexual immaturity is most often associated with women, it is also true that men, in spite of the premium placed upon sexual virility by most cultural norms, frequently harbor ideas that sex is unclean. Hence

[8] Harriet R. Mowrer, "Sex as a Factor in Domestic Discord," *American Sociological Review*, 1, No. 2 (April, 1936), pp. 252–263.

they remain unduly attached to a mother or sister all their lives, use escape mechanisms such as "illness" to avoid sexual experiences, and develop serious personality conflicts as a result of the sexual role (in conflict with the traditional masculine pattern) which they wish to play in marriage. A number of typical cases in the writer's clinical files show this reversal of role, almost paralleling the so-called "neurotic" or escape-response type of married woman. Like many "neurotic" or frigid women, these men are physically normal, but early familial attachments or unpleasant experiences and incidents in their social milieu have led to the assumption of a role the reverse of that traditionally thought of as masculine.

Inhibitions which operate in the sexual-conflict realm are therefore not characteristic of only one of the sexes, but may occur in either husband or wife. In either instance, a characteristic type of marital conflict ensues which is reflected in the whole general pattern of interaction.

Sexual irregularities prior to marriage, like early inhibitions, often aggravate the tendency to look on sex in an unfavorable light. Particularly is this true in women who have had sexual experiences which were unwanted. The husband becomes identified with this earlier unpleasant experience, so that each sexual episode in marriage constitutes a rehearsal of the previous event. Where the experiences have been pleasant, on the other hand, whether in the case of the man or the woman, sex relations have been so closely identified with the particular person as to make later adjustment in marriage with a conventional partner difficult if not impossible. Even where the experience has been with the marriage partner, it often calls out attitudes of hostility and ambivalence arising out of earlier guilt-feelings and loss of respect.

CONFLICT IN THE RESPONSE RELATION

As we pass from our focus on what is more strictly sex toward the analysis of response, we see other differences become the center of conflict. The pattern of response relations within families in which the marriage partners grew up may range all the way from those where the child was given no attention and affection to those where constant solicitude and affection were the rule. Little show of affection frequently causes the child to become so emotionally inhibited as not to be able to give or to appreciate signs of affection when married. In those instances, on the contrary, where demonstrations of affection were marked, the childhood norm carries over into marriage. Thus a wife who has been an only child and has received warm affection from parents demonstrative toward each other may be unhappy with a husband who has been treated casually by parents never seen to display any mutual affection.

Close attachments to members of the family, whether parents or siblings, accentuate the normal difficulties involved in achieving the response role expected in marriage. Like sexual adjustment, harmonious response relations are the results of accommodation, into which some conflict inevitably enters. Part of this is the result of the fact that the marriage partner is a substitute for earlier sources of response, which very often have not been wholly abandoned, so that the two are in conflict. Response conflicts between wife and mother-in-law are quite common, although similar conflicts, in less marked degree, also exist between husband and father-in-law. Conflicts with siblings-in-law, likewise, are common in those instances where the in-law has assumed the role of parent more than that of sibling.

The basis for the conflict between wife and mother-in-law is obvious in our culture. Traditionally, marriage was not largely on an affectional basis; respectable women were more inhibited and restrained than men. The mother often realized through the intimate relations with her son the response, denied her by her husband, which she craved but did not dare express. The inhibited wife could secure the response-satisfaction (with its sexual sublimation) through the relation with her son, and at the same time be free of any guilt-feelings — indeed, she could count on social approval. She was often dominating in her son's choice of a wife, subconsciously, perhaps, preferring one who would not prove too great a rival. But when the wife did become a rival for the son's affections, the mother in advancing age could very often recreate her earlier response experience through contact with her young grandson.

The modern trend is to assume a more casual attitude toward one's married children. Women, too, are more independent, having a larger number of interests outside the home. Whereas in the past a woman was old at thirty-five, she now is often considered highly attractive even at forty-five or fifty. Her careful grooming and accomplishments in matters outside the home give her approval and recognition. She no longer is dependent on her son for emotional satisfaction, since her relations with her husband are more soundly affectional. She is regarded as the equal of her husband, her contacts are wide, she is no longer sexually inhibited. The love of son for mother is still portrayed far more touchingly than that of the daughter, and the commercialism of Mother's Day still appeals to the traditional conception that "There is no sweetheart like a boy's mother." Nevertheless, it is true that only the very old and the unadjusted in personality and marriage cling to the idea tenaciously.

Nevertheless, many parents, particularly mothers, are unadjusted, and project their conflicts and unreasonable if not irrational attachments on their children. The conduct of the parent making for conflict in response relations between husband and wife may vary all the way from the obvious but extreme cases in which a mother takes to her bed following her favorite son's marriage and remains an "invalid" demanding sympathy and attention, to the less obvious symbolic behavior of keeping her adult son furnished with underwear. In the latter case, the mother refuses to recognize the break in response relations which marriage normally necessitates. The continuity in the intimate relationship between mother and son is preserved from infancy (symbolized by diapers) to manhood (symbolized by underwear), and is carried on into his marriage.

Some tension between in-laws is of course inevitable and may be considered quite normal. This tension grows out of the fact that there is unfamiliarity with the new surroundings as well as uncertainty as to what behavior is expected. Thus a wife may be uncertain as to how she has been portrayed to her husband's mother, and it may be a perplexing question which part of herself she should put forth in order to please the new relative. She finds herself tense and unnatural, possibly even with a certain amount of resentment, since it is implied that she and not the mother (whose relation with her son is more fixed at this stage because it has lasted much longer) is the one "on trial." Furthermore, even the husband she thought she knew thoroughly seems different in his old familial surroundings. The wife, for example, may resent the fact that Jim's mother talks so unreasonably about cocktails and is so glad that "her boy" never touches them, while Jim, basking in adoration, plays the "good boy" role to perfection — never explaining that his attitudes have changed since he left home and that although he, like many others, takes an occasional cocktail, it does not mean that he is an alcoholic. "It is not like Jim to behave this way," the wife reflects. Can it be that he, too, is a stranger to her? Thus the husband or the wife, as the case may be, becomes identified with the unpleasant tension in the situation; the result is that greater demands are made upon him for demonstrations and reassurances of affection. If these are given with what seems to be even a slight hesitation, a further strain is put upon the newly established response relation.

Another basis for tension in the relation between in-laws may be the anomalous position of the newcomer in the family. Many things go on within the family which are not understandable to him because he is an outsider unfamiliar with many of the habits, rituals, and traditions understood only by its members. Yet because he has married into the family he is usually supposed to understand them automatically. What would be thought of as a serious breach of etiquette in "outside" social relations is perpetuated tenfold "inside" the family, while the newcomer sits by bored and perplexed, yet not daring to ask questions which might reflect his anomalous position since a high premium is put upon his rapid and complete assimilation.

Antagonism on the part of the newcomer may further develop out of the role assigned him by the acquired family, for this may be in direct contrast to that which he has in his own family and nonfamily contacts. In many instances this role may be similar to that of the marriage partner so that no distinction is made, the same role being assigned to both. The newcomer, however, may reject this definition of role which his marriage partner has accepted throughout the years.

It is quite natural for a parent to look a little wistfully at the establishment of a son's or daughter's new home because it normally means a definite break with the old and carries the implication that thereafter the new will play the more important role. When, however, the new home and the old are thrown into competition, tension is inevitable. Newly married couples are usually enthusiastic about their homes, no matter how unpretentious, probably because the planning and the furnishing of the home is the first large enterprise they engage in together. During this period there is normally a close identification and sharing of interests and enthusiasms and an intimate mutual reactiveness that has a deep emotional tone. Threats to the achievement of this type of relation often appear in the behavior of an in-law, who either symbolically refuses to accept the presence of the new home or regards it as in conflict with the old. All descriptions of the new home are met with "It will be nicer than your own home. You won't want to come home any more." Of course, the parent here is endeavoring to maneuver the son or daughter into the reassurance of "Oh no, nothing will ever take the place of my old home. It comes first." When such reassurance is not forthcoming the parent, in an effort to remain in the foreground, resorts continually to remind him of the desirable features of his early home. There is also a constant revival of the past by recalling events which occurred when he was a small child — always, be it noted, situations which existed prior to his marriage. A constant revival of early experiences which have an emotional content, with the implied premium on faithfulness to the old environment, often calls out guilt-feelings. The marriage partner, feeling the pull of the two emotional situations, is unable to choose between them and cannot completely "find himself" in his new response realm. The other person in the marriage may not approve the policy of appeasing the parent, realizing that appeasement is not suited to the situation, and yet he cannot cope with the inhibitions which prevent the marriage partner from liberating himself adequately from the early response ties.

Symbolic Response Conflict

This inability of one of the marriage partners to perform an overt act which will liquidate the conflict resulting from the necessary substitution of a new object of response for the earlier one is not unusual. The best examples of such conflict are seen in men who at the time of marriage are unable to make a transfer from their mothers to their wives as beneficiaries of their life insurance. Sometimes months go by before they are able to do so, and the writer has known men who never succeeded in the task. The transfer would denote in the son's mind, in many cases, an act of "unfaithfulness" to the earlier response object, so that he has strong inhibitions about making it. In other instances, the son continues to be under parental domination, which he finds so satisfying that he does not want to jeopardize it by making a change in the status quo. The never consummated transfer in beneficiary, then, becomes the symbol of a response transference which has never taken place — in other words, of a response adjustment which has never been completely achieved.

Although reorientation in response interaction may be achieved more readily where the marriage partners are able to perform some overt act which will symbolize to each other their emancipation from parental domination, other symbols making for conflict remain in the foreground, especially when they take the form of traits which become symbols of an unpleasant if not distasteful relation. The marriage partner may discover in his mate similarities or even apparent identities with the in-law for whom antipathy is felt. Accordingly, he responds to the mate with the same hostilities which characterize his response to the "unpopular" relative. These traits do not initially call out antagonisms and in most instances are not even noticed until they become defined in interaction with the in-law. Thus a wife's exacting habits may not make for conflict with her husband until they are recognized by him as virtually identical with those of the mother-in-law who interferes in his personal affairs by giving unsolicited advice and criticism. Similarities in daughter and mother are often quite striking, the former seeming to be only a younger edition of the latter.

Not only does conflict result from identification of traits or mannerisms of the marriage mate with those of a close member of his family, but it may also result from similarities between traits of a member of one's own family and those of the marriage partner. In these instances the identification is likewise one which calls out hate reactions because the earlier relations have been unpleasant. Thus a husband may identify traits in his mother which early antagonized him with what appear to be similar traits in his wife.

CULTURAL CONFLICT

A third realm of marriage interaction is the cultural. Here conflict grows out of differences in the standards — most of them in the realm of the sacred as dealt with in Chapter One — of the groups in which the two grew up. Differences in food, dress, language, education, religion, recreational interests, etc., make for conflict in varying degrees of intensity, depending on the range of these combining cultural elements. Cultural differences of this sort give rise to conflict largely because they symbolize obstacles to or lack of identification of the persons concerned, and thus impede harmonious response.

Cultural conflicts may be of two types. The first results from the marriage of persons coming from areas in which the cultures are different. This may be called a general cultural conflict. The second type of cultural conflict does not result from variations in general cultural background of the marriage mates, but rather from differing interpretations of culture superimposed on the general background by the specific family and nonfamily groups to which they belong. This is a specific cultural conflict.

The first type of conflict is common in the United States, and is readily understood and analyzed by "the man on the street." Examples are everywhere: the intermarriage of persons of quite divergent cultural backgrounds, such as Orthodox Jewish and Protestant, strict Catholic and Protestant, older American and recent immigrant; marriage in immigrant areas where one person becomes assimilated more rapidly than the other; marriage between the urban and rural dweller, between employer and employee, between Bohemian and Philistine, etc. Here is apparent the diversity of the combining elements of culture as reflected in religion, food habits, education, language, dress, philosophy of life, occupational status, and standards of conduct. So evident is the contrast, in many instances, that the partners are quite conscious of it, therefore striving to find common elements as a basis for adjustment. A difference in religion or in philosophy of life, for example, does not inevitably make for conflict if the couple is otherwise held together by common bonds of association, sympathies, and interests. In such instances, *like* rather than *unlike* elements in cultural backgrounds are stressed; the degree of conflict will depend on the extent to which adjustment in other realms tends to make up for lack of complete cultural harmony.

Adjustment between partners brought up in differing cultural areas is often complicated by the attempts of their respective families to continue to act as interpreters of culture. This is quite as might be expected in view of the similar attempts in this direction in almost every marriage. In the case of intermarriage of representatives of widely contrasting cultures this tendency is naturally heightened, because each family feels that its unquestionable role is that of saving its member from being absorbed by the competing culture, which, because it is strange and not understood, seems inferior. Furthermore, the intermarriage situation is often made more acute because parents often are not told of the engagement or even of the marriage until after it takes place. Accordingly, the most the family can do, once the marriage is an accomplished fact, is to lose no time in endeavoring to perpetuate its own particular culture — unless, of course, it "washes its hands" of the renegade. So drastic a step is rarely taken; usually, after disapproval that may or may not be apparent, the family endeavors to save the situation by taking the obvious step of converting the member of the "outside" group to its way of life. Of course, there are cases where the parents seem at once to incorporate the members of the other group into the family without opposition, but this is usually only a lull; there has not yet been time to organize their program of assimilation. All members of the family are supposed to cooperate in the enterprise. If the family is highly religious, while the acquired member is not, then they may assume the missionary role of saving a soul. The techniques used at first may be indirect, such as presenting the couple with a Bible, suggesting to a minister of the family's faith that he call upon the newlyweds, and the like. In these instances, the "outside" family member is likely to feel not only that such conduct is a criticism of his group but also of himself, with the result that he blames the marriage partner for the family's attitude. Since such a premium is placed upon assimilation, outwitting the family in all its attempts becomes a game, and all too often an opposition team is recruited from among the "outside" family. Inasmuch as both families may be "outside" in each other's eyes, the possibilities of trouble are manifold. For example, the birth of a child may be the occasion for a further attempt to initiate control through a particular baptismal ceremony. The result in many instances is that if marriage is to be successful there must necessarily be an estrangement from both cultures with but marginal participation in either.

An important fact to remember in intermarriage cases, however, is the extent to which obvious cultural differences provide a ready basis for rationalizing more fundamental conflicts; for example, in many clinical cases with which the writer is familiar, much of the cultural conflict would have been repressed had there been a greater identification in response relations. This is understandable; many persons feel the need of obvious "reasons" to furnish not only to their friends, but to themselves as well, a plausible explanation for tension and friction which is largely unverbalized. Cultural differences, being more readily recognized and expressed in language, provide a fund of "explanations" for conflicts growing out of interaction in other realms. Thus these cultural conflicts become the scapegoat for other more subtle and less clearly defined conflicts.

The second type of cultural conflict has been more generally overlooked. When there are no obvious differences in the cultural areas in which the partners have grown up, it is assumed that their cultural backgrounds are alike. Thus, for example, if both belong to the same religion, educational level, social class, geographical locality, and so on, their cultural backgrounds are spoken of as the "same." Such an apparent identity creates an illusion, for no consideration is given to the definitions of situations provided by the early play group, school, family, and similar settings; these create wide differences within the particular cultural pattern. Accordingly, two persons coming from closely comparable cultural areas may conflict in the realm of cultural interaction. Methodists, for example, may disagree radically on their church attendance. One may come from a family which has stressed the ritualistic aspects of the religion; the other from one which has emphasized Methodism as a system of philosophy or ethics. Again, although similar food prepared in similar ways may be shared, conflict may arise over how much time is spent in eating it and the manner in which it is eaten — aspects of the specific cultural pattern. Take the case of a husband whose family had never looked upon mealtime as anything more than an occasion for satisfying an elemental desire; meals were always eaten in a great hurry, with few words spoken. His wife's family, on the other hand, had always stressed the dinner hour as a time for conversation and expression of companionship and good-fellowship; it was looked forward to as the family's social hour. The wife naturally becomes violently irritated at her husband as he races through his meal, eating his dessert as she finishes her second course. Similarly, one person prefers the radio with the meal while the other may become upset because in his childhood home the radio was forbidden at mealtimes. Although coming from the same economic level, one marriage partner may carry over from his familial cultural pattern an emphasis on high-styled clothes and a new motorcar each season, whereas his mate's familial home emphasized an attractive house with servants.

Aesthetic and recreational interests likewise may be radically different in their specific cultural content because of the dissimilarity of the groups with which each has been associated. Both husband and wife may be fond of music, for instance, but the wife may have sung in the church choir before marriage, the husband with a jazz orchestra. In marriage, each becomes irritated at the other's efforts to gratify musical cravings. Both husband and wife may possess a strict moral code, yet one sees no harm in occasionally going out with a person of the opposite sex; the other feels that such practices end in real or imaginary infidelity.

Because marital partners usually share an illusion of likeness as to their interests and ideas, believing them to have been closely similar during courtship and early marriage, these specific cultural conflicts seem to develop suddenly. To the mates they appear to be symbolic of a widening breach caused by fundamental differences in personal traits or attributes. Now, although the suddenness is exaggerated, there can be little doubt that in many cases these specific cultural differences do in fact merge into the realm of conflict between personal attributes.

CONFLICT IN PERSONAL ATTRIBUTES

Complete resemblance in this realm is never found; in every marriage, therefore, some conflict of personal traits inevitably enters. Complete resemblance, however, might also make for conflict, for even the narcist must some time become bored with himself; he would therefore find his double quite uninteresting in the long run. Furthermore, few if any normal persons are satisfied with all their own characteristics (even though the narcist might be), so that the double would only remind him of traits which he had already found irritating and which he did not care to live with twofold. Of course, most marriage partners are not closely similar; their differences, especially when extreme, are the source of irritation rather than their similarities.

Irritations may arise out of a host of combinations of personal attributes at variance with one another. Thus a person who emphasizes perfection in appearance may be displeased by a mate who is careless in dress or personal habits, and vice versa. An energetic and enthusiastic wife may be goaded to wrath by an indolent and phlegmatic husband. A wife who is thrifty may be irritated by the extra money her husband spends when she sends him to do marketing. A husband may find a wife annoying who buys a hat for its shape or color without thinking, apparently, how she will look in it. A wife who dislikes cocktails will rebel at being maneuvered into situations where she has to drink or be the "wet blanket" of the party. A practical wife who has difficulty in making the budget balance may be extremely vexed by a husband who repeatedly invites unplanned-for dinner guests to the home, his desire to be a "good fellow" overshadowing any consideration of the extra expense entailed. Again, a wife may feel moved to an act of desertion when her music-lover husband continues to buy records although he has no machine on which to play them and their financial status is such that they can scarcely pay the grocery bill. A nervous husband, easily upset, is often angered by a wife who remains detached and poised on all occasions. A husband who has a flair for exotic and complex drama may be nettled by his wife's preference for Andy Hardy pictures. A wife's "get by" philosophy may irk her conservative "loss-of-status-fearing" husband. A husband may be exasperated because his wife spends the extra money from the budget for an imported cologne when he had contemplated spending it for champagne.

That these conflicts are basic to marital maladjustments, however, no experienced analyst or family clinician would ever contend. They find expression as the inevitable result of intimate association and day-by-day living together. Some of the same tensions may be felt at intervals between business partners, employer and employee, professor and colleague, physician and patient, between friends, and in many other pair-groupings, but are reinforced between husband and wife by continued close and intimate association in a wide variety of situations. In fact, the very multiplicity of associations throws these irritations into greater relief and makes them easily recognizable. It is because they are so easily recognized that the persons themselves often tend to exaggerate them and use them as rationalizations for other more fundamental conflicts within the complex of marriage relations. When differences in personal traits are strongly emphasized, only a very naive student of the family looks upon them as other than attempts to justify less "obvious" dissatisfactions in the marriage relation.

Hence, conflicts in the realm of the personal attributes are of little significance unless aggravated by personality conflicts and, particularly, by lack of harmony in the sexual and affectional realm. Without the soothing effect of harmonious response relations expressed through intimacies and demonstrations of affection, sympathy, and sharing of aspirations, these differences become constant irritants and furnish ready excuses to the marriage mates for their failure to get along together. It seems to be more flattering to the ego to speak of a "temperamental conflict," for instance, than to admit an exaggerated emotional attachment for a parent which is blocking a response adjustment with the partner.

ACCORD AS A BY-PRODUCT OF CONFLICT

Because of the premium our culture places upon complete accord in marriage, even slight differences between husband and wife are often interpreted as tension and conflict. Here no distinction is made between conflict patterns leading to disorganization and the normal disagreements which result from intimate interaction. The latter are of such a nature that accommodation is worked out and they never become involved in an intricate conflict pattern. This is equivalent to saying that a conflict *pattern* does not inevitably characterize all marriages but only those in which no accommodation or solution has been found. It is, furthermore, the equivalent of saying that conflict inevitably does result in all marriages, as it does in all human relationships, and as such is part and parcel of the adjustment process itself. Burgess and Locke speak of this process as the functional nature of conflict;[9] Waller refers to it as productive conflict.[10] Even quarreling is regarded by some students of the family as functional and productive. It is pointed out that quarreling furnishes opportunities for cathartic release of emotional tensions which otherwise would become repressed. Furthermore, it is a way of bringing issues out in the open after which there may be a redefinition of the situation. Burgess and Locke also make the distinction between conflict and tension, tension being defined as an unsolved conflict.[11] Thus marriage normally would be characterized by conflict, while the marriage *conflict pat-*

[9] Ernest W. Burgess and Harvey J. Locke, *The Family* (2nd. ed., New York: American Book Co., 1953), pp. 513–515.
[10] Willard Waller, *The Family*, rev. by Reuben Hill (New York: Dryden Press, 1951), pp. 353–356.
[11] *Op. cit.*

tern would be from their standpoint an accumulation of tensions or un-solved conflicts leading to complete disruption of unity.

Why conflicts are resolved in some marriages and not in others depends upon a number of factors, chief of which is the psycho-socio-cultural equipment of the mates. As we have already pointed out in this chapter, some individuals because of their psychogenetic background are better able to meet normal problems of adjustment than are others. Furthermore, reasons for marriage, the meaning of marriage in one's particular cultural and social group, social pressures, and so on, all tend to modify or accentuate tendencies toward accommodation.

It needs to be borne in mind that not all conflict elements are of equal significance and therefore do not produce the same intensity of emotional reaction. Those, for example, related to the realm of personal attributes are of less significance than those in the other realms described (pp. 376–384). Some conflicts, also, because they arise out of elements chiefly defined in overt behavior, are more readily resolved.

Since not all individuals have identical values, patterns of accommodation to conflict are more readily worked out than might be expected. Mowrer has described this process as follows:

> Each individual's personality is made up of a group of values which may be thought of as arranged in a series, the first value of which is the most precious and the last the least. Both husband and wife learn in a general way the rating of at least the upper end of this series in each other's personality. Then when problems arise calling for family activity the person whose values rate lowest with reference to this particular problem subordinates himself to the leadership or domination of the other. But again this same individual in another situation may find his most precious values involved and so become the leader in the solution of this problem. If the ratings of values which bear upon any specific problem are always different, no difficulty arises in determining who shall play the leading role. But if both find values of equal preciousness functioning in the situation, then there is discord.[12]

Intensive research with a large group of so-called successful marriages would undoubtedly reveal patterns of accommodation which could be classified quite as adequately and as advantageously as patterns of domestic discord in unsuccessful marriages. The data in these cases, however, would need to be comparable in fullness and intimate details to those in complicated domestic discord situations. Just as healthy persons are not so much inclined to visit the physician as are the ill, it will be considerable time before the successfully married will visit the clinician for a marital checkup.

Where there are not these compensating accommodations, the result is the emergence and development of the conflict pattern, the general nature of which has already been described (pp. 369–372), in which conflict in one realm quickly spreads to other realms in its circular interactional progress. In this pattern every phase of conflict is linked with every other in such a

12 Ernest R. Mowrer, *The Family* (Chicago: University of Chicago Press, 1932), p. 112.

way that those appearing later directly or indirectly modify or aggravate those appearing earlier — the familiar "vicious circle."

The most significant aspect of this linkage is the position and meaning that each phase takes. There results a wide variation in patterns by which conflict in any one realm becomes associated with that in other realms. To say, however, that any one phase, the escape response through illness, for example, is linked with sex maladjustment, another phase in the pattern, is not enough. Why? Because each pattern is made up of an intricate network of symbolic elements in terms of which the persons involved interact. In fact, much of the interaction in marriage goes on in terms of this symbolization which, as has already been pointed out, is intelligible only to the participants. Quarreling, for example, is never merely a response to an immediate conflict situation. On the contrary, the explosive reaction is in terms of a whole complex of past experiences which are symbolically called to mind by the more immediate features of conflict. Events, reconstructed situations, past experiences, words, gestures, tones of voice, traits, or personal belongings such as articles of clothing and jewelry have unique meanings to the participants in any marriage, and interaction goes on largely in terms of these meanings.

MECHANISMS OF DISPLACEMENT OF CONFLICT

Once marriage conflict crystallizes into a definite pattern, it rarely continues indefinitely but tends to take other forms. This results from the fact that either one or both of the mates seek some solution — conscious or unconscious. The significance of the unconscious solutions lies in the fact that the ensuing reconstruction is likely to be a temporary expedient; that is to say, the marriage becomes satisfactory through the use of a subterfuge or substitute adjustment.

One of the unconscious means by which this substitution or displacement of conflict is achieved is the escape mechanism. With some persons this is simply a reinstatement of earlier techniques of social adjustment which constitute the dominant note of the life organization. The marriage partner in such cases simply carries over into marriage the same type of habitual response with which he has met other crisis situations. In other cases, however, the escape does not constitute a general continuity of personality pattern from childhood onward but instead is a displacement mechanism arising in marriage through which the marriage partner finds some sort of solution to the conflict.

Illness is but one of these escapes, and is more often used by the wife than by the husband. The wife, in many instances, becomes "too ill" to face the conflict. Since she is too ill to face it, it does not exist for her. Her attention becomes centered on her imaginary illnesses and she lives in her realm of pains, pills, hospitals, and physicians. Thus one knows of mistress-keeping husbands with "invalid" wives. It is often erroneously assumed that acquisition of the mistress followed the "invalidism" of the wife, whereas in reality the "invalidism" is the wife's answer to the problem she could not solve in any other way.

Closely related to "illness" as a displacement technique is that of martyrdom. Through this mechanism the unadjusted in marriage may achieve personal satisfactions from dwelling on their misery and living in a world of wrongs and hurts. In this world of retreat, injuries are highly exaggerated and self-pity becomes the keynote. As in the case of the escape through "illness," attention becomes so centered on one idea as to erase from consciousness the real conflict situation. Through enjoyment of his role of "suffering" the martyr achieves emotional satisfaction which enables him to forget that such satisfaction is not forthcoming from his mate. Although martyrdom, like "illness," is more frequently the wife's device, it is occasionally utilized by the husband.

Another displacement mechanism is fantasy. Here the conflict is solved by forgetting marriage; in all his social contacts with the other sex the partner behaves as does a single person looking for romance. He imaginatively constructs and achieves a substitute relation in which these members of the other sex become collectively a surrogate for the spouse. Furthermore, just as an unattractive single person may compensate for his unpopularity by constructing in his imagination a phantom escort or lover who becomes so real that it protects him from his feeling of loneliness and failure, so the unhappily married individual, through this surrogate, is able to convince himself that an unhappy situation does not exist for him. His flirtations thus act as a cushion for his ego, helping to convince him, through his real or fancied success with the opposite sex in general, that he is not a failure with one of its members in particular. Such persons see in almost every social affair, business or professional contact, train trip, and so on, a potential source of romance which provides the opportunity of further reinforcing the satisfactions of the substitute-relation. They are rarely unfaithful to their mates, usually staying within the bounds of a fairly strict moral code. Often recognized as the "life of the party," the most popular teachers, or the most interesting professional men, they are usually spoken of as having, it is understood, an unsympathetic and even cruel spouse.

Still another mechanism, that of idealization, provides for the unadjusted partner a solution of marital conflict. Idealization may be any one of three types. In the first type, a few desirable and satisfying traits of the spouse, or elements of the marriage itself, are exaggerated so as completely to overshadow or blot out the undesirable aspects. The person then reacts to the entire marriage situation in terms of these few restricted but desirable aspects. This type of idealization operates to some degree in every marriage, and as such is a factor in accommodation.

In the second type of idealization, traits are assigned the mate which are so strongly desired as to make conflict with him impossible. But since conflict does exist, it must then be the fault of someone else — i.e., of a substitute source of conflict. The locale of conflict is thereby transferred from within to an element outside the marriage. This mechanism often operates in suits for alienation of affection; for example, the "other woman" is the person responsible for the conflict, for the husband is a perfect individual whom the unwanted siren just will not let alone. In other instances, the parents of the spouse are said to be responsible for the conflict by forcing him to follow their dictates against his will. In these cases the conflict between the marriage partner and the "outside disturbers" becomes so intense as to cause the former to forget entirely the nature and source of the original conflict.

A third type of idealization is found where the partner accepts a marriage pattern quite contrary to his earlier desires and expectations, assigning to it highly satisfactory elements which in reality do not exist. In this way he is able to convince himself that it is the type of marriage for which he has wished — indeed, has long been striving. Redefinition of values thereby takes place — redefinition in terms of a pattern imposed on the marriage and assumed to make for harmony. An extreme example of this idealizing mechanism is manifested by a husband who is at first shocked by his wife's extramarital affair but later convinces himself that a wife should experiment with other men, for in so doing she becomes a more satisfactory mate. He may even go so far as to afford opportunities for his wife and her "lover" to meet successfully — the classic example of the *mari complaisant.*

Deprecation, a form of subterfuge akin to but not identical with idealization, is that in which a reorientation takes place in regard to the marriage. The conflict is viewed in relation to other life problems or is compared with the marital conflicts of other persons. Viewed in its larger perspective the conflict then at times diminishes in importance, so that the marriage partner can deprecate it and thereby take a less emotional attitude toward it. Through his own deprecatory redefinition of the situation he initiates a process of accommodation.

Many times this self-reorientation is precipitated by a crisis situation such as death or accident in the family, a community or world catastrophe, etc. In this respect deprecation probably is the most temporary of all the mechanisms of displacement, although in some respects it lacks the degree of subterfuge found in most of the substitute adjustments.

Not all persons in the marriage conflict situation turn to unconscious mechanisms of solution such as those which have just been described; conscious solutions may be chosen. A conspicuous example is divorce as a gateway to remarriage — which often turns out to be disappointing.[13] This is particularly true when the person remarrying has an unadjusted life organization. He may find himself no better adjusted, for the equivalent length of time, than in his former marriage. In fact, like conduct may call out like responses — i.e., like those of the first marriage. There are, on the other hand, persons who have achieved harmony after divorce and remarriage. In many more cases, however, the second marriage is found to be unsatisfactory — in fact, as much so as the first. It is conceivable that there are other cases in which the partner either refuses to face the realization and admission of re-

---

[13] Cf. Harvey J. Locke, *Predicting Adjustment in Marriage* (N. Y.: Henry Holt & Co., 1951), pp. 298–309; Thomas P. Monahan, "How Stable Are Remarriages?" *American Journal of Sociology,* 18 (Nov. 1952), pp. 280–288.

peated failure, or accepts the situation (having learned to expect and be satisfied with less the second time). Where one partner has been "deserted" for another, he may be unable to face the blow to his ego — for as such it is considered by our culture — except by remarriage. A high premium is therefore placed upon success in the hope of erasing all sense of failure and its accompanying feeling of deflation. There are other cases where failure produces an orientation in regard to what marriage involves; hence the second experience results in a better adjustment. There is also the person who still remains attached to his first spouse, and when making a second venture marries someone resembling the first — if not in psychical traits, then in physical ones. If this marriage is successful he vicariously lives his first marriage as he wishes it had been. Likewise, remarriage with former mates is not uncommon.

CLINICAL TREATMENT

Another conscious solution in marriage conflict is clinical treatment; the marriage mates seek therapeutic benefits from a skilled family clinician. Here it is assumed that the clinician's program will be based on available scientific knowledge concerning the factors making for stability and instability within the marriage pattern and on a body of tested control techniques developed from wide research and clinical experience. Of course, these demonstrated and tested techniques, like the traditional "cures" in medicine, are not applied without experimental adaptation to the many variable situations. Thus the family consultant is both researcher and clinician.

Through the techniques of clinical treatment it is often possible for persons experiencing conflict in marriage to redefine their marriage situation and thereby achieve what to them is a satisfactory adjustment. Experiences in the various realms of interaction are recreated and recast into redefined patterns through a psychocultural analysis which extends over a period of months. No attempt is made by the clinician to urge or encourage them to continue the marriage relation or, if they are separated, to resume it. The patients alone make the decision. The larger percentage of those seeking therapy want to work out an adjustment, and these persons come from a wide range of cultural, economic, and social groups. The writer has found the so-called educated to be just as naive as the uneducated where their marital conflicts are involved. This is likewise true of the professional as over against the nonprofessional. Legal training, or success in the business or teaching world, for example, does not yield equipment for coping with one's own marital problems any more than it does in diagnosing and treating one's own physical ailments. Just as the family physician is needed for physical problems, so is the marital clinician needed for marriage conflict problems. With the increasing secularization of our society, or at least until the family succeeds in sacralizing itself to an extent much greater than is at present widely manifest, the marital clinician must take the place of the sacred sages.

SELECTED READINGS

Burgess, Ernest W., and Locke, Harvey J., *The Family* (2nd ed., New York: American Book Co., 1953), chap. 18.

——, and Wallin, Paul, *Engagement and Marriage* (Philadelphia: J. B. Lippincott Co., 1953).

Dickinson, Robert L., and Beam, Lura, *A Thousand Marriages: A Medical Study of Sex Adjustment* (Baltimore: Williams and Wilkins, 1931).

Folsom, Joseph K., *The Family in Democratic Society* (New York: Wiley, 1943), chap. 13.

Fromm-Reichmann, Frieda, *Principles of Intensive Psychotherapy* (Chicago: University of Chicago Press, 1950).

Glick, Paul C., "First Marriages and Remarriages," *American Sociological Review,* 14 (December, 1949), pp. 726–734.

Goode, William J., "Economic Factors and Marital Stability," *American Sociological Review,* 16 (December, 1951), pp. 802–812.

Hill, Reuben, *Families Under Stress* (New York: Harper and Brothers, 1949), chaps. 1–4.

Jacobson, Paul H., "Differentials in Divorce by Duration of Marriage and Size of Family," *American Sociological Review,* 15 (April, 1950), pp. 235–244.

Kirkpatrick, Clifford, "Factors in Marital Adjustment," *American Journal of Sociology,* 43 (September, 1937), pp. 270–283.

Koos, Earl L., *Families in Trouble* (New York: King's Crown Press, 1946).

Landis, Judson T., "Marriages of Mixed and Non-Mixed Religious Faith," *American Sociological Review,* 14 (June, 1949), pp. 401–407.

Levy, John, and Monroe, Ruth, *The Happy Family* (New York: Knopf, 1938).

Locke, Harvey J., and Karlsson, Georg, "Marital Adjustment and Prediction," *American Sociological Review,* 17 (February, 1952), pp. 10–17.

Mowrer, Ernest R., *Disorganization: Personal and Social* (Philadelphia: Lippincott, 1942), chaps. 17, 18.

——, *Family Disorganization* (Chicago: University of Chicago Press, rev. ed., 1939), chaps. 9, 10.

Mowrer, Harriet R., *Personality Adjustment and Domestic Discord* (New York: American Book Co., 1935).

——, "The Clinical Treatment of Marital Conflicts," *American Sociological Review,* 2 (1937), pp. 771–778.

——, "Sex as a Factor in Domestic Discord," *American Sociological Review,* 1 (April, 1936), pp. 252–263.

Nimkoff, M. F., *Marriage and the Family* (Boston: Houghton Mifflin, 1947).

Strauss, Anselm, "The Influence of Parent Images Upon Marital Choice," *American Sociological Review,* 11 (October, 1946), pp. 554–559.

Terman, Lewis M., and Wallin, Paul, "The Validity of Marriage Prediction and Marital Adjustment Tests," *American Sociological Review,* 14 (August, 1949), pp. 497–504.

——, and associates, *Psychological Factors in Marital Happiness* (New York: McGraw-Hill, 1938).

WALLIN, PAUL, "An Appraisal of Some Methodological Aspects of the Kinsey Report," *American Sociological Review*, 14 (April, 1949), pp. 197–210.

WHITE, R. W., *Lives in Progress* (New York: Dryden, 1952), chap. 8.

WINCH, ROBERT F., *The Modern Family* (New York: Henry Holt, 1952), chap. 15.

TOPICS FOR DISCUSSION OR REPORTS

1. Discuss order of birth and show how this factor has operated to determine your role in the family. How has this role made for conflict or adjustment with your acquaintances?

2. Explain what is meant by the statement that response relations form the matrix of the marriage relations.

3. Make personality analyses of yourself and of your prospective marriage partner, focusing on the factors which make for conflict as discussed in this chapter. (If you haven't as yet selected a marriage partner, make an analysis revealing the type of person who would constitute a good marriage risk for you, and explain why the risk would be good.)

4. Explain why the differentiation between the satisfactions of sex and of response may have led less frequently to marriage conflict in the past than at the present time.

5. Read and analyze three published autobiographies and show what childhood response relations described there would later make for marriage conflict.

6. What is meant by the marriage-conflict pattern?

7. Take a case of "intermarriage" with which you are familiar, using the term in the sense in which it is used in this chapter, and analyze it in terms of possible cultural conflict and accommodation.

8. Analyze your best friend, preferably of the opposite sex, enumerating and discussing the personal attributes which make for conflict with other persons.

9. Write a case history describing in detail the overt behavior of an unadjusted married person who uses one of the displacement mechanisms described.

10. Why do some marriages fail while in others conflict is resolved through accommodation?

11. Under what conditions can conflict in marriage be considered to be functional or productive?

12. Read Chapter Eleven, "Getting Along in Marriage" and compare the mechanisms of adjustment in marriage with those of discord as discussed in this chapter.

Chapter Thirteen

Financing the Marriage

HOWARD F. BIGELOW

MONEY ENOUGH FOR MARRIAGE

How much money does it take to get married?" is one of the questions most frequently asked by young men and young women who are seriously contemplating marriage. Of course, those who are asking this question want to know far more about costs than about the initial expenses of obtaining a marriage license and paying the preacher. They want to know on how small an income and with how little money in the bank they can safely launch a marriage and perhaps start a family. They are not necessarily seeking encouragement to hurry into marriage. Most intelligent young couples, no matter how anxious they are to start their new families, are seriously concerned lest they embark on this, their most important life venture, with economic resources which may prove to be inadequate.

Obviously this question has no single answer. In any marriage, money has no value in itself but is wanted only for what it will buy. Couples ask this question because they are trying to frame in simple form a whole complex of ideas. They ask about how much money they need because money is a master symbol for economic resources. It is the common denominator by means of which the sum total of a great variety of wants can be expressed. When couples ask how much money it takes to get married, they really want help in doing two things: first, in analyzing, appraising, and evaluating the relative importance of a great number of wants which they hope their new family will be able to satisfy; and second, in inventorying the resources of all kinds which they have or can make available for use in satisfying these wants. They want help in determining the minimum essentials for satisfactory family living, both in terms of the wants to be satisfied and of the resources which are needed to satisfy these wants.

When young people approach the problem in this way they are running true to form. All of us, young and old alike, are inclined to take our wants pretty much for granted, and spend most of our time and effort hunting for the means for their satisfaction. We really do not know whether or not it is our most important and most fundamental wants we are trying to satisfy, especially in times of reasonable prosperity when it is relatively easy to satisfy our wants in customary ways. It is only when we are faced with a radical change in our manner of living — as a result of personal misfortune, a severe business depression, or the outbreak of a world war, or sometimes even as a result of falling in love — that we take time to find out what after all is fundamental and what is superficial in our manner of living.

FAMILY WANTS

To list our fundamental wants in general terms is relatively easy. There are the three primary necessities of food, clothing, and shelter, and the almost equally important wants of facilities for transportation and communication, for good health, for education, and for recreation. In recent years we have come to realize that good living is impossible unless in addition to securing the material goods and services necessary for satisfying these wants we can also satisfy our wants for certain intangibles — companionship and affection, security in the present and in the future, freedom from the arbitrary domination of others which only security can bring, a chance for a bit of adventure now and then, social position and the recognition by others which social position implies and, most important of all, self-respect.

We usually think of these fundamental wants in terms of wants for specific goods and services: not food, but roast beef, or carrots, or oranges, or ice cream; not clothing, but a new dress or a pair of shoes; not transportation, but a bicycle, an automobile, or taxi service; not means of communication, but frequent mail deliveries, a telephone, a daily newspaper, or a radio; not recreation, but tickets to the theater or a ball game, a new set of golf clubs, a picnic or a dinner dance, or a trip to Sun Valley; not security in the abstract, but a bank account, some life insurance, a comfortable home owned free and clear, a social-security account, or a few reasonably safe investments; not social position as such, but a house on a certain street, an evening wrap from an exclusive shop, or membership in the proper club.

While it is easy to agree in general terms about our fundamental wants, no two people translate these fundamental wants into specific wants for the same list of goods and services. The first and inescapable problem which must be worked out by any couple who seriously want an answer to the question of how much money they need to make their marriage go, therefore, is to determine what are the most important and what are the least important of their specific wants.

During the courtship period men and women are continuously engaged in exploring the interests and standards of their fellows, each looking for a partner with interests sufficiently similar so that they can become good "pals," and sufficiently varied so that they can help each other to new and stimulating interests. During engagement, couples often unconsciously work out the answers to many of these questions concerning wants by exchanging opinions as to likes and dislikes, values and aversions, and by the expression of preferences when alternatives arise.

Of course, the process is only begun during the courtship and engagement stage of the family life cycle. The inevitable problems of adjustment within the family are kept at a minimum, and results are more satisfactory, if the partners have continued the process of deliberation which began in the engagement period and are consciously working out together a carefully integrated, harmonious, and personalized pattern of living for their family.

For this pattern of living then becomes the objective toward which all the family's work in money management may be aimed.

Satisfying Wants by Wise Expenditures

There are three principal ways in which families use money to satisfy their wants. (1) They spend part of their money in the market for goods and services which they purchase in a form which will immediately satisfy their wants. (2) Part of their money is spent for materials and equipment with which to produce for themselves goods and services which they either cannot afford to buy ready to use with the money at their disposal, or which cannot be found in the market in a form exactly suited to their needs. (3) Part of their money is turned over to various institutions, public and private, in the form of contributions, membership fees, and taxes, in return for which they receive the services which these institutions perform.

All families use their money in all three of these ways. But few families satisfy all their wants in exactly the same manner. There is no single item which all families buy ready for use in the market; nor for that matter, is there any item which all families produce for their own use. Most families get most of their meals at home, yet restaurants and cafeterias and tea rooms do a thriving business. Although we have compulsory education laws in most of our states and excellent public schools, many families still prefer to send their children to private or parochial schools, and a few hire tutors to teach them at home. Because in recent years there has been a marked increase in the sale of ready-to-wear clothing, it is easy to assume that families buy all their clothing ready-made. But sewing machine manufacturers continue to sell domestic sewing machines, and every department store has a piecegoods department selling fabrics and patterns to families that want to make their own clothing.

In planning the pattern of living for their family, therefore, a couple must consider not only the wants they are to satisfy, but the way or ways in which they are going to provide the goods and services called for in the pattern. In planning the best use of family funds it is necessary to decide how much money shall be apportioned for the purchase of what finished goods and services in the market, how much shall be used for the purchase of what raw materials and what equipment for home production, and how much needs to be set aside to pay for what community facilities and government services.

Each of these three ways of using the family's money presents its own peculiar problems. When the family spends its money in the market, it is faced with all the problems of wise buying. When it uses money in connection with its home production program, it is faced with the problems of estimating costs in order to know what pays best, of the selection of the type or types of home production in which the family is going to specialize, and of the efficient organization of production processes. Spending together for community facilities involves the whole problem of effective participation in community affairs.

THE PROBLEM OF INTELLIGENT BUYING

Good buying has been described as the art of securing goods which as nearly as possible satisfy a consumer's needs, with a minimum outlay of time, energy, and money. This involves, on the one hand, knowing how to determine what will best satisfy the buyer's wants, what characteristics are absolutely essential, what are highly desirable, and what are desirable but unnecessary. It involves, on the other hand, knowing how to find out about qualities of goods which are available in the market and the places where they are available in the most convenient form and at the lowest price — knowledge which may be gained by personal inspection, simple testing, and trial, or by gathering information from salesmen, from labels, and from advertising.

In some cases the buyer knows just exactly what will satisfy his wants. He knows it is available in the market. He has bought it before. His problem is to be sure that he gets such an article. In other cases he has a good idea of what he wants, but he is not sure just what article or qualities will be most satisfactory. So he shops about a bit, studies available commodities, and after determining what alternatives are available, he sets up his specifications and makes his selection.

For example, a homemaker knows that X's Supreme Brand of canned macaroni and cheese has just the flavor her family likes. Her problem is a simple one. She must be sure to get X's Supreme Brand, and no other. But suppose she needs a new dinner dress? Here the problem is different. She studies the fashion magazines to find out about the latest models, goes shopping to determine what the popular colors are, and then makes her selection in terms of personal suitability, her husband's preferences, and the demands of her social schedule.

In the course of a lifetime the members of a family must purchase a great variety of commodities and services, ranging all the way from the frequent purchases of beans and beefsteak and bread and butter, through the seasonal selection of clothing, the purchase of furniture, radios, refrigerators, and family cars, to the selection of the doctor and the hospital for maternity confinement, the purchase of bassinet and baby carriage, and the selection of the school, whether public or private, for the children's education.

In order to buy this long and varied list of items wisely, it is necessary to accumulate detailed information about a great variety of commodities and services, and about the markets and the types of market organization through which they are supplied. If possible, the buyer should learn about the various elements which enter into the cost of producing and distributing these goods and services, and the usual relation of these costs to the prices the consumer must pay. It helps to understand the relationship between wholesale and retail prices, and between various classes of goods which may be used as substitutes for each other. The efficient buyer will, therefore, acquire a large and varied working vocabulary of technical terms. He will learn the nature of many sorts of materials, and the relative desirability of the different qualities of these materials for particular purposes. In addition, he must develop keenness of perception when looking over goods in the market; he must learn to discriminate clearly between the essential and non-essential; and he must hold himself to constant, careful attention to detail.

The task of buying wisely is not an easy one, but it is possible. A great many of the articles which a family purchases at frequent intervals involve only small outlays. Here occasional mistakes are not too expensive. It is possible to learn how to make these purchases wisely simply by careful and continuous study of the results of experience in buying. Most of the purchases which the family makes only at long intervals involve an outlay large enough to justify spending time studying both the family's needs and the available market offerings.

While the members of a family must purchase this great variety of commodities and services in the course of a lifetime, there is no one year in which they must learn to purchase all of them. Nowadays, bride and groom bring to marriage buying skills acquired from years of personal experience in buying for themselves. In the first few months of married life, their immediate problem in buying is to learn how to make selections which will be mutually satisfactory. They must learn to plan their buying together, although they can, and in many cases they should, practice division of labor when it comes to actual market selection, each buying the goods and services which he knows best how to buy. Every year each one of them can, from one source and another, get together the information needed to buy wisely two or three new commodities or services. Every year each one of them can check on purchasing policies, studying particularly those articles in which there has been obvious technological progress, or in which there is reason to suspect that the family is not doing as well as it might with its buying.

The normal progress of the family will indicate clearly from year to year what new buying skills the members of the family must develop. Experience in family living will provide a constantly broadening background for analysis of family wants, just as repeated experience in buying brings increasing facility in market selection. A couple starting out in a furnished apartment can postpone the intensive study of the qualities of living room rugs until they are about ready to buy one for an unfurnished apartment or a new house. By that time they will have learned a good deal about rugs from their experience with the ones their landlord supplies. There is no need to spend a great deal of time on the details of the furnishings for a nursery until the approaching arrival of the first baby. Then furnishing the nursery can be worked out as part of the whole plan for welcoming the newcomer to the family circle.

The important thing is to know how to become an efficient buyer whenever the need arises. Especially in times of rapid technological progress, when the qualities of goods change from year to year and when new products are constantly coming on the market, and during periods of war emergency and reconversion, when old ones no longer are available, the "family buyer" needs to know where and how to get detailed and accurate information about current market offerings.

Numerous aids are available to the consumer buyer. Perhaps the one most immediately effective is the salesman who knows his merchandise and has the same ideas as the buyer about values and use. Usually the inexperienced buyer finds that it saves time to hunt up such a salesperson, and in the long run it saves both time and money to follow his advice.

Advertising can be of much help to the consumer-buyer especially if, when reading or listening to advertising, he understands what the advertiser is trying to accomplish in the particular advertisement. For example, national magazine advertising can call his attention to the product, tell him who makes it, what it is good for, and occasionally something about what it ought to cost. Local newspaper advertising more often tells where an article can be had, when it will be on sale, and the price at which it is offered. Radio and video advertising is for the most part reminder advertising of the repetitive type. Mail-order catalogs and dealer aids usually give more detailed descriptions of the product.

Labels are a good source of information. Brand labels enable the housewife to identify "X's Supreme Macaroni." Grade labels indicate the grade or commercial standard to which goods conform. Descriptive labels describe one or more features of the article usually in non-technical terms. Informative labels are designed to answer five questions that buyers want to know: what the product is made of, how it is made, what it will do, how to care for it, how to use it. These labels frequently give performance and quality of the article in question compared with other articles of better or poorer quality in the same line, or compared with a minimum standard. (Of course, most if not all labels must be "taken with a grain of salt.")

There is available to the interested student a constantly increasing volume of books, pamphlets, magazine articles, government bulletins, and other written materials dealing with specific buying problems. Some of the most helpful of this material goes out of date quickly, but new material of the same sort is constantly becoming available. To use this material effectively, the buyer must learn to evaluate it for accuracy, for timeliness, and especially for its applicability to the particular buying problems with which he is immediately concerned.

Finally, there are the consumer information services. Consumers Research, Inc., now located in Washington, New Jersey, was organized in 1929. Consumers Union of the United States, Inc., 38 East First Street, New York City, was organized in 1935 by a group who left Consumers Research because of differences over policy. Both organizations test and report upon consumers goods. Both publish monthly bulletins giving detailed reports on current research projects and an annual handbook or buyers guide listing in summary form their ratings on a long list of products. In addition to the product ratings, the monthly bulletins contain news items of interest to consumers.

Properly used, these services can provide a great deal of help, especially for typical families. From the detailed information about commodities in the monthly bulletins, the buyer can learn what to look for when comparing goods in the market. Used with discretion, the recommendations as to "best buys" are also helpful, though in using these recommendations families must keep two things in mind. First, none of these agencies can possibly include all of the available brands of any article, especially outside of the New York City area, though they try to include all brands having national distribution and a good selection of regional brands. Second, the family buyer must remember that in making these "best buy" recommendations, the evaluation involves the weighting of a number of factors, and that such weighting is of necessity biased. If the family is in the same socio-economic class as the families the rating group had in mind in determining their "best buy," probably the recommendation will hold. If, however, the family is not of that class or is living under different conditions, having different needs, it would be better to make an independent decision as to what will be the best buy.

In all buying each family must be the final authority as to what is the wisest use of their money. The family alone can know all the factors which are involved. All market aids available should of course be used. But decisions will have to be made in terms of the personal considerations involved. For example, there are times in the life of every family when the family buyer can afford to spend a good deal of time and energy shopping in low-service stores in order to save a little money. There are other times when it is necessary to pay higher prices for goods from full-service stores in order to conserve the definitely limited time and energy of the family members.

In short, buying techniques may be improved, but no family can ever hope to do a perfect job. The family buyer will be doing a good job if, with the money and time and energy available for buying, he gets from the market goods and services which satisfy well a reasonable number of the family's most important wants.

PRODUCTION BY THE FAMILY

Families usually engage in production for their own use for one or more of the following reasons: the commodity or service is not available on the market; it costs more than they can afford; they prefer the homemade to the commercially produced goods; they enjoy producing the article in question.

Home production makes it possible to use available resources, either material or personal, which would otherwise be wasted. Production for use has definite educational values. In deciding upon the best use of money in financing the family's home production program, each family tries to select the group of activities which will pay best both from the pecuniary and personal viewpoint. From the pecuniary viewpoint, what pays best can be determined by comparing the cost of home production and market purchase. There are two principal methods by which costs may be compared. One consists of the comparison of the total cost of carrying on a home production activity with the total cost of buying similar goods or services in the market. This method should be used whenever a family is deciding whether or not to undertake a particular type of home production activity. A different method is used when a family already has the equipment and facilities for a given type of home production, but wants to know whether or not to put these facilities to a particular use. Then the procedure involves computing only the additional costs which are entailed by the use, ignoring the fixed charges connected with the ownership and maintenance of the equipment, since these fixed charges must be met whether the equipment is put to use or not.

For example, a family is considering the purchase of a family car, to be used for local and long-distance transportation. Their first step is to determine the total cost of car ownership and operation, either for a year or for the life of the car. To do this, they must include both (1) fixed charges: interest on their investment in the automobile; its total cost if they are estimating cost for the life of the car, or adequate allowances for depreciation and obsolescence if they are estimating for the shorter period; insurance, taxes and license fees, and garage rent — and (2) operating expenses: gasoline and oil; greasing, washing, and repairs; replacements of tires, batteries, and other working parts; minor repairs and adjustments; and such incidental expenses as occasional fines for traffic violations and parking fees. Then they must estimate the cost of using the necessary amount of public transportation: bus, rail, and taxi. By comparing these two totals, they may determine whether it will be to their financial advantage to own an automobile or to depend on public transportation.

Suppose a family finds that the total cost of owning and operating a car will run about eight cents a mile for normal use. Most of the time it will be driven with only one passenger. This will make the cost of home-produced transportation run between seven and eight cents per passenger mile. If they live near a bus line which provides reliable and convenient public transportation at four cents a mile, on the basis of comparative cost this family may decide to do without a car. If they must depend largely on taxi service, the financial advantage may lie with car ownership.

Suppose, on the other hand, a larger family finds that its car will be driven most of the time with from two to five passengers. An average of three passengers per car mile will reduce the cost per passenger mile for family transportation below the four-cent-a-mile mark. Cost estimates indicate that it would pay this family to own and operate its own automobile, even though frequent and inexpensive bus service is available.

Suppose, however, that the family already has a car but wants to know whether or not to use it for a trip to a city one hundred miles away. In this case, the only costs to be considered are the additional costs which the trip will involve: expenditures for gas and oil, possible parking fees, allowance for additional wear on tires (no inconsiderable item nowadays), and possible minor repairs. Fixed charges do not need to be included, for they will go on whether the car is used or not. Suppose in this case the family finds that the cost of the trip will be $8.00, or four cents per car mile. If only one member of the family is to make the trip, he may decide to use either his own car or public transportation, whichever is more convenient. But if four members of the family are going, the cost would be only about one cent per passenger mile by car. This is a cost which few if any commercial transportation agencies can meet.

In estimating the cost of carrying on activities in which labor is an important element, it may or may not be necessary to add labor costs to the other costs which are involved. If labor is hired to carry on the work, the expenditure for hired help should be added. If members of the family spend time in home production which they could otherwise spend in earning money, the amount they could have earned should be added to the other costs of home production as labor cost.

Members of a family should place a cash value on their labor only if otherwise salable time is used in home production. If the wage-and-hour law prevents the head of the family from selling his services in industry for more than forty hours a week, his time outside working hours has no market value. If social convention prohibits a married woman from seeking gainful employment, her labor has no market value. But all this unsalable labor of the members of the family, if spent in home production, can have value in use. The amount of this value may be determined as follows: from the cost of similar goods and services purchased in the market, subtract the cost of materials used and the overhead expense involved in home production. This gives the *value created by home production,* or the *net value of home production.* (The method used is similar to, though not identical with, the method used to determine *value added by manufacture.*) To determine the return for the time and energy expended by the members of the family, divide this *net value of home production* by the number of hours spent on the work. This gives in dollar terms the *real wages earned per hour* in the type of home production in question.

Since, in most families, the time and energy available for home production is limited, as well as the money available for the purchase of goods and services in the market, it is usually wise for members of the family to spend their available unsalable time in whatever activities will yield the largest return per hour in real wages. By comparing the return per hour of time spent in various types of production activity, it is possible to determine where this financial advantage lies.

In making these estimates, a family often finds that time spent in home production yields a higher return per hour in real wages than the same amount of time spent in earning money outside the home. If this proves to be true, a family may decide that it will be to their financial advantage to divert part of the salable time of family members from earning to home production. If a family finds that time spent in certain types of home production activity yields a return much greater than the rate for which competent hired help can be had, they may decide to provide the goods and services in question by supplementing the work of the members of the family with the services of a hired helper, instead of using commercial facilities.

Table 8 shows the application of this method in estimating the *net value of home production* and *real wages earned per hour* in preparing and serving meals for families of various sizes under certain assumed conditions indicated in the footnote to the table. On the basis of these estimates, a girl

TABLE 8

ESTIMATE OF RELATIVE SAVINGS BY SIZE OF FAMILY OBTAINED BY PREPARATION OF MEALS AT HOME

Analysis	Estimates according to Number of Persons in Family					
	1	2	3	4	5	6
Food costs — 80 cents per person per day	$ .80	$1.60	$2.40	$3.20	$4.00	$4.80
Overhead — 60 cents per day for family	.60	.60	.60	.60	.60	.60
Cost of preparing and serving meals	1.40	2.20	3.00	3.80	4.60	5.40
Cost of purchasing meals of similar quality with similar service outside of home (breakfast, 40 cents; lunch, 65 cents; dinner, $1.15) — $2.20 per day per person	2.20	4.40	6.60	8.80	11.00	13.20
Net value of home production, i.e., saving in outlay by preparation of meals for family at home	.80	2.20	3.60	5.00	6.40	7.80
Hours spent in meal preparation, serving, and clearing away	4	4	4½	5	5	5½
Real wages per hour	.20	.55	.80	1.00	1.28	1.42

Basis of Estimates

Food costs

    Median expenditure for food for family as reported in Consumer Purchase Study for 1935–1936 *plus 100 per cent for recent price increases* — probably still too low in 1953.

Overhead

Gas for cooking and heating water	$4.00
Electricity for refrigerator	1.50
Electricity for lights	.50
Maintenance, repair, and replacement of equipment	12.00
	$18.00 per month or 60 cents per day

Maintenance, repair, replacement assumes the following equipment:

Refrigerator	$200.00
Stove	150.00
Table service: silver, dishes, linens	225.00
Dining room furniture	200.00
Electrical equipment	100.00
Miscellaneous equipment	125.00
	$1000.00

Average life of equipment 10 years	
Replacement allowance per year	$100.00
Interest on investment $1000.00 at 3 per cent	30.00
Incidentals	14.00
Overhead cost per year	$144.00
Overhead cost per month	12.00

    Time estimates — based on Hazel Kyrk, *Economic Problems of the Family* (New York: Harper, 1933), Table 13, p. 51.

living in a small apartment before marriage, or a woman whose husband was away on business, could, for approximately the same price, either buy her meals outside or prepare them for herself, depending on personal factors. For a couple after marriage, there would be a significant saving from preparing and serving meals at home, though not enough to make it extravagant for the couple to eat a good many meals out if the wife were working. A large family, on the other hand, would find taking its meals out much more expensive. If necessary, a family of five or six could hire a cook to prepare and serve meals at home and still keep the cost of feeding the family much below the cost of buying meals outside the home.

From the pecuniary viewpoint, then, a family usually selects those home production activities which will add most to the family's real income for the expenditure of time, energy, and money involved. Sometimes, however, if pressure on the family's money income is unusually high, the family adds other activities, which, while they do not pay well per hour of time spent, use unsalable time in conserving available materials that otherwise would be wasted, adding to the family's real income articles the members of the family would otherwise be compelled to do without. For example, a mother makes a new winter coat for her daughter out of a discarded coat. She spends fifty hours of her time and makes a cash outlay of fifteen cents for a pattern, and a dime for a spool of thread. A new coat would cost ten dollars and the family does not have the ten dollars. But by using time and salvaging available materials daughter gets a good-looking new coat instead of having to appear in an old one.

For personal reasons, families frequently select activities regardless of how much or how little they save in actual money outlay. They sometimes desire articles or services which are not available in the market, or they prefer the homemade to the purchased article. In other cases, family members do not count the cost of the time and energy spent because they like the activity itself. The work accomplished in pursuing a hobby is really a by-product. Many women knit for the sake of the emotional release which knitting brings; the fact that they have a dress or a scarf or a sweater to show for their work is simply something extra. Still other families, including the children, do certain things for themselves because of the educational values involved.

In most cases, probably both the pecuniary and the personal elements enter into the final decision of working out the family's home production program. When funds are limited, pecuniary factors control. When it is not necessary to plan quite so closely, personal considerations may play a major part in the decisions. For example, the cost of material for homemade clothing is usually from one third to one half the cost of a finished garment of similar quality. But the rate per hour of real income earned is frequently low. If it is important to stretch the family's money income to the maximum, as was the case with Alabama low-income farm families who were trying to clothe school girls adequately on ten dollars per year of cash outlay, pecuniary considerations alone would lead the family to make nearly all of the clothing, as these families did.[1] On the other hand, in a family with plenty of money to spend, the homemaker may decide to make clothing for any one of a number of personal reasons — because members of the family are hard to fit with ready-made clothing, because they like the garments she makes with a touch of individual styling better than those they can buy in the market, because she wants her daughters to appreciate the values in clothing construction, or just because she likes to sew.

In working out the family's home production program, it is usually desirable to specialize. The family is usually able to provide adequate equipment for carrying on effectively a few major activities. Concentration on these activities increases facility in doing the work, and brings savings large enough to pay good dividends even on expensive equipment. Where it is desirable to capitalize on various special abilities of the members of the family, definite division of labor can be planned for, with one member of the family responsible for one type of home production and another for another. In other cases, better results can be secured by planning projects which call for cooperation of all the members of the family in a common task.

In planning the proper division of work, the traditional distinction between man's work and woman's work should be ignored. In the modern cooperative family it is appropriate for each member of the family to do whatever he is best able to do. If the husband's work takes him away from home a good deal, the wife may take over complete responsibility for the upkeep of the house and grounds. If, on the other hand, his business gives him an advantage in buying food or clothing, he may do the purchasing which in most families is left for the wife. If both husband and wife are working outside the home adding to the family's money income, both may also properly share in the work of the home.

There is no one best way to work out a family's home production program. No family will want to make exactly the same division of its money between buying and financing home production from year to year. There are, however, a number of principles which may serve as a guide in making decisions concerning the home production program.

The larger the family, ordinarily, the greater is the pressure on the family's money income, and the greater is the amount of real income which can be added by home production. When a family is small and its income generous, there is a tendency to do less in the way of home production. When a family is large, with boys and girls in high school and college, and there is severe pressure on the family's money income, it is usually desirable to use the abilities of all the members of the family greatly to expand the family's home production program.

During periods of prosperity, opportunities for employment often make it desirable for the members of the family to earn more, and to buy more of what they need and do less for themselves. During periods of depression, on the other hand, it is possible to offset, at least in part, the decline in earnings by increasing the amount that the members of the family do for themselves.

In recent years, families have come to do less in the way of production of

[1] *Consumers' Guide*, Nov. 15, 1941, p. 9.

raw materials, and more final processing and providing of personal services for the members of the family. This is, of course, especially true of urban families. As the market has more and more adequately provided necessities at moderate cost, there has been a definite trend toward emphasizing recreational and avocational interests in the home production program, using unsalable time to do things for the members of the family which put the gilt edge on life.

During World War II many families were able by home production to cushion the impact of the war on the family's usual level of living. Home canning and victory gardens supplemented limited supplies of rationed food. When laundry service broke down, families with washing machines (and some without) took time off from essential war work to do their own washing and ironing. Mothers of small children used their time and sewing machines to supplement the short supply of children's garments, even buying old clothes of good quality at rummage sales in order to get the material they needed.

In the years immediately following World War II many families helped to combat inflation by doing many things for themselves; since everything they produced for themselves added to the short supplies of goods available for use, and everything which they did not have to buy reduced by so much the demand for goods that was a potent factor in inflating prices.

FAMILY USE OF COMMUNITY FACILITIES

Fundamentally, the problem of spending together for community facilities is a problem of effective citizenship. If a community is to provide the services which families want, the members of those families must participate in the direction and support of community agencies. In the case of government agencies, they must help to shape the will of the majority by the exercise of the franchise and the right of petition. They must accept the financial burdens which the maintenance of these community facilities impose. They must check to be sure that funds are spent with reasonable effectiveness for services which are worth to the families of the community somewhere near what they cost. And perhaps most difficult of all, families must insist that expenditures for community agencies be discontinued promptly when there is no longer need for the services those agencies were set up to render.

College men and women should be well qualified to assume leadership in the direction of community affairs. They will have a strong motive for effective community service if they see that their participation is something they are doing not only for the good of others, but also because their own families benefit from effective community housekeeping. However, while both time and money spent in improving community services can be made to pay dividends in the increased satisfactions which are available for the family, it is important to see this as part of a larger whole. Money can be spent only once. In apportioning the family's money among the three ways of providing for its wants, each way should get as much, and only as much, as will yield larger returns than if the same money were used in some other way.

The Problem of Financial Planning

If money is to be properly apportioned among purchase, home production, and community expenditures for the wide variety of goods and services
needed to satisfy the many and diverse wants of all the members of a family,
it is necessary for the family to have a more or less carefully thought-out
financial plan to guide its members in their spending of their common funds.
The plan may be a simple statement put down under large major headings
in general terms, or it may be worked out in meticulous detail, listing almost
every item for which the family is to spend its money for a year or more in
advance.

The informal type of budget procedure works well for some individuals,
especially those with regular incomes. They know exactly what they have to
spend. They do not need to consult anyone about the way they disburse their
money. Because they spend all their money themselves, they can easily keep
a mental record of where it goes, and they may make a good many minor
adjustments in their spending without any elaborate replanning of their
whole manner of living.

Many families, too, find that there are periods of considerable length in
the life of the family during which planning and spending can be made
largely a matter of routine. They have learned from experience what the
members of the family want, and what the family's money can be made to
do. They set up some simple but positive checks on their use of money, and
get along very well without putting any considerable amount of time on
either formal planning or record keeping. It is not that they do not plan.
Rather, they know each other so well and have their spending habits so
firmly established that a little dinner-table conversation or an occasional comment when reading the advertisements in the evening paper make it possible
for them to spend their family funds in ways which are mutually satisfactory
to all the members of the family.

On the other hand, people with only a moderate grasp of money values —
and that includes most of us — should make detailed written plans for the
use of their money. Because they have only a vague notion of what a given
amount of money will do, they may have to do considerable shopping as a
part of the planning process, in order to determine the cost of the types of
articles they desire. Instead of planning their spending in terms of allowances in round numbers for each of the principal budget headings and subheadings, they should set down exact allowances for each of the items they
are going to purchase in terms of the prices for which these articles can be
secured in local markets. Since they have very little realization of how much
money they are handling, and almost no notion of where it has gone once
they have spent it, they need to keep detailed records of their expenditures in
a form which can be checked easily and frequently with their spending plan.

Even families with a highly developed money sense find that they must
resort to carefully worked-out written plans and to the keeping of detailed
records of expenditures when conditions change radically either within or

outside the family. When they have had time to make the necessary changes in their spending habits, they may return to their less formal methods of financial planning and expenditure control.

For most young people, engagement and marriage mean radical changes in their manner of living and their methods of spending. Even for men and women who have had some experience in managing an establishment of their own, setting up a home brings unique problems. A few couples with experience in money management are able to handle financial planning effectively from the start without written plans. Usually they do this by turning over to one member of the new family the whole responsibility for family spending, or they divide between husband and wife both the money income and the responsibility for purchasing goods and paying the family bills. Most couples, however, do much better with their money management if they work out before marriage a rather detailed if somewhat tentative financial plan, and follow it through by keeping detailed records of all their expenditures for at least the first few months of their married life. One of the most effective ways of learning about likes and dislikes, about what wants the potential husband or wife considers absolutely fundamental and what things are desirable but unnecessary, is for the engaged pair to work out together, *before marriage,* a detailed financial plan. Then by keeping accurate records of their actual expenditures and comparing them with the original plan, it is possible for them to learn what they can or cannot make money do. Having thus come to a common understanding, they find it much easier to work out a mutually satisfactory basis for money management which will enable them to get the largest possible amount of satisfaction from the family's available money resources.

METHODS OF BUDGETING

Many systems of family budgeting have been advocated, and in all probability many more systems are actually in use. A family may begin by estimating the amount of their income, and keep their expenditures clearly within the limits set by the income which is sure to be available. Or they may begin by listing their wants, and then see how far it is possible to go in satisfying as many as possible of the most important of these wants by clever and effective use of money income supplemented by other available resources. Some people prefer to begin by dividing the family's probable income among perhaps a half dozen large groups of important expenditures, and then to work out in detail the items for which the money is to be spent, letting the original apportionment set limits to the expenditures for items under each of the principal budget headings. Other people find it easier to start with the details of their actual expenditures, planning month by month for the purchase of the goods and services they need or are accustomed to enjoy. Then they group these detailed expenditures in some more or less orthodox fashion which is both workable and convenient, in order to accumulate subtotals and totals which are few enough in number to be manageable when balancing income and expenditure.

Any method of financial planning will do which works well. If it is to work well, the method must let the members of the family see clearly in advance what resources they have to work with, what wants they have to satisfy, and what expenditures will probably give them the largest amount of satisfaction from the means at their disposal. It must contain positive checks upon actual expenditures sufficient to insure the use of the family's money and other resources in the ways which the members of the family have decided upon. Moreover, since it is never possible to determine exactly all needs in advance, it must be sufficiently flexible to allow for replanning from time to time as conditions demand. [2]

Many people find that making a financial plan is much more difficult than getting their money's worth once the plan is made. There are a number of reasons why this is true. Working out a spending plan for a family requires foresight and constructive imagination. In making a workable spending plan it is necessary to deal with a mass of detail, and somehow or other bring together a wide variety of diverse variables into a reasonably well-organized and not too unharmonious whole. It involves the expression of a great many concrete details of family spending in abstract symbols called numbers. For many people numbers are symbols in an unfamiliar language. As a result, the totals in many spending plans turn out to be broad but meaningless generalizations which fail to provide the guidance in actual spending for which they are intended.

People who are overwhelmed by the mass of detail which intelligent planning involves find that it helps to break the problem up into a series of separate problems, each one of which can be handled reasonably well by itself. Hence, budget headings are helpful: Food, Clothing, Shelter, House Operation, Health, Recreation, etc. People who find that figures have little meaning can use both words and figures in working out the details of their plan. If they work out a week's menus, plan the grocery lists, and figure the cost of buying the food required, they arrive at a total for food which means something to them. They may find it difficult to decide whether they need $350 or $400 for clothing. If they take an inventory of the clothes they have on hand, and consider the social functions they must attend, where they expect to go for their vacation, and what demands the job makes on their clothing supply, they can work out a list of articles which will fill their needs, and by a little shopping for prices and qualities, determine just what $350 and just what $400 will mean in terms of an actual wardrobe.

Some families find that they can handle fairly well the detail which is involved in planning the use of money for a single pay period, but find it difficult and confusing to try to plan in more general terms for a quarter or for a year in advance. To them a year's plan is simply the amounts in a month's plan multiplied by twelve, or a week's plan multiplied by fifty-two.

2 For detailed methods of financial planning and budgeting, see Howard F. Bigelow, *Family Finance* (revised, Philadelphia: Lippincott, 1953), chaps. 14, 15; S. Agnes Donham, *Spending the Family Income* (Boston: Little, Brown, 1933). For a simple, workable plan, see *Money Management, the Budget Calendar,* published by the Household Finance Co., 919 North Michigan Ave., Chicago, Ill.

This method leaves out of account many important expenditures requiring sizable amounts of money which must be made only once or twice during the year. If instead of multiplying the amounts opposite each item in the plan for a single pay period by the number of periods in a year, they should work out a series of plans, including in each plan the regularly recurring, the seasonal, and the occasional expenditures to be made in that particular pay period, they would then arrive, by adding the amounts opposite each item in these smaller spending plans, at a year's financial plan which has meaning and which will provide a working guide to their expenditures when they put it in practice.

Other families find it easy to work out a spending plan in general terms for a year in advance. Then they work out a plan for each month in the year by dividing by twelve the yearly allowances for each of the items in their yearly plan. This plan looks well on paper, but something always happens when they attempt to put it into practice.

Suppose a family has worked out such a plan, taking account of all income from all sources which will be available to spend during the year, being careful to include not only the regularly recurring expenditures for food and rent and utilities, but the seasonal and occasional expenditures as well, keeping totals of their expenditures well within the limits set by their estimates of yearly income. What happens when they try to follow their plan for January? Their monthly plan assumes they will have exactly one twelfth of the year's income to spend in January. This may or may not be true. Assume that it is. Their monthly plan provides one twelfth of the year's allowance for fuel. A cold snap the first week makes it necessary to spend in January a fifth of the year's allowance for fuel. The plan calls for one twelfth of the year's allowance for gifts. Yet there are bills for half of last year's Christmas gifts yet to be paid. The cost of the yearly license and a year's insurance for the automobile, added to the regular operating expenses and payments for a few unexpected minor repairs, requires nearly two months' allowance for transportation, with only one month's allowance available for expenditure. On the other hand, the plan provides for one twelfth of the clothing allowance, which is being saved to use in March for clothes for Easter; one twelfth of the vacation allowance, to be spent next July; and one twelfth of the allowance for the life insurance premium, which comes due next May. Suppose that instead of apportioning one twelfth of the income and one twelfth of each of these allowances to each month in the year, the family should allocate the income to the months in which it will be received, and the allowances for each of the items in their yearly plan to the months in which the expenditures are actually to be made. By adjusting the expenditures for each month until they are in line with the income then actually available, they would have a workable spending plan.

BUDGET PERCENTAGES

Many people are interested in knowing whether they are making the best possible apportionment of their income between the various large groups of expenditures in their financial plan. They want to know what percentage of their income should be spent for food or for clothing, or for insurance, or for the family car. There are several reasons why there can be no simple formula of budget percentages which automatically gives a satisfactory basis for a spending plan.

In the first place, no two families have exactly the same set of wants. One family prefers a big car, new every year, and is perfectly contented to live in a small apartment. Another prefers a large comfortable home, and drives an old car or depends on commercial transportation.

In the second place, families provide for their wants in different ways. One family prefers to buy most of its meals out, but makes most of the children's clothing. Another family buys its clothing, but raises a vegetable garden, does most of its own canning and baking, and seldom eats out. The first family will spend a larger proportion of its income for food and a smaller proportion for clothing. The family satisfying its wants for a particular group of expenditures by purchasing goods ready to use in the market must allot a larger proportion of its income to that type of expenditure than does a family producing most of its requirements for its own use.

In the third place, there is no year in which the relative prices of all goods are exactly the same. If food prices rise more than clothing prices, then a larger percentage of the family income will be needed for food and a smaller percentage for clothing. If the price of men's clothing rises more than the price of women's clothing, then it will probably be necessary to set aside a larger percentage of the family income for the man to spend on his wardrobe.

In the fourth place, there are no two years in the life of any family in which it buys exactly the same list of goods and services. The family's wants change from year to year. Market offerings change. Durable goods are purchased only at long intervals. Further, families buy first one thing and then another. One year they buy a new car. Another year they buy new furniture for the living room. Another year they take an expensive vacation. Another year they "buy" a new baby. The proportion to be alloted to the various divisions of the spending plan must change with these marked variations in the family's purchases.

Properly used, budget percentages compiled from the expenditures of a large group of families with similar incomes and similar wants, living under similar conditions, can provide a guide to probable requirements for various types of expenditures over a period of years. But it is important to remember that the figures are the result of averaging the expenditures of large numbers of individual families, and that in all probability no family in the group spent its income exactly as the composite indicates. In fact there is some reason to believe that for the very items for which averages seem to run most uniformly, the individual deviations in expenditures are frequently greatest.[3]

Clearly, then, there can be no hard and fast rule for financial planning based on budget percentages, especially in times when prices or family needs

[3] For discussion of some of the principles involved in the apportionment of income among the various items of expenditure, see Bigelow, *op. cit.*, Pt. 3.

are changing rapidly. The only practical way to make a satisfactory apportionment of funds among the major divisions of the spending plan is to work out the apportionment in terms of the wants themselves, determining what are the most important, the next most important, and the next most important of the family's wants, and then allotting available funds by assigning whatever amounts are necessary at existing price levels to satisfy these wants properly, including in the final plan as many of the more important wants as can be satisfied with the available income.

THE FAMILY LIFE CYCLE

To be sure that the family is satisfying its most important wants, the members should work out each year's spending plan as an integral part of a long-time financial program. But it is no more satisfactory to work out this long-time plan for ten or twenty or thirty years by taking a single year's plan and multiplying it by the number of years involved than it is to take a week's spending plan and multiply it by fifty-two and call it an annual budget.

The wants and needs of every family change from year to year, with the inevitable changes in the ages, interests, and even in the number of the family members. Similarly, the family's money income varies with the number and earning power of its gainfully employed members, and with the changes in the amount and yield of the family's investments. But the family income does not necessarily vary proportionately or even directly with the family needs. There are some families whose income increases as rapidly during the years in which it is bringing up its children as do the demands upon it. But most families find that the years when the children are in high school and college bring expenses which cannot be met out of current income. Even though the family has saved substantial sums in anticipation of these expenses, these years put a very heavy strain on the family's financial resources. If a family is to provide for all its important wants during the years of heavy expense, it is absolutely necessary to plan in advance for many of these expenditures. Otherwise the family may find that it has spent its money for nonessentials during periods of generous income, and as a result must do without many goods and services it wants very much during periods of heavy demand.

But in recent years it has been very difficult to plan even for a year in advance. Ever since the outbreak of the First World War we have been more conscious of the changing and uncertain elements in the world in which we must live than of the constant and dependable factors. How can a family know what its wants will be even next year, to say nothing of five or ten or fifteen or twenty years in advance? What basis does it have for deciding which of its future wants are more important than the present wants which it might satisfy with the same amount of money?

In the first place, we do know that every family passes through a definite life cycle, in which each stage has its characteristic wants, its characteristic patterns of expenditures. Figure 8 shows graphically the varying burden of family support in a middle class family. Most families have a similar life cycle.

First comes the establishment of the family.[4] During the first few years of family life, expenses for food and clothing and other current necessities are at

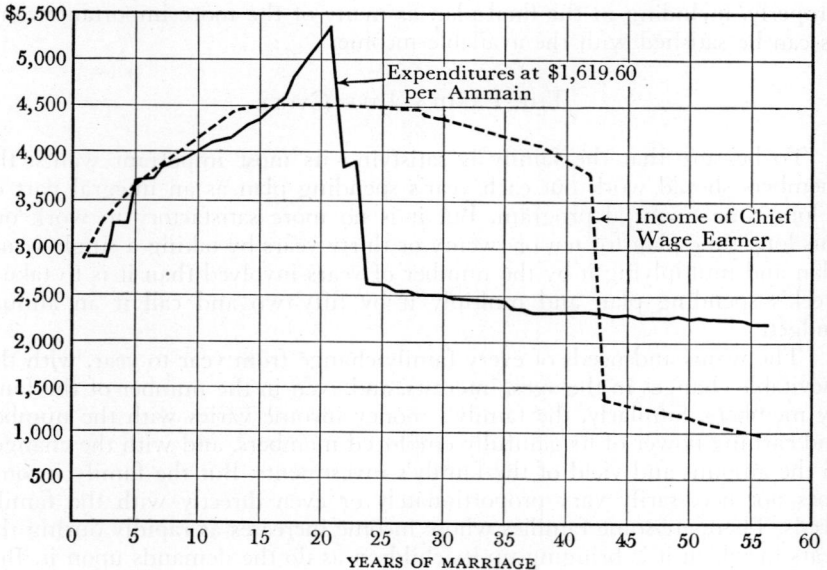

FIGURE 8. VARYING BURDEN OF FAMILY SUPPORT [5]

[4] In countries where the engagement is a formal legal ceremony involving formal property settlements, from the economic viewpoint the engagement period is part of the establishment stage of the life cycle. In countries where engaged couples have no clearly recognized social or legal status until the engagement is formally announced a few weeks before marriage it may be helpful to think of the engagement period as a separate stage in the cycle.

[5] The income line is annual income for a man with a maximum income of $4500. L. I. Dublin and A. J. Lotka, *The Money Value of a Man* (rev., New York: Ronald Press, 1946). The expenditure line is expenditure in dollars computed at $1619.60 per ammain.

The data on which this chart is based assume a family consisting of a husband and wife, married when he is 25 and she is 23, who rear two children, a boy born at the end of the second year, and a girl born at the end of the fourth year of their married life. It is further assumed that the family supports each of its children for nineteen years, providing them with a high school education. On the nineteenth birthday, each child leaves home and becomes self-supporting. The husband continues to work regularly until his sixty-seventh birthday, when he retires to live for fourteen years on his accumulated savings.

After the family has passed the peak of its expense, it continues to live at the same level, investing its surplus income at 3 per cent, until the retirement of the head of the family. The family's income after retirement consists of the interest at 3 per cent on its accumulated savings. During the retirement years, the family draws upon the principal of its savings each year for the amount needed to maintain its accustomed level of living. Even if both husband and wife live for fourteen years after the husband's retirement, according to this example there will still be left some $3200 of the family's accumulated savings to be passed on to the heirs. See H. F. Bigelow, *Family Finance* (rev., Philadelphia: Lippincott, 1953).

a minimum. There is then the possibility of saving money for investment in securities to supplement income in later years, in durable household equipment, or perhaps even in the home itself.

Next comes the childbearing and preschool period. Current expenses will begin to increase gradually during this period. The outstanding expenses will be for medical attendance and hospital bills — the acquisition cost of the children — and extra expenditures for household service necessary while the children are small.

Then comes the elementary school period. Current expenses continue to increase gradually during this period but are still far from their peak. Food costs are increasing somewhat; clothing costs are increasing decidedly. While actual education expenses are moderate, the children are beginning to bring pressure for higher standards at home in order that they may come up to the standards set by the other children in school who come from families with larger incomes.

For most families the high school period brings the largest demand upon the family income. Current expenses for food, clothing, books, and entertainment absorb a larger portion of the family income. In addition, social pressure on the family both at school and at home calls for improved standards at a time when it is most difficult to provide them.

If the standard of the family calls for a college education, the next period will entail even heavier expenditure. Some assistance from the children's earnings may be looked for here as the result of vacation employment. But even with some aid from this source, during this period comparatively few families are able to provide for current expenditures entirely from current income. Maintenance costs for the children are at their maximum. These expenditures are increased if it is necessary for the boy or girl to live away from home. Frequently educational expenses form the largest single item in the budget. In most cases the father and mother are spending more on each one of the children during this period than they are spending on themselves.

Of necessity a period of recovery follows. As one by one the children finish high school or college and become self-supporting, current expenses drop rapidly; but there is a great deal to be done by way of recouping the family fortunes. The family's original supply of furniture is worn out. The old house is usually too big and almost always out of repair. Savings are depleted, and old age is not so very many years ahead. In this period, for the second time in the life cycle of the family, accumulation for the future both in the form of investments and of equipment should take a large share of the family income.

Finally, there is a period of retirement. In this period current expenses are usually moderate and by necessity are scaled to what the individual fortune will permit. Travel and winters in Florida or California are desirable, but the longing for new thrills may have passed. Food needs and wear and tear on clothing are low. Usually a small, convenient apartment will provide more desirable housing than the large house which was necessary while the family was growing up. Adequate provision for personal service is the single item of expense which may run very high in elderly families.[6]

[6] Bigelow, *Family Finance*, pp. 15–17.

The length of each of the stages in the typical cycle and the extent to which there is overlapping vary from family to family, depending upon the age of the parents at the time of their marriage, the time of the arrival of the first child, the number and spacing of the children, and the amount and type of education with which they are to be provided. The time when a given family will enter each of these stages can be determined when the first child is born. When the family is complete, it is possible to determine within a year or two the time when the family will be free from the burden of the nurture and education of the children.

If a family will work out the approximate timing of its progress through the family life cycle, taking into account the age of the parents or other relatives who might become dependent,[7] it will be possible to get a fairly detailed idea of the wants to be satisfied year by year through the whole life of the family.

Determining the amount of money a family will have to use is a more difficult problem. The initial earning power and the opportunities for advancement in the occupation or profession in which the husband is engaged or for which he is preparing can be determined, as can the probable earning power of the wife if she is to work outside the home after marriage.[8] It is possible to estimate the probable income which the family, with reasonable care and average good fortune, should receive from such investments as the members of the family now own or can reasonably expect to accumulate or inherit. By combining these separate estimates, a family can determine in present dollar values the probable amount of the income which it will have to spend during the various stages of the life cycle.

PLANNING FOR CHANGING BUSINESS CONDITIONS

The family of course must recognize that both incomes and living costs are constantly changing. The only practical long-time approach is to plan in terms of *present price levels,* working out the plan so that it will be relatively easy to make corrections both on the income and the expenditure side as changes occur in income and prices due to postwar inflation and deflation and the swing of the business cycle.

[7] Are sons-in-law and daughters-in-law relatives? A family with the tradition of early marriage may find it necessary to plan for subsidizing its children during the period in which they are finishing their education and becoming established in their occupation. The government, in the so-called G.I. Bill, recognizes this need in the case of men whose education has been interrupted by war service.

[8] The wife brings no dowry to the marriage in the United States, but often is given a college or vocational education by her parents which she can use to earn the trousseau, furniture, and equipment which the dowry buys in other countries. The wife will find it advisable to work outside the home at two stages in the family life cycle: (1) between marriage and the first child, to pay for furniture and unusual initial expenses of setting up housekeeping; and (2) during the high school and college period, when she is freed from the care of her children and when her salary will help to defray the extra expenses at the peak of the expense cycle.

Families can do very little to overcome the impact of inflation. If they try to protect themselves by buying in advance of use, they only make bad matters worse. Their best procedure is to eliminate all unnecessary expenditures, facing the fact that if inflation is severe and continues long enough they will have to turn to their savings to provide even the necessities for their members.

Deflation also brings with it difficult problems of financial readjustment. When prices are falling, incomes may lag behind, but often the same forces that are pushing prices downward cause a great deal of unemployment, so that many families find it is not a question of whether prices are falling more rapidly than income, but rather of whether they can get any income at all. [9]

Making a long-time financial plan for a family is a good deal like planning a long cross-country vacation trip in the family car. In planning such a trip, the members of the family know that they have a limited amount of time and a limited amount of money to spend. They select a destination. This means they must average so many miles a day, driving more miles when the roads are good and the weather fine and fewer miles when the roads are bad and the weather unfavorable. The amount of money they have to spend determines the type of accommodation they can use en route. And they usually plan in terms of so many nights to be spent in hotels or tourist homes or cabins. They allow a moderate or a generous amount for meals along the way. They must also make some allowance for the hazards of the highway. If everything goes unusually well, they may be able to afford a couple of side trips to points of interest along the way. Although they know in advance that they will not follow out their plan in every detail, they make a plan, because by planning they can have a better trip with the time and means at their disposal.

A long-time financial plan is not a definite and detailed plan, nor one to be adhered to religiously no matter what happens. Rather it is a chart intended to give direction to the family's planning of its spending for shorter periods. Just as the plan for the vacation trip lets the family work out the details of the journey with the whole trip in mind, so the long-time financial plan lets the family see each immediate financial problem in its relation to the long life of the family.

In long-time planning, therefore, a couple try to get a picture of their family moving through the years. They estimate the probable cost of providing for the family's more important wants during each stage of the family life cycle. They take stock of their money income and of all other available pecuniary and nonpecuniary resources. They make due allowance for the ways in which the family will be affected by the hazards life holds, and allow adequate margins for adjustment. If they work out their original plan carefully and adapt it intelligently to conditions as they develop, at the end of ten or fifteen or twenty years the family will find that they have been able to get much more for their money than would have been possible under a system of unplanned random spending.

[9] See Chapter Twenty-One, pp. 616–623, for a discussion of family adjustments in the depression.

TYPICAL PROBLEMS OF POLICY MAKING

In handling its financial affairs, every family faces the necessity of making decisions upon a number of problems of fiscal administration and financial policy. Among the more important are the following: Who shall earn and who shall spend the family's money? Shall the wife work outside the home after marriage? How shall we provide the funds necessary for starting our family? What sort of financial records should we keep? At what level of living shall we start our family? How many children can we afford to have? How much and what sort of insurance shall we buy? Shall we always pay cash, or is it all right sometimes to buy on credit?

Each of these questions has to be decided in the light of the individual family situation. For example, there are a number of reasons why the wife may decide to work outside the home after marriage. She may like to work. There may be some special need for her services. In case of a serious epidemic, all the nurses in the community are expected to help until the emergency is past. If there is a temporary labor shortage in an essential local industry, there is often community pressure for married women to work till the rush is over. Or she may need the money she earns to meet personal or family financial obligations, such as the support of parents or other family members; or the support of her own family while her husband is in school or is getting started in his business or profession; or the payment of her own or her husband's school debts. She may want to earn money in order to enable the family to get ahead financially — by the purchase of furniture, a car, or a home; or by putting her earnings into a cash reserve against unexpected unemployment, or to defray the expenses of childbirth, or for working capital for the family business, or for future income for the family. Or she may feel that earning is the best way for her to help provide the family with a higher present level of living, especially when the husband's income is low or when family expenses are unusually high.

In deciding whether or not the wife should work outside the home after marriage, the answer depends in the last analysis on whether she can contribute more to the family by earning money or by working at home. If, in order to make it possible for the wife to be away from home, it is necessary to hire household help or to make extensive use of expensive community services, ordinarily to break even financially she must be able to earn at least twice as much per hour as she must pay for the help which she hires. She will find inevitably that working outside the home involves additional expenditures for extra clothing, for transportation to and from work, for lunches, for professional expenses or union dues, for more or less compulsory contribution to community projects, and for more expensive ways of buying and of doing her housework. Since her husband is already using her income tax deduction against the family income, whatever she earns will be subject to taxation at whatever rate applies to her additions to the family income. If she and her husband, and perhaps other members of the family, can among them do the housework, so that extra expenses are kept to a minimum, it is often possible for the wife, especially if she is a trained woman, to add substantially to the family's financial resources by gainful employment. But it is important that the family understands fully all the changes which her working outside the home involves. Decision in favor of employment should be made only in cases where it is clear she will add substantially to the family's net money income without overworking. For what she does for her family at home has cash value, and there is as yet no income tax to be paid on what she adds to the family's real income. And there are important, if sometimes intangible values, just in having a wife, and especially a mother, always around the house.

In deciding on whether to buy on credit or to pay cash, a family must decide whether they want the item badly enough to pay the price *plus* the financing charges. If, for example, by buying a washing machine on the installment plan and doing the laundry at home, a family can save enough on the laundry bill in two weeks to make a month's payment on the washer, they would do well to buy the machine on the installment plan.

In deciding upon how many children they can afford, many families base their decision on the relative importance of a standard of living which is high in material goods and services but low in family responsibilities, and one which is somewhat lower in material goods and services but much richer in personal interrelationships. Many families limit the number of their children, not because they want a higher material standard of living for themselves, but because they want to give their children advantages which they did not have. They should remember that a standard moderately high in material goods and services and rich in the personal interactions which life with many brothers and sisters can bring is an excellent preparation for effective living in adult life.

In deciding upon how much and what types of life insurance to carry, the family will need to consider the life expectancy of the family members, the occupational hazards which they run, and the relative importance of insuring against premature death or the possibility of a prolonged old age. Here many families find that the best policy is to use ordinary or whole life insurance, which usually provides protection at moderately low cost and at the same time has cash values which can be used to purchase a life annuity in case the insured lives to the retirement period.

Finally, we come back to the question with which we began: "How much money does it take to get married?" No one amount of money will guarantee success in marriage, though some studies seem to indicate that a moderate amount is better than either too little or too much. Happily married couples can be found at all income levels, and unhappy couples as well.[10]

How much money is needed depends upon the kind of families two people come from and the kind of family they expect to form. It depends on the income level of the parents' families, on the income level at which the young people are starting, and on the income level which they may reasonably ex-

[10] See E. W. Burgess and L. S. Cottrell, Jr., *Predicting Success or Failure in Marriage* (New York: Prentice-Hall, 1939), chap. 9, for discussion of the influence of income and economic status on marital happiness.

pect to attain. It depends on the occupation of the husband — and of the wife, should she decide to work outside the home after marriage — since different occupations bring varying financial and social demands. It depends on the type of community in which the new family will live, and on the standard of living they are expected to maintain. Usually a young couple find that the larger the city and the more exclusive the neighborhood in which they are living, the higher are living costs.

The amount of money required to get married varies not only with the index of living costs in different communities, but even more with the relative importance to the members of the family of material goods which cost money and nonmaterial values which do not. It depends on the age of the husband and wife at the time of their marriage, on the number of children they are planning to have, and on when they plan to have them. Much depends on what they are likely to inherit from their parents; this may be either a substantial addition to the family's money capital or, in some cases, added dependents to care for and support. It depends on the nonpecuniary resources which the two young people have available, such as furniture and equipment, an automobile, a house in which to live, stocks of clothing, a radio, equipment for sports and recreation.

In the light of all these varied factors, then, each couple must determine for themselves how much money they need if they are to marry. This is an important decision, for money is important in modern marriage. Not because money is an end in itself — let that be clearly understood — but because it is one of the essential tools with which a family may carve out a well-rounded and abundantly satisfying life for all its members.

SELECTED READINGS

BIGELOW, HOWARD F., *Family Finance* (rev., Philadelphia: Lippincott, 1953).

BONDE, RUTH L., *Management in Daily Living* (New York: Macmillan, 1944).

COLE, JESSIE V., *The Consumer-Buyer and the Market* (New York: Wiley, 1938).

DONHAM, S. AGNES, *Case Book in Family Budgeting* (Boston: Boston Cooking School Magazine, 1937).

——, *Spending the Family Income* (Boston: Little, Brown, 1933).

Household Finance Corporation, Chicago, "Money Management Series." Especially "Money Management — Your Budget"; "Money Management for Newlyweds."

——, "Better Buymanship Series."

KYRK, HAZEL, *Economic Problems of the Family* (New York: Harper, 1933).

NICKELL, PAULENA, and DORSEY, JEAN MUIR, *Management in Family Living* (rev. ed.; New York: Wiley, 1947).

RADELL, NEVA H., *Accounting for the Individual and Family* (New York: Prentice-Hall, 1940).

REID, MARGARET G., *Consumers and the Market* (New York: Crofts, 1938).

TROELSTRUP, ARCH W., *Consumer Problems* (New York: McGraw-Hill Book Co., Inc., 1952).

1. A young couple is just setting up housekeeping. They plan to have two children. They hope sometime to own their own home. They wish to give their children a high school education, and if possible to give one of them a college education. They wish to accumulate enough to be independent in their old age, and to be able to leave to their children an estate of at least $10,000 in addition to their home. When should they plan to buy their home? When should they accumulate money for the college education? When should they make provision for their old age? When should they plan to set aside the savings necessary to the accumulation of their estate?

2. List the ten most effective ways in which you can increase your efficiency as a buyer.

3. List all the activities you know which can, if necessary, be carried on in the home to supplement the family's money income. Classify these in three ways, as follows:

   (1) According to who may engage in them, as: (a) women's activities; (b) men's activities: (c) activities suited to either men or women; and (d) activities requiring family cooperation.

   (2) Activities suited to families living: (a) on farms; (b) in small towns or villages; (c) in single houses in cities; and (d) in city apartments.

   (3) According to skill and equipment, as: (a) activities which require special equipment; (b) activities which require special skill; and (c) activities which require neither special equipment nor special skill.

4. In what types of economic activity is there the greatest advantage in mass production? In what types of economic activity is there greater advantage in home production? For what types of commodities and service is there greatest saving in distribution costs by production for use at home?

5. What do you consider to be the relative importance of the following values which may be secured from production for use: (a) satisfying wants better; (b) satisfying more wants; (c) satisfying wants not otherwise possible; and (d) engaging in activity which is satisfying in itself? Are there any other values to be secured from home production which you feel should be listed with these? What are they?

6. In estimating the cost of feeding a family at home and comparing this with the cost of feeding it in a restaurant or a boarding house, ordinarily only the actual cost of the food purchased and in a few cases the cost of ice and fuel are included in the costs of the home-planned meals. (1) Is this a sound basis for deciding upon the relative advantage of boarding or of providing meals at home? (2) Should the housewife count a share of rent for the space used in the kitchen and dining room, a return on the family's investment in kitchen equipment, table service, and the like, along with a definite charge for her own labor, as part of the cost of feeding the family at home?

7. In what specific ways can individual families of your acquaintance increase the satisfaction they secure from their collective expenditures by more frequent use of the services the government or private agencies supply?

8. How many families of your acquaintance practice financial planning as it is

defined in this chapter? How many work according to an informal or unwritten budget? How many work out detailed spending plans? How many keep accurate account of their expenditures?

9. Give several examples of the way actual families of your acquaintance balance their budgets.

10. List at least ten devices used by families of your acquaintance to keep actual expenditures within the limits set up in their spending plan.

11. What kind of budget best suits your personal needs? Point out several specific ways in which this budget insures your securing the maximum of satisfaction from the money income and other resources at your disposal.

12. In families of your acquaintance, which member or members of the family group make the final decisions in planning family expenditures? What seem to be the advantages and disadvantages in each case? How can a budget be devised which will care adequately for the necessary common wants of a family, and at the same time allow each individual the largest possible amount of freedom in satisfying his personal preferences?

13. A young couple want advice in working out a financial plan for their family. Using the family life cycle method, indicate for them the probable expenses they must provide for in each of the stages of the family life cycle.

14. Make a list of all the elements in the current business situation which families should consider in planning their expenditures for the next month; in working out their next year's budget.

15. In what stage of the business cycle are you now living? Are prices rising or falling? Is the long-run trend of prices up or down? Is either inflation or deflation in immediate prospect? How do you tell?

Chapter Fourteen

Heredity and the Family

RAY D. OWEN

O NE of our first concerns in anticipating parenthood is the nature of the inheritance we will provide our children. Our legacy to them will fall into three quite different categories: material things, like money and property; the things our children will learn from us, like patterns of behavior, customs, and information; and their biological equipment and nature. All these will play an integral part in determining the directions in which our children will develop. And while the laws and processes of transmission from one generation to the next are quite different in the three categories, their effects are intermingled in a single individual in such complex ways that it is often impossible, with the information at hand, to distinguish the effects of original differences in one category from those in another. The primary concern of this chapter will be biological inheritance; but, lest this concern appear to be thought of exclusive importance in the discussion to follow, it should be emphasized at the start that no individual is the product of his biological inheritance alone. We inherit only potentialities — promises, more or less, to react in fairly specific ways to specific environments, but in many respects to react in a variety of ways to a variety of environments. This lability, developed to an unusual extent in human beings, explains in large part the success of our species.[1]

Limiting our consideration for the time being to inherent biological differences, the category usually implied in the term *heredity*, it is obvious that concern about our children in this connection takes a number of forms. We shall distinguish three. First, there is a normal curiosity as to "what Junior will be like." Will he have his daddy's blue eyes or his mother's brown; his grandfather's pattern of baldness or his father's curly, thick hair — and so on, almost without limit. This sort of curiosity is somewhat like that of the gardener who buys a packet of mixed seeds, and over his pipe that evening wonders what kinds and colors of flowers he will harvest. Like the gardener most of us are happy to take what we get, although we can enjoy speculating over the contents of our packages. Familiarity with the facts and laws of heredity can sometimes give us a fair idea of what sorts of seed we are planting, but the seeds of humanity are generally a complex mixture indeed.

A second form of concern over heredity is of much more serious significance because it is a source not of enjoyable speculation over a variety of possible happy harvests but of pain and fear, sometimes needless and pointless,

[1] See Bain's discussion of the same point, pp. 172–179.

in anticipating possible unhappy consequences. This is concern over defects and deficiencies that our children may inherit, over family "taints" and "blemishes," physical, mental, or emotional, thought by many, often mistakenly, to be fixed by heredity beyond correction and marring our children for life. Many elementary discussions of human heredity are limited to listing such heritable defects. This is probably in large part because many people do worry about them and because the better known inherited human differences are simply inherited characteristics of this sort. They are most likely to be noted and are most easily studied and followed through families in their passage from one generation to the next. We would be unwise to ignore the existence of such characteristics. We would also be unwise to ignore the facts (1) that almost all of them, as specific entities, are rare; (2) that not all of them are beyond correction in the individual possessing them; and (3) that not all the defects that look alike are inherited alike — some of them may not be inherited at all. This is not to minimize the importance of a rational consideration of possible unhappy harvests in particular cases but to suggest that the consideration should always be rational and based on an enlightened evaluation of the facts in each case.

Social, rather than individual, aspects of heredity represent the third sort of concern. This is the problem of "inherent population quality." It queries, "What sort of population will the next generation comprise? Will they as a whole be a small step forward or backward on the long slope of human evolution, or will they maintain the status quo? Will our children as a population be as responsive as we would have been to the better world we hope to provide for them, or will they be more or less so because of a different inherent constitution?" Here the interactions of material, cultural, and biological inheritance are particularly complex. None of these sources of human differences is static. Almost certainly, the details of the biological composition of tomorrow's human population will differ from today's. It will be affected by the decision of today's young men and women whether or not to marry, whether or not to have children, how many to have, and how soon to begin. It is related to these decisions as their statistical consequence, and it requires a statistical rather than a strictly individual frame of reference. It is also related to a variety of factors beyond immediate individual control: to the social patterns of our culture and the extent to which our population is subdivided in reproduction by political, geographic, economic, educational, racial, religious, or other barriers into more or less isolated groups; to the potential occurrence of new hereditary qualities, influenced perhaps by blind forces like those inherent in "atomic bombardment"; and to the equally blind operations of the laws of chance in sampling from the germ plasm of today's parents the basic materials with which tomorrow's population will be built.[2]

These, then, are complicated questions and their intelligent consideration will involve some familiarity with the laws and processes of biological inheritance. We shall deal for the most part, perforce, in generalities; of the considerable mass of data and specific information at hand we shall be able

[2] This problem is the primary concern of Woofter in chap. 25, pp. 743–772.

to sample only lightly. Such a procedure may be considered adequate for an over-all appreciation of the significance of heredity in marriage. For the solution of perplexing or worrisome individual problems, however, confident predictions must be based on more thorough and expert knowledge both of the principles of heredity and of the limitations of their application to the cases in question. At least one semester course in heredity is offered in almost every college; we cannot expect our cursory consideration here to take its place.

Principles of Heredity

Each human being begins life as a single cell, a fertilized egg. The individual at this stage has been formed by the union of two "half-individuals" — one from the father, the sperm cell, and the other from the mother, the egg. The fertilized egg is quite small; it has been estimated that all the fertilized eggs from which the present human inhabitants of the world developed had a total volume of about three quarts. Through this physically tiny bottleneck have passed all the biologically inherited characteristics and potentialities that serve to make us similar to but different from our ancestors. Our descendants will be connected with us by a bottleneck of comparable size.

It is not surprising, in view of the vital and complicated function of this physical connection between generations, to find it, in spite of its small size, complex, delicately balanced, and precisely organized. The germ plasm that forms the material basis of inheritance is, to begin with, neither a homogeneous fluid nor a mixture of blending fluids like coffee and cream, but is a motley of particles, like beads or marbles of many different colors, each particle with its own separate and virtually permanent integrity. We recognize the effects of these particulate differences when we speak of the specific inherited characteristics of people, like baldness or color blindness. We call these basic particles, the units of inheritance, *genes*. Thus an hereditarily bald man may be regarded as having a "gene for baldness"; a color blind man has a "gene for color blindness."

While no one has ever surely seen a gene, we have a considerable amount of knowledge about genes generally and therefore about the nature and structure of the germ plasm. Most of this knowledge has been derived from laboratory studies of plants and animals and is only in the process of being extended to human beings. The extension is greatly facilitated by the knowledge that the fundamental laws and mechanisms of biological inheritance hold for all sexually-reproducing organisms — human, plant, and animal.

An important characteristic of genes that might be anticipated from the way individuals are formed and how they differ, is that genes are ordinarily present *in pairs* in all persons. The individual originates from the fusion of two "half-individuals," the sperm from the father and the egg from the mother, and each of these elements generally contributes one member of each pair of genes — or, to put it differently, one complete set of genes. When the individual in turn forms reproductive cells (sperm or egg, depending on his sex), the paired genes separate without having modified each other in any way, one member of each pair (and therefore one complete set of genes) going into each sperm or egg. New "half-individuals" are thus formed, each with a sample half of the paired genes of the parent. These germ cells in turn form the next generation as those from the opposite sexes again fuse as fertilized eggs. The pageant of human generations and the variety of biologically inherited human differences thus resolve themselves into a scheme as simple and logical as one might conceive. They have their basis in a germ plasm that is, first, *particulate* — composed of many units, each with its own separate and virtually permanent integrity; and second, *duplicate* — so that the particles generally occur in pairs in any individual, one member of each pair coming from each parent, and one member of each pair going into each sperm or egg. These are the principles of heredity.

From Gene to Characteristic

The members of any given pair of genes in an individual may be alike and of one kind, or different, or alike and of another kind. For example, if we let *a* represent the gene for albinism, and *A* the alternative gene for normal pigmentation, most individuals in human populations are of genetic type *AA* and are normally pigmented. They receive the normal gene from each of their parents, and will transmit it to each of their children. A few people (about one in 20,000 in European countries) are of genetic type *aa* and are albinos, with white hair, rosy-white skin, and pink eyes. They received the gene for albinism from each of their parents, and will in turn transmit it to each of their children. The purpose of this example is to call attention to the third possible genetic type, *Aa*. Such individuals are normally pigmented and cannot at present be distinguished from those of type *AA*. Nevertheless, they receive the gene for albinism from one of their parents — it does not matter which — and will pass it on to half their children, on the average. They are "carrying" albinism, but they do not show it because the presence of the normal gene, *A*, masks or obscures the presence of the alternative gene, *a*. We describe this situation by saying that *A* is dominant to *a*, or that *a* is recessive (see Figure 9, Inheritance of Albinism, for a graphic description of this same point).

Dominance of one gene over its alternative is a very common (although not a universal) phenomenon, and it seems a simple enough "complication" indeed — one even to be expected on *a priori* grounds. The process of pigment development is probably a rather involved chain of chemical reactions. Under the influence of the *A* gene this process goes on normally. When no *A* gene is present, that is, when the developing individual is of type *aa*, the chemical chain is apparently broken somewhere along the line and no pigment is formed. Viewed in this light, it is not surprising that an individual with one *A* gene should produce normal pigment whether he has another *A* gene or only the *a* gene to complete his pair. But regardless of its reasonableness, dominance often confuses the genetic situation in human families. The recessive gene for albinism, for example, may pass unnoticed for generations in a family, occurring only in *Aa* individuals who have no way of knowing

IF ○ represents the gene for <u>albinism</u>, and
● is its normal alternative,

Since genes are in general present in duplicate, a person may be any one of three types:

(1) ●/●   (2) ●/○   (3) ○/○

Types (I) and (2) are indistinguishable in appearance: this illustrates DOMINANCE of the normal gene over its alternative.

The paired particles separate when an individual forms germ cells. Thus a man of type (2) forms two kinds of sperm in equal numbers:

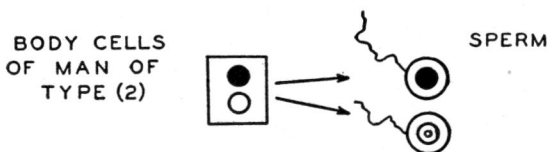

BODY CELLS OF MAN OF TYPE (2)   SPERM

The "defective" gene may be hidden for generations by its dominant, normal alternative:

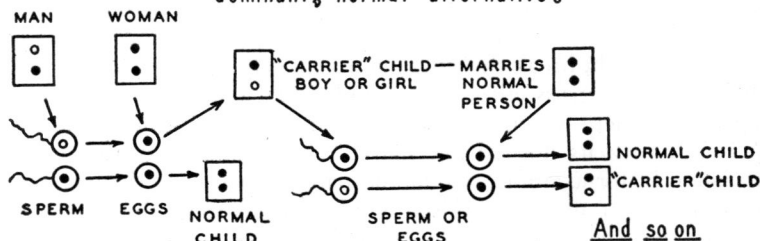

MAN   WOMAN

"CARRIER" CHILD — MARRIES BOY OR GIRL   NORMAL PERSON

SPERM   EGGS   NORMAL CHILD   SPERM OR EGGS   NORMAL CHILD   "CARRIER" CHILD

<u>And so on</u>

But when two "carriers" marry

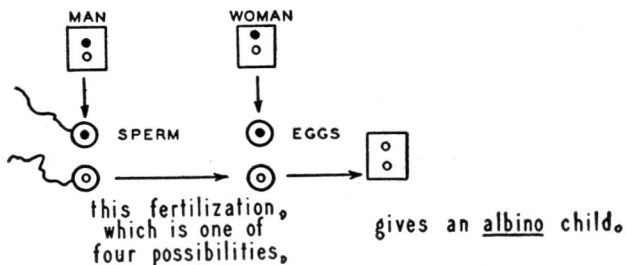

MAN   WOMAN

SPERM   EGGS

this fertilization, which is one of four possibilities,   gives an <u>albino</u> child.

FIGURE 9. INHERITANCE OF ALBINISM.

that they are carrying it hidden. But when such a person marries another Aa like himself with regard to this pair of genes, their children have a chance of receiving the a gene from each parent and therefore of being albinos.

In passing, we may note the effect that marriages between relatives have on the chance that recessive defects like albinism will appear in the children. Consider a marriage between first cousins (call them John and Alice) who have one set of common grandparents. Suppose that the common grandfather carried any recessive defect, hidden. One of John's parents, and one of Alice's parents, who are sisters or brothers, each had a good chance of receiving this hidden, undesirable gene and in turn transmitting it to John and Alice, again probably hidden. If the gene is rare in the population generally, and John and Alice married unrelated individuals, the chance of their choosing mates also carrying this particular gene would be small. But if they marry each other, it is quite possible that one or more of their children will receive the hidden gene from each of them and will be defective. The precise probabilities are easily figured. We may permit ourselves a generalization. Wherever a rare, recessive, hereditary defect appears in the population you can be sure there has been a relatively high incidence of cousin marriages among the parents of the defective individuals.

To return to the action of genes on pigment development, we can anticipate another sort of genetic complication that has been observed in a variety of connections. We noted that the synthesis of pigment probably involves a long chain of chemical reactions and that the gene a for albinism when present in duplicate apparently broke this chain somewhere before pigment was actually produced. Now it is entirely conceivable that another gene (call it c, for colorless) might break this chain at an entirely different point, but might produce the same gross effect on the individual that the a gene does. As a matter of fact, there is some evidence of two or more distinct genes for "albinism," each with its normal alternative.[3] The resultant confusion is easily appreciated. If, for example, two albino parents each have the same gene for albinism (aa x aa) all their children will be albinos (aa). But if one is albino because of the a gene and has the normal C gene in duplicate ($aaCC$), and the other is albino because of the c gene and has the normal A gene in duplicate ($AAcc$), the children will all be normal ($AaCc$). They have a normal gene to carry them past both potential breaks in the chemical chain of pigment synthesis. The geneticist's prediction would therefore be quite opposite in the two types of marriages, although to everyone else only one type of marriage would appear to be involved. Of course such complications with respect to albinism specifically are very rare. In other connections, however, comparable phenomena, involving entirely different genes with similar effects, may be most important to the individual and his family.

Many of the hereditary qualities of human beings are a great deal more complex, involving differences not in one or two distinct gene pairs, as in the example above, but in many. For the moment we may disregard the effects of environment on such qualities as height, weight, and intelligence, and consider only the biologically inherited human differences in these char-

[3] Lancelot Hogben, *Nature and Nurture* (New York: Norton, 1939), p. 61.

acteristics. We cannot separate all people into classes, like tall and short, or heavy and light, or dull and bright. These characteristics fall along a continuous curve, in general the normal frequency curve, most individuals clustering around an average value typical of the population. There are a few greatly different from this average, and more fall into each arbitrary class as we approach this average from either extreme. A tall person may have many more "genes for tallness" than a short person has, and consequently the children of tall people are on the average taller than those of short people. But so many gene-pairs are involved and they seem to interact in such complex ways that it has been impossible to single out particular genes and label them or to follow them specifically through human generations. Thus, while there is every reason to believe that such genes exist and that the basis of these hereditary differences of degree is particulate and duplicate just as that of the more clear-cut differences of kind is, the actual analysis and application of the science of heredity in the two classes of characteristics is quite different. In the case of *qualitative* differences, like albinism as distinct from normal pigmentation, genetic types may be defined, precise probabilities computed, and predictions made for the children of almost any marriage after careful study. When *quantitative* differences, like height, weight, or intelligence, are involved, a statistical treatment of measurement data is necessary and the conclusions are less precise in their application to individual cases. Much of our knowledge of quantitative inheritance has been drawn from studies of cultivated plants and domestic animals, where characteristics of economic importance are usually of this sort.

COMPLICATIONS DUE TO DEFICIENT ENVIRONMENTS

We have so far in this discussion largely ignored the fact that individuals developing in different environments may show contrasts comparable to those caused by heredity. For example, genes for chlorophyl deficiency are rather common in corn, acting somewhat like the albino genes in human beings to produce "albino" corn seedlings. These seedlings die, because they are unable to synthesize sugar. But by the simple expedient of growing corn seedlings in the dark, genetically normal plants can be made to look like albinos. These plants, too, die; they have no functional chlorophyl and, anyway, without sunlight they cannot produce sugar. If we consider the chain of chemical reactions resulting in the elaboration of chlorophyl, it is apparent that in the case of the hereditary albino seedling this chain has been broken somewhere by the existence in the plant of a defective gene. But the chain can also be broken by the absence of a specific environmental factor, sunlight, and it really makes little difference to the seedling whether it is a defective gene or a continuously defective environment that breaks the chain. The plant fails to elaborate chlorophyl in either case, and dies.

Comparable but somewhat less well-established examples may be drawn from human inheritance. To cite only one, we may consider differences in skin color among "whites." Some people are dark; others are fair. If we all enjoyed the same degree of exposure to sun and wind, our differences in skin color might well be primarily hereditary. On the other hand, if we all had the same genes for skin color, our differences might be the result of variable exposure to skin-darkening factors in our environments. But neither of these ideal situations exists; the great variety of degrees of apparent fairness or darkness among "whites" is really the result of an interaction among different genes and different environments. We could not study the inheritance of skin color in this population without some way of eliminating, controlling, or making allowance for the environmental variable. We would be stupid to conclude, from gross appearance alone, that farmers as a whole have *inherited* darker skins than have professors of philosophy. This is so obvious that it seems unnecessary even to mention it. But, in other connections, essentially the same sort of situation is much less obvious, and we must be critical if we are to avoid blundering. We shall return to this point later.

Not only may a specific environmental deficiency produce a close copy of an hereditary defect, but a specific material added from the environment may substitute for the action of a defective gene and result in the development of a normal individual even though he is genetically defective. The most critical work in this connection has been done with molds, some strains of which are unable to produce any one of a variety of chemical growth-factors normally synthesized by other strains. These particular deficiencies have been shown to be simply inherited. A strain unable to elaborate one of these materials for itself will grow little or not at all on a medium lacking the substance but may grow normally if the medium contains the critical materials. Similarly, ordinary diabetic humans cannot produce an adequate supply of insulin, a product of certain cells in the pancreas, and their defect is believed to be rather simply inherited. As we all know, such individuals may be supplied with insulin by injections, and under such conditions they no longer show the symptoms of diabetes. In this particular environment they can no longer be regarded as defective. Other examples are becoming increasingly numerous.

Correction of an hereditary abnormality in an individual does not, of course, change his genes; we have emphasized that these hereditary particles maintain a virtually permanent, unchanging integrity. There is, therefore, an essential difference between genically and environmentally produced abnormalities. Our hereditary albino corn seedling, for example, if it could be induced to flower and bear seeds, would pass its own genetic failings on to its progeny, while the chlorophyl-deficient plant produced by depriving a normal seedling of light, if it is restored to sunlight in time, can become green and produce entirely normal progeny. In the same way, a diabetic person, no matter how "normal" insulin injections have made him appear, will transmit unchanged genes to his children, and diabetes may therefore crop up among his descendants. These in turn will require insulin injections.

APPLICATIONS

Of the three kinds of concern over human heredity distinguished in the introduction to this chapter, probably the most common and the least serious is ordinary curiosity regarding the normal human differences our children may be expected to show. Such characteristics run the whole gamut of complexity of hereditary control. A few are known to be simply inherited and expressed in any environment that will support life, while many appear to depend on the interaction of numbers of genes, often in complex interplay with the environment. The reliability of predictions for the children of particular marriages varies correspondingly.

The simplest case is illustrated by certain chemical substances called *antigens*, found in human blood cells. One gene controls the development of an antigen called *M*, and its alternative a different antigen, *N*. These substances are not known to be of any advantage or disadvantage to anyone; they simply represent normal human differences. Dominance does not complicate the action of this pair of genes. If a person has the gene for *M* in duplicate he will have only antigen *M;* if the members of this gene pair are different in an individual he will have both *M* and *N;* or if he has the gene for *N* in duplicate he will have only antigen *N*. Thus the genetic formula of an individual can be determined for this gene pair directly from tests of his blood, and precise predictions for this characteristic can be made for the children of any marriage. Medicolegal applications of these and other inherited blood characteristics are familiar to many of us.

More commonly, dominance enters in as a complicating factor. This has already been discussed in connection with albinism. The difficulty in this sort of case is to distinguish between individuals carrying the dominant gene in duplicate, and those with only one dominant gene and the corresponding recessive. For example, Rife cites the use of a chemical compound called phenylthiocarbamide in the manufacture of ice-cube trays. Some customers complained of a bitter taste in their ice cubes; others noticed no such taste. Now it is known that ability to taste this compound depends on a simple dominant gene (T); "nontasters" have the alternative recessive gene in duplicate (*tt*). About 30 per cent of us are "nontasters." If both parents are "nontasters," all the children are expected to be "nontasters." But if one or both parents are "tasters," the types and the proportions of the types of children with regard to this characteristic will depend on whether the "taster" parents are *TT* or *Tt*. *All* of the children of any *TT* parent will be "tasters." The chances are that *half* of the children of a *Tt* parent and a "nontaster" parent will be "tasters," half "nontasters." On the average, *three fourths* of the children having both parents *Tt* will be "tasters," one fourth "nontasters." In some cases the determination of the genetic formula for a "taster," through testing his relatives, is easy; in other cases it is difficult or, at present, impossible. Knowing the frequency of this characteristic in the population, we can make averaged predictions for groups of marriages of the different types, but these statistical predictions may be of little significance in individual cases.

Still more difficult is it to make genetic predictions involving characteristics controlled by numerous genes. It is popularly believed, for example, that blue and brown eyes are controlled by a single pair of genes, the gene for brown being dominant to its alternative for blue. Thus two blue-eyed parents could have no brown-eyed children, while brown-eyed parents carrying the recessive blue hidden could have either brown- or blue-eyed children. In general this explanation of the inheritance of eye color seems to have been satisfactory. However, more careful study has shown that a number of genes influence the amount of pigment deposited in the human iris. Some people have so little brown color apparent that they may be classed as blue-eyed. Nevertheless, two such parents may have children with enough brown to justify their classification as brown-eyed. Needless to say, such children are disturbed if they are confronted with the simpler but erroneous popular concept of eye-color inheritance.

In the case of eye colors, we were dealing with a characteristic not known to be modified by the environment. But many of the most important questions we might ask about our children involve qualities obviously affected by their surroundings. Here we must go cautiously; we must know the environment in which the individuals on whose genetic type we are to base our predictions developed — and the effects of this environment on them; and we must anticipate the environments of their children. For most of us the attitude of the gardener mentioned earlier seems best: we will be happy to take what harvest we get; we may enjoy speculating as to its nature, but at any rate we resolve to provide it with the best environment possible, with the sort of care and surroundings that will encourage the realization of the most desirable of its varied potentialities.

This concept of *varied potentialities* is one of the most important to come out of genetic thought. It has two contexts: the first, emphasized above, is that in general any individual is molded to some extent by his environment. How much and in what direction will depend on the range and nature of environments possible and on the degree of fixed genetic control of the characteristics under consideration. The other is applied to the potentialities of different individuals rather than to the different potentialities of a particular individual. Here we recognize that no two individuals (except for identical twins that develop from a single fertilized egg) are inherently alike. When sample halves of the paired genes of a parent go into the germ cells he produces, successive samples of this sort may differ greatly in the particular genes they contain. This means that even brothers and sisters may get very different genes and therefore react differently to similar environments. Recognition of this basis of inherent individual variation, interacting with a variable environment to produce real human differences, is important in many matters of public policy; for example, education. We cannot for "All men are created *equal*" read "All men are created *alike*." We must recognize and respect individual differences.

"Family Taints" and Abnormalities

Not long ago the subject matter of human heredity was a collection of horrors; what was known was largely depressing and the unknown was threatening. The field has become more cheerful of late. Primarily responsible for this change is the growing realization that a precise knowledge of heredity does more to dispel individual fears than to increase them. This does not mean that heredity is becoming less important in human affairs or that we are learning to ignore it. But for a vague and restless suspicion of "tainted families" there is slowly being substituted a more dispassionate and objective definition of particular hereditary entities, a more clear-cut distinction between these and similar defects having little or no hereditary significance. An attack has been made on the old illusion that "hereditary" and "incurable" were necessarily synonymous terms, and it is recognized that, instead of blocking successful medical treatment of a particular defect, a knowledge of its heredity may assist in its early diagnosis and therefore promote its cure. The fact that such cures do not change the responsible defective genes bothers some of us more than others. Those who are concerned over this point are generally thinking in population, rather than individual, terms, and we will postpone its consideration to the final section of this chapter.

Just as the normal human differences our children may possess run the whole gamut of genetic complexity, so too their possible abnormalities may range from simple inheritance to very complicated genic and environmental interactions. Relatively few human defects are known to be simply inherited; that is, dependent on single, known, labeled genes that produce their undesirable effects in all environments that will support life. Furthermore, these genes are rare relative to their normal alternatives, so that the chance that any individual taken at random will carry any particular one of them is small. Finally, even should a "bad" gene be known to be present in a family, it is clear that some members of the family may possess it while others are completely free of it. It would then be unfortunate if all the members of the family worried unnecessarily about carrying it. An illustration may clarify the situation.

Most of us know of the rare condition called hemophilia, the "bleeder's disease." The blood of affected people clots very slowly, and if untreated they may bleed to death from a scratch. Until very recently, extraction of a tooth from such a person was almost equivalent to execution. The condition depends upon a single defective gene, but this gene violates one of the principles of heredity presented earlier in this chapter, and thus necessitates a brief digression here.

In referring to the particulate and duplicate basis of hereditary differences, we carefully hedged on the latter point and said that genes were "ordinarily" or "generally" present in pairs in any individual. The fact is that *certain genes*, while present in pairs in women, *are single in men*. Because these genes are associated in inheritance with factors that determine

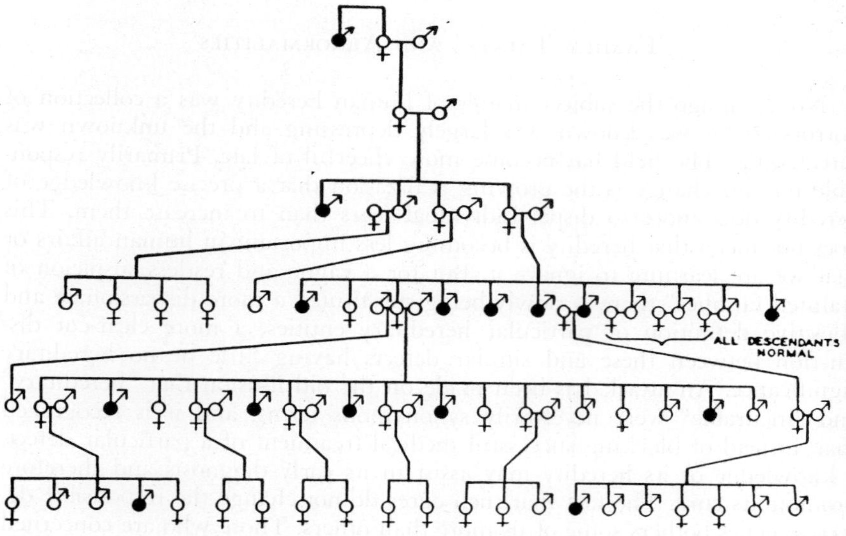

FIGURE 10A.   INHERITANCE OF HEMOPHILIA

In this actual human pedigree, ♂ = male; ♀ = female; black circles were "bleeders."
(*After Sturtevant and Beadle, from Mohr after Schloessman.*)

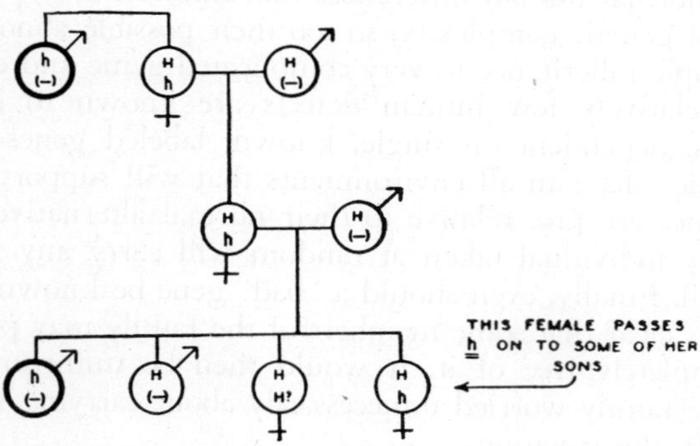

FIGURE 10B.   GENETIC TYPES FOR THE PEDIGREE IN FIGURE 10A.

For the first three generations, genes may be designated: H = normal; h = hemophilia; (—) convention showing male has only one gene of this pair which he receives
from his mother. He gets the (—) from his father.

the potential sex of an individual, they are called "sex-linked." The gene for
hemophilia and its dominant normal alternative belong to this class. If *h*
represents the defective gene for hemophilia, and *H* its normal alternative,
it is easily seen that women having a pair of these genes may belong to any
of three types: *HH*, *Hh*, or *hh*. Since *H* is dominant, the first two types
would be normal, and of the small number of women who have one *h*
gene only the very small fraction who have another like it to complete their
pair would be hemophilic.

Among men, however, the situation is quite different. If a man happens to have the defective *h* gene, he cannot have the normal alternative to hide it and he will be a "bleeder." Like ordinary red-green colorblindness and other sex-linked recessive traits, therefore, hemophilia is very much more common in boys than in girls.

Another qualification of a general statement made earlier is suggested by this consideration of hemophilia. We referred to the genes as "virtually" unchanging and emphasized that no known way exists of making any particular defective gene change into a normal one. Nevertheless, by a rare, uncontrolled, little-understood process known as *mutation,* genes do occasionally change. It has been estimated that about one in 30,000 normal *H* genes changes to the defective *h* gene each generation. One such change is believed to have occurred in Queen Victoria of England or in one of her immediate ancestors, and through her daughters the defective gene was introduced into certain of the royal families of Europe. Their subsequent history is interesting, but we shall not take space to tell it here (see question 4, p. 438).

To return to more immediate problems, how may hemophilia illustrate the value of a precise knowledge of heredity? First of all, it defines a specific medical entity, distinguishing it from most other superficially similar, basically different conditions. Other bleeder's diseases are known; only one of them shows an hereditary pattern like that of hemophilia. Secondly, having defined this entity, it makes possible the anticipation of cases in which a specific treatment or prophylaxis will be necessary. A substance that will temporarily restore normal clotting powers to hemophilic blood has been reported in recent work on human blood fractions. The extraction of a "bleeder's" tooth needs no longer to be dangerous. On the average, half of the boys whose maternal grandfather was hemophilic will also be "bleeders." Emergencies necessitating the special treatment of these children can be anticipated and provided for. Finally, and most important from our present point of view, individuals with hemophilic relatives can often be assured that they either do or do not carry the condition, and doubts and fears can then be replaced by certain knowledge of either alternative. For example, no man can transmit the gene for hemophilia to any of his children unless the man himself is a "bleeder," regardless of the frequency of the condition in his family. The sons of hemophilic men are as likely to be normal as are those of normal men. They receive their member of the *H* gene pair from their mothers, and their affected fathers can transmit no "taint" to them. On the other hand, the daughters of hemophilic men *all carry the defective gene hidden,* and half of the sons of these carrier daughters will be affected, *regardless of whom the carrier women marry.* Other situations with respect to this condition need not be illustrated here (cf. Figure 10, *Inheritance of Hemophilia*).

It should be emphasized that hemophilia was introduced into this discussion only as an example and that a consideration of other simply inherited defects would suggest similar conclusions. Some of these conditions depend on sex-linked genes like those for hemophilia; others show no association with sex. Some of the defective genes are dominant to their normal alternatives;

others are recessive; some are irregular in their dominance relations. Some produce uniform, well-defined defects; others vary greatly in their expression. But in each case, precise knowledge may cancel groundless fears or speed diagnosis and sometimes suggest precautions or treatments to be applied to affected individuals. An aim of medical genetics is to find the particular developmental reaction in which each defective gene fails to carry out the function of its normal alternative, and to substitute for the product of this gene by modifying or supplementing the individual's environment. A great deal remains to be learned in this connection.

The temptation is strong here to list the known simply inherited defects of human beings. Recalling the pitfalls enumerated earlier, however, will explain the advisability of avoiding such a list. Two or more different genes may cause grossly similar defects. An environmental deficiency may copy the effect of a defective gene; a defect so produced will not, of course, be transmitted by inheritance. A gene may be "bad" in one environment, harmless in another. It seems much better, therefore, to urge expert individual consideration of each worrisome case than to provide a table subject to uncritical misuse. "Heredity clinics" located mainly in university centers give qualified guidance to a few people; no doubt such clinics will become more common in the future.[4]

Heredity doubtless plays some part in many conditions more complicated than the simple abnormalities we have been discussing. The difficulty comes in evaluating the importance of the part it plays and in applying such knowledge to specific cases. It is as foolhardy, for example, to say that "cancer is inherited" or that "insanity is inherited" as it is to assert that inheritance plays no role in these or similar complex conditions. There are a great many kinds of cancer — hundreds of them. A few very rare kinds appear to be simply inherited and to develop in individuals of particular genetic types no matter what their environment. Other types of cancer seem vaguely to "run in families," as though there were an inherited greater susceptibility to these types present in these families. But other observations — like, for instance, that cited by Scheinfeld of the girls who were employed in painting watch dials with a luminous radium paint and almost all of whom died of malignant cancer — indicate that most human beings will develop some kind of cancer if sufficiently exposed to cancer-inciting agents. We gain very little by regarding the many diverse kinds of aberrant growth as if they were a single biological entity and frightening each other with tales of uniform transmission of this entity through biological inheritance. On the other hand, competent consideration of a consistent family history of a specific type of cancer may lead to its early recognition in an individual and thus to successful treatment. Again in this connection the science of heredity is being changed from a gospel of useless despair to one of useful hope. Remarks somewhat similar to those for cancer, with perhaps an increased emphasis on the environmental variable, might be made for mental defects.

---

[4] See the paper by Dice listed among the references on p. 437, for a discussion of heredity clinics. Institutions at present providing organized consulting service in this field include the Universities of Michigan, Minnesota, Oklahoma, Utah, Texas, and Toronto; McGill University, and the Bowman Gray School of Medicine, Winston-Salem, N. C.

POPULATION QUALITY

Relationships between the family unit and the population will be discussed more thoroughly in Chapter Twenty-five. A brief consideration of some of the possible implications of heredity relative to the biological quality of a population remains to complete the present chapter.

The success of plant and animal breeders in directing the evolution of their stocks toward desired ends has led some socially conscious people to support attempts toward a similar control of human evolution. Programs of socially "planned parenthood" designed to improve the inherent merit or to prevent possible deterioration of human populations have been classed as *eugenics*. Eugenics is thus a collection of action-programs and not a quest for neutral knowledge; it is for this reason fundamentally distinct from the science of human heredity.

Two essential sources of alarm for the future of human populations are cited by eugenists and reflected in two rather distinct aspects of eugenic programs. The first is the fact that humanitarian civilization, particularly as expressed in medicine, makes possible the reproduction of hereditary defectives that would, under more "natural" circumstances, fail to survive or to leave offspring perpetuating their defects. For example, severe diabetics before the development of insulin treatments probably did not often live long enough to have many children. There was thus a "pressure" acting to limit the frequency of the undesirable gene or genes for diabetes in the population. Insulin injections, however, make it possible for diabetics today to lead normal lives, to have as many children as other people do, and therefore to transmit their defective genes unchanged to another generation. Similar conditions have arisen in connection with other heritable defects. *Negative eugenics* would substitute a social factor in the form of "selective sterilization" of defectives or of some other mechanism discouraging their reproduction, for the decreasingly important "natural selection" in human populations. The second source of alarm has been a higher average birth rate among less effective fragments of intellectual and economic society than among those "classes" considered more "desirable." The basis of such desirability or undesirability has been presumed in part to involve biologically inherited characteristics, and it has been feared that under the present differential birth rate there will be a general lowering of population quality in succeeding generations. This has given rise to *positive eugenics*, a consideration of programs designed to encourage higher reproductive rates among presumably better prospective parents.

The common-sense plausibility of much eugenic thought is sufficient to render further discussion of points in its favor unnecessary here. The degree of stock-improvement achieved by plant and animal breeders is an impressive model, indicating the wide range of qualities that may be bettered through controlled or planned reproduction. It seems obvious that social action to minimize the spread of defective genes through human populations as well as to encourage larger families among people with better hereditary equipment would be wise. Even if strictly biological considerations be set aside, it remains evident that social inadequates on the whole are unable to provide the sort of homes and environments that offer their children opportunity to develop into effective citizens. But there seems at present to be some gap between the "common-sense plausibility of much eugenic thought" as expressed in the above generalizations and the probable effectiveness of certain eugenic programs as judged by the more precise and objective standards of the science of heredity. Returning to the case of diabetics, clearly the responsible genes can be classed as uniformly undesirable only in a society ignorant of insulin. Medicine has developed an environment in which the gene or genes for diabetes are no longer necessarily bad. In the face of rather numerous examples of leaders and thoroughly "desirable" citizens who are nevertheless diabetics, few among even the most ardent eugenists would advocate the wholesale sterilization of such "defectives." This seems to point to a dilemma for advocates of negative eugenics: if humanitarian society is unable to provide an environment nullifying the undesirability of defective genes, "natural selection" remains as powerful as ever; if such an environment can be provided, the defective genes need no longer be considered undesirable. There are, of course, flaws in this logic, and a whole borderland of cases in which selective sterilization or other eugenic measures may be wise. Our point is that easy and uncritical acceptance of plausible generalities is never wise.

Many other facts must be dismissed with scant consideration here. The genes for most recessive human hereditary defects are rare; this means that in a great majority of people carrying them they are hidden by their normal alternatives. Sterilization of individuals showing a particular defect of this sort will therefore eliminate from the population only a very small fraction of these unwanted genes, and we cannot hope to accomplish great improvements with respect to these characteristics through selective sterilization for a few generations. Other, differently inherited, defects may be either more or less subject to effective selection, depending on the type of inheritance involved. Meanwhile, other factors may be creating much more significant changes in the distribution of human genes. War, for example, may be regarded as a great experiment in the elimination of *desirable* genes, since we choose our best to be killed. We can derive scant comfort from the knowledge that war is becoming less selective in this respect.

Another factor is the breakup of isolates in our population. A small community, or a small subpopulation isolated from others in reproduction by racial, political, economic, or other barriers, may show a relatively high incidence of particular hereditary defects. If the barriers are somehow removed, thus increasing the effective population size of the isolate, the defective genes are spread among correspondingly more people. There is then less chance that a given child will receive any particular defective gene from both parents, and a consequent decrease in the incidence of hereditary defectives, permanent if the size of the subpopulation remains at the larger value. "In so far as we are concerned with rare defects, the social instruments which make for racial betterment are the bicycle and the omnibus, the flivver and the jazz band — in short, the collective enjoyments of town life." [5]

In positive eugenics, we need to be critical of the grounds for assuming inherent biological superiority as a property of any particular "class." We referred to the absurdity of concluding, from appearances alone, that farmers as a whole inherit darker skins than do professors of philosophy. What shall be our grounds for evaluating the inherent intellectual potentialities of the children of farmers as a population compared with those of professors? Here, too, unless we can reliably eliminate, control, or make allowance for the environmental variable we are not likely to draw a just conclusion.

Many of our population policies, many of our material discoveries, many of our social and political decisions may have effects on the inherent qualities of our population. We need to consider these effects as best we can, just as we need to consider the effects of our own family decisions against the broader social background. But we may lose, not gain, from oversimplification of these issues. They are not simple.

SELECTED READINGS

Dahlberg, Gunnar, *Race, Reason and Rubbish*. Translated from the Swedish by Lancelot Hogben (New York: Columbia University Press, 1943), chaps. 1, 4, 5, 10.

Dice, L. R., "Heredity Clinics: Their Value for Public Service and for Research," *American Journal of Human Genetics*, 4 (1952), pp. 1-13.

Dunn, L. C., and Dobzhansky, T., *Heredity, Race, and Society* (New York: The New American Library of World Literature, Inc., 1952).

Haldane, J. B. S., *New Paths in Genetics* (New York: Harper, 1942), chaps. 1-5.

Hogben, Lancelot, *Nature and Nurture* (New York: Norton, 1939), chaps. 1, 5.

Kemp, Tage, *Genetics and Disease*. Translated from the Danish by Elisabeth Aagensen (Copenhagen: Ejnar Munksgaard, 1951), parts 2, 3, 4.

Scheinfeld, A., *The New You and Heredity* (Philadelphia: Lippincott, 1950).

Srb, A. M., and Owen, R. D., *General Genetics* (San Francisco: W. H. Freeman & Co., 1952), chaps. 1, 2, 20, 24.

Stern, Curt, *Principles of Human Genetics* (San Francisco: W. H. Freeman & Co., 1949), chaps. 1, 2, 8, 23, 24.

TOPICS FOR DISCUSSION OR REPORTS

1. Leaflets to demonstrate heredity, including paper treated with phenylthiocarbamide for the "taster test," may be obtained from the American Genetic Association, 1507 M Street, N. W., Washington 5, D. C. (1953 cost: 10 leaflets for 25 cents; 50 for $1.00). Can you determine your genetic type for this pair of genes? Try tracing the genes through a family. What chance have you for a "nontaster" child? Does the sample of population represented by the members of this class fit the expected proportion of about 30 per cent "nontasters"? Why isn't the percentage exactly as expected?

[5] Gunnar Dahlberg, *Race, Reason, and Rubbish* (New York: Columbia University Press, 1943), p. 188.

2. What clear-cut normal human differences occur in your family or other families you know? What part does heredity appear to play in these differences?
3. Do you know of a simply-inherited abnormality among families of your acquaintance? How does it appear to be inherited? What counsel might you give a worried member of this family considering marriage?
4. With the aid of an encyclopedia, try to trace the gene for hemophilia from Victoria through the former royal families of Spain and Russia. What part in the histories of these countries may this defective gene have played?
5. Evaluate the following assertions (some of them are false; others may be partly true but require restatement or qualification).
   (a) Syphilis is inherited.
   (b) Cancer is inherited.
   (c) The children of a woman's second husband will be modified by the hereditary characteristics of her first husband.
   (d) A pregnant woman can make her unborn child into a music lover simply by listening to good music herself during pregnancy.
   (e) If you study hard, your children will inherit more intelligence.
6. Is the assertion that heredity plays an important part in human variation irreconcilable with our national declaration that "all men are created equal"?
7. Complete the pedigree begun in Figure 10B, p. 432.

Chapter Fifteen

Caring for Mother and Child
Before and After

ELIZABETH GENTRY

NATURE OF PRENATAL CARE

By prenatal care is meant the special medical supervision of the pregnant woman up to the time she goes into labor. The type of medical care is largely preventive in nature and is a recent addition to the practice of medicine. Not long ago the pregnant woman went to the physician only when she did not feel well, whereas now he aims to keep her feeling well throughout pregnancy. By attention to symptoms when they arise, moreover, he prevents their development into more serious difficulties.

The special medical supervision of the pregnant woman has developed into a well-systematized schedule of care. Certain procedures are followed at the first visit and at subsequent visits, the number of which is more or less uniform. This systematization has resulted in much less illness and fewer deaths for both mothers and children and has made pregnancy and childbirth much safer experiences.

As implied above, the purpose of prenatal care is to discover all signs of ill health present at the time when pregnancy is diagnosed, and to maintain the pregnant woman in as good health as possible by heeding danger signs early. This systematic care prepares the pregnant woman for labor so that she may be delivered of a normal baby and recover from childbirth rapidly.

Before beginning our discussion of prenatal care, it is well to suggest that just before marriage the woman should have a physical examination to determine whether she should become pregnant. If she practices contraception, another examination should come when she contemplates trying to become pregnant. A careful history of diseases, past and present, is necessary, for there are several which are made definitely worse by pregnancy and may be contraindications to the risk of pregnancy. Active tuberculosis, chronic kidney disease, certain types of heart disease, syphilis, and a type of epilepsy for which there is no known cause are all contraindications to pregnancy. Any diseases which "run in the family" should be discussed with the physician, for some are serious and others are not; most diseases do *not* run in the family — any family — in spite of folklore to the contrary.

A physical examination to determine the advisability of pregnancy involves not only a search for disease, but also measurement of the pelvis. Certain abnormalities of the pelvis will necessitate Caesarean section, and these may first be discovered at this time. Such abnormalities are not a contraindication to pregnancy, however, but an operation involves greater risk and also greater expense.

CHOICE OF PHYSICIAN

The choice of a physician for prenatal care and delivery of the child is one that is dependent to some degree on the pocketbook. Specialists (obstetricians) charge according to their training and the size of the city in which they practice. The fee is roughly twice that asked by a general practitioner, and may be even more. If the pregnant woman lives in a city large enough to support a specialist and is able to pay the increased charge, then she should go to him. But if she would have to go to another town, or go into debt, then the handicaps far exceed the advantages unless she knows beforehand that there will be complications.

To find an obstetrician the pregnant woman or her husband can ask a physician of their acquaintance or call the county medical society. Often physicians are not listed in the telephone directory according to the kind of work they do; the medical society will give this information.

SIGNS OF PREGNANCY

In the majority of instances the earliest sign of pregnancy is a missed menstrual period. In a small percentage of cases there is, after conception, one scanty menstrual period, but this is not repeated. In rare cases a slight flow of blood may occur at the time of the regular menses for two or three periods. This may be a sign of threatening miscarriage, and hence should be reported to the doctor.

About 50 per cent of pregnant women have nausea and vomiting to some degree. Nausea is usually present on awakening or shortly thereafter, commonly recurs at meal time, and infrequently is present all day; it usually disappears after the first three months of pregnancy. In a small number of cases it is necessary to hospitalize pregnant women for excessive vomiting.

One of the causes of excessive vomiting during this period is psychological — that is, fear or strong dislike of pregnancy. This factor is frequently prominent in unmarried pregnant women, but may also be present in married women.

Mrs. E. J. had been married only three months and was still working, with the plan of continuing to do so for a couple of years because her husband was a student and could not support her. She thought that she was practicing contraception correctly (for she had been following advice given by her mother) when she became pregnant. Her nausea began when she was three days late with her menses. When a test confirmed her pregnancy, her nausea became rapidly worse. By the third month it was necessary for her to enter the hospital, for she had lost weight rapidly and her body was deprived of fluids by the persistent vomiting. Her obstetrician had been unable to convince her that miscarriage or her death was worse than carrying the pregnancy to term. A psychiatrist was called in, and he was successful in changing her unfavorable feelings concerning pregnancy so that she stopped vomiting.

Two other early signs or symptoms of pregnancy which may be noted by the pregnant woman are increasing tenseness of her breasts and an increase in weight.

When the menstrual period has been missed two weeks the physician should be consulted if this is at all practical, for proper planning of the prenatal schedule can then be most readily set up. It is usually difficult to be sure of pregnancy at this early date, but the probabilities in favor of pregnancy in a young married woman who has always been regular in her menses and has not tried to prevent pregnancy are so great that it is wise for the physician to treat her as if she were pregnant. By the time the next visit is due, one month later, it is usually possible to confirm by physical examination alone the existence of pregnancy. If it is necessary for any reason that she know at the time of the first visit, a quite reliable biological test is usually available for an appropriate fee (ten to twenty-five dollars). Unless the matter is of great urgency, however, there is little purpose in such a test, for it merely gives a rather accurate diagnosis three to six weeks earlier than would otherwise be possible.

All of the signs of pregnancy mentioned above except the biological test are said to be presumptive, because they are not diagnostic; that is, they may occur in other conditions also. Later on in pregnancy other signs arise which are diagnostic; by the third month the doctor may feel a definite enlargement and softening of the uterus; by the fifth month he may be able to hear the heart tones of the baby; and by the sixth month he may be able to note the movement of the baby. Between the fourth and fifth months the mother usually feels the baby move — that is, she is said to "feel life"; this is presumptive, for it is merely an interpretation of a sensation. Further, the entire breast becomes fuller and more erect and the pigmented ring about the nipples becomes more darkly pigmented.

Thus the diagnosis of pregnancy can be said to be probable quite early in the process; if the biological test is performed and is positive, it is of course certain. A doctor who has taken care of many pregnant women is seldom in doubt as to the pregnancy by the time two menstrual periods have been missed.

THE FIRST VISIT

The first visit is the most important one of the first six months. It is at this visit that the doctor (1) makes the diagnosis of pregnancy and estimates the delivery date of the baby; (2) determines the health status of his patient and initiates treatment if this is necessary; (3) makes the pelvic measurements (often done at a later visit); (4) investigates the diet, making up for deficiencies; (5) advises about clothing and exercise; and (6) outlines in a general way the course of prenatal care. Let us discuss each of these items:

1. For the accurate diagnosis of pregnancy a complete menstrual history is ordinarily necessary. A history of marked irregularity means greater dependence on symptoms and signs other than a missed menstrual period for diagnosis of pregnancy. Without a biological test, the doctor, and hence the patient also, may be uncertain as to the existence of pregnancy for a month or two. This is particularly true where the irregularity is of too great or too frequent menstruations rather than of too slight or too few. Here the uterus may even be slightly enlarged and softer than normal, which further confuses the issue temporarily. Time, however, will bring the answer if the woman does not want to go to the expense of a biological test.

Mrs. C. F. had always been irregular in her periods, frequently skipping one, and several times, two. Now her menses were two and a half months late, and a suitable test confirmed her suspicion that she was pregnant. Due to her past menstrual irregularity, it is uncertain whether conception took place one or two months previously; the correct date will be suggested by the time at which movement of the child is first felt.

The estimated delivery date of the mother is merely an approximation based on the average, but it is very useful to both doctor and patient. Physicians used to think that gestation took 280 days, and it is true that they still count that many from the last normal menstrual period, but they have some reason to believe that conception usually takes place midway in a menstrual cycle. This would subtract twelve to sixteen days from the 280 for an average pregnancy. The end of the pregnancy is figured by subtracting three months from the first day of the previous normal menstrual period and adding seven days. Thus if the previous period began July tenth, April seventeenth of the following year is the "due date."

2. Determination of the present health of the woman requires first a careful past history, for the doctor wants to know all the experiences and factors that might influence her health now. A history of too frequent or too much menstruation, to say nothing of actual previous miscarriage, may indicate a persisting tendency on the part of a woman to miscarry. Hence she is cautioned to notify the doctor of any flow and to go to bed at the first sign of spotting.

Some diseases may not be noticeable under ordinary living but will cause difficulty during pregnancy. Of these, diseases of the heart, kidney, and lungs are among the most important, for all of these organs undergo an unusual amount of work at this time. A nephritis, for example, not uncommonly leaves some weakness which may interfere with adequate excretion of waste products. Since the mother's kidneys act as excretory organs for the waste products of the baby too, the additional load is evident. It is not possible to cut down on the amount of the fetal waste products, but it is possible to reduce those of the pregnant woman.

Young women with the commonest type of heart trouble (rheumatic) go through pregnancy and childbirth very well as a rule, but the amount and kind of anesthesia during labor will be determined by the degree of heart trouble that exists.

One of the most serious diseases that can affect pregnancy is tuberculosis. It is true that a considerable number of adults will show evidences of completely healed tuberculous infection in an X-ray of their lungs, though most of them do not know they ever had it; they either were not ill with the first infection or it simulated another disease and was not diagnosed. But if a woman has been ill with tuberculosis, particularly during the six or seven years previous to pregnancy, her pregnancy might reactivate a dormant infection. In the case of a history of tuberculosis, a woman would do better to ask her physician whether she should become pregnant rather than to go to him already pregnant. In the latter case she will be allowed to continue her pregnancy unless there are signs of present activity of tuberculosis. In either case she will be watched with great care.

Two other diseases of particular importance are gonorrhea and syphilis. Tests are always made for both, regardless of a negative history, for both can be passed on to the child and both can be present without the knowledge of the individual. Gonorrhea can infect the baby only when it is being born; the organisms enter its eyes and induce a severe eye infection. In the past a large percentage of our sightless were blinded in this manner, but today drops in the eyes of the baby immediately after birth is routine. This provides almost complete protection. If infection of the eyes occurs, treatment with penicillin is very effective.

Syphilis is another matter. The causative organism can pass into the child from the mother. Syphilis in an infant is always contracted from an infected mother, never from an infected sperm; hence the baby never gets syphilis directly from his father, although his father may have infected his mother. Syphilis is a disease so protean in its manifestations, affecting all parts of the body, that it is not to be ignored, regardless of whether the infected mother is having symptoms or not. Treatment is begun immediately. If she has not passed beyond the fourth month of her pregnancy, her baby will be spared an infection. The drugs used in the treatment of this disease are now very effective agents. Of course, if the mother is found to have syphilis, the father also should be tested for it.

One source of infant mortality that long baffled physicians is a disease called erythroblastosis, an anemic condition which was often lethal for second and third babies. Fortunately in 1941 the causes of and treatment for this condition were discovered. It is now known to be associated with the incompatibility of blood types, usually where an Rh negative woman is mated with an Rh positive man. (The Rh refers to the Rhesus monkey in which the blood types were first identified.) Although about 11 per cent of marriage combinations involve an Rh negative woman and an Rh positive man only about one out of 200 births exhibit erythroblastosis. In second and third pregnancies substances from the mother's blood may destroy red blood cells of the baby, producing the appearance in the newborn infant of anemia and excessive jaundice. Treatment consists of blood transfusion of the proper blood type and careful attention during the first few weeks.

In addition to obtaining a history of past diseases, the doctor should know whether the woman has had an abdominal operation, in that some pain may be anticipated with a stretching of parts involved when the uterus enlarges upward. An old fracture of the pelvis may in a few cases interfere with delivery of the baby by changing the contour of the birth canal. Any known present disease must, of course, be investigated in full and treatment given.

The physical examination itself is a well-systematized set of procedures; special attention is given to the heart, lungs, and kidneys of the pregnant woman. A blood pressure reading and urinalysis constitute an integral part of every prenatal visit to the doctor, because changes in these two tests are early danger signals. Examination of the blood for anemia and infection completes the laboratory procedures. Dental care is indicated if teeth or gums are diseased.

3. Pelvic measurements may be taken either at the first visit or later. The measurements affect the handling of labor, but have nothing to do with prenatal care. They are made before the last month, however, since at that time all vaginal examinations are avoided because of the chance of infection. The measurement of the internal size of the pelvis is the most important, as it helps the doctor to decide whether there is sufficient room for the baby to emerge safely.

4. The proper diet for a pregnant woman would keep the average person healthy too. There is a somewhat increased need for certain vitamins and minerals. Emphasis is laid on the fact that a good diet includes an abundance of milk, fresh fruits, and vegetables, and a moderate amount of meat and eggs. A multivitamin product is often added. It is not necessary that the pregnant woman eat more food; in fact, she may have to restrict the amount of fattening food, since she must not gain more than two pounds a month — twenty-five pounds at the outside, during the whole of her pregnancy. Smoking may be limited, and consumption of hard liquor is always limited or prohibited.

5. So far as clothing is concerned, the pregnant woman is advised to wear flat-heeled or moderately flat-heeled shoes most of the time, and during the last four months a supporting girdle is often recommended. It is important that she walk at least a mile a day but avoid all strenuous exercise. She should not do any heavy lifting nor endure any jouncing. She may take short motor rides, but should travel only on good roads.

6. Prenatal care comprises a definite number of visits with a definite spacing: every three or four weeks for the first six months, and every two or three weeks thereafter except during the last month, when visits are once a week. Visits become more frequent toward the end, because it is during the last two months that the majority of pathological conditions become clearly apparent.

THE OTHER VISITS

There are nine to twelve prenatal visits to the doctor if the pregnant woman makes her first one two weeks after a missed menstrual period. At these visits the doctor carries out at least three procedures: he weighs his patient, takes her blood pressure, and examines the urine specimen she brought. He asks her leading questions, the answers to which allow him to judge if anything is going wrong. Albumin in the urine, increasing blood pressure, swelling of the feet and ankles, bleeding from the genital tract are early signs of trouble. The first three may signify the onset of toxemia, the serious form of which is convulsions, a condition which twenty years ago occurred much more commonly than now. Early detection and medical measures have saved many lives which otherwise would have been lost from this cause. Bleeding in early pregnancy may be an indication of miscarriage; late in pregnancy, it may mean that something has happened to the placenta.

Mrs. B. M. had had an entirely uneventful pregnancy until the beginning of the ninth month. A urine specimen was being collected in the doctor's office when she passed some bright red blood, at least a tablespoonful. She was hospitalized and X rays were taken to determine if the placenta was lower in the uterus than is usual. Examination in the operating room as well as the X ray confirmed the diagnosis. A Caesarean section was performed, because if this patient had been allowed to go into labor normally, she would have had a severe hemorrhage which might have been difficult to stop.

In addition to asking questions about these matters, the doctor makes certain that there is not too much vomiting early in pregnancy and that vomiting has stopped altogether by the third month. He also asks about constipation, cramps, shortness of breath, dizziness, spots before the eyes, headache, worry, and sleep. Often a second test for syphilis is made at least three months after the first one.

Toward the end of pregnancy the question of home delivery or hospital delivery comes up. Hospital deliveries are becoming more and more common, but in towns and rural areas a small percentage of babies are still born at home. The doctor's fee is usually the same. He prefers the hospital, because there he has plenty of nurses to help him, and he can attain a degree of antisepsis approximating a surgical operation. Moreover, he has much better control over conditions affecting his patient when she is in a hospital. Consequently the question of home delivery is seldom raised.

[There is, to be sure, a vocal minority of physicians, and occasionally of patients, who insist on raising the problem of home care. They point out that even though the physician's fees are the same for either hospital or home, there are many areas remote from a hospital, and, moreover, that under any circumstances many patients find it difficult to pay the high hospital costs. The physician's insistence on hospital care, they claim, is primarily with reference to his own convenience rather than to the welfare of the patient. The result of such insistence, in the estimation of this minority, is that families are saddled with hospital bills that for them are tremendous, or they reluctantly consent to be handled as charity cases. Willingness of the physician to grant home care would save the family's pocketbook or the family's pride, and sometimes both. Hospital insurance, either physician- or government-sponsored, might be the solution — but *somebody* pays for the insurance. It is therefore best, say the home care advocates, to be as economical as possible — editorial *addendum.*]

When a woman discovers she is pregnant, she need not change her routine to any marked degree. If she is a housewife she may continue her domestic pursuits throughout pregnancy. If she is in a gainful occupation outside the home, how long she continues depends somewhat on her employer, somewhat on the way she feels, and mostly on whether her physician judges her to be in good health. Certainly, unless the activity is definitely harmful, she may continue it until the sixth month if she is able to get sufficient exercise and sleep and avoid fatigue. The important consideration is that she keep mentally occupied in order to divert her attention from the few unpleasant sensations which are common to most pregnant women. A great many pregnant women say they never felt better in their lives, but the majority have a few complaints, most of which are unimportant.

One of the great advantages of prenatal care is that it extends over such a long period and the visits are so frequent that the physician and the patient are able to become well acquainted with each other. He learns, first of all, whether she wanted to become pregnant. If she and her husband are happy about her pregnancy, her attitude toward the many aspects of pregnancy is much healthier; she considers any vexations as incidental to it and worth the price. But if she is unhappy about it for any reason, she is apt to magnify the vexations, an attitude which the doctor makes every effort to change, for his reward is a willing, cooperative patient instead of one who dislikes the whole procedure. Among the women who object to pregnancy the majority, fortunately enough, complain merely of "bad timing," and soon become reconciled to and happy in their pregnancy; some, however, must be persuaded of the rewards of bringing up a child. It is often the husband's attitude toward a family which needs changing. This is more difficult to effect, for the personal contacts between physician and husband are few if any. Fortunately most adults change their dislike of children once they become parents themselves. (For more details on the psychological aspects of pregnancy, see the next chapter, pp. 458-459.)

Even the mother who is happy about her expected baby must make some adjustments during pregnancy as well as afterwards. Both she and her husband must understand that there are many changes coming into their life. There will be much less freedom to do the multitude of things hitherto enjoyed together. There will be sleepless nights, and the wife will have less time to devote to her husband. It takes real effort and planning to be a good mother — and the same applies to being a good father.

[In case there is already a child in the family, another kind of prenatal preparation is necessary, or at least advisable: that of acquainting the firstborn with his or her sibling. Many mothers have adopted the practice of letting the child "feel the baby move" (whether movement can actually be felt is unimportant if only the child's imagination is suitably stimulated). In this and similar ways the firstborn is made ready for the deprivations almost certain to be experienced; they can be transformed into gratifications if properly anticipated — editorial *addendum*.]

FEAR AND FABLES

There are a great many fables about procreation, for to the untutored it is a great mystery. Even the biologist is awed by its complexity, but he has substituted facts for superstition in many of its aspects and is constantly adding more. Many myths have been passed on from one generation to another, and the pregnant woman brings many of them to her doctor who must explain their lack of factual foundation. He tells her there is no basis for the belief that certain foods exert specific effects on character or sex or that they produce birthmarks. He assures her that fright will not mark her child either. He informs her that she may lie down in any position which is comfortable to her because her position will not cause deformities in her child. He explains that it is impossible to diagnose the sex of the child from the rate of the heartbeat or from the position of the child. He refutes the claim that restriction of food limits the weight of the baby and states, rather, that restriction of food is for the mother's benefit alone. [Sometimes the physician will find it necessary repeatedly to stress the fact that many of the food cravings experienced by a minority of pregnant women are imaginary, and are often mere attention-getting devices. Pregnancy *is* accompanied by some discomfort and numerous unfamiliar internal sensations, and these can readily be interpreted, given the widespread folklore, as craving for "the food the baby needs." Unconscious resentment against the peacefully snoring husband can be transmuted into a demand that he rouse the nearby delicatessen keeper for the immediate purchase of a jar of dill pickles! This of course is not to deny that there may be genuine cravings — editorial *addendum*.]

PREPARATION FOR LABOR

Since most women have heard from someone that labor is painful, it is surprising that they usually do not dread the final act. In some communities there are doctors who have added to their prenatal care more instruction in the physiology of pregnancy, more opportunity to talk over attitudes toward pregnancy and parenthood, and exercises to induce relaxation (these last to be used during labor). In a considerable number of pregnant women these measures have resulted in less need of painkilling drugs. Some people call this natural childbirth. There is still a good deal of difference of opinion among physicians and people who have tried it. It is all right to talk it over with the physician and then to leave the decision up to him as to whether to try it.

There are those who claim they would not have another child because of the pain, but the majority have forgotten most of the unpleasantness by the time the baby is a couple of days old. In fact, as soon as the baby has been born, the mother's chief interest is in the child and whether or not it is normal.

Toward the end of pregnancy the doctor discusses the signs of labor. The first sign of labor is usually abdominal cramps or backache or both.

When the cramps continue, get closer together, last longer and get harder, the chances are that labor is beginning. Nevertheless, until the pains are ten to twelve minutes apart it is not necessary for the woman to go to the hospital.

Toward the end of pregnancy the bag of water may break before any pains have occurred, in which case the doctor should be notified immediately. Usually labor begins within twenty-four hours, particularly if much water has been lost. The woman should go to bed to prevent further loss of fluid, as continued loss may make the labor longer and harder, causing what is called a "dry labor."

LABOR AND DELIVERY

There are three stages of labor, each having a specific function; the first, opening of the womb; the second, birth of the baby; the third, expulsion of the afterbirth.

With the first baby, labor is usually longer than with subsequent children unless many years elapse between pregnancies. The first stage starts slowly. The woman often has cramps for eight or ten hours before they come near enough together and regularly enough for hospitalization.

Upon hospitalization, the nurses give the woman an enema and a sponge bath and take her temperature. The doctor ascertains her blood pressure and examines her internally by way of the rectum to determine if the mouth of the womb has undergone any changes. It is normally thick, but during pregnancy it becomes somewhat thinner and during labor becomes even thinner and opens up. These changes are due to the fact that its muscles slide up into the body of the uterus. The pains are caused by the contraction of the uterus as a whole. The pressure of the baby's hard head against the mouth of the womb increases the rate of progress of labor. If a softer part of the baby is over the outlet, the labor is apt to be longer and slower.

If the woman has received a drug she will sleep between contractions, rousing only when the pain comes, although later she may not remember any discomfort. All in all, the woman in labor does not require nearly as much encouraging as her husband does. The stories and cartoons are correct; he often needs to be told that everything is all right. It would seem from outward appearances that seventeen hours (the average duration of a first labor) is much longer to him. He feels helpless in that he can only wait, whereas the woman realizes that progress is being made. Another reason for her assurance is that she is well acquainted with her doctor by this time, and usually has complete confidence in him. It is up to the doctor to get better acquainted with the husband on this occasion and inspire confidence in him too.

The problems at this stage are the progress of labor, careful watch over the condition of the baby by observation of the quality and rate of the heart tones, and watchfulness over the strength of the mother. She is given fluids freely, especially fruit juice with sugar to keep up her strength.

At the same time that the mouth of the womb dilates, the head descends into the pelvis. When the uterus is sufficiently dilated the head slips through, and thus begins the second stage of labor, lasting two hours on an average.

When the head slips through the mouth of the womb, it exerts pressure on the rectum and makes the mother feel the desire to push, which she is encouraged to do in order that her abdominal muscles may assist in the process of expulsion.

When the baby is born, the umbilical cord is tied and cut. Mucous which the baby may have in its throat is cleared out and, if the baby has not cried by this time, it is stimulated by patting or pinching. Seldom are more strenuous measures necessary. As a prophylactic measure against gonorrhea, silver nitrate is put into his eyes. (This procedure was referred to earlier in the chapter.) This drug will kill any gonococcus organisms present.

The third stage of labor begins as soon as the baby is born. It is at this time that maternal hemorrhages may occur, due to incomplete separation of the afterbirth, which interferes with contraction of the uterus. Usually an extract of pituitary gland will cause sufficient contraction to stop the bleeding and assist in the separation. The less blood that is lost, the sooner the mother will recover her strength. Once the afterbirth is separated, it is expelled, and labor is at an end.

Postpartum Care

Postpartum care is the care given to a mother after her baby is born and up to her recovery from the immediate effects of pregnancy. It is terminated by the six weeks' checkup by the doctor to determine her condition at that time.

During the postpartum period several events occur. The uterus gradually decreases from the size of a newborn baby's head to that of a small pear. During this time there is a discharge from the uterus, consisting of blood and the sloughed off internal surface of the womb. The discharge gradually decreases during the first month and finally disappears.

Lactation is another event. During pregnancy the glandular tissue of the breast has increased tremendously, displacing the fat of which the breast was mostly composed before. At first the glands are filled with a watery fluid called colostrum, which has some nourishment and is slightly laxative to the baby. The third day the milk "comes in," engorging the breasts and making them painful for about thirty-six hours.

A common routine for breast feeding is the following: the baby is put to breast once during the first twenty-four hours, three times during the next twenty-four, and thereafter every three or four hours. The first two to three days he gets some colostrum as he sucks on the nipple, and by the time the milk comes in he is able for the first time to take his own nourishment.

The mother is often astonished at feeling so well after having a baby. She is able to have a regular diet, to turn over without distress, to read, to be visited by friends, and otherwise to enjoy life. This is in great contrast to the first few days following an operation.

However, if it is her first baby she may have some feelings of anxiety as to how she is going to take care of her child. The information from the doctor or nurse about what to expect regarding sleep, eating, crying, bowel movements, and other behavior is very helpful. In some hospitals the child stays in the same room with the mother, and she and her husband have the opportunity to become acquainted with their baby. This arrangement is called rooming-in. [It provides some of the advantages of home care without inconveniencing the physician or limiting facilities for care of mother and child — editorial *addendum*.]

The usual postpartum period in the hospital is five to seven days. During this time special attention is paid to the mother's breasts, the nipples being cleansed before and after each nursing. Special attention also is paid to the amount and type of vaginal discharge. The decrease in size of the uterus is checked every day because failure to contract may be due to infection. This is usually controlled by penicillin or other drugs.

The mother's diet in the hospital is usually liquid or soft the first day, and general thereafter. Forcing of fluid, with fruit juices and milk in abundance, is necessary to make possible an adequate supply of milk.

The care of the baby is concerned mainly with three things: (1) assuring antiseptic technique for the umbilical cord; (2) keeping the baby clean and warm; and (3) establishing adequate food intake. Every effort is made to establish an adequate supply of breast milk, for nursing aids in the regression in the size of the mother's womb besides being exceedingly important to the welfare of the baby. It gives him not only the best and the cleanest food but also protection against certain diseases. In addition, it provides him with a sense of security when he is held in his mother's arms. The psychological aspect of nursing is as important as the nourishment which the child gets.

A thorough physical examination of the baby is an integral part of the immediate postnatal care of the baby. He should also be given vitamin K shortly after he is born if his mother was not given it during her labor. This will prevent a disease which may cause hemorrhage in some babies. If his mother was Rh negative his Rh factor should also be determined. (The Rh factor has been discussed earlier in this chapter.) An obstetrician and some general practitioners turn over the care of the baby at this point to a specialist in child care, the pediatrician. His training is especially helpful in case the baby does not weigh five and a half pounds or if he is not doing well.

The mother is usually sitting up in bed the second day, may get out of bed that day or the next, and often is walking around by the time she goes home. She may have most of the responsibility of the baby from the first, if she started caring for him in the hospital. However, this does not mean that she is ready to go to work when she gets home. She should have help with the housework for at least the first two weeks.

At the six-weeks' checkup the mother is given an internal examination to determine the size and position of the uterus, the condition of the mouth of the womb, the vagina, and the outlet. Her heart, lungs, urine, and blood pressure are also tested.

SPACING FUTURE PREGNANCIES

The six-weeks' visit is the logical time to consider the problem of spacing future pregnancies. Following this visit, the mother may resume sexual relations for the first time after her baby is born. Spacing involves some method of contraception, a topic which has been discussed in Chapter Eleven.

Unless there is some urgency because of the advanced age of the parents, many physicians believe in a spacing of one and a half or two years. There are many reasons for this opinion, chief among them being the health of the mother. A period of freedom from pregnancy will give her body the opportunity to recuperate fully: her womb returns in size almost to that before pregnancy; her pelvic and abdominal muscles attain their former tone after the great stretching to which they were subjected during pregnancy and childbirth; organs such as the kidneys and heart are under decreased load. If she had any signs of undue strain such as increased blood pressure or albumin, it may be that the doctor will judge nine to fifteen months between pregnancies insufficient.

It is extremely important that the mother avoid pregnancy within the first six-month period, not only because of her own health. Pregnancy leads to cessation of breast milk formation, which would be detrimental to the best interests of the child just born. A good milk supply is dependent to a considerable extent upon happiness, rest, and freedom from worry.

There is a widely held misconception among laymen that nursing a baby will prevent conception. A doctor does not have to look far for instances of the falsity of this idea. The opposite is in fact the case; conception interferes with milk formation.

Another reason for spacing babies at least two years apart is to allow time for the many social-psychological adjustments that the presence of a child in the home requires of both the mother and the father. At first the mother tends to lose sight of her husband's claims on her. As the care of the baby becomes routine she should make an effort to regain her perspective, so that she not only devotes some time to her husband but also to her personal interests outside of the home. The father may be jealous of his own child; therefore he too should analyze his reactions to the changed situation.

COST OF PRENATAL CARE AND DELIVERY

At the first visit to a doctor the topic of cost should be brought up for discussion, preferably by the woman. The charge varies from one community to another and from general practitioner to specialist. The average charge by a general practitioner is seventy-five to one hundred dollars, which includes prenatal care. In general, a specialist charges one and a half to two times as much as a general practitioner does. If he is a full-fledged specialist, he has had three years of special training beyond the general internship, in addition to experience concentrated to a large degree on obstetrical cases.

Whether general practitioner or specialist, the physician's fee is usually the same for home as for hospital delivery.

In most communities of any size the hospital makes a regular charge for obstetrical cases, usually for five to seven days, which includes the care of the baby. This charge varies in different communities. It differs for private, semi-private, and ward quarters. The accompanying table, therefore, can at best be approximate within wide limits.

TABLE 9
COMPARATIVE COSTS OF HOME VERSUS HOSPITAL DELIVERY [1]

Home Delivery

Physician	$ 75.00 — $200.00
Practical nurse, 2 weeks	100.00 — 120.00
Housekeeper, 3 weeks	60.00 — 90.00
Baby's clothes, etc.	40.00 — 75.00
	$275.00 — $485.00

Hospital Delivery

Physician	$ 75.00 — $200.00
Hospital room, 6 days	60.00 — 120.00
Hospital delivery fee	15.00 — 30.00
Practical nurse, 1 week	50.00 — 60.00
Housekeeper, 2 weeks	40.00 — 60.00
Baby's clothes, etc.	35.00 — 70.00
	$275.00 $540.00

IMPORTANCE OF PRENATAL CARE

The obstetrician and pediatrician have been primarily responsible for the great decrease in the death rate among mothers and babies, resulting in the extension of the average life span of the individual. It is true that the most dangerous day of a person's life is his first day, the most dangerous week of his life is his first, and the most dangerous month is also his first. More children are now growing to adulthood and more mothers are able to give them the family life that only a mother can give.

SELECTED READINGS

CARRINGTON, W. J., *Safe Convoy* (Philadelphia: Lippincott, 1944).
CORBIN, HAZEL, *Getting Ready to Be a Father* (New York: Macmillan, 1939).
——, and VAN BLARCOM, C., *Getting Ready to Be a Mother* (New York: Macmillan, 1940).
EASTMAN, NICHOLSON J., *Expectant Motherhood* (Boston: Little, Brown, 1940).
ETS, MARIE HALL, *The Story of a Baby* (New York: Viking, 1939).

[1] These are estimates for 1954; various parts of the country will of course differ widely. Note that if friends or relatives can perform the services in brackets { }, the total for home care can be reduced to $115.00 to $275.00, and for hospital delivery to $185.00 to $420.00. It is only when friends or relatives provide help, plainly enough, that the home has any substantial cost advantage over the hospital — $70.00 to $145.00 saving.

Federal Security Agency, Children's Bureau, *Prenatal Care* (Washington, D. C.: Superintendent of Documents, 1950).

READ, GRANTLY DICK, *Childbirth Without Fear* (New York: Harper & Bros., 1944).

ROSENBERG, BERYL DAVID, *Special Delivery* (Chicago: Ziff-Davis, 1944).

ROWLAND, LOYD W., *Pierre the Pelican; Prenatal Series* (New Orleans: The Louisiana Society for Mental Health, 1950).

SHERBON, FLORENCE BROWN, *The Child* (New York: McGraw-Hill, 1941).

TODD, R. L., and FREEMAN, R. B., *Health Care of the Family* (Philadelphia: Saunders, 1946).

WHIPPLE, DOROTHY V., *Our American Babies* (New York: Barrows, 1944).

ZABRISKIE, LOUISE, *Mother and Baby Care in Pictures* (Philadelphia: Lippincott, 1935).

TOPICS FOR DISCUSSION OR REPORTS

1. What are the signs of pregnancy?
2. How soon should a woman go to her physician when she suspects pregnancy?
3. What is meant by a program of prenatal care?
4. What does the doctor look for, in particular, at the first visit?
5. How is the early diagnosis of pregnancy made?
6. Discuss the importance of prenatal care.
7. What are the stages of labor?
8. What is the role of the physician in prenatal care?
9. What is the healthy attitude toward pregnancy and childbirth?
10. How does one compute the date of birth of the child?
11. What is meant by the term "spacing pregnancies"?
12. What are the danger signs during pregnancy?
13. What is meant by "rooming-in"?
14. What is meant by "natural childbirth"?
15. Find out what the cost range of having a baby is in your locality, and compare with the range of incomes.
16. Present the case for and against home delivery, being sure to include the consideration of cost for "average families."
17. Do health insurance plans ordinarily cover the costs of childbirth? What are the special provisions, if any? Are there any health insurance plans specifically *excluding* childbirth benefits?
18. Compare procedures, etc. relating to childbirth in the United States and in some other country or countries having comparable rates of infant and maternal mortality.

Questions 15–18 are editorial addenda.

Chapter Sixteen

The Opportunities of Parenthood

KATHARINE WHITESIDE TAYLOR

Personality the Result of Family Experience

THE most important forces shaping the human personality are those surrounding it in infancy and early childhood, as Read Bain has so clearly pointed out in Chapter Six. Among these, relations with the members of the family group stand first. In contemporary America, at least, the parents are the small child's whole world. It is not surprising, therefore, that adults reflect in their lives the attitudes, beliefs, reaction patterns, and "emotional climate" of their childhood homes. One father observed recently: "Every time I see my own children disciplining my grandchildren I believe more strongly in education for family life! They are using the same tactics I used on them years ago — and I'm afraid their children will develop the same faults they have if we can't somehow break into the vicious circle."

The contribution of parents to the personalities of their children has long been recognized by philosophers and poets. Consider the Biblical pronouncement about "visiting the iniquity of the fathers upon the children unto the third and fourth generation," and the teaching of Confucius that if the parent-child relation is wholesome and good, every other relation will come right as a matter of course. Walt Whitman expresses it in these lines:

There was a child went forth every day,
And the first object he looked upon and received with wonder, pity, love, or
    dread, that object he became,
And that object became part of him for the day, or a certain part of the day,
    or for many years, or stretching cycles of years . . .
His own parents,
He that had fathered him, and she that conceived him in her womb and
    birthed him,
They gave this child more of themselves than that,
They gave him afterward every day — they and of them became part of
    him.[1]

Case histories explored by psychiatrists support the thesis that early experience is the most important factor in the formation of personality.[2] With different research techniques the recent studies of the psychologist Terman and of the sociologists Burgess and Cottrell come to agreement as to the primary importance of the parent-child relationship in later marital happiness.

---

[1] Walt Whitman, "There Was a Child Went Forth," *Leaves of Grass* (Boston: Thayer and Eldridge, 1860–1861).
[2] E. H. Erickson, *Childhood and Society* (New York: Norton, 1951); *A Healthy Personality for Every Child*, White House Conference Findings (Raleigh, N. C.: Health Publications Institute, 1951).

The latter report a striking tendency to repeat in adult life the patterns of the childhood home, not only in marriage but in all social contacts.[3] Terman's finding that "the degree of satisfaction which one finds in a marriage depends partly upon one's own characteristic attitudes and temperament," rather than upon "objective" factors, seems particularly significant here. In describing the traits of the unhappily married, he writes: "Most of these are items that in ordinary settings are interpreted as indicating neurotic tendency." [4] Terman also found the reverse to be true, namely, that persons who are "stabilized and socialized," i.e., emotionally mature, are most happy and successful in marriage.

Because the tie between parents and child is so close in our society the emotional climate generated by the parents deserves attention. The child absorbs the attitudes, aspirations, joys, anxieties, tensions he feels in his home and will tend to breathe out what he breathes in. If strains and conflicts are too prevalent, the child will not only be affected by the hostility in the voices he hears and the tension in the arms that hold him, but he will be drained emotionally by the unsatisfied longings in their hearts.[5] Psychiatric literature abounds in statements to the effect that disharmonies in the family are likely ultimately to find their reflection in the child, or "marital relationships with difficulties are not only detrimental to the happiness and efficiency of the man and woman, but capable also of throwing serious obstacles in the path of child life." [6] It has also been found in clinical work with children that where the parents are finding satisfaction in their married life or can be helped to find it by the clinical workers, it is possible in the vast majority of cases to overcome the child's problem, but that if the reverse is true, the majority of the cases are failures.[7]

In a study of early psychological needs based upon 100 cases of infants, evidence was found that the roots of unhappiness, ineffectual living, dependency, and unsocial behavior as well as of more extensive disorganization lie in maladjustments established during earliest infancy in personal relationships. Strong emotional attitudes in parents or nurses have been known to affect the rapid and sensitive personality development taking place in the very first year of life. We know now with relative certainty that the capacity for mature emotional relationships in adult life is an outgrowth of the amount and quality of mothering which an infant receives.[8]

[3] Ernest W. Burgess and Leonard S. Cottrell, Jr., *Predicting Success or Failure in Marriage* (New York: Prentice-Hall, 1939), chap. 17.
[4] L. M. Terman and associates, *Psychological Factors in Marital Happiness* (New York: McGraw-Hill, 1938), pp. 145–147, 165–166.
[5] J. Bowley, "The Influence of Early Environment in the Development of Neurosis and Neurotic Character," *International Journal of Psychoanalysis*, 21 (1940), pp. 154–178.
[6] Gardner Murphy, *Personality, a Biosocial Approach to Origins and Structure* (New York: Harper's, 1947). See also the whole issue of *Understanding the Child*, Oct., 1952, for summary of findings regarding effect of love starvation on infants.
[7] Helen Witmer and students, "The Outcome of Treatment in a Child Guidance Clinic," *Smith College Studies in Social Work*, 3 (June, 1933), p. 339.
[8] Margaret A. Ribble, *The Rights of Infants: Early Psychological Needs and Their Satisfaction* (New York: Columbia University Press, 1943), pp. 2 and 13.

If the parents are happy and serene in their relation with each other so that surface irritations are relatively unimportant, the baby is assured the best foundation for wholesome emotional growth. It is therefore highly desirable that the beginning of marital solidarity be achieved before any couple undertakes the profound responsibility and new adjustments inherent in the addition of a child.

Many couples have sought by the birth of a baby to cement a marriage that had symptoms of falling apart. In so doing, they usually insure its complete demolition, for they then confront these questions: Whose values and attitudes shall regulate the child's behavior? Who shall possess the child emotionally? Whose goals shall direct his future? On the other hand, if the partners are sufficiently mature to be able to focus wholeheartedly on someone outside themselves and if they have passed safely through most of the important adjustments of early marriage, the birth of a child may engender a feeling of fulfillment and a vital new interest that does deepen their sense of fusion. Just as Terman found in his study of marriage, it is perhaps true in all situations involving human sociation that the result is not determined by external factors alone. The *inter*action of internal readiness (or the absence of it) with external reality gives the clue. The meaning of the child to the parents is therefore determined, in part at least, by the meaning each parent has for the other, and the meaning of the marriage in the lives of both.

When people have achieved a really satisfying relationship in their love life and other phases of shared living, the carry-over of serenity and relaxation will help them bear the strains of continual care, wakeful nights, and the other exacting demands babies make. Equally important are their genuine acceptance of each other as persons, and the capacity of each to respect and assimilate the most important wishes of the other in creating values satisfying to both. Until married persons have learned to adjust to one another on a basis of equality, they are not ready to adjust to the powerful, primitive drives of a baby and to guide him safely toward the socially sensitive adulthood which may be termed emotional maturity.

EMOTIONAL MATURITY: PREREQUISITE FOR PARENTHOOD

So far, there has been no complete analysis of the characteristics of the emotionally mature personality, although there have been several good descriptions of the neurotic.[9] There is great need for further investigation in this important area. The two most helpful approaches to the problem so far may be called the dynamic, based upon the findings of psychoanalysts, psychiatrists, and clinical psychologists; and the cultural, based upon the studies of sociologists, anthropologists, and social psychologists. There has been at times some conflict between the two approaches, but each actually implies the other and both are essential in any complete delineation of the mature personality. A *human* being is formed by continuous interaction between his

[9] A. Adler, *Understanding Human Nature* (New York: Greenberg, 1927); also Karen Horney, *The Neurotic Personality of Our Time* (New York: Norton, 1937); and E. A. Strecker, *Their Mother's Sons* (Philadelphia: Lippincott, 1951).

developing drives and the restrictions, values, and expectations of the surrounding culture. Furthermore, the standards by which his maturity is judged are set by that culture. It is not enough that his goals are in harmony with his own inner needs; they must also be acceptable to the particular milieu in which he finds himself, if he is to be called mature in that culture.

Emotional maturity is characterized first by the capacity to see one's self and life objectively. It is to accept the reality of one's own endowments and environment and the responsibility for working out a satisfying way of life within the limits of that reality. It is to solve one's problems with a minimum of internal conflict or external friction by using one's own powers rather than by exploiting others. It includes a well-defined scheme of values which serves as a guide for making satisfying decisions. It means an ever-increasing capacity to respond with tenderness and sympathy to the needs of others, at the same time maintaining one's own selfhood.

The really mature person accepts the changes, privations, and frustrations inherent in the life process, and uses them as stimuli for further growth. He has found ways of releasing tensions through the arts, social relations, or other constructive outlets acceptable both to his needs and his conscience. Therefore, instead of "going to pieces" in the vortex of emotions generated by frustration and privation, he manages to direct the energy so liberated into new relations, creative activities, and constructive work.

When one's own life is adequate it is not necessary to "live through others." Therefore one is able to love for the delight one finds in another person and in giving of one's self, without making excessive demands on the beloved. In the marriage relation emotional maturity can be measured in part by a capacity for mature heterosexuality, for giving and sustaining mate-love on a give-and-take basis, as well as by the capacity to survive both good and ill fortune without either becoming emotionally dependent or sacrificing integrity.

The mature person sees all other people as ends in themselves rather than as means to ends. He has shifted from self-centeredness to other-centeredness, and finds his life integrated around tasks of social worth. He has achieved such mastery over himself that he wants and works for only those goals he believes to be good in the largest sense, and is capable of devoting himself to them even at great personal sacrifice. He not only affirms but lives his religion.

The prerequisite of all these attributes of maturity is emotional emancipation from parents, obviating the need for seeking parent-substitutes in other relationships throughout life.[10] It is only after the individual has outgrown the need for parental ministrations, affection, approval, and support, that he is emotionally capable of entering into mature personal relations. Not until he is freed from infantile erotic ties and has developed personal autonomy is he able to participate in a marriage relation on a give-and-take basis. Emotional self-reliance is also essential for sustaining the demands of parenthood — where for long years the scales are heavily weighted on the giving side.

[10] A discussion of the stages gone through in achieving this emotional emancipation will be found under Emotional Maturation and Adolescence, pp. 480–483.

In contrast, note the patterns of the emotionally immature person. He has not completely resolved all the basic conflicts that should be worked out during adolescence and is never quite sure of what he thinks or what he wants to be. He may vacillate continually between masculine and feminine roles, and always feel resentful of the supposed greater privileges of the opposite sex. He may still be a child in wanting all the privileges of every role he plays without accepting the responsibilities it entails; and like a child he will always blame others when things go wrong and will depend on them for everything, from getting to places on time to making major decisions. Beyond this, he will seek to manipulate others rather than use his own powers to obtain his major satisfactions, and will exploit them without giving much in return. Therefore, while this type of person has an excessive need for love and devotion, such as a parent gives a little child, he is perpetually afraid lest too much will be asked of him and he may actually run away from the very thing he wants. He is incapable of sustaining any relation on the terms of equal giving that are essential to adult love.

In addition, such persons resent any demands of reality interfering with the immediate and complete satisfactions of their wishes. When a small child is uncomfortable his first impulse is to cry for relief, regardless of whose sensibilities he offends. In the same way dependent adults want immediate relief from tension, and find it difficult to wait for a solution that is acceptable to others as well as to themselves. They are apt to feel strong antagonism to persons who fail to fulfill their needs, as well as to those who compete as rivals for attention. They are so completely absorbed in their own wishes and feelings that they cannot see any situation as a whole; their own part in it is all-engrossing. While they may claim to be altruistic, there is usually considerable discrepancy between their expressed ideals and what they really do, particularly in their person-to-person relations. A further complicating factor is that the really immature person fails to recognize his own immaturity and the unreasonableness of his demands.

We do not mean to imply, however, that there is a clean-cut division between the mature and the immature. Most of us are intermittently mature and immature, depending upon conditions. Even the best of us, when faced by too many frustrations and disappointments, have spells of being regressive (neurotic). The difference is that the relatively mature person finds ways of pulling himself out of the slump by arranging sufficient satisfactions to counteract some frustrations. He consciously seeks acceptable ways of relieving his tensions, and if possible works out a plan that will lessen frustrations in the future. The immature person, on the other hand, remains submerged in self-pity, depends upon someone else to come to his rescue as a mother does for a little child, and is enraged if the mother-substitute is not forthcoming or if her ministrations in any way fall short of his needs.

PREGNANCY AND THE MARRIAGE RELATION

With this background it is easy to understand why the advent of a child puts a severe strain upon the relation of immature partners from even the beginning of pregnancy. With the first baby especially, the wife is likely to be upset during the first few months, and during the last to feel somewhat unwieldy and uncomfortable. Add to this the embarrassment and distress she may feel at her ungainly figure and short breath, the curtailment of the pleasures and satisfactions she has taken for granted, and the not infrequent dread of childbirth, and it is easy to see why her life would seem overloaded with frustrations. Modern education for childbirth helps greatly, however.

Many women so helped find that the joy of expectant motherhood, the importance of the new role, the feeling of fulfillment and completeness, and the bond of increased tenderness with the husband keep the balance well weighted toward the positive side. Some psychiatrists report that women who are happy in their marriage relation and in their prospective motherhood often avoid nausea completely and find the whole nine months a time of added vitality and zestful living.

Similar contrasts may appear in the attitudes of men toward pregnancy. For the young man who has sought a mother-substitute in his wife, the pregnant woman's genuine need for extra consideration and tenderness is extremely irksome because the tables are thereby turned. He also may thoroughly resent the restrictions on the pleasures and freedom they have enjoyed together, and may assert that his wife feels ill or tired just when he is most wanting her ministrations or companionship. In her preoccupation with preparations for the expected infant he may also fear that he will have a secondary role in his wife's affection in the years to come.

To the young man who feels secure and adequate, however, the advent of a child may seem the most wonderful thing that could happen. For him parenthood comes as a real fulfillment, the validation of his manhood. He is delighted at the vigorous fetal movements his wife reports, and is sure his offspring will be a star athlete. Such a father enjoys wondering what the "little beggar" will look like only slightly less than planning his or her career from the cradle on through college. He feels occasional irritation at the curtailment of their activities as pregnancy progresses, to be sure, but this is counterbalanced by fatherly anticipations and the realization of a stronger bond between himself and his wife.[11]

Effects of the First Child on Parents

Much emphasis is rightly being placed on the effects of parents on the child's personality, but just as much could be written, and with as much warrant, about the effect of the child on the parents' development. From the moment he is born the child exerts an important influence upon them. The birth of the first baby is one of the most maturing of experiences for both parents, because of the powerful train of associations and the depth of emotions involved. It is one of the great crises of life.

When the pain is not too excruciating (and modern medicine has done much to reduce it), childbirth itself may be an exhilarating experience to a

[11] H. Miller and F. Flannery, "Education for Childbirth in Private Practice," *Child and Family Digest*, 6 (April, 1952), pp. 33–44.

woman. She may feel herself the instrument of a tremendous life force stronger than herself that compels her to utilize strength she never dreamed she had. The feeling of the young mother has been expressed in the lines:

"Where have I come from, where did you pick me up?" the baby asked its mother.

She, half crying, half laughing, and clasping the baby to her breast, —

"You were hidden in my heart as its desire, my darling . . .

As I gaze on your face, mystery overwhelms me: you who belong to all have become mine.

For fear of losing you I hold you tight to my breast. What magic has snared the world's treasure in the slender arms of mine?" [12]

But what of the young father? For the sake of sharing in one of life's deepest experiences as well as giving his wife invaluable support and hence strengthening the marriage bond, the father should be permitted to stand at her side during labor and the actual birth of the baby.[13] The effects of parenthood on him also are profound. He has a new status as father that brings sobering responsibility, a feeling of authority, and increased respect from relatives and friends. Since parenthood is in accord with one of our basic customs, community approval itself has a stabilizing effect, and a young man who never thought much about tomorrow finds himself sacrificing certain present satisfactions to take out life insurance for his family. He realizes that he has given hostages to the future and that his concern cannot stop with his own life.

The quality of the sexual communion of the mates may improve too. The relentlessly realistic biological experience the woman has been through may help her to overcome any unfortunately conditioned disgusts and improve her capacity for sexual enjoyment. Her new status as mother frequently helps her accept her biological role and increases her satisfaction with her role as a woman. Psychiatrists believe these to be the underlying reasons why in some cases women have overcome their frigidity and developed a normal orgasm capacity after the birth of a child.[14]

THE NEGLECTED FATHER

If the father has had an experience in his own childhood of a baby brother or sister who interfered with his rights, the experience may be reactivated and he may feel himself abandoned, and react with panic and

[12] Rabindranath Tagore, "The Beginning," *The Crescent Moon* (New York: Macmillan, 1913).

[13] The tendency among some doctors and hospitals to keep young fathers out of the delivery room seems to this writer unwholesome from a psychological point of view, though it may simplify things for the physicians. Many young couples have expressed satisfaction at having the father present during the birth for the comfort his presence brings to his wife, for his first hand understanding of the ordeal she has gone through, for his own emotional growth, and for a powerful initial welding of the new family unit.

[14] S. Freud, *Modern Sexuality and Modern Nervousness* (New York: Eugenics Publishing Co., 1931).

resentment quite without realizing the cause.[15] Therefore every effort should be made by the young mother to keep the husband reassured of her affection, in spite of her natural absorption in her baby. He should be restored to the key place that is rightfully his when the first flush of maternal ecstasy has passed and the manifold tasks involved in baby care have been mastered. As proof that the problem is recognized, the writer cites the title of a humorous but earnest lecture which was given recently: "The Care and Feeding of the Young Father."

It may help both young parents to realize that the mother's capacity to give the young child the quality of care and affection he needs depends primarily upon the quality of understanding and support she receives from her husband. If he feels rejected, he will find it difficult not to respond with hostility instead of affection; and if she feels isolated by his hostility, she cannot give the baby a sense of being supported on a vast sea of love essential to his wholesome growth. The emotional tone of the husband-wife relationship is the climate in which the child thrives or starves. Therefore husband and wife should continue to cherish and cultivate their own love relationship, both as the best source of fulfilling their primary need for love, and equally important as the essential strand determining the quality of all other family ties.

Too many American women make their children the emotional center of their lives, even after babyhood is passed. One woman who had become such a supermother to her two children that she refused to let anyone wait on them but herself writes as follows:

My babies were becoming an obsession. They threw all else so out of focus that the world, including my husband, had become little better than a blur — I was out of touch with my friends. I didn't read any more. I hardly knew who was running for president. And as for Jim, I didn't have any time or energy left for him. He'd become a part of the furniture.

One day a queer look he gave me when I made him turn off the radio in the middle of an important broadcast for fear it would wake the children set me to thinking. I realized how completely I was giving the children the right of way — regardless of his wishes or convenience.

It dawned on me that Jim had been the Superfluous Man ever since the day he paced the floor outside the obstetrical room at the hospital while I did the hard work. For several years he had patiently waited for me to let our own life together swing back to normal, while I had let the children separate us. It was time to take hold of myself.[16]

Since the whole initial adjustment to parenthood is so profound and of such basic importance in the lives of all concerned, there should be an abundance of discussion groups and classes for parents of both sexes to talk through the new problems of babies and frustrated parents. There is

[15] *Op. cit.*, p. 102.
[16] Wainright Evans, "Are Good Mothers Unfaithful Wives?" *Better Homes and Gardens* (July, 1941).

no better time to release the facts of parenthood than now, even for folks who have taken courses before marriage. The actual experience is likely to involve many pitfalls impossible to foresee.

PARENTAL ATTITUDES TOWARD THE CHILDREN

There seem to be four main ways of thinking about children: as a responsibility, as a nuisance, as compensatory sources of satisfaction, or as bundles of potentialities.[17] Although all four are found in the reactions of most parents at one time or another, the one which is dominant most of the time colors the whole relation and to a large extent determines the development of both parents and child. First of all, it is of course natural for parents to think of their child as an overwhelming responsibility. They realize that they alone are primarily responsible twenty-four hours a day until the child is fully mature, that his needs must always be met before they can think of their own. A child actually adds from 45 to 80 per cent to the household duties of the mother, with the heavier burdens coming in the earlier years.

There are financial burdens too. A nursery, added or improvised within the space available, is needed in the house. The new car or the long-planned vacation may have to be set aside. The extension of educational opportunities for children from nursery school through college and possibly into post-graduate work, the increasing services and recommendations of specialists in nutrition, medical care, recreation, psychology, and psychiatry, all tend to overwhelm parents with the ceaseless expenses involved in having a child. Children are far from the potential economic assets they were in frontier days; indeed, parents reconcile themselves today to continuous expense until the children are well past physiological maturity.

Parents who think of their children primarily as responsibilities are more likely to think of them also (subconsciously) as competitors for the good things in life, as rivals for the affection of others, as frustrating elements that stand between them and the satisfaction of needs and wishes; in fact, as nuisances. They tend to see their offspring as competitive siblings rather than as their own children.[18]

Since immature parents can seldom see reality as it is, they tend to blame their children for all the hardships in their lives. They may feel that if only there were no "pesky" child around they would come in for a larger share of the affections and attentions of the mate and of the family income and luxuries. This sense of being thwarted is often found among parents who have sought the birth of a child as a magic panacea. When it

[17] R. M. Bakwin and H. Bakwin, *Psychological Care During Infancy and Childhood* (New York: Appleton-Century, 1942), chap. 20; and M. Levine, *Psychotherapy in Medical Practice* (New York: Macmillan, 1942), chaps. 10 and 11.

[18] J. Silberfenning, "Mother Types Encountered in Child Guidance Clinics," *American Journal of Orthopsychiatry,* 11 (July, 1941), pp. 475–484, suggests that hostility toward a child is a displacement of earlier feelings of a mother toward her own parents or siblings. The anxious mother is projecting to her children some of her own earlier feelings, particularly fears of injury or death.

is found that the satisfactions of having a baby also entail heavy responsibilities and interference with rights and comforts, rather than unalloyed, effortless pleasure, immature parents may register their disappointment by complete rejection of the child — and it is the rejected children who develop personality disorders in their attempts to compensate for lack of security. Indeed, such rejected persons may continue throughout life to act like children in the hope of receiving thereby the long-retarded bestowal of love and they may in turn resent their children, thus continuing the vicious circle. They may be continually impelled to seek reassurance of their welcome and importance. The greater their needs for affection and recognition, the harder they struggle for attention, often in antisocial ways.[19]

Some parents may completely reject their children and show it by continually blaming, hurrying, punishing, and interfering with them. A recent study shows that children in such an atmosphere of continuous rejection are those who show the most crying, whining, and unpleasant aggressive behavior. Those children who receive the smallest number of affectionate responses from their parents show the most attention-getting behavior.[20]

Other immature or frustrated parents tend to think of the child primarily as an instrument for fulfilling their own needs for affection, recognition, and mastery, and seek to manipulate him to their own ends. They do this chiefly by two methods: overindulgence and domination.

The tendency toward overindulgence is particularly strong in maladjusted parents who clutch at the child to satisfy their own unsatisfied need for love. The child is to them an extension of themselves, and keeping him physically dependent is a most effective way of prolonging this illusion. A mother, for instance, may turn to her baby as her main source of emotional satisfaction, overwhelm him with solicitude, anticipate his every want, and seriously interfere with his growth toward independence. Herein lies the danger of "spoiling," technically known as overindulgence. The "spoiled" child never learns to adapt himself to the demands of the outside world, but remains childish, thinking his needs will be taken care of for him. He is in general characterized by inferiority feelings and tendencies to withdraw from social contacts. He may also develop an abnormal eagerness to please those in authority at a sacrifice of independence, or again he may show so much hostility to all in authority that he never really becomes adjusted socially. Fathers may employ similar tactics, or perhaps more frequently may seek satisfaction for balked ego drives by directing every move a child makes and demanding unquestioning obedience.

Overindulgence and domination both tend to frustrate the child's developing powers and to interfere with many quite normal, justifiable wishes. Moreover, frustration and aggression are frequently joined as response sequences.[21] It is therefore easy to understand why the typical family back-

[19] P. Symonds, *The Psychology of Parent-Child Relationships* (New York: Appleton-Century, 1939) pp. 3–53.

[20] G. G. Lafore, *Practices of Parents in Dealing with Preschool Children;* Child Development Monographs No. 31, Teachers College, Columbia University, 1945.

[21] John Dollard and others, *Frustration and Aggression* (New Haven: Yale University Press, 1939), p. 11.

ground for aggressive delinquents has been found to be an overindulgent mother and a cruel, domineering father.[22]

MATERNAL OVERPROTECTION

The findings in an important study [23] indicate that maternal overprotection may take the form of excessive and prolonged maternal care, or excessive and prolonged domination, or both. Levy found maternal overprotection always correlated with both past and present privation in the life of the mother. In extreme cases of both types, there was excessive fondling, feeding, caring for, and sleeping with the child long past infancy. In one case the child was fed on a bottle until he was three and a half and in another was helped with his dressing until he was fourteen. The child may be taken to and from school every day and allowed to play only in the mother's sight long after it is necessary. In some cases such treatment may last until the child is fifteen. Along with this the child is prevented from taking any responsibility even in household tasks for fear he may be injured and he is never allowed to fight his own battles.

The formation of friendships with other children is also in many cases unconsciously combated by such a mother. She typically reaches out to prevent any freedom of movement that jeopardizes her social monopoly of her offspring. In "pure" cases of overprotection, the mother also limits her own social life to companionship with the child. There is, normally, a distinct tendency toward increase in the number of companions of the child with the increase in the number of social contacts of the parents.[24]

By an intensive study of the extreme cases of maternal overprotection we can understand the danger of such behavior even though it appears in less exaggerated form in other mothers. We are also able to recognize and understand the selfish, undisciplined, explosive behavior of the overprotected child in later years as an effort to maintain or regain the originally favored position with the mother. He has been veritably robbed of the opportunity of developing his own potentialities, of relying upon his own powers, and has thereby been deprived of one of his major birthrights. A boy's best friend is *not* always his mother!

THE DEVELOPMENTAL APPROACH

Of the four basic sets of parental attitudes listed (children are responsibilities, nuisances, sources of satisfaction, and potentialities), the only set acceptable to qualified students of the family is that of looking on the child as a bundle of potentialities to be released through wholesome surroundings

---

[22] Symonds, *op. cit.,* pp. 10, 46.

[23] David Levy, *Maternal Overprotection* (New York: Columbia University Press, 1943), pp. 57 ff.

[24] Levy, *op. cit.,* 71 ff. For further discussion of parental overconcern, see Bain's analysis earlier in this book, "Parent-Child and Child-Parent Fixations," pp. 197–200, also Strecker, *op. cit.*

and wise guidance. This does not mean that none of the other attitudes are ever present, for of course they are to some extent even in the best of parents. All of us at times feel ambivalent toward those we love. The important thing is that parents should not reject their offspring even though at times they are irritating, nor are parents justified in using them as a compensatory source of joy. On the other hand the deepest and surest joy parents can feel comes from watching their children's personalities unfold in an atmosphere of love and freedom.

An important study [25] of the differential concepts of parenthood held by parents of different racial and cultural groups and different social strata in Chicago justifies our attention as we consider the developmental approach to parenthood.

Dr. Duvall found two main clusters of attitudes toward children, which she labeled *developmental* and *traditional*. The traditional parents saw the "good" child as a "mannerable" child who minded his parents and kept clean and neat. They wanted their children to conform so they would be well regarded in the neighborhood. The developmental minded parents saw him as a personality with needs of self-expression and of self-realization. They wished to foster in their homes a "permissive, growth-promoting form of guidance."

Dr. Duvall found that the developmental pattern occurred much more frequently in the upper and middle classes of all the racial groups, but particularly in the native white and among mothers of younger children. On the other hand the greater proportion of traditional concepts were found at the "lower middle" and "upper lower" class levels, because of burdens of drudgery, cramped living, recency of migration, and lack of contact with other modes of living. Another factor reinforcing the "traditional" approach in these classes is an effort to achieve respectability. On the other hand it was found that even among the more liberated parents of the middle and upper classes the developmental approach is affected by social pressure toward conformity as children become old enough for contacts with school and community. This pressure cramps the freedom and creativity of the growing child. It is a major problem both of enlightened parents and of school people to see that the developmental approach is maintained so that each child's unique potentialities may be liberated for happy and effective living. To keep this attitude dominant parents must have a thorough understanding of the fundamental needs of the child. Tho two bodies of knowledge are inseparable!

Understanding the Child's Basic Needs

Instructions concerning the physical needs of the child are now readily available. The excellent practice of monthly visits to a pediatrician or a well-baby clinic, now being followed by an ever larger number of parents,

[25] Evelyn Millis Duvall, *Differential Concepts of Parenthood* (Ph.D. thesis, Chicago, University of Chicago Library, 1946). For a digest of findings see "Conceptions of Parenthood," *American Journal of Sociology* (Nov., 1946), pp. 193-204.

is a great help toward adequate physical care. Materials describing the basic mental, social, and emotional needs of the child are also available but have not yet been so widely applied. Parents should keep abreast of the scientifically sound but simply presented literature in this field.[26]

A carefully worked-out succession of steppingstones to a healthy personality is given by Erickson. These are: a sense of trust, sense of autonomy, sense of initiative, sense of accomplishment, sense of identity, sense of intimacy, parental sense, sense of integrity. He holds that each must be firmly established before the next can grow.[27] It is significant that the three books just cited describing the psychological needs of infants are written by doctors of medicine who recognize that the early scientific physical care of infants failed to recognize some of the deeply hidden desires in the emotional life of the mother and baby now called basic human needs. The basic needs of every individual fall into three main categories: the need for emotional security, for a sense of achievement, and for orientation to one's world. All human beings have these needs throughout the life span, though they are satisfied in different ways at successive stages.[28]

The Need for Love

In fulfilling the need for security, love stands first.[29] It may safely be said that love is to the baby's personality what food is to his body. His conception of the world as cold, hostile, and frustrating, or as warm, friendly, and happy, is a direct reflection of the personalities about him. So, too, his evolving picture of himself as a person depends upon the responses given his smiles, his spirit of play, his vigorous demands to have his needs met, and his lusty joy in their satisfaction. He soon comes to feel either that he is a person whom people love and find delightful or one whom no one finds interesting or cares much about.

Studies of orphanage children have shown that babies do not develop friendly personalities, nor do they really flourish physically, until they are given personal affection and attention. The sense of touch is the most elemental form of communication and the one that babies understand best. Hence, all babies need a generous amount of kissing and caressing for the development of happy, assured personalities. "The fundamental need of every human being for caressing is nowhere as demonstrable as it is in

[26] Notably Charles A. Aldrich and M. M. Aldrich, *Babies Are Human Beings* (New York: Macmillan, 1938); Margaret A. Ribble, *The Rights of Infants: Early Psychological Needs and Their Satisfaction* (New York: Columbia University Press, 1943); and Benjamin Spock, *The Common Sense Book of Baby Care* (New York: Duell, Sloan and Pearce, 1946).

[27] Helen Witmer and R. Kotinsky, *Personality in the Making* (New York: Harper, 1952). This is based on the fact-finding report of the Mid-Century White House Conference on Childhood and Youth, including a condensation of the Erickson material.

[28] See Percival Symonds, *The Dynamics of Human Adjustment* (New York: Appleton-Century, 1946), chap. 2, and E. W. Burgess and H. J. Locke, *The Family* (New York: American Book Co., 1945), chaps. 7, 8, 10.

[29] L. K. Frank, "The Fundamental Needs of the Child," *Mental Hygiene,* 22, No. 3 (July, 1938), pp. 357–379; also D. A. Prescott, *Emotion and the Educative Process* (Washington, D. C.: American Council of Education, 1938), chap. 4.

young babies. . . . Loving care and consistent, prompt response to their needs is tremendously important to their successful progress." [30]

The old rocking chair and the singing of lullabies therefore need not be discarded but should be enjoyed by both parents and child. It is our thesis that every baby is entitled to a "honeymoon" period with his mother when he and his needs are of first importance to her. Her love for him and for his baby traits is somehow communicated to the child and acts as the foundation for a more secure adulthood. The double satisfaction of drinking warm milk from his mother's breast while being held caressingly in her arms symbolizes for the child being loved and wanted. From clinical observation David Levy holds that happy experiences in breast feeding do more to establish the child's emotional security than whole dictionaries of words can do later.

Three decades ago half of the deaths of infants were caused by a baffling disease called *marasmus,* a Greek word meaning "wasting away." The discovery was made that marasmus occurred in the best of homes and hospitals as often as in poverty-stricken ones where good mothers frequently produced bouncing babies. Analyses of these findings brought to light the fact that an infant has an emotional hunger for the activities involved in good "mothering" as real as his hunger for food and oxygen. In marasmus, the infant starves for mothering, and gradually his vital activities go out of order, first that of elimination, then that of breathing and circulation. Knowing this, today we move homeless infants out of institutions into good foster homes as rapidly as possible. Instructions are now given to nurses caring for the newborn in hospitals to give each child a bit of loving with each bottle-feeding. Some of the more psychologically advanced hospitals have broken completely with traditional practice and allow the baby to be kept in a little crib by its mother, who is encouraged to fondle it as often as she wishes.

According to this view, moreover, a baby needs, during the period directly after birth and for some weeks following, a frequent repetition of conditions similar to the prenatal state. He has a real need to be held in close contact with his mother's body and carried about by her, and beyond this to be touched and fondled, to be spoken to and sung to so that his whole socioemotional nature may awaken and flourish. Babies denied their right to such mothering in the earliest weeks and months may suffer throughout life from an impaired capacity for full emotional response.[31]

Further evidence of the supreme importance of the parent-child relations comes from a study of the reactions of British children to the frights and deprivations of war. Children were not too seriously disturbed as a result of undergoing even severe bombings if they were with their own parents and if the latter remained reasonably poised. On the other hand, when separated from parents, even though cared for under excellent conditions, the children regressed to infantile ways and showed little improvement until

[30] Aldrich and Aldrich, *op. cit.,* p. 103.   [31] Ribble, *op. cit.,* pp. 1–3.

put into "artificial" families where four or five children could be carefully "mothered" by the same adult most of the time.[32]

THE NEED TO FEEL ADEQUATE

"Won't people spoil their babies if they give them all this affection and attention, even rocking and singing to them? Isn't that a form of maternal overprotection?" some will ask. Such a query arises from a misconception of the "spoiled" child. Those children whose basic needs are not adequately met are the "spoiled" ones in the real sense. Their disagreeable behavior is usually an effort to wrench from an antagonistic world the satisfactions they have missed. A study carried out in New York City corroborates this. Kindergarten teachers were asked to rate their pupils as to adjustment in school, and case histories were made of the home situation of those who were most happy, friendly, and cooperative, as well as of those who were most "spoiled" and unruly. It was found that the "good" children came from homes where they were thoroughly secure in the affection of parents but had adequate opportunity both for self-expression and the discipline of cooperative group living. The "spoiled" children, on the other hand, came from homes where some or all of these elements were lacking. From his wide experience with delinquent children, August Aichorn formulates the principle that education will succeed with a child in direct proportion to the wholesomeness of the love he receives from his parents.[33] In the deeper sense, parents cannot love their children too much, but they can express that love in ways that interfere with the fulfillment of other needs, such as the need to feel adequate and self-reliant.

Perhaps the most important way many loving parents err is by trying to do everything for their child when he is eager and ready to do things for himself, thereby frustrating his need for a sense of achievement. Even well-adjusted parents may make mistakes because they lack understanding of the importance of readiness in the child's learning. For instance, when the baby is seven or eight months old, he shows he is ready to learn to use a spoon by reaching for it and trying to feed himself. An understanding parent will give the child just enough help to insure "success," to the end that the effort is repeated. The child will soon develop other self-help skills such as washing, dressing, and putting things away if encouraged properly. It invariably takes more time to help a child learn to do these things for himself when he is first ready than to go on doing them for him, but when parents continue to do for the child what he is ready to do for himself, they do him a disservice. *The final object of parents should be to see the child independent and self-reliant.*

On the other hand there are hazards in forcing a youngster before he is ready, as overly conscientious or ambitious parents are wont to do. Pavlov induced nervous breakdowns in healthy dogs by forcing them to try performances beyond their powers. When their capacities were strained to the

[32] Anna Freud and D. T. Burlingham, *War and Children* (New York: Medical War Books, 1943), pp. 156–157.
[33] Symonds, *op. cit.*, p. 9.

limit, the dogs went to pieces and had to be sent to the country to recuperate. Even at best, habit training entails considerable frustration of deep-
seated drives and primitive responses. Feelings of strain, inadequacy, and
even of permanent inferiority may result, for example, from too early or
too rigorous training in bowel and bladder control.[34] The over-reaction of
parents to "accidents" of elimination and excretion have left scars on many
a child's personality.[35] Another area which gives trouble to the too prudish
parent is the normal tendency to play with the genitals, which appears in
all young children at one time or another. Parental overconcern with this
problem has been known to interfere with normal personality development
— even with later sexual enjoyment in marriage. The child's "sex education"
really begins in infancy with the way his body is handled, with the way
basic habits of eating and excretion are established, and with parental reactions to sex play. Understanding here is basic to wholesome growth, as has
been shown by many recent studies.

As already pointed out, many parents seek to realize their own unfulfilled
needs through the child and demand perfection beyond the child's capacity.
Parents will find it helpful to study what children within certain age ranges
are able to do, remembering at the same time that every child has his own
unique pattern of development. Gesell has worked out detailed "average"
summaries for the first five years, and has made some interesting observations on the years from five to ten.[36]

Parents who study child growth can watch for signs that their own
child is ready for certain activities, and can then provide an environment
where they may be tried out in safety. (An Iowa study indicates that children who are exposed to books, pictures, music, people, tools, and trips
develop faster than children who do not have these opportunities.)

The child's rate of progress is determined in part by the interaction
of internal growth with stimuli from the external world. A baby cannot
crawl until his coordinations are ready, but when they are ready, the first
real crawl will be taken to reach a desired object just beyond his reach. If,
however, every time the child reaches for something it is handed to him, or
his hand is slapped, or he has the psychological "slap" of failure, he may
never learn to help himself with effectiveness and satisfaction. Throughout the child's life, a sufficiently rich and friendly environment is essential
if his maturing powers are to be given full play.[37]

THE NEED FOR ORIENTATION

Just as the child's need to develop his own capacities is a natural check
on parental tendencies toward overprotection, so the rights of other family
members and of the parents themselves form a natural check on too great

[34] Flanders Dunbar, *Your Child's Mind and Body* (New York: Random House, 1949).
[35] Dorothy Baruch, *One Little Boy* (New York: Julian Press, 1952).
[36] Arnold Gesell and F. L. Ilg, *Child Development* (New York: Harper, 1949). Contains two
useful earlier books.
[37] For a more detailed discussion of this point, see pp. 475–477.

freedom in the child's use of his developing powers. Out of interacting with his fellows the child is oriented to what is mine and thine. As he perceives the rights of others, he is meeting in part his need for orientation to the world of persons. His further need for understanding and feeling at home in other aspects of his world will be discussed in the section on "Home as an Educational Institution."

The foundation of good relations in the family and in all other groups — indeed the most important principle in all great religions — is sensitivity to the rights of other people. Furthermore, the prerequisite of social sensitivity in children is having their own needs met. It is difficult for anyone to be very sensitive to the rights of others if any of his own basic needs remain unsatisfied for any length of time. Conversely, people who feel secure in the love of relatives and friends and adequate in their own developing powers are freed from the necessity of struggling for their own rights and can more readily adjust to those of others. In her important study of sympathetic behavior in young children, Lois Barclay Murphy found that children whose needs for warm response, sympathetic help, and free activity were adequately met were those who most frequently showed sympathy for others.[38]

Children who have been treated with sympathy and affection from the very beginning, whose lives have held more satisfactions than frustrations, can accept the laws of human interaction about them and regard them as benevolent and kindly. Of importance in helping the child orient his own desires to the rights of others is explaining how we all must obey rules so that everyone can be happy. He needs to feel that love and authority are merged in the personalities of his parents to help him realize that rules and restrictions are to keep people happy with each other, not to interfere with happiness.

From the time he starts asking questions every child should also have help in working out answers meaningful to him. This is especially true in the area of religious concepts in facilitating his orientation to his world.[39]

COOPERATION WITH GROWTH AND CHANGE

The physical weaning of the baby from the mother's breast — and of the mother from the baby! — is only the beginning of a process which continues until adulthood has been attained. The child's main job is growing up, and the best parents are those who facilitate growth instead of blocking it. As Gesell observes, "Even in the prodigiously complicated field

[38] Lois B. Murphy, *Social Behavior and Child Personality* (New York: Columbia University Press, 1937); see also Dorothy Baruch, *New Ways in Discipline* (New York: McGraw-Hill, 1949).
[39] Sophia Fahs, *Today's Children and Yesterday's Heritage* (Boston: Beacon Press, 1952). [It must of course be borne in mind that "religious" may be interpreted in other than a supernaturalistic sense, although ordinarily this should not be done. Perhaps it would be better to say that children need orientation toward ultimate values that in some way or ways are bindingly sacred — whether of traditionally religious derivation or not — the editor.]

of personality formation, growth factors are primarily determining. . . . Growth is a key concept." [40]

Wise parents keep several jumps ahead of the child, welcome the changes in him, and help him discover the more mature satisfactions of each successive stage. These changes come with such rapidity and complexity, especially in the early years, that even the best parents feel their capacities of adjustment to be inadequate. No one who keeps up with a lively, growing child can get set in his ways.

The course of physical development is never a straight line, but consists of spurts upward, alternating with plateaus or even valleys. In socioemotional development, which in general follows the physical, there may even be regressions to earlier levels, followed by further upward growth. [41]

Significant studies by Stoddard and Wellman at the Iowa Child Welfare Research Station found three factors to be of basic importance in determining whether or not a child was reaching his mental ceiling; namely, (1) stimulation to mental effort by a rich environment, (2) further stimulation by extensions of environment through trips and explorations, and (3) the absence of prolonged emotional conflict.

The most serious conflicts any of us have are born of the frustration of our fundamental drives for love and acceptance on the one hand and for a sense of achievement on the other. When these drives are interfered with, the normal reaction is to strike out at the thing or person responsible. When aggression is prohibited by the need for love and approval and no substitute outlet is found, the thwarted person remains suspended between his conflicting needs with neither adequately fulfilled. Such conflict, then, is a double frustration, since each need rules out the satisfaction of the other. Moreover, if the person seeks first one and then the other, as in the vacillations of the neurotic, neither satisfaction is really enjoyed because of the fear of losing the other. For instance, a child may succumb to the temptation of eating forbidden cookies, but his enjoyment is spoiled, and he may even get indigestion, for fear of the parental disapproval that is about to descend.

Kurt Lewin [42] shows the effect of frustration upon the level of a child's performance. The constructiveness of a group of nursery school children during ordinary free play, ascertained on a seven-point constructiveness scale, was found to be correlated (0.81) with both mental and chronological age. These children were then sent into an experimental room where numerous fascinating play materials had been arranged at one end. The children were allowed to play freely with these for a set time. Then a wire screen was let down in front of the play materials while the children were all forced to go to the other end of the room where they could see but not reach them. They showed hostility and withdrawal tendencies in various

[40] Gesell, *op. cit.*, p. 9.

[41] A. T. Jersild, *In Search of a Self* (New York: Teachers College Bureau of Publications, 1952).

[42] Kurt Lewin, "Experimental Frustration in Children," *Proceedings, Second Biennial Meeting, Society for Research in Child Development,* 1936, p. 100.

ways. While in this state of frustration they were required to take the tests again. The results were then compared with those obtained when the children were in the relatively calm state of ordinary free play. It was found that on the average constructiveness regresses during frustration by an amount equivalent to 17.3 months' mental age, from an average of 9.6 months' in younger subjects to 21.5 months' in the older.

GROWTH THROUGH FRUSTRATION

If parents and teachers realized the effect of frustration upon the child's use of his powers, they would be more careful to keep the balance between frustrations and satisfactions weighted on the positive side. Some frustration is inescapable in life. Indeed, it is inherent in the normal processes of growth itself and stimulates new adjustment. If it comes in graded doses and is not too overwhelming at any one time, it may be a valuable spur to further effort and growth. One of the most important lessons any of us has to learn is how to put the emotions generated by frustration to constructive use in recreational or vocational activity. A major task of parents is to guide and facilitate this learning from babyhood on.

It is essential for the child's socialization and happiness that he learn to bend and channel his desires in directions that are both satisfying to him and socially acceptable to his social group. For instance, he must learn to adapt his hunger drive to the civilized requirements of a set time for dinner, of washing hands and face, and of a clean bib. He cannot be forced to all these requirements at once, but they must be learned gradually and motivated by the desire for social approval. To sense how fast any given child's drives can be directed into socially acceptable channels is one of the most desirable techniques in the art of child training. When parents have been too severe, the child tends to develop neurotic conflict; if they are too lenient, he is likely to remain unsocialized.

The child experiences his first severe frustration when he is forced to give up his mother's breast.[43] Although his food can be as adequate as ever, that was not the only important thing he was getting in the nursing process; and he needs extra companionship with his parents to appease his emotional hunger for the bodily intimacy that is gone. He is very much like a dog grieving for a lost master, for he cannot yet verbalize his sorrow for what he has lost. He is likely to be more irritable, have bad dreams, and awaken in the night — all of which in turn decrease his popularity with his parents. Actually a child is never so much in need of love as when he is most unlovable, and parents who understand will spontaneously rise to the occasion. He needs extra reassurances of love by demonstrated affection, and richer companionship until he has adjusted to the shifts demanded by growth.[44]

[43] See Dollard, *op. cit.*, pp. 59, 60; also D. M. Levy, "Hostility Patterns in Sibling Rivalry Experiments," *American Journal of Orthopsychiatry*, Vol. 6, pp. 183–257, and the same author's "Primary Affect Hunger," *American Journal of Psychiatry*, 94 (Nov., 1937), pp. 643–652; also Erickson, *op. cit.*
[44] M. Applegate, *Everybody's Business — Our Children* (New York: Row, Peterson, 1952).

Between the ages of two and four the child is said to go through a transition from babyhood to childhood called the "little adolescence." By the age of three he runs about freely; he tends to get into everything and is in everyone's way. He therefore comes in for more criticism from adults, and is told that he is a "big boy" now and must behave better, that he is no longer a baby. In addition to this change and frustration in his relationships, his coordinations usually develop less rapidly than his critical judgment, so that he wants to manipulate materials before his fumbling fingers are ready. He feels frustrated by his own lack of power just when more and more is being demanded of him. Because of this it is quite normal for the child of three to show considerable irritation and temper, even to the point of tantrums. Studies have shown that such crises are more the result of social factors than of physiological maturing and that they reach their highest incidence between the ages of two and four.[45] Throughout childhood he needs an atmosphere in which it is comfortable to make mistakes, where he is assisted to improve without fear of blame, and where he knows that suggestions are made to help him rather than to point out his failures and inadequacies.

Sibling Rivalry

The frustrations of the growing-up process are increased when a new baby is born into the family at the peak of the first child's "little adolescence." He sees the newcomer at his own mother's breast where the baby part of him still longs to be. Even if he has been carefully prepared for the new baby and on the whole accepts it with interest and even affection, there are likely to be times when he feels sorely left out and when he feels as if everyone expected too much of him. He may become regressive in an effort to satisfy his needs in ways earlier found effective, and compete with the baby for the attention of his mother. He may develop food finickiness and refuse to eat, so that mother will coax and possibly feed him again as she did when he was younger. He may even start wetting his clothing so that she will have to change him as she does the baby. Bursts of temper and night terrors are also likely to appear as symptoms of his insecurity. Parents too frequently fail to understand the basic causes of these symptoms and add insult to injury by scolding and nagging, even insisting that he share precious toys with the baby — who may break them.[46]

For example, one little girl of three had become virtually an outcast after the arrival of the little brother. The mother shut her up in a dark closet every time she was "mean" to the baby, thereby increasing her feelings of isolation and rejection; the parents could not understand why her spiteful behavior became worse and worse. A conference with a guidance worker proved helpful. It was agreed that the mother would take special pains to

---

[45] Studies reviewed in Jones, Conrad, and Murphy, "Emotional and Social Development and the Educative Process," *Thirty-eighth Yearbook, National Society for the Study of Education,* 1939, pp. 361–391.

[46] Edith Neisser, *Brothers and Sisters* (New York: Harper, 1951).

reassure the little girl in every way she could. The following scene was reported: "I was rocking the baby when Betty came in and scowled saying, 'There's that baby again!' I then turned to grandmother and said, 'Mother, will you hold the baby for a while? I want to rock Betty.' I took Betty on my lap and rocked her. Betty looked up in amazement, then smiled all over herself, snuggled against me, and from that vantage point said for the first time, 'Haven't we a cute baby?' " As such treatment was repeated the child developed a proprietary interest and cooperative attitude in place of the hostile one.

The little child must be helped to see that even though relations change they need not be lost. Beyond this, he needs to feel that he can go back for a time to the earlier types of behavior when frustrations pile up too much. When he has received the particular reassurances he needs, he will tend to slough off the regressive actions and go forward renewed by the reassurance he received in the security of earlier familiar ways.[47]

The father can be of particular help by strengthening his relation with the child during the little adolescence, and especially when there is a new baby to complicate things. He may be peculiarly well equipped to understand the child's situation because of some of the feelings he may have had when the first baby came. He can help the child learn through experience that the way to recover from a shift or break in a relation is to strengthen old ties and knit new ones.

A vital relationship between father and child can be of great value to both participants. A little child with his amazing questions and ceaseless interest in doing and learning is more fascinating to most men than a helpless baby. By capitalizing the child's need for new satisfactions and skills, the father can help him learn that growing up is really much more fun than remaining a baby. As father and child become closer companions, the father can evoke in the child quasipaternal attitudes and protective behavior toward the baby, and help him feel that the new member is less a competitor than a jolly new playfellow. We now know that a sense of solidarity between siblings lays patterns for happily fulfilling relationships with friends and coworkers as well as with the marriage partner in adult life.[48]

Beyond this the child can be helped to find new playmates with whom he can associate on a more equalitarian basis than with anyone in the family. Good nursery schools or supervised play groups are a great help at this point, both in providing opportunity for new relations and in developing skills and self-reliance. There is the additional advantage of giving the young mother respite from her twenty-four-hour-a-day job, so that she can

[47] D. W. Baruch, "Therapeutic Procedures as Part of the Educative Process," *Journal of Consulting Psychology*, 4 (1940), pp. 165–172.

[48] Excellent discussions of sibling relations are to be found in *Child Study*, Summer 1946 issue on "Jealousy and Rivalry in Children"; Susan Isaacs, *The Nursery Years* (New York: Vanguard Press, 1937); Anna W. Wolf, *The Parents' Manual* (New York: Simon and Schuster, 1941), chap. 4, "Brothers and Sisters"; David M. Levy, *Studies in Sibling Rivalry* (New York: American Orthopsychiatric Association, 1938); and James Marshall, "Psychological Maturity as a Basis for Democracy," *Mental Hygiene*, 26, No. 2 (April, 1942), pp. 218–226.

better maintain a personal life of her own. Nursery schools, play groups, and kindergartens are particularly important in providing city children with constructive outlets, socialization, and elemental learning experiences. Co-operative nursery schools, organized and partly staffed by mothers who spend about one morning a week assisting, are spreading rapidly. They have double value in educating and helping parents along with their children. Young mothers often feel less isolated and more competent by participating in such groups, and whole families benefit — as the mother is, so is the family.[49]

HOME AS AN EDUCATIONAL INSTITUTION

Schools are merely an auxiliary to parents in their job of educating children. Children spend on an average only 30 to 36 hours of the 168-hour week in school. Moreover, home experience sinks deeper because of the profound feeling involved. It comes first while the child's mind is most impressionable, and it continues year after year.[50] Homes therefore should consciously plan to meet certain important educational needs. All children need rich sensory experiences with the natural elements of earth, water, sand, sticks, and stones, with bird notes and rustling leaves and rippling water, with growing plants and living animals. The human child has a longer period of infancy and with it a far greater capacity for learning and improving on his elders than any other young animal. The ceaseless movements, manipulations, and explorations of the small child are his self-education and also the equivalent of recreation, work, exploration, and creativity in the life of the adult. Play is also the best means of keeping the balance between frustration and fulfillment weighted on the positive side, and the child is especially in need of it during periods of privation like weaning. What he cannot have in reality he can achieve symbolically through his play life. Therefore the child should be given the greatest possible freedom in his play life while he is learning to conform to the social restrictions of this world.

Enough has been said to show how large a value children's play has for all sides of their growth. How great an ally the thoughtful parent can find it! And how fatal to go against this great stream of healthy and active impulses in our children! That 'restlessness' and inability to sit still; that 'mischievousness' and 'looking inside' and eternal 'Why?'; that indifference to soiled hands and

[49] Gruenberg and Krech, *The Many Lives of Modern Women* (New York: Doubleday, 1952). Della Cyrus, "Why Mothers Fail," *Atlantic Monthly*, Mar., 1944, pp. 57–60; Morris May, College Women Ten Years After," *Mademoiselle*, Sept., 1950, pp. 88–93; K. W. Taylor, "Growth through Cooperative Play Groups," *Marriage and Family Living*, August, 1946; and ———, "Cooperative Nursery Schools Educate Families," *Teacher's College Record*, Mar., 1953.

[50] There was a growing concern with the importance of the home as an educational institution, culminating in three volumes on education for family life by leading educational associations during the year 1941. They were directed toward helping individuals of all ages to those skills and insights that make for wholesome family life, recognizing that these learnings cannot be acquired during any one term or year but must be assimilated throughout life. The appearance of these three volumes in one year marks a real turning point in educational philosophy. See Selected Readings, p. 490.

torn clothes for the sake of running and climbing and digging and exploring — these are not unfortunate and accidental ways of childhood which are to be shed as soon as we can get rid of them. They are the glory of the human child, his human heritage. They are at once the representatives in him of human adventurousness and hard-won wisdom, and the means by which he in his turn will lay hold of knowledge and skill, and add to them. . . . No experimental scientist has a greater thirst for new facts than an ordinary healthy active child.[51]

Since most of the child's play life takes place in his own home and play yard, time, energy, and money spent by parents in improving the play facilities may be considered an educational investment of first importance. Every family with children should live in a house with outdoor play space if it is humanly possible to provide it. Opportunity for elemental play experience should also be provided inside the home for winter months and rainy days.[52] A workbench with hammer and nails and a large box of odd-sized mill ends is also valuable for functional learning, as well as a variety of blocks, paints, uncut newspaper, clay, a trunk of old clothes for play-acting on rainy days, and dolls and housekeeping toys for imitative play. Such materials lend themselves to ever more skillful uses and are not outgrown until childhood itself is left behind.

Too often aesthetic standards rather than the functional needs of the child guide the planning of even his own quarters. A child's room should have, in addition to a sturdy table and chair adapted to his size, an indoor sandbox; it should have a sink with running water for water play, mixing clay and paint, and washing hands and utensils; and it needs a washable and durable floor and walls which the child himself will delight in cleaning if he has his own pail and soap flakes. One wall might well have a built-in blackboard, another a smooth surface for finger painting and removable murals, and another a covering of burlap for tacking cut-outs, pictures, and posters. The fourth side might have cupboards or open shelves for keeping materials and toys not in use. If this room can have an entrance that does not go through the adult living quarters, so much the better. Otherwise, arrangements for washing and for changing boots may well be provided in the kitchen or laundry to save wear and tear on good floors and carpets and mother's nerves. Families would do well to analyze their housing from a functional point of view.[53]

51 Susan Isaacs, *The Nursery Years* (New York: Vanguard Press, 1937), pp. 10, 11; Hartley, Frank, and Goldenson, *Understanding Children's Play* (New York: Columbia University Press, 1952).

52 For helpful suggestions see E. Kawin, *The Wise Choice of Toys* (Chicago: University of Chicago Press, 1938); Charlotte Garrison and Emma Sheehy, *At Home with Children* (New York: Holt, 1943); M. and K. Frank, *How to Help Your Child in School* (New York: Viking, 1950).

53 Svend Riemer, "A Research Note on Sociological Home-planning," *American Journal of Sociology*, Vol. 46. Much of what has been said above is, of course, bitterly ironical today in view of the fact that not even the famed "middle class" family can afford such "functional housing." See also Riemer's discussion of this problem in Chapter Seventeen.

When a whole room cannot be provided for the child or children, a corner of the kitchen, breakfast room, or even the dining room may be adapted. The child can, of course, use his room for sleeping and dressing as well as for play if it is planned accordingly. In addition, it is a help to have a fairly large box on wheels and stilts like a wheelbarrow, which can be pushed about from room to room where mother is working, having ample room inside for play materials, and sides which serve as easels for tacking paper to paint. The small child's need for much companionship with his mother should be respected and provided for in this way. While he needs an hour or so to play alone each day, both for relaxation and to build up self-reliance, he will thrive best and learn most through creative interaction with parents, his first teachers. Parents who make ample provisions for child needs in this way will find that the space and equipment for adult activities is much more likely to be respected too. When little Johnny is happily busy and near mother as he wants to be, he can let her go on with her work as he does with his, and just an occasional smile and appreciative word is enough to give him the necessary sense of belonging.

In addition to abundant opportunity for recreational activities in the home, every child needs, as an important part of his family life education, an opportunity to participate in group tasks. A child of three or four who wants to wash the dishes should be allowed to do so with common china that can be readily replaced. The sensory delight of foamy suds and shining glasses and the feeling of contributing something important to cooperative living are priceless ingredients that many formally arranged educational experiences lack. Often the same parents who refuse to have the child "mess with the dishes" when he is three and considers it a privilege force him to do so when he is thirteen and considers it a stupid bore.

From the time he is old enough to verbalize his thoughts and to understand those of others the child should be included in the family planning. This can be done at a special time each week in a family round table; or it may be done casually as the need arises. The important thing is that the planning be done at a time when everyone is feeling genial and relaxed, as around the fire after dinner.[54] The more each member of the group actively participates in genuine planning, the fewer will be the discipline problems, the greater the friendliness, cooperation, and the actual productivity of the group. And if group planning has become a family custom, adolescent adjustment can be more smoothly made. Then even such knotty and frequent problems as time in at night, number of nights out a week, allowances and budgeting, clothing and make-up, choice of friends and ways of entertaining them, may be solved with understanding and amity.[55]

[54] See the Watsons' discussion of family councils in Chapter Eighteen, and Ernest Osborne, *The Family Scrap Book* (New York: Association Press, 1951).

[55] See Regina Westcott Wieman, *The Family Lives Its Religion* (New York: Harper, 1941), chap. X, for an excellent discussion of this subject; also R. Dreikurs, *The Challenge of Parenthood* (New York: Duell, Sloan and Pearce, 1948).

THE MAJOR PROBLEMS OF ADOLESCENCE

Adolescence is the process of becoming adult, and extends roughly throughout the second decade of life. The dramatic event ushering in this process is the onset of puberty, with the physical and emotional changes involved. Youngsters who have been adequately informed as to the anatomy and functions of the two sexes in ways described earlier will make the adjustments with greater ease. Accepting the fact emotionally that they are now no longer children but potential fathers and mothers, is different from understanding the process intellectually. All young people should understand the physiology of both sexes and the meaning of menstruation and of nocturnal emissions. Girls should be prepared with the equipment needed for their first menstruation, and boys with a razor for the first shave, and they should be given the feeling therewith that they are being welcomed into adulthood.[56] Young adults who reach puberty without adequate information or other preparation are seriously neglected. Emotional disturbances, even neuroses in later life, may be caused in part by emotional shocks received in unprepared discovery of the manifestations of puberty in themselves.

In addition to his or her own physiological maturation, there are four major developmental objectives to be achieved before the process is complete: (1) attaining emotional emancipation from one's parents and developing genuine self-determination; (2) becoming an integral part of a group of one's peers; (3) making a satisfactory heterosexual adjustment; and (4) establishing himself as a person on his or her own outside the childhood home. Until these goals are reached, the person in question can scarcely be called a true adult no matter what his chronological age may be. Certain it is that the longer the solution of these problems is postponed past twenty-one, the greater the difficulty of working them out.

There is reason therefore to welcome the sometimes uncouth signs that growth is taking place, even though the parents' capacity to "take it" and grow themselves in the process is put to a very severe test. The emotional storms, inconsistencies, and fluctuations, flightiness, swings from aloofness to friendliness, from selfishness to altruism, from clinging dependence to crude self-assertion, are difficult for parents to take at best. The adolescent period is often rendered more difficult for both parents and child because the parents' adjustments to middle age usually coincide with adolescence in their children. Therefore adolescence may be considered a genuine part of parenthood as well as of youth. Parents also are wondering what lies ahead for them, are having to relinquish some of their earlier dreams, and are facing the gradual diminution of certain present satisfactions before they are sure that equally good ones can be found to replace them. Confronting the frustrations that come with the advancing years, it is only natural that some parents lean too heavily on their children for emotional support and satisfaction.

[56] Excellent references on this subject for young adults are Alice Keliher, *Life and Growth* (New York: Appleton-Century, 1938) and Marion Faegre, *Understanding Ourselves* (Minneapolis: University of Minnesota Press, 1945).

It is not easy at best for the young adult to grow into genuine independence and stop leaning on his parents. Many of his inconsistencies and vacillations are an expression of fundamental indecision: Is it really better and safer to be a child or an adult? Do I really want to grow up and accept adult responsibility, or return to the secure and easy ways of childhood? Part of him longs to forge ahead and part of him holds back and even retreats into childish conduct. If to his normal anxiety are added feelings of guilt at failing to meet his parents' unconscious demand for continuing dependence, the struggle may be more than he can manage.

The boy's unkempt appearance and unruly manners, the girl's silliness and irresponsibility are samples of this tendency to regress.[57] Parents can help most by maintaining unwavering faith in the child's capacity to grow and by responding to and reinforcing the more mature behavior when the strains become too severe. There is security for the adolescent in knowing that his parents will interfere before real harm comes and will protect him from his own immaturity. If he has had a happy experience with authority as a young child, he can the more readily accept it as protection at adolescence.

"Just how much freedom should an adolescent have?" is a question frequently asked by parents. The limits are set by his degree of maturity as evidenced in sound judgment and capacity to accept responsibility. It is necessary to respect his immaturity as well as his maturity, to make allowance for incomplete development, and to step in when necessary to avoid serious harm.

An intensive study of high school students[58] shows that it was the youngsters who were most secure at home and who were certain of their parents' affection and faith in them who worked out their socioemotional problems most successfully. There was also a high correlation between satisfactory progress in solving these problems and success in school work. When the adolescent was immersed in conflict and consequent frustrations, his grades dropped, and as he worked them out his school work improved. Concentration is not primarily a matter of free will but rather the evidence that developmental problems are not too distracting and are being worked through satisfactorily. It has been found by some investigators that because of the academic quality of much modern education, in many instances the more time an adolescent spends on his school work the less well fitted he becomes for meeting the problems of life. He may even use it as an escape from painful reality.[59] If this be true, parents have a twofold task: to cooperate with the school people who are trying to functionalize education and at the same time to make up for school deficiencies by their own understanding and the liberating quality of their love. The capacity to give love

[57] Peter Blos, *The Adolescent Personality* (New York: Appleton-Century, 1941), pp. 70, 71, 105–107, 279–283.

[58] Harold E. Jones, "The California Adolescent Growth Study," *Journal of Educational Research*, 31 (April, 1938), pp. 561–567.

[59] K. W. Taylor, *Do Adolescents Need Parents?* (New York: Appleton-Century, 1938, republished by Grosset and Dunlap, 1949).

with all the freedom the child can use wisely is an essential ingredient of good parent-child relations at every stage of the growth process.

The supreme importance of the quality of family relationships in the development of adolescents is emphasized in a report of the effect of World War II upon the youth of our country.[60] It was found that adolescents did not show evidence of serious strain where parental affection had been strong, even under the stresses of fathers and brothers in the service, of both parents working, of crowded housing, of financial anxiety, or of any combination of these.

On the other hand the enormous increase in sex offenses among girls under twenty-one was believed attributable to two causes: first, girls were not given an opportunity to serve their country in the armed services until three years later than boys in spite of the fact that girls at that age are more mature than boys; second, parents showed a woeful lack of understanding and acceptance of their budding womanhood. The increase of delinquency among girls reached 130 per cent according to the FBI and was not limited to the underprivileged socioeconomic levels of society. Furthermore it is reported by a leading psychiatrist that sex disturbances are the most sensitive indicators of tension throughout the whole life span rather than primary problems in themselves.[61] Parents should understand the stages of socio-emotional maturation that culminate in adolescence in order that their own feelings of guilt, fear, and embarrassment may not complicate or permanently retard the process. That is the task of the section which follows.

EMOTIONAL MATURATION AND ADOLESCENCE

According to psychoanalytic findings the baby's first love-object is his own body, because of the simple organic sensory satisfactions it brings him through feeding and through being warm and petted. This is known as the autoerotic stage. Soon his attention shifts to the mother as he comes to realize it is she who satisfies his bodily needs for food, bodily contacts, and comfort. The mother then becomes the first external love-object and remains so until the little adolescence is accomplished and the baby becomes a child. In order for a child to evolve successfully from one stage to another it is necessary that the emotional needs characterizing each stage be adequately met. It is not unusual, then, for children to be primarily focused upon their mothers until they are four or five.[62]

Even in the most normal and well-adjusted individual, however, earlier stages of development are not completely obliterated as he matures. It is rather a matter of shifting emphasis. Normal adults still enjoy pleasurable bodily processes and feel affection for parents, even though their main concern is elsewhere. So also, vestiges of later stages (to be described) remain in

60 "Adolescents in War Time," *The Annals of the American Academy of Political and Social Science,* 236 (Nov., 1944), p. 26.

61 *Ibid.,* p. 4.

62 R. Havighurst, *Adolescent Character and Personality* (New York: Wiley, 1949). See also O. S. English and J. H. J. Pearson, *Emotional Factors in Living; Avoiding the Neurotic Pattern* (New York: Norton, 1945), who discuss these stages in psychoanalytic terms.

adults, but only as subsidiary concerns. The term "fixation" is used only when an individual maintains a primary focus upon any love-object beyond the usual age for it; for example, a man of twenty-five still having his mother as primary love-object.

The next normal stage is the sturdy egocentricity of childhood, known as the narcissistic period. The child is his own primary love-object, and his main sources of delight are the ego-satisfactions to be found in developing skills and prowess. This stage is differentiated from the autoerotic in that the child's focus is on the image of himself as a person and on satisfaction through accomplishments, rather than on his bodily sensations. Youngsters who develop a sense of adequacy during this period are more ready to shift to the next stage on a genuine give-and-take basis, because they are sure they do have something to give. Achieving fulfillment at each level gives ground to stand on while growing into the next. "Adults" who have remained fixated at the narcissistic level, however, are very poor risks as marriage partners because they remain primarily in love with themselves.

Significant case studies made recently corroborate the Freudian theory that with the awakening of the sex impulses at puberty the early parent fixations, particularly on the parent of the opposite sex, are reactivated.[63] For a time the adolescent feels an intense devotion to parents, alternating with periods of hostility resulting from the necessary frustration of the impulses involved. Parents who understand what is behind this ambivalence will not be confused by it. Nor will parents whose own adjustments are sound exploit the youngster's turning toward them by responding too warmly, thereby retarding the psychological weaning that must take place. On the other hand, as already pointed out, it is only as the adolescent feels understood and accepted by those all-important people, his parents, even with all his conflicting and confusing emotions, that he can feel strong and free enough to turn his interest and affection toward the outer world where he must gradually learn to take his place as a participating adult.

If all goes well, this period is only a brief and temporary regression, followed by the important shift from parents and self as love-objects to others outside the home group. The typical shift in our culture is first of all to those most like oneself — the members of one's own sex. This is manifested in the tendency to form clubs and groups of the same sex, avoiding the members of the opposite sex for a time.

The development of group loyalty is significant, for it marks the beginning of other-centeredness (the baby's love for his parents is not affection for separate persons as such but rather for the satisfiers of his own needs) and is also an important phase in the transition from dependence on parent to the self-reliance of true adulthood. The youngster is not strong enough to face the adult world alone, but with the security born of group solidarity is able to stand up for his own needs and rights. Many of the extremes to which parents object are born of this need to

63 See Blos, op. cit., pp. 315–316, and F. B. Strain, But You Don't Understand (New York: Appleton-Century-Crofts, 1949).

stand with the group and be accepted by it. Parents find it hard, of course, to accept the child's shift from being home-dominated to being group-dominated. They should realize that the youngsters most likely to attain self-reliance and independence are those who are most thoroughly accepted in their own age and sex groups.

As the youngster matures through satisfying group experience, he is very likely to become enamored of one love-object of his own sex. The intense friendships rather derisively called "crushes" are typical and normal during this period. They are the youngster's first tryouts at a deep and meaningful relationship with someone outside his own family and are an important step toward emotional emancipation. Here again no one needs to be alarmed when "crushes" occur. Concern is justified only if a child fails to develop through the experiences and grow past this stage, thus remaining fixated at the homosexual level. Those who fail in this way are incapable of sustaining genuine mate love. Again, it is the adolescent who is insecure in the love of one or both parents who is most likely to cling to the "crush," which is frequently "on" an older member of his own sex who serves in part as parent-substitute.

With reasonable support at home and ample opportunity for meeting the opposite sex under wholesome conditions, young adults begin to transfer their main interest to the opposite sex about the middle of the adolescent decade. The first symptom is a generic interest in the whole opposite sex. The tendency to go together in groups, seen in the middle teens, is typical of this stage. So also are the "pin-up pictures" and dirty stories so horrifying to adults who do not understand their significance. Because of the many fears and taboos unfortunately still surrounding sex and because of the youngster's normal anxiety about his own changing status and relations, he feels safer in meeting the opposite sex in groups rather than singly. As his feeling of ease and comfort grows, he normally begins to have dates, and in time to start with short spells of "going steady." The rapidity with which he shifts his "steadies" at the beginning of this stage may be illustrated by a custom reported in one junior high school, where a couple was considered "going steady" if they were seen walking down the hall together three days in succession! Parents and young adults alike should understand that the tendency to "go steady" for longer and longer stretches is a very important part of the growing-up process.

Parents who know the sequences of emotional growth can accept their sons and daughters as fascinating and delightful persons whom they doubly enjoy because of their developing womanhood or manhood, without wanting to cling to them as love-objects of their own. How different is this liberating acceptance and enjoyment from the attitude, too often found, of trying to block and postpone all secondary manifestations of sexual development, of keeping boys or girls "pure" and "innocent" but definitely immature for their age!

The first flowering of the sex drive, derisively called "puppy love," is a real and great emotional experience for the boy or girl, no matter how unworthy the object that evokes this feeling. Even though it is transitory, it is an important step in the maturation process and should be respected as such. For many it is the first experience of loving another more than oneself, and signalizes the budding of altruistic impulses that extend beyond the love-object to all humankind. The young person's feeling that he "just can't do enough" for his beloved, that he wants to perform great deeds of unselfish service for her sake, is among the noblest sentiments of the human heart. Parents who try to smother this feeling, or who even good-naturedly mock and belittle it, may really injure their child and also lose their chance to remain his friend because they have failed him at a really crucial time. When, as so often happens, these first loves are unrealistic and short-lived, the youngster stands in acute need of an understanding friend to help him through the subsequent upheaval. He cannot always take refuge in books, pets, or "activities."

There is some tendency, by the way, for parents, teachers, and club workers to rely too much on "hobbies" as escapes for young people. Valuable as they are in keeping emotionally fit, they should not be used as excuses for the postponement of major adjustments. An important study shows two of the major complaints of young adults to be lack of respect from their parents and other adults, and lack of a real share in the adult world. Young adults need the respect of parents, which includes giving them full opportunity to use their capacities. When they are freed to seek tasks related to any of their major needs, be it preparation for marriage or for vocational proficiency, the intensity of their application is amazing to onlooking adults. Instead of prolonging the period of dependency, it is wise for parents to give the adolescent abundant opportunities to study and try out the vocations which attract him and to change if necessary until a satisfying one has been found.

In like manner, young adults should be helped to the fulfillment of marriage when they are emotionally mature and ready for it. Parents' objections to potential mates and to reasonably early marriage are frequently derived from reluctance to let their child go. It will be remembered that a capacity for mate-love is one index of maturity. The satisfaction of fulfilling this capacity in marriage helps stabilize many personalities at the adult level.

Some parents find it particularly difficult to respect their young adult's further needs to find the vocation of his own choice and to evolve a scheme of values and philosophy of life really his own. Such things as political loyalties, ethical values, and religious beliefs are at the very core of the integrated personality and must be worked out by every individual for himself. Yet it is hardest to respect a child's right to self-determination in the things that matter most.[64]

THE EMPTY NEST

For many parents it is the supreme and final test of their capacity for love and sacrifice to let their children go, not only physically but psychi-

[64] Particularly helpful here are the chapters "Faith to Live By," and "Light on Life's Mysteries" in J. E. Crawford and L. E. Woodward, *Better Ways of Growing Up* (Philadelphia: Muhlenberg, 1948).

cally; to let them pursue their own major values in a life which may be quite different from the one their parents would have chosen for them. Adjusting to the empty nest is as much of a stimulus to the growth of parents as is the birth of a new baby to the child next older, or the break-up of a first love affair to the adolescent boy or girl. The stimulus is greater for those who understand that it is not only their own growth which is at stake in the final liberation, but also the growth of the child they love.

Habits of protecting children, "doing for" them, and even thinking for them have been so ingrained and have given such real satisfaction to most parents that the readjustment at best is not easy. It is hard to give up one's place of authority and prestige in the lives of one's children. Everyone likes to feel indispensable, and parents, after all, are like other normal human beings in this respect.

Parents whose children have just left home are often as much in need of help as are adolescents who face a new and uncertain world. They too may temporarily lose their moorings. Young adults who see and understand their parents' plight may well accept the responsibility of helping them to new interests and satisfactions. With wise counsel most parents can be helped to recognize that the liberation goes both ways, that they too are released emotionally for fresh experiences and new endeavors. Parents whose lives are rich and full may actually look forward to the time when they will be relieved from exacting parental duties and have more time for each other and for their creative pursuits.

It is not uncommon for the quality of the love-life of middle-aged couples to become even richer and more spontaneous when the period of child-bearing is past. All anxiety as to possible unwanted pregnancy is gone, and there is often more energy left at the end of the day than when parental duties were heavier. Many couples find much joy in their marital relationships well into their sixties or even seventies. The fact that some women experience genuine sexual fulfillment for the first time after the menopause should give couples a new motive for working at this basic satisfaction. (See references on the menopause in the Selected Readings.)

Those interested in facilitating the two-way liberation may profitably recall that sexual maladjustment was one of the factors correlated with maternal overprotection and that the other factors were restricted social life and thwarted ambitions. What we learn from a study of the severely maladjusted may be put to use in improving the lives of all. Therefore by seeking realization in the outlets denied her earlier and by building up a richer personal and social life the middle-aged mother may not only enrich her own life but also smooth the path for her children.

Moreover, the fact that the parent-child relation has changed does not mean that it must be relinquished — quite the opposite. Parents relieved of the responsibility of guiding adult sons and daughters may find them delightful friends leading separate and interesting lives of their own. It is the parents who liberate their children most completely and who keep growing themselves who are best able to maintain continuing friendship with them. And they may discover that serving on a consultative rather than a dictatorial basis really carries with it greater dignity and significance.

Growth through change is a basic principle of human life, not only during childhood and youth but throughout the span of living. People who cling to attitudes and behavior appropriate during earlier years feel their age as a burden rather than as an accumulation of insight, skill, and experience to be used in ever-changing ways.

For example, it is appropriate for young parents to be emotionally focused on their own children and primarily absorbed with their nurture. But at middle age, when these children are grown, if parents are still so absorbed their development has not kept pace with the flow of their lives. There should have been throughout the children's development a turning of more and more of the parental interest outward, not only toward their own personal pursuits, but to a concern with making the schools and indeed the whole community a good place for their children to grow up in. As one mother put it, "Now that my children are in high school my responsibility extends as far as they can drive in a car." And as their own children are more able to carry on alone, this larger social concern may well extend to all children everywhere. Instead of feeling that their lifework is over when their children are grown, middle-aged parents may well feel that it has just begun, and use all they have learned through their own family experience to enrich their activities in wider circles for many years to come.[65]

FAMILY ADJUSTMENTS TO LATER MATURITY

While medical science is continually improving the health and increasing the life expectancy of our aged citizens, there is considerable evidence that the cultural pattern is making it more difficult for them to find these added years psychologically rewarding. During the years of later maturity, when vigorous and active service outside the home is no longer possible, the severest life adjustments come to the individual parents and often to the middle-aged sons and daughters who are responsible for helping them. The number of families affected by this problem is growing because the proportion of the population over sixty-five is steadily increasing. In 1943 there were nine million over sixty-five years of age, and it is estimated that by 1980 there will be twenty-six million.

The tradition of conflict between generations goes back before the dawn of history. In his great anthropological study, *The Golden Bough,* Sir James G. Frazer delineates the various ways the old priests and kings in prehistoric tribes were often put to death by their own eldest sons when they were no longer strong enough to defend "the golden bough" or other symbols of power. The story of David and Absalom and the struggle between King Lear and his daughters indicate that such conflicts have persisted from the dim past. In societies like ancient China and India,

[65] David Mace, *Marriage: the Art of Lasting Love* (New York: Doubleday, 1952).

it is true, where wisdom and spiritual development were placed at the apex of values, old age has been venerated and looked upon as an enviable state in which the individual receives more respect and adulation than he did even in the prime of life. But in our own pioneer society, where for generations the most highly prized virtues have been physical vigor, courage, and a capacity for enterprise, first in reclaiming the wilderness and later in building great industries, the riches of accumulated wisdom and the mellowness of ripened years have found little place.

In early frontier days the problem was solved in many families by the relatively early death of the old folks. This fact and the frequent migration of young couples to new areas have led to what might be called the typical American stereotype, a vigorous young family living either far away from the older kin or, if still in the same locality, certainly in a different domicile.

When two and three generations share the same dwelling, there is likely to be considerable friction not only because of the age-long struggle for status, power, and respect between generations but also because of a widened gulf brought about by rapidity of change. The general lack of appreciation of the potential contributions of age in our youth-oriented culture also results in tension and a reluctance on the part of the younger to identify themselves closely enough with the problems of the aged to help work them through to a constructive conclusion. A very usual attitude is, "These old folks ought not to be in our way, taking the room and money we want for the children. Their lives are about over anyway. We want to live our lives without being burdened by them. We want to give everything we have to our children. Besides, children are so much sweeter to live with and will carry what we give them so much farther into the future."

A deeper understanding even of the needs of children suggests that contact with wider family connections, particularly with grandparents, can give them a broader base of security and a sense of being more thoroughly rooted in their world. Reminiscences about happenings in earlier days, entertaining folk tales and fairy stories, and companionship without the ogre of discipline in the offing, are a great delight to many children. Furthermore, a sense of being loved and enjoyed unconditionally by persons who have grown tender with the accumulated experience of living may enrich the lives of the grandchildren immeasurably.

Characteristically, most parents find it easier to consider a problem seriously if it affects the children. But what of the old folks themselves and their rights as human beings? The frontier ruthlessness which tends to dump them into a psychological scrap heap is utterly inconsistent with the basic principle of democracy — respect for the essential dignity, worth, and preciousness of every individual regardless of race, creed, sex, or age. It is all to the good that children have come into their own in this "century of the child." May it not be at the expense of the needs and rights and feelings of our old folk!

In spite of a growing awareness of their increasing numbers and an accumulation of articles about their adjustment, it is often difficult to find trained case-workers who take the problems of older people seriously. They are too often considered just "among those present." [66] In spite of such statements as "It is terrible to grow old," "You know I'm living on borrowed time," "This house is all I have left," there is often a pathetically grateful response to a little affection, and deep appreciation of the good things of life.

Not only because of the possible contributions of the older generation to grandchildren and to family tasks, but in the interest of their own psychic comfort, middle-aged sons and daughters usually find time and energy spent in working out satisfying plans of living with their parents most rewarding. Strands of affection running back through the years to earliest infancy are a part of the warp and woof of everyone's emotional life. Therefore putting the old people away in a home may be a real psychic risk for sons and daughters as well as for the aged persons themselves. In some cases this may be the best solution possible and should be carried out; [67] but the tendency at present seems to be to think of this as the "best" solution too readily.

Scientific investigations [68] into family adjustments of the aged are illuminating. A study of Minnesota families indicates that the conflicts between aged parents and their mature married offspring had their beginnings in early parent-child relations, were aggravated by the universal struggle for status, but were also an understandable outcome of our cultural setting. The investigator explained that the present stresses are also due to the rapidity of social change within recent decades and to the cultural lag in providing for the needs of old folk both in families and in community agencies. The aged subjects had the impression that there had been greater harmony between generations in their childhood homes than they were now experiencing. Explanations offered included the following: there existed a stricter code of family authority, the generations shared similar views on morality, and there were more primary-group activities in which grandparents could participate. In the rural families of yesterday there were things the old folks could do to be useful. "When we were young, work and thrift were the primary virtues, but today young people are a money-spending, work-free group, who attend church rarely, drink liquor, and go to late parties. They don't even make their own kids mind."

The researchers found that the more dependent the old folk were upon their children economically or emotionally the more intense was the intergenerational conflict. Frequent statements were, "They're all I've got to live for," "I've often wondered what people do who don't have children," "They mean everything. What would I do without them!" When such emotional dependence was coupled with fundamental disagreement on

[66] E. Stern and M. Ross, *You and Your Aging Parents* (New York: Wiley, 1952).

[67] Margaret Ryder, "Case Work with the Aged Parent and His Adult Children," *The Family*, 27 (Nov., 1945), pp. 243–250.

[68] Robert M. Dinkel, "Parent-Child Conflict in Minnesota Families," *American Sociological Review*, 8 (1943), pp. 412–419, and "Social Problems of the Aged," *Sociology and Social Research* (Jan., 1943), pp. 200–207.

basic issues and with enforced intimacy because of shared housing due to economic dependence, it is not surprising that there were major conflicts in seventeen out of forty cases and minor quarrels in most of the rest. It was found that the elderly woman carries on more activities in the home and also has more problems. Her only proof that she is needed comes from the mending, darning, and ironing services she performs. Small wonder that she is reluctant to give them up to more nimble hands.

The study by Landis [69] corroborates the need of older persons for economic independence, for more opportunities to go on working at suitable tasks and to maintain emotional independence through hobbies and interests of their own. The happiness of aged persons having such outlets and economic independence was greater when measured on an adjustment score than those who were dependent and relatively idle.

One student reports that in his own family, the five middle-aged sons and daughters have worked it out for their mother to have a place of her own with each of them. She is financially independent but contributes so much to each family that there is a friendly rivalry between them for her time. She has made with external ease and graciousness the shift from being the center of a large home with rich and meaningful community contacts of her own to a life deriving its chief meaning from the families of her children. Her son believes that her capacity to make this final adjustment so well was developed by constructively working through the manifold problems of her own girlhood, wifehood, and motherhood.[70]

BASIC NEEDS OF THE AGED

Penetrating students of total life-adjustments point out that persons in later maturity have needs which differ from the needs of the middle years. For example, the aged need simple tasks related to daily living, such as household chores and gardening, to give them a sense of still being organically related to life processes. According to this view, families who keep their old folks from helping with home tasks rob them of a sense of belonging and cut themselves off from a source of genuine help. Two other great needs of the elderly are for a sense of being loved and wanted and for a room of their own to retreat to amid their own familiar belongings. However, they need to set their own pace and have sufficient time alone to assimilate the meaning of their lives and prepare for the adventure of death.[71] Above all, old age should include opportunity for individual meditation and any kind of religious expression found helpful in deepening spiritual growth. Persons who, as they face eternity, continue to grow in sweetness, radiance, and serenity, regardless of diminishing physical and even mental powers, provide the final validation of life itself. Their ex-

---

[69] J. T. Landis, "Some Observations on Special Problems Encountered in Studying the Aged," *American Sociological Review*, 10 (June, 1945), pp. 427–429.

[70] George Lawton, ed., *New Goals for Old Age* (New York: Columbia University Press, 1943).

[71] Esther Harding, *The Way of All Women* (New York: Longmans, Green, 1943), chap. 8, interprets the findings of Jung regarding adjustments in later maturity.

ample and benevolent influence during their last years is perhaps the greatest gift they have ever given their families and friends, the realization that human existence rightly lived can deepen in beauty and meaning to the very end.

SUMMARY

A happy and wholesome family is founded by two emotionally mature individuals who have achieved genuine heterosexuality and an independence of thought, action, and ideals uninhibited by infantile attachment to their parents. They are therefore happy to welcome children and do not see them either as potential rivals or as extensions of themselves which they may manipulate to their own end. Therefore, each child as he takes his place in the family group is not only tenderly loved and cherished but is also respected as a separate and unique personality and is given every opportunity and encouragement to develop to the limit of his potentialities, regardless of whether or not they fit into any preconceived pattern parents may have. There is affection and companionship among all family members, tempered by a normal amount of friction which the parents have learned to utilize for the growth of individual family members and also for the increase of family solidarity. No one person's needs are considered more important than another's, and out of the vortex of conflicting needs of all family members there has evolved a genuine consideration for the rights of others. Adolescent changes and crudities are understood and welcomed as signs that normal development is taking place. Young adults are given freedom with stabilizing responsibility, and genuine self-determination regarding choice of vocation and avocation. Parents grow along with their children through the kaleidoscopic changes inherent in the natural history of the family and, although enjoying their parenthood to the full, maintain their husband-wife relation as the centrally significant part of their emotional lives. Such middle-aged parents are not left stranded in futility, but as their children leave the nest empty find new satisfaction and significance in wider service outside the home. When roles shift further, as sons and daughters become middle aged and their parents elderly, there is a genuine place even for the old folks in the family circle and they both receive and contribute security and enrichment through interaction with the other family members. Such family living is a crucible which gives to society not only young men and women able and eager to assume their share of the world's work and life, but middle-aged parents deepened by family experience, who extend their ministrations to the wider family we call the world, and grandparents whose poise and radiance as they face the future is a source of strength and inspiration.

SELECTED READINGS

ALDRICH, CHARLES A. and M. M., *Babies Are Human Beings* (New York: Macmillan, 1941).

APPLEGATE, M., *Everybody's Business — Our Children* (New York: Row, Peterson & Co., 1952).

BARUCH, DOROTHY W., *New Ways in Discipline* (New York: McGraw-Hill, 1949).

——, *One Little Boy* (New York: Julian Press, 1952).

——, *Parents Can Be People* (New York: Appleton-Century, 1944).

BLOS, PETER, *The Adolescent Personality* (New York: Appleton, 1941).

CYRUS, DELLA, "Why Mothers Fail," *Atlantic Monthly* (March, 1944), pp. 57–60.

DREIKURS, RUDOLPH, *The Challenge of Parenthood* (New York: Duell, Sloan and Pearce, 1948).

DUNBAR, FLANDERS, *Your Child's Mind and Body* (New York: Random House, 1949).

ERICKSON, E. H., *Childhood and Society* (New York: W. W. Norton, 1950).

FAHS, SOPHIA, *Today's Children and Yesterday's Heritage* (Boston: Beacon Press, 1952).

Family Life Education Basic Books

 Education for Family Life, 19th Yearbook A.A.S.A. (Washington, D. C.: N.E.A., 1941).

 Family Living and Our Schools, N.E.A. and Society for Curriculum Study (New York: Appleton-Century, 1941).

 Youth, Family, and Education by J. K. Folsom for the American Youth Commission (Washington, D. C.: American Council on Education, 1941).

FRANK, L. K., "The Fundamental Needs of the Child," *Mental Hygiene,* 23, 3 (July, 1938), pp. 353–379.

FRANK, M. and L. K., *How to Help Your Child in School* (New York: Viking, 1950).

GESELL, A., and ILG, F., *Child Development* (New York: Harper, 1949). This includes the following earlier volumes: ——, *Infant and Child in the Culture of Today* (New York: Harper, 1943); ——, *The Child from Five to Ten* (New York: Harper, 1946).

GRUENBERG, S. M., and KRECH, H. S., *The Many Lives of Modern Woman* (New York: Doubleday, 1952).

HARTLEY, R., FRANK, L. K., and GOLDENSON, R. M., *Understanding Children's Play* (New York: Columbia University Press, 1952).

HAVIGHURST, ROBERT, *Father of the Man* (Boston: Houghton-Mifflin, 1947).

——, *Adolescent Character and Personality* (New York: Wylie, 1949).

ISAACS, SUSAN, *The Nursery Years* (New York: Vanguard Press, 1936).

JENKINS, GLADYS, *These Are Your Children* (Chicago: Scott, Foresman Co., 1948).

JERSILD, A. T., *In Search of a Self* (New York: Teachers College Bureau of Publications, 1952).

LAWTON, GEORGE, *New Goals for Old Age* (New York: Columbia University Press, 1943).

LEVINE, LENA, and DOHERTY, B., *The Menopause* (New York: Random House, 1952).

LEVY, DAVID M., *Studies of Sibling Rivalry* (New York: American Orthopsychiatric Association, 1938).

LEVY, JOHN, and MUNROE, RUTH, *The Happy Family* (New York: Knopf, 1938).

MACE, DAVID, *Marriage: The Art of Lasting Love* (New York: Doubleday, 1952).

MACKENZIE, CATHERINE, *Parent and Child* (New York: Sloane, 1949).

MENNINGER, KARL, *Love Against Hate* (New York: Harcourt, Brace, 1942).

Mid-Century Whitehouse Conference on Childhood and Youth: Fact Finding Report, *A Healthy Personality for Every Child* (Raleigh, N. C.: Health Publications Institute, 1950).

MORRIS, MAY, "College Women, Ten Years After," *Mademoiselle* (Sept., 1950), pp. 122–125).

MURPHY, GARDINER, *Personality, A Biosocial Approach to Origins and Structure* (New York: Harper, 1947).

MURPHY, LOIS, *Social Behavior and Child Personality* (New York: Columbia University Press, 1937).

NEISSER, EDITH, *Brothers and Sisters* (New York: Harper, 1951).

OSBORNE, ERNEST, *The Family Scrap Book* (New York: Association Press, 1951).

RIBBLE, MARGARET, *Rights of Infants* (New York: Columbia University Press, 1943).

SPOCK, BENJAMIN, M.D., *Pocket Book of Baby and Child Care* (New York: Pocket Books, Inc., 1946).

STERN, E., and Ross, M., *You and Your Aging Parents* (New York, A. A. Wylie, 1952).

STRAIN, FRANCES B., *But You Don't Understand* (New York: Appleton-Century-Crofts, 1949).

——, *New Patterns in Sex Teaching* (New York: Appleton-Century, 1934).

STRECKER, EDWARD A., M.D., *Their Mothers' Sons* (Philadelphia: Lippincott, 1951).

SYMONDS, PERCIVAL, *The Psychology of Parent-Child Relationships* (rev. ed.; New York: Appleton-Century-Crofts, 1951).

TAYLOR, K. W., *Do Adolescents Need Parents?* (New York: Appleton-Century, 1938).

——, "Cooperative Nursery Schools," *Teachers College Record* (March, 1953).

——, *Getting Along With Parents* (Chicago: Science Research Associates, 1952).

——, "Parent Growth Through Cooperative Nursery Schools," *Marriage and Family Living* (August, 1946).

WALLER, WILLARD, *The Family: A Dynamic Interpretation,* rev. by Reuben Hill (New York: Dryden Press, 1952).

WIEMAN, REGINA WESTCOTT, *The Family Lives Its Religion* (New York: Harper, 1941).

WITMER, H., and KOTINSKY, R., *Personality in the Making* (New York: Harper, 1952). Based on Fact-Finding Report on Mid-Century White House Conference on Children and Youth.

TOPICS FOR DISCUSSION OR REPORTS

1. Cite experiences from your own childhood which have had a permanent effect upon your attitudes.
2. If you were a guidance worker, what would you say to a young couple having serious marital difficulties who thought they could patch things up by having a baby?

3. Give instances of behavior you consider emotionally mature and immature which you have observed in real life.
4. Visit a nursery school during the early morning period when children are arriving, or at the end of school when they are leaving, and describe the various types of parent-child relations you believe to be evidenced as parents part from or meet their children.
5. Visit a young parents' study group in a church nursery or P.T.A. and list the problems they seem to be facing in rearing their children, as evidenced in questions and comments.
6. How can we account for differences among children of the same family in interests, attitudes, moral adjustment?
7. Discuss the importance of play in the life of the child, and ways of promoting constructive activities, both at home and at school.
8. Visit a local parent-teacher meeting and try to discover the ways in which the parents are contributing to the life of the school. Suggest other ways in which home-school cooperation could be developed for the lasting benefit of children.
9. From your own experience and from your reading, delineate the role parents should play in the life of their adolescent sons and daughters.
10. Listen in on the conversations of your associates and list the most usual conflicts between parents and their adolescent sons and daughters. Discuss possible ways of working them out with reduced friction and increased harmony.
11. When and how should parents begin the child's sex education? In what ways can they carry it on through the adolescent period? What are the most important factors to be kept in mind?
12. What obligations, if any, do young married adults have toward their middle-aged parents?
13. In what ways can women at various stages of life contribute most to the progress of their world?
14. How can young wives and mothers prepare for the constructive life in the "empty nest" period?
15. What do you believe to be the main causes of conflict between elderly parents and middle-aged sons and daughters?
16. Visit a home for the aged and write a description of the attitudes and feelings you find in the persons residing there.
17. Phone the council of social agencies or equivalent service in your locality and request an interview to learn about the facilities in your community for helping individuals and families with personal adjustment problems, and write a description of the available services.

Chapter Seventeen

Designing the Family Home

SVEND RIEMER

THE CULTURAL SETTING

MOST of man's life is spent in a man-made environment: in private dwellings, in buildings which accommodate his industrial and commercial and administrative activities, in edifices which serve his ceremonial needs, and in crude huts or palatial structures available for social gatherings or play and entertainment. This environment provides shelter against the vicissitudes of extreme climatic conditions. It prevents exposure to the heat of the South or the cold of the North. It encases man in an air-space more adapted to the requirements of the human body than the outside. Hitherto this has been generally true with regard to temperature and precipitation; today's techniques approach the problem of regulating humidity and light radiation. Modern technicians, however, do not rest content with the attempt to mitigate extreme temperatures; they aim at optimal conditions as defined by research in human physiology and hygiene.

From the cliffs and caves of primordial man to the model apartments of the metropolitan skyscraper, shelter or housing has always been one of the most important because one of the most elementary aspects of our material culture. Its importance increases where climatic extremes reduce man's ability to spend his hours of work and leisure in the out-of-doors and where requirements for protective shelter are necessitated by the growing complexity of his industrial, commercial, and administrative activities.

Shelter Reflects Culture

At all times a close relationship has existed between man's shelter and all other aspects of both material and immaterial culture. What housing of private and public activities is obtained in any particular cultural or historical situation is dependent upon available techniques such as the accessibility of materials and craftsmanship in the perfecting and handling of tools, upon traditional construction methods, and upon rational engineering devices. Simultaneously, however, housing conditions are affected by the requirements for shelter dictated by the way of life that predominates in a culture. Sociologists are interested in these needs as met by a given state of technology.

The entire system of shelter reflects in every minute detail the ramifications of a given culture. There are public and private buildings, churches and workshops and governmental offices and clubs and dance halls and factories. Interior design varies from simple, undifferentiated halls and

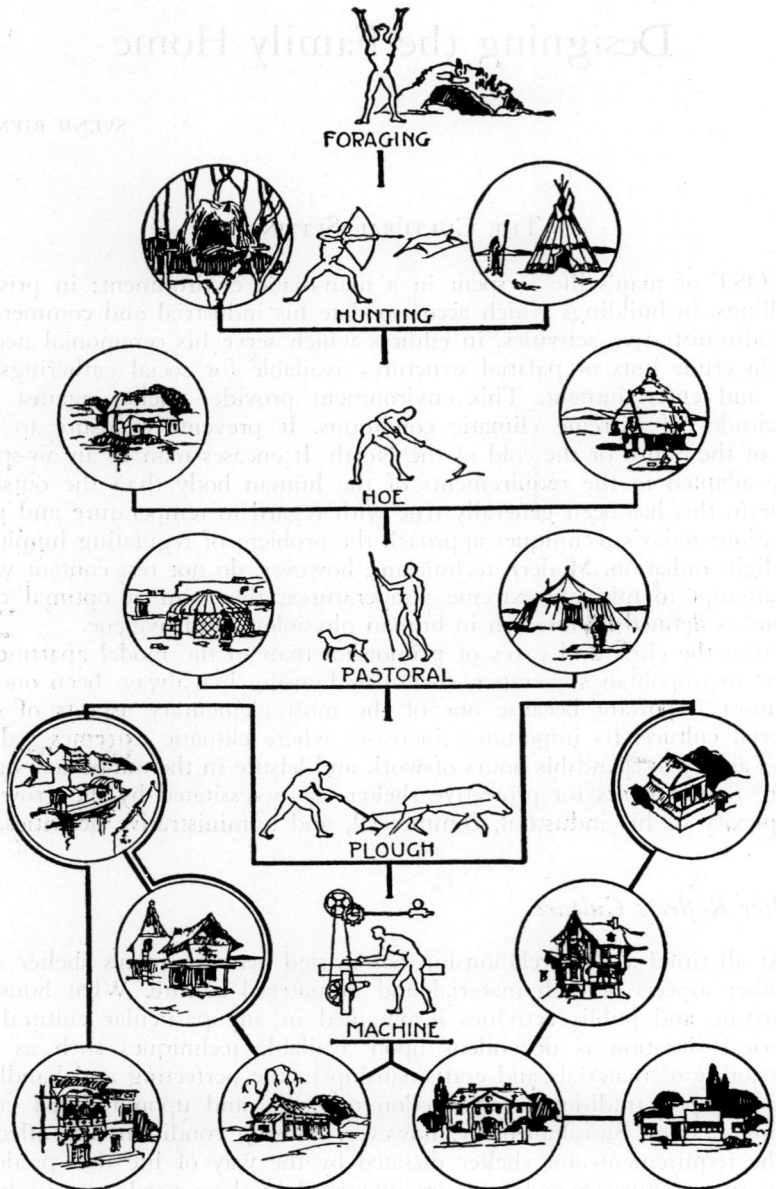

FIGURE 11. THE DEVELOPMENT OF MAN'S CULTURE AND HIS HOME

(From *The Evolving House*, by Albert F. Bemis; Cambridge, Mass., Technology Press, 1934)

cubicles with a minimum of partitions or none at all to the labyrinth of a government office building or a modern department store.

We talk about a system of shelter because human activities are distributed in different ways in relation to either private or public structures, and both types in turn have to be considered in relation to each other. On the midwestern farm, industrial and commercial activities as well as the private and social life of the family are sheltered within one and the same cluster of buildings. In the metropolitan area, all these activities are widely dispersed, connected with each other by various means of transportation, and housed in a welter of different constructions. Thus each culture displays its own characteristics. Any visual image of buildings, street layouts, open places, or village and city plans invites an understanding of the lives of the people who inhabit this man-made panorama.

The Family Residence

In our society, the selection and purchase of a dwelling unit to accommodate our private lives is in most cases a family problem.

A close relation exists between the family as a social institution and the physical structures available for family residence. The needs of the family influence both architect and contractor in their endeavor to produce a dwelling unit best fitted for the family. On the other hand, each existing structure molds family life according to the original intentions of the architect. With a minimum of subdivisions there is a minimum of privacy. Small cubicles separated from each other increase the opportunities for privacy, but they may impede or at least discourage social gatherings of the entire family group. The house as a physical structure squeezes the life of the family into a more or less rigid pattern. Nor is it a question only of more or less privacy. The floor plan tends to be suggestive with regard to the types of activities that are thrown together or held apart. A kitchen-diningroom combination or a study-bedroom combination indicates a way of life different from that in the home where such rooms are separate.

Deficiencies

Modern family life is not ideally accommodated in existing housing facilities. The majority of American families are forced to live in units that are not designed and built for the use to which they are put. One reason is simply the durability of the average dwelling. If buildings are kept in use for half a century, they lose in convenience and livability not only by a process of physical deterioration but also by simultaneous changes in our habits. Large homes of the nineteenth century, with the noise and clatter of the kitchen removed to the end of a long hall, are not attractive to the small modern family that has to get along without servants. But many of these structures are still in use despite the extra work they bring to the housewife who may prefer a compact bungalow.

Houses remain but the requirements of the American family are in a state of rapid change. Ironically, we might cite this as a case of cultural lag reversed. While patterns of interaction inside the family group undergo all those revolutionary changes which are discussed in other chapters, the products of material culture — i.e., the family dwellings available to the

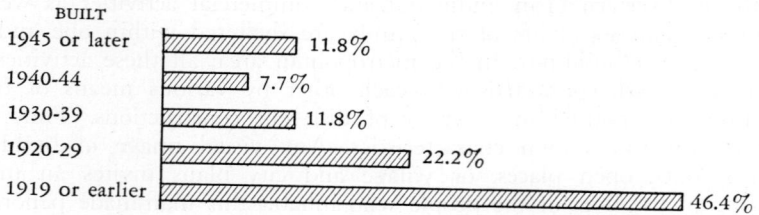

BUILT

1945 or later	11.8%
1940-44	7.7%
1930-39	11.8%
1920-29	22.2%
1919 or earlier	46.4%

FIGURE 12. THE AGE OF PRESENT NONFARM DWELLINGS

nation — remain unmoved and obsolete. Techniques and organization in the housing industry are unable to catch up with habits and attitudes, unable to reproduce the available stock of family housing as soon as it becomes functionally outdated.

Filtering-down

On the housing market, the severe competition for family dwellings adapted to contemporary needs leads to a process known as "filtering-down." Family homes are currently built for those who command the greatest purchasing power. Their particular needs attract the ingenuity of the architect and the solicitude of the contractor and the realtor. These wealthier groups are not only furnished with homes of modern design and equipment, but are given a wide range in choice of location. When the city expands and traffic starts roaring past the family residence, and when developments in construction and home equipment and in the pattern of family life convey the slightest tinge of obsolescence to the fashionable sections, they are abandoned for what are truly "greener pastures" and are sold at a discount to successive groups of the less wealthy.

As we proceed to the lower and lowest income groups, we find them housed in increasingly older residences. Not only are they forced to put up with advancing physical deterioration of the structure and lack of modern plumbing and equipment, but they are also compelled to accommodate themselves to dwelling units planned for a mode of life outdated by decades of social change. More than that, family habits and attitudes do not vary on a temporal basis alone; they are distinctly different in various strata of our society. Leisure time is spent differently, social entertaining assumes different forms, the family members congregate in different rooms of the home, and the extent to which domestic service can be employed demands different solutions of the home design. But the further we descend in the hierarchy of family incomes, the more often do we encounter families which are forced to make the best of a home planned for entirely different needs.

The most striking example of this state of affairs is to be found in the Negro districts of our large cities. Stately mansions in the path of the expanding Negro community are taken over, remodeled, and broken down into small apartments. Additional plumbing is installed wherever and however possible, and the minimum-sized "kitchenette," most frequently a single room crudely adapted to family living, takes the place of a full-sized home or apartment. These, to be sure, are extreme conditions, but they exemplify the process by which housing is supplied to those poor and weak in competitive power. The fact remains that only a minor section of the nation lives in houses which are built with the needs of the occupants in mind.

Economically there is nothing wrong with this situation and it has become acceptable as the natural course of events. But it has helped focus attention on the need for "functional" family housing, i.e., residential construction adapted to the everyday requirements of the occupants.

Housing for Family Needs

Since the depression of the 1930's attempts have been made to provide new home construction for the immediate use of all income levels. As far as the lowest incomes are concerned, construction has never been possible without government subsidy. Today, the housing industry is not unaware of the potentialities of a mass market in the middle income strata. The exploitation of these possibilities, however, is hampered by the necessity for revolutionary changes in production methods which will shift this section of our economy from a craftsman and small-shop basis to that of the large factory. Only in this way can cost levels be brought down to the purchasing power of the middle and the lower-middle income groups. The process is retarded by the inertia of contractors, realtors, architects, masons, carpenters — in short, by the organization of the financial transactions, the production processes, and the labor force in the building trades. The second-hand family residence is — and will be in the future — available on the market and will compete successfully in price and conveniences with the new homes built to measure. It is impossible to predict when this condition will be changed.

On "Functional" Architecture

Interest in "functional architecture" dates back to the beginning of the twentieth century and has encouraged us to ask the question how best the family residence should be designed and constructed for use.

The interrelationship of purpose and design had been forgotten by an era that built for show and conspicuous consumption rather than for convenience and utility. In a more general sense, to be sure, architecture

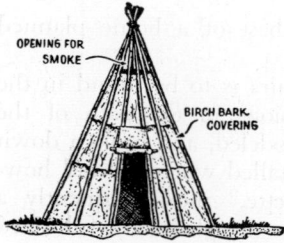

1. (above) PENOBSCOT BARK TIPI.

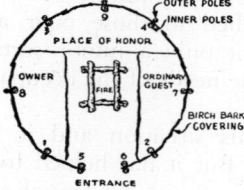

2. (above) CONVENTIONAL GREEK HOME HOMERIC AGE.

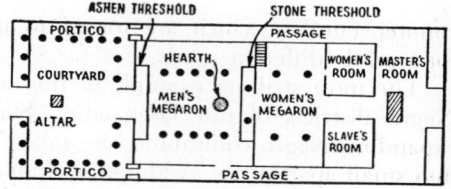

3. (above) PIONEER CABIN.

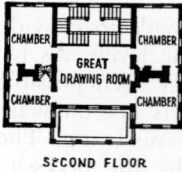

4. PLANTATION HOME.

5. (below) TYPICAL TWO-FAMILY HOUSE.

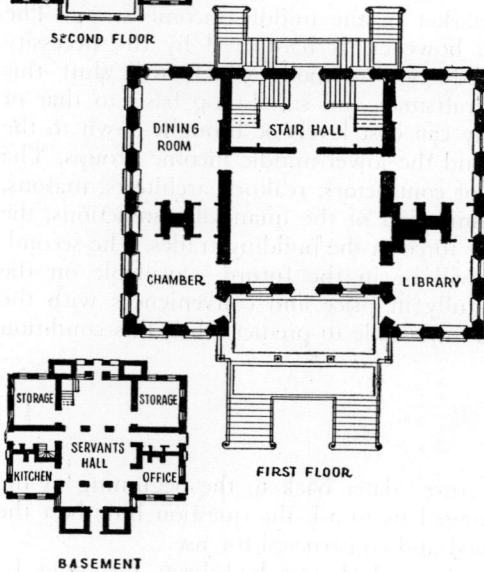

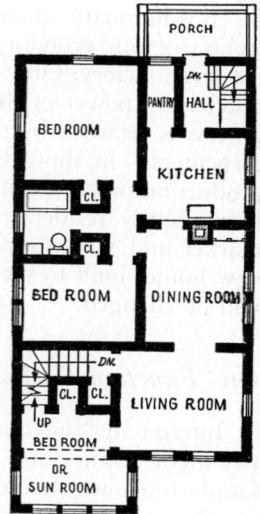

FIGURE 13. FLOOR PLANS AND PATTERNS OF FAMILY LIVING

(1, 2, 3, and 5 from *The Evolving House*. 4 from *Plantations from the Carolina Low Country*, by Samuel G. Stoney; Charleston, S.C., 1938)

was always "functional." It is bound to express both the state of available techniques and the specific needs of any given culture. The Greek temple, for instance, was not based upon a peculiar ideal of beauty but upon imitation of earlier wood construction and upon limitations in the means of handling the large marble blocks which were readily available for public and ostentatious construction. Similarly, the woodwork and the gable roof of the medieval house must be understood as a technique which remained visible and not as the offshoot of an ingenious search for the picturesque.

In architecture, however, as well as in literature, the arts, and music, we have become conscious of history. Research and conservation programs and pictorial reproductions of the architecture of the past and of foreign lands have made available for esthetic enjoyment the immense vista of private and public buildings built of stone or wood, in bamboo or even in snow blocks. All this has become our common property; but for the majority of us the social and economic and technological conditions which made these constructions at their time and at their proper location appear almost as a work of nature and necessity have faded into the background of consciousness. This wealth of three-dimensional constructions has lost social and cultural significance and appears only as a welter of fanciful creation and ornamentation today.

Architects became style-conscious; their attention was arrested by ornamental values. To be sure, they modified building methods according to improved techniques, but they retained ornamental features and blended the styles of varying periods. Willful play, however, broke the relation between beauty and basic construction, and the architect concentrated his attention upon the façade. While his creative imagination was thus engaged in exterior manipulation, the core of the building was neglected and fashioned by dull routine or possibly by a desire to provide a maximum of wall surface for a whimsical jumble of historical elements.

It was the mission of modern "functional architecture" to call attention to the need for purposeful construction in public as well as private buildings, in museums and school buildings, in office buildings and churches, and — last but not least — in the family residence. The reaction against the building history of the nineteenth century was violent and unrelenting. The charge of dishonesty was launched against the ostentatious and pompous mansions of the wealthy — dishonesty, because external appearance had become an end in itself. There were pillars for show that did not support anything; there were beams in the living room faked from two-by-eights and by no means part of the construction. Plantation mansions were sometimes fancied by Northern bankers; Gothic castles by cheap politicians. Neither technical necessity nor traditional symbolic values nor, finally, any personal affinity with either style or period determined the type of residence chosen for the family. On the contrary, requirements of style and ornament imposed decided inconveniences upon the occupants. Dark hallways, waste space, and useless rooms were placed inside turrets; or whimsical nooks and corners, crudely making their appeal for attention on the outside, were tacked on. And this sort of thing continues today!

To be sure, neither style nor ornament is entirely nonfunctional. The would-be palatial residences of the turn of the century, with their period bric-a-brac and stunts of whimsical inventiveness, are in themselves expressive of an era which stumbled into this maze of indiscriminate and somewhat barbaric appropriation of the historical past and of the "cultural" knick-knacks of the world. They reveal pride, possessiveness, and achievement. They serve excellently their purpose as showpieces that cannot be overlooked. They dominate the landscape and the street scene rather than blend harmoniously into the background. They wage a war for prominence with their neighbors, and their lack of taste does not offend the sensitivity of the self-made man to whom ornaments are gadgets and who uses them in his own fight for prominence. (See Figure 15.)

Functionalism in architecture, then, is strictly speaking neither new nor revolutionary. It has, rather, given a fresh emphasis to the *purpose* of

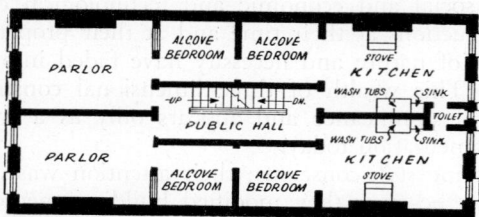

FIGURE 14. THE RAILROAD FLAT (From *The Evolving House*)

home construction. In line with the hedonistic values that prevail in our urban culture, the growing importance of leisure time and informal recreation in the residential areas of our large cities, the disappearance of abundant domestic service, and the need for labor-saving and utilitarian devices, there has been a complete reversal in the purpose for which the family residence is fashioned. There has been a shift from symbolic presentation and conspicuous consumption toward convenience in everyday life and a practical arrangement of rooms and equipment for the natural flow of indoor activities. This is the meaning of "functional" architecture as proclaimed in our housing literature.

Poverty and Economy Housing

The lack of "functional" home construction in the past has been caused by poverty as well as by unwisely dissipated wealth. In the immigrant sections of our metropolitan cities, particularly in New York, we are familiar with large apartment buildings containing so-called railroad flats. These consist of a row of individual rooms covering the entire long and narrow lot without any hall for purposes of communication. Rooms are strung in a line, and at remote locations they can be reached only by passing through the other rooms that block direct access. Such an arrangement provides a minimum of privacy and is now looked upon as a crime against the rules of functional design.

Even these apartments, so very undesirable at present, were not the result of negligence or lack of skill but of a situation in which the utmost economy was required to provide mere shelter to the masses migrating from abroad and from the rural hinterland into our urban communities. Halls were considered an unnecessary luxury because they represented a total loss for family living in the narrower sense. Purposes of economy overshadowed the purpose of providing privacy for individual rooms, for special home activities, or for the members of the family. Consideration of family functions requires a somewhat advanced standard of living and a willingness to accept utility rather than impressive appearance as a matter of primary importance.

FIGURE 15. AMERICAN PSEUDO-GOTHIC

Exaggerations

In the heat of pioneering and intellectual zeal, the early proponents of functional architecture seemed often negativistic and destructive in their appeal to the public. They wanted to "scrap the façade" and eliminate "false" ornaments. A building, they insisted, should bespeak its content and purpose and should be built from the inside out instead of with an eye to ornamentation.

These efforts were prone, in the beginning, to concentrate upon the elimination of false effects. Ingenuity and pleasing variety in utilitarian design for family living have developed slowly. There have been too many hasty attempts to abandon the sins of the nineteenth century by elimination only, by confronting us with the honesty of the blank wall, by furnishing us with those unimaginative "cigar boxes" or "chicken coops" which make us either yawn from sheer monotony as we pass by or which startle us to a reaction of disgust. It is sheer folly, of course, to build residences in which the family is meant to feel "at home" without due consideration of prevailing sentiments and traditions. Nor is it reasonable to assume that mere omission will necessarily create a pleasing esthetic effect.

The Place for Sentiment

The defensive reaction of the public against the rationally designed "machine for living" has its origin in a process which makes us associate comfort and warmth and friendliness and shelter with exactly the type of home environment we experienced in our childhood. The older generation "feels cold" in a modern apartment with light wall paper, and "sloppy" in the scientifically designed easy chair that flatters the spine of the younger set. Such childhood impressions, very naturally, have slowed up the general application of utilitarian principles to home design and equipment. Some of us cherish the hope of owning, one day, a Colonial house or a Cape Cod cottage or a log cabin with modern plumbing or one of those somewhat indefinite high-gabled brick structures which are not amiss in any American city. We may thus try to recover a feeling of security or youthful joy of life that is linked in our memories with such a residence — our own home or that of our envied companions or that of the most dignified and admired family in the neighborhood.

Such preferences, we have to admit, are often attached to superficial aspects of the family home. The basic structure, the floor plan in the miles and miles of one-family homes that extend into the periphery of our cities, is often monotonously the same. The contractor is well aware of the fact that there is economy in adherence to a limited number of model designs. Yet the consumer yearns for distinctive elements of "style," for something different that will make the family home stick out from its environment with characteristic features all its own.

At this point there is no longer any meaning in style as such. The ornamental surface is reduced to a mark of identification. Paradoxically, the symbols of individuality are repeated a thousand times all over the country. A modern cynic in the housing trade once offered to add to the basic structure — which as such we might have called either "clean" or "barren," according to taste — an ornamental surface which at slight additional cost would turn it into a residence representing the Middle Ages or antiquity, the Renaissance or the American frontier. The gist of the story is that style has lost symbolic significance; what remains is the desire for individual recognition and for a break in the monotony of family housing.

Individualization and Standardization

True individuality in a residential building must of course be expressed through design and construction, floor plan and equipment, and a location best adapted to the needs of the family that is going to fit itself into the house. Such individuality will be beyond the means of all but a small number in the higher income brackets. Nevertheless, in view of the standardization of our routines of family life and our attitudes toward the family home, there is considerable likelihood that the lower and middle income groups will be comfortably provided for in the model designs available at present and probably available in the future.

Under these circumstances, it might be well to abandon costly and superficial attempts at fake individuality by means of ornamental gadgets. We are still interested — and shall be as long as we cherish the idea and appreciate the economic and social values attached to individual home ownership — in some sort of exterior symbol of individual identity. Fortunately, well-balanced compromises between standardization and differentiation are approached in most modern real estate developments. We are not disturbed any more — remembering the jumble of willful style conglomerations of past decades — by private and public housing developments which lend the impression of unity to a neighborhood by emphasizing one type of structure and which may limit themselves to a small number of models or even to one structure repeated over and over again.

Differentiation is achieved by landscaping, by winding street-layouts, by exposing various sides of the house to the street front, by the choice of different additions to the basic structure (such as porches, extra rooms, or garages), and, finally, by the selection of different covers of paint which — wherever the neighborhood is well planned — will be carefully matched. In subdivisions of this kind, our present conditions are well expressed with an intermingling of individualistic and collectivistic attitudes, of personal responsibility and concerted action. Although the individual family home is clearly identified, it takes its place in a community of likeminded and congenial neighbors. As we motor past these modern residential sections, we readily become aware of the layout of the neighborhood as a whole. There is just as much variation as we are able to absorb at twenty-five miles an hour. The days are past when we promenaded on foot and enjoyed as individual museum pieces, placed in the parklike environment of extensive lots, the manifestations of patrician pride and whimsy.

Housing in Sacred and in Secular Society

In certain types of sacred society tradition determines the processes of production as well as consumption on a more or less permanent basis. The cultural setting of the housing problem, consequently, is not nearly as complex as in the contemporary scene. Techniques and esthetic embellishments are not subject to arbitrary choice. The general culture determines the tools available, the purposes of home design, and the manner in which activities are distributed between private and public structures. There is little room for inventiveness on the part of the individual builder. Customary procedures and construction methods are handed down through generations of craftsmen.

With the beginning of industrialization this security of craftsmanship, embedded in the very roots of culture and serving a traditional way of life, was abandoned for the freedom of experimentation. Mechanical discoveries contributed to these developments and so did an attitude that favored change for the sake of improvement as well as an end in itself. Many of the undesirable features of family housing in the nineteenth century were due to the abandonment of the fetters of tradition. In this era of laissez faire, we observe a playful and highly individualized grasp of the potentialities of new construction methods. Simultaneously building activities were reoriented toward new demands for sheltered space, particularly in growing urban communities. Esthetically, the lack of cultural norms invited a rather chaotic play with the style elements of the historical past and their whimsical adaptation for the purpose of conspicuous consumption.

Today we find ourselves at the end of a transition period. The purpose of home construction is more rationally considered. The everyday comfort of all family members is clearly proclaimed as the goal. The chaos of a confusing transition from the principles of sacred to the principles of secular society is being gradually replaced by purposeful design as far as the architects are concerned and by rational demands as far as the consumers are concerned. Home planning has become a matter not of tradition, not

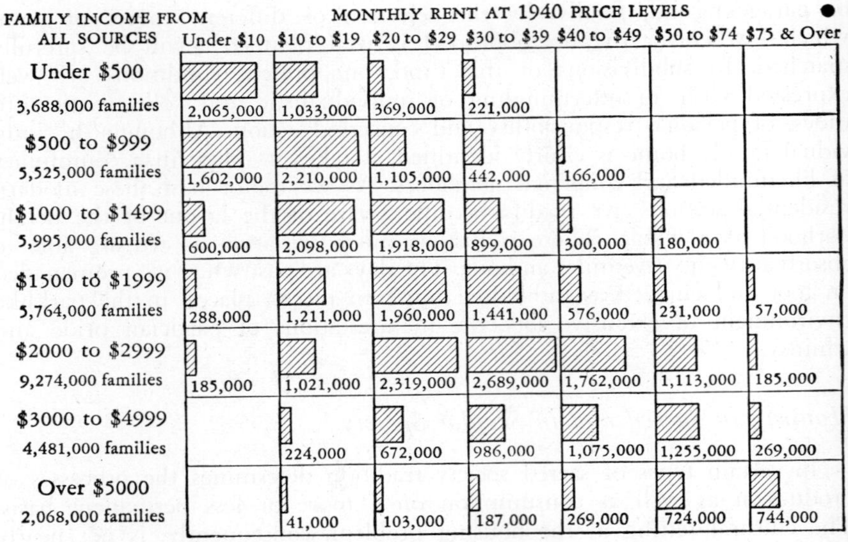

FAMILY INCOME FROM ALL SOURCES	MONTHLY RENT AT 1940 PRICE LEVELS						
	Under $10	$10 to $19	$20 to $29	$30 to $39	$40 to $49	$50 to $74	$75 & Over
Under $500 — 3,688,000 families	2,065,000	1,033,000	369,000	221,000			
$500 to $999 — 5,525,000 families	1,602,000	2,210,000	1,105,000	442,000	166,000		
$1000 to $1499 — 5,995,000 families	600,000	2,098,000	1,918,000	899,000	300,000	180,000	
$1500 to $1999 — 5,764,000 families	288,000	1,211,000	1,960,000	1,441,000	576,000	231,000	57,000
$2000 to $2999 — 9,274,000 families	185,000	1,021,000	2,319,000	2,689,000	1,762,000	1,113,000	185,000
$3000 to $4999 — 4,481,000 families		224,000	672,000	986,000	1,075,000	1,255,000	269,000
Over $5000 — 2,068,000 families		41,000	103,000	187,000	269,000	724,000	744,000

FIGURE 16. FAMILIES NEEDING HOUSING IN 1955 BY INCOME GROUPS
(Postwar Estimate)

of creative expression and arbitrary appreciation, but a matter of scientific procedures in which different professional disciplines make their own contributions. The very fact that the purposes of home construction are not taken for granted any more but are investigated by objective survey methods is sufficient indication that we have advanced to the threshold of a housing era that is entirely under the influence of the process of secularization predominant in our culture.

THE ECONOMIC SETTING

The National Outlook

Whether the American family is adequately housed depends not only upon our attitudes toward the family home but also upon our ability to afford adequate homes. In view of the uneven distribution of purchasing power the question will have to be answered with different income ranges in mind. The proportion of the national income that is diverted into housing investments is flexible. In our family budgets, the housing needs stand in competition with those for food, clothing, education, and other expenditures. In Swedish cities, it is quite customary to devote as much as one third of the entire family income for the rental of a modern apartment. In the American family budget, the housing item is generally limited to a smaller fraction of all expenditures and also varies with status, the size of the family, and regional customs. Only where the standard of living has advanced beyond the subsistence minimum is it possible to give attention to the need for more than the most primitive shelter. According to Engel's

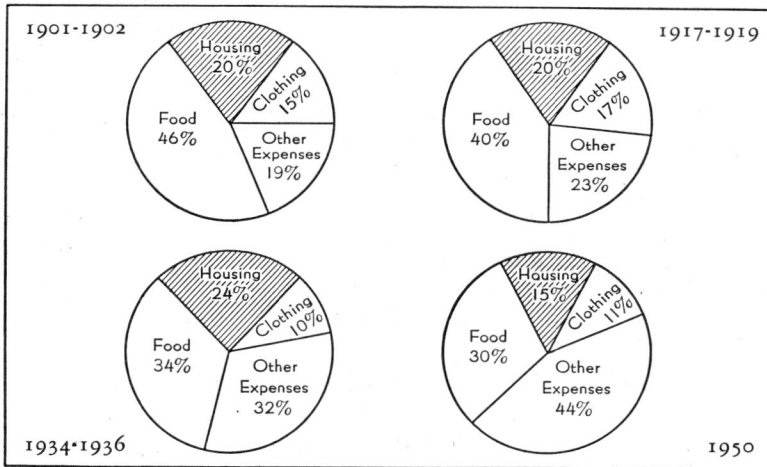

FIGURE 17. HOUSING IN THE CONSUMER'S BUDGET (1901 TO 1950)

well-known law, expenditures for food are relatively high in the lowest income groups, thus reducing the amount of money available for other items of consumption. No wonder, then, that "housing" as a movement that aims at certain minimum standards of privacy, plumbing, and neighborhood facilities for all citizens has only recently received public recognition.

Housing — a Public Utility

When we talk about "housing," we have in mind primarily the condition of that section in our community that is not able to obtain sanitary and wholesome family shelters with its own income. This is not a small section, nor is it a matter of a few extreme cases in the slums of our large cities. Under the circumstances some reformers, housing experts, politicians, and philanthropists have gone so far as to claim that housing should be considered a public utility and the community should be provided with adequate living quarters as a matter of civic responsibility just as it is provided with a sanitary sewage system, with waterworks, with gas and electricity, etc. This claim may go too far. It is rejected in any open discussion by all but a few progressive leaders. That the community as a whole has a certain responsibility in this matter, however, is widely accepted.

The need for better housing was first brought to public attention by journalists, by the so-called muckrakers of the turn of the century, and by social workers. In the early days the movement was carried on by contributions from philanthropists and charitable organizations and was limited to an experimental scale. Today it forms an important part of our federal, state, and municipal policies.

There are several reasons for this situation. In the first place, poor housing is expensive to the community at large. The social disorganization — delinquency, desertion, mental and physical illness — characteristic of slum areas,

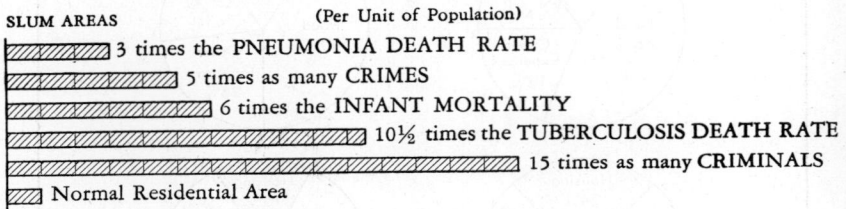

SLUM AREAS   (Per Unit of Population)

3 times the PNEUMONIA DEATH RATE
5 times as many CRIMES
6 times the INFANT MORTALITY
10½ times the TUBERCULOSIS DEATH RATE
15 times as many CRIMINALS
Normal Residential Area

FIGURE 18. SOCIAL ASPECTS OF SLUM AREAS IN DETROIT, MICHIGAN

necessitates heavy expenditures for relief services. That these costs would be eliminated by a thorough rehabilitation of such areas is a difficult assertion to prove, particularly to skeptical taxpayers. Although it is obvious that where living conditions are wholesome there is less misery and consequently less need for relief spending, we cannot conclude that proper housing is the sole factor making for adjustment in family life. Nevertheless it is an important factor.

In the second place, housing has a direct effect upon the growth and the decline of population and especially upon the quality of population. The community as a whole should be interested in securing for every child an environment that will develop him into a responsible citizen, healthy in body and mind. The gray wastelands beyond the railroad tracks and the overcrowded tenements of our great cities assuredly do not provide such an environment.

In the third place, the public is gradually becoming aware of the possibility that the lower-income and even many of the middle-income groups may be caught in an economic entanglement which is not of their own making and over which they have no control. Powerful and heretofore unmanageable social forces are at work in the housing industry. The individual who cannot extricate himself by his own efforts must have substantial public assistance to boost his purchasing power on this market.

Rural Farm Housing

So far we have given attention mainly to urban housing conditions. Actually the problem of rural housing is even more urgent. No less than two-thirds of all rural housing is inadequate for family living. Of the six and a half million rural farm homes, two million appear to be in need of major improvements and about the same number should be entirely replaced. In these figures, we have not even considered yet the exceedingly miserable living quarters of the migratory farm laborers.

The problem of farm housing is complicated by the fact that it is closely tied up with the operation of the farm as an economic unit. Frequently the farm cannot support a better house from its income. Improvements, even if subsidized, are sometimes not warranted because the farm may be

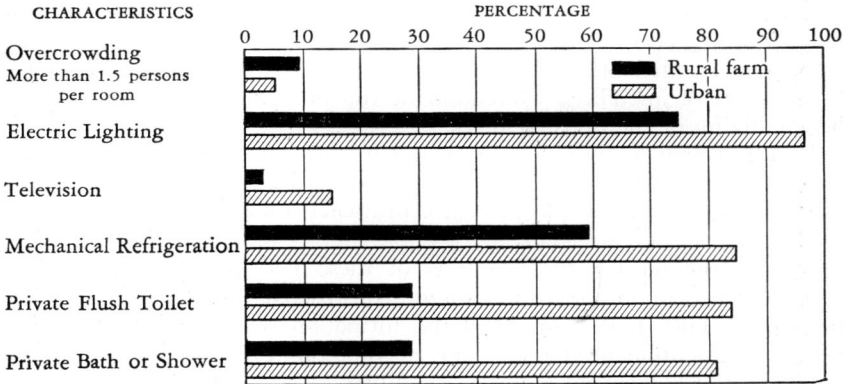

FIGURE 19. PERCENTAGE OF RURAL FARM AND URBAN DWELLINGS HAVING SELECTED CHARACTERISTICS, 1950

abandoned for economic reasons in the near future. Again, the house has no income value in itself. Whenever financial means are available for repair or building operations, the farmer is apt to invest the money in a barn or other economic units rather than in comfort for family living.

Under the circumstances the maintenance of the farm house is often neglected and equipment is lacking which would be considered absolutely necessary in most urban dwellings. One-half of our farm houses have no electricity, over 60 per cent have no running water, and close to 70 per cent have no private flush toilet and no private bath.

In many northern states, the farm houses are less crowded than the urban dwelling units. Unfortunately, however, the heating facilities are so inadequate that during the winter months all family members are crowded into a limited number of rooms for their waking hours.

Housing Agencies

Public assistance to urban housing has been offered in two ways:

(1) The former *United States Housing Authority* gave loans and offered outright subsidies to local housing authorities for slum clearance. Small, well planned neighborhoods were created to replace an equal amount of demolished slum housing. Eligibility to occupy the new houses was limited according to need (i.e., number of children, income, previous location, etc.) and to a certain extent also according to ability to take advantage of offered conveniences in the improvement of morale. Rents were adjusted on a sliding scale according to family income. The excess of costs over income was in part covered by funds of the Federal agency.

(2) The *Federal Housing Authority* limited itself to the insurance of loans made by various credit institutions for the purchase of family residences. This indirect means of assistance was aimed to help wide ranges of the middle classes, who were able to squeeze the purchase of a home into the family budget only on a long-term credit basis. The security of Federal insurance made it possible to offer loans at reasonable cost. Since loans were granted only when certain normative standards were met and on the basis of an official evaluation of the property, they contributed to the stabilizing of the housing market.

In adjustment to war conditions and to postwar inflationary tendencies on the housing market the services of these two agencies have undergone various changes. Both are at present coordinated under the *National Housing Agency*.

One of the most valuable effects of these Federal agencies has been their influence upon the formation of constructive local policies all over the nation. They have stimulated the formation of local housing authorities and have influenced real estate negotiations even beyond those cases in which FHA loans were in order. Furthermore, they have led to the formation of voluntary housing associations on a local basis. These have made it their purpose to survey conditions in their own locality, to call attention to blatant needs, and to use publicity and political pressure to ensure constructive action on the part of the municipal government.

The problem of rural housing has not been the main concern of any one government agency. As mentioned before, this problem is linked closely with the fate of the farm enterprise itself. In connection with economic rehabilitation or the distribution of special services, the following agencies have been involved: the Farm Security Administration, the Rural Resettlement Administration, and the Rural Electrification Administration.

The Housing Emergency

In the immediate postwar era the housing market was characterized, as we all know, by tremendous undersupply. Estimates of needed construction at fairly decent standards ranged all the way from ten to fifteen million homes to be built yearly for a period of about ten years. After World War II, an acute emergency existed which caused families to take advantage of inadequate shelters, to double up in crowded apartments and family homes, or to buy homes at inflated prices in order to remain secure from eviction. It retarded the formation of families by delaying marriage. It caused conflict and family tension in overcrowded quarters particularly where different generations found themselves piled up under the same roof and unable to realize their often widely different interests in leisure time activities and home arrangements.

The housing emergency forced upon American families inequalities in standards of living which were related neither to status nor to income but rather to accidental circumstances. Their general comfort depended upon whether they made their last move from one home to the other ten years, four years, or one year ago; upon whether they decided to buy a home at

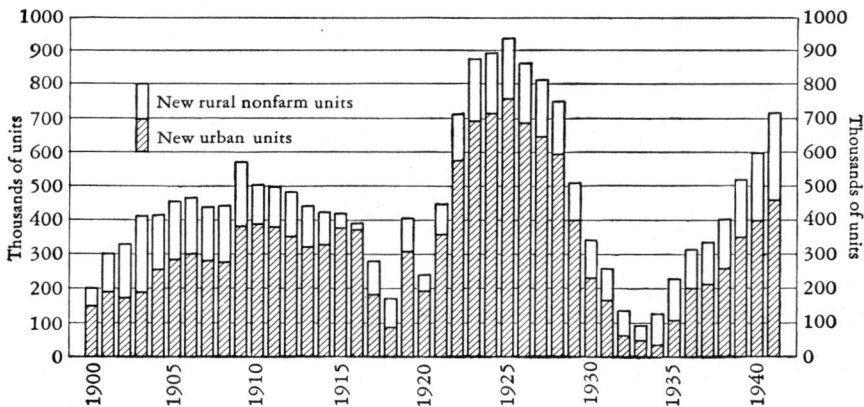

FIGURE 20. BUILDING ACTIVITIES 1900–1941
(From *American Housing;* New York, Twentieth Century Fund, 1944)

the right moment or decided to remain renters and were eventually forced into purchasing at a high price level. All this determines the proportion of the family income that is frozen by housing expenditures and consequently also the amount of income available for other needs.

Rent ceilings and ceiling prices for new construction on a local as well as federal basis were aimed at protecting family housing budgets against inflationary exploitation. They were apt to cause hardships to landlords, however, where rents were frozen on a fixed level while general prices rose. Thus the real income of property owners was artificially reduced. Sliding rent scales have been applied in other countries and may be proposed here in the future. With regard to ceilings on new construction, the old question arises whether excessive prices are a necessary evil, namely, as a necessary incentive to building activity; or whether the still unsatisfactory situation is due to abnormal market conditions which require interference by either local or federal government.

Trends of Home Construction

The postwar housing shortage was not the result of a merely temporary emergency. It was fundamentally due to the organization of building activities, the marketing of the product, and the structure of available labor.

Ever since the boom of the 1920's, the construction of family residences has not caught up with the demand for replacement, not to speak of the need for additional homes to accommodate the still growing number of families. Before the depression, the real estate market flourished on a speculative basis. From basic materials to finished product, speculative demand forced up price levels. Homes were bought not for need but for investment. It seemed wise to borrow money to finance the purchase of a home because its resale value would rise in the immediate future.

After the crash of 1929 careless methods of financing caught up with the consumer. With revolutionary changes in the income structure of the middle classes, millions of mortgages were foreclosed. Homes had to be sold or refinanced. Building activities shrank rapidly and have never fully recovered. The replacement of obsolescent homes has always been inadequate, and today the problem is compounded by the accumulation of doubled-up families from depression days and by the excessive marriage and birth rates following the war.

War Housing

In connection with the war boom, before as well as after Pearl Harbor, emergency housing became a necessity in those communities where war plants were located and where the additional labor force had to be somehow accommodated. Federal and municipal subsidies were accepted only with great hesitation. Local businessmen feared that any extension of available facilities might lead to a complete slump of property values in the community once the hastily assembled labor force dispersed again from the production centers to their place of origin. The shock of the last depression still affected the reactions of the businessman as well as the politician. Thus emergency housing was provided only under restrictive regulations. Priorities were limited. No action was taken until actual misery prevailed in trailer camps and in the single men's districts where members of the labor force spent lonely years without being able to have their families join them at their place of work. In many cases, emergency housing was constructed under the proviso that it be demountable or of sufficiently scanty quality not to affect the real estate market after the war.

No wonder then that we were, after the war, more crowded than ever before, that we were at times unable to continue the process of demolishing substandard housing, that we had to double up and pay an ever larger percentage of our income for housing needs.

Some of the difficulties of the war emergency have been overcome in recent years. Various bottlenecks in the form of missing parts and materials — which used to hold up construction at any point — have been cleared up. There remains the very elementary question, however, whether the costs of construction will ever again be reduced to a level where the money available in our family budgets for housing expenditures will command facilities as ample as those which characterized the living quarters of our grandparents or of those who bought a house in the twenties.

The Prospect of Housing Economics

We have to anticipate costs in the future which will reduce the space available for the individual family. We shall be compensated, on the other hand, by improved equipment which will to a certain extent alleviate the strain imposed upon us in the compact little family home. The reason for this expectation lies in the fact that the building process is still arrested at a stage of individual construction, that labor in the building industries operates on a craftsman basis. The advantages of industrial mass production, which are so obvious in the production of modern home equipment, cannot as yet be applied to the family residence itself.

The prospect that "prefabrication" will pull us out of this dilemma is not rosy, according to the judgment of housing experts, engineers, and architects. Prefabrication is based upon a shorter amortization period than that applied to the sturdier home of individual construction. To make it worth while for the consumer to buy a prefabricated house with a much shorter length of life, costs would have to be reduced to a much greater extent than we can hope for in the immediate future, in spite of the development of new materials and new methods of unit construction.

We are confronted here with a vicious circle. Great cost reductions can be expected only if prefabrication can proceed on a mass basis. We as consumers are hesitant, on the other hand, to accept prefabricated housing on more than an experimental basis. Our city ordinances prohibit the placing of prefabricated housing on the more desirable sites available in the community. Real estate lacks experience in handling the new product. Labor employed in the building industries joins the more conservative forces because the reshuffling from piece construction to factory work would entail difficulties in individual adjustment and, locally, the danger of temporary or even permanent unemployment.

The prospects, then, are uncertain at present. It is not impossible, however, that the future home of the American family will differ essentially from the accommodations of the past. It will be smaller and better equipped. We shall probably be more ready to change quarters in order to adapt ourselves to varying needs at different phases of the family cycle. For some time to come, the housing item in the family budget will consume a relatively large proportion. All these effects will be felt much less by those who acquired a home in the past under different circumstances.

The Private Outlook

The selection of a home presents a most important step in the life of the family. More is involved than in any other economic transaction. The family residence, its size and shape and location, should be chosen with the greatest care because it is bound to determine the way of life which the family is going to pursue. To put it somewhat differently: as you look around on the real estate market you are bargaining not only for one definite thing but for a whole bundle of things. You are bargaining for pleasant and easily prepared breakfasts in the morning, for sound sleep at night, for cheerful hours in good company in the evening, for a minimum of interference of your own activities with those of the other family members. You are, in short, bargaining for an environment in which your personality can thrive and where the family unit can develop to the best interest of parents as well as offspring.

These various purposes, woven into the intricate currents of family interaction, should be kept in mind even where we are concerned primarily with the economic aspects of the choice. The purchase of a home cannot be looked upon only as an investment. The lease of an apartment cannot be taken for a shrewd way of getting out of the responsibilities involved in home ownership. We must therefore scrutinize briefly how the individual family fits itself into the network of economic relationships on the housing market.

Home Ownership — When Is It Sound?

Whether home ownership is sound is a question that has been raised and thoroughly discussed in the recent literature. It has been pointed out, also, that the question should rather be: When is home ownership sound? In view of the great variety of family situations and market conditions that have to be met, there is no absolute answer.

The desirability of home ownership has been stressed frequently because of its effects upon responsible citizenship. It has been pointed out that it is apt to develop the appreciation of values centered around a stable family life, continuous gainful employment, and participation in community affairs. As a local taxpayer, the home owner is bound to follow with interest the course of local policies. He attends the school district meetings to weigh carefully the benefits resulting from additional property taxes for the education of his own children or those of his neighbors. Other tax assessments for local improvements such as sewerage, highways, and parks also strike home because they affect the pocket book, not necessarily in terms of immediate outlays only but also because neighborhood improvements are going to be reflected in the value of the individual property. Home ownership is the source of "grass roots" democracy. The family shares in the benefits and in the setbacks that befall the community at large.

This argument, to be sure, must be launched with caution. It has been used recklessly in the past. It has been used to tie labor down to a certain location in such a manner as to render it defenseless against exploitative wage arrangements. The idea of home ownership with all its sentimental overtones has been sold to families of low income who were not able to meet the necessary payments and actually to step from the stage of contract buying into the blessed state of clear ownership. Home ownership is apt to appeal to families of all strata of our society in times of expanding industrial activities and employment opportunities. During boom times, however, the purchasing contracts are written on a speculative basis at price levels that are unduly high. When a depression comes, it is impossible to live up to the financial commitments that were entered upon when things looked bright on the labor market. Buying a house means for most American families entering upon a financial program that will continue far into the future through the height of inflation as well as through the trough of economic depression.

Home ownership, then, ought not to be initiated during certain stages of the business cycle. If we buy on contract, we have to consider carefully how our commitments will fit into the future of the housing market. Unfortunately, the wise thing is to buy in the depression when nobody has any money anyway, and let the temptation pass us by while our incomes are riding high on the crest of the industrial boom.

Needless to say, sound home ownership can be based only on prospects of a more or less steady income. Periods of unemployment are apt to delay payments and to endanger not only ownership but also the investments of the past. The monthly installments of the purchasing contract have to be arranged not with maximum incomes, not with average incomes, but with minimum incomes in mind if the threat of mortgage foreclosure is to be avoided.

The Housing Item in the Family Budget

Even if we do not consider the catastrophic possibility of mortgage foreclosure and eviction, the amount of money spent for housing will be reflected in all other items of the budget. Every dollar that goes into housing expenditures will not be available for other necessities or luxuries, for educational advancement or travel or car or vacations.

There is a rough estimate that in the purchase of a home the total amount should never exceed twice the average yearly income available for family expenditures. This is a rule that rarely can be adhered to at present, certainly. There are some situations, for example, where home purchase is the only means of guaranteeing the family a roof over its head. Allowance will have to be made for emergencies. The commitment at a time of urgent need, however, will have to be paid for in later years, and the standard of living of the family will be affected forever after by the unfortunate need for a residence just as the calamity of a housing shortage strikes.

Some families may plan their entire leisure-time activities around the family home. For that reason, expenditures for commercial entertainment may be low. Some families may forego the expenses of higher education for their children. For some families, the home may be their hobby. It would be wrong to set rigid limits on what housing expenditures should be. There are other families who make unusually little use of their home: they may want books and classical records, they may want to take advantage of educational facilities and may like to travel, or they may simply like to eat so well and to entertain so frequently that these habits cut heavily into the budget. They will have to be careful in their decisions about housing and try to stay somewhere near the two-year-salary formula, which is after all a rule of thumb rather than a normal rate.

Home Ownership as an End in Itself

The ambition for home ownership is part of the American heritage. From pioneer days, from the days of large-scale immigration, it has been the dream of innumerable families to establish themselves on a piece of land of their own and to build their own house. There seems to be some intangible value in home ownership as such. It conveys a feeling of economic security, and the very fact that a certain residential structure stands forever available for family use, that nobody has the right to remove the family from its shelter, and that the memories of the family history will be closely linked to the home gives it a symbolic value that cannot easily be estimated in dollars and cents. If there is a willingness to accept economic sacrifices for the sake of emotional satisfactions, no outsider is justified or even competent to decide whether under such circumstances home ownership is sound. How much a person is willing to pay for the feeling of owning a home is a blunt fact that cannot be analyzed any further in terms of rational economic calculations.

Does Home Ownership Pay?

The abundant pamphlet literature on home ownership, on the other hand, frequently suggests that home ownership may be looked upon as an advantageous economic proposition. "You pay on the house just as you pay rent," so runs the customary argument, "but then at the end you own something; it is not all thrown out of the window." This argument, which treats home ownership as a saving device and investment, has to be taken with a grain of salt. It is not entirely false; but it would be wrong to assume that the monthly payments on the house represent so much saving nor would it be correct to forget the many hidden costs involved in home ownership in addition to the monthly payments on the contract.

While you pay for the house, it is being "amortized," and that means that it is being "used up." Depreciation may proceed at different rates. Whether you make a good buy or a bad one depends upon the speed with which the resale value decreases. Under no circumstances can the father hope to buy a home which will permit him to save for the end of his occupational career the amount of money that is being paid for the house. Short-term ownership and early resales on a seller's market may occasionally yield profits. The average home owner, however, is not necessarily out for a smart deal. He wants to live in a house and he has to pay for the occupancy. Whether he comes out in the long run with a better balance sheet of costs on the one hand and services on the other, is a question that requires detailed analysis in each individual case.

Consumer-purchaser studies have revealed that the home owner, as compared to the renter of the same income level, generally carries somewhat higher expenses. He also generally lives in a somewhat better house. There are hidden costs which tend to create the impression that home ownership is necessarily more profitable than a rental lease. The following are items that are often forgotten at the purchase of a family residence:

(1) Taxes
(2) Assessments
(3) Heating
(4) Water, light, and other utilities
(5) Repairs and other maintenance
(6) Labor used in upkeep and "fixing" things
(7) Depreciation

The last item is difficult to estimate because it depends upon the housing market in the far future, the solidity of the structure, the progress of "functional" obsolescence, and changes in the desirability of the neighborhood for residential purposes.

Under the circumstances it would be shortsighted to make an unqualified plea for home ownership as such. On the contrary, it may be wise to lean backward, in view of the way in which the American dream of "the little white house with the picket-fence" has been exploited by advertising and promotion literature.

Home Ownership as Responsibility

Quite apart from the type of house we buy and quite apart from the details of the purchasing contract, home ownership as such constitutes a challenge and a responsibility that are not desirable for everybody. Without the investment of occasional family labor in repair and maintenance, without anybody in the family who likes to "tinker" and who can swing a hammer, home ownership may after a few years become a source of irritation. Door knobs will be coming off, and nobody knows what to do with them. The plumbing gets clogged up or the cesspool is filled to the brim and a new one has to be excavated. The house may be sagging, but the owners may be unable to diagnose the situation and take adequate measures. For the uninitiated these dramatic emergencies mean repairs and repairs again. He will have no control over the final bill because he does not know what is amiss and whether the crew is actually working or just marking time while labor costs are running up. Indeed, home ownership is not everybody's business. There are those who make money by buying a house and remodeling it and selling it again on the market in improved condition. This, naturally, has nothing to do with home ownership. It means a part-time job in the housing business.

Home Ownership and Occupational Mobility

Home ownership defeats its end when the head of the family is not definitely settled with his occupational work in the community in which he happens to reside at a given time. He may buy and sell again, particularly if residences desirable for family living are not available for rent. He may come out even if he buys and sells on the same market. He may gain if the price trend is favorable; he may lose if it is unfavorable. But the average family father is no skilled operator on the real estate market. The family's standard of living is made dependent upon price fluctuations which the household head cannot foresee. It is doubtful whether the destiny of the individual family should be tied up with the hazards of an exceedingly unreliable market situation. Some will gain and others will lose. The responsible father will want to avoid risks that may force him into peonage for the rest of his life.

Home Ownership and the Family Cycle

Unfortunately the costs of home ownership tend to be highest when other financial responsibilities burden the family budget. It is seldom entered upon at an early age because a certain amount of security in the occupational career will have to be obtained first. Then the house is seldom paid for when expenditures for education and for social activities reach their peak in the family history. It is at this time, as a matter of fact, that the physical deterioration of the structure starts raising the maintenance costs. When finally the house is paid for and owned clear and when only taxes and maintenance have to be considered, the family cycle already draws close to its end. The children, by that time, have become independent. The house may have outgrown its usefulness. It may be too large for the aging couple, and the neighborhood in which it stands may no longer serve the needs of the occupants.

Buying vs. Renting

A minority only of all American families live in rented houses or apartments. Home ownership increases with income and security. In many sections of our society, home ownership is a symbol of respectability and responsible citizenship. Home ownership is desirable, therefore, from the viewpoint both of the individual and of the community as a whole. Likewise, it is important to point out that unwise commitments to home ownership are neither beneficial to the individual family nor to the community which has to cope with symptoms of maladjustment and social disorganization that may be caused by those who have overstepped their financial abilities in this all too adventurous field of conspicuous consumption.

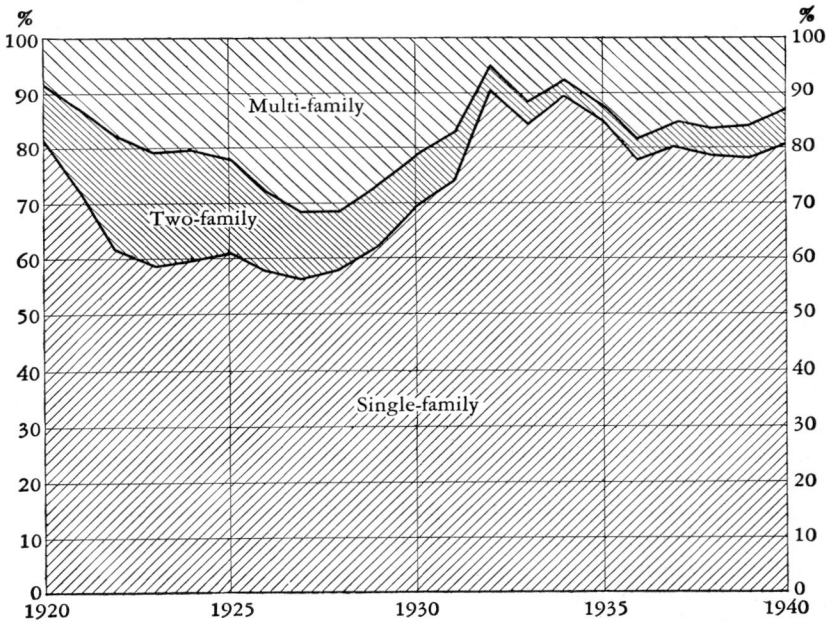

FIGURE 21. BUILDING OF SINGLE-FAMILY AND MULTIPLE UNITS 1920–1940

(From *American Housing;* New York, Twentieth Century Fund, 1944)

Renting and apartment house living, although more frequent in urban centers and in areas of disorganization and high mobility, do not necessarily imply lack of attachment to the family abode. Attitudes toward renting and buying are dependent upon tradition. In New York City, the center of wide-spread apartment housing and the homestead of European traditions, children are reared in one and the same apartment. There are many home owners, on the other hand, who move from house to house with gradually advancing or receding careers and with the specific requirements of the various phases of the family cycle. There are few who are able to realize the dream of the family home as a lasting center for a family unit covering its history from the birth of the first child to the solitude of the old and retired couple. Yet the dream may be worth fighting for, relentlessly and with ever-renewed optimism. It is part of the American tradition.

THE FAMILY'S HOME ADJUSTMENT

A house is not necessarily a home. It is a physical structure that may be designed for purposes of family residence. But if we talk about a home we have in mind not only the physical structure as such but also the manner in which the members of the family or the household have adjusted to it. In popular usage, the term "home" is burdened with evaluative connotations and means something like "a constructive family environment suitable for the rearing of children." As a matter of fact, the term is often used in such a manner as to exclude the possibility of any such thing as a bad "home." In the following discussion we shall try to keep ourselves detached from evaluations, but we shall include the interaction pattern of the family members and their adjustment to the physical structure.

What is the process of home adjustment? The answer involves an analysis of the relationship between the four walls, the interior subdivisions, and the equipment, on the one hand, and the interrelated or individualized family activities on the other. Here we are delving into the sociological aspects of "functional architecture" in the field of residential housing.

We want to know what aspects of the physical structure and what aspects of the family help in avoidance of friction. Both groups of aspects cooperate in the constitution of a home as we have defined the term. Both may be the source of maladjustment, and both may be instrumental in bringing about improvements in the home situation. We can make recommendations for the choice of a more suitable family residence, we may suggest the remodeling of certain parts of the present house, or we may recommend changes in the use of the house that will eliminate or mitigate friction or maladjustment.

As a guide we have developed a check-list of possible sources of friction that may arise in the process of home adjustment (see Table 10). This list may be used in questionnaire form or as a guide for interviews in the collection of case studies. More important, with the purpose of this text in mind, it can be used by the individual family in the search for a home. It may serve as an instrument that will offer a fairly good evaluation of the functional advantages and disadvantages that may be expected from the purchase or the rental of any variety of dwelling units available on the market. It may be used, further, in the diagnosis of a residence in which the family may be at present located. Suggestions for either remodeling or a rearrangement of family activities may result from the use of the check-list.

TABLE 10

CHECK-LIST OF INCONVENIENCES FOUND IN HOMES

Meals

1. Are you unduly crowded at mealtimes?
   a. every day ( )
   b. special occasions ( )
2. Are you apt to interfere with other activities when you set the table?
   a. kitchen work ( )
   b. recreation or study ( )
3. Is the distance too far between the dining table and the place where you prepare your food? ( )
4. Have you had difficulties in clearing out the odors after meals? ( )

Hygiene

5. Do you find the bathroom (shower, toilet) inadequate in regard to
   a. size
      1. for toilette and dressing ( )
      2. for housework ( )
   b. location
      1. consider accessibility ( )
      2. consider spread of noise ( )
   c. heating ( )
   d. noise insulation ( )
   e. ventilation ( )
6. Does the family's morning toilette and dressing interfere with
   a. kitchen work ( )
   b. breakfast ( )
   c. other members' toilette ( )
7. Is the bathroom equipment (shower, toilet) unsatisfactory because of
   a. lack of bathtub ( )
   b. lack of wash basin ( )
   c. lack of outlets for light ( )
   d. lack of shelves ( )
   e. lack of medicine chest ( )

Sleeping

8. Have you felt any inconvenience from the fact that you have not been able to provide separate sleeping rooms for
   a. the parents ( )
   b. the children of opposite sex ( )
   c. children of very different age ( )
9. Has there been any inconvenience in the arrangement of sleeping places in rooms which in daytime are mainly used as living room, dining room, kitchen, etc.? ( )
10. Have you missed the opportunity, because of size, to use any of the bedrooms in daytime for another purpose such as for a children's playroom, a study, etc.? ( )
11. Has there been any inconvenience due to the necessity of passing through a room in which somebody sleeps, either early in the morning or late at night? ( )
12. Does the lack of direct access from the bedrooms to bathroom or kitchen cause any difficulty? ( )
13. Are you crowded for dressing space in any of the bedrooms? ( )
14. Does the placement of doors or windows in the bedrooms hinder an otherwise desirable furniture arrangement? ( )
15. Is the sleep of anybody disturbed by
    a. noise from the street ( )

TABLE 10 (*continued*)

b. noise from neighbors ( )
c. noise from other rooms in the home
   1. bedrooms too close to kitchen, bathroom, or living room ( )
   2. generally bad insulation ( )
16. Has there been any disadvantage in the necessity of climbing stairs to the bedrooms for
   a. small children ( )
   b. ailing adults ( )
17. Are the light arrangements for dressing in the bedrooms unsatisfactory because of inadequate
   a. window placement ( )
   b. outlets for artificial light ( )
18. Are you dissatisfied with the ventilation of your bedrooms? ( )
19. Is your bedroom-closet space inadequate in regard to
   a. size ( )
   b. location ( )
   c. number ( )
   d. equipment ( )

Housework

20. Are there times when your kitchen work is interfered with by other activities, such as play, hobby, eating, washing, hanging around, etc.? ( )
21. Do you feel the kitchen is too small
   a. as an all-day center for your housekeeping activities ( )
   b. for others to help you with your kitchen work ( )
   c. for others to keep you company while you work ( )
22. Are you annoyed because the kitchen is badly insulated in regard to
   a. noise ( )
   b. odors ( )
23. Is your kitchen work made difficult by insufficient or badly located
   a. windows ( )
   b. artificial light ( )
   c. ventilation ( )
24. Is the kitchen badly located
   a. as a center for general house cleaning
      1. consider stairs ( )
      2. consider trespassing ( )
      3. consider distance ( )
   b. in relation to the entrance door ( )
   c. in relation to the bathroom ( )
   d. in relation to the laundry, etc. ( )
   e. for the supervision of children ( )
25. Is your work in the kitchen made difficult by cupboards or drawers that are inadequate in regard to
   a. size ( )
   b. location ( )
   c. number ( )
   d. equipment ( )
26. Is your work in the kitchen made difficult by inadequate equipment in regard to
   a. storage of perishable food ( )
   b. work space ( )
   c. stove ( )
   d. location of sink, stove, and work space in relation to each other ( )
   e. garbage disposal ( )
27. Do you feel urgent need for more storage space outside the kitchen, such as basement, attic, etc.? ( )
28. Is your housework strained by inadequate
   a. laundry facilities ( )

TABLE 10 (*continued*)

b. opportunities to dry your laundry ( )
c. space to iron your laundry ( )

29. Are the heating facilities inconvenient because
    a. you have to carry fuel ( )
    b. it is hard to start the fire ( )
    c. the living room is underheated ( )
    d. the bathroom is underheated ( )
    e. the bedrooms are underheated ( )
30. Are you severely inconvenienced by lack of hot water? ( )
31. Do you miss adequate garage or parking facilities? ( )

Children

32. Have you missed the opportunity of providing for your children
    a. a room of their own ( )
    b. a specially furnished corner for play, hobby, or study ( )
33. Have you missed a place to leave your infant unsupervised in the open air, such as balcony, porch, or yard? ( )
34. Have you felt the disadvantage of being unable to provide for your children
    a. an easily supervised space for play or study at home ( )
    b. an easily supervised place in the open air, right outside your home ( )
    c. a play space where they can be as noisy and careless as they want to be ( )
    d. open-air play space in park or playground ( )
    e. nursery school facilities ( )
    f. participation in clubs, etc. ( )
    g. supervision when you have to leave home ( )
    h. company of other children their own age ( )
35. Have you had difficulties in making adequate arrangements in case of illness in regard to
    a. isolation ( )
    b. supervision from the kitchen in daytime ( )
    c. supervision from the bedroom at night ( )

Leisure

36. Have you felt the desire for an extra room to which somebody might want to retire from the general living room in order to
    a. study ( )
    b. concentrate on a hobby ( )
    c. establish a workshop ( )
    d. be undisturbed by radio or listen to it alone ( )
37. Could you provide for the above activities by increasing the size of the following rooms
    a. living room ( )
    b. kitchen ( )
    c. bedroom ( )
    d. dining room or dinette ( )
    e. utility space such as basement, garage, etc. ( )
38. Have you been inconvenienced in the living room by noise due to
    a. insufficient insulation against neighbors ( )
    b. insufficient insulation between rooms ( )
    c. lack of doors ( )
39. Have you been inconvenienced by the necessity of passing through the living room in communicating between the kitchen, bedroom, bathroom, etc.? ( )
40. Have you been unable to place enough furniture in the living room or to arrange it adequately because of
    a. limited size
    b. inconvenient location of doors ( )
    c. insufficient or badly located light plugs ( )

TABLE 10 (*continued*)

41. Have you missed a comparatively private space out of doors for your leisure time, such as a balcony, porch, or pleasant and isolated back yard?   (   )

Social Life

42. When the parents have visitors in the evening, does it interfere with other members of the family in their
    a. recreation   (   )
    b. study   (   )
    c. bedtime   (   )
43. Would you like to let your children bring home friends, if only
    a. you had an additional room   (   )
    b. the living room, kitchen, bedroom, or dinette were larger   (   )
44. When you entertain visitors in the evening
    a. are you crowded at mealtimes   (   )
    b. do you therefore refrain from serving meals   (   )
    c. do you therefore refrain from inviting visitors   (   )
    d. are you annoyed by having to stay in the same room after dinner   (   )
45. When you have visitors in the evening, do you have to be careful in regard to noise
    a. for the sake of your neighbors   (   )
    b. for the sake of your sleeping children   (   )
46. Do you often feel the inconvenience of not being able to accommodate overnight guests?   (   )
47. Is the room in which you entertain convenient to the entrance door, making it unnecessary for visitors to cross rooms that are used for other purposes?   (   )
48. Have you been dissatisfied with the entrance to your home, because of
    a. lack of lighting   (   )
    b. lack of shelter against rain   (   )
49. Has there been any disadvantage in the necessity of climbing stairs to reach the entrance of your home, for
    a. small children   (   )
    b. ailing adults   (   )

Location

50. Is there any inconvenience in the distance from your home to
    a. occupational work   (   )
    b. schools   (   )
    c. playgrounds   (   )
    d. friends and relatives   (   )
    e. shopping   (   )
    f. movies   (   )
    g. club meetings   (   )

A Difficult Choice

The young couple that stand at the beginning of their family career have to choose from a tremendous variety of housing conditions. Superficially, we talk about one-bedroom, two-bedroom, and three-bedroom units, and often the young couple are satisfied in the beginning to step into any shelter which they can afford and which is not clearly too small for their needs. In the selection of the family home, however, much more is involved than the appropriation of so many square feet of sheltered space.

Somehow, in talking about *the* American family and about *the* American home, we go on the assumption that there is such a thing as a standard family type from which individual cases may deviate as exceptions only. Actually, American family and home life is composed of widely divergent and even sharply contrasting patterns. There is no such thing as *the* American home other than in terms of a crude and almost useless abstraction. Wherever research or personal experience leads us into contact with a large number of family homes, we may be surprised how little they have in common.

This is particularly true if we focus attention upon the process of home adjustment, which may vary both according to family attitudes and according to the physical structure of the residence. Moreover, the financial arrangements leading to the possession of the family home may vary greatly and — as we have seen — thereby affect the rest of the family budget and the standard of living.

Location and the Family Cycle

Americans are marrying today at a younger age than has been the case for many decades and before they are quite ready to settle down to the task of child rearing. Young couples tend to look for quarters close to the center of the city partly because they appreciate proximity to their places of work and to places of commercial entertainment and partly because low rentals in limited dwelling units may make it possible to save for the down payment on their future house. After a few years the young family settles down at the periphery of the city in a subdivision consisting of new homes that attract other families just about beginning to raise their children. In another few years the streets and backyards in this district will be filled with roaming children. In a few more, they will be sipping their ice cream sodas in the corner drugstore. Common experiences in such neighborhoods, where the phases of many family cycles run parallel, are apt to create a feeling of attachment to the district, which becomes sprinkled with acquaintances and friends of long standing. This pattern of planting the home in a new environment and growing up together with a gradually stabilizing community comes perhaps closest to what we have in mind when we mention the American family home. This pattern, however, is by no means the only one.

The neighborhood in which the family settles down may undergo changes while the children are growing up. It may lose desirability for family living. In the past, there were few guarantees for the stabilization of neighborhood qualities, and even today conditions are not foolproof either in the modern housing project or in the carefully zoned high-class residential district. Where the city extends rapidly, families will be forced to move repeatedly in order to retain a desirable house and congenial neighborhood conditions. The family may not be financially able to do so or may prefer to stay in order to permit the children to remain in the same school or in contact with an established playground. The family father will often have to make difficult decisions between varying financial and functional advantages and disadvantages. We must also consider the situation of the older couple. They may be living — after the children have left home — in a house too large for their needs, in a neighborhood which has lost its original meaning and to which they are attached by memory rather than by present requirements. They may consider moving closer to the center of the city once more.

Housing conditions may roughly approximate the above cycle. Deviations are probably frequent. There are children in the city streets and in the urban fringe. There are adolescents in the slums and in the staid middle-class neighborhood. The individual family may be higher in status and morale than its neighborhood, or it may be lower; on the road of seeking admittance to a better environment, or sinking to a lower level. Economic success or misfortune may determine the attitude toward the family home; it may be looked upon as an achievement, as the fulfillment of long-harbored ambitions, or as a comedown, in an environment to be loathed and contemptuously sneered at. And any urban environment contains families with mixed attitudes about the home base.

Structure and the Family Cycle

In most cases, the home is intended to serve the needs of the family through successive phases of the family cycle. It has to be large enough to accommodate the time of maximum requirements, when the children approach adulthood, and it has to be easily manageable when the children leave to establish homes of their own. The residence may be planned at an early stage for gradual additions. There may be sufficient rooms to provide private bedroom-study combinations for all the children, and these rooms may be converted to other uses at later phases of the family cycle. On the other hand, many families will be obliged to economize during the period of maximum needs in order to have funds for educational and other expenditures.

The main idea the father of a family should have in mind is that there will have to be compromise. There is no such thing as an ideal house for the middle-class or lower-class American family. Certain needs will have to be sacrificed for the sake of others. There are homes which provide a maximum of privacy to the individual members of the family, and others which are designed with emphasis upon the common living room space. The family will have to decide whether individualized activities or common gatherings shall be given preference.

The home may be looked upon as a makeshift city dormitory, compensated for by investment in and care for a family summer home; or the family may make its home its hobby and sacrifice other luxury items in the budget. The home may be pleasantly located for the enjoyment of the summer months, with certain inconveniences to bear in the winter, or it may be comfortable all through the year but not too well located for the enjoyment of out-door activities in the backyard or wider surroundings. The home may be designed to accommodate the needs of the father, who may want a study on the main floor while the children are crowded up-stairs for sleeping accommodations. It may be a home which favors the mother with a commodious kitchen, laundry, and utility room but with economy applied to the living room–dining room unit. Within a given rental or purchasing price, the family cannot have everything. If it is to be a home for the children with the living room practically turned into a nursery, then the parents will find themselves frustrated in their wish for privacy and entertaining.

Frequently the selection of a home is made with only one thing in mind: to avoid the greatest inconvenience experienced in present quarters. To meet the challenge requires intelligence as well as imagination: to pass in review, when selecting the family residence, the entire range of home activities and to consider their adaptability to a given physical structure.

The Contribution of Design and Equipment

The market at present is swamped with housing pamphlets, books, and magazines which leave most families unsatisfied with the quarters they occupy. We have come a long way in our ability to provide through "functional" design a floor plan that will make the family feel at home. In order not to be misled in the appreciation of different alternatives of design, it may be wise to define clearly what design and equipment can do and cannot do for the family.

The total floor space which the family commands within its budget is by and large delimited. An old structure, of course, will yield more space than a more recent one at the same price. We have to make up our mind whether we want to contend with a somewhat obsolete structure in perhaps not quite so good a neighborhood or whether we want to take advantage of the low maintenance costs of a modern structure and the optimistic spirit pervading a subdivision of new homes. This consideration will more or less decide how much total floor space we shall have available. Then comes the question of whether we favor privacy or space in the home. Do we want fewer but larger rooms, or more rooms at the cost of size? No skillful design can give us both spaciousness and privacy at the same time.

In viewing the manner in which the rooms are connected with each other, i.e., in considering the floor plan proper, we have to keep an eye on three things: transportation difficulties, the need for noise insulation, and readiness of communication between rooms related to each other by the nature of the activities that will be assigned to them.

Most modern families will want to have the dining space close to the kitchen in order to cut down on labor in connection with the setting of the table and the serving of food. Great attention is given at present to the breakfast nook in the kitchen. It saves transportation in the serving of informal meals in the routine of everyday life. While domestic service was readily available, there was an advantage in a long distance between kitchen and dining room because it kept the noise of the work space separate from the dining table and the living room.

Close proximity of activities invites needless interference. This concerns not only the clatter of dishwashing immediately after meals; it is just as relevant with regard to the relation of sleeping quarters and bathroom to each other. They should be close in order to accommodate a smooth functioning of the dressing and washing routine in the morning. As sleep-

DESIRABLE APARTMENT CHARACTERISTICS

THIS   NOT THIS

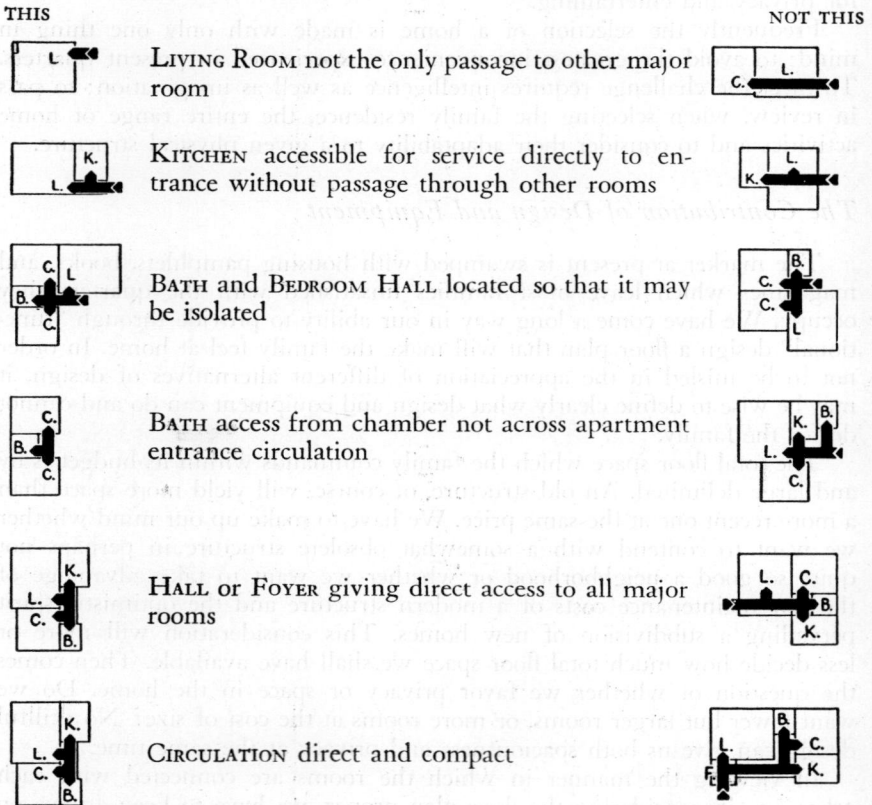

LIVING ROOM not the only passage to other major room

KITCHEN accessible for service directly to entrance without passage through other rooms

BATH and BEDROOM HALL located so that it may be isolated

BATH access from chamber not across apartment entrance circulation

HALL or FOYER giving direct access to all major rooms

CIRCULATION direct and compact

FIGURE 22. INCONVENIENCES AND CONVENIENCES IN DESIGN

(From "Rent to Space," by B. J. Harrison, H. D. Whitney, and Cloethiel Woodward; *Architectural Forum*, July, 1936)

ing and toilet activities of the family members overlap, however, irritation may be caused if the noise of flushing and the drawing of a bath penetrates into adjacent sleeping quarters.

In modern structures the rigidity of the alternative between convenient proximity and the avoidance of noise interference is broken down to a certain extent by insulation techniques. In the older structures, however, the floor plan should be studied carefully with both alternatives in mind.

The ideal arrangement of communications would make each individual room accessible directly to hall and entrance door without making the crossing of other rooms necessary. This cannot always be accomplished. Space is expensive and cannot be readily wasted on communications that are not absolutely necessary. Doors are generally desirable, but an excess of doors embarrasses the family by lack of wall space against which larger pieces of furniture can be placed.

To decide whether the flow of traffic is adequately arranged for by the architect, it will be necessary to imagine the home activities of the family fitted into the floor plan. For instance, one must anticipate whether there will be irritation because the living room has been placed directly at the entrance door so that neither kitchen nor dining room nor any of the bedrooms can be reached without crossing the common living room space. There are freak solutions, where a bedroom is accessible only through the kitchen or through another bedroom, or where the dining room is placed behind the kitchen. How much of this cross-routing of traffic will be acceptable will differ with the individual family.

There remains the decision, which in most cases runs parallel to the choice between an old or a modern structure, whether expenditures should go for space rather than modern equipment or vice versa. Where space requirements are urgent, as in families with many children, preference may be given to number and size of available rooms. Modern equipment, however, is a temptation to the housewife; and if proper arrangements can be made and the family members can be circumspect with regard to each other, or if there is a minimum requirement for privacy, a more compact home may be chosen in which an efficient setup of equipment makes life tolerable and convenient even in more limited quarters.

In considering structure and plan, both parents will have to weigh against each other the relative advantages of space and privacy, of accessibility of facilities and noise interferences, and finally of an increase of the total floor space and expensive but convenient and labor-saving equipment.

Techniques of Home Adjustment

Fortunately, there is a personal as well as a material side to the process of home adjustment. Sooner or later after the home has been selected, the need for special adjustments becomes apparent. It seldom fits like a glove. There may not be a sufficient number of rooms to keep interfering activities apart from each other. Inadequacies in the floor plan may have to be overcome by skillful arrangement of the routine of family life.

There are several ways by which the crowded homes of today are made more or less livable. Rooms may be furnished in such a manner as to accommodate not only one but two or more functions. The daily routine will then be established in such a manner that divergent activities will not be delegated to the same room at the same time but spread out over the twenty-four hours of the day without coming into direct contact with each other. Piano practice is reserved for the afternoon hours, while in the evening the living room stands available for less monopolizing activities. The children may do their homework in the dining room, but at dinner time they have to be through so that the housewife may set the table.

It is not always possible to separate mutually interfering home activities from each other by different time assignments. In that case the same activity may have to be assigned to different rooms at different times of the day. The members of the family then find themselves migrating through the residence in a consciously or automatically developed system of avoidance techniques.

The children's homework may begin during the afternoon hours in the living room, where more agreeable accommodations are available in the form of a writing desk or a radio that keeps the spirit entertained while the mind wrestles with arithmetic, and it may be continued in the evening hours in the bedroom-study combination to avoid the distracting chatter of the rest of the family and possibly their friends. Meals may be taken in the kitchen, but at times of cumbersome preparations for a social affair, on baking days, or when the mechanically inclined son has the kitchen littered with parts of a dismembered radio, they may be taken in the dining or living room. The variations of this general scheme are innumerable.

In many instances, of course, there is no other way out than to harden the family against irritations. The extent to which it is possible to concentrate on studies or reading while the radio is going full blast or while the living room is quivering with conversation, has only been touched upon by research. Casual observation shows that considerable tolerance for such conflicting stimuli can be obtained. We also know, however, that the ability to develop this kind of tolerance varies considerably from individual to individual. Nervous irritation and lack of efficiency may well be the consequence. Extreme sensitivity in some families may require the provision of more separate rooms, not only bedrooms but also acoustically separate units in the general living room space.

Problems arise frequently in connection with the entertainment of the special friends of individual members of the family. If no special recreation or rumpus room is available for the younger generation, or if the dining room cannot be closed off from the living room, or if some similar arrangement cannot be arrived at, we may have to resort to one of the two avoidance techniques that are applied in such instances: the rest of the family retires to their respective bedrooms or they plan these occasions carefully for evenings on which either the parents or the younger generation leave for the movies or some other activity outside the home. The desirability of a second living room is indicated by the frequency with which these conflicts occur in the average middle-class family.

There is a trend, as we know, toward the transfer of certain functions from the family home to neighborhood facilities or public institutions such as libraries, dance halls, restaurants, and places of commercial entertainment. This trend is not unrelated to the compression of the family home into structures of truly minimum size which allow only for the most informal and strictly relaxing type of leisure time activities. There is efficiency in arrangements which provide — albeit outside the individual home — specialized facilities for specialized activities. Fortunately this trend runs parallel to the increasing individualization of leisure time activities. Symptoms of maladjustment are apt to occur most frequently where the family home because of its compactness ceases to offer needed facilities, particularly for the younger generation — before community facilities have developed that will absorb the overflow from family residences. (See Fig. 23.)

The Family Home of the Future

The family home of the future will probably be smaller and more compact than that of the past. It will be far better equipped and in that manner

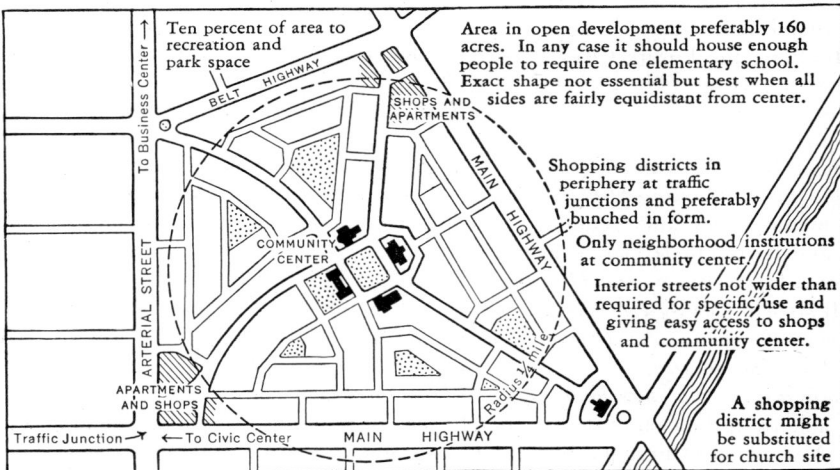

FIGURE 23. NEIGHBORHOODS FOR FAMILY LIVING

(From *Housing for the Machine Age*, by Clarence A. Perry; New York, 1939)

it will cut down upon the inconveniences involved in crowded living conditions. If prefabrication ever gains ground, this trend will be further reinforced. Homes will become highly mobile and more easily abandoned because of the lower unit price. But even without prefabrication, it is not unwarranted to expect further changes in our attitudes toward the family home. Whether prefabrication will be the deciding factor, or flexibility in economic arrangements of rental or contract of home purchase, or the mere insight that different types of homes and home environments are best suited for the needs in different phases of the family cycle, we may have to face the fact that the family residence as a firm center of the individual life-history is gradually fading out of the picture.

To be sure, we have to warn against any oversimplification of our views on family housing. The variety of patterns of home adjustment coexisting in this country is enormous. They reach from the shacks of the share-croppers in the South to the Long Island mansions of the aristocracy. But if any consistent trend of change in urban housing can be discerned in these past decades, it is in the direction of smaller and more mobile homes. The developments of the modern housing industry and the tendency toward individualization in the modern family are both contributing factors.

It is doubtful whether we shall be able to stem the tide by the proclamation of more conservative values. But we may conceive it as our task to avoid those symptoms of disorganization which originate in one-sided developments. Technological progress and the change in attitudes toward the family home have to be kept in balance with each other.

SELECTED READINGS

American Housing: Problems and Prospects (New York: The Twentieth Century Fund, 1944).

"Building the Future City," *Annals of the American Academy of Political and Social Science* (Nov., 1945).

CHURCHILL, HENRY, *The City Is the People* (New York: Reynal and Hitchcock, 1945).

DEAN, JOHN P., *Home Ownership — Is It Sound?* (New York: Harper, 1945).

The Farm Housing Problem, U. S. Department of Agriculture, Postwar Economic Policy and Planning, Hearings before the Subcommittee on Housing and Urban Redevelopment, p. 811.

FORD, JAMES, *Slums and Housing* (Cambridge: Harvard University Press, 1936).

MUMFORD, LEWIS, *The Culture of Cities* (New York: Harcourt, Brace, 1938).

PERRY, CLARENCE A., *Housing for the Machine Age* (New York: Russell Sage Foundation, 1939).

Planning the Neighborhood and *Planning the Home for Occupancy*. Both available from the Committee on the Hygiene of Housing, American Public Health Association (Chicago: Public Administration Service, 1938 and 1950).

SERT, I. L., *Can Our Cities Survive?* (Cambridge: Harvard University Press, 1944).

WRIGHT, HENRY, *Rehousing Urban America* (New York: Columbia University Press, 1935).

TOPICS FOR DISCUSSION AND REPORTS

1. Report the housing history of your own family.
2. Discuss and criticize the process of home adjustment in your own family home.
3. Indicate the type of family residence in which you hope to settle when you marry and start raising children.
4. Discuss different types of neighborhoods with regard to their value for family living.
5. Collect information from a specific family about composition, income, status, attitudes, and home activities; and use this information in proposing the type of residence which would best accommodate their needs.

6. Discuss, for a number of specific family situations, the question whether the families involved should buy or rent a home.
7. Discuss the different housing needs that are apt to arise in the life cycle of the type of family you are familiar with.
8. What are the advantages of apartment-house living for the family at specific stages of its development?
9. Investigate the "functional" aspects of the dwelling units used by a number of preliterate societies.
10. Discuss the effects upon other items of the family budget of increasing or decreasing housing expenditures and reflect upon the sociopsychological consequences.

Chapter Eighteen

Running Home and Household

FRANK D. AND AMEY E. WATSON

IN EARLIER days marriage was essentially a partnership. The woman spun and wove and produced many goods in the home. Neither husband nor wife supported the other. Each was in reality self-supporting, and the children also soon helped in the productive activities of the home. Today young people are raising seriously the following questions: Is it healthy for women to expect to be supported in idleness? Should women, on the other hand, prefer to be self-supporting a large part of their lives, even while they continue to carry their lessened home responsibilities? Is a woman supporting herself when she makes her contribution to the partnership through the competent management and work of the home?

Andrews expresses one point of view with vigor: [1]

> The American household, as its social ideal takes form, is an institution in which two adults form a partnership with equal responsibilities, make equal contributions to its support, and draw out equal returns not only in the daily physical services of food, clothing, and shelter but also in the broadening of experience and all the satisfactions of life. As junior partners enter the group, they are advanced as rapidly as possible to a full partnership relation. At its best the group provides for its members, adult and child alike, broad opportunity for the development of individual personality. As members of a social group that cares, the family supports each member as long as that is necessary and puts demands upon him when he can bear them, criticizes or encourages in turn as either is needed, and shapes the individual to take a place as a man or woman in the world.

It is the thesis of this chapter that sound principles of home administration and household management are essential to provide adequate physical care and psychological and emotional guidance to family members and that, moreover, it takes two alert and conscientious partners (both *father* and mother), equipped with understanding and fortified with the increasing scientific knowledge of child development and of skills in human relationships, to realize the full possibilities of family life at its highest level.

JOINT PLANNING FOR FAMILY LIVING

Most persons marry with certain goals in view and, consciously or otherwise, envisage to themselves the kind of family life which will harmonize with these objectives. If the couple are wisely mated, these objectives

[1] Benjamin R. Andrews, *The Economics of the Household* (New York: Macmillan, 1935), p. v.

532

will largely coincide — a happy circumstance, because the first years of marriage are concerned with the working out together of common values and aspirations. In some cases, however (and especially so during these hectic war and cold-war years), young people have rushed into marriage with little thought for the future, hoping that love will suffice and that the future will take care of itself.

All newlyweds who set up permanent homes must eventually face the problems of family administration and home management. If they wish to increase satisfactions in their home, plans and policies must be formulated and carried out competently. The formulation of plans and policies is called "family administration"; the execution of these policies is known as "the management of family life." Both of these terms are borrowed from industry but have a slightly different meaning when applied to the home. Some may object to bringing the concepts of the market place into home life, which all agree is primarily concerned with affection and the higher social and spiritual values. It is true that the objectives of homemaking are human satisfactions and development rather than increased production or profits. Yet the best type of family life doesn't just happen; it is the result of conscious planning and wise execution of details by husband and wife as two coordinate partners.

In the following discussion the larger aspects of *homemaking* are differentiated from the more routine business of *housekeeping*. Housekeeping is to be understood as comprising the productive work of the household, such as preparing food, clothing, and shelter for all those who live under a common roof. Housekeeping is concerned primarily with the mechanics of living. Homemaking is a broader term, specifying the direction of the personal life of the family group. In line with this distinction, the terms "family administration" and "management of family life" are to be differentiated from the terms "household administration" and "household management." Homemaking is here considered a joint enterprise of husband and wife.

Careful cooperative planning by both partners is necessary to achieve maximum enjoyment in a home. The realization by each mate that the responsibility for determining all major policies belongs to them *both* is perhaps the first important step in the sound administration of the home. Frequently the full responsibility, including even policy making, is left entirely to the wife. Yet the foundations of democracy in family life are laid in the skillful cooperation of two equal partners, using accepted techniques of family administration. The story is told of the couple who agreed early in their married life that all important decisions should be made by the man and all unimportant ones by the wife. The man chuckled a few years later when he told a friend that apparently all decisions were unimportant as his wife made them all! A man who is thus dominated by his wife may feel a pride in her ability, but difficulty lies ahead when growing sons and daughters refuse to accept the domination of their mother.

Homemaking as a partnership of two equals is considered impractical by such writers as Henry Carey,[2] who in an amusing article describes this type of family life as "a double-headed monster" which can have no unity. His description of the immature methods which some women use to attain their ends and of the low level of relationship which exists between some husbands and wives makes colorful reading but offers little constructive help toward sound and successful family relations.

TECHNIQUES FOR CREATIVE DECISIONS

In order that husband and wife may learn quickly to make decisions together, they should begin to work out common values and plans as soon as possible after they become engaged.

A concrete opportunity to plan together is given all young couples when they plan the wedding. This event, which should be a time for deep understanding and mutual satisfaction, is too often marred by the domination of parents (especially those of the bride) and by friction and over-fatigue on the part of both bride and groom. Although it is true that the wedding is the bride's *great* day, she should never fail to show consideration for the wishes of her partner. One couple became engaged when they were by no means young, and the ideas of both about marriage were already crystallized. The man in question, a free-thinker who liked simplicity, felt that a formal church wedding was out of the question for him. The bride and her father, however, as High-Church Episcopalians, felt that to have a fashionable wedding in their own church with all the usual formalities was the only possible plan. The groom tried to give in graciously to the wishes of the bride and her family but unconsciously felt deep resentment and unhappiness during the whole wedding. That no consideration was paid to his wishes in the matter meant that a real opportunity was lost for laying sound foundations for a harmonious honeymoon and for later successful accommodation.

The husband and wife as administrators of their joint lives may be compared to a board of directors of a company which formulates the policies of the concern. If the man thinks of the woman as a toy or as an incompetent, unable to think clearly and to make mature, responsible decisions, then joint policy making is impossible from the start.

The ability to think and plan creatively may be rare, but education for family life is seeking to develop more such creative personalities. Many young people have been overprotected by indulgent parents and hence find great difficulty in arriving jointly at any important decisions. Each mate must learn to view his own desires or wishes in relation to those of his mate if he is to achieve "creative accommodation,"[3] that is, the ability to work out solutions which will satisfy the wishes and purposes of both parties but which will give to each something more than either could have secured

[2] Henry R. Carey, "This Two-Headed Monster — The Family," *Harper's Magazine,* 156 (Jan., 1928), pp. 162–171.

[3] For a more complete discussion of creative accommodation, see Hornell H. Hart and Ella B. Hart, *Personality and the Family* (rev. ed.; Boston: Heath, 1941), pp. 320–338.

alone. Sait [4] adds: "Far more feasible for most couples is a working agreement as to the sphere in which one or the other is to be the leader and may count on willing cooperation. . . . Harmonious interdependence of the activities of husband and wife is scarcely possible without a fundamental agreement as to the goals they accept at the outset of marriage; the common objectives to the attainment of which they dedicate themselves."

The program worked out should be the result of joint decisions in which neither husband nor wife dictates the terms. All the major decisions must be measured and weighed carefully and skillfully so that each learns to play his part in the developing relation and in the resulting home life.

OBJECTIVES OF HOMEMAKING

The roles which husbands and wives are to play will depend largely on their skills, abilities, and personality make-up, as well as on their goals and objectives. Since the home is primarily the expression of the personalities of those who comprise it, one is not surprised to find many different objectives in homemaking. Some persons want home to be a quiet and peaceful place where they can rest and relax; others prefer much social life, with constant entertaining and gaiety. Some stress orderliness and punctuality, while others find an atmosphere of casualness essential to their happiness. If such apparently different objectives are to be combined into a harmonious whole, the spirit and practice of creative accommodation must be ever present, supported by mutual consideration, recognition of individuality, and genuine affection.

From such widely varying objectives in homemaking, can any general principles be formulated? Two authorities have attempted to answer this question. Groves states: [5]

There is only one test for a home. Does it send out its members well trained to play the game of life? If not, no matter how orderly and comfortable it may be, it is a mere shell of a home.

Richardson is even more explicit: [6]

We are more and more subordinating all other functions of the home to attaining its fundamental *raison d'être* which is to give refreshment and strength to body and spirit through experiences which family life alone is able to furnish, to provide activities, experiences and relationships, essential for the continued growth and all around development of both children and adults. . . . The type of home which today can succeed in maintaining its ideals must represent a democratic organization of its members, one in

[4] Una B. Sait, *New Horizons for the Family* (New York: Macmillan, 1938), p. 622. By permission of The Macmillan Company.
[5] Ernest R. Groves, quoted by Anna E. Richardson, "The Woman Administrator in the Modern Home," *Annals of the American Academy of Political and Social Science,* 143 (May, 1929), p. 24.
[6] Richardson, *op. cit.*

which each has a share in the determination of policies, a responsibility for carrying them out, and rights and privileges to be respected, as well as duties to perform.

In the light of these statements, can we not agree that while the objectives of individual homes may and should differ widely, all must conform to certain general underlying principles if the home is to be built on healthy foundations? To study these fundamental principles of sound homemaking and adjust their objectives accordingly is the responsibility of both partners. One family group known to the authors is emphasizing social climbing, with eyes constantly on the prestige value of every decision made. As a result, a car has been purchased well outside the amount set by the budget, and exclusive club memberships have been bought without regard to the fundamental and essential demands of paying everyday bills. In another home the emphasis is placed on very different values. Both husband and wife believe in freedom of expression for the children so far as this is consistent with consideration for others and the realities of life. Instead of one high-priced car, the needs of all the family were met by two low-priced cars, one of which was positively shabby but quite good enough for the youngsters to "run around" in and take apart when they wished. Are not the objectives of this family group healthier and socially more sound than those of the other?

RANGE OF CHOICE IN POLICY MAKING

Once their objectives are clarified, young people of imagination and resourcefulness find a wide range of choice open to them in planning their life together. Traditional patterns are easily followed but may cause the couple to miss much real happiness. We would advocate the laying out of plans which express the individuality of both partners. There are limitations, of course, within which every family must operate. For example, early planning would have first to consider the problems of self-support. Plans for building the home usually revolve around the man's career or job. If he is likely to be transferred frequently, it may be better to rent. The young man has usually decided on his profession or occupation before he becomes engaged, and a shift in his plans may often be both undesirable and impossible. Yet the decision as to where that living is to be made is frequently a choice which can be faced and made by young people together, as in the following instance:

A young college graduate fell in love with a young woman, also a college graduate, who was holding a job as secretary in a girl's private school in a large eastern city. He took a job in a business firm in the same city and they soon married. Neither liked city life. The wife was earning a little more than the husband but neither one had additional resources. If the wife had given up her job, their income would have been too small for their accustomed standard of living in the city. After a year of married life with both working, they decided that they wanted children and a more interesting life in some country community. Both of them gave up their jobs and moved to a New England community. There they set up a printing business in which both worked. Within a year they began to make good profits. The husband found that he could qualify as a teacher in the high school and still run their printing press on the side. They now could plan their first child. While both had to work as hard as in the city, they found life here more interesting. They had the courage to break from the traditional pattern of their many friends and to seek new pastures of their own choosing. Many young veterans and their wives are showing great originality in working out their life plans together.

Here are a few of the major problems that should be considered by engaged or early married couples as they plan their life together:

1. What are to be the sources of the family income? (a) the husband's earnings alone? or (b) the husband's and wife's earnings together? or (c) subsidies from one or both parental families, if such funds are available, if the families are willing, and if more professional training is needed? Does the GI Bill of Rights offer adequate income for further education, and does vocational rehabilitation offer a resource if the man or wife qualifies?

2. In the light of the probable family income for (a) the next year, and (b) the next five, ten, and fifteen years, what general level of living can best be set up to meet the needs of all? How shall the income be allocated to various items of the budget, including savings?

3. Are children desired by both parents? If not, how shall the cravings of the one who wishes parenthood be satisfied, if there is one such? If there are to be no children because of unsound heredity or for other reasons, should adoption be considered? If children are desired by both, are they to be planned for immediately? Should birth control methods be used? If so, which birth control methods are most satisfactory and healthful for both? How many children are desired and how should they be spaced?

4. Do the young couple want to buy a home eventually and if so, what housing arrangements can best be made temporarily, especially in the light of the present housing shortage? Must the couple live with relatives at first and if so just how should the expenses be shared? Do the young couple prefer to live eventually in city, country, or suburb? What type of house can they afford?

5. What general plans shall be made for the running of the home? (a) In the light of the wife's interests and abilities, and the exigencies of the budget, what is to be her role — primarily home manager with part-time assistance, or home manager and actual housekeeper, doing all or most of the work? (b) In the light of the husband's paid job and his interests, can he and does he wish to carry certain responsibilities in the home? If so, just what? (c) If and when there are children, what responsibilities can be delegated to each child at the appropriate age?

(d) If it is agreed that paid workers are to be employed, what are the personnel principles on the basis of which paid help is to be employed? Shall they live in or out?

6. What plans should be made for the best care of the health of the family in view of its needs and resources? What family physician or clinic shall be used? Shall the family take out some form of hospitalization or health insurance?

7. If children are planned for, should some provision be made in early marriage to start an educational fund for schooling, college, or later professional training? What schools shall the children attend — nursery school, public or private schools?

8. What provisions should be made for old age or premature death of either mate?

9. What leisure-time activities are enjoyed by both and therefore are to be carried on together and which are to be continued individually? As one example, to what type of summer vacation should the married couple and the family look forward? Do they prefer to travel and explore many new places, or do they prefer to get their roots into one community where the family may return year after year?

10. What contribution does the family as a unit wish to make to the church and to the community, (a) financially, (b) in terms of service?

The above list does not attempt to be all-inclusive. Many other vital policies will need to be formulated, such as the choice of church connections, the amount and type of entertaining, and the wise use of credit, including charge accounts at stores and installment buying.

CHILDREN AS JUNIOR PARTNERS IN POLICY MAKING

When a married couple has learned the pattern of mutual consideration and joint policy making, it is far easier as children arrive and grow up to give them a voice in family administration as junior partners, and to train them to consider and weigh the various factors that must be constantly faced when new plans are to be made. How soon can small children be brought into family plans, and how early can they have a real voice in determining family policies? Family councils of all members in which children are expected to discuss with their parents all important policies which concern them, are vital elements in democratic family life and should be encouraged and strengthened.[7] In the area of family finance, many fathers and mothers miss the opportunity to take their growing sons and daughters into their confidence, to tell them what the family income is and whence it comes. Here is a chance to think through as a family the ratio of allowances to yearly expenses and to see them in terms of the resources of the whole family for the year. At an early stage in their adolescent development, young people can and should be taught to respect the contribution which the mother makes by her daily services within the home and by her activities for others outside the home, whether paid

[7] See our earlier discussion of the family council, pp. 476–477.

or volunteer. They can also gain an interest in and an attitude of appreciation for their father's work outside the home, and a desire to carry their share of responsibility, both within and without the home.

The attitudes of a number of young women in a junior college toward the income sent them by their fathers was studied by one of the authors. None of the group knew any of the details of the family income. Their main idea was to "work" father for all they could get, and give little or nothing in return. As they learned to "work" their fathers, so will they use the same techniques with the husband at a later date!

The family has a real opportunity and a challenging responsibility to educate its young people in problems of money management and financial responsibility so that they may later manage successfully the finances and the productive work of their own homes. The ability to face a situation objectively, to analyze it into its elements, and to work through to a solution of the difficulties involved should be developed in children by practice at an early date in their development. This does not mean that children should be weighed down by family problems before they are old enough to understand them or before they can be trusted to keep confidential matters to themselves, but it does mean that they should not be shielded and overprotected from the realities of life.[8] They should be taught the actual value of human labor and should not be allowed to exploit their parents, the household employee, or any other persons. To this end they should be allowed to join in family judgments and to share in making family decisions as soon as they can really understand what is involved.

DIVISION OF LABOR IN HOME MANAGEMENT

Throughout the history of the human race, there has been a division of labor between the sexes, which has, however, varied from culture to culture.[9] In our Euro-American society, since industrialization removed domestic manufacture to the factory, men have been considered primarily responsible for earning the actual money for the family. To the wife was usually delegated the responsibility for the management of the home and the care of the children. Yet in millions of homes today mothers are sharing with the father the economic burden of earning the living. They have departed from the pattern which insists that woman's place is in the home. Moreover, the role of the father as copartner in the management of family

[8] See Bain's discussion of this point, pp. 176–177.

[9] See Margaret Mead, *Sex and Temperament in Three Primitive Societies* (New York: Morrow, 1935) as well as her other interesting reports in this field. See also Amram Scheinfeld, *Women and Men* (New York: Harcourt, Brace, 1944). Scheinfeld emphasizes that the division of labor between the sexes is largely determined biologically. One function is irrevocably and exclusively assigned to one sex, i.e., child bearing. Woman's biological function on the one hand and man's physical strength and athletic performance on the other are to him the outstanding causes of the sex division of labor and will continue to operate in the future. While Scheinfeld also discusses the cultural aspects of sex differences, he does not give them the importance that Margaret Mead does in her studies.

life is becoming increasingly important. To paraphrase Pearl Buck:[10] the home needs more of man, and the outside world needs more of woman.

No substitute can be found for the father-child relationship any more than one can be found for the relation of mother to child. Both parents are of vital importance in the emotional and social development of each child and neither relationship can be delegated to any other person. Only particular aspects of child care can be delegated to relieve both father and mother. It is in the continuity of the love and care of two mature parents that human personalities find security and stability. At different times and at different ages from infancy on through adolescence, one parent or the other may *seem* to be more important, but both are needed, at least in the background, until each child is psychologically weaned and finds his own independent existence.[11]

In the above discussion, the difference between the management of family life and the management of the household should again be emphasized. By the former term is meant the joint direction of detailed plans for the personal living of the family. The affectional side of family life is here emphasized, as contrasted with the work side. The father is as concerned as the mother in the direction of the educational life of the child. Discipline must be administered wisely and consistently by both parents working in harmony. The father who finds time to play games and enter into his child's fun is building a sound basis for the future. The emotional life of the child develops in a far more balanced way when there is a close affectional bond between father and child in addition to that between mother and child. The father has a vital role to play in interpreting community standards to his child and in helping his child build sound relations with his school, his church, and his community.

The responsibility for details of housekeeping and the problems of daily living is usually delegated to the wife as manager of the household, although in the upper income groups that responsibility is sometimes delegated to a paid housekeeper. In either case, a good manager executes these details within the limits decided upon by the partnership. Before she makes her schedules and plans for work, the manager must discriminate between the relative importance of the immediate, insistent tasks and the larger, often far distant, but more important goals. She must decide just *what* tasks must be done at home, just *how* they are to be done, and *by whom* they are to be done. If she has imagination and resourcefulness, she will find that many choices are open to her.

Whatever goal is chosen, the effective home manager will plan, direct, and guide the various detailed operations involved and will check the results against sound standards of performance. She will always keep in mind the fact that a plan or schedule is never an end in itself but only a means to satisfying and effective family living. Therefore any plan adopted will be

[10] See Pearl Buck, *Of Men and Women* (New York: John Day, 1941).
[11] See chap. 16, "The Opportunities of Parenthood," for discussion of the elements in a good parent-child relationship; also O. Spurgeon English, M.D., and Constance J. Foster, *Fathers Are Parents, Too* (New York: Putnam's, 1951).

flexible and subject to change whenever conditions in the home call for a revision of schedules. A good manager arranges her work in the sequence best suited to family needs, interests, work habits, and free time, and plans time and energy-saving combinations of tasks whenever possible. Furthermore, she does such tasks with the aid of the most effective tools available, arranged in the most efficient manner. The wise home manager will also utilize the findings of time and motion studies with layouts to save steps and to reduce fatigue from bad lighting and with studies of heights and postures as at kitchen sinks, laundry tubs, and work tables.

Just *what* tasks are to be carried on in any individual home will depend on many different factors. Certain processes, however, are carried on in every well-ordered home, with superficial differences depending on income level, educational standards, and other characteristics. These constant processes may be called the "invariables," the fundamental units of work in homemaking and housekeeping. If a job analysis were made in any home, these processes would inevitably be found to be present in greater or less degree. A list of these invariables will be found in Table 11.

In addition to the invariables which the authors believe every home must perform if it is to develop normally, a list of "variables" is also offered. When the management of the home is sound and the individual personalities within the home are developing in a wholesome way, the plane of living can be adjusted so that there may be a balance between income and outgo of money, time, and energy. For instance, the standard of food may be kept at a simple level if necessity demands, but it *must* contain the minimum elements of a healthy, well-balanced diet. The amount and style of clothing can be simplified or increased as the income and other factors change; yet there must be a minimum of clothing for warmth, comfort, and decency. The family which is living beyond its income is frequently in trouble and its members are likely to be nervous, irritable, and maladjusted. In a well-ordered society, the competent manager somehow finds sufficient money income to meet fundamental needs and still have time and energy for balanced living after the routine details of personal care are met. See Table 11 below for a list of the major invariables and variables met in the course of family administration and family management.

TABLE 11

MINIMUM ESSENTIALS IN THE ADMINISTRATION AND MANAGEMENT OF FAMILY LIFE,
INCLUDING THE HOUSEHOLD

Invariables	*Variables*
I. PLANNING STANDARD OF LIVING AND OTHER POLICIES	
1. Balance between income and outgo of money, time, and energy	1. More complex standard of living as money income and other resources increase
II. PHYSICAL CARE OF MEMBERS OF THE FAMILY	
1. Processes concerned with food	
a. Planning of meals	a. Planning of more luxurious menus
b. Purchasing of food or gathering it from farm or garden	b. Increase in elaborateness and amount

TABLE 11 (continued)

Invariables	Variables
c. Preparing of food, including regular meals and seasonal food such as pickles, jams, jellies, etc.	c. Increase in quality and elaborateness
d. Serving self and other members of family	d. Varying types and extent of service
e. Clearing away after meals	e. Clearing more complex, due to varying standards of entertainment
f. Refrigeration and other care of food	f. Quick freeze services, etc.

2. Processes concerned with clothing

Invariables	Variables
a. Planning clothing budget for each member of family	a. Planning for varying amounts and standards of style, neatness, and beauty
b. Purchasing clothing or buying goods for making	b. Increased quality, style, and beauty
c. Laundry	c. Frequency of changing and varying standards in regard to rough-dry or fine laundry work
d. Pressing and cleaning	d. Quality of materials and consequent care needed
e. Sorting, mending, and putting away; weekly and seasonal care	e. Varying amount of work depending on amount and quality of clothing

3. Processes concerned with shelter

Invariables	Variables
a. Selection of home and its equipment	a. Varying standards as to size, location, etc.
b. Continued care of property; daily care of bedrooms, bathrooms, and whole house; weekly care; special tasks; occasional care	b. Frequency and thoroughness of cleaning; type and amount of service
c. Laundry of house linens and other material	c. Frequency of changing house linens; quality of materials and consequent care needed
d. House furnishings and equipment; planning, purchasing, and replacing when worn; repairing and care	d. Type of house furnishings; extent and delicacy, with consequent care
e. Care of outside of house, grounds, garage, car, etc.	e. Extent of grounds, and standards of care of garden; type of car, etc.

4. Other processes concerned with physical care

a. Care of children

Invariables	Variables
i. Development of good physical habits; regularity of meals, food habits, bowel habits; sleeping habits; washing, bathing, and cleanliness; dressing; other habits	i. Varying standards in regard to health and habits
ii. Fresh air and exercise under supervision	ii. Amount and complexity of same
iii. Supervision of play, including music, art, literature, etc.	iii. Type of supervision and amount of creative expression possible
iv. Nursing in illness	iv. Use of clinic or private physician
v. Teamwork with physicians in planning child's regime	

b. Care of adults

Invariables	Variables
i. Nursing in illness	i. Extent and type of supervision; of medical care

III. BUSINESS ADMINISTRATION AND MANAGEMENT OF FINANCES OF FAMILY

Invariables	Variables
1. The making of a budget	1. Greater detail and complexity
2. Receiving and caring for income	2. Depositing income in bank

TABLE 11 (*continued*)

Invariables	*Variables*
3. Verifying all bills for accuracy	
4. Paying all bills and accounts, daily, weekly, and monthly	4. By cash, money order, or check
5. Paying taxes, federal, state, and local, when liable	
6. Savings, involuntary; Social Security	6. Savings, voluntary; life insurance, investments
7. Entering accounts and balancing income and outgo of money	7. Complexity of accounts

IV. PSYCHOLOGICAL, EMOTIONAL, AND EDUCATIONAL CARE OF FAMILY MEMBERS [12]

1. Constant oversight of infants and small children with understanding of their needs from the point of view of balanced growth of personality	1.–6. inclusive. Increased extent and more complex type of care and instruction to meet individual situations
2. Supervision of child's school work and cooperation with schools	
3. Supervision of recreational life of children and of family as a group	
4. Oversight of each child's development to adulthood with attainment of increasing self-reliance and independence	
5. Preparation for marriage and parenthood, including sound sex education	
6. Religious education in the home	

V. SOCIAL PROBLEMS INVOLVED IN CARING FOR THE FAMILY [13]

1. Adjustments of relationships within the home: grandparents, husband-wife, and children	1. Adjustment of relations with paid workers
2. Working out relationships of family to community and community institutions	

We recognize that the listing of the essential processes in maintaining a home is tentative and subject to criticism. Many persons would undoubtedly challenge some of the details which we have classified as invariables. The authors have endeavored, however, to include in this classification all the essential elements in sound family life. No matter how simply a family lives, meals that are appetizing and that meet the minimum requirements of a healthy diet must be served. This is an invariable. On the other hand, personal taste and income dictate the use of paper napkins or the most expensive and beautiful linens. Such complex and nonessential standards are called variables. In the same way, if a child is to grow and develop, he or she must receive constant supervision and care. This is an invariable. In giving this care, the mother whose income is limited may take her child to the well-baby clinic which the community offers without charge; the mother with adequate means may keep in constant touch with a

[12] See especially Chapter Sixteen.
[13] See especially Chapters Six and Twenty-Six.

pediatrician of her own choosing. The invariable is the medical care and guidance to which every mother and father should have access in a democratic society to ensure their child's healthy growth. The variable is the use of a private physician or specialist.

Every child of the lowest or highest income group has a right to individualized attention in the public school system of a democracy. A close relation between home and school is being strengthened by parent-teacher associations throughout the United States. This is essential for every child and is therefore considered an invariable. If the parent is financially able to send his child to a private school for even more individual attention, such a plan is considered a variable, not vital to the child's development.

In a democracy every home should include in its daily program all the invariables essential for the sound development of all members of the family. Unfortunately, ignorance, prejudice, and lack of intelligence prevent many persons from differentiating between the essentials and the non-essentials in homemaking. This is true in both the low and the high income families. Social waste and real tragedy result when persons of privilege use their large incomes to overindulge their children.

PERSONNEL PROBLEMS IN HOUSEHOLD MANAGEMENT

The management of the household is today the main occupation of between 29,000,000 and 33,000,000 women [14] as contrasted with 19,000,000 [15] women employed gainfully outside the home. These two groups are not mutually exclusive, as many homemakers also work outside the home either because they must support themselves and their dependents or because they enjoy the increased independence or for other reasons.

Any activity which consumes the time and energy of such a large percentage of the woman power of the nation deserves careful scrutiny. We need to make sure that it is organized efficiently and that it is conducted on sound scientific principles.

In planning just *who* are to do the tasks outlined in Table 11, each household manager should study her own situation and choose for each task the person best qualified for the work in question. The homemaker may decide to perform the tasks herself but as a good executive she will often delegate responsibilities to others who are better fitted than she for the particular piece of work. Increasingly she will find services available to her in the community which enable her to free herself from unnecessary drudgery, to contribute more to the higher values in family life, and to participate more freely in community affairs.[16]

[14] The Bureau of the Census gave 33,000,000 as the average number of women 14 years of age and over "keeping house" in 1949. (Current Population Reports, Series P-50, No. 19.) The number varies from time to time. It is safe to say that about 30,000,000 women are primarily engaged in homemaking.

[15] See Women's Bureau 1952, Handbook of Facts on Women Workers, Bulletin No. 242, U. S. Department of Labor, Women's Bureau, IX.

[16] See Nancy Barr Mavity, "The Two-Income Family," *Harper's Magazine,* December, 1951, which emphasizes the trend for both partners to work outside the home at times other than

The work of the home is now being performed by the following:

I. Unpaid workers (members of the family group)
   A. Mother as "chief cook and bottle washer," responsible for all tasks that she cannot effectively delegate. Time studies show excessive overwork if there are several small children, but not enough to do for self and husband in a modern apartment.[17]
   B. Father as her too frequently unwilling assistant, mixing the baby's formula when absolutely necessary but hoping devoutly that mother will soon be well enough to do it herself.
   C. Children of varying ages and varying temperaments but often *not* varying in their resistance and unwillingness to carry even part of their share of the load.
   D. Relatives sharing the home and — occasionally — informal guests. The former are not as frequent as they used to be because grandmothers more often have an income or receive social security payments adequate for their own needs. Maiden aunts who used to be such a resource generally have jobs and bachelor apartments of their own and cannot fit in as formerly.

II. Paid household employees, employed and directed by the household manager or the homemaker
   A. Housekeepers (managerial function)
   B. Household workers

III. Industrial workers, engaged, supervised, and paid by a commercial agency
   Window-washing agencies, caterers, commercial laundries, delicatessen stores, bakeries, and less-work-for-mother retail shops are illustrations. Also, in apartment hotels the management takes the responsibility of engaging and directing the workers who clean the rooms and render other services. These developments seem likely to expand greatly.

IV. Business persons, trained stenographers, or office secretaries
   Usually the home manager acts as office secretary for the family, although sometimes husband and wife keep accounts together and sometimes the husband is responsible for all business details. Again this is an individual matter, depending on the persons involved. Many businessmen, however, have their household bills paid and their accounts kept by their office secretary. Women of means, burdened by

child bearing. The home is no longer *primarily* an economic unit but is the center for emotional security. Democracy must supplement the home by community, state, national, and commercial assistance to build and protect a healthy, well-balanced future citizenry. See also Freda S. Miller, "Household Employment in the U. S.," Reprint from *International Labour Review*, 56, 4 (Oct., 1952), Geneva.

[17] Paulena Nickell and Jean M. Dorsey, *Management in Family Living* (New York: Wiley, 1942), chap. 5.

many community responsibilities, delegate much work to private secretaries. There are few families that do not need expert assistance when they make out their income tax returns.

V. Professional persons

The preparation of the food of small infants and the regime of older children are frequently guided by a private physician; trained nurses are called into many homes when there is severe illness; visiting homemakers and housekeepers are utilized by the lower income groups, under professional supervision, when the mother is unable for any reason to meet her home responsibilities. Specialists in employment problems are available to assist with job analyses and other personnel problems within the home.

From the above analysis it must be clear that the function of management within the home is a heavier and more important responsibility than is usually recognized. As in all other types of management, four main factors are utilized in meeting all the needs of the family group: (1) time; (2) money; (3) energy; (4) ability. It must be kept in mind that the goal of all is the emotional satisfaction of each and every member of the group.

1. The limits of time must be constantly kept in mind by the capable executive in the home. Family life must be scheduled, meals must be on time, appointments must be kept. Before children come, the time factor largely revolves around the business hours of the husband. The wife whose husband works all night or until four or five in the morning usually schedules her own time so as to have a good meal for him whenever he gets home, and keeps herself free in the late afternoon for companionship with him after his day's sleep. Later on, the baby's feeding schedule may have to take precedence. Still later the early morning schedule is set by school children who need to be encouraged to dress promptly, eat their breakfasts, and get off to school on time. Various studies of the amount of time home managers spend at their tasks show that many spend over fifty and some over sixty hours a week. Homemakers sometimes keep a time record and make time budgets in order to meet all the family's needs and yet keep their own hours within reasonable limits. As a higher plane of living is attained, home management grows more complex and paid employees are brought in, but the home manager must still keep the time element in mind, as household workers should not work longer than other industrial workers — certainly not more than fifty-four hours a week.

2. The limits of money are also accepted by a good executive, and she budgets her expenditures accordingly, as has been so clearly shown by Bigelow in Chapter Fifteen.

3. The third factor, energy, is not so generally recognized. Careful plans need to be made for the prevention of overfatigue. One homemaker may economize by doing her own family laundry — most couples do. But if she is frail and short of energy, she may find her economy of money counterbalanced by an exorbitant drain on her energy reserves. A maid may be employed who is an excellent cook and skillful in her care of the children, but

when she is asked to take care of the furnace or put on storm windows she may wisely object. On the other hand, a young son, aged sixteen, may be physically strong and able to do both jobs — if he can be persuaded that such work is not beneath the dignity of a prospective college freshman!

4. The fourth factor, ability, must also be considered in wise management, even though it raises all sorts of complex questions which can be answered only in terms of the particular situation. A woman who graduated from college and taught school three years before she married has developed certain skills and abilities as a teacher which have marketable value and, moreover, are socially valuable to society. How can these abilities be used to the greatest social advantage after marriage? Such problems of ability are not sex-limited. A man with potential ability as a social work executive needed a two-year training course in a school of social work. He and a young woman social worker decided to marry, with the understanding that she would hold her job for two years and enable him to complete his professional training. They did their own housework together after the day's work in order to live on their limited income while he attained secure professional status. In such ways does sound family management conserve and develop potential ability in every one of its members. Likewise any household workers employed by the family should be chosen carefully in terms of their ability to do the work which is to be done.

The work of the home, we conclude, includes many important, fundamental, and economically valuable processes which can be analyzed and assigned to different workers, very much as is done in an office or factory. In the majority of the homes of America, the daily work of the home is being carried largely, if not entirely, by members of the family group. First, the mother takes the money earned by her husband and any other gainfully employed members of the group, and by her processing services within the home transforms such money into real income. Many women thoroughly enjoy housework and prefer it to any other occupation. Such women are making a valuable economic and social contribution to the family's real income. Until recently, however, the pattern has been well entrenched in our culture that women should make their economic and social contribution only through the work of the home. Many mothers, however, have highly specialized gifts, and where the community responsibilities of the homemaker are large, it is neither practicable nor socially desirable that she should do all her own work.

The husband often assists in the actual work of the home by caring for the furnace, keeping the plumbing and electrical devices in repair, overseeing the care of grounds, paying the bills, and sharing accounting tasks. Some men find such activity about house and garden a great emotional release and an opportunity to express their own personalities.

In addition, the children of the family share in the actual work of the home when they keep their own rooms and toys in order, help with the washing of dishes and the care of the furnace, and share the care of younger members of the family group. A splendid sense of family solidarity can develop when all learn to work together as a team. Such productive activity has great educational value if allotted on the basis of sound educational procedure in accordance with interests, abilities, and needs of the individual personality.

The writers were recently entertained formally in a charming home where the youngest daughter of the house, aged fourteen, assisted in waiting on the table, at which there were ten guests. She did the job with such skill and poise that she met all the standards of the well-trained maid. At an informal meal in the same home, the mother and father and two daughters entertained the guests after dinner while another daughter of fifteen washed all the dishes alone. The mother explained that she herself loved to cook and do housework and that her daughters also enjoyed these tasks. These attitudes could well be adopted in other homes. In another instance of family cooperation, the grandmother stepped in as cook and waitress for a formal dinner party when the expected cook failed at the last minute.

In many families where the money income is sufficiently large (usually over $4000) paid workers are occasionally employed on part-time or full-time basis to assist the members of the family in performing the routine tasks of the home. Formerly not over 5 per cent of the homes in America employed such workers. Recently the number has greatly decreased.

In general the same principles of management and personnel practices should apply to domestic and industrial employees alike. Workers should be selected with care on the basis of their skills and personality qualifications; they should be trained; and after placement they should receive wise and sympathetic supervision. Household employment is the largest occupational field for women, involving as it does over two million women in normal times. At present this field is the most chaotic and least standardized of all occupations, except perhaps farming. The demand for skilled and reliable workers far exceeds the supply, and salaries for well-trained and capable workers are very high in the present market. Even unskilled and untrained workers receive a minimum of $20 weekly and others may expect as much as $200 a month in addition to board and room. Throughout the United States, women of leadership and social vision have formed in groups to study the problems connected with household employment and to improve relations between the employer and the employee in the home. The National Council on Household Employment once formulated a set of standards as to hours, wages, and labor policies known as "Proposals for a Voluntary Agreement in Household Employment." Many communities throughout the country are now adapting these standards to their local needs. Under the amended Social Security Act, Jan. 1, 1951, certain domestic workers are protected under old age and survivors' insurance.[18]

[18] See Women's Bureau 1952, Handbook of Facts on Women Workers, Bulletin No. 242, p. 84. For further information on standards and legislation in the field of household employment, write to the Director, Women's Bureau, U. S. Department of Labor, Washington, D. C.

Problems a Husband Meets and Skills He Needs

Three distinct combinations of marital roles are prevalent in modern family life according to Clifford Kirkpatrick. They are: (1) the masculine breadwinner and domestic homemaker type, with children; (2) the companionate type, with no children; and (3) the fifty-fifty partnership, with both parents gainfully employed in certain periods of the family cycle and with partial care of children delegated to competent employees or to social and educational agencies like the nursery school, day care centers, or city and country day schools.[19] To be a "good" husband and father requires different skills and abilities in each of the three combinations. Rights and duties of both husband and wife vary too!

Since the present chapter envisages as its norm the general pattern of a cooperative family based on a partnership of two equals, the wife working and making a distinct economic contribution either inside or outside the home, a special kind of husband and father is needed. Two prerequisites for fatherhood in a cooperative family are: (1) The modern husband must have the ability to think through a problem with his wife and arrive at a truly joint decision. For one whose father "ruled" the family and who when a bachelor had to consult no one about his decisions, this often represents a real achievement. (2) The second requisite for a modern husband is the ability to recognize the need for professional advice and the ability to put it to use. Life today has become increasingly complex. Any husband who assumes omniscience in matters affecting the health, finances, and legal rights and obligations of his family or who directs unaided the educational and vocational pursuits of his children is often inflating his own ego at the expense of the welfare of his family. The patriarchal pattern makes his word "law" in all such matters. In the new cooperative family, however, both husband and wife realize that there are situations in which they lack the necessary insight and knowledge to decide the best policy for the family. In a few favored communities, fortunately, qualified counselors are ready and eager to serve the best interests of the family group.[20]

A number of the major problems to be considered by the two marital partners as they plan their life together have already been listed. The solution of some of these may depend upon professional advice and guidance. In addition, both husband and wife frequently need special knowledge themselves of the issues and values involved in some of the decisions they must make. They will also find it necessary to develop new skills in order to handle new situations as they arise. In the management of family life, they should know, among other things, the following:

1. How to make a workable budget and how to keep reasonably simple accounts.

[19] For a more complete analysis of these roles, see Clifford A. Kirkpatrick, "Techniques in Marital Adjustment," *Annals of the American Academy of Political and Social Science,* 16 (March, 1932), pp. 178–185.

[20] See Chapter Twenty-Six for a discussion of Marriage Counseling.

2. How to choose intelligently the right location for a home and make a wise decision as to when it is better to rent and when to buy.
3. How to utilize available sources of information so as to purchase wisely both consumers' goods and capital equipment.
4. How to regulate the size of the family and the spacing of children after careful consideration of all factors.
5. How to guide children sympathetically and intelligently at home, in school, and at the various levels of play.
6. How to buy insurance wisely and make sound investments in view of the life cycle all families pass through.
7. How to draw up (with the aid of a lawyer) a will that is legally sound and adequate for all contingencies.

Many husbands will wish to share in the heavier physical and mechanical tasks involved in running a home, especially where the income is strictly limited. No hard and fast division of tasks can be made between husband and wife. Circumstances vary from family to family, depending not only upon the culture pattern of the country but also upon the individual interests, the training and capacities of husband and wife, and the number, age, and sex of the children. Although there is no universal rule, there are a number of items for which the husband is ordinarily held responsible. Bigelow lists them as follows: [21]

It may be his duty to provide the family with a place to live, to see that the house is kept in repair, and to provide for heat and light and other public utilities. Usually the husband is responsible for the care of the family car. He must plan for its purchase and maintenance, and he must take care of it himself, or he must supervise the work which is done upon it. In addition, in most families the husband, as well as the wife, makes substantial contributions in the form of household labor income. The husband may mow the yard, spade the garden, tend the furnace, clean the walks, repair the back steps, paint the kitchen, replace burned-out light bulbs, wash and grease the car, and mend the children's toys. And if his hours of work are limited, and his wife's home duties are unusually heavy, he may even take his turn washing dishes, helping with the heavy housecleaning, running the washing machine, or taking care of the children.

To accomplish these various tasks, the following skills and techniques, among others, seem desirable, if not essential:

1. A simple knowledge of carpentry, including the selection and care of tools both of hand and power types.
2. How to mix and thin paints and apply them and take the proper care of brushes, rollers, spray guns, etc.
3. Some knowledge of the principles of heating and cooling and the care of a furnace, oil or gas burner, and/or air conditioning unit.

21 Howard F. Bigelow, *Family Finance: A Study in the Economics of Consumption* (2nd ed.; Philadelphia: Lippincott, 1953), pp. 70–71.

4. Enough acquaintance with electricity so that he can easily make repairs to the doorbell, replace blown-out fuses, do simple wiring, and install new switches.
5. How to shut off the water supply of a house in case of emergency, replace a worn-out washer on a faucet, or knowledge of the simple details necessary to keep the electric pump running smoothly.
6. How to lubricate mechanical equipment requiring such periodic attention.
7. How to shut off gas and electricity in case of emergencies, and also how to read gas, electric, and water meters.
8. How to care for lawn, shade trees, and shrubbery, if there are such.
9. If houseman, gardener, or chauffeur is employed, a knowledge of the principles of the wise selection and supervision of such household workers.
10. Some skill in outdoor life, woodcraft, fishing, etc. This, with skill in one or two all-year-round hobbies, would be valuable assets, not only for family or personal recreation but also for the development of the father-child relation.
11. "First-aid in the home." Since a far larger number of accidents of all kinds occur in the home than is commonly supposed, both husband and wife should be prepared for all contingencies until professional help is available.
12. How to select technical magazines and handbooks for self-instruction.

Problems a Wife Meets and Skills She Needs

In the new equalitarian relationship which must develop between husbands and wives if the democratic family is to flourish, women need first to understand themselves and their roles in the family, in their communities, and in the nation. They must realize that in becoming *too* involved in their home duties, they inevitably fail to develop their all-round capacities and to become balanced, well-adjusted human beings, and they are therefore less adequate wives and mothers than they are potentially capable of being. Women must respect themselves and realize that like others they have rights, privileges, and duties. They must learn to be competent and to meet their responsibilities wisely. This, then, is perhaps the first problem which women must meet today in family administration: to play their role as an equal partner, not as Cinderella, the household drudge, nor as the prima donna asking constantly for the center of the stage. By finding their own particular place they can make their contribution through a rich and happy family life.

The woman learns to subordinate herself to the needs of her husband and her family when necessary, but the husband should also learn to make concessions and even sacrifices at times to meet the paramount needs of the family. Husband and wife seek to face situations objectively and impersonally, and to see the life of their individual family in its relation to the larger community — including the nation and the world society — of which they all form a part. Families which go on a "buyers' strike" and refuse to purchase any but the absolute essentials in order to prevent inflation are making a contribution, however small, to a better-ordered society. Parents and children who eat less to give more abroad are showing their understanding of these larger relationships. As wife and homemaker, the modern woman accepts the functions within the home upon which she and her husband agree. Usually she becomes the manager and worker in the home, devoting a large part of her time to the care of the house and the creation of a home atmosphere which will include charm and relaxation, at the same time giving constant affection while she meets the physical needs of the family group. Where the income is strictly limited, as it is in a large percentage of the homes of America,[22] the wife is usually faced with hard physical labor such as laundry work, scrubbing floors, and keeping the house reasonably clean, in addition to the daily routine of cooking, dishwashing, caring for members of the family when ill, and all the details listed in Table 11 above.[23] The wise purchasing of food and clothing and the artistic furnishing of the house give opportunity for taste and competence in buying within the limits of the family budget. In the systematic organization of the work of the household, in entertaining relatives, friends, and guests, the domestic wife finds many creative outlets. When the husband is a professional man, the wife often acts as his private secretary or makes important contributions to his career by entertaining persons who may contribute to his professional success.

When a woman assumes the responsibilities of motherhood, many new skills and abilities are called into play. The question of the correct food for the health of the child becomes a vital one even during pregnancy. Many women take up a study of dietetics at this time under the direction of the physician to whom they report regularly. Such knowledge continues to be of decided importance as children mature. The selection of the right diet for all members of the family group and its skillful preparation consume a large share of the mother's time and energy, whether she does the actual cooking herself or employs a cook whom she supervises. The right eating habits of all members of the family depend not only on the careful selection and preparation of food, but also on the mother's ability not to pay too much attention to the whims of any member of the group.

The mother soon finds that she requires new skills in order to understand the needs of her growing children, both in regard to their physical care and their emotional and social life. Many mothers today are turning to organized study groups where, under trained leadership, they find opportunity for continuing their education for family life. Equipped with insight and knowledge, they are more able to cope effectively with their children's quarrels and adjustments within the home and to assist their youngsters to build better community relations. Although she begins her domestic career by learning how to be a good cook and home manager, the competent mother also realizes that the social sciences have much to teach her through the new programs in child study and adult education. In such groups she learns that she must develop hobbies and outside interests so that family life may not become too

[22] In 1950, 11.5% of all families earned less than $1,000. 24.7% earned less than $2,000. U. S. Bureau of the Census, Current Population Reports, Series P-60, No. 9.

[23] For a discussion of the wife's contribution to the family income, see Bigelow, op. cit., p. 71.

ingrown, and that challenging community projects such as the League of Women Voters, church groups, and similar outlets are ready to absorb her attention when the time comes for the children to be emotionally weaned and to leave their parental home for homes of their own. As she realizes that her children must be left free to make mistakes and to develop as individuals, she fortunately discovers that her abilities are needed in the community as well as in the home, and she finds herself acting as treasurer of the local cooperative society or president of the parent-teacher association. Duvall and Hill point out [24] that "many women are really employed extensively outside their homes, but are not so regarded because they are not paid." Every wife, like every husband, needs to keep a wise balance between her responsibilities within the home and her volunteer responsibilities in the community, which should increase as her children mature.

The preceding discussion of the wife's skills in homemaking has been limited to those wives not gainfully employed. According to the Bureau of the Census, in 1951, about ten million homemakers worked outside the home. A recent survey made by the Women's Bureau of the U. S. Department of Labor reports that out of every hundred women who definitely intend to continue gainful employment, eighty-four are in the labor market for the purpose of supporting themselves and their dependents; eight work to pay for a home, to pay off debts, or to educate their children; and eight work primarily because of a career interest in the job.[25] Increasingly women are combining homemaking and gainful employment, although such a plan of life requires unlimited energy and great skill if one is to succeed. Needless to say, the entire family needs to participate to make this combined job an enjoyable one for the mother and homemaker.

When a mature woman decides to assume responsibility for a paid job outside the home in addition to her domestic responsibilities, she does not need to neglect the home. A good executive delegates many responsibilities to carefully selected and skilled assistants. As has already been stated, personnel problems in the home are now being studied in order that a supply of more skilled and competent workers may eventually be available.[26] For women who earn too small a wage to enable them to hire any assistance in the home, the problem is more serious and becomes a community responsibility through day care centers and other types of social and commercial aids.

Educational Backgrounds for Successful Family Administration

What is the responsibility of educators in a democratic country for the preparation of their students in the fields of marriage and family living? Educators differ among themselves on this question, but nevertheless a move-

---

[24] See Evelyn M. Duvall and Reuben Hill, *When You Marry* (rev. ed.; Boston: Heath, 1953, p. 226).

[25] See leaflet *Why Women Work* (June, 1946), Women's Bureau, U. S. Department of Labor.

[26] See Edith Barber, *Speaking of Servants: How to Hire, Train and Manage Household Employees* (New York: Whittlesey House, 1940).

ment is growing throughout the country to make education for marriage available to an ever larger number of young people. Writes one educator,[27] "Marriage problems are not new but their character reflects the changes of modern culture. There is also an unprecedented realization of their significance and a greater confidence than ever before in the value of science, both in preparing for marriage and in meeting the problems which it brings."

Many educators have believed that a broad cultural education for both men and women is necessary to lay the foundation for a fundamental understanding of human relations and of life situations. They claim that as men and women learn the best that has been thought and expressed in literature, philosophy, art, and religion and as they learn the basic elements in the natural and social sciences, they acquire attitudes and resources within themselves which make it possible for them to adjust intelligently to various life situations.

Other educators assert that specific techniques and skills must be taught to both men and women (but especially women) to prepare them for their important, differing roles in marriage and in family life. They cite the mounting divorce rate as evidence of family breakdown. They place emphasis upon the importance of more training in the field of home economics and the skills needed in homemaking and housekeeping. Only in this way, these educators assert, can future homemakers be adequately prepared to meet their daily responsibilities.

The authors would like to reconcile these two conflicting points of view and recommend a program of education which will include the best elements of both, emphasizing possibly an additional element. In our democratic society, where women are citizens and the political and social equals of men, it is important that women be educated and equipped to take their places not only in their homes but also in their communities, in the nation, and in the international society which must develop. We agree therefore with the first position, that all children should have as broad a cultural education as their aptitudes and abilities warrant, without discrimination as to social class, race, economic level, or sex. After this basis has been laid, however, there should be added further training in specialized skills to enable each individual to contribute his best to society, as a producer, as a consumer, as a marriage partner and parent, and as a citizen. Vocational or professional adjustment and preparation for marriage and family life are two fields which call for education in such specific skills and techniques. It is particularly important for marriage and family life that the emotional development of the individual should have been understood and assisted by parents, teachers, and other counselors.

Concretely, the parental home is the first educational agency which has the opportunity to build attitudes of far-reaching effect on the life organization of the adult.[28] In addition, the home should early begin to teach those skills which are later essential for marriage and family life. Mothers often

[27] See Ernest R. Groves, "Professional Training for Family Life Educators," *Marriage and Family Living,* 8 (May, 1946), pp. 25-26.

[28] See "Home as an Educational Institution" earlier in this book, pp. 476-477.

overprotect their children and give them every "advantage," such as music and dancing lessons, but fail to give them "opportunity" to learn by doing. When such mothers do all the hard work themselves or expect a paid worker to do it all, their children are encouraged to develop unsound and undemocratic attitudes. On the other hand, wise mothers and fathers agree that as early as possible children should wait on themselves and learn to work as a team in carrying their full share in family life. Specific skills should be taught by both father and mother: cooking for both sexes; carpentry and building and care of furnace for boys; sewing, child care, and all the skills essential to home management for girls. Although apartment and tenement-house living makes such education more difficult than in the early days of farm and rural life, yet much sharing of home responsibilities and education in actual skills are possible where both parents carry their share and see themselves as educators of their children. Much depends on the attitude with which responsibilities are carried. If work can be taught as a normal, healthy, satisfying, and creative activity, half the battle of life is won. Parents today also have a responsibility to understand and guide the development of the emotional life of their children to ensure all-round growth of personality at each stage of development.

Second, the school has a responsibility to teach attitudes and skills which will later contribute to a sound and happy family life. In the state of Oklahoma all boys and girls in the public school system are receiving education in homemaking. In the Philadelphia and Detroit public schools on the senior high school level, courses in foods, home management, and family relations are offered as electives to boys as well as to girls. The number electing this work increases each year. Thus the school as well as the home can teach both men and women to contribute to the maintenance of standards in home life.

Third, the Scout and kindred movements, settlements, the Y.W.C.A., the Y.M.C.A., and other recreational groups also contribute much in developing attitudes and teaching skills which will later be valuable in family life. Boys learn to cook willingly when they are camping. The above groups are doing much and can do even more to develop in boys healthier attitudes toward women and a willingness to carry their share of responsibility in home and community.

Fourth, the growing movement throughout the country for specific courses on marriage and family relations at the college level is making a most important contribution to a new understanding of the potentialities of the marital relation. There will be more on this in the last chapter.

Fifth, supplementing the preceding four sources of specific education for family life, the need for the broadest possible cultural background for everyone must again be emphasized. Appreciation of art, music, and literature (especially the drama) provides creative outlets for the leisure of all members of the family and thus supplies resources which may prevent family conflict and enrich family life. Such cultural education also furnishes insight into human problems and life situations which should give perspective and be applied in everyday living. Adult education of this kind should be available to all families regardless of economic level. Everyone needs the inspiration and relaxation that art and music can supply.

Finally, intelligent homemakers will find that there are many skills they must learn on the job, and that there should be and often are in the community centers to which brides and even older homemakers as well as household employees can go in order that all may learn new skills or strengthen those in which they are weak. The parent education movement is a striking illustration of society's meeting the need for education at the adult level of fathers and mothers on the job. No preparental education can be so vital as that given to parents after their children come, when under the guidance of skilled teachers and counselors pressing problems of human relationships can be studied objectively and solutions found.

SELECTED READINGS

ANDREWS, BENJAMIN R., *The Economics of the Household* (rev. ed.; New York: Macmillan, 1935).

APPLEBAUM, STELLA B., *Working Wives and Mothers* (Public Affairs Pamphlet No. 188, 1952. See p. 32 of this pamphlet for further material on What to Read).

BARBER, EDITH, *Speaking of Servants: How to Hire, Train and Manage Household Employees* (New York: Whittlesey House, 1940).

BIGELOW, HOWARD F., *Family Finance: A Study in the Economics of Consumption* (2nd ed.; Philadelphia: Lippincott, 1953).

BURGESS, ERNEST, and LOCKE, HARVEY J., *The Family: From Institution to Companionship* (2nd ed.; New York: American Book Company, 1953).

Department of Home Economics of the National Education Association, *Family Living and Our Schools* (New York: Appleton-Century, 1941).

DUVALL, EVELYN M., and HILL, REUBEN, *When You Marry* (rev. ed.; Boston: Heath, 1953).

ENGLISH, O. SPURGEON, M.D., and FOSTER, CONSTANCE, *Fathers Are Parents, Too* (New York: G. P. Putnam's Sons, 1951).

International Labour Office, *The Status and Conditions of Employment of Domestic Workers* (Geneva: Report of Meeting of Experts, July, 1951).

KYRK, HAZEL, *Economic Problems of the Family* (New York: Harper, 1933).

MAVITY, NANCY BARR, "The Two Income Family" *Harper's Magazine* (December, 1951).

MILLER, FREDA S., "Household Employment in the United States," *International Labour Review* (Geneva, October, 1952).

NICKELL, PAULENA, and DORSEY, JEAN M., *Management in Family Living* (New York: Wiley, 1942).

SCHEINFELD, AMRAM, *Women and Men* (New York: Harcourt, Brace, 1944).

Women's Bureau, *Handbook of Facts on Women Workers* (Bulletin No. 242, United States Department of Labor; Washington, D. C.: U. S. Government Printing Office, 1952).

Women's Bureau, *Women Workers and Their Dependents* (Bulletin No. 239, United States Department of Labor; Washington, D. C.: U. S. Government Printing Office, 1952).

1. What is meant by sound principles of administration and management? Distinguish between each as used in industry and apply to family life.
2. How do you differentiate between homemaking and housekeeping? Give illustrations to throw light on your answer.
3. Does sound organization call for a single responsible head? If you decide affirmatively, how are business partnerships conducted? Does a family offer an analogous situation? Why or why not?
4. To what extent does a knowledge of the family life cycle (marriage, birth of children, schooling, adolescence, maturity and departure of children later, middle age, old age, and death) help the two heads of a family to work out their problems of family management and finance?
5. When should children be included in family councils? What are the advantages of doing so? What is the difference between giving them a voice and giving them a vote? Which do you think wiser? Why?
6. What is meant by a time budget? an energy budget? Why are these two types of budget often overlooked when a money budget is not? What are the frequent consequences of this neglect?
7. Do you believe that "woman's place is in the home" or do you prefer Pearl Buck's statement, "The home needs man, and the outside world needs woman"? Discuss both these statements in the light of modern conditions and present your own point of view.
8. Why is it sometimes both necessary and advantageous for a young couple to live with relatives when first married? What are some of the disadvantages and dangers of such a plan? If the wife needs to work outside the home to make it possible for her husband to complete his professional education, is it wiser for the coming of children to be postponed or is there danger in such a plan? Is it frequently possible or desirable for the grandmother to contribute by caring for the child when both parents have to be absent from home? Discuss in detail, with case illustrations.
9. Discuss the role of play and the importance of leisure time activities, both (a) within the family group; and (b) in both parents' and children's relation to the larger community life.
10. When does a home need paid assistance to help the homemaker in carrying on the work of the home efficiently? Is this entirely a matter of the size of the family income or do other factors enter in? If the latter, what are those other factors? When possible, cite actual case material.
11. Do you believe that the principles of sound personnel relations apply in some ways in the work of the home? If so, explain more fully what is involved. Is there any relation between the training and efficient placement of workers? Does such relationship apply to the homemaker as well as to paid employees? Discuss in some detail the kind of training that you believe should be given both to unpaid and paid workers in the home.

Chapter Nineteen

What Family Members Should Know about Law

JOHN S. BRADWAY

THE FAMILY ALSO FUNCTIONS IN A LEGAL CONTEXT

ONE may think of the family as having a sort of life cycle. There are periods of this cycle that correspond roughly to birth, maturity, and dissolution of the individual. During its life the family not infrequently is confronted by crises. Some of these crises are so serious that to provide a solution outside help is needed — whether or not it is requested. The best source of such outside aid appears to lie in the field of the professions. Originally professional aid may have been remedial; but today both families and members of the professions are coming to see the value of preventive programs.

Among these family crises are many situations in which the resources of the field of law alone, or the combined resources of the law and one or more other professional fields, are necessary to resolve, or better still, to prevent the impending complications. Because the public relations programs of the physician and the clergyman long have been well established, members of a family find it easy to tap sources of medical and spiritual aid. The social distance between the family and the lawyer has not always been so readily bridged. Since it is unethical for the lawyer to advertise for business, the first step toward an accord would seem to be a responsibility of the individual family and its members.

From the cradle to the grave the family functions in a legal context. The lawyer is the man who makes rules of law available to all and sundry. The sooner the family brings its legal problems to the lawyer, the better. There is no occasion for a lay member of the family to set himself up as a lawyer. The task of practicing law for one's self is highly technical and, for an untrained person, full of pitfalls. Moreover, if the latter practices law for another, it is usually against the law.

In an earlier and less highly specialized day the "family lawyer" was a very real personage who performed a wide variety of indispensable services. It is to be hoped that in time it will again become possible for a substantial number of lawyers to specialize in family problems. The "divorce" lawyer is not unknown. If there is enough demand for his services, the "family" lawyer can be counted on to reappear on the domestic scene.

CAUTIONS ABOUT THIS CHAPTER

The present chapter is designed to inform the reader of some of the occasions when he should consult a competent lawyer with respect to the legal aspect of family problems; it may be thought of in terms of a discussion of legal first aid. A more technical treatment would not be readily understood by non-lawyer readers and would consume more space than is presently available. In view of the effort to simplify the material, however, the reader should be cautioned about several matters:

There is a distinct body of family law for each state in the United States. In this chapter we are talking about law on the national level. It is no substitute for information made available when a particular lawyer in a particular state is advising a particular client about a particular problem.

Legal language is hard reading for the layman. When one attempts to translate technicalities into lay words, the writer can never be sure that he has succeeded in getting across to the reader the precise shade of meaning.

It is said that "the law is unknown to him who knoweth not the reason thereof. . . ." Since space is lacking even to set down all the relevant rules, it is obvious why no efforts have been made to explain the reasons, historical and otherwise, behind any of them. We are not attempting to write a legislative handbook on what the law ought to be. We are merely generalizing on a national level as to what it appears to be.

THE LEGAL FAMILY

Many definitions of the word "family," varying with the purposes for which they were framed, are available in dictionaries, encyclopedias, and other books.[1] For the purposes of the present chapter a family will be treated as a group of persons held together by a bond recognized by the law. Our concern is with these questions: What are the "bonds" that are recognized by law? In what sort of situations does the law find it necessary to define a family?

The legal "bonds" that link together a family are indicated by words such as blood, ceremony, common shelter. If we think in terms of "blood," it is easy to include grandparents, parents, children, grandchildren, brothers and sisters, uncles, aunts, nieces, and nephews in an ever-widening circle. Under certain circumstances, relationship by the half-blood is recognized as a valid test. Stepchildren may be as much members of some families as other children. If we think in terms of a "legal ceremony" (marriage or adoption), a husband and wife and an adopted child are a family. But what about a man and woman living together illicitly with one or more illegitimate children? If we think in terms of a group of people living "under the same roof" and held together by economic considerations, we may agree that orphan brothers and sisters in the same house are a family. But what about the inmates of an orphan asylum?

The need to define the word "family" arises in a variety of situations:

[1] *Bouvier's Law Dictionary* (3rd revision, 8th ed., St. Paul: West, 1914) gives the following definition: "Family, father, mother and children. All the individuals who live under the authority of another, including the servants of the family. . . . All the relations who descend from a common ancestor or who spring from a common root. . . . In common parlance it consists of those who live under the same roof with the pater familias."

homestead exemptions, voting rights, and support provisions. In a will the testator may make provision for his "family" and a question may arise as to whether a mother-in-law or a second cousin or somebody else comes within the meaning of the word. Again, the paper before the court containing the words to be interpreted may be an insurance policy or certificate of a beneficial association. Members of a family interested in homestead statutes, wills, insurance policies and the like will do well to see a lawyer beforehand rather than afterwards to make sure that the language means what they think or want it to mean.

Families may be conventional or otherwise. Space prevents a discussion of the law relating to the unconventional type.[2] Generally, the legal rules discouraging the nonconformist unions will be found in statute books under the heading "crimes."

The conventional family begins with a promise to marry that results in an engagement. It comes to maturity with a more or less formal wedding ceremony. It reaches dissolution: naturally, by death of one of the members; or by separation; or legally, by annulment and divorce.

The Promise to Marry and Breach of Promise

The law generally becomes interested in the promise to marry when it is broken and one party, usually the woman, desires to sue the other for damages. In those states where such a suit may be brought, the plaintiff (that is, the person who brings the suit) is generally expected to prove: (a) a mutual promise to marry; (b) a breach of the promise by the adverse party; (c) damages on that account to the plaintiff.

The orthodox promise to marry may occur in written or oral or even less definite form. In effect one party says to the other: "Will you marry me?" The orthodox binding answer is: "Yes." Thereafter each party is legally under obligation to go through a marriage ceremony with the other within a specified, or at least within a reasonable, time. The word "obligation" is used advisedly. The sanction — money damages — is similar to that which would have arisen in law if the parties, instead of referring to marriage, had been discussing the sale of an automobile, a labor management contract, or a commercial partnership agreement.

Some people refer to this principle of the legally binding effect of a promise to marry as the "trap" theory. The words are spoken or written, and instantly the trap springs shut on both of the parties alike. Such a theory may be based on the idea that young people should engage in "courting" before they make more serious commitments. Other groups contend that the engagement period itself is essentially the time for each prospective partner to find out whether the two are suited to each other and likely to produce a family that will endure in the face of future stormy weather. Where the reason behind a rule

---

[2] In *Schwingle* v. *Keifer,* 105 Tex. 609, 153 S.W. 1132 (1913), the evidence showed an agreement, not to marry but to live together as husband and wife as long as they might desire to do so, with the privilege of dissolving the relationship at any time. The court held this was not a marriage agreement but something of an illicit nature.

of law changes, one may anticipate that in due course the rule itself will change. Not many laymen today think of an engagement to marry as a trap.

It is not hard to prove in court a written promise to marry if one has the writing in hand. An oral promise presents further problems of evidence. The witnesses may no longer be available; they may have forgotten; the jury may not believe them. In a situation in which no formal words of engagement are spoken or written, the jury sometimes may be asked to find as a fact from the mere conduct of the parties that they acted so as to make a reasonable man believe they were engaged.[3]

A *breach* of a promise to marry occurs when one party writes or tells the other, "I will not marry you," or where his conduct adds up to this conclusion. If, for example, the wedding is scheduled for January 1, at 12 o'clock noon, at the First Church and the groom does not appear, the legal results of his conduct may have to be reviewed. If it develops that he has a legally good excuse such as an unavoidable illness, his failure to be present may be treated as a postponement rather than a breach. A more considerate groom will consult his prospective bride a reasonable time in advance and secure her consent to a mutual postponement. Failure of the man thus to protect himself may put the bride in a legal position where she may make a choice. She may decide to treat the engagement as continuing, or she may regard it as broken and sue for damages.

Damages for a breach of a marriage promise are generally in the discretion of the jury. It would appear that some juries have allowed wide latitude to their imaginations in this field.[4]

There are two sorts of these damages: compensatory and punitive. Compensatory damages are an effort to reimburse the plaintiff for pecuniary loss. Punitive damages are intended to punish the defendant. They may include loss of opportunities during the engagement for contracting a suitable marriage with another, the disappointment of her reasonable expectations of material and social advantages resulting from the intended marriage, injury to plaintiff's health, feelings, wounding of her pride, blighting of her affections, the marring of her prospects in life.[5]

The defendant, usually the man, has three general defenses available to him depending upon the circumstances of the case: I never made a promise to marry this woman; I made the promise but I did not break it; I made the promise and I broke it, but I was justified legally in doing so.

Examples of the sort of situation in which the law may find the breach justified are: infancy of the defendant (until he reaches the age where the

---

[3] In *Munson v. Hastings*, 12 Vt. 346 (1839), the man for seven years gave his attentions to the girl constantly and exclusively, knowing that she understood they were to be married. No actual promise was proved. The court held that a promise to marry could not be inferred from mere attentions even though exclusive, long-continued, and manifesting an apparently serious and settled attachment between the parties. The length of time itself without a marriage rather tended to negate the idea of a promise.

[4] In *Garmony v. Henderson*, 114 Me. 75, 95 A. 409 (1915), the jury gave the woman a verdict of $116,000.

[5] See *Hahn v. Bettingen*, 81 Minn. 91, 83 N.W. 467 (1900).

law holds him to his promises); [6] where the two parties are so closely related by blood that the law will not permit them to marry in any event; where one's physical or mental health is below the standard required by law for married persons; where he is a married person at the time he makes his promise; where the woman is unchaste and the man does not discover the situation until after the promise.

There is considerable difference of opinion as to whether the law should allow breach of promise suits. Those who favor abolishment argue that the practice tends to become a racket. When such a suit is begun, or even threatened, the reputation of the male defendant suffers even though he may never have made a promise. An experienced and attractive woman plaintiff has opportunities to impress the jury, which may never be available to her more timid and retiring sister who might be more definitely victimized. A number of states have passed laws abolishing the right of action.[7]

We may well ponder whether the traditional concept of the law — that an engagement to marry is comparable to a commercial contract — is socially sound. Is an engagement to marry a relationship to be approached in the shrewd spirit appropriate to a business transaction where the rule is, "Let the buyer beware"; or is it properly a period when the two parties should be free of legal rules and permitted without obligation to consider whether or not their prospective marriage will result in the creation of an enduring family?

OTHER ANTENUPTIAL PROMISES

The promise to marry is the most obvious point at which the law of the family comes home to the two parties before the marriage ceremony takes place, but it is not the only one. Other legally significant antenuptial promises fall into two categories: (a) those relating to personal affairs; and (b) those relating to property matters.

Antenuptial contracts between the parties relating to personal affairs are not uncommon. Among them are agreements as to matters of sex, or not to live together at all or for a period of time,[8] or to live at a special place, or the

---

[6] In *Sawicki* v. *Slahor*, 11 N.J. Misc. 604; 167 Atl. 691 (1933), the two parties were under the age when they might legally marry. The boy told the girl that he had $300 and asked her to marry him. Relying on this statement of his economic condition, she consented and they had illicit intercourse. She became pregnant and he then stated he had never intended to marry her. When she sued, he pleaded infancy as a defense. The court recognized the general rule that infancy is a defense, but took the position that the boy by his fraudulent conduct had gone beyond the protection of the rule.

[7] For comments on this matter see 35 *Minnesota Law Review* (1951); 8 *Washington and Lee Law Review* (1951).

[8] In *Miller* v. *Miller*, 132 Misc. (N.Y.) 121 (1928), the parties had an antenuptial agreement that they would refrain from marital intercourse for a time but that after the expiration of the agreed period, they would establish normal marital relations. After marriage, the woman refused and continued to refuse. The court granted an annulment saying that marital intercourse (so that children may be born) is an obligation of the marriage contract.

religious education of the children. In general, the law declines to enforce such arrangements, holding that the public policy relating to the marriage state may not be varied by individuals to suit their own convenience. Sometimes the court grants an annulment of the marriage because one party has in mind certain personal plans that do not accord with the generally accepted ideas of marriage. And occasionally, the law will enforce such an agreement.[9]

At common law, the father and not the mother could decide how the child should be educated. The statutes in this country usually give the parents equal powers in this respect. With few exceptions, courts have generally refused to enforce antenuptial contracts regarding religious education of the children.[10]

A second group of antenuptial contracts deals with property. These may be divided into two categories. In one of them, the prospective husband tries to avoid the traditional obligation to support his future wife. In the other, there are property settlements.

The prospective husband who anticipates relieving himself of the continuing legal duty to support his wife is generally doomed to disappointment.[11]

In the ordinary property settlement antenuptial agreements, the contract generally will be upheld after marriage provided certain factors are present. The agreement must have been made in contemplation of a valid marriage. That is to say, it should not be susceptible of interpretation as a means of facilitating separation or divorce. It should be executed only after full adequate disclosure by each prospective partner as to the full extent of the property of the other. It should also, in the light of all the surrounding circumstances, be fair to both parties. These last two safeguards are primarily for the benefit of the woman. Traditionally the woman before and during marriage has been regarded by the law as one who is in need of special protection.[12]

Again, the woman, who is assumed to be less familiar with business affairs and more likely to be subject to overpersuasion, must have some reasonable information given to her of the nature and value of the man's property. But if the woman has this knowledge, her complaint that she did not know her legal rights in the matter will not be heard. This principle makes it desirable to re-emphasize the importance of consulting a lawyer before rather than after.

---

9 In *Ramon v. Ramon*, 34 N.Y.S. 2d 100 (1942), the parties had agreed that if children were born to them, they should be brought up in the Roman Catholic faith. After marriage, the woman refused to permit this sort of religious education. The woman left the man and sued him for support. He raised the antenuptial agreement as a defense. The court held that this contract was enforceable and that the woman had broken it.

10 See James E. Carty, "The Enforceability of Antenuptial Agreements for the Religious Instruction of Children," II, *Duke Bar Journal*, 70 (1951).

11 See Jacobs and Goebel, *Cases and Materials in Domestic Relations* (1952), pp. 639 ff.

12 F. V. Harper, *Problems of the Family* (Indiana: Bobbs-Merrill, 1952), pp. 45 ff.

A third sort of antenuptial contract brings together one or both of the engaged parties and a third person. There are two general groups of examples of this class: contracts (or provisions) in restraint of marriage, and contracts encouraging marriage. Contracts or wills or other dispositions of property, the effect of which is to restrain marriage, are held to be against public policy.[13] Marriage brokerage contracts are examples of the other group. The essence of these arrangements is a financial inducement to some person to encourage marriage. The money may come from a person desiring to be married or, for example, from a parent to help a child into matrimony. Again, however, the courts view with alarm efforts to make the marriage choice depend upon the salesmanship of third persons.[14] Orthodox Jewish groups, however, employ a person known as the *shadchan,* to all intents and purposes a marriage broker, and in rural Ireland a "go-between" frequently performs a similar function.

ENGAGEMENT PRESENTS

Engagement presents fall into two groups: those given between the engaged persons and those donated by third persons. Ordinarily in law a gift is a gift; once the transaction of giving is complete, the donor cannot recover. But there are circumstances under which the law allows recovery. So far as gifts between engaged couples are concerned, ordinarily there are four classes: gifts to attract attention or to improve one's position — for example, tickets to a football game; personal gifts as a matter of sentiment on anniversaries or holidays — for example, a birthday gift of flowers or jewelry or clothing; presents intended to be used in the future home, such as furniture, china, silverware, rugs; and the engagement ring. Znaniecki would call these "social instruments" bound up with the general "social method" of courtship persuasion.

No doubt there are presents which are given with the express understanding that, upon the happening of a contingency, they are to be returned. Recovery in such cases depends upon the ability of the donor to prove the agreement and the happening of the contingency. Odd as it may seem, there are some persons whose courtship procedure has been sufficiently cold-blooded to enable them to provide such proof!

Most of the litigation which occurs with respect to such matters, however, arises in cases where the intent of the parties is not express. In such

---

13 In *Knost* v. *Knost,* 129 S.W. 665 (1910), a will contained the following provision: "In the event of the marriage of my said daughter Anna Marie Louisa she is to receive only the same proportion of my estate as each of the other children." The court held that this provision was in restraint of marriage and therefore was contrary to public policy and void.

14 In *Packerman* v. *Shuster,* 12 Penna. D & C 717, a father offered a third person $500 for procuring for the daughter a young man inclined toward matrimony. The third person then sued for his $500. The court held that he could not recover because it is essential that marriage be voluntary and free from the influence brought to bear on either of the parties.

event the court must infer the meaning from the actions of the parties or from the class of article to which the gift belongs. Obviously, if the man takes the girl to a dance, the cost of the evening's entertainment, unless expressly stipulated, is not likely to be a matter as to which he may later sue her for reimbursement. Similarly, if the man gives the girl a wrist watch for a Christmas present, the idea that it is to be returned does not spring naturally to mind. It is something to be demonstrated by testimony of competent witnesses.

But with respect to the third and fourth classes of gifts — items to be used in the future home, and engagement rings — perhaps different presumptions may arise. It is clear that the event which touches off the suit may have something to do with the matter of recovery. Where the girl breaks the engagement, sympathy may swing to the jilted man and it may be argued that he should have these gifts back. If the man breaks the engagement, perhaps there is less reason to consider his feelings. If the parties mutually agree to disagree, still a third situation is present.

The cases generally allow recovery of the presents for the home by a young man when the girl has broken the engagement without legal justification. It is in the field of the engagement ring, however, that the greatest controversy has arisen. When the woman is not at fault, she usually may keep the ring; and a similar decision has been reached where she died before the marriage took place. Where the man is guilty of breaking the engagement, he usually may not recover.

But the gift is not necessarily between the parties. Relatives and friends may make donations. Wedding presents generally belong to the bride. Whether they could be recovered if the engagement was broken and the bride refused to return them would depend upon the circumstances of the case. In theory, the court might well find a condition implied in the transaction that the articles were given only because there was a wedding. But unless conditions pointed to some such implied understanding, a gift would be a gift.

A series of cases illustrative of court actions on suits involving engagement presents follows:

(1) In *Ruehling* v. *Hornung,* 98 Pa. Super. Ct. 535 (1929), the woman was required to return the engagement ring, a wrist watch, and a medallion.

(2) In *Seiler* v. *Funk,* 32 Ont. L.R. 99, the man was allowed to recover the items purchased for the home, but not personal items or Christmas presents.

(3) In *Cohen* v. *Sellar* (1926), 1 K.B. 536, the man gave the woman an engagement ring. She sued him for breach of promise and he filed a countersuit for the return of the ring. The jury found that the man had broken the engagement without cause and allowed the woman to keep the ring.

(4) In *Urbanus* v. *Burns,* 20 N.E. (2d) 869 (1939), the gifts were a dinner ring, a wrist watch, an onyx ring, and a diamond ring. Each gift was made on Christmas Eve. It appeared the parties were engaged. She died

and the man sued the estate. The court allowed the estate to keep the gifts because the woman had not broken the contract to marry.

(5) In *Beer* v. *Hart,* 274 N.Y.S. 671, the man was held at fault for the breach and could not recover the ring.

(6) In *Yubar* v. *Witaski,* 95 Pa. Super. Ct. (1929), the girl was a minor. The boy gave her a ring with the express understanding that if she should break the engagement, she would return the ring. She did breach her promise and refused restitution. The court, because she was a minor, allowed her to retain the ring.

(7) In *Wilson* v. *Riggs,* 196 N.E. 584 (1935), the engagement was broken by mutual consent and the court allowed the man to recover the engagement ring.

INTERFERENCE WITH CONTRACTS TO MARRY

After two persons are engaged, both are likely to receive quantities of advice, particularly with respect to the other person. Some of that advice will be in the direction of cautioning against the particular marriage, and this may result in a breach of the engagement. A number of cases have been devoted to a consideration of the question as to who may advise in such situations and what advice is permissible. One would assume that parents should be given every opportunity short of slander and libel to advise their children. The law seems to support this idea.[15] Even if the advice is maliciously given, there are cases which hold that there is no liability. Friends of the engaged couple may also give advice freely. In one case, the employer of the lady was permitted to persuade her not to marry.

In *Clarahan* v. *Casper,* 296 Pac. 140, the employer raised her salary from $150 a month to $250 a month and showered her with gifts and attentions, and the court said that no suit for persuading the woman to break the contract would be entertained. Of course, if there had been slander or libel, another problem would be presented.

THE MARRIAGE CEREMONY

If the premarital period seems to the student to be complicated by a large number of legal rules, such complication is slight indeed when compared to those which relate to the other phases of the life cycle of the family. The marriage ceremony is a time for the assembling of friends, a procession down the aisle of the church, appropriate organ music, a clergy-

---

[15] In *Leonard* v. *Whetstone,* 68 N.E. 197, the boy was a minor. He had seduced the girl and was ready to marry her when his father threatened to disinherit him if he did not immediately break off the proposed marriage. The father also sent the son out of the state to avoid the consequences of a suit for breach of promsie. The girl then sued the father for inducing the son to breach the engagement. The court held that she might not recover. A parent has a perfect right to advise his child.

man, responses, a reception, and an escape in a duly placarded car amid a shower of rice. It may also be an elopement with a hasty visit to a justice of the peace who brings in some witnesses, reads the ceremony, and accepts his fees. In some religious groups it may be a matter of the two parties' standing in the presence of the congregation and stating their mutual intentions. Here again, as in the case of the engagement, the acts of the parties have diverse implications depending upon the point of view of the observer. As our present effort is to see the ceremony through the eyes of the lawyer, it is necessary to mention the legal significance of the marriage ceremony.

The state, in what is known as a "democracy," is interested in the development of stable and enduring families because they have definite functions to perform in connection with the ownership of property, the orderly adjustment of the relations between the sexes, and the rearing of children. Laws relating to marriage have a definite bearing upon efforts of the state to further these and similar social and economic aims and objectives.

The state wants a record of these families so that the legitimacy of children and the ownership of property and the orthodox character of the union may be publicly available. Hence the parties are required to procure a license to marry. The issuance of the license is in the discretion of a public official. By law his authority and powers are set forth. Penalties are imposed for departure from the rules.

As a guard against marriages which might not properly be entered into, the state requires not only a record but publicity for a reasonable time in which to enable interested parties to take action. The traditional practice of publication of the banns has in many states been superseded or supplemented by statutes requiring the giving of advance notice. The catastrophe of hasty and ill-advised marriages calls for some such preventive measure.

The idea that a certain degree of physical or mental fitness should be a prerequisite to marriage has resulted in laws in thirty-five of our jurisdictions requiring a physical examination as a preliminary step to securing a license.[16]

The place of the marriage and the question as to who has the right to solemnize the ceremony are matters considered by the law. Clergymen and justices of the peace often are legally empowered to officiate. Determination of the authority of a justice of the peace is comparatively simple. But there have been cases in which the authority of the clergyman has been the subject of judicial inquiry.

Limitations of space forbid us to include here copies of all the marriage laws of the various states, but it is possible to include the text of the Uniform Marriage Act. This Act is issued by the National Conference on Uniform State Laws, a group of persons appointed by the Governors of the respec-

---

[16] In *Peterson* v. *Uidule,* 147 N.W. 966, the constitutionality of one of these earlier statutes was proclaimed by the court against objections that the law constituted an unreasonable restriction on the right to marry, that it was an interference with the constitutional right to life, liberty, and the pursuit of happiness, and other objectives.

tive states. They meet annually to consider acts drafted by committees. They have approved some seventy-five Uniform and Model Acts. With the endorsement of the American Bar Association they urge the enactment of these laws in each state. In consequence, some order and uniformity is appearing in the fifty-one jurisdictions composing the United States of America.

The Uniform Marriage and Marriage License Act was adopted in Wisconsin in 1917. The Uniform Marriage Evasion Act was adopted in Illinois, Louisiana, Massachusetts, Vermont, and Wisconsin. Both Acts were withdrawn from the active list at the meeting in 1943. However, their scope and content provide us with worthwhile illustrations of the general problem.

The Uniform Marriage and Marriage License Act deals in section one with the marriage contract and how it is made. The language is mandatory and indicates that the "only" way to contract a valid marriage is that prescribed in the statute. It also provides for a ceremonial marriage before designated officials; and a religious ceremonial marriage where the parties proceed "in accordance with the customs, rules, and regulations of any religious society, denomination, or sect to which either of the parties may belong."

Section two. Provides for the issuance of a marriage license.

Section three. Regulates the application for marriage license with a waiting period of "at least five days."

Section four. Covers identification of the parties and a statement of qualification and information to be gathered. This includes ". . . the legality of the contemplated marriage, the date of same, the names, relationship, if any, age, nationality, color, residence and occupation of such as are under the age of legal majority, any prior marriage or marriages of the parties, or either of them, and the manner of dissolution thereof . . ."

Section five. Covers consent of parent or guardian if either "of the contracting parties be under the marriageable age of consent as established by law . . ."

Section six. Requires a public notice of the intention to marry and prescribes the manner in which any one who objects to the marriage may legally present his grounds and have them passed upon by a court.

Section seven. Imposes a penalty upon one who swears falsely "in regard to any material fact relating to the competency of either or both of the parties . . ."

Section eight. Penalizes the clerk for unlawfully issuing a license.

Section nine. Prescribes records and blanks.

Section ten. Outlines the contents of the license — covering such points, for example, as where and when and by whom the ceremony may be performed.

Sections eleven and twelve. Specify the contents of the license (a) when the ceremony is before an official, (b) where the parties marry themselves.

Section thirteen. Treats the marriage certificates in similar fashion.

Sections fourteen and fifteen. Direct the delivery, filing, and recording of the certificate.

Section sixteen. Penalizes the officiating person for unlawful solemnization of the marriage.

Section seventeen. Punishes the parties for unlawful solemnization.

Section eighteen. Prescribes fine and imprisonment for one who "not being duly authorized by the laws of this state, shall wilfully or knowingly undertake to solemnize a marriage in this state."

Sections nineteen and twenty. Punish the failure to file the certificate, and violation relating to records.

Section twenty-one. Allows an action to recover "any fine or forfeiture accruing under the provisions of this act. . . ."

Section twenty-two. Makes a marriage license and certificate "prima facie evidence of such marriage. . . ."

Section twenty-three. Nullifies "all marriages hereafter contracted in violation of any of the requirements of Section one of this act except as to immaterial irregularities which are covered by Section twenty-four (immaterial irregularities as to want of authority of person officiating) and Section twenty-five (other immaterial irregularities)."

Section twenty-six. Deals with the marriage which is invalid at time of performance because of some obstacle. If the parties after the obstructing conditions are removed "continued to live together as husband and wife in good faith on the part of one of them" they shall "be held to have been legally married from and after the removal of such impediment. . . ."

Section twenty-seven. Provides for the legitimation of a child by the subsequent marriage of his parents.

Section twenty-eight. Calls for an annual report.

The usual sections as to interpretation and construction of the law and as to fees are included.

In the matter of evasion of the regulatory provisions of marriage law, a favorite device is to go to some other state where the obstacles are fewer, get married, and return home, trusting that the courts, if a case should ever arise, will apply the rule that a marriage valid where celebrated is valid everywhere. To remedy this situation several states have adopted antimarriage-evasion statutes.

Consequences of Failing to Comply with the Law

The parties may not go out of the state to evade the law but may stay where they are, counting upon a ceremony less formal than that prescribed by law to render their union legal. There is a difference of opinion among the states as to whether these less formal common-law unions should or should not be recognized. In a number of states there exist statutes which the courts have construed as prohibiting these common-law marriages. In other states common-law marriages are recognized as necessary and valid.

In *Caddy* v. *Relief Association*, 196 Atl. 590 (1938), a Pennsylvania court was called upon to determine the status of the following marriage. The parties were engaged and several times planned to be married but untoward events always interrupted. On one such occasion their car broke down. They took it to a garage and went to a motion picture while it was being repaired. In the theater the man produced a ring and suggested that they live together as "common-law people" without ceremony or priest or preacher. She said she was satisfied with the arrangement. He put the ring on her finger and she continued to wear it. After the motion picture was over they ate supper, got the repaired car, and drove to the home in which they had planned to live together. They did live together for several years till the man died. The woman now claims the insurance as his wife. The court held that common-law marriages were good in Pennsylvania and that this was a valid marriage.

The requirements of a valid common-law marriage vary from state to state. The points around which the cases revolve include a mutual agreement by the parties in terms of the present tense to take each other as husband and wife; cohabitation, a living together and a holding out of each by the other as man and wife to friends, neighbors, and the general public; repute, a recognition by the community of the two as husband and wife.

Once a common-law marriage is recognized as valid, the parties to it are as much husband and wife as though it had been signalized by the most elaborate ceremony and compliance with the statute.

SHOULD THE LAW RECOGNIZE COMMON-LAW MARRIAGE?

In a frontier society where people could not readily go to court houses and where preachers came by only occasionally, a device like common-law marriage was a necessity. Present-day legislatures are progressively extending prohibitions against the practice and requiring substantial compliance with the process involving a license, examinations, a ceremony before an authorized official, a record, public notice, and similar precautions. If one starts with the argument that marriage is a desirable status, that the law should encourage it and should therefore attempt to find that relations between men and women are legal rather than illegal, it is easy to reach a conclusion supporting common-law marriage. On the other hand, one may argue that marriage is so important a relationship that only specially qualified persons are entitled to share in it, that just as it is made difficult for people to become members of learned professions, so the way to marriage should be planned to keep out the unfit. By such reasoning one may justify an elaborate ceremonial. It is difficult to harmonize the two lines of reasoning. Perhaps it will be necessary for us to go through a longer period of trial and error before we decide upon the most satisfactory way to prevent undesirable marriages and to encourage those promising more stable families. One thinks, of course, of education, of work by properly trained marriage counselors, as one device which may be helpful.

Is This Marriage Valid?

Even after the marriage ceremony is proved to have been in accordance with the law there is still a question as to whether the parties are really married. Marriages are annulled for reasons existing before or at the time of the ceremony. Divorces are secured for events which occur after the wedding. An annulment declares that there never was a valid marriage. A divorce proclaims that a marriage formerly came into being but from and after the divorce decree it no longer has legal effect. In the case of both annulment and divorce the parties are back pretty much where they started from.

Space permits merely a statement of the usual grounds for annulment, with a few illustrations. These grounds depend in some states upon statutory authority, and elsewhere upon principles of equity derived perhaps from medieval ecclesiastical law at a time when divorce was not permitted and legal ingenuity was called in to extricate unhappy spouses from an intolerable situation. The major categories are: situations where the consent of the parties was not obtained; fraud; and situations in which the public policy of the state is involved.

Marriage is in many respects like a commercial contract; and consequently a meeting of minds, an intent to enter into such an agreement, is essential. Where this intent is lacking, the court frequently finds that the formalities do not count because a basic element was missing. The following are examples:

A. *A marriage in jest.* Occasionally persons marry as a climax to a "party." Realizing the next day that they have gone through a ceremony which may involve legal implications, they seek legal advice. Often, to keep the record clear, an annulment is requested and sometimes granted.

B. *A marriage of an insane or feebleminded person.* Some courts have held such marriages void, and others voidable subject to ratification by the insane person if and when he recovers his sanity. Here as in other cases where the law deals with a mental condition, the test to be applied is generally expressed in terms of the ability of the party to understand the nature of marriage and its consequences. The medical profession would surely not regard this as an adequate test.

C. *Where one or both of the parties is under the influence of intoxicating liquor or drugs.* The determining of the validity of a test is again a medical question. How much intoxication is needed to justify the court in recognizing the plea?

D. *Mistake as to the identity of the other party.* If a man marries Mary believing she is Eleanor, the courts may grant an annulment. But many of the cases which are brought under this heading do not result favorably for the plaintiff.

E. *Duress or force.* A person acting under the impulse of fear or threat of bodily harm is not exercising his own intent in the acts which he commits, and if at a later time and on a safe occasion he asks the court for relief, it may be expected.

F. *Fraud.* There are varying degrees of fraud, and a number of test cases reveal the types of fraud which may or may not be most likely to bring about annulment:

Adequate Basis	Rejected as Basis
Concealed pregnancy by another	Concealment of mental incapacity
Concealment of serious, incurable, or venereal disease	Lack of love and affection
	Misrepresentation of character
Concealment of sterility	Misrepresentation of race and nationality
Fraudulent intention not to consummate the marriage	Misrepresentation as to wealth

G. *Actions contrary to public policy* such as consanguinity, miscegenation, bigamy, prior marriage, and not divorced.

MARRIAGE STATUS

Having now considered engagement to marry, the marriage ceremony, and defects in the marriage which may be grounds for annulment, we come to those persons who are validly married. The first question regarding them is the nature of the relationship which they have taken upon themselves. The law refers to marriage in terms of *status* and contrasts it with the engagement to marry, which is like a contract, and with the marriage ceremony which, as the service indicates on its face, is another contract.

The marriage service is, in a sense, a three-party contract — the third party being either the church or the state, depending upon whether the official who celebrates the nuptials is a clergyman or a justice of the peace. It is spoken of as a sacrament or a special kind of contract which cannot properly be dissolved without the consent of all three parties.

But the marriage ceremony also creates a relation to which the state has attached certain factors which make it different from a contract. A few of the differences may be noted.

In a contract the parties may agree upon the terms and conditions. Unless these happen to be contrary to law or morals, the courts generally will enforce them or reward damages for their breach. In a marriage the law usually lays down the terms and conditions, and the right of action between the parties for a breach is in the direction of annulment or divorce and not in terms of money damages.

In *Gavin* v. *Gavin,* 264 S.W. 529 (1924), the woman alleged cruel and outrageous treatment by the husband, but contended she did not want a divorce. Instead she set forth her condition before marriage as the proprietress of a millinery business, and the representations of the man that he was wealthy and would supply her every want. She said she married him in reliance on these promises, and when they failed to materialize she brought the suit. She asked the court for loss of benefits, comforts and emoluments. The court said that in the absence of a statute permitting such an action it could not allow her to proceed. The man had agreed to marry her and had done so. His further promises were merged in and superseded by the marriage. The woman's right of action was therefore only that allowed married people against each other.

In a contract the parties may mutually make a new agreement at any time and abolish the old one. In a marriage, dissolution is permitted only by action of the state; and *a relationship which permits mutual dissolution by act of the parties alone is not marriage. Legally there is no basis for divorce by mutual consent!*
Ordinarily a contract that is valid where it is entered into, is valid everywhere. This rule does not hold good as to marriages. Miscegenous marriages have already been referred to. Polygamous unions also cause trouble.

In *Reynolds* v. *U.S.*, 98 U.S. 145 (1878), the idea of marriage as being a union of one man and one woman to the exclusion of all others was developed. The defendant was prosecuted under a statute prohibiting polygamy. He contended that he was a Mormon and that as a member of this group polygamy was enjoined upon him. He urged that since his act was the performance of a religious duty and since the Bill of Rights guaranteed religious freedom, he should not be prosecuted. The court said that religious freedom meant only the right to hold beliefs and did not extend to overt acts. The court further held that polygamy was recognized as antisocial among Christian peoples, so the man was convicted.

A contract is a device protected by Article I, Section 10 of the Constitution of the United States, which declares that "No state shall . . . pass any . . . law impairing the obligation of contracts." Marriage, on the other hand, is a creature of statute in the various states and may be modified only by the legislature.
In the eyes of the law, marriage is somewhat like a contract and yet it is considerably different. The rules are technical, but behind them is a picture in the minds of the judges to which they consciously or unconsciously refer in deciding the cases which arise.

Rights and Obligations of Married Persons

There is a great deal of law relating to the property of married persons. It is embodied in two systems. One of these stems from the common law of England and is characterized by a legislative effort to get away from the original idea which submerged the legal identity of the wife in the husband and gave him extensive control over her property. The statutes in this country embodying the changes begin about 1830 and mark a revolution in legal thinking. They are called Married Women's Statutes. As they differ in each state, it is impracticable to do more than refer to them here. The other system of law — known as community property — is in effect in several states of the West and Southwest. It comes to us from the civil law of France and Spain. Its distinguishing feature is a division of property into three classes: that of the husband, that of the wife, and a remainder called "the community" owned by the husband and wife in a form of partnership, with the husband acting as manager. Here again the details of the system vary from state to state, and space forbids more than mention of a substantial field of legal rules which deserves more adequate examination.

But there are rights and obligations of married persons of a different sort.

RIGHTS OF THE HUSBAND WITH RESPECT TO THE WIFE

Among the rights of the husband at common law were those of determining the domicile, enjoying consortium, and using his wife's earnings.

The word "domicile" is defined as "that place where a man has his true, fixed, and permanent home and principal establishment, and to which, whenever he is absent, he has the intention of returning." At common law the husband had a right to fix or to change the place of abode of the family. If the wife refused to accompany him, the act could be treated as a desertion on her part. Remedies of various sorts were open to him in that event. Whether it was ever an absolute right, today it is certainly qualified by reasonableness. Both parties should act reasonably. If the husband demands that the wife reside in a place which the court thinks is unsuitable, she will be excused for refusing to obey him.[17] If the wife, however, is unreasonable in her stubborn attitude, the court may refer to the original rule. The question seems to depend upon the reason for the wife's refusal. Exceptions to the rule that a wife's domicile is and should be with her husband are found in instances where the husband abandons the wife or, by his conduct, compels her to leave him; where the husband and wife agree that the wife for certain purposes may live elsewhere; and where the wife sues for divorce.

The word "consortium" is defined as "the right of the husband and wife respectively to the conjugal fellowship, company, cooperation, and aid of the other." It follows that if some outside person interferes with the right of the husband or the right of the wife to this consortium, the aggrieved spouse may sue the intender and recover damages. The question is as to the ways in which the third person may encroach upon the consortium. Obviously, if the wife is injured physically — for example, in an automobile accident — the husband is deprived of the society and companionship of the wife. Perhaps he must pay hospital and doctor bills. The offender should be made to pay. Under the statutes the usual problem

---

17 In *Powell* v. *Powell*, 29 Vt. 148, the husband asked for a divorce from the wife on the ground of desertion. They had lived together in Vermont. They then moved to New York and lived as man and wife for several years. The husband returned to Vermont, but the wife refused to follow him because she did not want to "live with him near his relatives." After failing to induce her to return, he sued. The court decided that the husband's right to determine a domicile was not an arbitrary power and the wife's refusal did not amount to desertion.

is whether there should be two suits or just one. Under one type of statute, the woman would sue for her own damages and sufferings as if she were unmarried. Under another type of statute, the husband or the husband and wife together would sue.

A second type of situation is where the loss of consortium is caused by "criminal conversation." This phrase is defined as "the act of adultery in a suit brought by the husband of the married woman with whom the act was committed, to recover damages of the adulterer."

A third type of loss occurs in cases where the basis of the action is alienation of affections. The wrongdoer has alienated the affections of one spouse and thereby deprives the other of the aid, comfort, assistance, and society which consortium gives him. In some states which have abolished breach of promise of marriage actions, the statute includes the prohibition against alienation of affections suits.

Another right of the husband gave him control over the wife's earnings. At common law, a husband was entitled absolutely to his wife's earnings. Modern statutes generally have given her a right to money she earns in enterprises apart from the household or the husband's business.

RIGHTS OF THE WIFE

The wife, on the other hand, has certain rights with respect to the husband. She is entitled to support, and she can act as his agent under certain circumstances.

The duty of the husband to support the wife is generally recognized and is sometimes prolonged to cover cases where the parties are divorced. The money paid is then often spoken of as alimony. This duty of the husband is not entirely absolute. If he is unable to support her, the judge may excuse him.[18] If the parties have made an agreement as to the support he should pay her and he complies with the agreement, the judge may refuse her further financial aid. If the wife does not abide by her marital vows and do her share in the work of the family, the judge may refuse to allow her support.

When the husband fails to fulfill this obligation, the wife has several remedies. One of them is a criminal prosecution for nonsupport. The various states have laws making this failure on his part a crime.

But there is another means by which she may obtain relief. She may incur certain obligations which the husband is called upon to pay. The wife may be an agent of the husband where he expressly authorizes her to act. She may also be an agent through necessity.

Where the husband and wife are living together and the wife makes purchases or incurs obligations, the presumption is that the wife acts as agent of the husband. A third person who advances credit to the wife under

[18] In *Roberts* v. *Roberts*, 125 S.W. (2d) 199 (1938), the wife sued for divorce and separate maintenance. The husband had become impoverished and moved to his mother's home, stating that he would return when he could find work. The court denied the divorce and the prayer for separate maintenance.

such circumstances expects the husband to pay. If the husband is to escape liability he must show rebuttal to the presumption.

In *Saks* v. *Huddleston,* 36 Fed. (2d) 537, a wife of a representative in Congress bought a fur coat for $235 and a scarf for $18 at the plaintiff's store in Washington. Plaintiff sued the husband alleging that it relied on his credit but as a matter of convenience to its customers kept the account in the wife's name. The store also had a promissory note signed by the wife. If nothing further had appeared among the facts, the court might well have found that the wife was the implied agent of the husband; that the articles purchased were reasonably necessary to her standard of living; and that the husband was liable. The husband, however, urged that the presumption should be rebutted because of the following facts. He gave her $75 a month for clothing which, in his opinion and having regard to his financial resources, was reasonable. During the preceding year he had given her an additional $2000 for personal expenses. He had told her not to run any accounts at department stores in Washington. He knew nothing about this debt until it was started.

The court was inclined to feel that a husband should provide for his wife according to his station in life, and if he does not she may contract debts on his credit — but in this case held for the husband.

Under certain statutes the wife is made personally liable from her own estate for debts, and in such a situation the question may be whether the wife is acting as an agent or on her own account. If she is acting as the agent of her husband, he is liable; otherwise she must pay for the debt from her own funds.

Where the husband and wife are living apart through the husband's fault, the presumption continues that the wife is acting as his agent. Where the separation is the fault of the wife, the presumption is that she acts on her own responsibility.

In cases of this sort the question is often raised as to whether the particular article purchased is or is not a necessary. The court in answering the question applies such tests as the health and comfort of the wife and the station in life and financial position of the husband.

Creditors have found the operation of these rules, whether under the common law or under married women's acts, quite uncertain. They contend it is not proper to place upon them the duty of an extensive investigation of the legal status of each feminine customer to determine who is to pay the bill. In some states they have been successful in having passed what are called Family Expense Statutes. Under them the husband and wife are jointly liable for family expenses. But the husband is still primarily liable where third parties have sold the wife "necessaries."

THE DISSOLUTION OF THE FAMILY

A family may come to an end in a variety of ways. Informally there may be desertion or abandonment by one of the spouses. At law there may be a separation recognized by an agreement, a limited divorce, and absolute divorce — for causes arising after the marriage. An annulment may be granted for cause arising before the moment of the wedding. Finally dissolution may come about from natural causes — death and the arrival at maturity of a child. Dissolution by divorce has received adequate attention in another chapter, and will not be discussed here. There is, however, much law relating to the other types of dissolution.

In an *abandonment* one spouse leaves, at least without the legally valid consent of the other. Where the husband is the "guilty" party the problem of support for the wife and the children becomes acute. At common law the duty of the husband to provide proper support for his wife and family was clearly recognized. The statutes have definitely improved the position of the wife in this respect, giving her criminal as well as civil machinery to enforce her demands. She may sue him civilly in a number of jurisdictions, either because the status of marriage imposes such obligation upon the husband or because failure by the husband to perform may throw the responsibility upon the state to provide support. The criminal law marks the greatest change in this respect. Modern statutes indicate ingenuity and resourcefulness of the draftsmen. The two most difficult problems are: (a) how to find the elusive spouse, who may have fled to another state; and (b) how to deal with the spouse who either because of handicaps cannot earn enough to support himself and family or who stubbornly prefers to spend some time in jail. Mention should be made here of the Uniform Desertion and Non-Support Act. From early in the present century the National Conference of Commissioners on Uniform State Laws has been seeking to provide a degree of uniformity in the statute law of the various American jurisdictions. The Act dealing with desertion, abandonment, and nonsupport has been adopted in a variety of states.

Separation as a means of dissolving a family usually involves an agreement between the parties. When that agreement is in writing a series of legal problems is presented. At common law husbands and wives could not contract or make gifts or deed property one to the other. To get around this rule they sometimes employed the device of giving the property to a third person with instructions as to how he should use it. Such person was sometimes a trustee. Exceptions to this general rule were worked out by courts of equity, so that conveyances by the husband directly to the wife were held good provided a fair and reasonable arrangement was made to protect the wife.[19] Today under the new statutes separation agreements are generally recognized, provided certain conditions are complied with. The separation must have actually taken place or must immediately follow the signing of the agreement. If the agreement looks toward a future sep-

[19] In *Leham* v. *Leham*, 244 N.Y.S. 265, the wife asked for a divorce with alimony; the husband contended that the parties had entered into a separation agreement which provided for payments to the wife in lieu of alimony. It appeared that the husband had not fully performed his part of the agreement. The court held that the wife was not limited in such a case to her rights under the separation agreement but could also ask for alimony in the discretion of the court. If the husband had performed his part of the contract, the court might have held that the payments were fair to the wife.

aration, it may be held void. If the agreement contains a provision that the parties may live apart, this is not enforceable by the courts. If the parties do come together again and live as man and wife even for a short time, the agreement is of no further legal effect.

ALIMONY

Alimony is related both to the problem of nonsupport and to family dissolution. It is defined as "the allowance which a husband, by order of the court, pays to his wife, being separate from him, for her mainte-nance. . . . It is also commonly used as equally applicable to all allowances, whether annual or in gross, made to a wife upon a decree of divorce." Four conditions usually must be satisfied before a court will award permanent alimony: the marriage must be legally valid; the marriage must have continued to the present time; the spouses must be separated by judicial decree; and the petitioning wife must be legally innocent.

Alimony developed originally in the ecclesiastical courts in England in connection with the law of divorce. In the United States every jurisdiction, except South Carolina, which does not grant divorces, has a statute respect-ing alimony. It is granted by the court and, in general, cannot be altered after the signing of the decree unless the statute expressly so provides. This discretion of the court ordinarily determines the form and amount of an award. The problem of enforcement involves requiring security for performance (a factor with which impecunious husbands can seldom comply) and the judicial power to seize his property or his person in order to enforce compliance.

In several states the statute authorizes the court in its discretion to award alimony to the husband — although the term "alimony" under these cir-cumstances is a misnomer.

Involved in the problem of alimony and the general dissolution of marriage is the matter of property settlements. Still others present a com-bination of the two.

Where the court has full or partial discretion, the idea of fault or of penalizing the offending spouse plays a part, and the judge has an oppor-tunity to apply to the parties in the case opinions of right and wrong which have come to be an important part of his thinking. It is a question whether a system of law based upon unrestricted personal judgment is de-sirable, however conscientious and able individual judges may be. On the other hand, a distribution of property based upon a rigid rule of law might work hardship in individual cases. The subject deserves general study in the light of the effect upon people of taking away from them or giving them family property. Violations of the divorce law such as adultery, cruelty, desertion may be punished by the criminal law. Is there reason to add to this punishment unlimited power to deprive a person of his prop-erty or to discourage him from desiring to accumulate it? *Should there not be in the case of dissolution of a family through divorce the same general plan for the dissolution of the family property as now obtains when the dissolution is caused by death?*

The Family and Death

When a family is confronted with the death of one of its members, the *legal repercussions* are largely in the field of property. The question is, "Who gets what property?"

It is difficult to discuss this matter: first, because there is some difference in the general approach of the law as between the common-law states and the community property states; second, because the law is statutory and varies materially from state to state. Perhaps the most that can be done here is to discuss various phases in the process of settling an estate and illustrate the points by reference to the statutes of a particular state arbitrarily selected.

From the point of view of the family and its interest in property, the following topics deserve mention: homestead, dower, curtesy, the procedure for settling an estate of a deceased person, including executors and administrators and the will.

"Homestead" is defined as "the home place — the place where home is." It is further described in terms of the laws covering it. "The homestead laws of various states are constitutional or statutory provisions for the exemption of a certain amount or value of real estate occupied by a debtor as his homestead from a forced sale for the payment of his debts. In some cases restraints are placed upon the alienation by the owner of his property, and in some cases the exempt property, upon the death of the owner, descends to the widow and minor children free from liability for his debts."

It is because of the restraints upon alienation and the rules of descent that the subject of homesteads should be mentioned here. The homestead is a valuable asset which under the laws of some states may not be given away by the person who makes a will. It may not be taken by creditors of the member of the family who dies. If there is no will, it descends in special fashion as the law provides.

Dower is defined as "the provision which the law makes for a widow out of the lands or tenements of her husband, for her support and the nurture of her children."

Curtesy is defined as "the estate to which by common law a man is entitled, on the death of his wife, in the lands or tenements of which she was seized in possession in fee simple or in toil during their coverture, provided they had lawful issue born alive which might have been capable of inheriting the estate."

These two words, "dower" and "curtesy," represent claims which husband and wife may make upon the estate of the other spouse after his or her death. The words are taken from the old law but are still in use by lawyers. In many states the old common-law dower and curtesy are abolished by statute and in their places are certain rights more recently created and dependent for their existence and nature upon the will of the legislature.[20] This problem is not met with in the same fashion in community property states. The community property upon the death of one spouse is divided and the surviving spouse takes a share in it.

It is necessary to mention these various rights which the surviving spouse has in the estate of the deceased, because unless proper provision is made beforehand the estate is lessened by these items, and results may be produced quite different from what the parties intended. Much disappointment and misunderstanding can be avoided in the family group if the members have a reasonably clear picture of what happens to the estate of a deceased member.

Mention has here been made of a situation in some states where certain property cannot be affected by previous agreement or deed or will — the homestead. Mention has also been made of dower and curtesy, which with the advice of a competent lawyer can be employed to aid in the welfare of the family. Without such expert advice difficulties are almost certain to arise. The present intent is to suggest the value of family planning so that the advantages of intestacy and testacy (see below) both may be weighed and a solution framed to meet a particular need. Each family has its own problems and these change from time to time; so no plan can be assumed adequate for any great period of time. It should be re-examined periodically.

The property which a person owns at the time of his death is called his estate. If he leaves a will he is *testate*. If there is no will he is said to die *intestate*. An estate consists of real estate, tangible personal property, and certain other valuables such as uncollected debts, which the law calls "choses in action." Land and the house on it is an example of real estate. Furniture, clothing, jewelry are examples of personal property. Among the other kinds of valuables are the right to money in bank, to the property represented by stocks, bonds, life insurance policies. Sometimes the person who owns the property is the exclusive owner. Other property is held jointly. A man and wife may own the home in both names, and upon the death of one of them the law in certain states gives the entire property to the survivor. This is called "tenancy by the entirety," and is very helpful to the survivor, who usually does not have to pay inheritance tax on this transfer of title. In other instances the ownership is joint or in common, and upon the death of one of the owners the property must be divided. The share of the deceased owner becomes part of his estate. A bank account may be held in joint ownership if arrangements with the bank are made.

A person who is planning the disposition of his property and affairs after death may look forward to the following procedure:

[20] In Massachusetts (Annotated Laws, Vol. VI, chap. 189) provisions are made.
    Sec. 1. A husband shall, upon the death of his wife, hold for his life one third of all land owned by her at any time during coverture. Such estate shall be known as his tenancy by curtesy, and the law relative to dower shall be applicable to curtesy. . . . A wife shall, upon the death of her husband, hold her dower at common law in her deceased husband's land. Such estate shall be known as her tenancy by dower.

A. Someone must be appointed by law charged with the responsibility and endowed with the authority necessary to settle the estate. This person is called an *executor* if the estate is settled under a will [21] and an *administrator* if there is no will. The appointment of an administrator involves a question as to who is entitled to preferential consideration by the court if more than one person wishes to undertake the task or if no one wishes to act.[22]

Four major situations may be recognized:

1. The decedent may leave lineal descendants, children, issue.
2. The decedent may leave no lineal descendants.
3. The decedent may leave no blood relations, kindred, heirs.
4. The surviving spouse may be forced to decide whether to take what the will provides or to choose the share allowed under the intestate laws, dower, curtesy, and similar substitute laws.

In any event some orderly procedure must be outlined to secure a competent administrator.

B. The executor or administrator must gather the assets of the estate. He gives notice of his appointment, usually by advertisement in the newspapers,

[21] In the Annotated Laws of Massachusetts, Chapter 192, are found the provisions for the probating of wills and the appointment of executors. Sec. 1 provides for a petition to the probate court, a proceeding which starts the process. The interested parties may agree "in writing" that the will may be probated, or they may contest its probate. In this latter event a lawsuit is begun to determine whether the will shall or shall not be admitted to probate.

Sec. 4. If a will has been duly proved and allowed the probate court shall issue letters testamentary thereon to the executor named therein, if he is legally competent and a suitable person and accepts the trust and within thirty days gives bond to discharge the same. . . .

In Deering's California Probate Code, Division III, Sec. 300, the community-property state provides: "When a person dies, the title to his property, real and personal, passes to the person to whom it is devised or bequeathed by his last will, or, in the absence of such disposition, to the persons who succeed to his estate as provided in Division II of this Code; but all of his property shall be subject to the possession of the executor or administrator and to the control of the Superior Court for the purposes of administration. . . ."

The law then proceeds to indicate how executors are appointed.

[22] Chapter 193 deals with the appointment of administrators, and here the law establishes a schedule of priorities among persons who may act in this capacity.

Sec. 1. Administration of the estate of a person deceased intestate shall be granted to one or more of the persons hereinafter mentioned and in the order named, if competent and suitable for the discharge of the trust and willing to undertake it, unless the court deems it proper to appoint some other person:

First, the widow or surviving husband of the deceased.

Second, the next of kin or their guardians or conservators as the court shall determine.

Third, if none of the above are competent or if they all renounce the administration or without sufficient cause neglect for thirty days after the death of the intestate to take administration of his estate, one or more of the principal creditors, after public notice upon the petition.

Fourth, if there is no widow, husband, or next of kin within the Commonwealth, a public administrator.

Sec. 7. If no executor is named in a will, or if all the executors therein named are dead or incompetent or refuse to accept the trust, or if, after being duly cited therefor, the executor neglects to accept the trust, or if he neglects for thirty days after the probate of the will to give bond according to law, the court shall commit the administration of the estate, with the will annexed, to any person interested in the will of said deceased, to any creditor of the deceased or to any suitable person . . .

and requests or demands or even sues to recover property belonging to the estate.[23]

C. A correct and authoritative inventory and appraisement of the property in the estate and its value must be made. This is to provide a basis for taxation and for the distribution of the estate to those entitled to it.

D. Eventually the executor or administrator, having collected the assets, verified the correctness of claims, and done the various tasks associated with his position, is prepared to make distribution of the funds and other property in his hands. He is guided by the terms of the homestead and dower and curtesy laws if such are in effect. If there is a will it supplies directions more or less effective. But if there is no will it is necessary to seek information from the law relating to distribution.

When the law comes to distribute the estate of a man who has not made a valid will, it is again faced with the possibilities mentioned above.

1. There may be lineal descendants who have at least a moral claim upon his estate.

2. There may be no lineal descendants, but there may be members of the family more distantly related who also have some claim.

3. There may be no family at all; in this case the estate goes to the state. The process is called escheat.

4. There may be a spouse, and rules of homestead, dower, and curtesy apply.

Where lineal descendants survive.

a. Some states do not mention the surviving spouse, who thus must claim dower or curtesy or the substitute for it.

b. Other states give the widow or widower equal shares in both real and personal property. The amount of the share varies.

c. In some states the widow and widower have equal rights but the share of real property and the share of personal property differ.

d. In still other states the widow, under certain circumstances, has a larger amount.

No lineal descendants survive.

a. In some states, the surviving spouse takes the whole estate, whether real or personal.

b. In other states the surviving spouse takes the entire real and personal property up to a certain value and in addition half of the property in excess of such value.

c. In other states the surviving spouse gets half of the estate, whether real or personal.

d. The other states provide in various ways.

[23] Chapter 195 contains General Provisions Relative to Executors and Administrators, under Massachusetts Law.

Sec. 1. The executor or administrator gives public notice of his appointment.

Sec. 5. He makes a true inventory of the real and personal property of the deceased.

Sec. 6. He provides for appraisers.

Sec. 7. He may secure authority to continue the business of the deceased for the benefit of the estate for a period not exceeding one year.

Sec. 11. He may be removed if he becomes insane or otherwise incapable of performing the trust.

Sec. 13. He may resign his trust.

No relatives survive.

a. Some states give the surviving spouse the entire estate, real and personal, with certain exception as parents.

b. Other states give the surviving spouse the entire estate if there is no issue, parent, brother, sister, or descendant of deceased brother or sister.

c. Other states give the surviving spouse the entire estate if there are no blood relatives or heirs.

d. There are miscellaneous provisions in other states.

Perhaps the foregoing is sufficient for a general preview of the vexed problem of settling decedents' estates.

The Will

A will is defined as "the disposition of one's property to take effect after death." It is one of the most important documents a man can sign because it is to direct others to do acts which the signer no longer can perform. The right to make a will is dependent upon statute. Limitations upon the right are found in the homestead laws already noted, dower and curtesy, the obligation to keep the provisions of the will consistent with the laws and the policy of the state, and the age of the testator.

Problems of execution of a will are as significant as the contents. There are three kinds of wills with respect to these problems of execution, and the law makes special provisions for each of the three. A nuncupative will is defined as "an oral will, declared by a testator in extremis, or under circumstances considered equivalent thereto, before witnesses, and afterwards reduced to writing." A holographic will is defined as "what is written with one's own hand."

The number of witnesses and their qualifications are generally regulated by statute. If an unqualified person's name appears as witness, the court may strike it out, and unless there are enough approved witnesses, the will may be declared invalid. Persons who are named in the will to share in the distribution should not serve as witnesses, because it may be suspected that some form of undue influence was used in the execution of the document.

The ceremony of execution should not be taken lightly. In general it consists of the following parts. The witnesses and the testator are brought together in the same place at the same time. The witnesses should be made known to the testator and he to them. He then should tell them that the document he holds in his hand and intends to sign is his last will and testament. Usually he need not reveal to them its contents — merely its nature and significance. He then asks them to serve as witnesses. They assent. He then signs the document at the end. They each sign the document after his signature and append their addresses. If at a later occasion the witnesses to the will are called upon, they usually go no further than to acknowledge their signatures. But they may be required to give opinions as to the mental condition of the testator and whether there were events which the law might construe as duress. Duress is defined as "personal restraint, or fear of personal injury or imprisonment." Undue influence is defined as "the use by one, in whom a confidence is reposed by another who holds a real or apparent authority over him, of such confidence or authority for the purpose of obtaining an unfair advantage of his weakness of mind, or of his necessities or distress . . . or to constrain him to do that which he would not have done without the exercise of that control. . . ."

The contents of the will, of course, represent individual needs and desires. In general, however, topics like the following are to be found in wills:

1. A description of the document as a "last will and testament." A letter may be received as a will under some circumstances, particularly if it shows an intent to dispose of property after death. But there is seldom reason to make a will if one expects it to be broken or attacked. If the document is not clearly a will, it may be successfully attacked.

2. An instruction to pay "all my debts and funeral expenses." The law provides for such payment anyway, but some people regard this as a business-like method of indicating a desire to discharge one's obligations. Sometimes provisions for the funeral or the tombstone are included.

3. Directions for the distribution of jewelry, clothing, household furniture, and personal belongings and small gifts by way of remembrance rather than as a division of the estate.

4. Directions for the distribution of money in bank, stocks, bonds, and other substantial items. Sometimes these bequests are direct to the recipient. At other times the property is given to a trustee or guardian to be used for the benefit of the donee.

5. Directions for the distribution of real estate owned by the testator. This also may be given outright or in trust or with conditions attached.

6. A residuary clause disposing of whatever has not been specifically given before. This is important; otherwise it may be necessary to have an administrator appointed to care for the items not covered by the will; this may mean more expense and trouble.

7. The appointment of an executor and provisions as to whether or not he shall be required to file a bond to insure the honesty of his conduct in this representative capacity.

8. The concluding clause — perhaps in the following form: "In witness whereof I, ———, the above named testator, have hereunto set my hand and seal this ——— day of ———, 19 ——."

9. The signatures of the testator and the witnesses. Where the will covers more than one page, it is good practice for the testator and witnesses to sign or initial each page. Then the provision in paragraph 8 above would recite the number of pages and the fact that each had been signed. This prevents the elimination of certain pages or the substitution of a new page.

To one who has not considered the matter it must appear very formal to require attention to all these points. Experience indicates, however, that unless they are attended to successful attacks upon the will may be made, and then the work has gone for nothing and the plans of the testator have been rendered difficult or impossible of completion.

The question may well be asked, "Why make a will?" The answer depends upon the individual circumstances of the testator. Two obvious advantages of a will are: the right to leave property as one wants to; and the right to name the person who shall have charge of settling the estate — the executor. In practice, however, the question is not one to be settled properly without conferences with a lawyer. The individual should consider first in which group of persons he belongs. Is he

1. A married man or woman who anticipates that upon his or her death he or she will be survived by a widow or a widower and children?

2. A married man or woman who anticipates that upon his or her death he or she will be survived by a widow and no children or a widower and no children?

3. A man or woman unmarried who anticipates leaving no widow or widower, no children or grandchildren or great-grandchildren, but who may be survived by brothers and sisters, aunts and uncles, cousins, nieces, and nephews?

4. A widow or widower who anticipates leaving no spouse, but a child or children or issue of children?

5. A man or woman without next of kin?

There is no space available here to attempt to answer each of these questions for all the states. The individual confronted with the question should ask himself, "If my estate were to be divided, under the intestate laws of my state, would the result satisfy me?" If the answer is "No," then a second question is whether a will can be drawn making a more satisfactory disposition. Naturally these are matters for a lawyer to consider. But the client, before approaching the lawyer, can do a number of things which will be helpful both to him and to the lawyer. The following are suggested:

1. A list of all property owned divided into the categories of real estate, personal property tangible, and personal property intangible, is a good first step. If values can be placed upon each item, the result will be helpful to the lawyer in determining taxation problems — local, state, and Federal. If the location of the real estate is set down, it will help to determine the law applicable to it because property in another state may have to be disposed of according to the laws of the other state. If there are stocks and bonds, the location of the corporation issuing them may be important for several reasons. If there are debts due, a list of the names and addresses of the debtors and information surrounding the transaction may be helpful. It is difficult to think of the family group with oneself no longer a member of it, but an effort in this direction is an essential to a useful will. If there are life insurance policies, it is well to see who the beneficiaries are and whether they should be changed. Proceeds of life insurance policies may or may not be made a part of the estate, depending upon the naming of beneficiaries.

2. A list of all persons whom the prospective testator may desire to remember in his will. Such a list should contain the items of property to be given to each person and the information as to whether the gift is to be absolute or conditional or in trust. The preparation of a plan of this sort requires much careful thinking. It is well to make several drafts and allow time for the implications of each draft to be considered before adopting or rejecting it. The first question is what is the testator's desire with respect to the persons to re-

ceive his bounty. The second is how best to accomplish the planned goal. Attention should be given to various future possibilities, and the testator should ponder — if so and so happens — how well this plan will function. The will speaks as of the day of the testator's death. Every day after that, the conditions with which he was familiar change. He cannot be there to make corrections in the plans. They remain as he laid them down. He cannot anticipate all the changes and events, but he should devote careful thought to the subject.

3. The testator should take the list of property and his carefully thought-out plan to a lawyer and ask the lawyer to talk the matter over and prepare a draft of a will. Only in the case of simple wills — such as leaving everything to one's wife and making her the executrix — is it safe to dash off a will. In many cases, several drafts are necessary to reach a plan which will carry out the testator's desires and a grouping of words which will stand up against attacks.

Attacks upon wills are made under a variety of conditions. A subsequent will or codicil may make the first one invalid. Evidence of undue influence, fraud, force, or lack of age or mental capacity may result in striking down the document purporting to be a will. The matter of improper formalities attending the execution — not enough disinterested witnesses — has already been referred to. The will may have been destroyed by the customary methods of cancellation, tearing, burning, etc., with the intent to revoke it. Or it may have been mutilated by someone without the authority of the testator or by mistake, and the question arises as to whether it is still a will. The language of the will itself may be confusing and require judicial interpretation. The property indicated in the will to be given to A may already have been bestowed upon B in the lifetime of the testator. Persons may be omitted by mistake from the will or given less than they could expect to get otherwise. They may decide to take against the will.

Considerations of this sort render it desirable that the testator should not make a will and then dismiss the subject from his mind. Every so often the testator should consult his lawyer again. A new tax law may have been passed in the meantime, some devisee may have died, children may have been born, property may have been sold or acquired; hence a new will or codicil may be called for.

The will itself should be kept carefully. A safedeposit box or a lawyer's safe are two recognized places of deposit. Some states, however, provide a special procedure by which a will may be lodged with a public official or even probated before the death of the testator. If the document is in public custody, one need not fear that it will be stolen or destroyed. If it has already been probated, there is no occasion at a later stage for anyone to claim its invalidity due to undue influence or force or fraud.

While one is discussing the matter with his lawyer, it is not a bad idea to consider whether it would be better to give the property right away instead of waiting until death. Considerations of taxation as well as other items may determine the answer.

Limitations of space preclude the possibility of a discussion of the operation of the tax laws upon family property. Since the laws change frequently, the only intelligent step to take is to consult a competent lawyer about the matter.

ADOPTION, CUSTODY, GUARDIANSHIP

Adoption is a proceeding by which a child is taken from one family — usually his natural family — and legally established as a member of a second family. Adoption, originally thought of as for the benefit of the adopting parent, in recent years has been hedged about by many precautions. The following preamble to the North Carolina Adoption Statute, Sec. 48-1, deserves to be quoted:

> The General Assembly hereby declares as a matter of legislative policy with respect to adoption that —
> (1) The primary purpose of this chapter is to protect children from unnecessary separation from parents who might give them good homes and loving care, to protect them from adoption by persons unfit to have the responsibility of their care and rearing, and to protect them from interference, long after they have become properly adjusted in their adoptive homes, by natural parents who may have some legal claim because of a defect in the adoption procedure.
> (2) The secondary purpose of this chapter is to protect the natural parents from hurried decisions made under strain and anxiety, to give up a child, and to protect foster parents from assuming responsibility for a child about whose heredity or mental or physical condition they know nothing, and to prevent later disturbance of their relationship to the child by natural parents whose legal rights have not been fully protected.
> (3) When the interests of a child and those of an adult are in conflict, such conflict should be resolved in favor of the child; and to that end this chapter should be liberally construed.

Adoption is statutory and those interested in investigating it should consult a competent lawyer.

Custody differs from adoption. In adoption, the child is taken bodily and completely from one family and legally made a part of another. He no longer is regarded as a child of his natural parents. In custody matters, the care and *control* of the child are taken bodily from one or both of the natural parents or from someone *in loco parentis* and placed with somebody else. In adoption the child's name and his right to inherit are changed. In custody cases it is only the responsibility for his care, food, clothing, shelter, training and general preparation for life as an adult which are transferred.

Custody is generally accomplished by juvenile court proceedings; but it may also be effected by a divorce court.

One example of a statute dealing with custody of a child and showing both the mutual rights of the parents to custody of the child and the limitation of those rights is New York Domestic Relations Law, Sec. 70, which reads:

Habeas corpus for child detained by parent. A husband or wife, being an inhabitant of this State, living in a state of separation, without being divorced, who has a minor child, may apply to the supreme court for a writ of habeas corpus to have such minor child brought before such court, and on the return thereof, the court, on due consideration, may award the natural guardianship, charge and custody of such child to either parent for such time, under such regulations and restrictions, and with such provisions and directions, as the case may require, and may at any time thereafter vacate or modify such order. In all cases there shall be no prima facie right to the custody of the child in either parent, but the court shall determine solely what is for the best interest of the child, . . . and make award accordingly.

Finally, in the case of guardianship of minors, we are dealing with a concept which has aroused little interest among the legislatures. If we are talking about guardianship in general, the meaning of the term overlaps "custody." There are, however, a number of specific types of guardianship in which the accompanying descriptive words confine the phrase to within usable limits. Thus, a parent may be *guardian of the person* of his child until the latter reaches twenty-one years. There are guardianships of the estate of minors — that is, persons appointed by the court to exercise controls over property. A guardian *ad litem* is appointed to represent children in litigation.

The importance of the concept that every child should have a guardian is pointed up in a report "Guardianship, a way of fulfilling public responsibility for children." In the introduction appears the following summary:

Problems that have long existed have been joined of late by others growing out of recent developments. For example, as a result of war casualties and wartime and postwar disturbances of family life, great numbers of children have been separated from their parents, with consequent increasing need for their care and supervision away from home. Then, too, more and more children are becoming eligible for financial benefits under social security and veterans' legislation: to ensure that payments are used for the children's benefit, safeguards are increasingly necessary — especially when the children are not living in their parental homes. And, finally, public welfare agencies of the States and of local communities are taking more responsibility for children; to clarify public responsibility, greater attention must be given to the legal status of children.[24]

A guardian may be appointed by the court or in some instances by will of the parent. His duties, depending upon the particular sort of guardian he may be, are to supervise the interest of the child in his personal life or his property or both. Generally, the guardian reports periodically to the court. In the case of guardian of the estate, he usually turns over the estate to the minor when the latter reaches the age of majority. The parent may be thought of as the primary guardian. The court may constitute a child-care agency a guardian, in a secondary sense, of the same child. The agency may place the child in a foster home and then the foster parent also becomes a guardian.

[24] U. S. Children's Bureau Publication #330 (1949).

RELATIONS BETWEEN THE CHILD AND THIRD PERSONS

The relations involved between a child and third persons may lie in the field of tort or in contract. The present problem is the extent to which the child is responsible in his own right and where the parent is involved.

If a child wilfully or negligently injures a third person, that third person generally must obtain satisfaction from the child himself. The parent is not generally liable.

In *Steinberg* v. *Conchor,* 293 N.Y.S. 147, Child A operated his bicycle in a careless way while on a public sidewalk and injured child B. Suit was brought by child B to recover damages for personal injuries and by B's father to recover for the loss of her services. The suit was against the parents of A for negligence in that they knowingly permitted him to operate his bicycle in a careless manner on the sidewalk in violation of a municipal ordinance, after receiving notice that he had done so on prior occasions and in that they failed to take steps to prevent such operation. The court held A's parents were not liable merely by reason of his or her relationship for the torts of the child. In the absence of a statute imposing such liability, parents may be held responsible under the following circumstances:
(1) Where the child is agent of the parent and acting in the scope of his agency.
(2) Where the parent negligently entrusts to the child an instrument which because of its nature, use, and purpose is so dangerous as to constitute in the hands of the child an unreasonable risk to others.
(3) Where the parent negligently entrusts to the child an instrumentality, which though not necessarily dangerous in itself, is likely to be put to a dangerous use by the child.
(4) Where the parent's negligence consists entirely in his failure reasonably to restrain the child from vicious conduct imperiling others, when parent knows of child's propensity toward such conduct.
(5) Where the parent participates in the tortious act by consenting to it or ratifying it.

None of these exceptional situations is inferable from the evidence in this case.

If the child commits a crime, the relationship of parent and child does not render the parent liable.

The liability of the parent for wrongful acts of the child is only one side of the picture. Third persons may do wrongful acts to the child, and the question arises as to whether the parent or the child, or both, have a right to claim redress. It is clear that in many situations the child may sue for injuries done him, and such suit is governed by the usual rules. That is to say, if the child is guilty of contributory negligence, he may not be able to recover. But the degree of care required of a child in such cases is often less than the law would expect of an adult.

In addition, the father may sue the third person for loss of services of the child and for incidental expenses. The theory behind this is that the child is the servant of the parent, and if it is shown that the relationship is that of master and servant as well as parent and child, recovery may be had. The relation of master and servant is assumed to exist if the child is a minor living at home. Temporary absence from home will not prevent the relation from continuing. And in many states, even if the child is actually working for someone else, the parent may still sue as master if he can reclaim the child's services at any time. But when the parent has permanently relinquished the right to the services of the child, he must find some other theory if he expects to recover. If in the wrongful act the child is killed, the right to recover depends upon the existence of a statute especially permitting such action.

Two sorts of action by a parent for loss of services of a child are especially significant — for seduction of a daughter and for abducting a child. In cases of seduction, the parent may sue the wrongdoer for such varied damages as loss of service of the daughter while incapacitated, incidental expenses, shame and disgrace to the family, the corrupting example to the other children. If there are aggravating circumstances, the suit may be for punitive damages to deter others from attempting similar actions. Even if the daughter is an adult, the father may recover by showing that the daughter was in his service.

SECURING JUSTICE ACCORDING TO LAW

Heretofore in this chapter, attention has been paid to the rules of law relating to the family. Rules of law are not self-enforcing. It is proper, therefore, to devote brief space to the related problem of how the individual member of the family sets the machinery of the law in operation. It is well for the reader to realize that the administration of justice according to law is one of the most important as well as one of the most complex and difficult problems of our civilization.

There are various kinds of justice — some reached as a result of highly emotionalized and others by coolly detached thinking. Justice according to law is based on the theory that ours should be "a government of laws and not of men." In our efforts to approximate this ideal, the law has arranged a system of checks and balances on the judgment of the individual. If a certain human problem passes through the legal machinery designed for the purpose, the result is justice according to law.

This legal machinery for administering justice consists of a series of agencies and persons trained in certain types of thinking. Let us approach them from the standpoint of the member of a family who wants help on a problem. First, he must know that his problem is one for which the law may provide a remedy. A reading of the material in the earlier part of this chapter should suggest some of the circumstances with which the law deals. It should give reasonable indication of the fact that a visit to a lawyer may not be a waste of time.

Specifically, it is worth while to secure legal advice:

1. Before entering into an engagement to marry. In jurisdictions in which breach of promise suits are permitted, the consequences to the man of the starting of proceedings, or the threat of proceedings, are serious. Failure to understand the law may involve a variety of expensive and unpleasant consequences.

2. Before the marriage takes place, assuming that we are interested in stable families, it is clear that conditions which might lead to annulment, separation, divorce, and the resulting broken homes, should be avoided. The time to avoid them is, if possible, before rather than after. Recognizing that marriage involves the assumption of obligations of a legal nature, it is a matter of good sense to understand them before assuming them. Marriage affects property rights. An antenuptial agreement as to property may be a most helpful solution to what may otherwise develop into a source of discontent.

3. Periodically, during the continuance of the marriage, a legal check-up should be requested. The analogy is to the perfectly healthy patient who visits the physician in order to be kept healthy. Preventive law is as important as preventive medicine.

4. Whenever difficulties arise which threaten to disturb the normal life of the family, legal advice should be sought. If the trouble can be averted, so much the better. If it cannot, then the problem is to limit the extent of the catastrophe to a minimum.

5. In anticipation of dissolution of the family by death, the law obviously should be consulted.

The foregoing statement should not be taken as an indication that the members of the family should consult no one but a lawyer. They certainly should secure at every stage all the help which is available in the community and through the services of the various professions. But they should remember that the lawyer also may have something to contribute.

Having decided that a lawyer is worthy of a visit, the next question is, "Which lawyer?" A layman who already knows a lawyer has this question answered for him. Corporations have found it a matter of sensible business procedure to have either a legal department or a special law firm to keep them out of legal entanglements. The average family has not taken this precaution. It is time it did so. Many individuals never do go to a lawyer's office, but secure legal advice from someone else who may or may not know what he is talking about. The risks involved in such a course of conduct are obvious.

The question of which lawyer depends in part upon the ability of the client to pay. If he can pay no fee at all, he should locate the nearest Legal Aid Society or Legal Aid Committee of a bar association. These organizations, now operating in most of the larger cities, handle only cases and clients where no fee can be paid. If none is available in a particular locality, the family should ascertain which lawyers are prepared to render similar service on a nonfee basis. In time one may expect organized legal aid in each county, but unless there is evidence of a need for it, few persons are willing to undertake the labor and responsibility of attempting to establish it.

If the family can pay a nominal fee, not one commensurate with the work involved but at least a minimum fee, it should locate the nearest Legal Service Bureau. This type of organization, which came into existence in a variety of forms just before the outbreak of World War II, is designed for the intermediate group of clients. At present it exists in only a few places. Elsewhere, the family should seek information as to which lawyers are prepared to render service in return for a nominal fee.

If the family can pay a full fee, any lawyer might be available to take the case, but there is still a problem — how to find a lawyer experienced in the particular field of law which the situation requires. A license to practice law is not limited to a particular field. The attorney is authorized to handle anything which may come to him. It is clear that few lawyers have time to become equally experienced in every branch of practice. Ordinarily, a lawyer will tell his client if he is not prepared to handle a particular kind of work and will suggest calling in another lawyer to care for some special part of the task.

After the family has found the lawyer, the next question of interest is what the lawyer can do. What he can do depends, of course, upon the terms of a particular case. But there are certain general classes of service which he can render.

Legal Advice. Perhaps half the persons applying to Legal Aid Societies for assistance require nothing more than advice. This may consist of a statement of the rights of the client or the law on a particular point. The client does not want to do anything; he merely wants knowledge; or he may plan some action and desire to see that it is within the spirit and letter of the law.

Adjustments out of court. Perhaps one quarter or more of the cases coming to a Legal Aid Society call for more than advice, but may be settled without recourse to litigation. A conference between the contending parties is enough.

Litigation. A small percentage of cases must go to court, but many of these do not necessarily involve controversy. For example, an adoption proceeding may be arranged with everyone in an amicable mood, but the signature of the judge on the decree is necessary to make it legally binding. Another example would be a test case in which the purpose is to have the court determine the constitutionality of a statute.

Changes in legislation. In matters of advice, adjustment, and litigation, the lawyer employs existing law. There are times when the existing law is not adequate for the purpose. Then new law must be made or the old law amended. Lawyers do this sort of work.

Interprofessional cooperation. There are many problems in which the law supplies a part but not the whole of the remedy. In such cases the lawyer works with others in a composite solution.

Perhaps the most dramatic part of the lawyer's work occurs in the courtroom when a controversy is being litigated. Mention should be made of the process and the nature of the contribution toward a solution made by the different persons.

The court system in the various states is similar to the grouping of Federal courts. It consists of three classes of tribunals.

1. The so-called lower courts, with which the layman ordinarily comes in contact, handle either specialized problems or the preliminary stages of litigation. A domestic relations or juvenile court handles certain phases of family matters. A police court deals with the first stage of the criminal law process. A small claims court adjudicates disputes where the amount of money involved is small (perhaps not more than $50).

2. The courts of general jurisdiction. These are called the trial courts. In them one meets the jury in many cases. Matters are tried here unless some special court is set up to care for them. They are known by different names in different states, but one exists in each county.

3. The appellate courts. These are established to check the work of the lower courts and trial courts and to correct errors.

The lower courts are generally staffed by a judge, court officials such as stenographers, persons to keep order, and sometimes specialized persons such as social case workers, psychiatrists, and others.

The trial courts employ a judge, court officials, and a jury.

The appellate courts include judges, law clerks, and court officials.

The process of litigation involves steps like the following:

1. The lawyer for the family must decide whether there are benefits to be derived from the litigation process to justify the risks, delay, and expense involved. This is often a difficult and grave decision to make.

2. In a civil case the lawyer for the aggrieved party, the plaintiff, prepares a statement of the complaint and files it with the Clerk of the Court and an order of the court, often called a summons, is issued, directed to the defendant requiring him to answer the complaint. This is given to the defendant; frequently this is the sheriff's duty.

In a criminal case the matter is usually begun by a warrant. The aggrieved party swears to the facts indicating that someone else has committed a crime. A justice of the peace or other officer issues the warrant which may be served on the accused by the sheriff or the police.

3. In a civil case the attorney for the defendant files another document answering the complaint of the plaintiff. These papers are called the pleadings. They raise the issues and show what matters must be settled in court.

There is no similar proceeding in the usual criminal case.

4. Eventually the case comes on for trial. The lawyers see that evidence is presented for their respective clients and argue points of law.

If there is a jury, it determines the facts.

The judge presides, acting as a sort of umpire in the proceedings, and states to the jury the law relative to the facts.

The mental process in such a proceeding is sometimes thought of as comparable to an accounting. The plaintiff's credits and debits are set down and evaluated; so likewise are the defendant's. The various columns are totaled and a balance struck. The winner is the party in whose favor the balance appears. It is this balance which we call justice according to law.

SELECTED READINGS

"Legal Aid Work," *Annals of the American Academy of Political and Social Science,* 124 (March, 1926).
———, "Law and Social Welfare," 145 (Sept., 1929).
———, "Frontiers of Legal Aid Work," 205 (Sept., 1939).
BRADWAY, JOHN S., *Law and Social Work* (Chicago: University of Chicago Press, 1935).
BRECKENRIDGE, SOPHONISBA P., *The Family and the State* (Chicago: University of Chicago Press, 1934).
———, *Social Work and the Courts* (Chicago: University of Chicago Press, 1934).
BROWN, ESTHER LUCILLE, *Lawyers and the Promotion of Justice* (New York: Russell Sage Foundation, 1938).
CLARKE, HELEN I., *Social Legislation* (New York: Appleton-Century, 1940).
GOLDSTEIN, JONAH J., *The Family in Court* (New York: Clark Boardman, 1934).
KOEGEL, OTTO E., *Common Law Marriage and Its Development in the United States* (Washington: Byrne, 1936).
"Alimony," *Law and Contemporary Problems,* 6 (Spring, 1939).
———, "Children of Divorced Parents," 10 (Summer, 1944).
MADDEN, JOSEPHINE, *A Handbook of the Law of Persons and Domestic Relations* (Minneapolis: West, 1931).
MAGUIRE, JOHN M., *The Lance of Justice* (Cambridge: Harvard University Press, 1938).
MAY, GEOFFREY, *Marriage Laws and Decisions in the United States* (New York: Russell Sage Foundation, 1928).
SMITH, R. H., and BRADWAY, J. S., "Growth of Legal Aid Work in the United States," U. S. Bureau of Labor Statistics, Bul. 607.
VERNIER, CHESTER G., *American Family Laws* (5 vols., Palo Alto: Stanford University Press, 1931–1938).

TOPICS FOR DISCUSSION OR REPORTS

1. Discuss the work of the clerk in the marriage license bureau with him and report your findings to the class.
2. Write a paper on the subject, "The Legal Concept in Marriage Is in the Field of Status."
3. Write a paper on the subject, "How Much Law Should a Marriage Counselor Know?"
4. Make a study of the nearest Gretna Green and report on the devices employed to encourage hasty marriage.
5. Visit courts which handle domestic problems and report on the cases cared for.
6. Make an analysis of court procedure in the juvenile court.

7. Arrange a meeting with a lawyer to discuss "Support of Wife and Child."
8. What are the legal steps taken to accomplish legitimation of children of unmarried parents in your state?
9. If a wife wishes to secure support from her husband who has escaped over the state line into another jurisdiction, how should she proceed? Look up the law on this point and report on it.
10. What are the legal provisions for adoption in your state?
11. In what ways has common law been supplemented, extended, or abrogated with regard to the rights, duties, and liabilities of parents in relation to their children? Of children to parents?
12. Why is annulment rather than divorce sometimes the preferred procedure?

Chapter Twenty

Religion in Family Life

ROCKWELL C. SMITH

THE preceding chapters of the text have been devoted to making the meaning and nature of the family explicit, hence it seems appropriate to begin this chapter with some statement as to the nature and meaning of religion. Religion represents man's effort to orient his life to final realities, his search for an ultimate meaning within the changing flow of his experience — a meaning which can at once bring order out of what is apparently chaos and promote within man a sense of security and dignity in the midst of a daily life that often renders him insecure and mean. Once man finds this ultimate meaning, religion becomes his effort to preserve and promote that meaning on every level and in every act of his life. This latter statement of course describes the religion of the self-aware and thoughtful person. Many sincerely religious people accept the interpretation of the meaning of the universe offered by someone else and act as they are instructed without being intimately involved in the transaction. The motive which feeds such piety as they have, however, is essentially the same as that which motivates the saint; both are seeking to ally their lives with the significant meanings of the universe around them.[1]

Religion as defined above expresses itself typically in three ways or on three levels. First of all, it is "thought," i.e., a fundamental philosophy of the world and man's place therein. This thought expresses itself in creed, dogma, holy books, doctrine, teaching, theology. In the second place, it is rite and ritual. There are proper ways of acting with reference to the ultimate reality and these are regarded as divinely sanctioned. Third, religion develops a unique fellowship involving not only the human participants but the divinity or divinities as well. Entirely apart from our opinion as to the reality of the objects of worship — of God or the gods — there remains the fact that a fellowship which, in the minds of the participants, brings in not simply the visible but also a divine company is a unique kind of fellowship. It is, to echo Chapter One, sacred in a special way, i.e., *holy*.

The importance of marriage and the family in the eyes of religious persons is indicated by a study of families representative of the best in their several religious groupings in rural Wisconsin. Members of Catholic, Lutheran, and Reformed churches were interviewed in relatively equal numbers. When they were asked about their social interaction with other

---

[1] See Harris Franklin Rall, *Christianity, an Inquiry into Its Nature and Truth* (New York: Scribner's, 1940), chap. 1, for a summary discussion of the nature of religion; J. Milton Yinger, *Religion in the Struggle for Power* (Durham, N. C.: Duke University Press, 1946), chap. 1; and Howard Becker and H. E. Barnes, *Social Thought from Lore to Science* (2nd ed., Washington, D. C.: Harren Press, 1952), chap. 1 *et passim*.

religious bodies the following answers were given. Only 9 out of 58 traded exclusively with members of their own denomination; 19 enjoyed recreation exclusively within their own church group; 23 visited socially within their own denomination exclusively; but 52 insisted that their children should marry within their own church. Thus 89 per cent indicated their opposition in theory and practice to intermarriage between differing faiths, whereas only 39 per cent indicated their similar opposition to social visiting among differing faiths.[2]

RELIGIOUS RITE AND FAMILY LIFE

Perhaps we are all most conscious of the interaction of religion and family life on the level of rite and ritual. All religions provide special ceremonies through and by which family life and marriage have been dignified. One great branch of the Christian church has elevated the marriage ceremony itself to the height of a sacrament — that is, an occasion for the unique revelation and impartation of the grace of God to man. The fact that no other human contract is so dignified by religion indicates something of the importance which is attached to marriage and the family by religious persons. Most religions continue to attend the family with special religious ceremonies after it has once been formed. Among Christians there is the rite of baptism, by which the child or young adult is recognized by the church. Among the Hebrews there are the rite of circumcision and other ceremonies upon the occasion of the child's wider participation in religious affairs. All these ceremonies and rites have a familiar background and are ceremonies which involve not the detached individual but the family as a religious unit.

It is obvious that by these ceremonies and rites the church is seeking to dignify and make permanent the individual marriage and family relation. Thus rite and ceremony become a means of furthering family life and promoting marital accord. If, however, the partners to a marriage come to their married life from diverse religious backgrounds and with differing ceremonial experiences, it is equally obvious that the religious practices originally designed to strengthen marriage may result ultimately in weakening it. People with differing ceremonial backgrounds may find that these rites and ceremonies become the center of irritation and dissension; this applies not simply to those rites with which the church has surrounded marriage but to all rites. Common prayer may be a profound reinforcer of family unity, but if one member of the married pair is accustomed to prayer after the formal fashion of the Episcopal Church and the other is used to the silent devotion of the Friends, there exists the possibility that their praying may in a real sense serve to separate them. In the following case we see the profound unifying power of common rites and ritual.

[2] Rockwell C. Smith, "Religion as a Social Differentiator in Rural Wisconsin" (unpublished Ph.D. thesis, University of Wisconsin, 1942).

Doris and Kenneth were school teachers in separate communities. They had become acquainted as young people in high school and had maintained their friendship through their college days until it ripened into an engagement. They had attended a small teachers' college in a small community. After their first year of teaching they decided to marry early in the summer and to spend their summer together as graduate students at a large urban university. Since Doris was an orphan, they decided not to be married in their home community but in the city in which the university was located. All these decisions, except the decision to marry, were made by correspondence or on week end visits during the busy spring term of teaching.

Kenneth preceded Doris by several days in arriving in the metropolis and secured an apartment for the summer. Both the activity and the metropolitan situation were new to him and left him with a feeling of confusion. When Doris came she likewise developed a sense of confusion, in part in reaction to the emotional state of Kenneth and in part from the novelty of the situation. The novelty to which they had both looked forward so confidently as exciting proved rather depressing, and at the same time its strangeness intruded into their relation with each other. They did not feel at ease together; their married life seemed about to begin in an atmosphere of doubt and emotional distress.

Kenneth had arranged that they should be married by the local minister of their denomination. They were to be married in the evening and went in the afternoon to make the final arrangements. In the interview the pastor proved friendly and sympathetic. He knew several of their friends who were pastors of the denomination and conversed with them first about these mutual acquaintances. He then went through the marriage service with them, a service with which they were already familiar, answering their questions and ending the interview by taking them to the little chapel in which the marriage was to take place. Throughout the whole conversation was the suggestion that they were making this new and important commitment under the auspices of an institution which had been their familiar associate for years.

When the service did take place, it served to restore them to an old and familiar social setting and situation. The strangeness of the city was put into the background of their experience, while the social loyalties and the religious attitudes which they shared were brought to the fore. At the close of the service their self-confidence and their feeling of dependence upon each other were restored, and they were able to begin their married relation with a complete sense of trust in each other and with emotional balance and personal poise. Here the religious ritual and the services of the pastor functioned to provide balance in a new and strange social situation at a time when such balance meant the happy beginning of a married relation. Had this function not been performed, it is highly probable that the attitudes of confusion and doubt produced by a new social situation might have carried over into the marriage with unfortunate results.

When a member of the Roman Catholic Church marries a non-Catholic or when a Jew marries a Christian, marriage ritual and ceremony become matters of discussion and issue rather than unifying factors. The couple may even forego a religious ceremony entirely to be married by a judge, which means either that religious convictions have ceased to matter very much to either one or else that they are entering marriage without developing mutual understanding at the point of life's greatest loyalties. But the marriage ceremony is not the last point at which religious ritual will prove a divisive matter. When children are born, are they to go through the religious practice of circumcision or baptism? To which church or synagogue school shall they be sent? When other children are celebrating holy days, with which group shall they join?

A section of the journal *Lumen Vitae* in 1949 was given to the topic "Interfaith Marriage and Religious Life."[3] Therein Professor Murray H. Leiffer reports finding approximately 12 percent of the families in a middle-class Chicago community were composed of husband and wife who had diverse church backgrounds. The Rev. Thomas F. Coakley reports approximately 30 percent of marriages performed in 1947–49 in Sacred Heart Parish, Pittsburgh, were mixed. Thirteen percent of the Catholics who married in Holland 1935–38 made mixed marriages. In Switzerland mixed marriages rose from 3.1 percent in 1870 to 11.7 percent in 1941. The authors agree: (1) that mixed marriages are characteristically an urban phenomenon; (2) that they result in fewer children than religiously homogenous marriages; (3) that they end more frequently in divorce; (4) that the members of mixed marriages participate in church less than others; available evidence also points to the fact that where divorces occur they are likely to occur at an earlier date in mixed marriages than in marriages between persons of the same faith.[4] In the case of mixed marriages involving Roman Catholic and Protestant or Roman Catholic and Jew, the marked tendency is to a Roman Catholic ceremony.[5] Burgess and Cottrell point out that among their couples those married by civil ceremonies showed a much poorer adjustment than those married by religious observances.[6]

Socialization and Religious Fellowship

Again, on the level of religion as fellowship, religion and family life are intimately related. The period of courtship and engagement is one in which the partners are satisfied with their own exclusive society. But after their relation has culminated in marriage, there comes a desire to reunite with the general social world. In a word, the marriage pair desires to socialize its relationship. It is not difficult to understand that the avenues of socialization which the new pair will follow are those which were

[3] *Lumen Vitae*, International Review of Religious Education, 4, 3 (July–September, 1949), International Centre for Studies in Religious Education, 27, rue de Spa, Brussels, Belgium. See also Milton L. Barron, *People Who Intermarry* (Syracuse: Syracuse University Press, 1946).

[4] Ernest R. Mowrer, *Family Disorganization* (Chicago: University of Chicago Press, 1939), p. 104.

[5] See Ruby Jo Reeves Kennedy, "Single or Triple Melting-Pot?" *American Journal of Sociology*, 49 (Jan., 1944), p. 331.

[6] E. W. Burgess and L. S. Cottrell, Jr., *Predicting Success or Failure in Marriage* (New York: Prentice-Hall, 1939), p. 126.

familiar to them before their marriage. The church — that is, the religious society — is one of the important avenues of socialization.

In the excitement of the courtship period young people are likely to underestimate the importance of religion and the church to their married happiness. The exclusiveness and intensity of their interest in each other make the more general and prosaic fellowship of the church seem trivial and unimportant. But when they are married and the euphoria of the honeymoon is over, they will find themselves faced with a problem of integrating their lives with the life of the community of which they are a part. The roles which they have found so congenial in the exclusiveness of their previous bond will now appear to be in need of alteration and adaptation in the face of a wider society which does not share their private meanings. The pair must face out to the world. This process of socialization may be an extremely difficult one — one in which private meanings are discarded at great loss to the pair holding them, because they seem to be inappropriate to the new role which the pair must assume. But if the pair can make its adjustment within the sympathetic bonds of a religious fellowship, the socialization becomes a natural and an easy process; the private meanings which have already attached to the marriage are not discarded, but are preserved and supplemented instead.

It should be obvious that persons coming from differing religious backgrounds are here faced with a handicap. They do not share a single religious fellowship in which they can socialize their new relation. Instead they are torn between two fellowships; each, in a sense, competes for their loyalty. In such a case the religious fellowship becomes not an avenue of socialization but an additional obstacle. Religion may bring not help but hindrance. Consider this instance:

Mary and Marvin were married after a courtship of several years, during which she taught school in the rural community in which he owned and operated a small business. She was a member of the Presbyterian Church and he a Mennonite. Between their two faiths there was no great theological difference, and Mary was particularly impressed by and eager to participate in the pacifist position of the Mennonites. Their marriage had every expectation of success by reason of their maturity, their long acquaintance, their sharing of common values. When Mary married Marvin she became a member of the Mennonite congregation to which he belonged, taking pride not simply in becoming a member of her husband's church but in becoming a member of a movement which had maintained a vigorous and idealistic peace testimony in the face of persecution for hundreds of years.

But soon her feeling toward the church and toward her husband suffered a change. Although she had been accepted with every sign of friendliness by the members of the church and although all the activities of the church were open to her, she felt herself alternately left out of or oppressed by church activities. Mennonite congregations are family affairs; persecution has given them an intense in-group solidarity which is the strength of the individual Mennonite in a hostile social environment. Mary could feel this intense group loyalty; she could hear the older people talking of events and persons which meant nothing to her.

It was natural for Marvin and herself to take dinner with his family on Sunday when he was courting her. To him it was equally natural to maintain that custom when they had a home of their own. It seemed to her, however, that they did not have a home of their own, but rather that the clan into which she had married simply had another stopping place in town. Their private lives and all their intimate aspirations were going down in a sea of family and kin.

Yet at the same time, she hated to complain to Marvin about the matter since it seemed foolish. Why shouldn't they go out to the farm for dinner after church on Sunday? She had enjoyed doing it in their courtship days. The attentions given them by the clan seemed so friendly that she began to wonder whether she was becoming "queer."

Marvin could not but notice the emotional tension under which Mary was laboring. Coming from the stern background of the Mennonites, he did not think of talking the matter over with her. Rather he concluded that she was angry with him, that he had unintentionally failed her in some subtle way. Thus within a year and a half a young couple beginning with many advantages had arrived at mutual distrust and guilty self-condemnation.

The student will note that Mary's difficulty lay not in entering the new fellowship, a step she had been eager to take, but in what that involved with respect to other fellowships in which she had formerly participated. As a Presbyterian she had been free to enter into whatever recreation groups she might choose. As a Mennonite she was expected to refrain from activities in certain recreational groups. Thus entering a different religious fellowship involved a readjustment of her entire system of group allegiances, a matter which she had not bargained for when she entered the Mennonite church. Since her marriage to Marvin was the cause of her entry into that church, and since his long membership there had made him so familiar with its restrictions as to be unaware of them, he had offended her twice: once, by bringing her into a restricting fellowship; and again by failure to perceive the fact that it was restricting for her.

Cases like this are not uncommon in the United States, with its peoples gathered from all over the world. Jew and Gentile or Catholic and Protestant, to name no other varieties of religious contrast, provide familiar examples of the clash of not only ceremonials but also of fellowship and belief. Such clashes apart, however, it seems fair to say that the binding force of the religious fellowship is much to be desired as a reinforcement of the family tie.

RELIGIOUS BELIEF: CONFLICTING LOYALTIES

But religion is more than rite and fellowship, it is a comprehensive philosophy of life or world view. As such it represents a conception of the nature of the universe from which there may be deduced conceptions of human nature, of human good, and of human development. (The process is of course reciprocal, and in some instances the subordinate notions may appear first.) Out of these ideas spring ethical precepts and moral codes — standards by which the individual is to guide his life. Here, of course, the interaction of religion and family life is extremely intimate.

First of all, religion sets an ideal for the family in the light of its ultimate philosophy of reality. All religions of a developed nature describe the privileges, duties, and responsibilities of husband and wife to each other, to their children, and to society in general. Virtually all religions describe the proper relations of children to parents, both as to what children owe and may properly accord to their parents and also what they ought to expect from their parents. These various duties and rights are interpreted as springing not out of social convention or the customs of any given society but out of the nature of ultimate reality itself.

But family relations carry farther than this. Even in our minutely subdivided and complex society the family is still a very real unity in numerous ways. Economically it is at least a unit of consumption; biologically it is the reproductive unit; and educationally it continues as the unit in which the fundamental humanizing influences are brought to bear on the infant organism. The fact that the family is a unit does not prevent a division of labor or differences of opinion within the family circle. But it does require that there should be common values and a common point of view as to what is ultimately meaningful. This common ideological unity is supplied by religion. The married partners find that they are dedicated not to private ends alone but that they also hold certain values in common — values which in their command over conduct and devotion surpass all others. This common loyalty to values which are outside the limits of the exclusive family circle is a strong cement for family relations. Again, however, we must remind ourselves that partners coming to marriage from markedly diverse religious backgrounds will often find in their religious loyalties and standards a ground for conflict rather than for unity. At the risk of offering a one-sided view we present the following case:

> Earl and Madge were born on neighboring farms, grew up, and passed through the common school in the same community. Earl's family consisted of his mother, his father, and himself. His father died when Earl was in his late teens, leaving him to care for his mother and operate the farm. Earl's family had always been reserved, living to itself. They were known as good neighbors from a negative point of view. They did not offend against neighborliness, but they certainly did not volunteer in acts of neighborly good will.
>
> Madge, on the other hand, came from a large family with a marked inclination to social life. They belonged to the church and to the Grange and were to the fore in all neighborhood social activities. Their piety was simple and crude, but it did involve a lively regard for and effort to secure the good will of their neighbors.
>
> Madge was an active girl, center of the neighborhood "crowd." She was flattered when Earl, who was known for his indifference, began to pay rather

vigorous court to her. Her parents were also pleased, as previously Madge had been looking with some favor upon a Catholic young man whereas they were Protestants. "At least Earl goes to our church when he goes anywhere!" they said. Under the stimulation of courtship Earl did attend church on several occasions, and the wedding, which came after but a few months of engagement, was a church affair.

After he had achieved his end and married Madge, however, there seemed to Earl no further reason for attendance. After all, church for him did not represent the center of abiding loyalties but rather a means to an end — marrying Madge. His fundamental system of values was limited to the family. Madge, on the other hand, looked to the church and to religion as permanent elements in her life; her system of values was oriented to others. Earl looked to Madge for certain specific physical and personal satisfactions. He expected her to rear a family to carry on his name. But with the family and the name as extensions of his own personality the matter ended. For Madge, however, family and children were not independent and self-maintaining but were the primary unit of the neighborhood, the church group, and the wider community.

It is obvious that here was the making of marital discord and disaster. Madge attended church by herself; Earl interpreted that attendance as neglect of himself and the family. In this he was supported by his mother, who lived with them. Yet when Madge tried to understand what "family" meant to him and to his mother, she entered a realm of attitudes which was alien to her. She soon gave up church attendance to secure peace at home and to avoid the embarrassment attached to attending church without her husband. But while her action in ceasing to attend church restored something like order in their home life, it made her profoundly dissatisfied with her husband.

Two children were born to the marriage, but their advent did nothing but increase Madge's dissatisfaction. To see her daughters growing up so differently from the way she had grown up in her parents' home served only to emphasize her helpless and unhappy condition. Pride kept her from leaving her husband and thereby admitting publicly the failure of their relation. Privately, however, she blamed him for her increasing sense of frustration.

During her young womanhood Madge had done some practical nursing in the neighborhood. An opportunity for what she regarded as honorable relief came when a neighbor woman was taken ill and asked her to come over to help about the home for a few days. The sickness proved to be chronic; the few days lengthened to months. Earl asked Madge to return home several times, but on each occasion she pointed out that she could not leave a sick woman without disregarding the duties of neighborliness. Finally Earl lost patience and told her never to come home again. This satisfied Madge, for it put the burden of their separation on him. They are still separated.

In this case we have marital discord arising out of conflicting loyalties in the realm of ultimate values. The personalities of Earl and Madge were organized about different ideals. Each could accommodate his life to the other only by a profound reorganization, naturally preceded or at the very least accompanied by disorganization, of his own personality structure. For mature persons, such unmaking and remaking of basic modes of conduct is frequently difficult and sometimes all but impossible. Certainly the latter was true of Earl and Madge. Given their situation, adjustment could come only by the disorganization of the personality of one of the parties to the marriage or the disorganization of the marriage structure itself. Madge maintained some adjustment in the situation rather than break off the marriage relation, because her personality organization involved respect for the good opinion of the community, which would have been lost by an open break. She preferred to accept the breakup of the family as soon as it could be brought about by means which would not cause her to offend community standards. The ultimate philosophies of life of the parties to the marriage were so discordant as to give them no universe of discourse.

NONRELIGIOUS DIFFERENCES AND CHURCH AFFILIATION

There is a fourth level on which religion and family living are related, but this level is not so obvious as the other three. Students of society have discovered that in a heterogeneous society such as ours differing religious bodies have a differential appeal. Some churches are middle-class churches; others represent the wealthier families; still others are working-class churches. This differentiation is often manifest among the local churches within a single denomination: there will be a wealthy down-town church, a middle-class church in the residential section, and a mission in the slums. But the differentiation also takes place generally as between denominational or sectarian groups. For example, Boisen has pointed out that Pentecostal or Millennial sects are a product of economically depressed populations which more standardized churches do not serve.[7] There is some recent evidence that among poorer families the contemporary churches have less effective appeal than among the wealthier.[8] Sewell's Oklahoma data indicate that the percentage of persons within economic categories who participate in church activities is lowest in the poorest category and rises directly with improving socioeconomic status.

This and like evidence points toward the fact that membership in a particular religious organization cannot be regarded as an index of the member's religious purpose only; it reveals also certain things about his social status. If two persons within the same "congregation of the faithful" marry, the chances are that they have much more in common than their common religious faith. If two persons from different religious organiza-

[7] Anton T. Boisen, "Economic Distress and Religious Experience," *Psychiatry*, 2 (May, 1939), pp. 185–194.

[8] William H. Sewell, *The Construction and Standardization of a Scale for the Measurement of Socio-Economic Status of Oklahoma Farm Families* (Stillwater: Oklahoma Agricultural and Mechanical College, Technical Bulletin No. 9, 1940).

tions marry, it is equally certain that the differences between them are much wider than the special field of religious faith and loyalty alone. Because religious affiliation appears to be associated with other fundamental social differences, such affiliation may be looked upon as one test of common cultural and social background. Other things being equal, young people coming to marriage from the same or closely similar religious affiliations will bring to their marriage a common store of belief and standards in nonreligious as well as in religious matters which will promote their happy adjustment in their later married life.[9]

In this connection the student should recall the case of Mary and Marvin discussed earlier in the chapter. Their difficulty was in part the difficulty associated with Mary's entrance into a new religious fellowship. But it also involved certain nonreligious social situations and customs associated with that fellowship. For instance, there was the custom, so oppressive to Mary, of the young folks' going out to the farm for Sunday dinner after church. The Mennonite attitude toward certain amusements and recreations which she had always considered innocent was also a force making for resentment in Mary against her husband's church, his people, and ultimately himself.

It is becoming increasingly clear that religion may affect us in still another way; that is, religious standards inculcated in childhood may dominate our lives and conduct long after we have consciously given up those standards. This fact goes a long way to explain difficulties now being faced by returning service personnel who, in the abnormalities of camp and combat, have indulged in types of conduct which their early religious training condemned. It also explains marital incompatibilities developing in partners whose lives have been influenced by behavior under war stresses, even though they themselves remained at home.

DEPENDENCE OF RELIGION ON THE FAMILY

Thus far we have indicated the dependence of family life on religion and the church. We may well recognize the fact, however, that the dependence is *inter*dependence. The relation between religion and family living is not one-sided. The church and religion have much to give to the family, but they also look to the family for gifts in return. Between family life and religion there is a constant and never-ceasing interaction; both are at one and the same time benefactor and benefited.

In our culture Christianity and Judaism are the dominating religions. Their relationship of common ancestry and development is well understood.[10] Both of these religions depend, in the final analysis, on a family metaphor in describing the relation of man to ultimate reality. God is our Father, men are His children, all men constitute the family of God and are

---

[9] A. B. Hollingshead, *Elmtown's Youth* (New York: Wiley, 1949), chap. 10. See also W. Lloyd Warner and Paul S. Lunt, *The Social Life of a Modern Community* (New Haven: Yale University Press, 1941), chap. 17.

[10] See our earlier discussion, Chapter Three, "Ancient Past and Living Present," pp. 84–103.

brothers one to the other. This is so commonplace to all of us that we do not realize how completely religion of this kind depends on the family. It is within the family circle that the child learns the meaning of such words as "father" and "brother." It is perhaps to be doubted whether a child who has not found a sense of security in his relation with his own father or father symbol, or a sense of affection and dignity as one among several real or symbolic brothers and sisters, can without great intellectual and emotional revolution become religiously a Christian or a Jew. And this of course explains part of the interest of the church in the family. Unless within individual families a happy and constructive relation prevails both between wife and husband and between parents and children as well as among the children themselves, the cogency of the religious interpretation of the universe and of man will be lost. If a child looks with hatred or with disgust upon his own father, it is difficult to see how he can learn to pray "Our Father" with any degree of helpfulness to himself. Thus religion depends on the family to give a background experience in social relations upon which the interpretation of the universe and the ultimate ends of life may be built.

The dependence of religion and the church on the family goes even farther than this. The church depends on the family to develop within the child those habits of piety and conduct which the church will later rationalize and interpret in its teaching. Logically, our world view is the basis for our standards and our conduct. Psychologically, we develop habits before we are capable of understanding the logic underlying them. We learn to pray, to worship, to participate in other religious behavior, and to conduct ourselves as moral persons before we have any clear idea of what these various items of conduct mean logically, or why we are engaged in them. Indeed, few men ever approach religious conduct through religious thought alone. The church, then, depends upon the family to establish within the child such standards and disciplines as will conform to the ideology later to be taught by the church.

When Children Ask Religious Questions

Parents approach the responsibility of inculcating religious habits and attitudes in the child in a variety of ways. A common method is to allow all matters of religious practice and idea to wait upon some question of the child. A question directed at where babies come from or where dead people go is often answered with a reference to God. How ineffective such a procedure of answering a mystery by a mystery is! Unless the child has become familiar with God, a reference to Him thoroughly confuses the situation.[11]

Other parents leave the religious nurture of the child exclusively to the church or synagogue, feeling that they have discharged their responsibility when they have exposed the child to religious teaching. As a matter

11 See Margueritte Harmon Bro, *When Children Ask* (Chicago: Willett, Clark, 1940).

of fact, for the young child there is no authority so final as that of his parents. What other people say and do is always much less important than what his parents say and do. To leave religious nurture to those outside the family circle is to relegate religion to a role of decidedly minor importance in the experience and valuation of the child. Unless parents themselves regard religion as of minor importance and wish their children to participate in religious institutions for conventional reasons only, they should consider the importance of commending religion to their children by their own practice and example.

Parents who are concerned to share their religious heritage with their children discover a series of ways for doing so on the level of the child's experience. Fully as important as practices which the child carries out by himself (bedtime prayers, for example) are religious activities in which he participates as one member of the family along with others. Grace at meals, with various family members alternating in speaking the words, is a case in point. One young couple, concerned that their little girl should have every religious as well as every medical and educational advantage, developed and used successfully the following program. Just after the child's six o'clock evening feeding, at a time when the baby was full, warm, relaxed, and happy, the mother or father (sometimes both) stood beside her crib, took her hand in one of theirs, and offered a short spoken prayer. They made this an unfailing ritual. Long before the child could speak or understand language, she was reaching out her hand to take that of her mother or father in the nightly ritual. In this manner she became a religious participant. As she began to learn to talk, any new word she had learned during the day was made a part of the prayer that night. Thus this child can never remember the time when her day did not end in a period of prayer. This ritual was one of the most familiar parts of her routine; it required no explanation to her. When words began to have meaning she already had a fund of experiences, attitudes, and activities to which to refer the word "God." Later, more complete and intelligent participation in family and church religious life was built upon this emotionally fundamental experience.

Parents who have been forced by mature experience to change the ideas of religion which they learned in childhood often do not wish to put the burden of such a change upon their children. To protect the children from such conflict they deliberately refrain from offering them any religious teaching at all. Their argument is: "We want Jimmie and Betty to choose their religion for themselves, to join whatever church they choose when they are old enough to decide for themselves." Fortunately or unfortunately, such a course is impossible. We cannot, in the first place, protect our children from all the dangers of life. Risk-taking is part of living. To safeguard a child from every possible source of danger is to prevent him from developing any sense of responsibility. Furthermore, children learn about religion anyway. They readily pick up religion as superstition and semimagic unless we supply them with a better and more wholesome type of religion. It is certainly not easy in a day of rapid change to share with others a vital religion; but the alternate course of bringing children up with no reference to or practice of religion in the home is one involving even greater risks for them as well as for us.

Happy Married Living and the Content of Faith

Thus far we have indicated the nature of religion, the areas in which the achievement of a happy marriage is helped or hindered by religion, and the areas in which religion shows special dependence on the family for its own maintenance. From what we have said it is apparent that a common religious faith and church adherence will serve as a force making for family unity and marital happiness irrespective of what that religious faith may be. The unifying powers which we have described are not so much the inherent powers of religion and the church as they are powers which we might discover in any social reality having the force which the church has in our culture. It is only reasonable to continue, however, by indicating that within the content of the Judaeo-Christian tradition to which most of us pay our religious tribute there are strong forces making for happy marriage and home life.

The first of these strengthening forces inherent in the Judaeo-Christian tradition is its estimate of the worth of personality. Persons are the great values in the universe according to the religions sharing this tradition, and a person, in Kant's classic phrase, is always to be treated as an end and never as a means. No one would maintain, however, that either in their interpretation of the marriage relation or in their general ethical programs the religions within that tradition have always maintained this point of view thoroughly and consistently. In the history of the Christian church alone there are many occasions upon which the essential rights of persons as persons have been denied, even with cruelty and persecution. But the ideal has nevertheless been kept alive by religious forces. If the churches can succeed in making this ideal real in the lives of their adherents, then young people under their tutelage will come to marriage looking upon the relation not as an opportunity for exploitation or for the achievement of private ends at the expense of the other member of the pair, but as a cooperative enterprise and adventure.

It has already been stated in other chapters that nothing so quickly brings failure in the marriage relation as the attitude that marriage is an opportunity for getting purely personal satisfaction. The chances of failure in marriage are very slight if the partners have learned in previous experiences to treat other people as ends in themselves and not as means to their own private ends. Thus the content of the Judaeo-Christian tradition makes for family unity and happiness.

A second requirement for the foundation of a happy and an enduring home is flexibility in personal adjustment. Marriage, because of its intimacy and inclusiveness, requires a multitude of adjustments on the part of the couple if the relation is to be happy or even endurable. These adjustments *must* be made or the relation will be broken. If one partner does all the yielding and the other assumes and maintains a universally dominant role, the bond between them may maintain itself but scarcely with the greatest happiness for all concerned. The ideal is that adjustments should be mutual, that there should be genuine give and take. Whether this give and take is possible depends on the character of the partners. The religious ideal inculcates attitudes which encourage adjustment. Central to the religious ideal is the teaching of the importance of humility. The Beatitudes of Jesus carry the classic statement of that point of view. The first four as recorded by Matthew [12] (blessed are the poor in spirit, the mourners, the meek, and those who hunger and thirst after righteousness) pronounce blessings upon persons whose only possession is their knowledge of their own need, their will to seek and to make an adjustment. In this religious tradition the ideal character is a malleable one. The person who is praised is the person who is teachable, willing and able to learn and change; the morality is not static but dynamic, exactly the kind which is required for successful married living in a day of change like our own.

Reference has been made in other chapters to the important role of the home in providing security for the child. It is becoming increasingly evident that a sense of security is one of the inherent needs of man as man. This need for security should not be confused with a desire for physical safety or bodily comfort. The security which men need seems rather to be a social security in the sense of an assured status within a social group and a sense of being wanted and necessary. In this connection the statement is made that the root trouble in almost every psychosis is the sense of isolation.[13] One of the overwhelming tragedies, one which can and does overtake men, is the sense of not being wanted or needed by the world of which they are a part, of being outside the support and fellowship of any significant and meaningful group life.

In cultures more static than our own, economic and political institutions and class and caste relationships are able to give people a sense of security and meaning in life. The recurrent crises of our modern dynamic cultures, however, have rendered economic and political institutions so unstable as to afford little inner assurance to the individual. We sensed in the vigor and rigor of totalitarian political institutions the passion with which people everywhere are seeking for some ultimate security and meaning in life. Indeed, it seems possible that the ruthlessness of political despotisms varies directly with the sense of insecurity of their adherents.

Under such a cultural environment it is extremely difficult for the family to discharge its function of providing felt security for the child. Enmeshed in an impersonal secular society,[14] it can give no guarantee to its members of either physical support or safety, to say nothing of social

[12] Matt. 5:3–6.
[13] Anton T. Boisen, *The Exploration of the Inner World* (Chicago: Willett, Clark, 1936), pp. 142–162.
[14] Regina Westcott Wieman, *The Modern Family and the Church* (New York: Harper, 1937), chap. 1.

status. The parents, conscious of this fact, reflect in their treatment of their children their own inner sense of insecurity. Though they may be providing an adequate house and diet for the children and customary educational advantages, their own inner lack of assurance and confidence robs their children of precisely that sense of security which the home alone can give. It is here that religion renders what is probably its most significant service to the family. All religions worthy of the name insist that our final security rests not in physical or material possessions or in social position, but in confidence in the underlying reliability of our universe and its fundamental regard for the values which we cherish most. We are "saved" — that is, rendered personally secure and serene — by faith, by confidence in an unseen order of righteousness around us.

It is not the province of a chapter such as this to argue the intellectual acceptability or validity of such a hypothesis. Those are theological and philosophical questions. It is the province of this chapter to point out that such confidence in a meaningful world is one of the sole remaining sources of security for family living in a society changing so rapidly as ours. When parents under the guidance and with the help of the church *live* such a faith, they provide in their own lives, both by example and precept, a sense of security for their children which can stand against the assaults of our societal confusion.

A further word along this same line with reference to the parents themselves: Earlier it has been pointed out that one of the patterns of adjustment which the married pair may develop is the complete dominance of one of the partners. Another possible development is the total dependence of one of the partners on the other. When one member of the pair seeks security in such dependence an unfair and in time an intolerable burden is placed upon the member who provides the security, while the dependent member is maintained in a permanently infantile state. No adult human personality has the right to achieve security through slavish dependence upon another; to do so is to put an unreasonable burden on the partner and to rob oneself of maturity. This unhappy situation is avoided when the married partners find their security in faith in the ultimate reliability of their universe rather than in a faith in human or physical resources.

By "faith" in this connection we mean the commitment of the personality to certain judgments as definitive for living. These judgments may not even be stated in intellectual terms. But they are the vital hypotheses implied in living itself. Ordinary usage, particularly in religious circles, defines faith as the personal acceptance of certain judgments about reality as correct. It is largely a matter of belief, and often of mere verbal repetition, rather than of a commitment to a scale of values. Faith as the intellectual acceptance of specific dogmas or doctrines carries no promise of security whatever; a living faith goes far beyond intellectual acceptance, and security is found in a living faith alone.

From time to time we have indicated that religious differences may become the basis of an unhappy and ill-adjusted home. It should be said, however, that even in cases where religious disparities exist the religious spirit carries within itself the attitudes necessary to a happy adjustment. Adjustment is necessary in such cases, which means that *another* adjustment is added to those which every young couple entering marriage has to face. But a successful and creative adjustment is possible wherever a devout religious attitude exists, as the following case shows:

Roger and Edith came from Protestant and Roman Catholic homes respectively. Each home was religiously strict, and no love was lost for members of the other faith. Roger and Edith met while they were both employed in a large school. They were congenial and began to go out together with no thought of any relation beyond simple friendship. Their friendship did increase with time, however, and after a courtship period of some two years, they became secretly engaged. They kept their engagement unannounced because they did not wish to face any issues with their respective families before their own decisions were made.

Both were extremely religious persons, though not in an aggressive sense. They decided that the taking of a religious attitude toward their problem, both as to their own action and their parents' reaction, was the sensible procedure. They studied each other's faith, and on the basis of study and discussion, together with kindly religious advice, decided to join the same church. This they did, and announced this fact and the fact of their engagement to their families at the same time. Of course, a great furor developed, with a spilling-over of emotions on all sides. Wisely, however, Roger and Edith decided for themselves and could stand by to help their parents to an adjustment, for they were not so seriously involved in the disturbance as they would have been if they were still making up their own minds.

They proceeded to be married in the church they had chosen and to take an active part in its program, thus indicating to their parents the sincerity of their decision. After the first emotional splurges and threats of disinheritance, the parents calmed down to the realization that they were facing a fact. After all, they did not wish to lose their son and daughter, so they made overtures of friendliness which were returned, and harmony was restored. After a period of several years the marriage appears to be an exceedingly happy one on all sides, including even the two sets of parents.

Several salient facts should be underlined in this case: (1) Both partners agreed to take a religious attitude to a religious problem. (2) They agreed to settle their problem before marriage and as a step to marriage. (3) They appreciated that they were dealing with two problems: their own decision as to a common faith, and their parents' reaction to the decision. (4) They settled their own problem as to a common religion first and acted upon that decision. (5) They then turned to their parents, to help them with the ensuing problem of adjustment. (6) They dealt with the emotional threats of their parents as a separate problem and did not consider them in reaching a decision as to a common religion. (7) Throughout they refused to let the difference in religion become the cause of a loss of all religion.

CHURCH EDUCATION FOR FAMILY LIVING

Some mention should be made of the activities which churches are promoting in the strengthening of marriage and family life. Most if not all religious bodies are making conscious efforts to develop in youth an understanding and appreciation of marriage and family relations, as well as to offer to married couples and to families advisory and clinical services. These activities take the form both of preparation for marriage and family life and of assistance in meeting difficulties and making adjustments if home life is threatened after marriage. The agencies used are publications, church school classes, discussion groups, special lectures, summer camps, sermons, activity programs, and finally, clinics to which unadjusted or maladjusted persons may bring their marital problems. Subjects dealt with include virtually all those discussed in this book. In addition to the attempt to inculcate certain points of view and to impart information, there is a constant effort to provide social situations in which young men and young women may meet one another and may develop friendships under such conditions as will make the growth of happy and constructive family and home relations probable.

The following program carried on by a Protestant church in a community of some twelve hundred persons is not typical,[15] but indicates the sort of work being done by many local churches concerned about the problems of the modern family:

I. Education
    A. Parent education in child rearing, behavior difficulties, personality growth, etc.
    B. Discussions of boy-and-girl relations in high school young peoples' group
    C. Similar training for older youth
    D. Occasional sermons by pastor on the ideal family life, frequent illustrations in other sermons drawn from family experience, and application to family situations of ethical truths

II. Activity Program
    A. Social parties for youth
    B. Emphasis on the home as a place for such parties and carrying out of those parties in homes of parents
    C. Social activities for young parents specially devised to meet their situation and needs

III. Correctional Program
    A. Counseling by pastor both at his initiative and by request of families involved
    B. Services in correction of physical disease or malfunctioning through denominational hospital located in a near-by urban center

[15] Among Roman Catholics, Cana Conferences offer a similar program in many dioceses. See also a series of pamphlets "Parents — Teachers of Religion — In the Home," published by Board of Education, The Methodist Church, P. O. Box 871, Nashville, Tennessee.

C. Financial or legal aid to families
D. Service by pastor to families as intermediary to various political and social agencies with which the disorganized family might have to work

It is obvious that the above program leaves much to be desired, but it is carried on by only one trained individual, the pastor of the church. Elements which might well be added are sex education for youth by a qualified physician, and special counseling for seriously maladjusted couples by someone with psychiatric training and experience. This much can be done, however, by an ordinary church in an ordinary community — given a trained pastor.

RELIGION AND MATRIMONIAL RISKS

The foregoing discussion has undoubtedly raised in some student's mind the question: "But what of persons who have no religion?" We can discuss the question with more clarity if we ask first the somewhat more limited but related question: "What of persons who are affiliated with no church?" Beyond doubt, any answer to this question cannot help but be colored by religious preferences — those of the writer included. Nevertheless, it is possible to say with considerable objectivity that the unaffiliated are not particularly "good risks" in matrimony. This conclusion grows out of the data of the Burgess and Cottrell study.[16] As to why this is so we may offer two tentative suggestions.

One reason for not affiliating with any church is that the person in question can find no existing church with the belief and practice of which he or she can agree. This very fact indicates that we are dealing with a highly individual personality, with someone who finds a maximum of difficulty in expressing his impulses and attitudes in the normal social framework. If a man or woman cannot find a religious group in which he secures adequate religious expression, it is probable that he has peculiar beliefs and practices which would make difficult his adjustment in the family as well. It should be noted, of course, that the saint as well as the sinner may find the belief and practice of the churches alien to his own point of view — but saints as well as sinners have been notoriously poor marriage risks.

The second reason for not being affiliated with a church, and possibly the more common one, is indifference to the issues which the church raises. Such indifference means that fundamental life satisfactions are being secured on a relatively low level. Not to see issues means ultimately not to sense values, and the man who is indifferent to religious issues and for this reason is unaffiliated with any church is a man whose general insensitivity to values makes him a poor marriage risk.

There remains the class of persons who not only claim no church affiliation but insist that they have no religion whatever. If religion be interpreted

---

[16] Burgess and Cottrell, *op. cit.*, pp. 112–116, 345–346.

in narrow traditional terms, their claim is probably correct; but if religion be thought of as a fundamental interpretation of life, together with a working out in living of the practical implications of that interpretation, then even these persons have a core of belief and attitude which, because it controls their decisions and conduct, should be called religious. Two persons who claim to have no religion and who contemplate marriage ought to strive to make explicit to each other their controlling loyalties in order that they may assess the possibility of fitting these two systems of values into the foundations of an enduring home.

SELECTED READINGS

BARRON, MILTON L. *People Who Intermarry* (Syracuse: Syracuse University Press, 1946).
BOISEN, ANTON T., *The Exploration of the Inner World* (Chicago: Willett, Clark, 1936), chaps. 5–7.
BRUEHL, CHARLES, *The Evil of Mixed Marriages* (New York: Schaefer, 1927).
BURGESS, ERNEST W., and COTTRELL, LEONARD S., JR., *Predicting Success or Failure in Marriage* (New York: Prentice-Hall, 1939), chap. 8.
CARRIER, BLANCHE, *Church Education for Family Life* (New York: Harper, 1937), chap. 1.
HOLT, ARTHUR E., *The Fate of the Family in the Modern World* (Chicago: Willett, Clark, 1936), Pt. 4.
JOYCE, GEORGE HAYWARD, *Christian Marriage* (New York: Sheed and Ward, 1933).
KAPLAN, MORDECAI M., *The Meaning of God in Modern Jewish Religion* (New York: Behrman's Jewish Book House, 1937).
MACINTOSH, DOUGLAS CLYDE, *The Reasonableness of Christianity* (New York: Scribner's, 1925).
NIEBUHR, REINHOLD, *The Nature and Destiny of Man* (New York: Scribner's, 1941).
RALL, HARRIS FRANKLIN, *Christianity, an Inquiry into Its Nature and Truth* (New York: Scribner's, 1940).
SHERRILL, LEWIS JOSEPH, *Family and Church* (Cincinnati: Abingdon Press, 1937).
WIEMAN, REGINA WESTCOTT, *The Modern Family and the Church* (New York: Harper, 1937), chaps. 1, 5, 8, 13.
YINGER, J. MILTON, *Religion in the Struggle for Power* (Durham, N. C.: Duke University Press, 1946).

TOPICS FOR DISCUSSION OR REPORTS

1. No solution is suggested for the case of Marvin and Mary in the chapter discussion. Considering their general social situation and the fact that they are both religious persons, suggest possible procedures for the adjustment of their differences and the development of a harmonious family life.
2. Consult the pastors of several local churches to discover what programs of education for family life they are sponsoring. What criticisms would you offer of the programs as they stand and what suggestions would you make

for improving them? Compare the programs with those surveyed by Carrier and Wieman (see Selected Readings).

3. What role does religion play in the marital adjustment of the two or three most successfully married couples that you know?

4. Two young people come to you for advice. Coming from very different religious backgrounds they have met at college and now desire to be married, as the young man has a teaching position in a rural community. They say: "We've outgrown religion since we've been in college so that our different religious backgrounds do not matter to us." What advice would you offer to such a couple and why? Compare your advice with that offered by Bruehl (see Selected Readings).

5. It is often said that the birth of a child brings a common interest into the home and unites the parents. Why was this not true in the case of Earl and Madge? In what cases can the birth of a child be expected to provide a basis for unity?

6. Mrs. S. is a woman who has failed to make a successful adjustment in her home life. She hides her failure from herself by being extremely active in the work of the church and by posing as an extremely religious woman. In the meantime she neglects her husband and children. Recognizing that her interest and activity in the church are abnormal, what procedures would you use, if you were her pastor, to restore her to a happy home life and a normal religious life? What would Boisen say of her case (see Selected Readings)?

7. In the light of your study and reading, what role do you think the church and religion should play in helping persons to successful married life in a changing culture like our own? Compare your conclusions with those of Holt (see Selected Readings).

8. Compare the ideal of marriage discussed in Joyce, *Christian Marriage*, with that set forth in Wieman, *The Modern Family and the Church*. What elements of possible conflict do you see between marriage partners holding these differing views? What does Bruehl have to say about such matters?

9. Secure a copy of the marriage ritual of some religious body. List personal characteristics and attitudes required of the parties to the marriage by the ritual. Are personal qualities important for successful marriage omitted? Are nonessentials included?

10. Can anyone relatively ignorant of theology, as many sociologists and most students are, arrive at justifiable conclusions about the role of religion in family life? Is a "social gospel" a good substitute for knowledge of religious history and theology? Why, or why not?

Chapter Twenty-One

Handling Family Strains and Shocks

THOMAS D. ELIOT

Preconditions of Family Integrity

PREPARATION for marriage should include some foreknowledge of its risks. Sooner or later every family is dissolved, with or without ensuing disaster. It is naive always to assume that "they lived happily forever after." (It is equally fallacious to assume that all marriages are unhappy.) Disillusion threatens a too romantic image or ideal of family life; with such a conception minor incidents may produce shock and crisis which, if expected and prepared against, might have been "taken in stride."

It is normal for all of us, and especially for married people, to have problems; problems become abnormal only if the persons concerned lack the personal and social resources to solve them — that is, to reduce tensions to tolerable, stabilizable limits. When increasing conflict is felt within or between persons or groups and the problem situation begins to involve increasing areas or to call for outside intervention, a problem is becoming socially (and perhaps psychically) "pathological."

A family which establishes its structure on weak foundations is threatened from the start. In our culture the solidarity of family life rests on four bases: (1) It should have sound heredity.[1] (2) Its morale should be healthy; that is, the emotional attitudes and ethical values of its members as they interact must include fundamental loyalties, affections, and hopes for the family as a continuing group. (3) There should be income from some source adequate for maintenance of a normal standard of living.[2] (4) It should be organized and launched on a pattern acceptable to the current mores and sanctioned by law: the respectability and self-respect of its members, in the communities from which most college students are drawn, will depend upon reasonable conformity to the family pattern expected of middle-class status.

In family living there are biological, emotional, moral, economic, and legal elements, all interacting at any given time, though some of them have become constant while others are more conspicuous because they are changing. Each precondition of family integrity just described needs, furthermore, the support and encouragement of appropriate agencies in the organization of modern communities.

---

[1] See Chapter Fourteen, Heredity and the Family.
[2] Thomas D. Eliot, ed., *American Standards and Planes of Living* (Boston: Ginn, 1931), chaps. 6–11 and pp. 16–21. Income may, in general, derive from pay, investments, taxes, loans, philanthropy, or legal or illegal theft.

MAJOR FAMILY CRISES

If any of the preconditions for the integrity of a family is lacking or is allowed to sag or break down, the resulting strains may sooner or later produce a family crisis.[3]

In the analyses of family conflicts[4] we have already seen how sequences of minor crises are precipitated and may cumulate into major crises. The major family crises are those which involve dismemberment, with or without demoralization[5] such as bereavements, hospitalizations, military service, imprisonment, desertion (and runaways), and divorce.

Dismemberment is an event, a *de facto* situation; demoralization is a process. By "demoralization" is here implied no moralistic judgment;[6] it is used to mean de-*morale*-ization, the gradual loss of morale and thus of family solidarity. Any human group, to qualify as a functional group, must operate as a "system of interacting personalities."[7] The family in demoralization loses this character. As long as family demoralization is proceeding, it means recurring crises. It is at critical points where decisions are made by or for the parties concerned, that people cut a cross section through the demoralization process, take stock of the changed situation, and redefine it. Family dismemberment (voluntary or otherwise) may occur at such crises or may be postponed. But if, in a previously normal family, a dismemberment is the initial

[3] Sociologists define "crisis" as a stage in any given interactional process where a person or group is involved in a problem that has proved insoluble by whatever habits, customs, or routine practices have been depended upon, and attention is suddenly focused upon the crossroads or the impasse. Any problem makes one stop and think; that is, the competition or thwarting of motives, goals, habits, attitudes, or roles creates bodily and neural tensions that send messages to the brain, demanding "intelligent" choice, direction by the ego, and conscious mobilization of accessible resources to resolve the tension. Crisis occurs when such messages find latent personal resources inadequate. Yet "time marches on" and decision and action are forced; one gropes for inspiration, invents a new solution, guesses at random, seeks to escape, or reverts to primitive reactions. As in a bridge, overstrain at one point may be carried to other points; the break occurs where strains meet at some spot in the family which happens to be inadequate to the load. Economic shock, for example, may break down standards or morale and distort or truncate the family pattern; or character breakdown may lead to economic failure.

[4] See Chapter Twelve, especially pp. 369–372.

[5] Family breakdowns in our culture may be grouped as follows: (1) Demoralization only (morale precondition impaired): (a) nonsupport, (b) cumulative conflict, (c) adultery; (2) Dismemberment only (family pattern amputated): (a) childlessness (voluntary or involuntary), (b) loss of child, (c) widowhood, (d) orphanhood, (e) hospitalization, (f) conscription; (3) Demoralization plus dismemberment: (a) illegitimacy (incomplete family pattern), (b) runaway situation, (c) desertion (or enlistment as escape), (d) divorce, (e) imprisonment, (f) suicide or murder, etc.

[6] Since the word "demoralization" is clearly evaluative, it is apparent that in presenting possible alternatives and preventives we are in the field of applied sociology, of application of means to ends through the use of norms. The "abnormal" is here not merely the variant from average, but the variant from the tolerable-in-our-culture. Social normality is reasonably harmonious adjustment in our changing culture. Pathology is but discomfort within or between persons or groups, but discomfort is the internally perceivable phase of physical tensions which are partly conditioned by culturally imparted norms and pressures.

[7] Henry Jones, "The Working Faith of a Social Reformer," *Hibbert Journal*, 4 (Apr., 1906), p. 550.

shock, a consequent series of crisis situations may involve demoralization, with or without further dismemberment later.

Most published studies of family breakdown are concerned chiefly with the causes and processes leading up to family dissolutions. At that point the members are supposed to "live unhappily for ever after," but how they do so we are seldom told.

The occasions of crises differ in certain obvious respects. Some are more or less revocable; others, notably death, are irrevocable. In some situations dismemberment causes the shock or strain, e.g., bereavement and most cases of hospitalization, imprisonment, or conscription. In other cases a dismemberment follows unsuccessful efforts to readjust to shock or strain by other means, e.g., desertion, divorce, suicide, commitment, enlistment.

We should always remember that no family can last forever; that dissolution may be normal (i.e., serve to complete a painless, peaceful process of separation); and that efforts to prevent some dissolutions caused by death, separation, or achievement of independence may actually defeat themselves by producing misery, strains, crises, and loss of morale. Foreknowledge of typical reactions to family dissolutions, whether happy or unhappy, may help to forestall some of the abnormal possibilities [8] latent in anybody's marriage. "Forewarned is forearmed."

OUTCOMES OF CRISES

Personal reactions to crises vary widely with the total situation at the place and time. In time of *collective* disaster other family crises get less attention, not only from others but from oneself. If all are losing sons and fathers, loss of income seems a minor shock. Moreover, a shock similar to that which great numbers of people are suffering is easier to bear. In a fire, flood, or financial panic, to have "lost everything" may actually be a badge of entry to status in a new fellowship.

Merrill analyzes adjustments to crises in terms of roles: broken, restored, or revamped. He notes differing cultural patternings of such roles in crises, quite aside from national differences in ritual matters.

It is a temptation to evaluate the several results of reactions to crises as "good" or "bad," as "success" or "failure." This is admissible only when we refer these words to the standards of the particular group or culture being used as a criterion. History and ethnography present ample evidence of cultures in which, for example, the widow who ceases to grieve is *not* considered a "success." Indeed, one can discover lags of this kind in our own crosshatched culture. Remarriage, for example, is shunned by some widows as a matter of "pride" or "loyalty." Divorce, again, may be considered either as a solution or as a failure.

The efforts of family members to adjust themselves to crises, whether or not growing out of conflict, are processes of social accommodation and, within the personality, of gradual, more or less successful "assimilation of

[8] Francis E. Merrill, *Courtship and Marriage* (New York: Sloane, 1949), pp. 286–313.

experience." [9] Evidences of successful assimilation of a shock would include: (1) thorough catharsis of feeling; (2) acceptance of those elements in the situation clearly beyond control, with a minimum of self-deception, self-pity, self-satisfaction, or self-repression; (3) relaxation of tensions, with life back in its channel moving on, and with reasonably sympathetic understanding and forgiveness of oneself and others; (4) reorientation to the new situation-process as it emerges; (5) ability to use all one's experiences as fully as before the crisis; (6) ability to refrain from such behaviors as one repents; that is, re-establishment of stable habits, self-control, reorganized economic life, and normal social life.

The emotional tensions resulting from unadjustment in crises cannot be maintained at height; in the absence of a solution the ensuing state of mind is downgrade. Secondary or delayed effects begin to appear in the behavior: resources, physical and moral along with financial, begin to "peter out"; momentum subsides, resistance relaxes. When immediate efforts to stand up to the crisis do not solve the situation, brand-new reactions, alien to previous patterns of life organization, rarely appear. Instead, people fall back on old alternatives: tantrums, drink, running away, earlier skills, vestigial or latent personal resources. Demoralization following crises is often traceable to actual or incipient demoralization *before* the events which forced the crisis and reinforced the strains.

What major family crises should college students be prepared for? It is not easy for a couple in love to conceive that their marriage may be broken into. Certainly, their future family is unlikely to present a desertion or an imprisonment situation — but one never can tell. Because divorce and legal separation are costly, desertion is associated with the poor; yet it frequently precedes divorce in middle-class marriage. Since the depression of 1929–1939 we can no longer consider unemployment and impoverishment as a merely lower-class "problem." Separation by war is still imminent for many prospective spouses. A glance at increasing rates for chronic diseases, physical and mental, shows separation by hospitalization as a hazard more real than it is easy for youth to realize. Not for nothing are the conventional marriage vows "for better, for worse, in sickness and in health." We here single out for fuller consideration (1) sudden impoverishment, (2) desertion, (3) divorce, and (4) bereavement, believing that families' reactions to these major crises are sufficiently representative of other such situations.

SHORT-TIME REACTIONS TO IMPOVERISHMENT

The shock and strain to which families were most conspicuously subjected during the depression of the thirties was unemployment. At that time several studies were made of the reactions of families to this type of crisis, which may reappear in any current postwar depression. Cavan and Ranck,[10] studying a hundred families intensively, have traced some typical unfavor-

[9] This phrase has been attributed to Adolph Meyer.
[10] Ruth Shonle Cavan and Katherine Howland Ranck, *The Family and the Depression* (Chicago: University of Chicago Press, 1938), pp. 55–149.

able sequences of attitudes following impoverishment. Immediate responses are those of fear: fear of loss of status, loss of savings, loss of "necessities." Fear of going on relief is a special bogey. Fears bring worries. Discouragement and resentment are both prevalent — the latter being projected upon various scapegoats. Worry, whether it be considered "normal" or "excessive," arises where there is still effort or hope to maintain former status and roles. Hope, pride, shame, and fear reflect tensions between old habits and new facts.

Cavan lists recourses of the unemployed: Seeking a similar (or *any*) job; postponing trips, investments, etc.; cutting expenses; selling assets; borrowing; moving; admitting failure, i.e., loss of goals and self-respect. If the family's morale was already faulty, those formerly respected as breadwinners and purse controllers have frequently found themselves losing status in the family. Roles begin to shift, and unless there is easy acceptance of such shifts, new roles clash with old.[11] Resistance against the lower role may result in quarreling, evasion, breakdown, even crime. Suicide "due to poverty" is seldom found to be due to that exclusively. Other escape mechanisms are more frequent, such as continuing to spend as if nothing had happened ("prosperity just around the corner"); stretching one's purchasing credit or personal borrowing; gambling, drinking, daydreaming about the past or the future; reversion to religious solace; focusing upon children's affections; hysterical illnesses and "nervous breakdowns";[12] projection of blame. Concentrating on children may help one to forget one's own frustrations; but it may also impose an unwise proxy wish-fulfillment upon some child. Runaways may be made in order to escape an intolerable situation; but they may also be made with the idea (or rationalization) of relieving the family of a burden. If a spouse is made the scapegoat for loss of income, desertion or divorce may ensue. One type of crisis thus merges into another, and this in turn may lead to further crises.

None of these devices, alone or in combination, really solves or even avoids the actual situation, unless it be suicide. Fantasy-thinking may postpone the facing of reality, but may even aggravate the problem, as running away, deserting, and frequent moving may also do.[13]

Drawing on one's future (liquidating savings, investments, or insurance) in order to persist in present roles and habits is equally a refusal to face reality. It may be admitted that, between loss of savings (by inflation, or business or bank failures) and loss of current income, the latter is the more trying crisis to deal with; the present rather than the future has to be faced. Sudden loss of savings, however, may discourage subsequent savings. "What's the use?" is a natural though unwise reaction to such a shock. So is radicalism or cynicism.

Hobbies saved some people's morale when the job was gone, for although hobbies are on the ragged edge of escape mechanisms, many of them have some inherent productive or recreative values.

---

[11] Ruth Shonle Cavan, *The American Family* (New York: Crowell, 1953), p. 539.

[12] See Mirra Komarovsky, *The Unemployed Man and His Family* (New York: Dryden, 1940); R. C. Angell, *The Family Encounters the Depression* (New York: Scribner's, 1936), pp. 48–49.

[13] If migration is to an actual job, or to a helping relative, it is of course no evasion.

Evasions may be considered as efforts to avoid disorganization of worse-feared kinds, but some evasions may result in or be considered as in themselves processes of personal or familial disorganization. If evasions fail or worse than fail, the alternatives of relief and crime loom up. The taboo on relief is occasionally the more repellent. But even acceptance of relief may constitute a new crisis, since it involves a new status. At this juncture, therefore, there may be a succession of new evasions, especially the rationalization that relief is just temporary. The threat to status may seem greater than the fear of physical suffering.

Angell, analyzing only fifty depression families, largely those of college students, found that the ultimate results of loss of income depend heavily (1) upon two variables within the family itself, which he calls (a) "integration" (affectional or practical) and (b) "adaptability" (collective flexibility), and (2) upon degrees of outside pressure. If the crisis involves no changes of economic position, family roles are not greatly strained. By contrast, in the York family [14] the husband was totally out of business; the wife, formerly of the leisure class, became a bridge teacher and earned $2500 a year. The economic positions of the two were reversed. Angell found that if the pressure is not sufficient to change the economic positions in the family, the family's "vulnerability" depends upon its degree of solidarity ("integration"). "For a decrease with modified or changed positions adaptability becomes of overwhelming importance. This, after all, is common sense, since these are the situations which call for readjustment of roles and hence for family flexibility." [15]

The kinds of habits and attitudes that make a family vulnerable to economic shock are listed by Angell. If a middle-class family identifies its social standing with materialistic standards of living — mere possessing and spending — it is threatened. If there be insistence upon maintenance of traditional family roles and their associated mores — the husband-provider, the wife-ornamental, the child-dependent, for example — then watch out. And, of course, a stubborn habit of happy-go-lucky irresponsibility is a third type of hazard.

Economic shock, when it consists of sudden change of economic position, causes one kind of strain if the consequent changes of role are accepted, another if the new role is resisted. "Adaptability" may consist of successful devices for *resistance* to change of role (such as quick securing of a new job, or even a different occupation). Or adaptability may mean easy adjustment in new roles. The family subjected to sudden changes of economic position is temporarily or permanently vulnerable if neither kind of adaptability is evinced.

In general, adaptability is found to be more essential to maintenance of family normality during a critical period than is previous integration itself, for crises often bring out unsuspected capacities for solidarity, latent loyalties by which persons bolster each other's morale. Momentary initial demoralization, or even one member's anxiety, may be the needed stimulus. It may also be said in general that the lower the standard of living, the less is the shock

[14] Angell, *op. cit.*, pp. 49–50.   [15] *Ibid.*, p. 263. See also pp. 44–45.

of lost income; but that the higher the plane of living, the more resources and capacities are available to buffer the shock. There are many possible sacrifices to choose among.

SECONDARY ADJUSTMENTS TO IMPOVERISHMENT

Adversity may increase family solidarity, or even heal old conflicts between relatives, spouses, and siblings. Angell and Cavan and Ranck agree on this point with each other and with the students of bereavement. If the strain cracks the health or morale of some one member of a family, the others may rally together for that crisis better than they did when, dependent upon that member in the initial crisis, they shared only his own impaired morale.

Angell notes certain secondary strains, due to special incidents which may accompany families' efforts to adjust. For example, the consolidation of two households is apt to generate friction. Change of residence in order to escape one set of strains may produce another set.

On the other hand, he warns that some of the apparent shifts from demoralization to recovery may be due, not to pure family integrity and family adaptability, but to the maturing of certain members who thus increase their adaptability and outgrow their vulnerability to impoverishment.

Bakké, apparently defining similar situations in his own terms, says that most unemployed workers avoid going on relief because that act represents to them a failure of life goals which they do not lose merely upon disemployment.[16] Workers' rationalizations of their relief status are, then, efforts to disguise this failure. Such loss of status is, however, mitigated by the wholesale similar plight of others. Occasionally a worker's family uses its adaptability to revise its goals — realistically, cynically, intelligently, according to its own lights but not according to ours. It learns to get all it can get by with; to tell a tale of woe to "prove need"; to conceal assets; to control the social worker; to demand relief, or more relief, as a right; to feel that the town owes it a living. Such attitudes and techniques are called pauperization — one form of demoralization. They may also be redefined, says Bakké, as symptoms of continued wishes for independence, for a feeling of self-direction. The more successful are one's techniques of initiative or clever individualism in intriguing for public relief or private charity, the more is one accused of losing individual initiative and personal competence! And the more difficult is the secondary crisis for such families — the shock of finding legitimate work again! Relief may actually become or seem more secure than employment.[17]

On the positive side, secondary adjustments begin with the ability of the family to control their feelings, to re-establish a set of habits (whether new or old), and to rationalize their new status and roles by a mutually acceptable definition of the new situation. Major concessions, such as resigning from clubs, abandoning plans for children's education, avoiding childbearing, post-

---

[16] E. Wight Bakké, *The Unemployed Worker* (New Haven: Yale University Press, 1940), pp. 317–318, 383.
[17] *Ibid.*, pp. 384–385.

poning marriage in order to support one's own family, may enable current routine habits to be maintained with less sense of debacle.

Rational efforts to face and solve problems of impoverishment may or may not prove adequate in a major depression, but some persons prove amazingly resourceful. Take the following case:

> Mr. C. had been in business for himself and went bankrupt. Except for his furniture, he lost . . . everything. . . . Fortunately for this family, the wife was a versatile as well as charming and well-poised woman, and her sewing kept the family looking well dressed.
>
> After about three months of relief, the wife secured a small clerical job at a salary which would just cover their living expenses, but not the rent. The husband, not willing to rust, in addition to keeping house, cooking, doing the washing and ironing, organized some of his fellow townsmen into a group for mutual help on a non-financial basis. Because there were nearly a hundred of them scurrying around and cooperating in an organized way, they succeeded, in addition to saving face and maintaining morale, in paying an occasional month's rent.
>
> When last heard of, the group, under this man's leadership, had taken over a dilapidated property with the understanding that if they did all the work of repairing it and making it available for profitable use at the end of a year, a certain number of families could live there rent free, for one year.

When a wife pitches in and earns, it may be merely as a loyal helpmate; it may wholesomely raise her status in the children's eyes. There need be no usurping dominance; yet there remain subtle effects on the family life.

Other realistic resources are: taking lodgers, putting the mother or children to work, joint occupancies, moving back to a cheaper former neighborhood. All involve risks of further crises or demoralization.

DESERTION A FAMILY CRISIS [18]

Rough estimates indicate at least 50,000 desertions per year — and more during depressions. Such figures, however, are not easy to prove; many desertions never publicly appear as such, and there is also this perplexing question: how many days' absence constitutes desertion? Yet, except as a forerunner of divorce, desertion is relatively uncommon in the middle class; the word does not even appear in the index of Waller's middle-class text.

Desertion is distinguished from separation in that separation includes some arrangement or understanding (voluntary or compulsory) for support of the deserted, or some "agreement to disagree." Both are relatively revocable; there may be hope (or fear) of return on either side.

Some women apply for relief as soon as they are deserted — because the

[18] See also Francis E. Merrill, *Courtship and Marriage* (New York: Sloane, 1949), pp. 297–300; Jacob T. Zukerman, "A Socio-Legal Approach to Family Desertion," *Marriage and Family Living,* 12 (Summer, 1950), pp. 83–84; Ruth Reed, *The Modern Family* (New York: Knopf, 1929), pp. 121–127.

desertion itself was a reaction to acute demoralization or to a hopeless impoverishment, or because of inadequate health and strength, or because of a large family, or because of a habit of dependency, or because of some combination of factors. A few, for similar reasons plus some resentment against the deserter or naive confidence in the arm of the law, turn first to the police. A few are already on relief when deserted. A few women seek outside help after a spasmodic effort to find a job. But the majority eke out a living for several weeks or months or years; from many deserted wives our social agencies presumably never hear at all.

Among the economic recourses of deserted mothers are most of those already listed among the expedients of wives confronted by impoverishment due to unemployment of the husband or other purely economic causes. First resorts are, naturally, use of savings and credit, moving to cheaper rooms, earning in or outside the home, taking in boarders who may or may not help in the home. In large families, deserted mothers may work the children. They may get help from employers; or they may "borrow" from friends and neighbors, church or relatives; or they may even beg or steal before (or besides) using "charity." Some return to the grandparental roof, or move to another town for a job or for economy. Some place the child in an institution, day nursery, or elsewhere, or hire a caretaker; others merely leave the child in neglect. A few seek a new mate, legally or illegally, for support.

A few seek redress through the courts, usually with legal aid from a relief agency. Such cases are rare, however; patient endurance is more usual. If a woman is quick to seek legal action, one suspects at once that conflict had been sufficiently acute to "justify" separation of some sort. That court action is so seldom spontaneous is due not only to its cost and its formalities, so terrifying for the poor and ignorant, but to various combinations of hopelessness, hopefulness, contrition, loyalty, relief, resignation, carelessness, fear, shame, and occasionally collusion. Many a case is complicated (and hopes are raised) by the deserter's unheralded return. The majority of deserted mothers seem to "manage" until to desertion is added childbirth or some other new crisis which without the desertion might not have happened or might have been weathered. By the time the wife's resistances are broken down to the point of legal procedure against her husband, it is anyone's guess whether any treatment, with or without court action, can be as helpful as before.

It is of course plain that such conditions in a deserted family cannot be attributed exclusively to the desertion; the desertion emerged from a previous total situation and itself was only part of a total situation out of which the current situation emerged. Manifestly components of such total situation-sequences vary tremendously. There are, of course, cases where the sexual element is dominant, and the man is found living with another woman, or is discovered to have secured a legal divorce "by publication" in order to remarry.

Interesting variants are the "repeaters" and the "pregnancy deserters," who run away from the family situation during (to them) intolerable crises; the desperate debtors or other fugitive types; those who, from whereabouts unknown, keep in touch with their families, directly or through a third party and with or without the wife's knowledge, or even send money more or less dutifully for the children's support.

The deserter is apt to regret the loss of his children more than that of his wife; this may motivate his return or his efforts to support the family. Many are willing to return if the wife will "behave"; this is the basis of many pre-court "reconciliations." But a hasty pseudo-reconciliation in court, under pressure, may be as disastrous as hasty desertion. Only when ambivalent emotions — however recessive — are still accessible, can a measure of family unity really be restored through the good offices of a tactful third party, legal or social. To prevent resentment against compulsory punishment one must cultivate in the client a sincere sense of guilt and expiation, or a sense of fatalism, or a belief that the treatment is really impersonal like a disagreeable but therapeutic medicine or operation. Not easy!

The dismembered family, if it retains a modicum of the other preconditions of integrity (sound heredity, income, morale), is better than continued demoralization with merely nominal preservation of the accepted family pattern. But the stabilizing of a truncated family is by no means an easy task to undertake.

READJUSTMENTS AFTER THE DIVORCE CRISIS

Demoralizations of family unity proceeding through a sequence of crises toward divorce have been described in Chapter Twelve by Dr. Mowrer. Divorce itself as legal and social process is to be discussed in Chapter Twenty-Three. But divorce as a dismemberment is a springboard as well as an end-product. The parties go on living. Their continued reaction to the changed situation has been examined by a few sociologists, notably Waller, who himself experienced what he wrote about.

It should be noted that divorce as an act leads to divorce as a status. The difficulties of the divorced state, if better known, would probably be enough to deter most couples from entering upon it lightly. Where they are less than the miseries of a really unhappy marriage, the couple is at most jumping from the fire into the frying pan. The longer the marriage, however, the more difficult the postdivorce adjustments tend to be.[19]

The goals and tests of recovery from divorce may not be conscious in the divorced persons, but they are observable under the following heads: the salving of wounded pride; the rechannelizing of living habits; the re-establishment of friendship groups; the relaxation of tensions; the reorientation of sexual affection or substitution of love-objects. Let us take the rechannelizing of living habits, especially the mode of gaining a livelihood, first.

A divorcée has several options: she may secure alimony, she may get a job, she may rely upon relatives or relief, she may secretly or overtly become

---

19 *cf.* Edmund Bergler, *Divorce Won't Help* (New York: Harper, 1948). Bergler lists 6 types (pp. 179–187): (1) Naïvely resolves against remarriage unless perfect. (2) Despises all of opposite sex, seeks marriage of convenience. (3) Resolves against remarriage, espouses career or cause, and rejects sex with contempt. (4) Seeks sex on own free terms without love. (5) Virtuously writes off any further "sex," devotes future to children. (6) Defines situation and role as hopeless.

a kept mistress or prostitute. Mowrer, much of whose published work deals with predivorce interaction, merely summarizes the career of Miriam Donavan after the final separation:

> [With no skill for home and no vocation other than sex,] Miriam follows the scarlet path, making an easy living, but always restless and despairing. Later she enters into a free alliance with Robert Timmins, a married man who lives a double life. The same cycle of dreams, disillusionment, and despair which had characterized her life with Alfred Donavan are repeated, and finally end in suicide when she realizes that she is losing Robert Timmins.[20]

A new job may represent humiliation to the divorcée; but it may be her social as well as financial salvation — through its distractions, its routine, its steadying responsibilities, its new human contacts and status. It is usually a much better means of adjustment than is alimony.[21]

The ordinary divorced man, while not so hard hit as the divorced woman, usually has to support the costs of two domiciles, not to mention the court costs; and his earning power is apt to be more or less subtly impaired besides. Paying alimony may reduce a man to a state of hermitage; but refusal to pay it may land him in jail. That it may prevent or wreck a second marriage is obvious. Clearly, alimony (unless voluntary) aggravates rather than heals wounds already angry.

Personality readjustments after divorce include compensatory behaviors, substitutive or defensive or aggressive, which may or may not prove satisfying or relax tensions. Reaction processes in the postdivorce situation may be classified for convenience as transitional unadjustments, demoralizations, callosity, rebound, rebalance, remarriage. Full recoveries are rare.

Divorced persons, as has been suggested, seek outlet, refuge, or distraction in their old work or in a new career. They may blame themselves and do some form of penance, or they may blame some scapegoat; or, as radicals, they may "take it out on" some social situation or "system" or code. They may turn to religious solace, or invoke religious sanctions; or on the other hand they may repudiate all religion because their own has let them down.

As in other group crises, the reactions of family members to a crisis depend upon their previous roles and conceptions of roles: who was dominated and whether he liked it; who was complex and who was simple; who was analytic and who lacked insight; who took the initiative in escape by divorce and who in conflict. Much of the behavior of the divorced is, naturally, *compensatory*, i.e., consists of efforts to restore balance, to regain one's social standing, to brace up, to save face, to justify self, to take revenge, or sometimes to reinstate the memories of happier days.

"The memory of a person is dear after the person is dear no more," [22] or, as Korzybski might put it, Mary (1936) is still loved, despite one's repulsion from Mary (1946). A husband may thus be emotionally aware of the dis-

[20] Ernest R. Mowrer, *Family Disorganization* (Chicago: University of Chicago Press, 1927), p. 251.

[21] For detailed discussion of alimony see chap. 19, pp. 578–579 and chap. 23, pp. 701–703.

[22] Willard Waller, *The Old Love and the New* (New York: Liveright, 1930), p. 135.

crepancy between the two "Mary's" but be unable to accept realistically that the discrepancy is irremediable, or at least unfavorable to wishful thinking. Such a state of mind may leave the bride-image as a sort of dissociated complex. The wish to escape from the present disagreeable reality to the earlier image then produces a regressive trend, a drag-back to the "old love," or a hopeless quest for some substitute for it (the Don Juan type).

It stands to reason that two persons who have just been through an unhappy marriage and an unhappy legal process are not suddenly happy. Most of them have grief as real as do the widowed, though of different quality.[23] Women apparently take the shock harder than do men — though this is a very broad generalization. The difference is attributable to the greater development of the "romantic complex" among women in our culture [24] and to the so-called "natural polygamy" or easier transference mechanism found in many males.

Shand has noted that sorrow is greater when the object of deprivation or substantial reminders thereof (in this case the children, the house, the former spouse, etc.) remain to refresh the sense of loss of the relationship.[25] The divorce itself is suddenly discovered to be, not a solution or haven, but merely a turnstile into new and thorny paths, which must be walked with still aching bruises and ill-healed scars. Some divorced people "blow up and go to pieces" after divorce. In protest or escape or revenge, they turn to drink or promiscuity or Bohemianism, to radicalism, or even to brutal frankness, egotism, and spitefulness.

In marital interaction the sharing of mental content often leads to interchangeability of complexes and associations of ideas. Where there are ambivalent attitudes toward some value situation, both parties share also both poles of the ambivalence, so that whichever one starts conversation on whichever side of a dilemma, the other can and does supply the expected dialectic response. Let marital conflict develop, however, and each party will fixate upon one pole of such complexes and identify the opposite pole with the enemy mate. This mechanism probably explains the occasional reversion of divorced persons to the very habits, opinions, etc., which they had ostensibly resented in the other spouse before divorce.[26] Another explanation is that in the original resentment there was an element of self-repression which is later released in the general shakeup of controls in the postdivorce period. That is, if one has repressed or suppressed one's own impulses, the spouse's overt expression of the same impulses arouses one's own repressed complex and one's own conflict attitude is then projected upon the self-indulging mate. Later, one may feel that since the estranged mate "got away with it," one has been cheating oneself, and "it shall go hard but we shall better the instruction." [27]

Occasionally modern sophistication or friends' advice will induce a di-

23 Meyer F. Nimkoff, *Marriage and the Family* (Boston: Houghton Mifflin, 1947), p. 641; Willard Waller, *The Family,* rev. by Reuben Hill (New York: Dryden, 1951), pp. 500–530.
24 Nimkoff, *op. cit.*
25 Alexander F. Shand, *The Foundations of Character* (London: Macmillan, 1914), pp. 320–323.
26 Waller, *op. cit.,* pp. 528–529.
27 Freud's, Faris's, and Mead's interpretations are suggested by Waller, *op. cit.* As is often the case, Waller is unduly eclectic here.

vorced person to seek psychoanalysis as a *deus ex machina* to solve or resolve all emotional conflicts. If such service has efficacy, its insights might rather be sought before and during marriage than after divorce!

A simple person may become complex in the divorced state; but paradoxically, a personality which was complicated by marriage may also become simple, if life is for some reason relatively simplified by the divorce. Readjustment is easier for one whose conscience is clear — and this, regardless of whether others *think* him to blame. Restored complacency is often aided or bolstered by rationalizations of personal fictions or "life-lies," [28] serving as self-justifying myths.

The category of "unforgivable" marital offenses is more or less neatly defined in many cultures. If there is cultural unanimity with respect to the unforgivable in conjugal conduct, the situation is simple compared with situations where, for example, the culture of one party leads him to consider it unforgivable that he is unforgiven for a "venial" offense which the other party considers intolerable according to *his* mores.

Delayed Personal Reactions of the Divorced

The overt behavior of the divorced, together with their personal autobiographical data, gives varying evidence of profound internal unadjustment: suppressions, repression, regressions, ambivalent motivations, blockages, cleavage between lust and love, loss of self-confidence and ambition, doubts, indecision, nightmare, morbidly transferred attachments or aversions — all these and more. Old emotional patterns may carry on or recrudesce to complicate the new situation. Formerly successful adjustive habits if continued may become ill adapted. Yet suppressed complexes seem actually to magnify their own insistence through suppression. The energy of suppression is wasted against the energy of rebellion, leaving little for efforts at external readjustment.

Divorced persons have to deal with a sense of failure, for they may well question their own judgment and adaptability. They may indulge in secret self-reproach or remorse. They are lucky if they do not develop inferiority feelings or overcompensate by aggressiveness. They suffer from loneliness; even wrangling was not lonely! They have to repattern their habits of daily routine, of sex, of food, even of sleep and work.[29]

The divorced may fluctuate between craving sympathy and dreading pity, between revenge and remorse. They may crave enlightenment but resent advice. They may wonder what they lacked, yet fear the sense of inferiority that might come if they admitted their own shortcomings in the marriage relation. Resentment of curiosity, like fear of publicity, may make divorced people reticent, though longing to unburden. A pose of cheer, efficiency, indifference, even of coquetry, license, or boasted recovery,

[28] Cf. Ibsen, *Rosmersholm.* Also Douglas Gordon Campbell, "Structural Implications of a Semantic Analysis of Group Fictions and Personal Memories," *Bulletin,* Society for Social Research (University of Chicago), 15 (March, 1936), pp. 4–5.

[29] Nimkoff, *op. cit.,* pp. 639–640. See also Merrill, *op. cit.,* pp. 304–313.

may conceal melancholy and reveal lack of rebalance. Wit may be an outlet for despair.

Many divorced persons feel under social compulsion to suppress their regrets and *seem* happy, to show that they "don't care": there is a sporting code in their set. Disillusion may help them to take this pose. But they may still secretly cherish *the values they thought they had*. This forlorn hope, together with uncertainty of status, nevertheless maintains the continued struggle of readjustment.

Occasionally traits alleged to have caused the break are suddenly reversed, or traits condemned in the other spouse are suddenly adopted. With the refined aspect of love remaining fixated to the former wife-image, the crude physical impulses, released, may regress to vicious channels. Sexual "conquests" may be a salve to pride, an effort to restore the sense of masterfulness in the ego — male or female.

Other ambivalent reactions are: the writing of abject letters of longing which are destroyed in anger or pride and shame; total recall of certain episodes with emotional blockage of others associated with the shock; a wish for unburdening "guilt" to someone (abreaction, catharsis), restrained by a defensive reticence or self-justifying pride.

Restlessness and irritability are carried over to the details of dwelling or shopping as scapegoats. Emotional tensions may affect the viscera and appear as physical illnesses, or may affect the musculature and appear as hysterical symptoms. To withdraw into a numb sulk over a deprivation is, like "throwing a tantrum," a familiar infantile device for wish-getting. In an adult divorced person such behavior may therefore be considered a sort of regression to infantile behavior patterns. Regression to adolescent patterns may be represented by resort to gambling, hilarity, drink, vice. To give these love-objects the right of way is also a subtle insult and revenge against the lost spouse, a demonstration of physical and moral independence: one secretly hopes that the former mate will hear of it and be hurt. There may also be a hope of drowning love with lust, to satisfy with "phony" substitutes the frustrated wish for response. Or, if formerly accused by the partner of impotence or coldness, one thus registers virility and gaiety and thus "proves" to the world that alleged impotence or frigidity was "actually" based upon personal distaste.

Revenge may also take the form of efforts to force the offending partner to be the suppliant — to beg for a reunion. Threats to marry another, to commit suicide, etc., are attempts to force the divorced mate into line, at least to prevent a second marriage. There is a further tendency or temptation to belittle the former spouse; even to project upon all members of the opposite sex characteristics such as estranged one from the lost mate — and occasionally to take sexual "revenge" upon them.

Waller seemed to imply that subjects who have regressed to promiscuity during divorce achieve some sort of purgation thereby or somehow free their spiritual affections to seek a new love-object on a higher level. This is not, however, clearly demonstrated. A few divorced couples have occasional sexual recourse to each other, succumbing on the physical level or finding it possible to "love together but not live together." The attempt to reunite may renew hate and revive physical revulsion, despite roused sexuality.

The struggles of the divorced to compensate for all their difficulties may produce or lead to the acceptance of new rationalizations, personal philosophies, myths, or religions. If either sex more frequently than the other develops a defense of cynicism, it is the disillusioned woman, perhaps because among women, as we have already noted, the romantic complex has in our culture greater prevalence and persistence.

Any anxiety over status which developed before divorce and was per-haps contributory to the divorce, is likely to be intensified by it. Unfortu-nately for our sense of "poetic justice," the self-respect of the injured party is apt to be impaired as much as is others' respect for the offending party. If divorced people discuss their problems in self-justification (and many of them do), there will always be those who will listen and seem sympa-thetic, if only to get the "low-down on the gossip." Real sympathy is rare and seldom seeks to intrude. Most people would rather listen to and talk about the divorced than to befriend them.

Among the friends of any couple there are those who tend to range themselves especially as friends of one or the other. When divorce has come, most of them must or do maintain contact with one or the other, seldom with both. Each group of friends, accepting its own definition of the situation, then acts as a polar magnet drawing the couple further apart. Separation once thus confirmed commits each party to further separation because of the groups' interaction and the need of each to "keep face" in the chosen role of injured party. Misinterpretations by one party, reported back by grapevine gossip, may be imputed to him as deliberate lies by the other. Indeed, if there are "nonpartisan" friends, the warring couple may compete for their confidence, each hoping to estrange them from the other. Efforts of such friends to mediate are apt to be resisted. A stranger with prestige or professional skill is apt to be more successful, being an agent not already so personally enmeshed in the situation as are friends or relatives.

Occasionally a divorced person, continuing in contact with the same social circle, may try to compete for the old mate with later rivals, or for some new mate, by trying to act or appear young, gay, etc. Again, it often happens that the divorced person, feeling need of status and response, seeks such friends as he thinks will bolster his ego.

If a divorced spouse returns to the parental home, the earlier emotional weaning of adolescence may be undone — especially if the father or mother, as parent-in-law, has been a competing factor in the domestic discord. Both the divorced and the parent may regress to an earlier level of parent-child interdependence, or one of them may struggle against such dependence.

Occasionally there is the peculiar situation of a divorced person backed up cordially by his or her former spouse's relatives. To the *amour-propre* of such a person, rear-guard support from in-laws must be very welcome!

DIVORCE AS STATUS VERSUS DIVORCE AS ACT

Normal interpersonal relations develop habits, recognized roles, orbits of accepted social distances, and confidence based thereon. The divorced find these relations and reliabilities upset, tangled, unreliable. Gossip, unconsciously or deliberately malicious; imputations of conduct or attitude on both sides; stereotyped assumptions about the divorced — these are only a few of the complicating factors. Even efforts to escape from the tangled skeins may enmesh the divorced in further misunderstandings.

Awkwardnesses arise when someone hasn't yet heard about the divorce, or when the divorced person doesn't know whether the others know. Fear of such embarrassments, rather than any unfriendly attitude, may lead a hostess to omit invitations to divorced persons. And then, too, convention indicates for such a guest an unattached guest of opposite sex, and the hostess may not have a suitable partner handy, or she may fear the imputation of matchmaking. Being left out of formerly congenial groups hurts.

Stigma on the divorced derives in part from the historic prohibition of divorce by the Roman Catholic Church. The adverse sanctions were such as to produce an assumption of serious delinquency. Such stigma is unreasonable in two definite respects. (1) The defendant is most apt to have been the offender against the actual marriage, yet stigma attaches to the plaintiff! The one whose adherence to some *ideal* of the marriage state has made him the "injured party" is treated as offender against the matrimonial institution; it is he who has "committed the divorce." [30] (2) The stigma subtly assumes that "concealment" (merely due to a wish for privacy) is a confession of evil; and stigma works behind the backs of its victims, leaving them helpless. Thus "friends" and employers — past or prospective — may avoid admitting that divorce still is really a cause for social rejection.

Because of the association between divorce and scandal artificially maintained by newspapers, any ordinarily newsworthy acts — and some commonplace ones — become suddenly "spicy" if connected with a divorced person. The same events in a married person's life, if publicized, would not be headlined; we do not read, for example, "Married Woman Loses Jewels."

To contemn one's former mate or to "take it out on" the mores or institutions of our culture may be a temptation, especially if one's case is "justified" by facts and by others' opinions; but it seldom makes for good readjustment, personal or social. Those who explode and become demoralized after divorce stand to lose, of course, the contacts by which they formerly held social status; even if personal equilibrium is regained afterward it is hard to recover this lost social acceptance. Ostracism is then all too apt to relegate its victims to the cynical or vicious groups which were about to be outgrown, and to destroy any newly recovered poise.

[30] See Waller, *The Family*, p. 537 and citation there of Karl Llewellyn, "Behind the Law of Divorce, II," *Columbia Law Review*, Vol. 33, p. 293, footnote 113. This by no means exhausts the list of contradictions and inconsistencies involved.

CHILDREN OF THE DIVORCED

A divorcée who might otherwise have reverted to her maiden name to conceal her divorce may retain her married name if there are children, in order to save them from possible greater humiliation or sense of social insecurity.

No matter which party is awarded the children, their existence, and often their resemblance to father or mother, serves to remind each party of the other — and of their past happiness and miseries. Parental attitudes are then apt to be correspondingly ambivalent. Morbid attachment or morbid aversion to a child as spouse-identified-image may develop. A child's disliked traits may be blamed by each parent upon the other's "heredity"; or traits like those of the hated spouse may, though inherently innocent, produce antagonism in the other parent. Praised and blamed alternately, a child may find his values wretchedly confused.

The fear of the other's "lies" becomes for each parent a motive for prying into the child's interaction with the absent parent, as well as a stimulus to defensiveness and self-justification. Such defensiveness against actual or supposed criticism is interpreted by the other parent as an attack, to be met by further defense. The child is caught in a vicious circle of reprisals; or perhaps of competition for his confidence and bribes for his affection; or of jealousy, especially when the child is pleased with his visit or gifts at the other parent's home. Cases such as the following are all too frequent:

> Mrs. T., daughter of a prominent urban minister, a lonely schoolteacher, married Mr. T., a rural minister, on a romantic-poetic level. Later divorced, she struggled to support her children, and resented bitterly his ability (during the children's annual short visit) to lavish special gifts on them which, as youngsters, they noticed more than they noticed the daily food and care which she provided during the rest of the year.[31]

Solomon threatened to split a baby between contending "mothers." The real mother wished to give up the child to save its life. Selfless parental devotion might actually prefer to leave the child altogether to the other parent rather than ask a judge to divide a child's spirit by two.

Reactions of a child to such situations are apt to be unfortunate. If Junior enjoys fast driving and mama blames his father for it, just that may confirm his love for the other parent and for the fault. As revenge papa may indulge the child in the behavior punished by mama. As in an undivorced family, a child may learn to exploit both parents by playing them against each other for favors or freedoms. Yet the child gets from such experience no basic sense of security or responsibility. He senses, perhaps, that he is not loved for himself but as a symbol of victory or defeat for each parent. In any event, the feeling of insecurity and absence of authority is likely to wreak havoc.

When a child does take sides between his divided parents, he often

[31] Personal correspondence.

seems perverse in his choice. If each parent presents the child with a conception of the other parent's role which to the child seems incompatible with that parent's own definition of the situation, the parent who is the more simple, forbearing, judicial, scrupulous, or sporting toward the other, or stricter in standards of upbringing, may lose out.

Child guidance clinics often deal with the aftermaths of divorce, and occasionally reorient, not the marriage, but the mental hygiene of a divorcée as well as of the child. In any peculiar parent-child relation the child is not only confused and disillusioned as to his *parents'* status, but comes to feel insecure as to how he himself stands with his parents and with his companions. If these problems are complicated with a step-parent, such a child may feel doubly cheated and rejected, and may project his unhappiness into his own uncertain future — through distrust of all marriage and avoidance of the other sex.[32] Or, if the children of the divorced do marry, memory of their parents' experience may inhibit a whole-hearted, self-giving attitude — an inhibition which handicaps the relation and thus tends to corroborate the skepticism.[33]

A divorced mother may transfer all her starved affections to a child who resembles her own father, or to her idealized memory of her former spouse as she once loved him, identifying the child with the lost image and fixating her own and the child's affections by hovering and dependence until the child's normal adolescent break-away and eventual marriage are badly complicated, hindered, or even prevented. Or she may seek proxy wish-fulfillment through a child temperamentally unfitted for the role she conceives for him.[34] In the marriage of such a child, we might expect to find in his choice of a mate strong traits of the parent-image, either of the idealized absent parent or of the doting one who has tried to monopolize his affections.

Where there are children of a second marriage, the competing roles of the children of the different marriages — competing between themselves, in the affections of each of the new pair, and especially for the affections of the joint parent — are unenviable. Yet some step-parents have had sufficient insight and self-control to handle the situation successfully, and occasionally one finds a child to whom parents' conflicts have proved a salutary lesson or a stimulus to achievement.[35]

SECOND MARRIAGES OF THE DIVORCED

Remarriage of the divorced pair itself occasionally occurs, spontaneously or (still more rarely) through mediation by friends or social workers. A

[32] Nimkoff, *op. cit.,* pp. 643–648.

[33] Cf. Thomas D. Eliot, "Reactions to Predictive Assumptions," *American Sociological Review,* 2 (Aug., 1937), pp. 508–517. Entering marriage with fingers crossed is like entering a boxing match in the same position! Marriage is not merely an experiment but an *experience:* one is himself a participant in the experiment and the experiment is invalid unless one throws one's *self* into the balance with the other ingredients.

[34] Similar problems may arise also, of course, in an unhappy marriage without divorce.

[35] Thomas D. Eliot, "Why Family Harmony?" *Mental Hygiene,* 16 (Jan., 1938), pp. 85–100.

divorced couple should beware of pseudo-reconciliations, and so should a third party, more than in desertion situations. Only less dangerous is it to advise the speeding up of a divorce. Both divorce and remarriage are end results of slow-maturing processes which may be complicated and distorted by "forcing."

A remarriage of the same parties is never quite the same, and to expect it to be so is to court redisillusion. Usually the faults of each persist or recrudesce in response to old stimuli. Too many heartburnings and gossips and new differences have intervened. Jealousy in respect to any amours of the divorced interval is just one example. Yet successful remarriages are known, where both parties had really gained insight in the interim.

The divorced person who clings to a beloved memory is less likely to marry again than the one who had come to hate the former spouse, or (by identification) to hate *all* members of the opposite sex; but indulgence in fond memories is not a facing of reality.

It should be remembered that approximately 50 per cent of the divorced do *not* marry again. Whether many who do not would if they had the chance has not been ascertained. Persons who seek or welcome divorce with deliberate intent to remarry another already selected mate suffer less trauma than others, of course; but the former spouses of such persons may suffer all the more.[36]

If a second marriage is not actually the purpose of a divorce, if it represents recovery from the crisis of separation and not a mere rebound, the divorced person, being older and having been "burnt," may be more cautious, less romantic and self-abandoning, than in the courtship of his or her earlier "mistake." This is probably true whether the new spouse in some respect fits the earlier image or on the other hand appeals to some other "self" or contrasting phase of the divorced personality. The remarried person may keep some anchor to windward, spiritually and even financially. The fear of "getting burnt a second time" accounts in part for the deliberate avoidance of spiritual intimacy in the more or less cynical free unions or mistress relationships attempted by some divorced persons. In these relations, love is divorced from reciprocal responsibility, at least theoretically. But often one or the other party *does* get "burnt," i.e., really falls in love when the other has not, and in consequence suffers when the other party "loves and leaves."

When separation eliminates the irritations which caused it, love may revive and the disillusioning miseries of "freedom" may pall. But if divorce has already occurred, return to the spouse has thereby been made difficult. If, then, a divorced person lacks insight into his own basic conflicts and develops a nostalgic reillusion about the married state, the combination prepares the way for "escape" into a second marriage.

Remarriage "on the rebound" (love at next sight) is dangerous because it is apt to result from a desperate need for status and security, and for confessional, confidential, or sexual response, leading the divorced to develop a violent "transference" of affection to some relative stranger to whom

[36] Nimkoff, *op. cit.*, pp. 640–642.

are imputed all the qualities missed or lost in the former spouse. A second marriage may fail because the divorced member is constantly expecting, imagining, or trying to see in the new spouse the qualities of the old, or making disillusioned comparisons of the new spouse with a now idealized first mate.

The increased age of both parties to a second marriage may be sufficient to reduce the actively sexual elements in the second courtship and marriage, at least for the previously married party. But it is notable that most divorcés select mates definitely younger than their former wives.

Waller noted that while the divorcé is considered a poorer risk in marriage than a bachelor or widower, he is considered "fair game" sexually by the Bohemian crowd. He is considered "experienced"; but, if the results of his experience are egotistic or cynical, that will not make him a better mate. Whole-heartedness will not be easy for one who is not yet free from lurking fixations on the predisillusioned image of the ex-mate.[37]

Waller was one of the few writers to provide any public insight into the postdivorce period. But even in his *The Old Love and the New* there is little about "the new." He shed little light on the processes of reconditioning, displacement, projection, identification, dissociation, compensation, and even revenge which may enter into postdivorce and postbereavement courtships and second marriages — a scientifically fascinating yet practically unexplored field for research.

When one of a divorced pair remarries, while the other has not done so, there is likely to be in the act of remarriage a new twinge of irrevocability added to the latter's feeling about the divorce even if he or she imagines by that time that recovery has progressed to successful readjustment. The second marriage may seem to seal the divorced person's sense of previous failure, or the humiliation of the still unremarried former spouse; and this added chagrin might be felt whether the new spouse of the remarried person seems to the unremarried one to be superior to himself or inferior. Full recovery would be marked by sincere friendly interest in or indifference to the other's remarriage. Incomplete recovery is sometimes revealed by a sudden interest in, more or less subtly competing with or humiliating, the second spouse. Merely as ex-spouse one has less chance of full recovery; but successful second marriage depends again on being able to attach one's full affections to a new mate with a minimum of lurking love or hate.

One who continues to blame *all* the trouble on the other party, without insight into his or her own share in the situation, or even one who blames himself exclusively, may in a second marriage find himself repeating the same or new errors through misconception of his roles. On the other hand, we have observed second marriages in which the formerly divorced partner seems to have learned by bitter experience the greater insight, tolerance, and equanimity which make for compatibility.

Locke [38] has rated the "happiness" of second marriages of the divorced.

[37] Waller, *The Family, op. cit.*, pp. 540–542.
[38] Harvey Locke, *Predicting Adjustment in Marriage* (New York: Holt, 1951), pp. 305–308.

Of 146 remarried divorced persons, 65 (44.5%) reported themselves "very happy," 47 (32.2%) "happy," and only 16 (11%) unhappy. Locke's hypothesis became: "There is no significant difference in the degree of marital adjustment of divorced persons in subsequent marriages and the adjustment of persons married only once." Locke and Clausner's study [39] of 47 such persons (with a control group of 64) corroborated this hypothesis except for remarried divorced men: they remain less good risks.

A second marriage need be delayed out of "decent regard for the opinions of men" only as long as these opinions are themselves so indecent and imperious that the status of the new marriage is threatened by gossip. But on inherent grounds of mental hygiene, second marriage should be delayed until reasonable emotional stability has been regained.

In rare cases one party unselfishly releases the other "freely" in divorce, and "knowing all forgives all" but remains "faithful" to the old love; such devotion, while it may be considered romantic, is itself a barrier to remarriage. By contrast, people whose first marriage was on an immature level may both acquire sufficient insight not only to outgrow the marriage but to outgrow the divorce, find new spouses on an adult level, and retain a valid though distant friendship with the first spouse. More often, however, such mates, though callow at the start, mature together and find roles in ordinary marriage, with tension or friction, but without divorce.

HELPS TO RECOVERY AFTER DIVORCE

Waller saw some hope that the miseries of divorce in our present culture may be reduced by better marriage laws and more open-eyed marriages, by better education for marriage and better child management — in other words, by better men and better women.[40] Nimkoff also noted that the after-effects of divorce, as of bereavement, depend partly upon the public's attitude toward and treatment of the victims.[41] The stigma upon the divorced has certainly relaxed during recent decades. Reducing the public and antagonistic *ex parte* features of the legal process would reduce the shock.

We should be able, moreover, through sound mental hygiene, mental clinics, and public education, to make it easier for many divorced persons to "assimilate the experience," which at best is traumatic. Here and there in the literature and case records one finds suggestions of helpful practice in the direction indicated. A person should avoid avoiding his problem. One's past is *there* — irrevocable, undeniable reality; yet *not there*, in that one can't have that of which he has been deprived. Yet *as past* it can be used in the present for the future. Indeed, the only way to rid one's self of a walled-off repression is so to release it that present experience can absorb it, use it up, incorporate it, so that it loses its identity as a separate conflicting complex within the personality. "From now on" is the motto.

---

[39] Harvey Locke and Wm. J. Clausner, "Marital Adjustment of Divorced Persons in Subsequent Marriages," *Sociology and Social Research*, 33 (Nov.–Dec., 1948), pp. 97–101.

[40] Waller, *The Family*, pp. 535–537.

[41] *Nimkoff, op. cit.*, p. 650.

The experience can be shared — but with the right people, those of discretion and insight, who are neither condemning nor too condoning or condoling; people who judge not, that they be not judged. "Unburdening" may help one to organize and appraise his crisis more objectively. But mere catharsis is not enough; there must be some faith in one's possibilities of life and some arousal of energies and attitudes ("will") toward mastery of the difficulty through replanned habits and goals.

CLASS DIFFERENCES IN CRISIS REACTIONS

How families deal with shocks and strains is partly patterned by class culture. In a competitive society with a tradition that projects divine disfavor in the form of poverty, illness, etc., on moral inadequacies, but rewards charity and *noblesse oblige* with prestige and religious merit, there is cultural ambivalence. It is better to give than to receive. If one has status or ambition, one conceals one's troubles. One feels shame in "begging" or asking help. One must *seem* successful. This is the middle and upper-class attitude, and in the U.S.A. it goes on far down the scale as the upper lower class. This is the group formerly referred to as the "worthy poor," whose "self-respect" must be preserved by the philanthropists — perhaps by letting them feel that they have solved their own problems.

Whether or how agents of another class or of the community should intervene in families' troubles is a basic problem in social pathology that cannot be discussed here. Families of the lower classes are more accustomed to sharing their troubles and accepting help, and the literature of social case work reveals increasing skills and insights in therapeutic measures — from Frederic Almy's "Adequate Relief," [42] through Mary Richmond's *Social Diagnosis*,[43] Karl De Schweintz' *The Art of Helping People Out of Trouble*,[44] Virginia Robinson's *Changing Psychology of Social Case Work*,[45] to Ada Sheffield's *Social Insights in Case Situations*.[46] But a study of Koos [47] confirms a general and perennial realization that social agencies reach few of people's problems. Koos was not using situational analysis, but he was successful in interview-rapport. Of his 62 families in a "lower class" area only 14 had no "troubles" during the two-year period of study, but only a fraction of the families got help from social agencies.

Koos let his families tell him what they mean by "a trouble." It is not ordinary chronic worry, but worry accentuated by a *jam,* emergent when everything has been tried and failed, and they don't know where to turn. This description fits the word crisis as sociologically defined; but the actual

---

[42] *National Conference of Charities and Correction, 1911:* pp. 281–291.
[43] Russell Sage Foundation, New York, 1917.
[44] Houghton Mifflin, Boston, 1924.
[45] University of North Carolina Press, Chapel Hill, 1930.
[46] Appleton-Century, New York, 1937.
[47] Earl Lomon Koos, *Families in Trouble* (New York: King's Crown, 1946). The findings would make a good case for a "family policy" (*familiepolitik* as Scandinavians call it) of extended social services through the social insurance, health, and educational agencies.

situations listed show that Koos' term refers primarily to the *subjective* effects of the exigencies. The latter are classified as *causing* the "troubles," but include far more than the conventional categories of major crises, discussed in this chapter. The latter might be considered classes of massive *outcomes,* but are themselves crises in turn. Of his 62 families, 36 had financial troubles due to illness, unemployment, death, etc. The rest were troubles of personal interaction — intrafamilial or interfamilial or extrafamilial.

Koos finds that most middle-class families also have troubles, but there is a higher threshold of vulnerability, slower impact, less "bunching of hits," fewer crisis-prone cases, shorter duration. A half are solved in two weeks, a quarter in one week. In 36 low-income cases the crisis was financial; 73 cases were interpersonal. No case had received aids from outside agencies, and few were available.[48] R. S. Lynd commented:

> Not until one reaches the wealthy who can pay — and pay handsomely enough to be impersonal about it — for the services of child psychologists, psychoanalysts, lawyers, divorce courts, and so on, does seeking help become a relatively matter-of-fact affair. Wherever there is a middle class, there our type of society augments the fact of human trouble with an extra loading of shame. The anxious distinction between "respectable" trouble and disgrace . . . tends to disappear among the middle class. There all human trouble except sickness and death is a thing to be kept secret.[49]

Cavan, distinguishing between "external" and "internal" aspects of crisis, finds that external crises, especially economic, vary inversely with income level; internal crises increase with income. Middle-class crises tend to be interpersonal; interfamily conflict being reduced by residential separation, "good breeding," and pride, less unemployment and more savings and earning power, and greater adaptability in both goals and means. On the other hand, there are greater aspirations, greater sensitivity, and vulnerability, and reluctance to confide in relatives or friends. The "lower" classes are more relaxed toward accepting philanthropy and seek it sooner, before crises have lowered the plane of living and savings. They have more delinquencies, runaways, illnesses, confinements, and cash emergencies, with less savings. They have neighbors and talk freely — but being poorly equipped to talk, their words may worsen the trouble.[50]

It is a characteristically human power to transmute into higher values any experience, however catastrophic. Assimilation is not enough. Family crises can become stimuli to strengthening and enrichment of personal character and familial solidarity. Such a predictive assumption tends to prove itself true. Yet it is also true that conduct in crisis is as apt to be a function of previous crisis experience as it is a forecast of later character. Grappling with a family crisis, one feels as if one had changed completely, especially if there has been dissociation and repression — but not so. Even

---

[48] Earl Lomon Koos, "Middle Class Family Crises," *Marriage and Family Living,* 10 (Spring, 1948), pp. 25, 40. Koos' promised book in this field was not accessible at the time of writing.
[49] *Ibid.,* preface, p. ix.
[50] Cavan, *op. cit.,* pp. 153–154, 167–168, 175–176, 185–186.

if one's behavior proves to be a mirror image of that prior to the shock, the ambivalent opposite trend was probably latent. To be free of one's past one must be able to be free with it, not against it. That is even more true for the divorced or deserted person, whose unpleasant past is apt to be unpredictably or even obstreperously thrown up to him by himself and others, than for the bereaved or the impoverished.

"The Lord turned the captivity of Job when he prayed for his friends." If upon advice, insight, or spontaneous response, a person afflicted by a life crisis feels under sincere compulsion to help others, this distraction from egoistic anxieties, his shift of focus to a larger unity in which he participates, may free him from the burden he bears — even though that burden be an Old Man of the Sea with seven devils.

SELECTED READINGS

ANGELL, ROBERT COOLEY, *The Family Encounters the Depression* (New York: Scribner's, 1936).

BAKKÉ, E. WIGHT, *The Unemployed Worker* (New Haven: Yale University Press, 1940).

BERGLER, EDMUND, *Divorce Won't Help* (New York: Harper, 1948).

BOULDING, ELISE, "Family Adjustments to War Separation and Reunion," *Annals of the American Academy of Political and Social Science*, 272 (November, 1950), pp. 59–67.

CAVAN, RUTH SHONLE, *The American Family* (New York: Crowell, 1953), pp. 153–186, 532–571.

——, and RANCK, KATHERINE HOWLAND, *The Family and the Depression* (Chicago: University of Chicago Press, 1938), pp. 4–9.

COLCORD, JOANNA C., *Broken Homes* (New York: Russell Sage Foundation, 1919).

ELIOT, THOMAS D., *American Standards and Planes of Living* (Boston: Ginn, 1931), Introduction.

——, "Why Family Harmony," *Mental Hygiene*, 16 (Jan., 1932), pp. 85–100.

EUBANK, EARLE, *A Study of Family Desertion* (Chicago: University of Chicago, 1916).

FOLSOM, JOSEPH K., *The Family* (New York: Wiley, 1934).

FOSTER, ROBERT GEIB, *Marriage and Family Relationships* (New York: Macmillan, 1944), pp. 212–240.

GOODE, WILLIAM, "Problems in Post-Divorce Adjustment," *American Sociological Review*, 14 (June, 1949), pp. 394–401.

HALL, CALVIN, "The Instability of Post-War Marriages," *Journal of Social Psychology*, 5 (Nov., 1934), pp. 523–530.

HILL, REUBEN, *Families under Stress: Adjustment to the Crises of War Separation and Reunion* (New York: Harper, 1949).

IGEL, AMALIA, "Effects of War Separation on Father-Child Relationships," *Family*, 27 (March, 1945), pp. 5–9.

KOMAROVSKY, MIRRA, *The Unemployed Man and His Family* (New York: Dryden, 1940).

KOOS, EARL LOMON, "Class Differences in Family Reactions to Crisis," *Marriage and Family Living*, 12 (Summer, 1950), pp. 77–78, 99.

Koos, Earl Lomon, "Middle-Class Family Crises," *Marriage and Family Living,* 10 (Spring, 1948), pp. 25, 40.

Locke, Harvey J., and Clausner, William J., "Marital Adjustment of Divorced Persons in Subsequent Marriages," *Sociology and Social Research,* 33 (November–December, 1948), pp. 97–101.

——, *Predicting Adjustment in Marriage* (New York: Holt, 1951), pp. 298–309.

Merrill, Francis E., *Courtship and Marriage* (New York: Sloane, 1949), pp. 286–313.

Mowrer, Ernest R., *Family Disorganization* (Chicago: University of Chicago Press, 1927).

Nimkoff, M. F., *Marriage and the Family* (Boston: Houghton Mifflin, 1947), pp. 610–623, 639–648.

Owen, J. Z., *Widows Can Be Happy* (New York: Greenberg, 1951).

Patterson, Samuel H., *Family Desertion and Non-Support* (California: Whittier State School, 1922).

Raines, Shirley, "Personality Traits of Persons Who Divorced and Remarried," *Family Life,* 10 (June, 1950), pp. 1–2.

Reed, Ruth, *The Modern Family* (New York: Knopf, 1929), pp. 121–127.

Rosenbaum, Milton, "Emotional Aspects of Wartime Separations," *Family,* 24 (Jan., 1944), pp. 337–341.

Roulston, Marjorie Hillis, *You Can Start All Over: A Guide for the Widow and Divorcée* (New York: Harper, 1951).

Sheffield, Ada Eliot, *Social Insight in Case Situations* (New York: Appleton-Century, 1937).

Truxall, Andrew G., and Merrill, Francis E., *The Family in American Culture* (New York: Prentice-Hall, 1947), pp. 632–639.

Ullman, A. D., *et al.,* "Does Failure Run in Families?" *American Journal of Psychiatry,* 107 (March, 1951), pp. 667–676.

Waller, Willard, *The Family,* rev. by Reuben Hill (New York: Dryden Press, 1938, 1951), pp. 453–469, 515–527, 525–591, 531–561.

——, *The Old Love and the New* (New York: Liveright, 1930).

Zukerman, Jacob T., "A Socio-Legal Approach to Family Desertion," *Marriage and Family Living,* 12 (Summer, 1950), pp. 83–84.

TOPICS FOR DISCUSSIONS OR REPORTS

1. What laws does your own state have on desertion? How are they enforced?
2. What is the current trend of social-work practice in dealing with desertion?
3. Do the people writing the Dorothy Dix, Beatrice Fairfax, and similar syndicated columns say much about the aftermaths of divorce?
4. Is there much popular discussion of postdivorce problems?
5. Try to discover, from magazines written two generations ago, what the stereotypes supposedly depicting the divorced woman were like.
6. If you have a close friend who is a child of divorced parents, get him to write for you an account of his adjustment to the divorce situation.
7. Would formal social announcement of the divorce help in later adjustments?
8. Report findings of studies of the aftermath of wartime separations.

Chapter Twenty-Two

Bereavement: Inevitable but Not Insurmountable

THOMAS D. ELIOT

Is MR. HESSERT in this class? . . . There is an urgent message from his home to go to his mother at St. Luke's Hospital at once." This might have happened to the student who reads this; it might happen to you today. Strictly speaking, death is never prevented: it is postponed.

Bereavements are usually unexpected, often a shock, and seldom planned for either personally or by the family. Yet they are the most widespread form of family dismemberment and must be considered, potentially at least, as the normal form of family dissolution. It therefore behooves the educated person to have some knowledge of the actual dangers and possible adjustments characteristic of such family crises.

A quarter of all American marriages are in a widowed state at any given time. Probably five times as many families are broken by death as by all other forms of dismemberment combined. One in thirteen among persons of marriageable age — a total of six million or more — is widowed. Four fifths of the broken homes are fatherless.[1]

Studies of pauperism, delinquency, neglect and other behavior problem-situations often discover as "causes" of the trouble homes broken by deaths inadequately coped with. But the social psychology of bereavement as such has been slow to draw scientific attention.

That bereavement has been so little studied can be attributed to inertia, taboo, and inherent methodological difficulties, not to the obscurity of the problem. The normal death rate bereaves two American families every minute — and this quite aside from war. A problem involving so profoundly a million or more persons at all times deserves our attention, however reluctant and however ignorant or helpless we may feel about it. If there be any counsels of wisdom or comfort, they should be made accessible to the bereaved and to the advisers of the bereaved. "Science rather than silence" should be the watchword when confronted by a problem of such universality.

Religion and poetry have attempted to shed light upon the experience of bereavement, but the shadow is still there. There is a bond of sympathy between those who have gone through it, but as yet the survivors offer little to guide those not acquainted with grief.

Too often the individual has been left to face the ordeal unprepared and alone. We do not even know to what extent the old rites and beliefs continue

---

[1] M. F. Nimkoff, *Marriage and the Family* (Boston: Houghton Mifflin, 1947), pp. 613–618. The disproportion of widows to widowers is due to (1) higher death rate of men, (2) higher remarriage rate of widowers, (3) greater male age at marriage, and (4) war deaths.

to mean what they did. The changes in religion, science, commerce, and urban life have brought such a medley of new ideas and tastes in funeral rites and practices that nobody really knows what he or anybody else really needs in the crisis of bereavement. As a result we may fall back upon the habits of friends, our memories of others' behavior, or the suggestions of the mortuary salesman.[2]

Taboo versus Need

Within recent years the taboo upon speaking of death has been abated, much as has been the case in the fields of sex and insanity; people are increasingly willing to discuss their own and others' experiences objectively and analytically. Certain typical patterns of the mourning period, though as yet unpredictable, are recognizable; and to a minor extent there begins to be a mental hygiene for grief. The subject, instead of being a matter of ceremonials and silence, of gruesome horror or grim humor, has become respectable and relaxed. Yet the taboo is still strong.

[Taboos are blessed *and* cursed.] . . . Because death is too much feared to be faced, our defense is to *joke* about it . . . as in other respects, there is a striking analogy between the field of behavior in response to death, and the field of behavior in response to sex. Each represents a life-crisis, calling out intense emotions which seek expression in unusual actions. Around every such common crisis, repeated, imitated, or inculcated practices have accreted: folkways, culture traits, taboos, sacraments, beliefs, compulsions — a whole culture complex. The breakdown of the sex taboo, whatever other results it may have had, has made it possible to face the facts squarely, to study them with some relaxation, and probably to improve social techniques in this field. Sex is no longer exclusively associated with its morbid aspects. . . .

[Where death is concerned, there] is, in some respects, a heavier load of taboo and resistance than in the case of sex. Yet it is hoped that the relaxation of the conventional repression of death may make it easier to face the fact, to study its social aspects, and to guide our attitudes and our techniques more satisfactorily. . . . If proper sex education is important, delicate, and subtle, so is proper death education.[3]

The accumulation of further case studies may be increasingly helpful in the guidance of patients, parishioners, clients, friends, and one's own family in the crises of bereavement. It is to be hoped that increasing foreknowledge of the emotional problems of bereavement may enable the art of mental hygiene to provide more fruitful ways of conserving the values

[2] Thomas D. Eliot, "The Liberal Viewpoint," *New York World-Telegram,* April 10, 1933; adapted. See Howard Becker and D. K. Bruner, "Some Aspects of Taboo and Totemism," *Journal of Social Psychology,* 3, 3 (Aug., 1932), pp. 337-352.

[3] Thomas D. Eliot, "The Adjustive Behavior of Bereaved Families," *Social Forces,* 8 (June, 1930), pp. 544-545. See also Sylvia Anthony, *The Child's Discovery of Death* (London: Kegan Paul, Trench, Trubner, 1940).

of one's loved ones: viz., the social relation of love and the purposes of that love.

FACTORS IN THE INITIAL SHOCK SITUATION

Physically, one must recognize bereavement as a major shock, often requiring physical or even medical care like any other illness or accident, with time for physical recovery. The viscera, under the effects of emotion, are subject to various spastic and circulatory conditions which are beyond my competence and beyond the scope of this paper, though by no means unrelated thereto. There are possible analogies, in certain respects, to child-bearing: pregnancy and childbirth, like bereavement, are normal but profound organic crises from which recovery is necessary though also normal.

Some physicians routinely offer a sedative to the bereaved at the time of the death, to dull shock and lessen exhaustion. Perhaps for acute cases we shall one day use prolonged narcosis therapy as in cases of operational fatigue from combat shock and stress. On awakening, the lapse of time subconsciously felt may in itself have a therapeutic value.

Psychologically, bereavement is a major type in the general class of traumatic frustration-situations. Arrested impulse or thwarted habit is at the root of all sorrow. Bereavement is one's blocked wish for response following death of the love-object. The loved one is gone, but the associated memories and habits and needs remain alive as a real complex in the mind of the bereaved. Variations of bereavement reactions from case to case are attributable in part to degrees of love and in part to degrees of energy and habitual temperament in the bereaved person, as well as to external variables. In the crisis, energy and attention are apt to be focused narrowly on the immediate: on one's own suffering, needs, anxieties, loss, or on those of the deceased. This concentration tends to drain off energy, interest, or attention from all other affairs ordinarily important to the bereaved person. Distraction from grief is difficult even when willingly sought as "escape."

Sociologically, bereavement is the dismemberment of an affectional group by death, and the questions are: What happens in such groups? How are the structure and the social relationships of families affected when a beloved member is irrevocably torn away? What shifts and substitutions of the former roles of family members occur during readjustment? Bereavement is thus a problem in intrapersonal conflict, accommodation, and/or assimilation — disorganization — and in interpersonal accommodation and group reorganization — disintegration.

MOURNING AS A PERSONAL ADJUSTMENT PROCESS

Bereavement is obviously for the most part a phase of familial relations. There is a period of emotional disturbance [4] and, normally, some gradual accommodation (relaxation of unpleasant tensions) in the situation. To

---

[4] Including not only grief but resentment, anxiety, upset routine, or actual hardship.

this period has been given the term "mourning process" in a new, sociological sense. During mourning the attachments of the survivor to the dead person are gradually relaxed and transferred to new objects or channels; this process has also been called the "sublimation of grief." [5]

One interpretation of the "work" of mourning is that each unit of affectionate attachment to the deceased, upon being revived in memory and grief, is diffused and reattached, or at least loosened ready for transference to new objects. As the emotional ties are relaxed and redirected, the experience of bereavement is, in sociological terms, assimilated by the person, accepted (introjected) into the personality, relegated rather than repressed. The psychic wound gradually heals. This psychic work may be consciously expedited by appropriate ideology, mental hygiene, and common sense, but this work of inner healing cannot succeed if deliberately attempted exclusively on the self-conscious level. The work of reorientation to the new situation goes on inevitably day and night — by daydreams and night dreams.

"It takes a strong light to cast a sharp shadow." Since we cannot abolish death we cannot assuredly avoid bereavement without obliterating all past joy and love, or entirely immunizing ourselves to love. Once sorrow sincerely disappears, the tension of the love that gave rise to it has likewise been liquidated. Intensity of sorrow tends to vary directly as intensity of prior joy and love. Every person is unique, and to the extent that affection for the deceased also was personalized it is irreplaceable. Such sorrow actually increases love for the lost personality, whose satisfying attributes are recalled.

Family members who have become deeply dependent in any way upon the deceased member will, because of this dependence, have their grief intensified by the sense of emptiness, helplessness, or fear. But such dependence may seek all the more quickly the solace of persons as substitute love-objects accessible for relief of the intolerable strain.

In general, children, being less habituated, recover from mourning soon; their energies and affections are easily transferred. Only where the new situation presents new hardship or "guilt" may a child brood over his memories, fixated upon the lost parent or protector.[6] An adult, on the other hand, not easily reoriented, may have to live over an entire life, painfully bringing to consciousness and renouncing as now nonexistent each beloved experience, before the tensions of mourning are neutralized.[7]

As in recoveries from other crises, adjustments to bereavement seem to be easier for those who were normally adjusted before bereavement, as evidenced by physical and emotional stability, social-economic normality, and education. On the other hand, conflicts of culture, as in the families of the foreign born, complicate adjustments to bereavement.

It is also alleged that a second or third bereavement in a family is borne

[5] Thomas D. Eliot, *op. cit.* in fn. 3, p. 544.

[6] See Anthony, *op. cit.*

[7] Willard Waller, *The Family*, rev. by Reuben Hill (New York: Dryden Press, 1951), p. 476. The fact that mourning usually eventuates in recovery led Waller actually to use the word "mourning" positively for the whole recovery process (e.g., *ibid.*, pp. 480–498, esp. 481–482).

with more equanimity than the first, at least if the wounds (traumata) of the first have in some measure healed. If a family is bereft simultaneously of more than one member, it may be that something like Weber's "law" of sensation may be observable: beyond a certain degree of shock, additional severity reaches diminishing returns in pain or capacity to react.

In the reactions of the bereaved, the "last days" and attitudes of the dying person may prove to be important factors. If death is feared or foreseen, crisis is present for the survivors even before death. The shattering of one's vital confidence, previously based upon spontaneous faith in the possibilities of life or upon our protective taboos against thoughts of one's own mortality, may produce considerable reorientation of life organization. Serious illness as well as bereavement in a family may have this "sobering effect." In one case, return of a foster child to its own family produced a trauma in the foster parents definitely comparable to bereavement.

"Being prepared for the worst" is apparently a mitigation for the bereaved if not accompanied by prolonged strain or exhaustion. But even when expected, the arrival of actual death of a beloved person, being unique for that particular interpersonal relation, is a new experience and a shock. A refusal to accept the foresight of death tends to increase the shock of it.

IMMEDIATE REACTIONS: DISBELIEF AND DEFENSE

A common first reaction, especially if death was sudden or the news unforeseen, is disbelief; the actual is rejected as unreal. There may be temporary but stubborn inability or refusal to believe or to accept the actuality of the death or of its consequences, i.e., the differences in the actual situation already and inevitably present and in process as results of the death. Unless otherwise indicated, all illustrations are from the writer's case files:

1. Her reaction to the news was disbelief — for about a month after, since she felt that many come out alive due to misinformation or some mistake on the part of observers. Then no other word came, and she finally gave in and accepted it as a fact.

2. I felt as if I had turned to ice, I was so chilly. I don't remember crying at first, but did not think it had actually happened. . . . I said, "It can't be true."

In people's refusal to accept the fact of death there is an obvious element of wishful thinking or defense, but much of it must be on a subconscious level. One's habits, powerfully reinforced by needs and satisfactions, may prove to be incapable of rapid readjustment. Numbness, the refusal to realize, may have a protective function — as a buffer to a shock which taken all at once would be too devastating. The sense of unreality seems to be a common symptom of general psychophysical shock. It may explain some cases of preternatural calm or apparent detachment during crises. This may amount to a sense of exaltation.

Spontaneous inability to believe is to be distinguished from active effort *not* to believe.

When I heard an M.D.'s opinion, given to me over the phone . . . I was unutterably shocked. My heart began pounding and kept it up all thru the night as I uttered over and over, "God is man's life." . . . Then I decided to fight harder than ever against death. Toward the end I did not believe he was going, although as he lessened his hold upon me, my spirits soared into a state of exaltation. . . . I felt it was because the battle was won and he would get well and stay here. . . . At first I could not bear to leave the body or have it taken, I was so confident that my love was strong enough to hold him, to bring his life back. I could not believe that he had slipped away and left me freed. I did not believe in his death. (Christian Scientist, whose Methodist husband had been painfully ill for four years with bone tuberculosis.)

More frequently observed initial reactions are physical prostration, daze, prolonged weeping, poor appetite, insomnia, rigid stoicism, efforts to console others.

Certain metaphorical euphemisms, such as "joined the clouds," "over the horizon," "on the long trail," "faded into the mist," are ways of evading the blunt fact of death.[8]

If there are any possibly questionable circumstances surrounding the death, moreover, or if there are similar situations in which the supposed death proved to be an error, the bereaved may spin fantastically thin webs of hope and lean upon them. Deaths reported from overseas occasionally lend themselves to such efforts.

The deceased may appear in "veridical" dreams, so vivid that in the peculiar double-awareness of such dreams, the bereaved is momentarily persuaded (if only in sleep) that it is the death, not this dream, which is an illusion.[9] Such dreams serve a double purpose of denying the death and of perpetuating the loved one and the satisfactions of affection. There is also the occasional experience of "invisible presence" of the deceased.

A paradox of bereavement is the intellectual recognition of the irrevocability of the death and protean struggles to circumvent this irrevocability. Bereavement is full of the ambivalent conflict of despair and craving, "that incomprehensible contradiction of memory and nonexistence."[10] The essence of sorrow is frustration of impulse and deprivation of satisfaction or of the means of satisfaction; and its intensity is a function of the ratio between the person's energy and the degree of resistance to his desires. Since in bereavement the opposition to realization is absolute, no energy opposed can overcome it. The very memory which is invoked as the nearest approach to restitution is also a reminder of the impossibility of that restitution. The sense of irrevocability comes — sometimes after hysterical efforts — when one realizes that no resources of his are adequate to resist or replace the loss.

Efforts to avoid grief by repressing the fact of death are one thing. It is a further step to try to forget the deceased entirely. The effort here is to re-

---

[8] "Morbid," *Time,* 42 (Oct. 25, 1943), p. 46.
[9] Randall Jarrell, "The Lost Love," *Atlantic,* 169 (Apr., 1942), p. 493.
[10] Marcel Proust, *Cities of the Plain* (New York: Random House, 1934), vol. 1, p. 235.

duce the sense of loss by devaluing the thing lost, or to remove from consciousness the event of loss by removing from consciousness the thing lost. When the fact of death is accepted, there may still be effort to escape from it by forgetting, by distraction, by pretenses and fantasy, or by suppressing all reminders.

1. I returned to work after four days. The girls at the office (Washington, D. C.) were surprised. I returned because I thought it was best for me. . . . I put away everything that suggested my husband. [Later in Evanston] I avoided places where we had been together. I don't play the record of his voice. I quit buying the perfume I used to use. . . . I put away my black dresses for at least a year. This she says she did, not because of his wish nor to seek a new mate, but to avoid the pain of reminders, and as being "sensible." [Presumably this young war widow would not have felt the need to avoid reminders if memories had not been besetting her. Men were still being compared mentally with her husband.]

2. Still more surprising, after he was gone and there was the awful vacancy of not having Dad there to tell things to, we still had our many interests outside — our Boy Scouts or Girl Scouts, our music lessons, our church club, our little jobs for earning money. . . . Best of all Mother was not suddenly left in an empty home filled with memories. She had her innumerable clubs and they called to her more and more.

THE MASOCHISM OF SORROW

The occasional opposite case, that of willful effort to keep grief fresh, is perhaps less easy for some of us to understand. Distraction. consolation, and recovery may actually be resisted by the "voluptuaries of grief." If one *wishes* to grieve, condolence is welcome; consolation is resented,[11] if there is energy to resist.

If there had been elements of estrangement or petty conflict during life, there may be an element of self-punishment for repressed guilt feelings. The bereaved then feels a constant though unverbalized need to demonstrate to himself his role as mourner. There may be also a touch of masochism in it, or of pride, or of some conventional conception of the proper role of widow or gold star mother.

[A year after the death] time has not helped alleviate her [the mother's] sorrows. She has many crying spells and keeps insisting that her life on earth will be very short. [In this case the husband is a drunkard and the dead sailor son had drawn a strong mother-attachment.]

In two cases, the actual or alleged fact that the death could have been avoided — in one case by more care by a fellow sailor, in the other by more personal caution — were especially aggravating to grief. One may interpret obsession with memories as a form of attempted wishfulfillment — not merely as escape from present pain but as a regression to and fixation at the

[11] Seneca, *Consolations.*

period when the loved one was there. Intense longing for the irrevocably gone, the thwarted wish for the love-object, accompanies all these overt symptoms.

THE AMBIVALENCE OF GRIEF

It is possible to interpret the blocking off of the past as an *escape* from fixations, lest one become a self-impaled martyr.

1. The significance of her child's needing her brought Mrs. J. on back to reality, so to speak, and from then on her condition rapidly improved.
2. A Christian Scientist mother avoided answering the door bell before the funeral, and stayed for two weeks in a relative's home in another city afterward, because she could not stand the sympathizing by friends. "S. is alive, carrying on . . . bravely behind the veil." She continued to work over her religious books and was under counsel from a practitioner.

The armed services are remarkably efficient, under the circumstances, in returning personal effects of the war dead. How has this affected the survivors? The reactions reported are ambivalent: the family craves them, is much upset on their arrival, and either displays or conceals them; seldom uses them.

1. A father and daughter traveled a long distance to the Navy Base from which the man had flown, "for his effects and a talk with someone who had been on the scene of the crash."
2. Father was overwhelmed by the trunk with photographs of the family and pictures of him with his friends. Later the Purple Heart, brought by a fellow officer, broke him up. It was framed on the wall, still later.

There is a definite similarity of pattern in the reactions toward these objects and the reactions toward other post mortem reminders — letters, eye-witnesses, etc. — and in the ambivalent cravings for the dreaded certainties of detailed accounts.

That grief may be ambivalent in attraction and avoidance is further shown in the following from a young widow:

I like to recall the many things we did together — trips we took, saving for something special, his demonstrations of affection, what a promising future he had . . . our plans for getting a house, etc., etc. It is sometimes so un-bearable being reminded . . . that I try to keep occupied and to have people around.

There follows a self-protective attitude that I have observed only twice, though it is quite understandable:

Feeling now that one should not "put all of one's eggs in one basket," as it were. It might be better not to learn to depend upon only one person — keep back some reserve of self so that you won't be so hurt or lost.

Perpetuation of the Love-Object

Note, please, a distinction between efforts to perpetuate one's *sorrow* and the very different effort to perpetuate either *the love-object* itself or the purposes and significance of the deceased. The former seems like futile morbidity to most of us: it is bad mental hygiene. Perpetuation of the love-object, on the other hand, may be attributed to the natural wish for reunion, i.e., the "wish for response," or to a fear of admitting one's own mortality, or to identification of the body with the person. This last may take physical forms, such as elaborate embalming or the sealing of caskets, or the exhuming, transport, and reburial of bodies from overseas.

Some few make a fetish of the ashes either by preservation in a shrine or by elaborate ceremonial dispersion or spot-burial. Naturalism, whether of the "dust to dust" type or of the "resurrection through germination" type or based merely on a sentimental wish to associate memories with a spot through a sort of contact magic, motivates such cases. It may even stem from a wish to *escape the thought of continuity after death.*

The Rev. Francis L. Hilditch . . . knew a woman who carried her daughter's ashes everywhere. . . . People will give extraordinary directions about the taking of their ashes to a particular spot or out to sea. . . .

Canon Francis J. Edmond agreed that burial requests are sometimes blasphemous: "One man left instructions that his body should be burned and his ashes scattered over his potato patch. That man was really trying to show his contempt for his own body." [12]

Preservation of the body, of mementoes, and of habitats of the deceased is considered a symbol of loyalty, but is also evidence of a fear of forgetting, a pleasure-pain.

Immortality and Religion

The quality of immediate reactions to death, as of all subsequent reactions to bereavement, is markedly affected by whatever cultural definition of the situation is shared by the bereaved. Special beliefs in regard to immortality, such as those of the Mormons, the Christian Scientists, the Spiritualists, the Hindus, the Moslems, and certain nonliterate peoples, or, by contrast, those of materialists, agnostics,[13] atheists, Calvinists, undoubtedly affect the attitudes of the bereaved, in mitigation or aggravation, and influence the nature of their compensatory efforts, if any, during the crisis.

A belief in immortality, whether unquestioned or accepted as a last resort against intolerable despair and grief, is of course an important element in the attitudes of many bereaved persons, especially of those religions that make such doctrines cardinal elements of faith.

[12] "Morbid," *Time,* 42 (Oct. 25, 1943), p. 46.
[13] Corliss Lamont, "A Humanist Funeral Service," *Unity,* 94 (Dec. 2, 1940), pp. 108–109.

My idea of death and eternity have changed since [the] death. Heaven isn't half as far away or half as vague as it was before. I feel that now that mother is there everything will be ready for me when I come to the end of my days. This has been a great comfort to me . . . a land of good — a land of re-union — a place to see mother and F. [the dead fiancé] . . . Now I believe that it is greed that tries to keep a dying soul on earth.

Beliefs in immortality serve to transcend by faith the barrier of death. Grief tends to vary inversely as the hope of meeting hereafter; directly as despair of reunion. The wish for reunion with the loved one projects itself, of course, through beliefs in immortality conceived as future life. Here is a letter from a Christian Scientist:

We know that the experience you are going through now lies ahead of all of us . . . insofar as we see those dearest to us as individuals to whom we are privileged to help on their way — as they in turn help us on our way — that sense of "mine" is kept out and it is easier to lose them and let them go.

What John wrote in his first letter became a clue to me when he said that Mark seemed to have lived as much in fourteen years as some people do in forty. . . . He laid his body down but he is alive forevermore, loving you just the same, and when the time comes for you — and us — to lay down our sense of body, I am perfectly sure he'll be just as happy to see us and have a lot to show us and tell us about — things he knows about and we don't. I re-member saying to Mrs. Hard (a Chicago practitioner) once that the problem of separation from Arthur seemed a very real and difficult one to me and I asked her how she worked it out for herself and Mr. Hard, for he is such a nice man and they work together all the time. " Why," said she, "which-ever one stays will have such a lot to do that the time will not seem long." [14]

The wish of the bereaved *to die* may be a wish to escape intolerable grief, but it may also be a wish to beat the irrevocable, to achieve reunion. In rare cases belief in immortality might contribute to a suicide, through the ration-alization that those bereaved of each other would be thus reunited (Romeo and Juliet pattern). Life "alone" being considered "intolerable," suicide might also be logical for a disbeliever. Both of these are distinct from the wish to die (or to have died) *instead* of the deceased.

His fiancée was inconsolable. She had to be continually watched so that she would not harm herself. [From a war case.]

In still another direction, the wish for perpetuation and reunion takes the form of seeking spiritualistic séances, or at least the examination of spiritistic literature. Many persons not conventionally religious will make, shortly after a bereavement, a more or less vigorous inquiry into spiritualism, which offers on a pseudo-physical level assurances which merely scriptural theology lacks.

[14] Arthur James Todd, ed., *Life and Letters of Martha Gaddis Todd* (Chicago: Art Institute of Chicago, 1940), p. 203.

A few are carried away by their own wishful thinking as much as by the tricks of the séance.

"Unbelievers" have different problems in bereavement, but not necessarily more serious ones, than those who are not sure or those who "believe":

1. As to immortality I had no positive belief or disbelief, just a feeling that in a universe as well ordered and marvelous as this all things are possible. Certainly our influence and spirit live on in the lives of those about us. Whether death of the body brings eternal rest for our inner spirit or whether it frees our spirit for a new adventurous living elsewhere in the universe I cannot know. I did not care. I was ready to trust that to Divine Will and have faith that whichever it was, it would be good. Now when I have seen a life that was so full of potential beauty and love take on a growing feeling of despair and end without renewed hope, I wish that I could be sure that P. still lives and has found greater understanding and hope. I *hope* he does live and understand; I'm not sure.

2. I am agnostic regarding life after death and frankly most skeptical of the continuity of my ego, and I accept death as a final parting. Naturally there is shock and pain, which must be met just as any other shock or loss.

3. One thing I know — Mat is gone, he is dead, but, so long as people who loved him live, he lives.

Without religion, grief becomes unpatterned; variations are tolerated.

PROJECTIONS OF MEMORY, PERSONALITY, AND PURPOSE

Again, the wish for perpetuation of the deceased may take the form of substitute fulfillment through a child of the deceased, who may be (unwisely) expected by the bereaved to grow up in the dead parent's image, to fill his role, and to complete the hopes of the deceased or the bereaved.

Expressed or imagined wishes of the deceased may or may not affect bereaved behavior, either in the immediate crisis or in later adjustments. "He would have wanted me to remarry"; or, "We had agreed that Junior would need a mother's care"; or, "She would have wished this work to carry on" — such expressions occur. Fixation on the deceased or a spouse's known expectations or promises against remarriage may cause resistance to all possible new love-objects. Or they may cause conflict and/or recurrent remorse when a new love is admitted.

To offset the sense of possible *waste of life* or *loss of values,* or as a substitute for spiritual immortality or memory, many have the impulse to perpetuate memory in *memorials.*

The great number of new public monuments and private memorials following every war is also ample evidence of the *wish for recognition* — recognition of the bereaved. Many express their gratification over press notices as well as over resolutions, memorial gifts, and large attendance at services.

1. We were thrilled to think that our mother was so well known and dearly beloved to have so many friends (700) paying tribute to her. . . .

They are starting a memorial plaque now. The D.D.N—— [deceased's name] Shelf at the public library will be maintained by a woman's organization. The symbolism of this is very great. Mother was a learned woman, a student, and a reader.

2. Announcement was made in the . . . Faculty Bulletin and college paper; it was broadcast over the radio in the news (I was later told); the flag on the campus was at half mast on Wednesday; his picture and account of his life were in the [city] papers; the school sent notices to cities where X—— had gone to school and taught — it appeared in *Science;* Graduate Magazine; it appeared in [eight other cities, including] two places where he had lived as a child. The tone was very complimentary. Since the notifications were made by friends, and many people who perhaps otherwise would not have known and would be interested were thus informed, we were pleased and have kept copies.

For many persons there comes an active wish to perpetuate the interests of the deceased and help to fulfill his or her hopes cut off by death.

Self-Centered and Regressive Patterns

One of the frequently found bereavement reactions is extreme self-centeredness. Even the immediate reactions of the bereaved do not take place in a social vacuum; the more self-centered a personality is, however, the more apt it is to isolate itself in grief without consideration for others except to crave their corroborative comfort.

The bereaved tends to imagine that his grief is unique. "There is no sorrow like unto my sorrow." If this serves to increase one's sense of importance it may be in a sense welcomed by the bereaved personality. It may also convince the bereaved that he has been singled out for unexampled injustice or that nobody else can understand.

1. A bereaved fiancée in college resented well-meant efforts of sorority mates to "be with her" and "distract her" — and they considered her as eccentric or putting on a false front of indifference because (like Job) she felt her comforters could not understand. Informant tended to feel that her grief was unique and greater than others; that those who tried to comfort could not understand.

2. One friend tried to tell me that Time would heal my sorrow — I thanked her but felt that she just did not understand.

A unique bereavement, which seems to single out some person "irrationally," is like sudden bereavement often felt to be "unfair," especially if preceded by happiness now keenly recalled. Egotic behavior under such conditions is not to be taken as evidence of blameworthy or unusual selfishness, though a prior habit of unselfishness may inhibit it. It is understandable as a self-defense of the personality against a mortal attack on its inner integrity, a conflict within one's central citadel of values and of control. In an habitually selfish personality, however, it may lead the bereaved to seek attention to the exclusion of others.

One case has been reported to me in which a mother seemed to be "putting on an act." The tantrum is distinct from a sincere breakdown in grief: it implies an ulterior purpose. It is not necessarily conscious or deliberately staged but it is dispelled by attention rather than by exhaustion and it betokens a felt need for pity or for recognition of one's importance. It may be interpreted as a regressive outbreak of a childhood pattern or device for getting help when injured or deprived.

I think it likely that, were it possible to make thorough inquiry, it would be found it is cyclothymic (mercurial) and extrovertive personalities who tend to break out in overt paroxysms of weeping, protest, etc., especially if the culture in which the family has been reared offers permitted patterns of this extrovertive sort. Seizures of grief or rage, however they may be motivated, are physically exhausting, and therefore are apt to be followed by temporary episodes variously described as blank, mute despair, stolidity, inability to act or even move, indifference to stimuli. As realization bears in upon consciousness, periods of abandon may supervene, passively expressed in weeping or self-centered self-pity, aggressively expressed in resentment, cursing, self-blame, even self-injury.

Since the sheer drain upon energy precludes indefinite continuance of either frantic manifestations of grief or its rigorous repression, each of these is apt to give way shortly or intermittently to its opposite.

Some people "rise to the occasion," are integrated or reorganized by a family crisis. Shand has noted that sorrow can make or break a person. Occasionally a person fails to rally from the first shock of a bereavement and actually dies or goes insane or permanently melancholic. Collapse is less frequent than a sudden rally; but after exaltation, watch out for a slump. Certain religious fears or self-blame culturally conditioned by moral beliefs may complicate such cases.

On the other hand there are those whose temperament, habits, and culture combine to prevent overt expression of grief, at least in public. Conscious self-control represents internal consumption of nervous energy, which is also exhausting and may produce spastic visceral tensions and even physical illness or nervous collapse. It is a widespread observation that those who express their grief violently may more quickly recover from it.

If the ambitions and sense of worthwhileness of the bereaved have been dependent upon response from the deceased or upon status in that person's eyes, there may be a sudden sense of deflation; of disillusion as to the importance of the bereaved; of the futility even of his own loves and hates.

A common observation of the bereaved is that the *meaning* drops out of everything that previously had importance. Various expressions recur which seem to describe a similar subjective experience: emptiness, deadness, futility.

When she heard the news [withheld for two weeks after childbirth] she cried very little and seemed to go off into a stupor, not caring whether she lived or died. She just appeared to give up, but the family convinced her that she should live for her daughter's sake. [The girl was named "Georgia" for her soldier father.]

A more introvertive form of the collapse of values occurs when the bereaved feels that he *himself* is valueless, has lost motivation, and therefore imagines he can no longer contribute or create, has no one to live for, or is now merely a burden. Whether or not complicated by self-blame or sheer loneliness, the sense of the worthlessness of self, of life in general, or of life without the deceased to motivate it, might lead to thoughts of suicide. Shand [15] attributed this sort of reaction to the concentration of the person's energy in the conflicts of sorrow, which distract his interests. In psychiatric terms, we might say that sorrow drains off all "affect" from other complexes of the personality. Closely related to this is behavior or feeling of the bereaved that she or he has no will, no effective wish or ability to act. *Apparent* calm may be due to "freezing pressure" — repression — either spontaneous or self-controlled; but also to a sort of attitudinal paralysis or *aboulia,* characterized less by tension than by weakness, lack of energy.[16]

> Lately I have seen one of the boys for the first time since the mother's death. The change in him is very apparent. He looks older. His attitude toward life is "What's the use?" He remarked to me that he never heard such true words as Shakespeare's " All the world's a stage," etc. Nothing seems to interest him anymore, while last year he was in all the school activities and entered into the spirit of things.

Reluctance and indifference toward one's usual habits, appearance, or enterprises reveal to one that these had previously been motivated at least in part by loyalties to the deceased or to values cherished by the deceased; that they depended upon the discipline of the deceased or were efforts to appear worthy of the esteem of the loved one. Activity on the part of the bereaved is not the answer here. What activity would replace the love of books and of record-collections, since love of the objects is present but their tie with the dead is too great to permit enjoyment, especially in the immediate period of bereavement, which is the time when they will be most missed? Some point could be made here about resentment-reactions toward these objects, and a suggestion of allowing time to elapse for overcoming the feeling which these objects provoke.

I have also observed bereaved persons preternaturally buoyed up, apparently in full command of themselves and everyone else, and even consciously surprised over their own condition in this respect. Exceptional activity, care for others, assumption of new responsibilities, even a sober cheerfulness, may characterize this type of reaction. Elements of "necessity," deliberate mental hygiene, common sense, pride, imitation, conception of role, temporary overstimulation by the fatigue poisons of emotional strain,

[15] See Alexander F. Shand, *The Foundations of Character* (London: Macmillan, 1914), pp. 301–369. Most of Shand's findings have been checked against actual case histories in my own or students' files. See also Howard Becker, "The Sorrow of Bereavement," *Journal of Abnormal and Social Psychology,* 27 (Jan.–March, 1933).

[16] Shand, *op. cit.,* and 77th "Law."

the dependence of others less competent, may enter into the situation. Such people may reserve their weeping for their pillows.

One widow believes it helpful to let the bereaved talk of the deceased if it eases their minds; but not to encourage them. She agreed that one should give rein to grief occasionally, but reserved hers for her own privacy.

Routine duties proved helpful in keeping her on keel. She thinks it good to place the bereaved where the situation will rouse his interest and focus his attention outside of himself, but nobody did that for her. Hovering and obviously accompanying her merely focused her self-attention further. To meet another person who has successfully readjusted after bereavement might have been helpful; she did not think of that at the time.

There was no obsession with memories after the first month. Memories continued to come but were not allowed to become introvertive. They were allowed to pass in review, to herself, but not fixated. There was no wish to forget the deceased, however.

THE CRAVING FOR EXPLANATIONS AND SCAPEGOATS

The bereaved often insistently demand *explanations* of the death. Curiosity for details may indicate a craving for the relaxation that results from an adequate natural explanation or even from a confirmation and consequent acceptance of the death. This is found in the pitiful eagerness with which war-bereaved families receive the painful letters from the front after a death overseas, and reconstruct the scene in imagination.

An insatiable desire to know all the details and actual or possible causes of the death, may also be traceable to a subconscious wish to exculpate one's self, possibly because of some still more deeply repressed hates or "death wishes" surviving from frustrations or momentary quarrels of the past. Such material would require psychoanalysis to uncover and prove. One may suspect it when a bereaved person is too obviously defensive or seeks to blame others, as well as when he turns upon himself his own irrational accusations. But such blame-reactions may be more simply attributed merely to a jealous or sometimes extrovertive personality or, on the other hand, to an introvertive, masochistic personality.

An habitually rebellious person, who may on occasion have got results or satisfaction from angry response to frustrations, may add anger to grief. One may seek a personal scapegoat — a nurse, a family member, a commanding officer, or a national leader — Roosevelt, Churchill, Stalin, or Hitler — to lay blame upon. Gropings for an object for one's resentment, and efforts to rationalize one's irrational anger, seem thus to interact with the craving for *explanations,* which in turn may be inseparably linked with the curiosity of survivors. Blame may even express itself in revenge.

On the death day of Mr. Roosevelt . . . I saw one flag flying at the full height of the mast . . . so I asked the person responsible . . . why he had it so; his reply was, "I'm flying this flag to show that I have one, but I'm keeping it all the way up . . . because I ain't paying no honor to that guy that got us into this war and got my two sons killed at Pearl Harbor!"

In civilized, sane situations one would rarely find direct violent reprisals. But the situation may leave room for permanent grudges or lead to a carry-over of prejudices to other situations where the grudge is irrelevant and unfair. In wartime, revenge may be turned against the enemy as a whole, a generalized hate-object substituting for some unknown actual killer to whom in turn his victim was unknown. A soldier bereaved of his buddy, or a family member bereaved by a sailor's death, may channelize resentment of the loss against *any* "Nip" or "Kraut" — one is as bad as another; in fact "a Jap is a Jap is a Jap," as the late Gertrude Stein might have put it.

MOURNING, SYMPATHY, AND RECOVERY

The urge which a bereaved person feels to go over the bereavement crisis in detail may thus be due to mere morbid curiosity, to a secret fear of guilt, or to search for a scapegoat. In may also be a way of giving the mind a chance to accommodate itself to the new situation; to realize, accept, reorient, and assimilate the actual sequence of events in a way which the speed and shock of the moment had made impossible at the time. I have observed a comparable phenomenon during a patient's recovery from electric shock treatment after profound depression.

The writing down of the details in a diary or case study or even a formal interview with a minister or social worker or friend may not be without pain of refreshed grief; but it may also prove to be a relief so far as it helps the recovering person to stand off objectively from the event, to realize that time has begun to make a difference, or to redefine the situation. Or it may help the bereaved to select, organize, rationalize, and accept the version of the events which he is going to assimilate as part of his recovery. This is similar to the familiar catharsis effect of the confessional or of "abreaction" in psychoanalysis. The gradual re-examination and redefinition of each situation as it comes to recollection tends to relax and reorient the personality.

Do the bereaved want sympathy; and if so, how? One suspects that even those who claim that they would prefer to be left alone, would be embittered if their friends did so. "Misery loves company," and sorrow is lessened when others are simultaneously afflicted. To be bereaved with need for concealment or with none about who are aware of one's grief, is peculiarly poignant. Expressed sympathy simultaneously releases and relieves sorrow; on the contrary, in the rare case of anyone's gloating over a death or over the grief-stricken, sorrow and shock would of course be aggravated.

Some of the bereaved have the grace to appreciate the good will of even these "Job's comforters" who are maladroit and malapropos. Most express great comfort or even gratification from all the expressions of sympathy, or show special response to specific acts, phrases, or gestures.

1. My friends and my minister helped, not in saying anything but in giving me the feeling they knew I was going through a hard time and that they would do anything they could.

2. A hand clasp of understanding and the letter of sympathy are very helpful. We were surprised that such busy people in a *city* where we had lived only a year and a half were so concerned and friendly. Made one realize how warm hearted and good people are. . . . Realization of how many friends we had made me feel not quite so alone.

3. So you carry on . . . you start climbing the next hill. And then you find something you weren't prepared for. Your pain eases . . . warmth creeps through your chilled heart. Suddenly you realize what has happened. It is the letters. They come from close friends and from old but distant ones; from those you had thought indifferent or hostile; from strangers; from the great and from the humble. This fragrant bloom of sympathy fills you with awe. . . .[17]

The attentions which come to the bereaved, however conventional, may help in the work of recovery if they rouse a sense of status and of self-justification. If manifestations of sorrow bring such attentions, such manifestations may be thereby prolonged but may thereby also cure the original grief; whereas pride in not "showing weakness" or in not asking for help may increase the length of inner mourning.

To have others to comfort and support in family bereavement is, as in other family crises, a distraction from one's own grief. Evidence of the sympathy of others, as shown by funeral attendance and the like, may be profoundly comforting.

THE ROLE OF CUSTOMS AND RIGHTS

Funeral customs vary widely not only from culture to culture but (through lag, innovation, and diffusion) within our own culture. They all have, or once had, some motivation. Many of them still serve to cushion the shock, to comfort, distract, or encourage; they help to carry along the bereaved into less troubled waters. Where salable goods or services are involved, commercial motives may even elaborate such customs. Other traditional items are being streamlined out of the funeral by urbanism and mechanization.[18] The subjective reactions of survivors toward both material traits and nonmaterial traits of the funeral complex are beginning to be studied; the findings should be helpful to all those who try as professionals or as friends to be helpful at such times.

The public functions of the funeral period are those of initiation reversed. At adolescence various group rites give recognition to the entry of a new person into full participation in church and state. At death, a

---

[17] Howard Vincent O'Brien, "All Things Considered," *Chicago Daily News,* reprinted in *Reader's Digest,* " 'So Long, Son,' " (June, 1944), pp. 1-2.

[18] W. P. Hohenschuh, *The Modern Funeral* (Chicago: Trade Periodical Co., 1900), and current trade magazines.

person is apt to be thought of as still "there" until the rituals required by convention give recognition, by public farewells and "decent burial" or other disposal, that the deceased has formally departed the community. Many such rituals also serve as initiation into the heavenly community, which is comforting to survivors and helps in their reorientation if it does not induce a wish for reunion-by-death.

The emphasis of embalmers upon the "memory image" of the deceased has positive mental-therapeutic value in helping to replace or offset distressing memories of the body as actually dying.[19]

"Something to be done" is often a healing blessing for the bereaved. Even the routine of providing for physical necessities may serve, like a flywheel, to carry people past a dead center and on their way again. "Blessed be drudgery." During the first days of the bereavement crisis, the ceremonials, visitations, and symbolisms of the funeral period serve to keep the bereaved family busy. In fact, many customs which to the unbereaved or "sophisticated" observer may seem useless, conventional, irrational, outworn, or even superstitious may have certain values as evidences of affection and as distractions. Ceremonials have always been recognized as effective in the channeling and release or relaxation of the tensions to be dealt with in crises, quite aside from belief in immortality. Sincere rites may have profound psychological effects, either disturbing or comforting.[20]

SHIFTS OF FAMILY CONFIGURATIONS AFTER BEREAVEMENT

So far we have viewed the reintegration of roles chiefly from the side of personal reactions to bereavement situations. The interpersonal aspects, however, are of quite as much importance, for the configuration of interactions necessarily changes when a family group member is reft away, just as every line of stress in an entire spiderweb changes simultaneously and topologically when a single supporting strand is nipped. New roles may be accepted in a new consensus, or new conflict may arise out of disagreement as to status within the family or as to the role of the family as a whole in the community under the new conditions. Waller stated well the readjustment of family pattern to the amputation of a member:

The sociological structure of the group has been altered; although the original pattern may seem to continue to exist for a time, the fundamental pattern of the dyad or triad later establishes itself; it is at first an all-but-one configuration, and later the absent member is out of the picture entirely. For the group which is left the loss of a member may none the less be a sentimental asset; it happens sometimes that parents are woven more closely together by the loss of a child, or the whole family is given a rallying point by the loss of a central member. As we have seen, the life of the departed is always

---

[19] *The Embalmers' Monthly, passim.*
[20] Scott M. Buchanan, "Some Unnoted Aspects of Therapy," in *A Contribution of Mental Hygiene to Education* (Chicago: Illinois Conference on Public Welfare, 1933), pp. 50–64.

idealized; we may say that the family loses a member but gains a collective representation.[21]

Nevertheless, conventional roles in the family structure must be filled by some survivor, with or without rivalry:

1. Aunt attempts to take the place of my grandmother as a homemaker for my grandfather. He is now living with my aunt. He could not stand to live alone.

2. For the husband and five-year-old daughter, this death meant a complete readjustment of their home life. They took a smaller apartment, and now have a housekeeper, who will never be able, even in a small way, to make up for the absent one.

Should we expect greater or less family solidarity as a result of bereavements? The answers are about as one would expect.

Where marriage is recent the widowed bride is reabsorbed in her family, and if not remarried will usually take a job and renew or increase her family loyalties. With recovery she tends to escape from her in-laws to regain her freedom and avoid embarrassing reminders.

Family solidarity was, at first, definitely increased by the bereavement. The daughter in-law became closer to the family, and family interests were centered on the grandchild, Georgia. . . . There were difficulties concerning the insurance — the usual army red-tape — and this soon became the center of a quarrel between the girl and her parents. They wanted the insurance money in exchange for her "room and board," and the girl began to feel abused, as her mother still expected a great deal from her (housework, etc.). This drew her even closer to her husband's family, though she did not consent to live with them when she was invited to. Family solidarity gradually became decreased, however. . . . She gradually became estranged from her "in-laws" . . . they were quite hurt about their daughter-in-law's actions — not so much that she married again, but that she had severed all relationship with them.

Where it is an unattached son who has been killed, the families I have studied seem to have been bound more closely together by the loss.

The K's showed a realignment of roles — a younger brother falling heir to his parents' attentions, the daughters closer together than ever before, and more frequent family parties.

During mourning each interpersonal relation, having been developed under the subtle influences of all other intrafamilial relationships including those with the deceased, is revised and rehabituated. This is in some measure true even where for the dead member is shortly substituted his personified memory. The actual person, had he lived, would have changed with the march of time in a different way.

[21] Waller, *op. cit.*, pp. 491–492. For a *general* dyadic analysis, see Howard Becker and Ruth Hill Useem, "Sociological Analysis of the Dyad," *American Sociological Review*, 7, 1 (Feb., 1942), pp. 13–26.

1. To all of us, for a long time, it merely seemed as if my father were away on one of his lecture tours and that he would soon be home again. . . . Our family life has gone on in the same way. My brother, who is at home, has taken over some of the duties of head of the family, but mother is still really head of us all. There is a stronger family unity than ever before, but this is the only change. . . . We continue to go back to our summer cottage . . . it is dearer to us now than ever. It was his own favorite place, he built it and everything about the place speaks of him.

2. Mrs. C. did not give the children too much hope of an actual reunion with their father but tried to have them feel he still exists, in the influence which his personality and works have had. With this definition, Mrs. C. said she believed her husband had achieved life and that he would still go on living through his work, ideals, and attitudes created among his family, friends, and associates.

Where survivors identify themselves or some other family member with the dear departed, the results may be unhappy, especially if one member's conception of his own or another's new role proves incompatible with the others' conception of that role:

Our family was a very strongly knit primary group based upon the patriarchal prototype of the Old Testament . . . [After mother's death] my father seemed very unhappy and alone in the world; at the same time he became more dominating over us. Father perhaps felt that he must assume a double role as disciplinarian.

On the other hand, if a death breaks up a family triangle of jealous attachments ("Oedipus," or other) or a set of previously conflicting conceptions of role, family harmony may be increased by the death without conscious realization of the nature of the process:

Much closer to his father after death of his mother. Father had never been harsh to him but he had always been afraid of him. Was 21 at his mother's death. "Since then we've been like a couple of boys." The father seemed to open up to him more because of loneliness.

Mourning and recovery are complicated and hastened or retarded by family interaction. Ambivalent phases of mourning, such as release and repression, dependence and freedom, self-pity and self-solace, may be assumed as overt roles by different persons in the bereaved home, or alternately they may comfort and need comfort. Recovering at different paces, some may feel the need to prolong or simulate grief, others to shorten or suppress it. Family conversation hastens the process of rehabituation to the new situation. The "realism" of "modern" attitudes may sometimes accentuate shock, sometimes hasten an acceptance which conventional sentimentalities might postpone.

A family member may always have secretly coveted the role of the deceased, possibly as symbol of victory or adulthood. Conversion of personality through identification with the role of the deceased is thus neatly explained in Waller's words: "Complete fulfillment of the parent's role has been prevented precisely by the presence of the parent, which has imposed the filial role as a limiting factor." [22]

If the family's activities and affectional life were organized chiefly by or around a certain member, the death of that person may disorganize the family's living pattern. Or his "memory" may hold them together, at least during gradual establishment of other orientations. Solidarity may be increased by greater interdependence. Or latent centrifugal interests previously restrained by loyalty or by authority may await the death for their expressions. This is especially and naturally true for married and marriageable children.

An integrated family may resolve to live "as if" the lost member were still with them. If such motivation be kept on a high spiritual plane and not too specific, it may provide a valuable momentum — probably tapering off normally as it ceases to be a felt need. It may, however, become a "dead hand," the known habits or supposed wishes of the deceased being cited by a new family head as a device of supernatural sanction comparable to the "Thus spake the Lord" of the ancient prophets. Or the family may split over conflicting interpretations of "what mother would have said," each side quoting this authority to rationalize his own wishes.

Because many people have never developed full visualization of absent persons, the deceased personality may be remembered only fragmentarily, yet missed quite as much or more for that reason. The dead person may be rebuilt in composite memory by the family, yet each may give him a different role in retrospect, and therefore a differing influence in the ongoing family life. Competing images of the lost one may accentuate a family change.

> One family had to postpone the placing of a memorial tablet because of inability of its members to agree on the relative importance of certain roles and traits to be included or omitted in the tribute to be inscribed.

Projection of wished-for qualities upon the memory of a dead family member is encouraged by our folkways. "Speak well of the dead" is derived from ghost-fear or an unconscious sense of guilt.[23] The practice also serves to justify and support a grief which otherwise would be wearing off too soon to suit other drives or habits of the bereaved person or requirements of the culture.

One must recognize that in thousands of "normal" families, affection is mixed with indifference or with other less attractive sentiments which are ignored in our cultural stereotypes of family life. Bereavement may be cut across by more or less admitted realizations: of a sense of relief

---

[22] Waller, *op. cit.*, p. 494.

[23] See Howard Becker, "A Social-Psychological Study of Bereavement" (unpublished M.A. thesis, Northwestern University, 1926), chaps. 5, 7, 10; —— and David K. Bruner, "Attitudes toward Death and the Dead and Some Possible Causes of Ghost Fear," *Mental Hygiene,* 15 (Oct., 1931), pp. 828–837; and —— and —— "Some Aspects of Taboo and Totemism," *Journal of Social Psychology,* 3 (Aug., 1932), pp. 337–352.

from expense, labor, or domination, or of increased status, or of new freedom, or of financial deprivation or gain. If the family is highly conventional, the repression of such motives may develop guilt as compensation, with overcompensation in the form of excessive expressions of sorrow, or idealization.

Even toward living loved ones our attitudes are often mixed, and, conversely, even the death of a rival or a habitual quarrel-mate may cause emotional upset of habits which can be included as a phase of bereavement. Where convention requires silence and repression in respect to antagonistic feelings toward the deceased, the alternate ambivalent sentiments, i.e., love and grief, being reinforced by guilt-feelings, may be exaggerated.[24] Such feelings probably account for elaborate propitiations of ancestral spirits, whether "primitive" or "civilized," as well as for some morbid mourning.

The interaction of family life, especially with children, is a corrective for certain dangers of mourning, such as the overvaluation of the deceased, the loss of personal ambitions, the tendency of grief to discolor everything else and "take the joy out of life."

The Urge to Remarry: A Mark of Recovery

There may be, in later stages of recovery, an effort on the part of family members to reconstruct or perpetuate the satisfactions of the earlier situation by substituting a new love-object in the role of the old.

The thwarted craving in bereavement is to some extent a craving for a duplicate individual or for an equivalent relationship; recovery therefore will be found when this relation is restored with another person. Within the family this may be a new spouse, a new baby, or an adopted child.[25]

Prompt remarriage after widowhood may be a tribute to the soundness of conjugal relations of the first marriage. On the other hand, idealization of a deceased spouse may postpone remarriage in the search for perfection. But widows, being more isolated by financial and domestic necessity, by convention, by age, and perhaps by quality of desires, than are widowers, less often remarry. Nevertheless, on the "rebound" especially, "a little widow is a dangerous thing" — especially for a widower!

Then, too, widowers tend to remarry because a man's environment is apt to be more sexually stimulating and because, if there are children, a widower's domestic need of a woman's help is more exigent than a widow's need for a man. Widowers take residence with relatives more frequently than do widows. If widows are young, most of them go to work; if they can't work themselves, they may work their children or work the charities.[26]

---

[24] Anthony, *op. cit.*

[25] In Rotterdam, where planned parenthood had been generally encouraged, it was found that in families apparently closed, the death of a child was, on the average, followed by a birth after an appropriate interval. See J. Sanders, *The Declining Birthrate in Rotterdam* (The Hague: Nijhoff, 1931), p. 120.

[26] Nimkoff, *op. cit.*, pp. 613 ff.; Francis E. Merrill, *Courtship and Marriage* (New York: Sloane, 1949), p. 295.

Remarriage is probably happier where there is no identification of new with former spouse such as would lead to repeated jolts of disillusion when the actual role is revealed instead of the expected. The new marriage should be recognized as that of a later and different phase of the widowed personality. A similar remark will apply to children's attitudes toward stepparents: they should not constantly be comparing them to the lost parent-image. Nor should a parent conceive a younger child's role in the image of a dead brother or sister. Feeling that he is only a substitute, such a child may acquire a subtle but profound sense of insecurity.

Social Relations after Bereavement

Formal mourning, during which for an announced period the family neither accepts nor gives social invitations except to intimates, and wears black, is rarely practiced nowadays. People are apt in these matters to follow their own feelings and tastes, which may prevent their interest and enjoyment of gaiety for some time. Later, their social and civic life is apt to be normal. Widows and widowers for the most part must continue daily to mingle with their kind. Apart from earning a living there usually are civic and congenial groups in which they have readjustments or contacts to make in the single role. Each will discover whether their friendships and prestige were their own or primarily for the lost spouse. Since the conventions of entertainment often call for pairs, the widowed will sometimes feel left out, but often too will be included to "fill out" a party to which they would not formerly have been invited. They may again be acceptable in bachelor crowds or as popular and still eligible chaperons.

Occasionally an abrupt repression of a lost love may release and reinforce (in a bereaved personality) extrovertive and egotic drives — acquisitive, dominative, or combative — as compensatory trends. Since such drives, though self-centered, call for social interaction, they depend for their satisfaction on the presence of others. This may contribute to gradual rebalance, relaxation, and recovery. To the extent that sexual love has egotic components, however, bereavement may give rise to deliberate diffusion (temporary promiscuity) or groping experimentation with substitutes before a satisfactory reattachment is found.

In community relations, bereaved family members if adult may become more individualized (at least temporarily). Having a necessary or interesting job is, as we saw, itself a curative factor in bereavement. The widow without children may achieve a new freedom; the widower is a bachelor again; the supporting or supported child is at last "on his own." For these roles the community may provide some more or less ill-fitting stereotypes, accepted by the bereaved with more or less good grace, depending on the rate of mourning and recovery.[27]

Since grief is intensely self-centered and introvertive, any attachments

[27] "The Widow's Plight," *Harper's Magazine*, 167 (July, 1933), pp. 228–238. An anonymous article.

or attractions to other persons, or almost any kind of group demands upon the bereaved, however irksome or incongruous they may seem at the moment, may serve a therapeutic purpose in detaching the fixation from the deceased and refreeing the energies of the bereaved from self-absorption. One may never feel a "decision" to take up life again; it is, in a sense, life which takes one up again. Mourning may never be absolutely finished, but it gradually approaches zero as a limit.

REINTEGRATION OF ROLES AFTER BEREAVEMENT

When condolences cease to arrive and the world moves on, there is apt to be a slump. Secondary reactions begin to appear; new sets of attitudes, habits, roles, are accepted, rejected, accommodated, reintegrated.

If grief is combined with energy enough to rebel against people, fate, heaven, self, or other scapegoats, the resultant is embitteredness, envy, even destructiveness. One may self-centeredly resent the deprivation of one's satisfactions in the loved one, and the intrusion of anyone who opposes one's grief; or, having "escaped" into vice or drink, one may turn against oneself for trying to forget, punish oneself, and then even proceed to be sorry for oneself when so punished. If, on the other hand, one lacks energy or "will" to rebel, the result may be despair, melancholy, fretfulness, indifference or, more congenially, resignation, insatiable craving for sympathy, sublimation.

Recovery of a sort is seen in the formal use of stereotyped formulae or symbols of resignation, fatalism, stoicism, religion, or sentimentality; the intensification of love for one's family or a general increase in kindliness; attempts to "escape" from grief through daydreaming, or gaiety, or by removing all reminders, or moving to a new residence, or overworking; compensating for the loss of a loved one through devotion to his memory; or subjecting one's memories to deliberate suppression which may or may not be permanent.

The impulsive grief which characterizes the early stages of mourning tends to become patterned by rationalization, by convention, by habit, becoming the sorrow of sentiment. Sadness is secondary sorrow, implying memory or sympathy.

Acceptance of what we might now consider an old-fashioned loyalty to the dead may give a person a sense of guilt if he discovers himself no longer grieving. Such remorse may itself perpetuate grief and resist comfort. As a milder form, we have the hasty assurances to an interviewer lest the inadvertent use of some word such as "recovery," "healing," "forgetting," or "happy," be misinterpreted: "Of course I don't mean really happy, but . . . ," or "Not that one can really forget, but you know what I mean," etc.

That a condition of apparently full self-control and insight can conceal incomplete recovery should always be borne in mind. The complexities are intricate.

Truly successful recovery from bereavement means gradual relaxation of its tensions and frustrations in favor of some more satisfactory or at least tolerable patterns of behavior. The bereaved find someone else through whom they can satisfy their affectional needs; or they find religious beliefs which fully reconcile them; or they reabsorb their energies and redevote their affections in some life work as an alternate channel; or they assume the role of the deceased or project his personality by some conspicuous service in his name or through creation of some appropriate and constructive memorial. Even gradual relaxing through "forgetting," i.e., through the competition of unplanned new habits, may produce "successful" recovery.

Mourning Compared with Postdivorce

In his excellent treatment of the mourning period,[28] Waller brought out a number of similarities and differences between readjustment after divorce and recovery from bereavement. The first three of the following are, however, additional differences between the two classes of crises:

1. From death of older relatives there is often economic gain (inheritance, or release from expense) exceeding the current expenses of illness and funerals; whereas alimony from divorce seldom rises to the point of economic gain, as compared to the predivorce period.

2. In bereavement, convention expects mourning and occasionally creates mental conflict when the bereaved ceases to grieve or feels ambivalent motives of relief or revenge and tries to conceal or repress them. Divorced spouses likewise are often subject to inner stress because of ambivalent motives — hate of mate versus hate of hate — which tear them. But here, convention imputes to afflicted persons a sense of relief which they seldom feel. They *do* feel the public's expectation and may try to play the role. The longing for the lost mate is like a bereavement and mourning process, but more tantalizing because the love-object continues to live though in new roles. It differs from bereavement in that convention makes opposite demands, opposite to impulse.

3. In bereavement the mind is free to idealize the deceased. The divorced or deserted person may daydream, but he is all too easily jolted back into the reality or worse; in self-justification the divorced may actually diabolize each other — the opposite of idealization.

Waller also noted the following differences:

4. Divorce is less final and convincing. The love-object remains actually or potentially present to refresh the trauma.

5. Culture provides for the divorced no definite conventional period of protection and recovery, though the ordeal is in some cases more difficult than that of bereavement.

6. The misery of the postdivorce period is complicated by wounded pride, which seldom affects the bereaved.

[28] Waller, *op. cit.*, pp. 480–498, and 552–559.

7. The attitudes of and toward one's circle of friends are far more complex and unpredictable to all concerned in divorce than they are in the bereavement situation.

8. The widowed, like the divorced, must reorganize their friendship groups on a "single" basis, but for the former there are no estrangements nor is their status rendered ambiguous.

9. Bereavement in our culture may bring favorable attention, ego enhancement. Both parties gain status rather than lose it. There still exists to handicap the divorced, personally and vocationally, a stigma which does not afflict the bereaved. Yet recovery is obviously frequent; sometimes, indeed, too rapid for safety.[29]

10. We do not find in the bereaved the phenomenon of overcompensatory aggressiveness, or self-enlargement.

11. In some bereavements the survivor may identify himself with the deceased, and try to carry on his role; not so for the divorced, who must justify himself by denying such identification even if it sneaks in occasionally.

12. Far less resort to Bohemianism or vice is found among the widowed than among the divorced.

Similarities noted between the experiences of the divorced and the bereaved are often far-reaching:

1. In both there is the loss of a former love-object which changes the whole life situation.

2. Internal and (usually) external adjustments are slow, and largely unplanned, uncontrolled, automatic. The main outlines of these adjustments are essentially similar. The slower the adjustments the more apt they are to be thorough, permanent, and satisfactory.

3. There are similar yearnings, frustrations, and sense of emptiness.

4. There are many similar insistent habits and impulses to be reconditioned, broken, or transferred piecemeal, and some of these may prove persistent beyond control.

5. The reintegration of new habits into some new system of living is often similar.

6. In both experiences there is dream-work and fantasy formation as a phase of unadjustment or reorientation of attitudes.

7. In each there is a gradual piecemeal canceling of memory by actuality; the facts of each memory are checked off with a twinge as no longer actual.

8. The divorced and the bereaved may both reactivate roles played *before marriage* — though this is probably more frequent for the divorced than for the bereaved.

9. For both the bereaved and the divorced there is apt to be an increase of self-centeredness; one would be driven in on self even in the absence of self-conscious uncertainties and defenses.

10. Either group may find recovery through work or routine or ceremonials, which are the first activities to regain meaningfulness after the period of "emptiness."

[29] Waller, *op. cit.*, pp. 515–517.

11. Either may indulge in "confessional" confidences, or in forced pleasures, in hope of escaping from or relieving tensions.

12. In both, the habit of conceiving one's role as unhappy may outlast the tensions which constitute the unhappiness. When spontaneous pain is gone, mourning if continued may then become merely ritual or patterned auto-suggestion.

13. In both there is often the gradual discovery of new love-objects — for the divorced oftener than for the widowed, it may be a series of substitutes.

14. For both there are similar patterns of personal disorganization or re-organization of life habits, with some new philosophy of life emerging therefrom.

SELECTED READINGS

Most items referred to in the footnotes also belong here, but space is not available; the student should take account of this.

BENDANN, EFFIE, *Death Customs* (New York: Knopf, 1930).

BENJAMIN, LOUISE PAYNE, "Meet a War Widow," *Ladies' Home Journal,* 62 (Jan., 1945), pp. 97–101, 105–106.

BLACKWOOD, ANDREW W., *The Funeral* (Philadelphia: Westminster, 1942).

CURTISS, MINA, "The Midst of Life," *Atlantic Monthly,* 151 (Jan., 1933), pp. 114–123; (Feb., 1933), pp. 240–250; (Mar., 1933), pp. 372–380; (Apr., 1933), pp. 476–487.

ELIOT, THOMAS D., "The Bereaved Family," *The Annals of the American Academy of Political and Social Science,* 160 (Mar., 1932), pp. 1–7.

———, "Bereavement as a Problem for Family Research and Technique," *Family,* 11 (June, 1930), pp. 1–2.

———, "War Bereavements and Their Recovery," *Marriage and Family Living,* 8 (Feb., 1946), pp. 1–6.

ELIOT, WILLIAM GREENLEAF, *The Discipline of Sorrow* (St. Louis: Metcalf, 1858).

FAHS, SOPHIA L., and SPOERL, DOROTHY T., *Beginnings of Life and Death* (Boston: Beacon, 1950), pp. 141–149.

FLANNER, FRANK BATES, *Funeral Services and Hymns* (Chicago: Trade Periodical Co., 1906).

FOLSOM, JOSEPH K., *The Family and Democratic Society* (New York: Wiley, 1943), pp. 406–407.

FRITZ, M. A., "A Study of Widowhood," *Sociology and Social Research,* 14 (July–Aug., 1930), pp. 553–559.

FULCOMER, DAVID MARTIN, *The Adjustive Behavior of Some Recently Bereaved Spouses,* unpublished Ph.D. Dissertation, Northwestern University, 1942.

GUNTHER, JOHN, *Death Be Not Proud* (New York: Harper, 1949).

HARKNESS, SAMUEL, "No More Funerals," *Scribner's,* 90 (Oct., 1931), pp. 393–396.

HEDIN, A., "Funerals without Flowers," *Forum,* 93 (May, 1935), pp. 306–307.

HOHMAN, LESLIE B., "The War Department Regrets . . . ," *Ladies' Home Journal,* 62 (Jan., 1945), pp. 102–103.

KLEIN, MELANIE, "Mourning and Its Relation to Manic-Depressive States" (1938–39), in *Contributions to Psychoanalysis, 1921–1945* (London: Hogarth, 1948), pp. 311–338.

Koos, Earl Lomon, *Families in Trouble* (New York: King's Crown, 1946), pp. 75–76.

Locke, Harvey J., *Predicting Adjustment in Marriage* (New York: Holt, 1951), pp. 298–309.

Mansfield, Katherine, "The Daughters of the Late Colonel," in *The Garden Party* (New York: Knopf, 1923), pp. 83–115.

Merrill, Francis E., *Courtship and Marriage* (New York: Sloane, 1949), pp. 286–297.

Owen, J. Z., *Widows Can Be Happy* (New York: Greenberg, 1951).

Rogers, William Fred, *Ye Shall Be Comforted* (Philadelphia: Westminster, 1950).

Shaler, Nathaniel Southgate, *The Individual: A Study of Life and Death* (New York: Appleton, 1905), pp. 203–250.

Tigner, High Stevenson, "A Foray into Funeral Customs," *Christian Century,* 54 (Oct. 13, 1937), pp. 1263–1265.

Wilson, Arnold, and Levy, Hermann, *Burial Reform and Funeral Costs* (London: Oxford University Press, 1938).

TOPICS FOR DISCUSSIONS OR REPORTS

1. Visit a number of local "funeral parlors," "funeral homes," and "morticians." Find out the range of funeral expenses currently regarded as neither indecently low nor ostentatiously high in the locality in question.
2. Read the chapter on bereavement in Willard Waller's *The Family: A Dynamic Interpretation,* rev. by Reuben Hill. Do the case materials in that chapter help to illuminate our discussion here? Why, or why not?
3. Read the chapters on sorrow in A. F. Shand's *The Foundations of Character.* Are any of the phenomena there recounted "foreign-sounding"? Do you know of American parallels?
4. Study an authentic account of a family bereft of father or mother. Analyze the ways in which the configuration of member roles changes.
5. If some type of bereavement reaction in the text reminds you of an actual case, write it up in detail.
6. Report on the more or less successful readjustment processes of some family following a bereavement, using Eliot's outline (A Step toward the Social Psychology of Bereavement) listed in the Selected Readings.

Chapter Twenty-Three

The Scope and Meaning of Divorce

MABEL A. ELLIOTT

I T'S TIME we looked into divorce," was the comment of a sensitive editor of a national magazine as the recent census releases reporting increased divorce rates reached his desk. Looking into divorce, however, consists of more than noting the phenomenal increases and interviewing the most colorful cases of breakup. It is necessary today for the student to look behind divorce to marriage itself for explanations. Several chapters of *Family, Marriage, and Parenthood* have been devoted to this task.

There is some evidence that divorce rates are high in this country precisely because marriage is highly esteemed. Take Sweden or France, whose divorce laws we shall discuss in more detail later. Their divorce rates have been much lower than ours; yet their laws regulating divorce are much less restrictive. What do you find accompanying the relatively lower divorce rates of the Swedes? You find that the number who marry is very low, that marriages are postponed until the thirties, and that the rates of illegitimate births are high. America has high divorce rates but there is no repudiation of marriage.

Looking at the contemporary American situation even more closely, we discover that divorced persons of both sexes are more likely, age for age, to marry again than are the single to marry for the first time. There is no rejection of marriage by those who divorce; their remarriage in such large numbers shows that. They know even better than single persons that married life is satisfying and they return to it. Compared with desertions, informal separations, exchange of partners, and births out of wedlock, divorce is at least legal and aboveboard.

When people cease to bother to divorce, marriage and family life will be really threatened. From all reports that day now appears far distant. Having cleared away the notion that divorce is something to condemn without examination, and the idea that disintegration of family life is indicated only by divorce, perhaps we are ready to examine in some detail the scope and meaning of divorce today.

WAYS OF VIEWING DIVORCE

Divorce may be viewed as a social problem, a legal dissolution of marriage bonds, a personal tragedy, or an evidence of disregard of one of God's holy ordinances. As the final outcome of family disintegration, divorce is merely the process by which legal status is given to a relationship already shattered by unkept pledges, broken faith, bitter tensions, and painful disillusionment. Since the state insists upon regulating relations between the sexes, provisions for release from the responsibilities and obligations incurred by marriage must also be laid down by the state.[1] Therein we have the social logic embraced in divorce legislation. All societies, whether primitive or civilized, through formal or informal controls define the terms upon which the marriage ties may be severed with the sanction of the group.

The relatively rigid controls which all societies exert over marriage and divorce represent a rationalization of human experience into customs and practices which purport to advance the welfare of all concerned. Since the emotions are so much a part of marriage, it is only natural that the group controls which govern marriage should also be invested with great feeling. Sacred values are really those aspects of our culture that concern us most, or those about which we feel most deeply. They represent some of our greatest intimacies when they refer to marriage or its dissolution. Therefore, men and women everywhere find it difficult to dissociate prejudice from fact, emotion from reason, or custom from the eternal verities in reviewing the issues of divorce. Established practices take on a sacred character and tend to persist with a compulsive power. So far as one may view marriage objectively, there seems to be no escape from this dilemma. Acceptable marriages are hedged in by social notions of respectability, by the economic dependence of woman and her need for care during pregnancy and childbirth, by the child's needs for love and protection, as well as by the state known as "being in love" and the imperious urges of sex.

Marriage, according to the cynic, was invented by woman to hold her man. There may be as much truth as humor in his viewpoint, for the lot of wife and mother entails so many sacrifices that women may be justified in demanding a certain amount of material and emotional security before they barter the favors of sex. When we review the history of matrimonial institutions we find that the trend of development in marriage laws generally represents a gradual restriction of the license of men and a concomitant increase in the responsibilities imposed upon husbands and fathers, with penalties attached for failure to accept them.

All divorce codes are an index to the position of woman. We have come a long way; the oldest known divorce regulations were incorporated in the Assyrian code of Hammurabi, drawn up around 2300 to 2500 B.C., and this ancient code provided that man might divorce his wife at will, with no need for stating his reasons. The early Hebrews had a similar privilege of handing their wives "bills of divorcement" whenever they so fancied. We must credit the Hebrews, however, with recognizing that some compensation should be granted the wives thus summarily dismissed. Even in primitive tribes some form of payment is usually made when a wife is rejected. It seems obvious to simple peoples that the matter requires some sort of adjustment. In the patriarchal society of the ancient Hebrews,

---

[1] See Chapter Nineteen for a more detailed account of the legal philosophy underlying legislation concerning marriage and divorce, pp. 572–579.

we may presume that it was men *in their position as fathers* who wrote the divorce codes protecting their daughters against the fickleness of masculine impulses. Thus the parental love of a man for his daughter has been the source of most of our protective legislation for women, even for that which survives today.

With woman's advance to a position somewhat resembling equality with man, modern divorce regulations have changed their emphasis. In recent years the whole trend of legislation has been a matter of facilitating release from unbearable marriages, with little attention to the matter of protecting the helpless female.

TYPES OF DIVORCE

Today, provisions for divorce differ with nearly every political unit, but in most nations divorce laws are uniform throughout the particular country. In the United States the provisions for divorce are many and varied, as we shall discuss later. In all political jurisdictions the types of divorce may be subsumed, however, under two categories. (1) Absolute divorce, known in Roman law as *a vinculo matrimonii,* provides full and final dissolution of the marriage and leaves both partners free to marry again. Their status is that of single persons, i.e., the same as if they had never wedded. (2) Legal separation or partial divorce is known technically as *a mensa et thoro* (separation from bed and board). This estate prohibits any further marital relations unless there is a reconciliation.[2]

Ordinarily legal separations or partial divorces are sought at the insistence of the wife. In some instances it may be true that both husband and wife wish to establish separate residences and both have no thought or desire for remarriage. Often, however, it is a matter of an outraged wife demanding support from an erring husband and at the same time seeking to prevent him from marrying his mistress. While legal separations may be justified by such moralistic considerations, there is little gain in such an arrangement since the innocent person could usually secure better protection by an absolute divorce. Consider the husband's dilemma. The ousted man feels committed to lifelong adultery. Frustrated by such an arrangement, he may seek divorce in another jurisdiction and leave his legal wife in the doubtful position of contributing to a quasi-bigamous marriage. On the other hand, conservative social opinion supports a legal separation of marriage partners where continued living together is no longer tolerable. The Roman Catholic Church allows such a separation in case of adultery. If a Roman Catholic secures an absolute divorce he is not allowed to remarry. Twenty-five states, the District of Columbia, and Hawaii grant such partial divorces or legal separations.

In Louisiana no absolute divorces can be obtained without a year's lapse, except for adultery, in which case the decree may be granted im-

[2] Helen I. Clarke, *Social Legislation* (New York: Appleton-Century, 1940), pp. 139–140, and Mabel A. Elliott and Francis E. Merrill, *Social Disorganization* (third ed.; New York: Harper, 1950), pp. 422–423.

mediately. In case of legal separation, the party to whom such a partial divorce is granted may petition for absolute divorce at the end of the waiting period in case there is no reconciliation.[3]

Interlocutory decrees (decrees *nisi*), which involve a period of waiting, usually a year, before an absolute divorce is granted, are in effect in sixteen jurisdictions. Such decrees prevent hasty divorces and remarriages as well as fraud and aim at promoting reconciliation. If there is a reconciliation during the waiting period, the divorce becomes null and void.

AMERICAN DIVORCE RATES SINCE 1866

Our high divorce rate is a relatively recent phenomenon. While divorce legislation was liberalized markedly in the period from 1830 to 1850 during the rise of the Woman's Rights Movement, we have no record of any accompanying rise in divorce. At any rate, no one thought divorces important enough to tabulate any national statistics on the subject during the colonial or federal period.[4] Following the Civil War an antidivorce sentiment arose which was evidenced in the tightening of divorce provisions. Business conditions and political morality were both in such a chaotic condition that men apparently decided to preserve the family and make at least one institution fairly secure. During this conservative reaction there was a demand to know what the divorce situation actually was. The first statistical report of divorces was kept in 1866 and a ten-year report was published by the Census Bureau in 1876, indicating a total of 122,261 for the decade. For the next ten years 206,595 divorces were granted. From 1886 to 1896 there were 352,363. With the turn of the century the numbers grew. For the decade 1896–1906 there were 593,362, and from 1906 to 1916 there were 975,728. For the first fifty years for which we have figures more than 4,500,000 persons were divorced.

By 1920 the rate had mounted rapidly, with 170,509 for the single year. In 1929 there were 201,468. People began to talk about the disappearance of the family. Some said that marriage was an outmoded institution. With the depression the divorce rate declined. In 1930 there were only 191,591 divorces. In 1932 there were still fewer, only 160,338. "This is one of the good results of an economic upset," we were gravely reminded. Apparently such a pleasant conclusion had little basis in fact. Divorces were merely too expensive. After the Federal Emergency Relief Administration was well organized, divorces shot up. In 1934 the estimated rate was 204,000; it rose to 218,000 in 1935; to 236,000 in 1936; and to 249,000 in 1937.[5] Accurate current statistics for divorce are lacking because states follow no uniform

[3] Chester G. Vernier, *American Family Laws* (5 vols; Palo Alto: Stanford University Press, 1931–1938), Vol. 2, p. 152; and Ray E. Baber, *Marriage and the Family* (New York: McGraw-Hill, 1939), p. 492.

[4] Of course some of the colonies and states kept statistics but this was by no means universal.

[5] From 1932 to 1937 no divorce statistics were gathered by the Census Bureau because of the economy program of the Department of Commerce. Estimates for these years were calculated by Samuel A. Stouffer and Lyle M. Spencer; see their article, "Recent Increases in Marriage and Divorce," *American Journal of Sociology*, 44 (Jan., 1939), pp. 551–554.

plan in reporting their divorces. The best figures are the estimates of the National Office of Vital Statistics, from which we can make a rough approximation of divorce trends in America. The estimates of divorces for World War II, 1941 to 1945, were particularly tentative because they were based on incomplete information.[6]

As Table 12 shows, a tremendous increase in divorce occurred from 1939 to 1946. In 1939 there were approximately 251,000 divorces and annulments; in 1946 the number rose to an estimated 610,000. For the year 1946 there was, in fact, a 25.8 per cent increase over 1945. This rising tide of divorce had been predicted by sociologists early in the war. They knew that the war would place abnormal strains on normally suitable marriages on the one hand, and would promote obviously unsuitable marriages on the other. During the years 1947–1948 the rate declined markedly and tapered off significantly in 1949–1950. Incomplete returns since 1950, when hostilities began in Korea, indicate a new upsurge in divorce.

TABLE 12

ESTIMATED DIVORCES IN THE UNITED STATES: 1939 TO 1950
(Includes annulments. Minus sign (—) denotes decrease)

Year	Estimated divorces	Per cent increase over preceding year	Rate per 1000 total population*
1950	385,144	—3.0	2.6
1949	397,000	—2.7	2.7
1948	408,000	—15.5	2.8
1947	483,000	—20.8	3.4
1946	610,000	25.8	4.3
1945	502,000	25.5	3.6
1944	400,000	11.4	2.9
1943	359,000	11.8	2.6
1942	321,000	9.6	2.4
1941	293,000	11.0	2.2
1940	264,000	5.2	2.0
1939	251,000	2.9	1.9

* For the war years, 1940 to 1945, population base includes armed forces overseas.

DIVORCE RATES AS A BAROMETER OF SOCIAL CONDITIONS

Thus we see that the decline in the divorce rates during the depths of the depression from 1930 to 1933 cannot be attributed to any strengthening

[6] The national estimates for 1941–1944 are based upon incomplete data representing 49.1 per cent to 49.5 per cent of the civilian population. Estimates were computed on the assumption that the areas which did not report contributed to the divorce rate in the same proportion that it had contributed in 1937 to 1940. During the depression and during the war years the Government did not have facilities for gathering complete statistics. See *Marriage and Divorce in the United States, 1937 to 1945*, and *Summary of Marriage and Divorce Statistics, United States, 1950*, National Office of Vital Statistics, Federal Security Agency, Special Reports, Sept. 10, 1946 and Oct. 29, 1952.

of family ties but rather to the restraining influence of poverty itself. The family has been called the microcosm of the macrocosm, society; or, as it was stated in the first chapter of this book, changing societies are family contexts. Societal change runs parallel with familial change; as the smallest social unit, the family registers in miniature the various stresses and strains to which the larger social structure is subjected. The rate of family disorganization and divorce is of course only a partial index to family stability. The family may reflect other social and economic changes as well.

Economic depressions seem to lower the divorce rate, as we have seen. In families in which tensions have not reached an acute stage, meeting the common problem of stretching a lowered income may bring unity of purpose. Some families were already torn by conflicts and incompatibility, however, and often found increased irritation in their marital relations. In any event we are safe in believing that the divorce rate declined chiefly because of two facts. (1) Divorces are relatively expensive to obtain, and many deferred suing for legal severance of the marriage bonds simply because they could not afford to pay the price. (2) The marriage rate declined during the same period, and since many divorces are secured within the first few years of marriage, some of the bad marital risks were at least temporarily eliminated.

Prosperity, on the other hand, is accompanied by an increase in both marriages and divorces. We must presume that the financial ability to hazard the risks in each instance is related, at least, to the rates.

Other economic factors are obviously related to family stability. The economic status of women is unquestionably a factor in the rate. Indeed, the whole question of women's status in general is involved in family disorganization, as we shall point out later. But the relatively superior ability of the modern woman to earn her own livelihood has been a factor in increased divorce. When women had few vocational opportunities outside of homemaking, a wife put up with an unhappy and distasteful marriage. With increased opportunities for work outside the home, however, a woman was no longer beholden to her husband. If she could provide herself with sufficient income she could even tell her husband "to go to hell," as was the case in *The Constant Wife*.

Despite the wide opportunities available to women for employment, a prejudice against married women's working has persisted. For many wives this has been a source of mental conflict; economic dependency carries with it a status of subordination and inferiority which no amount of lip service to a theory of "What is mine is yours" can ever erase.

Where the husband makes a small or insufficient wage the wife may decide to retain her status as a wage earner. Sometimes she may even decide that her marriage possesses no advantage if she must contribute more than her husband does to the upkeep of a house or an apartment.

Occupations themselves seem to contribute to marriage hazards. At least an earlier study made on this topic in this country shows wide disparity in divorce rates in various occupations.[7] Sometimes a person may be irritated by a hated vocation. Thus the husband may project his dislike of a job on his family. Certain occupations, by their very nature, are more conducive than others to fragility of the marriage tie. It is well known, for example, that divorce rates are high among actors and traveling men.

The theatrical world subjects men and women of the stage to the continual emotional stimulation of glamorously attractive persons. This is, in itself, important in breaking down family ties, but there are additional factors. Actors live continually in an unreal world, in which normal values are hard to achieve on any objective basis. Furthermore, they live a public existence, with their every move watched closely by the press and the fawning public. A misunderstanding becomes a rift, partially because it is so interpreted by the news-hungry reporter.

There are further explanations for the higher rates among certain occupational groups. Both the actor and the traveling man lead a highly mobile life and are removed from the primary group controls. The traveling man has a less glamourous existence. His marriage hazard is a result of his absence from home and the temptation to extramarital excursions which his job entails. There must be other explanations for the high divorce rates of barbers, cigar operatives, and bartenders.

Physicians have the highest divorce rate among the learned professions. Divorce rates run high not merely because the physician has numerous contacts with attractive women, but also because the physician's wife is forced to lead a restricted social life. If she and her husband go to a dinner party or a concert, he may receive an emergency call in the midst of it. If they are hosts to their own friends, there is no certainty that he can enjoy any normal role toward his guests. A physician's wife can contribute much to her husband's success by a little self-abnegation and a willingness to sacrifice her social life. But it is easy to feel neglected and to conjure up nonexistent love interests on the part of her hard-working husband. And, occasionally, the physician justifies her suspicions and takes solace in his "understanding" friend.

If a young woman wants to be relatively certain she is marrying for keeps, she should marry a farmer or a preacher. They are the two best risks in marriage. Farmers virtually have to have a wife to run a farm successfully, and their wives are practically bound to be helpmates. Frequently, the farmer's wife owns the farm or they live on her father's farm; and economic considerations, as well as affection, are conducive to the farmer's good behavior. Farmers also have few opportunities to meet women more attractive than their wives.

Clergymen probably meet more foolish and attractive women than any other occupational group. Yet the occasional erring man of the cloth furnishes a newspaper headline, chiefly because he is so unusual. Religious

[7] *Marriage and Divorce, 1867–1906* (Washington, D. C.: Bulletin 96 of the Twelfth Census of the United States, 1909), p. 46.

belief and the moral leadership entrusted to the minister are important factors in controlling his behavior. Divorce is low among the clergy of virtually all denominations. Remarriage is forbidden among the Episcopal clergy.

Mechanics and laborers also ranked in the lowest quartile so far as divorce rates are concerned in the earlier study. A study made in Spokane in 1943 showed that professional men had the lowest divorce rate, with a significant increase through the occupational categories of proprietors, clerical workers, and skilled workers, with semiskilled workers having the highest rate. With unskilled workers the rate declined precipitately, although unemployed men had a relatively high rate.

Ability to pay for a divorce is greater among mechanics and laborers today, and this is undoubtedly a factor in the divorce rate itself.[8]

War and the Divorce Rate

Divorces in wartime are much the same as peacetime divorces. But divorce in wartime is speeded up both because of the impact of socially disorganizing influences on existing marriages and because war itself is a stimulation to an increase in the types of marriages which are doomed to fail. In addition, wartime prosperity seems to play a large part in speeding up the rate of divorce.

In an effort to secure all-out production, wages are always advanced rapidly in wartime. This is especially true of wages for the women who invade the ranks of workers. Because women war-workers have adequate means to pay the necessary legal costs of a divorce, many seek release from an unhappy marriage. Such women often would be reluctant to ask for a divorce in peacetime, for the expense entailed would mean a definite cut in the family budget. William Fielding Ogburn thinks this increase in prosperity is in all probability the major factor in increased wartime divorces.[9]

There are other reasons, however. War is socially disorganizing on many counts. Women are quite generally earning money, and they are often separated from their families. Husbands go to distant cities to work in war plants, to undertake scientific research, or to work in a governmental agency. Mature men and women are often separated for the first time in their married life. Sometimes they are surprised to find out how much they enjoy separations. Frequently these shifts in work and residence result in new attractions and love interests. Every personnel director in America has known instances of the woman war-worker who became involved with a fellow war-worker while her husband was overseas.

[8] H. Ashley Weeks, "Differential Divorce Rates by Occupation," *Social Forces,* 21 (March, 1943), p. 336.
[9] Mabel A. Elliott, "The Rising Tide of Divorce," *National Parent-Teacher,* 38 (Sept., 1943), pp. 7–9; William Fielding Ogburn, "Marriages, Births and Divorces in the American Family in World War II," *The Annals,* 229 (Sept., 1943), pp. 27–28.

The housing shortage during the war undoubtedly created many tensions. Families crowded into trailers must have experienced new irritations, occasioned by the lack of privacy, lack of space, lack of room to work, to read, or to put anything. Sometimes the housing shortage meant a long separation of husband and wife. The wife got a job in which she became so much involved that interest in her marriage began to wane. The bread-and-butter aspects of marriage were, for the time being at least, of no importance.

Consider the case of Evelyn Straight. Evelyn's husband was a scientist, who undertook some important research on the famous Manhattan Project. His job involved traveling from one scientific laboratory to another and, in consequence, he was seldom home. When he came home, he could not discuss what he was doing. Frequently he held hurried, unintelligible telephone conversations and then dashed out the door.

Evelyn knew it was all important secret work, but even so, she became very bored. Their only child had just finished college and had gone to work in a distant city. Evelyn decided to get a job. She mentioned the fact to a friend and was told that there was an excellent opportunity for a woman with her background in a city some three hundred miles away.

Evelyn had been a dress designer before her marriage and there was an opening as head designer with a well-known firm. She accepted. When her husband came home on his next trip, she was not there. He spent a miserable five days. At the end of this time he became furious and called her by long distance telephone. She insisted that she had promised to finish certain designs and could not possibly return home.

Mr. Straight felt his whole position was outraged. There wasn't even a maid to cook his meals at home. His laundry was a problem; he tried to wash out his socks and handkerchiefs himself, but they looked like a pathetic mess.

He called his wife again and told her he was going out to the West Coast and that he would expect her back at the end of ten days when he returned, for his vacation would start then. When he returned, Evelyn was not there, but she came home thirty-six hours later in none too cheerful a mood herself. They had planned to spend the vacation on Prince Edward Island with the Grays, who were friends of long standing. The Grays soon realized the tensions between the Straights. Mr. Straight could see no sense in his wife's "perverse" interest in her job. She thought him wholly unreasonable. Both made acrimonious remarks. One thing led to another and, finally, there was suit for divorce. A marriage which would have undoubtedly endured the peacetime stresses of academic life, folded up on the shoals of the war on the home front.

On the surface it would seem that the Straights should have been able to solve their marriage problems. Here were two mature, well educated, intelligent people. Actually both were working under terrific strains. Professor Straight's long absences from home created resentment. His mysterious behavior with reference to his secret research project created suspicions his wife could not overcome. Driven by patriotic and personal anxieties each was irritated by the other's conduct. Yet the conduct of each was in a special sense a direct outgrowth of wartime conditions.

A survey made of marital status of the civilian population in the United States in February, 1946, showed some striking facts with reference to husbands and wives who were away from home (Table 13). This survey was made on a sampling basis of 25,000 households in 68 areas in 42 states and the District of Columbia. From these figures estimates were compiled for the marital status of the total population over 14 years. They indicate that 650,000 wives were living away from their husbands in February, 1946, and that 1,150,000 men not in the armed forces were living away from their wives.

TABLE 13

MARITAL STATUS OF PERSONS 14 YEARS OLD AND OVER, BY SEX, FOR THE UNITED STATES: ESTIMATED CIVILIAN POPULATION NOT IN INSTITUTIONS, FEBRUARY, 1946 AND 1944, TOTAL POPULATION, APRIL, 1940 [10]

Marital Status and Sex	1940	1944	1946
Total Male	50,553,748	41,260,000	47,290,000
Single	17,593,379	9,320,000	12,520,000
Married	30,192,334	29,690,000	32,070,000
Wife present	28,657,820	—	31,420,000
Wife absent	1,534,514	—	650,000
Widowed and divorced	2,768,035	2,250,000	2,700,000
Total Female	50,549,176	52,300,000	53,520,000
Single	13,935,866	12,630,000	12,310,000
Married	30,090,488	32,850,000	33,810,000
Husband present	28,516,937	28,630,000	31,420,000
Husband absent	1,573,551	4,220,000	2,390,000
In armed forces	—	2,760,000	1,240,000
Other	—	1,460,000	1,150,000
Widowed and divorced	6,522,822	6,820,000	7,400,000

All told, 1,800,000 husbands and wives were living apart. For the years 1940 and 1944 the proportion was even higher. Unquestionably some of these couples were living apart because they preferred to do so and, in any case, marital ties must have been weakened by such absences.[11] Personal behavior is always relaxed in wartime, partially as a release from the tensions of war. When victory came things were not improved, for just as in the first World War normal conditions were not restored simultaneously with the cessation of hostilities. There was a moral letdown. Men in uniform became restless. They had won the war, but they could not go home.

At home women were often bitter and jealous. Sometimes they too cheated in the marriage game. Sex impulses, we must remember, are not limited by marriage vows. Thus it often happened that it was the soldier

[10] Bureau of the Census, Population Series, P-5, No. 10, Washington, D. C., October 14, 1946, p. 3.
[11] For more detail see Bossard's account of war-induced family disorganization in chap. 24 pp. 716–730.

who kept the faith, only to return home to a philandering wife. Many a dis-illusioned husband accused his wife of adultery.

Yes, war exacts a heavy toll in disorganized families. J. P. Marquand's story of the young Navy officer and his reactions at the news of his wife's infidelity was poignant, chiefly because the man seemed to be so much re-lieved at the escape which her infidelity allowed him. Even the opportunity to file suit for divorce may seem salutary when a man of character might otherwise feel the necessity for holding true to marriage vows.

Many wartime marriages were born to die and indeed might never have been contracted in peacetime. In the emotional excitement of war, young people seem to grasp at temporary security with no consideration of the un-certain years ahead.

Elspeth Harding was such a war bride. She was nineteen and a junior in a midwestern university when she married Jack Harding, a young lieutenant in the Army Air Corps. He was twenty and had lied about his age to secure the license. It had all happened very quickly. Elspeth King had been at the dance at the USO as a junior hostess. He thought he had never seen anyone half as lovely. He said, "Where have you been all my life?" and it sounded like an original question to Elspeth.

The next week they met again and Jack told her he had shipping orders and he would probably never see her again.

"Oh, no," she said softly. But Jack knew the statistics. The chances were against his coming back. The German pilot fighters were ace airmen. Both were touched more by the thought of annihilation than by any real attraction of kindred souls. But it all happened. They were married without veil, orange blossoms, or wedding march. As Elspeth ruefully recounted, "I did have a corsage. We spent three days on an Ozark honeymoon and then we parted, as we had met, strangers, afraid of life ahead."

"It was wicked," she went on, "but I virtually prayed he would meet a hero's death. Then I should have received his Distinguished Service Medal. It would have been romantic. What I could not face was Jack's return. I did not even know his family. I knew no more of his goals or ambitions. He was only a handsome face with pleading eyes."

For Jack, piloting a bomber through flak-filled skies, the marriage was a different thing. As he aimed his ship toward the target, he could close his eyes and see Elspeth. She was his vision of loveliness, his escape from the mockery of war. He fulfilled his missions. He was cited for bravery. Yes, he received a medal and then he flew back to the West Coast, where Elspeth had gone when she finished college.

Elspeth seemed in a daze. She did not talk. She even cried when Jack asked her what was the matter. "Was there someone else?"

"No, of course not," she replied. Jack was stunned. "You did not write to me, except for three letters," Elspeth said weakly.

"How could I?" exclaimed Jack. "One can't write love letters after ex-peditions into shellfire."

The case had been duplicated many times. Two young people mistook sympathy and need for sympathy for some deeper and more abiding affection. Both were intelligent enough to recognize that it was a mistake and took the legal steps for divorce.

Divorce in wartime is like peacetime divorce, only more so! All the factors which make for marital difficulties are accentuated. The pressures to remain married, called social controls, warrant further attention. They were breaking down for World War II, as we shall see.

Divorce and the Status of Women

V. F. Calverton has asserted that the new freedom for women has been mainly responsible for divorce. In a sense this is true, but there is still the well known if unverifiable fact that a large percentage of divorces are demanded by husbands even though the husks of chivalry are preserved by allowing the wife to press the suit in such instances. Even so, the political enfranchisement of women has increased the wife's demand for equality before the law in the marriage relation itself. The recognition of women as legal persons has lowered their willingness to submit to unhappy domesticity. Concomitantly, the greater social freedom of women has more or less inevitably led to a greater degree of sexual laxity, a freedom which strikes at the heart of family stability. Yet for all the vaunted liberalism of the modern generation, any failure to abide by traditional notions of morality entails great risks for all women, married and unmarried alike.[12] Men "rarely marry their mistresses," nor are they willing to accept laxity on the part of their wives.

Strictly speaking, one cannot say that divorce has been increased by the freedom symbolized by higher education for women, since divorce has been relatively negligible among women college graduates. Nevertheless, it has been the college woman who has been most articulate in her demand for reasonable and humane divorce laws, and indirectly the increase in women's rights has been a factor in the increasing divorce rate. It may well be true that women actually want divorces more often than do their husbands. For, as Pearl Buck has pointed out so emphatically, a woman is not equal in status to her husband. Modern marriage imposes frustrations on women, and the whole traditional patterning of marriage opposes her fulfillment in some respects, however much it may permit her fulfillment on a biological basis. Few homes, despite their variety of activities and responsibilities, offer sufficient scope for the trained energies of an intelligent, educated woman.[13]

Decline in Religious Sanctions

Increase in divorce, however, cannot be directly or exclusively attributed to the emancipation of women. The increased divorce rate is also a barometer

[12] In this connection see Judith Kelly, *Marriage Is a Private Affair* (New York: Harper, 1941). This prize novel discusses the risks of sex liberalism and infidelity in an upper middle-class family.

[13] Pearl S. Buck, *Of Men and Women* (London: Methuen, 1942), especially chaps. 3 and 4.

of declining social controls and notably of the decline of religious authority over the state of matrimony. In both the Protestant Reformation and the Puritan Revolt there was a rejection of the Roman Catholic and the Anglican doctrine of divorce. Protestant churches, it is true, have continued to emphasize the need for stable and decent family relations, and most of them accept a quasi-sacramental doctrine of marriage. Yet the rejection of the belief in marriage as a true sacrament led to an interpretation of marriage as a contractual relationship. This in turn led to the inevitable conclusion that if one person failed to live up to his part of the contract, the innocent party or spouse might also be relieved of any further responsibility. There can be no doubt that the great increase in divorce in recent years registers the decline of rigid religious controls. So long as men and women regard divorce as a deadly sin and remarriage as unthinkable they will suffer gross indignities before running the risk of excommunication or eternal punishment. When men and women reject such ideas as medieval or as untenable, divorce is much more an index of social change than it is an index of increase in marriage tensions.

For the majority of Roman Catholics there can be no serious questioning, among either the clergy or laity, of the Church's rigid divorce canon. At the same time, the more liberal element of the Protestant Episcopal (Anglican) Church has made several attempts to revise the rulings on divorce and divorced persons within its communion. Because the conservative group has outnumbered the liberal, no effective change has been made until recently. The canon proposed at the general convention of that Church held in Kansas City in October, 1940, provided that while the clergy could not remarry a divorced person with a living former spouse, persons whose former marriages had been dissolved might, in case of remarriage, seek a blessing for their union, if the spiritual welfare of the parties and the good of the church and society seemed to be served thereby.[14] The clergy were not ordinarily allowed to marry such persons but merely offered prayers for their divine blessing, which seemed incongruous to many thoughtful church members.

Despite many demands for a more liberal attitude no further alterations in the canon were made until September, 1946, when the triennial convention of the Protestant Episcopal Church was held in Philadelphia. This new canon permits remarriage of communicants in case of divorce or annulment if evidence is presented through the bishop which shows that certain "impediments" to matrimony existed before the earlier marriage was performed. The impediments accepted are (1) marriage between certain categories of blood relations, (2) mistaken identity, (3) mental deficiency, (4) insanity, (5) failure of either party to achieve puberty, (6) impotence, (7) sexual perversion, (8) venereal disease, (9) bigamy, and (10) "such defects of personality as to make free consent impossible." The bishop in his diocese has final decision with reference to the admissibility of remarriage in each case. In other words, the Episcopal Church is making what have generally been acknowledged as impediments to marriage in the first place, suitable grounds

[14] *Report on the Joint Commission on Marriage and Divorce to the General Convention* (Kansas City, Mo., 1940), pp. 3–6.

for its dissolution.[15] What the Episcopalian canon fails to recognize is that alleged and real reasons are seldom the same, as we shall discuss later.

While the Roman Catholic Church has adhered tenaciously to its belief in the inviolability of marriage, it has not been notably successful in maintaining the canon in case of mixed marriages. Of course, mixed Protestant-Roman Catholic marriages are technically forbidden by the church but in ordinary instances are allowed by dispensation of rules if the non-Catholic signs an Antenuptial Agreement.[16] In this each party indicates consent to be married by the church and to rear any children in the Catholic faith.

Despite these precautionary measures and the stress on the sacramental character of marriage, such mixed marriages have a far higher rate of failure than in cases where both parties are members of the same church, whether Protestants or Catholics. Howard Bell's study of 12,000 young people shows that 15.2 per cent of the homes were broken in case of mixed marriages. In contrast only 6.8 per cent of the Protestant homes were broken and slightly fewer, 6.4 per cent, of the Roman Catholic homes were broken.[17] Thus the pattern of divorce has crept into Roman Catholic as well as Protestant families, in spite of earnest attempts to prevent it.

Decline in the effectiveness of nonreligious social controls is also apparent in divorce rates. The stabilizing influence of the larger kith and kin groups has gone with the passing generation. Today families are so scattered that a high degree of family solidarity is a rarity. The Smiths and the Browns no longer may be thought of as families "with a solid front." The mobile character of our economic and social life means that members of the larger families are sometimes as strange to each other as foreigners. Young people "live their own lives" a thousand miles from their parents. They no longer feel much concern about how father and mother would react to a divorce. Young people might be more stable if they could discuss their marriage problems with an older relative; mobility lessens the interference of in-laws in modern marriage, but it also removes a safety valve. One cannot let off steam so well to strangers, and if Mary cannot go home to mother for a bit of consolation when John hurts her feelings, she may walk out for good. If mother can point out that "dear old dad" has not always been easy to live with, things may not seem so bad after all. And on the other hand, if John's father can talk with him he may come to realize that "all women are difficult at times," and he may not resent Mary's outbursts of temper so much.

Urban life has meant that community controls in family life have also declined. Community controls in matters of marriage tend to be most rigid in sacred societies, to which our closest present-day approximations are small towns and rural neighborhoods where there is great homogeneity in cultural background, religious beliefs, and social and economic classes. Where the population in a given community belongs to one religious group, the church

---

[15] Note on "Remarriage," *The Churchman* (Oct. 1, 1946), p. 12.

[16] Pope Pius XI, *Casti Connubi*, sections 82 and 85. See our Chapter Nineteen on the legal enforceability of such agreements.

[17] Howard M. Bell, *Youth Tell Their Story* (Washington, D. C.: American Council on Education, 1938), p. 21.

and the community are one for all practical purposes. This is true whether we are considering a Roman Catholic settlement or a Dunkard or Church of the Brethren community. Where there are a great many widely varying controls and affiliations representing every type of religious connection, the divorce rate tends to rise markedly. Lack of consensus in the basic definitions of the purpose and function of the family must inevitably be disruptive of stable family life. The consequences are extreme secularization, with its demoralized, marginal, and decadent personality products.

MOBILITY AND MATERIALISM

We have mentioned the effect of mobility in reference to primary-group controls in realms of marriage. Mobility as a significant aspect of modern life has other profound repercussions upon the life organization of every individual and hence inevitably registers itself in the shared existence which we call family life. As has often been remarked since Becker coined the term "mental mobility," mobility is not merely a spatial matter.[18] Life for sizable numbers of college students, skilled laborers, professional people, business executives, marginal workers, and dispossessed persons has taken on a mobile character. Residence in one section of the country is succeeded by life under markedly varying conditions in another part of the country. Often there is a shift from country to city, from small town to metropolis. This shift from one location to another involves a series of adjustments to new points of view and new experiences as well, even in peace times. Often the conservative becomes liberal, the liberal becomes Bohemian. The exposure to so many new situations invites tolerance but it also results in a decline in the rigidity of old values, including that of a permanent monogamy. Thus mental mobility is often a concomitant of physical mobility.

Quite aside from all the other disruptive impacts of war on the family, the unparalleled mobility of young men, marriageable and married alike, has inevitably affected the family. Young men from Keokuk and Kalamazoo, Shanghai and Stalingrad, have traveled to the four corners of the globe. In every hamlet young men from high schools, stores, farms, and offices became virtually a displaced generation, far from home, friends, and familiar controls. Faced with new attractions, not to mention ever-present dangers, these young men reached out for whatever sympathy they might secure from young women from strange, or at least different, cultural backgrounds. Many were genuinely attracted by these young women, with little recognition of the importance of cultural values in building stable family organization. Some of these marriages will endure but many of them will end as sadly, if not as tragically, as that of the European bride who shot her American husband when he deserted and tried to divorce her on his return home.

For those who stayed at home, mental mobility was furthered by the far-

---

18 Howard Becker, "Forms of Population Movement: Prolegomena to a Study of Mental Mobility," *Social Forces*, 9, No. 2 (Dec., 1930), pp. 147–160, and 9, No. 3 (Mar., 1931), pp. 351–361; and Elliott and Merrill, *op. cit.*, chap. 27, "Mobility."

flung increases in mental contacts provided by the press and in particular by the radio. The so-called "soap dramas" gave many women something to think about, for there usually was a family tension or a divorce to heighten the interest. Easy television solutions of family tensions have raised new questions. "Should I too seek a release from my marriage?" has been a question which many an onlooker has undoubtedly asked himself. Consciousness of the tensions which perplex modern husbands and wives has probably increased. This must have resulted in greater self-diagnosis and increased the visits to lawyers and the divorce courts.

But ours is not only a generation of speed and mobility; ours is also a generation which worships at the shrine of materialism. Never before in man's history has the gratification of material wants and the multiplication of those wants taken so significant a place in the average person's manner of living. Undoubtedly this has contributed to the physical well-being of our generation. At the same time it has created an emphasis on material values above matters of spiritual or ethical import. This fact is evidenced in every aspect of community, national, and international existence. So far as families are concerned, materialism has set standards of consumption above standards of family security. Women have sought work outside the home to increase the family income, often at the risk of endangering the fabric of the family itself. Women have sued for divorce because their husbands could not support them in their accustomed fashion. One cannot live on love alone, but a major emphasis on economics may drive out love. In giving advice to a younger woman, many an older matron has reasoned, "Do not marry if you cannot improve your status." Lack of material things does not always lead to estrangement but emphasis on materialism distorts the affectional function of the family which is its basic contribution to human welfare and happiness. Wherever there is dissatisfaction, for whatever reason, emotional relationships tend to be strained.

DIVORCES AND THE DIVORCED

Divorce, most sociologists would agree, is part of the American way of life. In our country permanent monogamy constitutes the most desirable form of marriage relation; but for those, especially urban residents, who can no longer find any durable satisfaction in marriage and for whom a continued relation offers only frustration, hypocrisy, and deterioration of both personalities, divorce has become a respectable solution. Whereas divorce was formerly looked at askance by the solid members of society, very little stigma is attached to divorce or the divorced persons today outside the most conservative religious groups. In some communities, notably Hollywood, divorce has become virtually "normal." One of the usual questions when a movie star marries is, "How long will it last?"

Nevertheless, even for movie stars a divorce is usually a trying and bitter experience. It is the final revelation of broken faith, an open admission of a marriage which failed. And often enough it is the prelude to other social disasters. For there must be adjustments after divorce. Habits of living must be altered. Children must be cared for while they suffer the deprivation of one parent's love and attention. The economics of divorce is seldom satisfactory. Alimonies are hard to collect. Two families are difficult to support. Rates of suicide, insanity, crime, and delinquency, and other evidences of personal disorganization are all high in families torn asunder by divorce. Divorce is thus not so much a final solution to a bad marriage as it is an earmark of one. Of course divorce is by no means disorganizing to all who secure final papers; like everything else, its disruptive character depends on the capacity of the given personality to meet crisis situations effectively. But for a sizable share of ex-husbands and ex-wives, it is a thoroughly disillusioning experience.

Are there any distinguishing characteristics among those who secure divorces? From personal observation most of us recognize that the divorced, like those who solve their marriage problems otherwise, represent a cross section of human society. Basically, divorces grow out of problems of sex and emotional adjustment, both of which are no respecters of class or creed. A divorcée, Mrs. Harding, for example, became the first lady of the land. An Episcopalian minister was sued for divorce by his wife, who refused to give up her Baptist affiliations. A well-known authority on the family asked his wife to divorce him so that he might marry his secretary. A Negro maid who resented her husband's spending his hard-earned cash for alcohol brought suit against him. A world-famed professor told his students, "We can adjust to any situation if we make up our minds to do so," but made up his own mind not to adjust to the tyranny of his wife's jealousy. A refined young woman who loved her husband dearly saw him carried away by the devotion of his nurse during a serious illness. A doctor found one of his patients more attractive than his grubby wife who had worked so hard to help her husband through his expensive years in the medical school. A banker's wife sought release from her marriage when she discovered her husband's "love nest." An Italian woman discovered that American women did not need to submit to periodic beatings; imbued with the fervor of her new rights, she asked release from what had become an intolerable marriage.

As great as the social differences found among divorced people is the range of personality characteristics, but there are no very extensive studies of the ways in which the characteristics of divorced persons are distributed throughout this range. We can name, however, a few rather impersonal differences which seem to be socially significant.

SIGNIFICANT FACTS ABOUT AMERICAN DIVORCE

Most divorces take place within the first few years of marriage. In fact, the greatest period of risk is the first five years of marriage, according to census data.[19] The risk diminishes sharply after the fourteenth year. Approximately two-thirds of the divorces occur in the first ten years. Of

[19] *Statistics on Divorces and Annulments, Specified States,* 1949. U. S. Public Health Service, Federal Security Agency (Aug. 3, 1951), p. 105.

course, as newspaper items bear witness, marriages are occasionally dissolved after husband and wife have passed their threescore years and ten. There are always instances of older men who wish to take a younger and more attractive wife when they have passed middle age. Nevertheless the vast majority of marriages which last ten or more years are seldom dissolved in the divorce court. Love may not always have remained but the force of habit and mutual dependency makes life without the other unthinkable.

Age at marriage seems to bear some relation to the difficulties encountered. We have no figures relating to the ages of all persons granted divorce, but several studies shed light on the subject. Hart and Shields discovered that marriages in which the bride was under twenty-one and the man several years her senior seemed to entail greatest risks.[20] Burgess and Cottrell found that marriages in which the bride was under twenty-two and the groom over thirty-one showed the greatest number of maladjustments.[21] A study by Marshall and May based on divorced persons in Ohio showed 54.5 per cent of 8773 litigants to have been minors at time of marriage. Moderately early marriages, on the other hand, they concluded to be less hazardous than those contracted very early or very late. Differences between the ages of husband and wife have generally been assumed to be a source of friction. In the Ohio study, however, in 61 per cent of the cases the difference was only four years or less. Where husbands and wives were the same age the marriages lasted longest. When the husband was older than his wife the risk was slightly higher. When the wife was the elder the hazard was greatest of all.[22] We have no control data for the general population, however, and hence can draw no completely satisfactory conclusions. Differences in age may not be important where compatibility exists.

Women are the plaintiffs in approximately three fourths of the divorce suits. In 1932, to be exact, women received 73.5 per cent of the divorces granted. In 1950 data for twenty states shows women received approximately the same number, or 72.2 per cent.[23] Even where husbands demand a divorce, they usually wish to appear gallant and are reluctant to start the proceedings. However unseemly a man's conduct may be, he apparently prefers to do the conventionally chivalrous thing and let his wife press suit. When the wife's conduct has been of a scandalous type, the husband is less concerned about appearances. In nearly all other instances few men wish their wives to suffer from the stigma of being a defendant in a divorce trial. There are of course further explanations of the fact that women are the plaintiffs in the majority of cases. Fathers often oppose a divorce, because it usually means separation from their children. Unless a man is interested in remarriage, divorce presages a lonely existence. Men seem to be less nourished on romance and tend

[20] Hornell Hart and Wilmer Shields, "Happiness in Relation to Age at Marriage," *Journal of Social Hygiene,* 12 (Oct., 1926), pp. 403–407.

[21] Ernest W. Burgess and Leonard S. Cottrell, Jr., *Predicting Success or Failure in Marriage* (New York: Prentice-Hall, 1939), pp. 115–117.

[22] Leon C. Marshall and Geoffrey May, *The Divorce Court* (Baltimore, Johns Hopkins Press, 1932–1933), vol. 2, and Baber, *op. cit.,* pp. 453–454.

[23] Statistics on Divorces and Annulments, Specified States, 1950, *Vital Statistics Special Reports,* Public Health Service, Federal Security Agency, Dec. 9, 1952, Washington, p. 68.

to take a more realistic view of the advantages which even a dull marriage may entail.

In 1931, childless couples were granted 62.2 per cent of the divorces. Furthermore, 70 per cent of all childless couples are estimated to dissolve their marriages in divorce, whereas only 8 per cent of couples with children secure divorce.[24] Most parents thus seem to take their responsibility toward their children seriously. Even so, many children suffer from homes broken by divorce.

Despite the Hollywood pattern the Mountain States, not the Pacific Coast, lead in the number of divorces granted in proportion to total population. The easy divorce laws of Nevada and Idaho probably account for part of the difference, since migratory divorce is encouraged in those states. Nevertheless the sectional differences must be explained by differences in social attitudes rather than in the mere laws themselves. Table 14 shows that the rates increase

TABLE 14

AMERICAN DIVORCE RATES BY REGIONS, 1940 [25]

Region	Divorce Rate per 1000 Persons
Middle Atlantic	0.9
New England	1.2
East North Central	2.0
Pacific	3.4
Mountain	4.1

markedly as we go from east to west. Perhaps the best explanation is that divorce for women is easiest where marriage opportunities for men are lowest. Men tend to be chivalrous where women are scarce.[26]

DIVORCE PROVISIONS IN OTHER COUNTRIES

Legal provisions for divorce in any group are directly related to other aspects of the society. In modern Western civilization, attitudes toward divorce vary with religious affiliation and social conservatism. Hence we may well expect to find legal provisions for divorce to be a barometer of dominant social opinion. In Europe there is wide variance in the laws because there have been so many cultural differences in the shape of religious controls and in the social, political, and economic enfranchisement of women.

The Scandinavian countries have been completely Protestant in religious tradition and dominantly liberal in their economic and social philosophy. It is not surprising, therefore, to find divorce by mutual consent a basic provision of their divorce code. In case both parties desire a divorce, they are required to present their case either to their pastor or to a designated govern-

[24] Ray E. Baber, *Marriage and the Family* (New York: McGraw-Hill, 1939), p. 489.
[25] Data taken from "Summary of Marriage and Divorce Statistics, United States, 1949," *Vital Statistics Special Reports*, Public Health Service, Federal Security Agency, Washington, June 5, 1951, p. 23.
[26] Elliott and Merrill, *op. cit.*, p. 745.

mental official, who tries to work out a reconciliation. If this is not possible, a legal separation is granted. In Sweden the waiting period is one year; in Denmark, a year and a half; in Norway, one to three years. Other allowable reasons for divorce include adultery, six years' absence without word, insanity for a period of three years, threat to life, life imprisonment, neglect of domestic duties, and exposure to venereal disease.[27] In addition there are also provisions for divorce by royal prerogative in case of sentence for grave crime or on evidence of violence, insobriety, or prodigality.

Italy, whose population is more than 98 per cent Roman Catholic, has no provision for absolute divorce. For the Roman Catholic, absolute divorce is unthinkable because divorce is not recognized by the church. Legal separations are authorized when marriages are unendurable, but even in case of adultery no remarriage is possible. No one supposes that such rigid restrictions are wholly successful in promoting marital fidelity. Indeed, it is a well-known fact that there are many illicit unions in Italy, much marital infidelity, and a great deal of prostitution.

In the United Kingdom previous to 1857, absolute divorce was reserved for the upper classes and it could be granted only by Act of Parliament. In that year a Divorce Act was passed which allowed men to obtain divorce from their wives on grounds of adultery. Wives, however, could not rid themselves of guilty husbands unless such husbands were also guilty of cruelty. Apparently there was no thought that the fact of unfaithfulness on the part of the husband might also be considered cruelty. These regulations were in force until 1923, when the law was revised, making it no longer necessary for a woman to produce evidence of cruelty in case of an erring husband. The law was repealed in 1924 but re-enacted in 1925.[28] The dramatic events leading up to the divorce of Wallis Simpson and her marriage to the former King Edward VIII convinced many people that the rigid British divorce law must be altered. The English Matrimonial Causes Act was thus amended in 1937 to permit divorce on additional grounds. As revised in 1950, the act provides that divorce may be obtained for adultery following marriage, desertion for three years, cruelty such as to injure mind and body, insanity for five years. The wife may also obtain divorce for sex perversions on the part of her husband.

During the short-lived Spanish Republic the traditional Catholic ban on divorce was replaced by more liberal provisions. With the defeat of the Loyalists the Fascist government re-established the canon law. Absolute divorce is no longer granted but legal separations may take place according to the special regulations of the Roman Catholic Church.[29]

During the Vichy regime in France there was marked tightening of di-

---

[27] See Elliott and Merrill, *op. cit.;* James Thorsten Sellin, *Marriage and Divorce Legislation in Sweden* (Ph.D. thesis, University of Pennsylvania, 1922), pp. 72–85; and H. S. Tillotson, "Scandinavia's Solution to the Divorce Problem," *Current History,* 34 (July, 1931), pp. 551–554. Cf. also *Martindale-Hubbell Law Directory* (Summit, N. J., 1953), for data on these countries. (This directory is alphabetized, but not paginated.)

[28] A. P. Herbert, *Holy Deadlock* (London: Watt, 1934).

[29] The author is indebted to the Spanish Embassy, Washington, D. C., for this information.

vorce procedures. By the law of April 2, 1941, which was designed to strengthen the birth rate, no one was allowed to apply for a divorce for three years. In certain cases, separations were allowed, with the proviso that divorce would be automatic after three years had elapsed.

When France was freed from Nazi occupation, prewar divorce procedures were restored, but have since been revised. In divorce cases the judge asks the defendant to appear in an effort to secure reconciliation. If he does not appear a decree by default carries a waiting period of 8 months. In any case a woman must wait 300 days after the decree before remarrying unless she meanwhile bears a child.[30]

Although many conservatives have bemoaned "liberal" provisions for divorce in France, the rate has actually never been alarming. In the years before World War II divorces totaled about 20,000 annually. The French rate per 1000 population was less than one third that of the United States in 1935. For although the intellectual Frenchman may disown religious affiliations and religious ideals, France is essentially Catholic in its background and tradition. As one Frenchman would have it, "A French atheist is a *Catholic* atheist." The *tradition* in France is thus strongly opposed to divorce. The economic status of women outside the family is difficult, and respectable Frenchwomen are inclined to accept the necessity for overlooking what their husbands consider mere peccadilloes, however painful these infidelities may be. Many American sociologists err in thinking that the average Frenchwoman does not mind her husband's having a mistress or two. As a matter of fact, she is usually deeply hurt by such unfaithfulness, but her social and economic status has made her more or less powerless to object.[31]

In Germany, with the enactment of the Nazi laws of 1935 and their subsequent alterations, marriages between Jews and Aryans were forbidden under the Nürnberg interracial laws "protecting German blood and honor." Marriages between Jews and Gentiles were declared invalid. Although couples had sometimes been married as much as fifteen years or longer, Nazi courts accepted complaint of mistaken identity as a ground of annulment but with the proviso that all children be considered legitimate. Both divorces and annulments were a product of the Nazi philosophy permeating the interpretation of the law rather than the provision of the code itself.

By Law No. 1, issued by the Control Council for Germany, September 20, 1945, all laws of a political or discriminatory nature upon which the Nazi regime rested, and all laws, ordinances, and decrees explanatory thereto were repealed.[32] The present divorce law of Germany is not, however, a re-enactment of the laws antecedent to the Nazi regime, but the Nazi divorce law expurgated of all discrimination and political provisions.[33] Divorce is allowed on grounds of adultery, violation of marital obligations, insanity, and venereal disease (if the latter two grounds can be morally justified), and desertion

30 Cf. "France, Law Digest, Divorce"; *Martindale-Hubbell Law Directory,* Part III, 1953.

31 The author is indebted to Marie Louise Bannelier for this interpretation of the Frenchwoman's attitude. Naturally, proof one way or the other is difficult.

32 *Official Gazette of the Control Council for Germany,* Number 1 (Berlin, Oct. 29, 1945), pp. 6–7.

33 The author is indebted to Dr. V. Gvoski of the Library of Congress for this interpretation.

for three years. The right to divorce is thus based chiefly on the guilt of the partner, but such a right is abnegated if the injured partner has condoned the violation of marital responsibilities. The right to divorce on grounds of guilt is lost if the partner does not file suit within six months.

Germans take the matter of establishing guilt seriously and the judgment expressly mentions that the defendant is guilty if a divorce is granted for such a reason. If the defendant also makes a countercharge of guilt and this is established, both parties are declared guilty. A former wife who is found guilty of a serious lapse in conduct following her divorce may be forbidden the right to retain her former husband's surname. Property divisions under present divorce laws are in accordance with older provisions of the *Bürgerliches Gesetzbuch*.[34]

The Soviet government by one stroke sought to abolish all ties between church and state. To this end the religious marriage ceremony was declared invalid and the civil marriage became the only legal one. Divorce was declared a purely personal matter; dissatisfied partners were allowed complete freedom in seeking release from marriage. Naturally, to be divorced, one must first have been married.

When a young couple wished to marry, they had only to sign their names in the official marriage register and have their passports stamped with a statement to the effect they had been married; but a large number of people never bothered to have the state thus sanctify their union, and as late as 1935 at least 50 per cent of the "marriages" were unregistered. Divorce procedure, however, was as simple as marriage. One simply applied for it, signed the divorce register, paid three rubles, and had his passport stamped to indicate his divorce status. With such possibilities for freedom at hand, almost any marital disagreement afforded a reason for a trip to the Divorce Bureau.

By 1920 divorce rates in Russia were the highest in the world. In 1935 Soviet leaders became alarmed by the problem and during the summer of that year an official edict went out to the effect that petitions for divorce must state some reason for desiring it and that the officer at the Marriage Bureau was in duty bound to attempt to dissuade applicants. Both husband and wife were required to sign the divorce document and everyone was required to have his marriage or divorce entered in his passport. Alimony was required for the support of all minor children, and the alimony dodger was dealt with rigidly. Two years' prison sentence might be exacted in such cases. Alimony was automatically deducted from the wages paid in Russian prisons.[35]

The provision for support of children has always been a check on Soviet divorce. The early Soviet marriage code required a man to contribute from 25 to 35 per cent of his earnings for their care. On the other hand, women who have had no children have never been eligible for support unless unable to work. Today, if a woman has any physical disability acquired after marriage, she may be supported for a year. If she is not employed but is capable

[34] *Official Gazette of the Control Council for Germany*, Number 4 (Berlin, Feb. 28, 1946) (printed in parallel French, Russian, English, and German texts), Law 16 (Marriage Law), pp. 77–94.
[35] *New York Times*, Nov. 10, 1935, Section 7, p. 12.

of working, she may be supported for a period of six months.[36]

Following the new restrictions a tremendous decline in divorce was reported. In Moscow, for example, there were approximately 9000 divorces in 1937, in contrast to 16,000 in 1936.[37] For the central area in which Moscow and Leningrad are located the number decreased from 82,001 for the first four months of 1936 to 24,331 for the same period in 1937.[38]

Further changes in the Soviet law were made by a decree published by the Presidium of the Supreme Soviet of the U.S.S.R. on July 28, 1944, and are still in force. This decree provided there be no obstacles to a divorce if there were "good grounds," but every attempt must be made to prevent unfounded divorces and to promote reconciliation between man and wife.

The appeal for divorce is heard by the People's Court. The appellant makes application for divorce, stating his motives. The defendant is then summoned and acquainted with the charges. Witnesses may be called. In any event, the court is charged with the task of attempting to reconcile the estranged pair. If this fails, the case goes to a higher court.

Interestingly enough, there is no statement of specific grounds for divorce in the new Soviet law. Each case is considered on its merits and what may be allowed as sufficient grounds in one instance may be disallowed in another. This, in Soviet opinion, allows greater democracy in the particular decision than would be possible if divorce were granted only on specific grounds. Obviously, this allows for a measurable difference in the acceptance of alleged reasons for divorce. But, as everyone knows, it is tense relationships rather than the alleged reasons which are actually responsible for divorce.

When a divorce is granted, appropriate entries are made in the passport of each party. The court determines the custody of children, whether one or both parents shall assume responsibility for their maintenance, and how the property shall be divided.

The cost of a Soviet divorce has been greatly increased, and this, presumably, has some deterrent effect on the rate. Today an application fee of 100 rubles is charged and when a divorce is granted, a further sum of from 500 to 2000 rubles must be paid.[39]

In Latin America absolute divorces are not permitted in Chile, Colombia, Paraguay, Argentina, and Brazil. These countries allow legal separation, and Chile is lenient with annulments. In Argentina and Brazil, restrictions are rigid, and legal separations are seldom permitted. In Brazil, marriages may be annulled in case of mistaken identity or essential error as to the honor or good name of the other partner. *Desquite,* or legal separation, may be conceded in cases of adultery, attempted homicide, grave injury, or desertion for two years, or by mutual consent after two years of marriage. In no case, however, may those legally separated be remarried legally. The restric-

---

[36] Julius Holzberg, "Divorce in Russia and America," *The Nation,* 128 (June 29, 1929), pp. 734–735.

[37] *New York Times,* Jan. 9, 1938, p. 40.

[38] *Moscow Daily News,* June 27, 1937, p. 2.

[39] Grigorii Markovich Sverdlov, *Legal Rights of the Soviet Family,* published by *Soviet News,* London, 1945, pp. 35–38. Cf. also "Russia, Law Digest, Divorce." *Martindale-Hubbell Law Directory,* Part III, 1953.

tions against divorce do not mean that there is an absolutely rigid system. After one year of marriage, a man may live with another woman quite legally by signing a contract known as a *casamento*. This amounts to legal concubinage. Children of such a union are legitimate but have no right of inheritance.

Despite extreme opposition by the Catholic Church, fourteen South American countries now permit absolute divorce. Of these, Bolivia, Costa Rica, Cuba, the Dominican Republic, Haiti, Mexico, Panama, Uruguay, and Venezuela had adopted such provisions before the war. In 1941, both Peru and Nicaragua adopted measures for securing complete divorce.[40] Many unhappily married persons from countries where no absolute divorce is obtainable seek divorce across the border. Such migratory divorces often present legal complications, just as they do in the United States, since many suits contesting such divorces have occurred and children of a marriage following such a divorce have been ruled illegitimate and denied inheritance rights. For example, many alienated persons from neighboring countries secure divorce in Uruguay, where divorce is surprisingly simple. All an Uruguayan wife needs to do to secure a divorce is to request one. No grounds need be stated. Such a divorce may be granted only after two years of marriage and a person may start a divorce action only once in each marriage. After application there is a waiting period of six months, during which time a reconciliation may be effected. If the wife still desires a divorce after six months, she is ordered to return in one year. If there is still no reconciliation, a final decree is granted. This law aims at preventing undue embarrassment and eliminates the necessity of securing witnesses. In Latin American countries it is considered especially distasteful to air one's marital troubles in public or to ask one's friends to present sordid testimony.

Divorce by mutual consent is also permitted in Uruguay. In such a case both parties appear to file the suit. Six months later, they are asked to present themselves to the court if no reconciliation is established. A final decree is given in six months after that. Divorces are also granted in Uruguay by alleging the usual grievances of adultery, incompatibility, or desertion, but such divorces require eight months. No terms of residence are required. The complainant has merely to show he has a domicile, and foreigners have no difficulty in acquiring a domicile.

In Mexico, divorce restrictions vary within the different provinces from conservative provisions to very radical. Mexico professes a nominal adherence to the Catholic Church but left-wing political movements have done much to undermine its authority. Consequently Mexico, in common with most countries emerging from a revolution, has witnessed a marked relaxation of the social controls over divorce. In one state, Chihuahua, the commercialization of divorce has proceeded along fantastic lines; all told, seventeen grounds of divorce are allowed. There is no residence requirement, and divorces have been obtainable by mail for the paltry sum of sixty

[40] Data obtained through the courtesy of Manuel Canyes, Chief of the Division of Law and Treaties of the Pan-American Union, March 23, 1953.

dollars. All this, however, is chiefly for the benefit of foreigners who wish to secure an easy divorce. Mexican women were given a theoretical freedom with the Revolution. Absolute divorce is now legal, but the old cultural norms have not thus far been uprooted for the masses. The Roman Catholic tradition still holds, particularly for women, who form the bulk of the active church membership. Most daughters would be disowned by their parents if divorced. The adoption of legal divorce in Mexico is thus a far cry from its social acceptance.[41] For the Mexican peasants who live in rural villages, legal divorce is scarcely a matter of concern, for most of them have had no legal marriage anyway. The Indian men hesitate to enter a binding church marriage or legal contract, choosing instead to be united in marriage by the tribal rituals.

After the revision of the British divorce laws in 1937, there was an unsuccessful attempt in the Canadian parliament to alter the Dominion divorce laws to conform with those of the mother country. A law so drawn passed the Canadian Senate in 1938 and was more or less expected to be adopted, but failed in the House of Representatives. As matters stand, the Dominion parliament still retains jurisdiction over divorce for Newfoundland, Quebec, Yukon, and the Northwest Territory. Parliament has authority to grant a divorce for any ground deemed sufficient in these provinces, but in general adultery is the only cause recognized. The parliamentary fee, exclusive of legal fees, is $210; hence only the well-to-do can afford to seek release from marital ties. In the other provinces, courts may grant decrees, but adultery is the generally recognized ground. Sex perversion is also recognized as a ground in several provinces, and Nova Scotia adds cruelty.[42]

DIVORCE LAWS IN THE UNITED STATES

The United States has lagged behind European countries in making no provision for divorce by mutual consent. Technically, a "friendly divorce" is collusion, a criminal offense. In this land of the free, release from marriage bonds may be allowed only because one party has grounds against the other party, who is guilty of reprehensible conduct.[43] In consequence, defendants in divorce trials are the willing victims of perjured testimony. Judges, however, are generally not disposed to question the testimony and consider perjury a lesser offense than the adultery or cruelty which might be encouraged by other legal requirements.[44]

Because our several states and territories retain sovereignty in matters of marriage and divorce we have confusing disparity in the provisions allowed. Divorce statutes, as Vernier points out, are not a product of logic alone

---

[41] Verna Carelton Milan, *Mexico Reborn* (Boston: Houghton Mifflin, 1939), chap. 7, "Freedom for Mexican Women."

[42] *Martindale-Hubbell Law Directory*, Part III, "Digests of the Laws of the Dominion of Canada" (Summit, N. J., 1953).

[43] Louis Harris, *Love, Marriage and Divorce in History and Law* (Boston: Stratford, 1939), p. 99; cited by Elliott and Merrill, *op. cit.*, p. 723.

[44] Vernier, *op. cit.*, vol. 2, p. 7.

but a confused combination of religious ideas, social attitudes, and historical accident.[45] In some states the legal grounds are substantially an outgrowth of the old canonical laws for legal separation, and divorce is conceived of much as a legal remedy for the status of a person injured by his or her spouse's reprehensible conduct.[46] New York alone adheres to the rigid religious restrictions and permits absolute divorce only for adultery, although New York permits dissolution of the marriage after an absence of five years — where the missing party is not located for five years — by assuming that the party is legally dead. For cruelty and abandonment, legal separation (divorce *a mensa et thoro*) is allowed. In some states, on the other hand, as many as eleven grounds are permitted.

Despite our much-vaunted democracy, our laws tend to reflect the points of view of a specific class, the lawmakers. These are generally representative of the middle class. In consequence, divorce laws, as Llewellyn points out, are "patterned upon bourgeois marriage conditions." The unpropertied and the impecunious are affected, however, by the bourgeois pattern. They make use of it and are on occasion forced to conform to it, but they do not to any great extent have any voice in determining its nature.[47] Divorce laws thus tend to be representative of the opinion of the articulate middle class, which in any society tends to be "the backbone of morality." The underlying pattern and ethics of marriage upon which the structure of modern divorce has been reluctantly erected, Llewellyn summarizes pithily as: "Live with your husband, go with him if he moves, attend to the social functions, support your wife, don't mortgage house or homestead without her consent, let her run the house (or the two-room kitchenette and bath)."[48]

Since modern marriage entails many adjustments to new situations, modern divorce must be recognized as an end in a process of adjustment and readjustment. While we have a noteworthy increase in the legal grounds for which divorce may be granted, it is more significant that the real reasons for seeking a divorce seldom coincide with the formal legal grounds.

Table 15 shows that in 1949 most divorces in the nine states tabulated were granted on charges of cruelty and desertion. Adultery, although it is usually considered the gravest breach of marital vows and is permitted as grounds for divorce in every state in the Union, accounted for very few divorces. Very little correspondence exists between grounds most generally admissible, however, and those for which divorces are granted. Even where adultery occurs, most husbands and wives hesitate to have their family scandals exposed.

Cruelty was the charge most frequently pressed by women in most North-

[45] Vernier, *op. cit.*, vol. 2, p. 7.
[46] *Ibid.*, p. 9.
[47] K. N. Llewellyn, "Behind the Law of Divorce, I" *Columbia Law Review*, 32 (Dec., 1932), pp. 1281–1308.
[48] K. N. Llewellyn, "Behind the Law of Divorce, II," *Columbia Law Review*, 33 (Jan., 1933), p. 33.

TABLE 15

Grounds for Which Divorces Were Granted in Ten States with Percentage Distribution, 1949[49]

CAUSES OF DIVORCES GRANTED	DELAWARE	FLORIDA	MICHIGAN	MISSISSIPPI	NEBRASKA	OREGON	SOUTH DAKOTA	VIRGINIA	WYOMING	IOWA
Adultery	6.9	9.8	0.1	6.2	0.5	0.1	0.4	9.0	0.1	0.9
Cruelty	20.0	27.0	89.5	44.0	75.2	82.6	7.6	0.4	81.9**	88.6
Desertion	67.2	55.4	5.5	42.0	6.4	12.1	12.8	87.0*	9.1	7.0
Neglect	0	0	4.1	0	6.3	0	6.0	0.0	6.1	0.4
Separation	0	0	0	0	0	0	0	0	1.5	0
Drunkenness	4.4	7.4	0.3	5.5	0.6	0.2	0.8	0	0.5	2.0
Illegal Divorce	0	0.4	0	0	0	0	0	0	0	0
Illegal Marriage	0	2.5	0	0.8	0	0	0	0	0.2	0
Fraud	0	0	0.8	0	0	0	0	0	0	0.0
Impotence	0	0	0	0	0	0.0	0	0.6	0.1	0
Imprisonment	7.3	0	0.1	0.5	0.4	0.6	8.	1.9	1.6	0.9
Insanity	0	0	0	0.2	0.4	0	0	0	0.3	0
Incompatibility	0	0	0.0	0	0	0	0	0	0.2	0
Other Causes	0.3	9.1	0.3	0.8	0	0.6	4.0	0.6	0.4	0.1

[49] Data in table computed by author from Table 3, Vol. 36, *Vital Statistics, Special Reports*, Public Health Service, Federal Security Agency, August 5, 1951, pp. 99–102.

* Includes 294 cases in which other causes were also alleged.

** Includes "intolerable indignities."

ern states in 1949. This alleged reason conveniently includes almost any sort of conduct which may be called offensive. Wives press cruelty charges because their husbands have criticized their cooking, stayed up late at night, brought home unwelcome guests, made fun of their religion, or been unwilling to pay for extensive additions to their wardrobe. Cruelty tends thus to be "mental cruelty." Very infrequently it is a matter of black eyes and bruises. All states except New York permit divorce on a cruelty charge. North Carolina and Iowa limit cruelty, however, to conduct endangering life, and the former permits only legal separation in such case.[50]

According to common law a man assumes liability for his wife's support upon entering the state of matrimony. When he fails to provide for his wife, over half the states authorize divorce. Even so, only a small per cent of those for whom we have statistics in 1950 are for neglect. Where women have independent means or are earning or are capable of earning their own living, such grounds are invalid. In no case may an unemployed husband or one who is ill be made defendant on such a charge. Cruelty charges are, however, often substantiated on the husband's failure to support.[51]

When women had less opportunity for self-support, desertion was the most frequently alleged charge, since it carried the implication of nonsupport. Today desertion ranks second among the causes for which divorces are granted. It is often the first cause in the South. The charge is usually purely formal and is considered in many circles as the least offensive charge. Women who deliberately leave their husbands often allege desertion. The charge is also characteristic of cases where both husbands and wives are anxious to make an end of the marriage. Where husbands initiate proceedings, desertion is the most frequent charge. All states except New York permit divorce on such grounds. In New York, however, as has been said, absence for five years without news allows an individual to be declared legally dead. This permits dissolution of the marriage and may amount substantially to divorce by desertion.[52]

Drunkenness is a penal offense in all states, and habitual drunkenness is an admissible reason for divorce in all but a few. No wife, however, can secure a divorce from a husband who is drunk only occasionally. The defendant must be a confirmed alcoholic who has given repeated evidences of extreme intoxication. In a few states (Oregon, Tennessee, and West Virginia) no spouse can divorce a mate who was a heavy drinker before marriage because of the presumption that these habits were known and accepted when the vows "for better or worse" were taken. Divorce laws do not recognize the chronic alcoholic for the neurotic or allergic individual that he is.[53]

Insanity is universally recognized as an impediment to marriage both by church and state, and all states allow a marriage to be dissolved or annulled if one mate was insane at the time of marriage. There is, how-

---

[50] Cf. *Martindale-Hubbell Law Directory*, 1953.
[51] Clarke, *op. cit.*, p. 125.
[52] *Ibid.*, p. 123.
[53] *Ibid.*, p. 122.

ever, great disparity of opinion as to the suitability of granting a divorce to the husband or wife if the mental breakdown occurs after the marriage. Nevertheless the trend is toward granting a divorce on such grounds, and more than half the states now authorize it. Since an insane wife is patently exempt from guilt, five states (Colorado, Minnesota, Mississippi, Nevada, and Pennsylvania) provide alimony. Pennsylvania does not allow divorce on grounds of insanity, as a matter of fact, but merely protects the insane wife who is divorced on other grounds.[54]

In any case of fraud, duress, or mistaken identity (even in case of marriage while intoxicated) most states allow either annulment or divorce. There is, however, no uniformity as to how these causes are defined. A man who has been previously divorced may conceal the fact from his fiancée without endangering his subsequent marriage. A woman who is pregnant by some man other than her husband at the time of her marriage may be divorced by her husband. A man, on the other hand, may not allege duress when he is an unwilling party to a "shotgun marriage."

Most states authorize additional grounds for divorce, although they do not bulk large in the causes for which divorces are granted. Bigamy, for example, is ground for either annulment or divorce in all states. Since sex relations are a basic aspect of marriage, impotency — or the incapacity to have such relations — is a ground for divorce in two-thirds of the states. Unwillingness to have sex relations, on the other hand, is usually considered a special form of cruelty, or else the specific unwillingness is recognized as a ground. Sterility, although a frequent cause of divorce in earlier societies, is no longer an allowable ground.[55] Even so, many sterile marriages end in divorce on some other charge.

These, then, are the major technical reasons which must be alleged if one seeks a divorce. The actual reasons for dissatisfaction in marriage might be better summed up, however, in the term "incompatibility." Thus New Mexico, Idaho, Wyoming, and Alaska have adopted legislation frankly acknowledging this fact.[56] However, these statutes legally recognize the trend toward divorce by mutual consent. Incompatibility as ground for divorce accepts the fact of personality differences and makes needless the absurd charges of grave offenses where no blame can be laid honestly.

MIGRATORY DIVORCE

Differences in statutory provisions have led to migratory divorce. By establishing a short and fictitious residence in another state, persons unable to secure a divorce at home may be released from the bonds of matrimony with relative ease. Although divorces are granted to nonresident couples in one-fourth of the cases, Cahen holds that only 3 per cent of divorces

[54] Cf. *Martindale-Hubbell Law Directory,* 1953.
[55] Clarke, *op. cit.,* p. 123.
[56] Alaska adopted such a statute in 1933, New Mexico in 1935. Others have adopted the provision more recently.

in the United States can be considered *truly* migratory. Twenty-two per
cent of the entire population is actually nonresident.[57] The publicity and
commercialization attached to migratory divorces, plus their importance
in certain divorce issues, have made them assume a significance out of all
proportion to their number.

In 1861 Nevada adopted marriage and divorce legislation copied almost
entirely from the civil code of California. By these provisions seven grounds
for divorce were permitted: impotency, adultery, willful desertion, conviction of felony or infamous crime, gross habitual drunkenness, extreme
cruelty, and nonsupport. There was obviously nothing distinctly "lenient"
in these provisions, since most of them were in line with liberal developments in many states. The real innovation lay in a residence requirement
of only six months before divorce proceedings might be instituted. No
great publicity was made of this residence provision, however, until 1909.
Then a lawyer with an eye to its commercial possibilities conducted an advertising campaign in New York City, where he pointed out the advantages
of securing a respectable divorce after a short residence in Nevada. The
lawyer was subsequently disbarred, but the seeds of migratory divorces
had been sown.[58] When New Yorkers began to seek Nevada divorces, the
shocked citizens of Nevada recoiled from the publicity; a revision of the
divorce statute in 1913 stipulated that divorces could be granted only to
those who had a bona fide residence of one year. In 1915 the earlier residence
of six months was restored. The grounds patently have little effect on the
trek to Reno; it is the short residence requirement which exerts the pull.
With the idea of stimulating a greater divorce trade the legislature shortened the period from six months to three months in 1927.

Other states saw the possibilities of profiting from a divorce business
among tourists. In 1931 Arkansas lowered its residence requirement to
three months with an idea of capitalizing upon the potential divorcées who
came to her resort capital at Hot Springs. Within a week Idaho enacted a
"ninety-day law." Not to be outdone, Nevada reduced her required residence to six weeks, and Idaho later adopted the same provision.[59] Perhaps
as much with an eye to enforcing some economic return for their lenient
residence requirements both Nevada and Idaho require genuine residence
and enforce this requirement rigidly. Partly because Reno has developed
all the facilities for making the period of residence as pleasant as possible
and partly because all its legal machinery is in effective operation, the Idaho
divorce laws do not attract any sizable number of people from outside the
state.[60]

In May, 1935, the Florida legislature established provision for legal
residence after ninety days.[61] This made it possible to combine the

[57] Cahen, *op. cit.*, chap. 5.
[58] Frank M. Ingraham and G. A. Ballard, "The Business of Migratory Divorce in Nevada,"
Law and Contemporary Problems, 2 (June, 1935), pp. 302–309.
[59] Rollo Bergeson, "The Divorce Mill Advertises," *Law and Contemporary Problems*, 2 (June,
1935), pp. 348–359.
[60] Gordon Gaskill, "Divorces While You Play," *Reader's Digest*, 39 (Oct., 1941), pp. 12–14.
[61] Bergeson, *op. cit.*

Easterner's favorite vacation with escape from matrimony for those who can afford to take three months off. In consequence, the divorce capital has been shifting to the eastern seaboard. In 1940 Reno granted a mere 2300 divorces, while Miami turned out 4000. The semitropical climate, with the relaxation which beach life affords, is no explanation for this shift. The fact is that most of the plaintiffs have no evidence save their perjured testimony as to a ninety-day residence in Florida, and certainly very few have any intention of becoming the permanent residents which they swear they intend to be. In this respect Florida divorces are open to the question of validity far more often than is the case in Nevada divorces. In consequence, many honest Florida lawyers have been outraged by the loss of dignity suffered by the Florida courts.[62] The Virgin Islands provide greater privacy and permit divorce after six weeks' residence.

South Carolina, prior to 1949, had contributed significantly to that peculiarly hypocritical collusion known as "fictitious" residence. As Brearley points out, all divorced persons among South Carolinians were in the broad sense migratory, since absolute divorce was not permitted for any cause within the state. Divorcees residing in the state either had to leave the state to secure the divorce or moved to the state after a divorce was obtained elsewhere.[63] Most South Carolinians seeking divorce apparently did so in neighboring states. Fictitious residences were often established by perjured testimony in Virginia and Georgia. Such subterfuges as that of a physician who sent his laundry to Georgia and thereby established residence while still maintaining his medical practice in South Carolina have been recounted.[64] Such migratory divorces were sternly rejected in South Carolina courts on the ground that any divorce which could be legally recognized according to the "full faith and credit" clause of the Constitution had to be granted by a state in which the plaintiff had valid domicile.[65] Nevertheless, the number of divorcees living in South Carolina mounted rapidly. In 1930 there were 4085 divorced persons in South Carolina in contrast to 1079 in 1900. In line with changing attitudes, South Carolina finally adopted a divorce statute in March, 1949, permitting divorce on grounds of adultery, desertion for one year, physical cruelty, and habitual drunkenness. The need for migratory divorce thus declined.

While any decent person may object to the commercialization attached to making divorce the leading business of Reno or any other divorce capital, migratory divorce is meeting a human need denied in those jurisdictions which have very rigid legal restrictions. Certainly we have ample reason to suppose it is far better for married couples who have come to the parting of the ways to do so without destroying the morale or self-respect of either party. The so-called divorce mills are making it possible to secure a respectable release from an unbearable marriage for those who can secure a divorce

---

[62] Cf. Gaskill, *op. cit.*, pp. 12–14. Cf. also *Martindale-Hubbell Law Directory*, 1953.
[63] H. C. Brearley, "A Note upon Migratory Divorce of South Carolinians," *Law and Contemporary Problems*, 2 (June, 1935), pp. 329–334.
[64] *Ibid.*
[65] *Ibid.*

only on scandalous grounds in New York. Moreover, the divorce grounds permitted in the more lenient states emphasize the essentially emotional and psychical attributes of marriage, whereas the more conservative jurisdictions place the physical aspects on a pedestal. While the church, especially the Roman Catholic and Anglican branches, has always held marriage to be a spiritual union, it has seen fit to penalize only the physical aberrations. Migratory divorce should make us all aware of the real reasons for divorce.

Migratory divorce, in the words of the late Ernest R. Groves,[66] may be considered as a safety valve. For the unhappy marriages of those who have not stooped to make use of the grounds allowable in New York, it allows an escape outside the fiction of legal separation. On the other hand, migratory divorce has probably forestalled a concerted attack on rigid divorce laws in New York, since it seems reasonable that those who have sought divorce elsewhere would have otherwise raised their voice in protest at home. It must therefore be a challenge to our social thinking. Unhappily, migratory divorce is available only to those who can afford the time and expense of travel.

Aside from the diverse attitudes with reference to the ethics and expediency of migratory divorce, two very practical problems remain. One is the question of whether migratory divorces are valid. This point has never been satisfactorily settled. There have been numerous decisions by New York courts holding that such divorces were not legal because they were secured without the parties' becoming actual residents of the states in which the divorces were granted. In the majority of instances, however, the issue as to whether or not the divorce is legal is never raised, and by virtue of social practice the divorce is acceptable.

Migratory divorce also raises the problem of the custody decree and of what becomes of the children. A custody granted to the father in one state, for example, may seem unwarranted to the mother. She may go to another state and ask to have the decree set aside. Judicial opinions vary as to which state has jurisdiction. Some states hold that the father, even though adjudged "guilty" by the divorce trial, still has the right to determine domicile for his children. Other courts have held that only the court of original jurisdiction has the right to modify the original decree. This is only one of the ways in which the legal aspects of migratory divorce are complicated.[67]

THE JUDGE AND THE DIVORCE COURT

Divorce proceedings, in most instances, tend to be a matter of formality. The couple previously has come to the parting of the ways and the average judge is realistic enough to know that the law cannot compel a man and wife to live together. As a matter of fact, after a judge has listened to the

[66] Ernest R. Groves, "Migratory Divorces," *Law and Contemporary Problems*, 2 (June, 1935), pp. 293–301.
[67] "Jurisdictional Bases of Custody Decrees," *Harvard Law Review*, 53 (April, 1940), pp. 1024–1030.

grievances of unhappy mates, he is usually convinced that divorce is more of a blessing than a necessary evil. Even so, there are a few judges who assume a counseling attitude toward the estranged couple, and these judges are sometimes instrumental in promoting a reconciliation.

In any event, judges must bear a major responsibility for the legal severing of the marriage tie. It is by the judge's decision that a divorce is granted, although frequently he makes no great effort to determine the reliability of the testimony presented. Nor is there any cross-examination of the witnesses to prove or disprove the validity of alleged grievances. Royal D. Rood, a Detroit lawyer, makes a trenchant indictment of the judicial procedure in divorce cases. Judicial decisions, he maintains, are the personal indictment of "social workers, policewomen, and gossipmongers" who influence the judge to such decisions.[68]

Unquestionably, Mr. Rood's attitude toward the social worker is unfair. Social workers, on occasion, may have been too active in breaking up families. Nevertheless the average social worker today recognizes the importance of maintaining the family during stresses and strains, and public money is often expended at the social worker's direction to keep the family intact. Earlier it was true that a widow or divorcée could secure financial assistance for her children, whereas the wife of an unemployed or sick husband was ineligible for "mother's assistance" or a widow's pension. Social workers may have thus favored divorce as a means of securing support in certain instances. Today the Social Security Act provides aid to dependent children wherever family income is insufficient, whether or not the family is widowed. This should eliminate any tendency on the part of social workers to secure divorces in order to facilitate the support of the family.

Rood accepts the ancient principle of common law that the "head" of the family has the prerogative of authority in family relationship. He is right in holding that modern divorce procedure is not much concerned with the interests of the defendant, who is usually the husband. Ancient common law gave the husband the right to command obedience from all who ate the food which he provided. Rood contends that the interests of the husband are ignored in depriving him of the services of those whom he has been required to maintain and support. In so doing, he apparently ignores the large body of sentiment which looks askance upon regarding either children or wives as the servants of the head of the family.

ALIMONY

Almost anyone can start an argument if he brings up the subject of alimony. There is a wide range in attitude. Some believe any woman so unfortunate as to be divorced should have some compensation; others condemn the whole business as a "racket."

The unwillingness of many men to pay continual tribute to women

[68] Royal D. Rood, *Matrimonial Shoals* (Detroit: Detroit Law Book Company, 1939), p. 12.

who have renounced them has been evidenced in the so-called "Alimony Clubs." Some of these men have fought payment of alimony to the extent of going to jail for refusal. They have recently organized for the purpose of reforming domestic relations laws.[69]

Alimony originally was the term applied to the support which was due a wife. When the ecclesiastical courts of England had jurisdiction over marital disruptions, there developed the practice of awarding permanent alimony to wives in case of judicial separation — or divorce *a mensa et thoro*. This was easily justified, since the woman was still her husband's legal wife; she was merely permitted to live apart from him because of his misconduct. When the husband was the plaintiff there was, of course, no alimony, since the wife was the guilty party. The ecclesiastical courts authorized no absolute divorce. Anyone who secured an absolute divorce before 1857 had to have a private Act of parliament.[70] Eventually the plight of wives who were divorced by their husbands was recognized. The so-called guilty woman often had no means of support and was forced into prostitution. In consequence, parliament later stipulated that financial support be arranged for the wife irrespective of her conduct and as a condition for granting a divorce to her husband.

The antecedent of modern alimony thus lies in the permanent alimony formerly awarded in legal separation. Because such alimony was enforced on guilty husbands, it partook of the nature of a penalty. The practice of extending alimony to guilty wives, on the other hand, enhanced the wife's invested interest in marriage and in a sense attached a penalty to committing a divorce as well as to committing adultery.[71] Out of the background of ecclesiastical law, common law, and parliamentary practice modern alimony developed. Today the term has come to mean the support which a former husband is required to give his wife, according to stipulations laid down by the court at the time the decree is granted. In general, the award of alimony has depended on the wife's innocence and her need and that of her children. Similarly, her husband's guilt and his ability to pay have been factors in determining the award.

Since their inception, alimony patterns, like those of divorce, have been based on the bourgeois marriage pattern. To pay alimony one must have some wherewithal. According to the Federal reports on marriage and divorce, only 16 per cent asked for and 12 per cent received alimony for the period 1867–1886. From 1887 to 1906, 13 per cent asked for support and 9 per cent were awarded it. In 1931, 9 per cent requested alimony and 6 per cent were given it. There are no current figures for the country as a whole, but in 1943 alimony was awarded to 32.8 per cent of the wives where they were granted the decree — a significant reversal of trend.[72]

[69] Baber, *op. cit.*, p. 470.
[70] Chester G. Vernier and John B. Hurlbut, "The Historical Background of Alimony and Its Present Statutory Structure," *Law and Contemporary Problems,* 6 (Spring, 1939), pp. 107–212.
[71] *Ibid.*
[72] *Vital Statistics* — Special Reports, Bureau of the Census, Vol. 17, No. 25 (June 9, 1943), p. 143.

So far as financial settlements are concerned, these are often agreed upon outside of court. On the other hand, they are not always satisfactory since they are even more difficult to enforce than a court award. Apparently the average modern woman seeking divorce prefers to sever all relations with her former mate, although women with children are more apt to ask for alimony than are childless women. Alimony is also more regularly sought where husbands are in the upper income brackets. Out-of-court settlements make possible an amicable arrangement and do not create as much antagonism as is usual in court awards.

Although independent women often refuse to accept anything from their former husbands, it would be socially undesirable to abolish provision for alimony. Rather, it would be a better public policy to award alimony to a much greater number of wives. There are a large number of divorced women who have insufficient means of support for themselves and children.[73] While alimony occasionally works a hardship on the husband, the wife has an economic interest in a marriage which has endured for any considerable period. Any earning power she might have had has been reduced by her years of marriage. She may even be justified in asking something in the way of damages for "taking the best years of her life." Remarriage, if she has children, is well-nigh impossible. Her husband, since he seldom has custody of the children, experiences no such handicap. In general, the amount of alimony granted should be based on practical considerations. The wife's need for support in relation to her own income and capacity for self-support should be taken into account and balanced with relation to the husband's income and property. Support for children should always be allowed, unless the wife's income is unusually ample, and even then a father should contribute to his children's support, if financially able.

Kelso makes three basic suggestions for the improvement of alimony laws. (1) Considerations of guilt or innocence should be eliminated and the whole matter adjusted on a basis of need for support and re-allocation of property. In this connection the welfare of the children should always take precedence over that of the contending spouses. (2) If the wife remarries, alimony should automatically stop, but some provision should be made for the children. (3) The court should have the right to amend alimony awards when it is later of interest to the state, or the parties concerned, especially the children.[74]

UNIFORM DIVORCE LEGISLATION

What the solution is to the disparity in our divorce laws none can say authoritatively. The lack of uniformity in the statutory regulations is in-

[73] Catherine Groves Peele, "Social and Psychological Effects of the Availability and the Granting of Alimony on the Spouses," *Law and Contemporary Problems,* 6 (Spring, 1939), pp. 283-292.
[74] Robert W. Kelso, "The Changing Social Setting of Alimony Law," *Law and Contemporary Problems,* 6 (Spring, 1939), pp. 186-196.

herent in differences in population and mores in the various parts of the United States as well as in our system of Federal government. For years some form of national divorce legislation has been urged by reformers, clergymen, and civic groups. Such legislation has much in its favor, for a uniform law would put an end to the abuses of easy divorce and the divorce marts.

No attempt to enact such a law has ever been successful, since the matter of deciding what should be its provisions is no easy matter. Apparently there is no pattern of marriage and divorce acceptable at once to such diverse groups as Catholics, Protestants, and those who are not church members. Furthermore, different sections of the country vary in their population, age and sex ratios, cultural traditions, and dominant religious adherence. An early compromise on uniform law thus seems unlikely. Perhaps the experimentation in various parts of our country may later yield a law acceptable to us all.

Once the possibility of absolute divorce is admitted, the legal reasons tend at best to be formal; the real reasons cannot be encompassed in the law unless we accept incompatibility as a broad subsuming basis for legally severing the marriage bonds. No one supposes that the marital problems of men and women conform to the disparity in divorce laws. Husbands and wives who are residents of New York undoubtedly have problems and grievances similar to those of unhappy mates in other states. The real reasons for any divorce arise out of the conflicts or tensions which develop between marriage partners which have been discussed in Chapters Fourteen and Fifteen. At present marital difficulties as attested to in the divorce courts usually bear very little relation to the basic reason for wishing to terminate marriage.

Friendly Divorce

In sophisticated circles there is often much talk of "friendly" divorces, of ex-husbands and ex-wives being on the best of terms, and of divorces secured amicably. Actually such cases are probably rarer than the parties involved maintain. In most states friendly divorces are technically illegal. One must secure a divorce not because the marriage is unhappy but because one party has been guilty of offensive conduct. As a result we have reason to believe that much of the testimony in divorce hearings, other than that pertaining to residence, is perjured. Most judges are of the opinion that there is no point in forcing people to live in an intolerable relationship, but greater honesty in divorce legislation would permit incompatibility as a general ground for divorce and eliminate this hypocrisy.

On the other hand, we all know that many cases in which there are serious tensions or "real" reasons for divorce do *not* end in the divorce court. A sense of honor, a sense of responsibility for the children, and economic reasons prevent many such marriages from breaking up. When a marriage yields only frustration and disillusionment, however, divorce may offer the only solution. Eventually the laws of our several states may make greater provision for the subtler aspects of marital tensions. To insist upon the sanctity of a union which is destructive to the personalities of both parties and their children can have no valid justification. Divorce in such cases may be like the surgeon's healing knife.

POSSIBILITY OF RECONCILIATION

Where a man finds the integrity of his personality threatened by the wife who distrusts him, or where she is humiliated by living with a husband who scorns her very being, there is little hope of rebuilding a satisfactory life together. Readjustment is possible only where there is a complete change of attitude, and unfortunately such a possibility is rare.[75]

Not all estrangements are irreparable, however. Often a man or woman may be unhappy over his job or be suffering from some other irritation and be so confused by the experience that he assumes his marriage is at fault. Minor tensions often occur which should not threaten the marriage.

Many divorces have occurred where the persons have mistakenly presumed their love was dead. The prolonged pain and suffering in the postdivorce period gives them proof of their deep-seated affection. If divorce is postponed or a period of waiting required before the decree becomes final, many couples find satisfaction in reconciliation.

THE CHILDREN'S STAKE IN DIVORCE

Most of our discussion has centered on the problems of divorce. The adjustments and maladjustments of the postdivorce period have been covered in Chapter Twenty-One. We are justified in considering here, however, certain facts about the children of the divorced.

According to Paul H. Jacobson, two-fifths of the divorced couples in 1948 had children. In the 421,000 divorces granted there were 313,000 children. Children are thus no preventive of divorce. Kingsley Davis estimated that there were roughly 1,533,000 children with divorced parents in 1940. The number of children affected by divorce 1933–1946 has also been estimated by Dr. Davis (Table 16). Through no fault save accident of birth, such children are made the unwilling parties to their parents' frustrations while suffering from emotional insecurity themselves.[76]

What becomes of the child of divorce? We have no adequate statistical studies dealing specifically with this topic. We know that children who come from broken homes bulk large in juvenile court cases and among the inmates of orphanages and correctional institutions. But these children, as

---

[75] Sidney E. Goldstein, *Marriage and Family Counseling* (New York: McGraw-Hill, 1945), pp. 188–189.

[76] Paul H. Jacobson, "Differentials in Divorce by Duration of Marriage and Size of Family," *American Sociological Review*, 15 (April, 1950), pp. 235–244; and Kingsley Davis, "Sociological and Statistical Analysis," Children of Divorced Parents, *Law and Contemporary Problems*, 10 (Summer, 1944), pp. 711–720.

TABLE 16

ESTIMATED NUMBER OF CHILDREN AFFECTED BY DIVORCE IN THE U.S., 1933–1946 [77]

Year	Children	Year	Children
1933	110,000	1940	176,000
1934	136,000	1941	192,000
1935	145,000	1942	205,000
1936	157,000	1943	218,000
1937	166,000	1944	209,000
1938	162,000	1945	254,000
1939	167,000	1946	307,000

Waller points out, are chiefly from families in the lower income group.[78] Such families seldom have money enough for "bourgeois divorce." The husband deserts, or the wife "walks out."

The suffering of a child who is deserted by one or both parents is probably more acute than that of a child with divorced parents. The emotional upset which the deserted child experiences is further complicated by low living standards, poor neighborhoods, unfortunate leisure-time habits, and all the disabilities and handicaps which accompany poverty. Nevertheless, divorce also often lowers the economic status of all persons concerned. If the husband remarries, he cannot support two families on the same plane on which he supported one. If the wife assumes responsibility for supporting her children, her earnings are seldom high enough to maintain the previous standard of living.

In any event, general experience points to the disruptive force of divorce on children. Probably every boarding school in the country harbors some young persons whose parents have deposited them there when the home was broken up. Any adviser in school or college can cite numerous incidents of students who have failed in school or have been brought up for breaking rules of conduct because they were overwhelmed by their parents' divorce. Such demoralized or marginal youngsters provide striking instances of the effects of an over-rapid shift from sacred to secular.

The emotional maladjustments which divorce occasions for children do not end with maturity. Instead, these maladjustments tend to carry over into their adult life and make for difficulties in their own marital ventures. Burgess and Cottrell's extensive research in factors responsible for success or failure in marriage showed that children of divorced parents are bad risks in marriage themselves.[79] Naturally, no one supposes that all children from such broken marriages possess difficult personalities or are unstable, neurotic individuals. If divorced parents are sensible and intelligent — and there are surely some who are — they make every effort to make their children happy, and in a measure these efforts probably compensate for the unfortunate effects of divorce.

What we need in the final analysis is not more liberal divorce laws but

[77] From estimates made by Kingsley Davis described in *Law and Contemporary Problems, op. cit.,* pp. 700–721.

[78] Willard Waller, *The Family: A Dynamic Interpretation* (New York: Dryden Press, 1938), p. 569.

[79] Burgess and Cottrell, *op. cit.,* p. 103.

better education for marriage and better marriage counseling. Only in this way can we lower the incompatibility which develops among many hopeful married couples in America.

SELECTED READINGS

"Alimony," *Law and Contemporary Problems* (June, 1939). A symposium.

BURGESS, ERNEST W., and COTTRELL, LEONARD S., JR., *Predicting Success or Failure in Marriage* (New York: Prentice-Hall, 1939), chap. 17.

CAVAN, RUTH SHONLE, *The American Family* (New York: Crowell, 1953). "Children of the Divorced," *Law and Contemporary Problems,* 10 (Summer, 1944). A symposium.

CLARKE, HELEN I., *Social Legislation* (New York: Appleton-Century, 1940), chap. 6.

"Divorce, A Re-examination of Basic Concepts," *Law and Contemporary Problems* (Winter, 1953). A symposium.

ELLIOTT, MABEL A., "Divorce Legislation and Family Stability," *The Annals of the American Academy of Political and Social Science,* 272 (Nov., 1950), pp. 134–147.

——, and MERRILL, FRANCIS E., *Social Disorganization* (Third ed.; New York: Harper, 1950).

GROVES, ERNEST R., and OGBURN, WILLIAM F., *American Marriage and Family Relationships* (New York: Holt, 1928), chaps. 22, 23.

HARRIS, LOUIS, *Love, Marriage and Divorce in History and Law* (Boston: Stratford, 1930).

LICHTENBERGER, JAMES P., *Divorce: A Social Interpretation* (New York: McGraw-Hill, 1931), chaps. 4, 5, 10, 14.

"Migratory Divorce," *Law and Contemporary Problems* (June, 1935). A symposium.

NIMKOFF, M. F., *The Family* (Boston: Houghton Mifflin, 1934), chaps. 10, 11.

SELLIN, JAMES THORSTEN, *Marriage and Divorce Legislation in Sweden* (Ph.D. thesis, University of Pennsylvania, 1922).

TRUXAL, ANDREW G., and MERRILL, FRANCIS F., *The Family in American Culture* (New York: Prentice-Hall, 1953).

VERNIER, CHESTER G., *American Family Laws* (5 vols.; Palo Alto: Stanford University Press, 1931–1938), vol. 2.

WALLER, WILLARD, *The Family: A Dynamic Interpretation,* rev. by Reuben Hill (New York: Dryden Press, 1951), chaps. 20, 21.

——, *The Old Love and the New* (New York: Liveright, 1930).

TOPICS FOR DISCUSSION OR REPORTS

1. Arrange an appointment with the judge who presides over divorce cases in your community and discuss the divorce problem with him. In this connection secure the statistics for divorce cases over a three-year period in his court, and make an analysis of trends.
2. Make a case study of a divorced couple whom you know intimately enough

to secure data with reference to the tensions, "real" causes, "alleged" causes, and readjustments following divorce.

3. Write a paper on The Economic Factor in Alimony Trends, making a special study of alimony in the various states in connection with your general conclusions.

4. Write a paper summarizing the statistical data on divorce since 1900. Compare trends from 1900 to 1910 with trends from 1940 to 1950.

5. Write a paper on The Roman Catholic Doctrine of the Inviolability of Marriage. Arrange to discuss the matter with a local priest. Discuss also the impact of the Protestant churches on divorce. Consult Willystine Goodsell, *Problems of the Family.*

6. Consult Martindale-Hubbell's Law Directory for the current year and compare divorce legislation in the various states with that of 1920.

7. Make a study of divorce in primitive societies. In this connection consult a number of standard texts on primitive family life, and also several monographs or studies of special Indian tribes, Oceanic peoples, African tribes, etc. If there is an anthropology department in your college, consult the faculty of that department.

8. Study all the allusions to divorce in the Old and New Testaments (consult a Biblical concordance for the references) and then trace the development of trends in the attitude toward masculine prerogatives in the matter of divorce.

9. Make a study of Scandinavian divorce legislation. (Consult Sellin's monograph, *The Encyclopedia of the Social Sciences,* etc.).

10. Correspond with several directors of marriage clinics as to (1) the types of cases they handle, (2) the adjustment treatment they use, (3) the success of such adjustments. See Duvall and Hill, *When You Marry* (Boston: Heath, 1945), for a directory of these clinics.

11. Make a study of the divorce statistics during the Korean hostilities (or following) with reference to those granted to soldiers and wives of soldiers in your home county.

12. Locate the residences of all persons divorced in your county in the last year. What proportion are rural residents? What proportion are urban residents? How many are in the upper economic residential areas? How many were among relief clients? How does the distribution of cases compare with the divorce rates in different areas in Chicago? Cf. Ernest R. Mowrer, *Family Disorganization* (rev. ed.; Chicago: University of Chicago Press, 1939).

13. Compare the divorce legislation of your state with the proposed uniform divorce law (look up your own law in the state statutes and secure a copy of the proposed uniform divorce law from your senator in Washington).

14. Review Burgess and Cottrell's book, *Predicting Success or Failure in Marriage,* and Terman's book, *Psychological Factors in Marital Happiness,* and then construct a statement of important factors to observe in preventing divorce.

15. Collect a bibliography on sex adjustments and divorce. Analyze the conclusions from these studies and compare them with Terman's conclusions in *Psychological Factors in Marital Happiness.*

Chapter Twenty-Four

War and the Family

JAMES H. S. BOSSARD [*]

A Foreword

IN June, 1950, the United States became involved in military conflict in Korea. In the months that followed, war was not formally declared, but, from the standpoint of the military personnel involved, the duration of the conflict, the scope of the fighting, and the number of casualties that have resulted, the struggle had all of the realities of war.

Moreover, the so-called "cold war," stemming from the ideological conflict between Soviet Russia and her satellites on the one hand and the rest of the world on the other, has prevailed virtually since the end of World War II. Furthermore, there are no signs of its abatement, and the nature of the struggle is such that it is a moot question whether it will abate for many years to come.

Since such an international situation results in the militarization, at least in part, of the life of all of the peoples concerned, the impact of war and such militarization upon the family remains, and seems destined to remain, a vital problem both now and in the future.

METHODOLOGICAL REMARKS

Four basic ideas inhere in any intelligent approach to the study of the family, war, and its aftermath, and it seems pertinent to examine them by way of preface to the present chapter.

1. The first of these emphasizes the fact that the family, despite its fundamental importance in society, is part of a closely intertwined civilization. Family life functions in reciprocal relation with larger social structures, and each is inevitably and vitally affected by changes in the other. Now war is not just a clash of armed might. Viewed dynamically, it is a complex of social changes, involving often the readjustment of the institutionalized arrangements by which men live. The economic structure is focused upon producing the sinews of war. Educational institutions

[*] AUTHOR'S NOTE: Mrs. Eleanor S. Boll, Research Associate of the William T. Carter Foundation, has contributed the section on "Headline Postwar Family Problems" as well as aided in the assembling of the material on which this chapter is based. The author has also drawn upon his previous publications dealing with war and the family. Acknowledgment for the privilege of reproducing this material is made to the *American Sociological Review*, *The Annals of the American Academy of Political and Social Science*, *Psychiatry*, and the *Journal of Home Economics*.

train personnel and foster morale. Preachers present arms. Population is redistributed: some areas grow phenomenally, others contract correspondingly. Large masses of people are shifted from their customary abodes, occupations, and preoccupations; and the family, as the institutionalized intermediary between individual and society, serves as a sort of funnel through which flows the stream of these everyday changes.

2. Second is the devious and often long drawn out relation between cause and effect. Herbert Spencer wrote about this years ago. In assessing the objective difficulties in the establishment of a social science, he referred to those which arose from the distribution of facts over time. "Those who have risen to the belief," he writes, "that societies are evolved in structure and function, as in growth, will be made to hesitate on contemplating the long unfolding through which early causes work out late results." [1] Contemporary sociologists pay tribute to this fact in their distinction between immediate and ultimate effects. In the case of war and the family, examples of the former would be the increase of war marriages and wartime separations of families; changed attitudes toward sex patterns or the status of women in the postwar period would be indicative of the latter. Thompson, the historian, for example, in writing of the Crusades, which must be considered as a series of wars, points out that their indirect stimulation, by changing the atmosphere of Europe and by shaking from end to end the highly localized life of eleventh-century Europe, may have been of far greater positive effect than any obviously direct consequences. [2] Similarly, reference should be made to distinctions between primary results and those called derivative. Contemporary sociologists have been much impressed with the chain of subsequent consequences growing out of an original factor, thus emphasizing the importance of a long-range point of view. Consideration of these long-range derivative consequences becomes particularly important when the aftermath of World War II is considered, for in the numbers of persons and the variety of epoch-making changes involved, few historic events can compare with it.

3. Third is the importance of historic perspective. Basic to this is an appreciation of the recurrence of war in human history. Beginning with our own experience, one finds that each generation in the history of the United States has witnessed the reality of war. From 1776 to 1953 we have been engaged in eight major wars, an average of one for every twenty-two years. We have been at war during twenty-six of the 177 years of our national existence. Our longest interval of peace has been thirty-three years — the period between the Civil War and the Spanish-American War.

This record of a peace-loving, relatively isolated people, preoccupied with the exploration of a virgin continent, is curiously paralleled by the experience of the leading nations of Europe during their much longer histories. An analysis of 950 years in the history of France shows that the French were at war in more than 80 per cent of those years, and that of thirty-four quarter-

[1] Herbert Spencer, *The Study of Sociology* (New York: Appleton, 1873), pp. 92–93.
[2] James Westfall Thompson, *An Economic and Social History of the Middle Ages* (New York: Century, 1928), p. 433.

centuries in this period, only one was free from an important war. Similarly, of thirty-five quarter-century periods in English history, only one was without a major war.[3]

When we delve into still earlier periods, the frequency of war becomes even more evident. Warfare was both constant and inevitable in the less settled areas of antiquity. To primitive groups it was the corollary of food getting; subsequently it became an essential mechanism in group consolidation, nation building, business investment, and commercial expansion. To many historic peoples, like the Greeks for example, war was considered the natural condition; peace had to be established by special treaty.

Not only is war a constant factor of periodic recurrence but, with the passing of time, it comes to play an increasing role in society. Quincy Wright, in his comprehensive two-volume work on war,[4] after acknowledging various difficulties resulting from incomplete historical data and oscillations in the lives of particular nations, identifies the following long-range trends: (1) armies have tended to become larger, absolutely and in relation to the population; (2) war tends to become more costly in life and wealth; (3) military activity becomes more concentrated in time; and (4) war tends to become more extended in space, with fewer places of safety and with more inconvenience to civilians. (Vol. I, pp. 119–125.) He finds that among the majority of primitive people, war is essentially conservative but that modern warfare becomes more dynamic and disorganizing and produces greater social effects (*ibid.*, p. 126). The destructiveness of war has had an upward tendency (*ibid.*, p. 378), standing out more and more as a recurrent catastrophe in civilized human existence. The more prolonged and destructive a war has been, the more changed is the world when it is over (*ibid.*, p. 128). It is well, then, to remember that the family has survived many wars.

4. Finally, the specificity of the problem needs to be emphasized. Especially is this the case whenever any historical or comparative approach is made. Historic events, as MacIver reminds us,[5] are unique configurations that do not recur as such. In studying the effects of war upon the family, it is necessary to recognize a number of differentials, of which the following seem to be the more important: (a) the nature of the war; (b) character and longevity of participation; (c) relative success or failure; (d) nature of the family life at the time of the war; (e) community and regional configuration; and (f) age or stage of the development of the culture.[6] From this follow two important facts: first, that the impact of World War II upon the American family had its own distinctive features; and, second, that these varied considerably from one area and population element to another within the nation.

[3] P. Sorokin, *Social and Cultural Dynamics* (New York: American Book Co., 1937), vol. 3, pp. 309, 316, 360–362.

[4] Quincy Wright, *A Study of War* (Chicago: University of Chicago Press, 1942).

[5] Robert M. MacIver, *Social Causation* (Boston: Ginn, 1942), p. 257.

[6] Space does not permit the merited discussion of each of these, but brief analyses of some can be found in the author's article, "The Family in Past Wars," in *The Annals of the American Academy of Political and Social Science* (Philadelphia: Sept., 1943), pp. 3–5.

The Sequence of Wartime Familial Changes

The more one considers the over-all relationship between war and the family, the more does a fourfold sequence of fairly measurable consequences seem to emerge. Stated in the order of their development they are: (1) changes in the nature and rate of marriage; (2) changes in the birth rate; (3) changes in the field of family problems; and (4) changes in the social responsibility for child care. Each of these will be examined briefly with particular reference to the United States during and after World War II.

1. Changes in the nature and rate of marriage

The Second World War began in Europe in September, 1939, and one immediate effect upon this country was an upswing of the business cycle. In September, 1940, the Selective Training and Service Act was passed, and our own defense preparations began. In December, 1941, a state of war was declared, which terminated in the summer of 1945. In June, 1950, hostilities began in Korea. With these dates in mind, it is interesting to consider Table 17, showing marriage rates since 1938.

TABLE 17

MARRIAGE RATES, PER 1000 POPULATION, 1938–1950 [7]

1938	10.2	1945	12.4
1939	10.5	1946	16.4
1940	11.9	1947	13.9
1941	12.6	1948	12.4
1942	13.1	1949	10.6
1943	11.8	1950	11.1
1944	10.9		

From this table and supplementary data examined it is evident that, first, wartime prosperity and, second, our entrance into World War II, resulted in a marked acceleration of the marriage rate. This began in the closing months of 1939 and reached its height in 1942, when the marriage rate was 13.1, the highest ever recorded for the United States. Similarly the rate for 1941 (12.6 per 1000 population) was higher than that for any prior year. Between 1940 and 1943, a total of 6,579,000 marriages took place, a surplus of about 1,118,000 over what could have been expected under normal peacetime conditions.[8]

Following the end of the war in Europe in May, 1945, and the beginning of the return of veterans to the United States, the marriage rate took a

---

[7] Federal Security Agency, National Office of Vital Statistics, *Summary of Marriage and Divorce Statistics*, 37, 3 (Oct. 29, 1952), p. 57.

[8] *Ibid.*, p. 57. See also W. F. Ogburn, "The American Family in World War II," *The Annals of the American Academy of Political and Social Science* (Philadelphia: Sept., 1943), pp. 20–29.

sharp upturn. For cities of 100,000 and over, the number of marriage licenses issued in July, 1945, was 22.2 per cent over the corresponding month in 1944, and by November, 1945, the increase was 37.1 per cent. The number of provisional licenses issued for the entire year 1945 was 1,632,156, an increase of 11.3 per cent over 1944. This marked increase continued to the summer of 1946. For the first quarter of 1946, the total number of licenses granted was 527,866, an increase of 57.1 per cent over the same quarter in 1944. For cities of 100,000 population and over, the increase for April and May was 59.8 and 64.3 per cent over the number for the corresponding months of 1945. For the entire year of 1946, the marriage rate reached a high of 16.4. Beginning with 1947, the rate declined until the summer of 1950, when, following the outbreak of hostilities in Korea, a sudden and dramatic upswing again occurred. Later in the year 1950, and during 1951, the rate resumed its downward trend.

Wartime changes in the age at marriage merit special reference because of their significance for the marriage pattern. One of these was the sharp increase in the number of young men entering marriage. Records for New York State, exclusive of New York City, show that almost three times as many boys under twenty were married in 1942 as were married in 1939. The rise was particularly marked in 1942, the first full calendar year of participation in the war. Both the Selective Service Act and wartime prosperity were significant factors in bringing this about. Striking, too, was the increasing tendency of these young men to marry women older than themselves. A second change in the age of marriage was the relative increase of marriages among persons thirty-five years of age and over. In New York State, from 1939 to 1942, the increase among women marrying in that age span was 73 per cent; for men, 65 per cent.[9] In a later chapter, the population problems introduced by these and similar facts are carefully considered.

Brief reference to the trends in the marriage rates during the war period among other nations is also in order. Marked variations prevail here. Among the English-speaking Allies, marriage rates increased appreciably with the outbreak of the war, until in each country an all-time high level was reached. This happened first in England, Wales, and Scotland (1940), and later in Canada and the United States. In the occupied countries, marriage rates fell during the early years of the occupancy but made marked recoveries subsequently, in spite of the recruiting of young men and women for labor in Germany and elsewhere. Among the Axis powers, the rates declined markedly during the war period — Germany dropping from 11.1 in 1939 to 7.4 in 1942; Italy from 7.2 in 1939 to 6.3 in 1942. Following the war, rates rose generally.[10]

Having postwar problems in mind, it is well to inquire briefly into the nature and range of these war marriages. Objective examination suggests that they fall into at least five groups. First were those culminating normal processes of courtship and planning, unique perhaps only in the incidental

[9] *Statistical Bulletin* (Metropolitan Life Insurance Company, May, 1944), pp. 5–7.
[10] *Ibid.* (Nov., 1944), pp. 3–4. See also Dec., 1951, Bulletin.

aspects of time, place, and other circumstances. Happily, these constituted a large proportion of the total. By way of contrast were those where cool calculation played its part, growing out of the direct, tangible, material advantages to be gained by marrying a member of the armed forces. The wife of an enlisted man received $50 a month, regardless. National Service Life Insurance, provided by the government, could be taken to the amount of $10,000. As of March 15, 1943, the average amount per life insured was $6,857. After the war, there were the possibilities of pensions, bonuses, and other grants. Without detracting from the legitimate purposes of such financial arrangements, the fact remains that marriage to a serviceman was a quick and direct way for women to supplement their incomes; that some women anticipated these advantages unduly is shown by the recurring appearance of those who married more than once, obviously for purposes of revenue. A third group of war marriages made matrimony a conventional cloak for sex satisfactions during periods of leave. The soldier has his leave. The future is uncertain. Does not life owe him something? And marriage is the covenant which the girl, her family, his background, and the customary mores demand. Akin to this is a much larger group where the wartime marriage satisfies some psychological need, with the particular choice of the mate as a secondary consideration. The homesick soldier who wanted solace and the frustrated private who needed to regain his ego were obvious illustrations of this type. Once the wave of such war marriages got under way, the movement generated its own fervor and claimed its victims among young men and young women alike. This suggests a fifth type: the partly imitative, partly compulsive marriage. War marriages are the vogue, everyone else is doing it; why not we? The pressure upon young people merely to marry, somewhat regardless of whom they married, was a tremendous one during the war years. This pressure operated at the induction center, in the platoon, on the ship, in the ground crew, in the girls' sorority, in the crowd, in the clique — everywhere the contagion of example. It came to be, at times, like shopping at a bargain counter. One might not exactly want the article offered, but sales are rapid, and if one doesn't purchase it, the next person in line will. Besides, one might be able to utilize the article later on, who knows. Some of these marriages, sudden in conception and execution and popularly referred to as love-at-first-sight marriages, obviously were of a compulsive sort — a kind of psychological mechanism by which one forced oneself to accept a bargain as the best bargain possible under the circumstances. Basic to at least the last two types is a conception of marriage as a status-achieving device, elsewhere developed by the author of this chapter.[11]

From the foregoing analysis, two conclusions may be drawn. First is the fact that many war marriages proceeded from motives which do not ordinarily make for permanent marital success. To be sure, unfortunate and unworthy matrimonial choices are always being made. Since mar-

---

[11] James H. S. Bossard, *Marriage and the Child* (Philadelphia: University of Pennsylvania Press, 1940), chap. 8; also, "Marriage as a Status-Achieving Device," *Sociology and Social Research* (Sept.–Oct., 1944), pp. 1–10.

riage has been romanticized and individualized in our culture, mate selection has not been conspicuous for exercise of intelligence. The whole current literature on the family emphasizes this. But war unmistakably increases the proportion of unwise marriages: marriages between persons not sufficiently known to each other, of differing cultures, from dissimilar social levels, and proceeding from motives that do not lend themselves to permanently satisfying attachments. This in turn suggests the second conclusion: that postwar developments and problems will be, in corresponding degree, the product of the types of marriages contracted during the preceding years. War marriages dictate the shape of postwar family relations and problems. Further, there is more than a little indication that the present state of high tension, whether called "cold war" or whatever, brings with it many of the marital consequences of "hot war." In particular, some of the changes in birth rate, recounted below, may well be attributable to "cold war" circumstances.

2. *Changes in the birth rate*

The second part of the sequence pattern consists of changes in the birth rate. The course of these changes follows, at the natural biological interval, changes in the marriage rate, modified by such other factors as the disposal of the armed forces, the length of the war, and the nature of the national economy. In the United States these factors produced, during the period of the Second World War, the following series of changes. A small increase manifested itself during 1940, chiefly in the second half of the year. The passage of the Selective Service Act (September, 1940) in proper course of time gave it a decided spurt, as did the declaration of war (December, 1941). By 1943, the birth rate was almost 23, a third higher than in 1933. Small fluctuations occurred until 1946, when the earlier rise of the marriage rate manifested itself in a marked increase of the birth rate. Table 18 shows annual estimated birth rates, corrected for underregistration, by selected years, 1915–1950.

TABLE 18

BIRTH RATES, CORRECTED FOR UNDERREGISTRATION, UNITED STATES, 1915–1950 [12]

1915	29.5	1943	22.7
1920	27.7	1944	21.2
1925	25.1	1945	20.4
1930	21.3	1946	24.1
1935	18.7	1947	26.6
1940	19.4	1948	24.9
1941	20.3	1949	24.6
1942	22.2	1950	23.5

[12] Federal Security Agency, National Office of Vital Statistics, *U. S. Summary of Vital Statistics, 1949*, 36, 22 (Sept. 10, 1952), p. 472.

The general trends of reproductivity on the basis of the age of the mother and the size of the family, manifest in the years before 1939, were continued during the war years. These can be summarized briefly. First, young mothers, in the age groups 20–29 years, were chiefly responsible for the rapid wartime rise in the birth rate, continuing a trend manifest since 1933; second, women at ages of 40 and over continued to show the downward trend evident among them for many years; third, the birth rate in large families (with five children or more) also continued its downward trend, an obvious correlate of the facts on the ages of mothers; and fourth, with the decline of the marriage rate after 1942 and the decline of the birth rate beginning with November, 1943, a drop in the birth rate of younger women became inevitable. It is significant to note, too, that comparing 1940 and 1943 birth data the largest relative increase of births was in families in which the father was under 20 years of age. The percentage of the rise for these years was 65.5, varying with the age of the wife and being highest when the wife was between 20 and 24 years. In this male group, anticipated military service was undoubtedly responsible in large measure for this marked increase.

These references to the age of the parents and the size of the family are of importance: first, as indications of family structures formed during the war period; second, as proof that the marked wartime rise of the birth rate must not be interpreted to mean a reversal of the long-time trend toward the small family system; and third, as evidence that, from the standpoint of the national population, the wartime surplus of births must be considered as a moving forward of births which would have occurred in ensuing years in the normal course of events.

3. Changes in the field of family problems

First the marriage rate, then the birth rate, then the divorce and other rates of family disorganization change under the impact of war. Scarcely had the spurt of war marriages begun than students of the family began to predict a marked rise in the rates of family problems. Such predictions centered chiefly on the divorce rate and forecast that it would approximate from one third to two fifths of the marriage rate. These predictions are now in process of fulfillment, although the measurable evidences of it are, at the present writing, just beginning to emerge. By agreement between the respective authors the data on divorce are presented by Dr. Elliott in the chapter devoted to that topic (see pp. 676–680).

A too exclusive reliance upon the data on divorce as a measure of postwar family problems obviously needs to be avoided, and for a number of reasons. First, there is a substantial element in the population whose religious affiliations, convictions, or community traditions make divorce an unacceptable way out of family difficulties. Second, for another large proportion of the population, the financial cost of divorce is prohibitive, or is considered to be. This cost of divorce is different, it will be realized, from the difficulty or ease in securing it. Third, by the pattern of social values of many people, divorce is not necessary for a dissolution of a marriage. A couple agree, or one member so determines, and they go their respective romantic ways regardless of earlier legal commitments. Living together by persons previously married and not divorced is quite common, especially among the lower classes in our urban areas. Finally, the rate of legal terminations is only one of many indices of marital difficulties, as the whole recent literature on family tensions, marital discord, and family conflict so clearly reveals.

4. Changes in the social responsibility for child care

Relatively little attention has been paid thus far to the fourth part of the sequence of changes suggested in this chapter; yet it must be evident that what happens to the family reacts in turn upon its children. The family is, from one point of view, the intermediary institution between the child and society, and when it does not function, the larger society must. It is the contention of this chapter, then, that the postwar period will witness a marked increase in the proportion of children that will need to be cared for by agencies other than their parents. This judgment is based upon three groups of facts. The first of these is historical. A careful reading of the history of child care in this country shows that, during the periods following two of our major wars, the Revolutionary and the Civil, there was considerable development in the social care of dependent and neglected children. After the Revolutionary War, New York, for example, in 1784 took the control of pauper children from church authorities and gave it to the overseers of the poor. A number of the larger cities enlarged or changed the location of the almshouse during these years, the almshouse being customarily used for institutional care of dependent children. In the decade after the Civil War, there was in particular a great deal of activity in the public care of children. In 1866 Massachusetts established a state primary school for the care of "unsettled" poor children and passed a law providing that children under sixteen years of age who, by reason of the neglect, crime, drunkenness, or other vices of parents, were suffered to be growing up without salutary parental control, might be committed by the court to the proper designated place. In 1866 Ohio authorized the establishment of the County Children's Homes system. In 1867 New York created its State Board of Charities, which found on its first examinations a total of 2231 children in almshouses. In 1869 Michigan appointed a Commission to make "exhaustive inquiry into the condition of children in county poorhouses" and in 1874 established its well-known State School system. In various other states conditions which developed during this decade in the public care of children led to reforms in subsequent years.[13]

Two other groups of facts are important relative to the proportion of children in need of public care. One is the marked increase in family dis-

[13] The reader will find an excellent summary of the history of these and other changes in Homer Folks, *The Care of Destitute, Neglected and Delinquent Children* (New York: Macmillan, 1902).

organization and disintegration that are the aftermath of war, conditions that lead finally to problems of child care. The second group of facts relate to the changing roles of the immediate and the extended or kinship group. Davis has pointed out the significance of these changes for children of the divorced, showing how in other societies the wider use of the kinship group solves problems which the greater reliance upon the immediate family intensifies in our own.[14] With our characteristic reliance upon the immediate family, the typical young child in America today views the world from a very narrow ledge, so to speak, and when that ledge of security wobbles or disintegrates, there is so often no family or other support save that of the agency arms of the larger society.

SOME IMMEDIATE POSTWAR PROBLEMS

Certain family problems resulting from World War II were quick to appear. In large part these have resulted from the processes of family separation and reunion; others, such as the inadequacy of housing facilities, have been due to sudden large-scale population transfers against the background of wartime shortages. Brief consideration will be given to the more important of these immediate changes.

Wartime Separations

War involves the mobility of people on a scale of tremendous proportions. The calling of millions of men to the colors for military service is but the more spectacular phase of such mobility. Others are called to the tributary activities of war; in this war the services of men and women of all mature ages have been utilized. This involves large-scale movement of civilian as well as military populations. From the standpoint of the family, the basic consideration in these movements of people is the separation of members of the family from one another under the conditions which war engenders. Three types of such separations may be noted as of outstanding frequency and importance. First and most obvious was the separation of husband and wife, involving the breakup of a crystallized relationship and the creation for both of the problem of adjusting, for the time being, to a nonfamily pattern of living. Second was the separation of parent, usually father, from younger child, involving a shift from biparental to maternal rearing of the child and the loss of the father's contribution to the child's continuing personality development. In many cases the absence of the father meant the loss of the family disciplinarian, such loss coming at a time when other members of the family, particularly the mother, were already disturbed. The general atmosphere in many homes in which wartime separations were made was one compounded of

[14] Kingsley Davis, in "Children and Divorced Parents," *Law and Contemporary Problems,* vol. 10, No. 5 (Durham: Duke University, 1944), pp. 700–710.

anxiety, confusion, hysteria, worry, and sentimentality, in varying proportions from case to case. Finally there was the separation of grown sons and daughters from older parents. Relatively little has been said of these separations, yet in many cases these have been of major importance, breaking up relationships which had developed and taken root during the years and severing ties of emotional and financial interdependence.

Reunion in the Postwar Family

With the cessation of war, new husbands return to the destiny of their choice; changed husbands are reunited with changed wives. Here in briefest outline is the basis of the reunion problems in the postwar family. Selected aspects will serve to identify some of the typical cases and processes involved.

First there is the reunion of couples married in the atmosphere and tempo of war. Perhaps most of these couples were separated prematurely, meaning that they were separated by the exigencies of war before the essential marriage relations were fully established. In some instances the separation occurred before the marriage was consummated; in some, before there was a basis of personal acquaintance; in many, before there could be a modicum of personality adjustment; in virtually all, before there could be the requisite emotional integration. The net result was to leave many of the persons with a sense of uncertainty, futility, disillusion, frustration, anger, and even hate. For such persons there was the natural tendency to project on the other the inadequacies which resulted from the situation. Moreover, the longer the separation, the greater the tendency to rationalize the inadequacies which it created. Contrariwise one hears of wartime marriages where a brief and happy interlude of marital experience created earnest longings for its resumption after the war. Reunion in the postwar family has its special meaning for each of these war marriages.

In some of these cases there is the added problem of reunion with one's civilian status. The military is a different world from the civilian, and in times of war it becomes the more important and, for the young and more romantically inclined, the all-engrossing world. In this military world the serviceman, already removed from his civilian setting, gains a military status. The girl he meets and marries (unless they have known each other reasonably well in civilian life) marries him as of this military status. When the war is over, he returns to his civilian status and setting. The colonel in the Army Air Force in sunny California is again a garage attendant, living on the wrong side of the railroad tracks. The farm boy who married the city good-time girlie takes her after the war to his pappy and mammy in the mountains of Tennessee. The girl who "looked good" as a canteen hostess does not fit into your family's modest bungalow. Reunion with civilian status and setting may precipitate difficult and often tragic problems.

Then there are the reunion problems of couples whose wartime separations were a therapeutic experiment or a welcome marital holiday. War, like a career in public life, offers many a family a socially acceptable way out of domestic difficulties. Through the long centuries it is a way which has been used extensively in wartime. Especially has this been true in the case of *mariages de convenance,* where neither divorce nor desertion is feasible. Today, in spite of the availability of other arrangements, war offers to many couples the opportunity for an experimental separation, the temporizing solution of delay, the mathematical chance of the more tragic end, or the honorable rationalization for the *coup de grâce.* For these couples, where the war brought no solution, the peace demands its own decisions.[15]

For many married couples there is reunion after the simple but trenchant fact of separation. Mere separation creates many problems. Perhaps the basic one for many wedded mates is that of rerouting the affectional outgo. When war separates a married couple, a face-to-face relationship gives way to a letter-to-letter relationship. The two are vastly different. They differ in content, in spontaneity, and particularly in clarity. Some people have a letter personality, some do not; some can verbalize well enough to convey or transmit their affections, their emotional attitudes, the whole distinctness and flavor of their personalities; and others manifestly cannot. This letter-to-letter relationship presents its own problems at each socio-intellectual level. Even at so high an intellectual level as the membership of an erudite scientific society, a letter may say now more, now less, than was meant, with no way often of realizing or correcting the misapprehension. The problem is most keen, of course, at the level of those who cannot write or who do so with extreme difficulty. Just what, for example, is the letter-to-letter relationship of those who write and say: "I am well. How is Mom? It is raining. How are you?"

Moreover, in all correspondence, one writes to the "last time I saw you" personality. In other words the serviceman and his wife each carry a picture of the other based on memories, with the last contact looming very large, and it is to this mental image that each writes. It is important to realize this because what happens with the passing of time is that each person changes, so that there develops a difference between the personality "as is" and the "last time I saw you" personality, which in turn may bring a sense of unreality or irrelevance into the correspondence, each writing to a conception of the other which is different from the person as he or she now is. One cannot live on letters alone. The major task of rerouting the face-to-face affectional outgo remains. For the wife there are the following obvious possibilities. She may return to her family and the earlier parent-daughter relationships may be reestablished, albeit on a new basis. If there is a child, or children, she may center her affection there. There may be homosexual developments. Sublimating forms of activity may be accepted. Finally, affectional relationships may be developed with other men with or without sexual exchange and with or without subsequent feelings of guilt. There is ample evidence from this and previous wars that all these reactions occur, and again it is important

[15] George K. Pratt, *Soldier to Civilian* (New York: McGraw-Hill, 1944), pp 41 ff

to remember that the longer the separation continues, the longer the new affectional lines have a chance to crystallize.

There is one feature of the wife's position in World War II which calls for especial comment. Many wives of servicemen were employed in industrial defense positions, earning sizable wages. In addition there was the fifty-dollar monthly allowance. Perhaps her whole family was enjoying war prosperity. If this wife was 22 years old, it meant that she was eight years old when the depression began. Other ages varied correspondingly. What this meant was that these young wives grew up during the depression decade and, if reared in working-class families, the mathematical probability of their having been on relief was very high. More than half the families inducted into military service in eastern urban areas were known to the social service exchanges in their areas. The point is that wartime prosperity brings to such young women a tremendous release from the shadow of economic sorrow, against the background of a World War. This, too, has its implications for the wife's behavior and for wife-husband-in-the-army relationships.

While the wife has been readjusting life, so has her husband. In terms of social process, the first thing that happens when the civilian turns soldier is the passing of the primary-group controls. He is withdrawn from his family, his neighborhood, his church, and all other stable, intimate groups which have exercised the chief controls over his conduct. As he loses his membership in these groups, he frequently shakes off his identification with the erstwhile moral code. He is on his own now, in a behavioristic sense. While he does not reject immediately the old mores, he is likely to think of them as being suspended for the time being. He is on vacation from the mores of his group.

"You're in the army now!" The new soldier joins a military unit, large in size and not operated primarily to accentuate his personal distinctness. He is in a man's world. The old-time feminine controls are gone. There exists an occupational and an attitudinal homogeneity. His new "buddies" are all engaged in the same pursuits, unusual, exciting, and with a stirring rendezvous ahead. What sociologists call an *in-group* has come into being.

Various factors make for new patterns of conduct in this in-group. Army life is rigid. It directs your movements and controls your thinking much of the time. It is a life of routine. When there is temporary release from the schedule, various vagaries of conduct become emotionally satisfying, a phenomenon most striking among the privates and noncommissioned officers. They take the orders. They are the underdogs. An affair with a woman serves to restore status. Moreover, the soldier's military life gives new opportunity; there are no womenfolk to check his hours of pursuit. The uniform has its own appeal in wartime. The government furnishes prophylactics. There is no local court to apprehend him. The girl knows he is in the army; she knows what to expect. And the soldier rationalizes his need. He is serving his country. Indeed, the wearing of the uniform is rationalized as conferring on the soldier a new set of morals.

The former mores continue to have his approval, to be sure, but they hold for folks who stay at home, particularly for his womenfolk. The moral code has to be changed to meet the needs of a unisexual group which is serving the country in time of crisis and danger. For the soldier to "cut loose" at appropriate times and in varying degrees becomes traditional. To drink, to engage in amours, is to behave as the group does. No disgrace is involved in the assumption of certain liberties. The soldier's new in-group approves, for the time being, new forms of conduct. Such transvaluation of the moral code may be temporary; it may last only as long as he is in the army; when he returns to civilian life, he may take up somewhere near where he left off; *but* this is what the situation tends to be as long as the in-group persists.

The mobility of wartime mores has been portrayed in terms of process, centering about the person. This process must be viewed, however, against the general background of war mentality. War is a stirring phenomenon. It stimulates the emotions. It shakes individuals out of the routines of their behavior and their thinking. It emphasizes new experiences and precipitates new judgments. Implied in all this is the loosening of the hold of customary inhibitions. Traditional ways of doing and thinking give way to new desires; impulses long latent find opportunity for release. The social threshold of inhibition is lowered. The mores of the entire society pass into a stage of active transition. New forms of conduct come to be approved, based on a present that seems unreal and a future that is obviously uncertain. Why, then, not take the cash and let the credit go? "Tonight, who cares: tomorrow, who knows?" As Waller has put it, war involves "hedonistic life adjustments on a short-term basis."[16] It is therefore secularizing to an extreme degree; no other set of processes exerts so disruptive an effect on sacred patterns.

Perhaps the most important fact about such couples is that each member of a pair is sharing different life experiences during the period of separation. Mates are not filed in secluded portfolios when war separates them. They go on living in their respective worlds. Their experiences may be red with infidelities or pink with prospects thereof; the essential fact is that they are living in worlds which are different, often glaringly different, from each other.

What war does to husband and wife comes to a focus with their peacetime reunion. The basic problem, pictured in terms of process, is somewhat as follows. When a couple marry, they begin usually with a number of common interests. These pertain, for instance, to matters of home, children, sex, and leisure-time activities. There is a substantial area of agreement in interest and in life values. Then a man goes to war. He may see his comrades shot to pieces. He lives in a foxhole amid muck and filth and insects and disease. He sees blood spilled and human life sacrificed. He sees commanding generals broken; states are dissolved; empires may crumble. The whole cosmos changes.

Then the soldier returns home. He is not the same and never can be

16 Willard Waller, *War and the Family* (New York: Dryden Press, 1940), p. 13.

the same again. His perspective has changed. His values are different. He and his wife resume housekeeping. She too may have changed, but not in the same directions. This girl, this woman, once so sensible and attractive, now seems to him silly and superficial. The things that are important to her seem now to him to be the essence of the trivial. They are measuring life by wholly different yardsticks.

Or, perhaps, he does not get into active combat. He stays chained to a desk. Here he learns to look at the world from a worm's-eye view. To the extent that he has been a good soldier at this job, he has made this an important part of his life. Thus he becomes the small time, triplicate ordering, mimeographing bureaucrat who tries men's souls in so limited a transaction as the purchase of a three-cent stamp. It is this type that the war bride of yesteryear finds herself living with in the peace of tomorrow, through the endless succession, not of stamp purchases, but of three meals a day, common bed, and other domestic accompaniments. Or he may go on chow or laundry detail in Florida or Iceland or Australia so long and so completely that he loses all perspective of his relation to the army, the war, and his family.

Another aspect of wartime separations of husband and wife, which has significance for their peacetime reunion, rests in the fact that a great many servicemen have had opportunities for personal development much greater than have their wives. Many of them have received considerable instruction, both technical and cultural. Some were made officers and placed in charge of other men. This often changes even the most intimate relations of a man. Thousands of husbands went and lived in distant parts of the world. They have come in contact with different cultures, learned new ways of living, formed new values. Travel, in war as in peace, is a great educator. Meanwhile the wife has remained at home on the Tennessee farm, in the Carolina mill town, or on the New Hampshire homestead. Her mental horizon has remained the same, changing only with the slower tempo of her home community.

Special mention must be made of the reunion of American servicemen with foreign war brides. By an Act of Congress (December 28th, 1945, Public Law 271) it was provided that alien spouses or children of United States citizens serving in or honorably discharged from the armed forces, might be admitted to the United States for permanent residence without meeting many of the usual immigration requirements.[17] It is estimated that by the end of July, 1946, when the program of the War Department to transport war dependents had ceased, about 70,000 foreignborn brides and children entered the United States. Of these, 52,500 were brides and 17,500 were children. Although they came from practically every country in which our armed forces were located, about 60,000 hailed from the European and Mediterranean areas and the remainder from the Pacific theater of operations. Of the former, about three-fouths came from Great Britain; about 15 per cent from France and Italy; and the remainder from Belgium,

[17] Ernest E. Salisbury, "The Immigration of G.I. Brides," *Monthly Review* (Immigration and Naturalization Service, U. S. Department of Justice, May, 1946), pp. 305–308.

Ireland, North Africa, and other countries, with a total of more than thirty nationalities represented. Of the Pacific area brides, most (about 85 per cent) were from Australia. The age concentration of these brides was in the early twenties, with a considerable proportion in the late teens. About one-third of them were mothers. Comparison with the statistics of overseas marriages in World War I indicates that the present situation is one of much greater extent and variety. For the years 1946 to 1950, inclusive, a total of 333 husbands, 114,691 wives, 4,669 alien children were admitted into the country as the result of marriages contracted by members of the armed forces with persons of foreign countries.[18] More recent figures, which take into account our Korean and related overseas enterprises, show an even greater range of "entangling alliances."

Relatively little has been written of the reunion of the serviceman with his family other than his wife. There is, for example, the teen-age lad who went away as a schoolboy, perhaps dominated by his father or pampered by a solicitous mother and more than likely spoken of by the neighbors as "that kid next door." Now he returns a veteran, perhaps an officer, possibly the holder of a medal. He has come of age, he has matured, he has been places and seen things. "Something new has been added." The old relationships obviously cannot be resumed, but in the beginning only he may be aware of it.[19]

The Returning Father and His Family

Hill and his associates have shed significant light on the stresses of wartime separation and reunion adjustment.[20] Obviously the father has his distinctive role in the family and for the child constitutes the complementary half of its biparental rearing. When the father leaves the family, his contributions are lost to the child and to the mother. Faced with this situation, both child and mother make compensatory adjustments. These may or may not be mentally or socially sound. When, now, the father returns to his family, there are not only the customary relations with the child to be established, but also the compensatory relationships between the child and the mother (and/or others) to be terminated or readjusted. The two following cases, which might be multiplied indefinitely, will serve to illustrate some of the difficulties encountered.

Mr. Smith was a Lieutenant Commander in the Navy, who came home to his wife and his three-year-old son, whom he had seldom seen. His wife had

[18] *Statistical Bulletin* (Metropolitan Life Insurance Company, June, 1946), pp. 1–2. See also, Bureau of the Census, *Statistical Abstract of the United States, 1952* (Washington, D. C.: Government Printing Office), p. 100.

[19] Ethel Ginsburg, "Veteran into Civilian: The Process of Readjustment," *Mental Hygiene,* (Jan., 1945), pp. 7–19.

[20] Reuben Hill, *Families Under Stress* (New York: Harper, 1949); Elise Boulding, "Family Adjustments to War Separation and Reunion," *The Annals of the American Academy of Political and Social Science* (November, 1950), pp. 59–67.

lived alone with the son during her husband's absence. The boy was at a difficult and important age so far as discipline is concerned. The mother had been doing fairly well, though she was more lenient than strict. But Mr. Smith was appalled that his young son did not jump to his command at the moment of the command. He had been used to that in the service. His method of punishing the baby when the baby misbehaved was to shout, "Come here!" Then when, and if, the baby came, he would slap him. The baby was afraid of his father, and the mother was very much annoyed at the whole situation. She understood, and was sympathetic with both, but could not do anything with her husband. Only the passage of time and the resumption of something approaching civilian routine bettered the situation.

The wife of Commander Jones spent the two years of her husband's absence trying to make up to his two teen-aged boys for the loss of their father. She also was set upon not letting the fact that they were growing up in an era of war prevent them from having the same kind of irresponsible adolescence that she had enjoyed. She painted up their father as "the man who was winning the war," and the boys could hardly wait till this hero returned. When he did, they were sadly disappointed. Instead of sitting around the fire telling them tales of gory naval engagements, he set out on a program of curtailing their liberties and giving them jobs to do to prepare them for the serious sort of world they were going to have to live in. In short, they got more than a taste of "good navy discipline."

Headline Postwar Family Problems

Another way to approach family problems in the postwar world is through the recordings of the daily press. True, these are "news" items which include the exceptional, the startling, the dramatic, the seamy, and the publicly discussed aspects of family problems; but what boils over the sides of the kettle is made up of the ingredients still within the kettle. The boiling over is simply a matter of temperature. Presented herewith, then, is a summary of news clippings on postwar problems with particular reference to war veterans, covering the ten months' period from September 1, 1945, to July 2, 1946. The material is limited, as far as is possible, to situations which seem to have been the product of wartime and postwar conditions. The two newspapers utilized were the *Philadelphia Evening Bulletin,* the largest evening newspaper in America, and *The Philadelphia Inquirer,* third largest morning newspaper. The June, 1946, circulations of these newspapers were 719,000 and 606,000 respectively, thus indicating a wide coverage, as well as dissemination, of news. This assemblage of newspaper material is part of a two-year study of postwar family problems that was made under the auspices of the William T. Carter Foundation of the University of Pennsylvania.

The summary here presented is partial and tentative, but includes the following items.

I. *Reunion and Family Relationships*

1. *Enoch Arden Marriages.* Shortly after the cessation of hostilities, the most dramatic news items concerning family relationships were those surrounding the servicemen who had been listed as missing or killed and who were found alive, usually as prisoners of war, after long internment. Between September 1, 1945, and February 21, 1946, seven cases of Enoch Arden marriages appeared in Philadelphia newspapers. These were direct results of war. The women, because of notifications from the Army and Navy, had assumed that they were free to remarry. The hasty remarriages may themselves have been partly attributable to the wartime atmosphere in which men and women met, courted, and married quickly. Aside from these common elements, the special problems of family readjustment and the personal reactions were unique in each case. Of greatest significance to the families were the four cases in which the husband, released from internment, was expecting a quick and happy reunion and in which the shock to their wives was equally great. Three of these couples had the second marriage annulled. Of these, one husband came home to attempt reconciliation with his nineteen year old wife who had "married" his own uncle, another to recourt the mother of his son whom he had never seen, the third to adopt the child of his wife by her second husband. In the fourth case, the woman attempted suicide under the weight of her decision; the three concerned talked over their problem seriously and could reach no agreement because the woman did not want to give up either husband. The other Enoch Arden marriages showed a different face. In two instances, the legally married couples had been estranged before the war separation. Divorce and remarriage were solutions here. And finally, the girl who wanted to keep her second "husband" was disowned by him. It was not a marriage, he said, but just one of those service acquaintanceships. These cases are the spectacular results of the return of "dead" men from the war. Others escape publicity but undoubtedly the people concerned do not all escape many of the elements of the situations described. Thought-provoking is the fact that soon after V-J Day, 3483 of such missing men were found alive. A total of 19,584 unfound cases remained, as of that date, on the casualty lists. (The state of mind of those who still cling to the belief that the missing may yet reappear is better imagined than described.)

2. *Bigamy.* Between September 18th and April 12th, eight cases of bigamy committed by or with servicemen were featured in the newspapers studied. Although bigamy is not in itself a phenomenon of wartime society exclusively, these cases either were entered into because of war conditions or were easily facilitated because of them. In all instances discovery came when peacetime brought the expectation of normal family life once more. Loneliness, the fear that they would never again see their former mates, and the opportunity afforded by long-distance separations precipitated both men and women into bigamy.

3. *Extramarital Relationships.* Precipitated and facilitated by the same

wartime conditions as were the bigamous relationships were those alliances, found in the study, that were entered into more loosely, without benefit of certificate. One woman explained that she had always leaned heavily upon her husband for advice. When he was taken away from her, she leaned on another man, with the result that they entered into a more intimate and less intellectual relationship. A returned veteran writes for advice. He had been so lonely at camp without his charming wife. Then he had met a girl "just like her." He had neglected to tell the girl that he was married, and now that he was home again his conscience hurt. Should he tell his wife?

These relationships showed significant differences from the bigamous ones. They occurred more generally. The story of infidelity appeared in feature articles, in reports of suits for divorce and custody of children, in legal proceedings over money, in servicemen's question columns, in letters to editors, and in columns answering personal problems. Also, these relationships were often temporary and frequent. Husbands and wives returned to each other to discover that their mates had indulged in a series of affairs during separation. Again, though few children were reported as figuring in the bigamous marriages, many were involved in these affairs. Frequently, illegitimate children were the cause of discovery. A London war bride came to America on money sent by her husband, but upon arrival she went to the serviceman who had remained in London after her husband had left and whose child was subsequently born to her at his relatives' home. A Navy enlisted man and his wife abandoned a baby because the baby was hers but not his.

Significant was a statement of Mrs. Lois Parsons, chairman of the Council of Social Agencies Committee on Unmarried Parenthood, who reported that one out of every twelve children then born in Washington, D. C., was illegitimate. She said that for the period 1943-45 an entirely different type of person was becoming the unmarried mother. A surprising number of illegitimate babies were being born to women in professional or semiprofessional fields, including teaching, nursing, and secretarial work. She blamed wartime loneliness and the fast tempo of the capital.

4. *The "Lesser" Problems.* It is behind the front page that one finds those problems of reunion that are less sensational but that are visited upon the largest number of people.

In the columns offering advice on personal troubles one finds some of the situations confronting plain Mary Smith and John Brown when they are reunited after wartime separation. The drafting of husbands was admittedly a godsend to some women. But wars do end. Four women wrote that they had hoped war would change their men but that, alas, they had come home just as difficult to get along with. The women had become used to a pleasant life without these detriments to happiness. How could they now take them back? Other women, eagerly awaiting the return of their husbands, were shocked to find them different men from the ones they had remembered. The large majority of letters to these columns are of this type. And of these, the greatest number of complaints deal with the seeming inability of the men to settle down to normal domestic life. They want to go out every night, and do so though wives have to stay home with children. They do not want to assume responsibility, or to care for children, or to look for work; they are content to sit, or go out, or gamble, and let the in-laws pay the bills. They are shiftless and lazy. They are not affectionate. They chafe at domestic ties. All these complaints come in a few weeks or months after the veterans' return, and although many writers think they may be expecting too much too soon, yet they are already experiencing a feeling of hopelessness about establishing satisfactory relationships.

In a good many instances, the readjustment was taking place in the home of the wife's parents. Here, the wife wants to know how she can adjust her parents and husband to each other; how she can get away from her parents without hurting their feelings; or how she can persuade her husband to make his own home. Two veterans complain that their wives have become opposed to, and unfitted for, keeping house, because of having lived with mother and father during the war. They refuse to accept the responsibilities of wifehood. And a young girl tells that since his return her husband is completely tied to his mother's apron strings, and wants to build a house right next door!

There are the formerly happy wives who have been careful and faithful during long years of separation and who have been shocked into distrust. "He tears up his letters carefully." "He has his mail forwarded to another address." "I found a picture of a girl in his wallet." "He says everything is all right. But I keep wondering." And there are the girls whose men are sent home as psychoneurotics. Those girls are worried and frightened at every sign of moodiness, temper, or illness. The burden is too great for one who does not quite understand but who has been charged with the responsibility for his adjustment to civilian and marital life.

Also behind the front page one discovers that poor stewardship is a cause for disillusion upon reunion. Provident servicemen have sent money home to their families during their years overseas in order that they might have a fund on which to start their civilian life. When they come home, they are sometimes disappointed. Some wives have been careless and have simply spent the money. Some have been sly, using the funds to buy homes in their own names. Others have quite maliciously tied up the money, insurance, or bonds, and refuse to accept their husbands back. Parents as well as wives are guilty of this sort of conduct, either using or refusing to part with the money sent to them by their sons for safekeeping. All these situations are revealed in actual suits brought by servicemen for return of their savings. The amounts involved range from a few hundred dollars to thirty thousand dollars.

5. *The Disabled Veteran.*[21] Headlined in the newspapers are reports of the courageous adjustment to civilian life of maimed and blinded

[21] For an excellent analysis of problems of the disabled veteran, see Ernest R. and Harriet R. Mowrer, "The Disabled Veteran in the Family," *The Annals of the American Academy of Political and Social Science* (May, 1945), pp. 150–159.

veterans, of their courageous wives who welcome them back, and of the women who marry them upon their return. Wives assist in setting up businesses, in buying chicken farms, and in starting out new lives with handicapped mates. A Master Sergeant who lost parts of all four limbs starts out on a vacation with his wife in a car built for his special use. Nurses marry their blinded patients and plastic surgery cases whose real faces had been blown away. A British girl flies from London to marry her fiancé who was paralyzed from the waist down. And a girl marries her childhood sweetheart who lost both hands in the war. These people are featured as making fine adjustments. But in a brief and unfeatured article in October, 1945, one reads this story: there are 83,000 men currently in Administration hospitals. A peak load of from 200,000 to 250,000 is estimated by 1965. This compares with 61,000 hospitalized twenty years after World War I.

6. *International Marriages*. Reference to this type of marriage has already been made. It is significant to add that their first problem, that of getting to the United States, aroused more controversy in letters to editors than any one other type during the ten months of the study. The GI's wanted their wives brought home. The wives wanted to come. American women wanted their own GI husbands given first priority on ships and thought American men should not have married foreign women at all. The foreign brides often had to wait, and some are still waiting for reunion with their husbands. This necessitates long separations while husbands are again in a congenial and familiar atmosphere, very different from the situation in which they met and married these girls. Some of the wives will never reach the States. The application for their passage must be made by their American husbands, whose ardor for foreign entanglements has long since cooled.

Once here, the newspapers follow their adjustments. Some of them glow with contentment over their new country, their American in-laws, their husbands, and the neighbors who welcome them with teas and receptions. Some do not. American GI's have a reputation for idealizing their country when they are away from it, and many foreign girls have taken their words literally. One English girl whose GI had bragged about the two homes he owned in America fled from him and demanded a divorce when she found she had to live in a "shack" with him and his small sister and brother. Fifty Australian brides who returned to Australia said that they were homesick; that they were disappointed because America was not like the movies; that American women resented them and said they had "pinched" their men; that American life was bedlam after the quiet of Australia; and that the cost of living was much higher. A group of British wives also complained about the living costs but were chiefly appalled by the rudeness of the people in New York City, the pushing and jamming into vehicles of transportation, the ill-mannered children and dirty living quarters. Others, less vocal, found life over here very bewildering. The food is peculiar. Their husbands like coffee but not the way their wives know how to make it. Americans have no reverence for the British ritual of tea-brewing. The money is different and hard to get used to. Two young brides got lost, one on a train and one in the subway. They spoke no English and could not ask their way. One little Italian bride committed suicide. She had been homesick and increasingly despondent ever since her arrival. Mentioned in the papers, though their special problems are as yet undisclosed, are the marriages of 150 American girls who went abroad to live with the British servicemen they met here during the war, and the marriages between American servicewomen and foreign-born men, for whose speedy entry into the United States Congress had to pass special legislation.

7. *Ex-Servicewomen.* New in our nation's history is the problem of the readjustment of the servicewoman to civilian life. About 400,000 of them, most of whom are potential family-makers, had to come back to parents, careers, or marriage. In interviews, some of them tell of their change to civilian life. First of all, they feel like "forgotten women." No such machinery has been set up to help them as there is for the men, and the men get preference everywhere. They miss the confidence the uniform gave. A uniform marked them as special, as someone in authority. Now they are but one of the crowd. They had not been living in family groups but in barracks with lots of girls their own age. They miss this companionship. They had been the center of attention of many men. Now they are back in a land where men are relatively scarce. Their lives had been exciting and glamorous. Now they must descend to the normal. Some of them want to postpone marriage and keep on living glamorous lives while they are still young; others want to marry as soon as possible. But they feel that their service careers have in some ways made them better fitted for wifehood. They have learned order, patience, and adaptability to discipline; to know all kinds of people; to take an active part in world problems; to understand men's problems and to make adjustments. Individual reactions to changes between military and civilian moral codes are shown in two cases. One ex-servicewoman, who cannot face the stigma of her baby born out of wedlock, abandons it. Another accepts hers as a responsibility and claims a dependency allotment for it when she applies for college tuition under the GI Bill. A special problem is that of the 123 disabled servicewomen who were entered in the vocational rehabilitation program of the Veterans Administration to be fitted for jobs.

II. *The World in Which They Live*

The veterans, who on their return must somehow begin living intimately with people who are slightly strange to them, are also confronted with a world that has become changed in some of its most fundamental aspects. If there were only the problems of adjustment to one's closest associates to concentrate upon, there might be fewer failures. But the veteran cannot simply sit down and learn to live over again with his family. He must have a roof over his head, he must find work of training to equip him for work, and he must meet the day-to-day exigencies of life as they come along relentlessly whether or not he is settled in mind, home, and occupation. All these things must be faced immediately and at the same time by most veterans.

1. *Housing.* Many veterans complain to the papers about the red tape surrounding GI loans for homes. They had been led to dream of coming home, getting money, and buying or building a home — just like that. Many have found that the world of finance is still run on the basis of good risks and bad risks rather than of who fought for freedom and who did not. The major problem, however, is the simple fact that there *is* no place to live. This problem has been increasing dangerously. In November, 1945, an *Evening Bulletin* poll in Philadelphia showed one veteran out of five having housing trouble. On June 8, 1946, the Veterans Administration reported that 60 per cent of a sample of veterans polled were still looking vainly for homes or apartments three or four months after their discharge. One reads of veterans and their families living in tents, in jails, in railroad stations, in converted chicken houses, in automobiles, in Quonset huts, and in caves; and of discharged veterans of months' standing still separated from their wives and children for lack of a place to live. These spectacular abodes are usually very temporary. Someone "moves over" and lets the family in. But far from temporary has been the crowding of families into a few rooms and the wholesale amount of living with in-laws. Barbara Barnes, columnist for the *Bulletin,* discloses that at the Philadelphia Homes Registration Office practically everyone interviewed is having trouble with relatives. Miss Ann Coyle, in charge of the office, says: "This in-law problem has been bothering the majority of the men who are house-hunting today. They stress their need for privacy above everything else. Privacy, and a stove on which to cook. Ninety-nine out of every 100 servicemen whom we interview have children. They are looking for a place to start housekeeping in a normal manner." A case cited as fairly representative was that of a Marine Corps officer, his wife, and four children, staying with friends in a five-room apartment. There are nine people, two bedrooms, one bathroom. Three people sleep in one bed; one boy, on two chairs. Coat hangers are suspended from every available ledge; otherwise they live out of suitcases. In the morning the hostess wakens each person by turn — by "bathroom turn." And this cannot be considered as temporary. Though the guests have tried every resource, there is still no serious prospect of their obtaining a home.

2. *Employment.* A second essential to the veteran upon his return is profitable work, and that right quickly in most cases. Few have sufficient funds to support their families long during a period of inflated prices. Furthermore, a job is a psychological necessity to many. Their letters to editors show that, just as they had expected homes as rewards for service, they also expected jobs. And they had thought in terms of the high-paying positions that their civilian friends took during the war, as well as of a position fitting the advancement in life that many of them had made while in the service. Many are still wondering what has happened and who has let them down.

Furthermore, to the veteran it is not only the question of a job but of the right job. Paul Trescott, reporting a survey of Philadelphia's returning vets, shows that only one-third want their old jobs back. Their reasons are these; no future in it, 21 per cent; job no longer exists, 17 per cent; no longer interested in that type of work, 14 per cent; miscellaneous, including not enough pay, 14 per cent; didn't like former job, 10 per cent; not physically able, 8 per cent; want to be self-employed or use new skill, 5 per cent; couldn't get old job back, 5 per cent; going to school, 6 per cent.

This necessity of finding a job is a second problem that is increasing in intensity. By the end of 1945, more than 225,000 ex-servicemen were receiving readjustment allowances, totaling, for the week ending November 17th, $5,233,209. In June, 1946, for Pennsylvania's servicemen alone, more than 949,000 checks were issued, totaling $18,954,718, the highest outlay for one single month.

3. *Education*. A happy solution to the employment problem for many veterans was a return to school or college, financed by the GI Bill of Rights, with a dependency allotment for families, and training for a better job than they are now equipped to take — a happy solution, that is, if they can get into a school, if they can find a place for themselves and their families to live, if they can support themselves on the allotment, and if the employment situation is such at the end of their training that they can find the type of employment they desire.

In December, 1945, there were in college classes 125,000 veterans financed under the GI Bill. Thus began the most extensive development in higher education known to history. By the end of June 30, 1951, a total of 7,600,000 veterans, or nearly one-half of those who served in World War II, received training under the provisions of this act. Of these, 2,200,000 had gone to colleges; 3,300,000, to schools below the college level; 1,400,000 had been given on-the-job training; and 700,000 had studied under the farm training program. Many, in excess of a quarter of the students, were married. About one-tenth of them had children. Housing was a serious problem for many, with overcrowding and/or temporary housing as the only immediate solution. Living within the allotments was a second serious problem. In some cases, wives were employed; in other instances, both husband and wife did extra jobs, meanwhile taking turns in caring for the baby. A third major problem was the combination of educational application with domestic duties. Fathers cut classes when babies were born; brought children to class when mother was ill or at work; tried to study amid the confusion of family life in a trailer.

SOME LONG RANGE CONSEQUENCES

Reference has been made previously in this chapter to the mobility of the mores, meaning by that phrase the modification in the mores that occurs when people change their place of residence or their status. Such modification is part of the larger fact that people's minds become as mobile as do their bodies in wartime. Just as they change the external circumstances of their lives, so they tend in varying degrees to change their ideas, ideals, values, judgments, and codes of behavior. Becker's general term for this social-psychological concomitant of physical migration is mental mobility.

These modifications of attitudes and values are of particular significance in any attempt to assess the long-range consequences of a world war. The great changes in human history are not those which occur in the mechanical gadgets which men use nor even in the institutionalized arrangements by which they live but in the attitudes and values they accept. The revolutions of the past which have had great meaning for mankind are those which have taken place in the minds of men. Changes of this kind are selected, then, as indicative of the long-range effects of war upon the family, to which we turn in the concluding section of this chapter. To emphasize a certain tentativeness in the nature of the ensuing discussion, the selected aspects are stated in the form of questions.

1. *How will the military experience of millions of American men affect their postwar attitudes as parents and mates? Will the coming years see the emergence in this country of the military male?*

It has been the experience of the past that great nations engaged in continuing warfare tend to produce a single definitive type of citizen which reflects the qualities essential for military success. This type, a product of military discipline, finds its expression in the dominant male, emphatic in the authority of the father over his children, of the master over his workers, and of the husband over his wife. Historians have identified this type among the warlike nations of the past, just as more recent students identify it among the Germans and the Japanese.

The military male, once his type crystallizes, tends toward hardness and firmness of character. Lecky wrote years ago,

> War accustoms men to the abnegation needed for simultaneous action, compels them to repress their fears, and establish a firm control over their affections. Patriotism, too, leads them to subordinate their personal wishes to the interests of the society in which they live.[22]

In times past, this type has held no high regard for women. In many of the qualities which he prized, women were indisputably inferior, with the inevitable result that he placed them in a subject status.

Much is said in historical records of the crude-mannered male which constant warfare created. Many men were gathered together over long periods of time, without the presence of women. They lived and talked a salty life. By way of indirect proof there are the statements by various historians of the Middle Ages that with the decline of constant devastating warfare, knights and lords had time to improve their manners and their relations with women. In speaking of the Crusades, Thompson states that

[22] William E. H. Lecky, *History of European Morals*, vol. 1 (New York: Appleton, 1869), p. 182.

"the rough and ready ways of the feudal, fighting West gave way to the politeness and address of the East. The man of war, the typical fighting baron, was humanized into a gentleman of culture, and good, though not soft, manners." [23]

During World War II, more than ten million fathers and husbands, present and prospective, were submitted to military discipline, many of them over an extended period of time and during an impressionable period of their lives. In the years since, military training and conflict experience in Korea and elsewhere have been the lot of many young Americans, and there is no prospect of much change in this respect. This involves the introduction of a new set of influences in the conditioning process of the maturing American male, on a scale of extensive proportions. Its consequences are destined to be enormous and, judging by the past, at least will bear in the direction of the military male.

2. *How did World War II, and continuing militarization, affect the status of women? What changes in the attitudes of women may be expected in the years ahead?*

Perhaps no other phase of the relationship between war and the family is covered so adequately in the historical material as the effect of war on the treatment and status of women. The available material may be divided into two parts. First is the treatment of women in conquered lands. Traditionally, women have been a spoil of war, with both their labor and their sex exploited by the conqueror. Several historic forms of this may be noted. Wife capture, for example, has been one of the recognized forms of obtaining a mate. It has existed among the Plains Indians of America,[24] the Amerinds, the Polynesians,[25] the early Germanic tribes, and various other groups. Both logic and anthropological research suggest that wife capture existed extensively in a day of constant warfare, woman labor, and female infanticide.

Again, concubinage results from war. As early as the time of the Homeric epics, the distinction between wife and concubine was this: the wife was purchased from her father, while the concubine was a prize of war.[26] Similarly, among the Romans concubinage was rare until the Punic Wars. During the Renaissance, both in France and in Italy the custom was common of buying captured women in the markets of Venice to serve as concubines.

Third, slavery was a customary fate of women in conquered countries in earlier wars, especially of the absolute or total type, such as the Greek wars against the barbarians or the Christian wars against the infidels.

The second part of our historical material deals with the effects of war on the status of women as a class. Two kinds of effect are noted. In the

23 James Westfall Thompson, *An Economic and Social History of the Middle Ages* (New York: Century, 1928), p. 435.

24 Robert Lowie, *Primitive Society* (New York: Boni and Liveright, 1920), p. 23.

25 Robert Briffault, "Concubinage," *Encyclopedia of the Social Sciences,* vol. 4 (New York: Macmillan, 1931), p. 172.

26 W. Goodsell, *A History of Marriage and the Family* (New York: Macmillan, rev. ed., 1934), p. 96.

earlier stages of cultural development, life was nomadic, war and the chase were man's chief pursuits, "the ascendancy of beauty is faint," and the life of women was one of hard and continuous toil. In addition to the duty of supplying the family with food and other necessities, motherhood was continuous and exhausting. To these duties, war added further burdens and anxieties. On the other hand, with a more highly developed economy, war proved a liberating influence, especially to women in the upper classes. Here the absence of the husband created the immediate necessity of having the wife assume greater responsibility and leadership in family matters.

What a prolonged war may mean is shown in the considered effects of the Punic Wars. First, for the thirty or more years of actual warfare, a large proportion of able-bodied Romans saw service in the field. Husbands were away from home for years at a time. As a consequence, the management of estates and households devolved upon their wives, many women receiving a training in self-reliance and efficiency in responsible positions. This in turn led such women to submit with ill grace to the restrictions in their daily lives and interests that their husbands imposed upon them on their return from the wars. Before long the *manus,* i.e., the power of the Roman husband over his wife, came to be indicted by these women as tyranny. After the second Punic War the controversy was compromised, and the practice of marriage without *manus* grew up. It was this sad circumstance that led the elder Cato to remark: "All men rule over women, we Romans rule over all men, and our wives rule over us."

Two later wars tell the same story. A recent writer has this to say about the effects of the American Civil War upon the Southern wife:

> In 1860, the South became a matriarchy. The men went away from home to other battlefields, leaving the women free to manage farm and plantation without their bungling hindrance; when they returned, those who had escaped heroic death found their surrogates in complete and competent charge and liking it. Four years had fixed the habit of command which, when I first began to know them, thirty had not broken.[27]

Perhaps most clearly revealed are the effects of the First World War in this respect. This war changed the employment of women "from a shameful business to heroism" overnight; it opened up new fields of employment, especially for women in the middle and upper classes and in many other respects it put the finishing touches on the "emancipation of women." Complementary to the right to behave like a man came, too, the right to misbehave as he does, thus bringing about a change in many of the mores.[28] As Burgess and Locke have so well put it, "World War I gave women the outward symbols of equality with men: namely, the suffrage and a social freedom."[29]

[27] John A. Rice, "My Father's Folks," *Harper's Magazine,* Sept., 1940, p. 426.
[28] Frederick Allen, *Only Yesterday* (New York: Harper, 1932).
[29] Ernest W. Burgess and Harvey Locke, *The Family* (2nd ed.; New York: American Book Co., 1953), p. 635.

The relationship between war and women has taken on new meaning in modern times as war has increasingly involved the efforts of women. In World War II, both Germany and Great Britain conscripted women for wartime service, thus putting the stamp of official approval, as it were, upon what large numbers of them were already doing. The change in warfare from a clash between professional armies to a struggle between entire populations, the addition of economic to military phases of conflict, the development of totalitarian warfare, all have combined to make the efforts and contributions of women of greater importance.

In the United States, World War II continued the equalizing processes of World War I, only more so and for a longer duration. Of dramatic significance in this connection was the opening up of four branches of the armed forces to women. Thousands of women enrolled in these auxiliary corps, serving with credit and demonstrating their value to the nation's military effort.

More extensive, even if less dramatic, was the marked increase in the employment of women during the war. The over-all extent of this increase is revealed by the annual reports on women workers, made by the Women's Bureau of the U. S. Department of Labor. From May, 1940, to May, 1945, the total number of women employed rose from 11,310,000 to 17,940,000. After the cessation of hostilities, the number naturally declined, but by May, 1946, it still stood at 16,260,000, which was 29.4 per cent of the total number of women fourteen years of age and over.[30] In April, 1951, the number stood at 18,602,000, thus indicating that the increase of World War II has remained. More than half of these were married women.

Evidence of a great many kinds is accumulating to show that whereas the First World War gave women the symbols of equality, the second one has given them an increased measure of the substance of it. With economic independence comes not only equality with the male, both within the home and outside, but also a sense of assurance and security in many aspects of human relationships. While the period immediately after the war will witness some recession in the number and proportion of those gainfully employed and in the assumption of roles of leadership and responsibility, on the whole an appreciable net gain in the status of women may be anticipated as a long-range result of World War II.

3. *What changes in the pattern of husband-wife relationships may be anticipated by way of aftermath of war? What, in other words, will happen as the militarily trained young male and the emancipated young woman unite in marriage?*

Before attempting to answer this question, three facts should be recalled. First, before the war the family was moving with fair rapidity in the direction of a person-centered, democratic form in which each marital partner gave increasing recognition to the individuality and interests of the other. A second fact is that, as a result of a World War of the magnitude and duration of the recent one, millions of men and women passed through

[30] *Facts on Women Workers* (Washington: U. S. Department of Labor, June, 1946).

widely differing experiences, so that thereafter many of their values, definitions of situations, memories, and preoccupations were quite different. Third, during the period of their life apart, many men and women became habituated to living their own lives.

In combination, these three facts suggest the answer to the questions proposed. At worst, they suggest increased conflict and discord, with rising rates of family disorganization and reorganization. At best, they promise an increasing personal schematization within the marriage relationship. More and more, marriage will become a personalized relationship in which each of the partners will live — within limitations, of course — his or her own life. This, as has been said, is not a new but simply an increasingly prevalent pattern. It is the inherent complement of the democratic family. It is the inevitable product of secondary rather than primary group life; of the increasing employment of women, especially of married women; of the growing participation of women in civic and community affairs; of a rapidly secularizing society. The Second World War obviously did not create, it merely augmented, personal schematization in marriage. In many cases this will prove troublesome, making for conflict, tension, infidelity, and misunderstanding; in others, and one believes the larger proportion of marriages, it will make for a fuller and richer relationship. Where there are the deepest valleys one finds also the highest mountains.

4. *What changes in the biosexual role of the family and in the patterns of sex behavior in general may be expected as an aftermath of war?*

Wars invariably affect the sex behavior of large segments of the participating populations. One finds much historical evidence on this point. The sexual misbehavior of soldiers with women in invaded lands is referred to in the histories of most wars. On the other hand, while there are cases of outstanding faithfulness of war "widows," like the "unwearied fidelity of Penelope, awaiting through the long, revolving years the return of her storm-tossed husband," contrasting instances are not infrequent, as the literature and news grist of many a postwar period reveals.

There are many reasons why war breaks the crystallized patterns of sex behavior. First, it removes young people from their primary group controls, and for young people, particularly for young men, such freedom tends to find expression in experimentation with the sexual aspects of life. Sex experimentation is an inevitable aspect of the process of maturing, and wartime conditions tend to stimulate both. Second, war brings with it a general relaxation of certain social controls as people bend their efforts toward military goals. Perhaps this is a phase of what Waller identified as the making of "hedonistic life-adjustments on a short-time basis." Third, for separated couples war means an interruption of regularized affectional relationships, with the consequent problems of adjustment behavior. Fourth, war means contact with exotic mates, and people of other groups and cultures often offer the added charm of novelty. Fifth, the general pattern of army life includes an increase of the so-called "manly pursuits," such as drinking, gambling, and the like. Finally, as wars continue and end, many

couples find it necessary to overlook wartime infidelities. To do this satisfactorily, there must be a certain depreciation of the idealized significance
of sex and an appreciation of its basic nature as a hunger of the organism and its role as a form of emotional catharsis. All these and other
factors make new attitudes toward sex an inevitable accompaniment to
war, their specific expression and degree being a matter of time and circumstance.

The changes which emerged after 1918 set the course for much that has
developed since World War II. At least six changes in the patterns of
sex behavior manifested themselves after the First World War. One of these
was the general lifting of the taboos upon sex, including on the positive
side a recognition of its significance in the life of the individual and its
role in social relationships. Second, and as a consequence of the first, there
was a marked growth in the movement for sex instruction, for both child
and youth. Third was the emergence of birth control as a social movement,
respectable, significant, and dynamic. Particularly did this movement make
tremendous strides among the poorer classes. Fourth was the increased
knowledge of the role of venereal infection and of prophylaxis, both growing
out of the soldier's wartime experience and his military instruction and
discipline. Fifth was the increase of premarital sex relationships, revealed
by statistical evidence and emphasized by the comments of informed
students in recent years.[31] Sixth, and perhaps as a pervasive change interrelated with most of the others, has been the passing of the double standard
of morals. This has already been referred to in connection with the changing
status of women.

Other students might modify or enlarge the foregoing list. Possibly the
sexualization of marriage, in contrast to its procreative role, and the emphasis upon the role of sex in the realm of mental hygiene might be
enumerated as additional specific changes.

The impact of the Second World War must be considered against the
background of present-day developments in (a) public education in the
field of human relationships, (b) the control of the venereal diseases
through the recently developed "wonder drugs," (c) the increased availability of contraceptives, (d) the lowered age of marriage, and (e) the
increasing emphasis upon the romantic aspect of marriage. Out of this
complex of social forces, there seems little doubt but that in the years
ahead this country will witness the continuation and intensification of
the changes following the First World War. Emphasis upon the extra-
procreative aspects of sex is destined to increase. Planned parenthood will be
more and more accepted as a part of family life mores, as well as of a
community's health and social program. Premarital sex relationships may
increase, with sex instruction and early marriage as possible counteracting
influences. A single standard of morals will be assumed as a matter of
course.

---

[31] Lewis M. Terman, *Psychological Factors in Marital Happiness* (New York: McGraw-Hill,
1938), pp. 319–324. See also especially the analysis by Alfred C. Kinsey, *Sexual Behavior in
the Human Male* (Philadelphia: Saunders, 1948).

5. *What changes in the economic bases of family life may be expected as an aftermath of war?*

As a preface to this discussion, two economic consequences of modern warfare must be noted. One of these is a dislocation of the price level, invariably upward and with relative rapidity. Second is a huge governmental expenditure for military purposes. Both of these have developed to a marked extent in the United States since 1940.

Resulting from these two factors in combination is the appearance of two types of economic families. One of these is *war rich* families, who profit from wartime expenditures. From December, 1941, to July, 1944, two hundred billion dollars were earmarked by the U. S. Government for expenditures for war purposes. The major share of the consequent increase of the national income went into increases of incomes of wage-earning families. Some of these were families experiencing prosperity after a decade of economic depression.[32] A large number were families who had been on relief rolls during the nineteen-thirties. Others were new families, forming their first conceptions of *family* incomes and expenditures.

The second type of economic family is those who have been *war poor*. These are families whose incomes were fixed, relatively or absolutely; teachers, public officials, clerks, and persons living on fixed incomes, such as interest on invested funds, pensions, etc. The particular wartime economic problem of these families grew in part out of increases in the cost of living; in part from the very marked increases in tax burdens, especially in federal income taxes; and in part, often, from the assumption of fixed economic responsibilities, such as insurance, amortizing mortgages, and the like.[33]

The long-range status and problems for both types of families will depend upon the national economic prospects. One's judgment of what these will be depends upon what school of politico-economic philosophy one adheres to. If one finds it possible to anticipate that a people, 150 million strong, can spend their resources with riotous abandon in a worldwide war, pile up a huge public debt, control production, dole out public funds through a variety of political devices, and then pull itself by its own bootstraps into a dream-like economic prosperity, then one can foresee a bright economic prospect for both types of families during the coming decades. To these ideas, the author of this chapter can in no way, nor in the slightest degree, subscribe.

War is a costly business. It destroys wealth. It withdraws labor from socially productive ends and diverts it to destructive purposes. Modern warfare is especially expensive because of its technical nature, which means

[32] Frederick L. Allen, "Who's Getting the Money?" *Harper's Magazine*, June, 1944, pp. 3–4; also James H. S. Bossard, "Family Backgrounds of Wartime Adolescents," *The Annals of the American Academy of Political and Social Science*, Nov., 1944, pp. 33–34.

[33] Elbert D. Thomas, "Twenty Million Forgotten Americans," *American Magazine*, May, 1944; *The Monthly Labor Review* (Bureau of Labor Statistics, U. S. Department of Labor, May, 1944); Ruth Okey and Mary G. Luck, *Wartime Food for Four Income Levels*, Heller Committee for Research in Social Economics (Berkeley: University of California Press, 1943); Bossard, *op. cit.*, pp. 35–36.

relatively costly equipment. Coupled with this factor is the relatively low casualty rate suffered by American military forces. Speaking with cold objectivity, this means the survival of more persons, with fewer reserves of wealth. Taxes must remain high for many years after the war, and the danger of inflation is more than a political bugaboo. These are the grim realities of the situation. Short-range stimulation and financial legerdemain may delay the operation of the inevitable, particularly in a land capable of taking so much economic punishment; but in the long run the financial prospect for large portions of American families is not bright.

6. *Are all the effects of war upon the family of a disorganizing or problem-creating kind?*

Not all the effects of war upon the family are problem-provoking. War, like other adversities, often binds families closer together. Suffering welds relationships as nothing else can. The realities of war dwarf into insignificance many of the trivialities of life, and this helps to reveal its abiding fundamentals. War calls forth a spiritual rejuvenation which may re-create the inner meaning of family life. Many a married couple, casual in the indifferent intimacy of the years, are bound together again in a common anxiety for children in their country's service. Other couples find life anew in the idealism of wartime service and translate this psychic renewal into their marital relationship. The background of a national crisis places in proper perspective the domestic squabbles and triangles which seemed so important in more placid days.

Not all wartime separations produce tension or defensive coolness. A man and wife separated by half the world may come, perhaps for the first time, to assess their true devotion to each other. Just as one learns to skate during the summer and to swim in winter, so good husbands may be born in the discomfort of military barracks, and more forbearing wives be resolved in the loneliness of their wartime estate. War tries people's souls, and if some are weighed and found wanting and if others are lost in the process of weighing, there still are legion who find themselves anew in meeting the trial.

The historical evidence on the positive side is scant. Only, it must be so. If war were so devastating for family life as some students have indicated, then the family could not have survived its own history. The resiliency of the family — this is its answer to the wars of the past. The family has survived many wars.

SELECTED READINGS

ABRAMS, RAY H., "The American Family in World War II," *The Annals of the American Academy of Political and Social Science,* Sept., 1943.

BECKER, HOWARD, "After the Deluge," in symposium edited by Henry P. Jordan, *Problems of Post-War Reconstruction* (Washington, D. C.: American Council on Public Affairs, 1942).

BOSSARD, JAMES H. S., *Marriage and the Child* (Philadelphia: University of Pennsylvania Press, 1940), chap. 5.

———, "War and the Family," *American Sociological Review* (June, 1941), pp. 330–344.

———, "Family Problems in Wartime," *Psychiatry* (Feb., 1944), pp. 65–72.

———, "Family Problems of the Immediate Future," *Journal of Home Economics* (Sept., 1945), pp. 383–387.

———, and BOLL, ELEANOR S., "Adolescents in Wartime," *The Annals of the American Academy of Political and Social Science* (Nov., 1944).

BURGESS, ERNEST W., and LOCKE, HARVEY, *The Family* (2nd ed.; New York: American Book Co., 1953), chap. 21.

CUBER, JOHN F., "Family Readjustment of Veterans," *Marriage and Family Living* (Spring, 1945), pp. 28–30.

DUVALL, EVELYN M., and HILL, REUBEN, *When You Marry* (rev.; Boston: Heath, 1953), chaps. 20 and 21.

GOODSELL, WILLYSTINE, *A History of the Family as a Social and Educational Institution* (New York: Macmillan, 1915).

GRUENBERG, SIDONIE MATSNER, *The Family in a World at War* (New York: Harper, 1942).

HALL, CALVIN, "The Instability of Post-War Marriages," *Journal of Social Psychology*, 5 (1934), pp. 523–530.

HILL, REUBEN, "The Returning Father and His Family," *Marriage and Family Living* (Spring, 1945), pp. 31–34.

———, *Families Under Stress* (New York: Harper, 1949).

HILTON, JAMES, *Random Harvest* (Boston: Little, Brown, 1941).

KUPPER, HERBERT I., *Back to Life: The Emotional Adjustment of Veterans* (New York: Fischer, 1945).

McDONAUGH, EDWARD, "The Discharged Serviceman and His Family," *American Journal of Sociology* (Mar., 1946), pp. 451–454.

MENDELSSOHN-BARTHOLDY, ALBRECHT, *The War and German Society* (New Haven: Yale University Press, 1937).

PRATT, GEORGE K., *Soldier to Civilian* (New York: McGraw-Hill, 1944).

WALLER, WILLARD, *War and the Family* (New York: Dryden Press, 1940).

———, ed., *War in the Twentieth Century* (New York: Dryden Press, 1940).

———, *The Veteran Comes Back* (New York: Dryden Press, 1944).

TOPICS FOR DISCUSSION OR REPORTS

1. Compare the effects of war upon courtship and marriage with those of a major depression like that of the 1930's.
2. Why did the effects of the First World War upon the marriage rate in Britain differ so markedly from the effects in the European countries allied to Britain?
3. How prevalent has war been through the centuries? What does this suggest concerning its effects upon the family?
4. How do wars differ as to their nature and rate of casualties?
5. What is the extent of cultural intermarriage in the United States? What is its significance for children?
6. Identify the effects upon family life of large-scale civilian disasters, such as earthquakes, floods, etc. How do these differ from the effects of military disasters?

7. What elements in the population are penalized most by relatively sudden dislocations of the price level during wartime?
8. What are the characteristics of war mentality? How may war mentality affect family life?
9. What changes in the social care of children resulted after the Civil War? What changes may be expected after the Second World War?
10. What is the value of newspaper reports for the study of the effects of war upon marriage and the family?
11. What evidences of antagonisms between the sexes can be found in contemporary novels? In the drama? In industrial employment?

Chapter Twenty-Five

Larger or Smaller Families for America?

T. J. WOOFTER

THE size and structure of the family have changed radically in the past century. The large colonial family has been replaced by a much smaller unit. There are fewer children but more old people. More couples remain childless. More families are broken by divorce but fewer by premature death. First children are born later, and middle-aged parents have fewer children. Thus the childbearing period has been shortened at both ends. These changes are still in process, which means that in the future these characteristics will be still more exaggerated.

If we define families to include young people who have had no children and old people whose children have started families of their own, it is apparent that the responsibility for rearing children is unequally distributed. Half the families have no children under 18 years of age, and half of the children are in one seventh of the families, those families including three or more children apiece. The other half are in one- and two-child families (Fig. 24).

In view of these facts we may ask: (1) Will the family continue to fulfill one of its primary functions, the maintenance of the race? (2) What

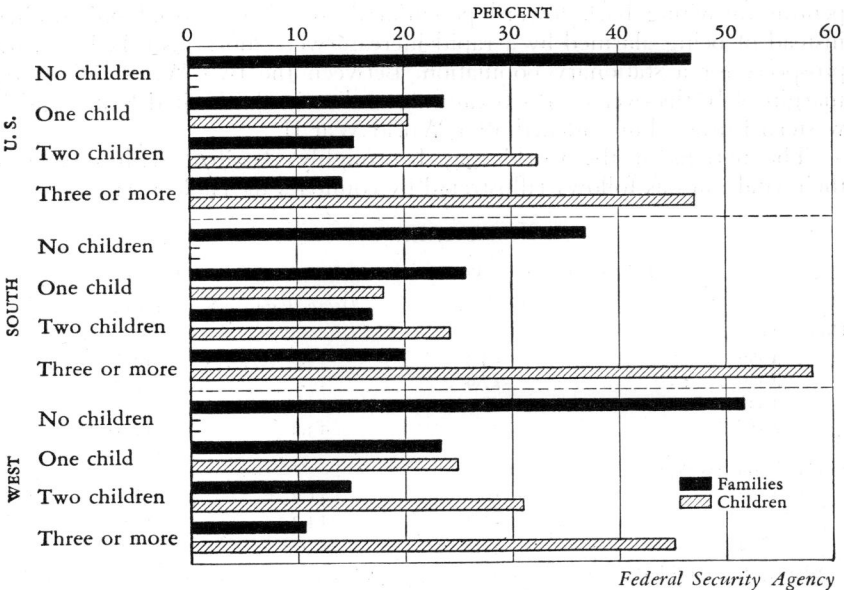

Federal Security Agency

FIGURE 24. PERCENTAGE OF FAMILIES AND CHILDREN IN FAMILIES BY TYPE AND REGION, 1940

are the basic causes of this smaller number of children? (3) What will be the effects upon economic life; upon social institutions? (4) What policies are appropriate to meet the situation?

WORLD TRENDS IN POPULATION

Underlying the changes in the family are fundamental changes in birth and death rates. The persistent and widespread decline in the birth rate which has been characteristic of all industrialized nations has been one of the most far-reaching social forces in the past hundred years. It has affected the rate of total population growth, family size and structure, age composition, social attitudes, economic development, and relative military strength.

A reduction in the death rate has also accompanied industrialization. During the early 1800's, saving of life was more marked than slight changes in the birth rate, with the result that people of European stock trebled from two to six hundred million in a century. The consequent pressures at home sent streams of colonizers all over the world, peopling the Americas and establishing outposts in Africa, Asia, and the Pacific. At that time Malthus and the economists of his school were alarmed at the seeming ability of population to expand more rapidly than production. Alongside the dramatic reduction in the death rate, forces working toward the reduction of the birth rate were gathering momentum, so that during the latter part of the nineteenth century and the first of the twentieth the pendulum swung back toward potential decrease, and social philosophers instead of being alarmed by a rapid increase were more disturbed by early prospects for a stationary population. Between the two World Wars, the margin of births over deaths became very slim in the United States and in western Europe, but widened after World War II.

The nations of the world may be roughly classified with respect to their vital rates as follows (illustrated by countries in Table 19):

TABLE 19

VITAL RATES PER 1000 POPULATION IN SELECTED COUNTRIES [1]

	Birth Rate	Death Rate	Natural Increase
United States:			
1950	23.4	9.6	13.8
1940	17.9	10.7	7.2
1930	18.9	11.3	7.6
1915	25.0	13.2	11.8
England and Wales:			
1950	16.1	11.7	4.4
1910	25.2	14.2	11.0
1870	35.3	22.2	13.1

[1] Adapted from Tables 28 and 57, pp. 123 and 175, Warren S. Thompson, *Population Problems and Vital Statistics of the United States* (New York: McGraw-Hill, 1930) and UN *Demographic Yearbook*, 1951.

TABLE 19 (*continued*)

		Birth Rate	Death Rate	Natural Increase
France:				
	1950	20.4	12.6	7.8
	1930	17.7	16.4	1.3
	1910	19.4	18.5	.9
	1890	22.6	22.2	.4
	1850	27.0	23.5	3.5
Russia:				
	1950 (estimate only)	—	—	15.0
	1930	43.8	18.9	24.9
	1910	45.6	28.9	16.7
	1890	48.6	35.8	12.8
	1870	48.9	36.9	12.0
Rumania:				
	1940	26.5	19.1	7.4
	1930	34.8	20.7	14.1
	1910	41.5	25.6	15.9
	1890	40.6	30.2	10.4
	1870	33.5	26.5	7.0
Japan:				
	1950	28.4	11.0	17.4
	1930	33.0	18.8	14.2
	1910	33.8	20.8	13.0
	1890	28.8	20.4	8.4
Chile:				
	1950	32.4	15.7	16.7
	1930	38.8	24.1	14.7
	1910	39.5	31.7	7.8
	1890	35.5	35.0	.5

Western Europe (except Italy and Spain): Low birth rates; low death rates; sluggish rate of natural increase.

Eastern Europe (including Russia): High but slightly declining birth rates; death rates still somewhat higher than western Europe; substantial rate of natural increase; prospects for continuing vigorous increase in population for a number of decades, especially in Russia.

Spain and Italy: Rates between those of eastern and western Europe.

United States: Rates approaching those of western Europe in the inter-war period, but recovering *very* rapidly from 1945 to 1950.

South America, Asia, and Africa: High birth rates with some signs of decrease; death rates high in most countries, medium in Japan, Philippines, and Argentina, substantial reduction since 1910; vigorous natural increase which will persist for a number of decades unless there is a sudden reduction in birth rates.

Thus nation after nation had become concerned over the effects of declining natural increase. Some students held that modern industrialization is self-destructive since it is not conducive to the future replacement of the population. As a result, increased attention has been centered upon positive population policies planned with the hope that the decline can be checked.

DECLINING NATURAL INCREASE IN THE UNITED STATES

In the United States in 1940 the proportion of the population represented by children under five years of age was only one-third of what it was in 1800. This is a clear illustration of the extent to which the falling birth rate has offset the saving of life in early childhood. The large families prevalent in colonial days in spite of a high infant death rate have become rare. Childless couples are not uncommon, and among families with children the one- and two-child patterns predominate. The most rapid reduction in fertility has occurred from 1900 to 1940.

The downward trend in fertility was fairly steady in all industrialized nations up to 1940. War and postwar prosperity caused a reversal, or at least an interruption in the trend, especially in the United States. The decennial rate of increase in the United States was only 7 per cent from 1930 to 1940. From 1940 to 1950, however, it was over 14 per cent, more rapid than in 1915 but slower than before 1900. Here the low depression birth rates increased nearly 30 per cent, with the result that the number of children under 10 years of age increased 30 per cent from 1940 to 1950. The number of children per family did not, however, increase so rapidly because one of the factors underlying the increase in the birth rate was an increase in the marriage rate, forming a larger number of families.

The present discussion of family size is centered more on the long-time trend than the pattern of the immediate present, which may or may not indicate a stabilization of the birth rate. Only time can determine whether family planning will result in a stationary or continued downward trend.[2]

If we examine certain correlative facts, some conclusions as to recent changes in family practice stand out. It is generally agreed that there has been no noticeable biological change in the capacity for childbearing. In fact, vigorous campaigns against venereal disease, malnutrition, and disabilities arising from childbirth would lead to the conclusion that there is probably less involuntary sterility. The supposition that postponement of the age of marriage was a causal factor is also not borne out in recent years. Although this may have operated in the early part of the last century, there has been little change from 1890 to World War II. The percentages of all women who are married and of women under twenty-five years of age who are married have remained constant since that date. But the marriage rate actually increased sharply from 1940 to 1950.

While women marry as early as they did in 1890, there is a tendency to have the first child later. Likewise, an increasing proportion of married women remain childless. This is indexed in Table 20, which indicates

[2] For fuller discussion of the factors involved, cf. T. J. Woofter, "Factors Sustaining the Birth Rate," *American Sociological Review*, June, 1949.

TABLE 20

BIRTH AND SURVIVAL OF CHILDREN PER WOMAN WHO HAD BEEN MARRIED
AND WAS 35 TO 74 YEARS OF AGE, 1910 AND 1940

Date	Children Born	Children Surviving to Age 20	Per Cent of Women Who Were Childless
1910	4.66	3.49	10.0
1940	3.08	2.62	16.0

that in 1910 only 10 per cent of the married women over thirty-five years of age had remained childless and that in 1940 the percentage was 16. Increasing childlessness and the postponement of childbearing have resulted in a sharp reduction in the number of children per woman. Table 20 compares the women who had been married and had completed or almost completed their childbearing experience. In 1910 these women had averaged 4.66 children apiece; in 1940, only 3.08. Improved death rates, however, enabled the larger proportion of the later generation to survive. Only about 70 per cent of those born before 1910 lived to age 20, about 85 per cent of those born before 1940 lived to that age.

It is probable that this reduction is almost entirely attributable to the gradual extension throughout all areas and social classes of the practice of voluntary limitation of family size, the increased knowledge of and ability to use contraceptive practices. It will be recognized that this is a cause only in the immediate sense of providing a means. The basic causes — in the sense of motivation — are involved in the reasons why couples want fewer children.

The economic, social, and psychological reasons for the trend are complex and can only be suggested here. Postponement of the age at which men earn an independent living, due to prolonged schooling and training, has undoubtedly been one factor. The increasing tendency of young wives to work and contribute to the family budget has been another. A feeling of insecurity in an industrial economy has contributed. The relative level of living actually available to a young family in comparison with the one they would like to attain, i.e., the desire to "get ahead" in life, is influential. Difficulty in securing adequate housing accommodations for medium size and large families, together with the sacrifices of certain social freedom and privileges which are associated with child rearing, have also entered into the picture. Another factor, more difficult to measure, has been the increase in the divorce rate, which arises in part from the psychological stresses and strains characteristic of many modern marriages.

It has long been recognized that the motivation for small families is weaker in rural areas than in cities. Not only have the means for family limitation been less available to farm families, but the difficulties of providing at least a minimum of food and shelter for larger families are not so acute as in congested cities. In some types of farming a large family is actually an economic asset. The farm family, therefore, has always been characterized by more children. As late as 1940 there were 1.6 children per family in farm areas as against .9 of a child per family in cities. One influential factor in the decline in the total birth rate has been the increasing proportion of urban dwellers in the whole population. After migration, rural families tend to adopt the city-family pattern rather than continue their rural customs.

It has likewise been recognized that even though foreign immigrants usually settle in cities, they have constituted a high-fertility group. This is attributable partially to the fact that the majority have come from rural areas. Drastic control of immigration after the 1920's has caused this element in the population to age beyond the childbearing period without large annual increments of young marriageable immigrants. This elimination and aging of the high-fertility, foreign-born groups has been another factor in the reduction of the over-all birth rate, since the second and third generations of children of foreign parentage tend to conform to the urban pattern of their new home.

In the past, the Negro has been characterized by a relatively high birth rate and by disproportionately high mortality. Within the past few decades the decline in the Negro birth rate has been more rapid than the decline in the death rate. As a result the effective fertility, or the number of surviving children per thousand women, is not appreciably greater in the Negro group when other factors are held constant than it is in a comparable white group. That is to say, the effective fertility in the Negro urban and the Negro rural elements is little different from the corresponding white rates. As a whole, however, the Negro population still exhibits a somewhat higher net reproduction ratio because it is still more concentrated on farms than the white population.

Notwithstanding these differentials between rural and urban, foreign-born and native-born, Negro and white, the downward trend of the birth rate has been a common characteristic of all classes. The rate of decline has, however, varied. The decrease in fertility of the formerly high-fertility groups has been proportionately more rapid than in those groups which had already reached a fairly low fertility level, with the result that over the past few decades the urban-rural, foreign-native, Negro-white differentials have been narrowed.

Future Fertility and Total Population

Whether this decline in the birth rate will be projected into the future at the rate that has prevailed in the past thirty years has been a matter of speculation among experts. Considerable light may be thrown on the question by a comparison of trends in the United States with those in other nations which are farther along in the population cycle, on the assumption that, unless some unexpected reversal occurs, the United States will follow these other nations. Likewise, comparison of differential rates within the United States in the heavily industrialized regions where fertility is already low with the South and West where the reduction has not been so great, presents some evidence upon which predictions may be based if it is assumed that the latter regions will in the future follow the trends that have prevailed in other sections.

Long-range population projections have, in the past, proved tricky and have been subject to drastic revisions. For instance, the predictions of a decline in the United States population within a few decades, which were based on depression conditions, have been abandoned. From recent trends it appears that there are two main prospects for the growth of the United States population: (1) That the present high birth rates (see Figure 25A) will continue and the death rates will further diminish. In this event a declining or stationary population would be postponed at least to the end of the century. (2) That present high birth rates will prove to be the result of temporary postwar factors and that they will gradually resume the prewar downward trend. In this case, a population peak would be reached some decades hence. For the next few years, however, there would be no sharp drop in the rate of natural increase.

The economic and social effects of the approach of a stationary or declining population are difficult to forecast. The prospect need cause no undue pessimism, since the change will be sufficiently gradual to allow for appropriate adjustments. On the whole, the effect may be beneficial economically if increased productivity brings an accompanying rise in the level of living and if the adjustment in size of family to family resources brings about a better distribution of child rearing facilities, with the result that the oncoming generation will be more healthy and better educated.

Internal adjustments in the economic and social structure which will be necessitated by the change in age structure and by the slower rate of family formation will, however, be marked, and these will without doubt demand increasing attention from social scientists and from the managers of businesses whose expansion is dependent on an increase in number of consumers.

Changes in Age Structure

A declining population indicates a reduction in the proportion of children and an increase in that of old people. Continuation of present trends (see Figure 25B) with only slight reduction in the birth rate would, at least until the 1960's, result in the maintenance of the present proportion of children and about the same proportion of persons 15 to 65, with an increase in those over 65 years of age to nearly 10 per cent of the total.[3]

Unless the increasing proportion of aged in the population is accompanied by a prolonged period of employability in this older age group, there will be a marked increase in the proportion of dependents and pensioners at this upper end of the age pyramid. The provision of old-age

[3] Margaret J. Haygood and J. S. Siegel, "Projections of the Regional Distribution of the Population," *Agricultural Economics Research* (April, 1951).

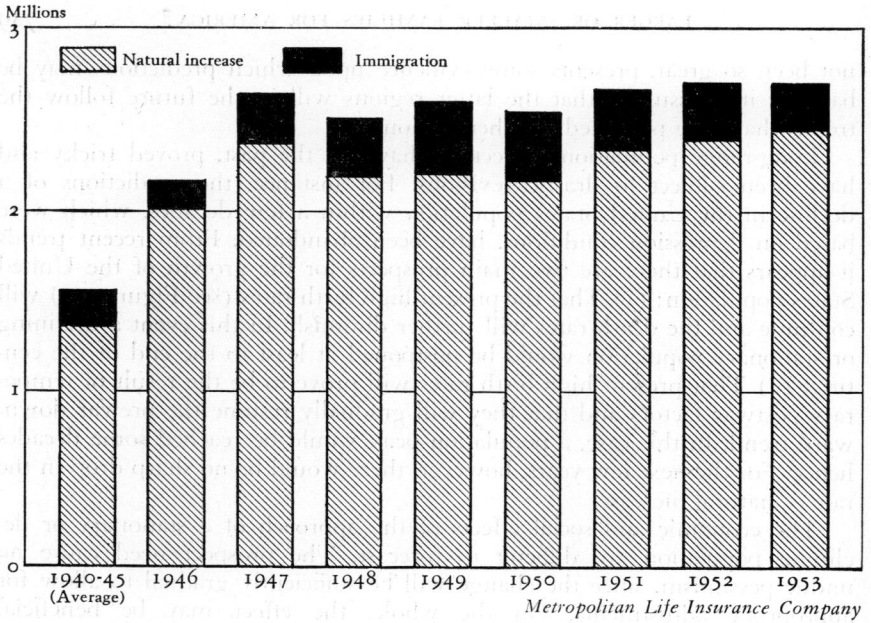

Millions

Natural increase   Immigration

1940-45 (Average)   1946   1947   1948   1949   1950   1951   1952   1953

Metropolitan Life Insurance Company

FIGURE 25A. ANNUAL POPULATION INCREASE IN THE UNITED STATES, 1940–1953

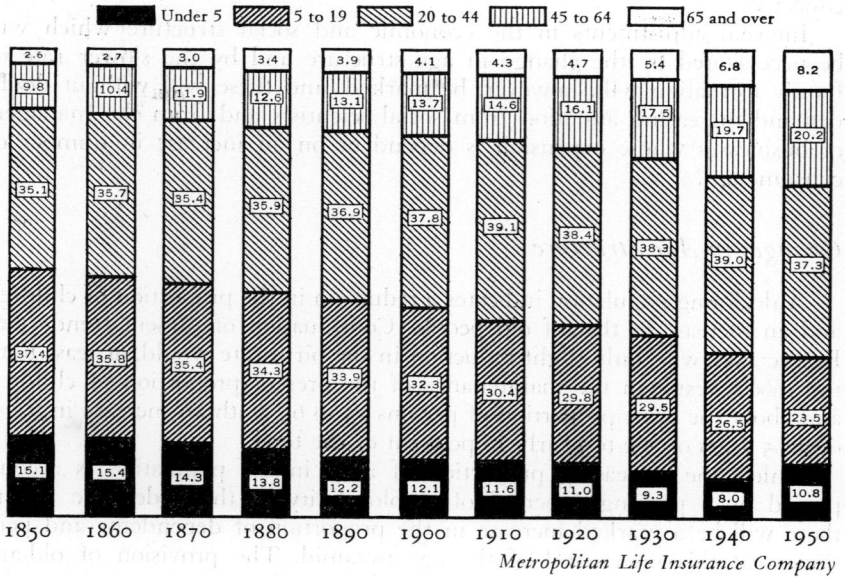

Under 5   5 to 19   20 to 44   45 to 64   65 and over

	1850	1860	1870	1880	1890	1900	1910	1920	1930	1940	1950
65 and over	2.6	2.7	3.0	3.4	3.9	4.1	4.3	4.7	5.4	6.8	8.2
45 to 64	9.8	10.4	11.9	12.6	13.1	13.7	14.6	16.1	17.5	19.7	20.2
20 to 44	35.1	35.7	35.4	35.9	36.9	37.8	39.1	38.4	38.3	39.0	37.3
5 to 19	37.4	35.8	35.4	34.3	33.9	32.3	30.4	29.8	29.5	26.5	23.5
Under 5	15.1	15.4	14.3	13.8	12.2	12.1	11.6	11.0	9.3	8.0	10.8

Metropolitan Life Insurance Company

FIGURE 25B. PERCENT DISTRIBUTION OF TOTAL POPULATION BY AGE
UNITED STATES, 1850 TO 1950

insurance and assistance under the Social Security system is an effort to cushion this future increase in old-age dependents.

Effects on Number and Size of Families

Changes in the total population structure will, in part, be reflected in the composition of the average family household in the country. Until the effects of the high birth rates of 1921–1924 have worn off, the rate of new family formation by young couples in their twenties and early thirties may be expected to continue at a high level. When the small number of children who were born from 1932 to 1937 reach maturity, there will be a pronounced decrease in family formation, followed by a temporary upswing after the babies born during the war attain the age of marriage. This may be followed by a slackening increase in new families until the total number reaches stability within a reasonably short time after the total population stabilizes.

If Social Security measures are successful in enabling an increasing number of old couples to continue maintenance of a separate household, family household groups may be expected to decrease in size as they increase in number, the decrease being associated of course with the decreasing proportion of young dependents.

If these results are inevitable or wholly desirable, then the only policies called for are those which will adjust economic and social institutions to a stationary population. Manufacturers of baby carriages, baby foods, and children's clothing must adjust to a stable market, and builders of residential accommodations and equipment should take into account the greater predominance of small families and a slower rate of family formation. The labor force will not expand so rapidly and the average age of available workers will increase. These are only a few of the economic adjustments which may be necessary; the social adjustments may have just as wide ramifications. Fortunately, if these adjustments must be made, there is ample time for the process, because basic population changes are slow and predictable within limits. Continuation of the present moderate rate of increase would require no specific economic adjustments as long as increasing production keeps pace with expanding population.

If, on the other hand, these trends are judged to be undesirable or alterable, then the United States can, along with other nations, attempt to evolve policies which will check the tendency to reduce family size.

POPULATION POLICIES

As has been pointed out, most industrialized nations have realized the situation. The policies advocated for improving it have varied widely. They have included marriage regulations, sterilization of the unfit, wide dissemination of contraceptive knowledge, encouragement of immigration, systematic development of services and subventions for families with children, propaganda campaigns, bachelor and spinster taxes, and actual payments on behalf of children either in the form of a bonus at birth or a continuing allowance as long as the child is under sixteen or under eighteen years of age.

In attempting to judge the effectiveness of these policies, we must keep in mind that with the exception of public education and public health services for children and public assistance for needy families with children, the inauguration of family assistance has been comparatively recent. Most of these systems were started during the depression of the 1930's. Any results have been difficult to disentangle from concomitant changes due to recovery from depression. For instance, in its early years the Hitler regime made spectacular achievements in increasing the birth rate for a year or two and then maintaining a fairly level trend up to the war. Students who have observed the Nazi policies closely conclude, however, that much of the initial spurt was due to rigid suppression of abortion at the expense of an increase in illegitimacy and that the later stability was due to improvement in employment. Russia had a similar spurt when abortion clinics were closed, but subsequent trends are confused with the stabilization of Soviet economy after the revolution. France with longer experience, while not able to increase the birth rate over a period of years, was seemingly able to check the decline between the two world wars. Another consideration which determines the effectiveness of these policies is that most of them have been modest in their beginnings and the state has assumed only a small proportion of the responsibility for financing child care. It should be said, however, that these provisions tend to become more comprehensive as time goes on.

Quantity and Quality

In the advocacy of population policies some planners emphasize improvement of the quality of the population; others, increase in the quantity. Some profess to see a conflict between these two objectives. On the other hand, some policies contribute to both objectives.

The economic argument for quality against quantity, stated in very general terms, is that, given a fixed amount of resources, per capita consumption can be higher for a stationary population than for an increasing population. If this is granted, it would mean that because there are fewer children, they could on the average be afforded superior advantages. This reasoning, however, overlooks the possibilities of changes in intelligence and technology. Improvements in production methods can within limits increase the per capita production of a larger population without changes in the total resources.

It is of course true that certain areas of the United States with limited resources are overpopulated in view of their present system of resource utilization. There is, however, no evidence that the country as a whole could not, even with the present status of knowledge and technology, support a considerably larger number of people. Some of the overcrowded areas, such as the South, might support a larger number with more efficient agriculture, more industrialization, more technical skill, and better distribution.

The social arguments for placing emphasis on quality rest primarily upon the desirability of discouraging child rearing by defective or incompetent parents and encouraging it in homes where superior advantages may be offered. The difficulty in translating these objectives into concrete policy lies in forecasting who will prove an incompetent parent. Aside from some manifestly undesirable hereditary traits, such as feeblemindedness and certain types of mental defect, our knowledge of the operation of biological heredity leaves much to be desired.[4] On the other hand, if social heredity in the form of advantages afforded by parents is considered, the way is open for the application of policies which will assure equal opportunity for the children of all families regardless of the social disadvantage of the parents.

Economic arguments for a vigorous increase in population rest on the assumption that such an increase is necessary to maintain an expanding economy. Here, again, it is not possible to be dogmatic, because increases in per capita consumption which accompany a rising standard of living may be as important in the maintenance of a healthy economy as are sheer increases in numbers without a rising standard of living. Success in the search for an optimum balance between population and resources will depend both upon continuing improvement in the techniques of production and trade and upon a healthy distribution of cash income and public service facilities designed for enhanced family living and development.

Health Policies

Most notable among the measures which were adopted primarily to improve the quality of the population and which serve likewise to maintain its quantity are public health measures, especially those designed to conserve the life and health of mothers and children. Within the past few decades about fourteen years have been added to the average expectation of life. This improvement has for the most part affected the ages below forty. This means not only that larger numbers survive but also that husband and wife families are not so frequently broken by death and consequently have a more extended child bearing period. In fact it is certain that, without this extension in the life span of the young and middle-aged, the decline in the birth rate would have been much sharper than it was over the past thirty years. The preservation of maternal lives has been especially influential in this respect, since many more women than men remarry after being widowed. Likewise, improvement in the general health of mothers has rendered them more capable of offering the advantages needed by growing children.

Recent preservation of life in the earlier years, especially the reduction in the infant death rate, has been outstanding. Since so much of the rate has been attributable to preventable causes, it is not likely that this sur-

4 Chapter Fourteen, Heredity and the Family, pp. 421–438.

vival has meant the perpetuation of any appreciable amount of biological unfitness. In fact the development of knowledge and skills in child care, both on the medical and on the nutritional front, has increased the probabilities not only that a child will survive to maturity but also that he will reach maturity in good health and with enhanced physical fitness. It may therefore be stated, without quibbling as to whether the objective is quantitative or qualitative, that the keystone of any population policy should be increased emphasis on public health measures, especially in the field of maternal and infant hygiene; for, remarkable as the progress in the past twenty-five years has been, there is still entirely too much preventable death and sickness which destroy life or efficiency before maturity.

Policies Primarily Qualitative

Among the measures designed primarily to improve the quality of the population at some slight expense to quantity are the recent stricter marriage regulations and the expansion of sterilization practices. Most states have some prerequisites for marriage which tend to discourage socially undesirable unions. These range all the way from a waiting period after a license has been obtained to a fairly rigid premarital examination. Eugenic sterilization of the mentally deficient and criminally insane is sanctioned in laws which have been passed by the majority of the states. Such programs, while obviously decreasing the extent of hereditary deficiency, have little ultimate effect on the total birth rate since they are applicable to persons so handicapped by deficiencies that they are not usually highly reproductive.

Other measures designed primarily to raise the quality of the population are involved in the movement to improve the knowledge of contraceptive methods and to make this knowledge widely available to families which for health or other reasons should be limited in size. Up to recent years the legal restrictions and the pressures of public opinion were such that this movement attained very little headway. However, the number of recognized birth control and planned parenthood clinics has increased substantially, and the extent to which doctors and others advise family limitation has probably increased also.

CHILDREN AND FAMILY INCOME

Aside from the policies which have as their principal objective the maintenance of health, the most widespread measures for the encouragement of large families have an economic basis or economic implications. Such policies are therefore aimed at a double objective — both the maintenance of a level of living by families with children which will be more nearly equal to that of families without children and the encouragement of larger families which might accompany such economic equalization. In other words, these two objectives may be promoted by the same policy so that equalization of the level of living of families with children and families without children will actually encourage larger families.

Before we can know to what extent such policies will serve this double purpose we must obtain more data about the operation of the economic motive in regulating family size. Our present knowledge on this point is not sufficiently definite, because economic motives are interrelated in various ways with the knowledge of and ability to use contraceptive devices, and with health status, moral convictions, and social and other psychological

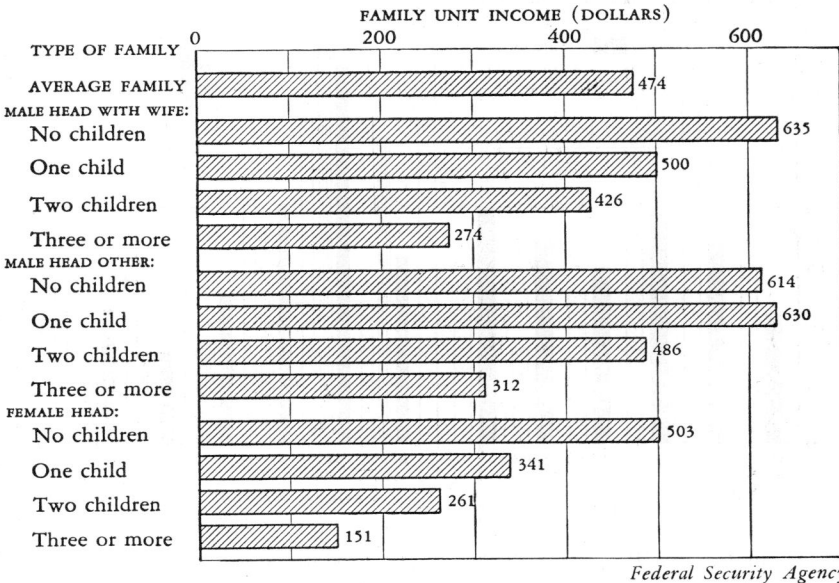

FAMILY UNIT INCOME (DOLLARS)

TYPE OF FAMILY	Value
AVERAGE FAMILY	474
MALE HEAD WITH WIFE:	
No children	635
One child	500
Two children	426
Three or more	274
MALE HEAD OTHER:	
No children	614
One child	630
Two children	486
Three or more	312
FEMALE HEAD:	
No children	503
One child	341
Two children	261
Three or more	151

Federal Security Agency

FIGURE 26. FAMILY UNIT INCOME OF NONFARM FAMILIES BY TYPE OF FAMILY. FAMILIES WITH WAGE OR SALARY INCOME ONLY, 1939

choices involved in the size of the family desired. Moreover, economic status is associated with family size in various ways at different age levels and on different levels of income.

The disadvantage in purchasing power of families with children as compared to families without children is apparent in Figure 26.[5]

In 1939 the per capita income of families of man, wife, and no children was $635, and that of man, wife, and three or more children, $274. Thus childless couples had more than twice the purchasing power of couples with three or more children. The per capita purchasing power of one-child families was about four fifths that of families without children. Figure 27 distributes families with respect to per capita income and number of children included. It will be noted that 70 per cent of all children

[5] In converting family income to per capita income, adults were assigned the value of 1 unit and children under 18 the value of ½ unit. See T. J. Woofter, "Children and Family Income," *Social Security Bulletin*, Jan., 1945. Actual amounts have changed but relationships are much the same.

were in families with per capita incomes below the national median of $474 and almost one third of the children were in families with per capita incomes as low as $150 to $300. This is simply an indication of the fact that family income usually increases slowly with the age of the head of the family. It cannot stretch as abruptly as family requirements are increased by each additional child.

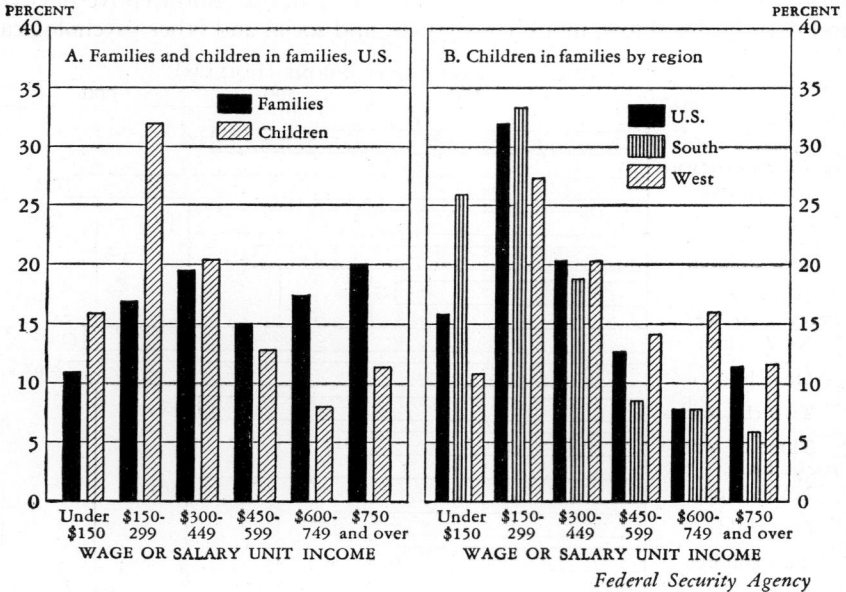

FIGURE 27. PERCENTAGE OF FAMILIES AND CHILDREN IN FAMILIES BY WAGE OR SALARY UNIT INCOME, UNITED STATES, 1939

Figure 26 indicates that the per capita income of nonfarm families of man, wife, and two children was $426. This does not give us a clearcut measure of the adequacy of such an amount for the support of such families. A measure for approximate determination of adequacy is afforded by the maintenance budget.[6] This budget includes the goods and services considered essential for a modest level of living for a man, wife, and two children. It is not a very liberal budget. It provides no expenses for operating an automobile, and only modest recreational, cultural, and miscellaneous outlays. This budget, priced by the Bureau of Labor Statistics in thirty-three principal cities in 1940, required an average per capita outlay of $427. This, it will be noted, is almost exactly the per capita income of all nonfarm, two-child families ($426). This can be interpreted as follows: The two-child family with the *average* income can support the modest level of living provided by the maintenance budget. Such a family with *less than average* income will have a level of living below this maintenance

[6] Margaret L. Stecker, *Intercity Differences in Costs of Living* (Washington: Works Progress Administration, 1937).

standard. The family with more than two children and no more than average income will likewise live below this maintenance standard. The one-child family with less than the average income, as is the case of many young couples, is under economic pressure not to add another member. The two-child family at or near the average income level is likewise inhibited from expansion.

The extent of maladjustment between per capita incomes for the support of families and per capita requirements as measured by the cost of the maintenance budget in cities is indicated by Table 21. From this table it is estimated that about 48 per cent of all children in these cities were in

TABLE 21

COMPARISON OF MEDIAN AND LOWER QUARTILE INCOME, 1939, AND COST OF MAINTENANCE BUDGET, 1940, 33 CITIES

City	Family Unit Income		Cost of Maintenance Budget	Per Cent of Families Living Below Maintenance
	Median	Lower Quartile		
United States, urban	$533	$321	$427	38
Washington, D.C.	704	435	461	27
San Francisco, Calif.	685	437	446	26
Seattle, Wash.	633	397	426	28
Portland, Ore.	630	388	402	26
Los Angeles, Calif.	620	400	407	26
Chicago, Ill.	612	395	447	31
New York, N.Y.	611	386	467	35
Detroit, Mich.	611	411	442	29
Minneapolis, Minn.	596	390	434	30
Milwaukee, Wis.	566	373	430	32
Buffalo, N.Y.	554	378	403	29
Boston, Mass.	540	350	444	38
Denver, Colo.	536	324	395	34
Cleveland, Ohio	527	341	429	37
Kansas City, Kans. & Mo.	523	300	385	34
Philadelphia, Pa.	519	341	407	35
Pittsburgh, Pa.	515	337	409	36
St. Louis, Mo.	514	309	426	36
Indianapolis, Ind.	508	313	395	35
Baltimore, Md.	505	321	408	35
Cincinnati, Ohio	494	304	411	39
Houston, Tex.	488	263	401	40
Richmond, Va.	484	253	408	41
Portland, Maine [a]	459	313	413	38
Manchester, N.H.[a]	458	296	416	44
Norfolk, Va.	416	235	407	48
Jacksonville, Fla.	412	222	398	47
Scranton, Pa.	411	245	424	52
Atlanta, Ga.	381	213	412	55
New Orleans, La.	355	198	393	56
Birmingham, Ala.	349	188	392	57
Memphis, Tenn.	309	179	399	67
Mobile, Ala.[a]	303	160	365	63

[a] Represents income for state urban population.

families with income which was insufficient to support the maintenance level of living. This 1939 situation has been improved by the rising level of income during the 1940's and by the more favorable distribution of income. On the other hand, the cost of living has also increased and there are more children per family. Thus, while the relationship of children to income may have improved to some extent, because incomes rose more rapidly than the cost of living, there are still large numbers who are disadvantaged, especially those in the larger families which are in the lower quarter of income size.

These maladjustments afford a general measure both of the financial sacrifice made by parents and of the relative disadvantage of children in larger families. They therefore constitute the basic justification for special aids for families with children. It is natural that farsighted couples who desire every advantage for their children should endeavor to relate family needs to family incomes as best they may. Such planning is rendered difficult, however, by two factors of time lag. First, the maximum expense of child care usually occurs a number of years before the family head reaches his maximum earning capacity. For instance, a father usually has his first child before the age of thirty but the average man reaches the peak of his earning capacity about the age of fifty-five, after most of the children are mature and self-supporting (Table 22). The second time lag is that

TABLE 22

MEDIAN TOTAL FAMILY INCOME AND AVERAGE NUMBER OF CHILDREN PER FAMILY, BY AGE OF MALE FAMILY HEAD

(Nonfarm Families, 1940, with only wage or salary income in 1939)

Age of head (years)	Median total family income	Average number of children
Under 25	$ 902	0.73
25–29	1,230	1.02
30–34	1,394	1.58
35–39	1,454 }	1.94
40–44	1,505 }	
45–49	1,536 }	1.46
50–54	1,540 }	
55–59	1,434 }	.69
60–64	1,326 }	
65 and over	1,238	.31

the maximum expense for the support of the child occurs some fifteen years after the child is born. The outlay for children from high school age onward is considerably above the outlay for infants. Therefore it may be said that so far as economic considerations enter into decisions as to the size of the family, they involve at least partially an effort to forecast the relationship between expense and income some years in the future. In this respect, temperament evidently plays its part, for some couples will think more in terms of future prospects than present status and, among these, some will be influenced by pessimism and some by optimism.

There is convincing evidence that, on a short-time basis, fluctuations in the birth rate are associated with changes in per capita income. Each pronounced economic cycle is accompanied by a retardation of the birth rate in a period of depression and its acceleration in a period of recovery. This relationship was particularly marked in the depression of the 1930's, when the birth rate reached an extreme low in 1933 of 16.6 per thousand, whereas by 1940 it had recovered to 17.9 per thousand, only to go on to still higher levels with the advent of high war incomes and other factors operating in the war period. These temporal fluctuations probably operate with different intensity at various income levels also. In the young low-income groups where lack of family planning is associated with poverty, the change in economic motivation from periods of depression to periods of prosperity is probably not so pronounced. Studies of relief families in the depression of the 1930's indicated that they maintained a high birth rate despite loss of private income. For the middle-income classes, a period of relative prosperity increases the possibility that wives can stop work without reducing the family level of living too sharply or that ambitions may be attained and children supported at the same time.

It may be argued that economic aids to families with children would not be effective because poorer families have the larger number of children. This assumption is partially based upon the age factor previously mentioned, namely, that children are usually in households when parents are young and have not reached their maximum earning capacity. As a matter of fact, in all families in 1940, 55 per cent of the urban children were in those with less than the median income (Figure 28); but by the time couples reach the age of thirty-five (Figure 29), the distribution of children is more nearly equal in the different income groups. The tendency of the younger couples in the poorer families to have more children may be accounted for in several ways. Manifestly it is not a direct causal relationship, since it is not realistic to suppose that couples will deliberately decide that because they are poor they will rear more children. It is rather to be supposed that the basic cause is the correlation of lack of education and lack of ambition with lower income.

In a large proportion of the middle-income group the family income of childless couples is augmented by the earnings of the wife. In the Consumer Purchase Study of 1935[7] about one fourth of the white wives and one half of the Negro wives without children were contributing to the family budget; whereas, among the white couples with one child, less than 10 per cent of the wives were working, and among the larger families even fewer wives were employed. In most instances, when an employed wife quits work to assume family responsibilities, the family income is curtailed.

There is also reason to believe that security of income may be as persuasive as absolute level of income in influencing the decision to assume family responsibility. Although this hypothesis needs more thorough testing, it is probable that the constant fear of periods of low wages, unemploy-

[7] Special tabulation for Lorimer, Winston and Kiser, *Foundations of American Population Policy,* (New York: Macmillan, 1934), p. 123.

ment, industrial accident, and early discharge from industry is one of the reasons why the prevalence of family limitation is associated with industrialization. There is a theory that one of the reasons why the early months of World War II produced a record crop of births was that the income of soldiers' families was relatively secure. Although military family allotments and allowances did not support a high level of living, that level was reasonably adequate and assured. In addition, the hazard of death or disability was partially provided against by insurance and compensation.

In view of these complex relationships between income and fertility, it is not to be expected that the effects of an economic policy will be readily measurable in terms of its influence in increasing family size. The case for economic assistance to families with children must, therefore, rest primarily upon the effects of these policies in increasing the ability of these

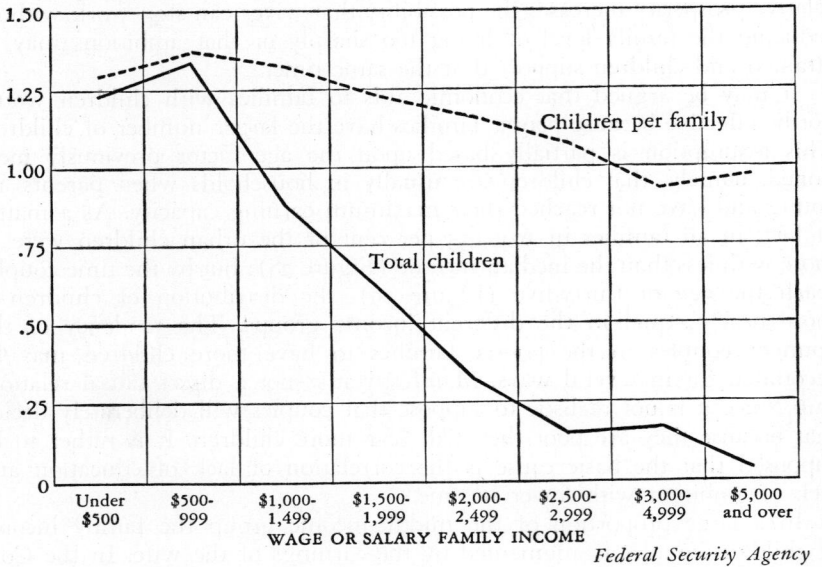

Federal Security Agency

FIGURE 28. CHILDREN PER FAMILY AND TOTAL CHILDREN IN FAMILIES BY WAGE OR SALARY FAMILY INCOME, NONFARM FAMILIES, SOUTHERN REGION, 1939

families to rear children and give them a good start in life. To the extent that such policies will actually encourage larger families or at least discourage smaller families, they may be considered also as measures for maintaining numbers.

Economic aid of this sort is generally known as a family allowance or a children's allowance. It is either a cash allowance or an allowance in kind made in the form of services directly to children, or subventions and privileges available to families with children. In one or the other of these forms, children's allowances, even though they may be limited to education, are practically universal.

Family Allowances — Cash

Cash allowances have been adopted by most European countries in the past few years. Such aids are usually based on the payment to each family of a stipulated monthly or weekly sum determined by the number of children in the family. The movement for cash allowances attained considerably greater momentum in the English-speaking world after the Report of Sir William Beveridge on Social Insurance and Allied Services in England and the adoption of cash allowances by Canada. The Beveridge Report placed less emphasis on the encouragement of larger families than on the equalization of income-level. In fact, Beveridge looked upon family allowances principally as a means of rounding out the system of social insurance. His argument was as follows: (a) normal wages are inade-

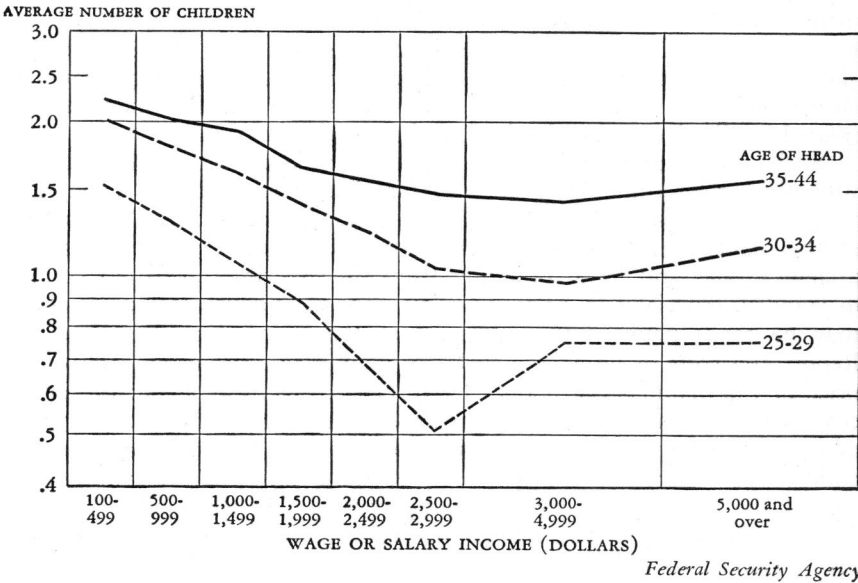

AVERAGE NUMBER OF CHILDREN

WAGE OR SALARY INCOME (DOLLARS)

Federal Security Agency

FIGURE 29. AVERAGE NUMBER OF CHILDREN PER FAMILY BY AGE OF HEAD AND FAMILY INCOME, UNITED STATES 1940 CENSUS

quate to support the larger families; (b) in periods of unemployment, unemployment benefits should be scaled below normal wages in order to encourage return to private employment; (c) if normal wages are inadequate for the larger families, the lower scale of unemployment benefits will be still more inadequate; (d) in order to correct this situation, the family with children should have an increased income regardless of whether the principal breadwinner is employed or unemployed.

Beveridge proposed an allowance for each child when the responsible parent was in receipt of any benefit or pension, and for each child after the first when the parent was self-supporting. The amount was to be graduated by the age of the child but to average eight shillings (roughly $1.60) per week. This was reduced to a flat five shillings ($1.00) when the legislation was enacted.

This proposal contains the basic principles of all family subventions in cash. A few countries extend the allowance per child to all children in the family, but the majority omit the first child from the computation and some begin to pay allowances only after the second or even third child. Some programs cover the whole population, and others are limited to particular groups. The amounts likewise vary, although comparisons from country to country are almost impossible because of fluctuation in exchange rates and purchasing power of various currencies.

The arguments in favor of cash family allowances are based on their tendency to equalize the incomes of families with children and those without children and the consequent possibility that they will encourage an increase in the size of families. The first contention is obviously correct. It may be said, however, that the second has not been demonstrated for various reasons. First, few countries have had allowances long enough or on a sufficiently universal basis to prove statistically whether they have increased family size or merely checked the tendency to decline.

Such allowances are in most cases so inadequate that they do not strengthen the economic position of families with children enough to provide a real offset to the economic cost of the larger family. Confirmation of this hypothesis, as pointed out above, is difficult because of varying exchange rates and levels of living from time to time and from country to country, especially in periods of inflation. Certain general comparisons may be made between the adequacy of the proposal in the Beveridge Report and costs of living in the United States in 1940, using the average price of the maintenance budget in thirty-three cities as a measure of the cost of living and reducing this cost to a unit basis by counting each adult provided for by the minimum budget as a full unit and the two children as one and one-fourth units. On this basis, the average annual cost of the maintenance level of living per child in the United States in 1940 was $215. The eight shillings per week allowance proposed by Beveridge amounts to $83.20 per year, which, even allowing for considerable differences in purchasing power in the two countries, is only about one third the American standard. The adequacy of this allowance is still further reduced by the failure to include the first child in the allowances. In other words, a two-child family receives only four shillings per child, since nothing is allowed for the first and eight shillings for the second.

The original Beveridge proposal of eight shillings is fairly representative of the usual family allowance provisions; it is somewhat less than scales recently adopted in Canada, Australia, and New Zealand and it is somewhat more than the allowance in some Continental countries. The postwar French measures are seemingly more liberal than the prewar scales, but their adequacy is difficult to assess because of inflation.

Further light on the adequacy of the usual amount of the allowance per child in other countries may be gained by an examination of the allowances made to dependents of soldiers in World War II.

As against the $83 proposed in the original Beveridge plan and the $52 finally adopted, the allowance for the first child of a man in the United States armed forces was $360 a year, with $240 for each subsequent child. These amounts were scaled approximately to the wartime cost of living in the larger cities; since they approximated the average per capita family incomes in these cities, they exceeded average per capita incomes in the lower-wage cities and rural areas.

A general scale of allowances of $9.00 per month for all the 45 million children in the United States under eighteen years of age would be only one third as adequate as allowances made to members of the families of men in the armed services. The cost would be about $4.5 billion annually. This would transfer a considerable amount from families with high incomes to families with low incomes; but families in the middle-income range, unless they included three or four children, would pay as much in taxes to support the plan as they received in benefits. For families who would eventually contribute about as much in taxes as they received in benefits, there would, however, be the advantage of spreading the cost of child support throughout the wage-earning period rather than concentrating it in the early years.

Thus, while it may be said that cash family allowances are undoubtedly of value in preventing undue hardship in large families with low incomes, it may also be said that there is no positive evidence that such allowances have contributed to an increase in the birth rate on a national scale. It may be that in some countries they have slowed down the decline. In a considerable number of countries the payment of allowances is not general but is restricted to certain classes, such as government workers or railroad workers; in other countries, the system has not been in effect long enough to produce reliable evidence as to what its effect on the trend in the birth rate is; and in most countries the allowance is such a small proportion of the total cost of rearing a child well that its payment probably does not have great influence on the economic motivation for increasing the size of the family. It has been pointed out that the larger families are usually those where the first child is born when the parents are young; therefore it would appear that the policy of paying no allowance for the first child, which is characteristic of so many of the schemes, would not constitute nearly so strong an inducement to assume family responsibilities early in life as would a system which began allowances with the first child.

On the other hand, one argument against family allowances is that systems that approximate adequacy will necessitate the transfer of a considerable proportion of national income to families that have children from families that have none. There is the additional consideration that allowances paid directly to the responsible parent do not constitute a guarantee that the whole benefit will accrue to the children. While an increase in the total family income normally results in increased expenditures for the children, in many cases such additional payments are merged with the total family budget and may be spent for other purposes. Another negative argument is based on the fear that allowances which are substantial may lead to "breeding for profit" by irresponsible couples.

Variations of the cash family allowances paid over periodic intervals are to be found in cash marriage bonuses and child bonuses or loans. Under such systems, a lump-sum payment alone is made to a couple getting married or bearing a child. Manifestly such a system emphasizes all the objections usually raised against family allowances. One cannot expect that a lump sum paid to the family at the time of a child's birth will be budgeted over the next sixteen or eighteen years of his dependent life; it is likely to be expended fairly soon after its receipt.

A somewhat negative and small-scale counterpart of family allowances is to be found in income-tax exemptions for dependent children. This is negative in the sense that the tax expenditure is decreased rather than the income increased, and small, since the exemption is small and the actual effect on the family net income is only a percentage of this exemption.

Family Allowances in Kind

Subventions to families with children in the form of special privileges or services exist in some form in almost every country, even in those which have systems of cash allowances. The most widespread is public education, with health services for mothers and children also fairly well accepted. Special aids for families with children do not represent a choice between cash allowances and subventions and services but a determination of the extent to which one or the other will be emphasized in a total system. Manifestly, the services should be basic and any cash allowances should be supplementary helps for the equalization of family income.

Educational policy in the United States has been directed toward the provision of free public education for all children of compulsory school age. The attainment of this goal, however, has been unequal as between the low-income and the high-income regions and especially between the urban and the rural districts. The quality of the educational offering is poorest in the areas in which most of the children reside.

It is true that some sort of tuition-free education is available to most children through the high school grades. On the other hand, the extra costs of schooling are a substantial drain on the family budget. They call for a critical examination of the extent to which education is really free and whether the costs of educating a child are equitably divided between parents and society. Even in the elementary grades there is some incidental cost for items like books and school lunches; the total for laboratory fees, library fees, athletic fees, and transportation becomes appreciably more in high school; and in college not only do these fees increase even more but tuition charges are added. Those young people who enroll in a college outside their home community must meet the additional expense of room and board. All these costs are undoubtedly a determining factor in the rapidity with which children drop out of school after the elementary grades. In low-income families there is a double incentive for young people to leave school when they reach working age. Not only are the costs thus eliminated, but the children are then able to contribute some of their earnings to the family budget. Recent studies have indicated that 50 per cent of the young people whose record in high school showed that they were among the most competent to go on to college failed to do so, and a large proportion of these assigned financial considerations as the primary reason. In the absence of more widespread and systematic programs of student aid, the nation is losing the increased skill and efficiency which would be derived from continued education of large numbers of young people who leave school prematurely.

Community services for the prevention of communicable diseases are fairly well developed in the United States; and for the needy, free medical and hospital services are to some extent available. In the middle-income groups the costs of adequate medical and dental care constitute a considerable drain on the resources of the larger families. A medical-care plan covering the whole population and financed on the basis of ability to pay would equalize the incidence of this cost between large and small families. Some nations which do not finance complete medical care provide maternity benefits to cover the costs of child bearing and medical care for infants. The most ambitious program of this kind which has been attempted in this country to date was the emergency program under which the wives of servicemen obtained free prenatal advice, hospitalization, delivery fees, and medical care of the infants.

In addition to free education and free or prepaid medical care, some countries, particularly the Scandinavian countries, have undertaken to supplement the budgets of families with children more directly through the device of allowing price discounts on commodities purchased for children, especially food, clothing, and rent. Such a device was adopted in this country during the depression for all families receiving public assistance, regardless of whether or not they had children. Under the food stamp plans these families were given the privilege of getting food free or buying it at considerable discount. The question of extending such subventions to the population as a whole, however, has never been seriously considered.

Free school lunches are an important segment of a nutrition program and provide some incidental reduction in the expense of education. The policy of our country has been to supply them almost entirely to children of needy families and to supply other children as nearly as possible at cost. Policy is governed by local practice. Federal funds can be used for free lunches for all children, but most communities finance their share of the costs by charging for the meals.

In Sweden the distribution of food to families with children was based in part on the necessity for the absorption of agricultural surpluses by the domestic population. Previously, subsidized dumping of these surpluses for cheaper prices abroad had been used to support prices. It was, however, argued that subsidy to families at home who needed an adequate diet was a sounder policy for supporting full agricultural production.

One of the major adjustments required when children are added comes in housing accommodations. It is difficult to say whether the recent trend toward the predominance of small apartment units which exclude children is the result of the increased proportion of small families or whether the decreasing inclination of urban families to have children is in a considerable measure attributable to the difficulties in securing adequate housing for larger families at a rental which can be afforded from the average income. Undoubtedly, much of the reluctance to start families would be removed by more widespread public housing facilities which would assure the admission of families with children, make available larger apartment units for families with children, and assure rents for these larger units within the reach of the average wage earner. Such a differential rent scale usually characterizes the few public housing projects which have been provided to date in this country.

Public housing available in the United States does not constitute a sufficiently large proportion of all housing to have a wide effect on the accommodations open to families with children. However, the housing projects that have been constructed are usually designed for larger families and do not exclude children.

To summarize the present development of social policy in the United States as it relates to family size, it may be said:

(1) Universal cash allowances for children have never received serious consideration but they have been recognized for segments of the population in need of public assistance and, in wartime, for families whose breadwinner has been inducted into the armed forces. The small negative allowance afforded by income tax exemptions is, however, a well-established policy.

(2) The nation has rather tended to develop free services which are directly available to children but has not systematically developed these services into a coherent pattern available to all areas and all income classes.

It is entirely possible that a comprehensive system of such services and subvention would not be subject to some of the objections offered as arguments against cash allowances but would in a large measure accomplish the same objective of equating the level of living for medium-sized families at a point now attainable only by childless or small families.

State Equalization of Opportunity

The services and facilities described in the previous section as family allowances in kind are, in the United States, largely planned, administered, and financed by state and local agencies. Equality of opportunity for all children to benefit by these programs is seriously hampered by uneven distribution of children and uneven ability to raise revenues. Broadly speaking, states with large agricultural populations have more children per family not only because of higher fertility on the farms but also because of higher fertility in their less industrialized cities. Such states have lower per capita incomes because of the high proportion of farmers and because of the lower wages in their urban areas. In 1940 the farm population was supporting 26 per cent of the nation's children on 7 per cent of the national income. Figure 30 shows the maladjustment of the distribution of children and income in the nonfarm population. New Mexico, with 1.46 children per nonfarm family, had less than $300 per capita income; California, with only half as many children per family, had over $525 per capita income.

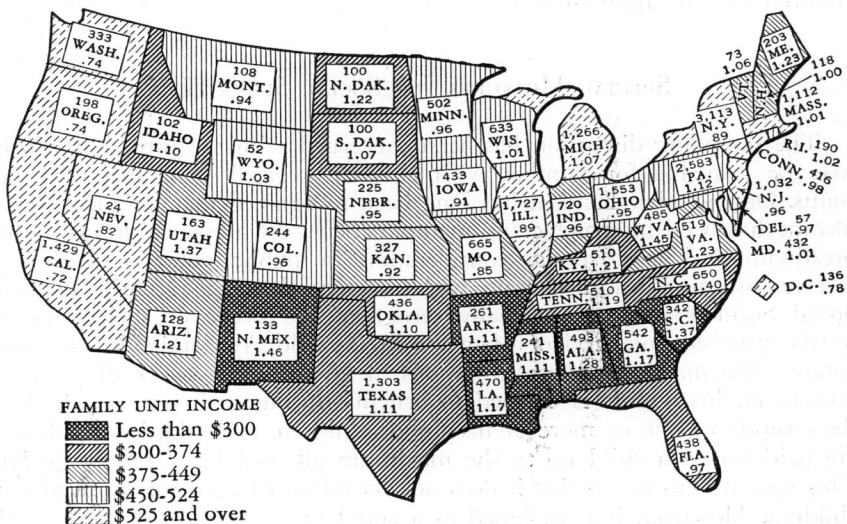

FAMILY UNIT INCOME
- Less than $300
- $300-374
- $375-449
- $450-524
- $525 and over

Social Security Board

FIGURE 30. CHILDREN UNDER 18 YEARS OF AGE AND UNIT INCOME OF NONFARM FAMILIES

Income, 1939; Children, 1940 U. S. Census; Upper figure — total nonfarm children in thousands; Lower figure — average number of children per nonfarm family.

This wide variation is an index of an equally widespread inability to collect taxes for public services and institutions. A predominantly rural state may tax its people more per dollar of wealth than an industrial state does and still produce less revenue per child. This means that children who grow up in some states have inferior health, education, and welfare facilities and are disadvantaged by state poverty as well as by family poverty.

This is not a problem of purely local concern. It is national in scope because our people move so freely from state to state. There are constant streams of migration from farm to city and from areas of disadvantage to areas of superior opportunity. A child educated in a backwoods community often lives eventually in a metropolis and sometimes exercises control over the affairs of the nation as a member of the Congress. The national stake in the development of every child into a useful citizen leads logically to the premise that the public support of programs and institutions for children should not rest entirely on the resources of the states but should be participated in by the national government. The support of some programs is now shared by federal aid to the states. Such grants are usually characterized by requirements that states and localities match a portion of the federal allocation and meet minimum national standards of performance. This device is in need of further extension and perfection in order that the interests of both the states and the nation may be properly advanced and the goal of equal opportunity for the development of all children may be approximated.

SPECIAL MEASURES FOR SOCIAL SECURITY

The preceding discussion has been concerned with the provision which may be available for families with children regardless of their income status. On the other hand, it has long been recognized that families whose income has been interrupted by unemployment, disability, or death of the breadwinner deserve special consideration in public policy and should receive assistance commensurate with their needs. The recently adopted Social Security measures partially recognize the needs of such families by the provision of survivors' benefits in the Old Age and Survivors Insurance system. Under these provisions, if an insured worker dies before retirement, his widow is entitled to benefits during such time as she has the custody of one or more of his minor children, and additional benefits are paid for each child up to the maximum allowed for a family group. This system is so recent that it does not yet affect a large proportion of the children. Moreover, it is designed as a supplement to other resources and not for full family support; hence families whose sole income is from such a benefit have hard sledding.

The number of children orphaned by death of the fathers is considerably larger than is usually realized. With the death rates prevailing in 1940, nearly 7 per cent of all children under eighteen had lost their fathers and nearly 16 per cent of those who had attained their eighteenth birthday had been previously orphaned. This meant that there were approximately 3,300,000 paternal orphans in the population. Even though large numbers of widows remarry, there were at the time of the 1940 Census over two million children in families with a female head whose male breadwinner was dead or divorced or incapacitated. Reference to Figure 26 shows the great disadvantage of women as family supporters. The per capita incomes of families headed by women were only about two thirds as large as those of the corresponding type of families with a male head. It will be many years before the insurance system covers enough of the population to provide benefits for a substantial proportion of the paternal orphans.

In the meantime, those who are in families whose income is so low that they are eligible for public assistance may receive benefits under the Aid to Dependent Children program. Since this is a state-federal program, the adequacy of the benefits varies considerably from one state to another. In a few states able to finance assistance programs the adequacy approaches an amount which would sustain a modest level of living. In low-income states the benefits are totally inadequate,[8] and even in the middle-income states these payments are inadequate when it is considered that unless the mother works, her maintenance as well as that of the children must be provided.

The problem of family benefits during periods of unemployment is particularly difficult. A few states have proposed to vary their scale of unemployment compensation benefits in accordance with the size of the worker's family. This, however, gives rise to the dilemma that the maximum unemployment compensation benefit is usually scaled below the previous wages of the worker in order to encourage return to private employment at the earliest opportunity. Under these circumstances, it is obviously impossible to pay an unemployment compensation benefit which will be adequate for a large family whose previous private income was already inadequate for a satisfactory level of living.

If, as we have indicated in previous sections, security of income is as persuasive a reason for assuming family responsibilities as the absolute level of income, it would appear that a more thoroughgoing system of social insurance and assistance, designed especially to give adequate protection to families with children against the hazards of income loss by reason of unemployment, ill health, or death, is a social policy of major importance both in protecting the quality of the population and to some extent in encouraging larger families.

IMMIGRATION

The foregoing discussion has been confined to the changes in the native population which are associated with the changes in the birth and death rates, because these are the changes which affect and are affected by changes in the family structure and attitudes. It must be borne in mind, however, that both qualitative and quantitative aspects of the total population can also be markedly changed by trends in migration. This applies both to shifts in international migration and to trends in internal migration. As long as the level of living in the United States is relatively high with respect to many other areas of the world, a substantial increase in numbers, at least for a temporary period, could be effected by loosening the restrictions on foreign immigration. In the past, increases in net immigration have had a double effect on population increase. The immigrants themselves constitute net increases in the total number, and they usually add to the segments of the population which have a relatively high birth rate, because immigrants are usually in the young adult ages and the majority come from rural areas of nations which have traditionally high birth rates.

[8] The increased federal contribution to these benefits which was enacted in 1946 may have the effect of raising the level of adequacy provided.

However, the considerations which are involved in change in immigration policy are not the same as those involved in efforts to influence the quality or quantity of the native population, although the two are related. Perhaps one reason why the slackening increase of the total population of the United States has not caused serious concern is the knowledge that at any time when it appears that the advantages of increased numbers would over-balance the disadvantages of uncontrolled immigration, quantity could be achieved in this way.

Conclusion

Population changes are so directly and fundamentally related to many other important social changes that they should, and probably will, command increasing attention as their true nature becomes more apparent. It is likewise obvious that our knowledge of the extent to which social policy can affect the quality and welfare of the population is more exact than the evidence as to the extent to which it can affect quantity, except in the case of those policies which are designed to conserve life. It is only within recent years that techniques of population analysis have enabled the student to predict with some degree of confidence what the trend in numbers will be a generation hence on the assumption of the approximate continuation of prevailing trends in birth and death rates. In the past, tendencies toward decline which have been inherent in the birth and death rates have been masked by immediate excess of births over deaths, and the changes have been so gradual that they cannot be accurately described except by observation over fairly long periods of time. It is safe to predict, however, that increasingly reliable methods of analysis, increasingly adequate basic data, and careful observation of the results of experimental policies will provide the means for choosing the most desirable measures in this field.

To admit inability of democratic economic and family structure to maintain at least a stationary population would savor of defeatism. It appears reasonable that a progressive nation can evolve a social system which will maintain numbers without impairment of the general standard of living or undue disadvantage to families with children. To reach this goal, certain present tendencies toward a declining rate of natural increase must be checked and at the same time average family income must be adequate to support an average sized family. The average family, in turn, must be large enough to replace each generation. To do so, some families must be larger than the average to counterbalance failure to marry, involuntary sterility, and other factors. In order that the parents of these larger families may not have to sacrifice too much and that the children may have equal opportunity, the nation needs a well-rounded system of housing, education, health, and welfare facilities and services specifically designed for the development of children. Payment for these services should come predominantly from public taxation rather than from the family income of parents.

SELECTED READINGS

CARR-SAUNDERS, A. M., *World Population — Past Growth and Present Trends* (Oxford: Clarendon Press, 1936).

Census, U. S. Bureau of, *Differential Fertility, 1940 and 1910* (Washington: 1943).

——, *Families — Family Wage or Salary Income, 1939* (Washington: 1944).

Children's Bureau, *Report of the White House Conference on Children in a Democracy* (Washington: U. S. Government Printing Office, 1940).

"Economic Measures in Favour of the Family," United Nations, Dept. of Social Affairs. Summarized by H. G. Hammons in *Eugenical News* (Dec., 1952).

GLASS, DAVID V., *Population Policies and Movements in Europe* (Oxford: Oxford University Press, 1940).

LORIMER, FRANK, and OSBORN, FREDERICK, *Dynamics of Population* (New York: Macmillan, 1934).

——; WINSTON, ELLEN; and KISER, LOUISE K., *Foundations of American Population Policy* (New York: Harper, 1941).

MYRDAL, ALVA, *Nation and Family* (New York: Harper, 1941).

MYRDAL, GUNNAR, *Population, A Problem for Democracy* (Cambridge: Harvard University Press, 1940).

National Resources Planning Board, *Problems of a Changing Population* (Washington: U. S. Government Printing Office, 1938).

Social and Psychological Factors Affecting Fertility, Milbank Memorial Fund, vol. 3, chaps. 11 and 13.

STECKER, MARGARET L., *Intercity Differences in Costs of Living in March, 1935, 59 Cities,* Research Monograph XII, Works Progress Administration (Washington: U. S. Government Printing Office, 1937).

WOOFTER, T. J., "Children and Family Income," *Social Security Bulletin,* vol. VIII (Washington: Jan., 1945).

——, "Children and Family Security," *Social Security Bulletin,* vol. VIII (Washington: Mar., 1945).

——, "Factors Sustaining the Birth Rate," *American Sociological Review* (June, 1949).

——, "Paternal Orphans," *Social Security Bulletin,* vol. VIII (Washington: Oct., 1945).

TOPICS FOR DISCUSSION OR REPORTS

1. What is the proportion of children and the per capita income in families with three or more children? What are the implications for maintenance of population numbers and for child development?

2. Why did the early years of the industrial revolution make it possible to increase population rapidly?

3. Compare the factors of natural increase in the United States with those in Russia and Japan.

4. Discuss in detail some of the social and psychological reasons for family limitation.

5. Discuss the social and economic adaptations which will have to be made if a stationary population is inevitable.

6. What are the difficulties in applying "eugenic" population policies?

7. The principal causes of infant death are premature birth, accidents in birth, diarrhea and enteritis, pneumonia, and influenza. To what extent would biological unfitness be perpetuated by reducing deaths from these causes?

8. What are the difficulties in determining the optimum size of population in relation to natural resources?

9. Outline the chief differences between a system of family allowances in cash and in kind or services.

10. Why is it difficult to prove that cash allowances have contributed to the maintenance of a high birth rate? Does this necessarily mean that they cannot accomplish such purpose?

11. The French system of family allowances provides a higher scale when the mother is not working and includes the first child in the calculation when the mother is not working. What are the advantages of this device?

12. What are the rural-urban differentials in number of children per family and income distribution? What effect do these have on health and education of the future population?

13. Can assistance to families, either in cash or in kind, be justified on grounds other than possibility of maintenance of numbers?

14. What special insurance and assistance provisions are now made for orphans and children whose fathers are incapacitated? How adequate are these provisions?

Chapter Twenty-Six

Plans for Strengthening Family Life*

REUBEN HILL

IN the preceding chapters has been told the story of family, marriage, and parenthood; it is one of growth, of strain and stress, of change, but of survival. Yet when we contemplate the future of these domestic institutions we perceive many paradoxes. Marriage in America has never been more popular, yet decisions to divorce are more numerous, too. It is now generally accepted as proper to put asunder by legal process those whom God obviously has not joined together. Moreover, the group of individuals between twenty-five and thirty-five most likely to marry is neither the single nor the widowed, but the divorced. Although disappointed in their first experiment, they affirm their approval of the married state by remarrying in record numbers.

Family living is no longer compulsory. A man can get his meals cooked and his clothes mended rather more cheaply without a wife than with one. Most able-bodied women can provide themselves with better clothes through their own efforts than out of the pay envelope of a husband. Economically, marriage has become a luxury and parenthood a positive expense. Most couples actually live more frugally together than they did separately; they economize to marry.

If marriage is uneconomical, if it is not compulsory, if it is often so painful that divorce ensues, why do people continue to marry and remarry in such numbers? Is family life just a perpetually transmitted bad habit?

A review of some of the facts presented in the rest of the book may make the task of answering these questions easier. Certainly we are going to need a perspective which includes both past and present if we expect to cast our eyes very far into the future.

A SUMMING UP

The introductory chapter called attention to the fact that the family is interwoven with two contrasting types of society, sacred and secular. As one pole is approached, kinship and neighborhood are paramount; toward the other extreme, individualism and anonymity hold sway. The shift from one to the other not only alters the functioning of the families involved, but also calls forth changes in the members of the families. Unmoral, demoralized, segmental, marginal, regulated, decadent, and liberated personalities appear; and the results of their actions affect, in turn,

* Special thanks are due Howard Becker, Evelyn M. Duvall, Sylvanus M. Duvall, and R. A. Schermerhorn for suggestions and constructive criticisms at crucial stages in the writing of this chapter. However, the use of "we" here and there, and especially in the paragraph concluding the chapter, indicates no shifting of final responsibility; the writer alone is to be blamed for any shortcomings.

their families and other social groups as well. Subsequent chapters expanded these basic concepts and brought evidence in support of them, so that our opening chapter served in part as an organizing pattern for later portions of the text.

Our search for family origins proved fruitless except as it demonstrated how varied family structure and function is among human and nonhuman groups. Common human elements were discovered, to be sure, such as the regulation of copulation and procreation, care and protection of the young, tuition and imparting of language to the child; but no amount of purely biological knowledge will enable us to predict the strikingly varied patterns which the human family takes. The social and cultural constituents of organization are the source of all the values and attributes which lend the family of a given society a distinctiveness of its own. To understand how a type got that way we must study its history. For each of the types listed in Table 2, p. 77, a history would have to be written for us to be able to appreciate its reason for being. Our own modern American family is of many hues, a heterogeneous mosaic at best, but it too made more sense as we followed its antecedents into prehistoric times. Thus ended our search for family origins, not with a protohuman family nor with the families of some primeval horde but modestly enough with our most ancient antecedent that kept records, the nomadic Hebrew family.

Our ideas of right and wrong, of morality and immorality, and our emphasis on the sanctity of the home and family were forged and hammered into their present form over many hundreds of years. Moving backward from the twentieth century we perceive contributions from a self-sufficient frontier family responsible for breaking the patriarchal authority of the father and also contributions from the emigrant families of Europe. Ideas which we have since termed "puritanical" came mainly from British settlers. From Britain we follow a trail to medieval centers where flowered many of our fantastic ideas about romantic love and the courtesies due women. From there we are impelled to go even farther back to the fusion of the early Christian with the Greek and Roman cultures. Back of the early Christian looms the forefather of them all, the Hebrew family of the Old Testament from which many of our religiously sanctioned values have come. The customs and laws of the early Hebrews with respect to marriage and the family have fortunately been preserved in the Old Testament of the Bible. Moreover, the Christian peoples have treated these Hebrew pronouncements as scripture, thereby crystallizing a family morality which otherwise might have been more flexible. Except where modified by the less dogmatic teachings of Jesus Christ, the "thou shalt nots" of the Mosaic law have survived to this day. There has been little invention of new ideas and much borrowing and modifying of old ones in this trek from the Hebrew patriarchal family of several hundred persons down to the typical American family of four. If our family organization is outmoded and ill-fitted for urban industrial living, the lag has been accumulating for some time. If American family design is breaking up, it may only mean that planning and reorganization are long overdue.

Varied family types in the United States compete for adherents. Regionally there are well defined types in the South, in the Spanish-American Southwest, in the Middle West, in the Ozarks, and in the Mormon country of the Rocky Mountains. Each of the forty-eight states legislates as a sovereign unit on matters relating to the family, and the legal norms differ sharply as a result. The rural family differs greatly from the urban, and there are great intrarural and intraurban variations. Sacred and secular trends cross and crisscross. Within a twenty minutes' drive from urban-secular Cedar Rapids, one drops into a relatively sacred Amana society with tightly knit family organization and unquestioning traditional familism. One needs only to cross a city like Chicago to pass successively through immigrant areas of sacred hue, slums with hosts of homeless men adrift in secular fashion, workingmen's areas where both the husband and wife work and children carry door keys about their necks. When one reaches swanky Suburbia he finds it has its own value system and family organization, often resembling a fatherless matriarchy since the husband leaves for work before the children are up and returns after they have gone to bed. Families vary tremendously, white and colored, rich and poor, native stock and immigrant; all serve to prove the folly of blueprinting family reformation uniformly for these United States. We are a multiverse rather than a universe!

Turning now to the points relevant to our problem in the later chapters of the book, we find pertinent the discussion of problems of courtship and mate selection and of husband-wife relations. We are told that courtship should be valuable for its own sake, as childhood is. Courtship should be enjoyed no more as preparation for marriage than childhood is enjoyed as preparation for adulthood. In the future we must meet the need for more companionship among young people and devise a more effective system of mate selection. More initiative for women in courtship is advocated, as is the removal of all restraints on employment of women so that they may be less hurried in their selections. A case is made for increased opportunities for circulation of young people among several groups for a more varied experience. These measures would make for less haphazard mating, which should in turn make life more tolerable within the American family.

The chapters on marriage phenomena emphasize the personal nature of that relationship rather than its institutional aspects. Evidences of marked secularization are given: growing sex freedom, instability of early marriage, startling increases in divorce, and a wide variety of conflict situations throughout the family life-cycle. The chapters on family crises and on the effects of war on family life remind us of the puny stature of the small conjugal family in confronting the tasks set for it. The effects of war speeded up many secularizing, disintegrating trends which were under way before the war. War is responsible for strange mismatings, for a great increase in aberrant sexual behavior, high illegitimacy, high mobility of population, and concomitant shifts in attitudes and values. The aftermath has been characterized by innumerable adjustments as families settle down to living together again. Estimates of family sociologists that a third of World War II marriages would dissolve and the partners rapidly remarry have proved accurate. These chapters leave a large measure of gloom and dismay as to the future of many individual families. Happily, one of the characteristics of the small modern family is its adaptability, as we shall point out later. As has already been said, "If wars were so devastating of family life as some writers would have us think, then the family could not have survived its own history." Again and again the family has operated as a sacred nucleus around which a more stable society could be organized. We suspect it has not yet lost its resiliency — indeed, it has shown great reorganizing power in this trying period after World War II.

These are just a few of the many points made in preceding chapters which we shall attempt to keep in mind in considering the planning and reorganization currently under way to improve the lot of people living in families. We will use them as points of reference in the discussion which follows.

How Fares the Family?

One of the gains of secularization has been the freedom given to critics of our social institutions. The family was one of the last institutions to lose its immunity to friendly as well as unfriendly criticism. Until fairly recently, few chose to brave the abuse which came to those who violated the traditional sanctity of the home by speaking out against what did or did not go on in it. Some of us wonder if the family today has not become public scapegoat number one as the floodgates of criticism have been opened. The family is blamed for juvenile delinquency, for truancy, for mental breakdowns, for physical deficiencies — for all of which community agencies should share responsibility. Men in their prime are found unfit for military service. Do physicians examine their outmoded system of providing medical services, or nutritionists their teaching techniques, or physical educators the lack of vitality in their program? Hardly. They all with one voice turn to the family: "If all parents would take care of their children, all would be well." Neat buck-passing but hard on the family groups that have to make the ultimate adjustments.

As we analyze the critics of the family we note that they divide between those who feel that the family is too sacred, unyielding, restrictive, and old-fashioned and those who feel that the family is quite unstable, disorganized, poorly ballasted, and vulnerable to all sorts of crises. Obviously during a period of rapid social change the family is bound to change and in so doing to displease those who like it as it is. The advocates of social change, who are discontented with things as they are, charge that the family is not adapting rapidly enough and is peculiarly restrictive in its maddeningly slow adjustments.

Representative of the proponents of greater and greater secularization and individualism are the Marxians and the free-love advocates. The

Marxians saw the family as the product of a decadent economic system, a bourgeois institution which sapped man's power and made him willing to stagnate in settled family living in preference to "throwing off his chains" in revolution. Family men were apparently poor revolutionists. Yet after twenty years of experiment with wide-open marriage and divorce arrangements in the Marxist Soviet Union, new restrictions were placed on divorce and abortion in 1936 and again in 1944. The few scattered attempts to separate children from parents and bring them up in children's cities have been abandoned. The objective of housing all families in communal living quarters is now questioned and the majority of Russian families live in private homes.[1] The criticisms of the Marxian extremists are no longer taken seriously, even by their own Marxist states.

Free-love advocates like Bertrand Russell find few who wish to spar with them any more. The issues they raised are almost dead. Changes in the sex mores between the two World Wars and during World War II have rendered meaningless their demands for additional freedom. If young people are irked by the restrictions of the family mores on their love life, they wink at the codes and make their own private adjustments.[2] The findings summarized by Folsom from recent studies emphasize the voluntary nature of virginity at marriage. Many of Russell's recommendations are already generally accepted in secularizing, romance-steeped America — the right to choose one's life mate for love alone, untrammeled by political or social expediencies and, if necessary, without the approval of parents, employers, and friends. Waller and others have shown the exploitation which goes on under the guise of expressing personality needs. The law of the jungle — exploit or be exploited — is an outgrowth of love relationships initiated without consideration of parents and friends. Actually the studies of marriage success indicate that marriages based on such headstrong love are poorer risks than more prosaic matchings.

The companionate marriage advocated by the late Judge Ben Lindsey for university students and others as a desirable prelude to a later more "serious" marriage in which children would be expected has actually arrived in fact.[3] Approximately 40 per cent of the returned servicemen on college campuses in recent years have been married, and the majority of these have been postponing children until graduation. Differences there are, to be sure, between Lindsey's proposal and present practice, but the major details are there. The period of the companionate has been lengthened within conventional marriages to allow couples to complete schooling, build up a surplus to provide for children, and enjoy "togetherness" before assuming parental responsibilities. As with other proposals made by

[1] Ernest W. Burgess and Harvey J. Locke, *The Family* (2nd ed.; New York: American Book Co., 1953), pp. 170–175.

[2] Austin L. Porterfield and H. Ellison Salley, "Current Folkways of Sexual Behavior," *The American Journal of Sociology*, 52 (Nov., 1946), pp. 209–217.

[3] Technically, companionate marriage is a proposed legal companionship between a man and woman qualified by a private agreement that no children are to come of the union and that the wife is to be economically independent of the husband. No state has yet legalized companionate marriage as here defined.

those who feel love should be emancipated from its fetters, this measure too is now generally accepted by conventional young people as a normal part of marriage.

On the other hand, Ruth Reed once pointed out that open experimenting with marriage forms has drawn violent objections and outright persecution. She deplored the unreasonable prejudice in America which cut short two of the most interesting experiments in polygyny and group marriage ever attempted in our society. She referred, of course, to the attempt at group marriage in the Oneida Community in New York State, 1848–1876, and the Mormon experiment with polygyny, 1843–1890.[4] Reared as monogamists, there were among the Mormons real difficulties in achieving satisfactory marriage adjustments. Neither husbands nor wives had any well-defined concepts of how to behave in a multiple-mate situation. Jealousy among wives and feelings of doubt, guilt, and inadequacy on the part of the husband were not uncommon. Compensations were evident in aggressive and dominant behavior and in expressions of anxiety feelings among both husbands and wives. Nevertheless Reed, in evaluating these experiments, stated that they were both successful "in that they accomplished the purposes for which they were undertaken, and in both cases the new form was apparently satisfactory to those who participated. In both cases the experiments were terminated in deference to outside pressure aimed at enforcing conformity to established standards."[5] The tendency to experiment on scriptural and theological grounds having been eliminated with such severity, all experimentation in recent years has been limited to those changes in family norms that could be brought into seeming conformity with legal requirements and to changes in the laws regulating marriage and divorce. Polygyny and polyandry are practiced today but on a strictly legal basis, one wife for one husband *at a time;* but, *in succession,* several wives and several husbands are not infrequently found today. Progressive polygamy, or serial monogamy!

Jessie Bernard offers an interesting criticism of the family system. She tests objectively the extent to which families are successfully performing each of the major functions and concludes that they are doing a competent job in the functions of reproduction, socialization, and providing an affectional milieu for the child. She sees, however, in our system of rearing children in families the negation of democracy. Theoretically, at least, all

4 Ruth Reed, *The Modern Family* (New York: Crofts, 1932), p. 161. See also an analytic but sympathetic description of both the Oneida and the Mormon experiments in Ruth S. Cavan's *The Family* (New York: Crowell, 1942), pp. 53–62. For additional insight into the social interaction and role playing within forty-seven Mormon polygynous families see the study conducted by J. E. Hulett, Jr., "Social Role and Personal Security in Mormon Polygamy," *The American Journal of Sociology*, 45 (1940), pp. 542–554, and "The Social Role of the Mormon Polygamous Male," *American Sociological Review*, 8 (1943), pp. 279–287, and of course Kimball Young's important book, *Isn't One Wife Enough?* (New York: Holt, 1954).

5 Reed, *op. cit.*, p. 169. As so often happens, having discontinued polygyny the Mormons have become stalwart defenders of monogamy. They are quite willing to help in the prosecution whenever any offshoot group or sect appears to be reviving plural marriage in the Utah-Arizona area. Recently undertaken were prosecutions involving members of a "Fundamentalist" cult who were arrested in 1953 on federal-state charges.

individuals are to have equal opportunity in a democracy, but our system of rearing children in families deprives many of them of this equality, since some have a far better start than others. She points out that children reared in homes varying widely in socioeconomic status have varying social inheritance, reflected in their intelligence, personalities, education, occupation, health, and opportunities in the industrial order.[6] The question then arises, "For the sake of our equalitarian ideology, should we abolish the family?"

In general each of the criticisms of the family discussed above conceives of the family as imposing unnecessary restrictions upon individual freedom and personality expression. If the criticisms were valid when they were made, we have shown that most of them are much less valid today. Family ties have loosened, and if anything the most telling criticism that can be made today is that families are unprotected in a rapidly secularizing world. The second set of critics who see the family as an institution of diminishing importance are hardest to meet if we squarely face the evidence.

Vanishing Functions of the Family

In our search for origins we found that in man's earlier history the family was virtually coterminous with society. All the vital problems of human existence were settled within the family. Only as man domesticated plants and animals and settled down into villages did competing associations develop, such as the state, the church, industry, and the school. Our discussion of the Hebrew family in its pastoral stage shows a complete identification of the patriarchal family, even at this date, with every major function of life in a sacred society. Some students of the family believe that this was on the whole desirable.[7]

The family of yesterday performed seven identifiable functions: (1) reproduction of population, (2) protection and care of the child, (3) economic production and consumption of family goods and services, (4) socialization of the child, (5) education of the child, (6) recreation, and (7) affection-giving, supplying love and a sense of security to all members of the family, and intimate emotional satisfactions.

Of these the economic, educational, recreational, and socialization functions have been particularly subject to transfer to other agencies. Actually, what are usually termed functions of the family are but names for large categories of concrete behavior, and the content of these categories is continually changing. It is doubtful whether any function of the family has been wholly or permanently transferred to another institution. The net picture of transfer may have been historically unfavorable to the family, but some of these functions are occasionally regained, and there always remain some sturdy families that never give them up.[8]

[6] Jessie Bernard, *American Family Behavior* (New York: Harper, 1942), pp. 538–544.
[7] C. C. Zimmerman and M. E. Frampton, *Family and Society* (New York: Van Nostrand, 1935).
[8] In many sacred societies in the United States families have successfully resisted the intrusion

Functions are in essence activities instituted to realize *taken values* rather than to meet *given needs*. The transfer of functions that has taken place probably reflects more a change in values than it signals the disappearance of the family as a source of influence in the western world. As its activities shift in emphasis, from one set of services to another, its members are freed to improve their performance in the areas of undisputed excellence where there is as yet little serious competition; namely, the reproductive, the child-care and the affectional. One measure of this would be the shift from predominantly housekeeping tasks by mothers to tasks that are predominantly homemaking and family-centered.

We are inclined to join Waller in his impatience with functionalism:

> The family, we hear, performs important functions in society; it provides for the perpetuation of the species and the training of the young; it performs economic and religious functions; and so on. Almost we are encouraged to believe that people marry and have children because they are eager to perform these needed societal functions. In fact, people marry because they are in love, or for other less romantic but no less personal reasons. The function of the family, from the viewpoint of individuals, is to satisfy their wishes. The function of the family or any other social institution is merely what people use it for.[9]

Activities carried on in the family represent the things family people regard as important in realizing their values. When someone makes a better mousetrap than father can improvise, he ceases to bother with his and buys it from the specialist. People continue to cook and dine in the home because it is pleasant to do so, but they also eat out in considerable numbers. When it becomes more pleasant to eat out than in the home it will not mean that the family has lost its anchor; it will just mean people are eating out! Quantitatively, the production element of the economic function left the home as industry moved from the home to the factory, but life has probably been quite as pleasant without the domestic workshop.

Both the informal and the technical education of the child take place increasingly in the school and on the playground. In spite of this, Hartshorne and May's studies of character development place the home ahead of the play group in character education, and place both ahead of the school and the Sunday school.[10] The trend of formal education is toward placing more responsibility on the home, as parent-teacher activities and home visits from teachers testify. Furthermore, the continued use of books, magazines, newspapers, and the new use of television in the home shows performance of educational functions by families. Many families, in fact, take these functions very seriously, and do not trust the school with everything.

---

of government and other agencies into areas traditionally dominated by the family. For a spirited criticism of the functionalist analysis of the family in this context, see Leonard S. Cottrell, Jr. and Nelson N. Foote, *New Directions of Research on the American Family* (New York: Social Science Research Council, 1954), Chap. 2.

[9] Willard Waller, *The Family* (New York: Dryden Press, 1938), p. 26.

[10] H. Hartshorne and M. A. May, *Studies in the Nature of Character*, vol. 1: *Studies in Deceit* (New York: Macmillan, 1928), chap. 3.

Much of the recreation of family members is rightly enough taking place outside the home where it can be adapted to the interests of age and sex groups; yet family picnics and "music fests" have not entirely disappeared. Family members continue to regard home as the favorite center for the practice of hobbies and craft work.

As for socialization, the process of fitting the child for living with his fellows, of designating what is proper behavior in social situations, has not so much left the family as it has changed in character. Once the task was to discipline the child so that he would mature quickly into a useful member of the family group for the family's sake (he constituted a capital asset and was desired for his contributions to the labor of the household and the farm). Today the task of socialization is directed at preparing the individual for independence of existence, to take his place entirely outside the family group. This is a more complex task; to produce self-sufficient, independent individuals who are vocationally, maritally, and morally competent to stand on their own feet and fend for themselves in a complicated urban society. To accomplish this end the family, as the child matures, shares the task of socialization increasingly with other groups in an ever-widening circle of personalities and acquaintances. The good family no longer prepares its members to live forever in close proximity to the family hearth. It helps its members one by one to assume an independent existence with families and friends of their own, competent to face crises without returning home for advice and direction. Socialization as a function remains vital to today's family. It differs widely, however, in objective and method from the socialization of the good old farm family of yore.

Granting some losses to competing associations, important segments of the economic, socializing, and educational functions remain in the home to support the three other major functions of the family which have not been seriously disturbed; namely, the reproductive, the protective (physical care of the child), and the affectional. These are probably enough to form the "intimately sacred nucleus" so essential to stable familial and societal structure and so basic to effective personality.

In this country approximately 96 per cent of the births are in wedlock, and there is no appreciable move toward separating the reproductive function from the family. While it is true that family size in the United States has declined in the last fifty years from 4.93 to 3.78, there is no evidence that another institution could perform this function as well. Some may feel that with added knowledge of human genetics we may be able to breed human stock in such a way that there is little likelihood of Rh factor blood incompatibility occurring or reproduction of hereditary weaknesses. The human stock might be greatly improved thereby.

None of these theoretical possibilities are likely to be adopted as long as the task of child rearing remains wedded so closely to the home. No substitute for the affectional atmosphere of a loving home has been found for the irreducible minimum of physical and emotional care of the infant and preschool child. Less than 2 per cent of the nation's children are

reared in foster homes or institutions. As a matter of fact, social workers
have come to encourage wherever possible the rearing of children by their
own parents in preference to foster-home placement or institutional placement. In commenting on the followup study of seventy-eight foster-home
children made by Anne Roe and Bela Mittelman, the editor of *Family Life*
infers that it is better for a child to have an intact home, even though not
a very good one, than to feel himself differentiated from other children
as a child without a home.[11]

AFFECTION-GIVING THE MAJOR FAMILY FUNCTION

Of all the services the family provides which bring members back to
the hearth night after night, the most apparent is the affectional warmth
shared by family members. As marriage has become more of a personal
relationship, the impelling tie that binds family members has become
affection. To be wanted, to be understood, to be appreciated, to be loved,
and to belong to someone are fundamental needs which parallel the needs
to possess, to love, and to respond to someone. Uniquely met in the intimacies of the family relationship, these needs should be listed among the
main sources of cohesion which sacralize families in America today.[12]
Most of our family habits and family routines which introduce security
and predictability to the family relationship are built around the affectional
activities and services of the family. Adults as well as children share the
needs for emotional security and love. They are basic needs which do not
disappear as one matures.[13]

There are also external reasons for the increasing emphasis on the family
as a bundle of personal relationships. Adults have turned to the family
for affection as their community contacts have become more and more
formal and segmental. Where yesterday they derived some affectional
satisfactions from neighbors and friends, today adults are emotionally
dependent on the few intense person-to-person relations found within the
family. Men and women require more affection to compensate for the loss
of other activities and satisfactions and to sustain them under strain and
anxiety. Men and women are marrying in record numbers today mainly
to achieve intimate response — the love of a man and a woman and their
love for their children. Taken largely for granted in the past as the normal
refuge from cold indifference, the family has become increasingly im-

[11] *Family Life,* vol. 6, No. 10 (Oct., 1946), p. 4.
[12] Evelyn M. Duvall and Reuben Hill, *When You Marry* (rev.; Boston: Heath, 1953), pp. 305–
306. These are not unlearned needs but are culturally defined within a sacred family tradition.
[13] As Strecker contends, however, it is true that an overvaluation of the affectional element may
lead to neuroticism and oversentimentality; see "What's Wrong with American Mothers,"
Saturday Evening Post (Sept., 1946). The discussion earlier by Bain, pp. 197–200, and by
Taylor, pp. 464–465, does show that the affectional value can be perverted. Families may
become hotbeds of emotional isolationism. Better by far is the practice of introducing children gradually to groups outside the family where the emotional ties may take more cooperative forms and where the bonds may be more diffused. Thus may family members avoid the
mistake of putting all their emotional eggs in one basket.

portant as the source of the affectional security that we all crave. The family has become love-in-action; this includes interest, respect, and affection.

ALTERNATIVES TO THE FAMILY SYSTEM

In our Euro-American society we are committed to the family system. To change to some other system would require the scrapping of most of our society's cultural equipment: individual family dwellings, family automobiles, family furniture, and hundreds of accessories and gadgets. It is possible, however, to conceive of a "brave new world":

> Eugenic colonies might take over the reproductive function. Governmental controlled nurseries might be assigned the task of protecting and socializing children. Separate living arrangements might be provided for men, women, youth, and children. . . . Men might live in separate barracks, or men and women in clubs; and children in schools.[14]

Many such arrangements might be imagined, but we are not likely to adopt them. The choice is not between some such fantasy and our present system. The alternative, as we see it, is between planned, guided functioning in terms of carefully specified goals and objectives and laissez-faire operation of the present system. Ideally any plan of action would conserve the binding forces which now tie family members together, but would also provide helps in adapting family practices to the demands of an increasingly secularizing society. What is needed is a family which combines integration of unique family values and loyalty to those values in the early years (sacred forces) with adaptability in the face of crises and high mobility (secularizing forces), producing a social form which can absorb the blows of social change without breaking under strain.

The stressing of unique family values was one of the forces which made the aristocratic family strong, although it is difficult to see why the practice should be limited to aristocrats. In fact, democratic families have unique and precious values which they have every obligation to stress. Consider, for example, the practice of sharing by all family members those elements which further good humor, fair play, respect for each other, common hobbies, and personality growth for all. There is even room for a few taboos, for that matter, say in the matter of family and personal privacy or in some devotion to a larger goal that is, in reality, a family ultimate. This latter could be interpreted in religious terms or in terms of a social ideal held sacred. Families that know what they stand for are fortunate, for they may well be held together in times of stress by these sacred objectives.

Perhaps this peculiar blend of integration and adaptability is the equivalent in family structure and organization of the "liberated person-

---

14 Bernard, *op. cit.*, p. 247. The Nazis moved in this direction, as did the Soviets in the earlier phases of their experiment.

ality" discussed briefly in the introductory chapter.[15] Using the formula for a liberated personality in family terms, we would get families in which the key attitudes and values are of sacred derivation, thus providing stability and persistence, and families in which traditional and supernaturalistic ways of achieving ends are replaced by actions that are principled and humane. In such families liberated personalities may be developed in earliest childhood, and if the external conditions are not too difficult they may be kept liberated throughout life.[16] We need to develop families which are ballasted less by unthinking habits of action and fixed ways of meeting needs than by timeless nonmaterialistic values. We are not there yet, indeed we may not even be traveling in that direction. All we know is that we are *in transition* from one fairly well defined sacred family form to another more secular form whose dimensions and duties we barely perceive. If we understood better the possibilities of a family which combines stability with adaptability, we might shape the future family accordingly. A further analysis of this transitional family is in order.

THE FAMILY IN TRANSITION

We witness today the growing pains of a transitional family that has had to change from the ways of pioneer and farm life to serve its members in quite different surroundings. It has changed its form and adapted its code of living to the cramped quarters of cities, to migration and trailer life, and to all the other terrific changes engendered and accentuated by the war. Moreover, we are living participants, we who are parents, as well as our children and quite possibly their children, in this period of transition. Waller eloquently describes the dilemma of those who are caught "in between":

All who live in a society which is changing from an old consensus to a new one must somehow mediate between the two moralities, and must bear the strain of their society's double life. The pioneers struggling toward the new norm pay heavily for the privilege; the cultural monadnocks who are left when the plain about them has been eroded away pay equally heavily; the average man pays least. When a society has moved a short distance toward a new consensus, the costs of conformity to the old norm are relatively slight and the costs of nonconformity are heavy indeed. When the new consensus has nearly been

[15] See especially pp. 44–46. For more detail see Howard Becker, "Processes of Secularisation," *Sociological Review* (British), 24 (Apr.–July and Oct. 1932), esp. pp. 138–154.
[16] See Margaret Park Redfield, "The American Family: Consensus and Freedom," *American Journal of Sociology,* 52 (Nov., 1946) p. 183. In commenting on the needed balance between integration and self-expression within families Redfield wrote, "Those whose personality has not been shaped by intimate attachments appear not only less human but also more vulnerable. Our complex civilization requires, it seems, a balance between the detachment which makes for adaptability — a detachment aided by the processes of mechanization, standardization, and secularization — and that inward attachment which gives some fixed values and creates some sort of moral order for the individual in spite of rapid changes in the environment."

achieved, the situation is reversed. In the intermediate stages, the choice between old and new norms is always difficult. . . .[17]

A certain amount of disorganization must precede reorganization. It may be that families in a transition period are always in a mild state of disorganization, the necessary price we pay for adjusting to changes about us. The life cycle of the transition family, moreover, is inevitably marked by a series of recurring upsets.[18] Each brings about a course of adjustment and maladjustment which runs approximately as shown in Figure 31.

I	
Pre-crisis patterns of meeting problems	Unified front
	Flexibility
	Rigidity
	Individuals first
	Closing of ranks
	Philosophy which fits
II	
Family meets a crisis	Loss of status through unemployment
	Death
	War separations
	Infidelity
	Desertion
	Divorce
III	
Disorganization, short time reactions	Refusal to face facts
	Fantasying crisis away
	Escape
	Fainting
	Apathy
	Compensation
IV	
Disorganization, long time reactions, accompanied by reorganization	Trial and error
	Search for solutions
	Struggle to attain a livable balance

V

Reorganization and attainment of permanent adjustment through formulation of new routines consistent with the new situation, reestablishment of stable habits, self-control, reorganized economic life, and normal social life; or

Fixation at one of the levels of stage III, in some form of escape, submission, or compensation

FIGURE 31. SCHEMATIC SERIES OF ADJUSTMENTS COMMON IN MANY FAMILY CRISES

[17] Waller, *The Family*, rev. by Reuben Hill (New York: Dryden Press, 1951), pp. 592–593.
[18] Handling Family Strains and Shocks, Chapter Twenty-One, pp. 616–640.

If our analysis depicted in Figure 31 is correct, the popular notion that all family disorganization is pathological requires revision. Disorganization mediates reorganization quite as frequently as it mediates family dissolution. Reorganization, moreover, is taking place not only within individual families in the innumerable adjustments of persons, but it is also apparent in the reformulation in public opinion of the conceptions of the family and of the roles of its members.[19]

We have maintained sturdily since frontier days that no family was a strong family until tested with crisis and trouble. Indeed we have evidence to show that sudden impoverishment in the depression strengthened families that were already well organized.[20]

Koos[21] tested this hypothesis in a special context. He lived rather intimately with some scores of families in one block of a New York tenement district for two years and observed a total of 109 family crises during that period. He confirms the course of adjustment depicted earlier in Figure 31 but finds that almost none of his families was better organized after a family upset than before. This may be expecting too much for low-income families. Out of 109 troubles, in only one case did the family appear to reorganize itself on a more solidified basis than it had before the trouble.[22]

Koos constructed profiles of trouble (see Table 23) to demonstrate how disorganized the families became immediately after the crisis (b), what their angle of recovery was (e), and at what level (d) of disorganization-reorganization they were able to stabilize themselves. The distribution of the 109 troubles are shown in Table 23, which we have adapted from Koos' study. It is pretty clear that his families experienced a net step downward in their attempts to reorganize. Life did not go on as before. For more than half of the troubles, 61 out of 109 (profile 3), reorganization failed to achieve the level of organization before the trouble. Twenty troubles followed the fourth profile of successively poorer organization as troubles accumulated. We might conclude that troubles at best are mixed blessings for low-income families.

Our main point — that family disorganization may mediate reorganization — is confirmed both by the studies of the effects of the depression on families and by Koos' findings, although the latter are not so convincing as the former. In their focus on disequilibrium American sociologists have overlooked the accompanying process of reorganization making for dynamic equilibrium.[23] This chapter offers an opportunity to rectify

[19] Burgess and Locke, *op. cit.*, p. 713.
[20] Ruth S. Cavan and K. H. Ranck, *The Family and the Depression* (Chicago: University of Chicago Press, 1938), and Robert C. Angell, *The Family Encounters the Depression* (New York: Scribner's, 1936).
[21] Earl Lomon Koos, *Families in Trouble* (New York: King's Crown Press, 1946).
[22] *Ibid.*, p. 110. Koos himself is careful to point out the inadvisability of making generalizations for all families from his findings. Sixty-two families are manifestly too few and too selected to be representative even of American low-income families.
[23] Gunnar Myrdal, *The American Dilemma*, 2 (New York: Harper, 1944), pp. 1055–1056.

TABLE 23

DISTRIBUTION OF PROFILES OF 109 TROUBLES AMONG 62 LOW INCOME FAMILIES
IN NEW YORK CITY, 1940–1943.
Source: E. L. Koos, *Families in Trouble* (New York: Kings Crown Press, 1946)

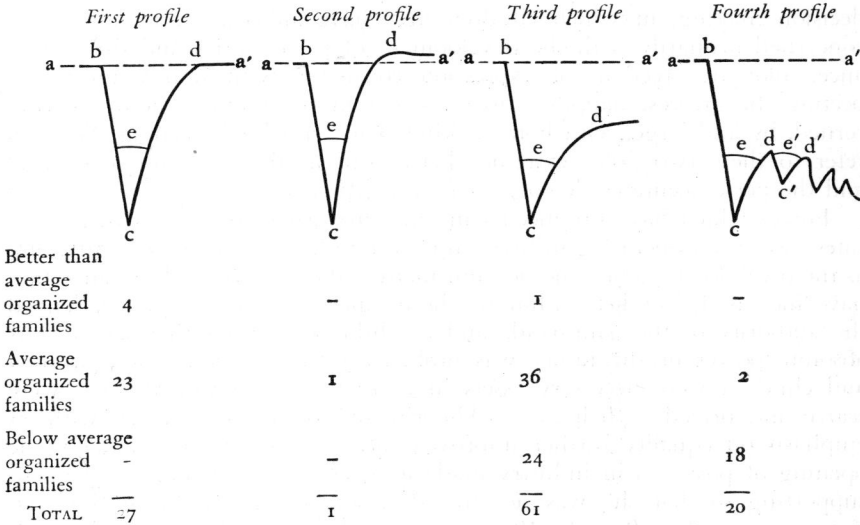

	First profile	Second profile	Third profile	Fourth profile
Better than average organized families	4	–	1	–
Average organized families	23	1	36	2
Below average organized families	-	–	24	18
TOTAL	27	1	61	20

Broken line a - - - a' represents level of organization before the trouble.
Solid line b——c——d—— represents course of adjustment after trouble hits family.
e represents angle of recovery.

that situation so far as family disorganization and reorganization are concerned.

In this conception of disorganization and reorganization as paired processes, we have the brush to add rosier tints to the somber picture of family life painted during this transition period. Record divorce rates, dwindling birth rates, evidences of parental irresponsibility, and widespread juvenile delinquency seem to point to a process of decay.[24] Yet these same trends represent not only disorganization but reorganization. The same forces which find expression in family instability are supporting a type of family unity based upon the binding affections and loyalties possible in a smaller, more personalized family association.

This point of view will be clearer if we contrast the known family form of yesterday with the possibilities inherent in its polar extreme. The family of yesterday described in its most extreme form was patriarchal, adult-centered, familistic, autocratic, concerned primarily with the production of things, and preoccupied with its own housekeeping. It was clearly incompatible in its value system with the notions of political

[24] The work of Carle C. Zimmerman is especially directed to this theme; see his *Family and Civilization* (New York: Harper, 1947) chaps. 5 and 29.

democracy, of the need for maximum expression of personality, of equality of opportunity, of the sacredness of personality which grew up in the educational, political, and philosophical circles of the time. Its polar extreme is impossible to achieve overnight, but it can be conceived as a workable form; namely, a family which is equalitarian, democratic in decision making, in which children may have an equal vote and voice, concerned primarily with the development of personalities and their guidance, allowing freedom of expression consistent with family unity, expecting the greatest happiness to be found in the family, and more concerned, by and large, with homemaking than with housekeeping. We will refer to these two polar extremes henceforth as the familistic-patriarchal and the person-centered-democratic family types, respectively.[25]

Forces which have produced pain and anguish to the status quo advocates have been operating to break up the familistic-patriarchal family, and as the breakdown gained momentum many indices of social disorganization have increased. Conflict within the home increased as women challenged the authority of their husbands and as children asserted themselves. The absolute power of the father was broken on the frontier, where women and children were necessary assets in a fight for survival. Women were scarce and prized as helpmates. The rise of political democracy with its emphasis on equality further improved the status of women. Finally the opening of positions in industry made it possible for a woman to be self-supporting so that she was not forced to marry just for a meal ticket. From a time when *Papa Is All* to a period which was characterized by the troubled, uncertain dominance in *Life With Father,* we have seen some family headships shift further still to the family council or committee ruled by its members. Such disorganization as appears to have developed mediated reorganization to bring us more democratic forms of family authority.

UNPREDICTABILITY OF FAMILY FORMS

But the transition to these more companionable forms is never complete nor uniformly compelling in a secularizing society. No pattern holds men and women in line very effectively as the old forms break up — here you may have a serial polygynist, there a budding patriarch, here a matriarchal arrangement, and there anarchy or a filiocentric family, depending often on the personal-social precipitates of early parent-child and courtship pair interaction.

There is considerable evidence that families are working out the form which appears most compatible with their particular personalities. They are taking advantage of the fact that there is no one compelling family

---

[25] Burgess and Locke, *op. cit.,* vii–viii. Burgess and Locke have popularized the terms "institutional" and "companionship" family for these polar forms. The terms are not satisfactory because all family forms are institutional if not matters of pure whim. The companionship family is no less institutional than its polar extreme. It is also often confused with the childless companionate family. We therefore reject them for the more descriptive terms "familistic-patriarchal" and "person-centered-democratic" family types.

form and are shaping their own. "In our family we handle the problem this way," is the proud explanation the young parent gives in a child-study meeting. Is this perhaps the answer?

Are not families growing into differentiated forms on the basis of their interpersonal experiences? Each party to a marriage brings to the relationship personal roles he has played which may not complement the personal roles of the other. Let us analyze the formation of a family pattern in a hypothetical pair, the Jack and Eileen Gordons. Jack Gordon has always dominated situations in his parental home, and has been encouraged thereby to play the dominant role in all other close relationships. His wife, by contrast, was reared in a home where no one person dominated all the time, and she desires to perpetuate such a pattern in her own marriage. Conflict there will be in the Gordon family as personalities strive for the balance that will prove most livable. The result may be an agreement that appears to be semi-patriarchal because Jack seems to make most of the decisions, but there will also be areas in which Eileen is dominant as well as areas in which they continue to challenge one another, ending with an embattled consensus. Disorganization and reorganization both appear in this marriage.

In other marital combinations, better matched in terms of the personal roles carried over from the parental families, the partners may quickly achieve agreement with one dominating and one subordinate or with any of several possible forms.[26] If there does not appear to be much uniformity in families during the transition period, we now see good reasons for the multiversity.

SEMIPATRIARCHIES STILL PREDOMINATE

If there is any modal type of family in America it is the semipatriarchal form in which a dominant husband brings in the bacon and a submissive woman plays a traditional wife-and-mother role. Child rearing and homemaking are primarily the responsibility of the wife, whereas the business contacts and political activities of the family remain the husband's province. This arrangement, midway between the familistic-patriarchal and the person-centered-democratic family, is constantly being challenged by insurgent mothers who rebel against the confining role of wife-and-mother and by a few fathers who feel strongly that it takes two to make a home. In spite of the dissidents it is our impression that the family form is stabilizing, temporarily at least, at this point.

Our cultural definitions continue to differentiate between masculine and feminine roles. The ladylike role shall be overtly subordinate, polite, and gracious. A manlike role must include self-assertion, initiative, and decisiveness. Moreover, many of our first and second generation immigrant families have never known any form except the patriarchal; for them the complementary roles of dominant father–submissive mother are culturally set.

[26] For an early empirical analysis of the phenomenon of transmission and formation of authority patterns see the research of Hazel Ingersoll, "A Study of the Transmission of Authority Patterns in the Family," *Genetic Psychology Monographs,* 38 (1948), pp. 225–302.

In census-taking and all official matters, the national, state, and local governments provide that the *family head* shall be the husband, if he is living. The law further supports the semipatriarchal arrangement in delineating the duty of the husband to support his wife and children and the wife's right to exact support.

Religion from the Hebrews down to the present has supported the familistic-patriarchal form. In a text for Catholic college students the official point of view of the Roman Catholic church is stated in forthright terms: "The man is the head, and the wife the heart of the home . . . the place of the woman is in the home." [27] And so it goes. Among the authoritarian religions there is little support for the other extreme, the person-centered-democratic family.

Money is a source of power that supports male dominance in the family. Unconsciously the most emancipated of women catch themselves saying, "I hate to spend his money." Money belongs to him who earns it, not to her who spends it, since he who earns it may withhold it. When the power of money is added to the cultural definition, it is no wonder that equalitarian personal-social arrangements give way to the culturally defined semipatriarchal roles. As more wives become competent to earn their living and choose that alternative throughout the family cycle, the power of money may be equalized between husband and wife. Meanwhile, even where both are working, the wife is usually paid less and her contribution is viewed as minor.

Finally there is the mating gradient, a demonstrable tendency for men to insure themselves a semipatriarchal authority by marrying mates of less education, younger, and less qualified to make decisions. Thus are husbands prepared to dominate the family intellectually. Moreover, if their quarrels came to blows, his greater physical strength would settle things.

The person-centered-democratic family advocated by most parent educators demands skill and understanding now possessed by few couples. Mature, equally matched personalities with rich experiences in give-and-take are needed to found such a family. Neurotic, egocentric, domineering, and submissive persons are handicapped. The so-called companionship family appears to have much in common with the ideal of "the brotherhood of man" as a millennial goal. Both may well be desirable but they are extreme polar types based largely on the opposite of *what is* to be found in society at a given time.[28] The likelihood of achieving either one seems remote at this writing.

A more pragmatic approach is to examine the weaknesses and strengths of families today and to attempt to formulate a national policy which

[27] Edgar Schmiedeler, *Marriage and the Family* (New York: McGraw-Hill, 1946).

[28] We hasten to point out that instances of close approximation to these polar ideals are not infrequent and help to keep them alive. The functional value of the person-centered-democratic family as an ideal has not been questioned in this essay. Indeed, those who have not attained this more democratic form can be perennially learning from it, admitting its desirability rather than remaining smug and complacent about their own less creative attainments.

would enable them to make the most of the impending changes in government, industry, and social relations. It is to that task that we now turn.

SOCIAL PLANNING FOR THE FAMILY

In an appraisal of the American family today, its most obvious strength is its physical health and resiliency, and its most obvious weakness is its relative insecurity. The external forces of social change are bound in the future to subject the family's resilient fiber to terrific strains and render it even more insecure. The family's insecurity is due to several factors: sociological, economic, and psychological.

Centered as it is about the husband and wife and their two or three children, the family is a precariously small and poorly structured unit to survive the stresses of life — divorce, desertion, war separations, sudden impoverishment, and death. Years ago family members could turn to the kinship group in time of need. But we no longer have easy access to innumerable relatives who can help us out in time of crisis. We have been separated from our kin by a peculiarly American custom which encourages newlyweds to establish a thoroughly independent household. Our very conjugal independence lays the basis for insecurity.

Facing the world alone, each conjugal unit finds itself vulnerable to the risks of unemployment, sickness, disability, and sudden death of the breadwinner. Today we do not make a living. We buy it. We make money, and that money determines the kinds of homes we live in, the food we eat and the clothes we wear, the security and independence we look to in hard times and trouble. The source of money may be stopped without warning and through no fault of the breadwinner by economic depression, accident, sickness, or death. This is the hard economic fact which produces insecurity in the typical American family.

Psychologically the family's insecurity is enhanced by the rapid changes in duties and roles of parents. Feelings of inadequacy surge up in parents reared under one school of discipline who are expected to function quite differently with their children today. Cut off from personal contacts with neighbors both of the friendly and/or prying variety and from the personal counsel of elders, young parents not infrequently face novel situations with anxiety and panic.

Another psychological lack is most apparent in city living. The anonymity of urban secularized societies may seem a welcome cloak to the prodigal runaway, but to the members of the typical American family it provides scant affectional fare. Living segmentally on a touch-and-go basis, which precludes becoming involved in the affairs of others, helps to maintain a sort of impersonal harmony, but psychologically leaves a void in the life of gregarious family people which heightens their sense of insecurity.

In some ways the insecurity of the American family is a paradox. No other country has a higher material level of living. Few countries have greater natural resources, yet millions of our families are living in insecurity. This feeling is particularly concentrated among urban families of lower than average income and education. Koos' study hypothesized that all low-income urban families "face troubles for which society has provided no particular means of solution or only solutions that lie beyond their level of income, education, and sophistication; these problems affect the structure and basis of the family both as an interacting group and as part of the community; as long as such problems fail of solution, the individual and the family will be unable to carry out their functions adequately and human wastage will result." [29]

As a background for our recommendations for a nationwide policy for family life, let us review some of the accomplishments that have already been made in reducing insecurity and improving the effectiveness of families in meeting their members' needs.

A FOLK MOVEMENT TO IMPROVE FAMILY LIFE

Virtually every basic science could make a contribution which would improve the lot of family members: biology, economics, physics, psychology, and sociology. Satisfactory home life requires better housing particularly among low-income groups, better public health facilities, more rational and careful legislation regarding marriage and divorce, a better distribution of the costs of illness, greater recreational facilities for children and adults and a larger measure of economic security for all classes.

These needs cannot be met by emergency reforms but require long-time planning. We have seen since 1900 a public awareness of family problems emerge from discussion by small groups of parents into an integrated movement for the improvement of family life. National organizations have grown up which have among their objectives the reducing of tensions and maladjustments within the home.

The history of the movement to improve family life is a record of several independent developments which at the start had little in common. Home economics, child study, social hygiene, mental hygiene, planned parenthood, and eugenics, as movements, all grew up to conserve some function which appeared in need of help.

The movement for the improvement of family life as it stands today strives for action on five fronts: (1) improvement of child care and training in the home through parent education and child study; (2) improvement of the health of family members through immunization, nutrition education, preventive medicine, and prevention of venereal diseases; (3) improvement of family stock by positive eugenics and planned parenthood programs among all strata of the population; (4) improvement of family solidarity through premarital, marital, and family counseling and education, as well as family case work in its broadest sense; (5) improvement of family administration and family integration through a variety of

[29] Koos, *op. cit.*, p. xiv.

family life education agencies. Obviously we cannot treat in detail these movements in a single chapter. Two of them, family counseling and family life education, are singled out for discussion because so little is known about them. We call attention to the other three to show the extent to which action has been taken already, both formally and informally, to conserve family values and improve the effectiveness of family activities in meeting the needs of members today.[30]

Marriage and Family Counseling

No area is more chaotic and none is riper with promise than the salvaging of families through skilled counseling. A husband and wife are worried about their heated tiffs; a parent feels that friction at home is producing anxiety in a child; a doctor has a patient whose home difficulties are delaying his recovery; a lawyer finds his client needs his marriage strengthened, not dissolved; an employer has a good workman who is falling down on the job because of personal problems; a minister desires advice regarding care for a member of a family in his church; an engaged couple wonder if they are ready to marry, they have so many doubts and mixed feelings — these are the grist of the marriage and family counseling mill which yesterday would have been solved over the backyard fence or with an older relative. Or worse, they are problems that might have been postponed indefinitely, never to be solved.

Fortunately, new skills and knowledges have arisen which are recognized as more effective than the trial-and-error approaches of the well-meaning relative or layman who handled these problems yesterday. Unfortunately the demand for help with personal and marriage problems far exceeds the supply of professional services, and commercial operators have filled in the void to exploit this vast reservoir of human need. Radio programs run by people of dubious background vie with magazine and newspaper columnists in giving advice to the lovelorn. Lee Steiner has ably exposed this racketeering in human anguish in her book, *Where Do People Take Their Troubles?*[31] She found no commericial operators trained in personality and family study and accused them collectively of offering advice without adequate investigation or case study of the individuals who came to them. Relying wholly on a vivid imagination and the gullibility of their patrons, the commercial "psychologists" make snap decisions which often prove disastrous to the client and to his friends and family. There is a big difference between this shoddy quackery and the reliable, modestly helpful professional counseling service which is becoming more widely

[30] For a much more complete discussion of these movements, see Joseph K. Folsom, *Youth, Family and Education* (Washington, D. C.: American Council on Education, 1941), pp. 47–159. See also Bess Goodykoontz and Beulah Coon, *Family Living and Our Schools* (New York: Appleton-Century, 1941), and American Association of School Administrators, The Nineteenth Yearbook, *Education for Family Life* (Washington, D. C.; National Education Association, 1941).

[31] Boston: Houghton Mifflin, 1945.

available. Evelyn Duvall has prepared a set of criteria by which you may judge a good counseling service:

A Good Counseling Service

1. Doesn't promise quick results or make snap judgments.
2. Doesn't diagnose until after a careful study has been made.
3. Keeps all information confidential.
4. May charge nominal fees which are frankly discussed.
5. May call in other trained specialists to help.
6. Uses only trained professional workers from reputable colleges specializing in such fields as social work, human development, psychiatry, and related areas. (At least a master's degree in the specialized area is the usual professional standard.)
7. Is affiliated with such reliable bodies as local councils of social agencies, and nationally with such professional organizations as the National Conference of Social Work, and the National Council on Family Relations.
8. Does not advertise or try to drum up business, relying instead on slowly building up a clientele of satisfied users through referrals from other agencies and professional persons.
9. May have a membership and a board of directors of reliable citizens who take the responsibility for supporting and interpreting the program to the community.[32]

Originally marriage counseling was an extraprofessional duty of the minister, the lawyer, and the teacher. Later it developed as a specialized service of family welfare agencies, child guidance centers, birth control clinics, and mental hygiene clinics. Tomorrow we may expect marriage counseling to emerge as a profession, occupying the full time of specialists situated in organized centers for marriage and family guidance. Professional training for these specialists is as yet only in the planning stages, although course work in counseling is offered as a vital part of the preparation for several professions, notably social case work, clinical psychology, and the ministry.

No family consultation center illustrates better than the Marriage Council of Philadelphia the basic objective of keeping well families well. Starting in 1932 with engaged and young married couples as clients, the center offered at the outset an opportunity to confer frankly and confidentially with a well-informed and sympathetic person on questions of sex, marital problems, or family relationships.

The Marriage Council is organized at present as a consultative and referral service. If treatment of emotional or specific problems is indicated, it offers contact with, and introduction to, organizations and individual specialists cooperating with the work of the Council. Because the needs of clients come foremost, the Council regards it as unwise to limit the practice of counseling to any one group of specialists. It is apparent that contributions in both points of view and techniques may be made by the members of many different professions.

[32] Duvall and Hill, *op. cit.*, p. 253.

Consultation service is rendered by trained social workers and physicians. In the judgment of the sponsors it is essential that counselors themselves have experienced marriage and that they have some knowledge of normal physiological processes, of organic disease, and of nervous symptoms and disorders. "But the attitude of the counselors, their philosophy of living, their own relationship to the place of sex in life are much more important than their knowledge in these fields, since much more depends upon the way in which a counselor talks than upon the content of what he says."[33]

The well-known American Institute of Family Relations of Los Angeles follows a pattern which differs somewhat from Philadelphia's Marriage Council. Organized somewhat earlier, in 1930, this center has a staff of medical, educational, and research directors, and directors of personal and social-psychological services as well as family relations counselors and lecturers. Approximately 3000 people are served by the center yearly, with the number increasing each year. The Institute's program of family life education has been extended through lecturing and bulletin services over a wide area. Recently a staff of regional consultants in twenty-six strategically located states has been added to provide consultation services for clients and teachers interested in furthering family life education. The Institute's program includes premarital examinations and conferences, adjusting of marital and family difficulties, and personal instruction gauged to meet the client's needs.

The typical procedure in a consultation center is for the client to be interviewed first by the secretary at the "intake" desk, then referred to the appropriate staff member or specialist. Several conferences may be held with the client before the complete picture of his problem becomes apparent. Often the counselor confers with fellow staff members in staff conferences about a difficult case in order to get suggestions for diagnosis and treatment. The client learns early that human relations are complex, that the solution of his problems may be painful and time-consuming, and that his cooperation will be required throughout the process. Far from being sympathetic in the traditional sense, the counselor may often seem detached in his search for the source of conflict. Just as the individual does not expect sentimentality from a doctor or nurse, he should not expect it from a counselor. What he can expect is understanding — and now and then that may hurt, just as medical treatment hurts. The counselor is not primarily interested in comforting the aggrieved one nor in placing blame but only in helping both parties reach as satisfactory an adjustment as possible.[34]

There is no question but that the need is great for an expansion of family counseling services, but we hope that their major function will soon become one of family life education; namely, keeping families well through a better

[33] Emily B. H. Mudd, "Marriage Counsel of Philadelphia," *Parent Education,* 3 (Apr.–May, 1936), p. 19.

[34] For a more complete discussion of the counseling process and techniques see John F. Cuber, *Marriage Counseling Practice* (New York: Appleton-Century, 1948); and Emily A. Mudd, *The Practice of Marriage Counseling* (New York: Association Press, 1951), pp. 112–210.

understanding of themselves. Just as health education has done much to teach us what to eat and how to keep physically fit and when to call a doctor, family life education at these centers would keep us in good family health. Regular checkups on the health of domestic relationships would operate as a preventive of major conflicts, separations, and divorces.

We can readily visualize families whose relationships are healthy handling the great majority of conflicts within their own circles. Keeping families well would keep the need for third-party mediators at a minimum. The sick family must perforce be willing to turn to a third party, just as a sick person turns to a physician. We need to recognize, however, that the pair relation is subtly but surely changed with the introduction of a third party, no matter how skilled. The fiction of solidarity, of pair unity, is shattered, and there is a feeling that public support of the fiction has been withdrawn. To rebuild that well-founded awareness of public support of the marriage becomes a major task of counselor and counselee.

Marriage and family counseling is a device for bringing family people with problems together with specialists who can apply the knowledges and skills of social and psychological science to the solution of family problems. The process becomes one of educating the client in these principles as they apply to his case and enabling him not only to solve his immediate problems but to carry over an understanding of himself and his family relationships so effectively that he can meet future crises with courage. This service ties in directly with our program of giving flexibility to families while conserving the unique values around which their life is organized.

EDUCATION FOR FAMILY LIFE

The American panacea for all social ills has been universal public education. Through the educational system we have expected to build a brave new world — and in spite of the cynics, we have not done badly. With education compulsory up to the age of eighteen in many states, it has been possible to accomplish a great deal through this medium.

Education for family living will be no exception, and its intricacies will make challenging subject matter for classes at any age level and add vitality to the traditional curriculum. In some communities the informal programs of churches, community agencies such as the Y.W.C.A. and the Y.M.C.A., the parent-teacher associations and youth groups, government agencies such as home economics extension, adult education departments, and others, actually outnumber the formal education courses of the elementary schools, the high schools, and the colleges. Wherever young people, parents, or grandparents congregate can be found a constituency eager for family life education. All that is needed is aggressive leadership and an organizational channel to build an active educational program.

In recent years family life education has been the means of rapprochement between the school and the family as they have cooperated on common problems. The school is justified in assuming part of the job because it is the chief repository of research findings and is better staffed than the average family could hope to be to teach young people the technical aspects of child development and parenthood.

The chief contributions of the nursery school and elementary school are three: (1) they aid parents in understanding the growing child through frequent conferences with teachers, whose observations of the child's development are more objective and extensive; (2) they aid the child to understand his home, to recognize its value in a vitalized curriculum which utilizes home activities as study materials; and (3) they supplement the family in its function of socializing the child for democratic family life.[35]

The first formal class work in marriage and family living is offered in high schools. Reference to the problems involved appear in classes in home economics, biology, social science, mental hygiene, and literature. Home economics departments have added to their traditional courses — in foods, clothing, housing, and household management — work in child study and family relationships. In Central High School at Tulsa, Oklahoma, about fifteen hundred boys and girls annually enroll in a homecrafts course which includes sex information, dating behavior, romantic love, divorce, and the personality development of children. In some schools the term "home mechanics" has been substituted for home economics, and boys vie with girls in learning the arts of homemaking. At Highland Park High School, Highland Park, Michigan, a course in sociology is taught to both sexes as Preparation for Marriage and Family Life and is climaxed by apprentice training in the nursery school.[36] Thus do some high schools propose to introduce boys to fatherhood!

Although formal course work in marriage preparation reaches as yet less than 20 per cent of students in high school, it is during this period that formal preparation will need to receive greatest attention. The high school is more nearly than any other the universal school for all marriageable youth.

It is in college that the most insistent demand for marriage preparation courses has come from students. Petitions have been circulated, editorials written, and student committees convened to bring pressure upon the faculty and administration for course work in marriage. Over the opposition of some members of the faculty and administration, courses have been introduced in several hundred colleges and universities which did not offer any instruction before. Table 24 shows the distribution of courses in this general field among colleges and universities as of 1945–1946. It is an impressive tribute to a grass-roots social movement among college students in the 1930's.

Changes in course content and emphasis have paralleled the increased

---

[35] For an evaluation of home and family life education in elementary grades see Elizabeth Stevenson, *Home and Family Life Education in Elementary Schools* (New York: Wiley, 1946).

[36] *Education for Family Living* (Detroit: Highland Park Board of Education, 1945); a picture and story interpretation of one area of work in the Highland Park High School.

TABLE 24

COLLEGE COURSES ON MARRIAGE AND THE FAMILY 1948–1949
CENSUS CONDUCTED BY THE NATIONAL COUNCIL OF FAMILY RELATIONS
AND THE AMERICAN SOCIAL HYGIENE ASSOCIATION [37]

Colleges Reporting	*Number of Colleges*
No such course offered	638
One or more courses offered	632

Enrollment in Courses	
	50,000 students
	(2 per cent of U.S. College Enrollment)

Nature of Courses	*Per Cent Reporting Such Courses*
Course limited to preparation for marriage only, or in combination with other courses on marriage and the family	64
Social problems of the family only, or in combination with other courses on family	45
History of marriage and the family only, or in combination with other courses on family	24

interest of college students in the know-how of married life. Attention in the more responsive schools is now directed toward the practical problems of courtship, factors in mate selection and marital solidarity, sex adjustments, and parenthood. Interest is maintained by starting with the questions dearest to the student and working outward, rather than presenting a logical, systematized organization of materials à la Chemistry 1. No course lends itself better to general functional education than marriage and the family, in that it meets all the criteria set up for general education courses: (1) it is designed explicitly to meet the needs of the vast majority of students, neither for an intellectual elite nor for a particular vocational group; (2) its content is essentially interdepartmental, with materials drawn from any source which throws light on the problem at hand; and (3) since the course is designed to produce more intelligent living, the topics and instructional methods are directed toward an ultimate goal of changed conduct rather than the mere intellectual grasp of information and concepts.

We have no standardized system of family life education and produce as yet no standard product.[38] Students who have had courses in this field in high school and college, however, may be expected to be more effective in

[37] For details about this census see Henry A. Bowman, "Collegiate Education for Marriage and Family Living," *The Annals,* 272 (November, 1950), pp. 148–155.

[38] Two of the most helpful journals for teachers in family life education are *Family Life* published by the American Institute of Family Relations, Los Angeles, California, and *Marriage and Family Living* published by the National Council on Family Relations, 5757 Drexel Avenue, Chicago, Illinois. A symposium, "Teaching College Marriage Courses," *Marriage and Family Living* (Spring, 1946), pp. 32–42, by Russell Cooper, Paul Popenoe, Judson T. Landis, Henry Bowman, Ralph G. Eckert, Lemo D. Rockwood, Noel Keys, and Lester A. Kirkndall, illustrates the varied resources available to the teacher of famliy courses in colleges today.

meeting the crises of married life because of superior insight into human behavior and a healthier attitude toward marriage and parenthood.

Too Little, Too Late

Yet we must face the fact that the general picture of family education in high schools and colleges is far from satisfactory. Too few students are reached to make any appreciable difference in the general stream of family living. There is more emphasis upon domestic skills than upon family relationships and getting along creatively with family members. More is taught about the family in other times and places than about our own, here and now; more about what is wrong with families than about how to improve one's own relationships. Moreover, there is too much neglect of the masculine role in the home and of educating boys for it. Home-making for boys is only a partial answer. It takes two to make a home, but the curriculum rarely recognizes that fact. Indeed, the typical high school and college curriculum ignores, by and large, the fact that most people will live out their days in family groups. Most curricula are designed for celibates and are quite as sterile as celibacy from a family life education point of view. Henry Bowman, whose views we have adapted here, writes:

> Successful marriage and family life must cease to be merely a by-product of our educational system and become one of its major objectives. This will involve not only courses, teachers, counselors in this area but also new emphases, new methods of coordination and integration, new foci, new perspective through the educational process. This implies more than a program. It implies a new social movement, which, indeed, is already under way. Its gradual evolution is probably inevitable; but it may be accelerated by the efforts of interested persons who are willing to face a great need.[39]

Family life education, which is a movement for the improvement of family life, begins in nursery school and extends through elementary school, high school, and college into adult education programs. It aims to encourage more compatible mate selection, right-sized families in keeping with capacity to provide for and ability to rear, and the development of ideals which make family life worth while for its own sake. Education aims to make family life and child rearing a genuinely growth-promoting experience, to be looked upon as a privilege rather than a burdensome duty. Here again we have the opportunity to sacralize the family structure, for education can help to impart the necessary values and ideals. We live in a secularizing society in which prescription is being replaced by principle, rigid "do's and don'ts" with flexible but firm patterns. Religion in the holy sense has less control than formerly; education can help us conserve older values and yet adopt the newer.

[39] Henry Bowman, "Education for Marriage and Family Life," *Marriage and Family Living,* 8, 3 (Summer, 1946), p. 64.

We started this section of the chapter asking ourselves the question: what are the accomplishments of this folk movement for the improvement of family life to date? We have seen that there are several well-organized programs operating, such as those of parent education, family welfare, marital guidance, maternal health, and family education. They are now finding common ground so that they may become integrated some day into one driving force with common aims and objectives — the improvement of family life through the critical utilization of modern science and social action. There yet remains much to be done. We turn now to a consideration of a nation-wide policy for family life.

Formulating a National Policy for Family Life

The President of the United States has twice called White House Conferences in recent years (the National Conference on Family Life in 1948 and the Midcentury White House Conference on Children and Youth) to deal with the problems of families, children and youth. These conferences have made only modest beginnings at formulating a national policy for family life, and almost none of their efforts have been translated into legislative enactments. The American family needs a bill of rights. We have done better in America by our hogs and field animals than we have done by our human resources, by our families and the children they are rearing. Few civilized countries have such a gap between abundance of natural and processed resources and distribution of these resources to its people.

We have reviewed the family's past, we have evaluated its present, and we now wish to shape its future. It is not enough that the family has survived; we wish it to be a positive force in producing competent and liberated personalities, in releasing creative energies to work at improving social relations among men. A democratic American family may be the crucible for creative democratic living just as the authoritarian patriarchal European family nurtured the acceptance of authority in the Old World. European researchers [40] claimed that the patterns of nurture characteristic of the patriarchal family prepared individuals for the unquestioning acceptance of authority in society and were in some measure responsible for the excessive growth of authority manifested in the totalitarian states. The patriarchal family was both cause and effect of the social order in which it flowered. To have cooperative families which in turn will foster cooperation in the social order we must first create conditions which will be congenial to the growth and development of cooperative living as the modal rather than the exceptional form.

A bill of rights for American families, stated as goals which lie within

[40] Max Horkheimer, editor, *Studien über Autorität und Familie* (Paris: Felix Alcan, 1936). But note that authoritarianism is not a one-way matter; families may be affected by a conscription system, for example. See Howard Becker, "German Families Today," in Hans Morgenthau, ed., *Germany in World Affairs* (Chicago: University of Chicago Press, 1951).

our grasp if we but use the knowledges available from social and psychological science, would include:

1. A minimum income to provide the essentials of the American standard of living to all families.

2. A system of protection against the risks of unemployment, accident, death, and old age.

3. Shelter so constructed that it is adapted to the needs and functions of family living.

4. Adequate medical care for all family members.

5. Health and nutritional education and checkups sufficient to keep family members well.

6. Vocational and recreational guidance and education for all children to allow maximum fulfillment and self-direction.

7. Minimum education for family life and for effective relations with others; assistance in utilizing new patterns for family functioning.

8. Adequate marriage and family counseling services for family checkups and remedial individualized treatment of domestic problems.

9. Provisions for family research to keep abreast of changing family needs and problems.

The writing of goals is the bare beginning of a policy. A second step is to discover at what points the goals established would, in the achieving, interfere with the goals and objectives of other associations in the national society. Each of these goals, if attained, is going to require programs of action and skilled personnel to implement them and will divert the energies of hundreds of thousands from the production of other more material things to the servicing of personalities.

To make the case, it will be necessary to make explicit the value of the family grouping in American life, a statement of faith, if you will, in the American Family. If it occupies first place in our hearts, a nationwide policy could be formulated which would put family welfare first in considering programs of action. The Committee on Family Life of the Woman's Foundation have prepared a statement which anticipates well the formulation of a national policy for family life. To them such a policy should include:

A considered formulation of the place and function of family living in American society, affirming the values and the aspirations which individuals are seeking in marriage and family life. . . .

An explicit statement of the meaning of the foregoing as it bears upon the programs, decisions, and objectives of all organized activities in the country, namely, government, business, and industry, labor organizations, education, religion, professional practices, and community life generally.

A declaration of the responsibility of all the above to recognize the impact of their decisions and activities upon the family, recognizing both their affirmative actions and their omissions and neglects as they help or jeopardize the family.

A long-term plan to protect and advance family living through the concerted utilization of all available agencies and professions and of all relevant instrumentalities needed to meet the necessary conditions and to aid the distinctive functions of the family.[41]

With such a broad statement of policy arrived at by the usual democratic procedures of discussion, investigation, debate, and consensus, a program of action might be worked out to guide change in such a way that the family is freed to advance under its own power. Families which are burdened with problems too large for them to solve because of their limited resources and understanding become ineffective instruments for rearing children, who often become public charges. If we are to sacralize the family we must create the conditions in which its values have some meaning and where its power of adaptation is not wasted in battling against the thick walls of entrenched privilege.

In concluding this section on family planning and social policy let us propose a modest program of action which with some much needed extending and broadening of the Social Security Act may enable us to attain most of the minimum goals for families formulated above (p. 801).

Starting with the family's reproductive function we propose that contraceptive information be freely distributed among all classes in order to give our population control over births. This service should be paralleled by infertility services to the involuntarily childless. The number of wanted children will hereby be kept at a maximum which will simultaneously improve the affectional function of the family. An unwanted baby is often a rejected baby, whereas a wanted baby may be the stimulus for improved affectional functioning if by any chance it was deficient before he arrived.

Secondly, we propose the provision of public services such as free obstetrical service, free maternity care, and housekeeping services during the first weeks after the mother returns from the hospital.[42] In the matter of child care alone, the provision of prenatal care, well-baby clinics, and child study classes has made it possible for the mother to protect and care for her child with a minimum of outside help. These services should lighten greatly the economic burden of rearing children without bringing the evils of direct subsidy.

Third, all families with more than one child are penalized economically in the realm of medical care and shelter. By organizing a system of country-wide medical insurance, by establishing low-cost housing projects with reduced rentals for families, and by instituting a system of public works and public employment the task of providing physical care and protection for children can be brought within the reach of the average family.

Fourth, the school and the family are able to carry out their joint

---

[41] Committee of Consultants on Family Life, *The Place of the Family in American Life* (New York: The Woman's Foundation, 1945), p. 14.

[42] Della Cyrus would extend socialized housekeeping services to all families in order to free mothers of small children from these tedious chores. She predicts that the husband-wife and parent-child relationships would be vastly improved. See her entire article, "What's Wrong with the Family," *Atlantic Monthly*, 178 (Nov., 1946), pp. 67-74.

educational and socialization functions most successfully only if a channel is provided for parents and teachers to get together. Parent education classes and clinics to which parents can bring problems are being provided in the Office of Education family life demonstration communities in Utah, which are being increasingly utilized by parents. Research in child development, disciplinary techniques, and delinquent conduct is being translated into family terms to show what conditions make for maximum socialization. Working together the family and the school make a fine team. Unfortunately such horizontal teaming of institutions occurs rarely in a secularizing society, and explicit arrangements have to be made, with substantial rewards for cooperation, before results can be expected.

Finally, we turn to the affectional function on which so much of the family's success as an institution is based. Research studies in the success and failure of marriage are revealing new ways of improving emotional security in the home. Lecturers and teachers are even now communicating the results of these studies to students, stressing the importance in mate selection of companionship, compatible temperaments, and similar home backgrounds. Hollywood should be encouraged to base more films on companionship and intention to found a family as the core element in married love and to minimize the infantile romantic notions of love at first sight which have brought disillusionment to countless couples.

To improve the affectional element in marriage we propose that premarital social-psychological examinations be prepared to determine the emotional eligibility of a person for marriage, just as we now give premarital physical examinations. Emotionally immature, dependent, or narcissistic persons who do not meet the minimum requirements for marriage might have access to rehabilitating clinics for treatment of their affectional and emotional deficiencies. Another test which should be standardized and further validated is the engagement adjustment scale. The engaged couple need to know how healthy their relationship is before marriage. They need to test the degree of unity, of solidarity which they have already achieved. These proposals may seem far-fetched to some but are suggestive of the helps which research and clinical agencies can give in improving the performance of the affectional function of the family. This is family planning that looks to the future!

In concluding this book we wish to affirm our faith in the ability of social science to produce the techniques and skills in social organization necessary to facilitate improvements in the family life of the future. Moreover, we see very few alternatives for the modern family in search of help. Secularization is far advanced; gone are the wise old men and the holy books with the accepted answers. Social technology with its clinics and classes and recommendations is a natural successor. Using the problem-solving approach, searching for causes which sometimes turn out to be both effect and cause, experimenting, recording results, taking little for granted until proved — these are the methods of social science and technology. A vital role is ahead for these disciplines, if not in changing family form or in creating new standards or norms, at least in predicting trends of significance to the family and in making additions to the knowledge of human conduct. We see the family, with these aids, surviving even the amazing technological developments now being forecast for the atomic age, and surviving the impact of urbanization, of social mobility, of wars and economic depressions, with a minimum of scars and a maximum of vitality. We see great possibilities in the family of tomorrow as an improved small-family organization, geared to assure maximum self-expression of family members while maintaining integrity and inner loyalty to the whole. Our optimism is predicated on the universality of the family phenomenon, on its survival powers in the past, on its present adaptability, and on the anticipated shape of things to come.

SELECTED READINGS

BERNARD, JESSIE, *American Family Behavior* (New York: Harper, 1942), chap. 22.

BURGESS, ERNEST W., and LOCKE, HARVEY J., *The Family: From Institution to Companionship* (2nd ed.; New York: American Book Company, 1953), chaps. 6, 16, 22.

CALVERTON, V. F., *The Bankruptcy of Marriage* (New York: Macaulay, 1928).

CAVAN, R. S., *The American Family* (New York: Crowell, 1953).

COHEN, WILBUR J., "Social Security and Family Stability," *The Annals,* 272 (November, 1950), pp. 117–127.

COSGROVE, MARJORIE, "School Guidance for Home and Family Living," *Marriage and Family Living,* 14 (February, 1952), pp. 26–31.

COTTRELL, LEONARD S., JR., and FOOTE, NELSON N., *New Directions of Research on the American Family* (New York: Social Science Research Council, in press), chap. 2.

CUBER, JOHN F., *Marriage Counseling Practice* (New York: Appleton-Century-Crofts, 1948).

CYRUS, DELLA D., "What's Wrong with the Family," *The Atlantic,* 178 (November, 1946), pp. 67–74.

DUVALL, EVELYN M., "Organization of Social Forces to Promote Family Stability," *The Annals,* 272 (November, 1950), pp. 77–86.

——, and HILL, REUBEN, *When You Marry* (rev.; Boston: Heath, 1953), chaps. 20, 21.

FOLSOM, JOSEPH K., *The Family and Democratic Society* (New York: Wiley, 1943), chaps. 7, 18, 20.

——, *Youth, Family and Education* (Washington, D. C.: American Council on Education, 1941), chaps. 2–9.

FORCE, ELIZABETH S., "High School Education for Family Living," *The Annals,* 272 (November, 1950), pp. 156–163.

GOODYKOONTZ, BESS; COON, BEULAH, et al., *Family Living and Our Schools* (New York: Appleton-Century-Crofts, 1941).

HILL, REUBEN, *Families Under Stress* (New York: Harper, 1949).

HOBBS, A. H., *Social Problems and Scientism* (Harrisburg, Pa.: Stackpole, 1953), chaps. 6 and 7.

HOLLINGSHEAD, AUGUST B., "Class Differences in Family Stability," *The Annals,* 272 (November, 1950), pp. 39–47.

Kirkendall, Lester A., and Handwerk, Esther, "Preparation of Teachers for Education in Marriage and Family Living," *Marriage and Family Living,* 12 (February, 1950), pp. 7-10.

Koos, Earl L., *Families in Trouble* (New York: King's Crown Press, 1946).

——, "Private Social Agencies and Family Stability," *The Annals,* 272 (November, 1950), pp. 110-117.

Mudd, Emily H., *The Practice of Marriage Counseling* (New York: Association Press, 1951), pp. 112-210.

——, and Preston, Malcolm G., "The Contemporary Status of Marriage Counseling," *The Annals,* 272 (November, 1950), pp. 102-109.

Mumford, Lewis, "Primary Orientation: The Family," *The Social Foundations of Post War Building* (London: Faber and Faber, 1943), pp. 32-37.

Myrdal, Alva, *Nation and Family: The Swedish Experiment in Democratic Family and Population Policy* (New York: Grove Press, 1952).

Redfield, Margaret Park, "The American Family: Consensus and Freedom," *American Journal of Sociology,* 52 (November, 1946), pp. 175-183.

Reed, Ruth, *The Modern Family* (New York: Crofts, 1932), chap. 18.

Seward, Georgene H., *Sex and the Social Order* (New York: McGraw-Hill, 1946), chaps. 13, 15.

Steiner, Lee R., *Where Do People Take Their Troubles?* (Boston: Houghton Mifflin, 1945).

Waller, Willard, *The Family: A Dynamic Interpretation,* rev. by Reuben Hill (New York: Dryden Press, 1951), chap. 25.

Westermarck, Edward A., *The Future of Marriage in Western Civilization* (New York: Macmillan, 1936).

Zimmerman, C. C., *Family and Civilization* (New York: Harper, 1947).

——, and Frampton, M. E., *Family and Society, A Study of the Sociology of Reconstruction* (New York: Van Nostrand, 1935).

TOPICS FOR DISCUSSION OR REPORTS

1. Write a paper giving your reactions to Della Cyrus's diagnosis of the modern family and her program of treatment. (See her article above.)

2. Make a list of the factors making for solidarity in your own parental family. Do you agree that domestic production activities are necessary to maintain family integrity? (See discussions of the problem by Zimmerman and Frampton, *Family and Society,* and by G. C. Homans, *The Human Group* [New York: Harcourt, Brace, 1951].)

3. Make a study of the families of your acquaintance that still have family reunions. How do they differ from families that have split into separate conjugal groups never having ritual get-togethers? Relate this to the discussion of sacred societies in Chapter One.

4. Discuss the implications of the homesteading movements and back-to-the-farm movements for urban families.

5. From your reading and observations, show why the family is to be preferred to the orphanage or nursery for meeting the vital needs of the child during the first years. What are its peculiar advantages?

6. Discuss the development of family life education programs in the high school. How can they facilitate the adjustment of adolescents within the parental family? What are the limitations of these programs at the present moment? (See articles by Cosgrove, Force, and Kirkendall-Handwerk in the Selected Readings.)

7. What steps might be taken to render American families less authoritarian? Why might this be debatable and/or desirable?

8. Make a study of six radio programs and as many motion pictures, noting the areas in which family conflict most frequently develops. Are the problems usually settled by outside counsel? What impressions of family life are left by radio, television, and motion pictures?

9. Interview a number of unmarried young people on the need for premarital counseling and matrimonial agencies or marriage brokers. Note the characteristics of those least interested in guidance. Would they make good marital risks?

10. In the absence of a family consultation center, which of the following do you feel is best equipped professionally to perform family counseling services: social case workers, physicians, ministers, lawyers, teachers? Explain the bases for your selection.

11. Discuss the pros and cons for requiring physical and psychological examinations before granting a marriage license to insure genetically, physically, and psychologically sound marriages in America.

12. Draft a design for family life which will allow the wife to develop as a person, the husband as a parent, and the children as distinct individuals, and show how such a family might achieve integration around timeless values. Relate if possible to Chapter One.

13. Criticize the proposals for a national policy for family life that have been made in this chapter from the standpoint of practicality. Rework them and write up a program as if you were preparing recommendations for a White House Conference on Family Life (see Swedish policy proposals in Myrdal's *Nation and Family* for the variables that should be considered).

Critiques of Kinsey Reports

Sex and Marital Adjustment:
A Critique of Kinsey's Approach †

HARRIET R. MOWRER

According to the repeated assertion of the authors, this extensive quantitative investigation of the reported sexual experiences of almost 6,000 white American females has far-reaching implications for our understanding of marital adjustment.

Attacks upon the problem of sexual adjustment in marriage have not proved as fruitful as they might have been, according to Kinsey, because no one has understood the basic physiology of sexual response, or the basic psychologic differences between female and male responsiveness.[1] (p. 8) Most of our past knowledge regarding these phenomena appears to be incorrect. (p. 12) The purpose of the study, he goes on to say, has been a fact-finding survey in which there has been an attempt not only to discover what people do sexually but what factors account for their patterns of sexual behavior and how these have affected their lives. We then see Professor Kinsey emerging from his purported role of the objectively oriented scientist studying the highly restricted physiological functioning of a human biological need to that of the bold, overly confident, often naive, occasionally moralistic counselor on marital affairs.

To accept the Kinsey findings without exacting scrutiny and numerous qualifications would be to perpetuate the error, which Kinsey implies has characterized the work of many, if not all, of the others in the field — both researchers and clinicians — namely, the acceptance and application of unsubstantiated findings, sometimes with harmful results to society.

METHODOLOGICAL INADEQUACIES

The possible methodological fallacies in the collection and analysis of the data of the sexual activities of the 5,940 white females are numerous and can only be briefly mentioned here.[2] There are obvious inadequacies in the sample of the females studied, particularly of the age groups over fifty, those of low educational levels, Catholics, rural and laboring classes. Almost all came from urban white collar or professional families. Twenty-four percent of those over thirty were still single. Of those over thirty who had married, 40% were either widowed, separated or divorced.

Likewise, the interviewing process is open to innumerable biases both from

† These three Critiques are reprinted from *SOCIAL PROBLEMS* by permission of the Society for the Study of Social Problems. An expanded version of these articles appears in *Sexual Behavior in American Society*, edited by Jerome Himelhoch with the assistance of Sylvia Fleis Fava (New York: W. W. Norton & Co., forthcoming).

[1] This and all subsequent references, unless otherwise specified, are to Alfred C. Kinsey, *et al.*, *Sexual Behavior in the Human Female* (Philadelphia: W. B. Saunders Co., 1953).

[2] The statistical methods used by Kinsey and his associates have recently been critically appraised by a Committee of the American Statistical Association and in general severely criticized. (2)

the standpoint of the technique of the interview; the phrasing, asking and sequence of questions, the purpose, speed, direction; attitude of interviewer (medical detective, fact-finder, or highly skilled scientific analyst); and the limitations
of the interviewee educationally, culturally, and particularly emotionally.

The momentous task of interviewing some 11,000 individuals (5,300 white
males and 5,940 females) and soliciting the report on their past actual sexual
behavior was accomplished by only two interviewers in sessions from one to two
hours. This meant going back as far as memory could recall to the occurrence of
the first sexual activity, the length of time required for the first orgasm, orgasmic
experience over five year periods, etc. — a considerable span of memory for the
middle and upper age group. The ability of the interviewers to acquire so much
data of this type in interviews of such short duration suggests a possible distor-
tion of the sample in several dimensions. First, toward those females who already had knowledge of the nature of the questions to be asked and had therefore reflected on their answers. This would be particularly true of those intimately
associated groups such as fraternal organizations, units of the armed forces, etc.
Second, those for whom sex had a distorted perspective because of feelings of
guilt, fear, or exaggerated curiosity would be anxious to discuss their sexual activities and might tend to give pre-structured replies. Third, such high premium
was placed upon rapidity of replies in the interview that any reply was given in
lieu of hesitation.

Thus there is no assurance that Kinsey's findings are representative and can
be extended to the general population. Kinsey is more concerned with frequency
data than with general patterns. Many of the general facts in the Kinsey report
have for several decades or longer been recognized by students of sexual behavior.
The critical question raised by the study, then, is not whether the data exist or
approach reality but the degree to which they do exist or the degree to which they
are reality. This question, then, the Kinsey statistical findings leave unanswered.
To discuss the implications of the Kinsey data for marital adjustment accordingly
does not imply that the writer accepts the data as accurate or that they have
demonstrable validity in the sense that Kinsey contends, either for the population
as a whole or for any fundamental segment of American society.

Orgasmic Experience as the Unit of Marital Adjustment

Although Kinsey acknowledges the importance of other factors (p. 11), he
places great stress on sexual adjustment as a factor in marital success. Sexual adjustment is measured by one unit — namely, orgasmic activity. Orgasm is possible
through six outlets: (a) masturbation, (b) nocturnal emissions, (c) premarital
petting, (d) coitus (premarital, marital, and extramarital), (e) homosexual contacts, (f) animal contacts. Females with premarital orgasmic activity [any or
total outlets] achieve marital sexual adjustment oftener and earlier than those
without. According to Kinsey, a considerable portion of maladjustment in marriage arises from the fact that the average female is aroused sexually less often
than the average male and that she frequently has difficulty in reaching orgasm
in her marital coitus. (p. 172) The most significant factor seems to be the female's inexperience prior to marriage. Some 36% of the sample had not prior to
marriage experienced orgasm on even a single occasion, from any outlet; only one
half had had a regular outlet. Calculations on the marital histories indicated, according to Kinsey, that those who had not responded to orgasm prior to marriage failed to respond after marriage three times as often as those who had had a

fair amount of orgasmic experience before marriage. About two-thirds of the married females had experienced orgasm prior to marriage from all outlets but only one-sixth had come from coitus. Fifty-three percent had had coitus with only a single partner, 34% with two or five partners and 13% with six or more. Eighty-seven percent had at least a portion of it with men whom they subsequently married. Forty-one percent had it with both the fiance and with other males.

There was a marked positive correlation between experience in orgasm through premarital coitus and capacity to reach orgasm after marriage. Among those who had never reached orgasm from any source prior to marriage, 44% had failed to reach orgasm in any of their coitus in the first year of marriage. Among those who had had premarital coitus without orgasm, 38–56% (sic) failed to reach orgasm in the first year of marriage. But among those who had reached orgasm at least twenty-five times before marriage, only three percent had not reached orgasm during the first year of marriage. Similar correlations were noted as long as fifteen years after marriage. Over half of those who had had coitus with orgasm had reached orgasm in practically all their coitus during the first year of marriage. Of those with no premarital coitus and no other orgasmic experience 29% had approached a hundred percent response in the first year of marriage. Kinsey concludes that " there is no sort of experience which shows a higher positive correlation with orgasmic success in marriage than coitus (leading to orgasm) before marriage." He goes on to say that avoidance of premarital sexual experience may lead to inhibitions which damage the capacity to respond so much that it may take years to get rid of them after marriage, "if they are ever dissipated." (p. 330) Furthermore, the learning early to respond emotionally to a sexual partner may contribute to the effectiveness of one's other nonsexual, social relationships.

It follows then from Kinsey's data: since the orgasmic activity is the unit of sexual adjustment, and since those having greatest orgasmic capacity before marriage also have it in marriage, and since premarital coitus shows a higher correlation with marital orgasmic success than any other premarital outlet, that the good or favorable marriage risks are those females who have had coitus with orgasm before marriage. The 47% of all the females who had premarital coitus with both fiance and other males would be good marriage risks providing they had had orgasm. Thus the female entering marriage without premarital coital experience, it would follow from Kinsey's findings, has a major hardship in achieving success. In fact, early orgasm becomes a panacea in reducing the incidence of unresponsiveness in marital coitus. He says, "it is doubtful if any type of therapy has ever been as effective as early experience in orgasm, in increasing the frequencies of response to orgasm in marital coitus." (pp. 385–386)

Where "regret after the experience of premarital coitus" is used as a criterion of its success, Kinsey's interpretation is open to serious question. Some 69% of the still unmarried females with coital experience insisted that they did not regret their experience. Another 13% had some minor regret. Some 77% of the married, according to Kinsey's interpretation, "looking back from the vantage point of their more mature experience," saw no reason to regret their premarital coitus. (p. 316) These figures, Kinsey says, differ from those usually presented and "illustrate the difference between wishful thinking and scientifically accumulated data." (p. 317)

Of this group, those females with the most experience regretted it the least. Twenty-five percent of those who had the smallest amount of premarital coitus regretted their experience while only 14% of those who had had it for two or three years and only 10% of those who had it for between four and ten years regretted it. The married females with their more extended coital experience regretted in only 11% of the cases, which Kinsey interprets as indicating that the data refute the statement that "the quality of a marital relationship is so far superior to a premarital relationship that women usually regret such experience."

But here Kinsey makes a grave error in his systematic and unscientific attempt to convince one of the benefits of premarital coitus for marital adjustment. It seems only reasonable to assume that those with the most premarital coital experience would have had the most premarital orgasmic experience which, according to Kinsey, leads to the highest orgasmic coital experience in marriage (Kinsey's criterion of marriage adjustment). Why, then, do these married women look wistfully to early premarital experience? Could it be that the more promiscuous a female is before marriage, the more unsuccessful and dissatisfying she finds her marriage?

THE KINSEY DILEMMA

The dilemma reappears in Kinsey's data on extramarital coitus. About 85% of those engaging in extramarital activity were responding at least on occasion to orgasm. For most age groups the incidences of response were about the same as those in marital coitus. Some females who had never or rarely reached orgasm with their husbands had responded regularly in extramarital coitus. (p. 432) Among the 514 females in the sample who had had extramarital coitus, over 68% had also had premarital coitus. Since only 50% of all the married females in the sample had had premarital coitus, Kinsey admits that those experienced in premarital coitus appear to be somewhat more inclined to accept extramarital coitus. (p. 427) If orgasm occurs as often (or more often) in extramarital coitus as in marital coitus, and if 68% of these women had coitus before marriage, where are the facts which substantiate Kinsey's repeated assertions, direct and implied, that premarital coitus leading to orgasm facilitates marital adjustment?

The females who had had extramarital coitus, according to Kinsey, seem to have been no more promiscuous in their extramarital experiences (81% with one to five partners as over against 80%) whether they had or had not had premarital coitus. (p. 428) But since, in Kinsey's definition, premarital coitus furnishes the climate most conducive to marital adjustment, his data then should show the group having had premarital sexual experience to have been much better adjusted in marriage and, therefore, to have been much less promiscuous. As far as the marriage relationship was concerned, there was a total of 71% for whom no marital difficulty with the spouse had yet developed, as reported by the female, because of her extramarital activity. Here Kinsey, seemingly for the first time, implies the possibility of a relationship between marital instability and extramarital relations. He concludes: "These data once again emphasize the fact that the reconciliation of the married individuals' desire for coitus with a variety of sexual partners, and the maintenance of a stable marriage, presents a problem which has not been satisfactorily resolved in our culture. It is not likely to be resolved until man moves more completely from his mammalian ancestry." (p. 436)

It is quite clear that Kinsey's data, despite his tendency to interpret and generalize far beyond and apart from his findings, do not establish a cause and effect relationship between premarital orgasmic activity and marital adjustment. The best that can most likely be said is that the stronger the sex drive of the females studied, the more likely they were to have had premarital, marital, and extramarital coitus with orgasm. The statistical findings of Burgess and Wallin (1) in their recent study of engagement and marriage, along with the earlier studies of Davis (3), Terman (7), and Locke (4), on the whole support the conclusion that husbands and wives with no experience of premarital intercourse have the higher probability of marital success, whereas couples in which husband or wife had premarital relations with spouse and others have the lower probability. The writer's clinical experience with a wide variety of couples experiencing marital conflict would further substantiate these findings. (5, 6)

This analysis of some of the major Kinsey findings as they relate to marital adjustment demonstrates the futility of studying the functioning of the sexual need or impulse in a purely physiological context. Cultural definitions of sexual experience transform both the character of sexual activity and of the sexual drive or need. The consequence is that sexual behavior can be adequately understood only in terms provided by the context of the cultural definitions and the psychological concomitants as these function in the experiences of socially oriented individuals.

The necessity for considering sex within the larger context is particularly important in the analysis of the functioning of the sexual factor in the dynamics of the marriage relationship because of the characteristic features which marriage has assumed in American society. These characteristic features consist of an overwhelming acceptance (albeit not unanimous) of the conception of marriage as a dynamic relationship in which the fundamental functions are those of providing a climate for the maximum satisfaction of the desires for affection, comradeship, sympathetic understanding and appreciation, emotional interdependence, and personality complementation. The sexual relationship in marriage represents one of the many ways in which these satisfactions are achieved and its significance lies in its dynamic linkage to the other sources of achievement available therein.

That is to say that as a factor in the marriage situation sex cannot be differentiated in its physiological aspects, but needs to be studied and interpreted in the light of its dynamic functioning in a socio-psycho-cultural framework. The physiological impulse becomes overlaid with social experiences, expressing itself in demonstration of affection and love, mutual identification, sympathy and companionship as well as in the release of physiological tensions. Sex in general takes on its meaning from the culture in which the individual lives, a culture in which sex is characterized by many conflicting values and notions, superstitions, romantic ideas, inhibitions, guilt feelings, etc. The meaning of sex to the individual, then, is the result of the orientation of his personal feelings, impulses, needs, experiences, attitudes, and wishes within this cultural maze. In marriage one sees the final orientation of this sexual definition and its functioning in relation to another individual. Thus the details of the sexual pattern achieved in marriage vary widely between couples even in the same cultural and social group. The crux of the relationship of the sexual pattern to happy and unhappy marriages lies in the degree of satisfaction this pattern furnishes to the particular couple involved. Furthermore, the sexual behavior is symbolically intertwined with the other aspects of marriage behavior so that it becomes both a mirror and a reflection of all the other phases of marital adjustment.

Studies such as Kinsey's, colossal as they may be in size, adequate or inadequate in methodology, which deal only with the discrete elements of sexual experience, their frequency and distribution, throw little or no light upon how sex actually functions in either a social or a marriage interactional context. There is still no scientific evidence to prove that the sex factor is in itself a significant determinant of marital success.

REFERENCES

1. ERNEST W. BURGESS and PAUL WALLIN, *Engagement and Marriage*, Philadelphia: J. B. Lippincott Co., 1953.
2. WILLIAM G. COCHRAN, FREDERICK MOSTELLER, JOHN W. TUKEY, "Statistical Problems of the Kinsey Report," *Journal of the American Statistical Association*, 264 (1953), 48.
3. KATHERINE B. DAVIS, *Factors in the Sex Life of Twenty-two Hundred Women*, New York: Harper and Brothers, 1929.
4. HARVEY J. LOCKE, *Predicting Adjustment in Marriage: A Comparison of a Divorced and a Happily Married Group*, New York: Henry Holt and Company, Inc., 1951.
5. HARRIET R. MOWRER, *Personality Adjustment and Domestic Discord*, New York: American Book Co., 1935.
6. ERNEST R. MOWRER and HARRIET MOWRER, "The Social Psychology of Marriage," *American Sociological Review*, 16 (1951), 27–36.
7. LEWIS M. TERMAN, *et al., Psychological Factors in Marital Happiness*, New York: McGraw-Hill Book Company, 1938.

Kinsey's View of Human Behavior

MANFORD H. KUHN

One would expect a zoologist, when he addresses himself to the study of some aspect of human behavior, to elect from the current assortment of theoretical orientations toward human behavior — such as psychoanalytic theory, field theory, symbolic interaction theory, and learning theory — that one which has the most in common with the zoological orientation toward organisms in general. It is therefore not surprising to find that Kinsey takes what is essentially the learning theorist's point of view, with its heavy reliance on physiological explanations for human (social) behavior. This much was evident in the first Kinsey report, but one had to infer it from his unit for analysis, his choice of language, his use of data from infra-human species, and from his interpretive statements scattered here and there throughout the book. In the second Kinsey report he has, in Chapter 16, "Psychologic Factors in Sexual Response," given a fairly explicit account of his view, one which corroborates the judgment that his is a learning theory position, at least insofar as he takes into account factors which are not patently physiological in the first place.

He makes it clear that he regards with misgivings the distinction between the physiologic and the psychologic.[3] He says, for example, "It might properly be contended that all functions of living matter are physiologic . . ." only regarding it as "customary" to regard "certain aspects of animal behavior as psychologic functions." (p. 642) This "customary" distinction he evidently regards as treacherous, for he suggests that an end product of the distinction encourages "the opinion that the psychologic aspects of human sexual behavior are of a different order

---

[3] He makes it abundantly clear in the subheadings he uses in Chapter 16 that he includes the social-psychological in the "psychologic."

4. *The physiologic act* vs. *the social act:* It is permissible for the scientist to "slice up" ongoing events in any way which appears to be useful in his endeavor to arrive at predictive statements of the regularity of behavior. It is, in the final analysis, the empirical — "Which conceptual scheme gives the most predictive results?" — which determines which unit for analysis will continue to be used. Again it was the drive-reduction paradigm of the learning theorist which apparently prompted Kinsey to take the physiological act, beginning with arousal and tumescence and ending with orgasm, as the basic unit for analysis in his over-all study of sexual behavior. If one is oriented, on the other hand, to look upon human beings as universally bringing their behavior under the control and direction of verbal plans of action, he would be inclined to take as his unit for analysis the acts as defined by the individual actors themselves, expecting this to yield more predictive results. I shall enlarge on this point later. It is sufficient here to note that Kinsey, having chosen his analytic unit, allows this unit to slip quietly over in his thinking to be a definition of what the actors themselves are in their own minds attempting to do.

5. *Learning = conditioning:* The development of preferences and avoidances may be construed to result from the vicissitudes of the drive during early experiences having to do with that drive. In short, the preferences and avoidances may be construed as mere overtones of physiological and neurological events, or mere cortical reflections of what is essentially a subcortical series of events. But if one holds the view that man's behavior is under the control of social (symbolic) recipes, one would look to the reference groups of subjects for evidence that these prejudices and avoidances were verbal importations, defining events and indicating positive and negative social objects.

6. *Initial acts crucial in switchboard theory of neural system:* Finally, if one takes the view that words and thoughts are mere epiphenomena which, after the fact, rationalize behavior for man, and if one holds further, that learning consists of neural modifications which result when behavior is successful in reducing a drive, then it follows logically that the first successful behavior, in this sense, is peculiarly important in establishing the form of subsequent behavior. This is the learning theory view, and it is Kinsey's view, at least regarding female sexual behavior. (The evidence he found for males was complicated and contradictory). If one holds the view, on the other hand, that behavior is organized and directed by means of shared symbols, then one proceeds to examine persistent behavior for evidence that it continues as associated shared norms persist, and changes when they change.

In sum, we may infer from these particulars that Professor Kinsey looks upon man's "true" nature as being his animal nature which would somehow find its most satisfying expression freed from the limiting and inhibiting norms imposed by culture. He treats culture implicitly, as Miller and Dollard do explicitly — that is, as a "maze." With this as a scientific orientation he goes beyond science (in the general tone which is apparent in the two volumes thus far published) to take what amounts to a moral position; an alignment, not just with the principle of a freer discussion and inquiry of sex, but with the principle of greater and freer sexuality, the superiority of quick responses, the desirability of 100% orgasm in the sexual activity of both sexes.

AN ALTERNATIVE VIEW

Before making such a sweeping and indiscriminate plea for change, Professor Kinsey might better have considered in how far the validity of his view of human nature, either in the broad or in the particulars with which he is dealing, has been demonstrated. We may agree with J. Robert Oppenheimer regarding the basic viewpoint of science that it is "a way of life in which the discovery of error is refined, in which almost all the ingenuity that goes into experimental, analytical, or mathematical techniques is devoted to refining, sharpening, making more effective the way of finding out that you are wrong: this is the element that creates discipline. The nature of the discipline of science is its devotion, its dedication to finding out when you are wrong, to the detection of error . . ." (1)

Let us consider an alternative structuring of sexual activity. A symbolic interaction view of sex would go something like this: Sex acts, sexual objects, sexual partners (human or otherwise) like all other objects toward which human beings behave are *social objects;* that is, they have meanings because meanings are assigned to them by the groups of which human beings are members, for there is nothing in the physiology of man which gives any dependable clue as to what pattern of activity will be followed toward them. The meanings of these social objects are mediated to the individual by means of language just as in the case of all other social objects. That the communications which involve these definitions are frequently — at least in our society — surreptitious and characterized by a high degree of innuendo does not in any wise diminish the truth of this assertion. In short, the sexual motives which human beings have are derived from the social roles they play; like all other motives these would not be possible were not the actions physiologically possible, but the physiology does not supply the motives, designate the partners, invest the objects with preformed passion, nor even dictate the objectives to be achieved. Furthermore, since sexual activity in the many hundreds of existing human societies involves a wide variety of differences in the reciprocal roles of the sexual partners, it is even most likely that differences between male and female sexual activity in our own society are attributable to the *social* sex role differentiation rather than to anatomical or physiological differences between the sexes.[6] And finally, one would expect to find that the attitudes toward sex, sexual partners, sexual rules, and sexual roles are inextricably related to attitudes toward the protection and rearing of children, toward the desired configuration of family life, and, in fact, toward all of the vast range of situations involving differential role playing on the basis of sex (and this includes just about all human activity in almost all societies).

With this orientation let us see what we might hypothesize regarding the differences Kinsey found between the sexes.[7]

It would follow from our alternative orientation that a "lack of susceptibility to 'psychological stimulation' " would result from a lack of communication — or at least from ambiguous communication — which would leave the individual without social objects. Without communication we would have no words. Without words we would have no objects. Without objects our fantasies could not be informed. Is it not at least impressionistically apparent that, despite the much heralded emancipation of women, communication in the female world and, for that matter, between the sexes, about sex, is very different in our society from the communication which is so very explicit about sex in the male world? Then it would seem

[6] Cf. Kinsey's own findings, including his inability to find physiological or anatomical differences between men and women of the sort which would possibly account for the differences between the sexes in their respective sexual behaviors (chs. 14–15, 17–18); note also that he found wider differences in sexual patterns among women than among men, a point which may pertain to this argument.

[7] And for which he was able to posit only the unsupported hypothesis that the differences must lie in the cerebral cortex. (pp. 710–712)

that the process of communication in the female subculture in our society needs to be investigated.[8]

It is also consistent with the hypothesis that the female world of communication about sex is different from that of the male world, that females are more variable in their sex lives, that their first experiences tend to define the activity for them in their subsequent behavior, and that they reach the height of their sexual "potential" later than do males. If there is a considerable lack of communication, then this whole area is, as we are in the habit of saying in social psychological circles, "relatively unstructured." Female behavior then would be somewhat analogous to the behavior of subjects in Sherif's well-known experiment on the auto-kinetic effect.[9] In the realm specifically of masturbation Kinsey's own data indicate that a much larger proportion of the male universe is involved in the activity, and a much larger proportion of the males who masturbate (75% of the males compared with only 43% of the females) *started as a result of communication from others about the activity.* (p. 173)

It is also consistent with our hypothesis regarding differential communication and its relation to the differences in the sexual behavior of the two sexes that males reach a peak of sexual activity in their late teens which is several times as high as the highest level reached by females. The communication about sex in the male subculture would be impressionistically judged to be at its height in the late teens.

As we previously noted, Kinsey chose as the unit for analysis what we called "the physiological act," ending with orgasm. As indicated earlier, any arbitrary unit for analysis by a scientist is defensible, for it will be tested in the final analysis by its utility in making empirical prediction. What Kinsey did which is not defensible was to let this definition of the objective of sexual activity slip quietly over to be *the* physiologically justified objective in sexual activity. By demonstrating that a significant minority of women regularly have orgasms in sexual activity he seems to have thought himself justified in assuming that all women ought regularly to "achieve" [10] orgasm. Our view of human behavior which we have contrasted with his indicates that men and women may very well have differing objectives in their sexual activity (even though most of the activity is conjoint) not because they are physiologically different but because their role definitions (and hence their conceptions of themselves) differ. It would seem reasonable to hypothesize that sexual activity is modally defined by and/or for women in our society as having a somewhat different relation to personal acceptance, love, marriage, offspring, and many other activities than it has for men. It may also be noted that, while sexual activity in the male much more regularly "ends" in orgasm, it would be a mistake to conclude without any further evidence that orgasm even for the male is *the* objective in all sexual activity.

If Kinsey had held this alternative symbolic interactionist view of human behavior, he would not have left his attempted correlations of differentials in sexual

---

[8] It might seem that this should have suggested itself to Kinsey from his having found many women who *are* psychologically stimulated and who do fantasy; had he not been looking for physiologic explanations he might have thought to see whether these females differed in their socio-experiential backgrounds from the majority.

[9] It might also be noticed in passing however that with respect to premarital intercourse our culture, in as far as it defines the matter, tends to suggest that the female loses all that she has to lose with the first act, a matter quite different from the definitions put upon male premarital sexual activity.

[10] "Achieve" used in this way would appear to be a loaded word.

activity of various kinds with social variables, particularly religion and educational level, where he did. For example, he made only the simple division of Protestant, Catholic, and Jewish (with subdivisions for Protestants and Catholics of "devout," "moderate," and "inactive"). Surely there is a tremendous difference in the definitions put upon sexual activities among, say, Episcopalians, Mormons, Holiness sects, Quakers, Methodists, and Jehovah's Witnesses — yet these are all presumably lumped together simply as "Protestants"!

A meticulous breakdown by reference groups rather than by gross imputed reference categories might have shed a great deal of light on, say, the problem of regret (or acceptance) regarding premarital coitus (pp. 316–321), or the many differences in so-called "psychological factors in sexual response" such as differences in arousal over observing the opposite sex (p. 651), observing genitalia (p. 655), exhibitionism (pp. 656–658), seeing movies (pp. 659–660), voyeurism (pp. 663–664), etc., which Kinsey found among females. Indeed, with respect to all the differences, whether among males or females, or between males and females, with respect to sexual activity in all its manifestations, the only way to have demonstrated that sexual variations are attributable to physiological variations (at least at this stage of our knowledge of and techniques for inquiry in physiology) would have been to have made a truly exhaustive study of human attitudes in terms of their possible derivation from reference groups. Having sustained the null hypothesis, he might then rightly have considered his view of human behavior validated. As it was he made attempts to test relations between sexual variations and only the most gross, superficial, and conglomerate of social categories.

It is pertinent to wonder how Kinsey conceives the purpose of addressing his report to human beings. If we behave essentially as do infra-human animals, if we are conditioned rather than informed and reflective, if our attitudes are *ex post* rationalizations of physiologic activity — then how could he expect the publication of this knowledge to affect materially our ability to control and re-direct our actions? One can only say that there appears to be a disjunction imputed by him between the (physiologically directed) subjects he studied and the (attitudinally controlled) human beings to whom he addresses his books.

REFERENCES

1. Quoted in a pamphlet "Science and Conscience," by Henry J. Cadbury (no place, date or publisher given), from Oppenheimer's paper, "The Relation of Research to the Liberal University," in *Freedom and the University,* Ithaca, N. Y., 1950, p. 110.

Kinsey's Challenge to Ethics and Religion

JOSEPH K. FOLSOM

"Maybe it's true, but it's not good policy to *broadcast* detailed truth without some consideration of how people are going to use it." Such is a common reaction to Kinsey. It is not peculiar to traditionalists nor to those lacking reverence for modern science. For example, Margaret Mead, in an eloquent Appendix on "The Ethics of Insight Giving" says: "When one writes in a way that is easily accessible to all interested citizens, I believe one should put oneself in those readers' place, and not force them either to accept or to reject [or to choose which to do?] interpretations, the implications of which they would not have chosen to hear had they been fully aware of them." "The sudden removal of a previously guaranteed reticence has left many young people singularly defenseless in just those areas where their desire to conform was protected by a lack of knowledge of the extent of non-conformity." (7) The most important aspect of the Kinsey studies is their challenge to re-examine the relation of science to ethics and religion and this connected issue of intellectual paternalism *versus* complete intellectual democracy.

The medieval harmony of science, ethics, and religion, documented by St. Thomas Aquinas, became more and more disturbed by the rapid development of science. In 1790 Kant seemed to solve the problem in a novel and revolutionary way, by making a complete separation of science and ethics. However, the ethics which actually operate in our society have never yet been reduced to any single principle, but are based on several different types of thinking. Wayne Leys has done a great service to social science by making explicit these ethical thoughtways. (6) He compares Kant's ethic of pursuing an ideal of social relations with the casuist ethic of following precedents, the Bentham utilitarian ethic of estimating the pleasant and painful consequences to all affected, the Hegelian ethic of loyalty to the larger whole, or destiny toward which history moves, and the Deweyan pragmatic ethic of solving the essential problem. The last seems like a kind of negative, objectivist, practical utilitarianism: doing what will most reduce complaints and conflicts.

The alarm over the Kinsey reports seems to be based on a fear that our fellow citizens are largely guided by an extremely realistic form of casuistry which says, "When in Rome do as the Romans *do* — read their laws — but also notice which laws are enforced." It is well known, of course, that many a person will thus appeal to custom when what the Romans do fits in with his felt needs, but when it does not, he may turn to an idealistic, utilitarian, or even a Hegelian argument. This is one of the commonest types of rationalization.

F. S. C. Northrop vigorously opposes this type of casuistry which would derive ethics from actual practice. Furthermore, Northrop sees a similar error in Hegelian and Marxian thinking. Hegel on the level of nations, and Marx on the level of classes, assume that in some important sense the "ought" can be derived from the "is." Yet Northrop rejects also the Kantian solution of making ethics independent of science. He believes that ethics can and should be derived from science. (8) The Kinsey reports would belong mostly to Northrop's descriptive "social science." Biology, psychology, and studies such as Kardiner's (5) which attempt to apply universal criteria to several cultures would seem to belong mostly to Northrop's "human and natural science," which he regards as a proper basis for ethics. However, while Kinsey's titles "Human Male" and "Human Female" seem to the anthropologist like a bit of ethnocentric conceit, there are many things in the reports which contribute to omni-human natural science in Northrop's sense. Such, for example, are the data on the tremendous age, sex, and individual differences.

There is a job to be done, and Northrop has suggested what it is. It is to translate our factual knowledge about human sexuality into ethics, legislation, social policy, and religious guidance. The time has now come to do it. Not because Kinsey has told us anything so very surprising, anything that was not known, in rough approximation, before. Rather, because he has told it so statistically to so many people that now there may be enough steam up to do what should have been done a long time ago.

This task should be done gradually through discussion. In this writer's view the discussion should be in no way secret, however benevolent and high-minded; but it should be *led* by men and women of unquestionable honesty, devotion to the general good, and free from any concealed personal motive or bias. Given the present organization of our intellectual life, these discussion leaders should be clearly distinguished from the factual researchers, although both groups require intellectual and moral integrity.

The kind of discussion we need is well represented by *Sex Ethics and the Kinsey Report* by Dr. Seward Hiltner (3), a clergyman and member of the University of Chicago theological faculty. Hiltner not only understands Kinsey's methods and results with uncommon acumen, but shows theoretical skill after the fashion of a Max Weber. He is interested in *patterns,* not of sex behavior and "outlets," but of sex attitudes and values. He constructs seven types, each logically consistent within itself, and most of them also well represented empirically. The first three are mass types correlated with Kinsey's three socio-educational levels: the "child-of-nature" attitude of the lower level, the "respectability-restraint" attitude of the middle level (especially before 1920), and the "romantic" attitude (romantic toward licit and illicit sex and not merely toward conventional courtship and choice of mate) of the upper level, now filtering down to other levels. Then there are three consistent patterns which Hiltner has observed among thoughtful individuals but which do not appear in the Kinsey data, either because Kinsey did not ask the necessary questions, or because the holders of these attitudes are too few. These are the "no harm" attitude, the "toleration" attitude, and the "personal-interpersonal" attitude. The last named is the one frankly admired by Hiltner. It is implied in the works of Erich Fromm. (2)

The person with this attitude "believes that the ordering of sex by society should be for the realization of personal and interpersonal values, not for the sake of control of such." It is neither legalistic nor libertarian, biologistic nor spiritistic, unreflectively conformist nor yet rebellious for the sake of proving non-conformity. "It does not consider naturalness or unnaturalness as adequate criteria." (3, p. 177) Hiltner measures all these six types against a seventh type as a standard. This is the *Christian view* [11] of sex, which Hiltner derives, in an objective, scholarly manner, from the Bible and Christian history, but also "taking into account the modern knowledge." The Christian view turns out to be essentially the personal-interpersonal attitude with the addition of Christian theological support. It is summarized in five points, here condensed: (a) sex is good if it serves the fulfillment of man as a total being, i.e., God's will for man, (b) the aim of all human interrelationships is to foster love, (c) the aim of sex is toward a progressive integration of the several necessary levels of sexual function, (d) human sex requires both intensity and steadfastness with a proper relationship between them, (e) the good of any sex act always depends in some measure upon the inner meaning to the persons involved, but the sole ultimate standard is the judgment and love of God. (3, pp. 179–180)

How is this Christian view different from the traditional sex mores? For one thing, it is adequate and inspiring on the positive side, whereas the traditional code emphasizes the negative, and the concrete. Hiltner thinks that Kinsey has distorted the Judaeo-Christian view by reading it through the ideas of his subjects. He asserts that this Judaeo-Christian tradition assigns more positive value to the sex act itself than is generally realized. He agrees in general with D. S. Bailey, an Anglican clergyman, who reads real flesh and not merely a symbol in the

[11] The Jewish view seems to be incorporated within this.

Biblical doctrine of "one flesh." (1) These scholars both seem to feel that although the sex act should be kept within marriage, yet it has a God-sanctioned value which is not dependent upon marriage as an institution nor upon the intention to procreate.

John J. Kane argues that the Catholic attitude toward sex has been seriously misunderstood by many Catholics as well as outsiders. Actually it is warmer, healthier, more positive than it seems. Catholic thought is not responsible for the identification of sex with the obscene or pornographic. But there is a certain caution in verbalizing it. "Since conjugal love is both a legitimate and beautiful kind of love, and since it is expressed in sexual union, the marital sex union should also be considered in that light." (4) If this approach differs significantly from the approach of the other branches of the Judaeo-Christian tradition, the difference, according to the present writer, involves a general tendency to leave many things publicly unsaid, to assume a benevolent, paternal control over the circulation of symbols and ideas. This may have had value in protecting the sex drive from fears and disgusts as well as guarding it against superfluous stimulation. This may account for a certain kind of healthy-mindedness in the Catholic attitude toward sex. The question is, can any such paternalistic control stand up indefinitely in the open ideological market of modern society, or must it be replaced by other controls?

Hiltner's Christian view, or in purely humanistic terms, his personal-interpersonal attitude, emphasizes "man as a total being." Two serious problems will arise: one has to do with the individual man as a total being, and the other with the total population of men as endowed with the same human needs and intrinsic worth.

In the total of needs, drives, and interests which make up the individual man, there is a class of *defensive* drives such as anger-and-aggression, and fear-and-escape. In a sense these are antagonistic to the rest of the personality; they are necessary evils, weapons held in reserve against emergencies, and they operate through a branch of the nervous system which is antagonistic to the branch concerned with hunger, sexual excitation, and the routine bodily processes. Anger does sometimes become linked with sexual desire, and the result may be sadism. Do we want more of that? Do we want to encourage the very natural linkage of sex with jealousy, a partly defensive emotion, because of the useful weapon this gives against sexual infidelity; or would we minimize jealousy as an evil and try to find adequate substitute weapons? We do wish to link sex more closely with tender love toward the mate, a linkage which seems to be deficient in some persons and cultures. Yet we fear that tenderness toward other love-objects such as children, one's own sex, or the spouse of one's friend, might lead to erotic feeling.

Perhaps no group of drives plays so large a part in the higher development of man as do the *exploratory* drives of curiosity, acquisition, construction, aesthetic creation, and the like. The full story of man as a total being is not understood until we recognize that man strives to make new connections, craves new experiences, strives to enter all fields he can within the limits of time, energy, and empirically adequate safety. Denis de Rougemont seems to recognize that sexual adventure provides some positive values which cannot be dismissed merely by calling them bad names. His answer is that marital fidelity is also a value, a faith chosen for its own sake, and to choose it means to renounce the values both of "spontaneity" and "manifold experience." (9)

Kinsey's outstanding discovery about sex differences is that males are erotically stimulated by a much greater variety of objects and mental images than are females. He thinks this is due to some biological difference. Hiltner is inclined to question this interpretation. That there is such a *biological* difference, however, is suggested by Slater and Woodside. "If the race were so constituted that female orgasm occurred before male, she might very well thereupon terminate coitus before the chance of conception had occurred. A male constitution that provided for ejaculation at the earliest possible moment after intromission would be a selective advantage." (10) More generally, we may theorize, nature is wasteful, and reproduction may be best assured by having an excess of male *excitement* present all the time, at the same time that the female, for short periods, may seem almost insatiable. Clearly ethics cannot be derived simply from natural law any more than it can from existing custom. But, on the other hand, an ethic of human fulfillment would continually seek harmless ways to use rather than waste, to integrate rather than to keep separate, the various and abundant potentialities of man.

The other serious problem is the problem of humanity as a whole population. Does the Christian view of sex hold that persons, when they cannot achieve the ideal, should renounce sex altogether? Must sex be used only during some limited period of one's lifetime, depriving especially men in youth and women in older years, often at the very times they are strongest in biological drive? Strange to say, these absolute deprivations would be much easier to endure were it not for the existence of a rather elastic supply of surplus sexuality in the non-deprived people of the opposite sex. Conversely, the surplus sexuality of these latter would not bother them so much were it not for their knowledge of the absolute deprivations existing among potential partners. One might almost say that sex, like "nature," abhors a vacuum, and that this characteristic is likely to increase the more we rationalize (in Max Weber's sense) and civilize our sexuality.

The problem is not a simple choice between two alternates. At least four distinct values are involved: (a) sexual exclusiveness, (b) permanence of marriage or intimate relationships, (c) male initiative in courtship and economic production, (d) better intersexual balance and wider satisfaction of the biological sex need. Any three of these can be attained better by sacrificing, or honestly subordinating and risking, the fourth. The least discussed possibility, though not necessarily the most hopeful, is the subordination of value three. That is, if boys were to marry soon after sexual maturity, taking wives a few years older, expecting more economic responsibility and courtship initiative from the girls, much of the problem as Kinsey portrays it might be relieved, and there would also be less widowhood.

But perhaps there are weightier considerations than these. If so, they will endure the strain of public exposure and discussion. Sex may be a dangerous thing, but now that we have radioactive dust floating about, any alarm over the insidious consequences of the "Kinsey bomb" should seem to be somewhat amusing.

REFERENCES

1. D. S. BAILEY, *The Mystery of Love and Marriage, A Study in the Theology of Sexual Relations*, New York: Harper and Brothers, 1952. See *Genesis* 2:24 and *Ephesians* 5:31.
2. ERICH FROMM, *Man for Himself*, New York: Rinehart and Co., 1947; *Psychoanalysis and Religion*, New Haven: Yale University Press, 1951.
3. SEWARD HILTNER, *Sex Ethics and the Kinsey Report*, New York: Association Press, 1953.

4. John J. Kane, *Marriage and the Family, A Catholic Approach,* New York: Dryden Press, 1952, p. 258.
5. Abram Kardiner, *et al., The Psychological Frontiers of Society,* New York: Columbia University Press, 1945.
6. Wayne Leys, *Ethics for Policy Decisions,* New York: Prentice-Hall, Inc., 1953.
7. Margaret Mead, *Male and Female,* New York: William Morrow and Co., 1949, p. 450.
8. F. S. C. Northrop, *The Meeting of East and West,* New York: The Macmillan Co., 1946, pp. 245, 256–258.
9. Denis de Rougemont, *Love in the Western World,* New York: Harcourt, Brace and Co., 1940, p. 290.
10. Eliot Slater and Moya Woodside, *New Patterns in Marriage,* London: Cassell and Co., 1951, p. 175.

Appendix Two

Marriage Prediction Scale†

ERNEST W. BURGESS AND LEONARD S. COTTRELL

DIRECTIONS: The man should read the part headed "Items for Prospective Husbands," mark his own score on each item, and add these figures together. For example, if he was the youngest of several children, this counts 15 toward the final score; but if he was an only child, his mark will be zero on this item. Similarly, the prospective bride marks her rating on each item under the heading "Items for Prospective Wives" and adds these figures to give her individual score. Then together the couple should answer the questions under the heading "Items Common to Both Husband and Wife," marking their rating on each. Adding the three totals — husband's score, wife's score, and items common to both — will give the "marriage prediction score." If this is above 700, there is a 98 per cent chance that the couple will be extremely happy. If between 540 and 700, there is a strong probability that they will be above average in happiness. But if the "prediction score" is below 300, the chances of unhappiness are almost 100 per cent.

SCORE

I. ITEMS FOR PROSPECTIVE HUSBANDS
  1. Your place in your family:
     Am only child — 0
     Am oldest child — 15
     Am middle child — 20
     Am youngest child — 15
     No reply — 0
  2. Most attached to which brother or sister:
     Only child — 0
     No special attachment but have brother or sister — 20
     Most attached to older brother — 20
     Most attached to older sister — 10
     Most attached to younger brother — 15
     Most attached to younger sister — 15
     No reply — 0
  3. Area of residence:
     City: * rooming-house area — 0
     City: * area of "first settlement" — 15
     City: * area of "second settlement" (newer neighborhoods) — 20
     City: * hotel area — 0
     City: * apartment and apartment hotel — 10
     City: * private homes of better class — 20
     City: * suburbs — 30
     Other city or town: above 10,000 — 10
     Small town (not city * suburb): below 10,000 — 20

† Used by permission of Prentice-Hall, Inc., publishers of *Predicting Success or Failure in Marriage* (New York, 1939).
* 200,000 population or over.

825

SCORE

Village and rural   15
No reply   5

4. Degree of education:

Grade school only   5
High school   0
Professional school (not collegiate)   0
College graduate   15
Graduate or professional work (beyond college)   20
No reply   0

5. Occupation:

None	0	Grocery-store owners	15
Accountants	15	High-school teachers	20
Advertising	15	Insurance salesmen	10
Architects	15	Laborers	0
Athletic coaches	20	Lawyers	15
Auto mechanics	5	Mail clerks	10
Automobile salesmen	10	Managers	15
Bank employees	10	Meat-market owners	10
Bankers	15	Mechanics	5
Barbers	5	Ministers	20
Bond salesmen	10	Musicians	5
Bookkeepers	10	Newspaper workers	15
Brokers	10	Office workers	15
Carpenters	5	Owners, large business	15
Chemical engineers	20	Plumbers	5
Civil engineers	15	Physicians	15
Clerks	10	Printers	10
Clothing-store owners	15	Railroad-office workers	10
Contractors	15	Real-estate salesmen	5
College professors	20	Salesmen (unclassified)	10
Corporation officials	15	Skilled workers	
Dentists	10	(unclassified)	5
Druggists	10	Small-store owners	10
Educational administrators	15	Store salesmen	15
Electrical engineers	15	Students	20
Electricians	10	Teachers	15
Engineers	15	Traveling salesmen	0
Factory foremen	10	Truck drivers	5
Farmers	10	Wholesale salesmen	15
Garage owners	10	All others	10
Gas-station employees	5	No reply	0
Government workers	15		

6. How long have you held your present position?

Less than one year   10
One to less than three years   0
Three to less than five years   10
Five to less than seven years   5
Seven years or more   0
No reply   0

SCORE

7. Your work record:
   Never worked because in school, or worked only at school
      vacation time   15
   Irregularly employed or continually changing jobs   0
   Regularly employed   20
   No reply   0
8. Present monthly income:
   None   10
   Under $150   0
   $150 to under $250   10
   $250 to under $350   5
   $350 or more   0
   No reply   0
9. Amount of savings:
   None   0
   Under $1000   10
   $1000 to under $2000   20
   $2000 to under $3000   15
   $3000 and over   10
   No reply   0
10. Financial index at marriage:
    Multiply your age (nearest birthday) by your present monthly
       earnings (example: 23 by $110 equals 2530). Then divide your
       total savings by this number (example: $1200 divided by 2530
       equals .47).
    If your index is:
    0 (no savings)   0
    Between .01 and .29   15
    .30 or over   20
    No reply   5
11. Family-background index (to obtain this, see Explanation A,
       page 814):
    Under 69   0
    70–89   5
    90–119   25
12. Present amount of religious activity (attendance at church,
       and so on):
    Member, but not stating amount of church attendance   5
    No attendance at church or church affairs   0
    Attend no more than once a month   10
    Attend two or three times a month   20
    Attend four or more times a month   15
    No reply   0
13. Age when you stopped going to Sunday School:
    Never went   10
    Stopped at 10 years or younger   0
    Attended until between 11 and 18 years of age   25
    Attended until 19 or more years of age   30
    No reply   10

SCORE

14. Number of social organizations of which you are a member:
    None — 0
    One — 10
    Two — 15
    Three or more — 20
    No reply — 0

15. Childhood and adolescence were spent chiefly in:
    City or town (10,000 or over) — 0
    Small town (less than 10,000) — 10
    Country — 30
    No reply — 0

16. Number of women you went with steadily before fiancee:
    None but fiancee — 10
    One — 5
    Two or three — 5
    Four or five — 5
    Six or more — 0
    No reply — 0

17. Number of men friends:
    Almost none — 0
    A few — 5
    Several — 20
    Many — 20
    No reply — 0

18. Marital status of your parents:
    Married, both living — 5
    Separated or divorced — 0
    Both dead — 5
    Father dead — 15
    Mother dead — 20
    No reply — 0

19. Your estimate of happiness of your parents' marriage:
    Very happy — 40
    Happy — 20
    Average — 10
    Unhappy — 20
    Very unhappy — 0
    No reply — 20

20. Amount of disagreement and conflict with your father:
    None — 40
    Very little — 30
    Moderate — 30
    A good deal — 15
    Almost continuous — 0
    No reply — 20

21. Do your parents favor your proposed marriage?
    Both "yes" — 20
    One "yes," the other "no" — 0
    Both "no" — 5
    No reply — 5

II. ITEMS FOR PROSPECTIVE WIVES
    1. Your place in your family:

Am only child	0
Am oldest child	10
Am middle child	10
Am youngest child	0
No reply	0

    2. Area of residence:

City: * rooming-house area	5
City: * area of "first settlement"	10
City: * area of "second settlement" (newer neighborhoods)	5
City: * hotel area	5
City: * apartment and apartment hotel	0
City: * private homes of better class	15
City: * suburbs	15
Other city: above 10,000	10
Small town: (not city * suburb) below 10,000	20
Village and rural	15
No reply	5

    3. Degree of education

Grade school only	0
High school	20
Professional school (not collegiate in grade)	20
College graduate	30
Graduate or professional work	40
No reply	10

    4. Occupation:

None	5
Domestic service	0
Unskilled industrial	0
Clerical and office, semiskilled operators, and so on	0
Skilled office secretaries, stenographers	10
Nursing	5
Professional — teaching	20
Professional — social work	5
Professional — law, medicine, and so on	0
Business women (high-paid)	10
Other occupations, such as student, and so on	5
No reply	10

    5. Is your present occupation in harmony with your vocational ambitions?

Have no special vocational ambition	0
Yes, in harmony with my ambitions	20
Slightly different from my ambitions	20
Greatly different from my ambitions	5
No reply	15

    6. If employed, how long held present position?

Less than one year	0

* 200,000 population or over.

	SCORE
One to less than three years	5
Three to less than seven years	10
Seven years and over	20
No reply	0

7. Your work record:

Never worked	0
Occasionally worked	5
Regularly employed	15
Housekeeper at home	10
Steadily engaged in outside activities (not gainful employment)	20
No reply	10

8. Your present monthly income:

None	10
Under $100	0
$100 to under $150	15
$150 to under $200	20
$200 and over	20
No reply	0

9. Amount of your present savings:

None	15
Under $500	5
$500 to under $1500	15
$1500 to under $2500	0
$2500 and over	20
No reply	5

10. Family-background index (to obtain this, see Explanation A, page 814):

Under 54	0
55 to 64	15
65 and over	25

11. Present amount of religious activity (attendance at church, and so on):

Member, but not stating amount of church attendance	5
No attendance at church or church affairs	0
Attend no more than once a month	5
Attend two or three times a month	5
Attend four or more times a month	10
No reply	5

12. Age when you stopped going to Sunday School:

Never went	0
Stopped at 10 years or younger	0
Attended until between 11 and 18 years of age	10
Attended until 19 or more years of age	20
No reply	0

13. Number of social organizations of which you are a member:

None	5
One	0
Two	10
Three or more	20
No reply	0

SCORE

14. Number of women friends:
    Almost none 0
    A few 20
    Several 10
    Many 30
    No reply 20
15. Your estimate of happiness of your parents' marriage:
    Very happy 20
    Happy 20
    Average 10
    Unhappy 0
    Very unhappy 0
    No reply 0
16. Amount of your disagreement and conflict with your father:
    None 10
    Very little 0
    Moderate 0
    A good deal 5
    Almost continuous 0
    No reply 5
17. Do parents favor your marriage?
    Both "yes" 20
    Father "yes"; mother "no" 15
    Father "no"; mother "yes" 0
    Both "no" 5
    No reply 5

III. ITEMS COMMON TO BOTH HUSBAND AND WIFE
    1. How long have you known each other?
       Under six months 0
       Six months to less than two years 10
       Two years to less than five years 20
       Five years to less than ten years 25
       Ten years or more 30
       No reply 20
    2. How long have you been "keeping company"?
       Under one year 0
       One year to under three years 5
       Three years and over 20
       No reply 5
    3. Difference between your ages (nearest birthdays):
       Same age 5
       Husband older by one to three years 5
       Husband older by four to seven years 0
       Husband older by eight or more years 10
       Wife older by one to three years 10
       Wife older by four or more years 30
       No reply 0

EXPLANATION A — FAMILY-BACKGROUND INDEX OF FATHER AND MOTHER

	HUSBAND'S SCORE	WIFE'S SCORE
a. Religious preference of father and mother (Catholic, Jewish, Protestant):		
Both parents same	20	10
Different	0	0
One or both not known	10	5
b. Education of parents:		
Both parents college	30	20
One college, one high school	20	15
Both parents high school	15	10
One college, one grammar school	15	10
One high school, one grammar school	10	7
Both parents grammar school	7	5
One no education	5	3
Both parents no education	0	0
One or both unknown	7	4
c. Order of birth of parents:		
Oldest and oldest	30	20
Oldest and middle	10	8
Oldest and youngest	10	8
Oldest and only	20	15
Middle and middle	10	8
Middle and only	20	15
Youngest and youngest	10	8
Youngest and only	0	0
Only and only	0	0
d. Number of brothers and sisters of parents:		
5 or more on both sides	20	10
5 or more on one side and 4 on the other	18	9
5 or more on one side and 3 on the other	17	8
5 or more on one side and 2 on the other	16	8
5 or more on one side and 1 on the other	15	7
5 or more on one side and 0 on the other	14	7
4 and 4	15	7
4 and 3	14	7
4 and 2	13	6
4 and 1	12	6
4 and 0	10	5
3 and 3	14	7
3 and 2	13	6
3 and 1	12	6
3 and 0	9	5
2 and 2	12	6
2 and 1	11	5
2 and 0	9	4
1 and 1	11	5
1 and 0	8	4
0 and 0	0	0
One or both not known	7	4

	HUSBAND'S SCORE	WIFE'S SCORE
e. Social status of parents' families in their community:		
Both parents of superior or reputable status	20	20
One parent of superior or reputable and another of inferior status	10	10
Both parents of inferior status	0	0

Engagement Adjustment Scale*

THIS is a method of appraising adjustment in engagement which has been devised and applied successfully by Dr. Ernest W. Burgess and Dr. Paul Wallin of the University of Chicago in a study of fifteen hundred married and engaged couples. Its merit is that you can compare yourselves as an engaged couple with these typical young people on whom the test was first standardized.

To maximize objectivity you should read the scale and score yourselves separately. When you have added up your scores you have a score of adjustment from the man's perspective and one from the woman's perspective. Add your individual scores together and divide by two and you have your score as an engaged couple. You are now ready to compare your score with the couples studied by Burgess and Wallin. The upper quarter of these fifteen hundred couples scored 163 or more. They are the best adjusted in engagement. The lower quarter scored 142 or below and are the least well adjusted in engagement. That means that half of the group ranged between scores of 142 and 163. If your score is in the lower grouping you should proceed cautiously because adjustment in engagement has been shown to be related to later adjustment in marriage.

	SCORE	
	Man	*Woman*
1. In leisure time do you prefer to be:		
"On the go" all or most of the time	3	3
Stay at home all or most of the time	10	10
Fifty-fifty reply or equivalent	5	5
Emphasis on stay at home	7	7
Man and woman differ	4	4
2. Do you and your fiance(e) engage in interests and activities together?		
All of them	10	10
Most of them	6	6
Some of them	2	3
Few or none	0	0
3. Do you confide in your fiance(e)?		
About everything	5	5
About most things	2	4
About some things	0	2

---

* Adapted for self-administration by Reuben Hill from the research scale presented in the report by Ernest W. Burgess and Paul Wallin, "Predicting Adjustment in Marriage from Adjustment in Engagement," *The American Journal of Sociology*, 49 (January, 1944), pp. 324–330. Used by permission of the University of Chicago Press, Publishers of *The American Journal of Sociology*.

	SCORE	
	Man	*Woman*
4. Does your fiance(e) confide in you?		
About everything	5	5
About most things	3	3
About some things	0	2
5. Frequency with which fiance(e) shows affection.		
Practically all the time	10	10
Very frequent	8	8
Occasionally	2	3
6. Are you satisfied with the amount of demonstration of affection?		
Both satisfied	7	7
Man satisfied, woman desires more	3	3
Woman satisfied, man desires more	3	3
Man satisfied, woman desires less	2	2
Woman satisfied, man desires less	2	2
One desires less, other desires more	1	1
Both desire more	4	4
7. See chart on opposite page.		
8. Do you ever wish you had not become engaged?		
Never	10	10
Once	5	5
Occasionally	1	1
Frequently	0	0
9. Have you ever contemplated breaking your engagement?		
Never	10	10
Once	5	5
Occasionally	1	1
Frequently	0	0
10. What things annoy you about your engagement? List them on a scratch pad and count them.		
Nothing listed	10	10
One thing mentioned	7	7
Two things	1	1
Three things	0	0
If "its length" only is mentioned	9	9
If "being separated" is cited	8	8
11. What things does your fiance(e) do that you do not like? List them on a scratch pad and count them.		
None	7	7
One thing mentioned	5	5
Two things	1	1
Three or more	0	0
12. Has your steady relationship with your fiance(e) ever been broken off temporarily?		
Never	10	10
Once	5	5
Twice	2	2
Three or more times	0	0
13. If you could, what things would you change in your fiance(e)? List them on a scratch pad checking		

7. Indicate your approximate agreement or disagreement with your fiance(e) on the following things. Do this for each item by putting a check in the column which shows your agreement or disagreement. To get the man's score, add the scale points for each check he made, e.g. every "Always agree" checked is worth eight (8) points, every "Frequently disagree" three (3) points, etc. To get the woman's score add the scale points for the items she has checked.

Score Value	8	6	5	3	2	0	
CHECK ONE COLUMN FOR EACH ITEM BELOW	ALWAYS AGREE	ALMOST ALWAYS AGREE	OCCASIONALLY DISAGREE	FREQUENTLY DISAGREE	ALMOST ALWAYS DISAGREE	ALWAYS DISAGREE	SCORE
Money matters							
Matters of recreation							
Religious matters							
Demonstration of affection							
Friends							
Arrangements for your marriage							
Dates with each other							
Table manners							
Matters of conventionality							
Philosophy of life							
Ways of dealing with your families							

	SCORE	
	Man	*Woman*

the following points and then count them: (a) in physical condition or appearance; (b) in mental or temperamental or personality characteristics; (c) in ideas; (d) in personal habits; (e) in any other way.

	Man	Woman
No change desired	10	10
One change mentioned	8	8
Two changes	6	6
Three changes	4	4
Four changes	2	2
Five changes	0	0

14. If you could, what things would you change in yourself following the same outline? List them on a scratch pad and count them.

	Man	Woman
No change desired	10	10
One change mentioned	8	8
Two changes	6	6
Three changes	4	4
Four changes	2	2
Five changes	0	0